SECOND EDITION

THE METHODS AND MATERIALS OF DEMOGRAPHY

SECOND EDITION

THE METHODS AND MATERIALS OF DEMOGRAPHY

Edited by

JACOB S. SIEGEL

DAVID A. SWANSON

ELSEVIER
ACADEMIC
PRESS

Amsterdam • Boston • Heidelberg • London • New York • Oxford
Paris • San Diego • San Francisco • Singapore • Sydney • Tokyo

Elsevier Academic Press
525 B Street, Suite 1900, San Diego, California 92101-4495, USA
84 Theobald's Road, London WC1X 8RR, UK

This book is printed on acid-free paper.

Library of Congress Cataloging-in-Publication Data
Application submitted

British Library Cataloguing in Publication Data
A catalogue record for this book is available from the British Library

ISBN: 0-12-641955-8

For all information on all Academic Press publications visit our Web site at
www.academicpress.com

Printed in the United States of America
04 05 06 07 08 9 8 7 6 5 4 3 2 1

Contents

Acknowledgments

Since its initial introduction in 1971, *The Methods and Materials of Demography* has served well several generations of demographers, sociologists, economists, planners, geographers, and other social scientists. It is a testament to both its strong fundamental structure and its need that the book has enjoyed such a long, successful run without substantive revisions. By the mid 1990s, however, a number of important methodological and technological advances in demography had occurred that rendered "*M&M*" out-of-date. These advances led to the commissioning of this revision of the 1976 Condensed version, an endeavor for which acknowledgments are due.

We first and foremost thank the authors of the individual chapters, who so generously gave of their time and expertise. We also thank Scott Bentley, Senior Editor, for his patience, suggestions, and steady guidance, and all the others at Academic Press who dedicated themselves to the task of seeing the work through to publication. A large debt of gratitude is owed to Tom Bryan for the long hours he spent "cleaning up" the original electronic files created from scanning the entirety of the 1976 Condensed version of *M&M*. Tom also provided several authors with formatting assistance and advice. His selfless generosity was instrumental in the completion of this project. Special thanks also go to George Hough and Juha Alanko for their assistance in resolving a myriad of technical problems ranging from corrupted files to software incompatibilities.

The present editors, the contributors to the new volume, and users, past and present, owe a great debt to Henry Shryock, Siegel's distinguished collaborator in the preparation of the original unabridged work. The present authors and editors also owe a debt of gratitude to Edward G. Stockwell, Emeritus Professor of Sociology, Bowling Green State University. In collaboration with the editors of the original work, he was responsible for abridging the original two-volume work published by the U.S. Census Bureau. In so ably carrying out the time-consuming and demanding task of condensing the longer text, he produced the volume

from which the present authors principally worked. We also owe much to the many contributors to the original unabridged version of *M&M*. They provided an enduring legacy that extends into this revision and likely well beyond. In this regard, we owe a special debt to many at the U.S. Census Bureau—past and present—but in particular, we want to thank John Long and Signe Wetrogan for their assistance in making this revision become a reality.

We also want to thank our friends, colleagues, and institutions for their forbearance, understanding, and assistance, and, in particular, our family members.

Jacob Siegel wants to thank his legions of students at the University of Connecticut, the University of Southern California, Cornell University, the University of California Berkeley, Howard University, the University of California Irvine, and especially, Georgetown University, his home base for almost a quarter century, for navigating with him through the earlier editions of the book and honing his knowledge of demography. He also wants to thank his friends and colleagues who invited him to join them in training the next generations of demographers at their institutions, Jane Wilkie, Judy Treas, Joe Stycos, Ron Lee, Tom Merrick, Frank Edwards, and Maurice van Arsdol. Further, he wants to pay tribute to Dan Levine, Jeff Passel, Greg Robinson, Henry Shryock, Bob Warren, Meyer Zitter, and the late Conrad Taeuber, all former colleagues at the U.S. Census Bureau, who contributed over many years to the high level of demographic scholarship in that agency. Finally, Siegel wishes to acknowledge his intellectual debt to Nathan Keyfitz and the late Ansley Coale, who contributed immensely to the development of demographic methods in our time and who trained and inspired a multitude of demographers in our country and abroad.

David Swanson is grateful for the training and mentoring he received while an undergraduate student at Western Washington University, a graduate student at the University of Hawaii, a staff researcher with the East-West Center's Population Institute and, subsequently, with the Washington

vii

State Office of Financial Management. To his wife Rita, David owes a lot, for not only putting up with several years of lost vacations, weekends, and evenings, but for her assistance with the Glossary. Sacrifices she made surpassed those of Dave and Jane, Milt and Roz, Nikole, Danielle, Gabrielle, and Brittany, in that the visits and activities they missed became many more boring and lonely occasions for her.

Jacob S. Siegel and David A. Swanson

Preface

LINDA GAGE AND DOUGLAS S. MASSEY

The original edition of the *Methods and Materials of Demography* was written between 1967 and 1970. The world of demography in the late 1960s was a far cry from the one we know today. Many of the methods we now take for granted had not yet been invented, and given the computational intensity of techniques such as multistate life tables and hazards modeling, some would have been impossible to implement in the early days of the computer era.

Although computers existed in the late 1960s, they were mainframes: big, costly, cumbersome, and expensive. If you wanted to run a computer program, you typically began by writing the code yourself, then keypunched the program onto a set of eighty-column cards, delivered the resulting deck across a counter to a computer operator, who then loaded it into a mechanical reader. Then your program entered a queue to compete with administrative jobs and other research applications for access to scarce "CPU" capacity, which never exceeded "640k." After working its way to the front of the queue, the program would finally run. If you hadn't made a keypunching error, violated the syntax of the programming language, or made a logical mistake that produced a mathematical impasse such as division by zero or some other nonsensical result, the program might successfully conclude and produce meaningful output. It would then be placed in a queue for printing on a mechanical line printer, and if the printer did not jam before getting to your output, it would be printed. It would then sit in a pile until the computer operator got around to separating it from other "print jobs" and then placing it in a specific cubbyhole associated with the first letter of your last name. There, hopefully, you would find your output. If all went well, the whole process might take four hours, but if the job was "big," it would be held in "batch" to run overnight, when competition for CPU access and memory slackened.

The foregoing represents a common historical scenario of demographic-data analysis for those fortunate enough to be working in a research university, a well-funded research institute, or the upper reaches of the federal bureaucracy in the 1960s (and into the 1980s). If one was unfortunate enough to be working at a teaching college, second-tier university, the middle echelons of the federal bureaucracy, or in most positions of state and local government, calculations had to be performed with electrical calculating machines that could handle only simple mathematical operations and limited bodies of data. Those even more unfortunate endured the tedium of performing error-prone calculations by hand, with pencil and paper.

Whether by electronic machine or by hand, even the simplest calculations were laborious, costly, and profligate with respect to time (hours spent adding, multiplying, and dividing dozens of numbers by hand), space (yielding file cabinets bulging with papers containing hand-entered data or columns of printed numbers), and personnel (squads of busy statistical clerks). Methodology was kept deliberately simple: descriptive rather than analytical, bivariate rather than multivariate, linear instead of nonlinear, scalar operations instead of matrix operations. In terms of analysis, demographers and statisticians worked to derive computational formulas that relied on simple sums and products and could be implemented in a series of easily transmitted steps. This all has changed. Happily since the "good old days," access to huge levels of computer power has become commonplace and software packages for a wide range of statistical and demographic techniques, both simple and complex, have become available to analysts.

With respect to data, the principal sources in 1970, especially in the more developed countries, were vital statistics and the census. In the United States, other than the Current Population Survey, little demographic data came from surveys. Today, there is a plethora of sample surveys, both general-purpose and specialized, relating to demographic, social, economic, and health characteristics, and covering both the more developed and the less developed countries. Vital registration systems have been improved and extended, and administrative data of many kinds are being exploited for their demographic applications.

The high cost of gathering and manipulating data in the late 1960s also meant that knowledge of the methods and materials of demography was not widely diffused. Expertise on most demographic techniques was confined to a few practitioners working in federal and state bureaucracies, the life insurance industry, or academia; and practically no one was familiar with *all* the methods and techniques employed to gather, correct, and analyze demographic data.

As a result, there was no single comprehensive source of information on demographic techniques, either for reference or for training purposes. During the first half of the last century a number of general textbooks on demography appeared, but they tended to focus on specific areas of the field or were too limited in the depth of their treatments. In 1925, Hugh Wolfenden's *Population Statistics and Their Compilation* was published by the Society of Actuaries; it focused on the compilation of census data and vital statistics and on mortality measures from an actuarial standpoint. The classic treatise on *The Length of Life*, published by Louis Dublin and Alfred Lotka in 1936 went into considerable detail on the methodology and applications of the life table but offered little on other methods. In the same year Robert Kuczynski published his monograph on *The Measurement of Population Growth*, which concentrated on fertility and mortality and their relation to population growth and included some international examples. A section on demographic methods was included in Margaret Hagood's *Statistics for Sociologists*, which was published in 1941. However, it was not until 1950, with the release of Peter Cox's *Demography*, that what many considered to be the first "comprehensive" textbook on demography appeared. This was followed in 1958 by George Barclay's *Techniques of Population Analysis*, which covered many of the principal topics of demography—and with an international orientation. Unfortunately, Barclay's work, like the work of those preceding him, also left many topics uncovered.

By the 1960s, a clear need had arisen for a current, comprehensive source of information on demographic methods and data that gave particular attention to the collection, compilation, and evaluation of census data and vital statistics. In the context of the Cold War, U.S. officials were working assiduously to capture the hearts and minds of people throughout the less developed world. As part of this effort, the U.S. Agency for International Development (AID) ran numerous training programs that brought officials from the less developed nations to the United States to acquire the technical expertise they needed to administer their rapidly growing states. The agency also sent out cadres of resident advisors to provide direct training and technical support.

An important focus of AID's training was demographic and statistical methods, designed to give officials in many newly decolonized states the technical knowledge they needed to implement a census, maintain vital registries, and staff an office of national statistics. In this effort, the lack of a text on demographic methods emerged as a serious handicap. AID subcontracted demographic training to the U.S. Bureau of the Census, but while its staff members had the demographic expertise, they too lacked teaching materials and readings. As an early interim solution to this problem, in 1951, Abram Jaffe (formerly of the Bureau of the Census, but at Columbia University by 1951) compiled a book of readings, with some introductory text, entitled *Handbook of Statistical Methods for Demographers*. In an effort to secure a more satisfactory training instrument, AID offered a special contract to the Census Bureau to allocate its personnel and resources to the task. Henry Shyrock and Jacob Siegel were named to coordinate the effort, which ultimately led to the completion of the two volumes known as *The Methods and Materials of Demography*, published in 1971 by the U.S. Government Printing Office for the U.S. Bureau of the Census. This two-volume work represents the first-ever systematic, comprehensive survey of demographic techniques and data.

Thus, the origins of *Methods and Materials* lay in a training imperative—the need for a comprehensive text that could be given to students, particularly those from the less developed nations, as part of an extended seminar on demographic techniques. It also was intended to serve as a reference guide for trained demographers to use after they returned to work in government, the private sector, or academia. The two volumes offered a detailed summary of the working knowledge of demographers circa 1970, drawing heavily on the day-to-day wisdom that over the years had been garnered by Census Bureau employees. In a very real way, it represented a systematic codification and extension of the inherited oral culture and technical lore of the Census Bureau's staff, recorded for general use by a wider public.

According to the preface, the original *Methods and Materials* sought to achieve

> . . . a systematic and comprehensive exposition, with illustrations, of the methods currently used by technicians or research workers in dealing with demographic data. . . . The book is intended to serve both as a text for course on demographic methods and as a reference for professional workers. . . .

Methods and Materials was intended to be used as the manual in a year-long training course, and given its didactic purpose was self-consciously written so as to assume little mathematical sophistication on the part of the reader. Each method was laid out in clear, step-by-step fashion, and computations were illustrated with examples based on actual demographic data.

Paradoxically, given the work's origins in the need to train students from the less developed countries, the examples were taken almost entirely from the censuses and vital statistics registries of the United States and other more developed countries. Shryock and Siegel were aware of this limitation and in their preface they lamented the lack of reliable data from the less developed nations and sought to assure readers that ". . . certain demographic principles and methods are essentially 'culture free,' and measures worked out for the United States could serve as well for any other country."

Whatever its shortcomings, the two volumes of *Methods and Materials* clearly addressed an unmet need and filled an essential niche in the field. The original publication run of 1971 was soon sold out, necessitating a second printing in 1973. But this printing also soon went out of stock, and a third printing was released in 1975 (followed by a fourth in 1980, shortly after which, the book went out of print). Clearly a bestseller by the standards of the Census Bureau and the U.S. Government Printing Office, the volume attracted the attention of the private sector, notably Professor Halliman Winsborough of the University of Wisconsin, who sought to publish a condensed version as part of his series entitled "Studies in Demography." To reduce the two volumes into a single compact work, he enlisted Professor Edward G. Stockwell of Bowling Green State University in Ohio and in 1976 Academic Press brought out its Condensed Edition of *Methods and Materials*.

Whereas the original Shryock and Siegel volume contained 888 pages, 25 chapters, and four appendices, the condensed version had 559 pages, 24 chapters, and three appendices. In preparing their original volume, Shryock and Siegel had each taken primary responsibility for writing eight chapters. For the remaining nine chapters they enlisted the help of 11 "associate authors." The two primary authors then read, edited, and approved all chapters before final publication. Conrad Taeuber, then Associate Director of the Census Bureau, also read and commented upon the manuscript. Among the associate authors were people such as Paul Glick, Charles Nam, and Paul Demeny. When these names are combined with those of Shryock, Siegel, and Taeuber, we find that *Methods and Materials* was associated with the labors of six current, past, or future Presidents of the Population Association of America, one indicator of its centrality to the discipline.

In the current volume, the number of chapters has been reduced to 22. Of these, 21 correspond to the original chapters delineated by Shryock and Siegel, and a new chapter on health demography has been added. As before, there are four appendices. Reflecting the greater scope and complexity of demography in the 21st century, however, is the expansion of the two primary and 11 associate authors of the first edition to two primary and 32 associate authors in the second. That the ratio of authors to chapters has virtually tripled, going from 0.52 to 1.55, may suggest something about the accumulation of methodological knowledge that has taken place over the past three decades.

Another perspective on the past three decades is offered by the concept of evolution—that gradual process in which something changes into a significantly different, especially

a more complex or more sophisticated form. It is imperceptible on a daily basis. After three decades it was time to take stock of *Methods and Materials* and assess how demography had changed. Those fortunate enough to have a copy of the original still turn to it for definitions, formulas, and general reference. The methods and materials of our discipline have changed so much that it was necessary to revise demographers' most cherished resource, the time-honored volumes that some refer to simply as "*M&M*."

In 1971, a "tiger" was a tiger and a "puma" was a mountain lion. Today a "TIGER" can be a Topologically Integrated Geographic Encoding and Referencing System and a "PUMA" can be a Public Use Microdata Area. In 1971, an "ace" was a playing card, now an "ACE" can be an Accuracy and Coverage Evaluation Survey. New alphabet combinations have entered the demographic vocabulary: ACS (American Community Survey), CDP (Census Designated Place), CMSA (Consolidated Metropolitan Statistical Area), GIS (Geographic Information System), and MAF (Master Address File). At the end of the 20th century, *M&M* was no longer widely available and it was no longer current. Many who teach and practice demography today were not yet born when the original work was printed. Yes, it was time to update the "old" version.

Much had changed in 30 years. The evolution of demography was fostered by the availability of more data and data sources, and improved tools to access, analyze, and quickly communicate information. The discipline responded to the opportunities created by the new computer technology, including the Internet, growth in data storage, and computing capacity; widespread availability of analytic software and Geographic Information Systems; and mass media interest in demography. The aging of the Post–World War II "baby boom" population, especially in the United States, also helped shift the focus of demography. Along with the intellectual progression of theories and improvements in and invention of demographic methods, the reach of demography expanded within other scientific disciplines, in state and local governments, community-based organizations, planning and marketing enterprises, and in the popular press.

The numerous authors selected to review and revise the chapters of *M&M* are specialists in their fields. They carefully preserved much of the original material, made major or minor modifications as needed, and brought the contents up to date by including recent research, references, and examples. Some chapters are little changed, while some changed significantly as new methods and improvements to previous methods were introduced. Other chapters and sections introduce topics, like health demography and geographic information systems, not included in the original.

The new chapter on Health Demography is included in recognition of the many questions on health that now appear regularly on population censuses and surveys, the close relation of health to the analysis of mortality changes, and the role of health as cause and consequence of various demographic and socioeconomic changes. This chapter defines the basic concepts relating to health and extends conventional life tables to measure "active" or "healthy" life expectancy. The importance of health issues to demography also is discussed in a chapter addressing estimation methods for statistically underdeveloped areas that reports on recent methodologies to incorporate the effects of the HIV/AIDS epidemic on life expectancy.

A Glossary is introduced that covers topics from abortion and abridged life table to zero population growth and zip codes. Appended to the Glossary is a "Demography Time Line," which records significant demographic events beginning with the Babylonian census in 3800 B.C., covers the 1971 publication of the *Methods and Materials of Demography*, and concludes with the release of United States Census results through the Internet in 2000.

Other new features include an appendix on Geographic Information Systems (GIS) that covers everything from the origins of GIS to the products of GIS. There are discussions about what GIS is and how it can be used by demographers to enhance analysis and aid communication of results. Techniques for analyzing spatial distributions are described. There is a very helpful section on practical issues to consider in developing a GIS, such as data-storage formats, attributes of reliable data, and dimensions of data display.

New chapter sections discuss the development of censuses and surveys over the last 30 years and provide guidelines on when is the most appropriate time to select neither, one or both. Many changes in the United States census are highlighted. The chapter on Population Size sets forth the evolution of enumeration techniques and coverage evaluation in the United States from the 1970 to the 2000 census. Specific techniques for data collection and methods for assessing coverage in the most recent decennial census are described. There is a candid discussion of the technical and political debates and tensions surrounding the issue of adjusting the U.S. census results for estimated undercounts. The chapter on Geographic Areas includes discussions of new statistical units in the U.S. and adds a new section on alternative ways of measuring an emerging concept of interest, namely "accessibility"—the relationship between distance and opportunities.

The chapter on Racial and Ethnic Composition describes how greatly the measurement of racial and ethnic composition has changed in the United States since 1970 and describes the two major efforts of the U.S. government to create standards for collecting data on race and Hispanic ethnicity. (The most recently adopted standard allowed people to select more than one racial identity in federal census, survey, and administrative forms for the first time.) There is a rich description of the new standards for collecting and tabulating data on race along with guidance to those who must "bridge" race data collected under the disparate standards of 1990 and 2000 for trend or time-series analysis.

Some chapters in the original were merged. Two chapters, one on Marital Characteristics and Family Groups and another on Marriage and Divorce were blended to reflect the current state of marriage, divorce, and living arrangements that include covenant marriages, cohabitation, living arrangements of adult children, grandparents as custodians of grandchildren, and a rise in the average age at first marriage. Previous chapters on Sex Composition and Age Composition also were combined and integrated into one chapter. The new chapter updates the previous materials with more current examples (usually through the 1990 round of census taking), including examples with international data, and provides references on computer spreadsheet programs that greatly simplify the application of many of the basic methods. The chapters on Educational Characteristics and Economic Characteristics chapters were also joined to address an increase in data sources, especially labor force surveys both in the United States and internationally, as well as new methodology since the early 1970s. As an example, this chapter contains a discussion of the World Bank's Living Standards Measurement Study (LSMS) that provides key information on income, expenditures, and wealth in the less developed countries.

Improvements in data collection, combined with an increase in computer capacity and analytic software, greatly simplify the application of many basic methods. They are referenced throughout the book but are especially emphasized in the chapters on Population Estimates and Population Projections. The chapter on Population Estimates presents the different types of estimation methods and a step-by-step approach for creating a population estimates program, from accessing data through selecting the appropriate methodology and finally applying evaluation techniques. In the chapter on Population Projections, new material on structural models is included that expands the treatment in the last version. This chapter also contains materials on economic-demographic models used to project growth for the larger areas such as counties, metropolitan areas, and nations and urban systems models for small area analysis, including transportation planning.

The demographic basics—birth, death and migration—are covered in several chapters. Discussions in the chapters on Fertility and Natality adopt more current terminology to describe measures of marital and nonmarital fertility and provide up-to-date examples of fertility measures. The discussion on research on children ever born and relationships between vital rates and age structure is expanded. Recent research on the use of multiple causes of death and the effect of the new international classification system of causes of death trends in the leading causes of death is addressed in the Mortality chapter. The construction of basic Life Tables has changed little in 50 years but life tables are more widely available today. As explained in the chapter on the Life Table, the forms, and range of applications, of life tables have been greatly expanded, particularly the use of multi-state life tables to measure social and economic characteristics in addition to mortality. Chapters on Internal Migration and Short-Distance Mobility and International Migration remain separate. Vastly improved sources of data on internal migration that became available over the last two decades are highlighted in the former chapter, especially longitudinal microdata that allow a more complete description of the moves that people make, the contexts surrounding moves, and the sequences of movement. In the latter chapter, there are discussions about the difficulty of measuring both illegal and nonpermanent immigration and the problems surrounding data on refugee populations.

This new edition keeps the best features of the earlier edition, updates the chapters, and develops new tables using real data to illustrate methods for data analysis. There is increased attention to sample survey data and international materials, particularly taking account of the new data on less developed countries. The new edition provides the academic references, methodological tools, and sources of data that demographers can both apply to basic scientific research and use to assist national, state and local government officials, corporate executives, community groups, the press, and the public to obtain demographic information. In turn, this demographic information can be used for advancing basic science as well as supporting decision-making, budget proposals, long-range planning, and program evaluation. This current work is consistent with the original in essential ways: careful definitions, detailed computational steps, and "real-life" examples. Concepts and methods are redesigned to state-of-the-art and updated with timely examples, current references, and topics not available in the original. This work, marking the significant evolution of demography since the original edition, is an invaluable reference for academic and applied demographers and demographic practitioners at all levels of training and experience.

1

Introduction

DAVID A. SWANSON AND JACOB S. SIEGEL

WHAT IS DEMOGRAPHY?

Demography is the scientific study of human population, including its size, distribution, composition, and the factors that determine changes in its size, distribution, and composition. From this definition we can say that demography focuses on five aspects of human population: (1) size, (2) distribution, (3) composition, (4) population dynamics, and (5) socioeconomic determinants and consequences of population change. Population size is simply the number of persons in a given area at a given time. Population distribution refers to the way the population is dispersed in geographic space at a given time. Population composition refers to the numbers of person in sex, age, and other "demographic" categories. The scope of the "demographic" categories appropriate for demographic study is subject to debate. All demographers would agree that age, sex, race, year of birth, and place of birth are demographic characteristics. These are all characteristics that do not essentially change in the lifetime of the individual, or change in a perfectly predictable way. They are so-called ascribed characteristics. Many other characteristics also are recognized as within the purview of the demographer. These fall into a long list of social and economic characteristics, including nativity, ethnicity, ancestry, religion, citizenship, marital status, household characteristics, living arrangements, educational level, school enrollment, labor force status, income, and wealth. Most of these characteristics can change in the lifetime of the individual. They are so-called achieved characteristics. Of course, some of these characteristics are the specialty of other disciplines as well, albeit the focus of interest is different. Some would include as demography all the areas about which questions are asked in the decennial population census. Our view of this question has a bearing on the subjects about which we write in this volume.

Narrowly defined, the components of change are births, deaths, and migration. In a more inclusive definition, we add marriage and divorce as processes affecting births, household formation, and household dissolution; and the role of sickness, or morbidity, as a process affecting mortality. The study of the interrelation of these factors and age/sex composition defines the subfield of formal demography. Beyond these demographic factors of change, there are a host of social and economic characteristics, such as those listed here, that represent causes and consequences of change in the basic demographic characteristics and the basic components of change. Study of these topics defines the subfields of social and economic demography. It should be evident that the boundaries of demography are not strictly defined and the field overlaps greatly with other disciplines. This book deals with the topics that we think essentially define the scope of demography today.

SUBFIELDS OF DEMOGRAPHY

The subfields of demography can be classified in several ways. One is in terms of the subject matter, geographic area, or methodological specialty of the demographer—for example, fertility, mortality, internal migration, state and local demography, Canada, Latin America, demography of aging, mathematical demography, economic demography, historical demography, and so on. Note that these specialties overlap and intersect in many ways. Another classification produces a simple dichotomy, but its two classes are also only ideal typical constructs with fuzzy edges: basic demography and applied demography. The primary focus of basic demography is on theoretical and empirical questions of interest to other demographers. The primary focus of applied demography is on practical questions of interest to parties outside the field of demography (Swanson, Burch, and Tedrow, 1996). Basic demography can be practiced from

1

either the perspective of formal demography or that of socioeconomic demography. The first has close ties to the statistical and mathematical sciences, and the latter has close ties to the social sciences. The key feature of basic demography that distinguishes it from applied demography is that its problems are generated internally. That is, they are defined by theory and the empirical and research traditions of the field itself. An important implication is that the audience for basic demography is composed largely of demographers themselves (Swanson *et al.*, 1996). On the other hand, applied demography serves the interests of business or government administration (Siegel, 2002). Units in government or business or other organizations need demographic analysis to assist them in making informed decisions. Applied demographers conceive of problems from a statistical point of view, investing only the time and resources necessary to produce a good decision or outcome. Moreover, as noted by Morrison (2002), applied demographers tend to arm themselves with demographic knowledge and draw on whatever data may be available to address tangible problems. However, it also is important to note that basic demographers and applied demographers share a common basic training in the concepts, methods, and materials of demography, so that they are able to communicate with one another without difficulty in spite of their difference in orientation.

OBJECTIVE OF THIS BOOK AND THE ROLE OF DEMOGRAPHERS

In this book, we focus on fundamentals that can be used by demographers of whatever specialty. We describe the basic concepts of demography, the commonly used terms and measures, the sources of demographic data and their uses. Our objective is twofold: (1) the primary objective is to give the reader with little or no training or experience in demography an introduction to the methods and materials of the field; (2) the secondary objective is to provide a reference book on demography's methods and materials for those with experience and training. Although the term "demographics" has become part of the public's vocabulary, there are relatively few self-described demographers. There are many more statisticians, economists, geographers, sociologists, and urban planners, for example.

Demography is rarely found as a independent academic discipline in an independent academic department. It is more commonly pursued as a subfield within departments of sociology, economics, or geography. However, practice of the field is relatively widespread among academic departments and is found not only in the departments named but also in such others as actuarial science, marketing, urban and regional planning, international relations, anthropology, history, and public health. Moreover, demographic centers are often found in affiliation with major research universi-

ties. These centers typically provide training and research opportunities as well as a meeting place for scholars interested in demographic studies but isolated in academic departments that have a different disciplinary focus.

In addition to those who would label themselves primarily as demographers, many who label themselves as something other than demographers are knowledgeable about demography and use its methods and materials. These would include, for example, many persons in actuarial science, economics, geography, market research, public health, sociology, transportation planning, and urban and regional planning. Few basic demographers work outside university settings, but many or most applied demographers do. In addition to those applied demographers employed in university institutes and bureaus of business research, there are those who work often as independent consultants or as analysts in large formal organizations. In the latter case, they collaborate with people representing a range of interests, from public health administration and human resources planning to marketing and traffic administration.

Typically, every country has a national governmental agency where demographic studies are the primary focus of activity. It is an organization responsible for providing information on population size, distribution, and composition to other agencies of government and to private organizations. In the United States, this organization is the Census Bureau. In other countries, such as Finland, it is the National Statistical Office, which in addition to providing information on size, distribution, and composition also provides information on births, deaths, and migration. In most cases, these governmental agencies prepare analyses of population trends as well as of the determinants and consequences of population change. Often, they are also the sources of innovations in the collection, processing, and dissemination of demographic data. In addition to national organizations, many countries have regional, state, and local organizations that compile, disseminate, and apply demographic information. In Finland, regional planning councils provide this service, and in Canada, most provincial governments as well as large cities do so. In the United States, most state governments have such an organization as do many counties and cities with large populations. While the service they provide is not as comprehensive as that of the national organizations, the subnational ones often provide more timely and detailed information for their specific areas of interest.

WHY STUDY POPULATION?

Demography can play a number of roles and serve several distinct purposes. The most fundamental is to describe changes in population size, distribution, and composition as a guide for decision making. This is done by obtaining counts of persons from, for example, censuses, the files of continuous population registers, administrative records, or sample surveys. Counts of births and deaths can be obtained from vital registration systems or from continuous population registers. Similarly, immigration and emigration data can be obtained from immigration registration systems or from continuous population registers. Although individual events may be unpredictable, clear patterns emerge when the records of individual events are combined. As is true in many other scientific fields, demographers make use of these patterns in studying population trends, developing theories of population change, and analyzing the causes and consequences of population trends. Various demographic measures such as ratios, percentages, rates, and averages may be derived from them. The resulting demographic data can then be used to describe the distribution of the population in space, its degree of concentration or dispersion, the fluctuations in its rate of growth, and its movements from one area to another. One demographer may study them to determine if there is evidence to support the human capital theory of migration (DaVanzo and Morrison, 1981; Massey, Alarcon, Durando, and Gonzales, 1987; Greenwood, 1997). Others, usually public officials, use these data to determine a likely "population future" as guides in making decisions about various government programs (U.S. Census Bureau/ Campbell, 1996; California/Heim *et al.*, 1998; Canada/ M.V. George *et al.*, 1994; George, 1999). As described earlier, demographic data play a role similar to that of data in other scientific fields, in that they can be used both for basic and applied purposes. However, demography enjoys two strong advantages over many other fields. First, the momentum of population processes links the present with the past and the future in clear and measurable ways. Second, in many parts of the world, these processes have been recorded with reasonable accuracy for many generations, even for centuries in some cases. Together, these two advantages form the conceptual and empirical basis on which the methods and materials of demography covered in this book are based.

ORGANIZATION OF THIS BOOK

The chapters of this book are grouped into three primary sections and a supplementary fourth section. The first part comprises Chapters 2 through 10 and covers the subjects of population size, distribution, and composition. The second part comprises Chapters 11 through 19 and covers population dynamics—the basic factors in population change. The third part comprises Chapters 20, 21, and 22 and covers the subjects of population estimates, population projections, and related types of data that are not directly available from a primary source such as a census, sample survey, or registration system. The fourth part is made up of several appendixes, a glossary, and a demographic timeline. The appendixes present supporting methodological tables and

set forth various mathematical methods closely associated with the practice of demography. The book concludes with a glossary (an alphabetic list of common terms and their definitions) and a demographic timeline (a list of events and persons, important in the development of demography as a science, in chronological order).

As in all recorded presentations of text material, we had to face the fact that the material in some chapters could not be adequately described without drawing on the material in a later chapter. This problem would arise regardless of the order of the topics or chapters followed. In the analysis of age-sex composition in Chapter 7, for example, it is necessary to make use of survival rates, which are derived by methods described in Chapter 13, "The Life Table." We have tried to minimize this problem so as to produce a volume that develops the material gradually and could serve more effectively as a learning instrument. A related problem is that a given method may apply to a number of subject fields within demography. Standardization, also called age-adjustment, can be applied to almost all kinds of ratios, rates, and averages: birth, death, and marriage rates; migration rates; enrollment ratios; employment ratios; and median years of school completed and per capita income. As a result, some topics have been repeated with different subject matters. We have tried to cope with this problem in a manner slightly different from that used in the preceding edition, which tried to avoid the repetition by describing different applications of the measures with different subject matter and which made frequent forward and backward references. To reduce this duplication, we assume that the reader will make judicious use of the detailed index to find the pertinent discussion.

Another issue we faced is the representation of the areas of the world outside the United States and the Western industrial countries both in terms of discussion materials and empirical examples. The majority of the authors reside in the United States. Given this fact, the authors and the editors made conscious efforts to "internationalize" the material in the book. We hope that we have succeeded at least as well as the authors and editors of the previous edition. Many new countries had to be brought into the fold, not only because of the proliferation of sovereign nations but also because of the recent availability of material for many important areas and countries (e.g., Russia, China, Indonesia).

In addition to discussing methods and materials, nearly every chapter contains a discussion of the uses and limitations of the data, materials, and methods, and some of the factors important in their use. Actual examples are often used to show how given methods and materials are developed and used. Of course, the illustrations do not cover every possible way in which a given method or set of materials can be used. Thus, the reader should be cognizant of the assumptions underlying a given method or set of materials. This becomes particularly important if he or she is considering the use of a given method in a new way. For example, a life table based on the mortality experience of a given year does not describe the mortality experience of any actual group of persons as they pass through life. Neither does a gross reproduction rate based on the fertility experience of a given year describe the actual fertility experience of any group of women who started life together. With due caution regarding their assumptions and limitations, however, these measures may be applied in many important descriptive and analytical ways.

Finally, as acknowledged in the "Author Biographies," there is the issue of material taken from the original two-volume set of *The Methods and Materials of Demography*. Virtually every chapter incorporates material from the original and, as such, this edition owes a debt to the original authors (listed in Table 1.1, presented later).

Having outlined the book's basic structure, we give a brief summary of the contents of each chapter, starting with Chapter 2, "Basic Sources of Statistics," by Thomas Bryan. This chapter covers both primary and secondary sources, at various geographic levels (international, national, subnational), as well as the quality of the data and related issues, such as confidentiality. Chapter 3, "Collection and Processing of Demographic Data," by Thomas Bryan and Robert Heuser, describes how demographic data are obtained from various sources, compiled, and disseminated. It covers data issues in more detail than Chapter 2, particularly those relating to standards and comparability. In Chapter 4, "Population Size," Janet Wilmoth discusses population as a concept, its various definitions, the issue of international comparability, and the various ways the population sizes of countries and their subdivisions have been measured. The next two chapters are concerned with the geographic aspects of population data and measurement. Chapter 5, "Population Distribution: Geographic Areas," by David Plane covers geographic concepts and definitions for the collection and tabulation of demographic data. In Chapter 6, "Population Distribution: Classification of Residence," Jerome McKibben and Kimberly Faust discuss the materials and measures associated with the dispersion of population in geographic space.

The next four chapters discuss a range of population characteristics. In Chapter 7, Frank Hobbs covers concepts, materials, and measures associated with "Age and Sex Composition," two characteristics of fundamental importance in demography because they are basic in the description and analysis of all the other subjects with which demography deals. Similarly, Jerome McKibben covers "Race and Ethnic Composition" in Chapter 8. This subject is fundamental in demography for a number of interrelated reasons, including the pronounced group variations observed, the relevance of these variations for understanding other classifications of demographic data, and their implications for public policy. In Chapter 9, "Marriage, Divorce, and Family Groups,"

Kimberly Faust deals with the concepts, materials, and measures pertaining to families and households and the processes by which they are formed and dissolved. William O'Hare, Kelvin Pollard, and Amy Ritualo also deal with socioeconomic or "achieved" characteristics in Chapter 10, "Education and Economic Characteristics." Educational attainment, school enrollment, labor force status, occupation, and income status are all associated with variations in socioeconomic status. This is the last of the chapters on population composition and concludes the first part of the book.

Part two of the book, "Components of Population Change," brings together a series of chapters dedicated to population dynamics, that is, the basic factors of population change—natality, mortality, and migration—but it supplements these with an introductory chapter on total change and with chapters on health, a factor associated with mortality change, and life tables, a specialized tool of mortality measurement. The discussion of marriage and divorce in Chapter 9 may also be considered as appropriate here for its role as a component of change in household formation and dissolution, and in natality. The section opens then with Chapter 11, "Population Change," by Stephen Perz. It is primarily concerned with the concepts and measurement of population change, particularly the alternative ways of measuring change. Assumptions may vary as to the pattern of change, and the basic data may reflect errors in the data as well as real change. The next two chapters are concerned with the topic of mortality, the first of the basic components of change. In Chapter 12, "Mortality," by Mary McGehee, this component is explored in terms of materials, concepts, and basic measures. Hallie Kintner extends the discussion of mortality in Chapter 13, focusing on "The Life Table," an important and versatile tool of demography that has applications in all of the subject areas we consider. This chapter informs us about how the life table expands our ability not only to measure mortality but also to measure any of the demographic characteristics previously considered as well as the other components of change. For example, Chapter 14, "Health Demography," authored by Vicki Lamb and Jacob Siegel, not only describes the materials, concepts, and measures of the field and their general association with mortality, but also introduces the reader to tables of healthy life, an extension of the conventional life table to the joint measurement of health and mortality.

The next two chapters explore natality, the second basic component of change, distinguishing those statistics derived from vital registration systems and those derived from census or survey data. Chapter 15, "Natality: Measures Based on Vital Statistics," by Sharon Estee, covers natality data from the first source. Chapter 16, "Natality: Measures Based on Censuses and Surveys," by Thomas Pullum, covers natality data from the second source. Chapter 17, "Reproductivity," by A. Dharmalingam, deals with those concepts and measures that link natality and mortality in the analysis of population growth, one phase of which is denominated population replacement. The third basic component of change, migration, is treated in the final two chapters of Part II of the book. The chapters distinguish the source/destination of the migration as foreign and domestic. These naturally fall under separate titles because of differences in sources, concepts, and methods. Chapter 18, "International Migration," by Barry Edmonston, and Margaret Michalowski, covers the first topic. Chapter 19, "Internal Migration and Short-Distance Mobility," by Peter Morrison, Thomas Bryan, and David Swanson, is concerned with domestic movements in geographic space.

The third part of the book covers the derivation and use of demographic materials that are not directly available from primary sources such as a census, survey, or registration system. This part comprises three chapters: Chapter 20, "Population Estimates," by Thomas Bryan; Chapter 21, "Population Projections," by M. V. George, Stanley Smith, David Swanson, and Jeffrey Tayman; and Chapter 22, "Methods for Statistically Underdeveloped Areas," by Carole Popoff and Dean Judson. The first two chapters build on reasonably acceptable demographic data from a variety of sources to develop estimates and projections. The third chapter sets forth the methods of deriving estimates and projections where the basic data are seriously defective or missing.

The final part of the book begins with four appendixes, which provide reference tables, general and specialized statistical and mathematical material, and, finally, specialized geographic material, designed to support the discussion in earlier chapters of the book. Appendix A, "Reference Tables for Constructing Abridged Life Tables," by George Hough, sets forth the reference tables for elaborating abridged life tables according to alternative formulas. Appendix B, "Model Life Tables," by C. M. Suchindran, sets forth the model tables of mortality, fertility, marriage, and population age distribution to support the discussions in Chapters 17 and 22. Appendix C, "Selected General Methods," by Dean Judson and Carole Popoff, describes general statistical and mathematical techniques needed to understand and apply many of the demographic techniques previously presented. Finally, Appendix D, "Geographic Information Systems," by Kathryn Bryan and Rob George, describe the specialized geographic methods for converting data into informational maps by computer.

Although the basic structure of this edition of *The Methods and Materials of Demography* and its five predecessors (the condensed version published by Academic Press in 1976 and the four printings of the original uncondensed version released by the U.S. Census Bureau, 1971, 1973, 1975, and 1980) remains the same, there are differences between this edition and the earlier ones. The first is the inclusion of new materials and new methods. Since the book in its various previous versions was released, the scope of demography, the sources of demographic data, and the methods have greatly expanded. It is not feasible in a single volume to present an exposition of this new material in detail, in addition to the basic materials and methods that must be covered if it is to serve as an introduction to the field. We have tried, however, to incorporate these new developments into the text insofar as feasible. We have already alluded to the developments in computer applications and geographic information systems (GIS). During the past three decades demographers have been busy tackling new issues, such as how "age," "period," and "cohort" effects interact in influencing variation and change in demographic and socioeconomic phenomena. While this issue is not confined to demographic phenomena, the cohort concept, linking a demographic characteristic or event and time, is central to the "demographic perspective." During the past several decades we have seen the flowering of mathematical demography and the development of "multistate" life tables of many kinds. This involves not only a considerable expansion in the application of the life-table concept to a wide array of demographic and socioeconomic characteristics, but a considerable expansion in the analytic products of such tables when the appropriate input data are available.

The need to find ways of filling the gaps or replacing defective demographic data for countries yet without adequate data collection systems has led to the development of model age schedules of fertility, marriage, and migration in addition to those for mortality and population previously available. The need to manage uncertainty in population estimates and projections has led to applications of decision theory, time series analysis, and probability theory to methods for setting confidence limits to estimates and projections—a process called stochastic demographic estimation and forecasting. There has been an expansion of the applications of demography in public health, local government planning, business and human resources planning, environmental issues, and traffic management. This expansion has helped to define the field of applied demography. The interplay of demography and a wide array of other applied disciplines has made its boundaries fuzzy but has given it a broad, even unlimited, field in which to apply demographic data, methods, and the "demographic perspective."

While the "demographic perspective" is largely a way of dealing with data, it is present when we (1) bring into play essentially demographic phenomena, such as population size, change in population numbers, numbers of births, deaths, and migration, and age/sex/race composition; (2) apply essentially demographic methods or tools, such as sex ratios, birth rates, probabilities of dying, and interstate migration rates, and their elaboration in the form of model tables, such as life tables, multistate tables, and model tables of fertility or marriage; (3) seek to measure and analyze how these demographic phenomena relate to one another and change over time, such as by cohort analysis or by analyzing the age-period-cohort interaction; and (4) construct broad theories as to the historical linkage or sequence of demographic phenomena, such as the theory of the demographic transition or theories accounting for internal migration flows. In these terms, the demographic perspective can be applied widely to serve a broad spectrum of applied disciplines as well as aid in interpreting broad historical movements. Burch (2001b) has stated that it is what we know about how populations work that makes demography unique. To a large degree, this knowledge is captured in the demographic perspective. It provides demographers with a framework within which data, models, and theory can be used to explain how populations work. As such, the perspective can contribute to the development of both models and theory, which Burch (2001a) and Keyfitz (1975), among others, argue is critical to the further development of demography as a science. The demographic perspective also aids in helping us to understand the implications of how populations work. That is, it furthers the aims of demography in its applied sense, not just its basic sense (Swanson *et al.*, 1996). As such, the demographic perspective is important to the further development of demography as an aid to practical decision making (Kintner and Swanson, 1994).

In addition to introducing new material, some reorganization of the book's original structure was carried out to reflect the changing concerns of demography and new technological developments. Chapter 14, "Health Demography," is new, and it reflects the growing interest in the interrelationship of health and demography, the recent application of demographic techniques to health data, and the emergence of the field of the demography of aging. Another example is Appendix D, "Geographic Information Systems," which deals with a technological innovation that occurred since the original version was written. In addition, some chapters in the original version were combined into single chapters. In the new edition, age composition and sex composition are combined, as are educational and economic characteristics. The book's reorganization is summarized in Table 1.1, which gives a "crosswalk" between chapters in the original (noncondensed) two-volume version of *The Methods and Materials of Demography*, last published by the Census Bureau in 1980 and this revision. It includes the names of the authors of the chapters in the original two-volume version published in 1971. The new authors had freedom to draw on the original texts insofar they deemed this useful in preparing the new texts; the extent to which they retained the original text was at their discretion. The inclusion of Table 1.1 is intended to obviate the need for attribution or co-authorship, given the variable retention of the original text by the current authors.

Although mentioned in several places in this book, one emerging area that we have not addressed in depth is the use of computer simulations in demographic analysis. This type of calculation has been receiving much attention recently and has the potential to be a powerful methodological development, but is so new that it is not yet possible to address it in detail. It has primarily been used as a tool for population projections (Smith, Tayman, and Swanson, 2001), but it has also received attention as a tool for theory building (Burch, 1999; Griffiths, Matthews, and Hinde, 2000; Wachter, Blackwell, and Hammel, 1997). Another area we have not addressed is demographic software. We decided against covering this topic in depth for several reasons. First, software technology seemed to be undergoing a period of rapid change as this volume was being prepared, and we were fearful that any specific demographic software we covered would be outdated by the time the book was published. The second reason is that we believed that the reader could implement any demographic method electronically, using standard, readily available spreadsheet and statistical software with only limited training and experience on computers. Third, we felt that, for the present purpose, it was more important to convey the logic of the methods rather than describe a device for accomplishing the result without thorough training as to its purpose and interpretation.

With respect to technological change, the reader should bear in mind that 30 years or so have passed since the original version of *The Methods and Materials of Demography* was first published (Shryock and Siegel, 1971) and 25 years have passed since the publication of the condensed version (Shryock and Siegel, as condensed by Stockwell, 1976). During this period, demography as a field of study, like other scientific disciplines and society in general, has been profoundly affected by technological change. In the 1970s, when the original and condensed editions were published, stand-alone mainframe computers run by "strange" computer languages were the norm. As both editors recall, these computers were found only in large institutions. This meant that access was profoundly limited and, even where possible, an often frustrating experience for a demographer because of the slow speed with which a demographic procedure could be carried out. Still, this was a major improvement over earlier days when an analytic procedure was carried out with electrical and mechanical calculators, and even paper and pencil. Today, networked personal computers run by easily grasped commands are the norm. They are found everywhere and access is virtually unlimited. Among other things, this means that demographers now have greater access to data and, with the expanded computing power, many types of demographic analyses can be done very quickly. The technological revolution, characterized by personal computers, online data sets, and tools for doing complex data analysis, has been responsible not only for methodological developments (e.g., computer simulation, which we discussed earlier in this section), but also for the diffusion of demographic data, materials, and methods. This trend is generally beneficial, but it can also contribute to an increase in the number of inadequately conducted analyses.

TABLE 1.1 Chapters in Original Two-Volume (Noncondensed) Version of *M&M*, by Author, Cross-Referenced to the Revised Edition of the Condensed Version

Chapter in original two-volume version of *M&M*		Corresponding chapter in revision	Author/co-author of original chapter
Preface		Preface	Henry S. Shryock & Jacob S. Siegel
1	Introduction	1	Henry S. Shryock
2	Basic Sources of Statistics	2	Henry S. Shryock
3	Collection & Processing of Demographic Data	3	Elizabeth Larmon, Robert Grove, & Robert Israel
4	Population Size	4	Henry S. Shryock
5	Population Distribution–Geographic Areas	5 & 6	Henry S. Shryock
6	Population Distribution–Classification of Residence	5 & 6	Henry S. Shryock
7	Sex Composition	7	Jacob S. Siegel
8	Age Composition	7	Jacob S. Siegel
9	Racial and Ethnic Composition	8	Henry S. Shryock
10	Marital Characteristics & Family Groups	9	Paul Glick
11	Educational Characteristics	10	Charles C. Nam
12	Economic Characteristics	10	Abram J. Jaffe
13	Population Change	11	Henry S. Shryock
14	Mortality	12	Jacob S. Siegel
15	The Life Table	13	Francisco Bayo & Jacob S. Siegel
		14 (Health Demography)	N/A
16	Natality: Measures Based on Vital Statistics	15	Jacob S. Siegel
17	Natality: Measures Based On Censuses and Surveys	16	Maria Davidson & Henry S. Shryock
18	Reproductivity	17	Maria Davidson & Henry S. Shryock
19	Marriage and Divorce	9	Charles Kindermann & Jacob S. Siegel
20	International Migration	18	Jacob S. Siegel
21	Internal Migration & Short-Distance Mobility	19	Henry S. Shryock
22	Selected General Methods	C	Wilson H. Grabill, John B. Forsythe, Margaret Gurney, & Jacob S. Siegel
23	Population Estimates	20	Jacob S. Siegel
24	Population Projections	21	Jacob S. Siegel
25	Some Methods of Estimation For Statistically Underdeveloped Areas	22	Paul Demeny
A	Methodology of Projections of Urban And Rural Population and Other Socio-Economic Characteristics of the Population	21	Jacob S. Siegel
B	Reference Tables For Constructing an Abridged Life Table by the Reed-Merrell Method	A	Francisco Bayo
C	Reference Tables of Interpolation Coefficients	C	Wilson H. Grabill & Jacob S. Siegel
D	Selected "West" Model Life Tables and Stable Population Tables, and Related Reference Tables	B	Paul Demeny
		D (GIS)	N/A
		Glossary/Demography Timeline	N/A
Subject/Author Index		Subject/Author Index	Rachel Johnson, Jacob S. Siegel, & Henry S. Shryock

We hope that this book will serve to reduce the frequency of such cases.

TARGET AUDIENCE

As described earlier, this book is aimed primarily at two groups. The first group comprises students in courses dealing with demographic methods. We believe that this book will be useful as the primary textbook focused on demographic methods. It will also be useful as supplementary reading or resource material for courses in which demography is covered in a short module. We believe that it is suitable for both graduate and upper-level undergraduate students. The second group at which this book is aimed comprises practitioners, both basic and applied, and persons working in a wide range of specialties in demography. This group includes not only demographers, but also sociologists, geographers, economists, city and regional planners, socioeconomic impact analysts, school-district planners, market analysts, and others with an interest in demography. We believe this book will give practitioners the tools they need to decide which data to use, which methods to apply, how best to apply them, for which problems to watch, and how to deal with unforeseen problems. Members of either of the two target groups should note that most of the book does not require a strong background in mathematics or statistics, although it assumes that readers have at least a basic knowledge of both subjects. Some chapters and appendixes, however, are quite mathematical or statistical in nature (i.e., Chapters 17 and 22, and Appendix C) and may require additional training and practice to comprehend fully.

References

Burch, T. 1999. "Computer Modelling of Theory: Explanation for the 21st Century." Discussion Paper No. 99-4. Population Studies Centre, University of Western Ontario, London, Canada.

Burch, T. 2001a. "Data, Models, Theory, and Reality: The Structure of Demographic Knowledge." Paper prepared for the workshop "Agent-Based Computational Demography." Max Planck Institute for Demographic Research, Rostock, Germany, February 21–23 (Revised draft, March 15).

Burch, T. 2001b. "Teaching the Fundamentals of Demography: A Model-Based Approach to Family and Fertility." Paper prepared for the seminar on Demographic Training in the Third Millennium, Rabat, Morocco, May 15–18 (Draft, January, 29).

California 1998. *County Population Projections with Race/Ethnic Detail.* By M. Heim and Associates. Sacramento, CA: State of California, Department of Finance.

Canada Statistics. 1994. *Population Projections for Canada, Provinces, and Territories, 1993–2016.* By M. V. George, M. J. Norris, F. Nault, S. Loh, and S. Dai. Catalogue No. 91-520. Ottawa, Canada: Demography Division, Statistics Canada.

DaVanzo, J., and P. Morrison. 1981. "Return and Other Sequences of Migration in the United States." *Demography* 18: 85–101.

George, M. V. 1999. "On the Use and Users of Demographic Projections in Canada". Joint ECE-EUROSTAT Workshop on Demographic Projections, Perugia, Italy, May 1999. ECE Working Paper No. 15, Geneva.

Greenwood, M. 1997. "Internal migration in developed countries." In M. Rosenzweig and O. Stark (Eds.), *Handbook of Population and Family Economics* (pp. 647–720). Amsterdam, The Netherlands: Elsevier Science Press.

Griffiths, P., Z. Matthews, and A. Hinde, 2000. "Understanding the Sex Ratio in India: A Simulation Approach." *Demography* 37: 477–488.

Keyfitz, N. 1975. "How Do We Know the Facts of Demography?" *Population and Development Review* 1: 267–288.

Kintner, H., and D. Swanson. 1994. "Estimating Vital Rates from Corporate Data Bases: How Long Will GM's Salaried Retirees Live?" In H. Kintner, T. Merrick, P. Morrison, and P. Voss (Eds.) *Demographics: A Casebook for Business and Government* (pp. 265–295). Boulder, CO: Westview Press.

Massey, D., R. Alarcon, R. Durand, and H. Gonzales. 1987. *Return to Aztlan: The Social Process of International Migration from Western Mexico.* Berkeley, CA: University of California Press.

Morrison, P. 2002. "The Evolving Role of Demography in the U.S. Business Arena." Paper presented at the 11th Biennial Conference of the Australian Population Association, Plenary Session on Population and Business, Sydney, Australia, October 2–4.

Shryock, H., J. Siegel, and Associates. 1971. *The Methods and Materials of Demography.* Washington, DC: U.S. Census Bureau/U.S. Government Printing Office.

Shryock, H., J. Siegel, and E. G. Stockwell. 1976. *The Methods and Materials of Demography,* Condensed Edition. New York: Academic Press.

Siegel, J. 2002. *Applied Demography: Applications to Business, Government, Law, and Public Policy.* New York, NY: Academic Press.

Smith, S., J. Tayman, and D. Swanson. 2001. *State and Local Population Projections: Methodology and Analysis.* New York: Kluwer Academic/Plenum Press.

Swanson, D., T. Burch, and L. Tedrow. 1996. "What Is Applied Demography?" *Population Research and Policy Review* 15 (December): 403–418.

U.S. Bureau of the Census. 1996. "Population Projections for States by Age, Sex, Race, and Hispanic Origin: 1995 to 2050." By P. Campbell. Report PPL-47. Washington, DC: U.S. Census Bureau.

Wachter, K, D. Blackwell, and E. A. Hammel. 1997. "Testing the Validity of Kinship Microsimulation." *Journal of Mathematical and Computer Modeling* 26: 89–104.

2

Basic Sources of Statistics

THOMAS BRYAN

To understand and analyze the topics and issues of demography, one must have access to appropriate statistics. The availability of demographic statistics has increased dramatically since the 1970s as a result of improved and expanded collection techniques, vast improvements in computing power, and the growth of the Internet.

Demographic statistics may be viewed as falling into two main categories: primary and secondary. Primary statistics are those that are the responsibility of the analyst and have been generated for a very specific purpose. The generation of primary statistics is usually very expensive and time-consuming. The advantages of primary data are that they are timely and may be created to meet very specific data needs. Secondary statistics differ in that they result from further analysis of statistics that have already been obtained. These are regarded as data disseminated via published reports, the Internet, worksheets, and professional papers. These data may be disseminated freely, as is the case with public records, or for a charge, as with data clearinghouses. Their benefit is that they generally save a great deal of time and cost. The drawback is that data are usually collected with a specific purpose in mind—sometimes creating bias. Additionally, secondary data are, by definition, old data (Stewart and Kamins, 1993, p. 2).

Statistics may be viewed as having two uses: descriptive and inferential. Descriptive statistics are a mass of data that may be used to describe a population or its characteristics. Inferential statistics, on the other hand, are a mass of data from which current or future inferences about a population or its characteristics may be drawn (Mendenhall, Ott, and Larson, 1974).

Whether the statistics are primary or secondary, or descriptive or inferential, the analyst must consider a number of issues. The first is validity, which asks, do the data accurately represent what they claim to measure? The next is reliability, which asks, are the data externally and internally measured

consistently? The third is that of data privacy and data suppression. As data users have acquired ever more sophisticated analytical techniques and computing power, resistance to access of private and government databases has been met. As the public faces a proliferation of requests for information about themselves and concerns mount about who may gain access to the information, resistance is building to participation in surveys and others data retrieval efforts (Duncan *et al.*, 1993, p. 271). In an era when theoretically "private" information about persons and their characteristics are easily available through legitimate data clearinghouses (as well as less reputable sources), the analyst must thoroughly consider whether the use of statistics is ethical, responsible, or in any way violates confidentiality or privacy.

These issues have come into focus with the advent of the Internet. In the electronic arena of the Internet, anyone can easily publish or access large quantities of social statistics. Unlike conventional publications and journals, these data can hardly be reviewed, monitored or regulated by the statistics professor. The challenge for the analyst, given the vast quantity and array of statistics available from official and unofficial sources on the Internet, is to be prudent in his or her selection of the appropriate statistics. This may be done by verifying the origin of the statistics, reviewing methods and materials used in creating the data, making determinations about the acceptable level of validity and reliability, then proceeding with considerations of ethical use and privacy. Analysts are warned to avoid unofficial statistical sources, as well as data that cannot be verified or are afforded no corresponding documentation.

TYPES OF SOURCES

The sources of demographic statistics are the published reports, unpublished worksheets, data sets, and so forth that are produced by official or private agencies through a variety of media. The sources may simply report primary statistics, or they may additionally include text that describes how the statistics are organized, and how the statistics were obtained, or an analysis that describes how valid or reliable the statistics are deemed to be. These sources may also contain descriptive or inferential material based on the statistics they contain. If the report is printed, descriptions or analysis of statistics may include graphical material, such as tables, charts, or illustrations. If the statistics have been released as part of an electronic package or are available on the Internet, it is oftentimes possible for the analyst to generate customized graphics, tables, or charts.

The same statistics may be selectively reproduced or rearranged in secondary sources such as compendia, statistical abstracts, and yearbooks. Other secondary sources that present some of these statistics are journals, textbooks, and research reports. Occasionally, a textbook or research report may include demographic statistics based on the unpublished tabulations of an official agency.

Many important demographic statistics are produced by combining census and vital statistics. Examples are vital rates, life tables, and population estimates and projections. Data gathered in population registers and other administrative records, such as immigration and emigration statistics, school enrollment, residential building permits, and registered voters, may also provide the basis for population estimates and other demographic analysis.

Primary Demographic Data and Statistics

Primary demographic data are most commonly gathered or aggregated at the national level. A country may have a central statistical office, or there may be separate agencies that take the census and compile the vital statistics. Even when both kinds of statistics emanate from the same agency, they are usually published in separate reports, reflecting the fact that censuses are customarily taken decennially or quinquennially and vital statistics are compiled annually or monthly.

In some countries, subnational areas such as provinces or states may have important responsibilities in conducting a census or operating a registration system. Data gathered by these regions may be for the sole use of the regions, or they may be gathered for a central national office. The central office may play a range of roles in the analysis and reporting of regional statistics, from simply collecting and reporting statistics that were tabulated in the provincial offices, to collecting the original records or abstracts and making its own tabulations. In either situation, both national and provincial offices may publish their own reports and tabulations. Statistics from different governmental sources may vary with respect to their arrangement, detail, and choice of derived figures. Moreover, what purport to be comparable

statistics may differ because of variations in classification or editing rules, varying definitions, or because of processing errors.

Demographic data may be collected either through censuses and surveys or through a population register. A population register in its complete form is a national system of continuous population accounting involving the recording of vital events and migrations as they occur in local communities. The purpose of the census or survey is simply to produce demographic statistics. The registration of vital events and population registers, on the other hand, may be at least as much directed toward the legal and administrative uses of its records. In fact, the compilation and publication of statistics from a population register may be rather minimal, partly because these activities tend to disturb the day-to-day operation of the register. Even though the equivalent of census statistics could be compiled from a population register, the countries with registers still find it necessary to conduct censuses through the usual method of enumerating all households simultaneously. This partial duplication of data-gathering is justified as a means of making sure that the register is working properly and of including additional items (characteristics) beyond those recorded in the register. There are often restrictions imposed on the public's access to the individual census or registration records in order to protect the privacy and interests of the persons concerned and to encourage complete and truthful reporting.

Statistics Produced from Combinations of Census and Registration Data

Some examples of data and measures based on combinations of population figures from a census with vital statistics were given earlier. Rates or ratios that have a vital event as the numerator and a population as the denominator are the most obvious type. The denominator may be a subpopulation, such as the number of men 65-to-69-years old (e.g., divided into the number of deaths occurring at that age) or the number of women 15-to-44-years old (e.g. divided into the total number of births). Moreover, the population may come from a sample survey or a population estimate, which in turn was based partly on past births and deaths.

Products of more complex combinations include current population estimates, life tables, net reproduction rates, estimates of net intercensal migration, and estimates of relative completeness of enumeration in successive censuses. The computation of population projections by the so-called component method starts with a population disaggregated by age and sex, mortality rates by age and sex, and fertility rates by age of mother. There may be a series of successive computations in which population and vital statistics are introduced at one or more stages.

All of these illustrative measures can be produced by the combination of statistics. A different approach is to relate the individual records. This is the approach taken in matching studies. By matching birth certificates, infant death certificates, and records of babies born in the corresponding period of time in the census, one can estimate both the proportion of births that were not registered and the proportion of infants who were not counted in the census. Other statistics of demographic value can be obtained by combining the information from the two sources for matched cases in order to obtain a greater number of characteristics for use in the computation of specific vital rates. For example, if educational attainment is recorded on the census schedule but is not called for on the death certificate, a matching study can yield mortality statistics for persons with various levels of educational attainment. When the same characteristic, such as age, is called for on both documents, the matching studies yield measures of the consistency of reporting.

In a country with a population register, matching studies with the census also can be carried out. Again, the resulting statistics could be either of the evaluative type or could produce cross-classifications of the population based on a greater number of characteristics than is possible from either source alone.

Secondary Sources

Secondary sources may be either official or unofficial and include a wide variety of textbooks, yearbooks, periodical journals, research reports, gazetteers, and atlases. In this section, only a few of the major sources of population statistics are mentioned. These statistics address the population and its components, as well as demographic aspects that can affect these elements, such as health and migration statistics.

International Data

Oftentimes demographic analysts are faced with the daunting task of gathering or relating information on a subject that they have never analyzed or on which they perhaps have limited knowledge of all possible sources. In these cases, it is best to pursue an index of statistics, which can provide information by subject, geography, author, or method. Many countries publish their own indices, while others provide a more comprehensive international perspective. An example is the *Index to International Statistics* (IIS), published by the U.S. Congressional Information Service. Begun in 1983, the IIS lists statistical publications on economics, industry, demography, and social statistics by international intergovernmental organizations, such as the United Nations, Organization for Economic Cooperation and Development, the European Union, the Organization of American States, commodity organizations, development banks, and other organizations. The United Nations also publishes *the Directory of International Statistics* (DIS). The directory is divided in two parts: The first part provides

statistics by subject matter and the second part provides an inventory of machine-readable databases of economic and social statistics by subject and by organization (United Nations, 1982a).

Additional indexes and resources may be accessed over the Internet. Conventions on the Internet may change over time, and hence the analyst is advised to use the references herein with caution.[1] If over time these addresses are modified, then the analyst is encouraged to use a "search engine" to find new addresses and reference material. Some of the best resources on the Internet are supported by the following three agencies: the United Nations (un.org), the Population Reference Bureau (prb.org), and the International Programs Center of the U.S. Census Bureau (census.gov/ipc/www).

Of all producers of secondary demographic statistics for the countries of the world, the United Nations is the most prolific. Its relevant publications include the following:

The *Demographic Yearbook* (published since 1948) presents basic population figures from censuses or estimates, and basic vital statistics yearly, and in every issue it features a special topic that is presented in more detail (e.g., natality statistics, mortality statistics, population distribution, population censuses, ethnic and economic characteristics of population, marriage and divorce statistics, population trends). Demographers, economists, public health workers, and sociologists have found the *Yearbook* a definitive source of demographic and population statistics. About 250 countries or regions are represented. The first group of tables comprises a world summary of basic demographic statistics. This summary is followed by statistics on the size, distribution, and trends in population, fertility, fetal mortality, infant and maternal mortality, and general mortality.

The *Statistical Yearbook* (published since 1948) contains fewer demographic series than the foregoing, but also includes four tables of manpower statistics. The *Yearbook*

---

[1] The Internet is a global collection of people and computers that are linked together. The Internet is physically a network of networks. It connects small computer networks by using a standard or common protocol (i.e. TCP/IP), which allows different networks worldwide to communicate with one another. Several important services are provided by the Internet. E-mail, allows users to send messages and electronic files via a computer that is connected to the Internet. File transfer protocol, or FTP, allows users to copy files from one Internet host computer to another. Telnet is a service that allows a user to connect to remote machines via the Internet network. Gopher is a program that allows a user to browse the resources of the Internet. The World Wide Web (www) is a graphics-based interface with which the user can access Internet resources through convenient "trails" of information. The development of the Internet through the 1990s has been rapid. With this growth, there has been no assurance that the Internet will maintain the same format or protocols for any period of time. Specific Internet addresses are given in this chapter in parenthesis, with a "www" precursor implied. To derive the most benefit from the Internet, analysts are encouraged to acquaint themselves with the organizations, concepts, and logic intrinsic to the Internet, rather than memorizing or referencing specific addresses.

is a comprehensive compendium of internationally comparable data for the analysis of socioeconomic development at the world, regional, and national levels. It provides data on the world economy, its structure, major trends, and current performance, as well as on issues such as world population, employment, inflation, production of energy, supply of food, external debt of developing countries, education, availability of dwellings, production of energy, development of new energy sources, and environmental pollution and management.

The *Population Bulletin* of the United Nations provides information periodically on population studies, gives a global perspective of demographic issues, and presents an analysis of the direct and indirect implications of population policy.

World Population Prospects provides population estimates and projections; it has been published irregularly since 1951. The most recent, *World Population Prospects: 1998 Revision*, presents population estimates from 1950 to 1995 and projections from 1995 to 2050. With the projection horizon extended to the year 2050, this publication presents a full century of demographic history/projections (1950–2050). Of the three parts, part I discusses fertility decline and highlights the demography of countries with economies in transition and the potential demographic impact of the AIDS epidemic in these countries, part II presents a world and regional overview of both historical and recent trends in population growth and their demographic components, and part III provides information on the more technical aspects of the population estimates and projections.

In addition to these international indices and compendia, numerous countries publish their own statistical abstracts, as seen in Appendix 1 (U.S. Bureau of the Census, 2003, p. 906). Several United States agencies also publish international population statistics. The primary U.S. producer is the Census Bureau. The International Programs Center (IPC), part of the Population Division of the U.S. Census Bureau, conducts demographic and socioeconomic studies and strengthens statistical development around the world through technical assistance, training, and production of software products. The IPC provides both published and unpublished reports, as well as interactive databases for numerous international demographic subjects, including the series listed here. Access to much of these data may be gained through the IPC website at census.gov/ipc/www.

The published reports of the IPC include the following:

World Population Profile, Series WP, published irregularly since 1985, presents a summary of world and demographic trends, with special topics (e.g., HIV/AIDS) and tables of data by region and country.
International Population Reports, Series IPC, (formerly P-95 and P-91) published irregularly, looks at different population topics in detail.

International Briefs, Series IB (formerly *Population Trends*, Series PPT) published irregularly, gives an overview of selected topics or countries.
Women in Development, Series WID, covers aspects of gender differentials.
Aging Trends, published irregularly, shows the impact of population aging on different countries.
Economic Profiles, published irregularly, focuses on the countries of the former Soviet Union. The profiles provide a description of the geography, population, and economy of the selected country.
Miscellaneous Reports

Unpublished reports of the IPC include the following:

Staff Papers, Series SP, published irregularly, examines subjects of special interest to the staff of the IPC.
Health Studies Research Notes, biannual publication, presents information on AIDS and HIV.
Eurasia Bulletin, published irregularly, examines and interprets new and existing data sets produced by statistical organizations of Eastern Europe, the former Soviet states, and Asia.

The International Data Base (IDB) is a computerized data bank containing statistical tables of demographic and socioeconomic data for all countries of the world. It is accessible through the IPC website. Data in the IDB are obtained from censuses and surveys (e.g., population by age and sex, labor force status, and marital status), from administrative records (e.g., registered births and deaths), or from the population estimates and projections produced by IPC. Where possible, data are obtained on urban/rural residence. These reported data are entered for available years from 1950 to the present. The U.S. Census Bureau analyzes the data and produces consistent estimates of fertility, mortality, migration, and population. Based on these analyses and on assumed future trends in fertility, mortality, and migration, population projections are made to the year 2050.

Of nongovernmental demographic and statistical resources, the Population Reference Bureau (PRB) is most prominent. Founded in 1929, the PRB is America's oldest population organization. The PRB, at PRB.org, publishes a monthly newsletter called *Population Today*, a quarterly titled the *Population Bulletin*, and the annual *World Population Data Sheet*. PRB also produces specialized publications covering population and public policy issues in the United States and in other countries.

The Population Association of America (PAA) is perhaps one of the best statistical resources and forums of discussion on international demography. The *Population Index*, which is published quarterly by the Office of Population Research at Princeton University (popindex.princeton.edu) for the PAA, has appeared since 1937. The editors and staff produce some 3500 annotated citations annually for the journal. The index covers all fields of interest to demographers, including historical demography, demographic and economic interrelations, research methlogy, and applied demography, as well as the core fields.

United States

As there are numerous data sources for the United States, it may be prudent for the analyst to review statistical indices prior to pursuing research and analysis. An example of such an index is the *American Statistics Index* (ASI), published annually, with monthly and quarterly updates, by the U.S. Congressional Information Service (CIS). The index is a comprehensive guide to statistical publications of the U.S. government. It features all publications that contain comparative tabular data, by geographic, economic, and demographic categories (Stewart and Kamins, 1993). Additional sources include the *Monthly Catalog of U.S. Government Publications* and the *Index to U.S. Government Periodicals*.

As with international statistics, there are also multiple indices and directories of United States statistics on the Internet. The Federal Technology Service maintains the "Government Information Xchange" on the Internet at info.gov; it links data users with resources from the federal government to local governments. The Federal Interagency Council on Statistical Policy maintains the Fedstats page on the Internet at fedstats.gov; it provides public access to statistics produced by more than 70 agencies in the United States federal government. Aside from these resources, searches for statistics may be conducted on the Internet using a search engine.

The U.S. Census Bureau is the most prolific producer of demographic statistics for the United States. It is commonly thought of only in the context of the primary statistics produced by the decennial census, but the U.S. Census Bureau is responsible for generating and publishing a great deal of demographic statistics of other types. These statistics are generally based on the series of ongoing surveys that it conducts. These include the Current Population Survey (CPS), the American Housing Survey (AHS), and the Survey of Income and Program Participation (SIPP), among others. The results of these surveys and other census data tabulations can be found in the following compendia:

Statistical Abstract of the United States. Published annually since 1878, the most comprehensive tabulation of statistics on the nation and states. Contains recent time series data at multiple geographic levels. Also includes "Guide to Sources," with references to statistical sources arranged alphabetically by subject.
County and City Data Book. Published approximately every 5 years since 1939, provides most recent population, housing, business, agriculture, and governmental data for small geographic areas.
State and Metropolitan Area Data Books. Patterned after the *County and City Data Book* and published in 1979, 1982, 1986, 1991, and 1998; provides state rankings for more than 1900 statistical items and metropolitan area rankings for 300 statistical items.
Congressional District Data Book. Similar to *County and City Data Book*, but provides data for congressional districts. Includes a congressional district atlas.
Access to these and other Census Bureau publications may be made by searching the Census Bureau's website at census.gov. For lists of publications, see the *Census Catalogue and Guide*, published quarterly.

CENSUSES AND SURVEYS

The distinction between a population census and a population survey is far from clear-cut. At one extreme, a complete national canvass of the population would always be recognized as a census. At the other extreme, a canvass of selected households in a village to describe their living conditions would probably be regarded as a social survey. But neither the mere use of sampling nor the size of the geographic area provides a universally recognized criterion. Most national censuses do aim at a complete count or listing of the inhabitants. Sampling is also used at one or more stages for purposes of efficiently collecting detailed characteristics of the entire population. When the U.S. Census Bureau, at the request and expense of the local government, takes a canvass of the population of a village with 100 inhabitants, it has no hesitation in calling the operation "a special census." The main objective of a population census is the determination of the number of inhabitants. The definition used by the United Nations is as follows: "A census of population may be defined as the total process of collecting, compiling, evaluating, analyzing and publishing or otherwise disseminating demographic, economic and social data pertaining, at a specified time, to all persons in a country or delimited part of a country" (United Nations 1998c, p. 3). In many modern population censuses, numerous questions are also asked about social and economic characteristics as well.

Most modern population censuses are associated with a housing census as well, which is defined by the United Nations as "the total process of collecting, compiling, evaluating, analyzing and publishing or otherwise disseminating statistical data pertaining, at a specified time, to all living quarters and occupants thereof in a country or in a well-delimited part of a country" (United Nations, 1998c, p. 3).

A survey, on the other hand, is a collection of standardized information from a specific population, or a sample from one, usually but not necessarily by means of questionnaire or interview (Robson, 1993, p. 49). The main purpose of a survey is to produce statistics about some aspects or characteristics of a study population (Fowler, 1993, p. 1). There are three distinct strands in the historical development of survey research: government/official statistics, academic/social research, and commercial/advertising research (Lyberg, 1997, pp. 1–2). Today, each brings to the field of surveys a unique perspective on approach, methods, errors, analysis, and conclusions.

The line between census and survey is further blurred by the concept of error. A census that failed to enumerate 100% of the population and its characteristics is, by definition, an incomplete census. Surveys have often been used in order to determine the amount of error in censuses. For example, following the 1991 population census in England and Wales, a census validation survey (CVS) was carried out to assess both the coverage and the quality of the census (Lyburg, 1997, p. 633). Similar evaluative measures were taken with the post-enumeration survey (PES) following the 1990 U.S. census and the Accuracy and Coverage Evaluation (ACE) Survey following the 2000 U.S. census.

The typical scope of a census or demographic survey is the size, distribution, and characteristics of the population. In countries without adequate registration of vital events, however, a population census or survey may include questions about births or deaths of household members in the period (usually the year) preceding the census. Moreover, even when vital statistics of good quality exist, the census or survey may include questions on fertility (e.g., children ever born, children still living, date of birth of each child) because the distribution of women by number of children ever born and by interval between successive births cannot be discovered from birth certificates.

Of special interest are the periodic national sample surveys of households that have been established in a number of countries. These may be conducted monthly, quarterly, or only annually. In some countries, they have been discontinued after one or two rounds because of financial or other problems. Usually the focus of these surveys is on employment status, housing and household characteristics, or consumer expenditures attributable to certain limited demographic characteristics, rather than the demographic information itself.

Both censuses and surveys have also tended to grow in the range of topics covered, in sophistication of procedures, in accuracy of results, and in the volume of statistics made available to the public.

History of Census Taking

Census taking began at least 5800 years ago in Egypt, Babylonia, China, Palestine, and Rome (Halacy, 1980, p. 1) Few of the results have survived, however. The counts of these early censuses were undertaken to determine fiscal, labor, and military obligations and were usually limited to heads of households, males of military age, taxpayers, or adult citizens. Women and children were seldom counted.

There may have been a Chinese census as early as 3000 BC, but only since 2300 BC have there been tax records and topographical data indicating the existence of formal records (Halacy, 1980, p. 17). The first of two enumerations mentioned in the Bible is assigned to the time of the Exodus, 1491 BC. The second was taken at the order of King David in 1017 BC. The Roman censuses, taken quinquennially, lasted about 800 years. Citizens and their property were inventoried for fiscal and military purposes. This enumeration was extended to the entire Roman Empire in 5 BC. The Domesday inquest ordered by William I of England in 1086 covered landholders and their holdings. The Middle Ages, however, were a period of retrogression in census taking throughout Europe, North Africa, and the Near East.

As Kingsley Davis pointed out, it is hard to say when the first census in the modern sense was undertaken since censuses were long deficient in some important respects (Davis, 1966, pp. 167–170). The implementation of a "first" census is obfuscated by conflicting definitions. Nouvelle France (later Quebec) and Acadia (later Nova Scotia) had enumerations between 1665 and 1754. In Europe, Sweden's census of 1749 is sometimes regarded as the first, but those in some of the Italian principalities (Naples, Sicily, etc.) go back into the 17th century. The clergy in the established Lutheran Church of Sweden had been compiling lists of parishioners for some years prior to the time when it was required to take annual (or later triennial) inventories. Whereas in Scandinavia this ecclesiastical function evolved into population registers and occasional censuses, the parish registers of baptisms, marriages, and burials in England evolved into a vital statistics system, as will be described later in this chapter.

Spain conducted its first true census in 1798, with England and France following shortly in 1801. Russia attempted a census in 1802, but failed to establish a working system until 1897. Though Norway had been performing population counts since 1769, its first complete census was not conducted until 1815. Greece soon followed, with a census in 1836, then Switzerland in 1860, and Italy in 1861.

In summary, the evolution of the modern census was a gradual one. The tradition of household canvasses or population registration often had to continue for a long time before the combination of public confidence, administrative experience, and technology could produce counts that met modern standards of completeness, accuracy, and simultaneity. Beginning with objectives of determining military, tax, and labor obligations, censuses in the 19th century changed their scope to meet other administrative needs as well as the needs of business, labor, education, and academic research. New items included on the census questionnaire reflected new problems confronting state and society.

International Censuses

In developing countries, the availability of data has improved greatly in recent decades. All countries have expanded and strengthened the capabilities of their statistical offices, including activities related to information on population. Most countries have started to take population censuses, as well as housing, agricultural, and industrial censuses (U.S. Census Bureau/Arriaga *et al.*, 1994, p. 1).

The classification and comparison of international censuses is a difficult task. Definitions of subjects, methods of data collection and aggregation, even language can all present problems in interpretation and use. The United Nations presents four major criteria for a census: individual enumeration, universality within a defined territory, simultaneity, and defined periodicity. Given these standards, there are valid reasons why some countries cannot strictly adhere to them and hence qualify as "census takers" (Goyer, 1980).

There are two excellent sources of international census statistics. The first is the Population Research Center (PRC) at the University of Texas. Founded in 1971, the PRC holds the results of over 80% of population censuses conducted worldwide. The PRC has an online international census catalog, available at prc.utexas.edu. The other comprehensive source of international census statistics is the *Handbooks of National Population Censuses* (Goyer and Domschke, 1983–1992). The handbooks provide a detailed analysis of the history of census taking in Latin America and the Caribbean, North America, Oceania, Europe, Asia, and Africa.

International Surveys

There are few true worldwide demographic surveys. The logistics of including all countries in a survey are simply too formidable. A few efforts exist, however. The World Fertility Survey (WFS), conducted by the International Statistics Institute (ISI), has reported cross-national summaries of fertility and other demographic characteristics from a wide range of countries since 1980.[2] Another well-known international survey program is the worldwide Demographic and Health Surveys Program. Funded by the U.S. Agency for International Development (USAID) and implemented by Macro International, Inc., the surveys are designed to collect data on fertility, family planning, and maternal and child health, and can be accessed through the Internet as well as

[2] Comparative studies are available through the International Statistical Institute, 428 Beatrixlaan, P.O. Box 950 2270 AZ, Voorburg, Netherlands.

in published reports. See info.usaid.gov and measureprogram.org. The DHS has provided technical assistance for more than 100 health-related surveys in Africa, Asia, the Near East, Latin America, and the Caribbean. Surveys are conducted by host-country institutions, usually government statistical offices.

Throughout the latter part of the past century, numerous health surveys related to particular health subjects and their effects (such as AIDS), as well as health studies particular to specific regions of the world, were taken. The analyst is encouraged to search the Internet or contact the agencies noted earlier for the latest information.

Demographic surveys around the world are reported by the United Nations in its *Sample Surveys of Current Interest* (United Nations, 1963). Surveys selected for the publication vary depending on the country or area represented, the subject represented, the amount of information provided, and the sample design. The publication is organized by country and subject matter, with detailed explanations of the surveys and their results.

Censuses in the United States

Population censuses developed relatively early in the United States. There were 25 colonial enumerations within what is now the United States, beginning with a census of Virginia in 1624–1625. The second census, however, did not take place until 1698. Colonial censuses continued throughout the New England and Mid-Atlantic area through 1767. Colonial censuses were distinguished from the first U.S. census in that they enumerated American Indians. Many colonies also enumerated blacks. The first census of the United States was conducted in 1790, and a scheduled round has never been missed since its inception.

Decennial Censuses

The U.S. census of population has been taken regularly every 10 years since 1790 and was one of the first to be started in modern times. At least as early as the 1940s, there have been demands for a quinquennial census of population—the frequency in a fair number of other countries—but so far no mid-decade census has ever been mandated and supported with appropriated funds by the Congress. The U.S. decennial census is currently mandated by the Constitution, Article I, Section 2, and authorized by Title 13 of the U.S. code, enacted on August 31, 1954.

Evolution of the Population Census Schedule

The area covered by the census included the advancing frontier within continental United States. Each outlying territory and possession has been included also, but the

TABLE 2.1   Questions Included in Each Population Census in the United States: 1790 to 2000

Census of 1790

Name of head of family, free white males 16 years and over, free white males under 16, free white females, slaves, other persons, and occupation 5 years ago, vocational training, and additional particulars designed to improve the classification of occupation.

Census of 1800

Name of head of family, if white, age and sex, race, slaves.

Census of 1810

Name of head of family, if white, age, sex, race, slaves.

Census of 1820

Name of head of family, age, sex, race, foreigner not naturalized, slaves, industry (agriculture, commerce, and manufactures).

Census of 1830

Name of head of family, age, sex, race, slaves, deaf and dumb, blind, foreigners not naturalized.

Census of 1840

Name of head of family, age, sex, race, slaves, number of deaf and dumb, number of blind, number of' insane and idiotic, whether in public or private charge, number of person in each family employed in each of six classes of industry and one of occupation, literacy, pensioners for Revolutionary or military service.

Census of 1850

Name, age, sex, race, whether deaf and dumb, blind, insane, or idiotic, value of real estate, occupation, place of birth, whether married within the year, school attendance: literacy, whether a pauper or convict.

Supplemental schedule: for slaves, public paupers, and criminals, persons who died during the year.

Census of 1860

Name, age, sex, race, value of real estate, value of personal estate, occupation, place of birth, whether married within the year, school attendance, literacy, whether deaf and dumb, blind, insane, idiotic, pauper, or convict.

Census of 1870

Name, age, sex, race, occupation, value of real estate, value of personal estate, place of birth, whether parents were foreign born, month of birth if born within the year, month of marriage if married within the year, school attendance, literacy, whether deaf and dumb, blind, insane, or idiotic, male citizens 21 and over, and number of such person denied the right to vote for other than rebellion.

Supplemental schedules: for persons who died during the year, paupers, prisoners.

Census 1880

Address, name, relationship to head of family, sex, race, age, marital status, month of birth if born within the census year, married within the year, occupation, number of months unemployed during year, sickness or temporary disability, whether blind, deaf and dumb, idiotic, insane, maimed, crippled, bedridden, or otherwise disabled, school attendance, literacy, place of birth of person and parents.

Supplemental schedules: for the Indian population, for persons who died during the year, insane, idiots, deaf-mutes, blind, homeless, children, prisoners, paupers, and indigent persons.

Census of 1890

Address, name, relationship to head of family, race, sex, age, marital status, number of families in house, number of persons in house, number of persons in family, whether a soldier, sailor or marine during Civil War (Union or Confederate) or widow of such a person, whether married during census year, for women, number of children born, and number now living, place of birth of person and parents, if foreign born, number of years in the United States, whether naturalized or whether naturalization papers had been taken out, profession, trade, or occupation, months unemployed during census year, months attended school during census year, literacy: whether able to speak English, and if not, language or dialect spoken, whether suffering from acute or chronic disease, with name of disease and length of time afflicted, whether defective in mind, sight, hearing, or speech, or whether crippled, maimed, or deformed, with name of defect whether a prisoner, convict, homeless child, or pauper, home rented or owned by head or member, of family, if owned by head or member, whether mortgaged, if head of family a farmer, whether farm rented or owned by him or member of his family, if owned, whether mortgaged, if mortgaged, post office address of owner.

Supplemental schedule: for the Indian population, for persons who died during the year, insane, feeble-minded and idiots, deaf, blind, diseased and physically defective, inmates of benevolent institutions, prisoners, paupers, and indigent persons, surviving soldiers, sailors, and marines, and widows of such, inmates of soldier's' homes.

Census of 1900

Address, name, relationship to head of family, sex, race, age, month and year of birth, marital status, number of years married, for women, number of children born and number now living, place of birth of person and parents, if foreign born, year of immigration to the United States, number of years in the United States, and whether naturalized, occupation, months not employed, months attended school during census year, literacy, ability to speak English.

Supplemental schedules: for the blind and for the deaf.

Census of 1910

Address, name, relationship to head of family, sex, race, age, marital status, number of years of present marriage, for women, number of children born and number now living, place of birth and mother tongue of person and parent, if foreign born, year of immigration, whether naturalized or alien, or whether able to speak English or if not, language spoken, occupation, industry, and class of worker, if an employee, whether out of work on census day, and number of weeks out of work during preceding year, literacy, school attendance, home owned or rented, if owned, whether mortgaged, whether farm or house, whether a survivor of Union or Confederate Army or Navy, whether blind or deaf and dumb.

Supplemental schedules: for the Indian population, blind, deaf, feeble-minded in institutions, insane in hospitals, paupers in almshouses, prisoners and juvenile delinquents in institutions.

Special notes: Not all of the 1910 census was indexed. Only the following states were indexed for 1910: Alabama, Arkansas, California, Florida, Georgia, Illinois, Kansas, Kentucky, Louisiana, Michigan, Mississippi, Missouri, North Carolina, Ohio, Oklahoma, Pennsylvania, South Carolina, Tennessee, Virginia, and West Virginia. Conspicuously absent are Massachusetts, New York, and a few other states in that area.

(continues)

TABLE 2.1 (*continued*)

Census of 1920

Address, name, relationship to head of family, sex, race, age, marital status, year of immigration to United States, whether naturalized and year of naturalization, school attendance, literacy, place of birth of person and parents, mother tongue of foreign born, ability to speak English, occupation, industry, and class of worker.

Supplemental schedule for blind and for the deaf.

Census of 1930

Address, name, relationship to head of family, sex, race, age, marital status, age at first marriage, home owned or rented, value or monthly rental, radio set, whether family lives on a farm, school attendance, literacy, place of birth of person and parents, if foreign born, language spoken in home before coming to United States, year of immigration, naturalization, ability to speak English, occupation, industry, and class of worker, whether at work previous day (or last regular working day), veteran status, for Indians, whether of full or mixed blood, and tribal affiliation.

Supplemental schedule: for gainful workers not at work on the day preceding the enumeration, blind and deaf-mutes.

(All inquiries in censuses from 1790 through 1930 were not asked of the entire population, only of applicable persons.)

Census of 1940

Information obtained from all persons: address, home owned or rented, value of monthly rental, whether on farm, name, relationship to head of household, sex, race, age, marital status, school or college attendance, educational attainment, place of birth, citizenship of foreign born, county, state, and town and village of residence 5 years ago and whether on a farm, employment status, if at work, whether in private or nonemergency government work, or in public emergency work (WPA, NYA, CCC, etc.), if in private or nonemergency government work, number of hours worked during week of March 24–30, if seeking work or on public emergency work, duration of employment, occupation, industry, and class of worker, number of weeks worked last year, wages and salary income last year and whether received other income of $50 or more.

Information obtained from 5% sample: Place of birth of parents, language spoken in home of earliest childhood, veteran status, which war or period of service, whether wife or widow of veteran, whether a child under 18 of a veteran and, if so, whether father is living, whether has Social Security number, and if so, whether deductions were made from all or part of wages or salary, occupation, industry, and class of worker, of women ever married—whether more than once, age at first marriage, and number of children ever born.

Supplemental schedule for infants born during the 4 months preceding the census.

Census of 1950

Information obtained from all persons: address, whether house is on farm, name, relationship to head of household, race, sex, age, marital status, place of birth, if foreign born, whether naturalized, employment status, hours worked in week preceding enumeration, occupation, industry, and class of worker.

Information obtained from 20% sample: whether living in same house a year ago, whether living on a farm a year ago, country of birth parents, educational attainment, school attendance, if looking for work, number of weeks, weeks worked last year, for each person and each family, earnings last year from wages and salary, from self-employment, other income last year, veteran status.

Supplemental schedule: for Americans overseas.

Information obtained from 31/3% sample: For persons who worked last year but not in current labor force: occupation, industry, and class of worker on last job, if ever married, whether married more than once, duration of present marital status, for women ever married, number of children ever born.

Supplemental schedules: for persons on Indian reservations, infants born in first three months of 1950, American overseas.

Special notes: The advent of the UNIVAC computer afforded the Census Bureau the opportunity to expand the sample from 5% to 20% of the total population.

Census of 1960

Information obtained from all persons: address, name, relationship to head of household, sex, race, month and year of birth, marital status.

Information obtained from 25% sample: Whether residence is on a farm, place of birth, if foreign born, language spoken in home before coming to United States, country of birth of parents, length of residence at present address, state, county, and city or town of residence 5 years ago, educational attainment, school or college attendance, and whether public or private school, whether married more than once and date of first marriage, for women ever married, number of children ever born, employment status, hours worked in week preceding enumeration, year last worked, occupation, industry, and class of worker, place of work—street address, which city or town (and whether in city limits or outside), county, state, zip code, means of transportation to work, weeks worked last year, earnings last year from wages and salary, from self-employment, other income last year, veteran status.

Supplemental schedule for Americans overseas.

Census of 1970

Information obtained from all persons: address, name, relationship to head of household, sex, race, age, month and year of birth, marital status, if American Indian, name of tribe.

Information obtained from 20% sample: Whether residence is on a farm, place of birth, educational attainment, for women, number of children ever born, employment status, hours worked in week preceding enumeration, year last worked, industry, occupation and class of worker, state or country of residence 5 years ago, activity 5 years ago, weeks worked last year, earnings last year from wages and salary, from self-employment, other income last year.

Information obtained from 15% sample: country of birth of parents, county, and city or town of residence 5 years ago (and whether in city limits or outside), length of residence at present address, language spoken in childhood home, school or college attendance, and whether public, parochial, or other private school, veteran status, place of work—street address, which city or town (and whether in city limits or outside), county, state, zip code, means of transportation to work.

Information obtained from 5% sample: whether of Spanish descent, citizenship, year of immigration, whether married more than once and date of first marriage, whether first marriage ended because of death of spouse, vocational training, for persons of working age, presence and duration of disability, industry, occupation, and class of worker 5 years ago.

Supplemental schedule: for Americans overseas.

(continues)

TABLE 2.1   *(continued)*

Census of 1980

Information obtained from all persons: address, name, relationship to head of household, sex, race, age, month and year of birth, marital status, if American Indian, name of tribe.

Information obtained from 15% sample: school enrollment, educational attainment, state or country of birth, citizenship and year immigrated, ancestry/ethnic origin, current language, year moved into residence, residence 5 years ago, major activity 5 years ago, veteran status, disability or handicap, children ever born, date of first marriage and whether terminated by death, current employment status, hours worked per week, place of employment, travel time to work, means of travel to work, carpool participation, whether looking for work (for unemployed).

Supplemental schedule: for Indian reservations.

Census of 1990

Information obtained from all persons: address, name, relationship to head of household, sex, race, age, marital status, and Hispanic origin.

Information obtained from 16% sample: school enrollment, educational attainment, state or country of birth, citizenship and year of entry, language spoken at home, ability to speak English, ancestry/ethnic origin, residence 5 years ago, veteran status/period served, disability, children ever born, current employment status, hours worked per week, place of employment, travel time to work, means of travel to work, persons in car pool, year last worked, industry/employer type, occupation/class of worker, self employment, weeks worked last year, total income by source.

Census of 2000

Information obtained from all persons: address, name, relationship to householder, sex, race, age, and Hispanic origin.

Information obtained from 15% sample: school enrollment, educational attainment, ancestry/ethnic origin, state or country of birth, citizenship and year of entry, language spoken at home, ability to speak English, residence 5 years ago, veteran status/period served, disability, grandparents as caregivers, children ever born, current employment status, hours worked per week, place of employment, travel time to work, means of travel to work, persons in car pool, industry/employer type, occupation/class of worker, self employment, weeks worked last year, total income by source.

statistics for these areas are mostly to be found in separate reports.[3] Beginning as a simple list of heads of households with a count of members in five demographic and social categories, the population census has developed into an inventory of many of the demographic, social, and economic characteristics of the American people.

A comprehensive account of the content of the population schedule at each census through 1990 is available from the Census Bureau (U.S. Census Bureau, 1989). A list of items included in each census through 2000 is given in Table 2.1. Two excellent cumulative lists of census publications exist. The first, *Dubesters*, lists all census publications from 1790 to 1945 (Cook, 1996). The second, the *Census Catalog and Guide*, covers subsequent years (U.S. Census Bureau 1985 and later).

The changing content of the population schedule has reflected the rise and wane of different public problems. Since the U.S. Constitution provided that representatives and direct taxes should be apportioned among the states "according to their respective numbers, which shall be determined by adding to the whole number of free persons excluding Indians not taxed, three-fifths of all other persons," early attention was directed to free blacks, slaves, and American Indians. The latter were not shown separately until 1870 and most were omitted until 1890. Increasing tabulation detail was obtained on age and race; but it was not until 1850 that single years of age and sex were reported

for whites, blacks, and mulattos. Interest in immigration was first reflected on the census schedule in 1820 in an item on "foreigners not naturalized"; but the peak of attention occurred in 1920 when there were questions on country of birth, country of birth of parents, citizenship, mother tongue, ability to speak English, year of immigration, and year of naturalization of the foreign born.

Attempts were made to collect vital statistics through the census before a national registration system was begun. Interest in public health led to a special schedule on mortality as early as 1850; but questions on marriages and births were carried on the population schedule itself, beginning in 1850 and 1870, respectively. A few questions on real property owned and on housing were included, beginning in 1850; but, with the advent of the concurrent housing census in 1940, such items were dropped from the population schedule. The topic, journey to work or "commuting," did not receive attention until 1960 when questions on place of work and means of transportation were included. New items added in the 1970 census included major activity and occupation five years earlier, vocational training, and additional particulars designed to improve the classification of occupation. Internal migration did not become a subject of inquiry until 1850 when state of birth was asked for, and it was not until 1940 that questions were carried on residence at a fixed date in the past. The first item on economic activity was obtained in 1820 ("number of persons engaged in agriculture," "number of persons engaged in commerce," "number of persons engaged in manufactures"). The items on economic characteristics have increased in number and

---

[3] Alaska and Hawaii, previously the subjects of separate reports, were included in the national population totals in the 1960 census (i.e., shortly after they became states).

detail; they have included some on wealth and, more recently, income. Education and veteran status were first recognized in 1840. Welfare interests in the defective, delinquent, and dependent were also recognized on the 1840 schedule. Such inquiries were expanded over the course of many decades and did not completely disappear from the main schedule until 1920. In 1970, again, an item on disability was introduced, and it was updated and improved in the 1980, 1990, and 2000 censuses.

Census 2000

Definitions of subjects used in the census are a reflection of the times. Changes in definitions are oftentimes necessary to make current terms and concepts more relevant. However, the changing of definitions must be done with caution, as census data are designed to be longitudinal—that is, comparable across time. A change in definitions cannot only be potentially confusing, but can make longitudinal definitions impossible. One example is that of race definitions and terms. The Office of Management and Budget (OMB) is responsible for the definition of race and race terminology. For Census 2000, the five major race categories included (1) American Indian or Alaska Native, (2) Asian, (3) black or African American, (4) Native Hawaiian or other Pacific Islander, and (5) white. In addition, respondents could identify themselves as Hispanic or Latino. The proliferation of interracial marriages in the latter part of the century has led to a considerable increase in the number of persons who could be considered to be of more than one race. In response to this, the OMB has not only refined the definitions of racial categories, but also decided to allow the use of multiple race categories in Census 2000. The benefit of this action is the opportunity for more individuals to accurately report their race. The drawback is that it will subdivide race into so many categories that it will be very difficult to compare the data with other census and survey data. Similar opportunities and drawbacks exist for the development of other census questions as well.

Questions currently asked by the census have been selected because they fill specific legislative requirements. The U.S. Census Bureau is central to this issue, not only because the Census Bureau asks questions many people consider personal, but also because proposals under serious consideration would allow the Census Bureau to use its authority to dip into other government records to gather population information. Many countries, including democratic nations, have long had population registers and/or national address registers to facilitate and even replace census taking, but the United States does not have such a register, in large part because of privacy concerns.

There has been rising public alarm over threats to privacy and confidentiality. These fears adversely affect people's perceptions of the U.S. Census Bureau. Persons in only 63%

of housing units promptly returned 1990 census questionnaires. This was below the 75% in 1980 and 78% in 1970. A Gallup poll taken a month before the census indicated that just 67% of Americans were fully or somewhat confident that census results would be kept confidential (Bryant and Dunn, 1995). By 2000 the return rate rose to 67%.

With the completion of the 2000 census, there are three broad areas with which users need to be acquainted to fully understand and effectively use the results: the geographic system, the structure of the data available, and the maps and geographic products available. These are fully described in the *Geographic Area Reference Manual* (U.S. Census Bureau, 2000a) and the *Introduction to Census 2000 Data Products* (U.S. Census Bureau, 2000b).

Data Products

The methods used for tabulating and disseminating data for Census 2000 differ significantly from previous censuses. For the first time, paper publications yield to electronic dissemination as the main census medium. Access to the Census 2000 data will be primarily through the "American Factfinder" at factfinder.census.gov on the Internet. The American Factfinder uses IBM parallel supercomputers, Oracle database capabilities, and ESRI geographic software to provide users with the capability to browse, search, and map data from many Census Bureau sources: the 1990 Population and Housing Censuses, the 1997 Economic Census, the American Community Survey, and Census 2000.

The union between the proposed Census 2000 data products and the American Factfinder can be depicted as a three-tiered pyramid (Figure 2.1). Each tier represents access to traditional types of census data as well as Census 2000 data. Each tier affords greater access to more detailed data while protecting confidentiality.

Most Census 2000 tabulations are also available on CD-ROMs or DVDs, with viewing software included, through the U.S. Census Bureau's Customer Services Center or by clicking "Catalog" on the U.S. Census Bureau's home page.

Data Available Electronically

Data available in an electronic format include the following:

1. *Census 2000 (P.L. 94–171), Redistricting Summary File.* These files contain the data necessary for local redistricting and include tabulations for 63 race categories, cross-tabulated by "Hispanic and not Hispanic" for the total population and the population 18 years old and over. Tabulations are available geographically down to the block level and are available electronically through the Internet and through two CD-ROM series (state and national files).

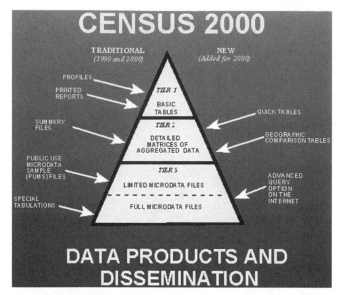

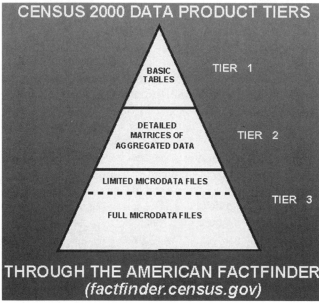

FIGURE 2.1

race and Hispanic-origin groups, as well as American Indians and Alaska Natives. The lowest geographic level in this file is the census tract, and there are minimum population-size thresholds before information is shown for a particular group.

4. *Summary File 3 (SF 3).* This file includes tabulations of the population and housing data collected from a sample of the population, with data provided down to the block group or census tract level. Data are also summarized at the ZCTA and congressional district levels.

5. *Summary File 4 (SF 4).* This file includes tabulations of the population and housing data collected from a sample of the population. As with SF 2, the tables in SF 4 are iterated for a selected list of detailed race and Hispanic-origin groups, as well as American Indians and Alaska Natives, and for ancestry groups.

6. *PUMS* (public use microdata samples). In addition to tables and summary files, microdata are also available. They enable advanced users to create their own customized tabulations and cross-tabulations of most population and housing subjects. There are two ways to access the microdata, through PUMS and the "advanced query function."

Even with the availability of voluminous printed and electronic publications, not all combinations and permutations of data are possible. To accommodate many specialized tabulations, the Census Bureau has provided microdata known as PUMS (public use microdata samples). PUMS data differ from summary data in that the basic unit of analysis for summary data is a specific geographic area, and for microdata the unit of analysis is an individual housing unit and the persons who live in it (U.S. Census Bureau, 1992).

PUMS contain records for a sample of housing units, with information on the characteristics of each unit and the people in it. The original PUMS data, however, are confidential until the unique identifiers of each record have been removed. Unusual data that could be attributed to a particular individual housing unit or person are also suppressed for confidentiality.

PUMS are taken from a unique geographic universe known as PUMAs, or public use microdata areas. The boundaries of PUMAs vary by state, but they are limited in that they must exceed 100,000 persons in a concentrated area. Two PUMS files are available; these represent samples of the 16% of households that completed the census long form, not samples of the entire population. These files are (1) a 1% sample: information for the nation and states, as well as substate areas where appropriate; and (2) a 5% sample: information for state and substate areas.

7. *Advanced query function.* The advanced query function in the American Factfinder is designed to help replace the Subject Summary Tape Files (SSTFs) and the Special Tabulation Program (STP) of the 1990 census. The advanced

2. *Summary File 1 (SF 1).* This file presents counts and basic cross-tabulations of information collected from all persons and housing units (i.e., 100% file). This includes age, sex, race, Hispanic origin, household relationship, and whether the residence is owned or rented. Data are available down to the block level for many tabulations and will be available at the census-tract level for others. Data are also summarized at other geographic levels, such as Zip Code Tabulation Areas (ZCTA) and congressional districts.

3. *Summary File 2 (SF 2).* This file also contains 100% population and housing unit characteristics, though the tables in this file are iterated for a selected list of detailed

query function will enable users to specify tabulations from the full microdata file, with safeguards and limitations to prevent disclosure of identifying information about individuals and housing units.

There are also two different files applicable to particular units in a geographic class rather than compilations for geographic levels per se. The first of these is the *Demographic Profiles*, which present demographic, social, economic, and housing characteristics. The second is the *Geographic Comparison Tables*, which contain population and housing characteristics for all geographic units in a specified parent area (e.g., all counties in a state).

Printed Reports

Though the scope of printed reports in 2000 is much smaller than in 1990, there are also three series of printed reports, with one report per state and a national summary volume. The report series are as follows:

1. *"Summary Population and Housing Characteristics" (PHC-1)*. This series presents 100% data on states, counties, places, and other areas. It is comparable to the 1990 Census CPH-1 series, "Summary Population and Housing Characteristics," and is available on the Internet.

2. *"Summary Social, Economic and Housing Characteristics" (PHC-2)*. This series includes tabulations of the population and housing data collected from a sample of the population for the same geographic areas as PHC-1, is comparable to the 1990 Census CPH-5 series, "Summary Social, Economic and Housing Characteristics," and is available on the Internet.

3. *"Population and Housing Unit Totals" (PHC-3)*. This series includes population and housing unit totals for Census 2000 as well as the 1990 and 1980 censuses. Information on area measurements and population density will is included. This series will include one printed report for each state plus a national report and is available on the Internet.

Maps and Geographic Products

To support the data and help users locate and identify geographic areas, a variety of geographic products are available. These products are available on the Internet, CD-ROM, DVD, and as print-on-demand products. These products include the following:

1. *TIGER/line files*. These files contain geographic boundaries and codes, streets, address ranges, and coordinates for use with geographic information systems (GIS). An online TIGER mapping utility is also available at census.gov.

2. *Census block maps*. These maps show the boundaries, names, and codes for American Indian or Alaska Native areas, Hawaiian home lands, states, counties, county subdivisions, places, census tracts, and census blocks.

3. *Census tract outline maps*. These county maps show the boundaries and numbers of census tracts and names of features underlying the boundaries. They also show the boundaries, names and codes for American Indian and Alaska Native areas, counties, county subdivisions, and places.

4. *Reference maps*. This series of reference maps shows the boundaries for tabulation areas including states, counties, American Indian reservations, county subdivisions (MCDs/CCDs), incorporated places, and census designated places. This series includes the state and county subdivision outline maps, urbanized area maps and metropolitan area maps.

5. *Generalized boundary files*. These files are designed for use in a geographic information system or similar mapping software and are available for most census geographic levels.

6. *Statistical maps*. Certain notable statistics are aggregated and presented in a special series of statistical maps.

Other Censuses: Special Federal Censuses

At the request and expense of local governments, many complete enumerations have been undertaken by the U.S. Census Bureau in postcensal periods. The local government almost invariably chooses to collect only the minimum types of information—name, relationship to the head of the household, sex, age, and race. A special census is usually taken to obtain a certified count for some fiscal purpose. Most of the special censuses are requested for cities; but counties, minor civil divisions, and annexations have also been covered and occasionally even an entire state. Results were published in *Current Population Reports*, Series P-28 (until 1985), and later in the PPL series.

Other Censuses: State and Local Censuses

The trend in the number of censuses taken by states and localities has been quite unlike the trend in the number of special censuses taken by the federal government. In or around 1905, 15 states took their own census; in 1915, 15 states; in 1925, 9 states; in or around 1935, 6 states; in 1945, 4 states; and in 1955 and 1965, only 2 states. The last survivors were Kansas and Massachusetts. Kansas needed its own census because legislative apportionment occurred in the ninth year of every decade, making it impossible to use federal decennial data. The Kansas census was abolished in 1979 after more than 100 years, but the constitutional requirement for a ninth-year reapportionment remained. A special law was enacted for a census in 1988, after which year the constitution was amended to revise the timing of reapportionment to the third year of each decade. Massachusetts also maintained a state census, conducted every 10 years in years ending with the number 5. After the last census was conducted in 1985, Massachusetts moved to abolish the state census and the change was ratified in 1990.

Censuses conducted by cities and other local governments are not currently, and never have been, very plentiful because of limited resources and considerable costs. Limited examples may be found in the State of California in the 1960s and 1970s. Rather, state and local agencies have worked with the Federal-State Cooperative for Population Estimates (FSCPE) to create necessary population and housing statistics. State representatives of the FSCPE supply selected input data for the Census Bureau's estimates program. Additionally, many members generate their own state, county, and subcounty estimates. The results of FSCPE estimates were historically published in the Census P-26 report series, but are now included in the Census P-25 series. Information on state and local agencies preparing population and housing estimates may be found in Census P-25 Series, No. 1063, or updates thereof.

Surveys in the United States

Compared to the situation in the other countries of the world, national sample surveys developed quite early in the United States. Government surveys are considered here first, followed by those conducted by private and academic survey organizations.

Government Surveys

The origins of U.S. Census Bureau surveys can be found in the Enumerative Check Census, taken as a part of the 1937 unemployment registration. During the latter half of the 1930s, the research staff of the Work Projects Administration (WPA) began developing techniques for measuring unemployment, first on a local-area basis and subsequently on a national basis. This research and the experience with the Enumerative Check Census led to the Sample Survey of Unemployment, which was started in March 1940 as a monthly activity by the WPA. In August 1942, responsibility for the Sample Survey of Unemployment was transferred to the U.S. Census Bureau, and in October 1943, the sample was thoroughly revised. In June 1947, it was renamed the Current Population Survey (CPS).

Today, the CPS is one of the most prominent demographic surveys. Estimates obtained from the CPS include employment, unemployment, earnings, hours of work, and other social, economic, and demographic indicators. CPS data are available for a variety of demographic characteristics including age, sex, race, and Hispanic origin. They are also available for occupation, industry, and class of worker. Supplemental questions to produce estimates on a variety of topics including marital status, school enrollment, educational attainment, mobility, household characteristics, income, previous work experience, health, and employee benefits are also often added to the regular CPS questionnaire (U.S. Bureau of Labor Statistics, 1998). Statistics are frequently released in official Bureau of Labor Statistics (BLS) publications, the Census Bureau's *Current Population Reports*, Series P-60, P-20, or P-23, or as part of numerous statistical compendia. The primary demographic data are released annually as a supplement. Additional supplements are available irregularly.

The special series of reports known as *Current Population Reports* usually present the results of national surveys and special studies by the U.S. Census Bureau:

P20, Population Characteristics. Intermittent summaries and analyses of trends in demographic characteristics in the United States.

P23, Special Studies. Intermittent publications on social and economic characteristics of the population of the United States and states.

P25, Population Estimates and Projections. Periodic estimates of the United States, states, counties, and incorporated areas; and projections of United States and subpopulations.

P26, Population estimates produced as a result of the Federal-State Cooperative Program for Population Estimates. Discontinued after 1988, and included with the P-25 series.

P28, Special Censuses. Reports of the results of special censuses taken by the Census Bureau in postcensal years at the request and expense of localities. No reports have been released in the series covering censuses taken since 1985, but listings of special census results appear for the later periods in the Population Paper Listing (PPL) series.

It should be noted that several of these reports may be discontinued in published paper format and may be presented entirely on the Internet.[4]

The U.S. Census Bureau also conducts other national surveys.[5] Among those most used is the American Housing

---

[4] Additional information on *Current Population Reports* may be found in the reports themselves (U.S. Census Bureau/Morris, 1996). The most recent publications may also be found on the Internet at census.gov/prod/www/titles.html#popspec.

[5] Principal demographic surveys conducted by the U.S. Census Bureau:

American Community Survey
American Housing Survey
Current Population Survey
Housing Vacancy Survey
National Health Interview Survey

Survey (AHS). AHS national data are collected every other year, and data for each of 47 selected metropolitan areas are collected about every 4 years, with an average of 12 metropolitan areas included each year. AHS survey data are ideal for measuring the flow of households through housing.

The most recent advance in Census Bureau surveys is the advent of the continuous measurement system (CMS). The CMS is a reengineering of the method for collecting the housing and socioeconomic data traditionally collected in the decennial census. It provides data every year instead of once in 10 years. It blends the strength of small area estimation from the census with the quality and timeliness of the current survey. Continuous measurement includes a large monthly survey, the American Community Survey (ACS), and additional estimates through the use of administrative records in statistical models. The ACS is in a developmental period that started in 1996. Beginning in 2003, over the course of each year, 3 million households are to be selected in the sample.

Data users have asked for timely data that provides consistent measures for all areas. Decennial sample data are out of date almost as soon as they are published (i.e., about 2 to 3 years after the census is taken), and their usefulness declines every year thereafter. Yet billions of government dollars are divided among jurisdictions and population groups each year on the basis of their socioeconomic profiles in the decennial census. The American Community Survey can identify rapid changes in an area's population and gives an up-to-date statistical picture when data users need it, not just once every 10 years. The ACS provides estimates of housing, social, and economic characteristics every year for all states, as well as for all cities, counties, metropolitan areas, and population groups of 65,000 persons or more. For smaller areas, it takes 2 to 5 years to sample a sufficient number of households for reliable results. Once the American Community Survey is in full operation, the multiyear estimates of characteristics will be updated each year for every governmental unit, for components of the population, and for census tracts and block groups.

The American Community Survey also screens for households with specific characteristics. These households

National Survey of Fishing, Hunting, and Wildlife-Associated Recreation
Residential Finance Survey
Survey of Income and Program Participation
Survey of Program Dynamics

Some economic surveys conducted by the U.S. Census Bureau:

Annual Retail Trade Survey
Annual Transportation Survey
Assets and Expenditures Survey
Business and Professional Classification Survey
Characteristics of Business Owners Survey
Monthly Retail Trade Survey
Monthly Wholesale Trade Survey
Women- and Minority-Owned Business Survey.

could be identified through the basic survey, or through the use of supplemental questions. Targeted households can then be candidates for follow-up interviews; this provides a more robust sampling frame for other surveys. Moreover, the prohibitively expensive screening interviews now required are no longer necessary.

The ACS provides more timely data for use in area estimation models that provide estimates of various special population groups for small geographic areas. In essence, detailed data from national household surveys (whose sample are too small to provide reliable estimates for states or localities) can be combined with data from the ACS to provide a new basis for creating population estimates for small geographic areas.

Finally, one of the largest national surveys conducted with assistance from the U.S. Census Bureau is the National Health Interview Survey (NHIS). The National Health Survey Act of 1956 provided for a continuing survey and special studies to secure accurate and current statistical information on the amount, distribution, and effects of illness and disability in the United States and the services rendered for or because of such conditions. The survey referred to in the act was initiated in July 1957 and is conducted by the Bureau of the Census on behalf of the National Center for Health Statistics (NCHS). Data are collected annually from approximately 43,000 households including about 106,000 persons. The survey is closely related to many other surveys sponsored or conducted by NCHS alone or jointly with the Census Bureau and private organizations.

Since most other federal agencies do not have their own national field organizations for conducting household surveys, they tend to turn to the U.S. Census Bureau as the collecting agency when social or economic data are needed for their research or administrative programs. In recent years such surveys have proliferated, partly in connection with programs in the fields of human resources, unemployment, health, education, and welfare. Federal grants have been made in large numbers to state and city agencies, and especially to universities, for surveys and research. Few of the surveys are concerned directly with population but they may include background questions on the demographic characteristics of the persons in the sample.

Research Surveys

There are a great many survey organizations in the United States, many of which conduct national sample surveys in which demographic data are collected. Demographic surveys conducted by universities in particular communities are legion, and their number grows at an accelerated pace. In recent years, other organizations such as Westat, Inc., and Macro, Inc., have stepped in to provide substantial research services as well. Most research surveys are funded, at least in part, by U.S. federal government agencies. Much of the data collected in these surveys is held in archives, such as the Inter-University Consortium for Political and Social Research (ICPSR) at the University of Michigan, and the Social Science Data Archives (SSDA) at Michigan State University and Yale University. Some of the larger survey research organizations are as follows:

1. The University of Chicago National Opinion Research Center (NORC) is an independent, not-for-profit research center that has been affiliated with the university for 50 years. NORC conducts more than 30 social surveys per year, including the General Social Survey (GSS) used in college and university teaching programs across the nation.

2. The University of Michigan Survey Research Center is part of the Institute for Social Research (ISR) at the University of Michigan and is the nation's longest-standing laboratory for interdisciplinary research in the social sciences (isr.umich.edu/src). It conducts, among other important work, two prominent surveys. The first is the Health, Retirement and Aging Survey (HRA), a result of the combination in 1998 of the Health and Retirement Study (HRS) and Asset and Health Dynamics Among the Oldest Old (AHEAD) and funded by the National Institute on Aging. The other is the Panel Study of Income Dynamics (PSID), funded by the National Science Foundation. Begun in 1968, the PSID is a longitudinal study of a representative sample of U.S. individuals and their family units.

3. The Ohio State University Center for Human Resource Research was founded in 1965 as a multidisciplinary research institution concerned with the problems associated with human resource development, conservation, and utilization. Among other substantial research work, the center has been responsible for the National Longitudinal Surveys of Labor Market Experience (NLS). The NLS began in 1965 when the U.S. Department of Labor contracted with the center to conduct longitudinal studies of labor market experience on four nationally representative groups of the U.S. civilian population. The project has involved repeated interviews of more than 35,000 U.S. residents, and it continues today.

4. The North Carolina Research Triangle Institute (RTI) is a nonprofit contract research organization located in North Carolina's Research Triangle Park (rti.org). RTI was established in 1958 by the University of North Carolina at Chapel Hill, Duke University, and North Carolina State University. Among numerous research projects, RTI's National Survey of Child and Adolescent Well-Being (NSCAW), sponsored by the U.S. Department of Health and Human Services, is the most prominent. The NSCAW is a 6-year study of 6000 children and adolescents who have come into contact with the child welfare system.

5. The University of Wisconsin-Madison Center for Demography and Ecology is another prominent national research center, whose largest responsibility has been to conduct the National Survey of Families and Households. The NSFH is a comprehensive, cross-sectional survey of 13,000 Americans in 1987–1988 and 1992–1994 (ssc.wisc.edu/nsfh).

6. Westat, Inc., has worked closely with numerous U.S. government agencies to conduct surveys, primarily in the areas of fertility, health, and military personnel. Ten American fertility surveys covering a 35-year period have been conducted by various organizations: the Growth of American Families in 1955 and 1960; the National Fertility Surveys in 1965, 1970, and 1975; the Princeton Fertility Survey (1957, with reinterviews in 1960 and 1963–1967); and the National Survey of Family Growth in 1973, 1976, 1982, and 1988. The latest of these surveys were sponsored by the National Center for Health Statistics (NCHS) and conducted by Westat. The most prominent national health studies Westat is involved in are the Continuing Survey of Food Intakes by Individuals and the National Health and Nutrition Examination Surveys (the latter also being sponsored by NCHS). Westat is also one of the few organizations that is responsible for gathering information on military personnel. It conducts the Communications and Enlistment Decision Studies/Youth Attitude Tracking Study and the Annual U.S. Army Reserve Troop Program Unit Soldier Survey.

Numerous other quality research organizations exist, and the analyst is encouraged to explore their work and become familiar with other national surveys not mentioned here.

REGISTRATION SYSTEMS

A registration system is the other common method for collecting demographic data. It differs from a census in that the registration system is conducted for both administrative and statistical uses and in other ways. For present purposes, a population registration system can be defined as "an individualized data system, that is, a mechanism of continuous recording, and/or of coordinated linkage, of selected information pertaining to each member of the resident population of a country in such a way to provide the possibility of determining up-to-date information concerning the size and characteristics of that population at selected time intervals." (United Nations, 1969).[6]

Definitions of the universal register, partial register, and vital statistics registration differ somewhat, but it is understood that the organization, as well as the operation, of all

[6] For a discussion of the various meanings of "civil registration" and the roles of local registration offices, ecclesiastical authorities, public health services, and so forth, see United Nations, *Handbook of Vital Statistics Systems and Methods* (1985).

are made official by having a legal basis. It must be noted also that the content, consistency, and completeness of population registration systems vary not only by country, but over time and within countries as well. Events such as war, famine, or even unusual prosperity that might last for short or long periods of time may create an impetus for greater or less registration or the linkage or destruction of existing records.

This chapter treats not only the possible statistics that are produced by registration of vital events and the recording of arrivals and departures at international boundaries, but also universal population registers and registers of parts of the population (e.g., workers employed in jobs covered by social insurance plans, aliens, members of the armed forces, voters). In most cases, one's name is inscribed in a register as the result of the occurrence of a certain event (e.g., birth, entering the country, attaining military age, entering gainful employment). Some registers are completed at a single date, some are repeated periodically, others are cumulative. The cumulative registers may be brought up to date by recording the occurrence of other events (e.g., death, migration, naturalization, retirement from the labor force).

History

The chronology of important events in the development of civil registration and of the vital statistics derived from it begins in antiquity. The earliest record of a register of households and persons comes from the Han dynasty of China during the 2nd century BC. The registration of households in Japan began much later, in the 7th century AD, during the Taika Restoration. It may be noted that the recording of marriages, christenings, and burials in parish registers developed as an ecclesiastical function in Christendom but gradually evolved into a secular system for the compulsory registration of births, marriages, deaths, and so on that extended to the population outside the country's established church. The 1532 English ordinance that required weekly "Bills of Mortality" to be compiled by the parish priests in London is a famous landmark. In 1538, every Anglican priest was required by civil law to make weekly entries in a register for weddings and baptisms as well as for burials, but these were not compiled into statistical totals for all of England. In fact, it was not until the Births, Marriages and Deaths Registration Act became effective in 1837 that these events were registered under civil auspices and a central records office was established. Meanwhile, the Council of Trent in 1563 made keeping of registers of marriages and baptisms a law of the Catholic Church, and registers were instituted not only in many European countries but also in their colonies in the New World.

Registration of vital events began relatively early in Protestant Scandinavia; the oldest parish register in Sweden goes back to 1608. Compulsory civil registration of births, deaths, stillbirths, and marriages was enacted in Finland (1628), Denmark (1646), Norway (1685), and Sweden (1686). The first regular publication of vital statistics by a government office is credited to William Farr, who was appointed compiler of abstracts in the General Register Office in 1839, shortly after England's Registration Act of 1837 went into effect.

For the Far East, Irene Taeuber's generalization that the great demographic tradition of that region is that of population registration may be cited (Taeuber, 1959, p. 261). This practice began in ancient China with the major function being the control of the population at the local level. Occasionally, the records would be summarized to successively higher levels to yield population totals and vital statistics. The family may be viewed as the basic social unit in this system of record keeping. In theory, a continuous population register should have resulted, but in practice, statistical controls were usually relatively weak and the compilations were either never made or they tended to languish in inaccessible archives.

The Chinese registration system diffused gradually to nearby lands. Until the present century, the statistics from this source were intended to cover only part of the total population and contained gross inaccuracies. Japan's adaptation of the Chinese system resulted in the *koseki*, or household registers. These had been in existence for more than a thousand years when, in 1721, an edict was issued that the numbers registered should be reported. Such compilations were made at 6-year intervals down to 1852 although certain relatively small classes of the population were omitted. Thus, this use of the population register parallels that in Scandinavia in the same centuries. The first census of Japan by means of a canvass of households was not attempted until 1920; it presumably resulted from the adoption of the Western practice that was then more than a century old. Fairly frequent compilations of populations and households were made in Korea during the Yi dynasty; the earliest was in 1395.

Vital Statistics

International View

According to the United Nations' *Handbook of Vital Statistics Methods*, "a vital statistics system can be defined as including the legal registration, statistical recording and reporting of the occurrence of, and the collection, compilation, analysis, presentation, and distribution of statistics pertaining to 'vital events', which in turn include live births, deaths, foetal deaths, marriages, divorces, adoptions, legitimations, recognitions, annulments, and legal separations" (United Nations, 1985). The end products of the system that are used by demographers are, of course, the vital statistics and not the legal issues of the document.[7]

Events Registered

As sugggesed earlier, events registered may include live births, deaths, fetal deaths (stillbirths), marriages, divorces, annulments, adoptions, legitimations, recognitions, and legal separations. Not all countries with a civil registration system register all these types of events or publish statistics on their numbers. Moreover, some types are of marginal interest to demographers. As is pointed out in the United Nations *Handbook*, other demographic events, such as migration and naturalization, are not generally considered part of the vital statistics system because they are not usually recorded by civil registration (United Nations, 1985). Moreover, these events are not considered "vital" events.[8]

Items on the Certificate

In discussing the items of information on the certificate or other statistical report of the vital event, those that are of demographic value and those that are of legal or medical value only may be distinguished. The former include the date of occurrence, the usual place of residence of the decedent or of the child's mother, age and sex of the decedent, sex of the child (birth), age and marital status of the mother, occupation of the father, order of the marriage (first, second, etc.), date of marriage for the divorce, and so on. The latter include such items as hour of birth, name of physician in attendance, name of person certifying the report, and date of registration. Some items such as weight at birth, period of gestation, and place of occurrence (instead of usual place of residence) are of marginal demographic utility but may be used in specialized studies.

Publications

Recommended annual tabulations of live births, deaths, fetal deaths, marriages, and divorces are outlined in the United Nations *Handbook of Vital Statistics* (United Nations, 1985). Rates and indexes, essential to even the most superficial demographic analysis, are also treated in the *Handbook* (United Nations, 1985). Inasmuch as many of the publications containing vital statistics also include other health statistics, the following discussion touches on both topics.

Compendia of world health statistics are prepared by the World Health Organization (WHO), a specialized agency of the United Nations. The WHO works in nearly 190 countries to coordinate programs aimed at solving health problems and the attainment of the highest possible level of health. Two important statistical periodicals are published by the WHO, *World Health Report* and *World Health Statistics*. Other important updates can be found on the WHO's Internet site at who.int.

The *World Health Report* annually presents detailed country-specific statistical data on mortality rates, causes of death, and other indicators of health trends at national and global levels. *Health statistics*, data for which are submitted to the WHO by national health and statistical offices, are compiled each year to help policy makers interpret changes over time and compare key indicators of health status in different countries.

World Health Statistics is a quarterly presenting intercountry comparisons together with information based on the assessment of trends over time. Articles also chart changes in such areas as morbidity and mortality, resource utilization, and the effectiveness of specific programs or interventions.

United States System: History

It has been mentioned that keeping records of baptisms, weddings, and burials was the function of the clergy in 17th century England. This practice was carried over to the English colonies in North America but was mostly pursued under secular auspices. As early as 1639, the judicial courts of the Massachusetts Bay Colony issued orders and decrees for the reporting of births, deaths, and marriages as part of an administrative-legal system, so that this colony may have been the first state in the Western world in which maintaining such records was a function of officers of the civil government (Wolfenden, 1954, pp. 22–23). Massachusetts also had the first state registration law (1842); but even under this program, registration was voluntary and incomplete. By 1865, deaths were fairly completely reported, however.

The other states gradually fell into line, and since 1919 all of the states have had birth and death records on file for their entire area even though registration was not complete. Several of the present states provided for compulsory registration while they were still territories. Most of the states and the District of Columbia now publish an annual or biennial report on vital statistics, but there is considerable variation in the scope and quality of these publications.

As previously mentioned, statistics of births and deaths (in the preceding year) were collected in some of the U.S. censuses of the latter half of the 19th century. Earlier in that century, the surgeon general of the army had begun a series of reports on mortality in the army (Willcox, 1933, p. 1). From the standpoint of civil registration systems, the role of

---

[7] The English-speaking reader should be aware that what is called "vital statistics" in English is roughly equivalent to the French "mouvement de la population" and the Italian "moviemento della popolazione." "Mouvement" is used in the sense of change, not migration.

[8] For a discussion of population and vital statistics, see United Nations, *Population and Vital Statistics Report*, 1998, Series A, Vol. L, No. 1, Department of Economic and Social Affairs.

the federal government begins with its setting up of the Death Registration Area in 1900. A comprehensive review of the history of the U.S. vital statistics system may be found in: *U.S. Vital Statistics System: Major Activities and Developments, 1950–95* (U.S. NCHS Hetzel, 1997).

It has been pointed out that the American system is fairly unusual in that states (and a few cities with independent registration systems) collect certificates of births and deaths from their local registrars and are paid to transmit copies to the federal government. In the beginning, the federal government recommended a model state law, obtained the adoption of standard certificates, and admitted states to the registration areas as they qualified. Only 10 states and the District of Columbia were in the original death registration area of 1900. The U.S. Census Bureau set up its birth registration area in 1915, with 10 states and the District of Columbia initially qualifying. In theory, 90% of deaths, or births, occurring in the state had to be registered; but ways of measuring performance were very crude. By 1933, all the present states except Alaska had been admitted to both registration areas. The territory of Alaska was admitted in 1950, the territory of Hawaii in 1917 for deaths and 1929 for births, Puerto Rico in 1932 for deaths and 1943 for births, and the Virgin Islands in 1924.

Historically, the registration of marriages and divorces in the United States has lagged even more than that of births and deaths. Indeed, national registration areas for marriages and divorces were not established until 1957 and 1958, respectively. The compilation of data on marriages and divorces by the federal government was discontinued in the mid-1990s and only national estimates of the marriage rate and divorce rate have been published in recent years by the National Center of Health Statistics. A complete discussion of the development of federal statistics on marriages and divorces in the United States may be found in *Vital Statistics of the United States* (U.S. National Center for Health Statistics, 1996).

Data on marriages and divorces are derived from complete counts of these events obtained from the states. From these counts, rates are computed for states, geographic divisions, regions, the registration area, and the United States as a whole. In fact, an annual national series, partly estimated, is available back to 1867 for marriages and to 1887 for divorces. Some of the underlying data represent marriage licenses issued rather than marriages performed. Characteristics of the persons concerned are obtained from samples of the original certificates filed in state offices.

United States System: Federal Publications

The primary federal publications on vital statistics in the United States are in the form of several series of annual reports. The U.S. Department of Health and Human Services (DHHS) is the United States government's principal agency for researching health issues. As a division of DHHS, the Centers for Disease Control and Prevention (cdc.gov) oversees 12 national agencies and programs, one of which is the National Center for Health Statistics (NCHS) (cdc.gov/nchswww).[9] The NCHS sponsors a number of national health surveys as well as state health statistics research. The NCHS is responsible for publishing provisional monthly vital statistics data and detailed final annual data. The volumes of mortality statistics began with 1900[10] and those of natality statistics with 1915. In 1937, the two series were fused into *Vital Statistics of the United States*. Inclusion of marriages and divorces in the bound annual volumes began in 1946 and ended with 1988 when NCHS stopped obtaining detailed data from the states. The last volumes of natality and mortality data were published in 1999 and 2002, respectively, with 1993 data. A reduced number of tabulations for subsequent years will be available electronically on CD-ROM. Additional tabulations are available on the Internet. Microdata files of births and deaths are also available on CD-ROM.

The organization of the annual reports is as follows:

Volume I: Natality
Volume II: Mortality
    Part A: General Mortality
    Part B: Geographic Detail for Mortality
Volume III: Marriage and Divorce

Volume I, Natality, is divided into four sections, Rates and Characteristics, Local Areas Statistics, Natality—Puerto Rico, the Virgin Islands (U.S.) and Guam, and Technical Appendix.

The two parts of Volume II, Mortality, are really continuous and are bound separately mainly because of the size of this volume. Part A contains seven sections, General Mortality, Infant Mortality, Fetal Mortality, Perinatal Deaths, Accidental Mortality, Life Tables, and Technical Appendix. Part B contains two sections, Section 8, Geographic Detail for Mortality, and Section 9, Puerto Rico, Virgin Islands (U.S.), and Guam.

Volume III, Marriage and Divorce, is divided into four sections, Marriages, Divorces, Puerto Rico and Virgin Islands (U.S.), and Technical Appendix.

---

[9] National Center for Chronic Disease Prevention and Health Promotion, National Center for Environmental Health, Office of Genetics and Disease Prevention, National Center for Health Statistics, National Center for HIV, STD, and TB Prevention, National Center for Infectious Diseases, National Center for Injury Prevention and Control, National Institute for Occupational Safety and Health, Epidemiology Program Office, Office of Global Health, Public Health Practice Program Office, and National Immunization Program.

[10] This is the year when the annual series began. Several States and cities had made transcripts of death certificates in 1880 and 1890 for use by the Census Bureau.

In addition to the *Vital Statistics of the United States*, the NCHS publishes two other series with voluminous vital statistics data for the United States and other countries. The first is the *National Vital Statistics Report* (previously the *Monthly Vital Statistics Report*), which has been published from January 1952 to the present. The report provides monthly and cumulative data on births, deaths, marriages, and divorces, and infant deaths for states and the United States. In addition, annual issues present preliminary and final data for states and the United States with brief analysis of the data.

The other set of publications is the *Vital and Health Statistics*, which has been published from 1963 to present. Containing 18 series of reports, this set of publications gives the results of numerous surveys, studies, and special data compilations. The series are as follows:

Series 1. Programs and Collection Procedures
Series 2. Data Evaluation and Methods Research
Series 3. Analytical and Epidemiological Studies
Series 4. Documents and Committee Reports
Series 5. International Vital and Health Statistics Reports
Series 6. Cognition and Survey Measurement
Series 10. Data from the National Health Interview Survey
Series 11. Data from the National Health Examination Survey, the National Health and Nutrition Examination Surveys, and the Hispanic Health and Nutrition Examination Survey
Series 12. Data from the Institutionalized Populations Surveys
Series 13. Data from the National Health Care Survey
Series 14. Data on Health Resources: Manpower and Facilities
Series 15. Data from Special Surveys
Series 16. Compilations of Advance Data from Vital and Health Statistics
Series 20. Data on Mortality
Series 21. Data on Natality, Marriage, and Divorce
Series 22. Data from the National Mortality and Mortality/Natality Surveys
Series 23. Data from the National Survey of Family Growth
Series 24. Compilations of Data on Natality, Mortality, Marriage, Divorce, and Induced Terminations of Pregnancy

Other Sources of Vital Statistics

Since some states and local governments were active in the field of vital statistics long before the federal government, it is not surprising that they also published the first reports. The state of Massachusetts inaugurated an annual report in 1843 (Gutman, 1959). Until 1949 the only tables giving the characteristics of brides and grooms were those published by a number of the states. A number of state health departments and state universities have also prepared and published life tables. On the whole, however, the annual reports on vital statistics published by state and city health departments do not represent a major additional source of demographic information. They are usually much less detailed than the federal reports. The corresponding figures in state and federal reports may differ somewhat because of such factors as the inclusion of more delayed certificates in the tabulations made in the state offices, different definitions and procedures, sampling errors when tabulations are restricted to a sample, and processing errors in either or both offices.

Another important nonfederal source of vital statistics in the United States is *Health and Healthcare in the United States* (Thomas, 1999). Providing summary data on all vital statistics components for county and metropolitan areas, *Health and Healthcare* provides both current estimates as well as projections of vital statistics.

Numerous religious institutions also track the vital statistics of their members and provide substantial insight into the characteristics of their members. For example, the Official Catholic Church Directory (annual) provides information on births, deaths, and marriages, the Catholic population, and the total population for each diocese.

Migration

Of the three demographic variables—fertility, mortality, and migration—procedures for the collection and tabulation of migration data are the least developed and standardized. As a result, there is a relative paucity of information on population movements between countries (i.e., international migration) and within the same country (i.e., internal migration) (United Nations, 1980). For countries without population registers, data on internal and international migration are difficult to obtain. International differences exist in defining what a migrant actually is, as well as in methods of collecting and tabulating the data necessary to generate migration statistics. Information regarding the number, sex, and ages of persons entering or leaving an area may be obtained from a census, population register, or border-control system. Migration is often measured, however, by using indirect information and methods, which may produce estimates with substantial error. Nevertheless, migration statistics are important for understanding the size and structure of a population in a defined place and time. Oftentimes, migration is the largest component of population change in an area and may transcend the other components of change.

International View

There has been a major shift in the direction of world migration in the past half century. Between 1845 and 1924, about 50 million migrants—mainly Europeans—settled permanently in the Western Hemisphere. In the past several decades the flows have become polarized on a north-south axis, with a majority of migrants coming from Asia, Latin America, and Africa. Though the preferred destinations are still the more developed countries, the rates of permanent migration to the more developed nations is stabilizing (United Nations 1982b, p. 3).

National governments often publish statistics on the basis of the records of immigrants arriving at and emigrants departing from the official ports of entry and stations on land borders. Migration statistics may also be generated from passports issued, local registers, and miscellaneous sources. All such records tend to be most complete and detailed for aliens arriving for purposes of settlement, and least so for the migration of the country's own citizens. Population registers of aliens may be of some value in studying immigration and emigration, assimilation through naturalization, and the characteristics of those foreign-born persons who have not become citizens. For the most part, a register mainly supplements other sources of information on these subjects (from the census and migration/border-control records).

The United Nations publishes information on the scope of international migration statistics, categories of international travelers, and types of organizational arrangements for collecting and processing data in this field (United Nations, 1980). The United Nations also produces detailed information on international migration policies, which affords the analyst an in-depth understanding of the role and characteristics of migrants around the world (United Nations, 1998b).

The United Nations *Demographic Yearbooks* carry numerous tables on international migration. Usually, statistics are given by countries, on major categories of arrivals and departures, long-term immigrants by country of last permanent residence, long-term emigrants by country of intended permanent residence, and long-term immigrants and emigrants by age and sex. The UN also regularly publishes specialized reports on the measurement of migration and reporting methods, as well as the results of research on individual countries.[11] Other valuable studies on migration have been conducted recently.[12]

[11] Two important United Nations publications on international migration are "National Data Sources and Programmes for Implementing the United Nations Recommendations on Statistics of International Migration." Series F, No. 37, 1986, and "Recommendations on Statistics of International Migration," Series M, No. 58, 1980.

[12] A valuable study of international migration was compiled by Charles B. Nam, William Serow, David Sly, and Robert Weller (Eds.) in 1990: *Handbook of International Migration*, Greenwood Press, New York. Detailed concepts of international migration are presented, with specific studies of Botswana, Brazil, Canada, China, Ecuador, Egypt, France, Germany, Guatemala, India, Indonesia, Israel, Italy, Japan, Kenya, the Netherlands, Poland, the Soviet Union, Thailand, the United Kingdom, and the United States. Another notable study is *International Handbook of Internal Migration*, Greenwood Press, New York, compiled by C.B. Nam, W. Serow, and S. Sly (Eds.) in 1990.

Perhaps one of the best sources of data on international migration is the Organisation for Economic Cooperation and Development (OECD.org), which comprises most industrialized countries, including the United States. Migration statistics are compiled, standardized, and compared annually for all member countries, giving the migration analyst one of the best portraits available of worldwide migration and migration internal to the member countries.

United States View

The history of U.S. migration statistics may be traced to the colonial period.[13] One of the more difficult types of population change to study is immigration and emigration, especially illegal migration. The U.S. Immigration and Naturalization Service (INS) (ins.usdoj.gov) is responsible for compiling data on alien immigration as well as on naturalizations in the United States. For purposes of classification, the INS divides those aliens coming to the United States from a foreign country into six categories and compiles statistics on all of them except one (U.S. INS, 1999):

1. *Immigrants.* Lawfully admitted persons who come to the United States for permanent residence, including persons arriving with that status and those adjusting to permanent residence after entry.
2. *Refugees.* Aliens who come to the United States to seek refuge from persecution abroad and who reside abroad.
3. *Asylees.* Aliens who come to the United States to seek refuge from persecution abroad and who are in the United States or at a U.S. port of entry.
4. *Nonimmigrant aliens.* Aliens who come to the United States for short periods for the specific purpose of visiting, studying, working for an international organization, and to carry on specific short-term business.
5. *Parolees.* Aliens temporarily admitted to the United States for urgent humanitarian reasons or to serve a

[13] There are only a few fragmentary statistics on immigration from abroad during the colonial period. The continuous series of federal statistics begins in 1820. The statistics were compiled by the Department of State from 1820 to 1874, by the Bureau of Statistics of the Treasury Department from 1867 to 1895, and by the Office or Bureau of Immigration, now the Immigration and Naturalization Service, from 1892 to the present, although publication was in abridged form or omitted from 1933 to 1942. Over this period, the coverage of the statistics has tended to become more complete, especially for immigrant aliens (those admitted for permanent residence). The series for emigrants began more recently—aliens deported (1892), aliens voluntarily departing (1927), and emigrant and nonemigrant aliens (1908). However, statistics on emigrant and nonemigrant aliens were discontinued in 1957 and 1956, respectively. For selected historical series and a good discussion of the development of the data, see U.S. Census Bureau, *Historical Statistics of the United States: Colonial Times to 1957*, 1960, pp. 48–66; *idem, Historical Statistics of the United States: Continuation to 1962 and Revisions*, 1965, pp. 10–11; Gertrude D. Krichefsky, "International Migration Statistics as Related to the United States," Part 1, *I and N Reporter*, 13(1): 8–15, July 1964.

significant public benefit, and required to leave when the conditions supporting their admission end.

6. *Illegal entrants.* Persons who have violated U.S. borders, overstayed their visas, or entered with illegally fabricated documents.

The INS also compiles information on naturalizations, and apprehensions and deportations of illegal aliens, and formerly compiled information on nonemigrant aliens.

The INS prepares numerous statistical studies on immigration and naturalizations. Data on legal immigration are compiled from immigrant visas issued by the U.S. Department of State and collected by INS officials at official ports of entry. (Aliens residing in the United States on whom legal residence ("adjustments") is conferred are also included in the immigrant statistics at the date of adjustment of status.) Data on visas and adjustments are collected by the INS Immigrant Data Capture (IMDAC) facility, yielding statistics on port of admission, type of admission, country of birth, last permanent residence, nationality, age, race, sex, marital status, occupation, original year and class of entry, and the state and zip code of intended residence.

The collection of statistics on emigrants was discontinued in 1957, and no national effort has been made to collect them since that year. Secondary statistics compiled in the United States and abroad suggest that the number of emigrants exceeded 100,000 per year between 1970 and 1990, and surpassed 200,000 every year in the 1990s. The U.S. Census Bureau currently uses an annual emigration figure of 222,000, representing both aliens and citizens, in the generation of national population estimates. This number, however, has typically been regarded as being substantially short of the actual volume of emigration.[14]

Just two publications of the Immigration and Naturalization Service provide the bulk of immigration statistics for the United States annually, and are available on the Internet at ins.usdoj.gov/stats/annual/fy96/index.html.

The *Statistical Yearbook of the Immigration and Naturalization Service*, published annually, is the most comprehensive publication on U.S. immigration statistics. Copies of each *Statistical Yearbook* (titled *Annual Report of the Immigration and Naturalization Service* prior to 1978) are available from 1965 to the current year. The 2000 report contains historical statistics on immigration and current statistics on arrivals and departures by month; immigrants by port of entry, classes under the immigration law, quota to which charged, country of last permanent residence, country of birth, state of intended residence, occupation, sex and age, and marital status; aliens previously admitted for a temporary stay whose status was changed to that of permanent residents;

refugees; temporary visitors; alien and citizen border-crossers over land boundaries; aliens excluded and deported by cause; aliens who reported under the alien address program and naturalizations by country of former allegiance, sex, age, marital status, occupation, and year of entry.

Another useful source of information on immigration is the *INS Immigration Reports*, which provide data on legal immigration to the United States and are available on the Internet at ins.usdoj.gov/stats/index.html. The format of the reports is as follows:

Section 1 Class of Admission

Table 1. Categories of Immigrants Subject to the Numerical Cap: Unadjusted and Fiscal Year Limits

Table 2. Immigrants Admitted by Major Category of Admission: Fiscal Years

---

Section 2 U.S. Residence

Table 3. Immigrants Admitted by State and Metropolitan Area of Intended Residence

Table 4. Immigrants Admitted by Major Category of Admission and State and Metropolitan Area of Intended Residence: Fiscal Year

---

Section 3 Region and Country of Origin

Table 5. Immigrants Admitted by Region and Selected Country of Birth: Fiscal Years

Table 6. Immigrants Admitted by Major Category of Admission and Region and Selected Country of Birth: Fiscal Year

Table 7. Immigrants Admitted by Selected State of Intended Residence and Country of Birth: Fiscal Year

---

Section 4 Age and Sex

Table 8. Immigrants Admitted by Sex and Age: Fiscal Years

Table 9. Immigrants Admitted by Major Category of Admission, Sex, and Age: Fiscal Year

---

Section 5 Occupation

Table 10. Immigrants Aged 16 to 64 Admitted by Occupation: Fiscal Years

Table 11. Immigrants Aged 16 to 64 Admitted by Major Category of Admission and Occupation: Fiscal Year

Table 12. Immigrants Aged 16 to 64 Admitted as Employment-Based Principals by Occupation: Fiscal Year

---

Other specialized reports are published irregularly as bulletins.

Internal Migration

Internal migration statistics for the United States have primarily been generated by decennial censuses, national surveys, and administrative records. While numerous state and regional studies have been conducted on the basis of these sources, it has been the responsibility of the U.S. Census Bureau to provide comprehensive and standardized migration statistics for the U.S. and subareas.

The decennial census has primarily been relied upon in two ways to provide migration statistics. First, general data collected by the census can be used to calculate migration

---

[14] For additional information on emigration, see Robert Warren and Ellen Percy Kraly, "The Elusive Exodus: Emigration from the United States," *Population Trends and Public Policy Paper*, No. 8, March, 1985, Washington, DC: Population Reference Bureau.

statistics.[15] Second, specific questions are contained in the census to determine migration patterns in relation to various population characteristics. These questions can include place of birth, place of residence 1 year ago or 5 years ago, and year moved to current residence.

Intercensal migration patterns are also measured by national surveys and administrative records. The main survey used to track migration in the United States is the Current Population Survey (CPS). The CPS presents information on the mobility of the U.S. population one year earlier. Data are provided for nonmovers; movers within counties, migrants between counties, states, and regions; migrants from abroad; movers within and between metropolitan and nonmetropolitan areas; and movers with and between central cities and suburbs of metropolitan areas. CPS data are released as part of the P-20 *Current Population Reports* series and are also available on the Internet at bls.census.gov/cps.

Another survey used for tracking intercensal migration is the Survey of Income and Program Participation (SIPP). First implemented in 1983, SIPP is a longitudinal survey of the noninstitutionalized population of the United States. Each SIPP panel also includes a topical module covering migration history. Though specific migration questions have varied from panel to panel, each migration history module has included questions on month and year of most recent and previous move, as well as the location of previous residences and place of birth. Data are available for nonmovers, movers within and between counties (though specific counties are not identified), movers between states, and movers from abroad. Some earlier modules contained questions on reasons for migration. SIPP data are released as special reports in the Census Bureau's P-70 *Current Population* Reports series.

Administrative records may also be used to measure migration. For example, the Census Bureau receives confidential Internal Revenue Service data on tax returns. After being stripped of the most sensitive data, the individual returns are linked to a county record and used to measure movement from year to year.

Population Registers

The United Nations definition of a population register as given earlier may be regarded as the "ideal type," to which some of the national registers described are only approximations (United Nations, 1998a). Population registers are built up from a base inventory of the population and its characteristics in an area, continuously supplanted by data on births, deaths, adoptions, legitimations, marriages, divorces, and changes of occupation, name, or address.

[15] The population component estimating equation, representing the relation between population at two dates and the demographic components of change during the intermediate period may be used. (See Chapter 19 of this volume and Alan Brown and Egon Neuberger, *Internal Migration*, Academic Press, New York, 1977, p. 105.)

The universal population register should be distinguished from official registers of parts of the population. It is true that the modern universal registers may have evolved from registers that excluded certain classes of the population (members of the nobility, etc.), but the intent of the modern registers is usually to cover all age and sex groups, all ethnic groups, all social classes, and so on. The partial registers, on the other hand, are established for specific administrative purposes and cover only those persons directly affected by the particular program. Examples are registers of workers or other persons covered by national social insurance schemes, of males eligible for compulsory military service, of persons registered as eligible to vote, of aliens, and of licensed automobile drivers. Most such registers are continuous, but some are periodic or exist only during a particular emergency. For example, there have been wartime registrations for the rationing of consumer goods. These may indeed include all or nearly all of the people; but, unlike the universal registers, they are temporary rather than permanent.

The UN has documented the history of population registers, their uses, general features (coverage, documents, information recorded, and administrative control), and their accuracy in their *Handbook on Civil Registration and Vital Statistics Systems* (United Nations, 1998a). It lists, by countries, both the date of establishment of the original register and the date of establishment of the register as then organized. This list, however, also contains a number of "partial registers" including some that exclude half or more of the population.

Universal Registers

The universal population register is now the least common, yet most comprehensive and timely statistical collection method. Until the 20th century, it flourished in only two widely separated regions—Northwestern Europe (mainly Scandinavia) and the Far East. The data from population registers are often available in separate sections because of many legal limitations and regulations, for example, personal privacy protection.

Population registers have historically been established primarily for identification, control, and police purposes, and often little use has been made of them for the compilation of population statistics. In a number of countries, data from the registers are used to produce one or more of the following: (1) current estimates of population for provinces and local areas, (2) statistics of internal migration and international migration, (3) vital statistics. Today, however, registers are used more expansively for such things as policy analysis and justifying the need for development of social services such as health care and education. Because of the prohibitively high cost of population and housing censuses, and even some statistical surveys, countries with population registers are experimenting with methods of combining their registers with other administrative records to conduct and improve their decennial censuses.

Currently, registers are maintained in Denmark, Finland, Japan, Norway, the Netherlands, Sweden, Bahrain, Kuwait, and Singapore. A substantial effort to conduct a registration system was once made in China, but essentially discontinued. China attempted to establish a population register based on domicile registration. This includes registration of total population, births, deaths, immigration, emigration, and changes in domiciles. When compared with census data, the registration data were shown to be inaccurate. China today relies on a decennial census and sample surveys to determine its population size and its characteristics. The Scandinavian countries all have historically established and well-developed central population registers, with personal identification numbers and unified coding systems for their populations. Bahrain also has a central registration system. In 1991, Bahrain conducted a national census and asked the enumerators to update the records of registration—essentially using one source to check the other. Kuwait had a relatively good population register before the 1991 Gulf War, though its future is uncertain. Singapore currently maintains an ongoing population register. As mandated by the National Registration Act of 1965, all persons who reside in Singapore are required to be registered and must file a notification of change of residence. The system is not, however, used in conjunction with or for the production of census data. Numerous other countries have lesser or noncentralized population registration systems.

Partial Registers

As indicated earlier, partial registers are set up for specific administrative programs and cover only those persons directly affected by the particular program or belonging to a particular group. Examples are registers of workers or other persons covered by national social insurance programs, of males subject to compulsory military service, of registered voters, and of licensed automobile drivers. Most such registers are continuous, but some are periodic or exist only during a particular crisis. For example, there have been wartime registrations for the rationing of consumer goods. These may indeed include all or nearly all of the papulation; but unlike the universal registers, they are temporary rather than permanent. It is best to consider each type of partial register separately for the international arena and the United States since the various types do not have many features in common.

Partial Registers: International Partial Registers

A wide variety of partial registers are maintained in different countries. The following are the most common:

1. *Social insurance and welfare.* Modern social insurance and social welfare systems (unemployment, retirement, sickness, public assistance, family allowances, etc.) had their origins in Europe and the British Dominions in the latter half of the 19th century. From the millions of records accumulated, statistics are compiled for administrative purposes. Some of these tables are of demographic interest, especially those relating to employment, unemployment, the aged, widows and orphans, mortality (including life tables for the population covered by certain programs), and births. From these records, moreover, special tabulations with a demographic orientation can be made; frequently such tabulations are based on a sample of the records. Finally, the statistics may be used in the preparation of population estimates or estimates of the total labor force. Likewise, life tables for a "covered" population may be used to estimate corresponding life tables for the total population.

Current social insurance and welfare systems vary widely in their administration and benefits, and this can substantially affect the quality of the data. In countries such as Finland, which also has a central universal register, the benefits and services included are universal entitlements. Accordingly, a person can receive benefits and services even if he or she has not been employed, is not married to an employed person, and does not have special insurance coverage.

Some countries, such as Ireland, have unilateral agreement with other countries. These agreements protect the pension entitlements of Irish people who go to work in these countries and they protect workers from those countries who work in Ireland. They allow periods of residence, that are completed in one country to be taken into account by the other country so that the worker may get a pension. These arrangements not only afford equitable disbursement of social benefits, but also can be used to create statistics of international labor and migration flows. Other countries that have little or no social insurance have few resulting data.

2. *Military service.* Countries that have compulsory military service ordinarily provide for the registration of persons attaining military age, and the person's record is maintained in the register until he passes beyond the prescribed maximum age. The U.S. Central Intelligence Agency (CIA) provides military manpower statistics annually in its world factbook (odci.gov/cia/publications/factbook/index.html). Data on current military manpower, the availability of males and females aged 15 to 49, those fit for military service, and those reaching military age annually, are presented for all countries. The University of Michigan serves as a comprehensive resource on military manpower around the world via its Internet page at henry.ugl.lib.umich.edu/libhome/Documents.center.

3. *Consumer rationing.* Rationing of food, articles of clothing, gasoline, and other consumer goods ordinarily represents an emergency national program in time of war, famine, and so on. Hence, registration of the population for rationing purposes is not to be considered as a permanent

source of demographic statistics. Nonetheless, some rationing programs have continued for a number of years, and important demographic uses have been made of the records. There are sometimes problems in the form of exempt classes and illegal behavior (e.g., duplicate registration, failure to notify the authorities of a death or removal); but these are often small and appropriate adjustments can be made in the statistics.

4. *Voters.* In countries where voting is compulsory for adults or where a very high proportion of all adults are registered as eligible voters, statistics of demographic value may be compiled. For example, in Brazil everyone eligible must vote. A certicate of proof of recent voting is one of the required legal documents for several situations, including simply getting a job. In other cases, even if a very high proportion of all adults are registered as eligible voters, little useful information may be derived from voting statistics as a result of national circumstances. In 1998, after a bitter civil war, Bosnia conducted national elections that were classified universally as the most complicated in this century, with more than 30 political parties and nearly 3500 candidates. Because many voting stations were located in "enemy" territory, many people were simply too fearful to cast their votes. Such challenges as voting irregularity, fraud, and the omission of data face the analyst when considering the use of voting registration data.

5. *School enrollment and school censuses.* School records management is an integral part of a local information system and hence forms part of a national information system. Data on school enrollment are important for measuring academic achievement and providing national school-age statistics for policy analysis and resource allocation. Most developed countries collect statistics of registered students according to grade—less often according to age—and often tabulate the demographic characteristics, geographic origin, and achievement of the students.

The primary source of international statistics on education is the United Nations Educational, Scientific and Cultural Organization (UNESCO). The UNESCO yearbook provides annual information on a wide range of educational statistics for the countries of the world. Selected educational statistics are available at the UNESCO site on the Internet at unesco.org.

The quality of international education statistics varies widely. Many developing countries have received assistance in developing a national education statistics system. For example, the Association for the Development of Education in Africa recently developed the National Education Statistical Information System (NESIS) in Sub-Saharan Africa and served first to create educational statistical systems in Ethiopia and Zambia based on sophisticated relational databases. Information about it is available on the Internet at nesis.easynet.fr. Other nations, which have established population registers, have chosen to arrange their data according to educational characteristics. For example, in 1985 Sweden initiated an education register, which comprises the 15- to 74-year-old population. Coordinated by Statistics Sweden (scb.se/scbeng/amhtm/ameng.htm), the system uses the National Identification Number to link key demographic and education data. The main demographic variables tabulated are age, sex, municipality of residence, country of birth, and citizenship. These variables are cross-tabulated with the education variables: highest education completed, completion year, and municipality of completion.

Since school census statistics are sometimes substituted for school enrollment statistics in making population estimates, this source is mentioned here. The school census is really a partial census rather than a register, however. There is a canvass of households either by direct interview or by means of forms sent home through the school children. Often the preschool children as well as the children of compulsory school age are covered.

6. *Judicial system.* Many developed countries employ rigorous registration of those involved in the judicial system, especially those regarded as being the most iniquitous. Extensive details about them, including social, economic, and physical characteristics, are recorded in comprehensive databases and communication networks. While most data are kept confidential, detailed characteristics of those involved in judicial systems are often tabulated, summarized, and published. These data may be used for both general demographic analysis as well as for describing the characteristics of the judicial system. As the judicial systems of individual countries widely vary, so too do judicial registration systems.

Partial Registers: U.S. Partial Registers

Although the United States has never had a universal population register, it has had several types of partial registers:

1. *Social insurance and welfare.* The U.S. social insurance and welfare program encompasses broad-based public systems for insuring workers and their families against insecurity caused by loss of income, the cost of health care, and retirement. The primary programs are Social Security, Medicare/Medicaid, workers' compensation, and unemployment insurance. In 1935, the Social Security Act was enacted to subsidize the retirement income of the elderly. Old-Age, Survivors, Disability Insurance, and Hospital Insurance, also known as OASDI and HI, are now parts of the program. As of 2000, there were over 45 million beneficiaries of the OASDI program. The program of health insurance for the elderly (Medicare-HI and SMI) in the United States affords statistics on registered persons 65 years old and over by county of residence beginning with 1966. Medicaid is a state-financed program of free medical care for the indigent, open to all ages. The program of health benefits for children and youth known as Child Health Insurance Programs (CHIP)

affords statistics on registered persons under 19 years of age. The Medicare and Medicaid Services Agency is the federal agency that administers the Medicare, Medicaid, and Child Health Insurance Programs (hcfa.gov/HCFA), which provide health insurance or free health care for more than 74 million Americans. It is assumed that virtually all Medicare- and Medicaid-eligible persons have registered, while registration in CHIP is more sporadic. Data derived from these programs may be accessed on the Internet at hcfa.gov.

Nearly all workers are covered by workers compensation laws, which are designed to ensure that employees who are injured or disabled on the job are provided with fixed monetary awards, eliminating the need for litigation. These programs are typically administered by states, which report compensation claims to the Occupational Safety and Health Administration (OSHA). OSHA publishes national statistics on injuries, illnesses, and workers' demographic characteristics on the Internet at osha.gov/oshstats/bls. Labor force, employment, and unemployment statistics are gathered by the states, and are submitted to the Bureau of Labor Statistics for publication on the Internet at bls.gov/top20.html. Additional national data are derived from the Current Population Survey, which provides comprehensive information on the employment and unemployment of the nation's population, classified by age, sex, race, and a variety of other characteristics. These data are available on the Internet at bls.gov/cpshome.htm.

2. *Military service.* In the United States, demographic statistics of those in military service are used in the construction of population estimates for the total and civilian populations. (See the following sections on "Estimates" and "Projections.") The useful characteristics have included age, sex, and race; geographic area in which stationed; and geographic area from which inducted. In estimating current migration, whether international or internal, it has been found desirable to distinguish military from civilian migration. An excellent source of statistical information on the Department of Defense is the U.S. Directorate for Information Operation and Reports (DIOR), and it can be accessed on the Internet at web1.whs.osd.mil/mmid/mmidhome.htm. Military manpower statistics are the responsibility of the Defense Manpower Data Center (dmdc.osd.mil), which was established in 1974 as the Manpower Research and Data Analysis Center (MARDAC) within the U.S. Navy. Some branches of the military provide their own demographic statistics, such as the Air Force. The Interactive Demographic Analysis System (IDEAS), available on the Internet at afpc.af.mil/sasdemog/default.html, provides data on active duty officers, active-duty enlisted personnel, and civilian employees.

3. *Voters.* Information on registration and voting in relation to various demographic and socioeconomic characteristics is collected for the nation in November of congressional and presidential election years in the Current Population Survey (CPS). Tabulations of voters in local districts are often made by local or state authorities. As few other data are gathered regularly at the voting-district level, data on voters can be used as a variable in a "ratio-correlation model" to generate estimates of population and population characteristics for voting districts and other small areas. These data may be useful in areas where service districts, such as fire and water districts and school districts, need population estimates for purposes of funding or planning. (See Chapter 20 on population estimates for further information.)

4. *School enrollment and school censuses.* Statistics compiled from lists of children enrolled in school are widely used in the United States because of their universality and pertinency for making estimates of current population. The National Center for Education Statistics (NCES) is the primary federal entity for collecting and analyzing data related to education in the United States and other nations (nces.ed.gov).

Besides their use in making estimates, education data are used by federal, state, and local governments that request data concerning school demographic characteristics, pupil/teacher ratios, and dropout rates. At the federal level, such statistics are used for testimony before congressional committees and for planning in various executive departments. Among the states, NCES statistics and assessment data are used to gauge progress in educational performance. The media use NCES data for reports on such topics as student performance, school expenditures, and teacher salaries. Researchers perform secondary analyses using NCES databases. Businesses use education data to conduct market research and to monitor major trends in educatuon (U.S. National Center for Education Statistics, 1999).

Among the voluminous statistics published by the NCES, the most relevant to the concept of a partial register are the Common Core of Data (CCD) and Private School Survey (PSS). The CCD is the primary database for basic elementary and secondary education statistics. Every year the CCD surveys all public elementary and secondary schools and all school districts in the United States. The CCD provides general descriptive statistics about schools and school districts, demographic information about students and staff, and fiscal data. The PSS provides the same type of information for private schools as does the CCD for public schools. The PSS is conducted every 2 years and includes such variables as school affiliation, number of high school graduates, and program emphasis.

The NCES founded the National Education Data Resource Center (NEDRC) to serve the needs of teachers, researchers, policy makers, and others for education data. Data sets for some 16 studies maintained by NCES are currently available through NEDRC. The purpose of NEDRC is to provide education information and data to those who cannot take advantage of the available NCES computer products or who do not have appropriate facilities to process the available data. Education data may also be found at the

National Library of Education (NLE), which is the largest federally funded library devoted entirely to education and is the federal government's principal center for information on education. As mentioned earlier, education statistics may be tabulated and published by religious institutions as well. For example, enrollment in the Catholic schools is reported in the Official Catholic Directory (annual).

5. *Judicial system.* The U.S. Department of Justice, Bureau of Justice Statistics (ojp.usdoj.gov/bjs) produces voluminous data on persons involved with the judicial system. As with education statistics, the registration of those in the judicial system may help localities with policy decisions on resource allocation and crime prevention.

MISCELLANEOUS SOURCES OF DATA

We list here some of the partial official registers that are less widely used for demographic studies, registers or other records maintained by private agencies, records that apply directly to things but indirectly to people, and the like. Again, statistics from these sources are sometimes used for population estimates. They include the following:

Tax office records of taxpayers and their dependents
City directories (addresses of householders published by private companies)
Church membership records
Postal delivery stops
Permits for new residential construction and for demolition
Utility records
Personal property registration and special licensing

POPULATION ESTIMATES

Even though population estimates have been alluded to a number of times, their importance as demographic source material calls for separate discussion. They are treated here in the last section of this chapter because they are not primary data but are largely derived from the other source materials already treated. The methodology of making population estimates as well as other aspects of the subject is treated fully in Chapter 20.

The use of statistical methods of estimating population in areas without population registers, and for time periods other than censal years, is a relatively recent phenomenon. Problems with defining geographic areas, a lack of data, and inadequate techniques have historically reduced population estimates to conjecture and speculation. One may identify essentially three types of population estimates. First, intercensal estimates "interpolate" between two censuses and take the results of these censuses into account. Second, postcensal estimates relate to a past or current date following a census and take that census and possibly earlier censuses

into account, but not later censuses. Third, historical or precensal estimates relate to a period preceding the availability of the census data.

While population estimates may be made for areas without supporting census or registration data, they usually involve censuses, registration data, and other data and techniques. Estimates may be made for age, sex, race, and other groups, as well as for the total population. Moreover, estimates may be made for other demographic categories, such as marriages, households, the labor force, and school enrollment.

In 1891, Noel A. Humphries alluded to one of the first statistical population estimation techniques. Citing an "inhabited house method," Humphries (1891, p. 328) concludes that "it is impossible to doubt that the increase in inhabited houses on the rate books affords a most valuable indication of the growth of the population." Shortly after Humphries's publication, E. Cannan suggested that by analyzing births, deaths, and population mobility in a particular area, demographic components could be effectively created with which to generate estimates (Cannan, 1895). What followed is the development of numerous techniques, each based on data as varied as population time series and administrative records. Today, the techniques used for intercensal and postcensal estimates are essentially the same, and differ only in their relationship to one or more censuses. Aside from censuses, population registers, and surveys, estimates may be produced in many ways, set forth in detail in Chapter 20 as mentioned (U.S. Census Bureau/Byerly, 1990). These include mathematical, statistical, and demographic techniques, and may employ one or more indicators of population change based on administrative records, such as tax data and school enrollment. Oftentimes, information is known about parts of a population, but not the population as a whole. In these instances, the benefits of different methods may be utilized.

International View

Estimates

Many of the international compilations of demographic statistics that were mentioned in this chapter (United Nations *Demographic Yearbook*, etc.) contain annual estimates of total population, mainly for countries. The tables of the *Demographic Yearbook* have copious notes indicating the sources of the estimates, the methods used, and qualitative characterizations of accuracy. More detailed estimates (especially in greater geographic detail) are usually published in national reports. These national reports may range from statistical yearbooks in which only a small part of the content is devoted to these estimates, to unbound periodicals that are restricted to population estimates.

Projections

International compilations of population projections are considerably less common than those of estimates. The

United Nations has at various times compiled projections made by national governments, modified them to conform to a global set of assumptions of its own devising, or made projections for regions or countries entirely on its own.

In the field of demography, there is a history of contention between the use of the terms "forecasts" and "projections." Producers of population "estimates" for future dates have typically preferred the term "projection," as different types of projections may be made conditional on the assumptions made. A forecast is typically taken as a factual, unconditional statement that the analyst concludes will be the most likely outcome. Needless to say, even when population figures are published as projections, they are oftentimes immediately interpreted and utilized as forecasts.

Many countries publish their own population projections and projections for other demographic categories. Included are population by age, sex, and race; households, families, married couples; marriages, births, and deaths; urban and rural population; population for geographic areas; school and university enrollment; educational attainment of the population; and economically active population, total and by occupational distribution.

Oftentimes, less developed countries are not equipped to make current population estimates, let alone projections. Several agencies have recently developed statistical packages to help prepare population projections for use in population analysis. One of these was a collaborative effort between the U.S. Census Bureau and the U.S. Agency for International Development that resulted in the creation of the manual *Population Analysis with Microcomputers* (U.S. Census Bureau/Arriaga, 1994).

United States View

Estimates

The history of population estimates in the United States began around 1900.[16] The Census Bureau is the primary agency responsible for the generation of official population and household estimates for the United States. Many current population estimates are prepared by state, county, and municipal statistical agencies; but the detail and the methodology are not uniform from one agency to another. Five major uses for the Census Bureau's population estimates (Long, 1993) may be enumerated:

Allocation of federal and state funds
Denominators for vital rates and per capita measures
Survey "controls"
Administrative planning and marketing decisions
Descriptive and analytical studies

Over the years, the population estimates have been published in a number of different series of reports. *Current Population Reports*, Series P-25, Population Estimates and Projections, is the primary publication reporting official population estimates. The series includes monthly estimates of the total U.S. population; annual midyear estimates of the U.S. population disaggegated by age, sex, race, and Hispanic origin; estimates for state population by age and sex; and population totals for counties, metropolitan areas, and 36,000 cities and other local governments. Several reports of the P-25 series are available on the Internet at census.gov/prod/www/titles.html#popest. Additional population estimates are also available on the Internet at census.gov/population/www/estimates/popest.html, along with a schedule of releases, estimates concepts, estimates methodology, and current working papers. These estimates are also available directly from the Census Bureau on CD-ROM. A series of household statistics and estimates is presented in *Current Population Reports*, Series P-20, which has provided data on household and family characteristics annually since 1947. Estimates of households, households by age of householder, and persons per household for states, as well as a schedule of releases and description of method-

---

[16] One of the first problems that confronted the United States Census when it was organized as a permanent bureau in 1902 was the need to make official estimates of population. Previously, the Treasury Department had been issuing estimates. The first annual report of the Census Bureau (U.S. Census Bureau, 1903, pp. 12–14) described plans for estimates and gave their projected frequency and scope.

Figures were to be issued as of the first of June for each year after 1900. These were for the continental United States as a whole, the several states, cities of 10,000 or more population, the urban balance in each state, and the rural part of each state. County estimates were also published for some years. This relatively ambitious program was based on the method of arithmetic progression, and the program gradually broke down as its inadequacies became apparent. The last city and county estimates under this program were published for 1926. After that year, efforts were concentrated on making more accurate estimates of national and state population by more refined methods that used postcensal data. A good deal of experimentation went on during the 1930s. In the 1970s, with more experience and more resources, the program was extended to cover all general purpose governmental areas, including counties, cities, and towns. Contracts with other federal agencies earlier made it possible to make occasional estimates in much more detail, such as the estimates for all counties as of 1966.

The modern era of population projections might be considered to have begun in the 1920s with two widely used sets of figures prepared by two teams of eminent demographers associated with private organizations. They were R. Pearl and L. Reed at the Johns Hopkins University and W. S. Thompson and P. K. Whelpton of the Scripps Foundation for Population Research.

The methodology of projections at the U.S. Census Bureau, however, has as its more proximate antecedents the projections made by the Scripps Foundation using the "cohort-component method" (i.e., a method applying separate assumptions concerning fertility, mortality, and net immigration to a current population age distribution). By this method, the future distribution of the population disaggregated by age and sex was obtained as an integral product of the computations. The first published projections from this source were presented in an article by Whelpton (1928, pp. 253–270). Three of the subsequent sets of projections (1934, 1937, and 1943) were published by the National Resources Board and its successor agencies. Thereafter, the U.S. Census Bureau assumed an active role in the field of national population projections.

ology, are available on the Internet at census.gov/popula tion/www/estimates/housing.html.

Informal cooperation between the federal government and the states in the area of local population estimates existed as early as 1953. In 1966, the National Governor's Conference, in cooperation with the Council of State Governments, initiated and sponsored the First National Conference on Comparative Statistics, held in Washington, D.C. This conference gave national recognition to the increasing demand for subnational population estimates. Between 1967 and 1973, a group of Census Bureau staff members and state analysts charged with developing annual subnational population estimates, formalized the Federal-State Cooperative Program for Local Population Estimates (FSCPE). The goals of the FSCPE are to promote cooperation between the states and the U.S. Census Bureau; prepare consistent and jointly accepted state, county, and subcounty estimates; assure accurate estimates through the use of established methods; afford comprehensive data review, reduce duplication of population estimates and improve communication; improve techniques and methodologies; encourage joint research efforts; and enhance recognition of local demographic work. The results of the FSCPE, county population estimates, appeared in *Current Population Reports*, Series P-26, during the 1970s and 1980s, as did estimates for the 39,000 general-purpose governments during the 1970s and 1980s. The P-26 series was discontinued and incorporated into the P-25 series in 1988 (see census.gov/population/www/coop/fscpe/html).

Projections

Official projections or forecasts of the population were essentially a much later development in the United States, although there were a few modest beginnings in the 19th century that did not develop into a continuing program. For the most part, these projections were based on the assumption of the continuation of a past rate of growth or used a relatively simple mathematical function that provided for a declining rate of growth.

As indicated above, *Current Population Reports*, Series P-25, is the primary publication for reporting official projections. Current practice is to publish new national projections every 3 or 4 years, while monitoring demographic developments for indications of unexpected changes. All the reports on state projections have also been carried in Series P-25. The first state projections for broad age groups were presented in August 1957 and the first for age groups and sex in October 1967. The reports on demographic projections (e.g., households, marital status) that are dependent on the basic population projections have been produced on an *ad hoc* basis, reflecting the availability of the national "controls," the expressed needs of users, and the extent to which earlier projections were out-of-line with subsequent demographic changes.

The P-25 series of population projections available on the Internet at census.gov/prod/www/titles.html#popest are as follows:

P25-1129, Projections of the Number of Households and Families in the United States: 1995 to 2010

P25-1130, Population Projections of the United States by Age, Sex, Race, and Hispanic Origin: 1995 to 2050

P25-1131, Population Projections for States, 1995 to 2025

P25-1132, Projections of the Voting-Age Population for States: November 1998

Additional population projections for the nation, states, households, and families, and the population of voting age, as well as a schedule of upcoming projections, descriptions of methods of projections, working papers, and special reports are available on the Internet at census.gov/ population/www/projections/popproj.html. For example, new national population projections, superseding those in P25-1130, were issued in year 2000.

As with the estimates program, the federal government and the states have worked together to generate state-level data. In August of 1979, the State Projections Task Force, the Census Bureau, the Bureau of Economic Analysis, and other agencies agreed to work closely in the preparation of state population projections, to facilitate the flow of technical information on population projections between states, and to establish formal communications for the development of population projections for use in federal programs. In 1981, the Federal-State Cooperative Program for Population Projections (FSCPPP) was created. State FSCPPP agencies work in cooperation with the Census Bureau's Population Projections Branch to exchange technical information on the production of subnational population projections. Information on the FSCPPP program may be found on the Internet at census.gov/population/www/fscpp/fscpp.html.

The advent of the electronic computer has notably facilitated the kinds of computations that are employed in making population projections. This technological change is leading to great expansion in the frequency, detail, and complexity of projections in those agencies that have such equipment. The vast improvements in computing power over the past years have also facilitated the generation of projections by many other governmental departments and private firms, often for very small geographic areas.

References

Bryant, B. E., and W. Dunn. 1995, May. "The Census and Privacy." *American Demographics*. Overland Park, KS: Cowles Business Media.

Cannan, E. 1895. "The Probability of a Cessation of the Growth of Population in England and Wales during the Next Century." *Economic Journal* 5 (20): 505–515.

Cook, K. 1996. *Dubesters U.S. Census Bibiliography with SuDocs Class Numbers and Indexes*. Englewood, CO: Libraries Unlimited.

Davis, K. 1996. "Census." *Encyclopedia Britannica*, Vol. 5. New York: Encyclopaedia Britannica.

Duncan, G. T., V. A. de Wolf, T. Jabine, and M. Straf. 1993. "Report of the Panel on Confidentiality and Data Access." *Journal of Official Statistics* 9(2).

Fowler, F. J. 1993. *Survey Research Methods*. Newbury Park, CA: Sage Press.

Goyer, D. 1980. *The International Population Census Revision and Update, 1945–1977*. New York: Academic Press.

Goyer, D., and E. M. Domschke. 1983–1992. *The Handbook of National Population Censuses*. Westport, CN: Greenwood Press.

Gutman, R. 1959. *Birth and Death Registration in Massachusetts: 1639–1900*. New York: Milbank Memorial Fund.

Halacy, D. 1980. *Census: 190 Years of Counting America*. New York: Elsevier/Nelson Books.

Humphries, N. A. 1891. *Results of the Recent Census and Estimates of Population in the Largest English Towns*. London: Royal Statistical Society.

Long, J. 1983. "Postcensal Population Estimates: States, Counties, and Places." *Technical Working Paper* No. 3, Washington, DC: U.S. Census Bureau, Population Division.

Lyberg, L. 1997. *Survey Measurement and Process Quality*. New York: John Wiley and Sons.

Mendenhall, W., L. Ott, and R. F. Larson. 1974. *Statistics, A Tool for the Social Sciences*. North Scituate, MA: Duxbury Press.

Official Catholic Directory Annual. New Providence, NJ: P. J. Kennedy and Sons.

Robson, C. 1993. *Real World Research*. Oxford, UK: Blackwell.

Stewart, D. W., and M. A. Kamins. 1993. *Secondary Research, Information Sources and Methods*. Newbury Park, CA: Sage.

Taeuber, I. B. 1959. "Demographic Research in the Pacific Area." In P. M. Hauser and O. D. Duncan (Eds.), *The Study of Population*. Chicago: University of Chicago Press.

Thomas, R. K. 1999. *Health and Healthcare in the United States*. Lanham, MD: Bernan Press.

United Nations. 1963. "Sample Surveys of Current Interest." Series C. No. 15 New York: United Nations.

United Nations. 1969. "Methodology and Evaluation of Population Registers and Similar Systems" Series F, No. 15. New York: United Nations.

United Nations. 1980. "Recommendations on Statistics of International Migration." Series M, No. 58. New York: United Nations, p. 1.

United Nations. 1982a. "Directory of International Statistics." Volume 1, Series M, No. 56, Rev. 1. New York: United Nations.

United Nations. 1982b. "International Migration Policies and Programmes: A World Survey." *Population Studies*, No. 80, New York: United Nations.

United Nations. 1985. "Handbook of Vital Statistics Systems and Methods." Series F, No. 35. New York: United Nations.

United Nations. 1998a. "Handbook on Civil Registration and Vital Statistics Systems." Series F. No. 69, New York: United Nations.

United Nations. 1998b. "International Migration Policies." ST/ESA/SER.A/161. New York: United Nations.

United Nations. 1998c. "Principles and Recommendations for National Population Censuses." Series M, No. 67. New York: United Nations.

U.S. Bureau of Labor Statistics. 1998. bls.census.gov/cps/ U.S. Bureau of Labor Statistics, October 5, 1998.

U.S. Census Bureau. 1903. *Report of the Director to the Secretary of Commerce and Labor*. Washington, DC: U.S. Census Bureau.

U.S. Census Bureau. Annual. *Census Catalog and Guide*. Washington, DC: U.S. Census Bureau.

U.S. Census Bureau. 1989. *200 Years of Census Taking: Population and Housing Questions 1790–1990*. Washington, DC: U.S. Census Bureau.

U.S. Census Bureau. 1990. "State and Local Agencies Preparing Population and Housing Estimates." By E. Byerly. Series P-25, No. 1063. Washington, DC: U.S. Census Bureau.

U.S. Census Bureau. 1992. "Census of Population and Housing, 1990: Public Use Microdata Sample U.S. Technical Documentation." Washington, DC: U.S. Census Bureau.

U.S. Census Bureau. 1994. *Population Analysis with Microcomputers*. By E. Arriaga, P. Johnson, and E. Jamison. Washington, DC: U.S. Census Bureau.

U.S. Census Bureau. 1996. "Subject Index to Current Population Reports and Other Population Report Series." By L. Morris. *Current Population Reports*, P23–192. Washington, DC: U.S. Census Bureau.

U.S. Census Bureau. 2000a. *Geographic Area Reference Manual* (GARM) Online at www.census.gov/geo/www/garm.html, on September 9, 2000.

U.S. Census Bureau. 2000b. *Introduction to Census 2000 Data Products*. Issued July 2000: MSO/00 CDP.

U.S. Census Bureau. 2003. *Statistical Abstract of the United States*. Washington, DC: U.S. Bureau of the Census.

U.S. Government Accounting Office. 1991. "Report to the Chairman, Subcommittee on Government Information and Regulation, Committee on Government Affairs, U.S. Senate." GAO/GGD-92-12. Washington, DC: USGAO.

U.S. Immigration and Naturalization Service. 1999. "Statistical Yearbook of the U.S. Immigration & Naturalization Service." Washington, DC: U.S. Immigration and Naturalization Service.

U.S. National Center for Education Statistics. 1999. nces.ed.gov/help. Washington, DC: U.S. National Center for Education Statistics. October 29, 1999.

U.S. National Center for Health Statistics. 1996. *Vital Statistics of the United States*. Vol. III, *Marriage and Divorce*. Hyattsville, MD: U.S. National Center for Health Statistics.

U.S. National Center for Health Statistics. 1997. *U.S. Vital Statistics System: Major Activities and Developments*, 1950–95. By A. M. Hetzel, (PHS) 97-1003, Hyattsville, MD: U.S. National Center for Health Statistics.

Whelpton, P. K. 1928. "Population of the United States, 1925 to 1975." *American Journal of Sociology* 34 (2): September.

Willcox, W. F. 1933. *Introduction to the Vital Statistics of the United States: 1900–1930*. Washington DC: U.S. Census Bureau.

Wolfenden, H. H. 1954. *Population Statistics and Their Compilation*. Chicago: University of Chicago Press.

Suggested Readings

Anderson, M. 1988. *The American Census, A Social History*. New Haven, CT: Yale University.

Bernstein, P. 1998. *Finding Statistics Online, How to Locate the Elusive Numbers You Need*. Medford, NJ: Information Today.

Chadwick, B., and T. Heaton. 1996. *Statistical Handbook on Adolescents in America*. Phoenix, AZ: Oryx Press.

Choldin, H. 1994. *Looking for the Last Percent: The Controversy over Census Undercounts*. New Brunswick, NJ: Rutgers University Press.

Courgeau, D. 1988. Méthodes de Mesure de la Mobilité Spatiale (Institut National d'Etudes Démographiques). Paris: INED.

Edmonston, B., and C. Schultze. 1995. *Modernizing the U.S. Census*. Washington, DC: National Academy Press.

Garoogian, R., A. Garoogian, and P. Weingart. Annual. *America's Top Rated Cities, a Statistical Handbook*. Boca Raton, FL: Universal Reference Publications.

Lavin, M. R. 1996. *Understanding the Census*. Kenmore, NY: Epoch Books.

Myers, D. 1992. *Analysis with Local Census Data*. San Diego, CA: Academic Press.

Onate, B. T., and J. M. Bader. 1989. *Sampling and Survey Statistics*. Laguna Philippines College.

Schick, F., and R. Schick. 1994. *Statistical Handbook on Aging Americans*. Phoenix, AZ: Oryx Press.

Stahl, C. 1988. *International Migration Today*. Paris: United Nations Educational, Scientific and Cultural Organization.

Thomas, R. K. 1999. *Health and Healthcare in the United States*. Lanham, MD: Bernan Press.

United Nations. 1985. "Handbook of Vital Statistics Systems and Methods." *Studies in Methods*. Series F, No. 35. New York: United Nations.

U.S. Census Bureau. 1989. *200 Years of Census Taking: Population and Housing Questions 1790–1990*. Washington, DC: U.S. Census Bureau.

Wright, C. D., and W. C. Hunt. 1900. *The History and Growth of the United States Census*. Washington, DC: Government Printing Office.

1

Guide to National Statistical Abstracts

This bibliography presents recent statistical abstracts for Slovakia, Russia, and member nations of the Organization for Economic Cooperation and Development. All sources contain statistical tables on a variety of subjects for the individual countries. Many of the publications provide text in English as well as in the national language(s). For further information on these publications, contact the named statistical agency that is responsible for editing the publication.

Australia
Australian Bureau of Statistics, Canberra.
Year Book Australia. Annual. 1997. (In English.)

Austria
Statistik Austria, Vienna.
Statistisches Jahrbuch Osterreichs. Annual. 2002. (In German with English translation of table headings.)

Belgium
Institut National de Statistique, Brussels.
Annuaire statistique de la Belgique. Annual. 1995. (In French and Dutch.)

Canada
Statistics Canada, Ottawa, Ontario.
Canada Yearbook: A review of economic, social, and political developments in Canada. 2001. Irregular. (In English.)

Czech Republic
Czech Statistical Office, Prague.
Statisticka Rocenka Ceske Rpubliky. 1996. (In English and Czech.)

Denmark
Danmarks Statistik, Copenhagen.
Statistisk Arbog. 2001. (In Danish.)

Finland
Statistics Finland, Helsinki.

Statistical Yearbook of Finland. Annual. 2001. (In English, Finnish, and Swedish.)

France
Institut National de la Statistique et des Etudes Economiques, Paris.
Annuaire Statistique de la France. Annual. 2002. (In French.)

Germany
Statistische Bundesamt, Wiesbaden.
Statistisches Jahrbuch für die Bundesrepublik Deutschland. Annual. 1996. (In German.)
Statistisches Jahrbuch für das Ausland. 1996.

Greece
National Statistical Service of Greece, Athens.
Concise Statistical Yearbook. 2000. (In English and Greek.)
Statistical Yearbook of Greece. Annual. 2000. (In English and Greek.)

Hungary
Hungarian Central Statistical Office, Budapest
Statistical Yearbook of Hungary. 2000. (In English and Hungarian.)

Iceland
Hagstofa Islands/Statistics Iceland, Reykjavik.
Statistical Yearbook of Iceland. 2001. Irregular. (In English and Icelandic.)

Ireland
Central Statistics Office, Cort.
Statistical Abstract. Annual. 1998–1999. (In English.)

Italy
ISTAT (Istituto Centrale di Statistica), Rome.
Annuario Statistico Italiano. Annual. 2001. (In Italian.)

Japan
Statistics Bureau, Ministry of Public Management, Tokyo.
Japan Statistical Yearbook. Annual. 2002. (In English and
   Japanese.)

Korea, South
National Statistical Office, Seoul.
Korea Statistical Yearbook. Annual. 2001. (In Korean and
   English.)

Luxembourg
STATEC (Service Central de la Statistique et des Etudes),
   Luxembourg.
Annuaire Statistique. Annual. 2001. (In French.)

México
Instituto Nacional de Estadística, Geografíae, Informática,
   Distrito Federal.
Anuario Estadístico de los Estados Unidos Méxicanos.
   Annual. 1993. (In Spanish.) Agenda Estadística. 1999.

Netherlands
Statistics Netherlands. Voorburg.
Statistisch Jaarboek. 2002. (In Dutch.)

New Zealand
Department of Statistics, Wellington.
New Zealand Official Yearbook. Annual. 1998. (In English.)

Norway
Statistics Norway, Oslo.
Statistical Yearbook. Annual. 2001. (In English.)

Poland
Central Statistical Office, Warsaw.
Concise Statistical Yearbook. 2001. (In both Polish and
   English.)
Statistical Yearbook of the Republic of Poland. 2000. (In
   both English and Polish.)

Portugal
INE (Instituto Nacional de Estatistica), Lisbon.
Anuario Estatistico: de Portugal. 1995. (In Portugese.)

Russia
State Committee of Statistics of Russia, Moscow.
Statistical Yearbook. 2001. (In Russian.)

Slovakia
Statistical Office of the Slovak Republic, Bratislava.
Statisticka Rocenka Slovensak. 2000. (In English and
   Slovak.)

Spain
INE (Instituto Nacional de Estadística), Madrid.
Anuario Estadístico de España. Annual. 1996. (In
   Spanish.)

Sweden
Statistics Sweden, Stockholm.
Statistik Arsbox for Sverige. Annual. 2002. (In English
   and Swedish.)

Switzerland
Bundesamt für Statistik, Bern.
Statistisches Jahrbuch der Schweiz. Annual. 2002. (In
   French and German.)

Turkey
State Institute of Statistics, Prime Ministry, Ankara.
Statistical Yearbook of Turkey. 1999. (In English and
   Turkish.)
Turkey in Statistics. 1999. (In English and Turkish.)

United Kingdom
The Stationary Office, Norwich.
Annual Abstract of Statistics. Annual. 1991. (In English.)

3

Collection and Processing of Demographic Data

THOMAS BRYAN AND ROBERT HEUSER

This chapter deals with the collection and processing of demographic data. This topic is closely related to that of the preceding chapter, which treated the important kinds of demographic statistics and their availability. The discussion covers censuses and surveys and also registration systems for the collection of vital statistics. Practices differ considerably from country to country, and it would not be practicable to cover in this chapter all the important differences in data collection methods. Instead, this subject is discussed mainly in terms of the norms as countries with a long history of censuses or registration systems recognize them and as they are presented in publications of the United Nations and other international organizations.

POPULATION CENSUSES AND SURVEYS

Since many of the procedures and problems of data collection are common to censuses and surveys, these two data sources are treated together. Some distinctions between censuses and surveys were mentioned in Chapter 2. The United Nations (UN) states, "Population and housing censuses are a primary means of collecting basic population and housing statistics as part of an integrated program of data collection and compilation aimed at providing a comprehensive source of statistical information for economic and social development planning, for administrative purposes, for assessing conditions in human settlements, for research and for commercial and other uses" (United Nations, 1998, pp. 4–5).

Essential Features of a Population Census

The essential features of a population census, as stated in a recent United Nations publication, are "individual

enumeration, universality within a defined territory, simultaneity, and defined periodicity" (United Nations, 1998, p. 3).

Individual Enumeration

The principle to be observed here is to list persons individually along with their specified characteristics. However, in some earlier types of censuses, the "group enumeration" method is employed, whereby the number of adult males, adult females, and children is tallied within each group or family. This procedure was widely practiced in most of the enumerations of the African populations during the colonial era. The first few censuses of the United States represented a variation of such group enumeration methods. The main disadvantage of this method is that no greater detail on characteristics can be provided in the tabulations than that contained in the tally cells themselves. Tabulation becomes a process of mere summation. It is impossible to cross-classify characteristics unless they were tallied in cross-classification during the enumeration.

Universality Within a Defined Territory

Ideally, a national census should cover the country's entire territory and all people resident or present (depending on whether the basis of enumeration is *de jure* or *de facto*). When these ideals cannot be achieved for some reason (e.g., enemy occupation of part of the country in wartime or civil strife), then the type of coverage attempted and achieved should be fully described in the census publications.

Simultaneity

Ideally, a census is taken as of a given day. The canvass itself need not be completed on that day, particularly in the

43

case of a *de jure* census. Often, the official time is midnight of the census day. The more protracted the period of the canvass, however, the more difficult it becomes to avoid omissions and duplications. Some of the topics in a census may refer not to status on the census day but to status at a specified date or period in the past, such as residence 5 years ago, labor force status in the week preceding the census day, and income in the preceding calendar year.

Defined Periodicity

The United Nations recommends, "Censuses should be taken at regular intervals so that comparable information is made available in a fixed sequence. A series of censuses makes it possible to appraise the past, accurately describe the present and estimate the future" (United Nations, 1998, p. 3). If the censuses are spaced exactly 5 or 10 years apart, cohort analysis can be carried out more readily and the results can be presented in more conventional terms. However, some countries may find that they need to conduct a census at an irregular interval because of rapid changes in their population characteristics or major geographic changes. In the interests of international comparability, the United Nations suggests that population censuses be taken as closely as feasible to the years ending in "0."

Periodicity is obviously not an intrinsic requirement of a census but sponsorship by a national government should be seen as such a requirement. The United Nations also emphasizes the importance of sponsorship of the census by the national government (United Nations, 1998, p. 4). A national census is conducted by the national government, perhaps with the active cooperation of state or provincial governments. While it is feasible to have a national sample survey conducted by a private survey organization or to have a small-scale census (for a limited area) conducted by a city government, university department, training center, or some other entity, only national governments have the resources to support the vast organization and large expenditures of a full-scale census.

Census Strategic Objectives

The development or substantial improvement of a census involves a considerable amount of work. The task should be undertaken with the goal of fulfilling specific strategic objectives. These objectives should include, but are not limited to, census content and cost-effectiveness, census impact on the public, and the production of results.

The content of the census should be examined to ensure that it meets the demonstrated requirements of the users, particularly national government agencies, within the constraints of a budget. While the "requirements" of users may be endless, they must be assigned priorities so that the legally mandated and most important data are gathered

before less essential data are sought. Not only must data priorities be established, but efficiencies and economies of scale in collecting, organizing, and disseminating results must be established as well. The impact on the public of conducting a census can be measured by the burden it creates, its compliance with legal and ethical standards, and its ability to protect confidentiality. Obviously, the impact can vary widely, but in most cases the results of the census are used for distribution of political representation and of public funds and as the backbone of a national data system. The aim of producing census results must be to deliver mandated products and services that meet established standards of quality and are released according to a reasonable timetable. This includes producing standardized outputs with a minimum of error for widely recognized and agreed-upon geographic areas (United Nations, 1998, p. 4).

Advantages and Uses of Sample Surveys

As vehicles for the collection of demographic data, sample surveys have certain advantages and disadvantages, and their purposes and applications differ somewhat from those of censuses. Generally, surveys are not nearly as large and expensive, nor do they have the legal mandates and implications of censuses. Yates (1981, 321) wrote, "surveys fall into two main classes: those which have as their object the assessment of the characteristics of the population or different parts of it and those that are investigational in character." In the census type of survey, estimates of the characteristics, quantitative and qualitative, of the whole population and usually also of various previously defined subdivisions of it are required. In the investigational type of survey, we are more concerned with the study of relationships between different variates.

Since surveys of either type rarely have the regimented, standardized requirements of censuses, one resulting advantage is the possibility of experimenting with new questions. The fact that a new question is not altogether successful is less critical in the case of a sample survey than in that of a census, where the investment is much larger and where failure cannot be remedied until after the lapse of 5 or 10 years. In a continuing survey, new features can be introduced not only in the questions proper but also in the instructions to the canvassers, the coding, the editing, and the tabulations. Since a national population census is a multipurpose statistical project, a fairly large number of different topics must be investigated, and no one of them can be explored in any great depth. In a survey, even when there is a nucleus of items that have to be included on the form every time, it is feasible in supplements, or occasional rounds, to probe a particular topic with a "battery" of related questions at relatively moderate additional cost.

In some instances, the data from a regular survey program may be superior in some respects to those from a census. The field staff for surveys is often retained from month to month or year to year. The smaller size of the survey operation makes it possible to do the work with a smaller, select staff and to maintain closer surveillance and control of procedures.

The shorter time interval between surveys makes them more suitable for studying those population characteristics that change frequently in some countries, such as household formation, fertility, and employment status. With observations taken more frequently, it is much more feasible to analyze trends over time in the statistics. The analyst can delineate seasonal movements if the survey is conducted monthly or quarterly. Even when the survey data are available only annually, cyclical movements can be delineated more precisely than from censuses, and turning points in trends are more accurately located. The response of demographic phenomena to economic changes and to political events can also be studied more satisfactorily.

Among disadvantages of surveys, sampling error is the major one. This disadvantage is offset to some extent by the ability to compute the sampling error for estimates of various sizes and thus describe the limits of reliability. On the other hand, the magnitude of nonsampling error in surveys is oftentimes undetermined and the size of the survey samples is usually such that reliable statistics can be shown only in very limited geographic detail and for relatively broad cross-tabulations. For the latter reason, the census is the principal source of data for small areas and detailed cross-classifications of population characteristics. There is also usually some sampling bias arising from the design of the survey or from failure to carry out the design precisely. For example, it may not be practical to sample the entire population and coverage may not be extended to certain population subgroups, such as nomadic or tribal populations or persons living in group quarters. Moreover, the public may not cooperate as well in a sample survey as in a national census, which receives a great deal of publicity with attendant patriotic appeal.

The uses of censuses and surveys are sometimes interrelated. The use of the sample survey for testing new questions has already been mentioned. New procedures may also be tested. Census statistics may serve as benchmarks for analyzing and evaluating survey data and vice versa. The census can be used as a sampling frame for selecting the population to be included in a survey or may be a means of selecting a population group, such as persons in specified occupations.

CENSUS RECOMMENDATIONS

Methods of data collection vary among countries according to their cultural and technical advancement, the amount of data-collecting experience, and the resources available.

Both the methods used and the practices recommended by international agencies are covered in a number of sources. The Statistical Office of the United Nations has produced a considerable body of literature on the various aspects of the collection and processing of demographic statistics from censuses and surveys.

Definitions of Concepts

One requirement of a well-planned and executed census or survey is the development of a set of concepts and classes to be covered and adherence to these definitions throughout all stages of the collection and processing operations. These concepts provide the basis for the development of question wording, instructions for the enumerators, and specifications for editing, coding, and tabulating the data. Only when concepts are carefully defined in operational terms and consistently applied can there be a firm basis for later analysis of the results. Definitions of all of the recommended topics for national censuses and household surveys are presented in the manuals of the United Nations and are recognized by many countries as international standard definitions for the various population characteristics (United Nations, 1998).

Organization of National Statistical Offices

The statistical programs of a country may be largely centered in one national statistical office, which conducts the census and the major sample surveys, or they may be scattered among a number of government agencies, each with specific interests and responsibilities. Considerable differences exist among countries in the organization and permanence of the national census office, which may be an autonomous agency or part of the central statistical office. The United Nations groups countries into three categories according to types of central organizations: (1) those with a permanent census office and subsidiary offices in the provinces, (2) those with a permanent central office but no continuing organization of regional offices, so that they depend on provincial services or officials or field organizations of other national agencies, and (3) those that have no permanent census office but create an organization for the taking of each census and dissolve it when the census operations are complete.

There are many advantages to maintaining a permanent census office. Much of the work, including analysis of the data from the past census and plans and preparations for the next census, can best be accomplished by being spread throughout the intercensal period. The basic staff retained for this purpose forms a nucleus of experienced personnel to assume administrative, technical, and supervisory responsibilities when the organization is expanded for taking the census. The maintenance of this staff helps assure the timeliness and maintenance of maps and technical documents necessary to conduct the census, as well as the security of historical census records.

Administration and Planning

The collection of demographic data by a census must have a legal basis, whereas a national sample survey may or may not have a legal foundation. The need for a legal basis is to establish administrative authority for the census. The administrative agency or organization is granted the authority to conduct a census and to use funds for this purpose within a specified time frame. The law must also provide for the conscription of the public to answer the census questions, and to do so truthfully. However, the legal basis that establishes the national program of census taking must also ensure the confidentiality of responses and ethical treatment of census respondents.

Any national census or major survey involves a vast amount of preparatory work, some aspects of which may begin years before the enumeration or survey date. Preliminary activities include geographic work, such as preparing maps and lists of places; determining the data needs of the national and local governments, business, labor, and the public; choosing the questions to be asked and the tabulations to be made; deciding on the method of enumeration; designing the questionnaire; testing the forms and procedures; planning the data-processing procedures; and acquiring the equipment to be used. Proper publicity for the census is important to the success of the enumeration, especially in countries where a census is being taken for the first time and the citizens may not understand its purpose. The public should also be assured of the confidentiality of the census returns—that is, that personal information will not be used for other than statistical purposes and will not be revealed in identifiable form by census officials.

Development of procedures for evaluation of the census should be part of the early planning to assure that they are included at the appropriate stages of the fieldwork and data processing and to assure that funds will be set aside for them. The funding of the census itself is one of many administrative responsibilities involved in the taking of a national census. Legislation must be passed to provide a legal basis, funds must be appropriated and a budget prepared, a time schedule of census operations must be set up, and a huge staff of census workers must be recruited and trained.

Quality Control

It is important from the outset of data collection to establish quality control measures for each step. Many of the processes for conducting and evaluating a census are similar to those of a large sample survey. Having quality control measures at each step of the process is important in order to recognize and identify problems as they occur, enabling proper intervention measures. In countries with only recent experience in conducting a census, a quality control program is necessary to measure how census operations are proceeding. Even in countries with long-established censuses and large surveys, fluctuating numbers and the quality of workers, differences in data across multiple geographic layers, multiple types of data inputs and outputs over time, and technological advances require a solid quality control program to be in place.

Geography

In a national census, the geographic work has a twofold purpose: (1) to assure a complete and unduplicated count of the population of the country as a whole and of the many subdivisions for which data are to be published; (2) to delineate the enumeration areas to be assigned to individual enumerators.

To successfully carry out censuses and surveys, a formal ongoing cartographic program should be established. An ongoing operation not only affords a greater degree of comparability over time, but also saves the resources necessary to create such a program every time it is needed.

The boundaries that must be observed in a census include administrative, political, and statistical subdivisions (such as states or provinces and smaller political units). In countries that have a well-established census program, the geographic work is continuous and involves updating maps for changes in boundaries (e.g., annexations), redefining statistical areas, and so forth. When maps are not available from a previous census, they may be developed from existing maps obtained from various sources such as military organizations, school systems, ministries of health or interior, or highway departments, or they may be prepared from aerial photographs. The materials from these various sources may be compiled to produce working maps for the enumeration.

Once the maps have been prepared, the enumeration areas are delineated. There are two requirements for the establishment of enumeration areas. First, the enumeration area must not cross the boundaries of any tabulation area. Second, in the case of a direct-interview type of census, the population of the enumeration area as well as its physical dimensions must be such that one canvasser can complete the enumeration of the area in the time allotted. In some countries, the preparation of adequate maps is not feasible because of a lack of qualified personnel or because of the cost of producing the maps. In these cases, a complete listing of all inhabited places may be made by field workers as a substitute for maps.

The geographic work is sometimes supplemented with a precanvass of the enumeration areas shortly before enumeration. A precanvass serves to prepare the way for the enumeration by filling in any missing information on the map, providing publicity for the census, arranging with village chiefs or town officials for the enumerator's visit, determining the time necessary for covering the area, and planning the enumerator's itinerary. Geographic work is equally important as a preparatory phase of sample surveys. The selection of the sample usually depends on the delineation of certain geographical areas to serve as primary sampling units, then subdivisions of those areas, and finally delineation of small area segments of suitable size for the interviewer to cover in the allotted time period.

One of the most difficult tasks in conducting a census or survey is to identify and delineate small areas. Not only do small areas pose problems for data collectors but for data publication as well. The refinement of a geographic base is usually closely related to available resources. Each finer level of geographic detail usually entails an exponentially greater cost in conducting a census or survey. With limited resources, the best method is to establish a hierarchical coding of all geographic, political, and statistical subdivisions. The smallest of these may be limited by a minimum population, oftentimes established as 1000 or 2500. In a technically more advanced setting, if more resources are available, it is possible to coordinate cartographic operations with specific geographic identifiers. In such geocoding, each census or survey record may be identified on a coordinate or grid system, such as latitude and longitude. More information on geographic information systems and geocoding are available in Appendix D.

Once a geographic base is established, records of living quarters and housing-unit listings should be established and preferably associated with unique geographic, political, or statistical codes. This is particularly helpful in establishing enumeration districts, regardless of the type of areas for which the data are tabulated. Address lists, group quarters, government housing, shelters, and the like may be found in population registers and the records of tax authorities and other administrative agencies.

Census Instruments

Census questionnaires may be classified into three general types: first, the single individual questionnaire, which contains information for only one person; second, the single household questionnaire, which contains information for all the members of the household or housing unit; and third, the multihousehold questionnaire, which contains information for as many persons as can be entered on the form, including members of several households. Each of these has certain advantages and disadvantages.

The single individual questionnaire is more flexible for compiling information if the processing is to be done without the help of mechanical equipment. The single household questionnaire has the advantage of being easy to manage in an enumeration and is especially convenient for obtaining a count of the number of households and for determining the relationship of each person to the householder. If part of the census questions is to be confined to a sample of households, a single household schedule is required. The multihousehold questionnaire is more economical from the standpoint of printing costs and is convenient for processing on conventional or electronic tabulating equipment, but it may be awkward to handle because of its size.

Another type of questionnaire is that described earlier for group enumeration of nomadic people, when only the number of persons for broad age-sex groups is recorded. Although these summarized data do not provide census data in the strictest sense of the term, the group enumeration procedure has been used to enumerate classes of the population for whom conventional enumeration methods are not practical.

Census Content

The census subjects to be included are a balance between needs for the data and resources for carrying out the census program. National and local needs are of primary importance, but some consideration may also be given to achieving international comparability in the subjects chosen. As a rule, the list of subjects included in the previous census or censuses provides the starting point from which further planning of subjects proceeds. In general, it is desirable that most questions be retained from census to census in essentially the same form to provide a time series that can serve for analysis of the country's progress and needs. Some changes in subjects are necessary, however, to meet the changing needs of the country. Advice is usually sought from various national and local government agencies. Advisory groups including experts covering a wide range of interests may be organized and invited to participate in the formulation of the questionnaire content.

Census subjects may be classified as to whether they are mandated, required, or programmatic, as does the U.S. Census Bureau. Mandated subjects are those whose need for decennial census data is specifically cited in legislation. Required subjects are those that are specifically required by law and for which the census is the only source that has historically been used. Programmatic subjects are used for program planning, implementation, and evaluation and to provide legal evidence (U.S. Census Bureau, 1995).

Given this context, the United Nation's list of recommended items for censuses is valuable as an indicator of the basic items that have proved useful in many countries and as a guide to international comparability in subjects covered (United Nations, 1998, pp. 59–60). Its list of topics to be included on the census questionnaire is as follows, with basic items shown in bold type:

1. Geographic and internal migration characteristics

Place of usual residence	**Duration of residence**
Place where found at time of census	**Total population (Derived)**
Place of birth	**Locality (Derived)**
Place of residence at a specified time in the past	**Urban and rural (Derived)**
Place of previous residence	

2. Household and family characteristics

Relationship to head or other reference person	**Household and family composition (Derived)**
Member of household	Household and family status (Derived)

3. Demographic and family characteristics

Sex	Religion
Age	Language
Marital status	National and/or ethnic groups
Citizenship	

4. Fertility and mortality

Children ever born	Maternal or paternal orphanhood
Children living	Age, date, or duration of first marriage
Date of birth of last child born alive	Age of mother at birth of first child born alive
Deaths in the past 12 months	

5. Educational characteristics

Literacy	**Educational attainment**
School attendance	Field of education and educational qualification

6. Economic characteristics

Activity status	**Status in employment**
Time worked	Income
Occupation	Institutional sector of employment
Industry	Place of work

7. International migration characteristics

Country of birth	Year or period of arrival
Citizenship	

8. Disability characteristics

Disability	Causes of disability
Impairment or handicap	

Regional interests are another consideration in the planning of census content. Organizations such as the Economic Commission for Europe, the Economic Commission for Asia and the Far East, the Economic Commission for Africa, ECLA, and the Inter-American Statistical Institute often conduct conferences with the United Nations to consider census content and methods and to make recommendations for the forthcoming census period. Neighboring countries sometimes cooperate in census planning through regional conferences or advisory groups for census subject matter

and practices. Public reaction to a subject also may influence the choice of census topics, since some questions may be too difficult or complicated for the respondent or the public may object to the substance of the question.

Survey Content

The contents of a survey are obviously significantly more guided by the objective and type of the survey than the standardization and continuity sought by a census. Although some sample surveys are multisubject surveys, it is more common for the survey to be restricted to one field, such as demographic characteristics or events, health, family income and expenditures, or labor force characteristics. One way in which sample surveys achieve multisubject scope is to vary the content from time to time. The UN *Handbook of Household Surveys* presents a list of recommended items for demographic surveys (United Nations, 1983). Content may also be determined by the type of survey being conducted, whether one-time (cross-sectional) or a series (longitudinal).

While the content of a census may be mandated, required, or programmatic, or combinations thereof, the requirements of specific survey questions are rarely well established and legal mandates for the content rarely exist. Therefore, consideration must not only be given to the value of each question in fulfilling the goal of the survey, but also the practicability of obtaining useful answers. Yates (1981, 58) wrote,

> If the information is to be furnished in response to questions, the points of consideration are whether the respondents are sufficiently informed to be capable of giving accurate answers; whether, if the provision of accurate answers involves them in a good deal of work, such as consulting previous records, they will be prepared to undertake this work; whether they have motives for concealing the truth, and if so whether they will merely refuse to answer, or will give incorrect replies.

Tabulation Program

Closely related to the choice of subjects to be included in a census or survey is the planning of the tabulation program. Potential cross-tabulations in a census are boundless. Therefore, the selection of material is dictated partly by the uses of the results. The capacity of the financial and human resources and equipment for processing the data and the available facilities for publishing the results (e.g., page space available) place some restrictions on the material to be tabulated. The tabulation plans, as well as the choice of subjects on the questionnaire, should undergo review by the public, governmental, and commercial potential users of the statistics. Recommended tabulations for each of the subjects covered in national censuses and in various types of surveys are listed in the UN manuals previously listed.

Part of the planning of the tabulation program involves determining the number of different levels of geographic detail to be presented. Data are usually presented for the primary administrative divisions of the country and their principal subdivisions and for cities in various size categories as well as for the country as a whole. For the smallest geographic areas, such as small villages, the results as a rule are limited to a report of the total number of inhabitants or perhaps the male and female populations only. At the next higher level, which may be secondary administrative divisions, the tabulations may provide only "inventory statistics." These statistics are simply a count of persons in the categories of age, marital status, economic activity, and so forth, with little cross-classification with other characteristics. For the primary administrative divisions and major cities, most subjects are cross-tabulated by age and sex, and often there are also cross-classifications with other social and economic characteristics, such as educational attainment by economic activity or employment status by occupation. Also, more detailed categories may be shown on such subjects as country of birth, mother tongue, or occupation. The greatest degree of detail, sometimes termed "analytical" tabulations as opposed to "inventory" statistics, is that in which cross-tabulations involve detailed categories of each of the three or four characteristics involved.

Conducting the Census or Survey

Recruitment and Training

One of the largest tasks in conducting a survey, and especially a census, is the recruitment and training of staff. Anderson (1988, p. 201) states of the 1950 U.S. Census,

> It was extraordinarily difficult to recruit in a number of months a reliable, competent staff of census enumerators and to guarantee uniform application of census procedures in the field. The 1950 evaluation studies indicated that on simple census questions, such as age and sex, the enumerators performed well. But in recording the answers to such complex questions as occupation and industry, two different interviewers recorded the answers differently in a sufficient number of cases to render the data suspect.

While retaining staff with the skills necessary for preparatory work (such as coding and data entry) is relatively easy, it is having a sufficient number of skilled workers conducting the enumeration that must be especially prepared for.

Pretesting

Pretesting of census content and methods has been found to be very useful in providing a basis for decisions that must be made during the advance planning of the census. This is especially so in countries without a long history of census taking. Such pretests vary in scope. They may be limited to testing a few new subject items, alternate wording of a question, different types of questionnaires, or different enumeration procedures. Most census testing includes at least one full-scale pretest containing all questions to be asked on the census itself and sometimes covering part or all of the processing phases as well. The suitability of topics that have not been tried before may be determined from a small-scale survey in two or three localities. With enough other questions on the questionnaire to achieve something close to a normal census situation, a reasonable assesment of the question may be made. A test involving only the employees of the census office and their families may sometimes suffice for this purpose. Countries having an annual sample survey sometimes use this survey as a vehicle for testing prospective census questions.

Enumeration

The crucial phase of a census or survey comes when the questionnaires are taken into the field and the task of obtaining the required information begins. The kinds of problems encountered and the procedures used for collecting the data are similar for censuses and surveys. In a census the procedures for enumeration are affected by the type of population count to be obtained. The census may be designed to count persons where they are found on census day (a *de facto* count) or according to their usual residence (a *de jure* count).

In a *de facto* census, the method is to list all persons present in the household or other living quarters at midnight of the census day or all who passed the night there. In this type of enumeration, there is a problem of counting persons who happen to be traveling on census day or who work at night and consequently would not be found in any of the places where people usually live. It may be necessary to count persons on trains and boats or to ask households to include such members on the census form as well as those persons actually present. In some countries all persons are requested to stay in their homes on the census day or until a signal announces the completion of the enumeration.

In a *de jure* census, all persons who usually live in the household are listed on the form whether they are present or not. Visitors who have a usual residence elsewhere are excluded from the listing but are counted at their usual residence. Provisions must be made in a *de jure* census for persons away from home if those persons think it is likely that no one at their usual residence will report them. The usual practice is to enumerate such persons on a special form, which is forwarded to the census office of their home address. The form is checked against the returns for that area and is added to the count there if the person is not already listed. This is a complicated and expensive procedure, and there still remains a chance that some persons will be missed and some counted twice.

There are two major types of enumeration, the direct-interview or canvasser method and the self-enumeration or householder method. In the direct-interview method, a census agent visits the household, lists the members living there, and asks the required questions for each person, usually by interviewing one member of the household. The advantage of this method is that the enumerator is a trained person who is familiar with the questions and their interpretation and he or she may assume a high degree of responsibility for the content of the census. Also, this method reduces the difficulty of obtaining information in an area where there is a low level of literacy. For these reasons it is considered possible to include more complex forms of questions in the direct-interview type of enumeration.

In self-enumeration, the census forms are distributed, usually one to each household, and one or more members of the household complete the form for all persons in the household. With this method of enumeration, there is less need for highly trained enumerators. The census enumerator may distribute the forms and later collect them, or the mail may be used for either the distribution or collection of the forms or for both. If enumerators collect the forms, they can review them for completeness and correctness and request additional information when necessary. In a mail census, the telephone may be used to collect information found to be lacking on the forms mailed in, or the enumerator may visit the household to obtain the missing information. In some cases the enumerator may complete an entire questionnaire if the household is unable to do so.

Self-enumeration has the advantage of giving the respondents more time to obtain the information and to consult records if necessary. People can supply the information about themselves, rather than having the information supplied by a household member who may not have complete or correct information. The possibility of bias resulting from a single enumerator's erroneously interpreting the questions is minimized in this method of enumeration. It is also more feasible to achieve simultaneity with self-enumeration because all respondents can be asked to complete the questionnaires as of the census day. Thus, in this respect, self-enumeration is the more suitable method if a *de facto* count is desired.

Self-enumeration is the more frequently used method in European countries, the United States, Australia, and New Zealand, whereas direct interview is the usual method in other countries. A combination of these two main types of enumeration is often used. The self-enumeration method may be considered appropriate for certain areas of the country and the interviewer method for others, or some of the information may be obtained by interview and the remainder by self-enumeration. In a census that uses the interviewer method as its basic procedure, self-enumeration

may be used for some individuals, such as roomers, when the head of the household cannot supply the information or when confidentiality is desired.

One of the goals of censuses and surveys is to minimize response burden. For years it has been possible to conduct surveys over the telephone, and more recently on the Internet. To make answering the census questionnaire easier and to ease respondent burden, many countries are exploring the possibility of allowing respondents to complete the basic demographic questions online over the World Wide Web, with Internet access to explanations about the questions asked in the census. Another innovation is telephone interviewing, whereby dedicated telephone lines are provided for the public to provide answers to the basic demographic questions, instead of their completing and mailing the census questionnaire.

Some special procedures for enumeration are required for certain groups of the population, such as nomads or people living in inaccessible areas (i.e., icy, mountainous, or forested areas). Levels of literacy may be low among certain social or geographically concentrated groups, who may have little understanding of the purpose of a census or interest in its objectives. A procedure sometimes followed is to request that all the members of such groups assemble in one place on a given day, since enumerating them at their usual place of residence might require from 4 to 5 months. For some of these, a method of group enumeration has been used. Rather than obtaining information for each individual or household, the enumerator obtains from the head of the group a count of the number of persons in various categories, such as marital status, sex, and age groups.

Enumeration of persons in hotels, *pensions*, missions, hospitals, and similar group quarters usually requires special procedures. Since some are transients, inquiry must be made to determine whether they have already been counted elsewhere. If a *de jure* count is being made, steps must be taken to assure that they are counted at their usual residence. Special individual census forms are usually used in group quarters, since the proprietor or other residents of the place could not provide the required information about each person. Another segment of the population that presents an enumeration problem is the homeless population, because people in this group have no fixed addresses and possibly occupy public spaces or temporary residences.

In some households the enumerator is unable to interview anyone even after repeated visits because no one is at home or, more rarely, because the occupants refuse to be enumerated. Since the primary purpose of a census is to obtain a count of the population, an effort is made to obtain information from neighbors about the number and sex of the household members. Neighbors may also be able to supply information about family relationships and marital status, which may, in turn, provide a basis for estimating age. Reliable information on other subjects usually cannot be obtained except from the members themselves, and these questions are left blank, perhaps to be supplied during processing operations according to procedures that are discussed in "Processing Data."

In a sample survey, it is less practical to get information from neighbors because the emphasis is on characteristics rather than on a count of the population. The usual procedure is to base the results on the cases interviewed and adjust the basic weighting factors to allow for noninterview cases when the final estimates are derived from the sample returns. The effect of this procedure is to impute to the population not interviewed the same characteristics reported by the interviewed population. Since this assumption may not be very accurate, the presence of numerous noninterview households may bias the sample.

When a conventional enumeration has been completed in the field, questionnaires are assembled into bundles, usually corresponding to the area covered by one enumerator. The number of documents, the geographic identification of the area, and other appropriate information are recorded on a control form, which accompanies the set of documents throughout the various stages of processing. The tremendous volume of records involved in a census or large survey makes the receipt and control of material a very important function. The identification of the geographic area provides a basis for filing the documents and a means of locating a particular set of documents at any stage of the processing.

Processing Data

Regardless of the care expended on the preparation of a census and the enumeration of the population, the quality and the usefulness of the data will be compromised if they are not properly processed. The processing of the data includes all the steps, whether carried out by hand or by machine, that are required to produce from the information on the original document the final published reports on the number and characteristics of the population. The extent to which these operations are accomplished by mechanical or electronic equipment or by hand varies among countries and among surveys and censuses within countries.

Recent innovations in data processing have advanced processing capabilities immensely. However, few censuses are processed entirely electronically. Usually, some of the data, such as preliminary counts of the population for geographic areas, are obtained from a hand count. Even data that are produced primarily by machine must undergo some manual processing to correct for omissions or inconsistencies on the questionnaire and to convert certain types of entries into appropriate input for the electronic equipment. Electronic output may undergo a certain amount of hand processing before it is ready for reproduction in a published report. Such factors as the cost and availability of equipment, the availability of manpower, and the goals in terms of tabulations to be made, reports to be published, and time schedules to be met determine the degree to which electronic processing is used. The data-processing operations to be performed in a census or survey usually consist of the following basic steps: editing, coding, data capture, and tabulation.

Editing

There are two principal points at which data errors may arise. The first occurs when a respondent provides erroneous or conflicting information, or an enumerator misrecords given information. The other occurs when data are coded and entered for computer processing. In both instances, concise rules should be established to determine how these errors should be edited. Census or survey procedures often include some editing of the questionnaires in the field offices to correct inconsistencies and eliminate omissions. Errors in the information can then more easily be corrected by checking with the respondent, and systematic errors made by the enumerator can more easily be rectified. Whether the editing is done in the field office or is part of central office processing, elimination of omissions and inconsistencies is a necessary step preliminary to coding.

A "not reported" category is permitted in some classifications of the population, but it is desirable to minimize the number of such cases. Where information is lacking, a reasonable entry can often be supplied by examining other information on the questionnaire. For example, a reasonable assumption of the relationship of a person to the head of the household or the householder can be made by checking names, ages, and marital status; or an entry of "married" may be assigned for marital status of a person whose relationship entry is "wife." Other edits may be made by comparing data entries with noncensus information, such as administrative records. For example, in 1980 the Census Bureau asked, "How many living quarters are in the building in which you live?" During editing, clerks were required to compare answers with the census mailout count for addresses with 10 or fewer units. If the clerk found that more units were reported in a building than questionnaires mailed, an enumerator was sent to investigate (Choldin, 1994, p. 57).

In manual editing, the clerks are given detailed specifications for assigning characteristics. Nonresponse cases may be assigned to a modal category (e.g., persons with place of birth not reported may be classified as native), or they may be distributed according to a known distribution of the population based on an earlier census. Since much of the editing for blanks and inconsistencies is accomplished by applying uniform rules, the use of electronic equipment for performing this operation is now commonplace. Electronic processing is designed to reject or to correct a record with missing or inconsistent data and assign a reasonable response on the basis of other information.

Problems with data entry and coding can lead to voluminous errors in raw data files, making testing and quality control procedures throughout the census especially important. Errors of this type are typically systematic and can lead to much more pervasive problems than erroneous individual records. Strict editing and error-testing rules should be established by data experts and operationalized by programmers to ensure a minimum of problems.

Coding

Coding is the conversion of entries on the questionnaire into symbols that can be used as input to the tabulating equipment. Many of the responses on a census or survey require no coding or may be "precoded" by having the code for each written entry printed on the schedule. For those that do, there are three different types of coding techniques possible. For questions that have a small number of possible answers, such as sex or marital status, and questions that are answered in terms of a numerical entry, the appropriate code may be entered directly. If there are multiple answers, then computer-assisted coding may be used. In this process, codes are stored in a database and are automatically accessed and inserted at the prompting of the operator. The third alternative is automatic coding, which may be used if the coding scheme is extraordinarily complex—such as when the codes for an answer need to be recorded in more than one place.

Data Capture

In most data-processing systems, there must be some means of transferring the data from the original document to the tabulating equipment. After going through editing and coding, the data on the questionnaire may be transferred to a format that is electronically recognizable. There is a lengthy history of improvements in this field. In the 1880s, the U.S. Census Bureau sponsored the development of punched-card tabulation equipment. By 1946, the Census Bureau had contracted with the Eckert-Mauchley Computer Corporation to design a machine for processing the 1950 census, and the result of this collaboration was the UNIVAC. Special equipment developed for the 1960 census of the United States "reads" microfilmed copies of the questionnaires and transfers the data directly to computer tape. This equipment, known as FOSDIC (film optical sensing device for input to computers), reads the schedule by means of a moving beam of light, decides which codes have been marked, and records them on magnetic tape. By the 1980s, optical mark reading (OMR) was being widely used. Akin to a "scan-tron," OMR dramatically improved the speed and

accuracy with which data were captured. However, OMR limited the format on which survey and census responses could be printed.

Today, there are three techniques commonly used to capture data. The first is simple keyboard entry by clerks. At an average rate of between 5000 and 10,000 keystrokes per hour (depending on equipment and the skill of the clerk), manual entry is reserved for only the smallest data-capture tasks. The second is optical character recognition (OCR). OCR devices are programmed to look for characters in certain places on a census or survey response and convert them to an accurate, electronically recognizable value. The third is electronic optical scanning, which can be especially useful for recording handwritten answers and especially voluminous data. Recent developments in OCR and scanning have led to substantial improvements in accuracy through better character recognition, higher rates of input, and the acceptability of a wider range of paper and other media for input.

It was noted earlier that during the planning stage of a census or survey, decisions are made about the tabulations to be produced, and outlines are prepared showing how the data are to be classified and what cross-tabulations are to be made. The outlines may be quite specific, showing in detail the content of each proposed table.

On the basis of these outlines, specifications for computer programs are written for the various operations of sorting, adding, subtracting, counting, comparing, and other arithmetic procedures to be performed by the tabulating equipment. The input is usually punched cards or computer tape, and the output is the printed results in tabular arrangement. In the most advanced systems of tabulation, the final results include not only the absolute numbers in each of the prescribed categories but derived numbers such as percentage distributions, medians, means, and ratios as well.

One of the most obvious indicators of the quality of the data from a census or survey is the nonresponse rate. Even when a nonresponse category is not published and characteristics are allocated for those persons for whom information is lacking, a count of the nonresponse cases should be obtained during processing. One advantage of performing the edit in the computer is that not only the number of nonresponses on a given subject but also the known characteristics of the nonrespondents may be recorded. This provides a basis for analyzing nonresponses and judging the effects of the allocation procedures.

The nonresponse rate for a given item has more meaning if it is based on the population to which the question applies or to which analysis of that subject is limited. The base for nonresponse rates on date of first marriage, for example, would exclude the single population, and nonresponse rates for country of birth would be limited to the foreign born. A problem arises in the establishment of a population base if the qualifying characteristic also contains a substantial number of nonresponses.

Planning the tabulations includes making some basic decisions about the treatment of nonresponses. Nonresponses may be represented in a separate category as "not reported" or they may be distributed among the specific categories according to some rule, ideally on the basis of other available characteristics of the person. Practices vary on the extent to which responses are allocated, but the elimination of "unknowns" before publication is a growing practice, partly because the greater capabilities of modern tabulating equipment have improved the possibilities of assigning a reasonable entry without prohibitive cost and partly because convenicncc to the user of the data favors the elimination of nonresponses.

Data Review

It has been mentioned that maintaining quality control and testing for errors while conducting a census or survey are imperative. Several steps may be taken to improve the accuracy and validity of results.

Supervisors should review samples of each enumerator's work for completeness and acceptability and accompany the enumerator on some of his or her visits. Progress-reporting of the enumeration enables census officials to know when an individual enumerator or the enumerators in a given area are falling seriously behind schedule and thus jeopardizing the completion of the census within the allotted time. Hand tallies of the population counted in each small area are compared with advance estimates, and the enumeration is reviewed if the results vary too widely from the expected number.

Reinterviewing is a common technique used for quality control of the data-collection process in sample surveys. A sample of households visited by the original interviewer is reinterviewed by the supervisor, and the results of the check-interview are compared with the original responses. Such checking determines whether the recorded interview actually took place and reveals any shortcomings of the interviewer.

Verification

Verification of the operation is an important element of each stage in the processing. Verification is not done for the purpose of removing all errors, as this is virtually impossible and does not justify the expense of time and resources. The purpose rather is (1) to detect systematic errors throughout the operation that can be remedied by changes in the instructions or by additional training of pcrsonncl, (2) to detect unsatisfactory performance on the part of an individual worker, and (3) to determine whether the general error rate of the operation is within tolerance. Therefore, it is seldom necessary to have 100% verification. A procedure often followed is to verify an individual's work until the worker is found to be qualified in terms of a maximum allowable error rate, and thereafter to verify only a sample of the individual's work. If during the operation, a worker is found to have dropped below the acceptable level of accuracy, his or her work units may be subjected to a complete review and correction process.

Verification may be "dependent," in which the verifier reviews the work of the original clerk and determines whether it is correct, or "independent," in which two persons do the same work independently and then a comparison is made of the results. Tests have shown that in dependent verification, a large proportion of the errors are missed. Independent verification, in which the verifier is not influenced by what was done by the original worker, has been found to be more successful in discovering errors.

The statistical tables produced by the tabulating equipment are usually subjected to editorial and statistical review before being prepared for publication. On the basis of advance estimates and data from previous surveys or other independent sources, judgments are made regarding the reasonableness of the numbers. Figures that are radically different from the expected magnitudes may indicate an error in the specifications for tabulation. Review at this stage may show the need for expansion of the editing procedure. For example, early tabulations of educational statistics occasionally showing impossible combinations of age and educational attainment may lead to an addition to the editing specifications to eliminate spurious cases of this nature. Tables are reviewed for internal consistency. It is not necessary that corresponding figures in different tables agree perfectly to the last digit, since minor differences are common in tables produced by different passes through the tabulating equipment. Arbitrary corrections for all small differences are not feasible, and such changes would add little to the accuracy of the data. If the tables printed out by the tabulating equipment are to be used for publication, the spelling, punctuation, spacing, and indentation are also carefully reviewed so that corrections can be made before the tables are reproduced.

Evaluation

The evaluation of census results is frequently cited as a requirement of a good census. An initial distinction must be made between the *products* of an evaluation program and the *uses* of these products. The products of an evaluation are measures of census error and identification of the sources of error.

Census errors may occur at any of the various stages of enumeration and processing and may be either *coverage* errors, that is, the omission or double-counting of persons, or *content* errors, that is, errors in the characteristics of the persons counted, resulting from incorrect reporting or recording or from failure to report. Methods for measuring the extent of error include reenumeration of a sample of the population covered in the census; comparison of census results with aggregate data from independent sources, usually administrative records; matching of census documents with other documents for the same person; and demographic analysis, which includes the comparison of statistics from successive censuses, analysis of the consistency of census statistics with estimates of population based on birth, death, and immigration statistics, and the analysis of census data for internal consistency and demographic reasonableness.

Uses of the results of census evaluation include guiding improvements in future censuses, assisting census users in interpreting results, and adjusting census results. Evaluation can identify certain geographic areas or persons with characteristics that made it problematic to enumerate them. The results of special enumeration efforts in relation to their costs may also be examined. Evaluation may also illustrate the usefulness and limitations of the census data, especially to novice users. It can alert the user to errors in the data and the magnitude of those errors. Moreover, the introduction of evaluation may inform users of additional sources of demographic data. Finally, evaluation may be used to adjust census results. Adjustment may be decided upon if evaluation indicates serious methodological, content, or coverage errors in the census (U.S. Census Bureau, 1985).

While there are a large number of methods for evaluating censuses, two predominant techniques have emerged. The first is the use of post-enumeration surveys, which employ case-by-case matching of the census and the survey to evaluate coverage and content error. The second is demographic analysis, which applies demographic techniques to data from administrative records to develop population estimates for comparison with the census.

Post-Enumeration Surveys

Post-enumeration surveys (PES) may be conducted in order to test census coverage and content error. While a PES may provide valuable insight into coverage and content error, caution must be used when designing and conducting a PES, as it is a statistically complex task. A simplified explanation of the method used by the U.S. Census Bureau in 1990 follows.

The Census Bureau's coverage measurement program in 1990 involving a post-enumeration survey was one in a series from 1950 to 2000. It was modeled after capture-recapture techniques used to estimate the size of animal populations. In essence, by sampling the population shortly after the census is taken and matching the two sets of data, estimates of census omissions may be derived. In the PES,

the traditional census enumeration corresponds to the original capture sample, and the PES to the recapture sample. However, equating the proportion of the PES sample not found in the census with the proportion of the census that was missed implicitly assumes that the chances of being counted in the capture sample and of being counted in the recapture sample are independent. It is known that the probability of being counted differs by age, sex, geographic area, and race, among other factors. For this reason, the results of the PES cannot be simply applied to the entire population, but instead must be stratified by small areas and various demographic and socioeconomic characteristics. In this way different coverage ratios are derived according to these factors.[1]

Demographic Analysis

In addition to the information afforded by a PES, simple demographic techniques can be used to evaluate a census for accuracy and reasonableness. Visually identifying results that are statistically improbable can be considered demographic analysis. However, much more refined demographic techniques are available not only for detecting error, but for identifying its source as well. The goal of demographic analysis is to provide population estimates that are independent of the census being evaluated, using data from other sources, including principally administrative records on demographic variables such as births, deaths, and migration, and demographic techniques such as sex ratio and survival analysis (Kerr, 1998, p. 1).

Demographic analysis can be used in two contexts. The first is to evaluate the quality of the results themselves, and the other is to provide measures of error for possible adjustment of the census. Countries may use different types and even different combinations of methods of demographic analysis to evaluate census results. The results of this analysis may be used not only to estimate the overcoverage or undercoverage, but also to provide a basis for adjustment to the official census population statistics. In cases where demographic analysis shows results similar to those of the census, confidence in the census may be increased.

Different formal procedures of coverage evaluation may be used, and in fact some may be more appropriate in certain countries, based on their record-keeping systems. In Canada, for example, a combination of a reverse record check (RRC) and an overcoverage study are used for evaluating the census. The RRC is a comprehensive record-linkage system, which entails taking a sample from various administrative

---

[1] Further information on post-enumeration surveys may be found in William Bell, "Using Information from Demographic Analysis in Post-Enumeration Survey Estimation." *Statistical Research Report* Series No. RR92/04, Washington, DC: U.S. Census Bureau, Statistical Research Division, 1992.

records of people who should have been enumerated and surveying for those who were missed. The overcoverage study involves reenumerating a sample of enumerated households to test whether the members should have been enumerated and where they should have been enumerated (Kerr, 1998, pp. 3–4). In Australia, the National Demographic Data Bank, established in 1926 to measure births, deaths, and international migration, is used to develop estimates, which are used in conjunction with a PES to evaluate that country's census (Kerr, 1998, p. 20).

In the United States, the Census Bureau applies demographic analysis, distinguished as being a *macro*level approach to measuring coverage, and a Post-Enumeration Survey distinguished as being a *micro*level approach. In the analytic method, estimates of the population below age 65 are derived from the basic demographic accounting equation, while Medicare data are used to estimate the population aged 65 and over. Some population groups, such as illegal entrants, have no associated administrative records and therefore must be estimated. While demographic analysis was not formally used to provide corrected populations in the 1990 U.S. census, it was used to measure net coverage error and "evaluate" the results of the PES (Robinson, 1996, p. 59).

The evaluation techniques of PES, RRC, overcoverage surveys, demographic analysis, and others are not without their shortcomings. The PES and RRC techniques are hindered by difficulty in measuring nonsampling error. Overcoverage is always difficult to measure, as in the case of *de jure* censuses, and the respondents often do not know that they have been recorded twice. The quality of demographic estimates declines in older age categories as the length of the times series for births used in estimation grows, and difficulty in measuring certain components (such as international migration) may compound error. Additionally, geographic detail is often lost, affording analysis only for large census regions or a nation as a whole.

The benefits of demographic analysis, however, are that it may be applied at a very low cost and that most of the administrative records necessary for demographic analysis oftentimes exist already and only need to be compiled and summarized for an evaluation. Demographic analysis is also easy to complete on a timely basis and works independently of the census, thus affording a quick and valid evaluation of census results. Finally, demographic analysis provides a benchmark of decennial census quality, affording the only consistent historical time series of measures of census net undercount for age, sex, and race groups (Robinson, 1996, pp. 60–61).

Dissemination

Once data are tabulated and reviewed, they are disseminated to users. Private, governmental, and other non-commercial groups rely on timely and convenient access to census data. Historically, census data have primarily been provided as a series of printed tables and more recently as data tapes and CD-ROMs. Recent advances in Internet technology now afford data users the opportunity to gather data online and to design data sets and tabulations not previously possible.[2]

Publication of Results

The output of the tabulation equipment may be used as the final statistical tables suitable for reproduction in the published reports, or it may be an interim tabular arrangement of the data from which the final tables will be produced. In the latter situation, typing of the final tables is either done directly from the machine printouts or requires preliminary hand posting of the data on worksheets to arrange them as required for the publication tables. These additional steps, of course, require verification, proofreading, and machine-checking.

Electronic Dissemination

The continuous improvement of computers and high-speed printers has made the automatic production of final tables both feasible and economical. The elimination of one or more manual operations in the production process reduces the burden of quality control, improves the timeliness of publication, and reduces manpower requirements. The use of high-speed printer output demands very precise advance planning of the content of each table, the wording of captions and stubs, and the spacing of lines and columns. The technical skill involved and the lead time required for such planning have led some countries to use a compromise procedure in which the machine printout is used for the body of the table but the stubs and captions are provided by means of preprinted overlays. The programming of the computer printout in these instances is designed to display the data in the desired arrangement and to include rudimentary captions, which identify the numbers.

As discussed in Chapter 2, the trend in the dissemination of survey and census data has been heavily toward electronic dissemination on CD-ROM and other high-capacity media, and it is now turning toward the Internet. There are many potential methods for data dissemination on the Internet, ranging from free public access of easily downloadable

---

[2] A valuable source of international census enumeration, data tabulation, and dissemination is *Diffusion: International Forum for Census Dissemination*, 1985, Statistics Canada. Published approximately every year, editorship rotates among participating countries. The journal provides international perspectives on testing forms, designs, topics, and questions. The journal also provides evaluation of data tabulation and dissemination methods.

data files and products, to interactive online software for the creation of customized data sets by the user to commercial "for a fee" data available by subscription only. Data security on the Internet is an important consideration, not only for users, but for data suppliers as well. Commercial data vendors often contend with security issues, such as unauthorized users' accessing their files without permission. In addition to the emplacement of sophisticated security systems, techniques have been devised whereby encoded/ encrypted data are placed on the Internet, and authorized users are privately given special software with which to access it.

Storage

In addition to these improvements in data dissemination, consideration must be given to the voluminous data in existence on other media. As already mentioned, many data have been stored on computer tape. Four alternate technological applications are used to replace traditional hard-copy records. These include microforms, computer-assisted microforms systems, optical disk systems, and computer-based systems (Suliman, 1996). It should be noted that these applications are used for a wide variety of data-storage purposes in addition to censuses and surveys, including civil registers, vital statistics, and population registers.

Microforms were one of the earliest replacements of hard-copy records and developed into both roll microfilm and flat microfiche. This application provides very long-term preservation of written information and often enhances written items on older records. An improvement of the microform system has been the computer-assisted microform system (CAM). If records already exist in a manual microform system, they can be indexed electronically, allowing very fast searches and record retrieval. If records do not already exist in a microform system, they may be filmed and placed directly into a CAM system. Shortcomings of both microform systems are the inability to evaluate the data statistically and to make any subsequent changes once the data have been filmed. The third application is known as an optical disk system. In this application, large volumes of records may be scanned electronically and stored on an optical disk. An electronic index may be created at the time of scanning, again allowing for very fast data searches and record retrieval. The optical disk system has the same limitations as microform, however, in that tabulations and calculations may not be made within the application, and revisions or corrections must be rescanned. The final system is the computer-based system. This has been described as the system in which data are entered directly via keystrokes or optical scanning systems that are compatible with software that enables conversion to an electronic format (Suliman, 1996).

Use of Sampling in Censuses

Although censuses as a rule involve a complete count of the number of inhabitants according to certain basic demographic characteristics, sampling is often used as an integral part of the enumeration to obtain additional information. As noted by the United Nations:

> The rapidly growing needs in a number of countries for extensive and reliable demographic data have made sampling methods a very desirable adjunct of any complete census. Sampling is increasingly being used for broadening the scope of the census by asking a number of questions of only a sample of the population. Modern experience in the use of sampling techniques has confirmed that it is not necessary to gather all demographic information on a complete basis; the sampling approach makes it feasible to obtain required data of acceptable accuracy when factors of time and cost might make it impracticable, or other considerations make it unnecessary, to obtain the data on a complete count basis. (United Nations, 1998, p. 25)

Many data items may have to be collected on a complete-count basis because of legal requirements or because of the need for a high degree of precision in the data on basic topics so as to establish benchmarks for subsequent studies. However, the need in most countries for more extensive demographic data has driven the collection of other items on a sample basis. This practice not only expands the potential coverage of subjects, but also saves time and money throughout the enumeration and processing stages as well.

Even when data collection is on a 100% basis, a representative sample of the schedules may be selected for advance processing to permit early publication of basic information for the country as a whole and for large areas. Many of the final tabulations in a census may be limited to a sample of the population; thus the cost of tabulation is reduced considerably, especially when detailed cross-classifications are involved. In addition to its use in enumeration and processing, sampling is important in the testing of census questionnaires and methods prior to enumeration, in the application of quality-control procedures during enumeration and processing, and in the evaluation of the census by means of a PES and field checks (United Nations, 1998, p. 47).

Sample Survey Methods

The role of sample survey methods in the collection of demographic data is well established. Some of the uses and advantages of sample surveys were discussed earlier in this chapter. While a complete discussion of probability, survey design, and sampling concepts is not presented here, it is important to consider three aspects of sampling. The first is the definition of the population. It is important for analysts to consider the population to be measured and characterized and to take precautions to ensure that the sample instrument affords generalizability to that population. The second is the sampling methods being used. The choice among convenience, typical-case, quota, or other designs in nonprobability sampling and among systematic, stratified, cluster, or other designs in probability sampling can have widely varying effects on the results of a survey. The third is the precision being sought. While the variance of sample estimates is inversely proportional to sample size, the cost, efficiency, and proposed uses of the data must also be considered (Henry, 1990).

When deriving census values based on sample census data, the sampling ratio itself determines the basic weights to be applied to each record (e.g., a sample of one in five leads to a weight of five). The figures produced by the application of these weights, however, are often subjected to other adjustments to obtain the final estimates. The adjustments may be made to account for the population not covered because of failure to obtain an interview. Also, independent population "controls" often are available to which the sample results are adjusted. In a census, the data obtained on a sample basis may be adjusted to the 100% population counts for the "marginal" totals by means of a ratio-estimation procedure. In this case the ratios of complete-count figures for specified demographic categories (e.g., age, sex, race) to the sample figures for the same categories are computed and used for adjusting the more detailed tabulations based on the sample. Similarly, the results of sample surveys may be adjusted to independent population controls, which are postcensal estimates derived by applying the basic population estimating equation to population figures from the previous census.

Other Demographic Record Systems

The administration of population registers differs somewhat from country to country, but basically it calls for registration at birth and entering specified subsequent events (marriage, change of residence, death, etc.) upon the individual or household record. A copy of this record, or an extract thereof, may be required to follow the person when she or he moves from one local jurisdiction to another. There are always local registers, and there may also be a central national register. The discussion of population registers in Chapter 2 gave an indication of their general nature and cited a number of publications concerning them.

Some aspects of the collection and processing of immigration data, particularly the registration system associated with border control, are discussed in Chapter 18. Here we consider, next, vital statistics registration systems in detail.

VITAL STATISTICS

Dual Functions of a Vital Statistics System

Vital statistics systems are designed primarily to accomplish the registration of vital events. Vital statistics, are the statistics derived from compiling vital events. Registration of births, deaths, marriages, and divorces was originally intended to meet public and private needs for permanent legal records of these events, and these needs continue to be very important. However, equally important are the demands for useful statistics that have come from the fields of public health, life insurance, medical research, and population analysis.

Viewed as one of several general methods of collecting demographic statistics, registration has certain advantages and disadvantages. If events are registered near the time of occurrence, the completeness of reporting and the accuracy of the information are potentially greater than if reporting depends on a later contacted by an official and recall of the facts by the respondent. Also, continuous availability of the data file tends to be assured by the dual uses of the information—for legal and for statistical and public purposes.

There are also certain limitations of the registration method. The fact that the vital record is a legal document limits the amount and kind of nonlegal information that can be included in it. The method is also affected by the number and variety of persons involved in registering the events. For example, birth registration in some countries requires actions by thousands or millions of individual citizens and hundreds of local officials. Thousands of physicians, nurses, or hospital employees may be involved, and all of these people have other duties that they consider more urgent. It seems inevitable that for the most part these many and diverse persons will have less training and expertise in data collection than the enumerators who interview respondents in censuses or other population surveys. The latter are usually given intensive training in which the importance, purposes, and exact specifications of the information sought are thoroughly explained.

Satisfactory conduct of registration, in terms of both the legal and the statistical requirements, is closely related to the completeness and promptness with which events are registered and the accuracy of the information in the registration records. Certain functions such as indexing and filing of certificates, issuance of copies, and amendment of records are important for their legal uses but do not significantly affect the statistics. However, if the legal functions are poorly performed, the statistical program will suffer because public pressures will demand that first priority be given to serving people's needs for copies of their personal records.

International Standards and National Practices

The *Handbook of Vital Statistics Systems and Methods, Volume I: Legal, Organizational and Technical Aspects* (United Nations, 1991) and *Handbook of Vital Statistics Systems and Methods, Volume II: Review of National Prac-*

tice (United Nations, 1985), published by the United Nations Statistical Office, are the principal sources of the material presented in this section on international recommendations for the collection and processing of vital statistics.

Definitions of Vital Events

As in all systems of data collection, clear, precise definitions of the phenomena measured are prerequisites for accurate vital statistics. Use of standard definitions of vital events is essential for comparability of statistics for different countries.

Live Birth

Most countries follow the definition of a live birth recommended by the World Health Assembly in May 1950, and by the United Nations Statistical Commission in 1953, which is as follows:

> Live birth is the complete expulsion or extraction from its mother of a product of conception, irrespective of the duration of pregnancy, which after such separation, breathes or shows any other evidence of life, such as beating of the heart, pulsation of the umbilical cord, or definite movement of voluntary muscles, whether or not the umbilical cord has been cut or the placenta is attached; each product of such birth is considered live-born. (United Nations, 1991, p. 17)

Under this definition a birth should be registered as a live birth regardless of its "viability" or death soon after birth or death before the required registration date. Although variations in the statistical treatment of "nonviable" live births (defined by low birthweight or short period of gestation) do not significantly affect the statistics of live births, they can have a substantial effect on fetal death and infant death statistics.

Death

Until very recently, there has been less difficulty with respect to the definition of death than with definitions of live birth and fetal death. For statistical purposes, the United Nations has recommended the following definition of death:

> Death is the permanent disappearance of all evidence of life at any time after live birth has taken place (postnatal cessation of vital functions without capability of resuscitation). This definition therefore excludes foetal deaths. (United Nations, 1991, p. 17)

Fetal Death

The definition of fetal death recommended by the World Health Organization (WHO) and the United Nations Statistical Commission is as follows:

> Foetal death is death prior to the complete expulsion or extraction from its mother of a product of conception, irrespective of the duration of pregnancy; the death is indicated by the fact that after such separation the foetus does not breathe or show any other evidence

of life, such as beating of the heart, pulsation of the umbilical cord, or definite movement of voluntary muscles. (United Nations, 1991, p. 17)

Marriage

The Statistical Commission of the United Nations has recommended the following definition of marriage for statistical purposes:

> Marriage is the act, ceremony or process by which the legal relationship of husband and wife is constituted. The legality of the union may be established by civil, religious, or other means as recognized by the laws of each country. (United Nations, 1991, p. 17)

Divorce

The United Nations Statistical Commission's recommended definition of divorce is as follows:

> Divorce is the final legal dissolution of a marriage, that is, the separation of husband and wife by a judicial decree which confers on the parties the right to civil and/or religious remarriage, according to the laws of each country. (United Nations, 1991, p. 17)

This definition excludes petitions, provisional divorces, and legal separations since they do not imply final dissolution of marriage and the right to remarry. In some countries, legal annulment is a statistically significant method of marriage termination. It is desirable in such countries to include annulments with divorces in determining the statistics of marriage dissolution. The *Handbook* defines annulment as "the invalidation or voiding of a marriage by a competent authority, according to the laws of each country, which confers on the parties the status of never having been married to each other (United Nations, 1991, p. 17).

Collection of Vital Statistics

Vital statistics systems differ in the amount of authority given to the collecting agency, the degree of national centralization of its organization, and the type of agency carrying out the program. The basic features of a vital statistics collection system are discussed in the following sections.

Civil Registration Method

This method of collecting vital statistics data is defined as the "continuous, permanent, compulsory recording of the occurrence and characteristics of vital events . . . in accordance with the legal requirements of each country" (United Nations, 1991, p. 16). The registration of all vital events must be done as they occur and must be maintained in order to be retrieved as required. This must be done by a permanent governmental agency with administrative stability. The underpinning, however, is that vital registration is legally required and there are penalties for failure to comply with the law. "The compulsion or legal obligation to register a vital event is the basic premise of the entire civil registration system. When registration is voluntary rather than compulsory, there can be no assurance of complete or accurate vital records or statistics" (United Nations, 1973, p. 159). Without specific penalties, the fact that it is compulsory is meaningless.

Governmental Organization

The registration systems may be classified as organized under centralized or decentralized control. Most nations have established a centralized national authority over registration. In some countries, it is the civil registration office, in others, the department of public health, and in others, the central statistical agency. Again, in some countries the same national agency is responsible for both registration and vital statistics, but in others two or occasionally three separate agencies control these two functions. Advantages of a central registration office include direct and effective control over the entire system, including a standard legal framework, uniform procedures, and consistent interpretation and enforcement of norms and regulations.

In a decentralized system, civil registration is administered by major civil divisions, for example, the state, province, or department. Many countries with federated political systems have decentralized registration systems.

The Statistical Office of the United Nations Secretariat undertook a Survey of Vital Statistics Methods during 1976–1979. Of the 103 countries reporting on the type of civil registration system, 88 were centralized and 15 decentralized (United Nations, 1985, p. 8).

Local registration areas are the basic units of a vital registration system. They must have clearly defined geographic boundaries and be small enough for the registrar to provide good registration services for the area and for persons reporting vital events to come to or communicate with the registration office without excessive difficulty. One of the most important responsibilities of the local registrar is to encourage the general population, physicians, midwives, and others to report occurrences of vital events promptly and to supply complete and accurate information about them.

Informants and Reporters

The person responsible by law for reporting the occurrence of a vital event may or may not also be the source of the facts associated with the event. In most countries, a family member is responsible for reporting the occurrence of a live birth, fetal death, or death, together with certain personal information, but the attendant physician or midwife is also responsible for reporting the event along with certain medical information. The officiant, civil or religious, at the marriage is required to report it in about one-half of the countries; in the other half, the participants, bride and groom, are responsible. Reporting of divorces is the responsibility of the court in slightly more than half of the

countries and of one or both of the parties to the divorce in the remaining countries (United Nations, 1985, pp. 20–22).

Place of Registration

The United Nations recommends and, with few exceptions, the countries of the world require registration of vital events in the local registration area where the event occurred. Statistics tabulated by the United Nations from the 1976–1979 survey of national practices show that the percentage of responding countries where vital events are registered by place of occurrence is 92 for births and deaths, 93 for fetal deaths, 90 for marriages, and only 55 for divorces (United Nations, 1985, pp. 29–30). Tabulations are frequently made by area of usual residence of the mother, decedent, and so forth; these are generally regarded as more useful for demographic purposes than tabulations by place of occurrence.

Time Allowed for Current Registration

The registration record usually calls for both the date of the event and the date of registration. National laws usually specify the maximum interval permitted between these two dates for each type of vital event. The 1976–1979 survey shows that the time allowed for registering deaths tends to be shorter than for births—94% within 30 days for deaths compared with 73% for births (United Nations, 1985, pp. 26–27). The United Nations recommends that final tabulations for any calendar period should be based on events that occurred during that period and not on those registered. Information from the 1976–1979 survey indicates that two-thirds to three-quarters of the countries tabulated the records by date of registration (United Nations, 1985, pp. 34–35).

Content of Statistical Records

The need for national vital statistics data is the primary determinant of what items should be collected on vital records. Another major consideration is international comparability. The United Nations has recommended lists of statistical items that should be included in the records of live births, fetal deaths, deaths, marriages, and divorces (United Nations, 1991, pp. 30–31). The World Health Organization recommended the form of the medical certificate of cause of death. Some of the recommended items are designated as priority items, that is, items all countries should include. Parallel listings of priority items for the various vital statistics records are shown in Table 3.1.

Compilation and Tabulation of Vital Statistics

The underlying purpose of a vital statistics system is to make available useful statistics for the planning, administration, and evaluation of public health programs and to provide basic statistics for demographic research. The documents undergo much the same processing that is required

TABLE 3.1   Priority Items Recommended for Inclusion in Statistical Reports of Live Birth, Fetal Death, Death, Marriage, and Divorce

Live birth	Fetal death	Death	Marriage	Divorce
Date of occurrence	Date of occurrence	Date of occurrence	Date of occurrence	Date of occurrence
Date of registration	Date of registration	Date of registration	Date of registration	Date of registration
Place of occurrence	Place of occurrence	Place of occurrence	Place of occurrence	Place of occurrence
Place of usual residence of mother		Place of usual residence	Place of usual residence[1]	Place of usual residence[2]
Sex	Sex	Sex		
Legitimacy status	Legitimacy status	Marital status	Marital status[1]	
Date of marriage (legitimate births)	Date of marriage (legitimate births)			Date of marriage
Age of mother	Age of mother	Age	Age[1]	Age[2]
Type of birth (single or multiple)	Type of birth (single or multiple)		Type of ceremony (civil, religious, etc.)	
Number of children born to this mother	Number of children born to this mother			Number of dependent children of divorcee[2]
	Number of previous fetal deaths to this mother			
Weight at birth				
	Gestational age			
Attendant at birth				
		Cause		
		Certifier		

[1] Of bride and groom.
[2] Of both divorcees.
Source: United Nations. 1991. "Handbook of Vital Statistics Systems and Methods," Volume I: "Legal, Organizational and Technical aspects." *Studies in Methods*, Series F, No. 35, pp. 30–31.

for census and survey data, and similar planning is required to produce the desired tabulations.

In a majority of countries, the central statistical office has been given responsibility for compilation of national vital statistics. In some countries, including the United States, this function has been located in the national public health agency. In other countries, responsibility has been divided between the health agencies and the statistical and registration agencies.

The United Nations has suggested four criteria for measuring the effectiveness of a national vital statistics program, (1) coverage of the statistics, (2) accuracy of the statistics, (3) tabulations of sufficient detail to reveal important relationships, and (4) timeliness of availability of the data (United Nations, 1991, p. 46). One of the basic premises of a vital statistics system is that every event should be reported for statistical purposes for all geographic areas and all population subgroups. The time reference for the data should be the date on which the event occurred. The geographic reference for the statistics may be either the place where the event occurred or the residence of the person to whom the event occurred. Final tabulations for subnational geographic areas should be by place of residence. This allows for computation of meaningful population-based rates. Tabulation by place of occurrence may also be useful for specific administrative purposes. Finally, the data and their analysis

need to be disseminated to be useful. Unless the data are available to the public, its willingness to support the system cannot be expected. A wide variety of dissemination media should be used, including printed publications, public use data tapes and disks, and the Internet.

It is also essential that statistics of births, deaths, and marriages be based on definitions and classifications that are identical to or consistent with those used in the population census. Computation of valid vital rates and use of these rates in population estimation depend on consistent treatment of vital statistics and population data. This objective is sometimes difficult to attain, however, especially when different agencies are responsible for the two statistical programs.

Other Methods of Obtaining Vital Statistics

Every nation has as a goal the coverage of all its states or other areas in its vital statistics system. This objective is often not achieved without a long period during which the registration system is being developed and its coverage gradually extended. Other data collection methods may supplement or be a substitute for the registration system. These may include surveys, censuses, and population registers.

Surveys

Vital statistics may be obtained from a household sample survey by questioning members of the household regarding vital events that occurred in that household in some specific past period. This method can be implemented in a relatively short time if the necessary technical skills can be mobilized to plan and conduct the survey; and it can be expected to provide some statistics rather speedily. Its success depends heavily on the willingness of persons in the sample to supply the information and on their ability to recall the vital events occurring during some past period of time, and the date, place of occurrence, and other facts about the events. Also, the considerable skills required for sample design, survey organization and operation, and questionnaire construction need to be available on a continuing basis.

Censuses

Information on vital events is sometimes obtained in the population census. Statistics on births, marriages, and deaths in the previous year are available from this source in some countries. This method is essentially a special survey, which includes the entire population rather than a sample. It is subject to the same limitations as surveys with respect to the recall of events.

Population Registers

In countries that maintain a population register, birth, death, marriage, and divorce registration may be an integral part of the register. The information obtained in the registration of vital events must not only serve the needs for statistics on these subjects but must also be consistent in definitions and classifications with the information to be kept in the population register on the entire population.

The United States Vital Statistics System

National-State Relationships

The United States system for collecting vital records is decentralized in that the legal authority over registration is located in each of the 50 states and the District of Columbia. New York City is an independent registration area that has its own laws and regulations and publishes its own reports, as do Guam, Puerto Rico, and the Virgin Islands of the United States. Many states are divided into local registration districts, for each of which a registrar is appointed. There are about 10,000 such registrars, appointed by the state governments or locally elected. Each state separately processes the statistics that it wishes for its own area and population. The processing of national vital statistics is centralized in the National Center for Health Statistics (NCHS), a federal agency located in the U.S. Public Health Service (US PHS). An extensive history of the U.S. vital registration and statistics system may be found in

History and Organization of the Vital Statistics System (Hetzel, 1997).

Uniformity of Reporting

Although registration of vital events is governed by state laws, a considerable degree of uniformity has been achieved in definitions, organization, procedures, and forms. Uniformity has been promoted primarily by the development of model laws and certificate forms that have been recommended for state use. The Model State Vital Statistics Law has been followed with variations in the laws enacted in the various states. It was first promulgated in 1907 and has been revised and reissued several times. The most recent version was promulgated in 1992 (US PHS, 1995). Standard certificates of the several vital events, issued by the responsible national agency, have been the principal means of achieving uniformity in the certificates of the individual states, which provide the information upon which national vital statistics are based. The last revision was promulgated in 1989 (US NCHS/Tolson et al., 1991). The next revision is being implemented gradually beginning in 2003.

The responsible national vital statistics agency (the Census Bureau, 1903–1946, NOVS, 1947–1959, and NCHS, 1960 to date) has actively assisted the state agencies in achieving complete, prompt, and accurate registration of vital events. Tests of registration completeness and intensive educational campaigns to promote registration have been joint federal-state efforts. The national office has developed and recommended to the states model handbooks designed to instruct physicians, hospitals, coroners and medical examiners, funeral directors, and marriage license clerks on current registration procedures and the meaning of the information requested in the certificates (e.g., US NCHS, 1987).

Functions Performed by State Offices

In the decentralized registration system of the United States, the primary responsibility for the collection of vital records rests with each state. This responsibility encompasses a number of functions that are carried out in each state's vital statistics office.

Planning Content of Forms

It is the responsibility of the state's vital statistics office to recommend the format and content of the vital records used in its jurisdiction. These recommendations are usually based to a large extent on the United States standard certificates but also often reflect special interests or needs not encompassed in the federal model forms. In spite of the efforts of the federal government to promote national uniformity, state and local uses of vital records, especially in the health field, produce differences in record content and format, which have an effect on the statistics. Some of the states have not included all of the standard demographic or health items on their vital records. Currently, however, all states have birth and death certificates that conform very closely to the U.S. standard certificates in content.

Confidentiality of Records

It is the responsibility of each sate or other registration area to determine the need for confidentiality and to maintain confidentiality of the vital records. In some areas, vital records are considered to be public documents; in other areas, the vital statistics laws and administrative regulations permit the release of information or certified copies of the record only to certain authorized persons.

Receipt and Processing of Records

One of the major functions of a state office is to serve as the repository for vital records of events occurring within the state, and thus to serve as a central source within each state for both the legal and statistical uses of the records. This function entails a number of related responsibilities, such as the handling of corrections, missing data, name changes, and adoptions and legitimations and issuing certified copies of records on file.

Electronic birth certificate (EBC) software has been developed for use in the capture of the information on the birth certificate at the reporting source (hospitals). This software has been designed to improve the timeliness and quality of birth registration. The information on the birth certificate is entered into the software by hospital personnel and transmitted to the appropriate registration authority within the state. Before transmission, it is checked for quality and completeness by an edit program designed and installed by the state. Currently all states are using EBC software and approximately 90% of births are currently registered through this process.

States are also in the process of developing Electronic death certificate (EDC) software. It is anticipated that within a few years most deaths will also be registered through an electronic process.

Tabulation and Publication of the Data

Just as each state prepares and processes its own vital statistics data, so does each state prepare an annual summary of its vital statistics. These summaries vary in analytic detail and comprehensiveness, but almost all states publish some kind of annual vital statistics report. Some of these reports merely present selected vital statistics data, whereas others contain, in addition to tabular material, an analysis and interpretation of the statistics.

Another activity of the state vital statistics offices is the transmittal of data to the National Center for Health Statistics (NCHS) for the purpose of assembling national statistics. The NCHS purchases the data in electronic form from each registration area through a contractual arrangement, which includes a guarantee of confidentiality prohibiting the center from releasing any data other than statistical summaries without the written consent of the state's vital statistics office.

In order to issue provisional statistics in its *National Vital Statistics Report*, NCHS receives reports from the states on the total number of records (birth, death, infant death, marriage, and divorce) received during the month regardless of date of occurrence. Characteristics about these events are not published in these provisional reports.

Functions Performed by the National Center for Health Statistics

The NCHS performs a variety of functions designed to improve the national vital statistics system. It exercises leadership in the revision of the standard certificates and in evaluating the completeness of birth registration; represents the United States in international conferences on the standard classification of causes of death; conducts a training program on vital and health statistics; and helps the states in developing forms, procedures, draft legislation, definitions, and tabulations.

The NCHS serves as the focal point for the collection, analysis, and dissemination of national vital statistics for the United States. Because of the diversity of practices and procedures existing in the decentralized U.S. system, the production of national statistics involves more than the combination of statistics from each registration area to produce national vital statistics.

Detailed data on births, deaths, and fetal deaths are obtained in electronic form through contractual arrangements with the states. The data are subjected to a series of computer edits that eliminate inconsistencies in the data and impute missing data for certain items. This is generally done only when the number of items with missing data comprises a very small proportion of the total. Sex, race, and geographic classification are assigned if not reported on the birth or death certificates, and age and marital status of mother are assigned if not reported on the birth certificate.

The final computer tabulations of national vital statistics appear in various publications prepared by NCHS and mentioned in Chapter 2, "Basic Sources of Statistics." Unpublished material and resource data for special investigations are maintained by the NCHS and made available on the Internet (*www.cdc.gov/nchs*). In addition, unit record data on births, deaths, and linked birth-infant deaths are available on CD-ROMs.

References

Anderson, M. 1988. *The American Census: A Social History.* New Haven, CT: Yale University Press.

Choldin, H. 1994. *Looking for the Last Percent: The Controversy over Census Undercounts.* New Brunswick, NJ: Rutgers University Press.

Henry, G. 1990. *Practical Sampling*. Newbury Park, CA: Sage.

Hetzel, A. M., 1997. *History and Organization of the Vital Statistics System*. Hyattsville, MD: National Center for Health Statistics.

Kerr, D. 1998. "A Review of Procedures for Estimating the Net Undercount of Censuses in Canada, the United States, Britain and Australia." *Demographic Documents*. Ottawa: Statistics Canada.

Robinson, J. G. 1996. "What Is the Role of Demographic Analysis in the 2000 United States Census?" *Proceedings of Statistics Canada Symposium, 96: Nonsampling Errors, Nov. 1996*. pp. 57–63, Ottawa: Statistics Canada.

Suliman, S. H. 1996. "Automation of Administrative Records and Statistics," http://www.un.org/Depts/unsd/demotss/tenjun96/suliman.htm, October 27, 1999.

United Nations, 1973. "Principles and Recommendations for a Vital Statistics System." *Statistical Papers*, Series M, No. 19, Rev. 1. New York: United Nations.

United Nations, 1983. "Handbook of Household Surveys." *Studies in Methods*, Series F, No. 10. New York: United Nations.

United Nations, 1985. "Handbook of Vital Statistics Systems and Methods," Volume II: "Review of National Practices." *Studies in Methods*, Series F, No. 35. New York: United Nations.

United Nations. 1991. "Handbook of Vital Statistics Systems and Methods," Volume I: "Legal, Organizational and Technical Aspects." *Studies in Methods*, Series F, No. 35. New York: United Nations.

United Nations. 1998. "Principles and Recommendations for Population and Housing Censuses." *Statistical Papers*, Series M. No. 67 / Rev. 1. New York: United Nations.

U.S. Census Bureau. 1985. "Evaluating Censuses of Population and Housing." *Special Training Document* ISP-TR-5. Washington, DC: U.S. Census Bureau.

U.S. Census Bureau. 1995. "Solicitation of 2000 Census Content Needs from Non-federal Data Users: November 1994–March 1995." Special report of the Decennial Management Division. Washington, DC: U.S. Census Bureau.

U.S. National Center for Health Statistics, 1987. *Hospitals' and Physicians' Handbook of Birth Registration and Fetal Death Reporting*. DHHS Pub. No. (PHS) 87–1107. Washington, DC: National Center for Health Statistics.

U.S. National Center for Health Statistics, 1991. "The 1989 Revision of the U.S. Standard Certificates and Reports," by G. C. Tolson, J. M. Barnes, G. A. Gay, and J. L. Kowaleski. *Vital Health Stat* 4(28). Hyattsville, MD: National Center for Health Statistics.

U.S. Public Health Service. 1995. *Model State Vital Statistics Act and Regulations*. DHHS Pub. No. (PHS) 95–1115.

Yates, Frank. 1981. *Sampling Methods for Censuses and Surveys*. New York: Oxford University Press.

Suggested Readings

Anderson, M. 1988. *The American Census: A Social History*. New Haven, CT: Yale University Press.

Edmonston, B., and C. Schultze (eds.). 1995. *Modernizing the U.S. Census*. Washington, DC: National Academy Press.

Hetzel, A. M. 1997. *History and Organization of the Vital Statistics System*. Hyattsville, MD: National Center for Health Statistics.

Hogan, H. 1993. "The 1990 Post-Enumeration Survey: Operations and Results." *Journal of the American Statistical Association* 88 (423), 1047–1060.

Robinson, J. G., B. Ahmed, P. Das Gupta, and K. A. Woodrow. 1993. "Estimating the Population Coverage in the 1990 United States Census Based on Demographic Analysis." *Journal of the American Statistical Association* 88 (423), 1061–1071.

United Nations. 1998. "Principles and Recommenolations for Population and Housing Censuses." *Statistical Papers*, Series M. No. 67/Rev. 1. New York: United Nations.

4

Population Size

JANET WILMOTH

The size of a population is usually the first demographic fact that a government tries to obtain. The initial censuses of a people are often a mere headcount. Particularly in premodern times, the emphasis in census taking was on fiscal and military potentials. Hence, women, children, aliens, slaves, or aborigines were usually relatively undercounted or omitted altogether (Alterman, 1969, Part I, Chapter 1). Modern censuses provide more comprehensive coverage, taking into consideration issues related to the individual enumeration of all persons living in a specific geographic area at a given time and the completeness of coverage.

CONCEPTS OF TOTAL POPULATION

In general, modern censuses are designed to include the "total population" of an area. This concept is not so simple as may at first appear. There are two "ideal" types of total population counts, the *de facto* and the *de jure* (Shryock, 1955). The former comprises all the people actually present in a given area at a given time. The latter is more ambiguous. It comprises all the people who "belong" to a given area at a given time by virtue of legal residence, usual residence, or some similar criterion. In practice, while modern censuses call for one of these ideal types with specified modifications, it is difficult to avoid some mixture of the two approaches.

Issues Related to National Practices

Specific National Practices

The practice followed in more than 220 national censuses is summarized in the United Nations *Demographic Yearbook: 1996*, Table 3, page 134 (United Nations, 1998). Since the *de facto* type of census is considerably more common

than the *de jure* type on a worldwide basis, the table merely notes which countries conduct a *de jure* census. For example, most African, Asian, South American, and Oceanic censuses are *de facto*. Notable exceptions include Algeria, Israel, Nepal, Philippines, Thailand, and Australia. The situation is mixed in North and Central America, with the following countries or dependent areas using the *de jure* approach: Canada, the Cayman Islands, Costa Rica, Greenland, Guadeloupe, Haiti, Martinique, Mexico, the Netherland Antilles, Nicaragua, Puerto Rico, the United States, and the U.S. Virgin Islands. A mixed situation also exists in Europe. The *de jure* approach is used in Austria, Belgium, Bosnia Herzegovina, Croatia, the Czech Republic, Denmark, the Faeroe Islands, Germany, Iceland, Luxembourg, the Netherlands, Norway, Slovakia, Slovenia, Sweden, Switzerland, and Yugoslavia (United Nations, 1998).

For many countries, the distinction between *de jure* and *de facto* would not be very important for the national total. Usually, however, the choice would appreciably affect the count for many geographic subdivisions. The effect would also vary according to the census date.

The United Nations regards the method used to allocate persons to a geographic subdivision of the country as being best determined by national needs. At first it seemed to favor the *de facto* principle, but later it recognized the complications of that approach for family statistics, migration statistics, and the computation of resident vital rates and other measures. The *de jure* concept seems to be rather ambiguous. Legal residence, usual residence, and still other criteria could be used to define the people who "belong" to a given area at a given time. In the United States, moreover, there is no unique definition of "legal residence." A person may have certain rights or duties (voting, public assistance, admission to a public institution, jury duty, certain taxes, and so forth) in one state or community and other rights or duties in another state or community. A citizen who has recently moved may not have some of these rights in any state. In certain Asian societies, the people have sometimes been enumerated at their familial or even ancestral home, where they actually may have lived only in childhood or never at all.

Thus, the relative difficulties of the *de facto* and *de jure* methods in census taking and their relative accuracy depend to some extent on the particular country. As a result, the *Handbook of Population and Housing Censuses* (United Nations, 1992, p. 91) recommends "that a combination of the two methods be adopted to obtain information that is as complete as possible." In such a situation, people may be listed in the field in a particular manner, but when the tabulations are made, some of them may be reassigned to other areas on the basis of recorded facts about where they spent the previous night or their usual residence. Whatever coverage method is used, it must be clearly spelled out for the benefit of those who report in the census, those who process the data, and those who use the statistics.

Inclusion of Certain Groups

Despite the coverage method used (e.g., *de jure*, *de facto*, or a combination of both), special consideration has to be given to certain groups because of their ambiguous situations. According to the United Nations (1992, pp. 81–82), these groups include the following:

(a) Nomads
(b) Persons living in areas to which access is difficult
(c) Military, naval, and diplomatic personnel of the country, and their families, located outside the country
(d) Merchant seaman and fisherman resident in the country but at sea at the time of the census (including those who have no place of residence other than their quarters aboard ship)
(e) Civilian residents temporarily in another country as seasonal workers
(f) Civilian residents who cross the boarder daily to work in another country
(g) Civilian residents other than those in groups (c), (e), and (f) who are working in another country
(h) Civilian residents other than those in groups (c) through (g) who are temporarily absent from the country
(i) Foreign military, naval, and diplomatic or defense personnel and their families who may be located in the country
(j) Civilian aliens temporarily in the country as seasonal workers
(k) Civilian aliens who cross a frontier daily to work in the country

(l) Civilian aliens other than those in groups (i), (j), and (k) who are working in the country
(m) Civilian aliens other than those in groups (i) through (l) who are temporarily in the country
(n) Transients on ships in harbor at the time of the census.

Particular attention is often given to providing separate counts of the civilian and military population for several reasons. In some ways, the civilian and military populations constitute separate economies. There are constraints on free movement from one to another. Moreover, they have different components of change, and their geographic distributions are very different. The most feasible methods of enumerating them may also differ. All these considerations have led a few countries to publish separate statistics for their civilian and military populations.

While specific countries may have different reasons for including or excluding specific groups in the total population, census documentation should clearly indicate which groups are included in the total population. In addition, estimates of the size of each nonenumerated group should be reported in the census documentation. This information can be gathered from administrative records or other sources. Alternatively, all of the people present in the country at the time of the census can be enumerated by using a census questionnaire that distinguishes these different groups. This information can be used later to include or exclude certain groups from the total population.

International Standards

The information regarding groups included or excluded is critical for comparing population size across different countries and regions, as well as for arriving at estimates of world population.

The United Nations (1992, p. 83) recommends that "groups, . . . , (a) through (f), (h) and (l) be included in, and (g), (i) through (k), (m), and (n) be excluded from, the total population." Even though this recommendation specifies issues related to civilian residents and civilian aliens quite clearly, it is consistent with earlier United Nations documents that advocate an "international conventional total" (also called a "modified *de facto* population"). This population count consists of "the total number of persons present in the country at the time of the census, excluding foreign military, naval, and diplomatic personnel and their families located in the country but including military, naval, and diplomatic personnel of the country and their families located abroad and merchant seamen resident in the country but at sea at the time of the census."[1]

---

[1] This recommendation appeared first in Statistical Papers, Series M, No. 27, *Principles and Recommendations for National Population Censuses*, 1958, p. 10.

Evidence of a Person

In addition to questions of whether certain classes of people are to be included in the national census count, and where a particular person should be counted, problems arise in actual practice as to whether there is sufficient evidence of a person. For example, even after repeated attempts to obtain the information by mail, telephone, or personal visit, there may remain a number of marginal cases where the only evidence consists of (1) names copied by the enumerator from mailboxes or (2) information from a neighbor that one or more people live at a given address. Decisions must then be made as to whether there is enough information to warrant listing these persons on the schedule. While specific decision rules vary across countries, it is recommended that census documentation clearly indicate the decision rules used regarding evidence of a person.

Method of Enumeration

The size of the total population can be determined through the use of several different methods.[2] The first is the canvasser method, which involves the use of trained enumerators who visit each housing unit to conduct an interview. During this interview, information is obtained about the housing structure and the characteristics of its occupants. The enumerator records this information on the appropriate census forms and then turns the forms in to his or her field supervisor. A primary advantage of this enumeration method is that the enumerators can be thoroughly trained in census procedures and instructions. This can increase the quality and consistency of the data, particularly in countries where a large proportion of the population is illiterate. The main disadvantages are that in practice not all of the household members can usually be directly interviewed and a misapplication of the rules by one enumerator can lead to misreporting in an entire enumeration area, i.e., enumerator-induced bias.

Another common method is the householder (or self-enumeration) method in which instructions and questionnaires are distributed to each housing unit before the census day. The census form is then completed by one member of the household, preferably the household head or another responsible household member. This method can improve accuracy by allowing the householder to consult with other members of the household at their convenience. It can also considerably lower costs, particularly when the mail-out/mail-back procedure of distribution is used extensively. This involves using the postal service to deliver and return the census forms, instead of an enumerator. The householder method is most effective in countries in which a high percentage of the population is literate and which have an efficient and universal postal system.

The census-station method involves developing a list of all housing units in an area and then establishing a centrally located census station. The population in that area is asked to report to the census station, where the enumerator records the relevant information on the appropriate forms. To ensure complete coverage, the enumerator is required to visit non-responding housing units. An alternative method involves assembling all of the residents of a given area in one place where the enumeration is conducted. In this situation, the head of the group often provides general information about the number of people living in the area. Detailed population characteristics are usually not collected. This method is particularly effective in enumerating individuals living in isolated areas and among particular groups.

In practice, a combination of methods is often used to ensure that the size of the total population is being accurately assessed. Furthermore, over time the balance of reliance on these methods can shift as the society changes. Changes in a population's literacy level, geographic location, and composition, as well as developments in the postal system, can call for a reassessment of the most appropriate enumeration method for a given census.

The United States Decennial Census

The Constitution of the United States requires (in Article 1, Section 2.3) merely that "Representatives . . . shall be apportioned among the several States which may be included within this Union, according to their respective numbers." The Constitution does not provide a unique prescription for the type of enumeration to be made. In the 18th century, there was considerably less difference between the *de jure* and *de facto* populations of an area than there was in the 20th, because the limited transportation facilities and the way of life tended to keep people at home. Hence, the framers of the Constitution probably were unaware of the ambiguity of their directive. Ordinarily, there would not be a great deal of difference at the national level, but in certain historical periods the two types of enumeration would have resulted in substantially different population totals. For example, during the peak of activity in World War II, a *de facto* count would have yielded about 9 million fewer persons than a count taken on a *strict de jure* basis. "The census has never been taken on a *de facto* basis, however: and it has come to be considered that such a basis would be inconsistent with the spirit, if not the letter, of the Constitution. The basic principle followed in American censuses is that of 'usual residence.' This type of census more nearly approximates the *de jure* than the *de facto*" (Shryock, 1955, p. 877).

---

[2] See United Nations (1992, pp. 88–90) for addition information. This section only summarizes the discussion presented there.

Definition of Usual Residence

The meaning of "usual residence" itself is not a simple matter and has to be spelled out in some detail for the benefit of enumerators and respondents. While the general spirit of "usual residence" has remained the same since the decennial census was established in the United States in 1790, the inclusion of specific groups has varied (Shryock, 1960). Usual place of residence is the "place where he or she lives and sleeps most of the time or the place where the person considers to be his or her usual home" (U.S. Bureau of the Census, 1992c). Since 1960 the procedures for conducting the census have depended more on self-enumeration and less on the canvasser method. As a result, the instructions to the householder on the mail-out/mail-back forms regarding whom to include on the household list are quite specific. The instructions on page 1 of the 1990 form asks the householder to "list on the number lines below the names of each person living here on Sunday, April 1, including all persons staying here who have no other home (U.S. Bureau of the Census, 1992d)". This list was to include newborns, members of the household temporarily absent on vacation, visiting, on business, or in a general hospital, as well as boarders or lodgers who usually slept in the housing unit. The instructions also covered a number of special cases, some of which are discussed in the sections that follow. Similar instructions were given for the census of 2000.

Enumeration of Special Populations[3]

Members of the Armed Forces within the United States

Persons in the Army, Navy, Air Force, Marine Corps, and Coast Guard of the United States were supposed to have been counted as residents of the place where they were stationed, not at the place from which they were inducted or at their parental home. Those members who lived off post were to be counted at their homes (with families, if any), whereas those who lived in barracks or similar quarters were considered as residents of those group quarters. One exception is the personnel assigned to the 6th or 7th Fleet of the Navy, who are counted as part of the overseas population. This information was collected in collaboration with the U.S. Department of Defense.

College Students

Beginning with the census of 1950, a student attending college has been considered a resident of the enumeration district in which she or he lives while attending college. That was also apparently the rule up to 1850; but, in most of the intervening censuses, the student was counted at his or her

[3] For more information, see U.S. Bureau of the Census (1993), Appendix D. Collection and Processing Procedures, and U.S. Bureau of the Census (1995a), Appendix 1C, Table of Residence Rules for the 1990 Census.

parental home. However, students away from home attending schools below the college level have been consistently counted at their parental homes.

Persons in Institutions

Persons in types of institutions where usual stays are for long periods of time (regardless of the length of stay of the person considered) were enumerated as residents of the institution. These include "Federal or State prisons; local jails; Federal detention centers; juvenile institutions; nursing, convalescent, and rest homes of the aged and dependent; or homes, schools, hospitals, or wards of the physically handicapped, mentally retarded, or mentally ill" (U.S. Bureau of the Census, 1992c). Individuals in general hospitals or other institutions for medical care where patients usually stay for only a short period are counted at their usual residences.

Persons with More Than One Residence

Persons with dual residences represent a variety of circumstances. In the U.S.'s affluent and mobile society, with its long vacations and early retirement, the occupancy of more than one home during the year is increasingly common. Many people change residences with the seasons. This group is to be counted in the household where the majority of the calendar year is spent. Of course, there have also long been classes of workers who changed their residences seasonally with the jobs—lumbermen, fishermen, agricultural laborers, cannery workers, and so on. The ordinary rule is to choose the residence where the person lives the greatest part of the year. However, if migrant agricultural workers or persons in worker camps do not report a usual residence, they are counted at their census-day location. Another class of dual residence consists of persons who work and live away from their homes and families, perhaps returning on weekends. In their case, the need for meaningful family statistics clashes with the need to include persons in the area where they are living most of the time. The residence rules for the 1990 and 2000 censuses are that individuals in this situation should be enumerated in the location where they live during the week.

Persons with No Usual Residence

Persons with no usual residence anywhere (migratory agricultural workers, vagrants, some traveling salespeople, etc.) have been counted where they were found according to a provision that goes back to the Act of 1790. To obtain a complete and unduplicated count of such persons, canvassing procedures like "T-night" ("T" for transient) and "M-night" ("M" for mission) were introduced some decades ago. Given the increased concern regarding the homeless population since 1970, the Census Bureau has expanded its efforts to enumerate the population living in shelters and public places such as bus and train terminals or outdoor locations. In the 1990 census, the "S-night" ("S" for streets and shelters) canvassing procedure occurred during the night of March 20–21. It involved trained census workers' going where homeless people were likely to be located, including streets, public parks, freeway overpasses, abandoned buildings, or shelters specifically serving the homeless population. This special enumeration effort counted approximately 240,000 people (U.S. Bureau of the Census, 1995b, Chapter 11). The 2000 census included a specific service-based enumeration (SEB), which counted people at community service organizations that typically serve people without housing, and targeted outdoor locations. In addition, census forms were available at various public locations such as post offices, community centers, and health care clinics (U.S. Bureau of the Census, 1999a).

Americans Abroad

This and the following category are of special interest from the standpoint of the United Nations' "international conventional total." It may be recalled that the recommendation called for the *inclusion* of the country's own military and diplomatic personnel stationed abroad or at sea. However, historically the enumeration of this group in the U.S. censuses has been inconsistent (U.S. Bureau of the Census, 1993). Only two censuses prior to 1900 (i.e., 1830 and 1840) attempted to enumerate this group. For those years in which Americans abroad were enumerated, the specific groups included (e.g., military personnel, federal civilian employees, crews of U.S. merchant marine vessels, and private U.S. citizens) and the countries considered as "abroad" have varied. This information is usually provided by several different federal agencies, including the Department of Defense. Table 4.1 presents the number of Americans overseas and summarizes the changes in residence rules.[4]

The 1990 and 2000 censuses enumerated overseas military personnel and federal civilian employees, as well as their dependents living with them. These groups, totaling 922,845 people in 1990, were included in the official counts that are used for congressional apportionment but omitted from other official statistics. Americans abroad only temporarily (as tourists, visitors, persons on short business trips, etc.) were supposed to be counted at their usual place of residence in the United States, whereas those away for longer periods (employed abroad, enrolled in a foreign university, living in retirement, etc.) were excluded from the basic count (U.S. Bureau of the Census 1993, 1995a, Chapter 1).

Foreign Citizens Temporarily in the United States

The U.S. census has adhered partially to the principle of the "international conventional total" by excluding foreign

military and diplomatic personnel and their families who are stationed here if they are living in embassies or similar quarters. In fact, such persons are not even listed. On the other hand, it fails to list all other citizens of foreign countries temporarily in this country. The American rules for inclusion or exclusion parallel those given in the preceding subsection (e.g., foreigners working or studying in the United States are counted). Failure to provide statistics on foreigners temporarily present and not on official assignments represents one of the points at which it is impossible to construct the "international conventional total" for the United States by the combination of published statistics.

Doubtful Cases

It may be apparent by now that these rules require a certain amount of judgment in some cases because such words as "temporary" and "usual" are not precisely defined. Attempts to use a time criterion, such as at least 60 days, have not been satisfactory. For one thing, both past and prospective length of stay must be considered. It may also be apparent that the nature and purpose of the stay are just as important considerations as the duration.

It should be noted that most of the specific decisions concerning where a person should be enumerated are not made in the central office, as is the case in some other countries, but are made in the field. In the United States, the Bureau of the Census formulates the general principles but leaves their application to the respondent or the enumerator. Except in the case of groups canvassed in certain special operations, the central office does not have the facts that would be needed to change the area to which the person is allocated.

Household Population

The allocation of these special groups can have a considerable effect on population counts in certain geographical areas. Thus, published counts often distinguish the size and characteristics of the "normal" population of an area, which excludes not only members of the armed forces stationed there and living in barracks or aboard ship but also persons living in institutions, college dormitories, and other group quarters. Table 1 of the 1990 census report, *General Population Characteristics* for the United States (U.S. Bureau of the Census, 1992b) indicates that 97.3% of the total population lived in households and 2.7% (more than 6 million people) lived in groups quarters. Table 35 in the same publication indicates that, among those living in group quarters, more than half are institutionalized while the remainder live in other group quarters. Although the concept of the "normal" population of an area is a social construction, the presence of a relatively large "nonnormal" population will distort its demographic composition and vital rates so as to obscure comparisons with other areas not

---

[4] See U.S. Bureau of the Census (1993) for a detailed discussion of changes in the residence rules regarding Americans abroad.

Wilmoth

TABLE 4.1 Americans Overseas, 1830–1840, 1900–1940, and 1950–1990 by Type (In 1850–1890 censuses, no figures were published for Americans overseas)

Year	Total U.S. population abroad[1]	Federal employees			Dependents of federal employees (armed forces and civilian)	Crews of U.S. merchant vessels	Private U.S. citizens
		Total	Armed forces	Civilians			
1990	925,845[2]	(NA)	529,269[3]	(NA)[4]	(NA)[4]	3,026[5]	(NA)
1980	995,546	562,962	515,408[3]	47,554[6]	423,584[6]	(NA)	(NA)
1970	1,737,836	1,114,224	1,057,776[7]	56,448[8]	371,366[8]	15,910[9]	236,336[10]
1960	1,374,421	647,730	609,720[11]	38,010[8]	506,393[8]	32,464[12]	187,834[10]
1950	481,545[13]	328,505	301,595[14]	26,910[8]	107,350[8]	45,690[15]	(NA)
1940	118,933[16]	(NA)	(NA)	(NA)	(NA)	(NA)	(NA)
1930	89,453[17]	(NA)	(NA)	(NA)	(NA)	(NA)	(NA)
1920	117,238[18]	(NA)	(NA)	(NA)	(NA)	(NA)	(NA)
1910	55,608[17]	(NA)	(NA)	(NA)	(NA)	(NA)	(NA)
1900	91,219[19]	(NA)	(NA)	(NA)	(NA)	(NA)	(NA)
1840	6,100[20]	(NA)	(NA)	(NA)	(NA)	(NA)	(NA)
1830	5,318[20]	(NA)	(NA)	(NA)	(NA)	(NA)	(NA)

(NA) Not available.

[1] Excludes U.S. citizens temporarily abroad on private business, travel, etc. Such persons were enumerated at their usual place of residence in the United States as absent members of their own households. Also excludes private, nonfederally affiliated U.S. citizens living abroad for an extended period, except for 1970 and 1960, which include portions of this subpopulation.

[2] Excludes 9460 persons overseas whose home state was not designated and 16,999 persons overseas whose designated home "state" was a U.S. outlying area.

[3] Based on administrative records provided by Department of Defense.

[4] Not shown separately. Total number reported of overseas federal civilian employees and dependents (of both military and civilian personnel) was 393,550. Based on administrative records provided by 30 federal agencies (including Department of Defense) and survey results provided by Department of Defense.

[5] Vessels sailing from one foreign port to another or in a foreign port. Overseas status based on Census Location Report.

[6] Based on administrative records provided by Office of Personnel Management and Departments of Defense and State.

[7] For members of the Army, Air Force, and Marine Corps abroad, based on administrative records provided by Department of Defense. Crews of deployed U.S. military vessels were enumerated on Report for Military and Maritime Personnel. Land-based Navy and Coast Guard personnel abroad were enumerated on Overseas Census Report.

[8] Enumerated on Overseas Census Report.

[9] Vessels at sea with a foreign port as their destination or in a foreign port. Enumerated on Report for Military and Maritime Personnel.

[10] U.S. citizens living abroad for an extended period not affiliated with the federal government, and their overseas dependents. Enumerated on Overseas Census Report.

[11] Enumerated on Overseas Census Report and Report for Military and Maritime Personnel.

[12] Vessels at sea or in a foreign port. Enumerated on Report for Military and Maritime Personnel.

[13] Based on 20% sample of reports received.

[14] Enumerated on Overseas Census Report and Crews of Vessels Report.

[15] Vessels at sea or in a foreign port. Enumerated on Crews of Vessels Report.

[16] Source of overseas count is unclear; see section on 1940 census.

[17] Enumerated on general population schedule.

[18] Enumerated on report for Military and Naval Population, etc., Abroad.

[19] Enumerated on report for Military and Naval Population and report for Civilians, Residents of U.S. at Military or Naval Stations.

[20] Persons on naval vessels in the service of the United States.

Source: U.S. Bureau of the Census, 1993, Table 2.

containing such a population. As a result, a distinction is often made between the total population, which includes all usual residents of an area, and the household population, which includes only the population living in households. For example, Table 57 of the 1990 census report, *General Population Characteristics* for Kansas indicates that Leavenworth County, Kansas, which contains a federal prison and a military post, contains a total population of 64,371 and a household population of 54,974 (U.S. Bureau of the Census 1992a). The difference between these two numbers (9397) represents the number of people living in group quarters.

Special Censuses and the Current Population Survey

For the most part, "usual residence" is defined the same way in the national sample surveys conducted by the U.S. Bureau of the Census. They have mostly been limited to the civilian noninstitutional population. A noteworthy exception is the March supplement to the Current Population Survey (CPS). That survey's focus on the labor force leads it to exclude people who are outside the market economy in the regular monthly survey, but the annual March supplement to the Current Population Survey covers the institutional population and members of the armed forces living off post or with their families on post. The CPS uses different residence rules for enumerating college students. They are counted at their parental homes, partly because counting them in the college communities during the academic year and at home (or where they are employed) during the vacation period would lead to seasonal variations in enumeration procedures and in the resulting statistics.

TIME REFERENCE

As noted by the United Nations (1992), two essential features of a population census are simultaneity and defined periodicity. Simultaneity refers to establishing a set census reference time during which census data are to be collected and recorded. Ideally, individuals should be enumerated on a given day and the information they provide should refer to a set time period. If a census has a specific official hour, it is usually midnight, a time when most persons are at home. However, the census day varies across countries as a result of seasonal fluctuations in weather, economic activity, and public observances. Considerations regarding the conduct of a de *facto* population census of an area can also influence the choice of a specific census time and day because such a population is subject to daily and seasonal fluctuations. These are relatively insignificant for most national totals, but particular areas could be greatly affected. Urban areas, especially the downtown districts of central cities, are particularly affected by daily fluctuations, while resort areas and certain types of agricultural areas are particularly affected by seasonal factors.

Once a day and time have been established that are favorable for conducting a census, subsequent censuses should also be conducted at the same time. However, the best day and time for taking a census may change over time because of shifts in a country's economic, social, and demographic characteristics. For example, the date of the U.S. census changed from the first Monday in August for the 1790 through 1820 censuses, to June 1 for the 1830 through 1900 censuses. The 1910 and 1920 censuses were conducted on April 15 and June 1 respectively. It was not until 1930 that the current census date of April 1 was established (U.S. Bureau of the Census, 1995a).

More important, the subsequent censuses should have a defined periodicity. In other words, they should occur at regular intervals. Even though some countries are able to conduct a census every 5 years, the United Nations (1992) acknowledges that this is not feasible for most countries and recommends that the established period between censuses should be no longer than 10 years.

A national census should not be taken by a crew of enumerators that moves from one district to another as it completes its work; nor, in general, should the enumeration begin on different dates in different parts of the country. Yet in practice, both have occurred. The enumeration in the earliest historic censuses and in contemporary censuses of the less developed countries typically extended over many months. If a day or month was cited, it meant nothing more than the time when the fieldwork began. The disadvantages of such protracted enumerations are that omissions and duplications are more difficult to avoid and it becomes increasingly difficult to relate the facts to the official census date.

At a more advanced stage of census taking, there are specifications like "the zero hour" (midnight) on July 1 (Li, 1987). Occasionally, exceptional starting dates may be justified by such considerations as gross variations in climate or the annual dispersal of nomads to isolated grazing grounds. For example, the census of Alaska is often conducted prior to April 1 to avoid canvassing Alaska during the spring thaw.

In some cases a serious attempt is made to complete the enumeration in a day's time. These censuses are characteristically on a *de facto* basis. Such rapid censuses are by no means limited to the more industrialized societies or the householder (i.e., self-enumeration) method of enumeration. The most dramatic enumerations are those in which normal business activities cease and the populace must stay at home until the end of the census day or until it has been announced that the canvass has been completed. However, the "one-day census" usually turns out to be an ideal or a figure of speech. One-day enumerations are often localized in coverage (e.g., focused only on particular geographic areas), based on previously collected information that is updated on the census day, or carried over into subsequent days.

COMPLETENESS OF COVERAGE

The completeness of coverage provided by a modern census is influenced largely by the degree of deliberate and unintentional exclusions. As has been mentioned already, countries often deliberately exclude from their censuses certain relatively small classes of population on the basis of the type of census being taken, whether *de jure*, *de facto*, or some modification of one of these. Other deliberate exclusions are based on feasibility, cost, danger to census personnel, or considerations of national security. Finally, some persons will be deliberately or inadvertently omitted from the population as defined, while others will be incorrectly counted. Official omissions by design then will be discussed separately from the net underenumeration (or overenumeration) that tends to occurs to some extent, in counting a sizable population, as a result of deliberate action or oversight on the part of respondents or enumerators.

Deliberate Exclusion of Territory or Group

It is not unusual for specific territories or various population subgroups to be excluded from a census for one reason or another. In some countries, for example, either the indigenous or nonindigenous population, or parts of them, may be omitted from the census count, or the two may be enumerated at different times. In addition to tribal jungle areas, censuses may omit parts of the country that are under the control of alien enemies or of insurgents. Some examples from the United Nations (1998) are as follows:

Country	Census date	Excluded Group or Territory
Brunei Darussalam	1991	Transients afloat
Brazil	1991	Indian jungle population
Ecuador	1990	Nomadic Indian tribes
Falkland Islands	1990	Dependent territories, such as South Georgia
Jordan	1994	Territory under occupation by foreign military forces
Lebanon	1970	Palestinian refugees in camps
Peru	1993	Indian jungle population

Attempts have also been made to estimate the population of the excluded territory or groups, and the more credible estimates are cited in the UN *Demographic Yearbooks*. The sources vary from sample surveys, projections from past counts, reports of tribal or village chiefs, and aerial photographs, to guesses by officials, missionaries, or explorers.

Exclusions and Duplications of Individuals and Households

The more sophisticated users of census data have long been aware that even census counts of the population size in a given area are not exact counts. The reader who has followed this discussion of the definition of population size will appreciate some of the uncertainties and the opportunities for omission or duplication. Some familiarity with field surveys will confirm the fact that it is not possible to make the count for a fair-sized area with absolute accuracy.

Two principal types of error influence the accuracy of census coverage: omissions and counting errors (Ericksen and DeFonso, 1993). Omissions include all of the people who were not counted but should have been counted. Counting errors include erroneous enumerations, such as a person being counted twice, counted in the wrong geographic location, or counted when he or she is not eligible to be included (i.e., "out-of-scope"). Counting errors also include

fabricated cases and those that have insufficient information. The sum of omissions and counting errors is designated gross coverage error. Typically, a census will contain more omissions than counting errors, with the result that there is a net underenumeration (i.e., net undercount). Most users of census data are more concerned with the net undercount. As a result, a variety of methods have been developed over the past 50 years to assess the degree to which a census underestimates the true population size.

Methods of Evaluating Census Coverage

Two general types of methods are used to evaluate census coverage (Citro and Cohen, 1985, Chapter 4; Siegel, 2002, Chapter 4). The first is a microlevel method in which individual cases enumerated in the census are matched to independent records or samples. The second is a macrolevel method in which aggregate census data are compared to other aggregate estimates of the population based on public records, such as vital statistics and immigration data. It also involves evaluating the census data for internal consistency and consistency with previous census results.

The United Nation's *Handbook of Population and Housing Censuses* (1992, p. 143) states the following:

> Errors in the census will have to be determined through rigorous and technically acceptable methods. These will include (a) carrying out a post-enumeration survey in sample areas; (b) comparing census results, either at the aggregate or individual-record level with information available from other inquiries or sources; and (c) using techniques of demographic analysis to evaluate the data by checking for internal consistency, comparing those data with the results of previous censuses, and checking for conformity with the data obtained from the vital registration and migration data systems.

The first recommendation is a microlevel method, the third is a macrolevel method, and the second is a combination of both. The basic features of each approach will be considered separately and then the implementation of these methods in the United States will be discussed in detail.

Post-Enumeration Surveys

The design of a post-enumeration survey (PES) is to gather two different samples that can be used to estimate net coverage error: the P sample and E sample (Citro and Cohen, 1985, Chapter 4; Hogan, 1992, 1993; U.S. Bureau of the Census, 1995b, Chapter 11). The P (or population) sample, provides insight into the number of omissions by serving as an independent sample that can be matched to census records. The P sample "recaptures" people through one of two methods. The first method involves a re-enumeration of select areas in which trained enumerators revisit households in a sample of census geographic locations. The second method uses an independent survey, such as the Current Population Survey (CPS), to identify the sample. The E (or enumeration) sample consists of a random sample of cases enumerated in the census. It provides estimates of erroneous enumerations. Together, these samples comprise the PES that is used to estimate net coverage error. The estimate is based on dual-system estimation or matching of the two records, the PES record and the census record.

In other words, dual-system estimation is the process of matching the PES sample to census records to determine the "true" number of people in an area (Wolter, 1986). It "conceptualizes each person as either in or not in the Census enumeration, as well as either in or not in the PES" (Hogan, 1992:261). For example,

	Census enumeration		
PES	**Total**	**In**	**Out**
Total	N_{++}	N_{+1}	N_{+2}
In	N_{1+}	N_{11}	N_{12}
Out	N_{2+}	N_{21}	N_{22}

Source: U.S. Bureau of the Census, 1995b, Chapter 11, p. 20.

Assuming that the probability of being in the census and the probability of being in the PES are independent, the estimated total population (N_{++}), is

$$N_{++} = (N_{+1})(N_{1+})/(N_{11}) \qquad (4.1)$$

The difference between the PES estimate and the final census count identifies the net undercount, and the ratio of these two results is an adjustment factor that can be used to correct for the net undercount (Hogan, 1992, 1993).

The strength of a post-enumeration survey is that, ideally, it can provide synthetic estimates of the corrected population for subnational geographic areas that are based on local area adjustment factors. These factors can be smoothed using regression techniques to reduce their variance (See Hogan, 1992 and 1993, for details). Even though these techniques continue to be developed and improved, the United Nations (1992, p. 145) recommends "that a post-enumeration survey be considered an essential component of the overall census operations" and notes "To be of maximum utility, the post-enumeration survey should meet three conditions. It should (1) constitute a separate count, independent of the original enumeration; (2) be representative of the whole country and all population groups; and (c) involve one-to-one matching and reconciliation of records."

Comparison with Other Data Sources

Information obtained from administrative or other records can also be employed to assess coverage error at the micro- or macrolevel. Similar to the logic of a PES, a sample could be drawn from administrative records, such as school enrollments, driver's license registrations, social security records, or Medicare enrollments; it is then matched with census records. This method is particularly effective when assessing coverage error in specific populations, such as children, young adults, or the elderly. A reverse record check, which has been extensively used in Canada, is another microlevel evaluation method. The Canadian method involves constructing the sample from four frames: (1) persons counted in the previous census, (2) births in the subsequent intercensal period, (3) immigrants in the subsequent intercensal period, and (4) persons determined through coverage evaluation to have been missed in the previous census (Citro and Cohen, 1985:123). These individuals are traced to their location at the census date and then census records are checked to see if the person was enumerated at that location. Interviews are used to verify census-day location and secure additional information that can be used to ascertain the characteristics of those not enumerated in the census. At the macrolevel, population registers, military service registries, or enrollment in entitlement programs (e.g., Social Security or Medicare) can provide information on the aggregate size of the population or of specific population groups that can then be compared to the final census counts for those groups. While these methods are useful for assessing coverage errors in the national count or among specific population groups, they are not useful in generating adjustment factors for local areas.

Demographic Analysis

Another method that is useful for assessing coverage at the national level is demographic analysis (DA). DA, developed by Coale (1955), is based on demography's fundamental population component estimating equation:

$$P_{t2} = P_{t1} + (B_{t1-t2} - D_{t1-t2}) + (I_{t1-t2} - E_{t1-t2}) \qquad (4.2)$$

which states that the size of a population at a given time is a function of the population size at an earlier time plus natural increase (i.e., births minus deaths) plus net immigration (i.e., immigration minus emigration). Given this, the size of a population can be determined by obtaining estimates of the various components of population change from different administrative sources. In practice, these estimates are constructed for subpopulations, usually specific age-sex-race groups, using direct and indirect methods (Himes and Clogg, 1992). Ideally, these estimates should come from independent sources, but this is often impossible. Commonly used sources of data include population registers, vital registration systems, immigration registration systems, enrollment records from social service programs, and even previous censuses. The quality of estimates derived from these sources depends on the accuracy and completeness of the particular source data (Citro and Cohen, 1985, Chapter 4).

While this method theoretically can be applied to subnational areas, the dearth of reliable independent data on internal migration often makes it impossible to generate accurate regional, state, or local estimates. This is the primary limitation of DA. Local estimates of net undercounts are usually preferred for adjusting for coverage errors since net undercounts tend to vary systematically across geographic locations. Other limitations of DA include the potential for error in the component estimates, the fact that it only provides estimates of net coverage error (i.e., omissions cannot be distinguished from erroneous inclusions), and the difficulty in assessing the uncertainty of the results. However, for national estimates of net undercount, it has several characteristics that make it a viable method. For example, it is a tested technique that is grounded in fundamental demographic methods, it provides estimates that are independent of PES estimates, and it is relatively cheap (Clogg and Himes, 1993).

Evaluation of Coverage in the United States

Although President Washington expressed his conviction that the first census, that of 1790, represented an undercount, no estimate of its accuracy was attempted. Although, for more than 100 years thereafter, most census officials never admitted publicly that the census could represent an under-enumeration, there were a few wise exceptions, such as General Francis A. Walker in his introduction to the 1870 census. He complained of the "essential viciousness of a protracted enumeration" because it led to omissions and duplications (Pritzker and Rothwell, 1968). Estimates of census coverage error during this period were low. For example,

> Francis A. Walker, Superintendent of the Ninth and Tenth Censuses, testified in 1892 to a select committee of the House: "I should consider that a man who did not come within half of 1 percent of the population had made a great mistake and a culpable mistake." Hon. Carroll D. Wright, Commissioner of Labor, who completed the work of the Eleventh Census, wrote in July, 1897: "I think that the Eleventh Census came within less than 1 percent of the true enumeration of the inhabitants," and authorized the publication of this opinion. (U.S. Bureau of the Census, 1906, p. 16).

Later evidence, however, indicates that these contemporary guesses regarding accuracy were too optimistic.

Yet such assessments from census officials were the best estimates available at the time. For example, Walter F. Wilcox in 1906:

> A census is like a decision by a court of last resort—there is no higher or equal authority to which to appeal. Hence there is no trustworthy means of determining the degree of error to which a census count of population is exposed, or the accuracy with which any particular census is taken. But no well-informed person believes that the figures of a census, however carefully taken, may be relied upon as accurate to the last figures. There being no test available, the opinions of competent experts may be put in evidence in support of this conclusion. (U.S. Bureau of the Census, 1906, p. 16)

As the 20th century progressed, and the U.S. Census Bureau was increasingly staffed with statistical and social science professionals, statistical methods designed to evaluate census coverage systematically were gradually developed (Anderson, 1988, Chapter 8; Choldin, 1994, Chapter 2; Citro and Cohen, 1985, Chapter 4). Before the middle of the century, the methods for evaluating census coverage primarily relied on comparing census results to other information sources. For example, checks against registrations for military service during World Wars I and II indicate some underenumeration in the censuses of 1920 and 1940, respectively (e.g., Price, 1947). The total number of registrants for ration books in World War II was also compared with the number expected from the 1940 census. The direction of the differences is consistent with underenumeration in the 1940 census. These amounts, however, are merely suggestive since there are reasons why the registration figures themselves may not have measured the eligible population exactly. There was even an attempt in 1940 to assess the percentage of people missed by the census through the use of survey methods. Shortly after the conclusion of the fieldwork for the 1940 census, the Gallup Poll of the American Institute of Public Opinion asked a sample of respondents whether they thought they had been missed in the census. About 4% replied affirmatively. Their names and addresses were supplied to the Census Bureau, which was able to find all but about one-quarter of the cases in its records; as a result, the number of missed persons was reduced to 1%. (This "find" rate is fairly typical for persons who claim they have been missed. Only a minority of the population is actually interviewed by the enumerators, and some of these do not understand the auspices of the interview.) The 1% under-enumeration is probably minimal since the quota sample then used by the American Institute of Public Opinion was likely to underrepresent the types of persons missed by census enumerators.

The first census of the United States to systematically and formally assess coverage with modern statistical methods was that of 1950. A detailed description of evaluation programs over the past 50 years will not be provided here. Rather, the key features and outcomes of each census' evaluation program will be discussed.

1950

The initial 1950 census evaluation involved a post-enumeration survey (PES) based on a combined sample of areas and individuals. The area sample was used to identify omissions of households while the individual sample was used to check for erroneous inclusions as well as exclusions (Citro and Cohen, 1985, Chapter 4). The PES yielded a net undercount of 1.4%. However, a chief shortcoming of the 1950 PES, was that it grossly underestimated the number of persons missed within enumerated living quarters. An additional evaluation, most notably Coale's (1955) demographic analysis, suggested that the PES estimate probably understated the true undercount. Demographic analysis indicated that the net undercount for 1950 was 4.1% for the entire population, with undercount rates being higher among men and blacks (Robinson *et al.*, 1993). On the basis of the available evidence, the Bureau of the Census set its final "minimum reasonable estimate" at 3.5% of the estimated true population.

1960

Checks on population coverage as part of the Evaluation and Research Program of the 1960 census were more varied and complex than those for the 1950 census. The 1960 coverage checks included (1) a post-enumeration study, (2) a reverse record check, (3) an administrative record match, and (4) demographic analysis (Citro and Cohen, 1985, Chapter 4).

The PES consisted of (1) a re-enumeration of housing units in an area sample of 2500 segments and (2) a re-enumeration of persons and housing units in a list sample of 15,000 living quarters enumerated in the census. The purpose of the first re-interview study was to estimate the number of missed households and the population in them. The primary purpose of the second study was to check on the accuracy of census coverage of persons in enumerated units. The net underenumeration for 1960 based on the PES studies was 1.8% of the estimated "true" population. The corresponding figure for the 1950 census was 1.4%, but it is possible that all of the difference is attributable to the better design of the 1960 PES. As in 1950 the 1960 PES grossly understated the number of persons in enumerated households.

The reverse record check was based on samples drawn from an independent frame of categories of persons who should have been enumerated in the 1960 census. The frame consisted of

1. Persons enumerated in the 1950 census
2. Persons missed in the 1950 census but detected in the 1950 PES
3. Children born during the intercensal period (as given by birth certificates)
4. Aliens who registered with the Immigration and Naturalization Service in January 1960

The objective, of course, was to establish whether the person being checked had died or emigrated during the intercensal decade, was enumerated in the 1960 census, or remained within the United States but was missed in the census. However, this frame was logically incomplete at several points, since it excluded persons missed in both the 1950 census and its PES, unregistered births, and 1950–1960 immigrants who were naturalized before January 1960 or else failed to register. It is thought that the bias in the estimated net underenumeration rate attributable to these deficiencies was not very great. However, other tracing and matching errors occurred, which also affected the results.

The final estimates of the net undercount based on this method ranged from 2.5 to 3.1% (Marks and Waksberg, 1966).

The administrative record check focused on estimating undercounts among two groups: college students and the elderly. A sample of college students enrolled during the spring of 1960 yielded an estimated undercount of 2.5 to 2.7%. Undercount rates for the older population were much higher, approximately 5.1 to 5.7%, based on a sample of persons receiving Social Security (Marks and Waksberg, 1966).

The 1960 estimates based on demographic analysis indicated a net undercount of 3.1%. However, the differences in the undercounts by gender and race persisted (Robinson *et al.*, 1993). On the basis of all the evidence, the Bureau of the Census concluded that the net underenumeration rate was probably lower in 1960 than in 1950.

1970

The 1970 census did not use a post-enumeration survey but instead relied primarily on the Current Population Survey, selected records, and demographic analysis. Three microlevel analyses were completed. The first involved matching the March 1970 Current Population Survey to the census, which resulted in an undercount estimate of 2.3% (Citro and Cohen, 1985, Chapter 4). The second and third analyses were both record checks. As in 1960, there was an interest in estimating undercounts for the elderly. However, the sample was drawn from Medicare enrollees aged 65 and over instead of Social Security benefiaries. This sample was matched to the census records, and an estimated undercount among the elderly population of 4.9% was obtained. An additional sample of men aged 20 to 29 was drawn from the driver's license records of the District of Columbia. Although this was primarily an exploratory study, it did find that a large proportion of the sample (14%) was missed in the census (Citro and Cohen, 1985, Chapter 4).

The demographic analysis in 1970 contained several changes that improved the method (Himes and Clogg, 1992). First, a new birth registration test indicated that birth registration was more complete than previously estimated. Also, more accurate estimates of the black population were constructed (Coale and Rives, 1973). Finally, better estimates of the population aged 65 and over could be obtained from Medicare records. The DA-estimated undercount was 2.7% overall; yet the relative undercount of men and the black population increased (Robinson *et al.*, 1993).

During the 1960s and 1970s there was increased interest in obtaining estimated undercounts for subnational geographic areas and specific population groups. This interest was driven by a variety of factors including the "one person, one vote" principle established by the Supreme Court in 1962, the increased spending in formula-funded federal programs, and state and local government's increasing reliance on these funds (Choldin, 1994, Chapter 3). However, as previously mentioned, demographic analysis cannot provide detailed estimates of coverage error that can be used to adjust local census counts; nor could a matching study based on a single Current Population Survey. As a result, the 1980 evaluation program reinstated the use of a post-enumeration survey.

1980

Once again, the Post-Enumeration Program (PEP) used a dual-system estimation technique to evaluate the census results. The P sample was based on the 1980 April and August Current Population Survey (CPS) samples, while the E sample included more than 100,000 census records (U.S. Bureau of the Census, 1987, Chapter 9). This analysis resulted in 12 sets of undercount estimates at the national level. The undercounts among the four estimates considered to be representative ranged from −1.0 to 1.7% (U.S. Bureau of the Census/Faye *et al.*, 1988).

The 1980 evaluation program also included demographic analysis, which was methodologically similar to the 1970 analysis. The major methodological change between the 1970 and 1980 analyses was the technique used to estimate the population aged 45 to 46 in 1980. Instead of carrying forward the Coale-Zelnik estimates, Whelpton's (1950) estimates were used (Himes and Clogg, 1992). While the reliability of the estimates of most demographic components improved between 1970 and 1980, the results of the 1980 demographic analysis overall are not considered as accurate as previous undercount estimates because of increased uncertainty regarding the net immigration component (Citro and Cohen, 1985, Chapter 4; Himes and Clogg, 1992). Still, the undercount estimated through DA (1.2%) fell within the range of PEP estimates. The evidence suggested that the 1980 census was the most accurate count yet, but this was possibly a spurious consequence of the numerous duplicate enumerations (Robinson *et al.*, 1993).

Ultimately however, these estimates were not used to adjust the census because, the Census Bureau argued, the available methods did not have a sufficient level of accuracy. Specifically, it maintained that there were serious limitations in both the PEP (e.g., correlation bias) and DA (e.g., immigration estimates). This decision generated a considerable amount of litigation and political controversy (see Choldin, 1994, Chapter 9; Ericksen and Kadane, 1985; Freedman and Navidi, 1986). Throughout the 1980s, the Census Bureau investigated ways to improve existing evaluation methods. However, in 1987 it was announced that the 1990 census would not be adjusted for coverage error. A coalition of states, cities, and organizations sued, with the result that there was an agreement to conduct a post-enumeration survey (PES) in 1990 that could potentially be used to correct for the undercount (Choldin, 1994, Chapter 9; Hogan, 1992; U.S. Bureau of the Census, 1995b, Chapter 11). The final decision regarding adjustment, however, was to be determined after the 1990 PES was completed.

1990

The 1990 PES was carried out under specific guidelines established prior to the census. It was similar to the 1980 PEP in that two samples were to be matched to the census. However, the P and E samples were based on 5290 block clusters that contained approximately 170,000 housing units. The P sample included all persons living in each block at the time of the PES, while the E sample included all census enumerations from each block (U.S. Bureau of the Census, 1995b, Chapter 11). The initial estimated undercount based on the PES was 2.1%, but it was subsequently reduced to 1.6% (Hogan, 1993). This adjusted estimate is reasonably consistent with the results of the 1990 demographic analysis, which showed a national undercount of 1.8% (Robinson *et al.*, 1993). Similar to previous evaluations, the estimates indicate that undercount rates are higher among men and "racial" minorities (i.e., blacks and Hispanics), particularly those living in central cities. A strength of the 1990 PES is that it provided detailed undercount estimates for 1392 post-strata based on region, census division, race, place/size, housing tenure (i.e., home ownership), age, and sex (Hogan, 1993). Not only does this provide adjustment factors for subnational geographic areas but, if the post-strata are relatively homogeneous, the problem of correlation bias is reduced (Schenker, 1993). These adjustment factors were further improved by smoothing them by generalized linear regression techniques. The resulting synthetic estimates were used to produce the adjusted census counts (Hogan, 1992, 1993).

Despite the improvements in the PES, there was considerable debate regarding whether these estimates should be used to adjust the census (see Choldin, 1994, Chapter 11 for details). Proponents of adjustment maintained that the adjusted census counts were more accurate than the unadjusted counts because the PES was able to partially correct for the differential undercount, particularly the undercount of black males. Opponents of adjustment argued that the PES contained several problematic aspects, including correlation bias and sensitivity of synthetic estimates to changes in the smoothing procedure, which increase the error of the adjustment factors. Both sides had different opinions regarding the relative accuracy of the census and dual-system estimates based on the PES. Extensive analyses of the estimates of error were conducted to inform this debate (U.S. Bureau of the Census, 1995b, Chapter 11; Mulry and Spencer, 1993). Ultimately, the director of the U.S. Census Bureau recommended adjustment, but the Secretary of Commerce—

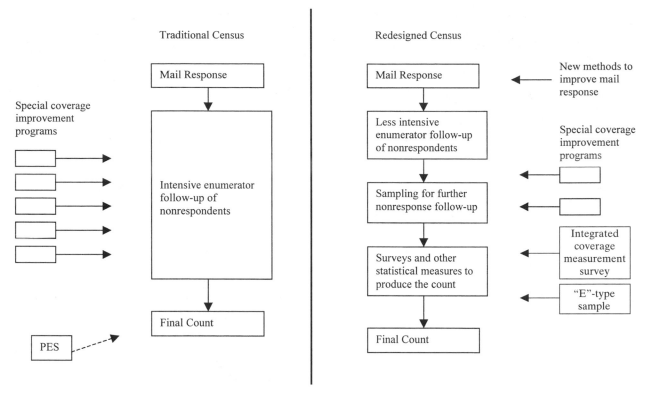

FIGURE 4.1 Schematic comparison of major design features for traditional and redesigned U.S. census
Source: Adapted from Edmonston and Schultze, 1995, Figure 5.1

who was to make the final decision—recommended that the 1990 census not be adjusted (Choldin, 1994, Chapter 11). This decision resulted in a variety of lawsuits (U.S. Bureau of the Census, 1995a, Chapter 1; Siegel, 2002, Chapter 12) and a renewed effort to study alternative methods for improving the 2000 census.

2000

The outcome of this research was the recommended "One-Number Census" or "Integrated Census Count." While the proposed plan was not accepted for Census 2000, for reasons explained at the end of this section, the basic features of this plan will be presented because they represent a fundamentally different approach to counting the population.[5] As noted by Edmonston and Schultze (1995, p. 76), "The traditional approach, used in the 1990 census, relies completely on intensive efforts to achieve a direct count (physical enumeration) of the entire population. The alternative approach, an integrated combination of enumeration and estimation, also starts with physical enumeration, but completes the count with statistical sampling and survey

techniques." Figure 4.1 highlights the essential features of each approach. The basic difference between these approaches is the degree to which resources are allocated to special coverage improvement programs and nonresponse follow-up. Another essential difference is the reliance on sampling techniques and statistical methods in generating the final census count.

For Census 2000, the U.S. Bureau of the Census (1997) distributed a mail-out/mail-back questionnaire using an improved Master Address File. Several methods were used to encourage people to respond, such as mailing two waves of questionnaires, mailing notices that remind individuals to respond, making forms available in various public locations, providing a toll-free telephone number for responding, sending forms in two languages (e.g., English and Spanish) to households in neighborhoods known to have a high proportion of people for whom English is a second language, and making available the census questionnaire in any of 6 languages. While these methods are designed to improve response rates, previous experience suggests that a substantial proportion of the population (more than 25%) will not respond. Furthermore, differential response rates may be reduced but will not be eliminated by these methods (Steffey and Bradburn, 1994, Chapter 3). In response to these anticipated problems, the Census Bureau developed

---

[5] Details regarding the proposed "One-Number Census" plans for Census 2000 using alternative census-taking methods can be obtained from the U.S. Bureau of the Census (1997).

an alternative method to count the population called the Integrated Census Count.

This method minimizes the amount of time and money allocated to follow up nonresponding households through the use of sampling. Two measures, based on independent samples, would be used to estimate the population size (U.S. Bureau of the Census, 1997; Wright, 1998). The first measure, based on the sample for nonresponse follow-up, is drawn after the mail-in phase is complete. This involves gathering a random sample of nonresponding households in each census tract that increases the direct contact rate to 90 percent of the households in each census tract. The size of the sample in each tract depends on the mail-in response rate. For example, if the mail-in response rate is 30%, then a sample of six out of seven nonresponding households will be required to obtain direct contact with 90% of all households in the tract. In contrast, a sample of at least 1 in 10 nonresponding households is needed if the mail-in response rate is 80%. Trained staff would enumerate the nonresponse follow-up sample through extensive field operations. Information regarding the characteristics of the sample household is then used to estimate the characteristics of the remaining 10% of households that were not enumerated (U.S. Bureau of the Census, 1997; Wright, 1998).

To illustrate how this method works, imagine a census tract that contains 1000 housing units but only 300 units mailed back a census form. The nonresponse follow-up sample for this census tract would consist of a random sample of 6 out of 7 of the 700 nonresponding households. The resulting sample would contain 600 households that would be enumerated by trained field staff. Together, the 300 mail-in responses and the 600 responses gathered through field operations would result in direct contact with 900 housing units in the census tract. The information from the 600 households in the nonresponse follow-up sample would then be used to estimate the characteristics of the remaining 100 households that were not enumerated.

The second measure, which provides a quality check, would be based on a nationwide probability sample of 25,000 census blocks (approximately 750,000 housing units) (U.S. Bureau of the Census, 1997). Households in this sample are contacted by trained interviewers to identify all residents of the households on the census day. No reference is made to information collected in the original census enumeration. The sample is then matched to the census enumeration to obtain the final census count. The match ratio established by the "PES" would be used to adjust the census count. "Specifically, the concept is to multiply the first measure (mostly based on counting) by the second measure (based on sampling) and divide this product by the number of matches, leading to an improved count—the *one number census*" (Wright, 1998, p. 248).

This plan received substantial support from the scientific community in the United States. It was constructed in accordance with the recommendations of three National Science Academy Panels (Panel on Census Requirements in the Year 2000 and Beyond, Panel to Evaluate Alternative Census Methods, and Academy Panel to Evaluate Alternative Census Methodologies). It also received the endorsement of numerous professional organizations including the American Statistical Association and the American Sociological Association (U.S. Bureau of the Census, 1997).

Yet the plan encountered considerable political opposition and was challenged in court. On January 28, 1999, the U.S. Supreme Court decided that the Census Bureau could not use statistical sampling to correct the census counts that are used for congressional apportionment (U.S. Supreme Court, 1999). However, the court's ruling did not prohibit the use of statistical sampling in census counts that are used for congressional or state redistricting and distribution of federal funds. While this ruling precludes the Census Bureau's plans for a "one-number census," it opened up the possibility of developing an initial count for congressional apportionment and a second count that corrects for coverage error.

In response to the Supreme Court's ruling, Kenneth Prewitt (1999), director of the Census Bureau, announced that the Census Bureau "will conduct the census for 2000 that provides the national apportionment numbers that do not rely on statistical sampling." The Census Bureau subsequently released "Census 2000 Operational Plans Using Traditional Census-Taking Methods" (U.S. Bureau of the Census, 1999a), as well as an updated operational plan (U.S. Bureau of the Census, 1999b). These plans are similar to those implemented in 1990 in that the Bureau's efforts would be focused on traditional nonresponse follow-up through the use of field enumerators and assessment of nonresponse through a program called "Accuracy and Coverage Evaluation (ACE)," which includes a post-enumeration survey. William Daley, the Secretary of Commerce (the Census Bureau's parent organization) supported this plan (Daley, 1999). The 2000 census has been completed employing the conventional methods. Moreover, analysis of the results of the ACE survey and demographic analysis led the Census Bureau to conclude that they would not necessarily improve on the initial counts and that no adjustments of these counts would be carried out for redistricting or distribution of federal funds.

While the short-term prospects for a "one-number census" based on sampling are no longer viable in the United States, the proposed alternative method has long-term potential to correct for the underenumeration problem. Even though a census using alternative methods based on statistical sampling for nonresponse did not take place in United States during the year 2000, the alternative methodology proposed by the Census Bureau is still a methodologically viable option for future censuses in other countries and even the United States.

References

Alterman, H. 1969. *Counting People: The Census in History*. New York: Harcourt, Brace & World.

Anderson, M. J. 1988. *The American Census: A Social History*. New Haven, CT: Yale University Press.

Coale, A. J. 1955. "The Population of the United States in 1950 Classified by Age, Sex, and Color—A Revision of Census Figures." *Journal of the American Statistical Association* 50: 16–54.

Coale, A. J., and N. W. Rives, Jr. 1973. "A Statistical Reconstruction of the Black Population of the United States, 1880–1970: Estimates of True Numbers by Age and Sex, Birth Rates, and Total Fertility." *Population Index* 39: 3–36.

Choldin, H. M. 1994. *Looking for the Last Percent: The Controversy over Census Undercounts*. New Brunswick, NJ: Rutgers University Press.

Citro, C. F., and M. L. Cohen (Eds.). 1985. *The Bicentennial Census: New Directions for Methodology in 1990*. Washington, DC: National Academy Press.

Clogg, C. C., and C. L. Himes. 1993. "Comment: Uncertainty in Demographic Analysis." *Journal of the American Statistical Association* 88: 1072–1074.

Daley, W. M. 1999. "Statement of U.S. Secretary of Commerce William M. Daley on Plan for Census 2000." U.S. Department of Commerce Press Release, February 24, 1999.

Edmonston, B., and C. Schultze (Eds.). 1995. *Modernizing the U.S. Census*. Washington, DC: National Academy Press.

Ericksen, E. P., and T. K. DeFonso. 1993. "Beyond the Net Undercount: How to Measure Census Error." *Chance* 6: 38–44.

Ericksen, E. P., and J. B. Kadane. 1985. "Estimating the Population in a Census Year." *Journal of the American Statistical Association* 80: 98–131.

Freedman, D. A., and W. C. Navidi. 1986. "Regression Models for Adjusting the 1980 Census." *Statistical Science* 1: 3–39.

Himes, C. L., and C. C. Clogg. 1992. "An Overview of Demographic Analysis as a Method for Evaluating Census Coverage in the United States." *Population Index* 58: 587–607.

Hogan, H. 1992. "The 1990 Post-Enumeration Survey: An Overview." *The American Statistician* 46: 261–269.

Hogan, H. 1993. "The 1990 Post-Enumeration Survey: Operations and Results." *Journal of the American Statistical Association* 88: 1047–1060.

Li, C. (Ed.). 1987. *A Census of One Billion People*. Boulder, CO: Westview Press.

Marks, E. D., and J. Waksberg. 1966. "Evaluation of Coverage in the 1960 Census of Population through Case-by-Case Checking." *Proceedings of the Social Statistics Section, 1966*. Washington, DC: American Statistical Association.

Mulry, M. H., and B. D. Spencer. 1993. "Accuracy of the 1990 Census and Undercount Adjustments." *Journal of the American Statistical Association* 88: 1080–1091.

Prewitt, K. 1999. "Statement of Kenneth Prewitt, Director of the U.S. Census Bureau, on Today's Supreme Court Ruling." U.S. Department of Commerce, Economics and Statistics Administration, Bureau of the Census Press Release, January 25, 1999.

Price, D. O. 1947. "A Check on Underenumeration in the 1940 Census." *American Sociological Review* 12: 44–49.

Pritzker, L., and N. D. Rothwell. 1968. "Procedural Difficulties in taking Past Censuses in Predominately Negro, Puerto Rican, and Mexican Areas." In D. M. Heer (Ed.), *Social Statistics and the City*. Cambridge, MA: Joint Center for Urban Studies of the Massachusetts Institute of Technology and Harvard University.

Robinson, J. G., B. Ahmed, P. D. Gupta, and K. A. Woodrow. 1993. "Estimation of Population Coverage in the 1990 United States Census Based on Demographic Analysis." *Journal of the American Statistical Association* 88: 1061–1071.

Schenker, N. 1993. "Undercount in the 1990 Census." *Journal of the American Statistical Association* 88: 1044–1046.

Shryock, H. S. 1955. "The Concepts of *De facto* and *De Jure* Population: The Experience in Censuses of the United States." *Proceedings of the World Population Conference*, 1954. Vol. IV, United Nations. E/CONF, 13/416.

Shryock, H. S. 1960. "The Concept of 'Usual' Residence in the Census of Population." *Proceedings of the Social Statistics Section*, 1960. Washington, DC: American Statistical Association, August 23–26, 1960.

Siegel, J. S. 2002. *Applied Demography: Applications to Business, Goverament, Law, & Public Policy*. San Diego: Academie Press.

Steffey, D. L., and N. M. Bradburn (Eds.). 1994. *Counting People in the Information Age*. Washington, DC: National Academy Press.

United Nations. 1992. *Handbook of Population and Housing Censuses: Part I. Planning, Organization and Administration of Population and Housing Censuses*. New York: United Nations.

United Nations. 1998. *Demographic Yearbook: 1996*. New York: United Nations.

U.S. Bureau of the Census. 1906. *Special Reports of the Twelfth Census, Supplementary Analysis and Derivative Tables*. Washington, DC: Government Printing Office.

U.S. Bureau of the Census. 1987. *1980 Census of Population and Housing: History. Part E*. Washington, DC: Government Printing Office.

U.S. Bureau of the Census. 1988. *The Coverage of Population in the 1980 Census*, by R. E. Fay, J. S. Passel, and J. G. Robinson. Evaluation and Research Reports, PHC 80-EA, 1980 Census of Population and Housing. Washington, D.C.: U.S. Bureau of the Census.

U.S. Bureau of the Census. 1992a. *1990 Census of Population and Housing. General Population Characteristics. Kansas*. Washington, DC: Government Printing Office.

U.S. Bureau of the Census. 1992b. *1990 Census of Population and Housing. General Population Characteristics. United States*. Washington, DC: Government Printing Office.

U.S. Bureau of the Census. 1992c. *1990 Census of Population and Housing. General Population Characteristics. United States. Appendix D. Collection and Processing Procedures*. Washington, DC: Government Printing Office.

U.S. Bureau of the Census. 1992d. *1990 Census of Population and Housing. General Population Characteristics. United States. Appendix E. Facsimiles of Respondent Instructions and Questionnaire Pages*. Washington, DC: Government Printing Office.

U.S. Bureau of the Census. 1993. *Americans Overseas in the U.S. Censuses*. Technical Paper 62. Washington, DC: Government Printing Office.

U.S. Bureau of the Census. 1995a. *1990 Census of Population and Housing: History. Part C*. Washington, DC: Government Printing Office.

U.S. Bureau of the Census. 1995b. *1990 Census of Population and Housing: History. Part D*. Washington, DC: Government Printing Office.

U.S. Bureau of the Census. 1997. *Report to Congress—The Plan for Census 2000*, www.census.gov/dmd/www/plansop.htm

U.S. Bureau of the Census. 1999a. *Census 2000 Operational Plan: Using Traditional Census Taking Methods*. Washington, DC: Government Printing Office.

U.S. Bureau of the Census. 1999b. *Updated Summary: Census 2000 Operational Plan*. Washington, DC: Government Printing Office.

U.S. Supreme Court. 1999. Nos. 98–404 and 98–564. Lexis-Nexis.

Whelpton, P. K. 1950. "Birth and Birth Rates in the Entire United States, 1909 to 1948." *Vital Statistics Special Reports* 33: 137–162.

Wolter, K. M. 1986. "Some Coverage Error Models for Census Data." *Journal of the American Statistical Association* 81: 338–346.

Wright, T. 1998. "Sampling and Census 2000: The Concepts." *American Scientist* 86: 245–253.

Suggested Readings

Alterman, H. 1969. *Counting People: The Census in History.* New York: Harcourt, Brace & World.

Anderson, M. J. 1988. *The American Census: A Social History,* New Haven, CT.: Yale University Press.

Choldin, H. M. 1994. *Looking for the Last Percent: The Controversy over Census Undercounts,* New Brunswick, NJ: Rutgers University Press.

Cohen, P. 1982. *A Calculating People.* Chicago, IL: University of Chicago Press.

Edmonston, B., and C. Schultze (Eds.). 1995. *Modernizing the U.S. Census.* Washington, DC: National Academy Press.

Himes, C. L., and C. C. Clogg. 1992. "An Overview of Demographic Analysis as a Method for Evaluating Census Coverage in the United States." *Population Index* 58: 587–607.

Hogan, H. 1992. "The 1990 Post-Enumeration Survey: An Overview." *The American Statistician.* 46: 261–269.

Steffey, D. L., and N. M. Bradburn (Eds.). 1994. *Counting People in the Information Age.* Washington, DC: National Academy Press.

United Nations. 1992. *Handbook of Population and Housing Censuses: Part I. Planning, Organization and Administration of Population and Housing Censuses.* New York: United Nations.

United Nations. 1998. *Priniciples and Recommendations for Population and Housing Censuses.* New York, NY: United Nations.

U.S. Bureau of the Census. 1977. "Developmental estimates of the coverage of the population of states in the 1970 census: Demographic analysis," by J. S. Siegel, J. S. Passel, N. W. Rivers, and J. G. Robinson. *Current Population Reports*, Series P-23, No. 65. Washington, DC: U.S. Bureau of the Census.

U.S. Bureau of the Census. 1985. *Evaluating Census of Population and Housing.* Special Training Document. ISP-TR-S. Washington, DC: U.S. Bureau of the Census.

U.S. Bureau of the Census. 2002. *Measuring America: The Decennial Census from 1790 to 2000.* Washington, DC: U.S. Census Bureau.

U.S. National Archives and Records Administration. 1997. *The 1790–1890 Federal Population Census, Revised.* Washington, DC: National Archives and Records Administration.

5

Population Distribution
Geographic Areas

DAVID A. PLANE

Since the first edition of *The Methods and Materials of Demography* was written in 1967 through 1970, a wide array of new uses for demographic analysis has arisen at the subnational and local scales. A booming "demographics" industry has developed that makes use of census materials and quantitative methods for the geographical analysis of population for private-sector marketing, business decision making, and public-planning applications. Thus today, more than ever, for many purposes information on the size and characteristics of the total population of a country is not sufficient. Population data are often needed for geographic subdivisions of a country and for other classifications of areas including smaller scale units with boundaries reflecting the settlements and neighborhoods in which people live. In most countries, the geographic distribution of the population is not even but is dense in some places and sparse in others, and the geographic patterns of demographic characteristics are often quite complex. This chapter treats the geographic distribution of the population by political areas and by several other types of geographic areas.

ADMINISTRATIVE OR POLITICAL AREAS

Political areas are not ordinarily created or delineated by a country's central statistical agency or its census office but instead are established by national constitutions, laws, decrees, regulations, or charters. In some countries, the primary political subdivisions are empowered to create secondary and tertiary subdivisions. Even with modern advances in methods for tabulating census data, it is still very challenging to do cross-country comparative work at the subnational level. Wide variations exist in the definitions of the fundamental geographic units for which data may be obtained for different countries.

The present discussion is confined to the major and minor civil divisions and to cities proper. ("Urban agglomerations" and "urban and rural" areas are discussed in the next major section of this chapter and in Chapter 6.)

Primary Divisions

Data on total population and population classified by urban/rural residence are given for the major civil divisions of most countries in several of the UN *Demographic Yearbooks*—for example, the 1993 *Yearbook* (United Nations, 1995) with data from 1985–1993 censuses. The generic names appear in English and French, and sometimes they appear in the national language as well. As shown in Table 5.1, the most common names in English for the primary areas are provinces, regions, districts, and states. The number of major civil divisions varies widely from country to country as shown in column 2 of Table 5.1. Just as countries themselves vary greatly in terms of their geographic areas and population sizes, so too are the areas and populations of major civil divisions highly variable. The average population size of the major civil divisions listed in the 1993 *Demographic Yearbook* ranges from just 1355 persons for the 13 separate Cook Islands to 37,683,688 for the 30 provinces, (independent) cities, and autonomous regions of China. Care should thus be exercised in comparing data between countries for major civil divisions.

Special Units

It is fairly common for the capital city to constitute a primary division in its own right and in a few countries, some of the larger cities are also primary political divisions. Countries that have been settled relatively recently or countries that contain large areas of virtually uninhabited land or land inhabited mainly by aborigines may have a

TABLE 5.1 Major Civil Divisions Used to Report Census Data in 1993 U.N. Demographic Yearbook

English generic name	Countries with number of units (and local generic name if listed in yearbook)	English generic name	Countries with number of units (and local generic name if listed in yearbook)
Primary Units		Regions	Aruba 9, Bahrain 12, Cote d'Ivoire 10, Czech Republic 7, Mali 7, Malta 6, Mauritania 13, Namibia 27, Oman 8, Philippines 14, Romania 40, Russian Federation 12, Senegal 10, Slovakia 3, Sudan 9, Tanzania 25
Cities and towns	Republic of Moldavia 49		
Communes	French Guiana 21, Martinique 33		
Counties	Norway 19		
Departments	Bolivia 9, Colombia 24, El Salvador 14, Paraguay 19, Uruguay 19	States	India 24, Malaysia 13, Mexico 31, Nigeria 31, United States 50, Venezuela 20
Development regions	Nepal 5	Subregions	Malawi 24
Districts	Belize 6, Brunei 5, Cape Verde 9, Cayman Islands 6, Gabon 9, Latvia 26, Lesotho 10, Madagascar 6, New Caledonia 31, Seychelles 5, Swaziland 4, Uganda 38	Towns	Macedonia 30
		Urban areas	Botswana 8
		Secondary Units	
Divisions	Bangladesh 4, Fiji 4, France 22, Tonga 5	Autonomous regions	China,[1] Iraq[1]
Governorates	Iraq 18, Yemen 11		
Islands	Comores Islands 3, Cook Islands 13, Turks and Caicos Islands 6	Capital	Bulgaria 1, Czech Republic 1, Paraguay 1, Poland 1, Slovakia 1
Local government regions	Vanuatu 11	Capital city/ rural area	Sierra Leone 2
Municipalities	Qatar 9	Cities	Bermuda 2, Egypt 4, Kazakhstan 1, Korea[1] 6, Kyrgyzstan 1
Parishes	Antigua and Barbuda 7, Bermuda 7, Isle of Man 17, Jamaica 14	Comisarias	Colombia 5
Popular republics	Yugoslavia 6	Districts	Mali 1, Sierra Leone 13, United States 1
Prefectures	Algeria 48, Central African Republic 16, Chad 15, Japan 47, Rwanda 11	Federal capitals	Argentina 1
Provinces	Argentina 22, Benin 6, Bulgaria 27 (Okruzi), Burkina Faso 30, Burundi 16, Canada 10, Chile 13, Ecuador 21, Egypt 15, Finland 12, Indonesia 27, Iran 24, Ireland 4, Kazakhstan 19, Korea 19 (Do), Kyrgyzstan 6 (Oblasts), Panama 9, Poland 48 (Voivodships), Sierra Leone 3, Solomon Islands 8, South Africa 4, Sweden 24 (Lans), Turkey 67 (Ili), Viet Nam 40, Zambia 9, Zimbabwe 10	Federal territories	Malaysia 2
		Frontier districts	Egypt 5
		Intendencias	Colombia 4
		Municipalities	China,[1] Romania 1
		Rural districts	Botswana 11
		Self-governing national states	South Africa 6
		Territories	Canada 2
		Towns	Isle of Man 4
		Union territories	India 7
Regional councils	New Zealand 13	Villages	Isle of Man 5

[1] Not separately identified in tabulations

Source: Prepared by the author; based on the U.N. *Demographic Yearbook*, 1993, Table 30.

different kind of primary subdivision that has a distinctive generic name and a rudimentary political character.

Secondary and Tertiary Divisions

To obtain data below the major civil division level, the statistical or demographic yearbook or the actual census reports for the specific nation will likely need to be consulted as the UN *Demographic Yearbook* generally does not give such detailed tabulations. The intermediate or secondary political divisions also have a wide variety of names. These include county, district, and commune. Some small countries have only primary divisions. Some large countries have three or more levels. Examples of tertiary divisions are the

townships in the United States, the *myun* and *eup* in Korea, and the *hsiang* and *chen* in Taiwan. For different administrative functions, a province, state, or other division may be divided into more than one set of political areas.

Municipalities

It is difficult to find a universal, precise term for the type of political area discussed in this subsection. The ideal type is the city; but smaller types of municipalities such as towns and villages are also included. (Incidentally, in Puerto Rico, a *municipio* is the equivalent of a county in mainland United States.) In some countries, these areas could be described as incorporated places or localities. In some countries, again, these municipalities are located within secondary or tertiary divisions; but in other countries, they are simply those territorial divisions that are administratively recognized as having an urban character.

The larger municipalities are frequently subdivided for administrative purposes into such areas as boroughs or wards (Britain and some of its former colonies), *arrondissements* (France), *ku* (Japan and Korea), and *chu* (China, Taiwan). These subdivisions of cities, in turn, may be divided into precincts (United States), *chun* (China, Taiwan), or *dong* (Korea). In China and Korea, even a fifth level exists—the *lin* and *ban*, respectively—for which "urban neighborhood" is as close as one could come in English. These smaller types of administrative areas are ordinarily not used for the presentation of official demographic statistics, but they are sometimes used as units in sample surveys.

Sources

Population totals for the major (primary) civil divisions are published in several of the *Demographic Yearbooks* of the United Nations, and fairly frequently there is a table showing the total population of capital cities and cities of 100,000 or more inhabitants.

The UN *Demographic Yearbooks* do not present statistics for smaller cities and other municipalities nor for the secondary, tertiary, and other divisions. For these, one must usually refer to the national publications.

Uses and Limitations

Statistics on the distribution of the population among political areas are useful for many purposes. For example, they may be used to meet legal requirements for determining the apportionment of representation in legislative bodies; they are needed for studies of internal migration and population distribution in relation to social, economic, and other administrative planning; and they provide base data for the computation of subnational vital statistics rates and for preparing local population estimates and projections.

A limitation of these political areas from the standpoint of the analysis of population distribution, and even from that of planning, is the fact that the boundaries may be rather arbitrary and may not consider physiographic, economic, or social factors. Moreover, the areas officially designated as cities may not correspond very well to the actual physical city in terms of population settlement or to the functional economic unit. Furthermore, in some countries the smallest type of political areas does not provide adequate geographic detail for ecological studies or city planning. Therefore, various types of statistical and functional areas have been defined, in census offices and elsewhere, to meet these needs. These may represent groups or subdivisions of the political areas, or they may disregard them altogether. Such areas are the subject of the second major section ("Statistical Areas") of this chapter and of Chapter 6.

Quality of the Statistics

Most of what can be said about the accuracy of total national population applies also to the country's geographic divisions. Furthermore, given a set of rules on who should be counted and where people should be counted within a country, there will be errors in applying these rules. Some people will be counted in the wrong area, others will be missed, and still others will be counted twice. Hence the accuracy of the counts for the areas will be impaired differentially.

Political Areas of the United States

The primary purpose of the census of the United States is the determination of the number of residents in each state for the purpose of apportioning the representatives to the Congress of the United States among the states. Within states, population must be obtained for smaller areas for determining congressional districts and for setting up districts (by various methods) for electing representatives to the individual state's legislative body or bodies and for other purposes required by state or local laws.

States

There are now 50 states and the District of Columbia within the United States proper. The number of states and some of their boundaries have changed in the course of American history; but from 1912 to 1959, there were 48 states. That area is typically called the "conterminous United States." For data presentation purposes, the Census Bureau treats the District of Columbia as the equivalent of a state. For some data the Bureau applies the same treatment to the territories under U.S. sovereignty or jurisdiction. The territories included for the 1990 decennial census were American Samoa, Guam, the Northern Mariana Islands, Palau, Puerto Rico and the U.S. Virgin Islands. With independence, Palau is no longer covered by U.S. population data.

The primary divisions of states are usually called counties. These in turn are subdivided into political units collectively known as minor civil divisions (MCDs). In most states, the places incorporated as municipalities are subordinate to minor civil divisions; but in some states, the incorporated places are themselves minor civil divisions of the counties. As will be shown, there are fairly numerous differences among the states in the nature and nomenclature of their political areas.

Counties

The primary divisions of the states are termed "counties" in all but two states, although four states also contain one or more independent cities. The county equivalents in Louisiana are the parishes. The primary divisions in the state of Alaska have been known as boroughs and census areas since the 1980 census (prior to that they were called election districts at the time of the state's formation in 1960 and census divisions for the 1970 decennial census). The independent cities are Baltimore (Maryland), Carson City (Nevada), St. Louis (Missouri), and 40 cities in Virginia. All in all, there were 3141 counties or county equivalents in the United States as of 2000 (with one new county under formation in Colorado).

Minor Civil Divisions

These are the tertiary subdivisions of the United States. The practice of reporting census data for county subdivisions goes all the way back to the first census in 1790, which reported data for towns, townships, and other units of local government. The minor civil divisions of counties have many kinds of names, as illustrated in Table 5.2, which shows the number of different types of MCDs used to report 1990 census data. "Township" is the most frequent. In the six New England States, New York, and Wisconsin, most MCDs are called "towns"; these are unlike the incorporated towns in other states in that they are not necessarily densely settled population centers. Some tertiary divisions have no local governmental organizations at all and may be uninhabited. Furthermore, in many states, some or all of the incorporated municipalities are also minor civil divisions. A further complication in some of the New England states is that all of the MCDs, be they cities or towns, are viewed locally as "incorporated" in that they exercise a number of local governmental powers. In the usage of Census Bureau publications, however, the term "incorporated place" has been reserved for localities or nucleated settlements and is not applied to other areal subdivisions.

In addition to the minor civil divisions shown in the census volumes, there are thousands of school and other taxation units for which separate population figures are not published. According to a recent (1997) census of governments, school districts numbered 13,726 nationwide and other specialized-function governmental units 34,683. Where more than one kind of primary subdivision exists in a county, the Census Bureau tries to select the more stable kind. In some states, however, no type of minor civil division has much stability. In some of the western states, for example, the election precincts may be changed after each election on the basis of the number of votes cast. Obviously, such units have practically no other statistical value. Even in states where the minor civil divisions do not change very

TABLE 5.2 Type and Number of County Subdivisions Used for the 1990 U.S. Census and as of 1999

	1990	1999
Townships	18,154	18,087
Census county divisions	5,581	5,581
Incorporated places	4,533	4,581
Towns	3,608	3,603
Election precincts	948	933
Magisterial districts	735	753
Parish governing authority districts	627	601
Supervisors' districts	410	410
Unorganized territories	282	285
Election districts	276	284
Census subareas	40	42
Plantations	36	33
Charter townships	N/A	26
Assessment districts	21	8
American Indian reservations	7	17
Grants	9	9
Purchases	6	6
Boroughs	5	5
Gores	4	4
Locations	4	4
Pseudo county subdivision	1	1
Road district	1	1
Total county subdivisions	35,298	35,274

Source: 1990 data from U.S. Bureau of the Census, *Geographic Areas Reference Manual*. Washington, DC: U.S. Government Printing Office, 1994. Currently available online at www.census.gov (U.S. Bureau of the Census, 2000a). 1999 data from Memorandum August 11, 1999, U.S. Bureau of the Census, Geography Division, List of Valid Entity Types and Number, by State.

often, they may have so little governmental significance that data published for them are also of limited usefulness. Here too the minor civil divisions may be so unfamiliar locally that it is very difficult for enumerators in the field to observe their boundaries. This is the situation in some southern states. At the other extreme are the stable towns of New England, which are of more political importance than the counties. For the 1990 census, 28 states had recognized minor civil divisions or equivalents.

A statistical solution to the problem of the evanescent or little-known minor civil divisions is the "census county division," which was first introduced in one state, Washington, in 1950 and then in many more states in the 1960 and subsequent censuses. For the 1990 census, the 21 census county division states were all in the West and Southeast.[1] The census county divisions, then, are the geographic-statistical equivalents of minor civil divisions; but because

---

[1] The state of Alaska has no counties and no minor civil divisions. Census subareas (CSAs) have been adopted as the statistical equivalents of MCDs. These are subdivisions of the boroughs and census areas that serve as the county equivalents.

they are not political areas, they are discussed in the next major section.

Incorporated Places

The generic definition of a "place" is a concentration of population regardless of the existence of legally prescribed limits, powers, or functions. While some incorporated places may serve as minor civil divisions, at the outset it should be clearly stated that place statistics and minor civil division statistics are two separate geographic schemes for tabulating census data. Depending on the vagaries of the various states' constitutions, laws, and local political structures, places may be either coterminous with or completely separately bounded from the county subdivisions. Whereas great pains are taken to provide a collectively exhaustive system of MCDs, MCD equivalents, and census county divisions, not everyone lives within a recognized place. At the time of the 1990 census, 66 million persons (approximately 26% of the total national population) lived outside of places.

Places are of two types: incorporated places and census-designated places. By definition, the incorporated places are the only ones that are political areas. All states contain incorporated places known as "cities."[2] Incorporated "towns" may be formed in 31 states, "villages" are permitted in 18, and "boroughs" in 3. New Jersey is the only state that permits formation of all four types. Where a state has more than one kind of municipality, cities tend to be larger places than the other types.

Unincorporated places that are defined for statistical tabulation purposes are now known as census-designated places (CDPs), with the criteria for designation based on total population size, population density, and geographic configuration. When CDPs were first recognized in 1950, they were called "unincorporated" places. CDPs are proposed and delineated by state, local, and tribal agencies and then reviewed and approved by the Census Bureau. There are only about one-fifth as many CDPs as there are incorporated places (4146 versus 19,289 at the time of the 1990 census.) However, a sizable fraction of the U.S. population (11.9% in 1990) lives in such settlements; without Census Bureau recognition, data tabulations would not exist for these commonly recognized localities.

Annexations

Beginning with 1970, the data shown for any area in a census report refer to the area's legally recognized boundaries as of January 1 of the census year. There are a great many changes in place boundaries through municipal annexations and detachments, mergers or consolidations, and incorporations and disincorporations. Since 1972, the Census Bureau in most years conducts a mail-out Boundary and Annexation Survey to track the changes.

Congressional and Legislative Districts

Congressional districts are the districts represented by a representative in the U.S. House of Representatives, whereas legislative districts are those represented by lawmakers serving in the state legislatures. At present, there are 435 congressional districts. The U.S. Constitution set the number of representatives at 65 from 1787 until the first census in 1790. The first apportionment, based on the 1790 census, resulted in 105 members. From 1800 through 1840, the number of representatives was determined by a fixed ratio of the number of persons to be represented. After 1840, the number of representatives changed with that ratio, as well as with population growth and the admission of new states. For the 1850 census and later apportionments, the number of House seats was fixed first, and the ratio of persons each representative was to represent changed. In 1911, the number of representatives in the House was capped at 433 with provision for the addition of one seat each for Arizona and New Mexico when they became states.[3] The House size, 435 members, has been unchanged since, except for a temporary increase to 437 at the time Alaska and Hawaii were admitted as states (U.S. Bureau of the Census, 2000a). The geographical boundaries of congressional districts are redrawn in each state by procedures specified by state legislatures, although now in some states bipartisan citizen's committees have been created in an attempt to blunt the influence of the controlling political party.

Except for Nebraska, every state legislature consists of two houses, each with its own districts, whose boundaries are also redrawn following each decennial census. These are all political areas, but they are not administrative areas.

General Considerations

The political uses of census data are so important that they go far to determine the basis of census tabulations of population for geographic areas. Fortunately, political units serve very well as statistical units of analysis in many demographic problems. In the realm where they are less satisfactory the Census Bureau has provided other types of area or residence classifications of population data with increasing usefulness over recent decades. A new tool in 1970, the address register, has subsequently been refined into a continuously maintained and updated national address database beginning with the 2000 census. That innovation, along with

---

[2] Strictly speaking, there are no incorporated places in Hawaii, only census designated places. The Census of Governments counts the combined city and county of Honolulu as a municipality.

[3] U.S. Statutes at Large, 37 Stat 13, 14 (1911).

the development of geographic information systems and the Census Bureau's TIGER system, has greatly facilitated the compilation of data for other types of units such as school districts, traffic zones, neighborhood planning units, and, indeed, for any other areas, political or otherwise, that can be defined or satisfactorily approximated in terms of combinations of city and rural blocks. The 1990 census was notable for being the first for which the whole national territory was "blocked." For the past several censuses, a "User Defined Areas" option has existed for localities to obtain special tabulations tailored to their own specific needs. The 2000 census for the first time provided standard tabulations for 5-digit zip code areas, though approximate data have been created for some time by private-sector firms doing allocations from, for example, block and block-group tabulations.[4]

The usefulness of demographic data for political areas of the United States for analysis of trends is greatest for the largest political subdivisions, namely the states. Counties and cities are probably next in order. Least satisfactory are the minor civil divisions, which, as we stated, change their boundaries frequently in some states. Another reason for the limited amount of analytical work done on population data for minor civil divisions is that many other types of data that one might wish to relate to census data are not available for geographic areas smaller than cities or counties. Moreover, the amount of detail and cross-classification of population data published by the census for minor civil divisions is quite limited.

For cross-sectional analyses that do not involve changes over time, counties, cities, and minor civil divisions, as well as states, may be very useful as units of analysis. In general, the smaller the geographic area with which one deals, the more homogeneous will be the population living in the area. Rates, averages, and other statistical summarizing measures are usually more meaningful if they relate to a relatively homogeneous population. However, if the geographic area and the population residing in it are very small, rates such as a migration rate or a death rate may be so unstable as to be meaningless. Here the total population exposed to the risk of migration or death may be too small for the statistical regularity of demographic events that is manifested when large populations are observed.

In publications of population statistics, data are often shown for a combination of political and nonpolitical areas, such as for the states and major geographic divisions, for counties and their urban and rural populations, or for incorporated and unincorporated places. The Census Bureau and other statistics-producing agencies present data for the states

sometimes listed in alphabetical order and sometimes in a geographic order. The usual geographic order conforms to the regions and divisions that are defined next.

STATISTICAL AREAS

For many purposes, data are needed for areas other than those recognized as political entities by law. Nonpolitical areas in common use for statistical purposes include both combinations and subdivisions of political areas. The most general objective in delineating such statistical areas is to attain relative homogeneity within the area, and, depending on the particular purpose of the delineation, the homogeneity sought may be with respect to geographic, demographic, economic, social, historical, or cultural characteristics. Also, groups of noncontiguous areas meeting specified criteria, such as all the urban areas within a state, are frequently used in presentation and analysis of population data.

International Recommendations and National Practices

There are several types of such statistical areas; for example, regions or functional economic areas; metropolitan areas, urban agglomerations, or conurbations; localities; and census tracts and block groups.

Regions or Functional Economic Areas

The terminology for this kind of geographic area is not too well standardized, but as used here, a "region" means a large area. It ordinarily means something more, however, namely some kind of functional economic or cultural area (McDonald, 1966; Odum and Moore, 1938; Taeuber, 1965; Whittlesey, 1954).[5] A region may represent a grouping of a country's primary divisions (e.g., states or provinces) or a grouping of secondary or tertiary divisions that cuts across the boundaries of the primary divisions. (There are also international regions, which are either combinations of whole countries or of areas which cut across national boundaries.) Among the factors on which regions are delineated are physiography, climate, type of soil, type of farming, culture, and economic levels and organizations. The cultural and economic factors include ethnic or linguistic differences, type of economy, and standard of living. The objective may be to create "uniform" (or "homogeneous") regions— which are delineated so as to minimize differences within regions and maximize differences among regions—or "nodal" regions—which feature a large city or urban

---

[4] Strictly speaking there is no such thing as a zip code area because zip codes are designated by the Postal Service for convenience of mail delivery. The Census Bureau units are "best approximations" delimited so as to provide a mutually exclusive and collectively exhaustive set of contiguous geographic areas for the national territory.

[5] As used in geography, a "region" may be an area of any size so long as it possesses homogeneity or cohesion.

complex functionally tied to and economically dominant over a hinterland. Some regionalizations may be based on statistical manipulations of a large number of indexes, for example, by cluster or factor analysis (Clayton, 1982; Morrill, 1988; Pandit, 1994; Plane, 1998; Plane and Isserman, 1983; Slater, 1976; Winchester, 1977). The regions defined and used by geographers, anthropologists, and so on are somewhat more likely than those defined by demographers and statisticians to ignore political areas altogether. The latter users have to be more concerned with the units for which their data are readily available and to use such units as building blocks in constructing regions. There may be also a hierarchy of regions; the simplest type consists of the region and the subregion.

Large Urban Agglomerations

The concept of an urban agglomeration is defined by the United Nations as follows: "A large locality of a country (i.e., a city or a town) is often part of an urban agglomeration, which comprises the city or town proper and also the suburban fringe or thickly settled territory lying outside of, but adjacent to, its boundaries. The urban agglomeration is, therefore, not identical with the locality but is an additional geographic unit that includes more than one locality" (United Nations, 1967, p. 51). (Discussion later in the chapter will show that this concept is broad enough to encompass both the metropolitan statistical areas and the urbanized areas used in the United States.)

A more detailed discussion of this concept is provided by Kingsley Davis and his associates (International Urban Research, 1959, pp. 1–17). According to them, the city as officially defined and the urban aggregate as ecologically conceived may differ because the city is either under-bounded or overbounded. Cities in Pakistan, for example, usually are "truebounded"—that is, they approximate the actual urban aggregate fairly closely. The underbounded city is the most common type elsewhere. Most of the cities in the Philippines are stated to be overbounded, in that they include huge areas of rural land within their boundaries. The *shi* in Japan are also of this type.

To define an urban aggregate or agglomeration, one may move in the direction of either an urbanized area or a metropolitan area. The former represents the territory "settled continuously in an urban fashion"; the latter typically includes some rural territory as well. Urbanized areas have been delineated in only a few countries. Their boundaries ignore political lines for the most part. In addition to the urbanized area in the United States, the conurbation in England and Wales is of this type. Metropolitan areas use political areas as building blocks and are based on principles of functional integration and a high degree of spatial interaction (such as commuting to workplaces) taking place within their bounds.

Although sometimes regarded as theoretically less desirable as the actual limits of urban agglomeration, metropolitan areas are often more feasible for both international and historical comparisons. They tend to be used more frequently than urbanized areas not only because of the greater stability and recognition of their boundaries but also because of the greater availability of social and economic data.[6] Data for urbanized areas have been limited to those provided by decennial census tabulations. Even if metropolitan areas have not been officially defined, they can be constructed in most countries from the available statistics, following standard principles, because metropolitan areas use standard political areas as their building blocks.

Localities

A "locality" is a distinct population cluster (inhabited place, settlement, population nucleus, etc.) the inhabitants of which live in closely adjacent structures. The locality usually has a commonly recognized name, but it may be named or delineated for purposes of the census. Localities are not necessarily the same as the smallest civil divisions of a country.

Localities, places, or settlements may be incorporated or unincorporated; thus, it is only the latter, or the sum of the two types, that is not provided for by the conventional statistics on political areas. The problem of delineating an unincorporated locality is similar to that of delineating a large urban agglomeration; but with the shift to the lower end of the scale, the areas required often cannot be approximated by combining several political areas because small localities are often part of the smallest type of political area. Just how small the smallest delineated locality should be for purposes of studying population distribution is rather arbitrary in countries where there is a size continuum from the largest agglomeration down to the isolated dwelling unit. In view of the considerable work required for such delineations, 200 inhabitants seems about as low a minimum as is reasonable.[7] In countries where there is essentially no scattered rural population but all rural families live in a village or hamlet, the answer is automatically provided by the settlement pattern. The rules for U.S. census designated place delineation have tended to set 1000 as the minimum population (and 2500 for designation as an "urban place"), although rural highway "sprawl" has made demarcation considerably more problematic than in lesser developed countries with a strong pattern of rural village settlement.

---

[6] The one governmental use of the U.S. urbanized area boundaries probably most visible to the general public is the federal requirement for lower speed limits on the portions of the interstate highways that lie within such continuously built-up territories around major cities.

[7] This is the class-mark between the lowest and the next to the lowest intervals in the table recommended by the United Nations, the lowest interval having no minimum.

Urban Census Tracts

The urban census tract is a statistical subdivision of a relatively large city, especially delineated for purposes of showing the internal distribution of population within the city and the characteristics of the inhabitants of the tract as compared with those of other tracts. Once their boundaries are established, not only census data but also other kinds of data, such as vital and health records, can be assembled for these areas. In Far Eastern countries and others where there are well-established small administrative units within cities, such special statistical subdivisions are unnecessary.

Statistical Areas of the United States

Regions

Two types of regional definitions of the United States are common—those that are groupings of whole states and those that cut across state lines. An older example of the former is the set of six regions of the South developed by Howard W. Odum (1936), and an illustration of the latter is the differing demarcations by geographers of the Middle West discussed by Fellmann, Getis, and Getis (1999, p. 16).

The greater convenience of the group-of-state regions for statistical compilations has led to their rather general adoption for presenting census data, although the greater homogeneity of regions that cut across state lines is well recognized.

Geographic Divisions and Census Regions

For its population publications the U.S. Bureau of the Census uses two levels of state groupings. Since the 1910 census, the states and the District of Columbia have been combined into nine groups, identified as "geographic divisions," and these in turn have been further combined into three or four groups, formerly called "sections" but since 1942 identified as "regions." The most recent changes to these long-standing groupings of the states were the additions of Alaska and Hawaii to the Pacific Division and West Region for the 1960 census and the renaming of the former North Central Region as the Midwest Region in 1984. Statistics may be presented for regions when the size of the sample does not permit publication for areas as small as states (for example with mobility data from Current Population Surveys). Figure 5.1 shows the states currently included in each division and each region. Commonly in

FIGURE 5.1   Maps of States, Divisions, and Regions of the United States

population research papers authors erroneously reference the divisions as "regions."

The objective in establishing these state groupings is described as follows: "The states within each of these divisions are for the most part fairly homogeneous in physical characteristics, as well as in the characteristics of their population and their economic and social conditions, while on the other hand each division differs more or less sharply from most others in these respects. In forming these groups of states the lines have been based partly on physical and partly on historical conditions" (U.S. Bureau of the Census, 1913, p. 13).[8] The use of the Mason-Dixon line, for example, as the boundary between the South and Northeast Regions (and of the South Atlantic and Middle Atlantic Divisions) is one example of the use of "historical conditions." Although a contemporary multistate regionalization based on a set of objectively chosen variables used to maximize internal homogeneity would doubtless differ from the groupings represented in the geographic divisions and regions, these have been retained to maintain continuity of data presentation from census to census as interest in historical comparisons has increased in recent decades.

Economic Subregions

The term "subregion" or "subarea" has been used in two senses in the United States: (1) to denote the subparts of a region (larger than a state), which may cut across state lines (e.g., Woofter, 1934), and (2) to denote subparts of states (Illinois Board of Economic Development, 1965). In either case, the delineation of the subregions may be based on any one or any combination of several types of criteria: agricultural, demographic, economic, social, cultural, and so on. Moreover, subregional boundaries may be coincident with county lines or they may cut across county lines.

The idea of the decennial census as a national inventory can be adequately implemented only by having material for examination and analysis for areas more appropriate for certain types of data than the conventional political units. This is especially important in the United States because of its large area, the great mobility of its population, and the fact that political boundaries in the United States offer little impediment to the flow of commerce and population across them. Because the political boundaries have so little effect in shaping the spatial patterns of economic and population phenomena, they are inadequate for delineating the most meaningful areas for portraying and analyzing these phenomena. Ideally, the delineation of economic areas should

not have to follow county or even township lines, but areas that did not do so would not be practicable or feasible for census purposes.

BEA Economic Areas

In recent years perhaps the most widely employed multicounty units have been the "economic areas" defined by the Bureau of Economic Analysis (BEA). In 1995 a new set of 172 BEA economic areas was redefined, replacing the 183-area set of units first defined in 1977 (minor revisions having been made to those units in 1983). The BEA economic areas are based on economic nodes—metropolitan areas or similar areas serving as centers of economic activity—and surrounding counties economically related to the node. Counties are the building blocks for these units, and commuting data from the 1990 Census of Population are the primary data used to assign outlying counties to nodes. The economic areas are collectively exhaustive and nonoverlapping. They may span state borders. The concept of the BEA economic areas is to provide a set of functional labor market areas that contain both the workplace and residence locations of the populations included, and about 80% of the 172 areas have net commuting rates of 1% or less.[9] Although the Census Bureau does not currently tabulate its data for BEA economic areas, because these units are collections of counties demographic data may be fairly readily aggregated to accompany the earnings by industry, employment by industry, total personal income and per capita personal income data provided by the BEA. For migration analysis, these units based on functional labor markets are much better units from a conceptual standpoint than, for instance, the states themselves.

State Economic Areas

Prior to the definition of BEA economic areas, the "state economic areas" (SEAs) were the most widely used, economically based, collectively exhaustive, multicounty, substate units. They failed, however, to enjoy the same history of successful recognition and widespread acceptance as did the concurrent efforts in metropolitan-area definition. The Bureau of the Census and the Bureau of Agricultural Economics commissioned Donald J. Bogue to develop a set of county groupings for the presentation of certain statistics from the 1950 Censuses of Population and Agriculture (U.S. Bureau of the Census, 1951; see also Beale, 1967). The state economic areas were relatively homogeneous subdivisions of the states consisting of single counties or groups of

---

[8] Chapter 6 in "Statistical Groupings of States and Counties" of the Census Bureau's *Geographical Areas Reference Manual* (available online at the Census Bureau's website; see U.S. Bureau of the Census 2000b) traces the history of the present regions and divisions back through each census and to statistical practices during colonial times. Additional details are given in Dahmann (1992).

[9] For more details about BEA economic areas and their 1995 redefinition, see Johnson (1995). This article and maps showing the boundaries of the 172 economic areas with the county constituents of each may currently be found on the Bureau of Economic Analysis website at: www.bea.doc.gov.

counties that had similar economic and social characteristics. There were two principal types of SEAs: the metropolitan and the nonmetropolitan. The former consisted of the larger standard metropolitan statistical areas (SMSAs; see the discussion that follows) except that when an SMSA was located in two or more states, each part became a separate metropolitan SEA. In nonmetropolitan areas, demographic, climatic, physiographic, and cultural factors, as well as factors pertaining more directly to the production and exchange of agricultural and nonagricultural goods, were considered. Census data were tabulated and reported for 501 SEAs for the 1950 census, 509 SEAs for 1960, and 510 for 1970 and 1980, after which they were dropped as official data-reporting units, ostensibly because of low usage.[10] One application for which the SEAs were quite useful was for reporting detailed area-to-area migration statistics. The origin-destination-specific matrices were considerably less clumsy to work with than the data-sparse county-to-county matrices that were made available through special tabulations from the 1980 and 1990 censuses (although county-to-county flow data have the virtue that they can be aggregated into any desired units—at least by the computer-sophisticated who are not intimidated by the task of manipulating quite large data files).

Metropolitan Areas

As this edition of *Methods and Materials* was being written, a major effort to review and refine metropolitan area definitions had just been completed. The units in use from 2003 forward, defined according to the recommended and adopted alternative, will be considerably different from the "metropolitan districts," "standard metropolitan areas" (SMAs), "standard metropolitan statistical areas" (SMSAs), "metropolitan statistical areas" (MSAs), and "metropolitan areas" (MAs) that represent the evolution of statistical practice over the past 90 years. Although originally intended merely as units to present more useful data tabulations, the officially recognized federal metropolitan areas have become rather extensively written into federal legislation for purposes of providing urban service, and the units have become not only widely recognized but also politically sensitive. This came about as suburban sprawl caused central cities to become less and less representative of the vast functional urban complexes that they had historically spawned, and no new governmental structures emerged on any sort of national basis to replace or supplement the incorporated cities and county governments.

Because of the widespread use of MAs throughout the federal agencies, these units are no longer considered within the sole purview of the Census Bureau. Currently the federal Office of Management and Budget (OMB) is charged with designating and defining metropolitan areas according to a set of official standards. The OMB is advised on these standards by the Federal Executive Committee on Metropolitan Areas (FECMA). By the late 1990s these standards, as the result of progressive bureaucratization of the process and several decades of political pressure and tinkering, had become so arcane and complex that they called into question the legitimacy of the entire concept, thus prompting the creation of a Metropolitan Area Standards Review Committee (MASRC) and the new system promulgated in the *Federal Registry* on December 27, 2000, that will be discussed shortly. Before turning to the future, however, let us first review the roots of the metropolitan area concept and the underlying bases for the criteria in effect through the 2000 census.

The "underbounding" of the major cities of the United States has long been noted—extending back even to prior to the Civil War. However, the first official recognition of the metropolitan concept was the Census Bureau's designation of metropolitan districts for cities with populations of 100,000 or more for the 1910 census. By 1930, metropolitan districts were extended down to cities with populations of 50,000 or more, so that by 1940 there were 140 recognized units. From 1910 through 1940, metropolitan district boundaries were drawn largely on the basis of population density, and minor civil divisions were used as the building blocks. In part because of the little-used MCD boundaries, other agencies and statistical groups did not make extensive use of the metropolitan district units. A major change was initiated by the federal Bureau of the Budget, which recognized that a more user-friendly metropolitan unit was needed. As a result, with the 1950 census, county-based metropolitan areas were first officially recognized (Shryock, 1957). At the same time, the Census Bureau launched the concept of the urbanized area (discussed shortly) to more accurately bound the actual physical extent of the functional urban region.

Since 1950, counties have been the building blocks for metropolitan units, except in New England where the towns are the more powerful units of government. Most of the standards for defining metropolitan areas date to the original set of rules agreed upon for the 1950 census when the units became known as "standard metropolitan areas," or SMAs. The general concept of a metropolitan area has been that "of an area containing a large population nucleus and adjacent communities that have a high degree of integration with that nucleus."[11] The definition of an individual metro-

---

[10] Shortly after the delineation of the state economic areas, Bogue and others combined them into a smaller number of economic subregions, which disregarded state lines. Still later these were further combined into 13 economic regions and 5 economic provinces. Bogue and Calvin Beale described the whole system in a monumental volume of more than 1100 pages. See Bogue and Beale (1953, 1961).

[11] *Federal Register*, Wednesday, October 20, 1999, Part IV, Office of Management and Budget, Recommendations from the Metropolitan Area Standards Review Committee to the Office of Management and Budget Concerning Changes to the Standards for Defining Metropolitan Areas; notice, p. 56628.

politan area has involved two considerations: first, a city or cities of specified population to constitute the central city and to identity the county in which it is located as the central county and, second, economic and social relationships with contiguous counties that are metropolitan in character, so that the periphery of the specific metropolitan area may be determined. Standard metropolitan statistical areas may cross state lines if necessary in order to include qualified contiguous counties.

Although the 1950 standards specified commuting as a major criterion on which to base the inclusion of counties outside the population nucleus, the first question on place of work was not included in the decennial censuses until 1960. The standard for minimum population of a central city to form the nucleus of an MSA in the 1950s was 50,000, although changes have more recently allowed exceptions so that smaller cities have been able to qualify. As the rules evolved, changes in nomenclature were also adopted. For several of the more recent censuses, the units were referred to as "standard metropolitan statistical areas" (SMSAs). Although since the 1980 census the first "S" has been dropped, the acronym SMSA is still widely (albeit, erroneously) used by researchers in refering to the official metropolitan areas. At present the units are known collectively as simply "metropolitan areas" (MAs). However, the individual units are designated by a complicated nomenclature beginning with the term for the basic units "metropolitan statistical areas" (MSAs) and continuing with the definitions of "consolidated metropolitan statistical areas" (CMSAs), primary metropolitan statistical areas (PMSAs), and New England County metropolitan areas (NECMAs). When revised MA rules were adopted in 1993 (which remained in effect through the 2000 census) there were 250 MSAs, 18 CMSAs consisting of 73 PMSAs, and 12 NECMAs. We shall now briefly summarize the step-by-step process for defining these units, which are those for which the 2000 decennial census data are being tabulated.

A metropolitan area is formed where there is a city of 50,000 or more *or* an urbanized area (discussed shortly) recognized by the Census Bureau with 50,000 or more inhabitants and if the included population totals at least 100,000 (or 75,000 in the six New England states). The county (or counties or towns in New England) that include(s) the largest city as well as any adjacent county that has at least half of its population in the urbanized area surrounding the largest city is (are) then designated as the "central county" (or "counties" or "towns") of the MSA. Additional outlying counties (or towns in New England) are included in the MSA on the basis of a set of rules relating to the percentage of in-commuting (15% being the normal minimum threshold) and other factors that are used to define "metropolitan character." These include population density, percentage of population classified as "urban," and percentage growth in population between the past two censuses.

For the 18 largest urban agglomerations, "consolidated metropolitan statistical areas" have been recognized that are composed of two or more constituent MSAs. When a CMSA is formed, the included MSAs then become known as "primary metropolitan statistical areas" (PMSAs). CMSAs must have minimum populations of 1 million or more.

Four size categories of MSAs are officially recognized: Level A, with 1 million or more total population; Level B, with 250,000 to 999,999; Level C, with 100,000 to 249,999; and Level D, with fewer than 100,000. Detailed rules also specify the conventions for naming MAs. An MSA's name can include up to three cities and names of each state in which it contains territory.

A multiyear process during the 1990s that involved the active participation of a number of demographers, geographers, and other experts resulted in the 1999 publication in the *Federal Registry* of new recommendations for a streamlined system of rules and a substantially revamped approach to metropolitan area definition. The proposal that was selected and promulgated in the form of the new official standards issued in December 2000 came after comment on and review of a number of alternatives that had been proposed exploring a wide spectrum of criteria and fundamental building blocks.

Although a return to minor civil divisions or the use of census tracts or zip code areas was contemplated, it was decided that the counties should be maintained as the fundamental structural elements particles for putting together metropolitan areas. It was concluded that the much greater availability and use of county data outweighed the disadvantages of using units that are (particularly in the western states) too large to very precisely delimit the functional urban realm. Only in New England will town-based units continue to be permitted, although under the new schema only as an alternative to the primary county-based units.

After considering a variety of other indicators, commuting was retained and strengthened as the basis for aggregating counties. The new definitions that have been put forward sweep aside the complex mix of other variables such as population density that had progressively crept into and excessively complicated MA definition. The recommendations seek to disentangle notions of *settlement structure* (as used in UA definition) from the criterion of *functional integration* has historically formed the basis for metropolitan-area recognition. The commuting threshold for qualifying outlying counties has been increased from 15% back to the 25% level used originally. The committee noted that since the journey-to-work question was added on the 1960 census, the percentage of workers commuting outside their county of residence increased from 15% to nearly 25% in 1990. Despite the increasingly non-nodal nature of many of our metropolitan complexes, the inward-commuting criterion has be retained. However, an important conceptual change is that an alternative qualification rule for outlying counties is that they will be included if 25% of their employed work-forces reside in the central county (or counties). Thus the decentralization of jobs and "reverse" commuting are explicitly recognized. Despite the recognition that commuting has fallen as a percentage of all trip making within urban areas, and that a majority of the total population may not be engaged in regular monetary labor, no publicly available alternative to commuting data has emerged.

Once again, a change in nomenclature is in the works, with the new system to be known as the "core-based statistical area" classification. The CBSAs to be defined will span the present metropolitan/nonmetropolitan continuum, with the term "metropolitan" no longer to be officially recognized. The proposed core areas for CBSAs are to be either Census Bureau defined urbanized areas (UAs) or new proposed units (also to be defined by the Census Bureau), to called "settlement clusters" (SCs). The SCs will have to encompass a population core of at least 10,000 inhabitants and extend the urbanized-area concept of a continuously built-up area to a lower level of the urban hierarchy. Rather than referring to the "central city" as has been the practice to date, the new term "principal city" is proposed because "central city" has become increasingly associated with "inner city."

The proposal as put forward envisions a four-level hierarchy based on total population size with the three types of CBSAs to be called "megapolitan," "macropolitan," and "micropolitan" areas, plus remaining non-CBSA territory:[12]

Core-based statistical areas	Population in cores
Megapolitan	1,000,000 and above
Macropolitan	50,000 to 999,000
Micropolitan	10,000 to 49,999

One million was conceded to be a well-established threshold for many of the highest scale urban functions. Proxying the geographic areas that may result with the proposed rules after the 2000 census data become available, the committee estimated that approximately 35 megapolitan areas may be formed. These would encompass some 45% of the 1990 U.S. population. After the OMB review, however, the proposed distinction between megapolitan and macropolitan areas was dropped in favor of retaining the single, more familiar "metropolitan" term. The smaller micropolitan areas were adopted, and that term is being added to the lexicon of official U.S. governmental statistical units.

Although the micropolitan and metropolitan areas to be defined will all be nonoverlapping entities, a two-tier hierarchical distinction has been adopted by the OMB, accepting the committee's recommendation to recognize

---

[12] An option still under consideration as of 2002 would split the broad macropolitan category into a separate "mesopolitan" category (50,000 to 249,999 population) and a (redefined) macropolitan category (250,000 to 999,999). This would not result in a five- rather than four-part division of the national territory.

some CBSAs clustering together to form "combined areas." In essence, the combined areas extend the current two-level PMSA/CMSA breakdown. Combined areas may be formed not only in the largest urban agglomerations but wherever adjacent CBSAs have moderately strong commuting linkages. Thus a combined area might include, for example, a metropolitan area plus two micropolitan areas, or even just two or more micropolitan areas. Rules for merging (eliminating separate designations) versus combining (retaining separate CBSA identities) are defined.

It will be interesting to watch the proposed CBSA system as it is implemented and refined. On the one hand, the new rules greatly simplify and clarify the definitions, and most of the decisions made opted to stick with more traditional practices rather than to substitute radical alternatives. On the other hand, the unfamiliar new nomenclature and the more detailed articulation of the national territory into the new metropolitan, micropolitan, and combined areas could further confuse statistical data users. As this edition was going to press, the critical 2000 commuting data needed to implement the new system had not yet been tabulated, and it thus remains to be seen exactly how the new standards will ultimately be implemented and accepted.

Urbanized Areas

The urban agglomeration known as the metropolitan district was replaced in 1950 not only by the standard metropolitan area but also by the urbanized area. The distinction between these two concepts was explained in the section on "Large Urban Agglomerations." In brief, the latter may be viewed as the physical city, the built-up area that would be identified from an aerial view, whereas the former also includes the more thinly settled area of the day-to-day economic and social influence of the metropolis in the form of worker commutation, shopping, newspaper circulation, and so on. Probably the greatest justification for setting up still another type of urban agglomeration, however, was the resulting improvement of the urban-rural classification.

Each urbanized area consists of a central city or cities and a densely settled residential belt outside the city limits that is called the "urban fringe." The basic criterion for defining the extent of the fringe portion of urbanized areas is a residential population density of 1000 persons per square mile. The boundaries of urbanized areas do not necessarily follow the lines of any governmental jurisdictions, and they are in principle subject to change whenever new development takes place. These are excellent units for many statistical purposes; however, noncensus data are generally unavailable and public awareness of their boundaries is virtually nonexistent. Urbanized areas are not stable in territorial coverage from census to census, and thus some forms of historical comparison may be difficult. Because of these limitations, metropolitan areas have been much more widely

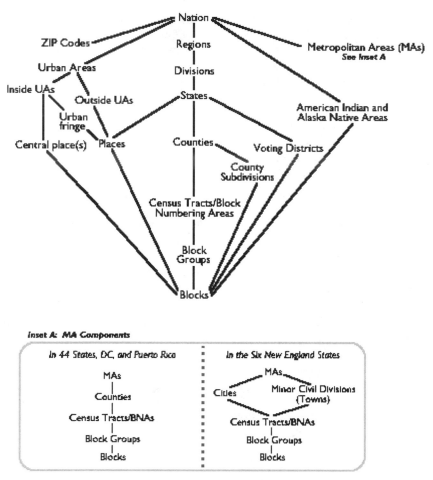

FIGURE 5.2   Graphic Structure in the U.S. Census

employed for both governmental and statistical purposes despite their tendency to "overbound" the functional built-up areas around major cities.

PUMAs

Public use microsample (PUMS) data from the 1990 census have been reported for a set of units known most commonly by their acronym: PUMAs. Public use microdata areas are special units for these data sets that somewhat approximate metropolitan areas. Unfortunately PUMAs have not been included on the Bureau's TIGER system. Analysts wishing to do GIS analysis of PUMA data have had to obtain geographic equivalency files to establish the location of the boundaries of PUMAs.

Subcounty Statistical Units

As shown in Figure 5.2, a hierarchy of statistical units have been developed to report census data below the county level. Census tracts and block numbering groups (BNGs),

block groups (BGs), and blocks provide progressively finer-scale units for carrying out geographical analyses. In general, the larger the area, the more data are available; for reliability reasons, only short-form data are typically obtainable at the block level. Formerly data were more readily accessible at the census tract than the block group scale (for example, for the 1980 census, printed tract reports were issued for each major metropolitan area, whereas microfiche or magnetic tape files were the only form for which block group information was provided.) Beginning with the 1990 census, however, block group information is as easily obtained as that for census tracts; for many analyses, the finer-scale geography of the BG may be more appropriate. Each of these three statistical units is now discussed in turn.

Census Tracts and Block Numbering Areas

Census tracts and block numbering areas are artificial units created strictly for the purpose of facilitating geographical analyses of population distribution at a more consistent and generally smaller scale than that afforded by political jurisdictions such as minor civil divisions. Census tracts are delineated by committees of local data users who are asked to designate units that follow recognizable boundaries and encompass areas that include between 2500 and 8000 persons. The boundaries are drawn based on principles of homogeneity; committees are asked to create units exhibiting, as much as practicable, uniform population characteristics, economic status, and housing conditions. Once established, usually only splits (or recombinations) of the tracts from a previous census are permitted. A major goal of the tracting program is to present units that can provide the basis for historical comparisons. The tracts from a more recent census are generally easily aggregated so as to re-create the areas encompassed by tracts designated for earlier censuses. The tract and BNA numbering systems used on recent censuses have been designed to facilitate such aggregation.[13] On the whole, the preservation of fixed boundaries is regarded as more basic than the preservation of homogeneity within a tract.

The census tract idea began with Walter Laidlaw, who divided New York City into tracts for the census of 1910. Census tracts were originally developed to subdivide the nation's urban areas. However, now, with the inclusion of block numbering areas, coverage of the entire nation has been achieved at this scale of analysis. Beginning with the 1990 census, block numbering areas became essentially the equivalent of census tracts. BNAs are created for counties (or their statistical equivalents) where no local committee exists to fix the boundaries. Typically state agencies and American Indian tribes, with a fair amount of Census Bureau involvement, designate BNAs.

For the 1990 census there were 50,690 tracts and 11,586 BNAs, with six states (California, Connecticut, Delaware, Hawaii, New Jersey, and Rhode Island) as well the District of Columbia being fully tracted. As of 2000, a total of 66,483 tracts/BNAs have been designated.

Block Groups

Block groups are subdivisions of census tracts or block numbering areas. They are created by the same committees or agencies that define tracts and BNAs. The block group is the smallest area for which census sample data are now reported. BGs replace the enumeration districts (EDs) that were sometimes formerly used to present small area data. A block group consists of several census blocks that share the same first-digit number within a census tract. For the 1990 census, 229,466 block groups were designated; as of 2000, there are 212,147.

Blocks

Beginning with the 1940 census of housing, blocks in cities of 50,000 inhabitants or more at the preceding census were numbered, and statistics and analytical maps were published using the block as a unit. In 1960, under special arrangements, the block statistics program was extended to 172 smaller cities as well. There was a total of about 737,000 blocks in the block-numbered areas. For the first time, the population total was also tabulated for blocks.[14] The 1990 census was the first for which the entire national territory was encompassed by official census block units. The Census Bureau published data for 7,020,924 blocks. Rapid advances in GIS and geocoding technology have made it sensible to begin the hierarchy of reporting units with blocks. A possible future (and perhaps ultimate step) would be the geocoding of the addresses of each housing unit. This would in principle permit complete flexibility in constructing the most appropriate small-area geographic units for any particular statistical purposes while still preserving the confidentiality of respondents through the establishment of minimum population or housing unit thresholds below which data would be suppressed.

Conclusions

We think of geographic elements as being relatively stable and unchanging. Yet this section has reported a picture of continuous change over the past few decades in the ways developed for presenting data on the geographic distribution of population in the United States. With a highly developed, expanding economy and a highly mobile population, the significant classifications for examining population distribution cannot remain static if they are to be functionally adequate. Governmental structures have proven slow to adjust to new realities leading to pressure to create more adequate units for statistical purposes. Settlement structures have evolved that look very little like the historical norms of just a few decades ago. Yet some degree of comparability of classification used in successive decades must be maintained to afford a basis of revealing trends and permitting historical analyses. This is an ever-present dilemma in the planning of population censuses that faces statistical agencies in other countries as well. If no changes were made, the concepts and definitions would increasingly fail to describe the current situation. If each census were planned afresh, with no regard to what had been done in the past, there would be no basis

---

[13] Census tracts and block groups are designated by up to four-digit numbers with optional two-digit decimal suffixes. Numbers are unique to each county and counties in the same metropolitan area may be requested to use distinct numerical ranges. When tracts are split, the two-digit suffixes may be used. For instance, tract 101 may be divided into tracts 101.01 and 101.02. Census tracts have numbers in the range 1 to 9499.99 whereas BNAs are numbered between 9501 to 9989.99. For more information see the *Geographic Areas Reference Manual* available at www.census.gov.

[14] *U.S. Census of Housing: 1960*, Vol. III, *City Blocks*, Series HC(3), Nos. 1 to 421, 1961 to 1962, Table 2.

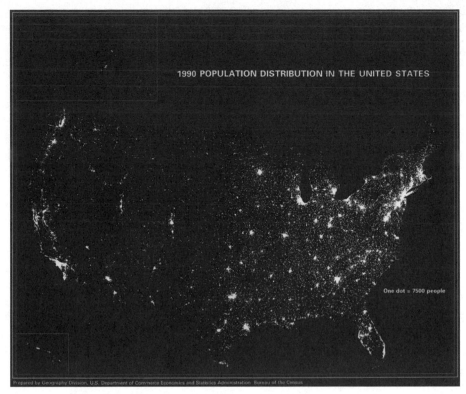

FIGURE 5.3   Population Distribution of the United States

for studying trends. An intermediate alternative is to introduce improvements, but in the year they are introduced to make at least some data available on both the old and the new basis.

A relatively new challenge in designing geographic units for data reporting has been the popularity of public use sample data. Privacy issues are even more a matter of concern in this area than they are when evaluating ecological data, yet for good geodemographic analysis such sample data must contain geographic identifiers at the smallest feasible scale. The use of special, ad hoc units such as PUMAs that do not correspond to any level of the primary census geographic hierarchy is certainly less than ideal. With the arrival of the American Community Survey data come further challenges for constructing the geographic concepts of reporting at the below-urban-area scale.

METHODS OF ANALYSIS

Figure 5.3 displays the population distribution of the United States. This "night-time" population map is an example of a population dot map. There are a number of measures for describing the spatial distribution of a population and many graphic devices other than dot maps for portraying population distribution and population density. The

interdisciplinary nature of demography is particularly displayed in this field. Geographers, statisticians, sociologists, and even physicists have contributed to it. In 1957 Duncan set out the following classification of measures, which he did not claim to be exhaustive or mutually exclusive:

A. Spatial measures
   (1) Number and density of inhabitants by geographic subdivisions
   (2) Measures of concentration
   (3) Measures of spacing
   (4) Centrographic measures
   (5) Population potential

B. Categorical measures
   (1) Rural-urban and metropolitan-nonmetropolitan classification
   (2) Community size distribution
   (3) Concentration by proximity to centers or to designated sites

In this book, topics B (1) and (2) are treated more fully in Chapter 6 than in this chapter. In this chapter, we shall discuss the others, combining treatment of A (5), population potential, with B(3) under the heading of the general concept of "accessibility" measures, of which we shall detail two types designated threshold and aggregate.

TABLE 5.3   Estimated Population, Area, and Density for
Major Areas of the World, 1993

Major area	Estimated midyear population (millions) (1)	Surface area (thousands of square kilometers) (2)	Density (1) ÷ (2)
World total	5,544	135,641	41
Africa	689	30,306	23
America, Latin	465	20,533	23
America, Northern	287	21,517	13
Asia	3,350	31,764	105
Europe	726	22,986	32
Oceania	28	8,537	3

Source: U.N. *Demographic Yearbook*, 1995, Table 1, p. 129.

Population Density

The density of population is a simple concept much used in analyses of urban development and studies relating population size to resources and in ecological studies. This simple concept has a number of pitfalls, however, some of which are discussed later. Density is usually computed as population per square kilometer, or per square mile, of land area rather than of gross area (land and water).[15]

The *1993 Demographic Yearbook* of the United Nations (1995) gives population per square kilometer for continents and regions (Table 1) and for countries (Table 5.3) as estimated using information from the 1990 round of censuses. Table 5.3 is abstracted from Table 1 in the *Yearbook*. By midyear 2000, with total population size up to approximately 6.080 billion, the world's density had increased to 45 persons per square kilometer. A few populous countries now have densities in excess of 250 persons per square kilometer (India, 274 persons / sq. km; Japan, 327; South Korea, 444; Belgium, 328; Netherlands, 375). From 500 to 2000, the country is likely to be a relatively small island (Barbados, 616; Bermuda, 1189; the Channel Islands, 749; and Malta, 1152); beyond 2000, the country is essentially a city (Singapore, 4650; Macao, 21,560; Monaco, 31,000; and Gibraltar, 4667).

At the other extreme, countries with considerable parts of their land area in deserts, mountains, tropical rain forests, ice caps, and so on have very low densities. The most thinly settled countries of all tend to be close to the Arctic or Antarctic circles. Even if we use the area of the ice-free portion of Greenland, its density is only about 0.1 per square kilometer (for the total surface area the density is only 0.02). Even Canada has a density of only 3.

These illustrations suggest that, for some purposes, more meaningful densities are obtained for a country or region by relating the size of its population to the amount of settled area. On this basis, the densities are often much greater, of course, than the "arithmetic" or "crude" densities we have reported here.

Another measure of population density has been suggested by George (1955). His measure relates to the "ratio between the requirements of a population and the resources made available to it by production in the area it occupies" (George 1955, p. 313). The ratio is $\Delta e = Nk/Sk'$, where N is the number of inhabitants, k the quantity of requirements per capita, S the area in square kilometers, and k' the quantity of resources produced per square kilometer. George concludes, however, that, "It is impossible to make a valid calculation of economic density in an industrial economy." Duncan, Cuzzort, and Duncan (1961, pp. 35–38) have discussed the conceptual difficulties in comparing the population density of different areas.

The most commonly employed alternative to crude density is "physiological" (sometimes alternatively called "nutritional") density, which is calculated as population divided by the quantity of arable land in a country. Data reported by Fellmann, Getis, and Getis (1999, p. 125), for example, show that the crude density of Bangladesh is substantially higher than that of Japan (921 versus 334 persons per square kilometer); however, a much greater percentage of Bangladesh's land area is devoted to agriculture than in highly urbanized Japan and thus the physiological densities are of reverse magnitudes: 2688 for Japan and 1292 for Bangladesh. A variation of physiological density is "agricultural" density, which is the farm population only divided by arable land; it gives a perspective on the labor-to-land intensity of agriculture. Note that agricultural density defined in this way reflects both the technological efficiency of farming as well as the labor intensity associated with the types of crops grown.

If there have been no changes in boundaries, the change in population density over a given period is, of course, simply proportionate to the change in population size. Thus, if the population has increased 10%, the density has also increased 10%.

United States

The population densities of the United States in midyear 2000 were as follows:

	United States
Crude density per square mile	78
Crude density per square kilometer	30
Physiologic density per square mile	376
Physiologic density per square kilometer	145

Percentage Distribution

A simple way of ordering the statistics that is appropriate for any demographic aggregate is to compute the

[15] Note that 1 square kilometer (km²) = 0.386103 square miles; 1 square mile = 2.58998 km².

percentage distribution living in the geographic areas of a given class. Table 5.4 is an illustration. Note that the change given in the last column is in terms of percentage points (i.e., the numerical difference between the two percentages). The percentages as rounded may not add exactly to 100. In such cases, however, it is conventional not to force the distribution to add exactly or to show the total line as 99.9, 100.1, and so on. Where there is a very large number of geographic areas and many would contain less than 0.1% of the population, the percentages could be carried out to two decimal places.

Rank

Another common practice is to include a supplementary table listing the geographic areas of a given class in rank order. Again, the rankings can be compared from one census to another and the changes in rank indicated. Table 5.5 gives an illustration for the "urban areas" of New Zealand. In cases of an exact tie, it is conventional to assign all tying areas the average of the ranks involved; for example, if two areas tied for seventh place, they would both be given a rank of $7\frac{1}{2}$. The choice of sign for the change in rank requires a little reflection. It seems more intuitive to assign a positive

TABLE 5.4 Percentage Distribution by Provinces and Territories of the Population of Canada, 1996 and 1999

Province or territory	1996		1999		Change in percentage, 1996 to 1999
	Number (thousands)	Percentage of total	Number (thousands)	Percentage of total	
Canada, total	29,671.9	100.0	30,491.3	100.0	NA
Newfoundland	560.6	1.9	541.0	1.8	−0.1
Prince Edward Island	136.2	0.5	138.0	0.5	—
Nova Scotia	931.2	3.1	939.8	3.1	−0.1
New Brunswick	753.0	2.5	755.0	2.5	−0.1
Quebec	7,274.0	24.5	7,345.4	24.1	−0.4
Ontario	11,100.9	37.4	11,513.8	37.8	+0.3
Manitoba	1,134.3	3.8	1,143.5	3.8	−0.1
Saskatchewan	1,019.5	3.4	1,027.8	3.4	−0.1
Alberta	2,780.6	9.4	2,964.7	9.7	+0.4
British Columbia	3,882.0	13.1	4,023.1	13.2	+0.1
Yukon	31.9	0.1	30.6	0.1	—
Northwest Territories	41.8	0.1	41.6	0.1	—
Nunavut	25.7	0.1	27.0	0.1	—

— Less than 0.05.

NA: Not applicable.

Source: Statistics Canada, CANSIM (online database), matrices 6367–6378 and 6408–6409 and calculations by the author.

TABLE 5.5 Population and Rank of Main Urban Areas in New Zealand, 1936 and 1996

	1936		1996		Change in rank, 1936–1996
	Population	Rank	Population	Rank	
Auckland	210,393	1	991,796	1	—
Wellington	149,382	2	334,051	2	—
Christchurch	132,282	3	325,250	3	—
Dunedin	81,848	4	110,801	6	−2
Napier-Hastings	36,158	5	112,793	5	—
Invercargill	25,682	6	49,403	9	−3
Wanganui	25,312	7	41,097	11	−4
Palmerston North	23,953	8	73,860	7	−1
Hamilton	19,373	9	158,045	4	+5
New Plymouth	18,194	10	48,871	10	—
Gisborne	15,521	11	32,608	12	−1
Nelson	13,545	12	50,692	8	+4

Sources: New Zealand, Census and Statistics Department, *Population Census, 1945,* Vol. 1, p. ix, and Table 6, *1996 Census of Population and Dwellings,* "Changes in Usually Resident Population for Urban Areas, 1986–1996", Statistics New Zealand website www.stats.govt.nz.

David A. Plane

sign to a rise in the rankings (movement "upward" toward number 1).[16]

Measures of Average Location and of Concentration

There has long been an interest in calculating some sort of average point for the distribution of population within a country or other area. Both European and American statisticians have contributed to this concept (Bachi, 1966). The most popular measures are the median point or location, or median center of population; the mean point, often called the "center of population"; and the point of minimum aggregate travel. A somewhat different concept is that of the point of maximum "population potential." There has been somewhat less scientific interest in measuring the dispersion of population. Here we will describe Bachi's "standard distance." Average positions and dispersion, density surfaces, and so on are treated systematically by Warntz and Neft (1960). Measures of population concentration (such as the Lorenz curve and Gini index) are discussed in Chapter 6.

Mediain Lines and Median Point

The "median lines" are two orthogonal lines (at right angles to each other), each of which divides the area into two parts having equal numbers of inhabitants. The "median point" (or median center of population) is the intersection of these two lines. The median lines are conventionally the north-south and east-west lines, but the location of the median point depends slightly on how these axes are rotated (Hart, 1954). Table 5.6 gives the location of the median center of population of the United States for each census year since 1880. The 1990 median center was located in Marshall Township, Lawrence County, Indiana, approximately 14 miles south of Bloomington.

Hart and others also mention that, in addition to median lines that divide a territory into halves in terms of population, other common fractions may be used, such as quarters and tenths. For the population and area of the United States, equal tenths ("decilides") have been computed in the north-south and the east-west directions (U.S. Bureau of the Census, 1963). These devices describe population distribution rather than central tendency, as does the median point.

Center of Population

The center of population, or the mean point of the population distributed over an area, may be defined as the center

---

TABLE 5.6 Median Center of Population of the United States, 1880–1990

Census Year	North Latitude °	′	″	West Longitude °	′	″
United States						
1990	38	57	55	86	31	53
1980	39	18	60	86	08	15
1970	39	47	43	85	31	43
1960	39	56	25	85	16	60
1950	40	00	12	85	02	21
Conterminous United States						
1950	40	00	12	84	56	51
1940	40	04	18	84	40	11
1930	40	11	52	84	36	35
1920	40	11	52	84	43	60
1910	40	07	33	85	02	00
1900	40	03	32	84	49	01
1890	40	02	51	84	40	01
1880	39	57	00	84	07	12

Source: "Population and Geographic Centers," U.S. Bureau of the Census website at www.census.gov (U.S. Bureau of the Census, 2000a).

---

of population gravity for the area, "in other words, the point upon which the [area] would balance, if it were a rigid plane without weight and the population distributed thereon, each individual being assumed to have equal weight and to exert an influence on the central point proportional to his distance from the point. The pivotal point, therefore, would be its center of gravity" (U.S. Bureau of the Census, 1924, p. 7). The formula for the coordinates of the mean center of population may be written as follows:

$$\bar{x} = \sum p_i x_i \Big/ \sum p_i \quad \text{and} \quad \bar{y} = \sum p_i y_i \Big/ \sum p_i \quad (5.1)$$

where p_i is the population at point i and x_i and y_i are its horizontal and vertical coordinates, respectively.

Thus, the mean point, unlike the median point, is influenced by the distance of a person from it. It is greatly affected by extreme items and is influenced by *any* change of the distribution over the total area. In the United States, for example, a population change in Alaska or Hawaii, which is far removed from the center, exerts a much greater leverage than a change in Missouri, the state where the center is now located.

Hart (1954, pp. 50–54) outlines a simple method of calculating the center of population from a map, which is parallel to his method for locating the median point. This graphic method is suitable for only a relatively small area where a map projection like a Mercator projection does not distort too much the relative distances along different parallels of latitude (i.e., where it may be assumed that equal distances in terms of degrees represent equal linear distances).

---

[16] Earlier editions of *The Methods and Materials of Demography* (e.g., Shryock and Siegel, 1973) adopted the opposite convention, using the sign of the difference between the ranks in the more recent and less recent years.

A more exact method for computing the center of population, and one that is required when dealing with a very large area, is described by the set of equations shown here:

$$\bar{x} = \left\{ \sum p_a \left(x_a - \overline{x'} \right) - \sum p_b \left(x' - \overline{x_b} \right) \right\} \Big/ \sum p_i + \overline{x'} \quad (5.2)$$

$$\bar{y} = \left\{ \sum p_c \left(y_c - \overline{y'} \right) - \sum p_d \left(y' - \overline{y_d} \right) \right\} \Big/ \sum p_i + \overline{y'} \quad (5.3)$$

where x' and y' are the coordinates of the assumed mean, x_{al} is any point east of that mean, x_b is any point west of it, y_c is any point north of it, y_d is any point south of it, and p_a, p_b, p_c, p_d are the populations in areas east, west, north, and south of the assumed mean, respectively.

The procedure is described in several publications of the U.S. Bureau of the Census. One such description is:

> Through this point [the assumed center] a parallel and a meridian are drawn, crossing the entire country.
>
> The product of the population of a given area by its distance from the assumed meridian is called an east or west moment. In calculating north and south moments the distances are measured in minutes of arc: in calculating east and west moments it is necessary to use miles on account of the unequal length of the degrees and minutes in different latitudes. The population of the country is grouped by square degrees—that is, by areas included between consecutive parallels and meridians—as they are convenient units with which to work. The population of the principal cities is then deducted from that of the respective square degrees in which they lie and treated separately. The center of population of each square degree is assumed to be at its geographical center except where such an assumption is manifestly incorrect; in these cases the position of the center of population of the square degree is estimated as nearly as possible. The population of each square degree north and south of the assumed parallel is multiplied by the distance of its center from that parallel; a similar calculation is made for the principal cities; and the sum of the north moments and the sum of the south moments are ascertained. The difference between these two sums, divided by the total population of the country, gives a correction to the latitude. In a similar manner the sums of the east and of the west moments are ascertained and from them the correction in longitude is made. (U.S. Bureau of the Census 1924, pp. 7–8)

For a large area, adjustments should be made for the sphericity of the earth.

The location of the center of population, unlike that of the median point, is independent of the particular axes chosen. The calculation of the center of population for a large country is well suited to programming for a computer. There it is feasible to introduce an additional refinement for the sphericity of the earth.

For illustrative computations of the center of population (and the median point), see the unabridged edition of *The Methods and Materials of Demography* (Shryock and Siegel, 1973, pp. 136–141).

Table 5.7 shows the movement of the center of population of the United States from 1790 to 1990. Note the difference between the locations for the "United States" (50 states) and "conterminous United States" (48 states). Notice that the mean centers tend to be farther south and substan-

tially farther west than the median centers shown in Table 5.6. Back in 1910, the mean center of population was in Bloomington, Indiana, the closest city to the 1990 median center. Although much more frequently seen than the median center, the mean center may actually be a somewhat less intuitive concept to explain to a nontechnical audience.

The definition of the "geographic center of area" is analogous to that of the mean center of population, but the computation is somewhat simpler. In some countries those two centers may be a great distance apart. Thus, in 1990, the mean center of population of the United States was in Missouri, whereas the geographic center of area was substantially to the northwest in Butte County, South Dakota, where it has been since the 1960 census after Alaska and Hawaii became states. The geographic center of area for the conterminous United States is in Smith County, Kansas.

In the last decades of the 19th and the early decades of the 20th century, there was great interest in the concept of center of population and in the mean location of many other units that are reported in censuses. For example, the *Statistical Atlas* published as part of the 1920 census of the United States gave the center of population for individual states, of the Negro population, and of the urban and rural population, and the mean point of the number of farms. This tradition has been revived to some extent by the Israeli demographer Roberto Bachi, who has computed or compiled centers of population for a variety of countries and population subgroups (Bachi, 1962).

The center of population, being merely the arithmetic mean of the population distribution, need not fall in a densely settled part of the country. In fact, the center of population of an archipelago may be in the sea. This is one of the circumstances that led the astronomer John Q. Stewart and the geographer William Warntz to regard the concept of center of population as being more misleading than useful (Stewart and Warntz, 1958; Warntz, 1958). Stewart's alternative concept of "population potential" is discussed below. Nevertheless, there seems to be real merit in Hart's view that the center of population is a useful summary measure for studying the shifts of population over time (Hart, 1954, p. 59).

Point of Minimum Aggregate Travel

This centrographic measure, sometimes called the "median center," is defined as "that point which can be reached by all items of a distribution with the least total straight line travel for all items," or "the point from which the total *radial* deviations of an areal distribution are at a minimum" (Hart, 1954, pp. 56, 58). Hart gives a graphic method for locating this point. This concept has fairly obvious applications to location theory (e.g., to estimating

TABLE 5.7 Mean Center of Population of the United States, 1790–1990

Census year	North latitude °	′	″	West longitude °	′	″	Approximate location
United States							
1990	37	52	20	91	12	55	Crawford County, MO, 10 miles southeast of Steelville
1980	38	08	13	90	34	26	Jefferson County, MO, ¼ mile west of DeSoto
1970	38	27	47	89	42	22	St. Clair County, MO, 5 miles east-southeast of Mascoutah
1960	38	35	58	89	12	35	Clinton County, IL, 6½ miles nothwest of Centralia
1950	38	48	15	88	22	08	Clay County, IL, 3 miles northeast of Louisville
Conterminous United States							
1950	38	50	21	88	09	33	Richland County, IL, 8 miles north-northwest of Olney
1940	38	56	54	87	22	35	Sullivan County, IN, 2 miles southeast by east of Carlisle
1930	39	03	45	87	08	06	Greene County, IN, 3 miles northeast of Lincoln
1920	39	10	21	86	43	15	Owen County, IN, 8 miles south-southeast of Spencer
1910	39	10	12	86	32	20	Monroe County, IN, in the city of Bloomington
1900	39	09	36	85	48	54	Bartholomew County, IN, 6 miles southeast of Columbus
1890	39	11	56	85	32	53	Decatur County, IN, 20 miles east of Columbus
1880	39	04	08	84	39	40	Boone County, KY, 8 miles west by south of Cincinnati, OH
1870	39	12	00	83	35	42	Highland County, OH, 48 miles east by north of Cincinnati
1860	39	00	24	82	48	48	Pike County, OH, 20 miles south by east of Chillicothe
1850	38	59	00	81	19	00	Wirt County, WV, 23 miles southeast of Parkersburg
1840	39	02	00	80	18	00	Upshur County, WV, 16 miles south of Clarksburg, WV[1]
1830	38	57	54	79	16	54	Grant County, WV, 19 miles west-southwest of Moorefield[1]
1820	39	05	42	78	33	00	Hardy County, WV, 16 miles east of Moorefield[1]
1810	39	11	30	77	37	12	Loudon County, VA, 40 miles northwest by west of Washington, DC
1800	39	16	06	76	56	30	Howard County, MD, 18 miles west of Baltimore
1790	39	16	30	76	11	12	Kent County, MD, 23 miles east of Baltimore

[1] West Virginia was set off from Virginia on December 31, 1862, and admitted as a state on June 19, 1863.

Source: "Population and Geographic Centers," U.S. Bureau of the Census website at www.census.gov (U.S. Bureau of the Census, 2000a).

the optimum central location for a public or private service of some sort).

Standard Distance

Measures of the dispersion of population have been proposed from time to time, but the one that has been most thoroughly developed is Bachi's (1958) "standard distance." The standard distance bears the same kind of relationship to the center of population that the standard deviation of any frequency distribution bears to the arithmetic mean. In other words, it is a measure of the dispersion of the distances of all inhabitants from the center of population.

If $\bar{x}$ and $\bar{y}$ are the coordinates of the center of population, say its longitude and latitude, then the distance from any item i, with coordinates x_i, and y_i, is given by

$$D_{ic} = \sqrt{(x_i - \bar{x})^2 + (y_i - \bar{y})^2} \qquad (5.4)$$

and the standard distance by

$$D = \sqrt{\frac{\sum_{i=1}^{n} D_{ic}^2}{n}} \qquad (5.5)$$

In practice, the distance would not be measured individually for each person but rather we should use data grouped by political areas (or square degrees), and it would then be assumed that the population of a unit area is concentrated in its geographic center. Here, then,

$$D = \sqrt{\frac{\sum_i f_i (x_i - \bar{x})^2}{n} + \frac{\sum_i f_i (y_i - \bar{y})^2}{n}} \qquad (5.6)$$

where f_i, is the number of persons in a particular unit of area.

Duncan, Cuzzort, and Duncan (1961, p. 93) pointed out that the standard distance is much less influenced by the set of real subdivisions used than are other measures of population dispersion (or concentration), such as the Lorenz curve (see Chapter 6). In general, however, the smaller the type of area used as a unit, the more closely will the computed standard distance approach the value computed from the locations of individual persons.

Standard distances can also be drawn on a map. Representing the standard distance by a line segment, we know the length of the line and its origin at the center of the population, but the direction in which it is drawn is purely arbitrary. One could appropriately draw a circle with the standard distance as its radius about the center of the population. Because the standard distance is equivalent to one standard deviation (1σ), the circle would indicate the area in which about two-thirds of the population is concentrated. The exact proportion would vary with the specific distribution.

Accessibility Measures

For many practical applications, such as for locating businesses or public facilities, it is desirable to attempt to measure the "accessibility" of various points with reference to a particular population distribution. The word "accessibility" is used in a variety of contexts, including sometimes as a proxy for "ease of interaction." Here, however, we shall restrict the usage to measures that attempt to portray the proximity of a mass of persons to particular geographic locations. Plane and Rogerson (1994, pp. 37–41) classified most commonly used measures into "threshold" and "aggregate" accessibility concepts. We examine each in turn.

Threshold Accessibility

One of the most widely employed forms of accessibility is simply to count the population resident within a circular area of radius R. Thus it may be reported that 3.2 million persons live within 50 miles of the proposed new major league ballpark, or 2000 households are located within 3 miles of the site for a new supermarket. As discussed in Appendix D, many GIS systems are now capable of aggregating geo-referenced census data at the block-group or block level to provide such estimates. For analytical purposes, one of the major uses of any accessibility measure is to compare the relative desirability of a number of different feasible sites for some activity. Sometimes a more refined measure might take into account configurations of road networks or even travel times so as to obtain the population residing within a (no longer circular) area defined by the outward bounds of travel with M minutes or H hours.

Threshold accessibility may be sensitive to the choice of the radius, R, selected. The relative accessibility of various locations may change depending on how far the analyst chooses to extend the threshold. Generally there should be some logically defensible rationale for the distance cutoff. It is possible to vary the R value continuously and to plot threshold accessibility curves that show the cumulative percentage of the population residing within any distance up until the radius encompasses the entire study area and 100% of the population. However, the virtue of the threshold-accessibility concept is its simplicity for communicating to a lay audience; so in most applications a single threshold would appear to be advisable.

Aggregate Accessibility

The principal alternative to threshold accessibility is a measure that weights all population resident within the study region by the spatial separation between each person and the location at which accessibility is being measured. The most commonly employed aggregate accessibility measure is known as "population potential," or sometimes "Hansen accessibility" after the author of a classic paper (Hansen, 1959) that popularized the concept in the city planning literature. The term "population potential" comes from the physics notion of a field measure (such as electrical or gravitational potential) and should not be invested with literal demographic meaning. As developed by Stewart, population potential applies to the accessibility to the population, or "level of influence" on the population, of a point on a map or of a small unit of area (Stewart and Warntz, 1959). If the "influence" of each individual at a point; is considered to be inversely proportional to his or her distance from it, the total potential of population at the point is the sum of the reciprocals of the distances of all individuals in the population from the point. In practice, of course, the computation is made by assuming that all the individuals within a suitably small area are equidistant from point j. Thus the formula for the potential at point j is

$$V_j = \sum_{i=1}^{n} P_i / D_{ij} \qquad (5.7)$$

where the P_i are the populations of the n areas into which a territory is divided, and the D_{ij} are the respective distances of these areas from point j (usually measured from the geographic center or from the approximate center of gravity of the population, in each area) (Duncan, 1957, pp. 35–36).[17]

Like the center of population (but unlike threshold accessibility), the population potential at any point in the territory is affected by the distribution of population over the entire territory. When the potential has been computed for a sufficient number of points, those of equal potential may be joined on the map to show contours or isopleths. It can be well appreciated that each computation involves a good deal of labor so that to produce a fine-grained map, the computations would need to be performed on a computer. On such a fine-grained map, there would be peaks of potential around every city that are not brought out on most of the available maps showing this measure.

To illustrate, we will show only the first few computations needed to calculate the population potential at one particular point. This is a hypothetical case. Let the "point" $j = 1$ in question be a capital city A with a population of 100,000. Let this population be P_1. Assume that the population is evenly distributed over the city. Because this "point" is a relatively populous area, it is necessary to take into

---

[17] The notation used in the formula has been changed from the original.

account the average distance of its own population from its geographic center. Let us say that this has been estimated from the city's map at 3 kilometers.[18]

Then measure the distance from the geographic center of every other political unit in the set being used to the center of the capital city. This set of units should account for all the national territory unless population potential is being studied for some other kind of area, such as a region. These geographic centers can be plotted by inspections but, where a primary unit has a very large and unevenly distributed population, the secondary divisions within it can be used for increased accuracy. Suppose we then have

Area (j)	P_j	D_{ij}	P_j/D_{ij}
1	100,000	3	33,333
2	25,000	8	3,125
3	10,000	10	1,000
...	...	...	
n	15,000	500	30

The population potential for the city is the sum of the last column. One does not have to work outward from the area in question while listing the areas; any systematic listing is acceptable. If the latitudes and longitudes of all the centers of geographic area (or, ideally, the centers of population of all the areas) are known, these can be programmed for a computer so that the distances to any point can be computed by triangulation.

Warntz and Neft (1960, p. 65) point out that "The peak of population potential coincides with the modal center on the smoothed density surface for the United States". The statement applied to 1950 but presumably it would still hold true.

The concept of population potential is more useful than that of aggregate travel distance and has sometimes proved valuable as an indicator of geographical variations in social and economic phenomena (e.g., rural population density, farmland values, miles of railway track per square mile, road density, density of wage earners in manufacturing, and death rates). Rural density, for example, tends to be proportional to the square of the potential.

Mapping Devices

There is a voluminous literature on the mapping of demographic data to which demographers, geographers, and members of other disciplines have contributed (see, e.g., Bachi, 1966; Schmid, 1954, pp. 184–222). Here we are concerned with mapping just the distribution of population and of population density.

---

[18] A "quick and dirty" method for estimating such contribution of "self-potential" (as it is sometimes endearingly called!) is to use one-half of the distance to the nearest neighbor.

Population Distribution

The commonest method of representing the distribution of the absolute number of inhabitants is a dot map (such as the one given previously as Figure 5.3). A small dot or spot of constant size represents a round number of people such as 100 or 1000. If a general impression is all that is wanted, the dots may be plotted more or less uniformly within the units of area given on the map. For a more exact portrayal, regard should be paid to any actual concentrations of population within the unit areas. This procedure calls for refering to figures for geographic subdivisions below the level of those outlined on the map. For example, with a county outline map of the United States, one could refer to the published figures for minor civil divisions or for incorporated places.

In maps of population distribution for a country or other area containing both thinly settled rural territory and large urban agglomerations, there is a real problem in the application of the conventional dot method. A black dot that represents few enough people to show the distribution of the rural population requires so many plottings within the limits of large cities that one sees only a solid black area, and even that may grossly underrepresent the actual number of dots required. To portray the population of large cities, one could use a dot of the same size but of a different color to which a higher value is assigned—for example, a black dot could represent 100 people and a red dot, 10,000. Another variation is to use circles of varying size for specific urban places. Such circles (or other graphic symbols) may be chosen in a limited number of sizes or forms, such as these:

- 2500 to 10,000
- 10,000 to 25,000
- 25,000 to 50,000

or, especially for larger cities, the circle may be drawn with the area proportional to the size of the population.

In the latter case, it is best to start with the largest place and determine the size of circle that can reasonably be accommodated on the map. (Because a number of the circles will overlap and will extend beyond the areas to which they apply, they should be either "open," that is, unshaded, or shaded in a light tint so that boundary lines can show through.) Suppose a circle with a diameter of 5 cm is chosen to represent a city of 500,000. Then, because the area of the circle is drawn proportionate to the population, and the area is πr^2, the radius required for a smaller population is solved by the following equation:

$$\frac{\pi r^2}{\pi \times 6.25} = \frac{P}{500,000} \tag{5.8}$$

or, alternatively

$$r = \sqrt{\frac{P}{80,000}} \, \text{cm} \tag{5.9}$$

so that, for a population of 100,000, a circle with a radius of 1.12 cm is needed. (Note that the radius varies with the square root of the population.)

To represent very wide ranges of population size, spherical symbols can be used instead of circles for the largest localities. The population of the large localities would then be proportional to the volume of the sphere implied. Other graphic devices are sometimes used to denote the population in a geographical area, for example, the heights of a rectangle (two-dimensional bar) or of a three-dimensional column shown in perspective. Such devices are convenient for only a relatively small number of areal units, such as the primary divisions of a country.

Population Density

A conventional way of indicating population density is that of shading or hatching, with the darker shadings representing the greater densities.[19] Such shadings may gloss over considerable internal variation within an area because they represent simply the area's average density. The contour or isopleth map also lends itself to the presentation of geographic regularities in population density. Some of the problems, considerations, and techniques in the construction of such maps are discussed by Duncan (1957) and by Schmid (1954). A more recent and somewhat detailed treatment of issues in population mapping is given by Schnell and Monmonier (1983, pp. 33–41).

References

Bachi, R. 1958. "Statistical Analysis of Geographic Series," *Bulletin of the International Statistical Institute* 36(2): 229–240.

Bachi, R. 1962. "Standard Distance Measures and Related Methods for Spatial Analysis." *Papers of the Regional Science Association* 10: 83–132.

Bachi, R. 1966. "Graphical Representation and Analysis of Geographical-Statistical Data," *Bulletin of the International Statistical Institute* (Proceedings of the 35th session, Belgrade, 1965) 41(1): 225.

Beale, C. L. 1967. "State Economic Areas—A Review after 17 Years." Washington, DC: *American Statistical Association, Proceedings of the Social Statistics Section*, 82–85.

Bogue, D. J., and C. L. Beale. 1953. U.S. Bureau of the Census and U.S. Bureau of Agricultural Economics, "Economic Subregions of the United States," Series Census-BAE, No. 19.

Bogue, D. J., and C. L. Beale. 1961. *Economic Areas of the United States*. New York: Free Press of Glencoe.

Clayton, C. 1982. "Hierarchically Organized Migration Fields: The Application of Higher Order Factor Analysis to Population Migration Tables." *Annals of Regional Science* 11: 109–122.

Dahmann, D. C. 1992. "Accounting for the Geography of Population: 200 Years of Census Bureau Practice with Macro-Scale Sub-National Regions." Paper presented at the Annual Meeting of the Association of American Geographers, San Diego, CA, April 18–22.

Duncan, O. D. 1957. "The Measurement of Population Distribution." *Population Studies* (London) 11(1): 27–45.

Duncan, O. D., R. P. Cuzzort, and B. Duncan. 1961. *Statistical Geography*. Glencoe, IL: The Free Press.

Fellmann, J. D., A. Getis, and J. Getis. 1999. *Human Geography: Landscapes of Human Activities*, 6th ed. New York, NY: WCB McGraw-Hill.

George, P. O. L. 1955. "Sur un project de calcul de la densité économique de la population" (On a project for calculating the economic density of the population), pp. 303–313, in *Proceedings of the World Population Conference, 1954* (Rome), Vol. IV, New York: United Nations.

Hansen, W. 1959. "How Accessibility Shapes Land Use," *Journal of the American Institute of Planners* 25: 72–77.

Hart, J. F. 1954. "Central Tendency in Areal Distributions." *Economic Geography* 30(1): 54.

Illinois Board of Economic Development. 1965. *Suggested Economic Regions in Illinois by Counties*, by Eleanor Gilpatrick, Springfield (Illinois).

International Urban Research. 1959. *The World's Metropolitan Areas*. Berkeley, CA: University of California Press.

Johnson, K. P. 1995. "Redefinition of the BEA Economic Areas," *Survey of Current Business* (February): 75–81.

McDonald, J. R. 1966. "The Region: Its Conception, Design, and Limitations." *Annals of the Association of American Geographers* 56: 516–528.

Morrill, R. L. 1988. Migration Regions and Population Redistribution. *Growth and Change* 19: 43–60.

Odum, H. W. 1936. *Southern Regions of the United States*. Chapel Hill: University of North Carolina Press.

Odum, H. W., and H. E. Moore. 1938. *American Regionalism: A Cultural-Historical Approach to National Integration*. New York: Henry Holt and Co.

Pandit, K. 1994. "Differentiating Between Subsystems and Typologies in the Analysis of Migration Regions: A U.S. Example." *Professional Geographer* 46: 331–345.

Planc, D. A. 1998. "Fuzzy Set Migration Regions." *Geographical and Environmental Modelling* 2(2): 141–162.

Plane, D. A., and A. M. Isserman. 1983. "U.S. Labor Force Migration: An Analysis of Trends, Net Exchanges, and Migration Subsystems." *Socio-Economic Planning Sciences* 17: 251–266.

Plane, D. A., and P. A. Rogerson. 1994. *The Geographical Analysis of Population: With Applications to Planning and Business*. New York: John Wiley & Sons.

Schmid, C. F. 1954. *Handbook of Graphic Presentation*. New York: Ronald Press.

Schnell, G. A., and M. S. Monmonier. 1983. *The Study of Population: Elements, Patterns, Processes*. Columbus, OH: Charles E. Merrill Publishing.

Shryock, H. S., Jr. 1957. "The Natural History of Standard Metropolitan Areas." *American Journal of Sociology* 63(2): 163–170.

Shryock, H. S., Jr., and J. S. Siegel. 1973. *The Methods and Materials of Demography*, 2nd rev. ed. Washington, DC: U.S. Government Printing Office.

Slater, P. B. 1976. "A Hierarchical Regionalization of Japanese Prefectures Using 1972 Interprefectural Migration Flows." *Regional Studies* 10: 123–132.

Stewart, J. Q., and W. Warntz. 1958. "Macrogeography and Social Science." *Geographical Review* 48(2): 167–184.

Stewart, J. Q., and W. Warntz. 1959. "Some Parameters of the Geographical Distribution of Population." *Geographical Review* 49(2): 270–272.

Taeuber, C. 1965. "Regional and Other Area Statistics in the United States," *Bulletin of the International Statistical Institute* (Proceedings of the 35th session, Belgrade, 1965) 41(1): 161–162.

United Nations. 1967. *Principles and Recommendations for the 1970 Population Censuses*, Statistical Papers, Series M, No. 44.

[19] For types of shadings available, see Schmid (1954, pp. 187–198).

United Nations. 1995. *Demographic Yearbook*. New York, NY: United Nations.

U.S. Bureau of the Census. 1913. *Thirteenth Census of the United States, Abstract of the Census*.

U.S. Bureau of the Census. 1924. *Statistical Atlas of the United States, 1924*, pp. 7–24.

U.S. Bureau of the Census. 1951. *State Economic Areas* (by Donald J. Bogue).

U.S. Bureau of the Census. 1963. "Zones of Equal Population in the United States: 1960." *Geographic Reports*, GE-10, No. 3.

U.S. Bureau of the Census. 2000a. www.census.gov/cao/www/congress/appormen.html#num.

U.S. Bureau of the Census. 2000b. *Geographic Areas Reference Manual*. www.census.gov/geo/www/garm.html.

Warntz, W. 1958. "Macrogeography and the Census." *The Professional Geographer*, 10(6): 6–10.

Warntz, W., and D. Neft. 1960. "Contributions to Statistical Methodology for Areal Distributions." *Journal of Regional Science* 2(1): 47–66.

Whittlesey, D. 1954. "The Regional Concept and the Regional Method." In P. E. James and C. F. Jones (Eds.). *American Geography: Inventory and Prospect*. Published for the Association of American Geographers by Syracuse University Press.

Winchester, H. P. M. 1977. *Changing Patterns of French Internal Migration, 1891–1968*. Research Paper No. 17. Oxford: Oxford University School of Geography.

Woofter, T. J., Jr. 1934. "Subregions of the Southeast." *Social Forces* 13(1): 43–50.

6

Population Distribution
Classification of Residence

JEROME N. McKIBBEN AND KIMBERLY A. FAUST

This chapter extends the geographic topics discussed in Chapter 5 by considering classes of geographic residence that are formed primarily for statistical purposes. The emphasis here is on geographic groupings that are not necessarily contiguous pieces of territory. The major focus is on the "urban-rural" classification. We start with a general discussion of this classification and then turn to international concepts and definitions dealing with it. We then discuss selected national level concepts, with a primary focus on the United States. We conclude this chapter with a discussion of commonly used measures of population distribution.

The working definitions of "urban" and "rural" vary greatly, not only according to nation, but also according to organization and research discipline. Urban settlements have been defined, for example, on the basis of an urban culture, administrative functions, percentage of people in nonagricultural occupations, and size or density of population (Palen, 2002). Rural areas are often defined as a residual category—that is, "areas not classified as urban"—but they may also be subdivided by criteria that vary according to nation, organization, and discipline. In spite of these problems, the urban-rural classification is widely used, as illustrated by Tables 6.1, 6.2, 6.3, and 6.4.

Table 6.1 shows the total population of selected countries around the world and the percentage in each country that is classified as urban. Over 96% of Kuwait's population of 1.97 million is classified as "urban," while only 17.6% of Papua-New Guinea's population of 4.9 million is so classified.

Table 6.2 shows the population of the United States counted in each decennial census from 1790 to 1990 classified by urban and rural residence. Notice that a major change in the definition of urban went into effect in 1950 and that data under the old and new definitions were made available for two censuses, 1950 and 1960. Under the earlier definition, the urban population of the United States in 1950 is 90.1 million, while under the revised definition it is 96.8 million in 1950.

Table 6.3 shows changes in the population of size-classes of towns of India between the census of 1981 and the census of 1991. The largest size class (Class I, towns having a population of 100,000 or more) experienced a 47% increase in population between 1981 and 1991, or an absolute increase of nearly 45 million people. The smallest size class (Class VI, towns having a population of fewer than 5000) experienced a 21% decline in total population from 1981 to 1991, or an absolute decrease of only 164,000 people.

URBAN-RURAL: INTERNATIONAL STANDARDS AND DEFINITIONS

United Nations Recommendations

In an effort to bring some level of standardization to urban/rural statistics, the United Nations (UN) has been developing and revising proposed standards for more than 40 years. The major purpose of this effort is to assist nations in both planning for and developing the content of censuses. Another goal is to improve international compatibility through the use of standardized definitions and classification, as noted in Chapters 2 and 3.

The most recent set of recommendations was developed within the framework of the *2000 World Population and Housing Census Program* adopted in 1995 (United Nations, 1998). Suggested topics to be included in censuses are divided into two types. The first, "core" topics, are subjects that all nations should cover in their censuses using the recommended definitions and classification listed. The second, "noncore" topics, are subjects that nations may wish to include in censuses. There are suggested definitions for some, but not all, noncore topics. Noncore topics are

TABLE 6.1 Urban Population of Selected Countries, 2001

Country	Percentage urban	Total population (thous.)	Definition of urban
Albania	42.9	3,145	Towns and industrial centers with population of 400 or more
Angola	34.9	13,527	Localities with a population of 2,000 or more
Argentina	88.3	37,488	Localities with a population of 2,000 or more
Bahrain	92.5	652	Localities with a population of 2,500 or more
Benin	43.0	6,446	Localities with a population of 10,000 or more
Brazil	81.7	172,559	Cities and towns as defined by municipal law
Costa Rica	59.5	4,112	Administrative centers of cantón, including adjacent areas with clear urban characteristics.
Czech Republic	74.5	10,260	Localities with a population of 5,000 or more
Denmark	85.1	5,333	Capital city plus provincial capitals
Dominica	71.4	71	Cities and villages with 500 or more population
Finland	58.5	5,178	Urban communes
Gambia	31.3	1,337	Capital city of Banjul
Germany	87.7	82,007	Localities with a population of 5,000 or more
Greece	60.3	10,623	Municipalities and communes in which the largest population center has 10,000 or more inhabitants, plus 18 urban agglomerations
Iceland	92.7	281	Localities with a population of 200 or more
Jordan	78.7	5,051	Localities with a population of 10,000 or more
Kuwait	96.1	1,971	Agglomerations of 10,000 or more population
Laos	19.7	5,403	Five largest towns
Madagascar	30.1	16,437	Centers with more than 5,000 inhabitants
Mauritius	41.6	1,171	Towns with proclaimed legal limits
Mongolia	56.6	2,559	Capital and district centers
Nigeria	44.9	116,929	Towns with 20,000 inhabitants whose occupations are not mainly agrarian
Norway	75.0	4,488	Localities with a population of 200 or more
Oman	76.5	2,622	Two main towns of Muscat and Matrah
Pakistan	33.4	144,971	Places with municipal corporation, town committee, or cantonment
Papua New Guinea	17.6	4,920	Centers with 500 inhabitants or more
Peru	73.1	26,093	Populated centers with 100 dwellings or more grouped contiguously and administrative centers of districts
Romania	55.2	22,388	Cities, towns, and 183 other localities having certain socioeconomic characteristics
Saint Kitts and Nevis	34.2	38	Cities of Basseterre and Charlestown
Suriname	74.8	419	Capital city of Greater Paramaribo
Uruguay	92.1	3,361	Cities as officially defined
Viet Nam	24.5	79,175	Places with 4,000 or more population
Zimbabwe	36.0	12,852	Nineteen main towns

Source: United Nations, 2002.

considered to be useful topics that are not necessarily of lesser importance or interest, but for which international comparability is more difficult to obtain.

The Recommendations for the 2000 Round of Censuses of Population and Housing (United Nations, 1998) lists "locality" as a derived core topic and "urban-rural areas" as a derived noncore topic. For census purposes, a locality is defined as a distinct population cluster—that is, the population living in neighboring buildings that either

1. Form a continuous built-up area with a clearly recognizable street formation; or
2. Though not part of such a built-up area, form a group to which a locally recognized place name is uniquely attached; or
3. Though not complying with either of the above two requirements, constitute a group, none of which is

separated from its nearest neighbor by more than 200 meters.

This definition is intended to provide general guidance to countries in identifying localities and determining their borders, and it may be need to be adapted in accordance with national conditions and practices. Further, it is recommended that the population be classified by size of locality according to the following classes:

1.0 1,000,000 or more
2.0 500,000–999,999
3.0 200,000–499,999
4.0 100,000–199,999
5.0 50,000–99,999
6.0 20,000–49,999
7.0 10,000–19,999

TABLE 6.2 United States Urban and Rural Population, 1790 to 2000

Date of Census	Total population (thous.)	Rural population (thous.)	Urban population (thous.)	Percentage of total population in urban areas
Current urban definition				
2000 (Apr.1)				
1990 (Apr.1)	248,709	61,656	187,053	75.2
1980 (Apr.1)	226,542	59,494	167,050	73.7
1970 (Apr.1)	203,302	53,565	149,646	73.6
1960 (Apr.1)	179,323	54,045	125,268	69.9
1950 (Apr.1)	151,325	54,478	96,846	64.0
Previous urban definition				
1960 (Apr.1)	179,323	66,259	113,063	63.1
1950 (Apr.1)	151,325	61,197	90,128	59.6
1940 (Apr.1)	132,164	57,459	74,705	56.5
1930 (Apr.1)	123,202	54,042	69,160	56.1
1920 (Jan. 1)	106,021	51,768	54,253	51.2
1910 (Apr.15)	92,228	50,164	42,064	45.6
1900 (Jun. 1)	76,212	45,997	30,214	39.6
1890 (Jun. 1)	62,979	40,873	22,106	35.1
1880 (Jun. 1)	50,189	36,059	14,129	28.2
1870 (Jun. 1)	38,558	28,656	9,902	25.7
1860 (Jun. 1)	31,443	25,226	6,216	19.8
1850 (Jun. 1)	23,191	19,617	3,574	15.4
1840 (Jun. 1)	17,063	15,218	1,845	10.8
1830 (Jun. 1)	12,860	11,733	1,127	8.8
1820 (Aug. 7)	9,638	8,945	693	7.2
1810 (Aug. 6)	7,239	6,714	525	7.3
1800 (Aug. 4)	5,308	4,986	322	6.1
1790 (Aug. 2)	3,929	3,727	202	5.1

Source: U.S. Census Bureau, 2002b.

8.0 5,000–9,999

9.0 2,000–4,999

10.0 1,000–1,999

11.0 500–999

12.0 200–499

13.0 Population living in localities with fewer than 200 inhabitants or in scattered buildings and population without a fixed place of residence

    13.1 Population living in localities with 50 to 199 inhabitants

    13.2 Population living in localities with fewer than 50 inhabitants or in scattered buildings

    13.3 Population without a fixed place of residence

In the most recent set of recommendations, the UN suggests that countries define urban areas as localities with a population of 2000 or more and rural areas as localities with a population of fewer than 2000. However, it notes that some countries may also wish to consider defining urban areas in other ways, such as in terms of administrative boundaries or built-up areas or in terms of functional areas. Further, the

TABLE 6.3 Population Change in Each Size-Class of Towns in India,[1] 1981–1991

Size-Class	Number of urban areas/ towns, 1991	Population change, 1981–1991		Percentage of total urban population	
		Amount	Percentage	1981	1991
All Classes	3,610	56,864,049	36.4	100.0	100.0
I	296	44,625,789	47.2	60.4	65.2
II	341	5,150,578	28.3	11.6	10.9
III	924	5,640,555	25.2	14.3	13.2
IV	1,138	1,676,425	11.2	9.6	7.8
V	725	−65,065	−1.2	3.6	2.6
VI	186	−164,233	−20.9	0.5	0.3

Note: The urban units have been categorized into the following six population-size classes:

Size-Class	Population
I	100,000 and above
II	50,000 to 99,999
III	20,000 to 49,999
IV	10,000 to 19,999
V	5,000 to 9,999
VI	Less than 5,000

[1] Excludes Assam, Jammu, and Kashmir.
Source: India (1991).

UN advises that countries may want to develop typologies of urban locations based on additional criteria, such as market towns, industrial areas, and central city or suburban.

The UN encourages countries that use the smallest civil division as the unit of urban classification to try to obtain results that correspond as closely as possible with those obtained by countries that use "locality" as the primary unit. Achieving this aim depends mainly on the nature of the smallest civil divisions in the countries concerned. If the smallest civil division is relatively small in area and borders a population cluster, it should be designated as part of the urban agglomeration. Conversely, in countries where the smallest civil division is a relatively large area and contains a population cluster, the UN suggests that efforts should be made to use smaller units as building blocks to identify urban and rural areas within the civil division.

National Practices

In spite of the UN's attempts to bring some degree of international standardization to the urban-rural classification, conformance to the standards varies substantially from one nation to another. Individual countries have usually designed and implemented criteria and definitions that address the administrative and policy needs of that country. (However, one point of general consistency is that most nations define rural as "all areas not urban" irrespective of the definition of urban used.) In sum, a majority of nations ignore the United Nations recommendations on locality and urban-rural classifications and use their own definitions and standards.

Most nations use one of five schemes when designating urban areas. The first and most widely used is simply establishing a minimum population size that acts as a threshold requirement for a town or city to qualify as an urban area. However, this minimum population prerequisite varies greatly from one country to another. Angola, for example, classifies any town with more than 2000 people as an urban area, while in Italy the requirement is 10,000 and in Nepal it is 9000.

There are other cases where population density is used in combination with population size to define an urban area. The Philippines requires that cities and municipalities have at least 1000 persons per square mile as well as a population minimum of 2500. In India, an urban area needs to have at least 5000 people and a population density of 1000 per square mile to qualify. The use of population density is usually seen in countries that have several geographically large municipalities.

Another popular classification system uses both population size and the primary economic activities of the area to determine if it is urban. For example, Estonia designates areas as urban on the basis of population size and the predominance of nonagricultural workers and their families. In Botswana, the standard is a population of at least 5000, where 75% of the economic activity is nonagricultural. Austria requires a commune to have 2000 persons and 85% of the active population to be engaged in nonagricultural/nonforestry work. These types of classification systems are often seen in nations that link the concept of rural status to the activity of farming.

There are several cases where cities and towns are legally defined or established as urban by official decree of the national government. Guatemala, Bulgaria, and the Republic of Korea are examples of nations that use this system. The exact requirements for urban designation vary greatly and frequently involve nondemographic and noneconomic factors

Finally, many nations have established "defined urban characteristics" that an area must possess in addition to population size in order to qualify for urban status. Chile, for example, states that a population center must have "certain public and municipal services" in order to attain urban status. Cuba requires an urban place to have a population of at least 2000. However, an area of lesser population can qualify if it has paved streets, street lighting, piped water, sewage, a medical center, and educational facilities.

Because of the complex and varied nature of these criteria for urban designation, researchers must use caution when conducting any comparisons of the level and extent of urbanization of one country with another. The United

Nations *Demographic Yearbook* lists the criteria that each country utilizes when designating areas as urban. Researchers should consult this volume to see the specific requirement each country uses and to keep informed of any recent definitional changes.

URBAN-RURAL DEFINITIONS IN THE UNITED STATES

Development of the Classification System

Since its inception, the definition of urban in the United States has always involved the number of residents (as counted by the census) in a given area although political criteria, such as administrative status, were also involved. As early as 1874, urban areas were defined as any incorporated place with a population of 8000 or more. The minimum size was officially reduced to 4000 in 1880 and reduced again in 1910 to the level of 2500. The practice of designating only incorporated places as urban (a standard that would continue until 1950) resulted in the labeling of many densely settled but unincorporated areas as rural, a practice that greatly inflated the rural population. Although the Census Bureau attempted to avoid some of the more glaring omissions by classifying selected areas as "urban under special rules," many large, closely built-up areas were excluded from the urban category (U.S. Census Bureau, 1995).

This practice proved to be particularly problematic in New England, where a town is equivalent to a minor civil division, much like a township in the Midwest. This led to the practice of classifying these areas in New England as "urban under special rules" (an application that was later extended to New York and Wisconsin). Thus, any such areas with a total population above the minimum threshold came to be considered as urban (Truesdell, 1949).

Recognizing the shortcomings of these criteria and practices, the Census Bureau implemented major changes in the definition and designation of urban areas after the 1950 census. The most important of these changes was the introduction of two new types of geographic units, the urbanized area (UA) and the census designated place (CDP) (U.S. Census Bureau, 1994). The introduction of the CDP resulted in classifying as urban, any densely settled area with a population of 2500 or more. The demarcation of CDP boundaries was determined by the Census Bureau after extensive fieldwork and mapping were conducted, with particular attention placed on the population density of the designated area. This represented a major shift in the concept of "urban." Instead of relying solely on legal boundaries and population size, factors such as population density and self-identification of place were now being taken into account as well (U.S. Census Bureau, 1996).

A further development was the UA concept, which includes built-up, but unincorporated areas, adjacent to cities and towns in the urban population. Initially, the base requirement for a UA was a central place with a population of 50,000 or more. Any area outside the city limits with at least 500 housing units per square mile or approximately 2000 persons per square mile (reduced to 1000 per square mile in 1960) would be included in that city's urban population count. These unincorporated areas had to be contiguous to or within one and a half miles of the core and connected to it by a road (U.S. Census Bureau, 1994). Given the rapid suburban growth that most cities were experiencing (and probably would continue to experience over the next several decades), this inclusion of the "urban fringe" population in the urban population would make the urban population counts much more reflective of the true urban-rural distribution of the population.

In 1970, the Census Bureau again modified the definition of urban with its introduction of the "extended city." During the 1960s, several cities in the United States began extending their municipal boundaries to include areas that were fundamentally rural in character. (e.g., San Diego, California, and Oklahoma City, Oklahoma). In addition, some cities adopted the "Unigov" system, whereby the city would annex the unincorporated areas of the county and then merge all city and county governmental functions in to one unit (e.g., Indianapolis, Indiana, and Columbus, Georgia).

To address the urban-rural classification in these situations, the Census Bureau developed criteria for identifying extended cities. An incorporated place would be considered an extended city if it contained one or more areas that

1. Are 5 square miles or more in size
2. Have a population density less than 100 persons per square mile and either
3. Comprise at least 25% of the total land area of the place or
4. Consist of 25 square miles or more.

To qualify, the first two conditions, and either the third or the fourth must apply. The rural portion of an extended city may consist of several separate pieces of territory, given that each section is at least 5 square miles in size and has a population density of fewer than 100 per square mile. If the extended city has low-density enclaves that are adjacent to its rural portions, these enclaves become part of the rural portion. There is no population minimum for UA extended cities; however, non-UA extended cities must have at least 2500 residents (U.S. Census Bureau, 1994). These specifications remained the same for the 1980 census. For the 1990 census, this classification system was also applied to certain places outside of UAs.

Despite their long history, urban-rural definitions in the United States are sometimes confused with those used to identify "metropolitan/nonmetropolitan areas (discussed in the previous chapter). Since the introduction of the "metropolitan statistical area" after the 1950 census, aspects of the

definitions for metropolitan-nonmetropolitan and urban-rural have overlapped and continue to do so.

There are several fundamental differences between the definitions of metropolitan-nonmetropolitan and urban-rural, even though the terms are frequently (and mistakenly) used interchangeably. Metropolitan areas are identified through criteria developed by the Office of Management and Budget (OMB). These criteria are primarily based on size of place, social and economic integration, and political boundaries. Urban-rural areas are identified through criteria developed by the U.S Census Bureau (2001b). These criteria primarily involve contiguous areas meeting certain requirements of population size and density.

Metropolitan areas can and, in fact, often do contain areas that have been classified as rural. As an example, consider the Mojave Desert, which is clearly a rural area, but one that lies within "metropolitan" San Bernardino County. Examples such as this have led the Office of Management and Budget (OMB) to stress that metropolitan statistical areas do not correspond to an urban-rural classification and should not be used in lieu of one (U.S. Office of Management and Budget, 2000).

This warning notwithstanding, one of the criteria that the OMB uses to identify counties as metropolitan central counties is the presence of a Census Bureau–defined UA. For example, immediately after the 2000 census was completed, the Census Bureau identified urbanized areas in the United States on the basis of its standards relating to population density. The OMB uses these results in developing its revised metropolitan area standards. It is precisely this use of an "urban" criterion in a "metropolitan" classification system that leads to much of the confusion of what is and is not considered an urban area in the United States.

Census Bureau Criteria for Urban Status in the 2000 Census

Soon after the first results of the 2000 census were tabulated, the Census Bureau began identifying and delineating the revised UA boundaries. The boundaries are based on finding a core of block groups or blocks that have a population density of at least 1000 per square mile and the surrounding blocks that have an overall density of at least 500 persons per square mile (U.S. Census Bureau, 2001b).

Territory that has been designated as urban is subdivided into two types: urbanized area (UA) and urban cluster (UC). The UC concept was introduced in conjunction with the 2000 census. A UA is defined as a densely settled core of block groups and blocks, along with adjacent densely settled blocks that meet minimum population density requirements, of at least 50,000 people, of whom at least 35,000 do not live in an area that is part of a military installation. A UC is defined as a core of densely settled block groups or blocks and the adjacent densely settled blocks that meet the minimum population density requirements and have a population of at least 2500 but less than 50,000. An area can also be designated a UC if it contains more than 50,000 if fewer than 35,000 of the residents live in an area that is not part of a military installation (U.S. Census Bureau, 2001b).

The idea of the UC was developed to help provide a more consistent and accurate measure of population concentration in and around places by eliminating the effect of state laws governing incorporation and annexation or the level of local participation in the CDP program. The vast majority of densely settled unincorporated areas are located adjacent to incorporated places. States with strict annexation laws (e.g., Michigan and New Jersey) will experience a higher proportion of urban population increases than will states like Mississippi and Texas that have more liberal annexation laws. UCs replace the provision in the 1990 and previous censuses that define as urban only those places with 2500 or more people located outside of urbanized areas (U.S. Census Bureau, 2002b).

The definition of both the urbanized area and the urban cluster are built around the concept of the "densely settled core." The Census Bureau begins its delineation of a potential urban area by identifying a densely settled "initial core." The initial core is defined by sequentially including the following qualifying territory:

1. One or more contiguous block groups that have a total land area less than or equal to 2 square miles and a population density of at least 1000 per square mile.
2. If no qualifying census block group exists, one or more contiguous blocks that have a population density of at least 1000 per square mile.
3. One or more block groups that have a land area less than or equal to 2 square miles, that have a population density of at least 500 per square mile, and that are contiguous to block groups or blocks that are identified by definition 1.
4. One or more contiguous blocks that have a population density of at least 500 per square mile and that are contiguous to qualifying block groups and blocks that are defined by definition 1, 2, or 3.
5. Any enclave of contiguous territory that does not meet the criteria above but is surrounded by block groups (BGs) and blocks that do qualify for inclusion in the initial core by the preceding requirements will be designated urban, provided the area of the enclave is not greater that 5 square miles.

There are several situations where the Census Bureau will include noncontiguous blocks and block groups in a core area that would otherwise qualify based on population density and landmass if the noncontiguous area can be reached from the core area using a "hop" or "jump" connection. The first step in this process is to identify all areas that qualify for "hop" connections. The "hop" concept, new

for the 2000 census, was developed to extend the urban definition across small nonqualifying census blocks. This avoids the need to designate the break in qualifying blocks as a "jump." A hop can be used if the distance from the initial core to the noncontiguous area is no more than 0.5 miles along the shortest road connection and the area being added has at least 1000 people or has a population density of at least 500 per square mile.

After all "hop" situations have been identified, the Census Bureau then begins to identify all areas that qualify for "jump" connections. A "jump" connection is used if the noncontiguous area is more that 0.5 mile, but less than 2.5 miles of a core (at this stage it is now referred to as an interim core), providing that the core has a total population of at least 1500. The territory being added to the interim core must have an overall population destiny of 500 per square mile and a total population of at least 1000. The Census Bureau selects the shortest qualifying road connection that forms the highest overall population density for the entire territory (jump blocks plus qualifying blocks) being added to the interim core.

These criteria also include several special rules to address the splitting of urbanized areas and designation of urban area titles. Researchers should consult "Urban Area Criteria for Census 2000, Proposed Criteria" (U.S. Census Bureau, 2001b) for in-depth and detailed instructions on the requirements and uses of hop and jump connections. For the revised and final standards used in defining urban areas, see "Urban Area Criteria for Census 2000" (U.S. Census Bureau, 2002a).

Differences Between the 2000 Census Criteria and the 1990 Census Criteria

The UA criteria used in conjunction with the 2000 census represents significant changes from the standards used in the 1990 census. In part this was due to technological advances, particularly in the field of geographic information systems. For example, it is now possible for the first time for all urban and rural delineation to be completely automated. This will not only speed the process, but also ensure that more standardized criteria will be used when designating urban and rural status.

The Census Bureau estimates that by using the new criteria, approximately 5 million more people will be classified as urban than was the case with the 1990 criteria. The majority of this increase will come from the reclassification of population residing outside of UAs. Under the 1990 standards, the urban population outside of UAs was limited to people living in an incorporated place and census-designated place having a population of 2500 or more. With the changes for 2000, many densely settled unincorporated areas will be designated as urban for the first time. This change will also include places with a population of fewer than 2500 that adjoin densely settled areas and, as such, bring the total population of the area to 2500 or more (U.S. Census Bureau, 2001b).

While the total urban population is expected to increase as a result of these definitional changes, these modifications are also expected to reduce the amount of territory designated as urban by as much as 7%. Part of this decrease is due to the removal of the criteria relating to "whole places" and "extended cities." Another factor is that the Census Bureau will not automatically recognize previously existing UA territory as part of the 2000 UA delineation process. In keeping with the goal of establishing a single set of rules for the designation of urban areas, UAs that had qualified in earlier censuses will not be "grandfathered." Areas that no longer qualify as UAs will most likely qualify as UCs for the 2000 census. States that have liberal annexation laws or overbounded places will notice the most significant decreases in total urban land area.

In addition to the aforementioned changes, there are several other major differences between the 1990 and 2000 census urban criteria (U.S. Census Bureau, 2002c). Some of the more important ones are the following:

1. For census 2000, the Census Bureau used urban clusters rather than places to determine the total urban population outside urbanized areas. Previously, place boundaries were used to determine the urban and rural classification of territory outside of urbanized areas. With the creation of urban clusters, place boundaries are now "invisible."

2. The extended-city (now called extended-places) criteria were modified extensively. Any place that is split by the boundary of an urbanized area or urban cluster is referred to as an extended place. Previously, sparsely settled areas were examined using density and area measurements to determine whether or not they were to be excluded from the urbanized area. The new urban criteria, based solely on the population density of block groups and blocks, provides a continuum of urban areas. This new definition, as is the case with the newly developed urban-cluster concept, was implemented primarily to reduce the bias in urban-area designation caused by the differences in state laws covering annexation and incorporation.

3. The permitted "jump" distance was increased from 1.5 to 2.5 miles. This increase was proposed as a means of recognizing improvements in the transportation network and the associated changes in development patterns that reflect these improvements.

4. The "uninhabitable jump" criteria are now more restrictive regarding the types of terrain over which an uninhabitable jump can be made.

5. The criteria relating to the central place of urbanized areas and their titles no longer follows standards predefined by other federal agencies. Previously, many central places of urbanized areas and their titles were based on definitions of central cities metropolitan areas set forth by the Office of Management and Budget.

Given the changes in the criteria governing the designation of urban areas, researchers must exercise caution when attempting any time series analysis of urban areas. The impact of these modifications will vary greatly, and the local effects of these changes should be examined before conducting any research.

Rural Definitions in the United States

The Census Bureau designates rural areas as "any areas not classified as urban." Within that definition the characteristics of rural areas can and do vary greatly, however. After the 1990 census, the Census Bureau reported rural populations in some subcategories. In "100%" data products, the rural population was divided into "places of less than 2500, and "not in places of less than 2500." The "not in places" category consisted of rural areas outside incorporated and census designated places as well as the rural portions of extended cities. In sample data products, the rural population was subdivided into "rural farm" and "rural nonfarm." The term, "rural farm," is defined as all rural households on farms in which $1000 or more of agricultural products were sold in 1989. All residual rural population was designated as "rural nonfarm" (U.S. Census Bureau, 1995).

Not surprisingly, several more comprehensive definitions of "rural area" have been developed. While some of these categorization schemes were developed to address issues related to a specific program or policy, several typologies have been used in various rural research programs and as tools in the formulation of policies specific to rural areas.

Two significant problems have emerged from these rural-classification typologies. The first issue is the sheer number and localized usage of "rural" definitions. For example, the state of Washington identifies no fewer than 10 different classification systems that are available for rural health assessments (Washington State Department of Health, 2001). In California, however, rural health assessment areas are defined as areas with a population density of fewer than 250 persons per square mile and excludes communities with a population greater than 50,000 (California Rural Health Policy Council, 2002). The Colorado Rural Health Center (2000) found that 20 different definitions of rural status were used by federal agencies, many in explicit grant applications.

This problem is not restricted to rural health. Most states have set their own standards on how to classify a school as "rural." The National Center for Education Statistics lists at least six different classification systems (U.S. National Center for Education Statistics, 2002). The state of New

York sets its own standard: A school district is considered rural if it has 25 or fewer students per square mile. Compare this with Arkansas, where a rural school is one with 500 or fewer students in grades K–12 (Rios, 1988). This patchwork approach to the definition of rural has led to a situation where numerous incompatible systems have been developed that make cross-state comparisons extremely difficult.

The second issues regarding rural definitions (as it is for urban definitions) is the fact that the majority of classifications schemes are based on county-level data frequently developed using the Office of Management and Budget's Metropolitan/Nonmetropolitan county designations. Despite a warning by the OMB that metropolitan statistical areas do not correspond to urban areas, several widely used rural classification systems have been developed based on non-metropolitan county descriptions. The primary reason for their development and popularity is their relative ease of use. As was mentioned in the previous chapter, most variables, from economic indicators to transportation data to service information, are not collected or maintained at geographic levels using the Census Bureau's rural definition. However, these data often are collected at the county level, and researchers are forced to develop typologies that use the OMB county-based nonmetropolitan system in their analyses of rural issues. For example, much of the research conducted in the 1970s, 1980s, and 1990s on the "Rural Renaissance" in the United States used MSA/non-MSA county criteria for classifying rural and urban areas (McKibben, 1992). This leads to the situation where the terms "rural" and "nonmetropolitan" are considered interchangeable and their respective uses depend on the conditions and research issues in question (Reeder and Calhoun, 2001).

The aforementioned concerns notwithstanding, several rural classification systems are now in wide use. Three of the most accepted are (1) the Rural-Urban Continuum Codes, (2) the Urban Influence Codes, and (3) the ERS County Typology. All three were developed and are used by the Economic Research Service of the U.S. Department of Agriculture. Whereas all three were formulated using the OMB nonmetropolitan county criteria, their very existence serves to underscore the diversity of classification schemes in rural areas.

The Rural-Urban Continuum Codes (also known as the Beale codes in honor of demographer Calvin Beale) were first developed in 1975, then updated in 1994 to reflect the metropolitan area changes after the 1990 census. This coding system distinguishes nonmetropolitan counties by degree of urbanization and proximity to metropolitan areas (Butler and Beale, 1994). These codes allow researchers to classify counties into groups useful for the analysis of trends involving population density and metropolitan influences. The definitions of the Rural-Urban Continuum Codes are as follows:

Metropolitan Counties

0 Central counties of metro areas of 1 million population or more

1 Fringe counties of metro areas of 1 million or more

2 Counties in metro areas of 250,000 to 1 million population

3 Counties in metro areas of fewer than 250,000 population

Nonmetropolitan Counties

4 Urban population of 20,000 or more, adjacent to a metro area

5 Urban population of 20,000 or more, not adjacent to a metro area

6 Urban population of 2500 to 19,999, adjacent to a metro area

7 Urban population of 2500 to 19,999, not adjacent to a metro area

8 Completely rural or fewer than 2500 urban population, adjacent to a metro area

9 Completely rural or fewer than 2500 urban population, not adjacent to a metro area

The Urban Influence Codes were developed primarily as a tool for measuring some of the differences in economic opportunity in rural areas, given their proximity to metropolitan areas. However, the primary difference of this system from the system of Urban-Rural Continuum Codes is the fact that the Urban Influence Codes account for the size of the metropolitan area to which the rural county is adjacent. The fundamental assumption is that the larger a metropolitan area, the greater the economic impact it will have on adjacent nonmetropolitan counties.

Economic opportunities in rural areas are directly related to both their population size and their access to larger, more populous areas. Further, access to larger economies, such as centers of information, communications, trade, and finance, allows a rural area to connect to national markets and be a working part of a regional economy (U.S. Economic Research Service, 2002a, 2002b).

The Urban Influence Codes divide the 3141 counties, county equivalents, and independent cities into nine groups. The code definitions are as follows:

Metro Counties

1 Large—in a metro area with 1 million residents or more

2 Small—in a metro area with fewer than 1 million residents

Nonmetro Counties

3 Adjacent to a large metro area and contains a city of at least 10,000 residents

4 Adjacent to a large metro area and does not have a city of at least 10,000 residents

5 Adjacent to a small metro area and contains a city of at least 10,000 residents

6 Adjacent to a small metro area and does not have a city of at least 10,000 residents

7 Not adjacent to a metro area and contains a city of at least 10,000 residents

8 Not adjacent to a metro area and contains a town of 2500 to 9999 residents (but not larger)

9 Not adjacent to a metro area and does not contain a town of at least 2500 residents

These codes attempt to measure the importance of adjacency to the large and small metropolitan areas and the importance of the size of the largest city within the county. Researchers should note that the coding structure of the Urban Influence Codes should not be viewed as reflecting a continuous decline in urban influence (Ghelfi and Parker, 1997).

The grouping of nonmetropolitan counties by the U.S. Economic Research Service (usually referred to as the ERS Typology) is a two-tiered system that classifies counties by economic type and by policy type (as explained in the discussion that follows). The county assignments were revised in 1993 to reflect population and commuting data from the 1990 census and again in 2003 to account for changes reported in the 2000 census. This typology is based on the assumption that knowledge and understanding of the different types of rural economies and their distinctive economic and sociodemographic profiles can aid rural policy makers (Cook and Mizer, 1994).

In the first step, nonmetropolitan counties are classified into one of six mutually exclusive economic types that best describe the primary economic activity in each county. The definitions and criteria of the six economic types are as follows:

Farming-dependent. Farming contributed a weighted annual average of 20% or more of the total labor and proprietor income over the 3 years, 1987–1989.

Mining-dependent. Mining contributed a weighted annual average of 15% or more of the total labor and proprietor income over the 3 years, 1987–1989.

Manufacturing-dependent. Manufacturing contributed a weighted annual average of 30% or more of the total labor and proprietor income over the 3 years, 1987–1989.

Government-dependent. Government activities contributed a weighted annual average of 25% or more of the total labor and proprietor income over the 3 years, 1987–1989.

Services-dependent. Service activities (private and personal services, agricultural services, wholesale and retail trade, finance and insurance, transportation, and public utilities) contributed a weighted annual average

of 50% or more of the total labor and proprietor income over the 3 years, 1987–1989.

Nonspecialized. Counties not classified as a specialized economic type over the 3 years, 1987–1989.

The second step in developing the typology is the classification of each nonmetropolitan county by one or more of five policy criteria. The inclusion of these overlapping policy categories helps to clarify the diversity of nonmetropolitan counties and improves the usefulness of the overall typology, while at the same time keeping the scheme from becoming dependent on geographic proximity to metropolitan areas as the primary factor for categorizing rural areas. Further, it helps reduce the wide range of economic and social diversity to a relatively few important themes of interest to rural policy makers (U.S. Economic Research Service, 2002a). The policy types and criteria for inclusion are as follows:

Retirement-destination. The population aged 60 years and older in 1990 increased by 15% or more during 1980–1990 through inmigration.

Federal land. Federally owned land made up 30% or more of a county's land area in the year 1987.

Commuting. Workers aged 16 years and over commuting to jobs outside their county of residence composed 40% or more of all the county's workers in 1990.

Persistent poverty. Persons with income below the poverty level in the preceding year composed 20% or more of the total population in each of the 4 years: 1960, 1970, 1980, and 1990.

Transfer dependent. Income from transfer payments (federal, state, and local) contributed a weighted annual average of 25% or more of the total personal income over the 3 years from 1987 to 1989.

Using the 1993 ERS typology, 2259 of the 2276 nonmetropolitan counties were classified into (one of) the six economic types and, as applicable, 1197 counties were classified into (one or more) of the five policy types (Cook and Mizer, 1994). Although the concept of population density (which is usually the centerpiece of any definition of rural) is absent from this typology, the typology is still very useful for identifying the wide diversity of nonmetropolitan populations. Further, the revision of the typology after every census ensures that it remains relevant and useful to policy makers.

Despite the popularity and wide use of the three aforementioned classification systems, their use still has not fully resolved the confusion surrounding the identification of an area as rural. As long as county-based nonmetropolitan criteria are used in the classification schemes, there will continue to be a high level of ambiguity and incompatibility in comparing and compiling data on rural areas in the United States.

MEASURES

Many of the measures presented in the preceding chapter can be applied to the distribution of the population according to residence classifications. However, the rapid rate of growth in urban areas of the world has created the need for specialized measures to address these developments. Some of these measures have been accepted immediately while others continue to be the subject of debate, as discussed next.

Percentage Distributions

Perhaps the simplest measure used to describe population distribution is the percentage distribution. It is often difficult to imagine the distribution of a population or the classification of residences if the absolute counts or numbers are used. In order for a reader to properly comprehend absolute numbers, he or she must relate them to the total population numbers. For example, stating that 250,000 residents are classified as urban is not as informative as stating that 50% of the residents are classified as urban.

When presenting populations as percentages, care must be taken in the choice of a base. Total population or a subtotal of population may be used. For example, Table 6.4 shows that 62% of the population of Poland is classified as urban. This value is calculated by dividing the number of people living in urban areas by the total population and multiplying the result by 100. Also from Table 6.4, we find that the number of people living in the cities of 200,000 or more in Israel as a percentage of the total population is 20%. However, if the same numerator is used but the total urban population is chosen as the denominator or the base, the resulting number for Israel is 22%. Likewise, if the percentage of people living in cities with greater than 50,000 inhabitants is of interest, the population of all cities with greater than 50,000 inhabitants could be summed and used as the numerator with the total population or total urban population as the denominator or base. Table 6.4 shows that 38% of the total Polish population and 54% of the total Israeli population live in cities of 50,000 or more inhabitants.

A close examination of Table 6.4 illustrates a point raised earlier in this chapter, namely that not all countries use the same definition of urban. In the case of these countries, Poland defines urban by type of locality, not by size. In Poland, any locality that exhibits a specific infrastructure is classified as urban. Israel simply uses the number of inhabitants to define urban, classifying any area with more than 2000 inhabitants as urban. Therefore, it was necessary to include urban areas with fewer than 2000 inhabitants for Poland but not for Israel. This point should be taken into account in any comparison of urban-rural percentages on the international level.

Although the use of percentages can be quite informative, it does not always present an accurate description of the urban-rural situation in a country. Given the variations in urban definitions, often an arbitrary minimum size limit is used to compare urban areas across countries. For example, if 2000 inhabitants is adopted as the minimum size limit, then some basis for comparison exists. However, use of a minimum size limit may mask real differences in the urban-rural distributions of the populations. If the calculations for two countries show that they have an 80% urban population by applying a minimum size limit, it may be falsely assumed that the urban-rural distribution of the two countries is quite similar. It could be the case that the an urban population of one country is distributed evenly among midsize cities, while the majority of the population in the second country is clustered in one megalopolis (see Chapter 5 for a discussion of definitions of cities by size).

Extent of Urbanization

According to estimates and projections produced by the United Nations (2002), future population growth will be

TABLE 6.4   Urban/Rural Population of Poland and Israel by Size of Locality, 1999

Size of locality	Poland		Israel	
	number	Percentage of total population	number	Percentage of total population
Urban'	23,894,134	61.8	5,675,800	91.4
200,000 and over	8,430,089	21.8	1,263,700	20.4
100,000 to 199,999	3,050,732	7.9	1,419,300	22.9
50,000 to 99,999	3,360,805	8.7	662,500	10.7
20,000 to 49,999	4,240,290	11.0	1,212,600	19.5
10,000 to 19,000	2,655,489	6.9	514,400	8.3
2,000 to 9,999	2,085,930	5.4	603,400	9.7
Less than 2,000	70,801	0.2	X	X
Rural	14,759,425	38.2	533,300	8.6
Total population	38,653,559	100.0	6,209,100	100.0

X: Not applicable.

[1] Poland defines urban population not by size of locality but by type of locality; therefore urban areas have no size limit. Israel defines urban population as any locality with more than 2,000 inhabitants.

Sources: Israel, Central Bureau of Statistics, 2002; Poland, Central Statistical Office, 2000.

mainly located in the urban areas of the world. The urban areas of the less developed regions will account for the majority of the growth projected from 2000 to 2030. The growth rate is expected to be 2.31% per year; this implies a "doubling time" of 30 years. This figure is in contrast with a growth rate of 0.37% per year in the urban areas of the more developed regions; the latter rate implies a "doubling time" of 186 years. (see Chapter 11 for "doubling time")

Conversely, growth of the rural populations of the world is projected to slow considerably. In the more developed regions, the "growth" rate between 2000 and 2030 is projected to be −1.19% and in the less developed regions it is projected to be 0.11%. Such a sharp difference in urban-rural growth rates will cause a fundamental redistribution of the world's population. The United Nations has projected that in the year 2007 the world's urban and rural populations will be equal.

It is interesting to note that the largest cities in the world are not necessarily those growing the fastest. Tokyo was reported to be the largest city in the world in 2000 (United Nations, 2001). In 2015, Tokyo is still expected to be the largest city in the world, although the growth rate will be near zero. Dhaka, Bangladesh, was ranked at 11th in world population in 2000. Its population is projected to double in the next 15 years; this would make it the fourth largest city by 2015. The high urban growth rates of less developed countries such as Bangladesh are being fueled by rural-urban migration and the transformation of rural settlements into cities (United Nations, 2001).

Not only is urbanization causing a redistribution of the world's population from rural areas to urban areas, but current urban growth rates are also causing an explosion in city size in the less developed regions. In the case of the more developed regions, urban population tends to be centered in small or midsize cities, whereas in the less developed regions the trend is toward a greater population concentration in cities of at least 1 million inhabitants. This trend is based on the continuation of the growth of "primate" cities in the less developed regions.

Primate cities are the urban giants that account for a disproportionate percentage of a country's population. According to Jefferson (1939), cities are classified as primate when they are at least twice as large as the next largest city and more than twice as significant. For example, Buenos Aires, Argentina, accounts for 33% of the entire country's population, while the second largest city accounts for less than 4% of the total population (Cifuentes, 2002). Table 6.5 shows the 20 cities with the highest degree of primacy in 2000.

Historically, primate cities developed as a consequence of the Industrial Revolution and the growth in employment opportunities in the public and private sectors of these cities. Today, in the less developed regions, migrants continue to move to the cities as a means of escaping the harsh conditions and poor economic prospects of the rural areas. Many

TABLE 6.5 Population of the Cities with the Highest Degree of Primacy in 2000

Rank	City	Country	Population (thous.)	Proportion of total urban population
1	Hong Kong	China	6,927	100.0[1]
2	Gaza Strip	Gaza Strip	1,060	100.0[2]
3	Singapore	Singapore	3,567	100.0
4	Conakry	Guinea	1,824	74.9
5	Panama City	Panama	1,173	73.0
6	Guatemala City	Guatemala	3,242	71.8
7	Beirut	Lebanon	2,055	69.8
8	Brazzaville	Congo	1,234	67.1
9	Santo Domingo	Dominican Republic	3,599	65.1
10	Kuwait City	Kuwait	1,190	61.8
11	Luanda	Angola	2,677	60.8
12	Port-au-Prince	Haiti	1,769	60.3
13	Lisbon	Portugal	3,826	60.1
14	Ndjamena	Chad	1,043	57.3
15	Phnom Penh	Cambodia	984	55.4
16	Bangkok	Thailand	7,281	54.9
17	Yerevan	Armenia	1,284	52.2
18	Kabul	Afghanistan	2,590	52.1
19	San Jose	Costa Rica	988	51.3
20	Ouagadougou	Burkina Faso	1,130	51.3

Source: United Nations, 2001.
[1] Before Chinese sovereignty in 1997.
[2] Under civil administration of Palestinean authority.

of these cities are unable to cope with the rapid population increases they are experiencing. The housing stock and sewage facilities are not adequate to accommodate the growing populations. High rates of inmigration coupled with high birth rates have resulted in the development in these cities of squatter settlements known variously as *barrios, bajos, barriadas, callampas, favellas, bidonvilles, bustees, gecekondu, kampongs,* and *barung-barong* (Macionis and Parrillo, 2001; Rubenstein, 1994). Kibera, a squatter's settlement on the outskirts of Nairobi, Kenya, represents one of the largest slums in Africa. More than 750,000 people live in an area of open sewers, primitive shelters, minimally functional toilets, and few water outlets (*Economist*, 2002).

Although primate cities in the more developed regions continue to thrive (e.g., Paris, France, and Madrid, Spain), an emerging trend in these areas is that of edge cities. Also known as suburban business districts, suburban cores, or perimeter cities, edge cities are located at the edges of large urban areas (Garreau, 1991). They are usually found at the intersection of major highways, and they represent the continuation of the suburbanization movement. As city dwellers moved beyond city limits, they created suburbs. Soon, retail outlets followed their customers to the suburbs. Eventually, the jobs moved to the places where people had been living and shopping for years. Garreau (1991) defined edge cities in terms of the following five characteristics:

A minimum of 5 million square feet of office space
A minimum of 600,000 square feet of retail space
A single-end destination for shopping, entertainment, and employment
Commuting of workers to the area for jobs with more people working in the area than living in the area
Growth of the area within the past 30 years, not simply the result of annexation of an existing city

Edge cities typically lack government structure. Most edge cities lie in unincorporated areas. For all intents and purposes they are cities, yet they are usually subject to the rule of county governments with few opportunities for self-governance.

Rank-Size Rule

Explaining the size and growth patterns of cities has always been of interest to researchers. Zipf (1949) put forth a "law" to explain the size and ranking of cities in a country. Simply stated, his law is that if the cities of a country are ordered by population size, the largest city will be twice as large as the second largest city, three times as large as the third largest city, four times as large as the fourth largest city, and so forth. His law is expressed by the following formula:

$$P_i = K/r_i \qquad (6.1)$$

where P_i is the population of the city, r_i is the rank of the city, and K is the size of the largest city. With an addition of a constant (n), this formula can be generalized to create the rank-size rule as follows:

$$P_i = K/r_i^n \qquad (6.2)$$

Therefore, Zipf's law is a special case of the rank size rule when n = 1. Zipf's law and the rank-size rule can be tested empirically by plotting the logarithm of the rank of the cities against the logarithm of their populations. The resulting slope should be −1, showing an inverse relationship between the logarithm of the size of city and the logarithm of its rank.

For years researchers have been trying to explain the consistency of Zipf's law. Although it does not always accurately describe the size and ranking of cities, it is, more often than not, correct (Brakman *et al.*, 1999; Gabaix, 1999; Reed, 1988) If cities follow Gibrat's law (Gabaix, 1999) and grow at the same rate regardless of size, the rank-size rule will at some point describe the size and rankings of the cities within a country. However, there is a tendency for the rank-size rule not to hold true in the case of primate cities that are national capitals (Cifuentes, 2002).

Gini Concentration Ratio and Lorenz Curve

The Lorenz curve is a graphic device for representing the inequality of two distributions. It is illustrated by plotting the cumulative percentage of the number of areas (Y_i) against the cumulative percentage of population (X_i) in these localities. In a country with a "perfectly" distributed population, the cumulative share of population would be equal to the cumulative share of the number of localities. Such equality of distributions is represented by a diagonal line. This diagonal line is compared to the actual distribution, and the gap between the ideal and actual lines is interpreted as the degree of inequality.

The Gini concentration ratio measures the degree of inequality or the size of the gap. The Gini ratio falls between 0.0 and 1.0. A Gini ratio of 1.0 indicates complete inequality, with all population located in one locality of a country and no population in the remaining areas. A Gini ratio of 0.0 indicates a perfect distribution of population in the areas of the country. Therefore, the higher the Gini concentration ratio, the greater the inequality between the population distribution and the number of localities. The measure may be computed as

$$\text{Gini Ratio} = \left(\sum_{i=1} X_i Y_{i+1} \right) - \left(\sum_{i=1} X_{i+1} Y_i \right) \qquad (6.3)$$

where X_i is the proportion of population in an area and Y_i is the proportion of localities in an area.

Table 6.6 shows the computations for Israel in 2000. The corresponding Lorenz curve is shown in Figure 6.1.

The Gini concentration ratio is calculated according the following steps:

Step 1. Post the number of localities in column 1.
Step 2. Post the population for each size of locality in column 2.

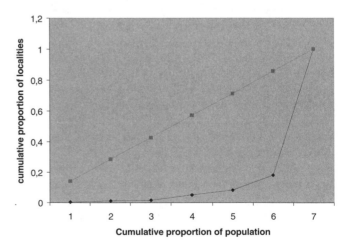

FIGURE 6.1 Lorenz curve for measuring population concentration in Israel, 2000, in relation to the number of localities. Source: Israel, Central Bureau of Statistics, 2002.

TABLE 6.6   Computation of Gini Concentration Ratio for Persons Living in Localities in Israel in 2000

Size of locality	Number of localities (1)	Population (2)	Proportion		Cumulative proportion		X_iY_{i+1} (7)	$X_{i+1}Y_i$ (8)
			Localities (3)	Population (4)	Localities (Y_i) (5)	Population (X_i) (6)		
All localities	1193	6,369,300	1.0000	1.0000	—	—	—	—
200,000 and over	4	1,484,700	.0033	.2331	.0033	.2331	.0023	.0014
100,000–199,999	8	1,243,200	.0067	.1952	.0100	.4283	.0075	.0053
50,000–99,999	9	676,400	.0075	.1062	.0175	.5345	.0268	.0128
20,000–49,999	39	1,267,600	.0327	.1990	.0502	.7335	.0590	.0410
10,000–19,999	36	526,300	.0302	.0826	.0804	.8161	.1463	.0736
2,000–9,999	118	631,800	.0989	.0992	.1793	.9153	.9153	.1793
Fewer than 2,000	979	539,200	.8206	.0846	1.0000	1.0000	—	—
Sum							1.1572	.3134
Gini ratio (difference of sums)							.8438	

Source: Israel, Central Bureau of Statistics, 2002.

Step 3. Compute the proportionate distribution of localities by dividing each number in column 1 by the total number of localities (e.g., 4 ÷ 1193 = .0033). Post the results in column 3.

Step 4. Compute the proportionate distribution of the population by dividing each number in column 2 by the total population (e.g., 1,484,700 ÷ 6,369,300 = .2331). Post the results in column 4.

Step 5. Cumulate the proportions of column 3 downward (.0033 + .0067, etc.). Post the results in column 5.

Step 6. Cumulate the proportions of column 4 downward (e.g., .2331 + .1952, etc.). Post the results in column 6.

Step 7. Multiply the first line of column 6 by the second line of column 5, the second line of column 6 by the third line of column 5, etc. (e.g., .2331 × .0100 = .0023). Post the results in column 7.

Step 8. Multiply the first line of column 5 by the second line of column 6, the second line of column 5 by the third line of column 6, etc. (e.g., .0033 × .4283 = .0014). Post the results in column 8.

Step 9. Sum column 7 (1.1572); sum column 8 (.3134).

Step 10. Subtract the total of column 8 from the total of column 7 (1.1572 − .3134 = .8438).

If the Gini concentration ratio is calculated as illustrated in Table 6.6, the resulting number can be used to describe the distribution of the population throughout the country. On the other hand, if the Gini concentration ratio is calculated for the total urban population by omitting the localities and their corresponding populations that fall outside urban limits, the ratio then becomes a measure of population inequality within the urban areas. The product of the urban Gini concentration ratio and the total urban percentage of a country is known as "scale of urbanization" (Jones, 1967).

Indices of Residential Separation

It is important to note the level and degree of residential separation and spatial isolation of groups, especially racial/ethnic groups, because of their possible long-term negative effects (Massey and Denton, 1988, 1998). An area that has a majority of racial minorities and, hence, of lower income households may experience an erosion of the tax base, resulting in underfunded schools or a loss of public services. White flight to the suburbs may result in physical or cultural isolation as well as the political isolation of minorities, creating unequal opportunities for the residents left behind.

Because of these and similar effects, researchers have continued to search for measures of "segregation". Over the years the validity of such measures has been a focus of considerable debate and analysis. Research presented by Duncan and Duncan (1955) led to the acceptance of the index of dissimilarity, also known as Delta (Δ), as the index of preference to use in the study of residential segregation.

As more data became available, computer analysis more sophisticated, and consequences of segregation better understood, researchers began to explore more refined indices of separation. A turning point was the publication of Massey and Denton's research in which they conducted cluster analyses of 20 indices of segregation. Their results showed that the various indices could be grouped into the five categories of evenness, exposure, concentration, centralization, and clustering (Massey and Denton, 1988). They recommended a single "best" index for each these five dimensions of residential segregation. This led to more debate and discussion of the use of indices to measure segregation. The ensuing articles challenged researchers to revise the indices, correct textual errors, and reexamine their uses and interpretations, especially in the cases of small minority populations or very large area subunits. (For a discussion of the debates, see Egan *et al.*, 1998; Massey and Denton, 1998; Massey *et al.*, 1996; St. John, 1995). The most popular indices in use today, following the classification system developed by Massey and Denton (1988), are presented next.

Evenness

This dimension measures the spatial segregation of various groups. Segregation is lowest when each area reflects the overall population share, considering minority and majority groups. Two measures of evenness are described here. The dissimilarity index measures the dissimilarity of two population distributions in an area, while the entropy index measures the diversity of the population within an area.

Index of Dissimilarity- Delta

This index measures the percentage of one group that would have to change residence in order to produce an even distribution of the two groups among areas. For example, a black-versus-all-other-races dissimilarity index of .4790 for Butler County, Ohio, as shown in Table 6.10 (presented later), means that 47.9% of blacks would need to move to another area subunit, such as another census tract, in order to eliminate racial segregation.

As stated previously, this measure has been one of the most popular measures of residential segregation. Criticisms are based on the fact that it measures only two groups at one time and that it is affected by the number and choice of area subunits used in the calculations (Siegel, 2002; p. 26). Typically, a minority group is compared to the majority group within a geographical area. Thereby, residential housing patterns of blacks can be compared to those of whites, or blacks could be compared to nonblacks, but blacks could not be compared to Hispanics and whites simultaneously. The index is computed by the following formula:

$$\Delta = \frac{1}{2}\sum_{i=1}^{N}\left|\frac{P_{ia}}{P_{Ja}} - \frac{P_{ib}}{P_{Jb}}\right| = \frac{1}{2}\sum_{i=1}^{N}|x_i - y_i| \qquad (6.4)$$

where a and b represent the members of the groups under study, *j* the entire geographical area (e.g., a county), P_i the population in area subunit i (e.g., a census tract or neighborhood), P_J the population in the parent area subunit J, N the number of subunits in the parent area, and x_i and y_i the proportions of the population in each group in each subunit out of the area total for the group. The index ranges from 0, indicating no residential segregation, to 1, indicating complete residential segregation. (see also Chapter 7.)

Several researchers have questioned the ability of this index to measure the level of segregation adequately. Morrill

(1991) and Wong (1993) have proposed alternative formulas that introduce spatial interaction components such as adjacency and length of common boundaries between area subunits.

Entropy Index

This index is also known as the Theil index or "diversity index." It too measures the differences in the distributions of groups within a geographical area. Unlike the index of dissimilarity, however, it allows for the calculation of measures for multiple groups simultaneously. Calculating the Theil index involves a multistep process in which an entropy score, a measure of diversity, is first calculated. The total area's (e.g., a state) entropy score is calculated from

$$E = \sum_{J=1}^{Z}(X_j)\ln[1/X_j] \qquad (6.5)$$

where X_J is the share for the population of the entire area in each category of the variable studied and Z is the number of categories. The resulting number is the diversity of the total area. The higher the number, the more diverse the area. The upper limit of the measure is given by the natural log of the number of groups used in the calculations. The upper limit is reached when all groups have equal representation within the area. Note, at this stage of the calculation, it is not possible to ascertain segregation because, although groups may be equally represented within the total area, they may still be arrayed in a segregated manner within the total area's boundaries.

The next step is to measure the individual subunits' (e.g., each county in the state) entropy score from

$$E_i = \sum_{J=1}^{Z}(X_J)\ln[1/X_J] \qquad (6.6)$$

where X_J is the share of the total in each category of the variable studied for in the area subunit $_i$.

Using the numbers generated from the preceding formulas, the Theil or entropy index can be calculated. This measure is interpreted as the weighted average deviation of each subunit's (e.g., county) entropy from the total area's (e.g., state) entropy. The final step is calculated from

$$H = \sum_{i=1}^{N}[t_i(E - E_i)]/ET \qquad (6.7)$$

where t_i represents total population of subunit $_i$ and T represents the total area population. The measure varies between 0.0—all subunits have the same composition as the overall area—to 1.0—all subunits contain only one group.

Tables 6.7, 6.8, and 6.9 illustrate the procedure for the computation of the Thiel index using data for the state of Rhode Island and its counties. In this case, the entropy of the areas is measured with respect to family composition. Analogous steps

TABLE 6.7   Number of Households by Type for Rhode Island and Its Counties (householders aged 15 to 64 years): 2000

	Rhode Island	Bristol Co.	Kent Co.	Newport Co.	Providence Co.	Washington Co.
Household type						
married couple	158,933	8,628	28,914	14,275	85,605	21,511
Other family	58,382	1,958	7,866	3,870	39,586	5,102
Nonfamily	94,889	3,432	14,382	9,023	57,685	10,367
Total	312,204	14,018	51,162	27,168	182,876	36,980

Source: U.S. Census Bureau, 2001a.

TABLE 6.8   Proportion of Households by Type for Rhode Island and Counties (householders aged 15–64 years): 2000

	Rhode Island	Bristol Co.	Kent Co.	Newport Co.	Providence Co.	Washington Co.
Household type						
married couple	0.509	0.615	0.565	0.525	0.468	0.582
Other family	0.187	0.140	0.154	0.142	0.216	0.138
Nonfamily	0.304	0.245	0.281	0.332	0.315	0.280

Source: Calculated from table 6.7.

are required to prepare the corresponding diversity measures used in the final calculation. The data chosen for the example are householders 15 to 64 years old disaggregated by type of household (married couple, other family, and nonfamily).

1. The entropy score for the state (E) is calculated by using the proportion of each family group within the state. The first step is to compute the proportion of each household type for the state (e.g., $158,933 \div 312,204$ = Proportion of married-couple households in Rhode Island).
2. The entropy score for the counties (E_i) is calculated by using the proportion of each family group within the counties. The first step is to compute the proportion of each household type for the county (e.g., $8,628 \div 14,018$ = Proportion of married-couple households in Bristol county).
3. Substituting the proportions from Table 6.8 into formula (6.6), the entropy score for the state (E) is as follows:

$$E = [(.509)\ln(1/.509)] + [(.187)\ln(1/.187)]$$
$$+ [(.304)\ln(1/.304)]$$
$$= 1.0192$$

4. Substituting the proportions from Table 6.8 into formula (6.6), the entropy score for Bristol county (E_i) is as follows (see Table 6.9):

$$E_i = [(.615)\ln(1/.615)] + [(.140)\ln(1/.140)]$$
$$+ [(.245)\ln(1/.245)]$$
$$= .9188$$

5. The Thiel or entropy index is now calculated using the E and E_i scores from each of the preceding counties with the total number of households of the counties and the state as described in formula (6.7). Using Bristol county as the example, its segment of the index would be figured as follows:

$$[14,018(1.0192 - .9188)] \div [(1.9192)312,204] = .0044$$

The results of all five counties, $[.0044 + .0142 + .0083 + (-.0178) + .0087]$, would then be summed, resulting in H, the measure of segregation of family types.

6. In this case, the resulting H = .0178. Thus Rhode Island has virtually no diversity throughout the state with respect to family types.

Exposure

These indices measure the extent of possible contact between group members. It is important to note that this measure is affected by the relative size of the two groups under study.

Isolation Index

This index measures the likelihood that a randomly chosen member of one group will meet another member of the same group. For example, in Table 6.10, the isolation index for blacks in Mahoning County, Ohio, shows that there is a 59.6% likelihood of one black person meeting another in that county. If there was no residential segregation, the likelihood would be only 15.9%, as indicated by the proportion of black population in the county. The isolation index is calculated as

$$P^{jm} = \sum_{i=1}^{N}\left[\left(\frac{x_i}{X}\right)\left(\frac{x_i}{t_i}\right)\right] \tag{6.8}$$

TABLE 6.9 Components of E and E_i (as calculated from formulas (5) and (6), respectively)

	Rhode Island	Bristol Co.	Kent Co.	Newport Co.	Providence Co.	Washington Co.
Household type						
Family	.3437	.2990	.3226	.3382	.3553	.3150
Other family	.3135	.2752	.2881	.2772	.3310	.2733
Nonfamily	.3620	.3446	.3567	.3661	.3639	.3564
Total	1.0194	.9188	.9674	.9815	1.0502	.9447

where *m* represents the members of the group under study (e.g., a minority group), *j* the entire geographical unit (e.g., a county), x_i the minority population in area subunit *i* (e.g., a census tract or neighborhood), X the total minority population of the entire area, and t_i the total population in area subunit *i*. The index ranges from 0, indicating no residential segregation, to 1, indicating complete residential segregation.

Interaction Index

This index measures the probability that a member of one group will meet a member of another group. When this index and the isolation index are used in an area with only two groups or when various groups are collapsed into a dichotomy, such as nonwhites as compared to whites, they sum to 1.0. Logically, lower values of interaction and higher values of isolation taken together indicate higher rates of segregation in an area. The index can be computed with the following formula:

$$P^{jm} = \sum_{i=1}^{N}\left[\left(\frac{x_i}{X}\right)\left(\frac{y_i}{t_i}\right)\right] \tag{6.9}$$

where *m* represents the members of the minority group under study, *j* the entire geographical unit (e.g., as a county), x_i the total minority population in area subunit *i* (e.g., a census tract or neighborhood), X the total minority population of the entire area, y_i the total population of the second group in area subunit *i*, and t_i the total population in area subunit *i*.

Concentration

The indices categorized as concentration measures introduce the idea of physical space. If groups have equal population size but occupy different amounts of space, the area would be considered as segregated. In addition to the index that follows, Massey and Denton (1988) have also proposed two additional measures—the absolute concentration index and the relative concentration index—that take into account the relative distribution of the various groups within an area.

TABLE 6.10 Black/African American Residential Segregation in Ohio's 15 Largest Counties, 1990–2000

	Proportion Black/African American		Index of dissimilarity		Isolation index	
County	1990	2000	1990	2000	1990	2000
Butler	0.0451	0.0527	.5892	.4790	.3167	.2293
Clermont	0.0086	0.0091	.3018	.2574	.0144	.0142
Cuyahoga	0.2480	0.2745	.8418	.7852	.8112	.7522
Franklin	0.1590	0.1789	.6546	.5985	.5370	.4870
Hamilton	0.2091	0.2343	.7091	.6796	.6252	.6020
Lake	0.0164	0.0199	.6490	.5985	.1075	.0969
Lorain	0.0793	0.0850	.5563	.5462	.2292	.2136
Lucas	0.1481	0.1698	.7113	.6750	.5834	.5408
Mahoning	0.1498	0.1587	.8146	.7802	.6210	.5958
Montgomery	0.1774	0.1986	.7747	.7476	.6756	.6462
Portage	0.0274	0.0318	.4694	.4586	.0593	.0706
Stark	0.0682	0.0720	.6122	.5772	.3289	.2840
Summit	0.1188	0.1319	.7010	.6674	.5183	.4840
Trumball	0.0668	0.0790	.6261	.6408	.3317	.3256
Warren	0.0212	0.0273	.6455	.5435	.3159	.1011

Source: Southwest Ohio Regional Data Center, 2001.

Concentration Index

This index, a derivative of the index of dissimilarity, is computed as follows:

$$C^{jm} = \frac{1}{2}\sum_{i=1}^{N}\left(\frac{x_i}{X} - \frac{a_j}{A}\right) \tag{6.10}$$

where *m* represents the members of the minority group under study, *j* the entire geographical unit (e.g., a county), x_i the total minority population in area subunit *i* (e.g., a census tract or neighborhood), X the total minority population of the entire area, a_i the land area of area subunits, and A the total land area of the entire geographical unit.

Centralization

Like the concentration indices, centralization introduces the aspect of physical space. In this dimension or category, the concern is the degree to which a group is near the center of the geographical unit. The nearness to the center of the area can be examined with absolute or relative measures.

Absolute Centralization Index

This index measures the distribution of the minority group around the center of the geographical unit. It has a range of -1 to $+1$. A negative score means a tendency for the minority group to live in the outlying areas, a positive score represents a tendency for minority members to live near the city center, and a score of 0 indicates that the group has a uniform distribution throughout the geographical area:

$$ACE = \sum_{i=1}^{N}(C_{i-1}A_i) - \sum_{i=1}^{N}(C_iA_{i-1}) \qquad (6.11)$$

where the N area subunits are ordered by increasing distance from the central business district, C is the cumulative proportion of the minority population up through subunit i, and A is the cumulative proportion of land area up through subunit i.

Relative Centralization Index

This index measures the area profile of the minority and majority groups. It represents the relative share of one group's population that would have to change their residences to match the centralization distribution of the other group. This measure typically has a range of -1 to $+1$, but in cases of a very small minority population in a large area, the range may drop below -1. A negative score means a tendency for the minority group to live in the outlying areas, a positive score represents a tendency for minority members to live near the city center, and a score of 0 indicates that the groups have the same spatial distribution throughout the geographical area:

$$RCE = \sum_{i=1}^{N}(x_{i-1}y_i) - \sum_{i=1}^{N}(x_iy_{i-1}) \qquad (6.12)$$

where the N area subunits are ordered by increasing distance from the central business district, x_i represents the cumulative proportion of the minority population in subunit i, and y_i represents the cumulative proportion of the majority population in subunit i.

Clustering

Racial or ethnic enclaves can be detected with the use of an index of clustering. It measures the extent to which the area subunits with minority members are grouped together or clustered. A high degree of clustering indicates a racial community. To measure this dimension adequately requires a two-step process. The first step is to calculate the index of spatial proximity, which is then used to calculate the index of relative clustering.

Index of Spatial Proximity

This measure is the average proximity between members of the same group and members of different groups. The average proximity between members of the same groups is calculated by

$$P_{xx} = \sum_{i=1}^{N}\sum_{j=1}^{N}\frac{x_ix_jc_{ij}}{X^2} \qquad (6.13)$$

and the average proximity between members of different groups is calculated by

$$P_{xy} = \sum_{i=1}^{N}\sum_{j=1}^{N}\frac{x_ix_jc_{ij}}{XY} \qquad (6.14)$$

where c_{ij} represents a negative exponential of distance between areas i and j, x_i the minority population in area subunit i (e.g., a census tract or neighborhood), x_j the minority population of area subunit j, X the total minority population of the entire area, Y the total majority population of the entire area, and N the total number of census tracts within the entire area. Therefore, the index of spatial proximity is calculated by

$$SP = (XP_{xx} + XP_{yy})/TP_{tt} \qquad (6.15)$$

where T represents the total population and P_{tt} the proportion of the population that is minority. If there is no differential clustering between X and Y, the index is 1.0. The larger the number, the nearer the members of the same group live to each other.

Index of Relative Clustering

Using the results from the calculations for the index of spatial proximity for both the minority population (x) and the majority population (y), the following formula is applied to compare the average distance between the minority and majority members. When both groups have the same amount of clustering, the score will be 0. A negative score indicates less clustering of the minority group as compared to the majority group while a positive score indicates more clustering of the minority group. The formula is

$$RCL = P_{xx}/P_{yy} - 1 \qquad (6.16)$$

The rapid urbanization of populations throughout the world has created a need for various measures to determine the scope, magnitude, distribution, and concentration of population growth. Many of the measures in this chapter have been subject to criticism, specifically in their application to the study of small minority populations and large metropolitan areas with numerous minority populations or very large area subunits. However, if used judiciously and interpreted properly, they are powerful tools when used to examine the latest trends in residential distribution and separation of groups.

References

Brakman, S., H. Garretsen, C. Van Marrewijk, and M. van den Berg. 1999. "The Return of Zipf: Towards a Further Understanding of the Rank-Size Distribution." *Journal of Regional Science* 39: 183–213.

California Rural Health Policy Council. 2002. California's Focal Point on Rural Health, www.ruralhealth.ca.gov/whatwearehome.htm, January 3, 2002.

Cifuentes, R. 2002. "Concentration of Population in Capital Cities: Determinants and Economic Effects." *Central Bank of Chile Working Papers*, No. 144.

Colorado Rural Health Center. 2000. *Am I Rural?* www.coruralhealth.org/publications, April 2, 2002.

Duncan, O. D., and B. Duncan. 1955. "A Methodological Analysis of Segregation Indices." *American Sociological Review* 59: 23–45.

Economist. 2002. "The Brown Revolution." *The Economist*, Print Edition, Reuters, May 9.

Egan, K. L., D. L. Anderton, and E. Weber. 1998. "Relative Spatial Concentration Among Minorities: Addressing Errors in Measurement." *Social Forces* 76(3): 1115.

Gabaix, X. 1999. "Zipf's Law for Cities: An Explanation." *Quarterly Journal of Economics* 114: 739–767.

Garreau, J. 1991. *Edge City: Life on the New Frontier*. New York: Doubleday.

Ghelfi, L., and T. Parker. 1997. "A County Level Measurement of Urban Influence." *Rural Development Perspectives* 12, (2).

India. 1991. *Final Population Totals. Census of India*. Office of the RGI and Census Commissioner, GOI, New Delhi.

Israel, Central Bureau of Statistics. 2002. *Statistics of the State of Israel. 2001: Projections of Israel's Population Until 2020*, www.cbs.gov.il/engindex.htm.

Jefferson, M. 1939. "The Law of the Primate City." *The Geographical Review* 29: 226–232.

Jones, F. 1967. "A Note on 'Measures of Urbanization,' With a Further Proposal." *Social Forces* 46(2): 275–279.

Macionis, J., and V. Parrillo. 2001. *Cities and Urban Life*. Upper Saddle River, NJ: Prentice Hall.

Massey, D., and N. Denton. 1988. "The Dimensions of Residential Segregation." *Social Forces* 67: 281–315.

Massey, D., and N. Denton. 1998. "The Elusive Quest for the Perfect Index of Concentration: Reply to Egan, Anderton, and Weber." *Social Forces* 76(3): 1123.

Massey, D., M. White, and V. Phua. 1996. "The Dimensions of Segregation Revisited." *Sociological Methods and Research* 25(2): 172.

McKibben, J. 1992. "The Rural Renaissance Revisited in Indiana." In *Proceedings of The 10th Conference of the Small City and Regional Community*. Western Michigan University, April.

Morrill, R. 1991. "On the Measure of Geographic Segregation." *Geography Research Forum* 11: 25–36.

Palen, J. 2002. *The Urban World*, 6th ed. Boston MA: McGraw-Hill.

Poland, Central Statistical Office. 2002. *Concise Statistical Yearbook of Poland*, www.stat.gov.pl/english/index.htm. March 27, 2002.

Reed, C. B. 1988. Zipf's Law. In S. Kotz, N. L. Johnson, and C. B. Reed (Eds.), *Encyclopedia of Statistical Sciences*. New York: Wiley.

Reeder, R., and S. Calhoun. 2001. "Funding is Less in Rural than in Urban Areas, but Varies by Region and Type of County." *Rural America* 16(3), Fall, 51–54.

Rios, B. 1988. "'Rural' A Concept beyond Definition?" Education Resource Information Center, www.ed.gov/databases/eric_digests/ed296820.html, April 12, 2002.

Rubenstein, J. 1994. *An Introduction to Human Geography*, 4th ed. New York: Macmillian.

Siegel, J. S. 2002. *Applied Demography: Applications to Business, Law, and Public Policy*. San Diego: Academic Press.

Southwest Ohio Regional Data Center. 2001, March. "Residential Segregation in Ohio's Counties, *Beyond the Numbers*," *Monthly Review*. Institute for Policy Research, University of Cincinnati, http://www.ipr.uc.edu/Centers/SORbeyond.cfm, August 1, 2002.

St. John, C. 1995. "Interclass Segregation, Poverty, and Poverty Concentration." Comment on Massey and Eggers. *American Journal of Sociology* 100(5): 1325–1335.

Truesdell, L. 1949. "The Development of the Urban-Rural Classification System in the United States: 1874–1949." *Current Population Reports*, Series P-23, No. 1, August. Washington, DC: U.S. Bureau of the Census.

United Nations, Department of Social and Economic Affairs. 1998. *Principles and Recommendations for Population and Housing Censuses*, Series M, No. 67, Rev. 1. New York: United Nations.

United Nations, Department of Social and Economic Affairs. 2001. *World Urbanization Prospects, The 1999 Revision*. New York: United Nations.

United Nations, Department of Social and Economic Affairs. 2002. *World Urbanization Prospects, The 2001 Revision, Data Tables and Highlights*. New York: United Nations.

U.S. Census Bureau. 1994. *Geographic Areas Reference Manual* (November).

U.S. Census Bureau. 1995. Urban and Rural Definitions. www.census.gov/population/censusdata/urdef.txt, January 24, 2002.

U.S. Census Bureau. 1996. Area Classifications, Appendix A. www.census.gov/1/90dec/cph4/, January 28, 2002.

U.S. Census Bureau. 2001a. *Profiles of General Demographic Characteristics 2000*. 2000 Census of Population and Housing, Table DP-1.

U.S. Census Bureau. 2001b. *Urban Area Criteria for Census 2000-Proposed Criteria*. Federal Register, Vol. 66, No. 60, March 28, 2001.

U.S. Census Bureau. 2002a. *Urban Area Criteria for Census 2000-*. Federal Register, Vol. 67, No.51, March 15, 2002.

U.S. Census Bureau. 2002b. Reference Resources for Understanding Census Bureau Geography, Appendix A. Census 2000 Geographic Terms and Concepts, www.census.gov/geo/www/reference.html, March 16, 2002

U.S. Census Bureau. 2002c. *Urban and Rural Classification*. www.census.gov/geo/www/ua/ua_2k.html, April 2, 2002.

U.S. Economic Research Service. 1994a. *Rural-Urban Continuum Codes for Metro and Nonmetro Counties*, by M. Butler and C. Beale.

U.S. Economic Research Service. 1994b. *The Revised EPS County Typology: An Overview*, Rural Development Research Report 89, by P. Cook and K. Mizer.

U.S. Economic Research Service. 2002a. *Measuring Rurality: County Typology Codes*, www.ers.usda.gov/briefing/rurality/typology/, February 20, 2002.

U.S. Economic Research Service. 2002b. *Measuring Rurality: Urban Influence Codes*, www.ers.usda.gov/briefing/rurality/urbaninf/, April 12, 2002.

U.S. National Center for Education Statistics. 2002. *What's Rural: Urban/Rural Classification Systems*, www.nces.ed.gov/surveys/ruraled/definitions.asp, April 12, 2002.

U.S. Office of Management and Budget. 2000. *Standards for Defining Metropolitan and Micropolitan Statistical Areas*. Federal Register, Vol. 65, No. 249, December 27, 2000.

Washington State Department of Health. 2001. *Guidelines for Using Rural-Urban Classification Systems for Public Health Assessment*, www.doh.wa.gov/data/guidelines/ruralurban.htm, April 2, 2002.

Wong, D. W. S. 1993. "Spatial Indices of Segregation." *Urban Studies* 30(3): 559–572.

Zipf, G. K. 1949. *Human Behavior and the Principle of the Least Effort.* New York: Addison-Wesley Press.

Suggested Readings

Bluestone, B., and M. Stevenson. 2000. *The Boston Renaissance: Race, Space, and Change in an American Metropolis.* New York: Russell Sage Foundation.

Chan, K. W. 1994. "Urbanization and Rural-Urban Migration in China Since 1982: A New Baseline." *Modern China* 20(2): 243–281.

Gugler, J. (Ed.). 1988. *The Urbanization of the Third World.* Oxford: Oxford University Press.

Jargowsky, P. A. 1997. *Poverty and Place: Ghettos, Barrios, and the American City.* New York: Russell Sage Foundation.

Massey, D., and N. Denton. 1993. *American Apartheid: Segregation and the Making of the Underclass.* Cambridge, MA: Harvard University Press.

Massey, D., and M. Eggers 1993. The Spatial Concentration of Affluence and Poverty during the 1970s. *Urban Affairs Review* 29(2): 299–322.

Reardon, S., and G. Firebaugh. 2000. "Measures of Multigroup Segregation. Population Research Institute." The Pennsylvania State University, Working Paper 00-13 (November 2000).

Squires, G. (ed). 2002. *Urban Sprawl: Causes, Consequences, and Policy Responses.* Washington, DC: The Urban Institute Press.

Theil, H., and A. Finezza. 1971. "A Note on the Measurement of Racial Integration of Schools by Means of Informational Concepts." *Journal of Mathematical Sociology* 1: 187–94.

U.S. Census Bureau. 2002. "Racial and Ethnic Segregation in the United States: 1980–2000," by J. Iceland and D. Weinberg. *Census Special Report, CENSR-4.*

7

Age and Sex Composition

FRANK HOBBS

INTRODUCTION

Uses of Data

The personal characteristics of age and sex hold positions of prime importance in demographic studies. Separate data for males and females and for ages are important in themselves, for the analysis of other types of data, and for the evaluation of the completeness and accuracy of the census counts of population.

Many types of planning, both public and private, such as military planning, planning of community institutions and services, particularly health services, and planning of sales programs require separate population data for males and females and for age groups. Age is an important variable in measuring potential school population, the potential voting population and potential manpower. Age data are required for preparing current population estimates and projections; projections of households, school enrollment, and labor force, as well as projections of requirements for schools, teachers, health services, food, and housing.

Social scientists of many types also have a special interest in the age and sex structure of a population, because social relationships within a community are considerably affected by the relative numbers of males and females and the relative numbers at each age. The sociologist and the economist have a vital interest in data on age and sex composition. The balance of the sexes affects social and economic relationships within a community. Social roles and cultural patterns may be affected. For example, imbalances in the number of men and women may affect marriage and fertility patterns, labor force participation, and the sex roles within the society.[1]

---

[1] For a cross-national analysis of the effect of sex composition on women's roles, see South and Trent (1988), and for a discussion of the demographic foundations of sex roles, see Davis and van den Oever (1982).

For such subjects as natality, mortality, migration, marital status, and economic characteristics, statistics are sometimes shown only for both sexes combined; but the ordinary and more useful practice is to present and analyze the statistics separately for males and females. In fact, a very large part of the usefulness of the sex classification in demographic statistics lies in its cross-classification with other classifications in which one may be interested. For example, the effect of variations in the proportion of the sexes on measures of natality is considerable. This effect may make itself felt indirectly through the marriage rate. Generally, there are substantial differences between the death rates of the sexes; hence, the effect of variations in sex composition from one population group to another should be taken into account in comparative studies of general mortality. The analysis of labor supply and military manpower requires separate information on males and females cross-classified with economic activity and age. In fact, a cross-classification with sex is useful for the effective analysis of nearly all types of data obtained in censuses and surveys, including data on racial and ethnic composition, educational status, and citizenship status, as well as the types of data mentioned previously.

Age is arguably the most important variable in the study of mortality, fertility, nuptiality, and certain other areas of demographic analysis. Tabulations on age are essential in the computation of the basic measures relating to the factors of population change, in the analysis of the factors of labor supply, and in the study of the problem of economic dependency. The importance of census data on age in studies of population growth is even greater when adequate vital statistics from a registration system are not available (United Nations, 1964). As with data on sex, a large part of the usefulness of the age classification lies in its cross-classifications with other demographic characteristics in which one may be primarily interested. For example, the cross-classifications of age with marital status, labor force, and migration make possible a much more effective use of census data on these subjects. Because these social and economic characteristics vary so much with age and because age composition also varies in time and place, populations cannot be meaningfully compared with respect to these other characteristics unless age has been "controlled."

Data on age and sex composition serve other important analytic purposes. Because the expected proportion of the sexes can often be independently determined within a narrow range, the tabulations by sex are useful in the evaluation of census and survey data, particularly with respect to the coverage of the population by sex and age. Furthermore, because the expected number of children, the expected number in certain older age groups, and the relative number of males and females at given ages can be determined closely or at least approximately, either on the basis of data external to the census or from census data themselves, the tabulations by age and sex are very useful in the evaluation of the quality of the returns from the census.

Definition and Classification

The definition and classification of sex present no statistical problems. It is a readily ascertainable characteristic, and the data are easy to obtain. The situation with respect to sex is in contrast to that of most other population characteristics, the definition and classification of which are much more complex because they involve numerous categories and are subject to alternative formulation as a result of cultural differences, differences in the uses to which the data will be put, and differences in the interpretations of respondents and enumerators.

Age is a more complex demographic characteristic than sex. The age of an individual in censuses is commonly defined in terms of the age of the person at his or her last birthday. Other definitions are possible and have been used. In some cases, age has been defined in terms of the age at the nearest birthday or even the next birthday, but these definitions are no longer employed in national censuses.

In some countries, individuals provide their age in terms of a lunar-based calendar. For example, in some East Asian countries, such as China, Korea, and Singapore, age may be reckoned on this basis (Saw, 1967). Under the lunar-based Chinese calendar system, an individual is assigned an age of 1 at birth, and then becomes a year older on each Chinese New Year's day. Furthermore, the lunar year is a few days shorter than the solar year. Accordingly, a person may be as much as 3 years older, and is always at least 1 year older than under the Western definition. Another example of a lunar-based system is the Islamic calendar (or Hejira calendar), but unlike the Chinese system, age is affected only by the shorter length (354 or 355 days) of the lunar year.

Even though individuals may be requested to provide a date of birth using the solar calendar, some respondents may only know their lunar birth date. Conversion from the Chinese system to the Gregorian (Western) calendar is possible, given the age based on the Chinese calendar, the "animal year" of birth, and information as to whether or not the birthday is located between New Year's day and the census date.[2] For example, in the 2000 census of China, enumerators were to fill in the Gregorian date of birth. If the respondent only knew the lunar birth month, enumerators were instructed to add one month to the lunar birth month to obtain the Gregorian birth month (with a note of caution that the 12th month in the lunar year is the first month in the next Gregorian year). Enumerators also were told to view the respondent's household registration book or personal identity card to find the Gregorian date of birth (China State Council Population Census Office, 2000).

The United Nations' (UN) (1998, p. 69) recommendation favors the Western approach, defining age as "the interval of time between the date of birth and the date of the census, expressed in completed solar years." Nevertheless, the elderly and the less literate residents of countries where other calendar systems are used would have difficulty in supplying this information.

Whatever the definition, the age actually recorded in a census may vary depending on whether the definition is applied as of the reference date of the census or as of the date of the actual enumeration, which may spread out over several days, weeks, or even months. If, as in the U.S. census of 1950, age is secured by a question on "age" and is recorded as of the date of the enumeration, the age distribution as tabulated, in effect, more nearly reflects the situation as of the median date of the enumeration than of the official census date. In the 1950 census of the United States, the median date of enumeration was about 1½ months after the official reference date. In the 1990 census of the United States, even though the respondents were requested to provide their age as of April 1, 1990, review of detailed 1990 information indicated that they tended to provide their age as of the date of completion of the questionnaire and to round up their age if they were close to having a birthday (Spencer, Word, and Hollman, 1992). In those censuses in which the enumeration is confined to a single day, week, or even month or where age is primarily ascertained on the basis of census reports on date of birth (e.g., United States, 1960 to 1980, and 2000), the age distribution given in the census reports reflects the situation on the census date quite closely.

Age data collected in censuses or national sample surveys may be tabulated in single years of age, 5-year age groups, or broader groups. The UN (1998, p. 159) recommendations

---

[2] The Chinese New Year always falls in either January or February; hence, there are always two animals in a Western solar calendar year. The first lasts for about 20 to 50 days and the second for the rest of the year.

for population and housing censuses call for tabulations of the national total, urban, and rural populations, for each major and minor civil division (separately for their urban and rural parts), and for each principal locality, in single years of age to 100. If tabulating by single year of age is considered inadvisable for any particular geographic area, then the age data should at least be tabulated in 5-year age groups (under 1, 1–4, 5–9, . . . 80–84, 85 and over). These data should also be tabulated by sex, and the category "not stated" should also be shown, if applicable. In order to fill the many demands for age data, both for specific ages and special combinations of ages, it is necessary to have tabulations in single years of age. Moreover, detailed age is required for cross-classification with several characteristics that change sharply from age to age over parts of the age range (e.g., school enrollment, labor force status, and marital status). However, 5-year data in the conventional age groups are satisfactory for most cross-classifications (e.g., nativity, country of birth, ethnic groups, and socioeconomic status). Broader age groups may be employed in cross-tabulations for smaller areas or in cross-tabulations containing a large number of variables.

When date-of-birth information is collected in a census or sample survey, the recommended method for converting it to age at last birthday is to subtract the exact date of birth from the date of the census or survey. The resulting ages, in whole years, could then be tabulated by single years or classified into age groups, as desired. Some countries, such as France (1994) in its 1990 census, "double classify" the data by date of birth and by age in completed years at the census date of birth and the year of the census. It is useful for some purposes to tabulate and publish the data in terms of calendar year of birth. Such tabulations are of particular value for use in combination with vital statistics (deaths, marriages) tabulated by year of birth.

Basis of Securing Data

Data on age and sex are secured through direct questions. The data on sex are simply secured by asking each person to report either male or female. Data on age may be secured by asking a direct question on age, by asking a question on date of birth, or month and year of birth (satisfactory if census day is on the first day of the month), or by asking both questions in combination. Inquiry regarding date of birth often occurred in European countries, and elsewhere a direct question on age was more common. In recent years, the use of both an age and a date-of-birth question has become more common.

In general, the information on age in the censuses of the United States had been secured by asking a direct question on age. However, in the 1900 census and in each census since 1960, the information was obtained by a question on age and date (or month and year) of birth, or by a question

on date of birth only (1960). The 1970 and 1980 censuses asked for age and quarter and year of birth, while the 1990 census asked for age and year of birth only. Census 2000 was the first U.S. census to ask for age and complete date of birth (month, day, year). The Current Population Survey secures information on age through questions on age and date (month and year) of birth.

The UN recommendations allow for securing information on age either by inquiring about date of birth or by asking directly for age at last birthday. The United Nations recommends asking date of birth for children reported as "1 year of age," even if a direct question on age is used for the remainder of the population, to obviate the tendency to report "1 year of age" for persons "0 years of age."

Direct reports on age are simpler to process but appear to give less accurate information on age than reports on date of birth, possibly because a question on age more easily permits approximate replies. On the other hand, the proportion of the population for which date of birth is not reported is ordinarily higher than for age, and the date-of-birth approach is hardly applicable to relatively illiterate populations. In such situations, where concepts of age have little meaning, individuals may be assigned to broad age groups on the basis of birth before or after certain major historical events affecting the population. Examples of countries using event calendars in their censuses include Papua New Guinea, 1980; Mozambique, 1997; and South Africa, 2001.

Sources of Data

The importance of age and sex classifications in censuses, surveys, and registrations has been widely recognized.[3] Wherever national population censuses have been taken, sex has nearly always been included among those subjects for which information was secured. Census or survey data for males and females are presented for nearly all countries of the world in a table annually included in the UN *Demographic Yearbook*. Recent census data or estimates of the age-sex distribution are also presented for most countries in another table of the *Yearbook*.

A classification by sex has been part of the U.S. census from its very beginning.[4] At first, data were collected and tabulated on the number of males and females in the white population only; but, from 1820 on, the total population and each identified racial group were classified by sex. Regional detail is available from 1820, and data by size of community from 1890. The first classification of sex by single years of age was published in 1880. Estimates of the sex distribution of the population cross-classified with age and color for the United States as a whole are available for each year

---

[3] See United Nations (1958, p. 9; 1967, pp. 40 and 67–69; and 1998, pp. 58–59 and 69).

[4] See U.S. Bureau of the Census (1965, Series A 23 and 24; and 1975, Series A 91–104; 1960a, Series A 23, 24, 34, and 35).

since 1900, and projections of the population by sex (also by age, race, and Hispanic origin) are available to 2100.[5] Almost every characteristic for which data are shown in the 1990 U.S. census reports was cross-classified with sex. This is true also of the U.S. Current Population Survey. Cross-classification with sex is also a common practice in the U.S. vital statistics tabulations.

For many countries, census counts or estimates of age distributions, both for single years of age and for broader age groups, are published in various issues of the United Nations' *Demographic Yearbook*. Such data generally are also available in the published census reports of the individual countries.

The U.S. Census Bureau has published data on the age and sex distribution of the population of the United States from almost the very beginning of the country's existence. Data for five broad age groups by sex are available for 1800. The amount of age detail increased with subsequent censuses until 1880, when, for the first time, data for 5-year age groups and for single years of age were published. Data classified by race and sex in broad age groups first became available in 1820, and subsequently the age detail shown was tabulated by sex and race. Tabulations for states accompanied the national tabulations in each census year.

Quality of Data

The principal problem relating to the quality of the data on sex collected in censuses concerns the difference in the completeness of coverage of the two sexes. At least in the statistically developed countries, misreporting of sex is negligible; there appears to be little or no reason for a tendency for one sex to be reported at the expense of the other. The reports on sex in the 1960 census of the United States and in the accompanying reinterview study differed by about 1% of the matched population. Because of misreporting of sex in both directions, the net reporting error in the 1960 census indicated by this match study was less than 0.5%.[6] In some countries, deliberate misreporting of sex may be more serious. Parents may report young boys as girls so that they may avoid the attention of evil spirits or so that they may be overlooked when their cohort is called up for military service. The same factors may contribute to differential underenumeration of the two sexes.

How complete are the census counts of males and females? Although there are no ideal standards against

[5] See U.S. Census Bureau (2000b), http://www.census.gov/population/www/projections/natproj.html.

[6] See U.S. Bureau of the Census (1964, p. 10). Although data on sex have continued to be collected in reinterview studies since 1960, the quality of these data has been assumed to remain very high and the subsequent census reinterview study reports did not include comparable analyses of the data on sex. A special tabulation of the 1990 reinterview data indicated that the gross differences in the reporting of sex amounted to about 1% of the matched population, with a net reporting error still less than 0.5%.

TABLE 7.1   Estimates of Net Underenumeration in the Census of Population, by Sex, for the United States: 1980 and 1990

Year and sex	Post-enumeration survey[1]		Demographic analysis[2]	
	Number (in thousands)	Percentage[3]	Number (in thousands)	Percentage[3]
1980				
Total	NA	1.0 to 2.1	3,171	1.4
Male	NA	1.2 to 2.6	2,675	2.4
Female	NA	0.8 to 1.7	496	0.4
1990				
Total	4,003	1.6	4,684	1.8
Male	2,384	1.9	3,480	2.8
Female	1,619	1.3	1,204	0.9

NA: Data not available.

[1] For 1980, implied range based on 9 of 12 alternative estimates from the 1980 Post Enumeration Program (PEP) provided in U.S. Bureau of the Census/Fay *et al.* (1988, Table 8.2). The remaining alternative estimates implied a net overcount of the population. For 1990, unpublished U.S. Census Bureau tabulations.

[2] For 1980, see U.S. Bureau of the Census/Fay *et al.* (1988, Table 3.2). For 1990, see Robinson *et al.* (1993, Table 1).

[3] Base is corrected population.

which the accuracy of census data can be measured, it is possible to derive some indication of both the relative and absolute completeness of enumeration of males and females. For the most part, these techniques are essentially the same as those used to evaluate total population coverage and would include reinterview studies, the use of external checks (e.g., Selective Service registration data and Social Security account holders), and various techniques of demographic analysis, such as the application of the population component estimating equation separately for each sex. Illustrative results for the United States in 1980 and 1990 are given in Table 7.1.

The errors in the reporting of age have probably been examined more intensively than the reporting errors for any other question in the census. Three factors may account for this intensive study: many of these errors are readily apparent, measurement techniques can be more easily developed for age data, and actuaries have had a special practical need to identify errors and to refine the reported data for use in the construction of life tables. Errors in the tabulated data on age may arise from the following types of errors of enumeration: coverage errors, failure to record age, and misreporting of age. There is some tendency for the types of errors in age data to offset one another; the extent to which this occurs depends not only on the nature and magnitude of the errors but also on the grouping of the data, as will be described more fully later in this discussion.

Before discussing the specific methodology of measuring errors in data on age, it is useful to consider the general features of errors in age data in somewhat more detail. The defects in census figures for a given age or age group resulting from coverage errors and misreporting of age may each be considered further in terms of the component errors. Coverage errors are of two types. Individuals of a given age may have been missed by the census or erroneously included in it (e.g., counted twice). The first type of coverage error represents *gross underenumeration* at this age and the second type represents *gross overenumeration*. The balance of the two types of coverage errors represents *net underenumeration* at this age. (Because underenumeration commonly exceeds overenumeration, we shall typically designate the balance in this way.)

In addition, the ages of some individuals included in the census may not have been reported, or may have been erroneously reported by the respondent, erroneously estimated by the enumerator, or erroneously allocated by the census office. A complete array of census reports of age in comparison with the true ages of the persons enumerated would show the number of persons at each age for whom age was correctly reported in the census, the number of persons incorrectly reporting "into" each age from lower or higher ages, and the number of persons incorrectly reporting "out" of each age into higher or lower ages. Such tabulations permit calculation of measures of *gross misreporting* of age, referred to also as *response variability* of age. If, however, we disregard the identity of individuals and allow for the offsetting effect of reporting "into" and reporting "out of" given ages, much smaller errors are found than are shown by the gross errors based on comparison of reports for individuals. Such *net misreporting* of a characteristic is also referred to as *response bias*. The combination of net underenumeration and net misreporting for a given age is termed *net census undercount* (net census overcount, if the number in the age is overstated) or *net census error.*

For example, the group of persons reporting age 42 in the census consists of (1) persons whose correct age is 42 and (2) those whose correct age is over or under 42 but who erroneously report age 42. The latter group is offset partly or wholly by (3) the number erroneously reporting "out of" age 42 into older or younger ages. The difference between groups 2 and 3 represents the net misreporting error for age 42. In addition, the census count at age 42 is affected by net underenumeration at this age (i.e., by the balance of the number of persons aged 42 omitted from the census and the number of persons aged 42 who are erroneously included in the census).

Where the data are grouped into 5-year groups or broader groups, both the gross and net misreporting errors are smaller than the corresponding errors for single ages because misreporting of age within the broader intervals has no effect. On the other hand, the amount of net underenumeration will tend to accumulate and grow as the age interval widens, because omissions will tend to exceed erroneous

inclusions at each age. For the total population, the amount of net underenumeration and the amount of net census undercount are the same because net age misreporting balances out to zero over all ages.

Many of the measures of error do not serve directly as a basis for adjusting the errors in the data. One may distinguish between the degree of precision required to evaluate a set of age data and the degree of precision required to correct it. Yet a sharp distinction cannot be made between the measurement of errors in census data and procedures for adjusting the census data to eliminate or reduce these errors; accordingly, these two subjects are best treated in combination. Some of the measures of error in age data are simply indexes describing the relative level of error for an entire distribution or most of it. The indexes may refer to only a small segment of the age distribution, to various ages, or to particular classes of ages (e.g., ages with certain terminal digits). Other procedures provide only estimates of relative error for age groups (i.e., the extent of error in a given census relative to the error in an earlier census in the same category or relative to another category in the same census). Still other measures of error involve the preparation of alternative estimates of the population for an age or age group that presumably are free of the types of errors under consideration. A carefully developed index for a particular age or age group, or an alternative estimate of the actual population or of its relative size, may then serve as the basis for adjusting the erroneous census count.

The techniques for evaluating and analyzing data on age and sex composition are related, particularly those for evaluating and analyzing age data. They often are best applied separately to the age distributions of the male and female populations. This chapter discusses these measures and methods under the following headings: (1) Analysis of Sex Composition, (2) Analysis of Deficiencies in Age Data, and (3) Analysis of Age Composition.

ANALYSIS OF SEX COMPOSITION

Numerical Measures

The numerical measures of sex composition are few and simple to compute. They are (1) the percentage of males in the population, or the masculinity proportion; (2) the sex ratio, or the masculinity ratio; and (3) the ratio of the excess or deficit of males to the total population. The mere excess or deficit of males is affected by the size of the population and is not, therefore, a very useful measure for making comparisons of one population group with another. The three measures listed are all useful for interarea or intergroup comparisons, or comparisons over time, because in one way or another they remove or reduce the effect of variations in population size. These measures are occasionally defined in terms of females, but conventionally they are defined in terms of males.

The *masculinity proportion* (or percentage male, or its complement, the percentage female) is the measure of sex composition most often used in nontechnical discussions. The formula for the masculinity proportion is

$$\frac{P_m}{P_t} \times 100 \tag{7.1}$$

where P_m represents the number of males and P_t the total population.[7] Let us apply the formula to Venezuela in 1990. The 1990 census showed 9,019,757 males and a total population of 18,105,265. Therefore, the masculinity proportion is

$$\frac{9,019,757}{18,105,265} \times 100 = 49.8\%$$

Fifty is the point of balance of the sexes, or the standard, according to this measure. A higher figure denotes an excess of males and a lower figure denotes an excess of females. The masculinity proportion of national populations varies over a rather narrow range, usually falling just below 50, unless exceptional historical circumstances have prevailed.

The *sex ratio* is the principal measure of sex composition used in technical studies. The sex ratio is usually defined as the number of males per 100 females, or

$$\frac{P_m}{P_f} \times 100 \tag{7.2}$$

where P_m, as before, represents the number of males and P_f the number of females. Given the male population as 9,019,757 and the female population as 9,085,508, the formula may be computed for Venezuela in 1990 as follows:

$$\frac{9,019,757}{9,085,508} \times 100 = 99.3$$

One hundred is the point of balance of the sexes according to this measure. A sex ratio above 100 denotes an excess of males; a sex ratio below 100 denotes an excess of females. Accordingly, the greater the excess of males, the higher the sex ratio; the greater the excess of females, the lower the sex ratio.

This form of the sex ratio is sometimes called the masculinity ratio. The sex ratio is also sometimes defined as the number of females per 100 males. This has been the official

practice in some countries in Eastern Europe, such as Bulgaria and Hungary, or in South Asia, such as India, but the United Nations as well as most countries follow the former definition.

The sex ratio of the Venezuelan population might be described as "typical" or a little above the typical level. In general, national sex ratios tend to fall in the narrow range from about 95 to 102, barring special circumstances, such as a history of heavy war losses or heavy immigration. National sex ratios outside the range of 90 to 105 are to be viewed as extreme.

Variations in the sex ratio are similar to those in the masculinity proportion. The sex ratio is a more sensitive indicator of differences in sex composition because it has a relatively smaller base.

The third measure of sex composition, the *excess (or deficit) of males as a percentage of the total population*, is given by the following formula:

$$\frac{P_m - P_f}{P_t} \times 100 \tag{7.3}$$

Again, employing the data for Venezuela in this formula, we obtain

$$\frac{9,019,757 - 9,085,508}{18,105,265} \times 100 = -0.4\%$$

This figure indicates that the deficit of males amounts to 0.4% of the total population. The point of balance of the sexes according to this measure, or the standard, is zero; a positive value denotes an excess of males and a negative value denotes an excess of females. It may be evident that the various measures of sex composition convey essentially the same information. Sometimes it is desired to convert the masculinity proportion into the sex ratio or the percentage excess (or deficit) of males, or the reverse, in the absence of the basic data on the numbers of males and females. These conversions may be effected by use of the following formulas, the application of which is illustrated with figures for Venezuela in 1990.[8]

Masculinity proportion

$$= \frac{\text{Sex ratio}}{1 + \text{Sex ratio}} \times 100 = \frac{.9928}{1.9928} \times 100 = 49.8\% \tag{7.4}$$

---

[7] The multiple of 10, or the *k* factor, employed to shift the decimal in this and other formulas, is often arbitrary and conventional. The particular *k* factor employed in a given formula may sometimes vary from one reference to another in this volume where there is no conventional *k* factor. Where there is a conventional *k* factor for a given formula, this factor has ordinarily been accepted for use here.

[8] In general, correct intermediate algebraic manipulation of the formulas presented requires that this manipulation be done on the basis of formulas omitting the *k* factor. For example, the sex ratio should be represented merely by $P_m \div P_f$ and the masculinity proportion by $P_m \div P_t$. The appropriate *k* factor may then be applied at the end. In general, in numerically applying a formula, one should carry in the intermediate calculations at least one additional significant figure beyond the number of significant figures to be shown in the result. Then the "result" figure may be rounded as desired.

Sex ratio $= \dfrac{\text{Masculinity proportion}}{1 - \text{Masculinity proportion}} \times 100$

$= \dfrac{.4982}{1 - .4982} \times 100 = \dfrac{.4982}{.5018} \times 100 = 99.3$ \hfill (7.5)

Percentage excess or deficit of males =

[Masculinity proportion $- (1 - $ Masculinity proportion)]

$\times 100 = [.4982 - (1 - .4982)] \times 100 = (.4982 - .5018) \times 100$

$= -.0036 \times 100 = -0.4\%$ \hfill (7.6)

Thus, if we divide the masculinity proportion (omitting the k factor) for Venezuela in 1990, .4982, by its complement, .5018, and multiply by 100, we obtain 99.3 as the sex ratio, the same value obtained earlier by direct computation. Or if we divide the sex ratio, .9928 by 1 plus the sex ratio, 1.9928, and multiply by 100, we obtain 49.8 as the masculinity proportion. A summary of each of these three measures of sex composition for various countries around 1990 is shown in Table 7.2.

There are few graphic devices that are designed specifically for description and analysis of sex composition. Principal among these is the population pyramid. Inasmuch as age is ordinarily combined with sex in the "content" of these devices, particularly in the case of the population pyramid, discussion of their construction and interpretation is postponed until later in the chapter. The standard graphic devices, including bar charts, line graphs, and pie charts,

TABLE 7.2 Calculation of Measures of Sex Composition for Various Countries: Around 1990

Continent or world region, country, and year	Population (in thousands)			Masculinity proportion [(1) ÷ (3)] × 100 = (4)	Sex ratio [(1) ÷ (2)] × 100 = (5)	Percentage excess or deficit of males [(1) − (2)] ÷ (3) × 100 = (6)
	Male (1)	Female (2)	Total (3)			
Africa						
Botswana (1991)	634	692	1,327	47.8	91.6	−4.4
South Africa (1991)	15,480	15,507	30,987	50.0	99.8	−0.1
Uganda (1991)	8,186	8,486	16,672	49.1	96.5	−1.8
Zimbabwe (1992)	5,084	5,329	10,413	48.8	95.4	−2.4
North America						
Canada (1991)	13,455	13,842	27,297	49.3	97.2	−1.4
Mexico (1990)	39,894	41,355	81,250	49.1	96.5	−1.8
United States (1990)	121,239	127,470	248,710	48.7	95.1	−2.5
South America						
Argentina (1991)	15,938	16,678	32,616	48.9	95.6	−2.3
Brazil (1991)	72,485	74,340	146,825	49.4	97.5	−1.3
Chile (1992)	6,553	6,795	13,348	49.1	96.4	−1.8
Venezuela (1990)	9,020	9,086	18,105	49.8	99.3	−0.4
Asia						
Bangladesh (1991)	54,728	51,587	106,315	51.5	106.1	+3.0
China (1990)	585,476	549,599	1,135,075	51.6	106.5	+3.2
India (1991)	435,208	403,360	838,568	51.9	107.9	+3.8
Indonesia (1990)	89,376	89,872	179,248	49.9	99.4	−0.3
Japan (1990)	60,697	62,914	123,611	49.1	96.5	−1.8
Malaysia (1991)	8,877	8,687	17,563	50.5	102.2	+1.1
Philippines (1990)	30,443	30,116	60,559	50.3	101.1	+0.5
South Korea (1990)	21,771	21,619	43,390	50.2	100.7	+0.3
Vietnam (1989)	31,337	33,075	64,412	48.7	94.7	−2.7
Europe						
Austria (1991)	3,754	4,042	7,796	48.2	92.9	−3.7
France (1990)	27,554	29,081	56,634	48.7	94.8	−2.7
Hungary (1990)	4,985	5,390	10,375	48.0	92.5	−3.9
Portugal (1991)	4,755	5,108	9,863	48.2	93.1	−3.6
Russia (1989)	68,714	78,308	147,022	46.7	87.7	−6.5
Sweden (1990)	4,242	4,345	8,587	49.4	97.6	−1.2
United Kingdom (1991)	27,344	29,123	56,467	48.4	93.9	−3.1
Oceania						
Australia (1991)	8,363	8,488	16,850	49.6	98.5	−0.7
New Zealand (1991)	1,663	1,711	3,374	49.3	97.1	−1.4

Source: Derived from U.S. Census Bureau (2000a, Table 4), www.census.gov/ipc/www/idbacc.html.

TABLE 7.3   Sex Ratios by Region and Residence, for the United States: 1990 (Males per 100 females)

Residence	United States Population (in thousands) Male (1)	Female (2)	Sex ratio [(1) ÷ (2)] × 100 (3)	Northeast (4)	Midwest (5)	South (6)	West (7)
Total	121,239	127,470	95.1	92.7	94.4	94.4	99.6
Urban	90,386	96,667	93.5	90.9	92.0	92.6	98.6
Rural	30,853	30,803	100.2	99.4	100.7	98.5	106.3

Source: Derived from U.S. Census Bureau (1992, Tables 14, 64, 114, 164, and 214).

are available, however, for depicting differences in sex composition from group to group or over time for a particular group.

The sex ratio is the most widely used measure of sex composition and we will give primary attention to it in the remaining discussion of the analysis of sex composition.

Analysis of Sex Ratios in Terms of Population Subgroups

Because the sex ratio may vary widely from one population subgroup to another, it is frequently desirable to consider separately the sex ratios of the important component subgroups in any detailed analysis of the sex composition of a population group. Account may be taken of these variations in the analysis of the overall level of the sex ratio at any date and of the differences in the sex ratio from area to area or from one population group to another.

For the United States in 1990, notably different sex ratios were recorded for the separate race, nativity, residence, regional, and age groups in the population (see Tables 7.3 and 7.4 for illustrative figures). The marked deficit of males in the urban population may be compared with the slight excess of males in the rural population. Historically, the urban population has had lower sex ratios principally because of the greater migration of females to cities. The sex ratio also varies widely among regions. Thus, the sex ratio is quite low in the Northeast and in approximate balance in the West. The marked excess of females for the black population may be compared with the marked excess of males among the Hispanic population.

Sex ratios for age groups vary widely around the sex ratio for the total population. For many analytic purposes, this variation may be considered the most important. The sex ratio tends to be high at the very young ages and then tends to decrease with increasing age. "Young" populations and populations with high birthrates tend to have higher overall sex ratios than "old" populations and populations with low birthrates because of the excess of boys among

TABLE 7.4   Sex Ratios by Race and Hispanic Origin, by Nativity, and by Age, for the United States: 1990 (Males per 100 females)

Race and Hispanic origin, and nativity	Sex ratio	Age (years)	Sex ratio
Total, all races	95.1	Total, all ages	95.1
Race and Hispanic Origin		Under 5	104.8
White	95.4	5 to 9	104.8
Non-Hispanic	95.0	10 to 14	105.0
Black	89.6	15 to 19	105.2
American Indian, Eskimo, and Aleut	97.5	20 to 24	103.5
		25 to 34	99.9
Asian and Pacific Islander	95.8	35 to 44	97.9
		45 to 54	95.6
Hispanic (of any race)	103.8	55 to 64	89.4
		65 to 74	78.1
Nativity		75 to 84	59.9
Native	94.9	85 and over	38.6
Foreign born	95.8		

Source: Derived from U.S. Census Bureau (1992, Table 16, and 1993a, Table 1).

births and children and the excess of male deaths at the older ages.

Analysis of Changes

It is frequently desired to explain in demographic terms the change in the sex composition of the population from one census to another. What is called for is a quantitative indication of how the components of population change—births, deaths, immigrants, and emigrants—contributed to the change in sex composition.

Unfortunately, such an analysis is complicated by the lack of perfect consistency between the data on the components of change and census data with respect to the intercensal change implied. It was pointed out earlier that coverage of males and females is likely to be different in a particular census and between censuses. Errors in the census data as reported and in the data on components of change affect the apparent change to be explained. It is desirable, therefore, in any analysis of changes shown by census figures, to take into account the errors in the census data and in the data on components. The errors in the census data cannot usually be determined very closely, however. If it can be assumed that the estimates of the components are satisfactory, the "error of closure" for each sex may be used as an estimate of change in the net coverage of each sex between the two censuses.

For simplicity, and in view of the lack of adequate information, we will generally assume in the following discussion that the data on components are substantially correct and reasonably consistent with the census figures as observed.

Change in Excess or Deficit of Males

The formula for analyzing the change between two censuses in the excess or deficit of males in terms of components may be developed from the separate equations representing the male and female populations at a given census (P_m^1 and P_f^1) in terms of the male and female populations at the preceding census (P_m^0 and P_f^0) and the male and female components of change (B_m and B_f for births, D_m and D_f for deaths, I_m and I_f for immigrants or in-migrants, and E_m and E_f for emigrants or out-migrants):

$$P_m^1 = P_m^0 + B_m - D_m + I_m - E_m \qquad (7.7)$$

$$P_f^1 = P_f^0 + B_f - D_f + I_f - E_f \qquad (7.8)$$

These are merely the usual intercensal or component equations expressed separately for males and females. Solving these equations for $P_m^1 - P_m^0$ and $P_f^1 - P_f^0$ (that is, the increase in the male and female population, respectively) and taking the difference between them, we have, for the intercensal change in the difference between the numbers of males and females:

$$(P_m^1 - P_f^1) - (P_m^0 - P_f^0)$$
$$= (B_m - B_f) - (D_m - D_f) + (I_m - I_f) - (E_m - E_f) \qquad (7.9)$$

Table 7.5 illustrates the application of this equation to the data for the United States in the period 1980 to 1990. Each item in Formula (7.9) is represented in Table 7.5, except that immigration and emigration are combined as net immigration. The table shows first that the excess of females decreased from 6,439,000 in 1980 to 6,231,000 in 1990, or by 208,000. The excess of males from net immigration outweighed the excess of females from the natural increase of the population. While 933,000 more males than females were being added through birth, 1,143,000 more males than females were being removed through death. This net excess of 210,000 females through natural increase was offset by the contribution of net migration, which added 325,000

TABLE 7.5 Component Analysis of the Change in the Difference between the Number of Males and Females in the United States: 1980–1990 (numbers in thousands)

Population or component of change	Male	Female	Difference[1]
Population (census)			
April 1, 1980	110,053	116,493	−6,439
April 1, 1990	121,239	127,470	−6,231
Change during decade			
Net change	11,186	10,978	+208
Births	19,280	18,346	+933
Deaths	(−)10,919	(−)9,776	(−)1,143
Net immigration	3,535	3,211	+325
Civilian	3,416	3,143	+274
Military	119	68	+51
Residual[2]	(−)710	(−)803	+94

[1] A plus sign denotes an excess of males. A minus sign denotes an excess of females.

[2] Difference between the intercensal change based on the two census counts and the intercensal change based on the "component" data (i.e., the error of closure).

Source: Derived from U.S. Census Bureau (1993b, Table F) and unpublished tabulations.

more males than females. The remainder (94,000) represents the difference between males and females in the error of closure.

Change in Sex Ratios in Terms of Components

It is of interest to analyze the difference, in terms of components, between the current sex ratio and a sex ratio of 100 representing a balance of the sexes (such as might result from the action of births and deaths in the absence of heavy migration).

Sex Ratio of Births

From an examination of the sex ratios of registered births for a wide array of countries, it is apparent that the component of births tends to bring about or to maintain an excess of males in the general population. The sex ratio of births is above 100 for nearly all countries for which relatively complete data are available and between 104 and 107 in most such countries (see Table 7.6).

Careful analysis relating to the sex ratio of births should take into account significant variations in this measure according to the demographic characteristics of the child and the parents. Among the important demographic characteristics that appear to distinguish births with respect to their sex ratio are age of parents, order of birth of child, and race. Studies based on data for the U.S. and other developed countries have shown, that there is an inverse relationship between the level of the sex ratio and the age of the

TABLE 7.6   Sex Ratios at Birth in Various Countries with Relatively Complete Registration (Male births per 100 female births)

Country	Period	Sex ratio	Country	Period	Sex ratio
Africa			*Asia*		
Egypt	1983–89	105.4	Japan	1983–91	105.6
Tunisia	1985–89	106.8	Malaysia	1983–92	107.4
			Sri Lanka	1983–87	104.4
North America					
Cuba	1983–88	106.9	*Europe*		
Guatemala	1983–88	103.8	France	1983–90	105.1
Panama	1983–90	105.4	Hungary	1983–91	105.0
United States	1983–88	105.1	Netherlands	1983–91	104.7
			Poland	1983–91	105.8
South America			Romania	1986–91	105.0
Chile	1983–91	104.7	United Kingdom	1983–91	105.2
Uruguay	1983–88	105.5			
Venezuela	1983–91	105.1	*Oceania*		
			Australia	1983–91	105.4
			New Zealand	1983–90	105.1

Source: Derived from United Nations (1994, Table 16).

father and the order of birth of the child, and that the sex ratio of white births exceeds that for the black population (Chahnazarian, 1988).[9] The difference between the sex ratio of births of whites and blacks has been observed more widely, based on comparisons of countries with mainly white populations and countries with mainly black populations.

Another factor that may affect the sex ratio of births is the socioeconomic status of the parents. A predominance of male births has been observed among higher socioeconomic groups in Western countries.[10] It may be explained in part by the predominance of lower order births when fertility is low and the lower rate of prenatal deaths. Similar information on the relationship between socioeconomic status and the sex ratio of births is not available for the less developed countries.

In recent years, the development and increased availability of the technology to identify the gender of a fetus has emerged as another factor affecting the sex ratio at birth, particularly in those countries with a strong cultural preference for sons. For example, Park and Cho (1995), Das Gupta and Bhat (1997), and Coale and Banister (1994), identified the importance of sex-selective abortion in the increase of the observed sex ratio at birth in South Korea, India, and China, respectively.

For areas with incomplete reporting of births, the observed sex ratio of births may be suspect. In some less

developed countries with a low level of literacy, a low percentage of the population living in urban areas, and a low percentage of births occurring in hospitals, male births are more likely to be registered than female births. Statistics on births occurring in hospitals and health centers in such countries generally result in more plausible sex ratios at birth.

Sex Ratio of Deaths

The sex ratio of deaths is much more variable from country to country than the sex ratio of births. Data for a wide range of countries indicate sex ratios well above 100 in many cases. Because this factor operates in a negative fashion, the component of deaths has tended to depress the sex ratio of most populations. High sex ratios of deaths (more than 120) occurred in recent years in Argentina, Cuba, Guatelmala, Mexico, and South Korea. Low ratios (less than 105) occurred in the Czech Republic, Denmark, Germany, and the United States. Intermediate ratios (105 to 120) occurred in Australia, Canada, Egypt, Japan, New Zealand, and Russia. National differences in the sex ratio of deaths may be accounted for partly by differences from country to country in the age-sex structure of the population and partly by differences in death rates for each age-sex group.

Demographic characteristics important in the further analysis of the sex ratio of deaths include age, race, ethnic group, educational level, and marital status. Sex ratios of deaths in the United States for broad classes defined by each of these characteristics for 1998 are as follows:

[9] Also see Ruder (1985), McMahan (1951), Myers (1954), and Macmahon and Pugh (1953).

[10] See Teitelbaum and Mantel (1971) and Winston (1931, 1932).

White	96.5	Married[a]	221.5
Black	106.2	Widowed[a]	32.3
All other races	123.3	All other[a]	134.8
Hispanic	131.1	Under 12 years completed	178.7[b]
Not Hispanic	96.8	12 years completed	156.4[b]
Under 65 years of age	166.1	13 years and over completed	161.5[b]
65 years of age and over	82.5		

[a] 15 years and over.

[b] 25–64 years of age; excludes age not stated.

There also are pronounced regional variations in the sex ratio of deaths in the United States. Figures for the several states ranged from 86.7 for Massachusetts to 139.6 for Alaska. As for countries, these variations are associated with differences in the composition of the population with respect to age, sex, and other characteristics, as well as with differences in death rates for these categories.

An important analytic question relates to the basis for the difference between male and female death rates. Both biological and cultural factors contribute to the sex differential in mortality (Gage, 1994). Historically, differences in the occupational distribution of the sexes illustrated the role of cultural factors; generally men worked at more physically demanding occupations. On the other hand, many women are exposed to the special risks of childbearing. The weight of biological forces is reflected in the higher mortality of male infants and fetuses. Since the 1970s, the sex differential in mortality has narrowed in some developed counties, including the United States (Trovato and Lalu, 1996). This may in part be due to a male-female convergence in some mortality-related behaviors, such as smoking (Waldron, 1993).

A special aspect of the relation of mortality to the sex ratio of a population is the effect of war. For the most part, males generally suffer the heaviest casualties because they alone tend to directly participate in battle. The estimated war-related deaths in Vietnam during the period 1965–1975 of men aged 15 to 29 were more than 7 times higher than expected in the absence of war, compared with 1.4 times for women aged 15 to 29. For men and women aged 15 and over, mortality was about twice as high as expected for men, but only about 20% higher for women (Hirschman, Preston, and Loi, 1995). Changes in the technology and conduct of wars, including particularly the bombing of industrial and administrative centers, may tend to equalize somewhat the extent of military casualties between the sexes. Further analysis of the relation of war to the sex ratio of deaths, designed to show the effect of the shifting number of males in the population at risk, would compare the sex ratio of deaths in the war years and in the immediate postwar period of various involved countries.

Special practices may affect the sex ratio of deaths. Female infanticide (such as in mainland China), the selective tribal killing of male captives, the provision of better care to the children of one sex than the other, and the suttee (in India) illustrate types of practices that have historically occurred in various areas of the world. Some countries in South Asia (e.g., Afghanistan) either recently showed or still show higher death rates for females than for males.

In recent years, HIV/AIDS-related deaths have become an important factor affecting the sex ratio (and the age composition) of deaths. An assessment model of the HIV-1 epidemic in sub-Saharan Africa indicated that large changes in the adult sex ratio and the age distribution of the economically active population were expected outcomes (Gregson, Garnet, and Anderson, 1994). In sub-Saharan Africa, more women than men are HIV-positive. Projections for South Africa, a country with a very high HIV prevalence rate, imply that by 2020 the mortality for women will peak during the ages of 30 to 34, while for men the projected peak is in the age group of 40 to 44 years (Stanecki, 2000).

Sex Ratio of Migrants

The sex ratio of migrants has been less uniform from area to area and has often shown more extreme values (above or below 100) than the sex ratio of either births or deaths. Immigrants to Colombia, Ecuador, and Italy in 1987 had sex ratios of 141, 149, and 152, respectively (United Nations, 1991, Table 30). The corresponding figures for Canada in 1989 and the United States in 1987 were 100 and 97, respectively. Most countries reporting immigration according to sex receive more males than females.

One or the other sex may be attracted in greater numbers to certain areas within countries, depending largely on the types of occupational opportunities and on various cultural factors, particularly customs regarding the separation of family members and the definition of sex roles. Patterns of sex-selectivity of internal migrants to cities differ among the countries and regions of the world. Women have become more predominant in the migration streams to large cities in Southeast Asia (such as Bangkok and Jakarta), for example (ESCAP, 1984). In India, men dominate the interstate migration flows. Women dominate the overall migration flows to rural areas in India, in part reflecting the cultural practice of a woman's moving to her husband's village at marriage (Skeldon, 1986). In Colombia (and other Latin American countries), women have dominated the internal migration streams to urban areas (Martine, 1975).

In the United States, the many office jobs and light factory jobs available in cities have historically attracted mainly women. The factor of internal migration has been an important element in the different sex ratios of the rural and urban populations of the United States. In the migration from rural to urban areas, females have substantially outnumbered males.

Specific cities show considerable variation in sex composition, largely as a result of differences in type of major economic activity. In 1990, the sex ratio was 86.9 for Albany, New York, a state capital; 91.2 for Hartford, Connecticut, a state capital and insurance center; and 105.8 and 115.7 for Anchorage and Fairbanks, Alaska, respectively, the two largest cities of a "frontier" state.

The sex ratio of an area may be affected by certain special features of the area that select certain classes of "migrants." A large military installation, a college for men or women, or an institution confining mainly or entirely persons of a particular sex may be located in the area. The sex ratios of Chattahoochee County, Georgia (193.1), and West Feliciana Parish, Louisiana (211.8), in 1990 illustrate, in part, the effect of the presence of a large military installation (Fort Benning Army Base) and a state penitentiary (Louisiana State Penitentiary), respectively.

It should be clear that the narrow bounds for acceptability of a national sex ratio do not apply to regional or local population or residence categories. Wide deviations from 100 should, however, be explainable in terms of the sex-selective character of migration to and from the specific area and the particular industrial and institutional makeup of the area.

Use of Sex Ratios in Evaluation of Census Data

Because of the relatively limited variability of the national sex ratio and its independence of the absolute numbers of males and females, it is employed in various ways in measuring the quality of census data on sex, particularly in cross-classification with age.

The simplest approach to evaluation of the quality of the data on sex for an area consists of observing the deviation of the sex ratio for the area as a whole from 100, the point of equality of the sexes. With, say, a fairly constant sex ratio at birth of about 105 and a sex ratio of deaths in the range 105 to 125, the sex ratio of a population will fall near 100 in the absence of migration. A sex ratio deviating appreciably from 100—say, below 90 or above 105—must be accounted for in terms of migration (both the volume and sex composition of the migrants being relevant) or a very high death rate, including war mortality. A sex ratio deviating even further from 100—say, above 110 or below 85— must be accounted for in terms of some unusual feature of the area, such as the location of a military installation in the area.

A theoretically more careful evaluation of the data on sex composition of an area at a census date would involve a check of the consistency of the sex ratio shown by the given census with the sex ratio shown by the previous census. For a country as a whole, a direct check can be made by use of the reported data on the components of population change during a decade.

Comparison can also be made between the sex ratio recorded in the census and the sex ratios shown by a post-enumeration survey and by independent estimates based on administrative records. In 1990 for the United States, the census sex ratio was 95.1 compared with a slightly higher 95.8 from the post-enumeration survey and 96.9 from demographic analysis. These figures both reflect a higher undercount of males than females.

ANALYSIS OF DEFICIENCIES IN AGE DATA

We shall consider the types of deficiencies in census tabulations of age under four general headings: (1) errors in single years of age, (2) errors in grouped data, (3) reporting of extreme old age, and (4) failure to report age.

Single Years of Age

Measurement of Age and Digit Preference

A glance at the single-year-of-age data for the population of the Philippines in 1990 (Table 7.7) reveals some obvious irregularities. For example, almost without exception, there is a clustering at ages ending in "0" and corresponding deficiencies at ages ending in "1." Less marked concentrations are found on ages ending in "5."

The figures for adjacent ages should presumably be rather similar. Even though past shifts in the annual number of births, deaths, and migrants can produce fluctuations from one single age to another, the fluctuations observed suggest faulty reporting. The tendency of enumerators or respondents to report certain ages at the expense of others is called age heaping, age preference, or digit preference. The latter term refers to preference for the various ages having the same terminal digit. Age heaping is most pronounced among populations or population subgroups having a low educational status. The causes and patterns of age or digit preference vary from one culture to another, but preference for ages ending in "0" and "5" is quite widespread. In some cultures, certain numbers may be specifically avoided (e.g., 13 in the West and 4 in East Asia). Heaping is the principal type of error in single-year-of-age data, although single ages are also affected by other types of age misreporting, net underenumeration, and nonreporting or misassignment of age. Age 0 is underreported often, for example, because "0" is not regarded as an age by many people and because parents may tend not to think of newborn infants as regular members of the household. In this section we shall confine ourselves to the topic of age heaping—that is, age preference or digit preference.

In principle, a post-enumeration survey or a sample reinterview study should provide considerable information on

TABLE 7.7 Population of the Philippines, by Single
Years of Age: 1990

Age (years)	Number	Age (years)	Number
Total	60,559,116	50	479,514
		51	346,367
Under 1	1,817,270	52	374,204
1	1,639,123	53	349,337
2	1,718,425	54	356,406
3	1,671,136	55	344,552
4	1,621,019	56	288,045
5	1,606,062	57	284,318
6	1,620,740	58	246,928
7	1,636,329	59	275,560
8	1,576,169		
9	1,621,708	60	322,233
		61	205,177
10	1,649,916	62	218,840
11	1,491,967	63	188,670
12	1,505,955	64	192,961
13	1,409,121	65	218,875
14	1,408,773	66	144,388
15	1,376,098	67	152,395
16	1,302,790	68	138,092
17	1,356,104	69	153,870
18	1,329,109		
19	1,276,550	70	182,814
		71	99,902
20	1,335,873	72	102,481
21	1,185,876	73	90,058
22	1,116,887	74	90,084
23	1,053,736	75	106,108
24	1,075,953	76	71,650
25	1,115,735	77	77,058
26	993,664	78	68,917
27	999,845	79	61,911
28	907,680		
29	928,327	80	67,699
		81	32,336
30	1,031,406	82	33,732
31	831,571	83	25,451
32	810,274	84	25,605
33	758,956	85	27,096
34	768,819	86	16,986
35	827,883	87	14,745
36	708,328	88	16,102
37	696,632	89	14,088
38	624,157		
39	644,621	90	9,330
		91	2,875
40	715,657	92	2,596
41	539,663	93	1,667
42	541,519	94	1,577
43	494,726	95	1,838
44	462,278	96	1,059
45	516,270	97	941
46	399,343	98	1,093
47	446,431	99	1,645
48	435,789	100	3,022
49	423,655		

Source: United Nations (1995, Table 26).

the nature and causes of errors of reporting in single ages. A tabulation of the results of the check re-enumeration by single years of age, cross-classified by the original census returns for single years of age, could not only provide an indication of the net errors in reporting both of specific terminal digits and of individual ages but could also provide the basis for an analysis of the errors in terms of the component directional biases characteristic of reporting at specific terminal digits and ages. In practice, however, the size of sample of the reinterview survey ordinarily precludes any evaluation in terms of single ages.

Indexes of Age Preference

In place of sample reinterview studies, various arithmetic devices have been developed for measuring heaping on individual ages or terminal digits. These devices depend on an assumption regarding the form of the true distribution of population by age over a part or all of the age range. On this basis, an estimate of the true number or numbers is developed and compared with the reported number or numbers. The simplest devices assume, in effect, that the true figures are *rectangularly* distributed (i.e., that there are equal numbers in each age) over some age range (such as a 3-year, 5-year, or 7-year age range) that includes and, preferably, is centered on the age being examined. For example, an index of heaping on age 30 in the 1990 census of the Philippines may be calculated as the ratio of the enumerated population aged 30 to one-third of the population aged 29, 30, and 31 (per 100):

$$\frac{P_{30}}{1/3(P_{29}+P_{30}+P_{31})} \times 100 =$$
$$\frac{1,031,406}{1/3(928,327+1,031,406+831,571)} \times 100 = 110.9$$
$$(7.10)$$

or, alternatively, as the ratio of the enumerated population aged 30 to one-fifth of the population aged 28, 29, 30, 31, and 32 (per 100):

$$\frac{P_{30}}{1/5(P_{28}+P_{29}+P_{30}+P_{31}+P_{32})} \times 100 =$$
$$\frac{1,031,406}{1/5(907,680+928,327+1,031,406+831,571+810,274)}$$
$$\times 100 = 114.4 \qquad (7.11)$$

In this case, the two indexes are similar whether a 3-year group or a 5-year group is used; both indicate substantial heaping on age 30. The higher the index, the greater the concentration on the age examined; an index of 100 indicates no concentration on this age. If the age under consideration is centered in the age range selected, the assumption regarding the true form of the distribution may alternatively be regarded as an assumption of *linearity* (that is, that the true figures form an arithmetic progression, or that they increase or decrease by equal amounts from age to age over the range). An assumption of rectangularity or linearity is less and less appropriate as the age range increases (e.g., greater than 7 years).

Whipple's Index

Indexes have been developed to reflect preference for or avoidance of a particular terminal digit or of each terminal digit. For example, employing again the assumption of rectangularity in a 10-year range, we may measure heaping on terminal digit "0" in the range 23 to 62 very roughly by comparing the sum of the populations at the ages ending in "0" in this range with one-tenth of the total population in the range:

$$\frac{\sum (P_{30} + P_{40} + P_{50} + P_{60})}{1/10 \sum (P_{23} + P_{24} + P_{25} + \ldots P_{60} + P_{61} + P_{62})} \times 100 \quad (7.12)$$

Similarly, employing either the assumption of rectangularity or of linearity in a 5-year range, we may measure heaping on multiples of five (terminal digits "0" and "5" combined) in the range 23 to 62 by comparing the sum of the populations at the ages in this range ending in "0" or "5" and one-fifth of the total population in the range:

$$\frac{\sum (P_{25} + P_{30} + \ldots P_{55} + P_{60})}{1/5 \sum (P_{23} + P_{24} + P_{25} + \ldots P_{60} + P_{61} + P_{62})} \times 100$$

$$= \frac{\sum\limits_{23}^{62} P_a \text{ ending in 0 or 5}}{1/5 \sum\limits_{23}^{62} P_a} \times 100 \quad (7.13)$$

For the Philippines in 1990, we have,

$$\frac{5,353,250}{1/5(23,844,399)} \times 100 = \frac{5,353,250}{4,768,880} \times 100 = 112.3$$

The corresponding figure for the United States in 1990 is 104.5. This measure is known as Whipple's index. It varies between 100, representing no preference for "0" or "5," and 500, indicating that only digits "0" and "5" were reported. Accordingly, the Philippines figure shows much more heaping on multiples of "5" compared with the U.S. figure. The population tabulated at these ages for the Philippines may be said to overstate the corresponding unbiased population by about 12%, compared with less than 5% for the United States.

The choice of the range 23 to 62 is largely arbitrary. In computing indexes of heaping, the ages of childhood and old age are often excluded because they are more strongly affected by other types of errors of reporting than by preference for specific terminal digits and the assumption of equal decrements from age to age is less applicable.

The procedure described can be extended theoretically to provide an index for each terminal digit (0, 1, 2, etc.). The population ending in each digit over a given range, say 23 to 82, or 10 to 89, may be compared with one-tenth of the total population in the range, as was done for digit "0" earlier, or it may be expressed as a percentage of the total population in the range. In the latter case, an index of 10% is supposed to indicate an unbiased distribution of terminal digits and, hence, presumably accurate reporting of age. Indexes in excess of 10% indicate a tendency toward preference for a particular digit, and indexes below 10% indicate a tendency toward avoidance of a particular digit.

Myers's Blended Method

Myers (1940) developed a "blended" method to avoid the bias in indexes computed in the way just described that is due to the fact that numbers ending in "0" would normally be larger than the following numbers ending in "1" to "9" because of the effect of mortality. The principle employed is to begin the count at each of the 10 digits in turn and then to average the results. Specifically, the method involves determining the proportion that the population ending in a given digit is of the total population 10 times, by varying the particular starting age for any 10-year age group. Table 7.8 shows the calculation of the indexes of preference for terminal digits in the age range 10 to 89 for the Philippines population in 1990 based on Myers's blended method. In this particular case, the first starting age was 10, then 11, and so on, to 19. The abbreviated procedure of calculation calls for the following steps:

Step 1. Sum the populations ending in each digit over the whole range, starting with the lower limit of the range (e.g., 10, 20, 30, . . . 80; 11, 21, 31, . . . 81).

Step 2. Ascertain the sum excluding the first population combined in step 1 (e.g., 20, 30, 40, . . . 80; 21, 31, 41, . . . 81).

Step 3. Weight the sums in steps 1 and 2 and add the results to obtain a blended population (e.g., weights 1 and 9 for the 0 digit; weights 2 and 8 for the 1 digit).

Step 4. Convert the distribution in step 3 into percentages.

Step 5. Take the deviation of each percentage in step 4 from 10.0, the expected value for each percentage.

The results in step 5 indicate the extent of concentration on or avoidance of a particular digit.[11] The weights in step 3 represent the number of times the combination of ages in step 1 or 2 is included when the starting age is varied from

---

[11] The effectiveness of the blending procedure is demonstrated by the results obtained by applying it to a life table stationary population (L_x), which is not directly affected by misreporting of age. If blending is not employed, the results are very sensitive to the choice of the particular starting age, and the frequency of the digits shows a substantial decline from 0 to 9. With blending, the frequency of the digits is about equal.

TABLE 7.8 Calculation of Preference Indexes for Terminal Digits by Myers' Blended Method, for the Philippines: 1990

Age range covered here is 10 to 89 years. Commonly, the same number of ages is included in the two sets of populations being weighted (cols. 1 and 2). The second set of populations (col. 2) can be extended to age 99 when figures for single ages are available. Ages above 99 may be disregarded.

| Terminal digit, a | Population with terminal digit, a | | Weights for— | | Blended population | | Deviation of percentage from 10.00[1] |
	Starting at age 10 + a (1)	Starting at age 20 + a (2)	Column 1 (3)	Column 2 (4)	Number (1) × (3) + (2) × (4) = (5)	Percent distribution (6)	(6) − 10.00 = (7)
0	5,794,442	4,144,526	1	9	43,095,176	11.52	1.52
1	4,735,734	3,243,767	2	8	35,421,604	9.47	0.53
2	4,706,488	3,200,533	3	7	36,523,195	9.77	0.23
3	4,371,722	2,962,601	4	6	35,262,494	9.43	0.57
4	4,382,456	2,973,683	5	5	36,780,695	9.83	0.17
5	4,534,455	3,158,357	6	4	39,840,158	10.65	0.65
6	3,926,253	2,623,463	7	3	35,354,160	9.45	0.55
7	4,028,469	2,672,365	8	2	37,572,482	10.05	0.05
8	3,767,867	2,438,758	9	1	36,349,561	9.72	0.28
9	3,780,227	2,503,677	10	0	37,802,270	10.11	0.11
Total	(X)	(X)	(X)	(X)	374,001,795	100.00	4.66
Summary index of age preference = Total ÷ 2	(X)	(X)	(X)	(X)	(X)	(X)	2.33

X: Not applicable.
[1] Signs disregarded.
Source: Basic data from United Nations (1995, table 26); and adapted from Myers (1940).

10 to 19. Note that the weights for each terminal digit would differ if the lower limit of the age range covered were different. For example, if the lower limit of the age range covered were 23, the weights for terminal digit 3 would be 1 (col. 1) and 9 (col. 2) and for terminal digit 0 would be 8 (col. 1) and 2 (col. 2).

The method thus yields an index of preference for each terminal digit, representing the deviation, from 10.0%, of the proportion of the total population reporting ages with a given terminal digit. A summary index of preference for all terminal digits is derived as one-half the sum of the deviations from 10.0%, each taken without regard to sign. If age heaping is nonexistent, the index would approximate zero. This index is an estimate of the minimum proportion of persons in the population for whom an age with an incorrect final digit is reported. The theoretical range of Myers's index is 0, representing no heaping, to 90, which would result if all ages were reported at a single digit, say zero. A summary preference index of 2.3 for the Philippines in 1990 is obtained.

Very small deviations from 100, 10, or 0 shown by various measures of heaping are not necessarily indicative of heaping and should be disregarded. The "true" population in any single year of age is by no means equal to exactly one-fifth of the 5-year age group centering around that age (nor one-tenth of the 10-year age group centering around the age), nor is there necessarily a gradual decline in the number of persons from the youngest to the oldest age in a broad group, as is assumed in the common formulas. The age distribution may have small irregular fluctuations, depending largely on the past trend of births, deaths, and migration. Extremely abnormal bunching should be most readily ascertainable in the data for the older ages (but before extreme old age), where mortality takes a heavy toll from age to age but the massive errors in the data for extreme old age do not yet show up. Past fluctuations in the number of births and migrants may still affect the figures, however. In short, it is not possible to measure digit preference precisely, because a precise distinction between the error due to digit preference, other errors, and real fluctuations cannot be made.

Other Summary Indexes of Digit Preference

A number of other general indexes of digit preference have been proposed—for example, the Bachi (1954) index, the Carrier (1959) index, and the Ramachandran (1967) index. These have some theoretical advantages over the Whipple and Myers indexes, but as indicators of the general extent of heaping, differ little from them. The Bachi method, for example, involves applying the Whipple method repeatedly to determine the extent of preference for each final digit. Like the Myers index, the Bachi index equals the sum of the positive deviations from 10%. It has a theoretical range from 0 to 90, and 10% is the expected value for each digit. The results obtained by the Bachi method resemble those obtained by the Myers method. The U.S. Census Bureau (1994) has developed a spreadsheet program, SINGAGE, that calculates the Myers, Whipple, and Bachi indexes of digit preference.

Although not widely used, Siegel has proposed a method of estimating digit preference that involves blending a series of estimates derived by osculatory interpolation. In his method, the average is taken of five different estimates of a particular age that are obtained by rotating the five-year age groups used in the interpolation. Siegel argues that it gives both a measure of terminal digit preference and a measure of the preference for particular ages. (See U.S. Bureau of the Census/Shryock, Siegel, and Associates, 1980, Vol. I., Table 8.6, for an example).

Reduction of and Adjustment for Age and Digit Preference

In the preceding section, we were concerned primarily with those measures that described an entire distribution or an important segment of it. We treat here those measures of heaping and procedures for reducing or eliminating heaping that are primarily applicable to individual ages. These measures and procedures include modifying the census schedule, such as by varying the form of the question or questions used to secure the data on age; and preparing alternative estimates or carefully derived corrections for individual ages, such as by use of annual birth statistics or mathematical interpolation to subdivide the 5-year totals established by the census and by calculation of refined age ratios for single ages. In some situations, it is also desirable to consider handling the problem by presenting only grouped data over part or all of the age distribution. In this case, the question of the optimum grouping of ages for tabulation and publication arises.

Question on Date of Birth

At the enumeration stage, a question on date of birth may be employed instead of a question on age, or both may be used in combination. When only a question on date of birth is used, the resulting pattern of age heaping is likely to be different, with preference for ages that correspond to years of birth ending in 0 or 5. For example, such heaping occurred in the 1970 and 1980 censuses of the United States, and both heaping on ages and on years of birth ending in 0 and 5 were evident in the 1990 census of the United States. Although the heaping on a few ages may continue to be considerable, the evidence suggests that the use of a question on date of birth, especially in combination with a question on age, contributes to the accuracy of the age data obtained (Spencer, 1987). In many cases, an enumerator may not ask both questions, but derives the answer to one by calculation from the answer to the other; yet it is believed that having both questions on the schedule seems to make the enumer-

ator and the respondent more conscientious in the handling of the questions on age. (The age question is also a useful source of an approximate answer when the respondent is unable or unwilling to estimate the date of birth.)

Calculation of Corrected Census Figures

Single-year-of-age data as reported may be "adjusted" following tabulation by developing alternative single-year-of-age figures directly. These alternative figures may replace the census counts entirely or, as is more common, provide a pattern by which the census totals for 5-year age groups may be redistributed by single years of age. There are several ways of developing the alternative estimates. These may involve the relatively direct use of annual birth statistics, "surviving" annual births to the census date, use of life table populations, combining birth, death, and migration statistics to derive actual population estimates, and use of various forms of mathematical interpolation.

The first procedure alluded to involves use of an annual series of past births, in the cohorts corresponding to the census ages, for distributing the 5-year census totals. For this purpose, annual birth statistics that have a fairly similar degree of completeness of registration over several years are required. The second procedure is quite similar, but the births employed are first reduced by deaths prior to the census date. A third procedure for replacing the tabulated single-year-of-age figures involves use of the life table stationary population (L_x column) from an unabridged life table (i.e., one showing single ages). The specific steps for distributing the 5-year totals according to three special sets of single-year-of-age estimates are illustrated for Puerto Rico in Table 7.9.

The use of birth statistics or of the life table stationary population to distribute 5-year census totals can easily result in discontinuity in the single ages at the junctions of the 5-year age groups, as may be seen by examining the age-to-age differences of the estimates in Table 7.9. A number of devices employing mathematical interpolation or graduation can be used to subdivide the 5-year census totals into single years of age in such a way as to effect a smooth transition from one age to another, while maintaining the 5-year totals and removing erratic fluctuations in the numbers (see last column in Table 7.9). In effect, these devices typically fit various mathematical curves to the totals for several adjacent 5-year age groups in order to arrive at the constituent single ages for the central 5-year age group in the set. The principal types of mathematical curves employed for this purpose are of the spline, osculatory, and polynomial form. In this method, various multipliers are ordinarily applied to the enumerated 5-year totals to obtain the required figures directly. It is important to note that each of the methods described also removes some true fluctuations implicit in the original single-year-of-age figures—that is, fluctuations not due to errors in age

TABLE 7.9   Calculation of the Distribution of the Population 25 to 29 and 30 to 34 Years Old by Single Years of Age, by Various Methods, for Puerto Rico: 1990

In each case, the census totals for age groups 25–29 and 30–34 are maintained. These are taken as the numerators of the distribution factors F_1, F_2, and F_3; the denominators are registered births, survivors of births, and life table stationary population in these groups, respectively. See footnotes.

| Age (years) | Census counts (1) | Estimates based directly on births | | Estimates based on survivors of births | | | Estimates based on life table population | | Estimates derived by mathematical interpolation[5] (9) |
		Registered births (2)	Estimated population $F_1^1 \times (2) =$ (3)	Survival rate[2] (4)	Survivors $(2) \times (4) =$ (5)	Estimated population $F_2^3 \times (5) =$ (6)	Life table stationary population[2] (7)	Estimated population $F_3^4 \times (7) =$ (8)	
25 to 29	270,562	385,367	270,562	(X)	372,099	270,562	482,762	270,562	270,562
25	57,814	79,024	55,481	.96987	76,643	55,729	96,987	54,356	55,142
26	54,404	77,746	54,585	.96784	75,246	54,713	96,784	54,242	54,722
27	53,677	76,853	53,958	.96566	74,214	53,963	96,566	54,120	54,241
28	52,758	75,842	53,248	.96335	73,062	53,125	96,335	53,991	53,599
29	51,909	75,902	53,290	.96090	72,934	53,032	96,090	53,853	52,858
30 to 34	254,287	383,726	254,287	(X)	365,605	254,287	476,422	254,287	254,287
30	54,170	75,204	49,836	.95835	72,072	50,128	95,835	51,151	52,198
31	48,988	75,829	50,250	.95568	72,468	50,403	95,568	51,009	51,598
32	50,067	76,083	50,419	.95293	72,502	50,427	95,293	50,862	50,937
33	52,005	77,650	51,457	.95009	73,774	51,312	95,009	50,710	50,180
34	49,057	78,960	52,325	.94717	74,789	52,017	94,717	50,555	49,374

[1] F_1 for 25–29 is $\dfrac{270,562}{385,367} = .70209$; F_1 for 30–34 is $\dfrac{254,287}{383,726} = .66268$.

[2] Life table for Puerto Rico, 1990.

[3] F_2 for 25–29 is $\dfrac{270,562}{372,099} = .72712$; F_2 for 30–34 is $\dfrac{254,287}{365,605} = .69552$.

[4] F_3 for 25–29 is $\dfrac{270,562}{482,762} = .56045$; F_3 for 30–34 is $\dfrac{254,287}{476,422} = .53374$.

[5] The specific method involved the use of Sprague osculatory multipliers applied to five consecutive 5-year age groups.

Source: Basic data from official national sources and from U.S. Census Bureau, International Programs Center, unpublished tabulations.

misreporting but to actual changes in past years in the number of births, deaths, and migration.

Residual Digit Preference in Grouped Data

In view of the magnitude of the errors that may occur in single ages, it may be preferable to combine the figures into 5-year age groups for publication purposes. This approach eliminates the irregularities within these groups, but the question is raised as to the optimum grouping of ages for tabulations from the point of view of minimizing heaping. (The optimum grouping so defined may still not be very practical for demographic analysis.) The concentration on multiples of five and other ages may have but slight effect on grouped data or the effect may be quite substantial. The effect of heaping is certain to remain to some extent in the conventional age grouping if the heaping particularly distorts the marginal ages like 0, 4, 5, and 9.

Serious obstacles exist to the introduction of the "optimum" grouping of data as a general practice. Different population groups (e.g., sex groups or urban-rural residence groups), different censuses, and different types of demographic data (e.g., population data or death statistics) may require different optimum groupings, so that difficulties arise in the cross-classification of data, in the computation of rates, and in the analysis of data over time; and the data may not be regularly tabulated in the necessary detail. In view of the fact particularly that the "decimal" grouping of data is the conventional grouping over much of the world, it may be expected that use of this grouping in the principal census tabulations of each country will continue. Illustrative calculations show, moreover, that there may be little difference between the 0 to 4 (5 to 9) grouping and other groupings in the extent of residual heaping and that the conventional grouping may show a relatively high level of accuracy even where preference for digit "0" is large.

Grouped Data

Types of Errors and Methods of Measurement

As indicated earlier, several important types of errors remain in age data even when the data are grouped. In addition to some residual error due to digit preference, 5-year or

10-year data are affected by other types of age misreporting and by net underenumeration. Absolute net underenumeration would tend to cumulate as the age band widens. On the other hand, the percentage of net underenumeration would be expected to vary fairly regularly over the age distribution, fluctuating only moderately up and down. Absolute net age misreporting error and the percentage of net age misreporting error should tend to take on positive and negative values alternately over the age scale, dropping to zero for the total population of all ages combined. For the total population, therefore, net census error and net underenumeration are identical. In general, as the age band widens, net age misreporting tends to become less important and net underenumeration tends to dominate as the type of error in age data.

The particular form that these types of errors take varies from country to country and from census to census. We may cite some of the specific types of errors that have been identified or described. Young children, particularly infants, and young adult males are omitted disproportionately in many censuses. The liability for military service may be an important factor in connection with the understatement of young adult males. It is possible that laws and practices relating to age for school attendance, child labor, voting, marriage, purchase of alcoholic beverages, and other such activities may induce young people to overstate their age, so that they may share in the privileges accorded under the law to persons who have attained the higher age. Responses regarding age may also be affected by the social prestige accorded certain members of a population, for example, the aged in some societies.

Ewbank (1981) identified several studies of age misreporting patterns in developing countries, and separately discussed such patterns for the age groups 0 to 14, 15 to 29, and 30 years and over. The ages of children tend to be reported more accurately than the ages of adults, although even children's ages show decreasing accuracy with increasing age of the child. Enumerators may frequently distort the reporting of age for women 15 to 29, in particular, by estimating age on the basis of the physical maturity, union/marital status, or parity of the woman. For example, in some censuses and surveys, as in those of the countries of tropical Africa, the number of females in their teens tends to be understated and the number of females in the adult age groups to be overstated. This bias has been attributed to a tendency among interviewers systematically to "age" those women who are already married or mothers on the assumption of a higher "typical" age of marriage than actually prevails (Brass et al., 1968, pp. 48–49). Among people aged 30 years and over, the problems of heaping on digits ending in 0 and 5 and age exaggeration are the most common types of age misreporting problems.

It is quite difficult to measure the errors in grouped data on age with any precision. It may be extremely difficult or impossible, in fact, to determine the separate contribution of each of the types of errors affecting a given figure and to separate the errors from real fluctuations (e.g., fluctuations due to migration) and, further, to identify the errors in relation to their causes. Some of the measures of error for age groups measure net age misreporting and net underenumeration separately, whereas others measure these types of errors only in combination or measure only one of them. Some of the procedures provide only indexes of error for entire age distributions or only estimates of relative error for age groups (i.e., relative to the error in the same category in an earlier census or relative to another category in the same census), whereas other procedures provide estimates of the actual extent of error for age groups.

As in the case of measuring coverage of the total population, the methods for determining the existence of such errors and their approximate magnitude may be classified into two broad types: first, case-by-case matching techniques employing data from reinterviews and independent lists or administrative records and, second, techniques of demographic analysis. The former techniques relate to studies in which data collected in the census are matched on a case-by-case basis with data for a sample of persons obtained by reinterview or from independent records. The latter techniques involve (1) the development of estimates of expected values for the population in age or other categories, or for various population ratios, by use and manipulation of (a) data from the census itself or an earlier census or censuses and (b) such data as birth, death, and migration statistics, and (2) the comparison of these expected values with the corresponding figures from the census. This method may also be extended to encompass comparison of aggregate administrative data with census counts.

Measurement by Reinterviews and Record Matching Studies

We consider first case-by-case checking techniques based on reinterviews and matching against independent lists and administrative records for the light they may throw on errors in grouped data. Case-by-case matching studies permit the separate measurement of the two components of net census error (or net census undercounts) in age data—net coverage error (or net underenumeration) and net age misreporting. Furthermore, this type of study theoretically permits separating each of these components into its principal components—net coverage error into omissions and erroneous inclusions at each age, and net misreporting error into the various directional biases that affect each age group. Thus, the results of a reinterview study, or administrative records may be cross-classified with the results of the original enumeration by 5-year, 10-year, or broader age groups, to determine the number of persons who were omitted from, or erroneously included in, the census, for the same age

TABLE 7.10 Indexes of Response Bias and Response Variability for the Reporting of Age of the Population of the United States: 1950 and 1960

CES represents the Content Evaluation Survey of the 1960 census reinterview program and PES represents the 1950 Post-Enumeration Survey.

| | Content Evaluation Study 1960 census match | | Post-Enumeration Survey 1950 census match | | Difference between 1960 census-CES match and 1950 census-PES match | |
	Index of net shift relative to CES class[1] (1)	Percentage in CES class differently reported (2)	Index of net shift relative to PES class[1] (3)	Percentage in PES class differently reported (4)	Index of net shift[2] |(1)| − |(3)| = (5)	Percent in class differently reported[3] (2) − (4) = (6)
Age (years)						
Under 5	−0.04	1.82	−1.64	2.98	−1.60	−1.16
5 to 14	+0.36	1.36	+0.54	1.58	−0.18	−0.22
15 to 24	−0.85	2.57	+0.93	2.59	−0.08	−0.02
25 to 34	+0.44	2.39	+0.22	3.67	+0.22	−1.28
35 to 44	+1.00	3.85	+1.07	4.48	−0.07	−0.63
45 to 54	−0.63	5.31	+0.11	6.42	+0.52	−1.11
55 to 64	−0.11	5.83	−2.18	6.91	−2.07	−1.08
65 and over	−0.79	3.21	−0.51	2.99	+0.28	+0.22

[1] A minus sign indicates that the census count is lower than the CES or PES figure.

[2] Represents the excess of the absolute figure (without regard to sign) in col. (1) over the absolute figure (without regard to sign) in col. (3). A minus sign indicates a lower level of error in the 1960 census than in the 1950 census; a plus sign indicates a higher level of error in the 1960 census.

[3] A minus sign indicates a lower level of error in the 1960 census than in the 1950 census; a plus sign indicates a higher level of error in the 1960 census.
Source: U.S. Bureau of the Census (1960b, Tables 1A–1E; 1964, Table 1; and 1980, Table 8–9).

groups, or who reported in the same, higher, or lower age group.

When the matching study is employed to measure misreporting of age, the comparison is restricted to persons included both in the census and in the sample survey or the record sample used in the evaluation (that is, "matched persons"), and the age of each person interviewed in the census is compared with the age obtained by more experienced interviewers in the "check" sample. (It may be desirable, also, to exclude from the analysis persons whose age was not reported in either interview.) Differences arise primarily in reporting, but also may occur in the recording and processing of the data. Because of problems relating to the design of the matching study, sample size and sample variability, and matching the census record and the "check" record, it is difficult to establish reliably the patterns of coverage error or age misreporting, or their combination, net census error, for 5-year age groups, or to separate net coverage error reliably into omissions and erroneous inclusions for age groups.

Reinterview studies designed to measure the extent of net coverage error and net misreporting error for age groups were conducted following both the 1950 and 1960 censuses of the United States. To evaluate the accuracy of age reporting and to measure the net coverage error for age groups in these two censuses, the data on age from the 1950 post-enumeration survey (PES) and the content evaluation study (CES) of the 1960 census reinterview program were com-

pared with the corresponding census data.[12] Table 7.10 illustrates how this type of data may be employed in the analysis of response errors in age data. The 1950 and 1960 census counts of the population for age groups are compared with the 1950 PES data and the 1960 CES data, respectively.

Measurement by Demographic Analysis

As mentioned earlier, numerous techniques of demographic analysis can be employed in the evaluation of census data for age groups. These techniques include such procedures as intercensal cohort analysis based on age data from an earlier census, derivation of estimates based on birth, death, and migration statistics, use of expected age ratios and sex ratios, mathematical graduation of census age data, comparison with various types of population models, comparison with estimates based on counts from administrative records, and other more elaborate techniques involving data from several censuses.

Ordinarily, these techniques do not permit the separate measurement of net underenumeration and net age

[12] Censuses taken after 1960 have included the collection of data on age in the respective post-enumeration surveys and content reinterview surveys, but the analyses of these surveys has been limited to "new" questionnaire items and to those items known to be more problematic than age. For the 1950 census-PES statistics, see U.S. Bureau of the Census (1960b). For the 1960 census-CES statistics, see U.S. Bureau of the Census (1964) and Marks and Waksberg (1966, p. 69).

misreporting for any age group; these errors are measured in combination as net census errors. Some of the techniques measure net age misreporting primarily and net underenumeration only secondarily or partly. Most of the techniques of evaluating grouped age data do not provide absolute estimates of net census error by which census data can be corrected.

The methods of measuring net census error as such can give some suggestive information regarding the nature and extent of net age misreporting, because, as we have previously noted, net coverage error should tend to be in the same direction from age to age and to vary rather regularly over the age distribution. A division of net census error into these two parts may also be possible by employing two or more methods of evaluation in combination. An estimate of net census error is itself subject to error because the corresponding estimate of the corrected population contains errors. These result from, for example, net undercount of the census figure for an age cohort in a previous census, error in the reported or estimated number of births, underreporting and age misclassification in the death statistics, and omission, understatement, or overstatement of the allowance for net migration.

The present discussion of the errors in grouped data on age by the methods of demographic analysis does not treat the measurement and correction of errors separately because, as we have noted, they are often two facets of the same operation. We will, however, particularly note those methods that directly provide corrections of census figures for net undercounts. The latter methods will be illustrated principally by a review of recent U.S. studies of net undercounts using demographic analysis. First, however, we consider the basic methods under the headings of (1) intercensal cohort analysis, (2) comparisons with estimates based on birth statistics, (3) age ratio analysis, (4) sex ratio analysis, (5) mathematical graduation of census data, and (6) comparison with population models. We also consider briefly (7) comparison with aggregate administrative data.

Intercensal Cohort Analysis

In this procedure, the counts of one census are, in effect, employed to evaluate the counts at a later census. Ordinarily, the principal demographic factor at the national level accounting for the difference between the figures for the same cohort at the two census dates is mortality. Migration will usually play a secondary, if not a minor, role, although even in this case the number of migrants may exceed the number of deaths at some of the younger ages. The figures from both the earlier and later censuses are affected by net census undercounts. In addition, it is possible that the level of migration and mortality may have been affected by such special factors as movement of military forces into and out of a country, refugee movements, epidemic or famine, and war deaths. The method of intercensal cohort analysis is illustrated with data for the United States from 1980 to 1990.

Table 7.11 sets forth the steps by which estimates of the expected population for age groups in April 1990 for the United States were derived. In this case, statistics on deaths, net civilian migration, and net movement of armed forces by age are available and have been compiled in terms of birth cohorts for April 1980 through March 1990. The expected population in 1990, derived by combining the 1980 census figures with the estimates of change for birth cohorts during 1980 to 1990, is compared with the corresponding 1990 census age counts.[13] The results reflect the combined effect of underenumeration and age misreporting (i.e., net errors) in the 1990 census, as well as the net errors in the 1980 census and errors in the data on intercensal change, particularly age misreporting errors in death statistics and coverage errors in the migration statistics. In more general terms, the method measures relative net census error for a birth cohort at two successive censuses.

The 3% deficit at ages 25 to 29 in 1990 (col. 9) suggests an underenumeration of persons of these ages in this census on the principal assumption that children aged 15 to 19 were rather well enumerated in 1980 (col. 1). The error of closure (col. 9) for the population aged 10 to 14 in 1990—1.4% of the population expected in 1990—suggests an underenumeration of the population aged 0 to 4 in 1980, perhaps combined with a coverage error in the migration statistics.

The method of intercensal cohort analysis may be applied in another way to evaluate the consistency of the data on age in two successive censuses when net immigration or emigration is negligible and death statistics are lacking or defective. Table 7.12 illustrates this method for South Korea for the 1985 and 1995 censuses. For South Korea, adequate death statistics or a life table to measure mortality between the censuses is not available; net migration is assumed to be negligible. First, the proportion surviving at each age between 1985 and 1995 (cols. 5 and 6) is calculated by dividing the 1995 population at a given age (terminal age) by the 1985 population 10 years younger (initial age). For example,

$$\frac{P^{1995}_{m20-24}}{P^{1985}_{m10-14}} = \frac{2,238,000}{2,311,000} = .96857$$

Second, the reasonableness of these proportions in themselves or in comparison with an actual set or a model set of life table survival rates is examined as a basis for judging the adequacy of the census data.

In the absence of net migration, proportions surviving in excess of 1.00 are unacceptable and suggest either net understatement in the 1985 census or net overstatement

---

[13] For details on the estimation of the population for age groups using birth cohorts, see U.S. Census Bureau (1993b).

TABLE 7.11 Calculation of the Error of Closure for the Population of the United States, by Age: April 1, 1980 to 1990

Age in 1980 (years)	Components of change, 1980 to 1990					Population, April 1, 1990		Error of closure		Age in 1990 (years)
	Census population, April 1, 1980 (+) (1)	Births (+) (2)	Deaths (−) (3)	Net civilian migration[1] (+) (4)	Net movement of Armed forces[2] (+) (5)	Expected (1) + (2) − (3) + (4) + (5) = (6)	Enumerated (census) (7)	Amount[3] (7) − (6) = (8)	Percentage of expected population, 1990[3] (8) ÷ (6) × 100 = (9)	
Total	226,545,805	37,625,917	20,695,518	6,559,049	187,707	250,222,960	248,709,873	−1,513,087	−0.6	Total
Births, 1985 to 1990	(X)	19,369,076	208,673	148,085	6,380	19,314,868	18,354,443	−960,425	−5.0	Under 5
Births, 1980 to 1985	(X)	18,256,841	258,197	441,156	3,448	18,443,248	18,099,179	−344,069	−1.9	5 to 9
Under 5	16,348,254	(X)	57,475	577,347	17,862	16,885,988	17,114,249	+228,261	+1.4	10 to 14
5 to 9	16,699,956	(X)	68,764	583,460	39,936	17,254,588	17,754,015	+499,427	+2.9	15 to 19
10 to 14	18,242,129	(X)	144,667	816,363	−148,129	18,765,696	19,020,312	+254,616	+1.4	20 to 24
15 to 19	21,168,124	(X)	238,011	1,160,659	−108,361	21,982,411	21,313,045	−669,366	−3.0	25 to 29
20 to 24	21,318,704	(X)	274,338	1,072,255	141,310	22,257,931	21,862,887	−395,044	−1.8	30 to 34
25 to 29	19,520,919	(X)	291,575	653,108	72,004	19,954,456	19,963,117	+8,661	(Z)	35 to 39
30 to 34	17,560,920	(X)	316,045	360,680	59,493	17,665,048	17,615,786	−49,262	−0.3	40 to 44
35 to 39	13,965,302	(X)	363,937	225,306	54,488	13,881,159	13,872,573	−8,586	−0.1	45 to 49
40 to 44	11,669,408	(X)	475,994	170,737	27,750	11,391,901	11,350,513	−41,388	−0.4	50 to 54
45 to 49	11,089,755	(X)	723,497	134,389	12,396	10,513,043	10,531,756	+18,713	+0.2	55 to 59
50 to 54	11,710,032	(X)	1,171,542	124,118	5,142	10,667,750	10,616,167	−51,583	−0.5	60 to 64
55 to 59	11,615,254	(X)	1,714,346	104,646	2,157	10,007,711	10,111,735	+104,024	+1.0	65 to 69
60 to 64	10,087,621	(X)	2,131,029	59,727	962	8,017,281	7,994,823	−22,458	−0.3	70 to 74
65 and over	25,549,427	(X)	12,257,428	−72,987	869	13,219,881	13,135,273	−84,608	−0.6	75 and over
55 and over	47,252,302	(X)	16,102,803	91,386	3,988	31,244,873	31,241,831	−3,042	(Z)	65 and over

X: Not applicable.
Z: Less than 0.05%.
[1] Minus sign denotes net emigration.
[2] Minus sign denotes net movement of armed forces from the United States.
[3] Minus sign denotes that census count is less than expected figure and plus sign denotes that census count is greater than expected figure.
Source: Derived from 1980 and 1990 enumerated census populations and unpublished tabulations from the U.S. Bureau of the Census.

TABLE 7.12   Evaluation of Consistency of Age Data from the 1985 and 1995 Censuses of South Korea, by Sex

| Age in— | | Population (census) (In thousands) | | | | Proportion surviving | | | | | | Male/female proportion surviving | |
| | | 1985 | | 1995 | | Census | | Model life table[1] | | Percent difference | | | |
1985 (years)	1995 (years)	Male (1)	Female (2)	Male (3)	Female (4)	Male (3)+(1) = (5)	Female (4)+(2) = (6)	Male (7)	Female (8)	Male $\frac{(5)-(7)}{(7)}$ ×100 = (9)	Female $\frac{(6)-(8)}{(8)}$ ×100 = (10)	Census data (5)+(6) = (11)	Model life table data (7)+(8) = (12)
(X)	All ages	20,228	20,192	22,357	22,196	(X)	(X)	(X)	(X)	(X)	(X)	(X)	(X)
(X)	Under 5	(X)	(X)	1,821	1,606	(X)	(X)	(X)	(X)	(X)	(X)	(X)	(X)
(X)	5 to 9	(X)	(X)	1,627	1,469	(X)	(X)	(X)	(X)	(X)	(X)	(X)	(X)
Under 5	10 to 14	1,923	1,780	1,914	1,798	.99534	1.01033	.98630	.99205	+0.92	+1.84	0.99	0.99
5 to 9	15 to 19	2,025	1,891	1,987	1,876	.98109	.99231	.99251	.99642	-1.15	-0.41	0.99	1.00
10 to 14	20 to 24	2,311	2,165	2,238	2,066	.96857	.95429	.99025	.99592	-2.19	-4.18	1.01	0.99
15 to 19	25 to 29	2,227	2,089	2,078	2,059	.93315	.98590	.98643	.99443	-5.40	-0.86	0.95	0.99
20 to 24	30 to 34	2,186	2,059	2,146	2,084	.98199	1.01191	.98351	.99265	-0.15	+1.94	0.97	0.99
25 to 34	35 to 44	3,617	3,569	3,683	3,522	1.01827	.98690	.97635	.98809	+4.29	-0.12	1.03	0.99
35 to 44	45 to 54	2,433	2,336	2,290	2,238	.94137	.95806	.95085	.97384	-1.00	-1.62	0.98	0.98
45 to 54	55 to 64	1,853	1,932	1,597	1,811	.86221	.93754	.88556	.93716	-2.64	+0.04	0.92	0.94
55 to 64	65 to 74	1,001	1,274	715	1,092	.71388	.85733	.74534	.84149	-4.22	+1.88	0.83	0.89
65 to 74	75 to 84	497	727	232	470	.46608	.64680	.51511	.63675	-9.52	+1.58	0.72	0.81
75 and over	85 and over	155	371	28	103	.18325	.27909	.21540	.26372	-14.92	+5.83	0.66	0.82

X: Not applicable.

[1]The model life tables employed here are from the United Nations' Model Life Tables, General Pattern, with male and female life expectancies at birth of 67.0 and 74.0, respectively.

Source: Basic data from Republic of Korea (1987, Table 2; 1997, Table 2) and from United Nations (1982).

(presumably due to age misreporting) in the 1995 census. This irregularity applies to the proportions for males with terminal ages 35 to 44 years, and to the proportions for females with terminal ages 10 to 14 and 30 to 34 years. The male-female ratios of the proportion surviving for South Korea are generally reasonable. Very different proportions surviving for males and females or higher proportions surviving for males than females except at the childbearing ages, as is shown for terminal ages 20 to 24 and 35 to 44 in Table 7.12, are slightly suspect.

Comparison with Estimates Based on Birth Statistics

Estimates of net undercounts of children may be derived by comparison of the census counts and estimates of children based on birth statistics, death statistics or life table survival rates, and migration statistics. If possible, the birth and death statistics, particularly the former, should be adjusted to include an allowance for underregistration. The method was illustrated with U.S. data in Table 7.11. Birth statistics for April 1, 1980, to April 1, 1985, and April 1, 1985, to April 1, 1990, are combined with death and immigration statistics for the same cohorts to derive estimates of the expected population under 5 and 5 to 9 years old in 1990. The difference between the expected population and the census count is then taken as the estimate of net undercount.

For the age group 0–4 in 1990,

$$B^{1985-1990} - D^{1985-1990} + M^{1985-1990} = P_{0-4}^{e1990} \quad (7.14)$$

$$P_{0-4}^{c1990} - P_{0-4}^{e1990} = E_{0-4}^{1990} \quad (7.15)$$

where P^c represents the census count, P^e the expected population, and E the estimated net undercount. The corresponding figures are

$$19,369,076 - 208,673 + 154,465 = 19,314,868$$

$$18,354,443 - 19,314,868 = -960,425$$

The census count of children under 5 years old, 18,354,443, falls below the expected population, 19,314,868, by about 960,000, or 5.0% of the expected figure. This difference is taken as the estimate of the net undercount of children under 5 in the census.

A special problem of calculation and interpretation of the difference between the expected population and the census count of children exists when the birth statistics or the death statistics are incomplete. In the absence of immigration, the comparison provides a minimum estimate of the net undercount of children when the expected population exceeds the census count (and a minimum estimate of the underregistration of births when the census figure exceeds the estimate based on births). It may be desirable or even preferable in this case to employ life table survival rates in lieu of death statistics because of the inadequacies of the reported death statistics or the convenience of using a life table.

The procedure is illustrated in Table 7.13, which compares the expected population under 10 years of age (single years under 5 and the age group 5 to 9) for males and females with the corresponding counts from the census of Panama taken on May 13, 1990. Registered births (col. 1), tabulated by calendar year of occurrence, were first redistributed to conform to "census" years (i.e., May to May) on the assumption that the distribution is rectangular (i.e., even) within each calendar year. Survival rates, representing the probability of survival from birth to the age at the census date, were then calculated from an abridged life table for Panama for 1990. The expected population excluding the effect of immigration (col. 4) was then derived as the product of the births in column 2 and the survival rates in column 3. The 4% deficit of the census count for children under 1 and the 1% deficit for children 1 to 4 years old in comparison with the corresponding expected populations may be taken as minimum estimates of the net undercounts of these groups. The method suggests a net census overcount of children 5 to 9 years old (about 5%). However, the survival rates from the 1990 life table may be too high, and, hence, the estimate of survivors may be too high. Even allowing for this possibility and the possibility of net emigration, the actual net undercounts may be greater than those shown for the ages under 3 to the extent that births are underregistered.

Age Ratio Analysis

The quality of the census returns for age groups may also be evaluated by comparing age ratios, calculated from the census data, with expected or standard values. An age ratio may be defined as the ratio of the population in the given age group to one-third of the sum of the populations in the age group itself and the preceding and following groups, times 100.[14] The age ratio for a 5-year age group, $_5P_a$ is defined then as follows:

$$\frac{_5P_a}{\frac{1}{3}(_5P_{a-5} + _5P_a + _5P_{a+5})} \times 100 \quad (7.16)$$

Barring extreme fluctuations in past births, deaths, or migration, the three age groups should form a nearly linear series. Age ratios should then approximate 100, even though actual historical variations in these factors would produce deviations from 100 in the age ratio for most ages. Inasmuch as, over a period of nearly a century, most countries have experienced not only minor fluctuations in population changes but also major upheavals, age ratios for some ages may deviate substantially from 100 even where reporting of

---

[14] Alternatively, age ratios have been defined as the ratio of the population in an age group to one-half the sum of the population in the preceding and subsequent groups, times 100. The definition given above is preferred.

TABLE 7.13   Comparison of Survivors of Births With Census Counts Under 10 Years of Age, by Sex, for Panama: 1990

Sex and year of birth	Births Registered (1)	Adjusted to "census year"[1] (1) redistributed = (2)	Survival rate from birth to census age[2] (3)	Expected population (2) × (3) = (4)	Census count (5)	Deficit or excess of census Amount (5) − (4) = (6)	Percentage (6) ÷ (4) × 100 = (7)	Age in 1990 (years)
Male								
1990	30,493	(X)	(X)	(X)	(X)	(X)	(X)	
1989	30,315	30,380	.97224	29,537	28,246	−1,291	−4.4	Under 1
1985–1988	119,383	119,417	(X)	115,020[3]	113,205	−1,815	−1.6	1 to 4
1988	30,253	30,276	.96624	29,254	27,465	−1,789	−6.1	1
1987	29,532	29,795	.96356	28,709	28,346	−363	−1.3	2
1986	29,724	29,654	.96195	28,526	28,620	+94	+0.3	3
1985	29,674	29,692	.96090	28,531	28,774	+243	+0.9	4
1980–1984	139,760	140,788[4]	.95907	135,026	141,203	+6,177	+4.6	5 to 9
Female								
1990	29,411	(X)	(X)	(X)	(X)	(X)	(X)	
1989	28,754	28,993	.97636	28,308	27,201	−1,107	−3.9	Under 1
1985–1988	112,616	112,758	(X)	109,179[3]	108,397	−782	−0.7	1 to 4
1988	28,206	28,406	.97108	27,584	26,068	−1,516	−5.5	1
1987	28,115	28,148	.96853	27,262	27,038	−224	−0.8	2
1986	27,931	27,998	.96715	27,078	27,755	+677	+2.5	3
1985	28,364	28,206	.96630	27,255	27,536	+281	+1.0	4
1980–1984	133,111	134,055[4]	.96499	129,362	135,729	+6,367	+4.9	5 to 9

X: Not applicable.

[1] Figures apply to period from May of year indicated to May of following year. Census was taken as of May 13, 1990.

[2] 1990 life table for Panama.

[3] Obtained by summation.

[4] Equals sum of (prorated) January–May 13 births in 1985, births in 1981–84, and (prorated) births May 14–December in 1980.

Source: Derived from basic data reported in United Nations (1988, Table 20; 1994, Table 16) and U.S. Census Bureau, International Programs Center, unpublished tabulations.

age is good. The assumption of an expected value of 100 also implies that coverage errors are about the same from age group to age group and that age reporting errors for a particular group are offset by complementary errors in adjacent age groups. In sum, age ratios serve primarily as measures of net age misreporting, not net census error, and they are not to be taken as valid indicators of error for particular age groups.

An overall measure of the accuracy of an age distribution, an age-accuracy index, may be derived by taking the average deviation (without regard to sign) from 100 of the age ratios over all ages. This is illustrated on the basis of data for Malaysia in 1991 in Table 7.14.

The sum of the deviations from 100 of the age ratios for males is 49.7, and the mean deviation for the 13 age groups is, therefore, 3.8. The average (3.9) of the mean deviation for males (3.8) and the mean deviation for females (4.0) is a measure of the overall accuracy of the age data of Malaysia in 1991, which can be compared with the same kind of measure for other years or other areas. The lower the age-accuracy index, the more adequate the census data

on age would appear to be. The results suggest that reporting of age is very similar, though slightly less satisfactory, for females in Malaysia to that for males. The results of similar calculations carried out for Australia, China, Hungary, Indonesia, Sweden, and the United States suggest that the quality of age reporting in Malaysia occupies an intermediate position:

Country (census year)	Age-accuracy index
United States (1990)	2.7
Australia (1991)	2.8
Sweden (1990)	3.8
Malaysia (1991)	3.9
China (1990)	4.7
Indonesia (1990)	5.3
Hungary (1990)	5.7

Sex Ratio Analysis

Several methods of evaluating census age data employ age-specific sex ratios from the census. One compares expected sex ratios for each age group, developed principally from vital statistics, with the census sex ratios. The

TABLE 7.14   Calculation of Age-Accuracy Index, for Malaysia: 1991

Age (years)	Population Male (1)	Population Female (2)	Male Ratio[1] (3)	Male Deviation from 100 (3) − 100 = (4)	Female Ratio[1] (5)	Female Deviation from 100 (5) − 100 = (6)
Under 5	1,150,221	1,084,179	(X)	(X)	(X)	(X)
5 to 9	1,152,353	1,091,915	104.6	+4.6	104.5	+4.5
10 to 14	1,001,605	958,663	99.2	−0.8	98.5	−1.5
15 to 19	875,587	868,013	98.7	−1.3	99.6	−0.4
20 to 24	782,941	787,241	96.8	−3.2	97.4	−2.6
25 to 29	767,471	768,927	102.1	+2.1	102.5	+2.5
30 to 34	704,377	695,016	102.3	+2.3	102.1	+2.1
35 to 39	592,796	578,116	100.0	—	100.2	+0.2
40 to 44	480,353	458,341	101.4	+1.4	101.1	+1.1
45 to 49	348,407	323,888	91.9	−8.1	89.7	−10.3
50 to 54	309,147	300,766	105.2	+5.2	105.9	+5.9
55 to 59	223,745	227,042	93.9	−6.1	94.5	−5.5
60 to 64	181,569	193,340	104.4	+4.4	105.9	+5.9
65 to 69	116,527	127,572	89.9	−10.1	90.2	−9.8
70 to 74	90,846	103,230	(X)	(X)	(X)	(X)
Total (irrespective of sign)	(X)	(X)	(X)	49.7	(X)	52.1
Mean	(X)	(X)	(X)	3.8	(X)	4.0

—: Represents zero.
X: Not applicable.

[1] The age ratio is defined as $\dfrac{{}_5P_a}{1/3({}_5P_{a-5} + {}_5P_a + {}_5P_{a+5})} \times 100$.

Source: Derived from enumerated census population as reported in U.S. Census Bureau (2000a, Table 4), www.census.gov/ipc/www/idbacc.html.

expected figures may be carefully developed estimates of the actual sex ratios at each age or theoretical figures based on a population model. Another judges the census age-specific sex ratios in terms of their age-to-age differences.

The first method involves developing estimates of the actual sex ratios at each age at a census date on the basis of the sex ratios of each of the components of change, particularly the sex ratio of births and the sex ratios of survival rates (i.e., the ratio of the male survival rate at a given age to the corresponding female rate, derived from life tables).[15] The basic calculations may be illustrated by the procedure for deriving the expected sex ratios at ages 0 to 4 and 5 to 9 at the census date. If the contribution of net migration is disregarded, the expected sex ratio at ages 0 to 4 equals the product of the sex ratio of births in the 5 years preceding the

census date and the ratio of (a) the male survival rate from birth to ages 0 to 4 $\left({}_b R^m_{0-4}\right)$ to (b) the corresponding female survival rate $\left({}_b R^f_{0-4}\right)$:[16]

$$\left(\frac{B^m}{B^f}\right)_{y-5\,\text{to}\,y} \times \frac{\left({}_b R^m_{0-4}\right)_{y-5\,\text{to}\,y}}{\left({}_b R^f_{0-4}\right)_{y-5\,\text{to}\,y}} = \left(\frac{P^m_{0-4}}{P^f_{0-4}}\right)'_y \qquad (7.17)$$

where y designates a given year and $y - 5$ to y refers to the preceding 5 years. The expected sex ratio for the age

[15] Full development of the estimates of expected sex ratios of this type requires a knowledge of the use of life tables and of techniques of population estimation. Both of these topics are treated in later chapters.

[16] The expressions in parentheses are calculated as units or are treated as single numbers in the calculations. For example, the sex ratio of births for a given period, whether calculated on the basis of reported births or assumed on the basis of the sex ratio of births for a later period, is treated as a single number in the "survival" calculations; and the sex ratio of the population is derived as a direct result, without intermediate figures for the absolute numbers of males and females.

group 5 to 9 would be derived theoretically as the joint product of the sex ratio of births 5 to 10 years earlier, the sex ratio of survival rates from birth to ages 0 to 4, 5 to 10 years earlier, and the sex ratio of survival rates from ages 0 to 4 to ages 5 to 9 in the previous 5 years:

$$\left(\frac{B^m}{B^f}\right)_{y-10 \text{ to } y-5} \times \frac{\left(R^m_b{}^{0-4}\right)_{y-10 \text{ to } y-5}}{\left(R^f_b{}^{0-4}\right)_{y-10 \text{ to } y-5}} \times \frac{\left(R^m{}^{5-9}\right)_{y-5 \text{ to } y}}{\left(R^f{}^{5-9}_{0-4}\right)_{y-5 \text{ to } y}} = \left(\frac{P^m_{5-9}}{P^f_{5-9}}\right)'_y$$

(7.18)

"Expected" sex ratios calculated in this way can then be compared to those calculated directly from the census data. An illustration of this procedure is presented in U.S. Bureau of the Census/Shryock, Siegel, and Associates, Vol. 1, Table 8.14 (1980).

The results of the method are directly applicable for judging the relative magnitude of the net census error of the counts of males and females; they do not indicate the absolute level of net census error for either sex. If the results of this method are to be used to derive absolute estimates of corrected population for either sex or both sexes combined, an acceptable, independently determined set of estimates of net undercounts or corrected census figures by age for either males or females is required. For example, if corrected census figures for females are available, the expected sex ratios would be applied to them to derive corrected figures for males. Because of the greater likelihood of deficiencies in the basic data and the greater dependence on the various assumptions made as one goes back in time, the estimates of expected sex ratios are subject to greater and greater error as one goes up the age scale.

When the detailed data required to develop a set of estimated actual sex ratios (e.g., historical series of life tables, historical data on births of boys and girls, net immigration or nativity of the population disaggregated by age and sex, war deaths) are not available or it is not practical to develop them, the expected pattern of sex ratios for age groups may be approximated by employing a single current life table to measure survival from birth to each age, in conjunction with the current reported or estimated sex ratio at birth. This method, in effect, assumes that there has been no net migration, either civilian or military, or excess mortality due to war or widespread epidemic. In addition, it assumes that the sex ratio of births and the differences in mortality between the sexes at each age have remained unchanged. To the extent that these conditions prevail, the approximation to the actual sex ratios will be closer.

Expected sex ratios at the early childhood ages are not far below the sex ratio at birth. Then, commonly, they fall gradually throughout life, not dipping below 100 until age 40 or later. The decline is gentle at first but becomes steeper at the older ages. The general pattern described results from

the usual small excess of boys among births and the usual excess of male over female mortality.[17]

The regularity of the change in the expected sex ratio from age to age that we have just noted provides a basis for elaborating the age-accuracy index based solely on age ratios described earlier to incorporate some measure of the accuracy of sex ratios. The United Nations (1952, 1955) has proposed such an *age-sex accuracy index*. In this index, the mean of the differences from age to age in reported sex ratios, without regard to sign, is taken as a measure of the accuracy of the observed sex ratios, on the assumption that these age-to-age changes should approximate zero. The UN age-sex accuracy index combines the sum of (1) the mean deviation of the age ratios for males from 100 (2) the mean deviation of the age ratios for females from 100, and (3) three times the mean of the age-to-age differences in reported sex ratios. In the UN procedure, an age ratio is defined as the ratio of the population in a given age group to one-half the sum of the populations in the preceding and following groups. The calculation of the UN age-sex accuracy index is illustrated in Table 7.15 for Turkey in 1990. The mean deviations of the age ratios for males and females are 5.5 and 5.5, respectively, and the mean age-to-age difference in the sex ratios is 4.0. Applying the UN formula, we have: 5.5 + 5.5 + 3(4.0) = 23.0. Comparable indexes for Turkey and a few other countries are as follows:

Country (census year)	U.N. age-sex accuracy index
Argentina (1991)	12.7
United States (1990)	14.7
Vietnam (1989)	22.9
Turkey (1990)	23.0
Hungary (1990)	26.0
Indonesia (1990)	31.0
India (1991)	39.6
Tanzania (1988)	47.7

The U.S. Census Bureau (1994) has developed a spreadsheet program, AGESEX, that calculates the United Nations age-sex accuracy index given the population in 5-year age groups, for males and females, as input data. Census age-sex data are described by the United Nations as "accurate," "inaccurate," or "highly inaccurate" depending on whether the UN index is under 20, 20 to 40, or over 40.

The UN index has a number of questionable features as a summary measure for comparing the accuracy of the age-sex data of various countries. Among these are the failure to take account of the expected decline in the sex ratio with increasing age and of real irregularities in age distribution due to migration, war, and epidemic as well as

---

[17] The variations in the theoretical pattern of expected sex ratios by age resulting solely from variations in the level of mortality, holding the sex ratio at birth constant and excluding the effect of civilian migration and military movements, may be shown by employing model life tables that have very different levels of mortality, such as those given in Coale and Demeny (1983) and United Nations (1982).

TABLE 7.15   Calculation of the United Nations Age-Sex Accuracy Index, for Turkey: 1990

Age (years)	Population Male (1)	Population Female (2)	Analysis of sex ratios Ratio [(1) ÷ (2)] × 100 = (3)	Analysis of sex ratios Successive differences ∈(3) = (4)	Analysis of age ratios Male Ratio[1] (5)	Analysis of age ratios Male Deviation from 100 (5) − 100 = (6)	Analysis of age ratios Female Ratio[1] (7)	Analysis of age ratios Female Deviation from 100 (7) − 100 = (8)
Under 5	3,052,255	2,902,489	105.16	(X)	(X)	(X)	(X)	(X)
5 to 9	3,541,409	3,357,800	105.47	−0.31	107.10	+7.10	107.74	+7.74
10 to 14	3,560,900	3,330,499	106.92	−1.45	106.19	+6.19	103.93	+3.93
15 to 19	3,165,061	3,051,408	103.72	+3.19	103.06	+3.06	104.41	+4.41
20 to 24	2,581,153	2,514,351	102.66	+1.07	92.17	−7.83	92.63	−7.37
25 to 29	2,435,765	2,377,362	102.46	+0.20	104.14	+4.14	105.57	+5.57
30 to 34	2,096,899	1,989,410	105.40	−2.95	99.38	−0.62	97.44	−2.56
35 to 39	1,784,121	1,705,943	104.58	+0.82	101.49	+1.49	101.57	+1.57
40 to 44	1,418,784	1,369,640	103.59	+0.99	98.01	−1.99	97.97	−2.03
45 to 49	1,111,113	1,090,046	101.93	+1.66	92.64	−7.36	90.52	−9.48
50 to 54	980,115	1,038,853	94.35	+7.59	93.14	−6.86	101.99	+1.99
55 to 59	993,402	947,119	104.89	−10.54	113.62	+13.62	100.46	+.046
60 to 64	768,547	846,746	90.76	+14.12	104.93	+4.93	115.30	+15.30
65 to 69	471,479	521,608	90.39	+0.38	93.26	−6.74	90.69	−9.31
70 to 74	242,572	303,519	79.92	+10.47	(X)	(X)	(X)	(X)
Total (irrespective of sign)	(X)	(X)	(X)	55.73	(X)	71.94	(X)	71.73
Mean	(X)	(X)	(X)	3.98	(X)	5.53	(X)	5.52

Index = 3 times mean difference in sex ratios plus mean deviations of male and female age ratios.
    = 3 × 3.98 + 5.53 + 5.52 = 22.99

X: Not applicable.

[1] The age ratio is defined here as $\dfrac{_5P_a}{1/2(_5P_{a-5} + _5P_{a+5})} \times 100$.

Source: Derived from enumerated census population as reported in U.S. Census Bureau (2000a, Table 4), www.census.gov/ipc/www/idbacc.html.

normal fluctuations in births and deaths; the use of a definition of an age ratio that omits the central age group and which, therefore, does not give it sufficient weight; and the considerable weight given to the sex-ratio component in the formula. In addition, the index is primarily a measure of net age misreporting and, for the most part, does not measure net underenumeration for age groups. An allowance for the typical decline in the sex ratio from childhood to old age can be made by adjusting the mean difference of the census sex ratios downward by the mean difference between the expected sex ratio for ages under 5 and, say, 70 to 74, derived from life tables. In spite of its limitations, however, the UN index can be a useful measure for making approximate distinctions between countries with respect to the accuracy of reporting age and sex in censuses.

Mathematical Graduation of Census Data

Mathematical graduation of census data can be employed to derive figures for 5-year age groups that are corrected primarily for net reporting error. What these graduation procedures do, essentially, is to "fit" different curves to the original 5- or 10-year totals, modifying the original 5-year totals. Among the major graduation methods are the Carrier-Farrag (1959) ratio method, Karup-King-Newton quadratic interpolation, cubic spline interpolation, Sprague or Beers osculatory methods, and methods developed by the United Nations. The U.S. Census Bureau (1994) has developed a spreadsheet program, AGESMTH, that smooths the 5-year totals of a population using most of these methods.

Other mathematical graduation methods have been developed that require more data than a distribution of the population in 5-year age groups at a single census. Demeny and Shorter (1968) developed a procedure requiring the population in 5-year age groups from two censuses enumerated 5 years apart (or a multiple thereof) and a set of intercensal survivorship probabilities, and the United Nations (1983) developed a procedure of fitting a polynomial based on a single-year-of-age distribution.

Comparison with Population Models

Still another basis of evaluating the census data on age is to compare the actual percentage distribution of the population by age with an expected age distribution corresponding to various population models. One such model is the *stable population model*. In the absence of migration, if fertility and mortality remain constant over several decades; the age distribution of a population would assume a definite unchanging form called stable. Such model age distributions are pertinent in the consideration of actual age distributions because nearly constant fertility and nearly constant or moderately declining mortality are characteristic of some less developed countries. The declines in mortality that have occurred in many populations affect the age distribution to only a small extent. Such countries have a relatively stable distribution (with constant mortality) or a quasi-stable age distribution (with moderately declining mortality). The age distributions of such countries may be represented rather well by the stable age distributions that would result from the persistence of their current fertility and mortality rates. The stable age distribution may then be used as a standard for judging the adequacy of reported age distributions (Coale, 1963; van de Walle, 1966).

With the limitations implied, the inadequacies of the age distribution in particular countries may be measured by comparing the percentage age distributions in these countries with the age distributions of the corresponding stable populations. Specifically, for each age group an index may be calculated by dividing the percentage in the age group in a given country by the corresponding percentage in the stable population. The choice of a stable age distribution to compare with the enumerated population is discussed in Chapter 22. The deviations of the indexes from 1.00 reflect the extent to which a particular age group is relatively overstated or understated as a result of net coverage error or age misreporting. For example, the indexes shown in Table 7.16 for Thailand in 1970 indicate a relatively high proportion of the male and female populations 5 to 14 years old and relatively low proportions in the age range 20 to 29 years (U.S. Census Bureau, 1985).

Comparison with Aggregate Administrative Data

Finally, we note the use of various types of aggregate data, compiled primarily for administrative purposes, to evaluate census data in particular age groups. This procedure assumes that the administrative records are free of the types of errors of coverage and age reporting that characterize household inquiries. It is assumed, for example, that a registration from which the aggregate data are derived is complete and accurate (without omissions, duplications, or inactive records, i.e., records for persons who died or are no longer eligible or obligated to remain in the file) and contains accurate age information, possibly involving formal proof of age. In these comparisons, no attempt is made at matching records for

TABLE 7.16   Comparison of the Enumerated Population of Thailand with a Stable Age Distribution, by Sex: 1970

Age (years)	Males			Females		
	Enumerated population (1)	Stable population[1] (2)	Ratio (3) = (1) ÷ (2)	Enumerated population (4)	Stable population[1] (5)	Ratio (6) = (4) ÷ (5)
All ages	100.0	100.0	—	100.0	100.0	—
0 to 4	16.7	17.3	0.97	16.2	17.0	0.95
5 to 9	15.7	14.4	1.09	15.1	14.2	1.06
10 to 14	13.5	12.3	1.10	13.1	12.1	1.08
15 to 19	10.7	10.5	1.02	10.9	10.3	1.06
20 to 24	7.7	8.8	0.88	7.9	8.8	0.90
25 to 29	6.4	7.5	0.85	6.6	7.4	0.89
30 to 34	6.1	6.3	0.97	6.2	6.2	1.00
35 to 39	5.6	5.3	1.06	5.6	5.3	1.06
40 to 44	4.5	4.4	1.02	4.4	4.4	1.00
45 to 49	3.5	3.6	0.97	3.5	3.7	0.95
50 to 54	2.8	2.9	0.97	2.8	3.0	0.93
55 to 59	2.3	2.3	1.00	2.3	2.4	0.96
60 to 64	1.8	1.7	1.06	1.9	1.9	1.00
65 to 69	1.3	1.2	1.08	1.4	1.4	1.00
70 or older	1.5	1.5	1.00	2.0	1.9	1.05

[1] Stable age distribution with "West" mortality, level 17, and r = .03.

Note: See Chapter 22 for details on methods of selecting particular stable age distributions.

Source: U.S. Bureau of the Census (1985, Figure 5-20).

TABLE 7.17 Percentage Net Undercount of the Census of Population of the United States, by Age and Sex: 1980 and 1990

Percentages relate to the total resident population. Base of percentages is the corrected population. Minus sign (–) denotes a net overcount in the census.

Age (years)	1980			1990		
	Both sexes	Male	Female	Both sexes	Male	Female
Total	1.2	2.2	0.3	1.8	2.8	0.9
Under 5	1.9	2.0	1.9	3.7	3.7	3.7
5 to 9	1.4	1.5	1.4	3.5	3.5	3.6
10 to 14	0.1	0.1	0.2	1.2	1.1	1.3
15 to 19	Z	0.3	–0.3	–1.7	–2.0	–1.3
20 to 24	1.9	3.3	0.5	Z	0.1	–0.2
25 to 29	2.6	4.3	0.9	4.1	5.6	2.5
30 to 34	1.5	3.2	–0.3	3.1	5.1	1.1
35 to 39	2.0	3.8	0.2	2.1	3.7	0.5
40 to 44	1.9	3.9	Z	1.0	2.4	–0.4
45 to 49	2.0	4.0	0.1	2.2	3.7	0.8
50 to 54	1.2	3.1	–0.7	2.1	3.8	0.6
55 to 59	0.8	2.6	–0.8	2.1	3.9	0.3
60 to 64	0.6	1.6	–0.2	1.5	3.3	–0.2
65 and over	–0.1	–0.7	0.3	0.8	1.5	0.3

Z Less than 0.05 percent.

Source: Robinson et al. (1991, appendix Table 2); and U.S. Census Bureau, unpublished tabulations.

individuals; only aggregates are employed. The aggregates may require a substantial amount of adjustment, however, to ensure agreement with the intended census coverage. These data may be a product of the Social Security system, the military registration system, the educational system, the vital registration system, immigration and naturalization programs, and other such programs.

The U.S. Census Bureau has used aggregate administrative data to derive estimates of the total population and corresponding estimates of net census undercounts, for the United States disaggregated by age, sex, and race in 1990, by the method of demographic analysis. The estimates of net census undercounts in 1990 by age and sex are shown in Table 7.17. The table indicates that most age-sex groups do in fact have net undercounts and that there is considerable variation in the size of the undercounts over the age distribution.

Extreme Old Age and Centenarians

Census age distributions at advanced ages, say for those 85 years old and over, suffer from serious reporting problems, with age exaggeration in older ages generally considered to be common (Ewbank, 1981). The extent of misreporting of age of household members due to ignorance

of the true age on the part of the respondent in the household may be considerable in this age range. The most serious reporting problems have been found among reported ages of 95 to 99 and 100 and over (Kestenbaum, 1992). There is a notable tendency, in particular, to report an age over 100 for persons of very advanced age, in part generally attributable to a desire to share in the esteem generally accorded extreme old age or from a gross ignorance of the true age. The exaggeration of the number of centenarians in census statistics is suggested by several considerations. First, if death rates at the later ages are projected to the end of life, the chance of death at age 100 would be extremely high and few persons would remain alive past 100. For example, even though mortality has improved dramatically at the oldest ages, at age 100 the probability of death in one year is in the vicinity of 0.30 to 0.35 according to several life tables (e.g., United States, 1989–1991; France, 1991–1995; Japan, 1991–1995; and Sweden, 1996–1999).[18] Second, the number of survivors 100 years old and over at a given census date, of the population 90 years old and over at the earlier census, tends to be smaller than the current census count of the population 100 years old and over. For example, the 1990 U.S. census count of the population 100 years old and over (37,306) exceeded the number expected on this basis by 8%.[19] Third, the number of centenarians is often disproportionately greater for groups with lower overall levels of life expectancy at birth. For example, about 16% of the 37,306 persons reported at age 100 or over in the 1990 U.S. census were black whereas blacks made up only 12% of the total population and only 7% of the population 85 years old and over.

The census count of persons of extreme old age may also be evaluated by Vincent's (1951) "method of extinct generations." The population 85 years old and over in a census taken in 1970 would have almost completely died off by 1990, so that it should be possible, by cumulating the appropriate statistics of deaths in the period 1970–1990, to reconstruct the "true" population 85 years old and over in 1970. Using an extension of this method incorporating some projected cohort deaths, Das Gupta (1991) estimated 15,236 centenarians in the United States in 1980 compared with an enumerated total of 32,194. Siegel and Passel (1976) had previously applied this method and other techniques of demographic analysis for 1950, 1960, and 1970, with similar results. Another method for estimating the number of centenarians and for evaluating the reported census count of this group is through the use of administrative records data,

[18] See United States 1989–1991 life tables produced by the U.S. National Center for Health Statistics (1997) and the Berkeley Mortality Data Base, http://www.demog.berkeley.edu/wilmoth/mortality/.

[19] A similar calculation is described in Myers (1966). Applying this calculation to 1980 census data results in an expected 34,480 centenarians in 1990.

specifically Medicare records. Estimates of the centenarian population using the Master Beneficiary Record File for Medicare also suggest that reported census totals of the population 100 years old and over represent an overcount of this group (Kestenbaum 1992, 1998).[20]

The thinness of the figures in the range 85 years old and over results in considerable fluctuation in rates based on them. Preston, Elo, and Stewart (1997) determined that several alternative patterns of age misreporting all led to underestimates of mortality at the oldest ages. However, it is necessary to compute rates for ages until the end of the life span for many purposes, such as to develop certain measures for the whole population or some particular age (e.g., computation of the value for life expectancy at birth or at age 40). Thus, even though in such cases the rates may not be correct in themselves, they are necessary to develop the other measures. Moreover, there is a direct interest in measuring the increase in the number of very old persons because of higher public health costs for this growing number and because of possible indications of increase in human life span.

Age Not Reported

Age is not always reported in a census, even though the enumerator may be instructed to secure an estimate from the respondent or to estimate it as well as possible while enumerating. In many national censuses, persons whose age is not reported by the respondent are assigned an age on the basis of an estimate made by the enumerator or on the basis of an estimate made in the processing of the census; or the category of "unknown" ages is distributed arithmetically prior to publication. As a result, census age distributions presented in recent UN *Demographic Yearbooks* often do not show a category of unknown age. The method used in national censuses to eliminate frequencies in this category is not always known, and hence it is not usually indicated in the UN tables. About one-half of the census age distributions (of about 75 countries with census age distributions reported) shown in the 1997 *Demographic Yearbook* have frequencies in a category of age not reported.

In population censuses of the United States since 1940, ages have been assigned to persons whose age was not reported on the basis of related information on the schedule for the person and other members of the household, such as the age of other members of the family (particularly the spouse) or marital status, and, for ages based on data from the long-form questionnaire, using information such as school attendance and employment status. In censuses since 1960, the allocation of age has been carried out by electronic computer on the basis of the record of an individual just previously enumerated in the census who had characteristics similar to those of the person whose age was not reported, whereas in 1950 and 1940 the allocation was made on the basis of distributions derived from the same or previous censuses. Because the age allocations are based on actual age distributions of similar population groups or the actual characteristics of the same individuals, the resulting assignments of age should be reasonable and show relatively little error.

The proportion of the total population whose age was not reported in the field enumeration of the decennial censuses of the United States was quite low until 1960. In each census since 1960, the assignment of age has been relatively more common, in part as a result of the shift of the census operation to primarily a "mail-out, mail-back" procedure. The reported percentages for each census since 1900 (with the separate percentages allocated and substituted[21] shown in parentheses, respectively) are as follows:

1900	0.3	1950	0.2
1910	0.2	1960	2.2 (= 1.7 + 0.5)
1920	0.1	1970	5.0 (= 2.6 + 2.4)
1930	0.1	1980	4.4 (= 2.9 + 1.5)
1940	0.2	1990	3.0 (= 2.4 + 0.6)

The recent procedures used to handle unreported age in the U.S. censuses are superior to those used generally in the censuses before 1940, when the number of persons whose age was not reported was shown in the published tables as a separate category, or in the 1880 census, when the "unknown ages" were distributed before printing in proportion to the ages reported. The pre-1940 procedure creates inconveniences in the use of the data, results in less accurate age data, and contributes to the cost of publication. Although simple prorating, like that in 1880, has its limitations (e.g., the results are subject to error and the procedure can be applied to only a few principal age distributions), it is about the only method feasible for eliminating the unknown ages from the age distributions of the censuses before 1940. This elimination is desirable not only for the reasons previously stated but also for making comparisons of the age statistics of two censuses.

To accomplish the arithmetic distribution of the unknown ages, it may be assumed that those of unknown age have the same percentage distribution by age as those of known age. The application of this assumption simply involves

---

[20] For a discussion of the quality of U.S. census data on centenarians, also see Spencer (1986) and U.S. Census Bureau/Krach and Velkoff (1999).

[21] In the 1990 census, for example, age was *allocated* for 2.4% of the enumerated population on the basis of other information regarding the same person, other persons in the household, or persons with similar characteristics reported on the census questionnaire. Age and all other population characteristics were *substituted* for an additional 0.6% of the population. Recall that substitution occurs as a part of the process of providing characteristics for persons not tallied because of the failure to interview households or because of mechanical failure in processing. The allocation ratio of 2.4% and the substitution rate of 0.6% combined imply that 3.0% of the 1990 census population had a computer-generated age.

TABLE 7.18   Procedure for Prorating Ages Not Reported, for Zimbabwe: 1992

Age (years)	Population as enumerated (1)	Population with ages not reported distributed over all ages (1) × f₁ = (2)	Population with ages not reported distributed over ages 20 years and over (1) × f₂ (ages 20 and over) = (3)
Total	10,412,548	10,412,548	10,412,548
Under 5	1,584,691	1,589,880	1,584,691
5 to 9	1,653,788	1,659,203	1,653,788
10 to 14	1,456,751	1,461,521	1,456,751
15 to 19	1,248,238	1,252,326	1,248,238
20 to 24	989,897	993,139	997,483
25 to 34	1,318,573	1,322,891	1,328,676
35 to 44	852,690	855,482	859,224
45 to 54	569,478	571,343	573,842
55 to 64	361,165	362,348	363,933
65 and over	343,291	344,415	345,922
Age not reported	33,986	(X)	(X)

Factors f_1 and f_2 are based on data in col. (1):

$$f_1 = \frac{\text{Total population}}{\substack{\text{Total population} \\ \text{of reported age}}} = \frac{\sum(P_a + P_u)}{\sum P_a} = \frac{10,412,548}{10,378,562} = 1.003274635$$

$$f_2 = \frac{\substack{\text{Population 20 years and} \\ \text{over + unreported ages}}}{\substack{\text{Population 20 years} \\ \text{and over}}} = \frac{\sum(P_a + P_u)}{\sum P_a} = \frac{4,469,080}{4,435,094} = 1.007662972$$

X: Not applicable.

Source: Basic data from U.S. Census Bureau (2000a, Table 4), www.census.gov/ipc/www/idbacc.html.

multiplying the number reported at each age by a factor equal to the ratio of the total population to the number whose age was reported; that is,

$$\frac{\sum\limits_{0}^{x} P_a + P_u}{\sum\limits_{0}^{x} P_a} \times P_a \qquad (7.19)$$

where P_a represents the number reported at each age and P_u the number whose age was not reported.[22] Table 7.18 illus-

[22] The numbers so obtained are the same as the numbers obtained by the longer procedure of computing the percentage distribution of persons of reported age, distributing the number of age not reported according to this percentage distribution, and adding the two absolute distributions together.

trates this procedure for distributing unreported ages in the case of the population of Zimbabwe in 1992. It may be more appropriate to distribute the unknowns among adults only. Table 7.18 also illustrates the procedure for distributing the unreported ages among the population 20 years old and over for the population of Zimbabwe in 1992.

The relative magnitude of this category reflects in a rough way the quality of the data on age. The existence of a very large proportion of persons of unknown age may raise a question as to the validity of the reported age distribution, although, as stated, this situation is quite uncommon.

ANALYSIS OF AGE COMPOSITION

General Techniques of Numerical and Graphic Analysis

Nature of Age Distributions

Data on age are most commonly tabulated and published in 5-year groups (0–4, 5–9, etc.). This detail is sufficient to provide an indication of the form of the age distribution and to serve most analytic uses. For some types of analysis, however, data for single years may be needed. In some parts of the age range (i.e., the late teens, early twenties, late middle age) changes in some of the characteristics of the population (i.e., labor force status, marital status, school enrollment status) are so rapid that single-year-of-age data are required to present them adequately. For other analytic purposes age data may be combined to obtain figures for various broader groups than 5-year groups. Age distributions consisting of combinations of 5-year age groups and 10-year age groups, or 10-year age groups only, may sometimes be published so as to achieve consolidation of masses of data and the reduction of sampling error, yet to provide sufficient detail to indicate variations by age and permit alternative combinations of age groups.

Further consolidation or special combinations are desirable to represent special age groups. For fertility analysis the total number of women 15 to 44 or 15 to 49 years of age (the childbearing ages) is significant; the population 5 to 17 (school ages) is important in educational research and planning; and the group 18 to 24 as a whole roughly defines the traditional college-age group, the group of prime military age, and the principal ages of labor force entry and marriage. For many purposes, the numbers of persons 18 and over and 21 and over are useful.

A classification of the total population into several mutually exclusive broad age groups having general functional significance may be found useful for a wide variety of analytic purposes. One such classification is as follows: under 5 years, the preschool ages; 5 to 17 years, the school ages; 18 to 44 years, the earlier working years, 45 to 64 years, the later working years; 65 years and over, the period of retirement. Any grouping of the ages into working ages, school ages, retirement ages, and so on is admittedly arbitrary and requires some adaptation to the customs and institutional practices of different areas or some modifications as these practices change. For example, in the early 19th century in the United States, the period of labor force participation was considerably longer than today, extending back into the current ages of compulsory school attendance and forward into the current ages of retirement.

Special interest also attaches to the numbers reaching certain "threshold" ages in each year. These usually correspond to the initial ages of the functional groupings described in the previous paragraph. On reaching these ages, new social roles are assumed or new stages in the life cycle are begun (e.g. birth and reaching age 5 or 6, 18, 21, and 65 in the western countries).

Percentage Distributions

In the simplest kind of analysis of age data, the magnitude of the numbers relative to one another is examined. If the absolute numbers distributed by 5-year age groups are converted to percentages, a clearer indication of the relative magnitudes of the numbers in the distribution is obtained. Conversion to percentages is necessary if the age distributions of different countries of quite different population size are to be conveniently compared, either numerically or graphically. The percentage distribution by age of the population of Mexico in 1990, for example, was quite different from that of the United States:

	Total	Under 5	5 to 14	15 to 24	25 to 34	35 to 44	45 to 64	65+
Mexico	100.0	12.6	25.9	21.7	14.6	10.0	11.0	4.2
U.S.	100.0	7.4	14.2	14.8	17.4	15.1	18.6	12.6

Percentage Changes by Age

An important phase of the analysis of age data relates to the measurement of changes over time. Most of the methods of description and analysis of age data to be considered next are applicable not only to the comparison of different populations but also to the comparison of the same population at different dates.

The simplest measure of change by age is given by the amount and percentage of change at each age. Table 7.19 shows the amounts and percentages of change for the U.S. population for 5-year age groups between 1980 and 1990.

Use of Indexes

Comparison between two percentage age distributions is facilitated by calculating indexes for each age group or overall indexes for the distributions. Age distributions for different areas, for population subgroups in a single area, and for the same area at different dates may be compared in this way.

Index of Relative Difference

The magnitude of the differences between any two age distributions, whether for different areas, dates, or population subgroups, may be summarized in single indexes from

TABLE 7.19   Population of the United States, 1980 and 1990, and Percentage Change, by Age, 1980 to 1990

Age (years)	Population		Increase[1]	
	1990 (1)	1980 (2)	Amount (1) − (2) = (3)	Percentage [(3) ÷ (2)] × 100 = (4)
Total	248,709,873	226,545,805	22,164,068	9.8
Under 5	18,354,443	16,348,254	2,006,189	12.3
5 to 9	18,099,179	16,699,956	1,399,223	8.4
10 to 14	17,114,249	18,242,129	−1,127,880	−6.2
15 to 19	17,754,015	21,168,124	−3,414,109	−16.1
20 to 24	19,020,312	21,318,704	−2,298,392	−10.8
25 to 29	21,313,045	19,520,919	1,792,126	9.2
30 to 34	21,862,887	17,560,920	4,301,967	24.5
35 to 44	37,578,903	25,634,710	11,944,193	46.6
45 to 54	25,223,086	22,799,787	2,423,299	10.6
55 to 64	21,147,923	21,702,875	−554,952	−2.6
65 and over	31,241,831	25,549,427	5,692,404	22.3

[1] A minus (−) sign denotes a decrease.

Source: Based on U.S. Census Bureau (1992, Table 14); and U.S. Bureau of the Census (1983, Table 43).

the individual age-specific proportions or indexes. Two such indexes are the index of relative difference and the index of dissimilarity. In the former procedure, (1) the deviations of the age-specific indexes from 100 are summed without regard to sign, (2) one-nth (n representing the number of age groups) of the sum is taken to derive the mean of the percentage differences at each age, and (3) the result in step 2 is divided by 2 to obtain the index of relative difference. The formula is

$$IRD = \frac{1}{2} \times \frac{\sum \left| \left(\frac{r_{2a}}{r_{1a}} \times 100 \right) - 100 \right|}{n} \qquad (7.20)$$

To reduce the likelihood of very large percent differences at the oldest ages, which are given equal weight in the average, a broad terminal age group should be used. The procedure is illustrated in Table 7.20 with the calculation of the index of relative difference between the age distribution of the United States and those of Norway and Mexico in 1990.

Index of Dissimilarity

Another summary measure of the difference between two age distributions—the index of dissimilarity—is based on the absolute differences between the percentages at each age. In this procedure, the differences between the percentages

TABLE 7.20 Calculation of Index of Relative Difference and Index of Dissimilarity of Age Distributions for Norway and Mexico Compared with the United States: 1990

Age (years)	United States (1990) Percentage of total (r_{1a}) (1)	Norway (1990) Percentage of total (r_{2a}) (2)	Norway (1990) Index $[(2) \div (1)] \times 100 =$ (3)	Norway (1990) Difference from United States, 1990 $(2) - (1) =$ (4)	Mexico (1990) Percent of total (r_{2a}) (5)	Mexico (1990) Index $[(5) \div (1)] \times 100 =$ (6)	Mexico (1990) Difference from United States, 1990 $(5) - (1) =$ (7)
Total	100.00	100.00	100.00	—	100.00	100.00	—
Under 5	7.38	6.48	87.81	−0.90	12.62	171.07	+5.24
5 to 14	14.16	12.27	86.65	−1.89	25.94	183.24	+11.79
15 to 24	14.79	15.25	103.15	+0.47	21.66	146.50	+6.88
25 to 34	17.36	15.10	86.98	−2.26	14.60	84.11	−2.76
35 to 44	15.11	14.66	97.03	−0.45	10.00	66.19	−5.11
45 to 54	10.14	10.80	106.49	+0.66	6.64	65.51	−3.50
55 to 64	8.50	8.95	105.25	+0.45	4.34	51.05	−4.16
65 to 74	7.28	9.28	127.51	+2.00	2.49	34.20	−4.79
75 and over	5.28	7.21	136.44	+1.92	1.69	32.03	−3.59
(1) Sum of percent differences without regard to sign = $\Sigma|$Index − 100$|$			120.36			467.70	
(2) Mean percent difference = $(\Sigma|$Index − 100$|) \div 9$			13.4			52.0	
(3) Index of relative difference = Half of mean percent difference = (2) ÷ 2			6.7			26.0	
(4) Sum of absolute differences without regard to sign = $\Sigma|r_{2a} - r_{1a}|$				11.00			47.81
(5) Index of dissimilarity = Half of sum of absolute differences = $\Sigma|r_{2a} - r_{1a}| \div 2$				5.5			23.9

— Represents zero.

Source: Based on U.S. Census Bureau (1992, Table 14; 2000a, Table 4), www.census.gov/ipc/www/idbacc.html.

for corresponding age groups are determined, they are summed without regard to sign, and one-half of the sum is taken (Duncan, 1959; Duncan and Duncan, 1955). (Taking one-half the sum of the absolute differences is equivalent to taking the sum of the positive differences or the sum of the negative differences.) The general formula is then

$$ID = \frac{1}{2} \sum |r_{2a} - r_{1a}| \qquad (7.21)$$

As noted in Chapter 6 the magnitude of these indexes is affected by the number of age classes in the distribution as well as by the size of the differences and, hence, the results are of greatest value in comparison with similarly computed indexes for other populations.

A third summary measure of differences between age distributions (illustrated in Chapter 6) is the Theil Coefficient (or Entropy Index). (See Reardon *et al.*, 2000, pp. 352–356.) It has the advantage that more than two distributions may be compared in a single measure.

Median Age

The analysis of age distributions may be carried further by computing some measure of central tendency. The choice of the measure of central tendency of a distribution depends, in general, on the logic of employing one or another measure, the form of the distribution, the arithmetic problems of applying one or another measure, and the extent to which the measure is sensitive to variations in the distribution. The most appropriate measure of central tendency for an age distribution is the median. The median age of an age distribution may be defined as the age that divides the population into two groups of equal-size, one of which is younger and the other of which is older than the median. It corresponds to the 50-percentile mark in the distribution. The median age must not be thought of as a point of concentration in age distributions of the population, however.

The arithmetic mean may also be considered as a measure of central tendency for age distributions. It is generally viewed as less appropriate than the median for this purpose because of the marked skewness of the age distribution of the general population. In addition, the calculation of the arithmetic mean is often complicated by the fact that many age distributions end with broad open-ended intervals, such as 65 and over or 75 and over. Because the calculation of the mean takes account of the entire distribution, however, it is more sensitive to variations in it.

Inasmuch as the general form of the age distribution of the general population (i.e., reverse logistic and right skewness) appears also in many other important types of demographic distributions (e.g., families by size, births and birthrates by birth order, birthrates by age for married women, age of the population enrolled in school, age of the single population), the median is commonly used as a summarizing measure of central tendency in demographic analysis.

Because of the importance of the median in demographic analysis, it is desirable to review here the method of computing it. The formula for computing the median age from grouped data, as well as for computing the median of any continuous quantitative variable from grouped data,[23] may be given as

$$Md = l_{Md} + \left(\frac{\frac{N}{2} - \sum f_x}{f_{Md}} \right) i \qquad (7.22)$$

where l_{Md} = the lower limit of the class containing the middle, or $N/2^{th}$ item; N = the sum of all the frequencies; $\sum f_x$ = the sum of the frequencies in all the classes preceding the class containing the $N/2^{th}$ item; f_{Md} = frequency of the class containing the $N/2^{th}$ item; and i = size of the class interval containing the $N/2^{th}$ item. If there is a category of age not reported, *N* would exclude the frequencies of this class. We may illustrate the application of the formula by computing the median age of the population of India in 1991, using the following data:

Age (years)	Population (in thousands)	Age (years)	Population (in thousands)
Total	838,568	55 to 59	21,473
0 to 4	102,378	60 to 64	22,749
5 to 9	111,295	65 to 69	12,858
10 to 14	98,692	70 to 74	10,554
15 to 19	79,035	75 to 79	4,146
20 to 24	74,473	80 and over	6,375
25 to 29	69,239	Age not reported	4,695
30 to 34	58,404		
35 to 39	52,399		
40 to 44	42,556		
45 to 49	36,134		
50 to 54	31,114		

Source: U.S. Census Bureau (2000a, Table 4).

The $N/2^{th}$, or "middle," person falls in the class interval 20 to 24 years. The formula may be evaluated as follows:

$$Md = 20.0 + \left(\frac{\frac{833,873}{2} - 391,400}{74,473} \right) 5$$

$$= 20.0 + \left(\frac{25,537}{74,473} \right) 5$$

$$= 20.0 + (.3429)5 = 20.0 + 1.7$$

$$= 21.7$$

---

[23] A continuous quantitative variable is a quantitative variable that may assume values at any point on the numerical scale within the whole range of the variable (e.g., age, income, birth weight). This type of variable should be distinguished from discontinuous, or discrete, quantitative variables, which may assume only integral values within the range of the variable (e.g., size of family, order of birth, children ever born).

Medians are regularly shown for the principal age distributions published in the decennial census reports of the U.S. Census Bureau, but this is not common practice in national census volumes elsewhere. The United Nations also presents median ages in its periodic reports on population projections for the countries of the world.

Measures of Old and of Aging Populations

The *median age* is often used as a basis for describing a population as "young" or "old" or as "aging" or "younging" (i.e., "growing younger"). An examination of the medians for a wide variety of countries around 1990 suggests a current range from 16 years to 38 years (Table 7.21). Populations with medians under 20 may be described as "young," those with medians 30 or over as "old," and those with medians 20 to 29 as of "intermediate" age. Kenya (15.9 years) and Bangladesh (17.9) are in the first category; Sweden (38.5) and France (35.5) are in the second; and India (21.7), Thailand (25.1), and Chile (26.3) are in the third. The U.S. population, with a median age of 32.9 years in 1990, is among the populations that are relatively "old". When the median age rises, the population may be said to be "aging," and when it falls, the population may be said to be "younging."

The *proportion of aged persons* has also been regarded as an indicator of a young or old population and of a population that is aging or younging (Table 7.21). On this basis, populations with 10.0% or more 65 years old and over may be said to be old (e.g., Japan, 12.1%, and Austria, 15.0%) and those with under 5.0% may be said to be young (e.g., Zambia, 2.6%, and Bolivia, 4.3%). Chile had 6.6%, India had only 4.1%, and Thailand only 4.6%. The examples of India and Thailand reflect the fact that the degree of "youth" or "age" depends to some extent on the measure employed and the classification categories of that measure. A still different indication of the degree to which a population is old or young and is aging or younging is given by the *proportion of people under age 15*. Again, let us suggest some limits for the proportion under 15 for characterizing a population as young or old: under 25.0% as old (e.g., Spain, 19.4%, and Belgium, 18.2%) and 35.0% and over as young (e.g., Bolivia, 41.4%, Uganda, 47.3%, and the Philippines, 39.6%). South Korea (25.7%) and Brazil (34.7%) fall, respectively, just at the lower and upper limits of the intermediate category.

A fourth measure, *the ratio of the number of elderly persons to the number of children*, or the *aged-child ratio*, takes into account the numbers and changes at both ends of the age distribution simultaneously. It may be represented by the following formula:

$$\frac{P^{65+}}{P_{0-14}} \times 100 \qquad (7.23)$$

TABLE 7.21 Summary Measures of Age Composition for Various Countries: Around 1990

| Country and year | Median age (1) | Percentage of total population | | Ratio of aged persons to children (per 100) (4) |
		Under 15 years (2)	65 years and over (3)	
Africa				
Kenya (1989)	15.9	47.9	3.3	6.9
South Africa (1991)	22.7	34.6	4.3	12.4
Uganda (1991)	16.3	47.3	3.3	7.1
Zambia (1990)	16.8	45.3	2.6	5.7
Zimbabwe (1992)	17.0	45.2	3.3	7.3
North America				
Canada (1991)	na	20.9	11.6	55.7
Mexico (1990)	19.8	38.6	4.2	10.8
United States (1990)	32.9	21.5	12.6	58.3
South America				
Argentina (1991)	27.2	30.6	8.9	29.0
Bolivia (1992)	19.2	41.4	4.3	10.3
Brazil (1991)	22.7	34.7	4.8	13.9
Chile (1992)	26.3	29.4	6.6	22.3
Ecuador (1990)	20.3	38.8	4.3	11.2
Venezuela (1990)	21.1	37.2	4.0	10.8
Asia				
Bangladesh (1991)	17.9	45.1	3.2	7.2
China (1990)	25.3	27.6	5.6	20.2
India (1991)	21.7	37.5	4.1	10.9
Indonesia (1990)	21.6	36.5	3.9	10.6
Japan (1990)	37.5	18.2	12.1	66.2
Malaysia (1991)	21.9	36.7	3.7	10.2
Philippines (1990)	19.7	39.6	3.4	8.6
South Korea (1990)	27.0	25.7	5.0	19.4
Thailand (1990)	25.1	28.8	4.6	15.9
Vietnam (1989)	20.2	39.0	4.7	12.2
Europe				
Austria (1991)	35.6	17.4	15.0	86.0
Belgium (1991)	36.5	18.2	18.5	101.7
France (1990)	35.5	19.1	14.7	77.4
Greece (1991)	36.1	19.2	13.7	71.1
Hungary (1990)	36.3	20.5	13.2	64.5
Portugal (1991)	34.5	20.0	13.6	68.1
Russia (1989)	32.8	23.1	9.6	41.7
Spain (1991)	33.9	19.4	13.8	71.3
Sweden (1990)	38.5	17.8	17.9	100.6
United Kingdom (1991)	36.3	19.1	16.0	83.8
Oceania				
Australia (1991)	32.4	22.3	11.3	50.6
New Zealand (1991)	31.4	23.2	11.3	48.5

Source: Basic data from U.S. Census Bureau (2000a, Table 4), www.census.gov/ipc/www/idbacc.html.

For India in 1991, the value of this measure is

$$\frac{33,933,000}{312,365,000} \times 100 = 10.9$$

Populations with aged-child ratios under 15, like India's, may be described as young (e.g., Kenya, 6.9, Bolivia, 10.3) and populations with aged-child ratios over 30 may be described as old (e.g., France, 77.4, and Japan, 66.2). Many less developed countries have so small a proportion of persons 65 and over and so large a proportion of children under 15 that it seems desirable to broaden the range of the numerator and narrow that of the denominator. If the age groups under 10 and 50 and over are used for India in 1991, the value of this ratio is (109,268,000 ÷ 213,673,000) × 100, or 51.1. In some more developed countries, the aging of the population has progressed rather far, and the aged-child ratio may approximate or even exceed 100. For example, the ratios in Sweden (100.6) and Belgium (101.7) indicate that the number of aged persons exceeds the number of children under 15. Of the summary indicators of aging we have mentioned—increase in median age, increase in proportion of aged persons, decrease in proportion of children, and increase in ratio of aged persons to children—the last measure, in one or another variant, is most sensitive to differences or changes in age composition and for some purposes may be considered the best index of population aging.

The four criteria of aging described may not give a consistent indication as to whether the population is aging or not. Because changes in the median age over some period depend merely on the relative magnitude of the growth rates of the total age segments above and below the initial median age during the period, the median age may hardly change while the proportions of aged persons and of children may both increase or both decrease. Accordingly, a population may in some cases appear to be aging and younging at the same time. A combination of a rise in the proportion 65 and over and a rise in the proportion under 15 would, of course, be accompanied by a decline in the proportion in the intermediate ages.

Aging of a population should be distinguished from the aging of individuals, an increase in the longevity of individuals, or an increase in the average length of life pertaining to a population. The latter two types of changes reflect declines in mortality and result from improvements in the quality of the environment, life-style changes, improvements in public health practices, and medical advances among other factors. The aging of a population is a characteristic of an age distribution and is importantly affected by the trend of the birth rate as well as by the trend of mortality.

Age Dependency Ratios

The variations in the proportions of children, aged persons, and persons of "working age" are taken account of jointly in the age dependency ratio (or its complement, the support ratio). The age dependency ratio represents the ratio of the combined child population and aged population to the population of intermediate age. One formula for the age dependency ratio useful for international comparisons relates the number of persons under 15 and 65 and over to the number 15 to 64:[24]

$$\frac{P_{0-14} + P_{65+}}{P_{15-64}} \times 100 \qquad (7.24)$$

Applying the formula to the data for India in 1991, we have

$$\frac{312,365,000 + 33,933,000}{487,575,000} \times 100 = 71.0$$

Separate calculation of the child-dependency ratio, or the component of the age dependency ratio representing children under 15 (i.e., the ratio of children under 15 to persons 15 to 64), and the old-age dependency ratio, or the component representing persons 65 and over (i.e., the ratio of persons 65 and over to persons 15 to 64), gives values of 64.1 and 7.0 (Table 7.22). The corresponding figures for the total-, child-, and aged-dependency ratios for Portugal in 1991 are 50.6, 30.1, and 20.5. As suggested by the figures for India and Portugal, differences (and changes) in age dependency ratios reflect primarily differences (and changes) in the proportion of the population under 15 rather than in the proportion of the population 65 and over.

Age dependency ratios for a number of countries around 1990 are shown in Table 7.22. In very young populations, ratios may exceed 100 (e.g., Uganda, 103; Kenya, 105); others are only about 50 (e.g., Canada, 48; France, 51). These figures reflect the great differences from country to country in the burden of dependency that the working-age population must bear—differences that are principally related to differences in the proportion of children and hence to differences in fertility rates. The figures for Northern and Western Europe, however, show a more even influence of the two components of the dependency ratio.

Variations in the age dependency ratio reflect in a general way the contribution of variations in age composition to variations in economic dependency. The age dependency ratio is a measure of age composition, not of economic dependency, however. The economic dependency ratio may be defined as the ratio of the economically inactive

---

[24] An alternative formula employs the population under 18 for child dependents and the population 18 to 64 for adults of working age. This formula is more applicable to the more developed countries where entry into the workforce typically comes relatively later than in less developed countries. Still other formulas employ the population 60 and over for the adult dependents and the population 15 to 59 (or 20 to 59) for adults of working age, especially for the less developed countries.

TABLE 7.22   Age Dependency Ratios for Various Countries: Around 1990 (ratios per 100)

Country and year	Total dependency ratio[1] (1)	Child dependency ratio[2] (2)	Aged dependency
Africa			
Kenya (1989)	104.9	98.2	6.8
South Africa (1991)	63.7	56.6	7.0
Uganda (1991)	102.5	95.8	6.8
Zambia (1990)	91.9	86.9	4.9
Zimbabwe (1992)	94.4	87.9	6.4
North America			
Canada (1991)	48.1	30.9	17.2
Mexico (1990)	74.7	67.4	7.3
United States (1990)	51.7	32.7	19.1
South America			
Argentina (1991)	65.1	50.5	14.6
Bolivia (1992)	84.0	76.1	7.8
Brazil (1991)	65.4	57.5	8.0
Chile (1992)	56.3	46.0	10.3
Ecuador (1990)	75.7	68.1	7.6
Venezuela (1990)	70.2	63.4	6.8
Asia			
Bangladesh (1991)	93.7	87.5	6.3
China (1990)	49.7	41.3	8.3
India (1991)	71.0	64.1	7.0
Indonesia (1990)	67.7	61.2	6.5
Japan (1990)	43.5	26.2	17.3
Malaysia (1991)	67.8	61.5	6.3
Philippines (1990)	75.5	69.5	6.0
South Korea (1990)	44.2	37.0	7.2
Thailand (1990)	50.1	43.2	6.9
Vietnam (1989)	77.8	69.3	8.4
Europe			
Austria (1991)	47.9	25.7	22.1
Belgium (1991)	57.7	28.6	29.1
France (1990)	51.0	28.8	22.3
Greece (1991)	49.1	28.7	20.4
Hungary (1990)	51.0	31.0	20.0
Portugal (1991)	50.6	30.1	20.5
Russia (1989)	48.7	34.4	14.3
Spain (1991)	49.7	29.0	20.7
Sweden (1990)	55.7	27.7	27.9
United Kingdom (1991)	53.9	29.3	24.6
Oceania			
Australia (1991)	50.7	33.7	17.1
New Zealand (1991)	52.6	35.5	17.2

[1] Ratio of persons under 15 years of age and 65 years and over to persons 15 to 64 years of age (per 100).

[2] Ratio of persons under 15 years of age to persons 15 to 64 years of age (per 100).

[3] Ratio of persons 65 years and over to persons 15 to 64 years of age (per 100).

Source: Basic data from U.S. Census Bureau (2000a, Table 4), www.census.gov/ipc/www/idbacc.html.

population to the active population over all ages or of nonworkers to workers (see Chapter 10).

Special Graphic Measures

This section describes two graphic measures that are particularly applicable to the analysis of age composition, supplementing those previously illustrated in earlier chapters applicable to age data.

Time Series Charts

The first, called the *one hundred percent stacked area chart*, may be employed to depict temporal changes in percentage age composition. Figure 7.1 shows the change in the percentage distribution of the population in broad age groups for the United States from 1900 to 1990.

Population Pyramid

A very effective and quite widely used method of graphically depicting the age-sex composition of a population is called a population pyramid. A population pyramid is designed to give a detailed picture of the age-sex structure of a population, indicating either single ages, 5-year groups, or other age combinations. The basic pyramid form consists of bars, representing age groups in ascending order from the lowest to the highest, pyramided horizontally on one another (see Figure 7.2). The bars for males are given on the left of a central vertical axis, and the bars for females are given on the right of the axis.

The number of males or females in the particular age group is indicated by the length of the bars from the central axis. The age scale is usually shown straddling the central axis, although it may be shown at the right or left of the pyramid only, or both on the right and left, perhaps in terms of both age and year of birth. In general, the age groups in a given pyramid must have the same class interval and must be represented by bars of equal thickness. Most commonly, pyramids show 5-year age groups.

A special problem is presented in the handling of the oldest age groups. If data are available for the oldest age groups in the standard class interval (e.g., 5-year age groups) until the end of the life span, the upper section of the pyramid would have an elongated needlelike form and convey little information for the space required. On the other hand, the bar for a broad terminal group generally is not used because it would not ordinarily be visually comparable with the bars for the other age groups. For this reason, pyramids are usually truncated at an open-ended age group where the data begin to run thin (e.g., 75 years and over, or 80 years and over, or higher).

Pyramids may be constructed on the basis of either absolute numbers or percentages. A special caution to be observed in constructing a "percentage" pyramid is to be

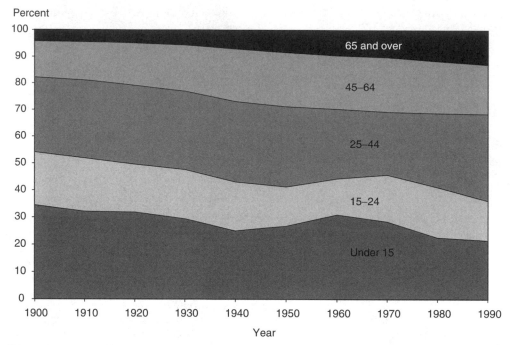

FIGURE 7.1   100–Percent Stacked Area Chart Showing Percent Distribution of the Population by Broad Age Groups for the United States: 1900 to 1990. Source: U.S. Census Bureau, census of population, 1900 to 2000.

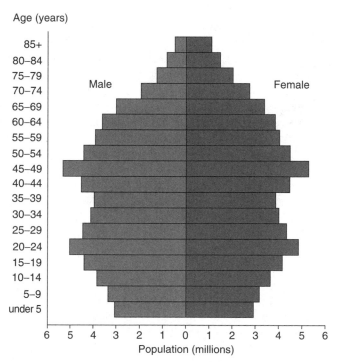

FIGURE 7.2   Population Pyramid for Japan: 1995. Source: U.S. Census Bureau (2000a).

sure to calculate the percentages on the basis of the grand total for the population, including both sexes and all ages (but excluding the population with age not reported). A percentage pyramid is similar, in the geometric sense of the word, to the corresponding "absolute" pyramid. With an appropriate selection of scales, the two pyramids are identical. The choice of one or the other type of pyramid is more important when pyramids for different dates, areas, or subpopulations are to be compared. Only absolute pyramids can show the differences or changes in the overall size of the total population and in the numbers at each age. Percentage pyramids show the differences or changes in the proportional size of each age-sex group. In general, pyramids to be compared should be drawn with the same horizontal scale and with bars of the same thickness.

Comparisons between pyramids for the same area at different dates and between pyramids for different areas or subpopulations may be facilitated by superimposing one pyramid on another either entirely or partly. The pyramids may be distinguished by use of different colors or cross-hatching schemes. Occasionally in absolute pyramids and invariably in percentage pyramids, the relative length of the bars in the two superimposed pyramids reverses at some ages. The graphical representation then becomes more complicated. For example, if one pyramid is to be drawn exactly over another and if the first pyramid is shown entirely in one color or cross-hatching scheme, then the parts of the bars in the second pyramid extending beyond the bars for the first pyramid would be shown in a second color or cross-hatching scheme, and the parts of the bars in the first pyramid extending beyond the bars for the second pyramid would be shown in a third color or cross-hatching scheme (Figure 7.3). An alternative design is to show the second pyramid wholly or partly offset from the first one. In this design, the first pyramid is presented in the conventional

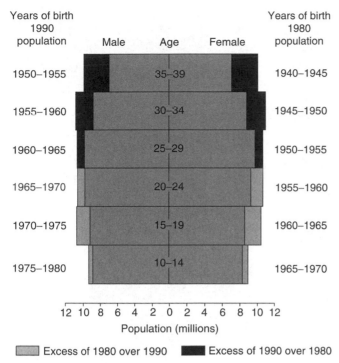

FIGURE 7.3 Section of the Pyramid for the Population of the United States: 1980 and 1990. Source: Table 7.19.

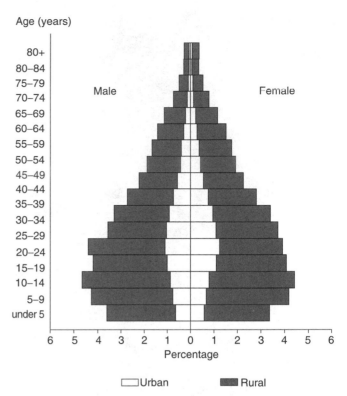

FIGURE 7.4 Percent Distribution of the Population of Thailand by Urban–Rural Residence, Age, and Sex: 1990. Source: United Nations (1999 Table 7).

way except that the bars are separated from age to age. The second pyramid is drawn partially superimposed on the first, using the space between the bars wholly or in part.

Any characteristic that varies by age and sex (e.g., marital status or urban-rural residence) may be added to a general population pyramid to develop a pyramid that reflects the age-sex distribution of both the general population and the population having the additional characteristic (Figure 7.4). Where additional characteristics beyond age and sex are included in the pyramid, the principles of construction are essentially the same. The bar for each age is subdivided into parts representing each category of the characteristic (e.g., single, married, widowed, divorced; urban, rural). It is important that each category shown separately occupy the same position in every bar relative to the central axis and to the other category or categories shown. Again, if percentages are used, they should be calculated on a single base, the total population. Various cross-hatching schemes or coloring schemes may be used to distinguish the various categories of the characteristic represented in the pyramid. When characteristics are added to a population pyramid, the age-sex distribution is shown most clearly for the innermost category in the pyramid and for the total population covered; the distribution of the other categories is harder to interpret. Population pyramids may also be employed to depict the age-sex distribution of demographic events—such

as deaths, marriages, divorces, and migration—during some period.

Pyramids may be analyzed and compared in terms of such characteristics as the relative magnitude of the area on each side of the central axis of the pyramid (the symmetry of the pyramid) or a part of it, the length of a bar or group of bars in relation to adjacent bars, and the steepness and regularity of the slope. (A pyramid may be described as having a steep slope when the sides of the pyramid recede very gradually and rise fairly vertically, and a gentle slope when the sides recede rapidly.) These characteristics of pyramids reflect, respectively, the proportion of the sexes, the proportion of the population in any particular age class or classes, and the general age structure of the population.

Populations with rather different age-sex structures are illustrated by the several pyramids shown in Figure 7.5. The pyramid for Uganda (1991) has a very broad base and narrows very rapidly. This pyramid illustrates the case of an age-sex structure with a very large proportion of children, a very small proportion of elderly persons, and a low median age (i.e., a relatively "young" population). The pyramid for Sweden (1990) has a relatively narrow base and a middle section of nearly the same dimensions, exhibiting a more rectangular shape. This pyramid illustrates the case of an age-sex structure with a very small proportion of children, a very large proportion of elderly persons, and a high median

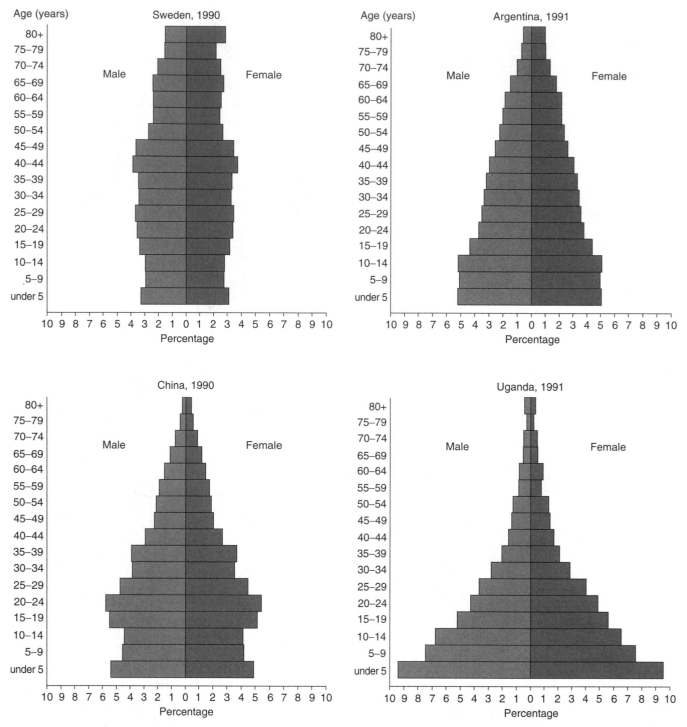

FIGURE 7.5 Percent Distribution by Age and Sex of the Populations of Sweden, China, Argentina, and Uganda: Around 1990. Source: U.S. Census Bureau (2000a).

age (i.e., a relatively "old" population). The pyramids for Argentina (1991) and China (1990) illustrate configurations intermediate between those for Uganda and Sweden. The pyramid for the population of France given in Figure 7.6 reflects various irregularities associated with that country's special history.

The pyramids of geographically very small countries and of subgroups of national populations—geographic subdivisions or socioeconomic classes—may have quite different configurations (i.e., they may vary considerably from the relatively smooth triangular and semi-elliptical shapes we have identified). For example, the pyramid for Kuwait

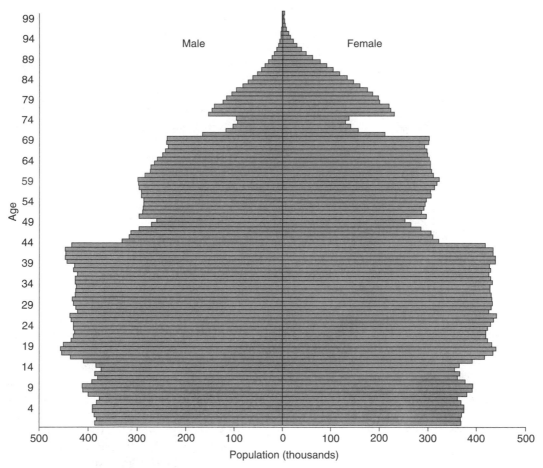

FIGURE 7.6   Population of France, by Age and Sex: March 5, 1990. Source: Basic data from Eurostat (1998).

distinguishing Kuwaitis and non-Kuwaitis in 1985 (Figure 7.7) shows that the foreign national population has a relatively narrow base (i.e., a small percentage of children), an extremely large bulge in the middle section (i.e., a high percentage of working age adults), and a substantial asymmetry (in this case, a large excess of males). The age-sex pyramids of the married population, the labor force, heads of households, and other groups have their characteristic configurations.

Analysis of Age Composition in Terms of Demographic Factors

Amount and Percentage of Change by Age

In this section we extend the analysis of age composition to consider in a preliminary manner the role of the factors of birth, mortality, and net immigration. These factors all operate on the population in an age-selective fashion, Births in a given year directly determine the size of the population under 1 year old at the end of that year, and because of the nature of the birth component and its magnitude relative to

the other components, it is also often the principal determinant of the size of older age groups in the appropriate later years. The deaths and migrants of a given year affect the entire distribution in that year directly, although deaths are usually concentrated among young children and aged persons and there is usually a disproportionately large number of young adults among migrants.

Number in Age Group

The number of persons in a given age group at a census date, and changes in the numbers between census dates for age groups, may be analyzed in terms of the past numbers of births, deaths, and "net immigrants." The number of persons in a given age group, x to $x + 4$ years of age, at a given date represents the balance of the number of births occurring x to $x + 4$ years earlier in the area, the number of deaths occurring to this cohort between the years of birth and the census date, and the number of migrants entering or leaving in this period with ages corresponding to this cohort. Any analysis of the factors underlying the census figures must also take into consideration the net undercount of the census figures. We may represent this relationship as follows:

Age (years)

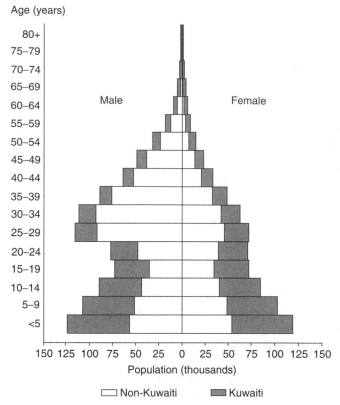

FIGURE 7.7 Population by Age, Sex, and Nationality for Kuwait: 1985
Source: Kuwait, Central Statistical Office (1986)

$$P_a = B_c - D_c + M_c - E_a \qquad (7.25)$$

where P_a is the population in the age group; B_c, births in the cohort; D_c, deaths occurring to the cohort; M_c, net migrants joining the cohort; and E_a, net undercount in the census figure. For purposes of the present analysis, we shall assume that there are no errors in the data on the components or that they have been satisfactorily corrected.

Generally, the younger the age group, the smaller the impact of death and migration in determining the size of the group and the greater the relative importance of births. Thus, the size of the population under 5 years of age on April 1, 1990, in the United States is very largely determined by the number of births occurring between April 1, 1985, and April 1, 1990. This number is modified only by the relatively small number of deaths occurring to these newborn children during the period and by the relatively small number of immigrant children in this cohort entering the country in the period. The net undercount of the census figure increases the potential gap between the births and the census figure somewhat further. Similarly, the population 5 to 9 years old on April 1, 1990, represents the births of April 1, 1980, to April 1, 1985, modified by deaths and migration up to April 1, 1990; the population 10 to 14 years old stems from the births of April 1, 1975, to April 1, 1980; and so forth.

The paramount importance of the past trend of births also applies generally in interpreting short-term changes in the number of aged persons. For example, the increase of 5.3 million, or 22%, in the population 65 years of age and over in the United States between 1980 and 1990 may be explained largely in terms of the rise in the number of births between 1895–1905 and 1915–1925.[25] Because the population aged 65 and over is largely made up of persons aged 65 to 84, we have used these ages to determine the birth years of the two groups of cohorts and then eliminated the years common to them. Once again, in spite of the considerable importance of deaths in determining the number of aged persons at each census date, the factor of mortality tends to be relatively secondary in explaining the change in the number of aged persons over a period as short as 10 years. As stated earlier, both groups of cohorts being compared have been exposed to the risk of death for the same number of years, albeit the considerable period of 65 to 84 years, and although some improvement in mortality may have occurred as the two groups of cohorts moved through life from infancy to old age 10 calendar years apart, this improvement was much less important than the fact that the number of years of exposure was the same.

The contribution of migration to the change in the aged population may be analyzed to some extent in the same way as the contribution of mortality. The two groups of cohorts have been "exposed to the risk" of migration for the same period of years (65 or more), but there may have been sudden shifts from year to year in the number of migrants affecting the two groups of cohorts.

A country's age profile may be affected by the events of war and postwar demobilization, as well as by peacetime mobilization. A war may be directly responsible for a short- or long-term deficit of (primarily) males of military age in the resident population, an increase in the death rate, a rise or fall in the birthrate, and the displacement of civilian population. To the extent that there are battle losses of military personnel, the deficit of males of military age will become permanent and may remain visible not only through the life span of the particular cohorts concerned but may also be reflected in later cohorts through the effect on the birthrate.[26] To the extent that the civilian population is directly involved in military activities and there are war losses of civilians (e.g., from bombing), the impact of a war will be more evenly distributed over the age-sex classes.

---

[25] The reference here is specifically to the number of births rather than to the birth rate. The absolute number of births may be rising while the birthrate may be falling because the total population is growing. For example, the U.S. birthrate decreased generally in the period 1895 to 1925, but the number of births increased during this period. These are the cohorts that entered the 65-and-over group during the 1960s, 1970s, and 1980s.

[26] For such effects in the Soviet Union, see Pirozhkov and Safarova (1994). Also see Metropolitan Life Insurance Company (1940a) and Smith and Zopf (1970, pp. 160–162).

The nature and extent of the effect of a war on the birthrate will depend in part on the duration and magnitude of the war, the degree to which families are separated by military service or destruction of civilian communities, and the impact of the war on the economy.[27] Although the birthrate may rise or fall during wartime, it is especially likely to rise during the immediate postwar demobilization period because of the reunion of married couples, a rise in the number of marriages, and the postponement of births. The sharp fluctuations in the birthrate usually associated with war tend to produce marked variations in the size of successive age groups in a population. These "hollow" and "swollen" age groups will grow older with the passage of time and reappear as hollow and swollen groups at successively older ages at various subsequent dates, possibly for decades to come (Figure 7.6).

As a direct result of war, the volume of ordinary civilian immigration or emigration is likely to fall off to a mere trickle while movements of military personnel into and out of the country and of refugees and expellees may be voluminous and erratic. With the end of the war, demobilization of military personnel or displacements of population may account for a tremendous rise in the volume of movement into or out of the belligerent countries. The changes described may have a considerable impact on the age profile of the population as well as its sex composition.

Percentage of Change

We turn next to a formulation of the contribution of each component of change to the total percentage change in an age group between two dates. We may represent the population at a given age in an earlier (P^0) and later (P^1) census in terms of its underlying components as follows:

$$P_a^0 = B^0 - D^0 + M^0 - E_a^0 \qquad (7.26)$$

$$P_a^1 = B^1 - D^1 + M^1 - E_a^1 \qquad (7.27)$$

Note that all the elements in each equation relate to the same birth cohorts. (These equations are of the same form as Equation 7.25.) The relative contribution of each component to the total change in population is obtained by taking the difference between these equations, grouping components, and dividing each side by P_a^0:

$$\frac{P_a^1 - P_a^0}{P_a^0} = \frac{B^1 - B^0}{P_a^0} - \frac{D^1 - D^0}{P_a^0} + \frac{M^1 - M^0}{P_a^0} - \frac{E_a^1 - E_a^0}{P_a^0}$$
$$(7.28)$$

Each term here, multiplied by 100, represents the contribution of a component in percentage points to the total percentage change.

Table 7.23 illustrates the application of this formula in analyzing the increase in the U.S. population for selected age groups between 1980 and 1990. First, determine the numbers of births, deaths, and net immigrants, as well as the net undercount pertaining to each cohort (cols. 1 and 2); second, take the difference between the amounts for the two cohorts (col. 3); and third, divide the difference by the population in the age group at the earlier census and multiply by 100 (col. 6). According to this calculation, of the 12.3% increase in the 0-to-4 age group, the increase in births "contributed" 16.3 percentage points and the decrease in deaths "contributed" 0.3 percentage point, for a combined positive contribution of 16.6 percentage points. The decrease in net migration and the increase in net undercount had a combined negative contribution of 4.3 percentage points, 0.4 percentage point attributable to the migration component and 3.9 percentage points to the change in undercount.

If only the contribution of births to total percentage change is to be measured, or can be measured because data on births alone can be developed, it is necessary simply to (1) determine the numbers of births corresponding to each cohort from the registration data or by estimation, (2) subtract the births of each cohort from the corresponding census counts, to obtain estimates for all other components combined, including the net census undercount, and (3) proceed as before (see Table 7.23).

An alternative procedure for computing the contribution of the components, which produces the same results, views the overall percentage change in the population as the weighted average of the percentage changes in the components. The percentage change in each component is shown in column 4 of Table 7.23. The weight attached to each component is derived by taking the ratio of a particular component for the earlier cohort to the census population at the earlier date. The weights are shown in column 5. The contribution of each component in percentage points (col. 6) is obtained by taking the product of the percentages in column 4 and the weights in column 5. The weights for births and net immigration are positive, and the weights for deaths and net undercount are negative. In the young ages, the component of births receives a relatively high weight in comparison with the other components. As one goes up the age scale, the *relative* weight of the birth component tends to fall and the *relative* weight of the other components taken together, particularly the death component, tends to rise. For example, at ages 0 to 4, the birth component has an *absolute* weight of 1.022 and the other components combined a weight of (−).022; but at ages 55 to 59, the birth component has an absolute weight of 1.277 compared with a weight of (−).277 for the other components combined. These figures indicate relative weights for births of 98% and 82%, respectively.[28]

---

[27] For the effects of World War I on the birthrate in several European countries, see Metropolitan Life Insurance Company (1940b).

[28] The relative weight of births may be given by $\frac{W_b}{2W_b - 1}$, where W_b represents the absolute weight for births. The value of this function declines with the rise in W_b.

TABLE 7.23 Calculation of the Contribution of the Components of Change to the Percentage Change for Selected Age Groups in the Population of the United States between 1980 and 1990

| Age and component | Number (In thousands) | | Change | | | Contribution of each component $[(3) \div P_a^{80}] \times 100$ or $(4) \times (5) =$ (6) |
	1980 (1)	1990 (2)	Amount (In thousands) $(2) - (1) =$ (3)	Percentage $[(3) \div (1)] \times 100 =$ (4)	Weight $(1) \div P_a^{80} =$ (5)	
Under 5 years:						
Births	16,711	19,369	+2,658	+15.91	+1.022	+16.3
Deaths[1]	(−)253	(−)209	+44	−17.39	−0.015	+0.3
Net migration	+213	+154	−59	−27.70	+0.013	−0.4
Net undercount	(−)324	(−)960	−636	+196.30	−0.020	−3.9
Population or total change	16,348	18,354	+2,006	+12.27	(1.000)	+12.3
5 to 9 years:						
Births	16,832	18,257	+1,425	+8.47	+1.008	+8.5
Deaths[1]	(−)365	(−)258	+107	−29.32	−0.022	+0.6
Net migration	+484	+445	−39	−8.06	+0.029	−0.2
Net undercount	(−)251	(−)344	−93	+37.05	−0.015	−0.6
Population or total change	16,700	18,099	+1,399	+8.38	(1.000)	+8.4
15 to 19 years:						
Births	20,909	16,832	−4,077	−19.50	+0.988	−19.3
Other components[2]	+259	+922	+663	+255.98	+0.012	+3.1
Population or total change	21,168	17,754	−3,414	−16.13	(1.000)	−16.1
25 to 29 years:						
Births	19,618	20,909	+1,291	+6.58	+1.005	+6.6
Other components[2]	(−)97	+404	+501	−516.49	−0.005	+2.6
Population or total change	19,521	21,313	+1,792	+9.18	(1.000)	+9.2
35 to 39 years:						
Births	14,445	19,618	+5,173	+35.81	+1.034	+37.0
Other components[2]	(−)480	+345	+825	−171.88	−0.034	+5.9
Population or total change	13,965	19,963	+5,998	+42.95	(1.000)	+43.0
55 to 59 years:						
Births	14,828	12,264	−2,564	−17.29	+1.277	−22.1
Other components[2]	(−)3,213	(−)1,732	+1,481	−46.09	−0.277	+12.8
Population or total change	11,615	10,532	−1,083	−9.32	(1.000)	−9.3

[1] As a negative component, "deaths" is assigned a negative sign. A positive amount of change in the number of deaths indicates a decrease in the number of deaths or in effect an addition to the population.

[2] "Other components" can have a positive or negative sign, depending on the combined contribution of deaths, net migration, and net coverage error.

Source: Based on U.S. Census Bureau, unpublished tabulations.

Changes in Proportions by Age and in Overall Age-Sex Structure

We turn next to a brief consideration of the demographic factors affecting the changes in the proportion of the population in a given age group between two dates or in the age-sex structure as a whole.

Changes in the proportion of the population in a given age group between two dates depend on the relative rates of growth of the age group in question and of the total population. In evaluating the role of natality in particular, it is useful to compare the percentage difference between the numbers of births corresponding to the two cohorts under study with the percentage difference in the numbers of births during the century or so prior to each of the two dates. For example, the proportion of the population 30 to 34 years old in the United States increased from 7.8% to 8.8% between 1980 and 1990 largely because (1) the relative excess of births occurring in 1955–1960 over births occurring in 1945–1950 (21%) was greater than (2) the relative excess of births in 1890–1990 over births in 1880–1980 (about 6%). The ratio of these ratios (1.21 ÷ 1.06) equals 1.14, suggesting a contribution of 14% due to births in the increase in the proportion of the population aged 30 to 34 between 1980 and 1990; this proportion actually rose by 13%. The increase in the proportion of aged persons in the United States between 1980 and 1990 resulted in large part from (1) the relative excess of births between 1905 and 1925 over births between 1895 and 1915 (when most persons 65 and over in 1990 and 1980, respectively, were born) in comparison with

(2) the slower average increase of births during the past century, which is responsible for the moderate rate of growth of the total population in the 1980–1990 decade. Thus, the longtime downward trend in the birthrate in the United States contributed to the increase in the proportion of persons in the older ages in recent decades.

A reduction in death rates contributes, as was stated earlier, to an increase in the *number* at an age group over a particular time interval (e.g., 10 years). Whether or not reductions in death rates contribute to an increase in the *proportion* of the population in any age group during such a period depends on the age pattern of improvements in death rates. More specifically, the effect of mortality on changes in proportions by age depends on the difference between (1) the relative improvement in survival rates from birth up to the specified age for the periods ending on each census date (e.g., 10 years apart) and (2) the relative improvement in survival rates from birth to census age over all age cohorts included in the total population at the census dates. In general, if the savings in lives are confined to childhood, the proportion of children will tend to rise and the proportion of older persons to fall; if the savings in lives are confined to older persons, the proportion of children will tend to fall and the proportion of older persons to rise. In the experience of the United States as well as of many other countries before about 1970, much more proportional improvement in mortality took place at the younger ages than at the older ages, and thus this factor contributed little or nothing to the increase in the proportion of the aged.[29] However, since the last quarter of the last century, the age pattern of death rates appears to have shifted in the United States and other low mortality countries (Preston *et al.*, 1989). To the extent that current and future changes in mortality are proportionally greater at older ages, this factor may be expected to assume greater weight, particularly in relatively "aged" countries (Caselli and Vallin, 1990).

The role of immigration can be analyzed in a similar way, but the specific impact on the age distribution may be quite different from that of deaths because the migrants have their own characteristic age pattern as well as a natural increase. Migrants change the prevailing age composition of the population to the extent that their age composition plus their natural increase differs from that of the general population. Because immigrants tend to be relatively young on arrival and may have a relatively higher natural increase, the usual short-term effect of immigration is to reduce the proportion of older adults and aged persons in the population. This "younging" effect will continue if the volume of immigra-

[29] Some earlier studies concerned with the theoretical and empirical analysis of the effect of mortality and natality trends on age composition are Coale (1956, 1972), United Nations (1954), and Stolnitz (1956). The relative contribution of fertility, mortality, and immigration to changes in the age composition of the U.S. population between 1900 and 1960 is analyzed in Valaoras (1950) and Hermalin (1966).

tion is maintained and the new arrivals continue to have a young age distribution. The younging effect will tend to decline, however, if the volume of immigration falls off or if the new arrivals begin having an older age distribution, as occurred generally in the United States in the first half of the 20th century.

Because the median age is the 50-percentile mark in the age distribution, changes in the median age may be analyzed in much the same manner as changes in the proportion at some age. The median age will rise during a period if the population above the median age at the beginning of the period grows at a faster rate than the population below the median (or the total population), and the median age will fall under the opposite conditions. Here again, the factors of mortality and migration have tended to be of considerably less importance than the factor of fertility in explaining a change in the median age, but, as stated, in recent decades in some countries the role of mortality has become more important than fertility.

Analysis of Population Pyramids

It is possible to infer a good deal about the demographic history of an area simply by examining the population pyramid depicting its age-sex structure. Because a pyramid does not identify the specific demographic factors that shaped it in a particular case, however, and because more than one factor contributes to the determination of the number of persons at each age, it is not possible to state exactly, especially without a knowledge of the history of the area, how demographic factors operated to give a particular pyramid its special form.

A pyramid with a very broad base suggests a population with a relatively high birthrate, and if, in addition, the pyramid narrows rapidly from the base up—that is, has a generally triangular shape with concave sides—a combination of high birthrates and high death rates is suggested. The pyramid for Uganda in 1991 shown in Figure 7.5 reflects such a demographic history. The beehive- or barrel-shaped pyramid for Sweden in 1990 shown in the same chart suggests a history of low fertility and low mortality. Irregular variations in the lengths of the bars point to past sharp fluctuations in the number of births or in the volume of migration, but they may also reflect a temporary rise in the number of deaths resulting from war or epidemic. The pyramid for France in 1990 shown in Figure 7.6 has a number of irregularities that may be explained on the basis of the fluctuations in the number of births and deaths caused by World Wars I and II. The pyramid has been annotated to indicate the age bands that were affected by military losses in World Wars I and II, deficits of births during these wars, and the post–World War II rise in births due to demobilization. If the bars for the youngest ages are shorter than those for the next higher ages, a recent decline in the number of births is suggested (Figure 7.2 for Japan in 1995), although some of such shortages may be due to relatively greater underenumeration of the youngest age groups.

Where the bars in the middle or the upper part of the pyramid are excessively long or short, heavy immigration or emigration of persons in these age groups in recent years, or of younger persons in the same age cohorts at an earlier date, is indicated. A pyramid with an asymmetrical shape in the primary labor force ages (e.g., 25 to 54) generally represents a population that is characterized by heavy sex-selectivity of recent immigrants, such as the foreign national population of Kuwait in 1985 shown in Figure 7.7.

Analysis of Age-Sex Structure by Use of Population Models

Earlier we referred to the use of various models of population structure in the evaluation and correction of census data on age-sex composition. These models are also useful in the analysis of the age-sex structure of populations. Comparisons of the structure of actual populations with the theoretical structure generated by various constant or variable conditions of fertility and mortality represented by these population models permits a fuller understanding of the role of these demographic conditions in age-sex structure. The pyramids of these population models may also be used as graphic standards for interpreting the pyramids of actual populations. Recall that the stable population model indicates the fixed age-sex structure of a population resulting from and consistent with constant birth and death rates (i.e., a constant growth rate, positive or negative) and no migration (a "closed population"). The quasi-stable population model corresponds to the stable population model except that mortality is assumed to be declining moderately. The stationary population model, identified previously as a special case of the stable population model, assumes a zero growth rate (i.e., constant and equal numbers of births and deaths each year and, hence, constant and equal birth and death rates each year). An alternative scenario for the stable population model incorporates immigration at a constant level by age (Espenshade et al., 1982). The pyramids of these models are smooth and regular.

Populations with high and relatively unchanging birthrates and with moderately high death rates, a type of population found in some less developed countries today, mostly in sub-Saharan Africa, resemble the stable population model with a high growth rate (e.g., Figure 7.5, Uganda). Populations with low birth and low death rates resemble the stable model with a low growth rate, or a stationary population with low birth and low death rates (e.g., Figure 7.5, Sweden). Low fertility-low mortality populations experiencing a steady flow of immigration or emigration (with a fixed age distribution) resemble a stationary population model incorporating migration (not illustrated.) The deviations of the age-sex structure of actual populations from the closely related models will give some indications of past

fluctuations in fertility and mortality, and the role of migration and war mortality.

References

Bachi, R. 1954. "Measurement of the Tendency to Round off Age Returns." *Bulletin de l'Institut International de Statistique* (Proceedings of the 28th Session, Rome), 34(3): 129–138.

Brass, W., A. J. Coale, P. Demeny, D. Heisel, F. Lorimer, A. Romaniuk, and E. van de Walle. 1968. *The Demography of Tropical Africa* (pp. 13–52). Princeton, NJ: Princeton University Press.

Carrier, N. H. 1959. "A Note on the Measurement of Digital Preference in Age Recordings." *Journal of the Institute of Actuaries* (Cambridge, England) 85: 71–85.

Carrier, N. H., and A. M. Farrag. 1959. "The Reduction of Errors in Census Populations for Statistically Underdeveloped Countries." *Population Studies* (London) 12(3): 240–285.

Caselli, G., and J. Vallin. 1990. "Mortality and Aging." *European Journal of Population* 6(1): 1–25.

Chahnazarian, A. 1988. "Determinants of the Sex Ratio at Birth: Review of Recent Literature." *Social Biology* 35(3–4): 214–235.

China, State Council Population Census Office (Ed.). 2000. *Di wu ci quanguo renkou pucha puchayuan shouce (Enumerator Handbook for the Fifth National Population Census)*, Beijing: China Statistics Press.

Coale, A. J. 1956. "The Effects of Changes in Mortality and Fertility on Age Composition." *Milbank Memorial Fund Quarterly* 34(1): 79–114.

Coale, A. J. 1963. "Estimates of Various Demographic Measures through the Quasi-Stable Age Distribution." *Emerging Techniques in Population Research*, Milbank Memorial Fund, pp. 175–193.

Coale, A. J. 1972. *The Growth and Structure of Human Populations: A Mathematical Investigation*. Princeton, NJ: Princeton University Press.

Coale, A. J., and J. Banister. 1994. "Five Decades of Missing Females in China." *Demography* 31(3): 459–479.

Coale, A. J., and P. Demeny. 1983. *Regional Model Life Tables and Stable Populations*, 2nd ed. with B. Vaughn. New York: Academic Press.

Das Gupta, M., and P. N. Mari Bhat. 1997. "Fertility Decline and Increased Manifestation of Sex Bias in India." *Population Studies* 51(3): 307–315.

Das Gupta, P. 1991. "Reconstruction of the Age Distribution of the Extreme Aged in the 1980 Census by the Method of Extinct Generations." *1990 Proceedings of the Social Statistics Section*. Washington, DC: American Statistical Association, pp. 154–159.

Davis, K., and P. van den Oever. 1982. "Demographic Foundations of New Sex Roles." *Population and Development Review* 8(3): 495–511.

Demeny, P., and F. C. Shorter. 1968. "Estimating Turkish Mortality, Fertility, and Age Structure," Statistics Institute Paper No. 2, Istanbul University, Istanbul, Turkey.

Duncan, O. D. 1959. "Residential Segregation and Social Differentiation." *International Population Conference*, International Union for the Scientific Study of Population, Vienna, pp. 571–572.

Duncan, O. D., and B. Duncan. 1955. "Residential Distribution and Occupational Stratification." *American Journal of Sociology* 60(5): 494.

ESCAP (United Nations Economic and Social Commission for Asia and the Pacific). 1984. "Internal Migration in the Countries of the ESCAP Region." *Third Asian and Pacific Population Conference: Selected Papers*. Asian Population Studies Series, No. 58, pp. 194–211.

Espenshade, T. J., L. F. Bouvier, and W. B. Arthur. 1982. "Immigration and the Stable Population Model." *Demography* 19(1): 125–134.

Ewbank, D. 1981. *Age Misreporting and Age Selective Underenumeration: Sources, Patterns, and Consequences for Demographic Analysis.*

Committee on Population and Demography. Report No. 4. Washington, DC.

France, Institut National de la Statistique et des Études Économiques. 1994. *Recensement de la Population de 1990, Population Totale, Résultats du Sondage au Quart*, INSEE Resultats #301–302.

Gage, T. B. 1994. "Population Variation in Cause of Death: Level, Gender, and Period Effects." *Demography* 31(2): 271–296.

Gregson, S., G. P. Garnett, and R. M. Anderson. 1994. "Assessing the Potential Impact of the HIV-1 Epidemic on Orphanhood and the Demographic Structure of Populations in sub-Saharan Africa." *Population Studies* 48(3): 435–458.

Hermalin, A. I. 1966. "The Effect of Changes in Mortality Rates on Population Growth and Age Distribution in the United States." *Milbank Memorial Fund Quarterly* 44(4): 451–469, Part 1.

Hirschman, C., S. Preston, and V. M. Loi. 1995. "Vietnamese Casualties during the American War: A New Estimate." *Population and Development Review* 21(4): 783–812.

Kestenbaum, B. 1992. "A Description of the Extreme Aged Population Based on Improved Medicare Enrollment Data." *Demography* 29(4): 565–580.

Kestenbaum, B. 1998. "Recent Mortality of the Oldest Old from Medicare Data." Social Security Adminstration, Working Paper. Baltimore, MD.

Kuwait Central Statistical Office. 1986. *1985 Census of Population.* (in Arabic).

Macmahon, B., and T. F. Pugh. 1953. "Influence of Birth Order and Maternal Age on the Human Sex Ratio at Birth." *British Journal of Preventive and Social Medicine* 7(2): 83–86.

Marks, E. S., and J. Waksberg. 1966. "Evaluation of Coverage in the 1960 Census of Population through Case-by-Case Checking." *Proceedings of the Social Statistics Section.* American Statistical Association. Washington, DC, pp. 62–70.

Martine, G. 1975. "Volume, Characteristics and Consequences of Internal Migration in Colombia." *Demography* 12(2): 193–208.

McMahan, C. A. 1951. "An Empirical Test of Three Hypotheses Concerning the Human Sex Ratio at Birth in the United States, 1915–48." *Milbank Memorial Fund Quarterly* 29(3): 273–293.

Metropolitan Life Insurance Company. 1940a. "The Cumulative Effect of Successive Wars on Age Composition of Population" *Statistical Bulletin* 21(4): 2–5.

Metropolitan Life Insurance Company. 1940b. "War and the Birth Rate," *Statistical Bulletin* 21(3): 3–6.

Myers, R. J. 1940. "Errors and Bias in the Reporting of Ages in Census Data." *Transactions of the Actuarial Society of America* 41: Part II (104): 395–415. (Reproduced in U.S. Bureau of the Census. 1951. *Handbook of Statistical Methods for Demographers*, pp. 115–125.)

Myers, R. J. 1954. "The Effect of Age of Mother and Birth Order on Sex Ratio at Birth." *Milbank Memorial Fund Quarterly* 32(3): 275–281.

Myers, R. J. 1966. "Validity of Centenarian Data in the 1960 Census." *Demography* 3(2): 470–476.

Park, C. B., and N. H. Cho. 1995. "Consequences of Son Preference in a Low-Fertility Society: Imbalance of the Sex Ratio at Birth in Korea." *Population and Development Review* 21(1): 59–84.

Pirozhkov, S., and G. Safarova. 1994. "Demographic Regularities and Irregularities: The Population Age Structure." In W. Lutz, S. Scherbov, and A. Volkov (Eds.), *Demographic Trends and Patterns in the Soviet Union Before 1991*, International Institute for Applied Systems Analysis (IIASA). Laxenburg, Austria.

Preston, S. H., C. Himes, and M. Eggers. 1989. "Demographic Conditions Responsible for Population Aging." *Demography* 26(4): 691–704.

Preston, S. H., I. T. Elo, and Q. Stewart. 1997. "Effects of Age Misreporting on Mortality Estimates at Older Ages." Population Aging Research Center, University of Pennsylvania, *Working Paper Series*, No. 98–01.

Ramachandran, K. V. 1967. "An Index to Measure Digit Preference Error in Age Data." Summary in United Nations, *World Population Conference, 1965* (Belgrade), Vol. III, pp. 202–203.

Reardon, S. F., J. T. Yun, and T. M. Eitle. 2000. "The Changing Structure of School Segregation: Measurement and Evidence of Multiracial Metropolitan-Area School Segregation, 1989–1995." *Demography* 37(3): 351–364.

Republic of Korea, National Statistical Office. 1987. *1985 Population and Housing Census Report, Whole Country*, Volume 1.

Republic of Korea, National Statistical Office. 1997. *1995 Population and Housing Census Report, Whole Country*, Volume 1.

Robinson, J. G., B. Ahmed, P., Das Gupta, and K. A. Woodrow. 1991. "Estimating Coverage of the 1990 United States Census: Demographic Analysis," paper presented at the American Statistical Association meetings, Atlanta, GA.

Robinson, J. G., B. Ahmed, P., Das Gupta, and K. A. Woodrow. 1993. "Estimation of Coverage in the 1990 United States Census Based on Demographic Analysis." *Journal of the American Statistical Association* 88(423): 1061–1071.

Ruder, A. 1985. "Paternal and Birth-Order Effect on the Human Secondary Sex Ratio." *American Journal of Human Genetics* 37(2): 362–372.

Saw, S. H. 1967. "Errors in Chinese Age Statistics." *Demography* 4(2): 859–875.

Siegel, J. S., and J. S. Passel. 1976. "New Estimates of the Number of Centenarians in the United States." *Journal of the American Statistical Association* 71(355): 559–566.

Skeldon, R. 1986. "On Migration Patterns in India during the 1970s." *Population and Development Review* 12(4): 759–779.

Smith, T. L., and P. E. Zopf, Jr. 1970. *Demography: Principles and Methods.* Philadelphia: F. A. Davis.

South, S. J., and K. Trent. 1988. "Sex Ratios and Women's Roles: A Cross-National Analysis." *American Journal of Sociology* 93(5): 1096–1115.

Spencer, G. 1986. "The Characteristics of Centenarians in the 1980 Census." Paper presented at the Population Association of America meetings, San Francisco, CA.

Spencer, G. 1987. "Improvements in the Quality of Census Age Statistics for the Elderly." *Proceedings of the 1987 Public Health Conference on Records and Statistics.* Washington, DC.

Spencer, G., D. L. Word, and F. W. Hollmann. 1992. "Discontinuities in Age and Race Data from the 1990 Census," Paper presented at the annual meeting of the Population Association of America, Denver, Colorado.

Stanecki, K. 2000. "The AIDS Pandemic in the 21st Century: The Demographic Impact in Developing Countries." Paper presented at the XIIIth International AIDS Conference. Durban, South Africa.

Stolnitz, G. J. 1956. "Mortality Declines and Age Distribution." *Milbank Memorial Fund Quarterly* 34(2): 178–215.

Teitelbaum, M. S., and N. Mantel. 1971. "Socioeconomic Factors and the Sex Ratio at Birth." *Journal of Biosocial Science* 3: 23–41.

Trovato, F., and N. M. Lalu. 1996. "Narrowing Sex Differentials in Life Expectancy in the Industrialized World: Early 1970's to Early 1990's." *Social Biology* 43(1–2): 20–37.

United Nations. 1952. "Accuracy Tests for Census Age Distributions Tabulated in Five-Year and Ten-Year Groups." *Population Bulletin* (2): 59–79.

United Nations. 1954. "The Cause of the Aging of Populations: Declining Mortality or Declining Fertility." *Population Bulletin of the United Nations* (4): 30–38.

United Nations. 1955. Chapter 3 in *Methods of Appraisal of Quality of Basic Data for Population Estimates.* Manuals on Methods of Estimating Population, Manual II. Series A, Population Studies, No. 23, pp. 31–54.

United Nations. 1958. *Principles and Recommendations for National Population Censuses*, Statistical Papers, Series M, No. 27. New York.

United Nations. 1964. *National Programmes of Analysis of Population Census Data as an Aid to Planning and Policy-Making.* Population Studies. Series A, No. 36.

United Nations. 1967. *Principles and Recommendations for the 1970 Population Censuses,* Statistical Papers, Series M, No. 44. New York.

United Nations. 1982. *Model Life Tables for Developing Countries.* Population Studies, No. 77. New York.

United Nations. 1983. *Indirect Techniques for Demographic Estimation.* Manual X, Population Studies, No. 81, Annex V.

United Nations. 1988. *Demographic Yearbook 1986.* New York: United Nations.

United Nations. 1994. *Demographic Yearbook 1992.* New York: United Nations.

United Nations. 1995. *Demographic Yearbook 1993.* New York: United Nations.

United Nations. 1998. *Principles and Recommendations for Population and Housing Censuses, Revision 1.* Statistical Papers, Series M, No. 67/Rev. 1. New York: United Nations.

U.S. Bureau of the Census. 1960a. *Historical Statistics of the United States: Colonial Times to 1957.* Washington, DC.

U.S. Bureau of the Census. 1960b. *The Post-Enumeration Survey: 1950.* Technical Paper No. 4. Washington, DC.

U.S. Bureau of the Census. 1964. *Accuracy of Data on Population Characteristics as Measured by Reinterviews.* Evaluation and Research Program U.S. Censuses of Population and Housing, 1960: ER 60, No. 4.

U.S. Bureau of the Census. 1965. *Historical Statistics of the United States: Continuation to 1962 and Revisions.* Washington, DC.

U.S. Bureau of the Census. 1975. *Historical Statistics of the United States: Colonial Times to 1970.* Washington, DC.

U.S. Bureau of the Census. 1980. *The Methods and Materials of Demography,* by H. S. Shryock, J. S. Siegel, and Associates. Vols. 1 and 2, Fourth Printing (rev.). Washington, DC.

U.S. Bureau of the Census. 1983. *General Population Characteristics, United States Summary, 1980.* 1980 Census of Population. PC80-1-B1. Washington, DC.

U.S. Bureau of the Census. 1985. *Evaluating Censuses of Population and Housing.* Statistical Training Document, ISP-TR-5, Washington, DC.

U.S. Bureau of the Census. 1988. *The Coverage of Population in the 1980 Census,* by R. E. Fay, J. S. Passel, and J. G. Robinson. 1980 Census of Population and Housing. PHC80-E4. Washington, DC: U.S. Bureau of the Census.

U.S. Census Bureau. 1992. *General Population Characteristics, United States, 1990.* 1990 Census of Population. CP-1-1. Washington, DC.

U.S. Census Bureau. 1993a. *The Foreign-Born Population in the United States, 1990.* 1990 Census of Population. CP-3-1. Washington, DC.

U.S. Census Bureau. 1993b. "U.S. Population Estimates, by Age, Sex, Race, and Hispanic Origin: 1980 to 1991," by F. W. Hollmann. *Current Population Reports,* P25-1095. Washington, DC.

U.S. Census Bureau. 1994. *Population Analysis with Microcomputers,* by E. E. Arriaga, with P. D. Johnson and E. Jamison (Associates). Volumes I and II.

U.S. Census Bureau. 1999. "Centenarians in the United States." By C. A. Krach and V. A. Velkoff. *Current Population Reports.* P-23-199RV. Washington, DC.

U.S. Census Bureau. 2000a. International Data Base, www.census.gov/ipc/www/idbacc.html.

U.S. Census Bureau. 2000b. "Population Projections for the United States by Age, Sex, Race, Hispanic Origin, and Nativity: 1999 to 2100." http://www.census.gov/population/www/projections/natproj.html.

U.S. National Center for Health Statistics. 1997. *U.S. Decennial Life Tables for 1989–91.* Vol. 1, Number 1, Hyattsville, MD.

Valaoras, V. G. 1950. "Patterns of Aging of Human Populations." Eastern States Health Education Conference (1949). *The Social and Biological Challenge of Our Aging Population.* New York: Columbia University Press, pp. 67–85.

van de Walle, E. 1966. "Some Characteristic Features of Census Age Distributions in Illiterate Populations." *American Journal of Sociology* 71(5): 549–557.

Vincent, P. 1951. "La Mortalité des Viellards" (The mortality of the aged). *Population* 6(2): 181–204, Paris.

Waldron, I. 1993. "Recent Trends in Sex Mortality Ratios for Adults in Developed Countries." *Social Science and Medicine* 36(4): 451–462.

Winston, S. 1931. "The Influence of Social Factors Upon the Sex Ratio at Birth." *American Journal of Sociology* 37(1): 1–21.

Winston, S. 1932. "Birth Control and the Sex Ratio at Birth." *American Journal of Sociology* 38: 225–231.

Suggested Readings

Anderson, B. A., and B. D. Silver. 1985. "Estimating Census Undercount from School Enrollment Data: An Application to the Soviet Censuses of 1959 and 1970." *Demography* 22(2): 289–308.

Bhat, P. N. Mari. 1990. "Estimating Transition Probabilities of Age Misstatement." *Demography* 27(1): 149–163.

Budd, J. W., and T. Guinnane. 1991. "Intentional Age-Misreporting, Age-Heaping, and the 1908 Old Age Pensions Act in Ireland." *Population Studies* 45(3): 497–518.

Caldwell, J. C. 1966. "Study of Age Misstatement Among Young Children in Ghana." *Demography* 3(2): 477–490.

Chu, C. Y. C. 1997. "Age-Distribution Dynamics and Aging Indexes." *Demography* 34(4): 551–563.

Coale, A. J. 1964. "How a Population Ages or Grows Younger." In R. Freedman (Ed.), *Population: The Vital Revolution* (pp. 47–58). Garden City, NY: Doubleday-Anchor.

Coale, A. J. 1991. "Excess Female Mortality and the Balance of the Sexes in the Population: An Estimate of the Number of 'Missing Females.'" *Population and Development Review* 17(3): 517–523.

Coale, A. J., and M. Zelnik. 1963. *New Estimates of Fertility and Population in the United States.* Princeton, NJ: Princeton University Press.

Das-Gupta, A. 1955. "Accuracy Index of Census Age Distributions." In United Nations, *World Population Conference, 1954* (Rome), Vol. IV, pp. 63–74.

El Badry, M. A. 1955. "Some Demographic Measurements for Egypt Based on the Stability of Census Age Distributions." *Milbank Memorial Fund Quarterly* 33(3): 268–305.

Eldridge, H. T., and J. S. Siegel, 1946. "The Changing Sex Ratio in the United States." *American Journal of Sociology* 52(3): 224–234.

Ghana Census Office. 1964. 1960 Census of Ghana, Vol. V, *Administrative Report, Post-Enumeration Survey,* Part II, and *Census Evaluation,* Part III, pp. 313–401. Accra.

Hull, T. 1990. "Recent Trends in Sex Ratios at Birth in China." *Population and Development Review* 16(1): 63–83.

James, W. H. 1987. "The Human Sex Ratio. Part 1: A Review of the Literature." *Human Biology* 59(5): 721–752.

Lorimer, F. 1951. "Dynamics of Age Structure in a Population with Initially High Fertility and Mortality." *Population Bulletin of the United Nations,* 1: 31–41.

Mason, K. O., and L. G. Cope. 1987. "Sources of Age and Date-of-Birth Misreporting in the 1900 U.S. Census." *Demography* 24(4): 563–573.

Myers, R. J. 1954. "Accuracy of Age Reporting in the 1950 United States Census." *Journal of the American Statistical Association* 49(268): 826–831.

Norland, J. A. 1975. "Measuring Change in Sex Composition." *Demography* 12(1): 81–88.

Notestein, F. W. 1960. "Mortality, Fertility, and Size—Age Distribution and the Growth Rate." In National Bureau of Economic Research, *Demographic and Economic Changes in Developed Countries*, Princeton, NJ: Princeton University Press, pp. 261–289.

Preston, S., I. T. Elo, A. Foster, and H. Fu. 1998. "Reconstructing the Size of the African American Population by Age and Sex, 1930–1990." *Demography* 35(1): 1–21.

Ramachandran, K. V., and V. A. Deshpande. 1964. "The Sex Ratio at Birth in India by Regions." *Milbank Memorial Fund Quarterly* 42(2): Part 1, 84–95.

Riley, M. W. 1987. "On the Significance of Age in Sociology." *American Sociological Review* 52(1): 1–14.

Rosenwaike, I. 1979. "A New Evaluation of United States Census Data on the Extreme Aged." *Demography* 16(2): 279–288.

Rubin, E. 1967. "The Sex Ratio at Birth." *American Statistician* 21(4): 45–48.

Siegel, J. S. 1968. "Completeness of Coverage of the Nonwhite Population in the 1960 Census and Current Estimates, and Some Implications." In David M. Heer (Ed.), *Social Statistics and the City* (pp. 13–54). Cambridge, MA: Joint Center for Urban Studies of the Massachusetts Institute of Technology and Harvard University.

Siegel, J. S. 1974. "Estimates of the Coverage of the Population by Sex, Race, and Age in the 1970 Census." *Demography* 11(1): 1–23.

Tien, H. Y. 1980. "Age-Sex Statistics for China: What Do Recent National Disclosures and Local Figures Reveal?" *Population and Development Review* 6(4): 651–662.

United Nations. 1953. "Population Structure as a Factor in Manpower and Dependency Problems of Underdeveloped Countries," by John D. Durand. *Population Bulletin of the United Nations* (3): 1–8.

United Nations. 1956. *The Aging of Populations and its Economic and Social Implications*. Series A, Population Studies, No. 26.

Valaoras, V. G. 1959. "Population Profiles as a Means for Reconstructing Demographic Histories." In International Union for the Scientific Study of Population, *International Population Conference*, 1959 (Vienna), pp. 62–72.

Yerushalmy, J. 1943. "The Age-Sex Composition of the Population Resulting from Natality and Mortality Conditions." *Milbank Memorial Fund Quarterly* 21(1): 37–63.

Yi, Z., T. Ping, G. Baochang, X. Yi, L. Bohua, and L. Yongpiing. 1993. "Causes and Implications of the Recent Increase in the Reported Sex Ratio at Birth in China." *Population and Development Review* 19(2): 283–302.

You, P. S. 1959. "Errors in Age Reporting in Statistically Underdeveloped Countries." *Population Studies* 13(2): 164–182.

Zelnik, M. 1961. "Age Heaping in the United States Census: 1880–1950." *Milbank Memorial Fund Quarterly* 39(3): 540–573.

Zelnik, M. 1964. "Errors in the 1960 Census Enumeration of Native Whites." *Journal of the American Statistical Association* 59(2): 437–459.

8

Racial and Ethnic Composition

JEROME N. McKIBBEN

Few areas of demographic research have undergone as much change in the past 30 years as race and ethnicity. While race and ethnicity were largely overlooked in the official statistics of most nations for the better part of the past century, the majority of the countries in the world today attempt to identify their populations by some type of racial or ethnic classification. These classifications and the population they are intended to represent are of interest to national policy makers, businesses, marketers, and researchers. Racial and ethnic groups frequently have different geographic distributions, demographic characteristics, socioeconomic attributes, and political views and affiliations. As more countries institute social and economic programs designed to assist and improve the socioeconomic standing of specific racial and ethnic groups, more complete and detailed statistics are likely to be developed.

In more than a few countries, programs have been created to address social and economic disadvantages that certain racial and ethnic groups have experienced. In the United States, for example, these programs include the Equal Employment Opportunity Act, Civil Rights Act, Voting Rights Act, Public Health Act, Fair Housing Act, Census Redistricting Act, and the Equal Credit Opportunity Act. To assist in the effective implementation of these and other social improvement programs, more detailed racial and ethnic statistics were developed through the programs of the Census Bureau and other federal, state, and local agencies.

There are, however, many areas in the world where racial and ethnic tensions make it politically and otherwise difficult to collect and report race and ethnicity data. Even the definition and classifications of the term "race" in a given nation can be a source of conflict and disagreement. Several countries have had violent and long-running disputes among racial or ethnic groups. If one group perceived that another ethnic group was experiencing a faster rate of population growth, this could lead to increased conflict among them. There are also cases where inequalities in the distribution of resources within nations would be highlighted if complete racial and ethnic statistics were tabulated. Again, this could lead to increased conflict.

Frequently, nations find that it is easier to avoid the issues of racial definitions and characteristics than to establish race categories and gather statistics. Mexico, for example, has not asked a race question on its census since 1921 (Sandar, 1998). Recently, the representatives of 23 Caribbean, Central American, and South American countries and territories met in Port of Spain to discuss issues concerning the year 2000 round of censuses. While the conference covered a wide range of topics, from housing questions to the environment, any discussion of race and ethnic questions was conspicuously absent (Latin American and Caribbean Demographic Center, 1998).

RACIAL, ETHNIC, AND NATIONALITY CHARACTERISTICS

The definitions of a "racial group" and an "ethnic group" are often muddled. Whereas two countries might use exactly the same term to describe a given ethnic group within their respective borders, the actual definition of membership could vary rather substantially. Similarly, people with the same racial background may be assigned different labels from one country to another. For example, a person who is one-quarter black and three-quarters white would most likely be categorized as black in the United States (at least prior to the 2000 census), while in Haiti he or she would be categorized as mulatto, and in Brazil as white (Murphy, 1998). While there may be certain physical differences among various groups, race and ethnicity are primarily socially defined constructs. Consequently, racial and ethnic

175

categories are less precise than many other demographic concepts and less generalizable across nations.

In demographic research, race tends to be narrowly defined. One useful definition is "a group that persons inside and outside the group decided to single out on the basis of real or alleged physical characteristics subjectively selected" (Feagin and Feagin, 1993). However, many nations, including the United States, depend on self-reporting in their censuses. Given the limited number of racial categories that respondents are typically permitted to choose from in a census, there tends to be a certain level of ambiguity in the definition of race. When respondents are given the freedom to choose multiple race categories (as was done in the United States for its 2000 census), the ambiguity increases.

The definition of "ethnic group" tends to be even more ambiguous than race, largely because it is used in both a broad and narrow context in demographic research. Some researchers prefer a narrow definition of ethnicity, one that is limited to groups distinguished primarily by nationality or geographic characteristics; others use a much wider definition, one that includes cultural factors such as religion and language (Feagin and Feagin, 1993). Often, in the case of a wider definition, several of these cultural characteristics are highly correlated within one group. For example, in Nigeria, the Hausas tend to be Moslem and speak Hausa while the Ibos are Christians and speak Ibo.

While nationality is sometimes closely related to ethnicity, it has a much more limited meaning. In regard to demographic research there are two primary types: (1) country of current citizenship and (2) country of origin. Countries with substantial immigrant population will frequently have persons who use both definitions to describe themselves. In Canada, for example, people may identify themselves as both Canadian and as Dutch. There also are cases where the majority of a nationality lives in one nation, but is a distinct minority. Examples of this are the Lapps in Finland, the Walloons in Belgium, the Sikhs in India, and the Basques in Spain. In these cases, members tend to use cultural factors, including language, to identify their nationality, as opposed to the country of citizenship. They suggest the distinction between "political nationality" and "ethnic nationality."

RACE AND ETHNIC GROUPS

National Practices

Over the past 30 years, there has been a marked decline in the movement to develop a "standardized" definition for both race and ethnicity that would be applicable across various cultures and nations. The United Nations (UN), for example, provides recommendations on questions and their wording, but the inclusion and scope of race and ethnic data in national statistics is now seen as a mostly local issue (United Nations, 1998). Consequently, each nation tends to develop a series of racial and ethnic definitions that reflect that country's cultural, social, and political system.

Because there is substantial variation in the racial and ethnic definitions used from country to country, cross-national comparative analysis is difficult. Researchers undertaking multinational analysis need to conduct an extensive review of each nation's racial and ethnic classification system to ensure that they are comparable. In addition, caution must be used when examining a given nation's racial and ethnic statistics over time because these definitions may have changed. Such has been the case for the United States over the past 50 years.

Racial Definitions in the United States

Until the 1970s, the racial classification and definitions used by the U.S. Census Bureau had been essentially the same for the preceding 40 years. Historically, the determination of race on U.S. censuses was made by the enumerator on the basis of observation or, more recently, by self-identification. Unfortunately, not all state and federal agencies used the same definitions. This led to some confusion, particularly when many of the "affirmative action" programs had to be implemented. To solve this problem, the Office of Management and Budget (OMB) developed *Statistical Directive 15, Race and Ethnic Standards for Federal Statistics and Administrative Reporting* (United States Office of Management and Budget [OMB], 1978). This directive was aimed at standardizing racial definitions for federal as well as state government agencies. In it, OMB identified four official race categories: (1) American Indian and Alaska Native, (2) Asian/Pacific Islander, (3) black, and (4) white.

Following the 1990 census, the OMB standards promulgated in 1978 came under increasing criticism. The primary complaints were that they (1) did not reflect the increasing diversity of the U.S. population, (2) used terms and concepts that did not have broad public acceptance, and (3) did not facilitate respondent self-identification. To correct these and other perceived deficiencies, the OMB established the Interagency Committee for the Review of Racial and Ethnic Standards in 1994. The members of the committee, who were from more than 30 agencies, spent 4 years developing new standards. In 1997, OMB (1997) released these new standards in its report, *Revisions to the Standards for the Classification of Federal Data on Race and Ethnicity*. The new standards were used in the 2000 census and adopted by all federal programs as of January 1, 2003.

The minimum categories for data on race for federal statistics, administrative reporting, and civil rights compliance are defined as follows:

White. A person having origins in any of the original peoples of Europe, the Middle East, or North Africa.

Black or African American. A person having origins in any of the black racial groups of Africa. Terms such as "Haitian" or "Negro" can also be used in addition to "Black or African-American."

American Indian or Alaska Native. A person having origins of any of the original peoples of North or South America (including Central America) and who maintains tribal affiliation or community attachments.

Asian. A person having origins in any of the original peoples of the Far East, Southeast Asia, or the Indian subcontinent including, for example, Cambodia, China, India, Japan, Korea, Malaysia, Pakistan, the Philippine Islands, Thailand, and Vietnam.

Native Hawaiian or Other Pacific Islander. A person having origins in any of the original peoples of Hawaii, Guam, Samoa, or other Pacific Islands.

In a move that reflected a major change from the 1978 standards, the new OMB 1997 specifications divided the former Asian/Pacific Islander category into two groups. The OMB felt that Native Hawaiians had presented a compelling argument that the racial categories needed to be amended in order to describe their social and economic situation. In order to identify Native Hawaiians separately in this new category, the choices of Guamanian (or Chamorro), Samoan, and "other Pacific Islander" were included in the 2000 census form.

It is important to note that the 1997 standards *do not* include an "other race" category. However, for the 2000 census, the OMB granted the Census Bureau an exception to use a category called "Some Other Race." The OMB (2000b) also granted a similar exception to the National Center for Health statistics to include "Some Other Race" on the U.S. standard birth and death certificates to maintain comparability between vital statistics data and those resulting from the 2000 census.

The most important change in the 1997 standards was the decision to allow respondents the option of selecting more than one racial category in responding to the question on race. This policy change was implemented so that federal agencies could collect information that more accurately reflected the increasing racial diversity of the U.S. population.

However, allowing people of a multiracial background to check two or more racial categories has created additional problems for researchers wishing to use race as a variable. With five different racial categories and the option of listing "Some Other Race," there are 63 different "combinations" (including single categories) of racial identification in the 2000 census. One problem with this is that the majority of the racial combinations (i.e., all except the single categories) were not available prior to the 2000 census, thus making

comparisons over time difficult. A second problem is that small geographic areas face a greater level of data suppression because many of the 63 possible combinations have insufficient numbers of respondents to allow for publication of the census results. While there is the option of collapsing all of the multiple race responses into a category called "Two or More Races," serious analytic problems remain. Provisional solutions to these issues provided by OMB will be discussed in later sections.

Hispanics and Latinos

In the United States, "Hispanic," is officially considered an ethnic group and not a race. According to the 1997 OMB reporting standards all federal agencies must maintain, collect, and present Hispanic data along with racial data. An "Hispanic" person is defined as a person of Cuban, Mexican, Puerto Rican, South or Central American, or other Spanish cultural or origin, regardless of race. The term "Spanish origin" can be used as an alternative to Hispanic, as can the term "Latino".

The primary goal of the new OMB standards is to establish a common criterion for the classification of Hispanic persons and to make the data consistent over time. However, problems will persist as long as there is disagreement and confusion among Hispanic respondents regarding their racial affiliation. In most cases, Hispanic respondents are classified as white, and exceptions are so identified (e.g., Hispanic-black, Hispanic-Asian). One issue that was expected to change the racial distribution of the Hispanic population in the 2000 census was the inclusion of South and Central American Indians in the American Indian/Alaska Native race category. Previous to this census, Hispanics who felt that their primary racial background was Central or South American Indian descent did not have the option of listing that as their race. Consequently, many of these people reported their race as "Other" on census forms.

The reporting of one's race as "Other" is very common among respondents of Hispanic origin. The overwhelming majority of the "Other" population in the 1980 and 1990 censuses were people of Hispanic origin. In 1980, 5.8 million of the 6.8 million "Other" respondents were Hispanic. In the 1990 census, these numbers had grown to 9.6 million out of 9.8 million (U.S. Census Bureau, 1991). As shown in Table 8.1, in the 2000 census, 14.9 million Hispanics, or 42.2% of the total U.S. Hispanic population, listed their race as "Other". Conversely, only 47.9% of the Hispanic population listed their race as white (U.S. Census Bureau, 2001). Thus, while most classification systems would list the majority of Hispanics as white, less than half of the U.S. Hispanic population identifies itself as white.

Because of refinements in census procedures and changes in the census questionnaire, data on the Hispanic population

TABLE 8.1   Hispanic Population by Race for the United
States, 2000

Race	Number	Percentage of total
Total	35,305,818	100.0
One race	33,081,736	93.7
White	16,907,852	47.9
Black or African American	710,353	2.0
American Indian and Alaska Native	407,073	1.2
Asian	119,829	0.3
Native Hawaiian and Other Pacific Islander	45,326	0.1
Some other race	14,891,303	42.2
Two or more races	2,224,082	6.3

Source: U.S. Census Bureau, Redistricting (P.L. 94–171) Summary
File Tables PL1 and PL2.

are not totally comparable across censuses. To address many of the inconsistencies between censuses and between racial and Hispanic data, the OMB (1978) included several changes in its revised Statistical Directive 15 relating to the issues of Hispanic/Latino classification.

Immigration and Emigration Statistics

The U.S. Immigration and Naturalization Service (INS) does not collect race and ethnic information on persons immigrating to the United States. Information on new arrivals is obtained from the U.S. Department of State's form OF-155, "Immigrant Visa and Alien Registration," and INS form I-181, "Memorandum of Creation of Record of Lawful Permanent Residence." Some of the useful variables collected on these forms include country of birth, country of last residence, and nationality (U.S. INS, 1999). In some instances, these can be used as proxies for ethnicity. However, researchers should use caution when using data from these two sources because there can be a notable difference between the official perception of an immigrant's racial/ethnic background, the immigrant's self-identification of race/ethnicity and country of birth and nationality.

Ancestry versus Ethnicity

The distinction between ancestry and ethnicity is often confusing in official government statistics. Question 10 on the U.S. 2000 census long form asks respondents to state their ancestry or ethnic origin. The Census Bureau defines ancestry as a person's ethnic origin, decent, heritage, or place of birth, or the place of birth of the person's parents (U.S. Census Bureau, 1990). Responses can range from national origins corresponding to the respondent's surname

(no matter how many generations the family has lived in the United States) to a specific subnational ethnic group such as Scotch, Ibo, or French Canadian. Further, the respondent has the option of listing more than one ancestry. Generally, only the first two responses were coded in 1990. If a response was in terms of a dual ancestry, such as Irish English, the person was assigned two codes, in this case one for Irish and another for English.

While ancestry and ethnic origin were asked on the 1980, 1990, and 2000 censuses, the usefulness of these statistics as descriptors of the ethnic composition of the population is questionable. Given that individuals that are of multiethnic backgrounds now constitute the majority of the nation's population, the accuracy of the census results is suspect at best. In most cases, the response given to the ancestry or ethnic origin question on censuses is valid only for those who are first- or second-generation Americans by birth.

PROCEDURES FOR USING THE 1997 OMB STANDARDS ON RACE AND ETHNIC DATA

Formats for Collecting Data on Race and Hispanic Ethnicity

The 1997 OMB standards provide for two formats that may be used for gathering information on race and Hispanic ethnicity. The first format is that of self-reporting or self-identification using two separate questions. The OMB states that this is the preferred method for collecting data on race and Hispanic ethnicity. This is the method that was used in the 2000 census. When race and Hispanic ethnicity are collected using this format, the OMB states that ethnicity should be collected first. For this two-question format, the minimum race and ethnic categories recommended by the OMB are as follows.

Race
American Indian or Alaska Native
Asian
Black or African American
Native Hawaiian or Other Pacific Islander
White
Ethnicity
Hispanic or Latino
Not Hispanic or Latino

The second format is designed for situations where self-reporting is not feasible. In such a situation, a combined race/ethnic format may be used. Data on both race (including multiple responses) and Hispanic ethnicity should be collected when appropriate and feasible. If the combined format is used, the OMB recommends at least six categories, as follows:

American Indian or Alaska Native
Asian
Black or African American
Hispanic or Latino
Native Hawaiian or Other Pacific Islander
White

Detailed instructions on the procedures for collecting race and ethnic data are provided in Chapter 2 of the OMB's (2000b) *Provisional Guidance on the Implementation of the 1997 Standards for Federal Data on Race and Ethnicity.*

Processing Census 2000 Data Using the 1997 Standards

As was the case for the 1990 census, the U.S. Census Bureau developed editing procedures for the 2000 census to impute race and Hispanic origin for people who did not provide this information (U.S. OMB, 2000b).

The editing and imputation procedures for race and Hispanic origin used in the 2000 census are as follows:

1. *Pre-editing.* This procedure detects and corrects out-of-range values, ensures that no more than eight race codes appear on the edited file, and resolves into one code multiple responses given to the question on Hispanic origin. (All original responses are preserved on the unedited files.)
2. *Within-household imputation.* When race or Hispanic-origin data are missing, responses are imputed from the responses for others within the same household who have reported race or Hispanic origin.
3. *Between-household imputation.* When data on race and Hispanic origin are missing for all household members, origin and race are assigned from other census records in surrounding blocks (or nearby households) with "similar" characteristics ("hot-deck" procedure).
4. *Substitution.* Characteristics are assigned for members of occupied housing units for which there is only a count of people and no characteristics are reported for anyone in the household ("hot-deck" procedure).
5. *Group quarters editing.* Characteristics are assigned to people in group quarters.

Detailed instructions on the procedures for processing and allocating race and ethnic data are provided in Chapter 2 of the OMB's (2000b), *Provisional Guidance on the Implementation of the 1997 Standards for Federal Data on Race and Ethnicity.*

Confidentiality and Data Suppression

To maintain confidentiality of information about specific individuals or households as required by law, the Census Bureau (and other federal agencies) use a "confidentiality edit" to ensure that published data do not disclose such information or make possible such disclosure. This procedure introduces a small amount of uncertainty into the data for small geographic areas to prevent identification of specific individuals or households. It was first implemented in the 1990 census. However, disclosure of confidential information has become a more serious issue for the U.S. Census Bureau and other federal agencies using the 1997 OMB standards, now that the number of race categories has been expanded to 63.

The OMB has instructed federal agencies to provide as much detail as possible while adhering to their own standards of data quality and confidentiality. Under a typical data-quality standard, a table cell cannot be published if its relative standard error or other measure of reliability is larger than some value specified by the agency. Such a cell would be suppressed—that is, withheld from publication. Under a confidentiality standard, a cell value must be suppressed if knowledge of the cell value might enable someone to gain knowledge about one of the respondents contributing data to the cell. If the cell is suppressed to preserve confidentiality, other cells must also be suppressed so that the cell value cannot be derived by subtraction. This procedure is called "complementary suppression." In either situation, information on subgroups that cannot appear separately in the table would be included in the appropriate subtotals and/or in the total (U.S. OMB, 2000a).

Because of confidentiality concerns, the Census Bureau chose to suppress a large amount of the detailed race and ethnic data gathered in the 2000 census. The March 2001 Redistricting Files, for example, are the only 2000 census product to report the total population for all 63 race categories at the block level. Detailed information on the definition of sensitive cells and the selection of cells for suppression is contained in *Statistical Policy Working Paper 22: Report on Statistical Disclosure Limitation Methodology* (U.S. OMB, 1994).

Tabulation and Bridging Data

The OMB has also developed standards and procedures for tabulating race and ethnic data that would allow for the production of as much detailed information as possible while adhering to the criteria for confidentiality and data quality. While different tabulation procedures might be required to meet the needs of different federal agencies, various agencies frequently need to compare race and ethnic data. To facilitate such comparisons, some standardization of tabulation procedures and categories is needed.

In addition to developing standards to establish consistency in tabulation procedures, the OMB has derived standards and procedures to govern the use of different "bridging" methodologies that have been developed for race and ethnic data. Bridging procedures are to be used during the temporary period of time (roughly the first 5 years after implementation of the 1997 standards) when data users may want to use different sets of race and ethnic data. The first set would be the data resulting from the use of the new 1997 definitions, and the second set would be a "bridging estimate" based on a method of predicting the responses that would have been obtained if the data had been collected using the 1978 definitions (U.S. OMB, 2000b). There are two principal purposes for using bridge estimates. The first is to help the user understand the relationship between the 1978 and 1997 definitions. The second is to provide consistent numerators and denominators for the transition period, before all data are available in the 1997 format.

Census data on the change in the distribution of the population by race in the United States between 1990 and 2000 are provided in Table 8.2.

The nine criteria that follow are designed to evaluate the technical merits of different bridging procedures. The first two criteria are used in the selection of a specific bridging method. The next six apply to both bridging and long-term tabulation decisions. The last criterion is of importance for the future tabulation of data collected using the 1997 standards. Researchers should consider each of these issues carefully when making decisions concerning the bridging and tabulation of race and ethnic data.

1. *Measuring change over time.* Differences between the new distribution and the old distribution should reflect the true change in the distribution itself as opposed to a methodologically induced change.
2. *Minimize disruption to the single-race distribution.* Ascertain how different the resulting bridge distribution is from the single-race distribution for detailed race under the 1997 standards. Differences should be kept to a minimum.
3. *Range of applicability.* Tabulation procedures that can be used in a wide range of programs and varied contexts are preferred.
4. *Meet confidentiality and reliability standards.* The tabulations must maintain confidentiality standards while also producing reliable estimates.
5. *Statistically defensible.* Tabulation procedures should follow recognized statistical practices.
6. *Ease of use.* Because the tabulation procedures must be capable of easy replication by others, it is important that they can be implemented with a minimum of difficulty.
7. *Skill required.* Individuals with relatively little statistical knowledge should be able to implement the tabulation procedures.
8. *Understandability and communicability.* The tabulation procedures should be easily explainable to the public.
9. *Congruence with respondent's choice.* Because of the changes in the categories and the ability of the respondents to list more than one race, the tabulation procedure must reflect to the greatest extent possible the full detail of race reporting.

Detailed instructions, definitions, and guidelines for tabulation procedures as well as bridging methodology are provided in Chapter 5 and Appendix C of the OMB (2000b) report, *Provisional Guidance on the Implementation of the 1997 Standards for Federal Data on Race and Ethnicity.*

Aggregation, Allocation, and Presentation of Race and Ethnic Data Using the 1997 Standards

Within the bounds of confidentiality and disclosure restrictions, the results of the 2000 census should be reported in as many different multiple race categories as possible. For agencies and organizations that collect and report race and ethnic data for civil rights and equal employment opportunity (EEO) programs, different presentation guidelines have been developed. OMB Bulletin No. 00-02 (U.S. OMB, 2000a) lists the governing rules for aggregating and allocating this type of data. An example is provided in Table 8.3.

TABLE 8.2   United States Population by Race, 1990 and 2000

Race	1990		2000	
	Number	Percentage of total population	Number	Percentage of total population
Total population	248,709,873	100.0	281,421,906	100.0
White	199,686,070	80.3	211,460,626	75.1
Black or African American	29,986,060	12.1	34,658,190	12.3
American Indian and Alaska Native	1,959,234	0.8	2,475,956	0.9
Asian	6,908,638	2.8	10,242,998	3.6
Native Hawaiian and Other Pacific Islander	365,024	0.1	398,835	0.1
Some other race	9,804,847	3.9	15,359,073	5.5
Two or more races	X	X	6,826,228	2.4

X Not applicable.

Source: U.S. Census Bureau; Redistricting (P.L. 94–171) Summary File, Tables PL1 and 1990 Census.

TABLE 8.3 Guidance on Aggregation and Allocation of Multiple-Race Responses for Use in Civil Rights Monitoring and Enforcement in the United States

Rank	Race
1	American Indian or Alaska Native
2	Asian
3	Black or African American
4	Native Hawaiian or Other Pacific Islander
5	White
6	American Indian or Alaska Native and White
7	Asian and White
8	Black or African American and White
9	American Indian or Alaska Native and Black or African American
10	>1%: Fill in if applicable
11	>1%: Fill in if applicable
12	Balance of individuals reporting more than one race
13	Total

Note: See text for explanation.
Source: United States Office of Management and Budget, 2000a.

The OMB guidelines state that a minimum of 10 racial categories should be presented. They are the five single race groups, four double race combinations, and one category to include the balance of individuals reporting more than one race. If applicable, in addition to these 10 categories, multiple-race combinations that constitute more than 1% of the populations of interest should also be included in the aggregation. The OMB allows responsible agencies to determine which additional combinations meet the 1% threshold for the relevant jurisdictions based on data from the 2000 census.

In terms of allocation of multiple-race responses for civil rights and EEO monitoring and enforcement, the OMB suggests that the following rules should be used.

1. Responses in the five single-race categories are not allocated.
2. Responses that combine one minority race and white are allocated to the minority race.
3. Responses that include two or more minority races are allocated as follows:
   a. If the enforcement action is in response to a complaint, allocate to the race of the alleged discrimination.
   b. If the enforcement action requires assessing "disparate impact," analyze the patterns based on alternative allocations to each of the minority groups.

It is important to note that the 1997 standards concerning the presentation of data on race and ethnicity under special circumstances are not to be invoked unilaterally by any federal agency or entity. If the standard categories are believed to be inappropriate, a special variance must be requested from the OMB. In-depth instructions for the presentation of race and ethnic data are provided in Chapter 4 of the OMB (2000b).

Vital Statistics

Periodically, the U.S. National Center for Health Statistics (NCHS) revises the U.S Standard Certificates and Reports, which set the standard on how race is reported on birth and death certificates, and fetal death reports. The most recent revision, now being put in effect (2003), deals with the timely implementation of the reporting classifications put forth in OMB Statistical Directive 15 as revised. However, there have been other changes in the reporting of race in vital statistics over the past 20 years that have had a major effect on the classification of a child's race and the comparability of vital statistics over time.

At no time have birth certificates included a question on the race of the child. Prior to 1989, the NCHS assigned a race to the child solely for statistical purposes. Births were tabulated by this assigned race of the child, which was inferred from information reported for the race of the parents on the birth certificate. When the parents were of the same race, the child was assumed to be of the race of the parents. If the parents were of different races and one parent was white, the child was assigned the race of the parent who was not white. When the parents were of different races and neither parent was white, the child was assigned, for statistical purposes, the father's race. The one exception to this rule was that, if either parent was of Hawaiian descent, the child was assigned as Hawaiian. If race was missing for one parent, the child was assigned the race of the parent for whom race was reported.

In 1989, the NCHS changed its editing procedures and began tabulating births according to the race of the mother. The primary reason for this change was the revision of the standard birth certificate, which was introduced in that year. However, a second and equally important reason was to address problems relating to the large proportion of births for which the father's race was not reported. The large percentage of births with the father's race not reported reflects the increase in the proportion of births to unmarried women and the resulting frequent lack of information about the father. Even before 1989, such births were assigned the race of the mother because there was no reasonable alternative (U.S. NCHS, 1999). A third reason was the rapid growth of interracial births in the United States. Between 1978 and 1992 the annual number of interracial births more than doubled to 133,000 (Population Reference Bureau, 1995). By tabulating all births according to the race of the mother, there was a more uniform approach to the tabulation, replacing an arbitrary set of rules based on the races of the parents.

If the race of the mother is not identifiable and the race of the father is known, the race of the father is assigned to the mother, whose race is then assigned to the child. If information on race is missing for both parents, the race of the mother is imputed using a "hot-deck" approach, which uses information from a nearby record in which the mother's race is known.

It is important to note that in the public use microdata files produced and disseminated by the NCHS, both the mother's and father's respective races are listed if they are reported on the birth certificate. Researchers may tabulate birth data by the race of the mother, the father, or some combination of the two. However, if the research is to be based on data from the birth certificate itself, it is suggested that the race of the child be assigned using the race of the mother. The NCHS, for example, has retabulated all of the annual birth data since 1980 by the race of the mother. Tables for years prior to 1980 show data by the race of the mother and by the race of the child using the previous algorithm of NCHS. The presentation of both sets of tabulations allows researchers to make a distinction between the effects of the definitional changes of a child's race from true changes in the data (U.S. NCHS, 1999). This precaution notwithstanding, particular vigilance should be used when conducting a long-term analysis of birth trends by race in substate areas that historically have experienced large numbers of multiracial births (McKibben *et al.*, 1997).

The aforementioned changes in the designation of the race of a child at birth has had a major impact on the calculation of infant mortality rates by race. The immediate effect of the 1989 revision was that a significant number of births previously recorded in the nonwhite categories was now classified as white. This problem is partially addressed by the Linked Birth and Infant Death File (LBIDF) project, a cooperative project of state vital statistics offices and the National Center for Health Statistics. With LBIDF data, it is possible to use the mother's race for both the numerator and denominator in the calculation of infant mortality rates because the mother's race is shown on the birth certificate, which, in turn, is linked to the infant death certificate (Weed, 1995). This data set notwithstanding, all analysis of death statistics by race over time should be conducted with great caution and researchers need to be sensitive to the varied number of race definitions used over the past 40 years.

INTERNATIONAL RACE AND ETHNIC CLASSIFICATIONS AND PRACTICES

Like the United States, many countries in the world count their citizens and collect vital statistics according to ethnic categories, but unlike the United States most countries do not compile data according to race. Apart from their demographic uses, the procedures and practices of counting racial or ethnic groups are central in each group's construction of its identity, both for those within a given group and those outside of it. Frequently, there is disagreement and conflict over the definitions used and their accuracy. Researchers need to be keenly aware of the social, political, and economic concerns each country has incorporated into its race and ethnic classifications.

The majority of Western nations today use the term "ethnicity" as a basis for dividing people into groups as opposed to the term "race." In many countries, ethnicity is regarded as being more scientifically defensible and politically acceptable than race. While there are some exceptions, many countries have, in fact, completely discontinued using the term "race" and instead use the term "ethnicity" alone in their classification systems. If any additional criteria are included along with ethnicity, they are often something relating to language or nationality (Kertzer and Arel, 2001).

In most countries, the definitions used in national censuses tend to make a person's racial or ethnic identity "official" or recognized, whether it is an accurate definition or not (Kertzer and Arel, 2001). In such cases, it is not uncommon for the self-perception of the respondent to differ greatly from the authoritative classification, leading to a large degree of ambiguity. Further, while the inclusion of an ethnic group into a nation's census categories may help legitimize a given group's standing in that country, it may also be used to identify its members for exclusion from some public programs or civil rights.

There are no universally accepted race concepts, ethnic concepts, or identities. Each nation develops and implements definitions and terms that address its own statistical and administrative needs. However, as we described in Chapter 2, for more than 40 years the United Nations (UN) has promulgated guiding principles on how nations should conduct censuses and collect demographic and vital statistics data. The primary objectives of the recommendations are to assist nations in planning the content of their censuses and to improve international comparability through harmonization of data, definitions, and the classification of topics.

The most recent edition of these recommendations was developed within the framework of the 2000 World Population and Housing Census Program adopted in 1995. The UN Recommendations for the 2000 round of censuses of population and housing (UN, 1998) does not mention the term "race" at all, and all questions on ethnic groups are regarded as noncore topics that is, useful topics for which international comparability is difficult to obtain. The UN regards an ethnic group (or a national group) to be composed of those people who consider themselves as having a common origin or culture, which may be reflected in a language or religion that differs from that of the rest of the population. Given this broad definition, the criteria for membership in a particular ethnic group can vary greatly. A group of people may believe that a certain characteristic identifies them as belonging to a particular ethnic group, while nonmembers who view the same characteristic of that group may tend not to assign them to that group, possibly assigning them to a different group.

Frequently, ethnic categories are constructed by national governments in response to public pressure. Where this has occurred, it has often been accompanied by tensions between the needs of researchers and the public. In France, for example, the need for greater precision in categories of analysis to distinguish between different racial and ethnic groups gave rise to passionate public debates over the country's current immigration policy and past colonial practices (Blum, 2001). As another example, Brazil has changed the race definition used in each of its past three censuses, and the public's perception of a race-free, nondiscriminatory Brazilian society clashes with the views of many researchers who try to demonstrate that there are social and economic differences based on racial and ethnic characteristics. Thus, over the past 30 years, the terms "race," "color," and "mixed" have had several different official meanings in Brazil (Nobles, 2001).

The issue of public pressure becomes even more complex when political influences from outside of the country affect what types of ethnic classification a nation uses. This is particularly the case when an ethnic group is located in several different countries. Table 8.4 shows how the ethnic composition of Macedonia was defined by four different nations in 1889 through 1905. Each nation classified the population in a manner that was best suited for its own political agenda. In Israel, where the official policy is that there are no real ethnic differences between Jews, the geographic area of the world from which a respondent's family has migrated is used in lieu of a direct ethnic classification (Goldscheider, 2001).

External political events can also affect how people identify themselves or how they want others to perceive them. During World War II, many Canadians of German descent listed themselves as Dutch on the census. As a result, that group's percentage of the Canadian population was substantially increased (Lieberson, 1993). More recently, many

Tutsi in Burundi identify themselves as some other ethnic group as they attempt to distance themselves from Hutu violence in neighboring Rwanda (Uvin, 2001).

In an effort to create classifications systems that are sensitive to the self-identity concerns of their citizens, several Western nations have gone to great lengths to expand the number of ethnic categories used in their official statistics. In Canada, for example, the number of ethnic categories in the 1996 census was increased over those used in 1991 to reflect the country's increased ethnic diversity. Several African groups such as Kenyans and Sudanese that had previously been listed as "African Black" were listed separately in Canada's 1996 census. In addition, many of the "Other Latin" respondents of earlier Canadian censuses were able to declare themselves as members of specific national groups, such as Peruvian and Honduran (Canada, Statistics Canada, 1996). While the expansion of ethnic categories in the data published by many countries has aided demographic researchers seeking to understand the interrelations of ethnic groups, it has also created problems with data comparability and for time series analysis. Until a classification system exists with little or no modification over several censuses, meaningful time series analysis and comparisons will be very difficult.

As stated earlier, a growing number of countries stopped using the term "race" altogether in favor of terms like "ethnic" and "minority group." Because of the political misuses of the term "race" by Germany under National Socialism, the word acquired a strong negative connotation, particularly in Europe. Consequently, a combination of elements of group identity, such as language, nationality, religion, and kinship, are increasingly used to designate an ethnic group and there is a reduced tendency to use physical characteristics to designate a "race." The 1991 census of the United Kingdom used a coding framework of 34 different ethnic groups. However, the terms for these ethnic groups ranged from commonly defined racial categories (e.g., white, black) to nationalities (e.g., Pakistani, Chinese) to geographic areas (e.g., Caribbean Islands, North Africa). Further, there were several separate categories for people who considered themselves of "Mixed" or "Other" backgrounds (Bulmer, 1995).

Uses and Limitations

In countries with populations that are not racially or ethnically homogeneous, statistics according to race or ethnic group are particularly useful for analyzing demographic trends, making population projections, and evaluating the quality of demographic statistics. In addition, government or private agencies seeking to target specific populations for social, economic, and health programs often have a keen interest in race and ethnic composition. Further, there is also a great need to cross-classify a wide range of socioeconomic

TABLE 8.4   Ethnic Designation by Source of Census Figures, Macedonia, 1889–1905 (Percent of total)

| Ethnic group counted | National group conducting the census | | | |
	Bulgarian	Serbian	Greek	Turkish
Bulgarians	52.3%	2.0%	19.3%	30.8%
Serbians	Z	71.4	0.0	3.4
Greeks	10.1	7.0	37.9	10.6
Albanians	5.7	5.8	Z	Z
Turks	22.1	8.1	36.8	51.8
Others	9.7	5.9	6.1	3.4
Total	100.0	100.0	100.0	100.0

Z Less than 0.05 percent.

Source: Kertzer and Arel, 2001.

and demographic characteristics by race and ethnicity: income, employment, education, immigration, age, and sex. The welfare of indigenous or minority groups is often of special concern to national governments, and information on the size and characteristics of such groups is needed to formulate and implement appropriate policies and lans for servicing these groups.

MEASURES

There are not many measures that are specific to racial and ethnic analysis. Simple percentage distributions are frequently used. The most commonly encountered measures used in racial and ethnic analysis are those based on either the Index of Dissimilarity or the "Segregation Index", both of which are discussed in Chapter 6. The Index of Dissimilarity can be used to compare the distribution by race (or some other characteristic of interest) in two areas or two groups of another type or, conversely, the distribution of two racial groups by some other characteristic, such as age or area.

Measures based on the Segregation Index deal with the geographic distribution of groups of interest relative to one another. These groups can be defined by race, ethnicity, language, and so forth. As discussed in Chapter 6, there are many variations of the "Segregation Index" because the measures have different strengths and weaknesses and because they are based on the more general measures used to describe the spatial distribution of populations.

Finally, because race and ethnicity are qualitative variables, they can be analyzed using measures designed expressly for use with qualitative variables—cluster analysis, discriminant analysis, and log-linear analysis, for example (Kaufmann and Rousseeuw, 1990; Tabachnick and Fidell, 1996).

COUNTRY OF BIRTH
AND CITIZENSHIP

Place of birth is one of the most frequently asked questions on population censuses. In most cases, it is asked of all respondents, both citizens and noncitizens. Country of birth is also usually recorded on entry documents by most immigration and emigration agencies for both permanent and temporary residents. Further, country of birth is frequently listed on death certificates, while the country of birth of parents is often listed on a child's birth certificate.

International Recommendations
and Practices

"Country of birth" has been included on the United Nation's recommended list of items for all the world census programs from 1950 to 2000. A person's country/place of birth is considered a core topic in the UN's (1998) Recommendations for the 2000 Censuses of Population and Housing. In these recommendations, place of birth is defined as the place of residence of the mother at the time of birth. For a person born outside the country, it is sufficient to ask for the country of residence of the mother at the time of birth. Information should be collected for all persons born in the country where the census is conducted as well as for all persons born outside the country. The UN also recommends gathering information on the place of birth of parents although this is considered a noncore topic. This information is essential to understanding the processes of integration of immigrants and is particularly relevant in countries with high immigration rates or much concern about the integration of their immigrants.

One of the key issues stressed by the UN is that a person's country of birth should be defined by current national boundaries and not the boundaries in place when that person was born. For purposes of international comparability as well as for internal use, it is recommended that the information on this topic be collected and coded in as detailed a manner as is feasible. The identification of the countries should be based on the three-digit alphabetical codes presented in the international standard, *ISO3166: Codes for the Representation of Names of Countries* (International Organization for Standardization, 1993).

However, it is important to note that country of birth does not necessarily mean country of citizenship. With the large number of refugees and displaced persons in the world today, it is not uncommon for a person to be born in one country and have citizenship in another. For example, many Palestinians were born in Middle Eastern countries but do not hold citizenship in their country of birth. Further, given the large number of new countries that have recently become independent—frequently due to the disintegration of other nation states—many persons' reported country of birth may not exist any longer.

An example of the distribution of a population by country of birth is given for Canada in Table 8.5, which shows how this distribution changed over three successive censuses between 1981 and 1996.

The UN (1998) recommendations list country of citizenship as a core topic that all nations should include in their censuses. The UN suggests that citizenship be defined as the particular legal bond between an individual and a nation state, acquired by birth or naturalization. Naturalization may be acquired by declaration, option, marriage, or other means. Information on citizenship should be collected for all persons and coded on the basis of the three-digit alphabetic codes presented in the International Standard (International Organization for Standardization, 1993). The UN recommends that countries ask questions on the basis of acquiring citizenship although this is considered a noncore topic.

TABLE 8.5 Foreign-Born Population by Country of Birth, Canada, Censuses of 1986, 1991, and 1996 (in thousands)

Country of birth	1986	1991	1996
United Kingdom	793.1	717.7	655.5
Italy	366.8	351.6	332.1
United States	282.0	249.1	244.7
Hong Kong (China)	77.4	152.5	241.1
India	130.1	173.7	235.9
China	119.2	157.4	231.1
Poland	156.8	184.7	193.4
Philippines	82.2	123.3	184.6
Germany	189.6	180.5	181.7
Portugal	139.6	161.2	158.8
Vietnam	82.8	113.6	139.3
Netherlands	134.2	129.6	124.5
Former Yugoslavia	87.8	88.8	122.0
Jamaica	87.6	102.4	115.8
Other and not stated	1178.9	1456.8	1810.6
Total	3908.0	4342.9	4971.1
Percentage of total population	15.4	16.1	17.4

Source: Canada, Statistics Canada, 1996.

In regard to demographic research and analysis, the primary concern for demographers is that country of birth or citizenship may not necessarily be a good indicator of a person's race or ethnicity. The most serious problem relates to people who come from multiracial or multiethnic countries. For example, a person who was born in Spain could consider his or her ethnic background to be Spanish, Basque, Catalan, or Galician. A person holding Mexican citizenship could consider himself or herself to be white, black, American Indian, or of multiracial background. Consequently, country of birth/citizenship may have little relationship to a person's racial or ethnic self-identification.

United States Practices

Because the United States was settled by immigrants and continues to be the recipient of large numbers of foreign migrants, there has been strong and persistent interest in the composition of the nation's population with respect to its nativity, ethnicity, and national origin. Research interests range from the size, location, and rate of growth of various immigrant groups, to their demographic and economic characteristics. This interest has grown substantially since the liberalization of U.S. immigration laws in 1965. After the repeal of national "quota restrictions," new waves of immigrants began arriving in the country. However, unlike the great migrations of the late 1800s and early 1900s in which the vast majority of immigrants came from Europe, the majority making up the new waves has migrated from areas in the Western Hemisphere, Africa, and Asia (Easterlin *et al.*, 1980).

Despite changes in the immigration laws (most recently, the Illegal Immigration Reform and Immigrant Responsibility Act of 1996), immigration trends in the United States have remained fairly constant in both numbers and characteristics over the past 10 years. The Immigration and Naturalization Service (INS) produces an annual report presenting data on ethnicity and nationality of legal immigrants into the country. This report lists country of origin and the U.S. state of intended residence (U.S. INS, 2000).

The U.S. Census Bureau (or its predecessor agencies) has asked for country of birth on census forms for more than 150 years. In the 2000 census, question 12 on the long form asks a respondent born in one of the 50 states or the District of Columbia to enter that state, while all others, including those born in Puerto Rico, Guam, and other U.S. outlying areas, are asked to list the country in which they were born.

The terms and definitions used by the Census Bureau and the INS regarding a person's country of birth have become similar over the past 10 years. One of the more important standards that was set is to record a person's country of birth on the basis of the accepted international boundaries of that nation in the year that the information was gathered. In many instances this has resulted in a closer relation between the country-of-birth data and the person's ancestry or ethnic background. For example, prior to 1991, a respondent who stated that he or she was born in the Soviet Union most likely would have identified Russian, Estonian, Armenian, or some other group as his or her ethnic background. Now, that person would identify the area in which he or she was born by its current name and boundaries. Thus, there is now a strong probability that a person listing his or her country of birth as Lithuania is actually a Lithuanian. This situation is also evident for people who have emigrated from the new countries that constituted the former Yugoslavia and the former Czechoslovakia.

In regard to data on the citizenship of residents of the United States, there are some notable differences between the definitions used by the Census Bureau and the INS. Question 13 on the 2000 census long form asks respondents if they are citizens of the United States. People responding yes to this question may chose from one of four categories: (1) born the United States, (2) born in one of the U.S. territories, (3) born abroad of an American parent or parents, and (4) citizen by naturalization. However, those who answer "no" are not asked their country of citizenship. While question 12 does ask a respondent's country of birth, it cannot be assumed that the country of birth is necessarily the country of citizenship.

The manifest focus of the INS is to ascertain who is a citizen and who is not. In this light, the INS is more concerned with the nation from which a person is emigrating than the person's racial and ethnic background. The laws and definitions on who is (and is not) a citizen established by the United States government are detailed and specific.

Consequently, the terms and definitions used by the INS regarding the country of emigration of a person are designed mainly to address questions of immigration law and policy rather than to provide data useful for conducting demographic analyses of immigrants' race and ethnic background.

The terms and definitions used by the INS to assign a nation of origin to a U.S. immigrant are as follows (U.S. INS, 1999):

Country of birth. The country in which a person is born

Country of chargeability. The independent country to which an immigrant entering under the preference system is accredited or charged

Country of citizenship. The country in which a person is born (and for which he or she has not renounced or lost citizenship) or naturalized, and to which that person owes allegiance and to whose protection he or she is entitled

Country of former allegiance. The previous country of citizenship of a naturalized United States citizen or of a person who has derivative United States citizenship

Country of last residence. The country in which an alien habitually resided prior to entering the United States

Country of nationality. The country of a person's citizenship or the country of which the person is deemed to be a national. (Note that the country of nationality can be different from the country of chargeability.)

Stateless person. A person having no nationality and unable to claim citizenship in any country

LANGUAGE

Language use or knowledge is a frequently asked question on national censuses and is recorded in many official statistics. Because language is a fundamental aspect of any culture, it is often used as a proxy for identifying a person's nationality or ethnic origin. This culturally based concept of nationality has become widely used in many countries over the past 75 years. The use of language to define a cultural or ethnic community has forced several nations to recognize the fact officially that many ethnic groups are not confined to the boundaries of one nation (Arel, 2001). While there has been a great expansion in the use and detail of language statistics, the classifications and function of these statistics are often the results of political considerations. Consequently, like all other definitions of ethnicity, there is a great variation in the definition of "language used" by different nations.

Three primary types of language inquires are made in censuses: (1) language first learned by the respondent, (2) language most commonly used by the respondent, and (3) knowledge of another officially recognized language (Arel, 2001). In countries with substantial multiethnic and multilingual populations, such as Nigeria and India, the language first learned may be used to address social policy issues and to identify minority-majority language areas. In nations that receive large immigrant populations, such as the United States and Canada, information on the language most commonly used is helpful for ascertaining the rate of assimilation of foreign nationals. For nations with a substantial and varied indigenous population, such as Mexico and Brazil, the knowledge of various languages can help measure the linguistic skills of a minority population. Because the manifest purpose of these language questions may be tied to specific political or economic issues, and are constructed to address those issues, the resulting data may be of limited use to researchers.

United States Practices

Except for 1950, there has been a language question on every United States census since 1890. However, the primary purpose for the question in the United States has been to measure assimilation, not to serve as a proxy for race or ethnic background. Originally, the question was whether or not the respondent could speak English. After 1930, the question was changed to determine instead the "mother tongue" of the foreign-born population (U.S. Census Bureau/Gibson and Lennon, 1999).

Since 1980, the language question on the decenial census asks, "Does this person speak a language other than English at home?" (question 11 a, b, and c on the 2000 census form). If the answer is yes, the respondent is asked to record the name of the language. In addition, the respondent is asked, "How well do you speak English?" The listed responsers are one: very well, well, not well, not at all. While the results of the language question on U.S. censuses are of great interest and have been cross-tabulated with many other variables, they have limited use describing race and ethnicity. This is because in the United States, census-based language questions have mainly been designed to gauge the level and extent of assimilation of first and second-generation immigrants and not to codify a person's national or ethnic background (or even to measure the country's linguistic resources). Given the number and scope of race and ethnic questions on U.S. censuses, there has never really been a need to use language as a proxy measurement.

International Practices

Many nations of the world have avoided the use of race/ethnic questions in their official statistics. Even in countries that do have a race/ethnic classification system, the definitions used are frequently restrictive or biased. Consequently language information is often used where reliable race and ethnic information is unavailable or of dubious quality.

This situation notwithstanding, language questions are considered to be noncore topics in the United Nations Recommendations for the 2000 round of Censuses of Population and Housing (1998). However, if a nation is going to collect data on language use, the United Nations recommends four questions felt to be most relevant:

1. What is your mother tongue, defined as the first language spoken in early childhood?
2. What is your main language, defined as the language that you command best?
3. What language(s) is (are) currently spoken at home?
4. Do you have knowledge of other language(s), defined as the ability to speak and/or write one or more designated languages?

In these recommendations, the UN suggests asking at least two questions, namely question 1 or 2 and question 3. It further suggests that for question 3, respondents should be allowed to list only one language.

In reality, the level and extent of language questions on national questionnaires vary greatly, as does their quality. India's 2001 census asks questions on the respondent's mother tongue and other languages known. The respondent can list up to two other languages in order of proficiency (India, Office of the Registrar General, 2001). An example of language distribution is given for India in Figure 8.1.

New Zealand first introduced a language question in its 1996 census. In its 2001 census, the language question offers a respondent the following five choices: English, Maori, Samoan, New Zealand Sign Language, and other. The respondent is instructed to list as many languages as is applicable (New Zealand, Statistics New Zealand, 2001). The reasons given by New Zealand for including a language question in its census are as follows:

1. To determine the usage and distribution of languages in New Zealand
2. To formulate and target policies and programs to promote the use of the Maori language
3. To assess the need for multilingual pamphlets and translation services
4. To determine the need for language-education programs

While this information has some usefulness to demographers, the manifest purpose of the question is to aid in social policy formation and not to ascertain race/ethnic classification (New Zealand, Statistics New Zealand, 1996).

The 1996 census of South Africa asks the following set of language-based questions: what language is spoken most often at home, does the respondent speak more than one language at home, and if so, what is it? With the wide range of languages spoken in the nation (e.g., English, Afrikaans, Xhosa, Zulu, Hindi), the main focus of the question is to ascertain the level and scope of multilingualism of residents in the nation as opposed to identifying specific geographic areas where one language predominates (South Africa Central Statistical Service, 1996).

As widely used as language questions are in national statistics, they are not found on all censuses, even in developed countries. The United Kingdom, for example, conducts an extensive census; yet its 2001 census contains no language question (United Kingdom Office of National Statistics, 2001). The census of Belgium had a language question until 1960, when Belgium dropped the language question. This was because the question was used as a proxy for ethnicity. It was removed under pressure from the Flemish portion of Belgium's population whose census counts showed dwindling numbers in the Brussels area, while substantial gains were shown for the Walloon portion of the population (Kertzer and Arel, 2001).

RELIGION

When considering a person's ethnic and cultural background, religion can be a useful identifier. The topic is of extensive political and social interest as well as of wide research interest; and it can be of special use to demographers. However, as was the case with languages, questions on religion are often used to address specific social and political issues. Any use of these statistics for research purposes must include an in-depth examination of their validity and reliability as a substitute for race or ethnic variables.

There has never been a religion question on the United States census. Although there have been calls periodically to include one, appals to the principle of separation of church and state have inevitably resulted in the exclusion of such a question from official statistics. (One exception is a special survey conducted by the Census Bureau in the late 1960s focusing on religion.) For the most part in the United

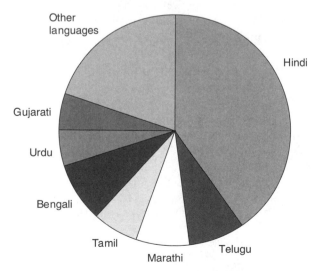

FIGURE 8.1   Distribution of the Population of India by Primary Language: 1991
Source: Census of India, 1997 (www.censusindia.net/datatable25/html)

States, information on the number and location of adherents to a particular religion are collected by the individual religious organization themselves or by private researchers.

International Practices

Religion is considered a noncore topic in the UN's Recommendations for the 2000 round of Censuses of Population and Housing (UN, 1998). If nations do choose to collect information on religion, the three most relevant areas of inquiry concern the following:

1. Formal membership in a church or religious community
2. Participation in the life of a church or religious community
3. Religious belief

When only one question is asked, it is suggested that the data be collected on "formal membership in a church or a religious community," allowing for respondents to state "none."

Examining a person's membership in a church or religious community fits into the concept of a cultural construction of identity and in many cases relates to the person's ethnic background. However, the connection between a person's religion and his or her ethnicity is one that a nation may not want to make. In Uzbekistan, there has been a great debate on whether or not to include a question on religion on its census. Proponents argue that its inclusion would send a message of religious tolerance and pluralism. Opponents charge that its inclusion could result in political tensions focusing on national and spiritual loyalties (Abramson, 2001). In some nations, information on religion is used as the primary distinction between different internal groups as opposed to ethnicity or nationality. Israel, for example, classifies non-Jewish residents inside its borders as Moslem, Christian, Druze, and other. Some maintain that the principal purpose of this classification is to deny Arab groups an ethnic or national identity. Thus, religion may be used as a proxy for ethnicity (Goldscheider, 2001). Figure 8.2 provides an example of the distribution of a population by religion with data for Australia.

Even in countries where a religion question is included for purely informational purposes, there has been a great deal of controversy over the usefulness of the question for researchers. Throughout the late 1990s, the United Kingdom grappled with the issue of including a religion question on its 2001 census. The arguments in favor included the need for information by religious orders to plan their social and welfare activities (Kosmin, 1999). One of the concerns voiced by religious minority groups was that the results could be used to target members of their religions for adverse purposes. The fact that this information would be available to people who may want to single out members of

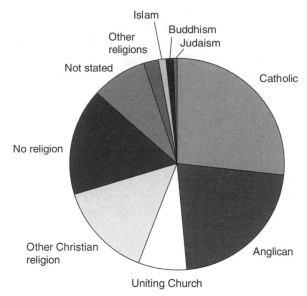

FIGURE 8.2 Distribution of the Population of Australia by Religion
Source: 1996 Australia Census of Population

particular religious groups led some religious organizations to strongly oppose the inclusion of any type of religion question (Weller and Andrews, 1998).

In 1999, it was decided to include the question "What is your religion" in the United Kingdom's 2001 census. However, in a compromise move to appease opponents, this question was made voluntary and is the only one that the respondent is not required to complete (United Kingdom, Office of National Statistics, 2001). Consequently, while there are now official government statistics on religious membership in the United Kingdom, there is also a great deal of concern about their completeness and accuracy.

The idea of allowing a respondent the option of answering questions concerning religion is not without precedent in a census. South Africa's census includes an optional question that allows the respondent to list the complete name of his or her religion, denomination, or belief. The New Zealand census form contains an extensive religion question, with detailed belief and denominational classifications, but the respondent again has the option of checking a box labeled "object to answering this question." Australia has asked an optional religion question on its censuses since 1971. Despite the voluntary nature of the question, the response rate has been fairly high over the past 30 years. In 1971, for example, 6.7% of the population did not state their religion and on the most recent (1996) census, that figure had increased slightly to 8.8% (Newman, 1998).

References

Abramson, D. M. 2001. "The Soviet Legacy and the Census in Uzbekistan." In D. Kertzer and D. Arel (Eds.), *Census and Identity* (pp. 137–155). Cambridge, UK: Cambridge University Press.

Arel, D. 2001. "Language and the Census." In D. Kertzer and D. Arel (Eds.), *Census and Identity* (pp. 79–96). Cambridge, UK: Cambridge University Press.

Blum, A. 2001. "The Debate on Resisting Identity Categorization in France." In D. Kertzer and D. Arel (Eds.), *Census and Identity* (pp. 97–117). Cambridge, UK: Cambridge University Press.

Bulmer, M. 1995. "The Ethnic Question in the 1991 Census of Population." In D. Coleman and J. Salt (Eds.), *Ethnicity in the 1991 Census, Vol. 1: General Demographic Characteristics of the Ethnic Minority Population* (pp. 23–46). London, UK: Her Majesty's Stationary Office.

Canada, Statistics Canada. 1996. "Comparison of Ethnic Origins collected in 1996, 1991, and 1986." *1996 Census Dictionary—Final Edition*. Ottawa, Ontario: Statistics Canada.

Easterlin, R. A., D. Ward, W. S. Bernard, and R. Ueda. 1980. *Immigration*, Cambridge, MA: Belknap Press.

Feagin, J. R., and C. B. Feagin. 1993. *Racial and Ethnic Relations*. Englewood Cliffs, NJ: Prentice Hall.

Goldscheider, C. 2001. "Ethnic Categorization in Censuses." In D. Kertzer and D. Arel (Eds.), *Census and Identity* (pp. 61–78). Cambridge, UK: Cambridge University Press.

India, Office of the Registrar General. 2001. *Census of India 2001, Household Form*. New Delhi, India: Office of the Registrar General of India.

International Organization for Standardization. 1993. *International Standard ISO 3166: Codes for the Representation of Names of Countries*, 4th ed. Berlin, Germany: International Organization for Standardization.

Kaufman, L., and P. J. Rousseeuw. 1990. *Finding Groups in Data*. New York: John Wiley.

Kertzer, K., and D. Arel. 2001. "Censuses, Identity Formation and the Struggle for Political Power." In D. Kertzer and D. Arel (Eds.), *Census and Identity* (pp. 10–32). Cambridge, UK: Cambridge University Press.

Kosmin, B. 1999. *Ethnic and Religious Questions in the 2001 UK Census of Population: Policy Recommendations*. London, UK: Institute of Jewish Policy Research.

Latin American and Caribbean Demographic Center. 1998. *Report on the Workshop on the Year 2000 Round of Population and Housing Censuses*. Santiago, Chile: CELADE.

Lieberson, S. 1993. *The Enumeration of Ethnic and Racial Groups in the Census: Some Devilish Principles*. In *Challenges of Measuring an Ethnic World*. Washington, DC: U.S. Census Bureau.

McKibben, J., K. Faust, and M. Gann. 1997. "Birth and Cohort Dynamics in the East South Central Region: Implications for Public Service Planning." Paper presented at the Population Association of America Annual Meetings, Washington, DC.

Murphy, M. 1998. "Defining People: Race and Ethnicity in South African Dictionaries." *International Journal of Lexicography* 11(1): 1–33.

Newman, G. 1998. "Census 96: Religion." *Research Note 27 1997–1998*. Canberra, Australia: Parliament of Australia.

New Zealand, Statistics New Zealand. 1996. *1996 Census Language Classifications. Classification and Standards Section*. Wellington, NZ: Statistics New Zealand.

New Zealand, Statistics New Zealand. 2001. *New Zealand Census of Population and Dwellings*. Wellington, NZ: Statistics New Zealand.

Nobles, M. 2001. "Racial Categorization and Censuses." In D. Kertzer and D. Arel (Eds.), *Census and Identity* (pp. 33–60). Cambridge, UK: Cambridge University Press.

Population Reference Bureau. 1995. "Multiracial Births Increase as U.S. Ponders Racial Definitions." *Population Today* 23 (4). Washington, DC: Population Reference Bureau.

Sandar, G. 1998. "The Other Americans." In M. Anderson and P. Collins (Eds.) *Race, Class, and Gender*, 3rd ed. (pp. 106–111). Belmont, CA: Wadsworth.

South Africa Central Statistical Service. 1996. *Census Form—1996*. Johannesburg, South Africa: South African Central Statistical Service.

Tabachnick, B., and L. Fidell. 1996. *Using Multivariate Statistics*, 3rd ed. New York: HarperCollins College Publishers.

United Kingdom Office of National Statistics. 2001. *Census 2001, England Household Form*. London, England: Office of National Statistics.

United Nations. 1998. *Principles and Recommendations for Population and Housing Censuses, Revision 1*. Statistics Division, Series M, No. 67, Rev. 1. New York: United Nations.

United States Census Bureau. 1990. Population Variable Definitions 1990 Census of Population, www.census.gov/td/stf3/append_b.html.

United States Census Bureau. 1991. *1990 Census Profile: Race and Hispanic Origin*. Washington, DC: U.S. Government Printing Office.

United States Census Bureau. 1999. *Historical Census Statistics on the Foreign-born Population of the United States*. By C. J. Gibson and E. Lennon. Population Division Working Paper No. 29. Washington, DC: U.S. Census Bureau.

United States Census Bureau. 2001. *Census 2000 Brief: Overview of Race and Hispanic Origin*. Washington, DC: U.S. Government Printing Office.

United States Immigration and Naturalization Service. 1999. *Statistical Yearbook of the Immigration and Naturalization Service, 1997*. Washington, DC: U.S. Government Printing Office.

United States Immigration and Naturalization Service. 2000. *Statistical Yearbook of the Immigration and Naturalization Service, 1998*. Washington, DC: U.S. Government Printing Office.

United States National Center for Health Statistics. 1999. *Vital Statistics of the United States: Natality, 1997, Technical Appendix*. Washington, DC: U.S. Government Printing Office.

United States Office of Management and Budget. 1978. *Statistical Directive 15, Race and Ethnic Standards for Federal Statistics and administrative Reporting*. Washington, DC: U.S. Government Printing Office.

United States Office of Management and Budget. 1994. *Statistical Policy Working Paper 22: Report on Statistical Disclosure Limitation Methodology*. Statistical Policy Office, Washington, DC: U.S. Government Printing Office.

United States Office of Management and Budget. 1997. *Revisions to the Standards for the Classifications of Federal Data on Race and Ethnicity*. Washington, DC: U.S. Government Printing Office.

United States Office of Management and Budget. 2000a. *March Bulletin No. 00–02. Guidance on Aggregation and Allocation of Data for Use in Civil Rights Monitoring and Enforcement*. Washington, DC: U.S. Government Printing Office.

United States Office of Management and Budget. 2000b. *Provisional Guidelines on the Implementation of the 1997 Standards for Federal Data on Race and Ethnicity*. Washington, DC: U.S. Government Printing Office.

Uvin, P. 2001. "On Counting, Categorizing and Violence in Burundi and Rwanda." In D. Kertzer and D. Arel (Eds.), *Census and Identity* (pp. 117–136). Cambridge, UK: Cambridge University Press.

Weed, J. A. 1995. "Vital Statistics in the United States: Preparing for the Next Century." *Population Index* 61(4): 527–539.

Weller, P., and A. Andrews. 1998. "Counting Religion: Religion, Statistics and the 2001 Census." *World Faiths Encounter* 21 (November): 23–34.

9

Marriage, Divorce, and Family Groups

KIMBERLY FAUST

Marriage or a similar institution exists in all societies, albeit with varying forms and functions. Special variations include consensual unions, common in many areas of Latin America, same-sex marriages now legal in Denmark and Sweden and among the Nandi of Kenya (woman-woman marriages), and polygamous marriages frequently found in sub-Saharan Africa. Given the wide range of possible marital situations, it is imperative to define marriage in terms of the laws or customs of individual countries or areas. Unfortunately, the national or provincial nature of marriage laws creates difficulties with respect to the international comparability of the data. The first half of this chapter examines the concepts and measures of marital status as well as those of marriage and divorce.

The principal source of data on marriage and divorce is vital registration systems and population registers, but such data can also be obtained from censuses and surveys. Information pertaining to marital behavior is usually derived from a civil registration system in the form of vital statistics. In nearly all areas of the world, marriages and divorces are certified by governmental authorities. These records can provide demographic information on persons as they move from one marital status to another. Censuses also may provide information that can be used to describe marital events and the resulting marital statuses. Data on marital status and marital characteristics are derived principally from censuses and surveys.

If registration data or census data on marriages are used to analyze marital behavior, then the data are said to be direct data. Conversely, if census data on marital status are used to estimate marital events, the data are said to be indirect. The data obtained from these two sources may relate to marital events within 1 year or other brief period of time—so-called period data—or they may apply to a long period of time for a group of persons whose experience is tracked over time—so-called cohort data for a birth cohort.

As the forms of marriage vary and change, so do the characteristics of households and family groups in which people live. Types of households and families may vary from the individual living alone to married couples (nuclear family) to extended families including related or unrelated individuals or subfamilies. The principal sources of statistical information on family groups are the same as those for marital characteristics, namely, censuses, surveys, and population registers. Family groups and household characteristics are the subjects of the second half of this chapter.

MARITAL STATUS

Concepts and Classifications

Basic Categories of Marital Status

In an effort to standardize the classification of marital status, most countries conducting a population census use the following general categories, which are applicable in nearly every culture: (1) single (never married), (2) married and not legally separated, (3) widowed and not remarried, (4) divorced and not remarried, and (5) married but legally separated. Occasionally, an additional category, (6) remarried, is used. This is a subcategory of married and reflects the move from widowed or divorced to married. Countries are requested by the United Nations to specify the minimum legal age at which marriage with parental consent can occur.

Other categories of marital status, although not as common, may be needed in countries where there are such special practices as concubinage, polygamy, levirate (marriage of her husband's brother by a widow), sororate (marriage of his wife's sister by a widower), and same-sex marriages. All of these marriage practices can be crucial to the understanding of the purpose of marriage. For example, in Denmark and Sweden it is now legal for two partners of the same sex to marry for no other reason than their desire to be together. However, among the Nandi of Kenya (Obler, 1980) and the Nuer of the Sudan (Burton, 1979), woman-woman marriages usually serve a more material purpose. Infertile women often become "female husbands" by marrying other women. The new wife then takes a male lover. The children that result from that union are said to belong to the biological mother and her female husband. Thereby, woman-woman marriages solve the problem of infertility as well as provide a marriage for a fertile woman who may not have been able to make a good marriage with a male because of a questionable history or status (Greene, 1998).

An annulment, or the rescision of a marriage, represents a special classification problem. Demographically it is akin to divorce and it is usually classified that way. Although only a low percent of all divorces (including annulments) in the United States are actually annulments, in areas where annulment is more common, it is recommended that a specific category be established for them. Annulments can be of a civil or a religious nature. Currently, most annulments are civil and involve the fulfillment of legal requirements. To annul a marriage, it is necessary to specify conditions that existed prior to the marriage that make the resulting marriage void or voidable. The most common conditions are bigamy, consanguinity of marriage partners, fraud or misrepresentation, impotence, or insanity (Faust and McKibben, 1999). Conversely, religious annulments must quality under church doctrine. Even though a religious annulment is secured, a civil annulment or a legal divorce also is necessary to end the marriage legally.

By further delineating the classifications of marital status, important information can be culled from the data that may facilitate the study of marriage and the impact of the various marital statuses on the demographic processes of fertility, mortality, and migration.

The frequencies observed in any of the marital status categories are highly dependent on the age-sex structure. For example, the decline in period marriage rates in the United States during the 1970s and 1980s appears to be inconsistent with the rise in median age at first marriage. However, during that period, the number of marriages per 1000 women aged 15 and over (i.e., the general marriage rate) declined at a faster pace than the number of marriages per 1000 total population (i.e., the crude marriage rate). The shifts in the U.S. population age structure were responsible for this phenomenon (Teachman, Polonko, and Scanzoni, 1999). As a result of the "baby boom," an increasing proportion of the population moved into the most common marriage ages. This caused the crude marriage rate to remain high while the general marriage rate fell. Likewise, the rates of marriages and divorces can appear to be inconsistent. Obviously, marriage licenses are granted only to people who are currently single (in the absence of polygamy), while divorce decrees are granted only to people who are currently married. If the size of one population changes in relation to the other, the rates can rise and fall without any real change in marriage/divorce behavior.

Legal and cultural factors can also affect the frequencies of the marital categories. The number of divorces and the ease of remarriage are to an important degree culturally based. Variations in these categories may also reflect the strictness or laxity of the legal system.

Additional Marital Status Concepts

Marital status often is further distinguished by making subdivisions or combinations of the standard categories. For example, the category "ever married" is simply a combination of "currently married" (including separated), widowed, and divorced. It is usually a counterpoint to "single" (i.e., "never married").

One variation in the development of family formation, cohabitation, has had a great impact on the classification of marital status. The practice of living together without a legal marriage is widespread and is on the increase worldwide. In some areas, it is a well-established practice; in other areas, it is fairly new. For example, in Bushbuckridge, a rural region of the Northern Province of South Africa, women are considered married when their male companions have paid the *labola* (traditional bride price), regardless whether a religious or civil ceremony was observed (Garenne, Tollman, Kahn, 2000). Given the large number of these type of unions, the creation of a separate marital status for couples living together who are not legally married can only improve our understanding of the marital and family characteristics of a population. Futhermore, important identifying information would be lost if they were combined with legally married couples.

The terminology used to describe these couples can vary and the individual terms carry different legal and cultural meanings. The three most common terms used are cohabitation, consensual union, and common law. Whereas these terms are often used interchangeably, caution is advised in making assumptions based on the terminology. For example, cohabitation is the term most frequently used in the United States. It specifies the sharing of a household by unmarried people who have a marital relationship. In Canada, the same type of union is referred to as a common-law union (Wu, 1999). Neither country awards many rights to, or imposes many obligations on, the couples participating in this type of living arrangement. Currently, in the United States it is estimated that there are 4.2 million opposite-sex cohabiting households and 1.7 million same-sex cohabiting households (U.S. Census Bureau/Saluter and Lugaila, 1998a.) Historically, cohabitation in the United States was most frequent among the lower income groups. At present, cohabitation crosses all income levels and is found in all "adult" age groups. Statistics Canada has also documented the number of Canadians in common-law unions (Wickens, 1997). In 1995, nearly 2 million Canadians, representing 14% of all couples, were living in common-law unions. Quebec has the largest number and share of cohabiting couples, who constitute 64% of all couples under age 30.

Consensual union is the term, common in Latin America, used to categorize couples who consider themselves to be married but have never had a religious or civil marriage ceremony. The legal meaning of this term can vary widely. In some countries, a consensual union is accorded all the rights, and is bound by all the obligations that legally married couples have; in other countries, the term is used to designate couples who may consider themselves married but are not legally married in the view of the government. Consensual unions are classified separately in most Latin American countries. In Puerto Rico, 12.8% of all women aged 15 to 49 were in consensual unions during 1995–1996. These women represented 23% of all women who were in a union (Davila, Ramos, and Mattei, 1998).

Common law is a third way to describe couples who are cohabiting without a legal marriage ceremony. Typically, a common-law union refers to cohabitation, as is the case in Canada. In the United States, a common-law marriage refers to a marriage that is recognized as legal although a legal ceremony was never preformed. Because there is no formal documentation of this type of marriage, a couple may be forced to prove the existence of their marriage if challenged. Currently, only eleven states in the United States (Alabama, Colorado, Iowa, Kansas, Montana, Oklahoma, Pennsylvania, Rhode Island, South Carolina, Texas, and Utah) plus the District of Columbia recognize this type of marriage. Although the requirements vary slightly among the states, the essential conditions are the same. First, in all cases, the couple must be free to marry legally; in other words, the members must be of legal age, currently unmarried, and of the opposite sex. Most important, they must conduct themselves in a way that leads to a reasonable belief that they are married. This may be accomplished by representing themselves to others as married. This representation may include cohabitation, but cohabitation alone cannot determine a legalized common-law marriage. Once the union is recognized as legal and valid, the only way to end the relationship is by a legal divorce decree. Whereas a marriage ceremony is not necessary, a formal divorce is necessary.

Recent changes worldwide in marriage and fertility practices, such as cohabitation, out-of-wedlock childbearing, delayed marriages, divorce, and remarriage, have changed the institution of marriage as well as the concepts embedded in marital status. Therefore, marital history can shed a great deal of light on the current and future behavior of mothers and children, including the timing of certain aspects of that behavior. In research on children, it is especially important to be aware of the marital history of their parents.

Because more children are expected to experience the divorce and remarriage of their parents as well as to spend some time in a cohabitating or single-parent household, an examination of the marital history of the parents may prove vital in helping to explain the children's current as well as future behavior.

Age at first marriage has been one of the most informative facts about women's marital history, especially for the study of their fertility. Because of the changing trends in family formation, age at marriage is not as directly related to fertility as it was a few decades ago. Instead, age at first union may be a more appropriate measure. For example, the United States Census Bureau (U.S. Census Bureau/Lugaila, 1998b) reported that in 1998 34.7% of all persons aged 25 to 34 were never married and 53.4% of blacks in that age group were never married. At the same time, 40.3% of all children who lived with an unmarried mother lived with mothers who had never been married. Clearly, the increase in proportions remaining single has led to an increase in out-of-wedlock childbearing. More than 30% of all births occur to unmarried women (U.S. National Center for Health Statistics, 1997). It is also estimated that 30% of all nonmarital births occur within cohabiting unions (Manning and Landale, 1996).

United States

Information on marital status has been published in the census reports of the United States for persons 15 years old and over from 1890 to 1930, and 14 years and over since 1940. At present, the Current Population Survey of the U. S. Census Bureau (1999) classifies persons by marital status into one of four major categories: never married, including persons whose only marriage was annulled; married, that is, persons currently married, whether spouse is present or living separately; widowed, that is, widows and widowers who have not remarried; and divorced, persons legally divorced and not remarried. The category "married" is further classified into (1) married, spouse present, (2) separated, (3) married, spouse absent. "Married, spouse present," includes everyone who shares a household with a spouse on a regular basis. Temporary absences, such as business trips, hospital stays, and vacations, do not change the classification. "Separated" includes everyone who has obtained a legal separation from a spouse, is living apart with the intention of securing a divorce, or is temporarily separated because of marital discord. The married, spouse absent, category is designed for couples who are currently married but are living in separate (nontemporary) residences. This would include, but is not limited to, cases of military service, imprisonment, and employment relocations.

A new type of marital status is being created in some states. The "covenant marriage" was first created in

Louisiana in 1997. In this type of marriage the couple signs a legally enforceable document in which the participants agree to undergo premarital counseling and predivorce counseling, and wait 24 months for the right to divorce without spouse's consent (Jeter, 1997).

Uses and Limitations

In spite of the changing nature of marriage, marriage, divorce, and marital status are useful and valid demographic variables for study because marriage is an expected event for nearly all of the world's population. To ignore marriage would be to ignore a major life course event directly affecting fertility and indirectly affecting a host of demographic social, and economic characteristics. Study of marital status allows us to examine the path to marriage by studying the characteristics of people never married as well as the characteristics of the newly married, and, of course, the study of marriage and divorce is directly linked to the study of marital status. We can study duration of marriage by comparing marriage and divorce data for the same cohorts. Socioeconomic and other circumstances before and after marriages can be studied to illustrate the forces at work in the processes of marital dissolution and remarriage.

Life course changes associated with marriage may be compared among racial, ethnic, and socioeconomic groups within and between countries. With the aid of marital status data, we may be able to ascertain the characteristics most closely associated with inequalities of income, education, employment, and longevity. By studying the movements between marital statuses, we may be able to predict the impact of changes in the legal system, the economy, and the social climate on families and children.

The use of marital status data does have some limitations. Census and survey responses on marital status are, for the most part, unvalidated responses. Respondents are rarely asked to provide legal documentation when completing surveys or censuses. The earlier discussion on cohabitation, consensual unions, and common-law marriages must be kept in mind when analyzing data classified by marital status. People reporting themselves as married may not be legally married. Although many cultural restrictions against cohabitation have been eased in both "modern" and "traditional" societies, many respondents may hesitate to report their status as cohabiting and report it as married instead. Alternatively, many persons who are cohabiting or living in common-law marriages may classify themselves as single, regardless of their real legal status and the guidelines of the census or survey.

Data on marriage and divorce obtained through a registration system for vital events may be of creditable quality and serve as numerators for marital rates of various kinds. Care must be taken in regard to the source of the data, however. Data on marriages may be compiled only for civil marriages, although religious ceremonies also may be recognized legally. Conversely, church registers may be the only source of data on marriages for some countries. In other countries, population registers serve as the principal source of data on marriages and marital status.

The type of census that is conducted in a particular country or area affects the data obtained for the marital status classes. A *de facto* enumeration may yield statistics on marital status (as well as on household characteristics) that do not reflect the usual situation of the persons concerned. Spouses may be temporarily absent for any number of reasons. This could cause the categories of "married, spouse present" to be understated and "married, spouse absent" to be overstated with respect to a *de jure* enumeration.

Quality of the Statistics

Response Bias

In reporting any type of personal information such as marital status, respondents frequently introduce several types of biases that tend to have a negative effect on the quality of the statistics. Interviewers and the processing operations introduce other types of biases. The biases introduced by respondents usually result from the respondent's unwillingness to admit marital difficulties, divorces, or separations. In general, people prefer to report themselves as married rather than single or separated. They may also report incorrect ages on marriage license forms in order to conceal their true age, such as when marrying without parental consent or when marrying in order to legitimate a child's birth.

One way to detect the underreporting of the "separated" category is to compare the number of separated women with the number of separated men. In a monogamous society, the numbers should be quite similar after the marital status of immigrants and emigrants is taken into consideration. A second way to check the validity of data on marital status is to compare (1) an estimate of the marital distribution at the census date based on (a) the marital distribution at an earlier census adjusted by (b) vital statistics data and immigration data with (2) the marital distribution at the current census. In general, the numbers of marriages and divorces should be consistent with the number of people claiming each marital status. The comparison of vital statistics and census statistics in the United States has become more difficult for researchers since the mid-1990s. The U.S. Department of Health and Human Services (1995) announced that, beginning January 1, 1996, payments to states and other vital registration areas for the compilation of detailed data from marriage and divorce certificates would be discontinued as a result of "tightened resource constraints," and that detailed statistics on marriages and divorces from individual states would no longer be obtained. The federal agency suggested that the information on marriages and divorces formerly gathered from states could be replaced by surveys conducted by the National Center for Health Statistics and by the Current Population Survey of the Census Bureau. In any case, estimates of marital groups from the Current Population Survey can be compared with corresponding data from the census.

Nonresponse and Inconsistent Responses

Nonresponse to questions on marital status and inconsistent responses involving marital status pose additional problems. Unlike age, which can be deduced from date of birth and the current date, marital status cannot be assumed or deduced readily from other answers of the respondent. Polygamy may cause confusion in the analysis of marital status and may be associated with inconsistent and unacceptable responses. In sub-Saharan Africa, polygamy ratios vary from 11.6% of married women in Burundi to 52.3% of married women in Togo (Speizer and Yates, 1998). If the proportions of marital categories for men and women are compared, more women than men should report being married. Yet when husbands' and wives' marital status responses in the 1989 Kenya Demographic and Health Surveys were matched, 6% of the husbands thought to be monogamous actually reported having at least two wives, while 8% of the husbands thought to be polygynous actually reported having only one wife (Ezeh, 1997). Likewise, if demographic variables such as mortality, fertility, or family planning are to be studied according to marital status, which wife should be used in the analysis? Should all of the wives be used, or the chronologically first wife, or a random sample of the wives? The selection of a wife at random may reduce the number of "incorrect" responses (Speizer and Yates, 1998).

MEASURES AND ANALYSIS OF CHANGES

Age and Sex as Variables

In spite of the errors that may occur in reporting, marital status classified by age and sex is useful in analyzing the marital and related behavior of males and females at various ages. By tracking marital status by age, it is possible to study the timing of marriage as it relates to other life course events such as education and employment. In addition, it allows for the study of marriage customs, particularly as they may affect males differently from females. Age at first marriage, likelihood of remarriage, interval of time between divorce and remarriage, and other such measures may not be the same for males and females. Furthermore, because of differing life expectancies within societies and among them,

and differences in the age and sex structure of populations, age at first marriage and age and rates of widowhood, as well as age and rates of remarriage, vary from one group to another.

Usually, the overall number of married men is about the same as the overall number of married women. However, great differences can be seen at each individual age group. In the United States and many other countries, the custom is for women to marry men older than they are. When that custom is combined with the longer life expectancy of women, great differences in marital status appear at the youngest and oldest age groups. More young women are married than are young men and fewer elderly women are married than are elderly men. When the numbers of men and women eligible for marriage at the customary marrying ages are grossly unequal, the phenomenon is termed the *marriage squeeze*. Given the customary gender difference in marriage ages, sharp fluctuations in the number of births tend to give rise to a marriage squeeze, to the disadvantage of one or the other sex depending on the direction of the change in the number of births.

Table 9.1 shows the marital distribution of the male and female population for two age groups, for three selected areas. The data presented illustrate the tendency toward early marriage for females in India and the propensity for

TABLE 9.1 Percentage Distribution of Males and Females Aged 20–24 and 65 Years and over by Marital Status, for Selected Areas: Selected Years, 1991 to 1998

Area, Year, and Marital Status	20–24 years old		65–69 years old[2]	
	Male	Female	Male	Female
India, 1991	100.0	100.0	100.0	100.0
Married	39.6	81.8	84.3	51.0
Divorced[1]	0.2	0.6	0.3	0.4
Widowed	0.3	0.6	13.4	48.0
Never married	59.9	17.0	2.0	0.6
West Bank and Gaza Strip, 1996	100.0	100.0	100.0	100.0
Married	27.6	62.4	87.5	34.3
Separated	0.1	0.3	0.2	1.1
Divorced	0.3	1.0	z	0.7
Widowed	0.0	0.3	11.6	61.1
Never married	72.1	36.1	0.7	2.8
United States, 1998	100.0	100.0	100.0	100.0
Married	15.9	27.8	80.4	55.9
Separated	0.9	1.9	1.1	1.3
Divorced	1.5	2.5	7.8	8.9
Widowed	0.0	0.2	8.8	31.9
Never married	83.4	70.3	4.1	4.3

z Less than 0.05.

[1] Includes separated.

[2] Ages 65–74 for the United States and 65 and over for the West Bank and Gaza Strip.

Sources: Palestinian Central Bureau of Statistics (1996); U.S. Census Bureau/Lugaila (1998b); United Nations (1997a).

Indian females to marry older males. The data for the United States show a modest tendency for women to marry older men. It is interesting to note the differences in the never-married category between the percentages for India and the United States. Indians, both males and females, are somewhat less likely to be never married, even at ages 65 through 69, than are their counterparts in the United States.

The data on marital status for age-sex groups can reflect the sex ratio of a country. As the reader may recall, the sex ratio represents the number of males for each 100 females in the population. If the sex ratio in the population is dramatically different from 100, the availability of marriage partners may become a problem. As a result of the "one-child" policy in China, which legally limits couples to a single child, and the preference of couples for sons, a tremendous shortage of female children, dubbed "missing girls," has occurred in that country. Eventually, this will result in a tremendous shortage of adult females, who may then be dubbed "missing brides." The imbalance in the age-specific sex ratios in China will greatly affect the marriage market and seriously skew the marital status distribution at each age.

Measures of Marriage and Divorce

As is characteristic of other demographic variables, there are many different measures of marriage and divorce. Some are easily confused and misinterpreted because they are rather similar in form and function. The most frequently cited statistic is the absolute number of marriages each year. While this statistic is useful in measuring gross changes in the number of marriages, it is not an analytically useful number because it does not take into account variations in population size or age structure. Increases (or decreases) in the number of marriages can result from a rise (or fall) in the population or an increase (decrease) in the number of young people in the population, such as resulted from the entry of the baby-boom cohorts into young adulthood in the 1960s and 1970s. Often, analyses of marriage are limited to men and women aged 15 and over. This is a rough way of "controlling" for age. By limiting the analysis to persons aged 15 and above, variations in the numbers at ages not eligible for marriage are excluded; persons under the age of 15 are at minimal risk of marriage.

Crude Marriage (Divorce) Rate

The simplest measure of marriage is the crude marriage rate, or the number of marriages in a year per 1000 population at midyear. Note that the crude marriage rate represents the number of marriages, not the number of people getting married. While this rate takes into account changes in the

size of the population, it is affected by segments of the population that are not at risk of marriage, such as minors or those people currently married. Crude marriage rates are used most effectively for gross analyses in areas that may not have the additional data to compute more refined measures. If M is the total number marriages in one year, and P is the average number of persons living in that year, then the formula for the crude marriage rate (CMR) is

$$CMR = \frac{M}{P} \times 1000 \qquad (9.1)$$

This same type of formulation can be used to calculate the crude divorce rate.

General Marriage (Divorce) Rate

In areas with more detailed data, a preferred measure is the general marriage rate (GMR). In this measure the population is restricted to persons of marriageable age. Most commonly the rate is expressed as the number of marriages per 1000 women aged 15 and over. The formula is

$$GMR = \frac{M}{P_{15+}^{f}} \times 1000 \qquad (9.2)$$

where M is the number of marriages and P_{15+}^{f} is the number of women aged 15 and older. A similar formula would be used to represent the general divorce rate.

Refined Divorce (Marriage) Rate

A common practice, employed especially by the news media, is to compare the number of marriages in a given year with the number of divorces in the same year, and to infer from this comparison the proportion of marriages ending in divorce. Although it is tempting to compare the numbers for each event in this way, it is misleading because it fails to relate the event of divorce to the population at risk. A better way to express the divorce rate in a year is to relate the number of divorces in the year to the number of married women or men at the middle of the year, or to the average number of married women and men. Currently, the U.S. National Center for Health Statistics uses the number of married women for such a computation. The formula is

$$RDR = \frac{D}{P_{mar}^{f}} \times 1000 \qquad (9.3)$$

where D is the number of divorces and P_{mar}^{f} is the number of married females. This measure is a type of *refined divorce rate*. A similar measure could be formulated for a *refined marriage rate*, wherein the number of marriages in a year is related to the number of single, widowed, and divorced women or men at the middle of the year.

Age-Sex-Specific Marriage (Divorce) Rates

It is often important to take account of the variations in the age and sex composition of a population and compute marriage and divorce rates for age groups separately for men and women. By restricting the measure to one age group (and one sex) at a time, it is possible not only to examine the rates for the individual age-sex groups but also to "control" for the size of the population in each age-sex group. Both marriage (*ASMR*) and divorce (*ASDR*) rates can be calculated in this way. The formula for the divorce rate at age 39 is

$$ASDR = \mu_{39} = \frac{D_{39}^f}{P_{39}^f} \times 1000 \tag{9.4}$$

where D_{39}^f refers to the number of divorces of females aged 39 in a year and P_{39}^f refers to the number of females aged 39 at the middle of the year.

It is useful to restrict the denominator of this measure to the married population in the age-sex group. This modification provides a more refined measure in that it relates the number of divorces in the age-sex group to the population exposed to the risk of divorce, namely, the number of married males or females in the age group, rather than the total number of males or females in the age group. A similar measure may be formulated for age-specific marriage rates wherein the number of marriages of females at a given age during a year is related to the number of single, widowed, or divorced women at the age at midyear. Unfortunately, the necessary data for computing these measures are not readily available for most countries.

Order-Specific Marriage (Divorce) Rates

Currently, it is predicted that 70% of separated and divorced Americans will remarry at some point (Faust and McKibben, 1999). Where, as in the United States, there are high rates of divorce and remarriage, it is important to distinguish between first marriage rates and remarriage rates. Remarriages, like first marriages, have a high probability of ending in divorce. Hence, there is interest in distinguishing between first divorces and second divorces. The residual categories may be given as third and higher marriages and third and higher divorces. Data on marriages and divorces of specific orders allow for the calculation of marriage and divorce rates of different orders. An order-specific marriage rate is defined as the number of marriages of a given order during a year per 1000 population 15 years and older at the middle of the year. The formula for the first-marriage rate is

$$\frac{M_1}{P_{nm}^{15+}} \times 1000 \tag{9.5}$$

where M_1 refers to the number of first marriages and P_{nm}^{15+} refers to the never-married population aged 15 years and older. The formula for second marriages is

$$\frac{M_2}{P_{W+D}} \times 1000 \tag{9.6}$$

where M_2 refers the number of second marriages and P_{w+d} refers to the (first-order) widowed and divorced population.

Standardization and Method of Expected Cases

The simplest and commonest way of describing the marital status of a population is to present a percentage distribution of the population by marital categories, i.e., to calculate general marital status ratios (GMSR). This calculation is carried out by dividing the number of persons in each marital category by the total population 15 years and over and multiplying the result by 100. This type of computation can be extended to each age-sex group. Percentage distributions by age may also be computed for each marital category.

A serious shortcoming of the GMSR is its dependency on the age structure of the population. If the general proportions in each marital class for two areas, or two different dates for the same area, are compared, this comparison would be affected by the fact that an old population would tend to have more people in the widowed category than a young population, and a young population would tend to have more people in the single category. A way to discount the effect of differences in the age structures of populations in such comparisons is to employ the same age distribution to weight the population at each age for the two populations being compared (i.e., to *standardize* the general percentages for each marital class). This technique uses one age distribution as the "standard" and then calculates how many persons would be in each marital class if all the populations being compared had the same age structure as the standard population. The choice of the standard population should be carefully considered. Any oddities in the age structure of the standard population will distort the comparison of the marital compositions of the populations under study.

Table 9.2 illustrates the procedure for standardizing the general percentage single, married, widowed, and divorced for age. The table shows how to prepare the age-standardized general percent in each marital status for males in 1890 by the direct method, using the number of males in 1998 in each age group as the standard. Analogous steps are required to prepare the corresponding age-standardized general percentage in each marital status for females.

TABLE 9.2 Calculation of Percentage Distribution by Marital Status for Males 15 years and over in 1890, Standardized by Age with the 1998 Age Distribution as Standard, for the United States

Age (years)	Males, 1998[2] (In thousands) (P_a) (1)	Distribution by marital status, 1890[1] (r_a)			
		Never married (2)	Married (3)	Widowed (4)	Divorced (5)
15 to 19	9,921	0.9957	0.0042	z	z
20 to 24	8,826	0.8081	0.1889	0.0025	0.0005
25 to 29	9,450	0.4607	0.5278	0.0099	0.0016
30 to 34	10,076	0.2655	0.7140	0.0181	0.0024
35 to 44	22,055	0.1537	0.8102	0.0327	0.0035
45 to 54	16,598	0.0915	0. 8440	0.0602	0.0043
55 to 64	10,673	0.0683	0.8245	0.1024	0.0048
65 and over	13,524	0.0561	0.7063	0.2335	0.0040
Males, 15 years and over, 1998 (ΣP_a)	101,123				
Expected number in marital status, 1890 ($\Sigma r_a * P_a$)		30,435	64,117	6269	297
Standardized percent in marital status, 1890 ($\Sigma r_a * P_a$)/ (ΣP_a) $*$ 100		30.1	63.4	6.2	0.3
Actual percentage in marital status, 1890		43.7	52.3	3.8	0.2

z Less than 0.00005.

[1] U.S. Census Bureau (1964).

[2] U.S. Census Bureau (1998d).

1. List the number of males in each age group 15 years and over in 1998 (P_a) in column 1.
2. Calculate the proportion of males in each marital status for each age group in 1890 (r_a) from the original census data. The results are shown in columns 2 to 5.
3. Multiply columns 2 through 5 by the corresponding number of males in 1998 in column 1. The result is the expected number in each marital status at each age ($r_a P_a$). (The results for individual age groups are not displayed in the table.)
4. Sum the results in 3 for each column. These are the total expected numbers for each marital status ($\Sigma r_a P_a$.).
5. Compute the general age-standardized percentage single, married, widowed, and divorced by dividing each column total from step 4 by the total male population in 1998 (101,123). [($\Sigma r_a P_a \div \Sigma P_a$) $*$ 100.] These are the standardized percentages for each marital status.

The results in step 5 are interpreted as the percent of males 15 years and over who would have been in each marital status in 1890 if the age structure of the male population in 1890 were the same as the age structure of the male population in 1998. Standardizing the general percents in each marital status in 1890 by the 1998 age structure results in lowering the percentage of single men and raising the percent married, widowed, and divorced. These adjusted percents for 1890 may now be compared with the observed percentages for 1998 (not shown) to reflect changes in marital status unaffected by the changes in age structure between the 2 years.

Total Marriage Rate

This is a measure of the total number of marriages for a specified cohort during its lifetime. The total marriage rate (TMR) for a synthetic cohort is calculated by summing the age-specific marriage rates over all age groups for other sex in a given year (compare with the total fertility rate). The total population at each age is used in the denominator (i.e., the denominator is not restricted to unmarried persons or only those at risk of marriage). When the age-specific rates are added in this way, they are weighted equally. In addition, this measure is not adjusted for mortality. The formula is as follows:

$$(TMR)^f = \sum_{a=15}^{\infty} \frac{M_a^f}{P_a^f} \times 1000 \qquad (9.7)$$

where M_a^f is the number of marriages of females aged a, and P_a^f is the total female population at age a.

A similar rate can be calculated for total first marriages (TFMR) by summing age-specific first marriage rates for either males or females. The formula is as follows:

$$(TFMR)^f = \sum_{a=15}^{\infty} \frac{M_a^{f,1}}{P_a^f} \times 1000 \qquad (9.8)$$

where $M_a^{f,1}$ is the number of first marriages to females aged a, and P_a^f is the total female population (including women in all marital categories) at age a.[1]

---

[1] These measures were originally proposed by Siegel and illustrated in U.S. Bureau of the Census/Shyrock, Siegel, and associates (1971). See Chapter 19.

Rates on a Probability Basis

Rates on a probability basis refer to a class of measures that indicate the probability that a marriage or divorce will occur in a specified limited population in a specified brief period, such as year. For example, the rates can focus on the likelihood of marriage for a person of a specific age, a specific duration of divorce or widowhood, or other characteristic, or a combination of these. This type of rate may be approximated by the central marriage rate at age a during the year (ASDR or μ_a). More precisely, we can allow for mortality during the year. The formula is as follows:

$$\bar{\mu}_a = \frac{2\mu_a}{2 + m_a} \qquad (9.9)$$

where $\bar{\mu}_a$ is an age-specific probability of marriage at age a during a year, μ_a is an age-specific central marriage rate and M_a is the central death rate for persons aged a. A first marriage probability for a particular age during a year can be measured by

$$\bar{\mu}_a^m = M_a^1 \div (P_a^S + \tfrac{1}{2} D_a^S + \tfrac{1}{2} M_a^S) = 2\mu_a^S \div (2 + M_a^S + \mu_a^S) \qquad (9.9a)$$

where P_a^s represents the midyear single population at age a, D_a^s represents deaths of single persons at that age during the year, and M_a^s represents marriages of single persons at the age. First marriage probabilities could be computed for the United States directly from the census of 1980 and several earlier censuses on the basis of the question on age at first marriage.

Nuptiality Tables

A more complex analytic tool is the nuptiality table (i.e., a marriage formation table or a marriage dissolution table). Nuptiality tables are specialized types of life tables designed to measure and analyze marriage and divorce patterns. (See Chapter 13, "The Life Table," for a detailed treatment of the anatomy, construction, and uses of the life table.) These tables can be constructed without regard to mortality (i.e., a gross nuptiality table) or with an allowance for mortality (i.e., a net nuptiality table.) In *marriage formation tables* (also called attrition tables for the single population), age-specific first marriage rates are used to reduce an initial cohort over the age scale by estimates of first marriages. In a gross nuptiality table, the persons who move to the next age are those males or females who did not marry in the age interval. In a net nuptiality table, the persons who move to the next age are those males or females who neither married nor died. These single survivors are then subject to the age-specific first marriage rates and mortality rates for the next age group.

Marriage formation tables also provide estimates of the median age at first marriage, the proportion of the initial cohort who remain single at each age, the proportion of the initial cohort who never marry, the chance of ever marrying from each age forward, and other measures. (See Shryock, Siegel, and Stockwell, *Methods and Materials of Demography: Condensed Edition*, Academic Press, 1976, Chapter 19, for an exposition of a complete net nuptiality table, based on probabilities of first marriage for 1958–1960 from the 1960 census prepared by P. C. Click.)

Marriage dissolution tables are computed in much the same way. Probabilities of divorce and death are used to calculate the number of marriages that dissolve. This type of table can provide information on the probability of a marriage ever ending in either divorce or death and the average duration in years of marriages.

Divorce Rates According to Marriage Duration

Because the length of marriage can affect the likelihood of divorce, it is of interest to calculate divorce rates for "each" duration or length of the marriage. The formula for a divorce rate specific for duration of marriage is

$$\frac{D_i}{P_{m,i}} \times 1000 \qquad (9.10)$$

where D_i represents the number of divorces of persons in a specific marriage-duration group (i), and $P_{m,i}$ represents the midyear married population of the same marriage-duration group (i).

Average Age at First Marriage

The average age at first marriage has received considerable attention as a means of describing and analyzing marital behavior. The measure has taken many specific forms, but the most common variation is the median age at first marriage computed from grouped data. This statistic represents the age below which and above which half of the population has married for the first time. In 1996, the estimated median age at first marriage in the United States was 27.1 years for males and 24.8 years for females (U.S. Census Bureau/Saluter and Lugaila, 1998a). These figures are approximately 4 years higher than the median age at first marriage for both males and females in 1970. The figure for males was at an historical high point. By 1997, the median age at first marriage had slipped to 26.8 for males but had risen to 25.0 for females. Table 9.3 shows the median ages at first marriage for males and females in the United States and Poland for the years, 1985 to 1997. We note that this measure has changed very little over this period in Poland, but has shown a fairly steady increase in the United States.

As stated earlier, period data represent information relating to a given year or short span of years. For example, the median age at marriage for all persons who married in 2001 is an example of a measure based on period data. A

TABLE 9.3 Median Age at First Marriage, for Ever-Married Males and Females, 1985 to 1997, for United States and Poland

Year	United States		Poland	
	Males	Females	Males	Females
1985	25.5	23.3	25.0	22.6
1986	25.7	23.1	25.0	22.6
1987	25.8	23.6	25.0	22.5
1988	25.9	23.6	25.0	22.5
1989	26.2	23.8	24.8	22.9
1990	26.1	23.9	24.9	22.7
1991	26.3	24.1	24.6	22.2
1992	26.5	24.4	24.6	22.1
1993	26.5	24.5	24.7	22.2
1994	26.7	24.5	24.8	22.4
1995	26.9	24.5	24.9	22.5
1996	27.1	24.8	24.9	22.6
1997	26.8	25.0	25.1	22.9

Sources: U.S. Census Bureau/Saluter and Lugaila (1998a); United Nations Statistical Office (1998).

TABLE 9.4 Percentage Never Married by Single Years of Age for Males and Females, United States, 1996

Age (years)	Males	Females
18	98.9	95.4
19	97.7	92.0
20	94.7	85.8
21	91.5	79.5
22	82.1	70.6
23	76.3	66.4
24	69.3	58.4
25	66.8	45.2
26	56.6	43.8
27	48.6	41.5
28	46.2	33.1
29	40.7	32.9
30	32.3	28.1
31	30.6	24.6
32	29.6	21.5
33	26.7	18.3

Source: U.S. Census Bureau/Saluter and Lugaila (1998a).

key attribute of this measure is that the data all pertain to the year 2001. Marriages during 2001 are arrayed according to age and the age above which and below which half of the newlyweds marry is the median age at marriage. Another method of ascertaining the median age at marriage is to reconstruct the marriage experience of persons born in each previous year or group of years from census data. This is possible where the census asks for age or date of first marriage, as was done in several U.S. censuses through 1980.

The median age at marriage can be calculated for all persons who were born in some prior year, say 1950, using cohort data. If the group of people born in 1950 is followed from birth to death, its cumulative marriage experiences can be used to calculate the actual median age at marriage for the birth cohort of 1950. The long period of time required for the entire cohort to reach old age and the fuzzy reference date make use of this measure problematic in spite of its verisimilitude.

Estimate of Median Age at First Marriage by an Indirect Method

Median age at first marriage can be estimated indirectly on the basis of census or survey data on marital status disaggregated by age and sex. The general method is as follows:

1. The proportion of people who will ever marry must be estimated first. (About 90% of the population in most countries will marry at least once. The remaining 10% never marry.) To ascertain this figure more closely, it is necessary to identify the age group at which the maximum proportion of people are married. For example, most people who will ever marry have been married by the time they reach ages 45 to 54. Therefore, the proportion married at this age group (45 to 54) is often used as the upper limit. Above this age group, death begins to drive the proportion down and the marriage rate is quite low.

2. We next need to divide this proportion in half to determine the proportion corresponding to the median age of first marriage. Assuming that 90% of men or women will ever marry, the proportion ever married corresponding to the median age of first marriage is 45%.

3. Next, locate the exact age at which 45% of the population is married. In most countries, this age is located somewhere between 25 and 29 years of age.

The procedure is illustrated here, first for single-year-of-age data and then for 5-year age group for U.S. 1996:

Step 1. For males, 95.53% of those aged 54 had ever married. For females, the corresponding value was 93.94%.

Step 2. One-half the value in step 1 is 47.76% for males and 46.97% for females. Subtracting these values from 100 yields 52.23% single for males and 53.03% single for females at the halfway mark. (This step is unnecessary for deriving the median age, but it may be more meaningful for those who interpret it as a measure of the attrition of the single population.)

Step 3. In Table 9.4, locate the ages at which 52.23% of the males are still single and the age at which 53.03% of the females are still single. It can be seen that the median age at first marriage for males falls between

TABLE 9.5 Percentage Never Married by 5-Year Age Groups for Males and Females, United States, 1996

Age	Male	Female
15–19	97.3	94.3
20–24	83.4	70.3
25–29	51.0	38.6
30–34	29.2	21.6
35–39	21.6	14.3
40–44	15.6	9.9
45–54	8.9	7.2

Source: U.S. Census Bureau/Saluter and Lugaila (1998a).

TABLE 9.6 Percentage Never-Married for Indian Women, by 50 Year Age Groups, 1991

Age (years)	Total	Never married	Percentage never married
15–19	36,803,855	23,654,821	64.27
20–24	36,958,481	6,280,927	16.99
25–29	34,692,671	1,450,149	4.18
30–34	28,486,719	505,122	1.77
35–39	24,840,570	233,959	0.94
40–44	19,714,094	191,862	0.97
45–49	17,179,239	125,345	0.73
50–54	14,208,702	107,651	0.76
Sum, 15–49-years			89.85

Source: United Nations Statistical Office (1998). *Demographic Yearbook*, Historical Supplement.

26.5 years, the midpoint of age 26 (where 56.6% of the males are still single) and 27.5 years, the midpoint of age 27 (where 48.6% of the males are still single). The target age is found among males at least 26.5 years but not yet 27.5 years of age. Therefore, the "median inteval" is 26.5–27.5 years of age. If we interpolate linearly between these midpoint values to the proportions noted earlier, the median age at first marriage is determined to be 27.0 years, slightly below the official figure.

Similarly, Table 9.4 shows that the median age for first marriage for females falls between age 24.5 (where 58.4% of the females are still single) and 25.5 years (where 45.2% of the females are still single). Again, using linear interpolation on the (cumulative) percents corresponding to the limits of the median interval, 24.5 and 25.5, we find the median age for females to be 24.9 years.

Table 9.5 shows the data in 5-year age groups corresponding to the single-year-of-age data in Table 9.4. The median age at first marriage can be estimated in the same way as with the data for single years of age. For example, the median age at first marriage for males is known to fall somewhere between the ages 20 to 24 and 25 to 29. Using the midpoints of each 5-year age group (22.5 and 27.5 years, respectively), we calculate the median age at first marriage to be 27.3 years for males and 25.2 for females by linear interpolation. (Note that within a few decimal points the results from single ages and grouped data are the same.) Care should be taken when using this procedure for populations with rapid age changes or irregular age distributions; in this case a linear progression of the percentages single over the five ages between the midpoints of the age groups may not be appropriate.

The median age at remarriage cannot confidently be estimated without specific data on marriages according to order and age at remarriage. The most accurate way to measure the median age of higher-order marriages is to ask the relevant questions on marriage certificates or census forms and to tabulate the data in the detail indicated.

Estimate of Mean Age at First Marriage by an Indirect Method

An indirect method may also be used to calculate the mean age at first marriage. Called the "singulate mean age at marriage," the measure represents the mean age at first marriage of those in a hypothetical or synthetic cohort who eventually marry by age 50 (Hajnal, 1953). A series of age-specific proportions of single persons for the age range 15 to 54 is used to calculate the hypothetical cohort's probability of remaining single (Islam and Ahmed, 1998). The basic assumption of the calculation is that the change in the proportion single from age x to age x + 1 is a measure of the proportion of a birth cohort that married at that age.

Another assumption of this method is that no one dies between the 15th and 50th birthdays. An example of this calculation is shown for females of India using data in Table 9.6.

The procedure results in an estimate of the average number of years lived in the single state by those who marry before age 50. The steps in the computations may be summarized as follows:

1. Sum the percentages single from age group 15 to 19 to age group 45 to 49 and multiply the sum by 5 (the use of 5 is required by the grouping into 5-year age groups):

$$89.85 \times 5 = 449.25$$

2. To this figure, add 1500 (15 × 100), the years lived by the cohort before the members' 15th birthday:

$$449.25 + 1500.0 = 1949.25$$

3. Average the percentages for ages 45 to 49 and 50 to 54:

$$\frac{1}{2}(0.73 + 0.76) = 0.74$$

4. Multiply the results in step 3 by 50:

$$0.74 \times 50 = 37.00$$

5. Subtract the result in step 4 from that in step 2:

$$1949.25 - 37.00 = 1912.25$$

6. Subtract the result in step 3 from 100:

$$100.00 - 0.74 = 99.26$$

7. Divide the result of step 5 by the result in step 6:

$$1912.25 \div 99.26 = 19.3$$

The number of years lived by those who did not marry before age 50 is calculated by multiplying the percent still single (0.74) by 50. This number (37.00) is then subtracted from the total years of single life to age 50 (1949.25), to obtain the adjusted total (1912.25). This is then divided by the percentage of women who have ever married (99.26). The result of the division is the singulate mean age at marriage. In the case of Indian women in 1991, the singulate mean age at marriage is 19.3 years.

Proportion Who Never Marry

The proportion of the population which never marries is of great interest in connection with the study of family structure and changes, fertility, and population growth. Historically, the terms bachelor and spinster were used for males and females, respectively, who had not yet married by age 35. Currently, we cannot safely assume that those who have not married by age 35 will never marry, even though first marriage rates after age 35 have tended to be low. In 1998, 13.6 million persons in the United States aged 25 to 34 years had never married. This represents 34.7% of all persons in that age group (U.S. Census Bureau/Lugaila, 1998b). It is projected that, by the year 2010, 28% of all persons aged 30 to 34 will have never married, as compared to 25% in 1996 (U.S. Census Bureau/Saluter and Lugaila, 1998a). As we saw in Table 9.5, for the United States in 1996 at ages 45–54, only 7.2% of the women had never married. (However, compare the corresponding figure for India in 1991 in Table 9.6—0.7%.)

It is not known whether those women will eventually marry or will choose to remain single. On the one hand, the leveling off in the age at first marriage may lead us to believe that they will marry at some time. On the other hand, there are many social changes occurring in the United States, as well as in other industrialized countries, that could lead to an increase in the proportion of persons who never marry. In these countries, out-of-wedlock childbearing is becoming more accepted. This decline in the stigma attached to non-marital births has been accompanied by an increase in divorce and cohabitation and an increase in the adoption of children by unmarried women. Furthermore, the improvement in methods of birth control is contributing to a reduction in the number of unwanted and unplanned pregnancies and the number of "forced" marriages resulting from unplanned pregnancies and childbearing.

Changing gender roles and broadened educational and economic options for women have been associated with lower marriage rates. Being employed outside the home introduces people to spousal alternatives (i.e., a wider group of friends, acquaintances, and coworkers). In addition, single women and men may feel that their independence and autonomy are threatened by marriage.

Group Variations

Understanding marital status as a demographic characteristic can be advanced by examining it in relation to other demographic and socioeconomic characteristics such as age, race, ethnicity, income, and education. It is known that the probability of marriage, age at entry into marriage, duration of marriage, probability of divorce, and likelihood of remarriage vary across social, racial, ethnic, and economic groups. For example, racial and ethnic groups in the United States differ in their tendency to marry early or late and in their lifetime percentages who never marry. In 1998, for example, 53.4% of blacks aged 25 to 34 had never married as compared to 35% for all persons in this age group (U.S. Census Bureau Lugaila, 1998b). Variations within ethnic groups are evidenced by marriage differences among the Hispanic groups. Cuban-American women tend to postpone marriage and childbearing while Puerto Rican women are much more likely to have children early and out of wedlock (Sanchez-Ayendez, 1988; Szapocznik and Hernandez, 1988).

FAMILY GROUPS

Historically, the United States census and other censuses have used the designation "household" to mark units of enumeration. Members of the household are not simply counted, however, but much data are also secured on the composition and structure of households. The relationships of the people within the household can document broad societal trends. For example, analyses of household composition during the 1990s showed an increasing proportion of children living in one-parent households as well as a large proportion of grandchildren living only with their grandparents. Likewise, the living arrangements of adults have been affected by societal changes. For example, there has been an increase in unmarried-couple households and households maintained by single adults living alone, including young adults maintaining their own households.

United Nations Concepts and Classifications

In its continuing series of recommendations for population and housing censuses, the United Nations (1997b) has recently produced a document that addresses most, if not all, of the permutations of living arrangements. Place of usual residence has been designated as the best method of associating persons with a particular household and housing unit and of grouping persons in households. Households may be single-person units or they may be multiperson units. Some countries use the "housekeeping-unit" concept of a household while others use the "household-dwelling unit" concept. The former concept focuses on the family relationships within the housing unit such as married couples or subfamilies, whereas the latter concept simply uses the aggregate number of persons occupying a housing unit. The United Nations suggests that the housekeeping-unit definition is more appropriate in areas where significant variations in household structure are believed to occur. For a complete listing of household concepts and definitions, the original document, *Principles and Recommendations for Population and Housing Censuses* (United Nations, 1997b) should be consulted.

Concepts Used in the United States

Households

According to concepts long used in the censuses and population surveys of the United States (U.S. Census Bureau, 1999),

> A household consists of all the persons who occupy a housing unit. A house, an apartment or other group of rooms, or a single room is regarded as a housing unit when it is occupied or intended for occupancy as separate living quarters; that is, when the occupants do not live and eat with any other people in the structure and there is either (1) direct access from the outside or through a common hall or (2) a kitchen or cooking equipment for the exclusive use of the occupants.

This definition of household includes the related family members and all the unrelated people who share the housing unit. The unrelated members include foster children, employees, and lodgers that share the housing unit.

Family and Nonfamily Households

Family households are households maintained by a family (as will be defined later). Family households include any unrelated people who may be residing in the same housing unit. Nonfamily households consist of a person living alone or a group of unrelated people sharing a housing unit, such as partners or roomers. For example, a widower living alone is designated in this way.

Householder

A householder is defined as the person, or one of the persons, in whose name the housing unit is owned or rented (also called the reference person). If the housing unit is jointly maintained (rented or owned) by a married couple, the householder or reference person may be either the husband or the wife, whoever is named first. The designation of the householder and the determination of each person's relationship in the household are made at the time of enumeration. The choice of the householder is important in that the relationship status of all other persons in the household is determined on the basis of their relationship to the householder.

Beginning in 1980, the Census Bureau ended its practice of automatically classifying the husband as the householder when the husband and wife jointly maintained the household. Historically, the Census Bureau employed the designation "head of household" or "head of family" for the person now designated as the "householder." Because of the greater sharing of responsibilities among family members, it was felt that the term "head" was no longer appropriate nor was it appropriate simply to assign the classification of householder to the male or oldest person in the household. By allowing household members to designate their own householder, it was hoped to bring the census into line with general social practice. However, self-designation does have drawbacks in specifying family relationships, as will be shown in connection with the definition of a stepfamily presented later.

Group Quarters

Groups quarters are the living arrangements of persons not living in households. These may be institutions, other recognized quarters for groups, or structures housing groups of 10 or more unrelated people. For example, a married couple and their two children living with five other persons in the unit or structure owned by the householder would still be considered a private household but a structure housing a married couple and nine other unrelated persons would be a group quarters. College dormitories and military barracks are also considered group quarters (regardless of the number of persons in the unit), as are institutions such as prisons and nursing homes.

Family and Related Concepts

The terminology relating to the family currently used by the Census Bureau was developed in 1947, and most of its categories have continued to be used to the present. However, it should be noted that specific changes in wording and definition have been required as a result of general societal changes such as the increases in cohabitation and non-marital parenthood.

Family

A family is a group of two or more persons in a household (one of whom is the householder) who are related by blood, marriage, or adoption. According to this definition, married couples, single parents and children, grandparents raising grandchildren, and two- or three-generation families are counted as one family if the members occupy the same living quarters.

Married couple

A married couple is defined as a husband and his wife enumerated as members of the same household (with or without children under 18 years old in the household).

Spouse

A spouse is a person married to and living with a householder. Common-law marriages as well as formal marriages both result in a spousal status according to this definition.

Subfamily

A subfamily is defined as a married couple (with or without children), or one parent with one or more own never-married children under 18 years old, in addition to the householder.

Related Subfamily

A related subfamily is defined as a married couple with or without children, or one parent with one or more own never-married children under 18 years old, related to the householder. An example is a married couple sharing the home of the husband's or wife's parents. A related subfamily is counted as part of the family of the householder, as the subfamily does not maintain its own household.

Unrelated Subfamily

Formerly called a secondary family, an unrelated subfamily is defined as a married couple (with or without children), or one parent with one or more own never-married children under 18 years old, living in a household but not related to the householder. These are now excluded from the count of families and the members are excluded from the count of family members.

Secondary Individuals

These are persons residing in a household who are unrelated to the householder. Those people residing in group quarters are also classified as secondary individuals. Examples of secondary individuals are a roommate, a boarder, a foster child, and residents of a halfway house.

Stepfamily

A stepfamily is defined as a married couple with at least one child under age 18 who is a stepchild of the householder. An accurate count of stepfamilies depends on the correct designation of the householder. For example, if the male is designated as the householder and he resides with his second wife and his own child from his first marriage, the unit is not counted as a stepfamily. However, if the wife is designated as the householder, the fact that she resides with her husband and his child from a former marriage would cause this family to be counted as a stepfamily.

Institutionalized Persons

Persons under authorized, supervised care or custody in a formal institution are designated institutionalized persons. All people living under these circumstances are classified as patients or inmates regardless of the level of care, length of stay, or reason for custody. Examples of such institutions are correctional facilities, nursing homes, psychiatric hospitals, and hospitals for the chronically ill, or physically handicapped. Institutions differ from other groups quarters in that persons in institutions are generally restricted to the institutional buildings or grounds.

Unmarried Couple

Two unrelated adults of the opposite sex who share a household (with or without the presence of children under 18 years of age) are referred to as an unmarried couple. There can be only two adults per household in this category.

Unmarried Partner

An unmarried partner is an adult who is unrelated to the householder but shares living quarters and has a close personal relationship with the householder. This partner can be of the same sex or of the opposite sex of the householder.

Unrelated Individual

An unrelated individual is a person living in a household who is not related to the householder or members of the family or related subfamily of that household.

Limitations and Quality

As suggested earlier, international comparability of household data is affected by the country's decision whether to use the housekeeping-unit or household-housing-unit concept of enumerating households and families. Even if we discount the official definition planned for an area, the statistics are also affected by how faithfully enumerators and respondents observe it. Considering the United States alone, changes in definition from one census to another limit comparability. For example, prior to 1980, group quarters were defined as living quarters containing six or more unrelated persons but, after that year, the definition was changed to include only groups of ten or more persons.

Analysis of Household and Family Statistics

Analyses of households and families are most often oriented in terms of family composition, characteristics of the householder, and characteristics of the other household members. Often, it is important to study households and families in terms of their characteristics as demographic units (e.g., their size, their type, the number of generations within the household, and the number and ages of children).

Size of Household or Family

A distribution of households by size is a discrete (i.e., in integers) distribution, beginning with one person as head of household living alone and continuing with each additional related and unrelated member of the household. The distribution of families is also a discrete distribution, but it begins with two (related) persons and continues with each additional related member of the household. In 2000, the average household size for the United States was 2.59 persons while the average family size was 3.14 persons (U.S. Census Bureau, 2000). The inclusion of the large number of the single-person households in the household total results in a lower average household size.

The pattern of the smaller (three to six persons on the average) nuclear family is not the norm in many societies of sub-Saharan Africa, as suggested in Table 9.7. Because of the complex kinship systems and polygyny in the area, one family may live in various households located within a compound (Garenne, 2001). Given the cultural and legal variations in marriage and residence rules, it is imperative to understand the composition of residences before assessing their size.

In computing the *mean* size of household, the numerator should be the total population located in households. This would exclude persons located in group quarters. However, if these data are not available—which may be the case in some areas that do not collect data on the number of individuals in households—the total population may be used. Therefore, the mean size of households may be computed by the following formulas:

$$\frac{\text{Population in households}}{\text{Number of households}} \quad \text{or} \quad \frac{\text{Total population}}{\text{Number of households}} \quad (12)$$

In computing the *median* size of households or families, the midpoint of the median class is the (exact) number itself. For example, size class 3 has a range from 2.5 to 3.5 and its midpoint is 3.0. This assumption is required because the distribution is discrete rather than continuous.

Number of Generations in a Family

Although the historical evidence on family size has pointed to smaller families, at least when the family is defined as part of a single household (Goody, 1972; Laslett, 1972), this may not be the case when families are defined in terms of consanguinity and may be found in more than one household. In many countries, including the United States, increased longevity has led to an increase in the proportion of "families" consisting of several generations, that is, to an increase in the average number of generations per extended family (Siegel, 1993). The "verticalization" of families so defined has occurred as multiple generations survive. This process is slowed to the extent that average age at childbearing, or the age of the mother when the first child is born, rises. At the same time, because of reduced fertility, families have fewer siblings, uncles, aunts, and cousins. The many Demographic and Health surveys have documented the variety of structures within extended families.

TABLE 9.7 Percentage Distribution of Households, by Size, for Selected Countries: Selected Years, 1996 to 2001

| Country | Year | Total households (thousands) | Percentage distribution by number of persons in household | | | | | |
			Total	1	2	3	4	5+
Canada	1996	10,820	100.0	24.2	31.6	16.9	17.0	10.3
Cyprus	2001	224	100.0	16.0	27.2	17.1	21.9	17.8
Norway	2001	4,486	100.0	16.5	23.9	18.0	23.8	17.9
South Africa	1996	9,060	100.0	16.4	17.6	14.6	15.2	36.4
United States	2000	105,480	100.0	25.8	32.6	16.5	14.2	10.8

Sources: Canada (1996); Cyprus (2001); Norway (2001); South Africa (1996), United States Census Bureau (2000).

Characteristics of Households and Families as Social and Economic Units

When studying families, it can be desirable to explore the social as well as economic characteristics of the household or family members. In this case, all the members are assumed to share the same characteristic. For example, household income is the combined total income of the householder and all other members 15 years old and over. This statistic would include the incomes of all subfamilies or unrelated individuals in the household. Family income is the total income of the related family members in the household. It would not include the income of the subfamilies or unrelated individuals in the household. Care must be taken when using these kinds of aggregate statistics. If families are to be compared on the basis of total family income, it may be necessary to consider the family type in the analysis. A family income of $43,000 per year earned by a single mother with three children may mean quite different economic circumstances than a family income of $43,000 per year earned by three adults in the same family. Likewise, it is useful to examine the differences between types of families and households by comparing them along racial, ethnic, and regional lines.

Characteristics of Persons by Characteristics of Their Household or Families

Conversely, it is sometimes beneficial to study individuals within the context of their households or families. This type of analysis is useful in ascertaining the effects of living arrangements on children's behavior. For example, it is common to compare the juvenile delinquency rates of children in one-parent households as opposed to two-parent households.

Another application of the study of the individual within the context of the household or family is the cross-classification of data for the reference person with data for spouses on the same characteristic. Age at marriage, age at remarriage, and presence of children may be cross-classified for the reference person and spouse. Other cross-tabulations on family or household status may include the following: marital status of adult children by the marital status of parents, ages of children by type of household, living arrangements of adult children by the marital status of their parents and other selected characteristics of parents, the marital status of the householder and subfamily members, and marital characteristics of persons by metropolitan residence and region of the household. These cross-tabulations may enable researchers to see the impact of family and household living arrangements on the individual family members.

Dynamics of Households and Families

In the United States as well as other countries, the analyses of households and families have had to change in order to adapt to the changes in marriage, divorce, household formation, and household dissolution. Studies can no longer be limited to the characteristics of the male householder and households headed by males, given the increase in single-parent female-headed families. They can no longer be limited to a couple's own children, given the increase in remarriages with children and blended families. They can no longer be limited to related family members, given the rise in consensual unions and same-sex unions.

Changes in Numbers of Households and Families

A rise in the number of housing units and households may lead one to believe that there is a rise in population, but growth in housing units is not necessarily associated with population growth. It may also be an indication of different configurations of families within those households, leading to a decline in average household size. Family types have undergone significant changes in the last few decades in the United States. In 1998 there were approximately 71 million family households and 32 million nonfamily households in the United States and only 49% of all U.S. family households contained children under age 18. At the same time, about 22 million adult children live with one or both of their parents (U.S. Census Bureau/Casper and Bryson, 1998c.) The large number of adult children living with their parents is matched by the large decline in young adults maintaining their own households. From 1990 to 1998, there was an 11% decrease in the number of 25-to-34-year-old Americans maintaining their own households (U.S. Census Bureau/ Lugaila, 1998b).

Historically, there had been a continuous decrease in the age at which children left their parental homes. Recently, however, that trend seems to be changing as adult children wait longer to leave home or return home after leaving for the first time (Settersten, 1998). Many theories have been put forth to explain the increasing trend of adult children living in the parental home. Soaring costs of education as well as inflated housing costs cause many adult children to remain at home while pursuing a college education (Setterson, 1998). Other researchers have suggested difficulty in finding employment, increased divorce rates, and a later age at marriage as factors contributing to this trend (DaVanzo and Goldscheider, 1990; Glick and Lin, 1986).

Often overlooked in demographic studies of households is the factor of housing stock, both its size and composition. If appropriate housing is neither available nor affordable, new households will not be established. Conversely, if housing is available and affordable, then the number of households may increase quickly. Checking the availability of housing is especially important when studying the changes in households over time or when comparing the number of households from one country or region to another. In a study of household composition in Vietnam, Belanger (2000) found that recently married couples in the south were much more likely to live with parents than recently married couples in the north. Belanger (2000) suggested that this may be due to the creation of small housing units in the north when the socialist government took over large urban houses and formed small apartments to accommodate more families. Because the apartments are much smaller in the northern region and financially manageable, it is more advantageous for newly married couples to procure their own housing rather than share tight quarters with other family members. An examination of the housing stock and housing prices would be important in comparing the number of households and families from area to area within the United States, given the wide range in the cost of living and in housing costs among regions. It is also important to consider the role of the housing stock in the growth or decline in the number of households in the United States.

Changes in Household and Family Composition

Dramatic changes in the rates of marriage, divorce, remarriage, marital and nonmarital childbearing, and survival have caused the composition of families within households to change as well.

Changes in Size of Household

One of the most obvious changes in household structure is the growing proportion of people living alone. Currently, in the United States about 13% of all adults live alone (U.S. Census Bureau/Saluter and Lugaila, 1998a) and the number of persons living alone is expected to increase for every age group (Figure 9.1). Of those adults living alone, 60% are female but the number of male householders living alone is also substantial and increasing. A large share of the elderly population of the United States consists of female householders living alone as a result of the premature deaths of men (or the greater longevity of women). Elderly married women are very likely to outlive their husbands. From an international perspective, this is generally true because life expectancies of women exceed those of men in the great majority of countries. Whether the elderly surviving women live alone rather than with others is affected by cultural beliefs regarding women's living arrangements as well as the availability of relatives and friends. Attention should be given, therefore, to the gender roles in a society when studying the living arrangements of elderly women and men, especially elderly single householders.

Changes in Households with Children

In 1998, only about 68% of all children in the United States lived with two parents. Of the remaining children, 28% lived with a single parent, as shown in Table 9.8. However, these figures may be misleading. For instance, "two parents" also includes stepparents. The single parent may be a never-married parent, a widowed parent, or a divorced parent. These are important characteristics to note as financial support of the children will vary according to the legal status of the child (e.g., whether a foster child or a stepchild) as well as the marital status of the parent.

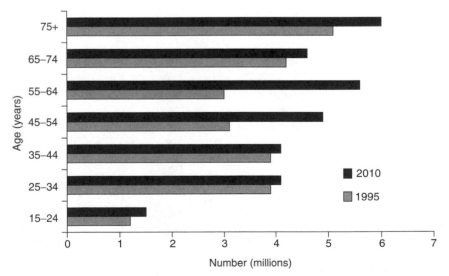

FIGURE 9.1 Comparison of Number of Adult Persons Living Alone, by Age Groups, Current, 1996, and Projected, 2000, for the United States
Source: U.S. Census Bureau/Saluter and Lugaila, 1998a

TABLE 9.8   Distribution of Children under 18 Years of Age,
by Presence of Parents, 1970 and 1998

Presence of parents	1970	1998
Children under 18 years, total (In thousands)	69,162	71,377
Percentage living with:		
Two parents	85.2	68.1
One parent	11.9	27.7
Mother only	10.8	23.3
Father only	1.1	4.4
Neither parent	2.9	4.1

Source: U.S. Census Bureau/Lugaila (1998b).

Researchers tend to ignore the living arrangements of children of single parents, focusing instead on the marital status of the parents (Manning and Smock, 1997). In the United States, many children of single parents do not live alone with the parent. Often there may be other adults in the household such as grandparents, cohabiting partners, or other nonfamily members. Furthermore, the presence of other adults in the household tends to be related to race and ethnicity; nonwhites are much more likely to be living in households with other adults in addition to the single parent than whites.

In conjunction with the decrease in two-parent households, there has been an increase in the number of grandparent-headed households. Legal changes begun in 1979 in the United States encouraged the placement of foster children in next-of-kin care and this was the starting point for the increase (Fuller-Thompson and Minkler, 2000). The legal changes, coupled with personal problems of some young parents such as drug use, prison confinement, health issues, and high unemployment rates, led to the need for grandparents to provide a home for their grandchildren with or without the children's parents. It is important to consider also the age of the parents or grandparents in the household. Because parental age at first birth has been increasing over the years, the likelihood that the children would be reared in families with older parents or older grandparents also has been increasing.

In the less developed countries also, the composition of households with children is dramatically changing, especially on the continent of Africa. As HIV/AIDS sweeps through many African countries and kills large numbers of parents, children are being forced into households that may not include family members. The number of children left orphaned by disease has been growing sharply, and care should be taken to examine the epidemiology of diseases in an area when looking for causes of changes in household composition.

The Life Cycle of the Family

It is apparent that family size and composition do not remain the same throughout the lives of the members. A family may experience the birth of children, their departure from the household, the return of adult children, divorces, remarriages, and widowhood, as well as other changes. These are so-called life cycle changes, the critical stages through which families may pass. There are many aspects of the life cycle of interest to analysts and service providers. Two periods of time in the life cycle of families are considered the most critical for a divorce to occur—the first seven years of marriage and the period when couples have young teenage children (Gottman and Levenson, 2000). A study in Norway (Villa, 2000) showed that the life stage of a family could be used to explain rural-urban migration. Families in, or entering into, the phase of having young children were much more likely to migrate to rural areas because of a perception of safety. Simply knowing the life cycles of families may help uncover reasons for societal trends in family transitions.

These illustrations suggest that the life cycle of the family can be quite important when studying the demography of families and households. The impact of these stages is compounded by the fact that there are cultural differences in the timing of the stages. In some cultures children are considered adults at age 12, while in others children are not considered adults until age 21. Researchers should therefore ascertain the variations in the life cycle of families from one society under study to another. In this way, explanations of demographic changes and characteristics, such as age at marriage and living arrangements of children and grandparents, may be more readily understood.

Illustrations of estimates of the principal parameters of the family life cycle for a series of birth cohorts are shown in Shryock, Siegel, and Stockwell, p. 175 (1976) and Siegel, p. 331 (1993). The stages are generally characterized by the median age or the mean age of the wife when the critical event occurs. The specific critical events that may be described in this way include age at first marriage, age at birth of first child, age at birth of last child, age at death of one spouse, and age at death of the second spouse. Other types of events characterize special types of life cycles.

References

Belanger, D. 2000. "Regional Differences in Household Composition and Family Formation Patterns in Vietnam." *Journal of Comparative Family Studies* 31(2): 171–196.

Burton, C. 1979. "Woman-Marriage in Africa: A Critical Study for Sex-Role Theory?" *Australian and New Zealand Journal of Sociology* 15(2):65–71.

Canada. Statistics Canada. 1996. "Private Households by Size." *Canada Census of Population 1996.*

Cyprus. Republic of Cyprus Statistical Service. 2001. *Census of Population 2001*.

DaVanzo, J., and F. Goldscheider. 1990. "Coming Home Again: Returns to the Parental Home of Young Adults." *Population Studies* 44: 241–255.

Davila, A., G. Ramos, and H. Mattei. 1998. *Encuesta de Salud Reproductiva: Puerto Rico, 1995–96*. Recinto de Ciencias Médicas. San Juan, Puerto Rico: Universidad de Puerto Rico.

Ezeh, A. 1997. "Polygyny and Reproductive Behavior in Sub-Saharan Africa: A Contextual Analysis." *Demography* 34(3): 355–368.

Faust, K., and J. McKibben. 1999. "Marital Dissolution: Divorce, Separation, Annulment, and Widowhood." In M. Sussman, S. Steinmetz, and G. Peterson (Eds.), *Handbook of Marriage and Family*, 2nd ed (pp. 475–499). New York: Plenum Press.

Fuller-Thompson, E., and M. Minkler. 2000. "African American Grandparents Raising Grandchildren: A National Profile of Demographic and Health Characteristics." *Health and Social Work* 25(2): 109–127.

Garenne, M. 2001. "Gender Asymmetry in Household Relationships in a Bilinear Society: the Sereer of Senegal." Paper presented for the virtual conference on African households: An exploration of census data. University of Pennsylvania, Center for Population Studies, November 21–23, 2001.

Garenne, M., S. Tollman, and K. Kahn. 2000. "Premarital Fertility in Rural South Africa: A Challenge to Existing Population Policy." *Studies in Family Planning* 31(1): 47–60.

Glick, P., and S. Lin. 1986. "More Young Adults Are Living with Their Parents: Who Are They?" *Journal of Marriage and the Family* 48: 107–112.

Goody, J. 1972. "The Evolution of the Family." In P. Laslett (Ed.), *Household and Family in Past Time*. Cambridge: Cambridge University Press.

Gottman, J., and R. Levenson. 2000. "The Timing of Divorce: Predicting When a Couple Will Divorce Over a 14-Year Period." *Journal of Marriage and the Family* 62(3): 737–746.

Greene, B. 1998. "The Institution of Woman Marriage in Africa: A Cross Cultural Analysis." *Ethnology* 37: 395–313.

Hajnal John, 1953. "Age of Marriage and Proportions Marrying." *Population Studies* (London) 7(2): 111–136.

Islam, M., and A. Ahmed. 1998. "Age at First Marriage and Its Determinants in Bangladesh." *Asia-Pacific Population Journal* 13(2): 73–92.

Jeter, J. 1997. "Covenant Marriages Tie the Knot Tightly." *The Washington Post*, p. A1.

Laslett. P., (Ed.). (1972) *Household and Family in Past Time*. Cambridge: Cambridge University Press.

Manning, W., and N. Landale. 1996. "Racial and Ethnic Differences in the Role of Cohabitation in Premarital Childbearing." *Journal of Marriage and the Family* 58: 63–77.

Manning, W., and P. Smock. 1997. "Children's Living Arrangements in Unmarried-Mother Families." *Journal of Family Issues* 18(5): 526–545.

Norway, Statistics Norway. 2001. "Persons in Private Households by Size of Household and Immigrant Population's Country," Table 3. *Norway Census of Population 2001*.

Obler, R. 1980. "Is the Female Husband a Man? Woman/Woman Marriage Among the Nandi of Kenya." *Ethnology* 19: 69–88.

Palestinian Central Bureau of Statistics. 1996. *The Demographic Survey of the West Bank and Gaza Strip*. Ramallah: PCBS, 1996.

Sanchez-Ayendez, M. 1988. "The Puerto Rican Family." In C. J. Mindel, R. W. Habenstein, and R. Wright, Jr. (Eds.), *Ethnic Families in America: Patterns and Variations*, 3rd ed. (pp. 173–198). New York: Elsevier.

Settersten, R., Jr. 1998. "A Time to Leave Home and a Time Never to Return? Age Constraints on the Living Arrangements of Young Adults." *Social Forces* 76 (4): 1373–1401.

Shryock, H. S., J. S. Siegel, and E. G. Stockwell. 1976. *The Methods and Materials of Demography*: Condensed Edition. New York: Academic Press.

Siegel, J. S. 1993. *A Generation of Change: A Profile of America's Older Population*. New York: Russell Sage Foundation.

South Africa, Statistics South Africa. 1996. "Census in Brief," Table 3.3. *South Africa Census of Population 1996*.

Speizer, I., and A. Yates. 1998. "Polygyny and African Couple Research." *Population Research and Policy Review* 17(6): 551–570.

Szapocznik, J., and R. Hernandez. 1988. "The Cuban American Family." In C. J. Mindel, R. W. Habenstein, and R. Wright, Jr. (Eds.), *Ethnic Families in America: Patterns and Variations*, 3rd ed. (pp. 160–172). New York: Elsevier.

Teachman, J., K. Polonko, and J. Scanzoni. 1999. "Demography and Families." In M. Sussman, S. Steinmetz, and G. Peterson (Eds.), *Handbook of Marriage and Family*, 2nd ed. (pp. 39–76). New York: Plenum Press.

United Nations Statistical Office. 1997a. *Demographic Yearbook*.

United Nations Statistical Office. 1997b. *Principles and Recommendations for Population and Housing Censuses*. Series M (67).

United Nations Statistical Office. 1998. *Demographic Yearbook*, CD-ROM, Historical Supplement.

U.S. Bureau of the Census. 1964. "Characteristics of the Population, Part 1, United States Summary," Table 177. *U.S. Census of Population: 1960*, Vol. 1.

U.S. Bureau of the Census. 1971. *The Methods and Materials of Demography, Vols. I–II*. By H. S. Shryock, J. S. Siegel, and Associates. Washington, DC: U.S. Government Printing Office.

U.S. Census Bureau. 1998a. "Marital Status and Living Arrangements: March 1996." By A. Saluter and T. Lugaila. *Current Population Reports*, Series p. 20–496.

U.S. Census Bureau. 1998b. "Marital Status and Living Arrangements: March 1998." Update by T. Lugaila. *Current Population Reports*, Series pp. 20–514.

U.S. Census Bureau. 1999. *Definitions and Explanations of the Current Population Survey*. Online at *http://www.census.gov/population/www/cps/cpsdef.html* (accessed on July 9, 1999).

U.S. Census Bureau. 2000. online at http://www.census.gov/population/www/census.

U.S. Department of Health and Human Services. 1995. "Change in the Marriage and Divorce Data Available from the National Center for Health Statistics." *Federal Register* 60(241): 66437–66438.

U.S. National Center for Health Statistics. 1997. "Advance Report of Natality Statistics, 1995." *Monthly Vital Statistics Report* 45 (11, supplement).

Villa, M. 2000. "Rural Life Courses in Norway: Living within the Rural-Urban Complementarity." *History of the Family* 5(4):473–491.

Wickens, B. 1997. "Shacking Up Now Respectable." *Maclean's* 110: 14.

Wu, Z. 1999. "Premarital Cohabitation and the Timing of First Marriage." *Canadian Review of Sociology and Anthropology* 36: 109–128.

Suggested Readings

Ayad, M., B. Barrere, and J. Otto. 1997. "Demographic and Socioeconomic Characteristics of Households." *Demographic and Health Surveys: Comparative Studies*, no. 26. Calverton, MD. Macro International.

Goldscheider, F. K., and C. Goldscheider. 1993. *Leaving Home before Marriage: Ethnicity, Familism, and Generational Relationships*. Madison, WI: University of Wisconsin Press.

Shryock, H. S., Siegel, J. S., and E. G. Stockwell. 1976. *The Methods and Materials of Demography: Condensed Edition*. Esp. Chapters 10 and 19.

Shorter, A. (1977). *The Making of the Modern Family*. New York: Basic Books.

Sigle-Rushton, W., and S. McLanahan. 2002. "The Living Arrangements of New Unmarried Mothers." *Demography* 39(3): 415–434.

Smith, S., J. Nogle, and S. Cody. 2002. A Regression Approach to Estimating the Average Number of Persons per Household. *Demography* 39(4): 697–712.

U.S. Census Bureau. 1998. "Household and Family Characteristics: March 1998 (Update)." By L. M. Casper and K. Bryson. *Current Population Reports*, p. 20–515.

U.S. Census Bureau. 1998c. "Growth in Single Fathers Outpaces Growth in Single Mothers, Census Reports." By L. Casper and K. Bryson. *Press Release*, December 11, 1998. U.S. Census Bureau. Online at *http://www.census.gov/Press-Release/cb98–228.html* (accessed on February 21, 2001).

U.S. Census Bureau. 1998d. *Current Population Reports*, Series P-20, "Marital Status of Persons 15 Years and Over, by Age, Sex, Race, Hispanic Origin, Metropolitan Residence, and Region: March, 1998."

10

Educational and Economic Characteristics

WILLIAM P. O'HARE, KELVIN M. POLLARD, AND AMY R. RITUALO

Some readers may ask why educational and economic characteristics should be addressed in a book on demographic methods and materials. There are several answers to this question. First, researchers routinely use educational and economic measures in the examination of demographic events and processes—particularly fertility, mortality, and migration (Christenson and Johnson, 1995; Macunovich, 1996; Rindfuss, Morgan, and Offutt, 1996; Rogers, 1992). Indeed, the underlying thesis of the demographic transition—perhaps the most central demographic paradigm—links changes in fertility and mortality to economic development (Coale, 1974).

Moreover, educational and economic characteristics are often the focus of demographic studies. For example, causes and consequences of differential educational attainment and the poverty status of the population are standard topics for demographers and demographic organizations, both in the United States and in other countries. Researchers trying to understand social structure and processes of stratification routinely use major demographic variables such as race, gender, and age to examine educational and economic differences.

Finally, the demography of educational and economic characteristics is fundamentally linked to public policy. For example, policy makers rely on such demographic information in the formation and evaluation of civil rights policies, gender equity efforts, and antipoverty programs. In addition, the educational and economic characteristics of states and communities are routinely used in funding formulas to distribute public funds. In fact, many policy goals—such as a lower high school dropout rate or a lower poverty ratio—actually are demographic measures of educational and economic characteristics. For example, countries adopting the Declaration on the Survival, Protection and Development of Children, announced at the 1990 United Nations World Summit for Children, set the following as two of their major goals for 2000. First, they wanted to reduce the adult illiteracy ratio by half its 1990 level. Second, they called for universal access to basic education and completion of primary education by at least 80% of primary school–age children.

In our efforts to update the original version of this publication, we have focused more on new sources of data (the *materials* of demography) rather than on new measures or analytic techniques (the *methods* of demography). This focus is based on our supposition that the sources of demographic data in these two topic areas have expanded much more rapidly than the analytical tools used in these areas. In some cases, new sources of educational and economic data have led to the development of subtopics within these areas that had received little attention in the past because of the scarcity of information. Recent work in the areas of wealth and poverty are examples of this development; these topics have become much more widely studied with the availability of new data sources.

This chapter treats educational and economic characteristics as if they were relatively unrelated. In fact, they are closely related in important ways. For example, an increase in education represents an increase in human capital; this in turn contributes to the productivity of the labor force; and a rise in labor productivity affects wages and salaries, hours of work, the demand for labor, and consumer behavior.

Under educational characteristics the principal topics covered in this chapter are school enrollment, educational progression, literacy, and educational attainment. The main topics considered under economic characteristics are economic activity and employment, income and poverty, and wealth.

EDUCATIONAL CHARACTERISTICS

School Enrollment

Perhaps the most fundamental educational characteristic is whether an individual is enrolled in an educational institution. The share of individuals, especially those in younger age groups, enrolled in school is a key indicator of a society's level of socioeconomic advancement. In more developed societies, most young people are in school, while a much smaller share of children and youth in less developed countries are enrolled in school.

Concepts and Definitions

According to the United Nations (UN), school enrollment refers to enrollment in any regular accredited educational institution, public or private, for systematic instruction at any level of education during a well-defined and recent time period—either at the time of a census or during the most recent school year. For the purposes of the International Standard Classification of Education, education includes all systematic activities designed to fulfill learning needs. Instruction in particular skills, which is not part of the recognized educational structure of the country (e.g., in-service training courses in factories), is not considered "school enrollment" for this purpose (United Nations, 1998). The United States employs that concept, defining school enrollment as attendance in any institution designed to advance a student toward a school diploma or collegiate degree (U.S. Census Bureau, 2000a). Where possible, the United Nations recommends that tabulations of school enrollment data be made according to age, sex, geographic division, and level of schooling.

In practice, the terms "school enrollment" and "school attendance" are often used interchangeably. Not everyone enrolled in a school attends every day, but typically the difference between enrollment and attendance is small and relatively stable over time. There may be situations, however, in which important distinctions are made between these two terms. For example, in schools where a large number of children are used to harvest crops at certain times during the year, enrollment and attendance figures for a given week may be quite different. In such situations it is important to be clear about the whether the figures in question concern attendance or enrollment.

School enrollment statistics often distinguish between enrollment in public or private educational institutions, between full-time and part-time enrollment, and between different levels of schools (primary, secondary, and tertiary). It is also common to find statistics shown for various types of educational institutions (e.g., college preparatory, vocational, teacher training) and by fields of study within a given level (e.g., law, engineering, medicine, social sciences).

Consideration must be given to the time reference for enrollment questions. An important factor in this regard is the opening and closing dates of the school year. If the question is about current enrollment, it should be asked only during a time when schools normally are in session and refer to the current school year or term. If a question is asked during a period when schools are not in session, it should refer to a time during the most recent school year. School enrollment questions should refer to a specific date or short period of time. Use of a broader time reference—for example, the previous 12 months or calendar year—may result in two different school years being covered. On this basis, counts of enrollment will be higher than would be expected on a specific date or during any single school year.

An inquiry on school enrollment is usually directed toward persons within certain age limits that must be selected carefully. If these age limits are narrow, it is likely that many enrolled persons will be excluded. If, on the other hand, the age limits are wide, the question on enrollment will be asked of many persons to whom it does not apply. Consequently, it is necessary to weigh the advantages and disadvantages of questioning some age segments of the population among whom there are few enrollees in order to count all who are enrolled, as opposed to limiting the enrollment question to age groups having a substantial number enrolled and thereby limiting response, burden, and cost. Moreover, recent social changes, especially in Western societies, complicate the analysis of age-specific trends in enrollment. Individuals often start school earlier in life (i.e., attending preschool before age 5) and continue going to school later in life than even a generation ago (i.e., returning to college or graduate school in their thirties).

Sources of Data

Most national censuses of population include some form of inquiry for measuring educational characteristics. A question on school enrollment has been included in the decennial census of the United States since 1840. There were no age limits for the enrollment questions in many of the censuses, but increasing emphasis in the tabulations was placed on the customary ages of school and university enrollment. In the censuses of 1950 and 1960, the question was confined to persons under age 30 and persons between 5 and 34 years old, respectively.

Since 1970, there have been no age limits for this item, but most of the tabulations have emphasized the age range from 3 through 34 years. Enrollment data are shown for fairly detailed age groups and are also cross-classified by level of school or grade enrolled (nursery school, kindergarten, elementary, high school, college or university) and by type of control (public or private).

The U.S. Census Bureau has collected data on school enrollment in the Current Population Survey every October since 1945. The resulting statistics are published in Series P20 of the *Current Population Reports* series. In addition, the U.S. Department of Education collects a standardized set of information known as the Common Core of Data (CCD), which is an annual survey that provides descriptive data for all public elementary and secondary schools in the United States. The CCD statistics are collected from education departments in all 50 states, the District of Columbia, Department of Defense schools, and outlying areas (i.e., Puerto Rico, the U.S. Virgin Islands, and Guam).

Internationally, the United Nations Educational, Scientific and Cultural Organization (UNESCO) collects school enrollment data from administrative agencies of United Nations member countries. It has published the data in an annual statistical yearbook since 1963. The UNESCO *Statistical Yearbook* is arguably the most widely used source for international education data, partly because it allows for comparisons of countries with widely different educational systems. Another international organization that collects school enrollment and other educational data is the Organisation for Economic Cooperation and Development (OECD), a group of 29 industrialized countries that share information used for formulating the public policies of their governments.

Measures

Measures of school enrollment usually relate to an exact date or a very short period of time. They may depend on either census or survey data alone or on a combination of these data with statistics from educational systems.

Crude and General Enrollment Ratios

The first measure, the *crude enrollment ratio* (often mislabeled a rate), may be expressed symbolically as

$$\frac{E}{P} \times 100 \qquad (10.1)$$

where E = Total enrollment at all levels and ages
       P = Total population

Because the constant multiplier employed with the various kinds of enrollment ratios is usually 100, the numerical results are usually labeled as percentages.

Preferably, the denominator of this ratio should be the population eligible to be included in the numerator. Whether or not an age limitation has been placed on the enrollment question, the population in ages at which persons are customarily enrolled may be employed in the denominator. In

this case, the measure calculated is called the *general enrollment ratio*. Using ages 5 to 34 as the age range in which people are customarily enrolled in educational institutions, it may be expressed symbolically as

$$\frac{E}{\sum\limits_{a=5}^{34} P_a} \times 100 \qquad (10.2)$$

where E = Total enrollment at all levels and ages

$\sum\limits_{a=5}^{34} P_a$ = Population 5 to 34 years of age

Age-Specific and Level-Specific Enrollment Ratios

Comparisons based on crude or even general enrollment ratios may be misleading because age distributions differ from one population to another. Caution must be exercised in interpreting enrollment trends on the basis of crude and general enrollment ratios because they may mask changes among specific groups. That is, overall trends may change very little while some changes in the population distribution among age groups undergo significant change. A shift toward a more youthful population can raise the crude enrollment ratio by placing more persons in the typical enrollment ages while age-specific enrollment ratios remain constant.

Age-specific enrollment ratios are better measures of effective enrollment than crude or general enrollment ratios because they focus on particular ages or age groups. The *age-specific enrollment ratio* may be expressed as

$$\frac{E_a}{P_a} \times 100 \qquad (10.3)$$

where E_a = Enrollment at age a
        P_a = Population at age a

The *level-specific enrollment ratio* may be expressed as

$$\frac{E_l}{P_a} \times 100 \qquad (10.4)$$

where E_l = Enrollment at school level l
        P_a = Population in age group a corresponding to school level in the numerator

In this measure, the numerator is not necessarily fully included in the denominator. Although most persons enrolled in high school or secondary school, for example, may be in the age range of 14 to 17 years, some will be below and some above that age range. Furthermore, some persons aged 14 to 17 may be enrolled in school but not at the secondary level (see Table 10.1 for the United States figures in 2000). An appropriate age range for the denominator can be selected by examining cross-classifications of age and school grade, and identifying the ages that are

TABLE 10.1   School Enrollment Status of the Civilian Noninstitutional Population 3 Years Old and Over, by Age, Sex, and School Level: United States, October 2000 (Numbers in thousands)

Age (years)	Population	Total enrolled	Enrolled by school level			
			Nursery and kindergarten	Elementary	High school	College
Male						
3 and 4	4,046	2,157	2,157	—	—	—
5 and 6	4,270	4,064	2,211	1,853	—	—
7 to 13	14,403	14,238	6	14,139	93	—
14 to 17	8,051	7,721	—	740	6,931	48
18 and 19	3,994	2,399	—	3	729	1,667
20 to 34	27,798	4,379	—	10	132	4,236
35 and older	63,240	1,024	—	14	57	953
Total, 3 and older	125,800	35,979	4,373	16,758	7,942	6,905
Female						
3 and 4	3,946	2,007	2,007	—	—	—
5 and 6	4,000	3,838	2,019	1,819	—	—
7 to 13	13,753	13,610	6	13,461	143	—
14 to 17	7,663	7,388	—	505	6,809	74
18 and 19	3,908	2,515	—	6	506	2,003
20 to 34	28,409	4,963	—	8	125	4,831
35 and older	70,633	1,808	—	17	58	1,732
Total, 3 and older	132,311	36,130	4,032	15,815	7,642	8,641

— Represents less than 500.

Source: U.S. Census Bureau, *Current Population Reports*, Series P20–521, "School Enrollment—Social and Economic Characteristics of Students: October 1998 (Update)," by G. M. Martinez and A. E. Curry (September 1999): table 1. Accessed online at http://www.census.gov/population/www/socdemo/school/98tabs.html on June 21, 2000.

typical for the school grade or level in the numerator.[1] The level-specific enrollment ratio can be calculated for other levels of school in addition to the principal level at which an age group is attending. (Sometimes the level-specific enrollment ratio is called the *gross enrollment ratio*.)

The next measure, the *age-level-specific enrollment ratio*, in effect, combines the specificity of both the level-specific enrollment ratio and the age-specific ratio. Sometimes referred to as the *net enrollment ratio*, it can be computed when both enrollment classified by age and enrollment classified by level are available. It may be expressed as

$$\frac{E_{al}}{P_a} \times 100 \qquad (10.5)$$

where E_{al} = Enrollment at age a and school level l
          P_a = Population at age a

This ratio tells us the relative frequency for persons aged a to be enrolled at level l. For the most part, this ratio would be computed for a particular age range in combination with a particular school level (e.g., elementary school level and ages 7 to 13). (The selection of the age range follows the same principle as for the level-specific enrollment ratio.) It would also be appropriate to compute ratios for a number of different grades, each in combination with a single age.

Age-Standardized or Age-Adjusted Ratio

What may appear to be differences or changes in enrollment participation when the general ratio is used may be partly or wholly a function of differences or changes in the distribution of the population by age within the age range

[1] The level-specific enrollment ratio is analogous to various measures that have different names, suggested by the United Nations: (1) total school enrollment ratio, which is the total enrollment in all schools below the third level as a percentage of the population aged 5 to 19; (2) primary school enrollment ratio, which is the total enrollment in schools at the first level as a percentage of the population aged 5 to 14; and (3) secondary school enrollment ratio, which is the total enrollment in all schools at the second level as a percentage of the population aged 15 to 19.

for enrollment. For comparative purposes, therefore, it is often desirable to have a single overall adjusted measure of enrollment (rather than a number of specific measures) that is based on a common age distribution, called the standard population. To derive such a measure, the general enrollment ratio can be "standardized" to take into account the common age distribution of the population within the age range for enrollment. In this way, the effect of the different age structures is eliminated in comparing different groups at one date or the same group at different dates.

The age-standardized enrollment ratio may be expressed as

$$\frac{\sum (E_a/P_a) \times P_{sa}}{P_s} \times 100 \qquad (10.6)$$

where E_a = Enrollment in age group a
        P_a = Population in age group a
        P_{sa} = Standard population in age group a
        P_s = Total standard population

The standard population may be the age distribution of one of the population groups being compared, an average of the age distributions of two or more population groups being compared, or the distribution of a specially selected population (e.g., a national population when geographic subdivisions are being compared). Enrollment ratios can be standardized for additional factors, such as sex, ethnic group, or urban-rural residence, depending on the purpose of the comparison. (For a more detailed description of the standardization procedure, including variations such as indirect standardization, see Chapter 12.)

Measurement of Enrollment Differentials

The concern with equality of educational opportunity has led to many studies of disparities in school and college enrollments among population groups. Here it becomes necessary not only to obtain comparable measures of enrollment for various geographic, ethnic, and socioeconomic groups, and for the sexes, but also to define what constitutes widening, stability, or narrowing of disparities. For instance, is a narrowing of disparities better indicated by a closing of the gap in absolute percentage points of enrollment or by a reduction in the ratio of percentages enrolled?

Enrollment Projections

The process of deciding future educational needs—particularly for schools, classrooms, and teachers—makes projections of future school enrollments very important to local and state agencies. Common projection methods, such as the cohort-component and land-use methods, are often employed in making such projections. Because public acceptability of the projections is essential to future planning, the projection process often involves a team effort between trained demographers and local school officials (Swanson *et al.*, 1998). (Chapter 21 provides more detailed information on the methods used in school enrollment projections.)

Uses and Limitations

Data on school enrollment are used to measure the extent of participation of an area's population in the school system, as well as the relative participation of different segments of the population. Those involved in educational planning utilize enrollment statistics to measure the current (or projected) trend in school participation in both absolute and relative terms. Most uses focus on changes over time, comparisons across groups, or comparisons across geographic units.

Educational statistics in most countries include more complete coverage of enrollment in regular, graded general public educational institutions than of enrollment in specialized, private, technical and vocational educational programs. As a consequence, they often understate the total involvement of the population in the educational system. Differences in reporting of enrollment status limit international comparability of the statistics. The time reference of the census enrollment question not only varies from country to country, but is not stated at all in many national publications (United Nations, 1998). Enrollment is not always limited to regular schools; for example, enrollment in commercial schools, dancing schools, or language schools may be included in some countries but not in others. Variations in the age range to which the enrollment question applies also may compromise comparisons. In addition, the number of completed years of schooling that correspond to particular levels of education varies across countries. In Austria, for example, a student will complete his or her primary education after finishing the first 4 years of schooling; however, a student in the Netherlands will complete his or her primary education after finishing the first 8 years of schooling (U.S. National Center for Education Statistics, 1996).

Quality of Data

Enrollment data from school systems vary in quality depending on the attention given to statistical collection and reporting systems in the country (or in some cases, the school district) and the adequacy of the number and skills of personnel assigned to amass the data. The quality of census and survey data on enrollment depends greatly on the completeness and accuracy of the census or survey as a whole and on the attention devoted to refining the questions used to gather this information. Census and survey data usually are more uniform across states or localities because they are collected by a single agency assigned to compile the data. Before using enrollment data, one should examine the questions used, the population covered, the information provided to assist interviewers in asking the questions and in answering respondents' questions, the response rates to the questions, and other aspects of the data. As with other types of data collected in censuses and surveys, much depends on the knowledge and cooperation of the respondents.

Errors in population coverage and in age reporting are especially important. They affect not only the count of the total persons enrolled for the age range covered but also the age-specific enrollment ratios.

Educational Progression

Measures of educational progression reflect how students move through the educational system. For example, normative expectations identify the following transition points in the United States education system:

1. From preschool to elementary school
2. From elementary school to middle school
3. From middle school to high school
4. From high school to college
5. From undergraduate school to graduate school (or professional school)

One can also examine progression through school, grade by grade. The proportions of students that make the transitions just outlined provide useful information about the educational system in a country or about a population subgroup.

Concepts and Definitions

Data on educational progression provide a basis for understanding the extent to which population groups continue in school and to what extent continuation in school is a reflection of normal grade progression. We are concerned here with the concepts of school retention and dropout and of scholastic retardation and acceleration.

School retention refers to the continuation of persons enrolled in school from one school grade or level to another or from one age to an older age. Leaving school before graduation—typically referred to as "dropping out"—is the most commonly used basis for assessing academic retardation. Dropping out of school can be viewed as the inverse of school retention. Dropping out is also related to the school enrollment measures discussed in the previous section.

Sources of Data

Administrative data from school systems provide one basis for measures of school retention. The most frequently found source of retention data are the reports of school systems that give annual distributions of enrollment by grade and annual statistics on the number graduating from high school. Censuses are not very useful for measuring school retention because they ordinarily are taken at 5- or 10-year intervals. However, annual demographic surveys that obtain data on school enrollment by grade or age provide the necessary statistics for the computation of retention measures. Longitudinal surveys, including panel studies, that follow a cohort through time also are very useful in providing this kind of information.

Interpretation of these data is confounded by the fact that students often move from one school or school system to another during an academic year or between academic years. Consequently, annual changes in the number of students enrolled may be a product of migration more than educational advancement. This is particularly problematic for smaller geographic units where small changes can have a big impact on ratios and rates and where the effect of migration may be pronounced.

Measures

The U.S. National Center for Education Statistics (1999) describes three types of dropout ratios, which we list next. While these ratios focus on United States high schools, the concepts are easily transferred to other countries and other school levels. These measures provide important information about how effective educators are in keeping students enrolled in school.

The *crude (central) dropout rate* describes the "proportion" of students who leave school each year without having completed a high school program. This measure treats dropping out as a specific event that occurs during a specific period, usually one school year, and expresses the number of such events in relation to total enrollment.

The crude dropout rate may be expressed as

$$\frac{D_y}{E} \times 100 \qquad (10.7)$$

where D_y = Number of dropouts (events) in year y
           E = Total enrollment at the beginning or middle of year y

The *age-specific dropout ratio* measures the total number of dropouts among all young adults within a specified age range. This measure reflects the *status* of a group of individuals at a given date rather than the *incidence* of dropping out over a period of time. To reflect this fact, we may also call this measure the age-specific percent of dropouts. It includes all dropouts, regardless of the period when the person last attended school. Because age-specific dropout ratios can reveal the extent of the dropout problem in the adult population, they also can be used to estimate the need for further education and training.

The age-specific dropout ratio may be expressed as

$$\frac{D_{al}}{P_a} \times 100 \qquad (10.8)$$

where D_{al} = Number of nonstudents in age group a who have not completed educational level l

P_a = Population in age group a

The *KIDS COUNT Data Book* (published every year by the Annie E. Casey Foundation in Baltimore, Maryland) includes a measure like this. The number of 16-to-19-year-olds who are not attending school and who have not graduated from high school is expressed as a percentage of all 16-to-19-year-olds and labeled the "high school dropout rate." For example, in 1999, the number of 16-to-19-year-olds in the state of New York that were not attending school and were not high school graduates was 94,000. The total number of 16-to-19-year-olds was 1,041,000. The dropout ratio (computed by using Formula 10.8) was 9.0% (Annie E. Casey Foundation, 2002).

The *cohort dropout rate* represents the relative number of dropouts occurring to a cohort of students over a period of time, such as a single year or a few years. This rate is based on repeated measures of a group of students who start an educational level (such as high school) at the same time and reveals how many students who started that level drop out over time. Typically, cohort rates, which are developed from longitudinal studies, provide more background and contextual data on the students who drop out than are available through more common data collection systems, such as the Current Population Survey or the Common Core of Data. We have defined here a grade cohorts for analysis with respect to its experience in school retention.

The cohort dropout rate may be expressed as

$$\frac{\sum D_c^y}{E_c} \times 100 \qquad (10.9)$$

where D_c^y = Number of dropouts from cohort c in year y or specified later years

E_c = Enrollment in cohort c at beginning of year y

Uses and Limitations

The statistics used in analyzing school retention are subject to the same limitations as those used in analyzing school enrollment. In addition, caution needs to be exercised in measuring school retention to assure that the data for different points in time are comparable and relate to the same cohort of persons. In analyzing retention in, or dropping out of, school, it is necessary to specify clearly the "population at risk." Is the interest in the number or in the proportion of an age group that stays in or leaves school by an older age? Is it in the number or proportion of enrollees in a school grade who continue on to a higher grade or drop out? Or is it some combination of these, such as the number or pro-

portion of those in an age group who leave school before attaining a certain grade level? In areas experiencing high levels of migration, one must take extra care in examining calculations of school retention to make sure the measures reflect the population actually "at risk."

It is important to recognize that a person can drop out of school, only to reenter at a later date. Such a person would show up as a dropout event in the year he or she left school, even though the person ultimately returned. The person would also be part of the dropout population in one year, but not in the next.

Literacy

Measuring the literacy of a population has become increasingly important as developed countries move from labor economies to information- and technology-based economies. The literacy levels of industrialized countries can be closely related to the country's economic performance. According to the Organisation for Economic Cooperation and Development (OECD), low literacy levels are "a serious threat to economic performance and social cohesion" (U.S. National Center for Education Statistics, 1998, p. 13).

Concepts and Definitions

The United Nations defines literacy as the ability both to read and write, with understanding, a short simple statement on everyday life (United Nations, 1998). A person who cannot meet this criterion is regarded as illiterate. An illiterate person, therefore, may not read and write at all, or may read and write only figures and his or her own name, or may only read and write a ritual phrase that has been memorized. The language (or languages) in which a person can read and write is not a factor in determining literacy. A resident of England who can read and write in French but not in English would still be considered literate.

The term "illiteracy," as defined here, must be clearly distinguished from "functional illiteracy." The latter term has been used to refer to the completion of no more than a few years of primary schooling. For industrialized societies today, functional literacy would require several more years of schooling than a few years of primary schooling, although in the past, 4 years of primary schooling was often used to denote this level of literacy. Cross-tabulations of literacy and years of schooling completed indicate that not all persons reported as illiterate lack formal schooling, and not all persons without schooling are illiterate. While literacy is sometimes viewed as being differentiated along a continuum, it is usually treated as a dichotomous variable.

The United Nations recommended that a question on literacy be included in national censuses to be taken in 2000.

It further recommended that data on illiteracy be collected for the population 10 years of age and older. Because reading and writing ability ordinarily is not achieved until one has had some schooling or has at least had time to develop these skills, it is not useful to ask the question for young children. In some countries, including literacy data for persons aged 10 to 14 years may overestimate the illiterate population because persons in that age group still have the potential to become literate through continued formal schooling. As a result, the United Nations recommends that cross-national comparisons of literacy be limited to persons aged 15 and over (United Nations, 1998). The United Nations also recommends that data on illiteracy be tabulated by age, sex, and major civil division (distinguishing urban and rural areas within a division). When not classified by specific age group, the tabulations on illiteracy should at least distinguish between persons under 15 years of age and those aged 15 and over.

The standard practice in obtaining literacy data is to ask respondents if they can read and write. Their answers to this question are usually accepted at face value. Some countries ask separate questions about reading and writing ability, classifying persons as semiliterate if they can read but not write. Increasingly, efforts at collecting literacy-related data have moved beyond the simple measurement of the person's ability to read and write, focusing instead on his or her ability to use written information to function on the job and in society. In industrialized nations in particular, "adults today need a higher level of literacy to function well, because society has become more complex and low-skill jobs are disappearing. Inadequate levels of literacy in a broad section of the population may therefore have serious implications, even threatening a nation's economic strength and social cohesion" (U.S. National Center for Education Statistics, 1998, p. 13).

Sources of Data

UNESCO's *Statistical Yearbook* contains data on adult illiteracy. In addition, literacy is included in an international database maintained by the International Programs Center of the U.S. Census Bureau. For some countries, literacy data are available for selected characteristics, such as age, sex, and urban-rural residence. Furthermore, nine governments and three intergovernmental organizations in North America and Europe participated in the first International Adult Literacy Survey (IALS) in the autumn of 1994.[2]

----

[2] Information on the development and methodology of the International Adult Literacy Survey (IALS) can be found in U.S. National Center for Education Statistics, 1998, *Adult Literacy in OECD Countries: Technical Report on the First International Adult Literacy Survey*, NCES 98-053, by T. S. Murray, I.S. Kirsch, and L.B. Jenkins (Washington, DC: U.S. Government Printing Office).

A question on literacy was included in the decennial census of the United States from 1840 through 1930. This question was dropped in the 1940 census in favor of the more informative item on educational attainment. Although the Current Population Survey carried a question on illiteracy intermittently through 1979, the U.S. Census Bureau does not use the concept any longer because only one-half of 1% of the U.S. population reported in that survey that they could not read or write.

In 1985, the U.S. Department of Education revised the definition of literacy for its Young Adult Literacy Survey (YALS). This definition moved beyond the simple ability to read and write, focusing instead on the ability to use written information to function in society. The department also measured three domains of literacy—prose literacy, document literacy, and quantitative literacy—and reported data for various levels of literacy within these three domains. The 1992 National Adult Literacy Survey was modeled and improved on the basis of the methodology used in the YALS to assess the literacy of the entire adult population in the United States.

The United Nations Children's Fund (UNICEF) has developed the Multiple Indicator Cluster Survey (MICS) as a household survey tool for countries to measure and monitor the goals set by the 1990 World Summit for Children. By 1996, more than 100 countries had conducted the MICS (including countries such as Albania, the Dominican Republic, Mongolia, Lebanon, Côte d'Ivoire, Zambia, Senegal, and Somalia). In addition to collecting information on education, maternal mortality, contraceptive use, and HIV/AIDS, almost every survey includes a question on adult literacy of persons 15 years of age and older (UNICEF, 2000).

Measures

General measures of illiteracy provide some indication of the educational status of the population, as well as an indication of the country's socioeconomic level, with which illiteracy is highly correlated. Illiteracy measures for subcategories of the population provide a basis for analyzing group differences and changes in literacy, particularly its spread from one segment of the population to another. Such measures also can illustrate social stratification in a community or a society. Two measures to be defined are the crude illiteracy ratio (often mislabeled a "rate") and the age-specific illiteracy ratio.

The *crude illiteracy ratio* may be expressed as

$$\frac{I}{P} \times 100 \qquad (10.10)$$

where I = Number of illiterates in population covered
          P = Total population covered

TABLE 10.2   Illiteracy Ratios by Age and Sex: Burundi, 1990

Age (years)	Both sexes			Male			Female		
	Total	Illiterate		Total	Illiterate		Total	Illiterate	
		Number	Percent		Number	Percent		Number	Percent
15 and over	2,824,942	1,757,984	62.2	1,343,775	691,703	51.5	1,481,167	1,066,281	72.0
15 to 19	493,643	207,270	42.0	243,314	91,587	37.6	250,329	115,683	46.2
20 to 24	433,976	220,644	50.8	204,321	88,518	43.3	229,655	132,126	57.5
25 to 34	772,734	466,307	60.3	370,919	178,757	48.2	401,815	287,550	71.6
35 to 44	450,272	302,514	67.2	217,184	113,000	52.0	233,088	189,514	81.3
45 to 54	275,913	206,256	74.8	124,287	71,568	57.6	151,626	134,688	88.8
55 to 64	189,874	160,859	84.7	85,282	61,452	72.1	104,592	99,407	95.0
65 and over	208,530	194,134	93.1	98,468	86,821	88.2	110,062	107,313	97.5
Age not reported	9,611	NA	NA	6,883	NA	NA	2,728	NA	NA

NA: Data not available.

Sources: United Nations, *Demographic Yearbook, 1996,* table 7 (total population); UNESCO, *Statistical Yearbook, 1998,* table 1.2 (illiterate population).

An age range—usually 10 years and over or 15 years and over—needs to be specified. With such an age restriction, the measure may be designated the *general illiteracy ratio.*

In countries where great advances in schooling have been made in recent years, the crude illiteracy ratio or the general illiteracy ratio may still be high because of the inclusion of the less literate cohorts of earlier years. Presentation of illiteracy ratios for age groups not only provides an indication of the magnitude of the illiteracy problem among different age segments of the population, but also gives some indication of the historical change in illiteracy.

The *age-specific illiteracy ratio* may be expressed as

$$\frac{I_a}{P_a} \times 100 \qquad (10.11)$$

where I_a = Number of illiterates in age group a
   P_a = Population in age group a

Using the data on the number of illiterates in Burundi for age-sex groups in 1990 (shown in Table 10.2), we may illustrate the computation of illiteracy ratios as shown there. As with enrollment ratios, these are numerically labeled percentages (disregarding the small number with ages not reported):

$$\begin{pmatrix} \text{General illiteracy ratio} \\ \text{for people aged 15} \\ \text{and over, both sexes} \end{pmatrix} = \frac{1,757,984}{2,824,942} \times 100 = 62.2$$

Age-specific illiteracy ratios (males)

$$15 \text{ to } 19 \text{ years} = \frac{91,587}{243,314} \times 100 = 37.6$$

$$65 \text{ years and over} = \frac{86,821}{98,468} \times 100 = 88.2$$

The general illiteracy ratio for both sexes in Burundi in 1990 was 62.2%—that is, more than three-fifths of the population 15 years old and over were illiterate. Although the youngest age group has the lowest percentage of illiteracy, that percentage is still relatively high (37.6% for males aged 15 to 19 years).

The fairly steady rise in age-specific illiteracy ratios for Burundi from the youngest to the oldest age groups shown in Table 10.2 indicates a general historical increase in literacy in the country and suggests the pattern and pace of this development. Assuming that very few people become literate after age 15, we may describe Burundi's achievement in literacy in 1990 in terms of the illiteracy ratio for persons aged 15 to 19 (42%). In comparison, the literacy achievement characteristic of the period around 1950 was the illiteracy ratio for those aged 55 to 64 years in 1990 (84.7%). The pace of improvement for females was about the same as for males. This type of analysis depends on the assumption that there has been little or no difference in the mortality level of literate and illiterate persons over this period and little or no selective migration according to illiteracy, as well as on the assumption that literacy is not achieved after age 15.

Uses and Limitations

Golden (1955) developed the thesis that the literacy ratio is a useful index of a country's level of socioeconomic development. Kamerschen (1968) later refined Golden's thesis, concluding that the statistics support a threshold theory rather than a continuous one. Such a relationship may be reflected in the fact that a number of the more industrialized countries no longer collect statistics on illiteracy because the problem has virtually disappeared.

A question on the ability to read and write is obviously subject to a variety of interpretations, and the collection of illiteracy data in a census may be handled with varying degrees of conscientiousness relative to any official standard. In the case of educational level, an 8-year primary-school program in one country cannot always be compared with an 8-year primary-school program in another country. In sum, demographic statistics on education, apart from inadequacies of the data, reflect the effects of a variety of cultural, social, and psychological factors that must be considered when analyzing the data. All these considerations necessitate interpretation of published statistics on education in only general terms.

For example, one might expect an understatement of illiteracy because some people are reluctant to admit they do not know how to read or write. However, in a country with high levels of illiteracy, there is presumably no real hesitation in classifying oneself as illiterate. On the other hand, in a country with a high level of literacy, people who are illiterate may be very hesitant to identify themselves as such.

Where tests of reading and writing ability have been administered in addition to a simple inquiry on illiteracy, the general accuracy of the simple inquiry has been confirmed.[3] Analysis of the reported illiteracy of age cohorts in a sequence of censuses in the United States showed a high degree of consistency from census to census (Folger and Nam, 1967). It would be helpful, however, to have more thorough and systematic evaluations of reported data on illiteracy for a variety of countries.

Educational Attainment

Educational attainment is a critical measure of education, particularly in more developed countries. As the economies of these countries became more technically sophisticated, their workforce needs moved beyond basic literacy. As a result, more detailed measures of educational performance—measures that reflect what people get out of the educational system—have become more widely used.

According to the United Nations, educational attainment is the highest level of education completed in the country where the education was received (United Nations, 1998). It recommends that educational attainment be included among the basic areas of census inquiry and that data on the subject be collected for all persons 5 years of age and older.

Typically, educational attainment is measured not by the number of calendar years that a person has spent in school,

but by the highest grade or level that he or she was able to complete. If the person was educated in the school system of another country and not in his or her country of present residence, it is necessary to convert that schooling into the equivalent highest grade completed in the country of present residence.

The inclusion of a question on educational attainment in the United States census dates back to 1940. From 1950 through 1980, the census asked respondents about the highest *grade* of school they had ever attended, followed by a supplementary question on whether the respondent finished that highest grade. Research has shown that the inclusion of this supplementary question reduced the tendency to report an unfinished grade as the highest grade completed and thus corrected for the upward bias that may have occurred in statistics calculated without the use of such a question. However, questions measuring the number of years of school completed increasingly did not correspond with the actual degree attained, particularly beyond the high school level, and specific degrees such as an associate or a master's degree could not be identified from the "highest grade completed" inquiry (Kominski and Siegel, 1987, 1993).

As a result, the 1990 and 2000 censuses asked respondents about the highest *level* of education they have completed (see Table 10.3). The change is especially noticeable in the categories for high school completion and beyond. Whereas the "old" census questions measured individual years of schooling (e.g., 13 years completed), the 1990 census question focuses on specific levels of degree completion (e.g., some college but no degree, associate degree, or bachelor's degree). These developments have implications for several measures; for example, it is no longer possible to calculate the mean and median years of school completed. This change in measuring educational attainment was also reflected in the Current Population Survey (CPS) questionnaire beginning in 1992. See, for example Figure 10.1, displaying CPS data for 1995.

For a long time inquiries were made about educational attainment in the Current Population Survey only at irregular intervals. Since 1964, however, the U.S. Census Bureau has published an annual report on the educational attainment of the population (*Current Population Reports* Series P20, *Population Characteristics*). In comparing decennial census and CPS statistics on enrollment and educational attainment for subdivisions of the country, it should be borne in mind that in the census, college students are counted where they actually live while attending college, whereas the CPS counts unmarried students at their parental homes (see Chapter 4).

Measures

The measures of educational attainment considered here are taken from publications of the U.S. Census Bureau

---

[3] Discussion of the accuracy of reports on literacy as well as gradations of literacy can be found in S. S. Zarkhovic, 1954, "Sampling Control of Literacy Data," *Journal of the American Statistical Association*, 49(267): 510–519; and C. Windle, 1959, "The Accuracy of Census Literacy Statistics in Iran," *Journal of the American Statistical Association* 54 (287): 578–581.

TABLE 10.3 Educational Attainment Question(s) Asked in the U.S. Decennial Census, 1980 and 2000

1980 Census Questions

Question 9. What is the highest grade (or year) of regular school this person has ever attended?
- Nursery school
- Kindergarten
- Elementary through high school (grade or year) = 1 through 12
- College (academic year) = 1 through "8 or more"
- Never attended school

Question 10. Did that person finish the highest grade (or year) attended?

2000 Census Questions

Question 9. What is the highest degree or level of school this person has COMPLETED?
- No schooling completed
- Nursery school to 4th grade
- 5th grade or 6th grade
- 7th grade or 8th grade
- 9th grade
- 10th grade
- 11th grade
- 12th grade, NO DIPLOMA
- HIGH SCHOOL GRADUATE—high school DIPLOMA or the equivalent (for example: GED)
- Some college credit, but less than 1 year
- 1 or more years of college, no degree
- Associate degree in college (for example: AA, AS)
- Bachelor's degree (for example: BA, AB, BS)
- Master's degree (for example: MA, MS, MEng, MEd, MSW, MBA)
- Professional school degree (for example: MD, DDS, DVM, LLB, JD)
- Doctorate degree (for example: PhD, EdD)

Source: U.S. Census Bureau, *1980 Census of Population,* Volume 1, Characteristics of the Population, "General Social and Economic Characteristics," PC80–1, Part 1, United States Summary (December 1983), p. E-8; and "United States Census 2000," official informational census form.

and the United Nations. In interpreting them, note that many persons under 25 years of age may still be attending school and that the measures for these persons would tend to understate their eventual educational attainment to some degree.

The *cumulative grade attainment ratio* may be expressed as

$$\frac{C_a^{g+}}{P_a} \times 100 \qquad (10.12)$$

where D_a^{g+} = Persons at age a who completed grade g or beyond
  P_a = Population at age a

This measure indicates the proportion of a population at age a that has completed a given grade (or level) of school or beyond, or the proportion that has ever completed that grade (or level). For example, the ratio may be computed for the population 25 to 29 years of age that had ever completed high school or college. One particular application of the cumulative grade attainment ratio is the *high school completion ratio,* which is applied to the population aged 18 to 24 (Federal Interagency Forum on Child and Family Statistics, 2001).

The cumulative grade attainment ratio is illustrated next for males and females in selected age groups using the data on single years of school completed for Mexico given in Table 10.4.

The cumulative grade attainment ratio for the fourth year of secondary school or higher level is obtained by summing the frequencies in the categories "secondary level—4 or more" with those in all the categories under the "third level," and dividing by the total population in the age group minus the "not reported" category:

$$\text{Males 15 to 24} = \frac{532,236}{8,498,020 - 168,741} \times 100 = 6.4$$

$$\text{Females 15 to 24} = \frac{555,483}{8,995,546 - 199,439} \times 100 = 6.3$$

$$\text{Males 25 and over} = \frac{1,708,037}{15,426,946 - 539,875} \times 100 = 11.5$$

$$\text{Females 25 and over} = \frac{1,066,650}{16,690,364 - 652,006} \times 100 = 6.7$$

Where educational attainment is measured in number of years of school completed, the distribution of the population by years of school completed can be summarized in terms of two averages: the median years of school completed and the mean years of school completed. The *median years of school completed* may be defined as the value that divides the distribution of the population by educational attainment into two equal parts, one half of the cases falling below this value and one half of the cases exceeding this value. It is preferable to have single years or grades of school completed in the distribution to calculate the median with as high a degree of precision as the quality of the reported data permits.

In calculating the median years of school completed, it is necessary to make assumptions about the boundaries of classes and about the distribution of persons within them. It is assumed, for example, that persons who reported completing the 9th grade are distributed evenly between 9.0 and 9.9—that is, students who completed the 9th grade dropped out at various stages of the 10th grade. In this case, educational attainment is treated as a continuous quantitative variable rather than a discrete variable. (For a description of the procedure for computing the median, see Chapter 7.)

This assumption is not entirely realistic and, hence, leads to a statistic that is sometimes subject to misinterpretation.

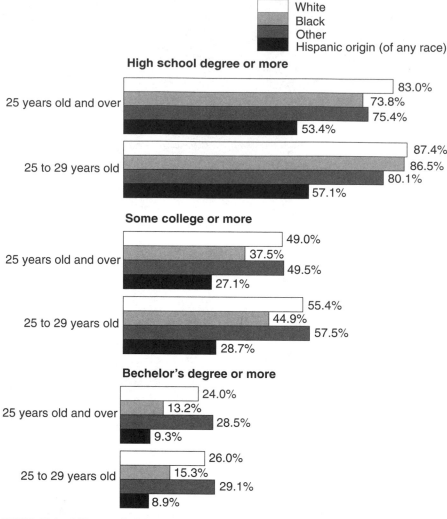

FIGURE 10.1 Differences in Educational Attainment by Race, Hispanic Origin, and Age: 1995
Source: U.S. Bureau of the Census, Current Population Survey

There is the basic question whether enrollment in a grade not completed is worth crediting for purposes of calculating educational attainment. Thus, should years of schooling be treated as a discrete variable rather than a continuous variable? In the United States, there is a tendency for persons who do not complete the highest grade they attend to drop out early in the school year and, therefore, to complete only a small fraction of the grade. Thus, although the stated class boundaries may describe accurately the limits of attainment (in the previous example, 9.0 years up to, but not including, 10.0 years), they do not describe accurately the distribution within the grade.

The form of the actual distribution for a reported year of school differs for those who are still attending at that grade level, on the one hand, and those who have graduated or dropped out of school, on the other hand. For the former, if one knows the date of the beginning of the school year and

the date of the census enumeration or administration of the survey, the number of years of school completed can be calculated to the decimal. For those who are no longer attending school, either because they completed a grade and left school or they dropped out of school (assuming they dropped out early in the year), it is reasonable to assume the "exact" grade (e.g., 9.0 years) as the midpoint of the grade interval. Hence, for a reported nine grades, the class limits for computing the median would be 8.50 to 9.49 for this group. Ideally, then, different assumptions should be made for the different groups.

In any event, care must be taken in interpreting the median number of school years completed as conventionally calculated. Given the assumption about the rectangular distribution of persons within the class limits, a median of, say, 9.3 years, should not be interpreted to mean that the average person in the population group for which the median

TABLE 10.4 Male and Female Population of Selected Ages by Years of School Completed and Corresponding Grade Attainment Ratios: Mexico, 1990

	Number						Percent					
	Male, 15 years and over			Female, 15 years and over			Male, 15 years and over			Female, 15 years and over		
Years of School Completed	Total	15 to 24 years	25 years and over	Total	15 to 24 years	25 years and over	Total	15 to 24 years	25 years and over	Total	15 to 24 years	25 years and over
Total	23,924,966	8,498,020	15,426,946	25,685,910	8,995,546	16,690,364	100.0	100.0	100.0	100.0	100.0	100.0
None	2,749,010	345,102	2,403,908	3,918,451	445,956	3,472,495	11.8	4.1	16.1	15.8	5.1	21.7
Primary Level												
1	522,374	59,887	462,487	532,767	62,888	469,879	2.3	0.7	3.1	2.1	0.7	2.9
2	1,268,166	161,908	1,106,258	1,335,811	179,110	1,156,701	5.5	1.9	7.4	5.4	2.0	7.2
3	1,789,960	287,177	1,502,783	1,921,758	327,169	1,594,589	7.7	3.4	10.1	7.7	3.7	9.9
4	1,062,485	273,193	789,292	1,236,504	314,111	922,393	4.6	3.3	5.3	5.0	3.6	5.8
5	762,725	291,486	471,239	856,493	308,249	548,244	3.3	3.5	3.2	3.4	3.5	3.4
6	4,539,035	1,559,482	2,979,553	5,014,128	1,782,749	3,231,379	19.6	18.7	20.0	20.2	20.3	20.1
Secondary Level												
1	1,403,652	977,812	425,840	1,299,951	909,406	390,545	6.0	11.7	2.9	5.2	10.3	2.4
2	2,009,812	1,233,666	776,146	1,942,903	1,176,477	766,426	8.7	14.8	5.2	7.8	13.4	4.8
3	4,868,858	2,607,330	2,261,528	5,153,566	2,734,509	2,419,057	21.0	31.3	15.2	20.8	31.1	15.1
4 or more	96,702	8,095	88,607	208,465	19,048	189,417	0.4	0.1	0.6	0.8	0.2	1.2
Third Level												
1	220,986	147,319	73,667	174,862	133,397	41,465	1.0	1.8	0.5	0.7	1.5	0.3
2	251,422	130,386	121,036	186,933	122,602	64,331	1.1	1.6	0.8	0.8	1.4	0.4
3	270,744	102,000	168,744	241,941	112,258	129,683	1.2	1.2	1.1	1.0	1.3	0.8
4	452,130	91,678	360,452	370,659	121,568	249,091	1.9	1.1	2.4	1.5	1.4	1.6
5	573,422	39,517	533,905	232,512	31,986	200,526	2.5	0.5	3.6	0.9	0.4	1.3
6 or more	374,867	13,241	361,626	206,761	14,624	192,137	1.6	0.2	2.4	0.8	0.2	1.2
Not reported	708,616	168,741	539,875	851,445	199,439	652,006	3.0	2.0	3.5	3.3	2.2	3.9
Median Years of School Completed[1]	6.8	8.2	6.2	6.5	8.1	5.7	(X)	(X)	(X)	(X)	(X)	(X)
Mean Years of School Completed[1]	6.7	7.7	6.2	6.2	7.6	5.4	(X)	(X)	(X)	(X)	(X)	(X)

(X) Not applicable.

[1] Disregarding cases not reported.

Source: Based on United Nations, *Demographic Yearbook*, 1994, table 34.

is computed has completed three-tenths of the 10th grade. Instead, it should be interpreted to mean that the average person in the group has completed the ninth grade and that some persons completing the ninth grade have attended the 10th grade. A median greater than 12, as in the United States, reflects primarily a very high concentration at high school graduation or higher. In some other countries, a median of 1 or even 0, likewise reflects a very high concentration at the initial grades of elementary school. If more precision in a summary measure of attainment is desired, then consideration should be given to using a cumulative grade attainment ratio.

The *mean years of school completed* can be defined as the arithmetic average of the years of school completed by all persons in a population reporting years of school completed. By contrast, the median shows the educational level that the middle person in a distribution has attained.

The procedure used in computing the mean years of school completed for grouped data is to (1) multiply the number of persons in each educational class by the midpoint of the number of years of school covered by the class, (2) sum the products for all classes, and (3) divide by the total population represented in step 1. The same considerations with respect to the determination of the boundaries of classes apply here as for the calculation of the median. If educational attainment is treated as a continuous quantitative variable, the midpoint of each class would then be at the center of each grade (e.g., 9.5). In calculating the mean years of school completed, it is necessary to assign a value to the highest educational attainment class if it is an open-ended class. For instance, if the highest level is 5 or more years of higher education (or 17 or more years of school), a value that represents the midvalue for persons in that category (perhaps 18) must be assigned.

While the mean is generally more sensitive to variations or changes in the educational distribution than is the median, the median is nearer the point of greatest concentration in the distribution. Therefore, the median is the more commonly used summary measure of educational attainment.

The median and mean years of school completed are illustrated next for males 25 years and over with data for Mexico shown in Table 10.4. (For a more complete description of the method of calculating the median for grouped data, see Chapter 7.) The median years of school completed is calculated by (1) dividing the total minus the age-not-reported category in half and subtracting the sum of the frequenies of the array in all the classes preceding the class containing the middle item; and (2) dividing the result in step 1 by the category containing the middle item (or in this case, primary level 6), which is larger than the result in step 1; (3) multiplying the percentage in step 2 by the size of the interval; and (4) adding the resulting quantity to the lower limit of the median class.

Median years of schooling for males aged 25 and over is shown as

$$\left(\frac{\frac{15,426,946 - 539,875}{2} - 6,735,967}{2,979,553} \right) = \frac{707,568.5}{2,979,553} = 0.2$$

$$\text{Median} = 6.0 + 0.2 = 6.2$$

For purposes of computing the median here, the distribution of years of school completed is regarded as continuous. The median for the group 25 years and over falls in the "primary level—year 6" category and, on the basis of the assumption of continuity, the median value is 6.2 years, as Table 10.4 shows.

Where most adults are high school graduates, as in the more developed countries, the median has become too insensitive an indicator of educational progress and more emphasis is given to cumulative attainment ratios at the higher levels. The U.S. Census Bureau has discontinued featuring the former measure.

The mean years of school completed by males 25 years old and over in Mexico is calculated by (1) multiplying the frequencies in each category in Table 10.4 cumulatively by the midpoint of each category and (2) dividing by the sum of the frequencies ("total" minus "not reported").

Mean years of school completed for males aged 25 and over is shown as

$$\frac{91,925,611.5}{15,426,946 - 539,875} = 6.2$$

Because the distribution of the population by years of school completed is concentrated toward the middle years of schooling, as for Mexico, the mean and the median have similar values. If the distribution were concentrated toward the lower levels of education, the mean years of schooling would be substantially higher than the median.[4] In general, as educational attainment rises, the gap between the two types of averages tends to fall until, as for most of the age-sex groups in Mexico in 1990, the median exceeds the mean.

As suggested by the discussion of illiteracy ratios, age-specific calculations of measures of educational attainment (for the ages beyond those at which formal education is normally obtained), if taken from a single census, may provide an indication of the historical changes in the level of schooling of a population. The measures used may be a cumulative attainment ratio (e.g., completion of elementary

---

[4] In 1961, the median years of schooling for Honduran males age 25 years and over was 0.9 years, while the mean years of schooling was 2.1 years. (H. S. Shyrock and J. S. Siegel, with E. D. Stockwll, 1976, *The Methods and Materials of Demography*, Condensed Edition: 187, San Diego: Academic Press.).

school or higher), or the median or mean years of school completed. For example, the percent with a bachelor's degree or higher for the United States population in 2000 shows a steady upward progression from the oldest to the younger ages among those aged 25 and over, although the measure peaks at 30.3 in the 45-to-49-year-old group. The assumption of stability of these figures over time is essentially corroborated by comparison with the figures for the same birth cohorts in 1995:

| Age | Percent bachelor's degree or higher | |
	2000	1995
25–29	29.1	24.7
30–34	29.5	25.3
35–39	27.4	25.5
40–44	26.7	27.9
45–49	30.3	30.2
50–54	30.2	25.3
55–59	25.0	20.2
60–64	21.6	17.8
65–69	18.5	15.2
70–74	16.4	13.0
75 and over	13.4	11.2

Source: U.S. Current Population Survey.

This type of analysis assumes that there is little or no difference in mortality levels, immigration rates, or coverage rates by level of educational attainment and that the educational attainment of individuals does not change after age 25. In some situations these assumptions may be tenuous, as for the younger ages in the table shown.

Uses and Limitations

Data on educational attainment may be used in several ways. First, one could study the productivity of the education systems in a country over time. Other phenomena that could be examined are the association of education with employment and occupational placement, the characteristics of the educated "manpower" supply, and the economic returns to education. Researchers could employ data on educational output to study the effects of education on fertility, mortality, migration, urbanization, and other demographic processes.

The United Nations regards education as one of the key factors determining the quality of life in a society and has long stressed the importance of data on educational status in government planning. Such data can reveal the disparity of educational opportunity between different segments of a population, for example, and can also be used to develop the educational system or to plan programs of economic development (United Nations, 1998).

In computing each of these measures, some account must be taken of nonresponses to the question on educational attainment whenever these are not allocated before publication. In the 1990 census of the United States 4.6% of adults (aged 25 and over) did not complete the question regarding the number of years of school completed. Unless there is a valid basis for distributing the nonresponses over the reported categories in a special way, it is customary to distribute them "pro rata" or, in effect, base the derived measures on the distribution for persons for whom reports on educational attainment have been received.

While the measures indicating years of school completed look like continuous ratio-level measures, the reality of educational attainment suggests that they are not. The 1-year difference between 12 years of school completed and 13 years of school completed (i.e., between those who end their education at high school and those who go on to college) is quite different than the 1-year difference between 9 years and 10 years of school completed.

Those using statistics on educational attainment should also recognize that they typically do not indicate the quality of education received or the resulting competencies of the persons involved. For example, trend analysis of educational attainment is complicated because we do not know how much better prepared scholastically a person may be after completing a given school level today than was his or her counterpart at an earlier period of time. Likewise, at any particular date, there may be variations among areas of a country in the types of school attended, the kinds of courses taken, and the quality of teaching, all of which make comparisons among groups difficult.

There is some degree of misreporting of highest grade or year of school completed; however, the difference generally only involves one or two grades. In addition, over-reporting of grade completion is somewhat greater than under-reporting, resulting in a small degree of net over-reporting. Misreporting of educational attainment can be intentional, as when a higher level than actually attained is reported for reasons of prestige. Misreporting may also be unintentional, as when recall of older persons is faulty, highest grade attended is mistaken for highest grade completed, or information is supplied secondhand by persons who did not have reliable information.

Changes in question wording in censuses and surveys often make it more complicated to present trend analyses. For example, when the U.S. Census Bureau in 1990 switched from collecting data for the highest grade or year of school ever attended to collecting data for the highest level or degree completed, it made trend analyses of decennial census data involving 1980 and future years more difficult. For some measures, this is only mildly problematic. By assuming, for example, that 12 years of completed education was equivalent to a high school degree, one could still produce a trend line on high school graduation. However, this is more difficult if one is trying to show trend data for receipt of a post-high school degree, such as completion of an associate's degree. In the 1990 and 2000 censuses, data were collected for persons who completed an associate's degree—a program that generally takes about 2 years of schooling after completing high school. It is impossible, however, to identify associate's degree holders using the 1980 census data, because it is difficult to determine whether persons who completed 2 years of college education earned an associate's degree or completed the first 2 years of a bachelor's degree program.

ECONOMIC CHARACTERISTICS

Economic Activity and Employment

Economic activity is vital to every society. How people organize themselves around productive activity and the stratification processes that are associated with differentiation of labor are fundamental characteristics of a society. This section focuses on several dimensions of work and the rewards of work (i.e., income and wealth).

Concepts and Definitions

Although all persons consume goods and services, only part of the population of a country is engaged in producing such goods and services. Most obviously, the youngest, the oldest, and the physically or mentally incapacitated do not engage in such economic activity because of an inability to do so. The *manpower* of a nation, then, is the totality of persons who could produce the goods and services if there were a demand for their labors and they desired to participate in such activity. The economically active (sometimes also called the labor force or workforce) is that part of the manpower that actually is working or looking for work.[5]

At any given time, an economically active person may be either employed or unemployed. (As we shall see, the distinction is not always clear-cut; some of the employed may be classified as underemployed.) Those not economically active may be subdivided according to their major type of activity—for example, going to school or keeping house. The economically active also may be classified according to the nature of their current, last, or usual job (e.g., occupation, industry, status or class of worker, or place of work). Other characteristics relevant to the economically active include the number of weeks worked in the past year, the number of hours worked in the past week or other

[5] See also A. J. Jaffe and C. D. Stewart, 1951, *Manpower Resources and Utilization*, chapter 2, "Definitions and Concepts," and chapter 3, "Socio-Economic Development and the Working Force" (New York: John Wiley & Sons).

reference period, and, for the unemployed, the duration of unemployment.

The United Nations (1998) has recommended that census information be collected that would allow persons to be classified according to *type of activity*—that is, either one's *current* economic activity (as of a certain date) or one's *usual* economic activity (during an extended reference period, such as the past 12 months). These data usually are collected for persons at and above a minimum age, depending on conditions in a specific country. For international comparisons, the UN recommends that tabulations (at a minimum) distinguish between persons under age 15 and persons aged 15 and older. In the United States, the monthly Current Population Survey (CPS)—the major source of official statistics on the labor force—collects data on employment for persons aged 15 and older. However, the official United States definition of the labor force relates to ages 16 and older.

Regardless of whether current or usual economic activity is used, the United Nations (1998) has recommended the following classification:

Economically active population
    Employed
    Unemployed
Not economically active population
    Students
    Homemakers
    Pension or capital income recipients
    Others

According to the International Labour Organisation's *Current International Recommendations on Labour Statistics* (International Labour Organisation, 2000), the *economically active population* "comprises all persons of either sex who furnish the supply of labour for the production of economic goods and services as defined by the United Nations system of national accounts and balances during a specified time-reference period." Included in this population are persons in the civilian labor force and those who serve in the armed forces. When compiling labor force data, some countries (for example, the United States) show persons in the armed forces in a separate category. In that way, armed forces personnel may be deducted from the total labor force whenever desirable for analytic purposes.

Within the economically active population, persons are categorized as either employed or unemployed. The *employed* population includes persons who either were engaged in paid (wage and salary) employment or were self-employed during the reference period. The employed also include persons with a job or business enterprise, but who were temporarily not at work due to illness, vacation, or some other specific reason. The *unemployed* population, by contrast, includes all persons who were without work but were available for work, *and* had taken specific steps to seek work during the reference period. (In many less developed countries, the criterion of actively seeking work often is relaxed to suit national circumstances.) Unemployed persons include persons without work but who have made arrangements to work or become self-employed after the reference period, and they may include persons who have been temporarily laid off from their regular jobs. The United Nations recommends that data on the unemployed distinguish first-time job seekers and those persons on layoff. It is important to recognize that those who are without a job, but are not seeking employment, are not included in the unemployed category under this definition. This latter group includes those who are sometimes referred to as "discouraged workers."

The *economically inactive population*—those persons of a minimum age not meeting any of the preceding characteristics during the reference period—consists of three main groups plus a residual category. Students are persons who attend any regular public or private institution for systematic instruction toward a diploma or degree. Homemakers are persons (either male or female) who are responsible for household duties in their own home. Pension or capital income recipients receive income from property, investments, pensions, or royalties. These persons are often elderly. The residual, or "other" category, includes those persons receiving public assistance or private support, volunteers, and other economically inactive persons who do not fall into the other three categories. (Students, homemakers, and pension or capital income recipients may also be classified as economically active if they meet the criteria for employed or unemployed during the reference period.)

The Labor Force and the Usually Active Population

As mentioned earlier, the term *economic activity* can refer to either the currently active population (indicated also by the term "the labor force") or the usually active population. The essence of all these terms involves the reference to time and the conduct of an activity from which the person derives, or attempts to derive, pay, profit, or family gain. The measurement of usual activity, based on a longer reference period such as past 12 months, is most useful when trying to include seasonal employment or in countries where a large proportion of the population participates in subsistence farming and cash cropping. The converse of the economically active population and the usually active population are the population not currently active and the population not usually active, respectively.

The collection procedures in the monthly Current Population Survey (CPS), the official source of U.S. labor force statistics, illustrate the labor force concept defined earlier. The CPS asks all persons aged 15 and over, excluding inmates of institutions and members of the armed forces living on a military installation, whether they worked for pay or profit during a specified week. Those who did so are classified as *employed*. Also classified as employed are those persons who had a job or business during the specified week but were absent from it because of vacation, illness, or related reasons. Persons who did not work for reasons other than those specified earlier were asked whether they sought work for pay or profit during the past four weeks and were available to take a job if offered. Those who answered yes to both questions are classified as *unemployed*. Also classified as unemployed are those persons who were on layoff from their job and expecting recall—regardless of whether or not they had actively sought work in the previous four weeks. All persons not meeting the criteria for classification as employed or unemployed are classified as *not in the labor force* (U.S. Census Bureau, 1994).

It is easiest to determine economic activity in a country or other area where practically everyone receives monetary remuneration for his or her labors. In situations where money does not change hands, such as in a subsistence economy or for self-employed persons, it can often be very difficult to decide who is and who is not economically active.

Job Characteristics

Three items of information that describe the economically active population are usually obtained when a census or sample survey is conducted. These are occupation, industry, and status in employment (for example, employee or employer).

According to the United Nations recommendations for population and housing censuses, "occupation refers to the type of work done during the time-reference period by the person employed (or the type of work done previously, if the person is unemployed), irrespective of the industry or the status in employment in which the person should be classified" (United Nations, 1998, p. 85). Examples of occupations are economist, secretary, vegetable grower, lawyer, dentist, and garbage collector.

Specific occupations are frequently consolidated in census and survey tabulations into conventionally defined broad groups. This often happens in the presentation of occupation statistics where the number of cases is small, as in the case of data for small areas, cross-classifications with other economic, social, and demographic variables (such as race and educational level), and data based on sample surveys.

In the United States, the Standard Occupational Classification (SOC) system is the universal occupational classification system used by all federal government agencies that collect occupation data. While data on occupation has been collected since the 1850 census of population, the SOC was first introduced in 1977. The SOC has undergone periodic revisions to accommodate new occupations—for example, computer software engineer, environmental engineer, and environmental scientist and specialist (including health). It was designed to cover all occupations for which work is performed for pay or profit, and to encourage all federal agencies (and private industries) to use one occupational classification system that would allow for comparability across data collection systems. The most recent revision of the SOC occurred in 1998; the Census Bureau used this revision to classify responses from the 2000 decennial census. Household surveys and other data collection systems began using the revised SOC system soon afterward (Levine, Salmon, and Weinberg, 1999).

The SOC has four hierarchical classification levels, designed to accommodate the ability and interest that various data collection efforts have for collecting and reporting occupational statistics.[6] The major occupation classification consists of 23 categories. This major grouping includes 98 minor classes, which can be disaggregated into 452 broad occupations and 822 detailed occupations (U.S. Bureau of Labor Statistics, 1999). The 23 major occupational groups of the revised SOC are as follows:

1. Management Occupations
2. Business and Financial Operations Occupations
3. Computer and Mathematical Occupations
4. Architecture and Engineering Occupations
5. Life, Physical, and Social Science Occupations
6. Community and Social Services Occupations
7. Legal Occupations
8. Education, Training, and Library Occupations
9. Arts, Design, Entertainment, Sports, and Media Occupations
10. Healthcare Practitioners and Technical Occupations
11. Healthcare Support Occupations
12. Protective Service Occupations
13. Food Preparation and Serving Related Occupations
14. Building and Grounds Cleaning and Maintenance Occupations
15. Personal Care and Service Occupations
16. Sales and Related Occupations
17. Office and Administrative Support Occupations
18. Farming, Fishing, and Forestry Occupations
19. Construction and Extraction Occupations
20. Installation, Maintenance, and Repair Occupations
21. Production Occupations
22. Transportation and Material Moving Occupations
23. Military Specific Occupations

For purposes of international comparisons, the United Nations recommends that countries compile their data in accordance with the latest revision of the *International Standard Classification of Occupations* (ISCO-88) from the

International Labour Organisation (ILO).[7] The UN recognizes, however, that many countries will want to use occupational classification systems that they believe are more useful for national purposes. Because of this fact, the recommendation also suggests that countries using a system other than the ISCO attempt to determine the ISCO equivalent to the occupational group of the specific countries (United Nations, 1998). Brazil, for example, uses a modified occupational coding list, Classificação Brasileira de Ocupações (CBO), which was created using ISCO-68 as a basis. For ease of international comparison, the Ministry of Labor provides the "crosswalk" between the CBO, ISCO-68, and ISCO-88 (Ministerio Do Trabalho, 1996).

In addition to information on the individual's occupation, it also is very important to know the person's industry of employment (industry), or the kind of establishment where the person is employed. As defined by the United Nations, "Industry refers to the activity of the establishment in which an employed person worked during the time reference period established for data on economic characteristics (or last worked, if unemployed)" (United Nations, 1998, p. 86). The term "activity of the establishment" means the kinds of goods produced or services rendered. Goods-producing establishments include, for example, a petroleum refinery, a pulp and paper factory, and a fruit or vegetable canning plant. Examples of service-providing establishments are a hospital, a bread and breakfast inn, a railroad, an elementary school, and a grocery store.

For purposes of international comparability, the United Nations recommends that "countries prepare tabulations involving the industrial characteristics of active persons according to the most recent revision of the *International Standard Industrial Classification of All Economic Activities* (ISIC) available at the time of the census" (United Nations, 1998, p. 86). As is the case with occupations, many countries use industrial classification systems that they believe are more useful for national purposes. The UN therefore recommends that these countries follow the same guidelines mentioned earlier with regard to occupations (United Nations, 1998). ISIC revision 3 is the most current industry classification system released by the ILO and consists of four levels of classification and 17 broad categories.

From the 1930s through the 1990s, U.S. national statistical agencies used the Standard Industrial Classification (SIC) as the classification system for industries. The SIC was revised periodically as the nation's economy changed, most recently in 1987. Since 1997, however, the United

---

[6] More information on the SOC system is available at the following website: http://stats.bls.gov/soc/socguide.htm.

[7] For more information, see International Labour Organisation, 1990, *International Standard Classification of Occupations (ISCO-88)*, Geneva: International Labour Office.

States has replaced the SIC with the North American Industrial Classification System (NAICS), which also will be used by Canada and Mexico (Saunders, 1999). As the economic structure of North American countries evolved from one based primarily on manufacturing to one increasingly dependent on services, many analysts considered the categories used in the SIC to be outdated. The implementation of the North American Free Trade Act, designed to create a single economic zone between the United States, Canada, and Mexico, also increased the attractiveness of a system that would be comparable for all three countries.

The NAICS system groups establishments according to a production-based concept. In other words, industries using similar processes to produce goods and services are classified in a single category. For example, newspaper publishers, radio stations, and data processing services—each of which would have been classified under a different sector under the SIC—are now classified into a single broad information category (U.S. Census Bureau, 2000b). The NAICS system lists 1170 specific industries in 20 different sectors. These sectors are as follows:

1. Agriculture, Forestry, Fishing, and Hunting
2. Mining
3. Utilities
4. Construction
5. Manufacturing
6. Wholesale Trade
7. Retail Trade
8. Transportation and Warehousing
9. Information
10. Finance and Insurance
11. Real Estate and Leasing
12. Professional, Scientific, and Technical Services
13. Management of Companies and Enterprises
14. Administrative and Support and Waste Management and Remediation Services
15. Educational Services
16. Health Care and Social Assistance
17. Arts, Entertainment, and Recreation
18. Accommodation and Food Services
19. Other Services (except Public Administration)
20. Public Administration

According to the United Nations, "status in employment[8] refers to the status of an economically active person with respect to his or her employment, that is to say, the type of explicit or implicit contract of employment with other persons or organizations that the person has in his/her job" (United Nations, 1998, p. 87).

_____
[8] The term used in the United States is "class of worker."

The international recommendations for classification of this economic characteristic and the definition of the categories follow:

(a) An *employee* is a person who works in a paid employment job, that is to say, a job where the explicit or implicit contract of employment gives the incumbent a basic remuneration that is independent of the revenue of the unit for which he or she works.
(b) An *employer* is a person who, working on his or her own economic account or with one or a few partners, holds a *self-employment* job and, in this capacity, has engaged on a continuous basis (including the reference period) one or more persons to work for him/her as employees.
(c) An *own-account worker* is a person who, working on his own account or with one or a few partners, holds a *self-employment job*, and has not engaged on a continuous basis any employees.
(d) A *contributing family worker* is a person who holds a self-employment job in a market oriented establishment operated by a related person living in the same household, and who cannot be regarded as a partner.
(e) A *member of producers' cooperative* is a person who holds a self-employment job in an establishment organized as a cooperative, in which each member takes part on an equal footing with other members in determining the organization of production, sales and/or other work.
(f) *Persons not classifiable by status* include those economically active persons for whom insufficient information is available, and/or cannot be included.

The United States and other countries often combine "employer" and "own account worker." In addition, they do not show "member of producers' cooperative" separately. This category has been common in socialist countries, such as the former Soviet Union and the Soviet bloc countries. In the United States in particular, few workers would fall under the category labeled "producers' cooperative."

Other Economic Characteristics of Workers

In addition to the basic questions on economic activity such as occupation, industry, and status, which are almost always included in population censuses and sample surveys that deal with economic characteristics of individuals, a large number of other economic characteristics have been included in various household surveys. Generally, population censuses can only accommodate questions on a few, if any, additional economic characteristics. However, many countries currently conduct special labor force sample surveys or economic sample surveys that often obtain information on additional economic characteristics of individuals. Examples of the additional items that may be included are as follows:

Number of hours worked in reference week
Normal or scheduled hours (or days) of work per week
Type of enterprise (household or nonhousehold)

Type of employing establishment (business, government,
    etc.)
Number of employees (asked of employers only)
Secondary occupation
Seasonal variations in time worked (asked of persons
    employed during the entire previous year)
Reason for part-time work during the reference week (only
    asked of persons who worked fewer than 35 hours or
    fewer than five days)
Whether respondent looked for more hours of work (only
    asked of persons who worked fewer than 35 hours or
    fewer than five days)
Whether respondent wanted more hours of work (only
    asked of persons who worked fewer than 35 hours or
    fewer than five days)
Kind of job sought (asked of unemployed persons)
Duration of unemployment
Migration for employment

Some of these items are designed to elicit information on the problem of underemployment. Though neither conceptually clear-cut nor easy to measure, underemployment is often a much more serious problem in underdeveloped countries than is unemployment.

Between "full" employment and complete lack of employment (i.e., unemployment) lies a continuum of working behavior. Any amount of work at any point on this continuum can be called "underemployment" (i.e., less than "full" employment). The International Labour Organisation (ILO) has defined the term as follows: "*underemployment* is the difference between the amount of work performed by persons in employment and the amount of work they would normally be able and willing to perform" (International Labour Organisation, 1957, p. 17).

Recent ILO conferences of labor statisticians have attempted to make this definition more concrete. As a result, the ILO has subdivided underemployment into two major categories: (1) visible, when persons involuntarily work part time or for shorter periods than usual, and (2) invisible, when persons work full time but the work is inadequate because earnings are too low or the job does not permit exercise of one's fullest skills.[9]

Despite much research on the measurement of underemployment, it has not been possible to develop procedures as precise as those used in measuring employment and unemployment. In large degree this difficulty stems from the fact that there is no uniquely correct measure or definition of "full" employment. For example, in the United States, 35 hours of work is considered a "full" week, but other coun-

tries use different thresholds. It is also impossible to discover a uniquely correct procedure for ascertaining invisible underemployment. The degree to which work is adequate or inadequate does not lend itself to easy definition and measurement.

Labor mobility is any change in a person's status that involves his or her economic activity or, more specifically, his or her job. The most common forms of labor mobility are as follows:

Entering or leaving the labor force
Shifting employment status
Changing occupation
Changing industry
Changing class of worker (status)
Changing employer
Moving from one geographic area to another (this topic
    also is addressed in Chapter 19, "Internal Migration."

Information on labor mobility can be obtained by asking persons about their economic characteristics at some previous date. They can be asked about their employment status, occupation, industry, and so forth. By comparing the previous and current activity, changes in economic activity can be noted. Information on gross changes (i.e., all movements) is obtained by such direct questioning. However, problems of memory recall, among other issues, have prevented much use of these questions. In countries like the United States, with a well-developed market economy, the labor force is not a static aggregate that changes only as the result of population growth. On the contrary, the labor force is subject to very high turnover, even in the short run.

Sources of Data

Information on economic activity is collected from households in population censuses or sample surveys, or from establishments through regular reporting in certain kinds of administrative programs or through special sample surveys. The data from sources other than households pertain to employment and unemployment but not to the economically inactive population.

Available national census statistics on the characteristics of the economically active population have been summarized in the UN *Demographic Yearbook*, most recently in 1994 (Tables 26 to 34). The ILO publishes labor force statistics from numerous sources, such as national labor force surveys and other related household surveys, in the annual *Yearbook of Labour Statistics*. In 1999, the ILO began a new publication series, *Key Indicators of the Labour Market*, which presents data and analyses of core labor market indicators at the country level (ILO, 2002a).

The United Nations has made efforts to select, arrange, and edit the statistics from member countries in order to increase international comparability. However, the number

---

[9] Also see International Labour Organisation, 2000, "Resolution Concerning the Measurement of Underemployment and Inadequate Employment Situations (October 1998)," data accessed online at www.ilo.org/public/english/bureau/stat/res/underemp.htm (July 23).

and nature of the footnotes on the tables in the *Demographic Yearbook* give one indication of the degree to which this objective could not readily be accomplished. Countries vary in terms of definitions, populations covered, and categories tabulated. Countries that conduct sample household surveys on a recurrent basis tend to use concepts and procedures similar, but not identical, to the UN recommendations.

As early as 1820, the U.S. census attempted to collect statistics on the economically active population. However, it was the 1870 population census that provided the first body of data adequate for a sophisticated profile of the

---

TABLE 10.5   Selected Questions on Economic Activity Asked in the 2000 United States Decennial Census

Questions on Labor Force Status

Question 21. LAST WEEK, did this person do ANY work for either pay or profit? (Mark the "Yes" box even if the person worked only 1 hour, or helped without pay in a family business or farm for 15 hours or more, or was on active duty in the Armed Forces.)
- Yes
- No—Skip to 25a

Question 25
a. LAST WEEK, was this person on layoff from a job?
  - Yes—Skip to 25c
  - No
b. LAST WEEK, was this person TEMPORARILY absent from a job or business?
  - Yes, on vacation, temporary illness, labor dispute, etc.—Skip to 26
  - No—Skip to 25d
c. Has this person been informed that he or she will be recalled to work within the next 6 months OR been given a date to return to work?
  - Yes—Skip to 25e
  - No
d. Has this person been looking for work during the last 4 weeks?
  - Yes
  - No—Skip to 26
e. LAST WEEK, could this person have started a job if offered one, or returned to work if recalled?
  - Yes, could have gone to work
  - No, because of own temporary illness
  - No, because of all other reasons (in school, etc.)

Question 26. When did this person last work, even for a few days?
- 1995 to 2000
- 1994 or earlizer, or never worked—Skip to 31

Questions on Industry, Occupation, and Work Status

Question 27. Industry or Employer (Describe clearly this person's chief job activity or business last week. If this person had more than one job, describe the one at which this person worked the most hours. If this person had no job or business last week, give the information for his/her last job or business since 1995.)
  a. For whom did this person work? (If now on active duty in the Armed Forces, mark box and print the branch of the Armed Forces.)
  (Name of company, business or other employer)

b. What kind of business or industry was this? (Describe the activity at location where employed—for example: hospital, newspaper publishing, mail order house, auto repair, shop, bank)

c. Is this mainly
  - Manufacturing?
  - Wholesale trade?
  - Retail trade?
  - Other (agriculture, construction, service, government, etc.)?

Question 28. Occupation
  a. What kind of work was this person doing? (For example: registered nurse, personnel manager, supervisor of order department, auto mechanic, accountant)

  b. What were this person's most important activities or duties? (For example: patient care, directing hiring policies, supervising order clerks, repairing automobiles, reconciling financial records)

Question 29. Was this person
- Employee in a PRIVATE-FOR-PROFIT company or business or of an individual, for wages, salary, or commissions
- Employee in a PRIVATE, NOT-FOR-PROFIT, tax exempt, or charitable organization
- Local GOVERNMENT employee (city, county, etc.)
- State GOVERNMENT employee
- Federal GOVERNMENT employee
- SELF-EMPLOYED in own NOT INCORPORATED business, professional practice, or farm
- SELF-EMPLOYED in own INCORPORATED business, professional practice, or farm
- Working WITHOUT PAY in family business or farm

Question on Activity in Previous Year

Question 30
  a. LAST YEAR, 1999, did this person work at a job or business at any time?
  - Yes
  - No—Skip to 31
  b. How many weeks did this person work in 1999? (Count paid vacation, sick leave, and military service)

  c. During the weeks WORKED in 1999, how many hours did this person usually work each week?

  Usual hours worked each week _____

Source: U.S. Census Bureau, "United States Census 2000," informational census questionnaire.

labor force. In the 1890 and 1910 censuses, substantial revisions were made in the collection and classification procedures so that it is difficult to construct a comparable series prior to 1930. In the late 1930s, the Works Progress Administration developed a standard set of labor force concepts and procedures that were used in the 1940 and subsequent population censuses and also in the monthly sample surveys. These surveys have been taken continuously since the 1940s.

In the population censuses from 1940 through 1960, persons aged 14 and over (except for inmates of institutions) were asked about their activities in the week preceding the census. Starting with the 1970 census, the Census Bureau began asking the employment question for persons aged 15 and over—a practice maintained in the monthly Current Population Survey (CPS) to this day. Table 10.5 shows the key labor force and employment questions asked in the 2000 decennial census. These questions were also asked of persons aged 15 and over. However, it should be noted that many agencies, such as the U.S. Bureau of Labor Statistics (BLS), report labor force data only for persons aged 16 and over.

The labor force concepts in the CPS are discussed in several reports (e.g., U.S. Census Bureau, 1994). The CPS obtains more detailed information on labor force status than does the decennial census. Data collected in the CPS make it possible to analyze several aspects of the work life of the employed, including full-time/part-time status, reasons for working part time (i.e., whether for economic or noneconomic reasons), and reasons for not working during the previous week. Similarly, the unemployed can be classified by such factors as duration of unemployment, occupation and industry of their last job (if they had worked before), class of work sought (full-time or part-time work), and reason for unemployment. Based on their reported activity, persons who are not in the labor force can be classified as homemakers, students, and other types (including retired, unable to work, etc.). Analysis of these categories is useful for studying the labor reserve and for making labor force projections.

Table 10.6 shows some of the regular statistics on labor force and employment status from the CPS. The annual figures represent averages of the monthly figures in a given year. Many monthly figures, including the ones in this table,

TABLE 10.6   Employment Status of the Civilian Noninstitutional Population 16 Years of Age and Over: United States, 1995 to April 2000 (Numbers in thousands)

Year and Month	Civilian noninstitutional population	Civilian labor force							Not in labor force
				Employed			Unemployed		
		Number	Percentage of population	Number	In agriculture	Nonagricultural industries	Number	Percent of labor force	
ANNUAL AVERAGES									
1995	198,584	132,304	66.6	124,900	3,440	121,460	7,404	5.6	66,280
1996	200,591	133,943	66.8	126,708	3,443	123,264	7,236	5.4	66,647
1997	203,133	136,297	67.1	129,558	3,399	126,159	6,739	4.9	66,837
1998	205,220	137,673	67.1	131,463	3,378	128,085	6,210	4.5	67,547
1999	207,753	139,368	67.1	133,488	3,281	130,207	5,880	4.2	68,385
MONTHLY DATA, SEASONALLY ADJUSTED									
1999:									
April	207,236	139,086	67.1	133,054	3,341	129,713	6,032	4.3	68,150
May	207,427	139,013	67.0	133,190	3,290	129,900	5,823	4.2	68,414
June	207,632	139,332	67.1	133,398	3,330	130,068	5,934	4.3	68,300
July	207,828	139,336	67.0	133,399	3,278	130,121	5,927	4.3	68,492
August	208,038	139,372	67.0	133,530	3,234	130,296	5,842	4.2	68,666
September	208,265	139,475	67.0	133,650	3,179	130,471	5,825	4.2	68,790
October	208,483	139,697	67.0	133,940	3,238	130,702	5,757	4.1	68,786
November	208,666	139,834	67.0	134,098	3,310	130,788	5,736	4.1	68,832
December	208,832	140,108	67.1	134,420	3,279	131,141	5,688	4.1	68,724
2000:									
January	208,782	140,910	67.5	135,221	3,371	131,850	5,689	4.0	67,872
February	208,907	141,165	67.6	135,362	3,408	131,954	5,804	4.1	67,742
March	209,053	140,867	67.4	135,159	3,359	131,801	5,708	4.1	68,187
April	209,216	141,230	67.5	135,706	3,355	132,351	5,524	3.9	67,986

Source: U.S. Bureau of Labor Statistics, *Employment and Earnings* 47: 5 (May 2000): table A-1.

TABLE 10.7 Occupation of Employed Persons 15 Years of Age and Over, by Sex and Marital Status: United States, 2001

Major Occupation Class and Sex	Number in thousands					Percent				
	Total	Never Married	Married	Widowed	Divorced	Total	Never Married	Married	Widowed	Divorced
Employed Males, 15 years and over	69,323	19,329	43,398	551	6,045	100.0	27.9	62.6	0.8	8.7
Executive, administrative, and managerial occupations	10,007	1,557	7,586	104	759	100.0	15.6	75.8	1.0	7.6
Professional specialty occupations	9,278	2,114	6,443	42	680	100.0	22.8	69.4	0.5	7.3
Technical, sales, and administrative support occupations	13,736	4,595	7,973	102	1,066	100.0	33.5	58.0	0.7	7.8
Service occupations	7,350	3,231	3,416	49	654	100.0	44.0	46.5	0.7	8.9
Farming, forestry, and fishing occupations	2,400	679	1,484	26	210	100.0	28.3	61.8	1.1	8.8
Precision production, craft, and repair occupations	13,150	2,698	9,000	99	1,353	100.0	20.5	68.4	0.8	10.3
Operators, fabricators, and laborers	13,402	4,452	7,496	129	1,324	100.0	33.2	55.9	1.0	9.9
Employed Females, 15 years and over	61,089	15,827	35,504	2,071	7,687	100.0	25.9	58.1	3.4	12.6
Executive, administrative, and managerial occupations	8,429	1,499	5,399	269	1,261	100.0	17.8	64.1	3.2	15.0
Professional specialty occupations	10,716	2,368	6,914	253	1,181	100.0	22.1	64.5	2.4	11.0
Technical, sales, and administrative support occupations	24,988	6,837	14,324	828	2,999	100.0	27.4	57.3	3.3	12.0
Service occupations	10,800	3,704	5,254	493	1,349	100.0	34.3	48.6	4.6	12.5
Farming, forestry, and fishing occupations	588	103	414	27	44	100.0	17.5	70.4	4.6	7.5
Precision production, craft, and repair occupations	1,146	209	731	30	177	100.0	18.2	63.8	2.6	15.4
Operators, fabricators, and laborers	4,423	1,105	2,470	171	671	100.0	25.0	55.8	3.9	15.2

Source: U.S. Census Bureau, March Current Population Survey, 1998.

are seasonally adjusted, because labor force statistics show substantial seasonal fluctuations.

In addition to the basic labor force statistics, the Census Bureau also reports labor force statistics that are cross-tabulated with a variety of demographic, social, and economic characteristics. Table 10.7, for example, shows how a key labor force characteristic (occupational category) can be used to study differentials in a demographic variable (marital status) among males and females.

Statistics from Establishments

The U.S. government compiles two major series of employment data from establishments. The Current Employment Statistics program, a joint venture of the U.S. Bureau of Labor Statistics and state employment agencies, collects monthly employment, earnings, and payroll data from 400,000 establishments. The resulting data yield state and national monthly totals on employment of nonfarm wage and salary workers.[10]

The other major series on employment comes from the Old Age and Survivors Insurance (OASI) records of the Social Security Administration (SSA). Each employer covered by Social Security provides quarterly information about each employee for the purpose of crediting the employee's pension fund. These records provide annual statistics at the national, state, and county level on the number of employees covered by the OASI. In addition, the SSA maintains a Continuous Work History Sample of 1% of covered workers. Through this data source, it is possible for analysts to study such issues as labor mobility (across estab-

[10] More information on the Current Employment Statistics program is available from the following website: www.bls.gov/ces.

lishments, industries, and geographic areas) and estimated earnings over time.

Several other specialized series on employment are compiled. For example, the censuses of manufacturing, mining, and construction ask the respective establishments for information on their employees. In addition, the U.S. Department of Agriculture collects data on farm labor. Probably the best known of the supplementary series is that of the unemployment insurance system. On a weekly basis, each state reports the number of persons receiving unemployment insurance to the U.S. federal government. This arrangement provides regular information on the volume of unemployment for counties, states, and the nation.

Establishment survey data typically differ from household survey data in several ways. First, household surveys cover all persons aged 15 and over in the United States, while establishment surveys cover only a portion of that population. For example, the BLS's Current Employment Series program excludes the self-employed, unpaid family workers, and farmers; it also lacks good coverage for persons employed in very small enterprises. Second, household data on unemployment cover any persons who were looking and available for work; the unemployment insurance series, by contrast, covers only persons who qualify for benefits under the laws of their state.

Other differences concern the availability of demographic and geographic information. In household surveys, for example, data are typically available for a variety of demographic and socioeconomic characteristics not generally available from establishment sources—age, sex, occupation, education, and so on. On the other hand, the establishment reports contain intercensal data for small geographic areas while subnational data from the household surveys are limited in geographic detail. Certain types of information—such as industry of employment, hours worked, and earnings—may be obtained more accurately from the establishment reports than from the household reports. Despite the differences, however, the two sources of statistics supplement each other enough so that the best analysis of employment trends can be made by the judicious use of data from both sources. Even so, the data obtained from the population censuses and the Current Population Survey are generally sufficient for most analytic needs, such as their use as benchmarks for labor force projections.

Measures

Economic Activity Ratios, Dependency Ratios, and Replacement Ratios

Many economic measures relate to the economically active population, the labor force, or gainful workers,

depending on the type of data available; however, we will refer to them generally as activity ratios. As with other demographic characteristics, crude, general, age-specific, and age-standardized ratios of economic activity may be computed. It is customary to show most ratios separately for males and females.

The *crude economic activity ratio* (conventionally called a "rate") represents the number of economically active persons as a percentage of the total population. It is also referred to as the *crude labor force participation ratio* ("rate") in countries where the labor force concept is applicable. For example, the crude economic activity ratio for Sweden in 2000 is computed as follows:

$$\frac{\text{Economically active population}}{\text{Total population}} \times 100 = \frac{4,815,000}{8,898,000} \times 100 = 54.1$$

Like all crude ratios, the age composition of the population greatly influences the crude activity age. This measure is useful primarily in comparisons where the analyst wishes to indicate simply the relative number of persons in a population who are working, regardless of any other factors involved. Examining changes in the crude economic activity ratio over time allows analysts to highlight the effect of different levels of natural increase and migration on economic activity.

Unlike the crude activity ratio, the *general economic activity ratio* is restricted to persons of working age. More refined than the crude ratio, this measure "controls" for the age structure of the population. We can calculate the general economic activity ratio for persons aged 15 years and over in Sweden in 2000 as follows:

$$\frac{\text{Population economically active } 15+}{\text{Total population } 15+} \times 100 = \frac{4,815,000}{7,201,000} \times 100 = 66.9$$

The minimum age for inclusion varies from country to country. For example, tabulations on economic activity have been shown for persons aged 12 and over in Uruguay and persons aged 7 and over in Bolivia (United Nations, 1996). Because of this fact, analysts making cross-national comparisons should consider the possibility that in many countries, a large number of economically active children might be arbitrarily excluded from the enumerated labor force because the minimal age may have been placed too high. Conversely, including an age group for whom the activity ratio is very low—the activity ratio for persons aged 7 and 8 in Bolivia was just 3.5% in 1990 (United Nations, 1996)—means a large number of economically inactive children will be included in the denominator, which may distort the rate.

Both the crude and general activity ratios are usually calculated separately for males and females. When calculated in this fashion, they are termed *sex-specific activity ratios*. Sex-specific activity ratios are calculated for two different reasons. First, the level of such ratios is usually much higher for men than for women, although that usually is less so in more developed countries. Second, variations in definitions and operational procedures that most often affect measures of economic activity have their greatest impact on figures for women because women's attachment to the labor force is more likely to be marginal and intermittent. Labor force participation ratios for women vary much more than for men over time and across countries. Ratios for men are less subject to temporary or spurious variations than ratios for women, and international comparison of ratios for men are considered more valid by many analysts. However, the female labor force is quite often the most dynamic part of the labor force, as has been the case in the United States since the 1960s; therefore, researchers who restrict their analyses to the male labor force may be ignoring very important current and historical trends.

The same warning should be given to analysts who conduct international and historical comparisons and restrict themselves to figures on activities of men in the prime working ages—20 to 59 years, for example. Just as with women, differences in definition and operating procedures (in the case of unpaid family workers or part-time workers, for example) often produce irregular or spurious variations in activity ratios for the very young and the old. Although analysts can make more valid comparisons by restricting their comparisons to the prime working ages, they may be ignoring age groups that have experienced the major changes in economic activity.

For the reasons mentioned earlier, analysts usually compare activity ratios for specific age-sex groups. In fact, *age-sex-specific activity ratios* (called labor force participation ratios when the labor force concept is used) are frequently the basic ratios that are studied in analyses of the economically active population. See for example, Figure 10.2.

An age-sex specific activity ratio is calculated using the following formula:

$$\frac{P^e_{as}}{P^t_{as}} \times 100 \qquad (10.13)$$

where P^e_{as} = Economically active population in age-sex group *as*

P^t_{as} = Total population in age-sex group *as*

For women 25 to 29 years of age in Canada in 1991, the ratio is calculated as follows:

$$\frac{P^e_{25-29f}}{P^t_{25-29f}} = \frac{884,825}{1,172,095} \times 100 = 0.755 \times 100 = 75.5$$

In addition to age and sex, one may calculate activity ratios for population groups defined by various other characteristics, for example, educational attainment, marital status, ethnicity, and economic level. The degree to which the activity ratios are made specific for such social and economic characteristics depends on two factors: the problems being studied and the availability of adequate data.

An *age-sex adjusted* or *standardized, activity ratio* is the ratio that would result for the "general" (i.e., adult) population if the age-sex specific ratios for a given date or geographic area were weighted by a standard age-sex population distribution (see Chapter 12). Often the standard used is the national age-sex distribution for some specified date.

A common practice in demographic analysis is to calculate an *age-dependency ratio* from statistics on the age distribution of the population without regard to actual participation in economic activities. For example, the commonly used age-dependency ratio (defined in Chapter 7),

$$\frac{P^t_{<15} + P^t_{65+}}{P^t_{15-64}} \times 100 \qquad (10.14)$$

considers all persons between ages 15 and 64 as producers and all persons under age 15 and over age 64 as dependents. This ratio is equivalent to the complement of the proportion of the total population 15 to 64 years old, a simple measure of age structure, but the term "dependency ratio" adds an aura of economic significance. This ratio is merely a measure of the role of age distribution in economic dependency.

The ratio of the economically inactive population to the economically active population is much more meaningful as a measure of economic dependency because it reflects not only the area's age-sex structure but also the economic activity participation ratios. Depending on which of these measures one uses, the results can turn out to be quite different, as data from Sweden's 1990 census show. In the age-dependency ratio, the combined number of persons under age 15 and persons aged 65 and over (3,070,565) is divided by the number of persons aged 15 to 64 (5,516,788), producing a ratio of 55.7 "age dependents" per 100 persons of working age. In the economic dependency ratio, by contrast, an economically inactive population (4,095,860), divided by the economically active population (4,491,493), yields the *economic dependency ratio* of 91.2 inactive persons per 100 active persons—more than one and one-half times larger than the age-dependency ratio.

The data in Table 10.8, which presents economic dependency ratios for selected countries, show how widely this measure can vary across countries. Several countries have economic dependency ratios of less than 100—meaning there are more economically active people than noneconomically active people. Jordan, on the other hand, has an economic dependency ratio over 200. Even within the same economic/geographic class (for example, "developed economies"), nations often show enormous variation in this measure.

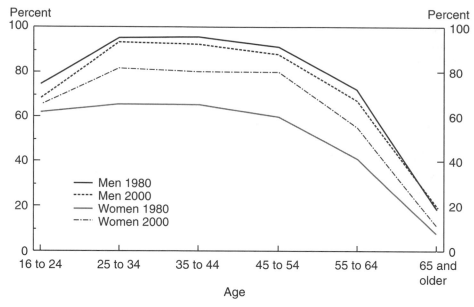

FIGURE 10.2   Labor force participation ratios for men and women. United States, 1980 and 2000
Source: U.S. Bureau of Labor Statistics, Monthly Age Labor Review Nov. 2001, 26. Primary source is the
Current Population Survey.

TABLE 10.8   Economic Dependency Ratios: Selected Countries, 2000

Country and region	Economically inactive population (1)	Economically active population (2)	Economic dependency ratio [(1)/(2)]*100 = (3)
DEVELOPED ECONOMIES			
France	22,335,514	17,574,760	127.1
Spain	32,401,260	26,836,408	120.7
Japan	58,727,298	68,369,016	85.9
TRANSITION ECONOMIES			
Hungary	5,198,509	4,769,046	109.0
Russian Federation	67,450,158	78,041,008	86.4
Ukraine	24,294,341	25,273,826	96.1
ASIA AND THE PACIFIC			
China	512,190,491	762,942,375	67.1
Indonesia	109,530,678	102,561,346	106.8
Nepal	12,172,293	10,870,411	112.0
LATIN AMERICA AND THE CARIBBEAN			
Argentina	22,035,369	14,996,445	146.9
Brazil	91,159,608	79,246,672	115.0
Jamaica	1,292,356	1,283,729	100.7
SUB-SAHARAN AFRICA			
Ethiopia	35,127,261	27,780,527	126.4
South Africa	25,280,845	18,028,352	140.2
Tanzania	17,030,890	18,088,365	94.2
MIDDLE EAST AND NORTH AFRICA			
Egypt	42,094,707	25,789,769	163.2
Jordan	3,346,903	1,566,212	213.7
Morocco	18,098,596	11,779,807	153.6

Source: International Labour Organisation, 2002.

Replacement ratios and rates for working ages indicate the potential population replacement during a specified future period, assuming the selected level of survival and the absence of any net migration. The *replacement ratio* is the number of expected entrants into a specified working age group during a period per 100 expected departures resulting from death or retirement for that same period. The *replacement rate* is the difference between the number of entrants and the number of departures in a given period, expressed as a percentage of the number of persons in the specified working ages at the beginning of the period.

The U.S. Department of Agriculture (USDA) has calculated such ratios for rural (or rural-farm) males for intercensal decades, with the following specifications.[11] The expected entrants are males 10 to 19 years old at the beginning of the decade who would be expected to survive to ages 20 to 29 at the end of the decade; the departures are the persons of working age who either reach age 65 or die during the decade. The USDA also has computed refined national-level measures based on actual ages of labor force entries and departures during the intercensal period, and of labor force participants disaggregated by age and sex as shown at the preceding census.

The basic method is illustrated by applying it to the 1991 census data for males in Canada (Table 10.9). Because labor force participation is shown for persons aged 15 and over, age 15 is used to begin the working ages. Moreover, because participation ratios drop dramatically after age 65 (to 15% for persons aged 65 to 69 and 8% for persons aged 70 and over), in the example, everyone is arbitrarily assumed to leave the labor force by age 65. Survival rates are computed from Canada's 1992 life table, as shown in the UN *Demographic Yearbook* for 1996.

The crude, general, age-specific, and standardized ratios of economic activity mentioned earlier have parallel measures for employment. Inasmuch as the former have been described in full, only a brief description of these employment-based measures is given. For example, the *employment ratio* is the number of employed persons as a percentage of the number of economically active persons or of the civilian labor force. Similarly, the *unemployment ratio* is the number of unemployed persons as a percentage of the number economically active persons or of the civilian labor force. Note that the employment ratio plus the unemployment ratio must equal 100% for any specified population.

The *proportion fully employed*, a measure of employment that is not widely used, is the total number of persons fully employed (i.e., the total number of employed persons minus

[11] See, for example, U.S. Department of Agriculture, Economic Research Service, 1966 *Statistical Bulletin* No. 378, "Potential Supply and Replacement of Rural Males of Labor Force Age: 1960–70," by G. K. Bowles, C. L. Beale, and B. S. Bradshaw (October).

TABLE 10.9 Procedures for Computing Replacement Ratios and Rates: Canada, males, 1991–1996

Age in 1991 (years)	Males, 1991 (1)	Survival, mortality, or retirement rate (2)	Estimated survivors, deaths, or retirements, 1996 (1) × (2) = (3)
(a). 10–14	962,920	0.99865[a]	961,617[a]
(b). 15–19	958,405	0.00439	4,204
(c). 20–24	985,225	0.00563	5,551
(d). 25–29	1,182,575	0.00576	6,810
(e). 30–34	1,237,685	0.00657	8,135
(f). 35–39	1,133,670	0.00816	9,246
(g). 40–44	1,042,185	0.01066	11,112
(h). 45–49	824,200	0.01686	13,892
(i). 50–54	663,285	0.02754	18,266
(j). 55–59	608,080	0.04612	28,047
(k). 60–64	571,945	1.00000[b]	571,945[b]

[a] Survival rates or survivors.
[b] Combined mortality and retirement rates or deaths and retirements.

1. Entrants (row a, 1996) = 961,617
2. Deaths and retirements (sum of rows b through k, 1996) = 677,209
3. Net available population, 1996 = 284,408 (= 961,617–677,209)
4. Males aged 15 to 64, 1991 (sum of rows b through k, 1991) = 9,207,255
5. Replacement Ratio (entrants/deaths & retirements × 100) = 142.0
6. Replacement Rate (net available population/total males 15–64 in 1991 × 100) = 3.1

Source: Original data from United Nations, *Demographic Yearbook*, 1993, table 26; and *Demographic Yearbook*, 1996, table 34.

the number of underemployed ones) as a percentage of the total (or civilian) labor force. A more commonly used measure, the *proportion underemployed* is the number of persons underemployed as a percentage of the labor force. Both of these measures also can be expressed as a percentage of the total number employed.

Tables of Working Life

Tables of working life (also referred to as "labor force life tables" or "tables of economically active life") are extensions of conventional life tables. They incorporate mortality rates and labor force participation ratios. They also describe the variation by age in the probability of entering or leaving the labor force, the average number of years of working life remaining, and related functions. Chapter 13 describes methods for constructing different types of life tables, including those of working life. Such tables facilitate the study of the labor force, including probable changes in its size and age-sex composition. They help in estimating expected lifetime earnings, in evaluating the probable effects of investment on education and training programs, and in measuring the economic effects of changes in either the age structure of the population or activity ratios.

As mentioned, a measure that can be derived directly from a table of working life is the expectation of active working life at birth or at any age. One may use working life tables to measure the aggregate number of entries into, as well as exits from, the labor force. Working life tables also measure the ages at which such events are likely to occur (Gendell, 1998; Gendell and Siegel, 1992). The expected active life at birth can be subtracted from life expectancy at birth to give a measure of the expectation of inactive life.

Factors in Analysis

In measuring economic activity and employment, the nature of the problem being studied determines the demographic factors to be included. For almost any analysis, employment and unemployment data should be tabulated and examined in age-sex detail. For specific problems, other population characteristics may be added.

For example, if the central problem is that of migration of the labor force and the reasons behind the phenomenon, it would be necessary to consider labor force status and employment status separately for migrants and nonmigrants. If the emphasis is on women in the labor force, then the analysis could consider their marital status, the number and age of their children, the employment status and earnings of the husband, and such other population characteristics as may seem relevant. If one were studying the relationship of education to employment status and type of job, many of the characteristics already noted, plus school attendance and educational attainment, would be relevant.

In countries containing both people living in a subsistence economy and those living in a market economy, it is important to distinguish the two sectors in the tabulations. This distinction may be approximated in terms of different ethnic groups, regions, urban-rural residence, or the major city compared with the balance of the country. In summary, many characteristics about which information is obtained in a census or sample household survey are useful in any analysis of economic activity. The primary problem toward which the study is directed will dictate the specific demographic and economic measures to be considered.

Projections of Economic Activity and Employment

Projections of economic activity (labor force) and employment provide a very useful planning tool for business leaders and government officials. Projections allow employers to gauge the future supply of and demand for labor in their industry. This in turn allows them to make informed decisions for their enterprises. Government officials also can use projections of labor force and employment in making decisions. For example, if "demand" projections of the occupational distribution of the labor force show a large expected increase in the need for technology-based jobs in a country, educational administrators can tailor their curriculum toward courses and programs that will prepare young people to take these jobs. Labor force projections also help businesses and government to prepare for changes in the composition of the workforce—for example, the changes in age, race, and education anticipated for the United States population in the first quarter of the 21st century.

Many international, national, and even some subnational agencies prepare labor force and employment projections. The International Labor Organisation (ILO) periodically releases world, regional, and national projections of the economically active population. In the United States, the U.S. Bureau of Labor Statistics (BLS) is the main source for such projections, preparing them every other year for the nation as a whole. BLS's program also encompasses biennial projections of employment with detail for industries and occupations. Using data from the BLS national projections, each state then produces its own occupational projections.

In the customary "prevalence ratio" method of projecting the labor force, analysts need to project ratios of economic activity (or labor force participation) as well as the size of the population. Specifically, projected age-sex–specific ratios of labor force participation are applied to the corresponding figures on the age-sex distribution of the population. Analysts preparing projections for ethnically diverse societies may wish to carry out the calculations for appropriate race and ethnicity groups. The scope of the projections is limited by the availability, detail, and quality of current estimates as well as the feasibility of projecting these elements. (For more information about projections of the labor force and employment, see Chapter 21.)

Uses and Limitations

Census and survey statistics on the economically active population are especially useful in those countries that do not have a highly developed system of economic statistics from establishment sources. Planning for economic development is an important use of such statistics, but it is only one of many uses. Labor force statistics provide much of the description of a nation's or a region's human resources. Statistics on occupational characteristics, particularly when cross-tabulated with educational attainment, provide an inventory of skills available among the people of a country. The UN *Handbook on Social Indicators* (United Nations, 1989) describes these and other uses at various levels of economic development.

There are key definitional and methodological limitations analysts must consider when examining statistics on the economically active population. First, data on economic characteristics based on population censuses may not be comparable with data from household sample surveys because of differences in concepts, definitions, field procedures, and processing procedures such as editing rules. For example, data from the U.S. decennial census differ slightly from Current Population Survey data for reasons such as relative training of the interviewers, differences in the reference period, and sampling variability. In addition, such data from consecutive censuses, or even time series data from the same household survey, may not be comparable. Statistics from different sources or the same source but different years may be affected by differences in definitions, question wording, coverage, time reference, and reporting errors. Various reports from the U.S. Census Bureau (for example, the P60 series of *Current Population* Reports) and the U.S. Bureau of Labor Statistics (such as its monthly journal *Employment and Earnings*) contain considerable information about the strengths and limitations of the labor force data.

The differences among countries in the definition of the economically active population may also adversely affect international comparisons on this subject. Countries vary in their treatment of categories such as inmates of institutions, members of the armed forces, persons living in special areas such as reservations, persons seeking work for the first time, persons engaged in part-time work, seasonal workers, and family workers. In some countries, all or parts of these groups are included among the inactive population, while other countries treat persons in the same categories as part of the economically active population. Even in the same country, the treatment of these categories may have changed between censuses or may differ between a census and a household sample survey, as alluded to earlier.

Generally, there are three major sources of noncomparability of census or survey data of which the analyst should be aware. They concern variations in (1) the length of the time period to which the questions on economic activity refer, (2) the definition and inclusion of unpaid family workers, and (3) the lower age limit of persons covered by economic activity questions.

Variations in Length of Time Period

Some questions on economic activity refer to the employment situation of the person on the day of the census or survey or during a brief period such as a specific week. In other cases, the question may refer to a longer period such as a month or year, whereas in still other cases (i.e., under the gainful worker concept), the questions refer to the usual activity of the person without reference to any specific time period. Such a variation in the time period affects the size of the economically active population, because more people would be considered as economically active under longer reference periods. The longer the reference period, the more likely someone will have been economically active at some point during the period. The length of a reference period also can affect the characteristics of the economically active population because a longer reference period is more likely to include marginal members

of the workforce (for example, seasonal workers, older persons, and full-time students). Such marginal members of the workforce are likely to have different demographic and socioeconomic characteristics from those of the "core" of the workforce, who would be included in a very short reference period.

Variation in Definition and Inclusion of Unpaid Family Workers

Another issue affecting comparability concerns variation in the classification of persons who are engaged in both economic activities and "noneconomic" activities (the latter including housekeeping or attending school). Perhaps the most important variation of this sort is the treatment of unpaid family workers—that is, persons who work without pay in economic enterprises operated by other members of their households. The United Nations (1998) has recommended that unpaid family workers who contribute to an enterprise be included in the employed population on the same basis as self-employed workers.

The question of receipt of money wages is a particularly important factor affecting the classification of persons as economically active. In industrialized countries and in the large cities of most other countries, the large majority of the workers receive money, usually wages and salaries. However, in many parts of the world, particularly in the less developed countries, people engage in activities for their own family's consumption—such as subsistence agriculture, home improvement, milking animals, and processing food—and do not work for money wages. Furthermore, because so many unpaid family workers (regardless of the type of economy) are women, statistics on female labor force participation are incomplete and often inaccurate (Anker, 1990). Variations in attitudes toward women and work complicate the issue even more.

Variation in Age Group Covered by Statistics on Economic Activity

Countries differ in the age range of the population for which the questions on economic activity are to be asked. In almost every case, the variant is the lower age limit. For example, in the United States, Canada, and Chile, questions of labor force participation are asked for persons 15 years of age and over (although in the United States tabulations are often presented for persons 16 years of age and over), while in other countries, for example, Colombia, Costa Rica, Mexico, and Portugal, persons 12 years of age are asked about their economic activity. In other countries such as Brazil, Indonesia, Namibia, and Pakistan, persons 10 years of age and over are asked about their economic activity, and in India the question is asked of persons 5 years of age and over (International Labour Office, 1990).

In order to permit international comparisons of data on the economically active population, the United Nations recommends that "tabulations of economic characteristics should at least distinguish persons under 15 years of age and those 15 years of age and over, and countries where the minimum school-leaving age is higher than 15 years and where there are economically active children below this age should endeavor to secure data on the economic characteristics of these children with a view to achieving international comparability at least for persons 15 years of age and over" (United Nations, 1998, p. 79). In the United States, the minimum age for tabulation of decennial census data was switched from 14 years to 16 years in the 1970s, even though supplementary labor force statistics were published for 14- and 15-year-olds for several years afterward.

Statistics on the workforce are subject to additional errors from various causes. Methods for measuring these types of errors (described earlier in this book), such as comparisons of aggregate statistics, matching studies, and re-interview studies, are applicable to a population's economic characteristics. Despite their limitations and their errors of measurement, labor force statistics have proven to be highly useful. Even in less developed countries, errors in responses seem to be less of a problem than conceptual difficulties.

Income, Wealth, and Poverty

Statistics on income, wealth, and poverty reflect the distribution of resources within a population or society. Although individual and family income have long been recognized as having important relationships to many of the demographic events and processes (such as mortality, fertility, migration, and marriage), income as an item was only introduced onto the U.S. population census schedules in 1940. Income data are much more widely collected in periodic and regular household surveys. Wealth and poverty are even more recent concepts. Measures of wealth have become useful because they often provide a more comprehensive picture of economic well-being than income measures do. As for poverty, few statistics were available before the 1960s, and data for international comparisons did not become available until the 1980s and 1990s.

Concepts and Definitions

Income is often meant to reflect the amount of resources received by individuals in a society. With regard to collecting data on it in censuses and surveys, the United Nations states, "income may be defined in terms of (a) monthly income in cash and/or in kind from work performed by each active person, or (b) the total annual income in cash and/or in kind of households regardless of source" (United Nations, 1998, p. 88).

What actually does constitute income depends on the individual society, however. In the United States, for

example, income includes salaries, wages, net earnings and profits from one's own business enterprise, and money earned from investments. Periodic payments received regularly from an inheritance or trust fund are also regarded as income, as are the following: alimony, pensions, annuities, cash benefits (such as Social Security benefits, family allowances, and unemployment benefits), sick pay, scholarships, and various other periodic receipts. On the other hand, the following items are usually not regarded as income: receipts from the sale of possessions, loan repayments, windfall gains, lump-sum inheritances, tax refunds, benefits on insurance policies, lump-sum compensation for injury and other legal damages received, and related items. This is the case even though the proceeds from these sources are sometimes spent on consumer goods and services.

Despite the lack of a universal standard regarding income data, there are some common principles that demographers should be cognizant of when dealing with this subject. First, the reference period for income data could be an hour, a day, a week, a month, or a year. Each choice has costs and benefits. Hourly wages provide evidence of returns to labor that may be masked by asking only about yearly income, but yearly income can overcome issues associated with seasonal work and provide a more realistic picture of well-being.

Second, to the extent that income is meant to reflect resources, cash, in-kind income, and noncash benefits should all be counted. However, in most contexts, only cash income is included for practical reasons. The decision on whether or not to include in-kind assistance or noncash benefits as money income can have important implications for certain types of analysis. For example, most government means-tested assistance in the United States is provided as in-kind or noncash benefits, such as food stamps or medical coverage; therefore income measures that do not include noncash benefits can overstate the level of poverty. Because the prevalence of noncash benefits varies between countries, one should make cross-national comparisons with caution (Blackburn, 1997).

There are three principal types of noncash benefits: those provided by the government, those provided by an employer (such as health insurance and child care subsidies), and those obtained through "goods in exchange" (such as growing crops for one's personal consumption or obtaining goods through barter). In subsistence economies, of course, practically all income is in-kind income. Procedures for collecting information about income in these circumstances are necessarily very different from those used in cash economies. In actual practice, censuses and surveys of many industrialized countries ignore noncash income, because it is a small part of total income and very difficult to measure.

A third important decision regarding income measures is whether to report pretax income or after-tax income. After-tax income is a better measure of disposable income (the actual resources available to a family to purchase necessities), but data on pretax income are much more readily available. Because tax rates differ widely among countries, one must be very careful in making cross-national comparisons based on pretax income.

It also is important to recognize the difference between earnings and income. Earnings represent money received in return for labor, but many types of income, such as interest from investments or government benefits, do not reflect a return on work. Most of the income received by the elderly, for example, is not earned income.

Finally, the unit used to gather and report income is important. One can look at income of individuals, families, or households. According to U.S. Census Bureau definitions, there is more than one person in a family and sometimes more than two generations in a household. Ideally, income data can be collected for each person in the household and then added to produce totals and subtotals for units such as households, families, and married couples. A less satisfactory approach would be to obtain family or household income by asking directly for the total income received by all family (or household) members combined. Income questions are rarely asked of children below working age, and adults living in certain types of group quarters, such as institutions, are often excluded as well.

For international comparisons, statistics on the incomes of persons are most useful for males of working age and, to a lesser extent, for females of working age. The socioeconomic status of a dependent child or spouse is reflected better by household and family income than by individual income. Where the household contains one or more persons unrelated to the head of the household, income statistics for the family are generally considered to be more useful than those for the entire household. However, this depends on customs and norms of the country involved; in large complex households it is often unclear how individual members of the household share income.

Wealth, typically measured as assets minus liabilities, represents the resources available to a person or family. These resources can be invested to increase a person's or family's economic well-being, for example, to purchase a house or to send a child to college. They can also be drawn on in times of need, for example, when family members experience unemployment or prolonged illness. While there is often a close association between income and wealth, the two concepts are very different. Wealth (or assets) is a more comprehensive measure of economic well-being because it includes resources not necessarily linked to current income. For example, wealth may include inheritance, savings, and appreciation of past investments that are unrelated to current income. In addition, wealth can reflect how much income has been saved rather than spent over time.

Poverty status signals a lack of resources and a state of destitution that is usually associated with material hard-ship. Poverty is often determined by comparing resources (usually income) with needs (often determined by family size and composition), but it is sometimes determined as a threshold relative to the income distribution in a society. For example, families who earn less than half the median income in a population are usually considered to be poor (Ruggles, 1990).

Poverty is usually based on money income. The official U.S. poverty threshold, established in the mid-1960s, compares the income of a family with a set of preestablished thresholds based on family size and composition. The official definition of poverty in the United States is derived by comparing the income for an individual or family to an assessment of needs based on family size and composition. For example, the poverty income threshold in 2000 for a family of one adult under age 65 and two related children under age 18 was $13,874, while the threshold for a family of nine or more people including eight or more children was $33,291 (U.S. Census Bureau, 2001c). Some researchers have argued that families or individuals may use savings or borrow money to make purchases beyond their yearly income and that consumption is a better gauge of poverty.

Sources of Data

Censuses and household surveys are the primary sources of income, wealth, and poverty data. However, data on income may also be available from establishment records (e.g., payrolls), income tax returns, and Social Security records. For example, the Statistics on Income (SOI) series from the U.S. Department of Treasury provides income data that are based on tax returns.

Statistics from administrative records are of limited value to demographers, however, because few demographic and social characteristics are recorded in these sources, the entire population is not covered, and administrative records data do not cover all income sources. For example, there is generally a cutoff point for income below which a tax return does not have to be filed. Moreover, Social Security records in the United States omit income above a legally specified amount and do not cover workers in certain industries or types of establishments. Establishment payrolls are of value mainly as a source of information about hourly, weekly, or monthly earnings, and these data are generally available only in the form of averages. Income data from administrative records may be particularly useful for evaluating the quality of the data collected in household interviews.

Income data used for international comparisons are often collected through sample surveys and censuses. However, the United Nations (1998) has recognized the difficulty of collecting good income data in a census, especially data on in-kind benefits and income from self-employment and investments, and recommends that sample surveys be considered for collecting this type of information. The data archives maintained by the Luxembourg Income Study (LIS) are derived from a set of such surveys. In 1980, the World Bank established the Living Standards Measurement Study, collecting detailed income and expenditure data in order "to explore ways of improving the type and quality of household data collected by government statistical offices in developing countries" and "to develop new methods for monitoring progress in raising levels of living, to identify the consequences for households of current and proposed government policies, and to improve communications between survey statisticians, analysts, and policymakers" (Grosh and Glewwe, 1995, 1). Currently more than 40 surveys have been completed, with additional surveys in various stages of implementation.

The 1940 U.S. census was the first U.S. census to contain a question on wage or salary income along with a question on whether the person had received $50 or more from other sources in the preceding calendar year. Income from all sources was first collected in the 1950 census.

The 2000 decennial census form includes questions on eight possible sources of income:

1. Wages, salaries, commissions, bonuses or tips from all jobs
2. Self-employment income from own nonfarm businesses or farm businesses
3. Interest, dividends, net rental income, royalty income, or income from estates or trusts
4. Social Security or Railroad Retirement benefits
5. Supplemental Security income
6. Any public assistance or welfare payment from state or local welfare offices
7. Retirement, survivor, or disability pensions
8. Any other sources of income received regularly such as veteran's payments, unemployment compensation, child support, or alimony

In the U.S. census, total income for a person, family, or household is the sum of amounts reported for all of these individual sources, less any losses.

The U.S. Census Bureau's Current Population Survey (CPS) first asked more detailed questions on income in 1945 for the calendar year 1944. The income concepts used in the CPS agree very closely with those used in the contemporary decennial census, although the CPS asks about many more specific sources of income compared to the eight asked about in the decennial census.

Family income and income of persons are associated with a variety of demographic, social, and economic characteristics. Table 10.10 presents the distribution of U.S. men and women according to age and income classes in 1998, as well as the mean and median income for each age-sex combination. The table shows that men have higher average incomes

than women at every age, and that average income increases with age until people reach the later working ages (with a peak at ages 45 to 54). Figure 10.3, also for the United States, shows how additional education enhances annual income.

In general, data on wealth are scarce, mainly because acquiring this information requires a large series of relatively complex questions. To obtain accurate information about assets and debts requires a set of questions about many possible sources of wealth. The accuracy of responses on these types of questions is problematic because of the sensitive nature of this type of data, as well as the lack of knowledge or faulty recall on the part of respondents. For example, estimating the equity in a home owned by the respondent requires that a person know (or estimate) the value of the property if it were to be sold and subtract the amount still owed on the property.

The Survey of Income and Program Participation (SIPP) has provided estimates of wealth for American families for the past 20 years. Reports can be found in the Census Bureau's P70 series of *Current Population Reports* ("Household Economic Studies"). In addition, the Consumer Finance Survey has provided some estimates of wealth. Private-sector vendors (e.g., Claritas) have provided some estimates of wealth for the United States based on statistical models.

Poverty data typically come from surveys that collect data on income, although they sometimes come from model-based estimates (i.e., estimates based on demographic or statistical analysis) and surveys on expenditures. In the United States, major sources of poverty statistics are the decennial census, the CPS, and the SIPP. All three collect data that can be used for estimating poverty, but many other surveys collect the information needed to construct measures of poverty. For example, both the National Survey of America's Families and the Panel Study of Income Dynamics gather data to determine poverty status according to the official government definition.

Measures

Measures of income, wealth, and poverty depend on how the data have been collected and their availability to researchers. Researchers who have access to exact dollar amounts from each respondent can easily construct many measures. Because of the sensitive nature of income data, however, such statistics often are gathered and reported in terms of a set of income categories or ranges. Under this method, respondents are allowed to select an income range rather than provide an exact amount. Generally, people are more willing to provide information of this type than give their exact income. Moreover, respondents can usually estimate the range of their income accurately, even if they do not know the exact amount.

TABLE 10.10 Income of Males and Females by Age: United States, 1998
(Numbers in thousands)

Sex and age (years)	Persons 15 years and over	With income									Median income ($)	Mean income ($)
		Total	$1 to $4,999 or loss	$5,000 to $9,999	$10,000 to $14,999	$15,000 to $24,999	$25,000 to $34,999	$35,000 to $49,999	$50,000 to $74,999	$75,000 and over		
MALES												
Total	102,048	94,948	8,360	9,142	9,548	17,620	14,718	15,234	11,763	8,562	26,492	36,315
15 to 24	19,131	14,079	5,019	2,778	2,057	2,557	971	477	160	61	8,190	12,343
25 to 34	18,923	18,330	893	1,104	1,639	4,117	3,955	3,604	2,085	931	28,117	33,334
35 to 44	22,156	21,539	786	1,232	1,245	3,482	3,944	4,600	3,668	2,582	35,177	44,191
45 to 54	17,144	16,821	608	938	995	2,196	2,648	3,424	3,341	2,671	38,922	49,910
55 to 64	10,967	10,678	556	908	913	1,705	1,510	1,826	1,678	1,583	32,776	46,257
65 and over	13,727	13,501	499	2,182	2,699	3,562	1,690	1,303	831	734	18,166	27,997
65 to 74	8,027	7,902	292	1,125	1,464	1,984	1,070	892	558	518	19,734	30,441
75 and over	5,700	5,599	207	1,058	1,235	1,578	620	412	273	216	16,479	24,547
FEMALES												
Total	109,628	98,694	18,146	18,463	14,113	19,018	12,504	9,149	5,094	2,208	20,462
15 to 24	18,791	13,875	5,761	3,100	1,944	2,106	686	203	49	27	6,534	9,271
25 to 34	19,551	17,773	2,860	2,174	2,384	4,135	3,137	1,976	844	263	18,257	21,537
35 to 44	22,588	20,970	3,271	2,457	2,594	4,197	3,378	2,884	1,517	671	20,285	25,518
45 to 54	18,088	16,915	2,138	2,016	1,948	3,383	2,834	2,319	1,622	653	21,588	27,081
55 to 64	11,943	10,968	2,089	2,114	1,367	2,026	1,331	1,068	617	355	14,675	21,369
65 and over	18,667	18,193	2,027	6,602	3,876	3,171	1,137	699	444	239	10,504	15,419
65 to 74	9,816	9,545	1,177	3,408	1,750	1,712	698	411	257	131	10,453	16,043
75 and over	8,851	8,648	849	3,194	2,126	1,459	440	287	186	107	10,545	14,729

Source: U.S. Census Bureau, "Money Income in the United States: 1998," *Current Population Reports*, P60–206 (September 1999): table 8.

Income data are frequently shown in the form of distributions, permitting analysts to measure the extent of income inequalities. Distributions also can be used to show the extent of poverty, whatever may be taken as the limit below which people are considered to be poor. Presenting data in a frequency distribution, however, complicates calculation of some measures.

Aggregate income is the sum of the income of all persons in a defined population. One can compute aggregate income from the frequency distribution of incomes by multiplying the number of persons in a particular class by the middle income value of the class. Allocation for cases of nonresponse would ordinarily have been done earlier in the process. In computing the aggregate for grouped data, one must make an assumption regarding the average value for the upper open-ended interval. Assigning a value to income responses above a certain level is often referred to as "topcoding." A value may be estimated by fitting a Pareto curve to the cumulative distribution (U.S. Census Bureau, 1967). The curve may also be used to introduce greater refinement in estimating the average for other very wide intervals. For example, for an interval ranging from $15,000 to $24,999, applying a Pareto curve might result in the use of $19,500 as the average value, rather than the middle value of $20,000. Persons with a negative income ("loss") constitute an open-ended interval at the lower end of the distribution, but they are conventionally combined with the lowest positive class, say "under $2000," and the middle value of $1000 is used for the combined classes. This procedure introduces a slight upward bias in the mean value of the distribution, although it does not affect the median.

Calculation of the aggregate income is shown at the bottom of Table 10.11. The result ($5,410,284,500,000) is derived by multiplying the number of persons in each class interval by that category's midpoint, then summing the results for each category. In this example, the midpoint of the highest income category ($75,000 and over) was calculated as 1.5 times the lower bound of the category, following the U.S. Census Bureau convention (U.S. Census Bureau, 1993b).

The *mean income of persons* is calculated by dividing the aggregate income by the total number of income recipients or total number of people. In the case of *mean family income* (or mean household income), aggregate income is divided by the total number of families (or households). In Table 10.11, mean individual income, $28,047, is derived by dividing total aggregate income, $5,410,284,500,000 by the total number of persons aged 15 and over, 192,902,000.

Mean income is also calculated in connection with national accounts statistics. Here the total national income (or that of a state) derived from administrative records such as tax returns may be divided by the total population to obtain per capita income, or by the total employed in order

TABLE 10.11   Distribution by Total Income and Selected Income Measures for Persons Aged 15 and Over: United States, 2000

Individual income (dollars)	Midpoint of interval (m_i)	Persons (in thousands) (f_i)
Total with income	X	192,902
Under $2,000	1,000	13,201
$2,000 to $2,999	2,500	4,170
$3,000 to $3,999	3,500	4,107
$4,000 to $4,999	4,500	4,289
$5,000 to $5,999	5,500	5,790
$6,000 to $6,999	6,500	6,689
$7,000 to $8,499	7,750	8,547
$8,500 to $9,999	9,250	6,579
$10,000 to $12,499	11,250	13,329
$12,500 to $14,999	13,750	10,327
$15,000 to $17,499	16,250	10,821
$17,500 to $19,999	18,750	8,369
$20,000 to $24,999	22,500	17,363
$25,000 to $29,999	27,500	14,683
$30,000 to $34,999	32,500	12,465
$35,000 to $49,999	42,500	24,209
$50,000 to $74,999	62,500	16,973
$75,000 and over	112,500[1]	10,992

Aggregate income ($\Sigma m_i f_i$) = $5,410,284,500,000

Mean income $\dfrac{5,410,284,500,000}{192,902,000}$ = $28,047

Median income = $20,067

Quintiles:

 Lowest fifth: Up to $7,059
 Second fifth: $7,060 to $15,031
 Middle fifth: $15,032 to $25,736
 Fourth fifth: $25,737 to $43,423
 Highest fifth: $43,424 or higher

X Not applicable.

[1] Estimated, using the U.S. Census Bureau's formula for calculating the approximate average value for an open-ended interval (1.5 times the lower interval boundary).

Note: Aggregate, mean, median, and quintile income figures calculated here differ from those in official tables, since narrower income intervals were used in those calculations.

Source for income distribution: U.S. Census Bureau, *Current Population Survey: March 1999 Technical Documentation* (Washington, D.C.: U.S. Government Printing Office, 1999): C-9, table 7.

to obtain average income per worker. Payroll data can also be used to determine mean earnings. For example, one can produce a mean earnings figure by dividing the aggregate income from the total payroll by the total number of employees. In the United States, the establishment payroll data and those obtained from economic censuses are used in this manner.

Median income is defined in a parallel fashion—that is, as the income value that divides income recipients (or families) into two equal parts, one higher and one lower than the median. It is highly unlikely that the median would fall in an open-ended interval; therefore, the problem posed by the mean of assigning an average value for the open-ended interval does not occur here. The median is often preferable to the mean for comparing population groups because extreme values do not affect the former, and it is closer to the point of concentration of the distribution. (For further details on how to calculate the median from grouped data, see Chapter 7). Because income distributions are typically skewed toward higher values, there is often a marked difference between the median income and the mean income for a group. For example, Table 10.11 shows that the *median* income of persons in the United States in 2000 was $20,067, while the *mean* income of persons for this group was $28,047.

When calculating the mean and the median, analysts must decide whether to use all persons or only those with income. Use of all persons provides a better assessment of the well-being of a population, but using only those with income provides a better assessment of the rewards of working.

In addition to the preceding measures of central tendency, measures of dispersion can be used to describe an income distribution. Quintiles (fifths) have come to be used extensively in the description of family and household income distributions, partly because they offer a simple way of describing income disparity. Quintiles provide information for groups on both the lower end and the upper end of the income distribution, as well as on the groups in the middle. In the United States, analysts often focus attention on the lowest and highest fifths and the share of the nation's aggregate income that each group receives. For example, U.S. Census Bureau data show that the top quintile of households received 49.7% of all money income in the United States in 2000, while the bottom quintile received 3.6% (U.S. Census Bureau, 2001b).

The computation of the four values defining the quintiles is similar to that for computing the median. One-fifth, two-fifths, and so on, of the total number of persons are first computed, and then the income values corresponding to these points are determined. Referring to Table 10.11, we note that the total number of persons is 192,902,000. We then proceed as follows:

$$\frac{192,902,000}{5} = 38,580,400$$

to determine the number of persons in the lowest fifth. Adding cumulatively, we determine that 38,246,000 persons have income below $7000. (The next frequency, 8,547,000—in the category $7000 to $8499—would put us over 38,580,400). The excess of persons at the first quintile position over the cumulative frequency is

$$38,580,400 - 38,246,000 = 334,400$$

The number of additional people that we need from the $7000-to-$8499 category to bring the cumulative total to 38,580,400 (in this case, 334,400) is divided by the frequency of the category to determine what proportion of the income category must be added to the lower limit of the category.

$$\frac{334,400}{8,547,000} = .0391$$

The width of the interval containing the upper bound of the first quintile is $1500 ($8500 minus $7000). Hence, we apply this proportion to that value as shown in the equation: $1500 × .0391 = $59. This step assumes that persons are distributed evenly across the entire income category. The upper bound of the first quintile is then computed by adding this value ($59) to the lower bound of the income range ($7000).

$$\$7000 + \$59 = \$7059$$

This is the first quintile's upper bound.

The U.S. Census Bureau has traditionally used quintiles to measure the extent of income inequality. It reports, for example, that the share of the aggregate household income that was received by the households in the top quintile increased from 43.8% in 1967 to 49.7% in 2000. During the same period, the share of aggregate household income received by the bottom quintile fell from 4% in 1967 to 3.6% in 2000 (U.S. Census Bureau, 2001b).

Both the *Lorenz curve* and the related *Gini concentration ratio* were described in Chapter 6 in connection with measuring the concentration of population in localities. They also can be used to measure the concentration of income, and they have received considerable application in this field. The *Gini ratio* (or *Gini index*) is a single statistic that summarizes the dispersion of income across the entire income distribution with a single number (U.S. Census Bureau, 2001b). It is a statistical measure of income inequality ranging from 0 to 1. A measure of 1 indicates perfect inequality—one person has all the income and the rest have none. Conversely, a measure of 0 indicates perfect equality—all people have an equal share of income. The Census Bureau shows that the Gini ratio for all U.S. households increased from .399 in 1967 to .460 in 2000 (U.S. Census Bureau, 2001b). These results are consistent with the findings on the shares of the aggregate income going to the highest and lowest quintiles of income recipients.

When any of the previous income measures are used to study changes over time, allowances should be made for changes in the cost of living. In the United States, for example, the annual income reports of the Census Bureau include time series in constant dollars using the most recent reference year as the base. Table 10.12 shows that the series in current dollars gives an exaggerated impression of the rise in family income since 1975. Current dollars are con-

TABLE 10.12   Median Income of Families in Current Dollars and Constant 1998 Dollars: United States, 1975–1998

Year	Current dollars	Constant 1998 dollars
1998	46,737	46,737
1997	44,568	45,262
1996	42,300	43,945
1995	40,611	43,436
1994	38,782	42,655
1993	36,959	41,691
1992	36,573	42,490
1991	35,939	43,011
1990	35,353	44,090
1989	34,213	44,974
1988	32,191	44,354
1987	30,970	44,438
1986	29,458	43,811
1985	27,735	42,015
1984	26,433	41,469
1983	24,580	40,226
1982	23,433	39,954
1981	22,388	40,502
1980	21,023	41,637
1979	19,587	43,144
1978	17,640	42,597
1977	16,009	41,289
1976	14,958	41,046
1975	13,719	39,790

Source: U.S. Bureau of the Census (online), available at http://www.census.gov/hhes/income/histinc/f07.html (July 10, 2 ••.

verted to constant dollars using the Consumer Prince Index (CPI) developed and maintained by the U.S. Bureau of Labor statistics.[12]

Finally, most cross-national income studies must put figures into a common currency. This requires access to data on international exchange rates.

Measures of Wealth

Data on wealth are relatively scarce because they require a large number of questions on a relatively complex topic. Measures of wealth are usually presented as a distribution of assets accompanied by average values, either collectively for all types of assets or for individual assets. For example, researchers may show what percentage of the population owns an asset of a particular type or what percentage falls into categories defined by a combination of assets.

Table 10.13 shows information on assets collected by the U.S. Census Bureau in the Survey of Income and Program Participation. While equity in a vehicle is the most common

---

[12] For a concise explanation of how current income figures are converted to constant dollars, see U.S. Census Bureau, 1999, "Money Income in the United States: 1998," *Current Population Reports* P60–206 (Washington, DC: U.S. Government Printing Office): Appendix D.

asset (owned by 85.7% of households), equity in a home is by far the biggest single source of wealth among Americans. It accounts for 44.4% of all net worth.

The highly skewed distribution of wealth in the United States is reflected in the tremendous differences between median wealth and mean wealth. The median U.S. household wealth in 1995 was $40,200 while the figure for mean household wealth calculated from the same source was more than twice as high at $102,626 (U.S. Census Bureau, 2001a).

Measures of Poverty

The *poverty ratio* is the most common measure of poverty. The poverty ratio is simply the percentage of a population that has income below a given poverty threshold. Some studies use multiples of the poverty line, such as 200% of poverty, to identify target populations.

Most measures of poverty fall into one of two types: absolute or relative. Absolute measures of poverty typically are based on an unchanging level of income or resources that are updated every year to account for inflation. Relative measures of poverty are based on the position of some group relative to the overall income distribution, for example, those with incomes that are less than half of the median income. Table 10.14 shows how the United Nations has applied a relative definition of poverty to children in countries. This table reflects the enormous variation in child poverty across 23 countries in the 1990s.

Table 10.15 shows poverty information for the United States in 2000. This type of presentation allows data users to glean a fuller picture of poverty by looking at the characteristics of individuals just above or just below the poverty line. It also allows researchers to identify those in extreme poverty, usually identified as those with incomes below 50% of the poverty threshold (Annie E. Casey Foundation, 2002). A growing practice in the United States labels those with income below 200% of poverty as "low-income," to distinguish them from persons in poverty (Loprest, 1999). This type of presentation also responds to critics who charge that most poverty measures treat poverty as a dichotomous variable (people are classified as either poor or not poor) when in fact poverty should be viewed as a continuous variable. Substantively, Table 10.15 shows that poverty varies by age. Children and young adults have the highest poverty levels, followed by the elderly, with those in the working ages (between ages 35 and 59) having the lowest poverty rates.

Uses and Limitations

Income statistics are of direct value to economists and others interested in the economy because they shed light on the distribution and sources of consumer income, wage and salary rates, and the effective employment of the workforce.

TABLE 10.13 Ownership Ratios, Median Value of Asset Holdings, and the Distribution of Measured Net Worth by Asset Type: United States, 1993

Asset Type	Percent of households that own asset type	Median values of holdings for asset owners (dollars)	Percent distribution of measured net worth
ALL ASSETS	X	37,587	100.0
Interest-earning assets at financial institutions	71.1	2,999	11.4
Saving accounts	60.1	NA	NA
Money market deposit accounts	12.6	NA	NA
Certificates of deposit	16.0	NA	NA
Interest-earning checking	36.9	NA	NA
Other interest-earning assets	8.6	12,998	4.0
Money market funds	3.9	NA	NA
Government securities	2.1	NA	NA
Corporate or municipal bonds	3.1	NA	NA
Other interest-earning assets	2.2	NA	NA
Checking accounts	45.9	499	0.5
Stocks and mutual fund shares	20.9	6,960	8.3
Own home	64.3	46,669	44.4
Rental property	8.4	29,300	6.7
Other real estate	9.3	19,415	4.6
Vehicles	85.7	5,140	6.4
Business or profession	10.8	7,000	6.4
U.S. savings bonds	18.5	775	0.8
IRA or Keogh accounts	23.1	12,985	6.7
Other financial investments	5.2	21,001	3.0

X Not applicable.

NA Data not available.

Source: U.S. Census Bureau, "Asset Ownership of Households: 1993," by T. J. Eller and Wallace Fraser, *Current Population Reports*, Series P70–47 (1995): table A.

Income is one of the best measures of economic well-being, and it is often used in conjunction with educational attainment and occupation to measure the broader concept of socioeconomic status. Although the concept of total income is not difficult to relate to the experience of persons, families, and households in most countries, obtaining good data on income is often a challenge. In many countries, one's income is a sensitive topic, while in other places the mix of cash and noncash income makes it difficult to get a true picture.

If one is considering primary data collection, conducting a small pilot study is often recommended to ascertain the possibility of obtaining reliable and valid information on income before any large-scale survey is undertaken. Income data obtained from household surveys should be verified against other available sources of such statistics. In the case of wage and salary income, such data can be checked against employers' records or establishment statistics when they are available. Unfortunately, for many other sources of income, there may be no means of verifying the responses.

Income is often underreported in surveys, particularly, income from certain sources like public welfare programs or investments, and rates of nonresponse to questions on income are often high because of its sensitive nature. One analysis of CPS data on income showed that the CPS underreported real income by about 12% (U.S. Census Bureau, 1993b). However, by comparing survey responses to national accounts, it was revealed that, for some particular sources of income such as interest and dividends, less than half the aggregate income was reported. In the 1990 decennial census, more than 13 million families did not provide data on income (U.S. Census Bureau, 1993a). This means that about 20% of all families had income data "imputed" by the Census Bureau because they either did not respond to income questions or did not fill out the census form appropriately.

Two groups that have posed major practical problems of income measurement are farmers and self-employed nonagricultural workers. For example, the food that these persons raise and consume enhances their well-being and standard of living, yet that food is not money income. Sometimes the imputed value of such noncash items can be estimated and added to cash profits to get total income figures for a farmer.

Data on income reported by the Census Bureau cover essentially money income (excluding, for example, capital gains) and exclude in-kind income, as previously stated. The fact that some farm families receive part of their income in the form of rent-free housing and goods produced and con-

TABLE 10.14 Percentage of Children Living in Poverty in Selected Countries by Rank: Various Years in the 1990s

Country (year)	Percent
Sweden (1995)	2.6
Norway (1995)	3.9
Finland (1995)	4.3
Belgium (1992)	4.4
Luxembourg (1994)	4.5
Denmark (1992)	5.1
Czech Republic (1996)	5.9
Netherlands (1994)	7.7
France (1994)	7.9
Hungary (1994)	10.3
Germany (1994)	10.7
Japan (1992)	12.2
Spain (1990)	12.3
Greece (1994)	12.3
Australia (1996–1997)	12.6
Poland (1995)	15.4
Canada (1994)	15.5
Ireland (1997)	16.8
Turkey (1994)	19.7
United Kingdom (1995)	19.8
Italy (1995)	20.5
United States (1997)	22.4
Mexico (1994)	26.2

Note: For this table, "percent of children in poverty" is defined as the share of children living in households with income below 50 per cent of the national median.

Source: UNICEF, "A League Table of Child Poverty in Rich Nations," *Innocenti Report Card*, Issue No. 1 (June 2000).

sumed on the farm, rather than in money, should be taken into consideration in comparing the income of farm and non-farm residents. Agriculture in the United States, however, has become so commercialized that in-kind income is now a minor factor in the income of most farm families.

It should be noted that many nonfarm residents also receive nonmonetary (in-kind) income. This noncash income often takes the form of business expense accounts, use of business transportation and facilities, full or partial compensation by business for medical and educational expenses, rent-free housing, and so on. In analyzing distributions of income, it should be recognized that capital gains tend to be concentrated more among higher income families than among lower income ones. However, many low-income families receive in-kind benefits such as food stamps, free school lunches, or medical assistance that also are not included in income figures.

The extreme case is that of subsistence (or semi-subsistence) farmers. Practically speaking, about all that can be done is to ascertain the approximate value of any produce that they have sold during a specified period. In some countries, many such farmers will have sold no produce whatsoever; whatever cash income they have during the year may be obtained from an occasional period of work off the farm or from some other member of the family who makes a monetary contribution. It is suggested, therefore, that data for subsistence farmers be tabulated and analyzed separately from data for nonagricultural workers, most of whom receive cash for their efforts.

TABLE 10.15 Low-Income Population as a Percentage of the Total Population, for Various Multiples of the Official Poverty Level, by Age: United States, 2000 (Numbers in thousands)

Age (years)	Total persons	Less than 50% of poverty level		Less than 100% of poverty level		Less than 150% of poverty level		Less than 200% of poverty level	
		Number	Percent of total	Number	Percent of total	Number	Percent of total	Number	Percent of total
TOTAL, all ages	271,059	13,914	5.1	34,476	12.7	58,316	21.5	83,379	30.8
Under 18	71,338	5,774	8.1	13,467	18.9	21,041	29.5	28,623	40.1
18 to 24	25,967	2,006	7.7	4,312	16.6	6,898	26.6	9,476	36.5
25 to 34	38,474	1,990	5.2	4,582	11.9	7,767	20.2	11,205	29.1
35 to 44	44,744	1,575	3.5	4,082	9.1	7,038	15.7	10,640	23.8
45 to 54	35,232	999	2.8	2,444	6.9	4,141	11.8	6,043	17.2
55 to 59	12,601	498	4.0	1,165	9.2	1,916	15.2	2,652	21.0
60 to 64	10,308	322	3.1	1,039	10.1	1,831	17.8	2,681	26.0
65 and over	32,394	750	2.3	3,386	10.5	7,685	23.7	12,059	37.2
65 to 74	17,843	413	2.3	1,616	9.1	3,645	20.4	5,633	31.6
75 and over	14,551	336	2.3	1,770	12.2	4,040	27.8	6,427	44.2

Source: U.S. Census Bureau, "Poverty in the United States: 1998," *Current Population Reports*, Series P60–207 (September 1999): table 2.

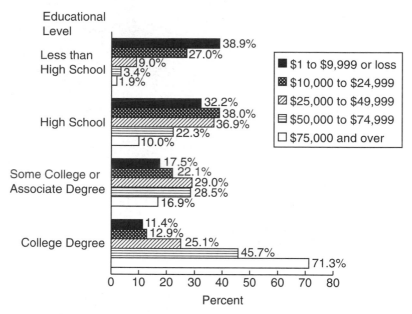

FIGURE 10.3 Percent Distribution of Males 25 Years Old and Over by Educational Attainment, According to Income in 1998: United States, 1999
Source: U.S. Bureau of the Census, "Money Income in the United States: 1998," *Current Population Reports*, P60-206 (September 1999): table 8

The self-employed persons in nonagricultural pursuits also present a problem, inasmuch as the true income from their work is the total amount of cash received minus the cost of doing business. Generally, the more developed the economy and the greater the amount of business performed by self-employed people, the more likely they are to have records that indicate the approximate cost of doing business, so that their true income is more accurately measured.

Because the amounts of income reported typically represent income before deductions for personal taxes, Social Security, savings bonds, and so on, it is not always an accurate measure of resources available to a family. Obtaining information on after-tax income is complicated, however. There are also large differences across countries in terms of taxes that must be considered in international comparisons.

In many ongoing surveys, such as the CPS and the decennial census, the income statistics refer to receipts during the preceding calendar year while the characteristics of the person, such as age, marital status, and labor force status, and the composition of the family refer to the survey date. Therefore, the income of the family does not include those amounts received by persons who were members of the family during all or part of the preceding calendar year but who no longer resided with the family at the time of enumeration. On the other hand, family income does include amounts reported by related persons who did not reside with the family last year but who were members of the family at the time of enumeration.

Scholars use measures of wealth to gain a better understanding of stratification within a population. Measures of wealth can shed light on the economic position of a group beyond that provided by income data. For example, the median income of elderly households in the United States (i.e., those with householders aged 65 years and over) is much less than the median for all households, but the median wealth of elderly households is much higher than the median for all households. The median income of elderly households in 2000 was $23,048 compared to $42,148 for all households (U.S. Census Bureau, 2001b), while the median net worth (wealth) of elderly households in 1995 was $92,399 compared to $40,200 for all households (U.S. Census Bureau, 2001a). In addition, examination of data on wealth offers a more complete perspective on economic inequality (Oliver and Shapiro, 1995). The median income of black households in the United States ($30,439) is 69% that of whites ($44,226), but the median net worth of households with a black householder ($7073) is just 14% that of whites ($49,030) (U.S. Census Bureau, 2001a, 2001b).

Because the poor population is often a target of public attention and public policies, data on poverty are useful because they identify the number, geographic distribution, and characteristics of those at the bottom of the income distribution. The U.S. Department of Education provides additional funds to schools on the basis of the number of children in poverty (U.S. National Research Council, 1997). Figures on poverty can also be used to estimate the number of persons who are likely to be eligible for government means-tested programs.

References

Anker, R. 1990. "Female Labour Force Participation in Developing Countries: A Critique of Current Definitions and Data Collection Methods." In R. Turvey (Ed.), *Developments in International Labour Statistics* (pp. 126–140). Geneva: International Labour Organisation.

Annie E. Casey Foundation. 2002. *KIDS COUNT Data Book: 2002*, Baltimore, MD: Annie E. Casey Foundation.

Blackburn, M. L. 1997. *Comparing Poverty: The United States and Other Industrial Nations*. Washington, DC: American Enterprise Institute.

Brazil, Ministerio Do Trabalho. 1996. *Trabua de Conversao CBO—IBGE—CIUO*. Ministerio do Trabalho. Secretaria de Politicas de Emprego e Salario-SPES: Brasilia.

Christenson, B. A., and N. E. Johnson. 1995. "Educational Inequality in Adult Mortality: An Assessment with Death Certificate Data from Michigan." *Demography* 32: 215–229.

Coale, A. J. 1974. "The History of the Human Population." In *The Human Population* (pp. 15–25). San Francisco: Scientific American.

Federal Interagency Forum on Child and Family Statistics. 2001. *America's Children: Key National Indicators of Well-Being, 2001*. Federal Interagency Forum on Child and Family Statistics, Washington, DC: U.S. Government Printing Office.

Folger, J. K., and C. B. Nam. 1967. *Education of the American Population*. Washington, DC: U.S. Government Printing Office.

Gendell, M. 1998. "Trends in Retirement Age in Four Countries, 1965–95." *Monthly Labor Review* 121: 8 (August): 20–30.

Gendell, M., and J. S. Siegel. 1992. "Trends in Retirement Age by Sex, 1950–2005." *Monthly Labor Review* 115: 7 (July): 22–29.

Golden, H. H. 1955. "Literacy and Social Change in Underdeveloped Countries." *Rural Sociology* 20(1): 1–7.

Grosh, M., and P. Glewwe. 1995. "A Guide to Living Standards Surveys and Their Data Sets." *LSMS Working Paper No. 120*, The World Bank (updated on March 1, 1996).

International Labour Office. 1990. *Statistical Sources and Methods. Vol. 3. Economically Active Population, Employment, Unemployment, and Hours of Work (Household Surveys)*, 2nd ed. Geneva: International Labour Office.

International Labour Office. 2002a. *Key Indicators of the Labour Market: 2002*. Geneva: International Labour Office.

International Labour Office. 2002b. *Yearbook of Labour Statistics: 2001*. Geneva: International Labour Office.

International Labour Organization. 2000. *Current International Recommendations on Labour Statistics*. Geneva: International Labour Organization.

International Labour Organisation. 1957. *Measurement of Underemployment*. Ninth International Conference of Labour Statisticians. Report No. 4. Geneva: International Labour Organisation.

International Labour Organisation. 2002. *Economically Active Population, 1950–2000*. Fourth Edition, Revision 2. Geneva: International Labour Organisation.

Kamerschen, D. R. 1968. "Literacy and Socioeconomic Development." *Rural Sociology* 33(2): 175–188.

Kominski, R., and P. M. Siegel. 1987. "Measuring Educational Attainment in the 1990 Census." Paper presented at the 1987 meeting of the American Sociological Association (August 17).

Kominski, R., and P. M. Siegel. 1993. "Measuring Education in the Current Population Survey." *Monthly Labor Review* 116: 9 (September): 34–38.

Levine, C., L. Salmon, and D. H. Weinberg. 1999. "Revising the Standard Occupational Classification System." *Monthly Labor Review* 122: 5 (May): 36–45.

Loprest, P. 1999, *How Families That Left Welfare Are Doing: A National Picture*. New Federalism: National Survey of America's Families, Series B, No. B-1 (August). Washington, DC: The Urban Institute.

Macunovich, D. J. 1996. "A Review of Recent Developments in the Economics of Fertility." In P. L. Menchik (Ed.), *Household and Family Economics* (pp. 91–157). Dordrecht, Netherlands: Kluwer Academic.

Oliver, M. L., and T. M. Shapiro. 1995. *Black Wealth, White Wealth: A New Perspective on Racial Inequality*. New York: Routledge.

Rindfuss, R. R., S. P. Morgan, and K. Offutt. 1996. "Education and the Changing Age Pattern of American Fertility: 1963–1989." *Demography* 33: 277–290.

Rogers, R. G. 1992. "Living and Dying in the U.S.A.: Sociodemographic Determinants of Death among Blacks and Whites." *Demography* 29: 287–303.

Ruggles, P. 1990. *Drawing the Line: Alternative Poverty Measures and Their Implications for Public Policy*. Washington, DC: The Urban Institute Press.

Saunders, N. C. 1999. "The North American Industry Classification System: Change on the Horizon," *Occupational Outlook Quarterly* (Fall).

Swanson, David A. *et al.* 1998. "K-12 Enrollment Forecasting: Merging Methods and Judgment." *ERS Spectrum* (Fall): 24–31.

UNESCO. 1998. *Statistical Yearbook, 1998*. Paris: UNESCO.

UNICEF. 2000. *Monitoring Progress Toward the Goals of the World Summit for Children: End-Decade Multiple Indicator Survey Manual*. New York: UNICEF.

United Nations. 1989. *Handbook on Social Indicators*. Series F, Studies in Methods, No. 49. New York: United Nations.

United Nations. 1996. *Demographic Yearbook, 1994*. New York: United Nations.

United Nations. 1998. *Principles and Recommendations for Population and Housing Census, Revision 1*. Series M, Statistical Papers, No. 67. New York: United Nations.

U.S. Bureau of Labor Statistics. 1999. *Revising the Standard Occupational Classification System*, Report 929. Washington, DC: U.S. Government Printing Office.

U.S. Census Bureau. 1967. Technical Paper No. 17. *Trends in the Income of Families and Persons in the United States: 1947 to 1960*. By M. F. Henson.

U.S. Census Bureau. 1993a. *1990 Census of Population*, "Social and Economic Characteristics," 1990 CP-2-1, United States. Washington, DC: U.S. Government Printing Office.

U.S. Census Bureau. 1993b. "Money Income of Households, Families, and Persons in the United States: 1992." *Current Population Reports* P60–184. Washington, DC: U.S. Government Printing Office.

U.S. Census Bureau. 1994. *Current Population Survey, March 1994: Technical Documentation*. Washington, DC: U.S. Government Printing Office.

U.S. Census Bureau. 2000a. Accessed online at www.census.gov/population/www/cps/cpsdef.html (July 17).

U.S. Census Bureau. 2000b. "North American Industry Classification System (NAICS)." Accessed online at www.census.gov/epcd/www/naics.html (July 23).

U.S. Census Bureau. 2001a. "Household Net Worth and Asset Ownership: 1995," by M. E. Davern and P. J. Fisher. *Current Population Reports* P70–71. Washington, DC: U.S. Government Printing Office.

U.S. Census Bureau. 2001b. "Money Income in the United States: 2000," by C. DeNavas-Walt, R. W. Cleveland, and M. I. Roemer. *Current Population Reports* P60–213. Washington, DC: U.S. Government Printing Office.

U.S. Census Bureau. 2001c. "Poverty in the United States: 2000," by J. Dalaker. *Current Population Reports* P60–214. Washington, DC: U.S. Government Printing Office.

U.S. National Center for Education Statistics. 1996. *Education in States and Nations*, 2nd ed., NCES 96-160, by R. P. Phelps, T. M. Smith, and N. Alsalam. Washington, DC: U.S. Government Printing Office.

U.S. National Center for Education Statistics. 1998. *Adult Literacy in OECD Countries: Technical Report on the First International Adult Literacy Survey*, NCES 98-053, by T. S. Murray, I. S. Kirsch, and L. B. Jenkins. Washington, DC: U.S. Government Printing Office.

U.S. National Center for Education Statistics. 1999. *Dropout Rates in the United States: 1997*, NCES 1999-082, by P. Kaufman, S. Klein, and M. Frase. Washington, DC: U.S. Government Printing Office.

U.S. National Research Council. 1997. *Small-Area Estimates of School-Age Children in Poverty*. Washington, DC: National Academy Press.

Suggested Readings

Blackburn, M. L. 1997. *Comparing Poverty: The United States and Other Industrial Nations*. Washington, DC: American Enterprise Institute for Public Policy Research.

International Labour Organization. 2000. *Key Indicators of the Labour Market: 1999*. Geneva: International Labour Organization.

Levy, F. 1998. *The New Dollars and Dreams: American Incomes and Economic Change*. New York: Russell Sage Foundation.

National Research Council. 1995. *Measuring Poverty: A New Approach*, edited by C. F. Citro and R. T. Michael. Washington, DC: National Academy Press.

Organisation for Economic Cooperation and Development. 2000. *Education at a Glance: OECD Indicators 2000 Edition*. Paris: OECD.

Ruggles, P. 1990. *Drawing the Line: Alternative Poverty Measures and Their Implications for Public Policy*. Washington, DC: The Urban Institute Press.

United Nations. 1998. *Principles and Recommendations for Population and Housing Censuses: Revision 1*. New York: United Nations.

U.S. Bureau of Economic Analysis. 1994. "Economic Concepts Incorporated in the Standard Industrial Classification Industries of the United States." Economic Classification Policy Committee Report No. 1 (August).

U.S. Bureau of Economic Analysis. 1994. "The Heterogeneity Index: A Quantitative Tool to Support Industrial Classification." Economic Classification Policy Committee Report No. 2 (August).

U.S. Bureau of Labor Statistics. 1997. "Employment Projections." In *BLS Handbook of Methods*, Chapter 13, Bulletin 2490 (April): 122–129.

U.S. Bureau of Labor Statistics. 1999. "Revising the Standard Occupational Classification System." Report 929.

U.S. Census Bureau. 1998. "Measuring 50 Years of Economic Change Using the March Current Population Survey." *Current Population Reports* P60–203. Washington, DC: U.S. Government Printing Office.

U.S. Census Bureau. 1999. "Experimental Poverty Measures: 1990 to 1997," by K. Short, T. Garner, D. Johnson, and P. Doyle. *Current Population Reports* P60–205. Washington, DC: U.S. Government Printing Office.

U.S. National Center for Education Statistics. 1996. *Education Indicators: An International Perspective*, by N. Matheson, L. H. Salganik, R. P. Phelps, M. Perie, N. Alsalam, and T. M. Smith. NCES 96-003. Washington, DC: U.S. Government Printing Office.

U.S. National Center for Education Statistics. 1996. *Education in States and Nations* 2nd ed., by R. P. Phelps, T. M. Smith, and N. Alsalam. NCES 96-160. Washington, DC: U.S. Government Printing Office.

U.S. National Center for Education Statistics. 1998. *Adult Literacy in OECD Countries: Technical Report on the First International Adult Literacy Survey*, by T. S. Murray, I. S. Kirsch, and L. B. Jenkins. NCES 98-053. Washington, DC: U.S. Government Printing Office.

Selected websites

The following is a list of selected websites that have general information or statistics pertinent to educational and economic characteristics, supplementing those websites noted in the text and References.

Academy for Educational Development (AED)

www.aed.org

AED is a nonprofit educational organization that addresses human development needs in the United States and worldwide. The site includes information about publications and programs.

International Labour Organisation (ILO)

www.ilo.org/public/english/index.htm

The International Labour Organisation is the United Nations' specialized agency that formulates international labor standards in the form of conventions and recommendations setting minimum standards of basic labor rights.

National Center for Education Statistics (NCES) (U.S. Department of Education)

www.nces.ed.gov

NCES is the primary federal entity for collecting and analyzing data on education in the United States and other nations.

Organisation for Economic Cooperation and Development (OECD)

www.oecd.org

The OECD groups 29 member countries in an organization that provides governments a setting in which to discuss, develop, and improve national and international economic and social policy.

U.S. Bureau of Economic Analysis (BAE) (U.S. Department of Commerce)

www.bea.gov

BAE is the principal federal agency responsible for analysing national and regional economic data and reporting on the state of the economy.

U.S. Bureau of Labor Statistics (BLS) (U.S. Department of Labor)

www.stats.bls.gov

The BLS site provides information about the labor market in the United States, including labor force statistics and other economic data, surveys and programs, publications, and regional information. Accessible publications online include the *Occupational Outlook Handbook*, *Occupational Outlook Quarterly*, and the *Monthly Labor Review*.

U.S. Social Security Administration (SSA)

www.ssa.gov

SSA is the federal agency compiles data on covered workers, beneficiaries, and benefits disbursed under the old-age security and disability programs.

United Nations Educational, Scientific and Cultural Organization (UNESCO)

www.unesco.org

Site contains several databases and selected statistics from the annual *UNESCO Statistical Yearbook*.

The World Bank

www.worldbank.org

This site includes information on recent, projects and publications as well as an electronic media center, which lists products and services. Covers developed countries as well as less developed countries.

11

Population Change

STEPHEN G. PERZ

DEFINITION AND TYPES

Directions of Change

Population change is measured as the difference between the size of the population at different dates. Partly because of the prevailing trend of population in the countries of the world, people often speak loosely of population "growth," when actually increase or decrease is possible. In census reports, increases are usually presented without a plus sign, while decreases are indicated by a minus sign.

Absolute and Percentage Change

One may obtain the absolute amount of change in the population at different dates by subtracting the population at the earlier date from the population at the later date. The percentage change over the period is obtained by dividing the absolute change by the population at the earlier date and multiplying by 100. In presenting information about population change, many census tables include columns with the following arrangement of captions:

Increase	
Number	Percent

Using the population at the earlier census as the base of the percentage of change is dictated partly by logic and partly by convenience. It is logical in that such a measure answers the basic question raised as to the rate of growth over an initial date. Many types of demographic rates are based on the population at the beginning of the period (e.g., survival rates and migration propensity rates). It is convenient in that this population is already at hand. While the calculation of vital rates uses the midperiod population, this alternative base would have to be estimated.

PITFALLS IN MEASUREMENT

In measuring population change, it is essential that the elements that enter into measurement be comparable over time. The geographic area to which the population refers should be constant, the definition of the population should be the same, and the completeness of coverage should not vary appreciably. This "rule" is not inviolable, however. There are cases, for example, where it is more realistic to measure changes for an expanding area, as explained later. Published population figures often refer to different areas or reflect different kinds of enumerations over time. However, adjustments are rarely feasible, and change is usually computed with published counts or estimates. Nonetheless, knowledge of these differences is important for analysis. Any attempt to measure population change must consider the following three pitfalls: (1) national or subnational areas may change, (2) definitions of the population to be counted may change, and (3) the completeness of coverage may vary.

Change in Territory

The national territory in which enumeration takes place may change as the result of conquest, treaties, advancement of the frontiers of settlement, and similar events. Within national boundaries, water areas may be transformed into land areas, and vice versa, as in the case of the Amazon River floodplain in Brazil. Often, it is possible to show the population within constant boundaries and then to compute the change for this area. Ordinarily, it is the present territory that is used when boundaries shift.

There are some cases when the use of an expanding area is preferable to that of a constant area. The total population of the United States is a case in point. There is relatively little interest in the population growth of the United States

253

within the territory of 1790. Fortunately, the territories purchased or annexed since that year contained few inhabitants prior to their inclusion and first enumeration. In contrast, the territorial shifts associated with the breakup of the Soviet Union created more complex problems for the examination of population change because western portions of the former USSR have been settled for centuries.

Within many countries, there are changes in the boundaries of states or provinces, secondary geographic subdivisions, cities, and townships, and in boundaries of areas defined mainly for statistical purposes, such as urban agglomerations or metropolitan areas. For example, ethnic conflicts within countries in Eastern Europe and Central Asia may lead to new subnational divisions. Among cities in any country, the change in the population may reflect annexations of territory. Because cities may grow by extending their land areas as well as by becoming more densely settled, the increase or decrease in the incorporated or expanding area is perhaps of primary importance.

While recent U.S. census reports do not include statistics for populations in annexed areas, these publications do afford some assessment of the area annexed in growing urban centers. Table 11.1 presents data on 1980 and 1990 populations and land areas of selected U.S. urbanized areas, ranked by percentage increase in land area during the 1980s (column 6). Columns 5 and 6 show that many areas with rapid population growth also experienced rapid growth in land area. In three cases, the geographic area grew as a result of annexation of other cities (column 7). Thus, it is often difficult to separate population growth from territorial annexation when assessing urban population change. Population growth in urban centers should always be treated with caution because the estimates may be biased upward as a result of increases in territory. There is often uncertainty or disagreement as to whether fixed territory or changing territory is conceptually more appropriate when measuring change in a particular situation. Given the importance of territorial annexation in growing urban areas, however,

TABLE 11.1   Growth of Population and Land Area, in Selected Urbanized Areas
in 1980, United States, 1980–1990
(Urbanized areas consist of the central place or places and the surrounding urban fringe)

Urbanized area	Population		Area[1]		Percent Increase[2]		Annexed cities, 1980–1990
	1980 (1)	1990 (2)	1980 (3)	1990 (4)	Population (5)	Area (6)	(7)
Norfolk-Portsmouth, VA	770,784	1,323,098	1,083	2,907	71.66	168.42	Hampton City, Newport News City, Suffolk City, Virginia Beach City
Antioch-Pittsburgh, CA	86,435	153,768	67	168	77.90	150.30	
Austin, TX	379,560	563,008	364	726	48.33	99.31	
McAllen-Pharr-Edinburg, TX	157,423	263,192	163	323	67.19	97.98	Mission
Fort Pierce, FL	70,450	126,342	143	279	79.34	95.38	
Melbourne-Palm Bay, FL	212,917	305,978	433	845	43.71	95.15	
Bremerton, WA	64,536	112,977	91	177	75.06	94.29	
Lancaster, CA	56,328	187,190	118	215	232.32	81.86	Palmdale
Raleigh, NC	206,597	305,925	255	461	48.08	80.82	
Simi Valley, CA	79,921	128,043	69	123	60.21	78.12	
Sarasota-Bradenton, FL	305,431	444,385	389	664	45.49	70.69	
Killeen, TX	88,145	137,876	104	172	56.42	65.10	
Fort Collins, CO	78,287	105,809	90	145	35.16	60.67	
Fort Myers-Cape Coral, FL	140,958	220,552	247	388	56.47	56.92	
Laredo, TX	94,961	123,651	56	86	30.21	53.93	
Durham, NC	157,289	205,355	188	275	30.56	46.06	
San Diego, CA	1,704,352	2,348,417	1,582	2,298	37.79	45.25	
Palm Springs, CA	66,431	129,025	164	233	94.22	42.07	
Olympia, WA	68,616	95,471	110	151	39.14	37.55	
Orlando, FL	577,235	887,126	808	1,104	53.69	36.60	

[1] Land areas are in square kilometres.
[2] Base is 1980 population or area; expressed per 100 population or area.
Sources: U.S. Bureau of the Census, 1983, Table 34, 1993a and 1993b, Table 1.

TABLE 11.2   De Jure and De Facto Population Growth in Hawaii, 1980–1990
(Population in thousands)

Census date	Resident (de jure) population (1)	Visitors present (2)	Residents absent (3)	De facto population (1) + (2) − (3) = (4)	Percent visitors (2) + (4) = (5)
1980 (April 1)	964.7	97.6	9.6	1052.7	9.3
1990 (April 1)	1108.2	158.5	18.4	1248.4	12.7
Change, 1980–90					
Number	143.5	60.9	8.8	195.7	3.4[2]
Percent[1]	14.9	62.4	91.7	18.6	X

X: Not applicable.
[1] Base of percent is 1980 population.
[2] Change in percentage points (= 12.7/9.3).
Source: Based on Schmitt (1992), table 1.

measurement of the part of the population change that is attributable to the change in territory demands attention.

Change in Definition

Populations may be defined in different ways, and changes from one definition to another over time hinder assessments of population growth. Populations may be redefined from *de jure* counts, which include only usual residents, to *de facto* counts of both residents present and visitors, or from *de facto* to *de jure* counts. A change from a *de jure* to a *de facto* basis in taking a census will not ordinarily have a great effect on the intercensal change at the national level, but it will often greatly affect the change in the population of certain geographic subdivisions. In any statistical area where substantial portions of the population are nonresidents, such as military personnel, students, or tourists, *de jure* and *de facto* enumerations will yield different results. Where a nonresident population grows at a different rate than that of residents, estimates of population growth on the basis of *de jure* and *de facto* enumerations will differ. Table 11.2 shows that the number of visitors in Hawaii grew as a percentage of the *de facto* population between 1980 and 1990. As a consequence, the increase of the *de facto* population was greater than that of the *de jure* population. If we had only a *de jure* enumeration in 1980 and a *de facto* enumeration in 1990, the percentage increase in the Hawaiian population would be 29.4%, much larger than percentage increases in both the *de jure* and *de facto* populations during the same period (i.e., 15% and 19%).

As another example of changing definitions of populations, the 1950 U.S. census counted college students living away from "home" at their college residences. The change in definition of "usual residence" is reflected in Table 11.3, which presents census figures for the town of Chapel Hill, the seat of the University of North Carolina.

TABLE 11.3   *De Jure* and *De Facto* Census Counts and Population Increase in Chapel Hill, NC, 1930 to 1990 (*De jure* counts, excluding students at the University of North Carolina)

Year	Population (1)	Percentage increase (2)
1930	2,699	(X)
1940	3,654	35.4
1950[1]	9,177	151.1
1960	12,573	37.0
1970	26,199	108.4
1980	32,421	23.7
1990	37,604	16.0

X: Not applicable.
[1] *De facto* count that includes students attending the University of North Carolina.
Sources: U.S. Bureau of the Census, 1983, Table 34, and 1993b, Table 1.

According to the U.S. Office of Education, 7419 students were enrolled in the university in the fall of 1949. If we assume that all of these students would not have been counted under the old rule, we obtain an adjusted count of 1758 for 1950. This indicates a population loss from 1940 to 1950. In the light of our knowledge of the place and the times, however, this loss looks unreasonable. It is possible that we have overadjusted by subtracting students who also had their parental home in the town or who had no usual place of residence elsewhere. It is also possible that a fairly large number of students lived in the outskirts of Chapel Hill and hence were properly not included in the 1950 total for the town and that some of the university students living in the town were missed in the 1950 census.

If we are examining the change in a particular subgroup of the population, we wish to be sure that the subgroup is defined consistently over the period considered. To illustrate, United Nations estimates of urban populations in Botswana included 341,000 persons on July 1, 1991, but 650,000 on July 1, 1992 (United Nations, 1998, pp. 161, 175). The 1991 estimate includes the urban populations of only seven town districts, while the 1992 estimate also includes populations of villages in other districts (Botswana/Central Statistics Office, 1991). Because such an appreciable alteration in the definition of urban areas prevents clear interpretation, change in urban populations should not be computed in this case.

Change in Coverage

Our last consideration of the pitfalls in measuring population change is whether the completeness of coverage has remained consistent. If the net undercount of the population varies among censuses, estimates of intercensal growth will be biased upward when coverage improves and downward when coverage worsens. If we know the percent undercount, we can obtain an adjusted population, which equals (1.000 minus the undercount proportion) divided into the enumerated population. Official estimates of net undercount are available for U.S. censuses from 1950 to 1990. Table 11.4 presents enumerated populations, undercount estimates, and adjusted populations in the United States for 1970, 1980 and 1990. Between 1970 and 1980, the net undercount declined (column 2), and as a result, the percentage increase in the enumerated population during the 1970s is greater than for the adjusted populations (columns 4 and 5). However, the net undercount rose from the 1980 to the 1990 census, and as a result the percentage increase in the adjusted population was higher than in the enumerated population during the 1980s. Thus, improvements in coverage will yield higher estimates of growth from enumerated than adjusted populations, while deterioration of coverage yields the opposite result.

POPULATION CHANGE AND POPULATION COMPOSITION

In addition to pitfalls of measurement, when estimating population growth over multiple time periods, it is important to recognize changes in population composition if different components of a population grow at different rates. If urban populations grow faster than rural populations, over time the aggregate rate of increase will rise because urban populations will account for ever larger proportions of the total population. Thus, a population's overall rate of change may vary because of changes in composition rather than changes in the growth rates of the components per se. Kephart (1988) shows that the nonmetropolitan "turnaround" in the United States during the 1970s did involve changes in rural and urban growth rates, offset in part by changes in rural and urban composition resulting from the emergence of new urban areas. The effects of changes in composition apply to other population segments that may have different growth rates, such as ethnic groups.

DESCRIPTION OF POPULATION CHANGE

It is often useful to describe the change that has taken place over more than one period (involving three or more dates on which the population has been measured) or to describe change during a given period. In the first case, the description summarizes the changes during a series of successive periods to track alterations in populations changes among periods. In the second case, one computes the change per year to see how change is distributed within the period. We may think of various logical, mathematical ways in which a population may change and then, using these logical formulations as models, see how actual change corresponds to them. The description of change is thus an example of

TABLE 11.4   Growth of Enumerated and Adjusted Populations of the United States, 1970 to 1990

Census year	Population (in thousands)		Percentage undercount (3)	Percentage increase in the preceding decade[2]	
	Enumerated (1)	Adjusted[1] (2)		Enumerated population (4)	Adjusted population (5)
1970	203,302	209,413	2.7	(X)	(X)
1980	226,540	229,264	1.2	11.4	9.5
1990	248,700	253,394	1.8	9.8	10.5

X: Not applicable.
[1] The adjusted population equals (1,000 minus the percentage undercount, divided by 100) divided into the enumerated population.
[2] The percentage increase equals the terminal population minus the initial population, divided by the initial population, multiplied by 100.
Sources: U.S. Bureau of the Census, 1983, Table 1, 1988, 1991, and 1993b, Table 1.

TABLE 11.5 Linear Change of Population in Brazil, 1980–1991 and 1991–1996

Census date	Population (1)	Increase since preceding date (2)	Years since preceding date (3)	Average annual increase[1], (2) ÷ (3) = (4)
1980 (September 1)	118,002,706	(X)	(X)	(X)
1991 (September 1)	146,825,475	28,822,769	11.000	2,620,252
1996 (August 31)	157,079,573	10,254,098	4.997	2,052,051

X: Not applicable.

[1] Equals the increase since the preceding census divided by the number of years elapsed since the preceding census.

Source: Based on Brazil, Instituto Brasileiro de Geografia e Estatística (Brazilian Institute of Geography and Statistics (IBGE), 1998.

interpolation or curve-fitting to time-series data. The techniques used in such descriptions are similar to those used in making intercensal estimates and projections by purely mathematical means.

Linear Change

Computing the average *amount* of change during a year or other interval of time is quite straightforward. One simply divides the total change by the number of years or other unit of time. Suppose we want to compare the average annual amounts of population growth of a country where the intercensal periods are of unequal length. Let us take the three most recent censuses of Brazil as an example, shown in Table 11.5.

In computing the average amount of increase during a period, we implicitly make an assumption about how the growth is distributed over that period. For the moment, let us assume that the growth is linear, or follows an arithmetic progression, which implies that there is a constant amount of increase per unit of time. While few demographic conditions cause populations to increase or decrease in an arithmetic progression, a straight line is frequently used not only to describe population growth in past periods but also to project it into the future for short periods of time. The general equation for a straight line is

$$y = a + bx \qquad (11.1)$$

where y is the height of the line from zero, x is the horizontal distance of the line from zero, a is the height of the line when x equals zero, and b is the slope of the line, which indicates the amount of change in y for a unit change in x. In the case of population change during a single period, we may express this as

$$P_n = P_0 + bn \qquad (11.2)$$

where P_0 is the initial population, P_n is the population at the end of the period (n years later), n is the time in years, and b is the annual amount of population change.

There are circumstances under which it is not particularly problematic to use a straight line in describing population change. When the time period between population enumer-

TABLE 11.6 Arithmetic Approximation of Population Growth Rates in Brazil, 1980–1991 and 1991–1996

Intercensal period	Arithmetic rate of increase[1] (1)	Average population[2] (2)	Arithmetic approximation to the geometric rate of increase[3] (3)
1980 to 1991	2.22	132,414,091	1.98
1991 to 1996	1.40	151,952,524	1.35

[1] Equals the average annual increase divided by the initial population, multiplied by 100. (Table 11.5, col. 4 ÷ col. 1 × 100.)

[2] Equals the mean of the initial and terminal populations of the period.

[3] Equals the average annual increase (Table 11.5, col. 4) divided by the average population (col. 2), multiplied by 100.

Source: Based on Table 11.5.

ations is short and the change relatively small, little error can be introduced by assuming that the population is changing arithmetically. When monthly estimates are available, one may assume that population change within a month follows a straight line. Even over a 5-year period between quinquennial censuses, barring a major catastrophe such as a war, epidemic, or forced migration, this assumption may be roughly applicable.

Rates of Change

More useful comparisons can be made with average annual *rates* of population change. This raises the question of how to express the rate, whether per unit, per 100, per 1000, or some other constant. For consistency, we will continue with the convention of expressing the rate as a percentage, or per 100.

Arithmetic Approximation to a Rate of Change

Let us continue with the Brazilian figures. We can use the average annual increase shown in column 4 in Table 11.5 to approximate an average annual rate of change that is simplistic but convenient. The arithmetic rate of increase, in column 1 of Table 11.6, is calculated dividing the average annual increase (column 4 in Table 11.5) by the population at the beginning of the intercensal period (column 1 in Table 11.5).

Arithmetic rates of increase are comparable only when the periods are of equal length. When the periods are of unequal duration, the longer period tends to have the higher arithmetic rate. In the Brazilian example, the 1980 to 1991 period is longer, and indicates a higher arithmetic growth rate than the 1991 to 1996 period. We must therefore choose a base for the rate that offsets the effects of unequal periods. To eliminate the bias due to unequal periods, an obvious choice for the base is the mean of the populations at the beginning and end of the periods. The average population appears in column 2 of Table 11.6, and the new rate, derived from this population and the average annual amount of change, is shown in column 3. When we compare columns 1 and 3 in Table 11.6, we see that the excess of the earlier over the later average rate is reduced from 0.82 to 0.63. Note that neither of these average annual rates, when applied annually to the successive populations, will produce the population at the end of the intercensal period. Nonetheless, they represent fairly close approximations to genuine average annual rates, particularly the second of these measures.

Because from formula (2) we know

$$b = \frac{P_n - P_0}{n} \qquad (11.3)$$

then the arithmetic approximation of the average rate is given by

$$r' = \frac{b}{1/2(P_0 + P_n)} \times 100 \qquad (11.4)$$

Geometric Change

A geometric series is one in which the population increases or decreases at the same rate during each unit of time, usually a year. If this constant rate of change is represented by r and the initial population is represented by P_0, then after n years the final population is given by

$$P_n = P_0(1+r)^n \qquad (11.5)$$

Suppose we observe the population at two dates and wish to find the annual rate of change on the assumption that the rate (rather than the change) is constant throughout the period. Let us return to our census data for Brazil. For the 1991-to-1996 intercensal period, $n = 4.997$ years, $P_0 = 146,825,475$, and $P_n = 157,079,573$. Then

$$1+r = \sqrt[n]{\frac{P_n}{P_0}} \qquad (11.6)$$

To solve the equation for r, take the natural logarithm of each side (ln), that is, the logarithm to the base e. The form

e represents the base of the system of natural logarithms, it is a mathematical constant that equals 2.71828 . . . The base of natural logarithms allows for computation of a constant rate of change, r, where the absolute amount of change varies over time. The base e serves as a mathematically efficient alternative to the base 10, commonly used in earlier years. To convert natural logarithms to ordinary numbers, use tables of natural logarithms or, more conveniently, a pocket calculator or computer.

$$\ln(1+r) = \frac{\ln\left(\dfrac{P_n}{P_0}\right)}{n} \qquad (11.7)$$

$$= \frac{\ln\left(\dfrac{157,079,573}{146,825,475}\right)}{4.997}$$

$$= \frac{\ln 1.069839}{4.997}$$

$$= \frac{.067508}{4.997}$$

$$\ln(1+r) = .013510$$

$$1+r = 1.013601$$

$$r = 0.013601, \text{ or about } 1.36\% \text{ per year}$$

For population change in Brazil during the 1980 to 1991 period, the assumption of geometric change yields a rate of about 2.01% per year.

If we had annual observations of the size of the population, and hence annual rates of population change, we could find the geometric mean of these annual rates:

$$r_{MG} = \sqrt[n]{\frac{P_1}{P_0} \times \frac{P_2}{P_1} \times \ldots \times \frac{P_n}{P_{n-1}}} = \sqrt[n]{\frac{P_n}{P_0}} \qquad (11.8)$$

Because the geometric rate is assumed to be constant throughout the period, this geometric mean would be identical with the geometric rate of change figured from the population at the beginning and end of the intercensal period.

Exponential Change

Geometric change is a type of change in which the compounding takes place at specified constant intervals, such as a year, and familiar to reader as "compound interest." However, the annual compounding is arbitrary. Why not compound semiannually or monthly? In an exponential series, the compounding takes place continuously (i.e., a constant rate of change is applied at every infinitesimal unit of time). For a fixed period, an exponential growth curve can be expressed as

$$P_n = P_0 e^{rn} \qquad (11.9)$$

Equation (11.9) allows for computation of change where the rate of change is compounded continuously. The term e is the base of natural logarithms. Solving for r, we get, first,

$$e^{rn} = \frac{P_n}{P_0} \tag{11.10}$$

Then,

$$r = \frac{\ln\left(\dfrac{P_n}{P_0}\right)}{n} \tag{11.11}$$

We will use Equation (11.11) to solve for the exponential rate of growth, r, for Brazil in its last two intercensal periods. For the 1980 to 1991 period, the computations are as follows:

$$r = \frac{\ln\left(\dfrac{146,825,475}{118,002,706}\right)}{11}$$

$$= \frac{\ln 1.244255}{11}$$

$$= \frac{0.218537}{11}$$

$$= 0.019867, \text{ or } 1.99\% \text{ per year}$$

For the 1991 to 1996 intercensal period, the average growth rate, derived by continuous compounding, is 1.35%. Note that the average rate of growth when the compounding is continuous is always less than when the compounding is between longer time intervals such as a year.

We will close this subsection by recapitulating the various estimates of the average annual rate of growth that we have computed by various formulas for the last two intercensal periods of Brazil. These estimates appear in Table 11.7. The geometric method tends to yield the highest estimates of growth, followed by the exponential method, then the arithmetic approximation.

TABLE 11.7 Arithmetic, Geometric, and Exponential Population Growth Rates in Brazil, 1980–1991 and 1991–1996

Formula	Growth rate	
	1980–1991	1991–1996
Arithmetic approximation[1]	1.98	1.35
Geometric—Annual compounding	2.01	1.36
Exponential—Continuous compounding	1.99	1.35

[1] Arithmetic approximation employed the midperiod population as a base.

Source: Tables 11.5 and 11.6, and text.

Population Change in Multiple Periods

The preceding section dealt with the computation of the average annual rate of change within a single period, specifically an intercensal period. Now we turn to the description of change over a number of periods. Here, some of the curves describing growth that we have already considered can also be applied, as can additional ones.

Describing the trend of population from a number of observations is usually a particular case of curve fitting, a topic that is dealt with more generally in Appendix C. In choosing the type of growth curve to fit to the population data, it is desirable both to examine the plotted points and to develop a demographic theory as to why population should be expected to change in the hypothesized way, given a particular set of historical conditions and in the light of demographic knowledge about the factors affecting the components of population change. The trend curve is of interest in its own right. It may also be used for purposes of interpolation (that is, to find the trend value at a given date within the period of observation) or for purposes of extrapolation (that is, to find the trend value at a given date beyond the observation period).

The Linear Trend

A straight line (that is, a polynomial of first degree) is represented by the following equation and can be fitted to three or more observations by the method of least squares:

$$P_t = a + bt \tag{11.12}$$

where t is the time in years elapsed between observations of population numbers.

Other Polynomial Trends

Population change is occasionally fairly well described by a polynomial of second or higher degree. The equation of a second-degree polynomial (or parabola) is

$$P_t = a + bt + ct^2 \tag{11.13}$$

and that of an nth degree polynomial is

$$P_t = a + bt + ct^2 + \ldots + kt^n \tag{11.14}$$

Exponential Curves

The general equation for an exponential curve is

$$y = ab^x \tag{11.15}$$

For population growth, this could be represented as

$$P_t = a(1 + r)^t \tag{11.16}$$

where P_t is the population at time t and r is the rate of change. The geometric growth equation, $P_n = P_0(1 + r)^n$, can be seen to be a special case of Equation 11.16.

When the rate of change is positive, the population described by such a curve would increase without any limit. Such a trend cannot continue indefinitely. An exponential curve may, however, describe population growth over a particular period of time. Demographers sometimes speak of such growth as "Malthusian growth" because of the well-known generalization by Malthus that population tends to increase in a geometric progression.

The Logistic Curve

One of the best-known growth curves in demography is the logistic curve. It was first derived by Verhulst around 1838 but was rediscovered and popularized by Pearl and Reed around 1920. Some species of animals and some bacterial cultures have been observed to grow rapidly at first when placed in a limited environment with ideal conditions of food supply and space for their initially few numbers, and then to grow slowly as the population experiences a pronounced scarcity of resources. There may be an upper limit to the numbers that can be maintained, whereupon the population ceases to grow. Considerations such as these have given rise to attempts to predict what the upper limit would be by fitting asymptotic growth curves to observed data. The equation of this curve is

$$Y_c = \frac{k}{1 + e^{a+bx}} \qquad (11.17)$$

where Y_c represents the computed value of Y, and k is the carrying capacity of a region, measured as the maximum number of persons that can be supported per unit of area.[1]

Like other growth curves, the logistic is used for projecting population growth as well as for describing its past course. Some writers have criticized the logistic as being too mechanistic in its assumptions (e.g., for not allowing for voluntary control over fertility or for migration) and for other reasons. The logistic cannot describe a population that is decreasing.

The Time Required for a Population to Double

It is often of interest to know the time required for a population to double in size if a given annual rate of increase were to continue. This interest reflects the problems confronting many rapidly growing countries, especially the economically underdeveloped ones.

For this purpose, we must return to Equation (11.9) for a constant growth rate, continuously compounded:

$$P_t = P_0 e^{rt}$$

where t is the length of the interval in years and P_t is the population at the end of the interval. We want to find the number of years it will take for P_t to equal $2P_0$:

$$2P_0 = P_0 e^{rt}$$

$$2 = e^{rt}$$

$$\ln 2 = rt$$

$$t = \frac{\ln 2}{r} \qquad (11.18)$$

For an example, we can calculate population doubling time in Brazil with the exponential growth rate for the 1991 to 1996 period. To find t, we evaluate Equation 11.18. The natural logarithm of 2 equals $0.693417\ldots$, and the annual rate of growth in Brazil between 1991 and 1996 was 1.35%.

$$t = \frac{0.693417}{0.0135}$$

$$t = 51.4 \text{ years}$$

Figure 11.1 shows the relationship between the annual rate of growth and the number of years for the population to double, and Table 11.8 presents this relationship in tabular form.

Cyclical Change

Most of the foregoing discussion concerns the description of secular trends in population size. In computing the average population change within an intercensal period, we were, however, dealing with the combined effects of secular and cyclical movements. In recent years, studies of cyclical population change have proliferated. Easterlin (1968, 1987) argued that large birth cohorts in post-war United States experienced lower incomes, resulting in later marriages and lower fertility. The large cohorts thus produced smaller cohorts, which in turn earned higher incomes and tended to have more children. These "Easterlin cycles" theoretically generate cyclical changes in rates of population growth across decades, though some authors have raised questions about their significance, particularly since 1980 (e.g., Pampel and Peters, 1995; Wachter, 1991). Short-term fluctuations in the components of population growth have become the subject of historical demography. Lee (1981) analyzed monthly data on wheat prices, mortality, and fertility in England from the 1540s to the 1840s. By removing secular trends, his analysis shows that cyclical rises in wheat

---

[1] The logistic curve is very similar to the Gompertz curve. One difference is that the growth increments of the logistic are symmetrical when plotted, closely resembling a normal curve, whereas those of the Gompertz curve are skewed. For the logistic curve, the differences between the reciprocals of the population values decline by a constant percentage. See pages 382–384 of the unabridged edition of *The Methods and Methods of Demography, published*, by the U.S. Census Bureau in 1980, for an illustration of the method of fitting a logistic curve.

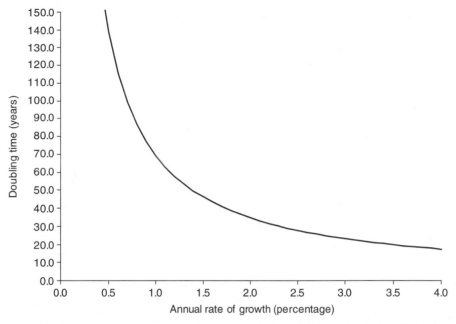

FIGURE 11.1   Number of Years Necessary for the Population to Double According to Specified Annual Rates of Growth. Source: Table 11.8

TABLE 11.8   Population Doubling Time at Different Annual Rates of Growth

Annual rate of growth	Doubling time	Annual rate of growth	Doubling time
0.1	693.1	2.1	33.0
0.2	346.6	2.2	31.5
0.3	231.0	2.3	30.1
0.4	173.3	2.4	28.9
0.5	138.6	2.5	27.7
0.6	115.5	2.6	26.7
0.7	99.0	2.7	25.7
0.8	86.6	2.8	24.8
0.9	77.0	2.9	23.9
1.0	69.3	3.0	23.1
1.1	63.0	3.1	22.4
1.2	57.8	3.2	21.7
1.3	53.3	3.3	21.0
1.4	49.5	3.4	20.4
1.5	46.2	3.5	19.8
1.6	43.3	3.6	19.3
1.7	40.8	3.7	18.7
1.8	38.5	3.8	18.2
1.9	36.5	3.9	17.8
2.0	34.7	4.0	17.3

Note: Computed by the formula for continuous compounding, $P_t = P_0 e^{rt}$, where $t = ln\ 2 \div r$.

prices led to rises in mortality along with declines in nuptiality, which reduced population growth for up to 36 months. Related work (e.g., Galloway 1988) extended these findings to eight other European countries and showed that cyclical effects of grain prices on mortality eroded by the 19th century. Similar methods have also been applied to the less developed countries experiencing economic growth followed by debt crises during the 1980s. Tapinos, Mason, Bravo, and colleagues (1997) analyzed annual data in nine Latin American countries and showed some decreases in nuptiality and increases in child mortality during years of declines in gross domestic product or immediately following such declines. Work on cyclical fluctuations in the components of population growth tends to find weak effects, but most authors admit to the need for refinement in the methods employed.

Seasonal Change

Because each of the components of population growth is subject to seasonal change, the growth of total population, especially the *de facto* population, may exhibit some degree of seasonal fluctuation. To observe this, we need fairly accurate estimates of population on a monthly or at least a quarterly basis. Data from the Consumer Confidence Survey of Floridians reveal a pronounced seasonal fluctuation of population in Florida due to temporary residents. Overall, 4.1% of Florida's population consisted of temporary residents in 1993. They numbered nearly 558,000 persons among the total for the state, estimated to be 13,609,000 on April 1, 1993. In January, however, the percentage of temporary residents peaked at 7.3%, or about 991,000 people. The temporary population declined in subsequent months, reaching a trough in September of 1.1%, or 143,000 people. This pattern, seen in qualified degree in many southern U.S. states, reflects an influx of temporary residents seeking warmer accommodations during the winter months (Galvez and McLarty, 1996).

ACCURACY OF MEASUREMENT

Because population change may be derived by subtraction from population counts or estimates, we must first consider the accuracy of these counts or estimates. If the estimates came from sample surveys (or from a sample of a complete census or a population register) and if sampling error were the only source of error, then the error of the change would be given by the ordinary formula for the standard error of a difference (assuming a random sample):

$$\sigma_{P1-P_2} = \sqrt{\sigma_{P_1}^2 + \sigma_{P_2}^2} + 2\, \text{cov}\, \sigma_1\sigma_2 \qquad (11.19)$$

That is, the variance of the difference in populations essentially equals the sum of the variances of the quantities themselves. In most situations, however, the bias of the population figure is much more important than its sampling error. Very often there is serial correlation among the biases, indicated by the covariance term. Because the successive population censuses and surveys are taken by essentially the same procedures, the bias is likely to be of roughly the same sign and percentage at successive censuses.

COMPONENTS OF POPULATION CHANGE

There are only four components of change in the total population, namely, births, deaths, immigration, and emigration. The algebraic excess of births over deaths is called natural increase. Note that natural decrease can also occur, however. The algebraic excess of immigration over emigration is called net migration, either net immigration or net emigration. Usually, as is the case in this book, the terms immigration and emigration are reserved for movements across international boundaries, whereas movements into or out of an area within a country are called in-migration and out-migration, respectively. In-migration and out-migration are collectively called internal migration. Sometimes we are interested in the total migration to or from an area, regardless of whether it is to (or from) another area in the same country or abroad. (The following chapters are concerned with the specific components of population change.)

These components, of course, may be measured and studied not only for the total population but also for subgroups of the population such as an age-sex group, the employed population, or the single population. In many such cases, we have to deal with changes in classification. The exceptions are fixed attributes of individuals such as sex and place of birth. Some of the changes (as in age) are entirely predictable if we are dealing with true rather than reported characteristics. Others, such as those in marital status, have

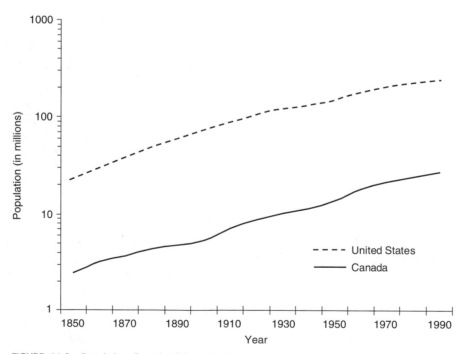

FIGURE 11.2 Population Growth of Canada, 1851 to 1991, and the United States, 1850 to 1990 (Semilogarithmic scale)

restricted paths; for example, a change from single status is irreversible and the only possible change from widowed or divorced is to married (excluding death). With some characteristics, however (e.g., occupation, income, or religion), it is theoretically possible to change from any category to any other category.

FACTORS IMPORTANT IN ANALYSIS

A great deal of demographic analysis is carried out in terms of comparisons of population change among different political units, residence areas, and groups having various demographic, social, and economic characteristics. Comparisons of percentage change are usually more meaningful than those of absolute change. If population changes in two countries with intercensal periods of different lengths are being compared, annual average rates should be computed, preferably with the assumption of exponential growth.

If two areas, or groups, of radically different population size (e.g., the United States and Canada) are being compared graphically, a better indication of relative rates of change is given by a semilogarithmic graph (Figure 11.2) than by an arithmetic graph. Here population is plotted to a logarithmic scale on the vertical axis, whereas time is plotted to an arithmetic scale on the horizontal axis. Then equal vertical distances will represent equal rates of change without regard to the size of the population. Further, on a semilogarithmic graph, a population increasing at a constant rate is represented by a straight line.

References

Botswana, Central Statistics Office. 1991. *1991 Population and Housing Census: Administrative/Technical Report and National Statistical Tables*. Gaborone, Botswana: Central Statistical Office.

Brazil, Instituto Brasileiro de Geografia e Estatística (Brazilian Institute of Geography and Statistics, IBGE). 1998. *Dados Históricos dos Censos— População, 1940–1996*, http://www.ibge.org/informacoes/estat1.htm, available June 1998.

Easterlin, R. 1968. *Population, Labor Force, and Long Swings in Economic Growth: The American Experience*. New York: National Bureau of Economic Research.

Easterlin, R. 1987. *Birth and Fortune: The Impact of Numbers on Personal Welfare*. Chicago: University of Chicago Press.

Galloway, P. R. 1988. "Basic Patterns in Annual Variations in Fertility, Nuptiality, Mortality, and Prices in Pre-Industrial Europe." *Population Studies* 24(2): 275–302.

Galvez, J., and C. McLarty. 1996. "Measurement of Florida Temporary Residents Using a Telephone Survey." *Journal of Social and Economic Measurement* 22: 25–42.

Kephart, G. 1988. "Heterogeneity and the Implied Dynamics of Regional Growth Rates: Was the Nonmetropolitan Turnaround an Artifact of Aggregation?" *Demography* 25(1): 99–113.

Lee, R. D. 1981. "Short-Term Variation: Vital Rates, Prices, and Weather." In E. A. Wrigley and R. S. Schofield (Eds.), *The Population History of England, 1541–1871* (pp. 356–401). Cambridge: Harvard University Press.

Pampel, F. C., and H. E. Peters. 1995. "The Easterlin Effect." *Annual Review of Sociology* 21: 163–194.

Schmitt, R. C. 1992. "Estimating Hawaii's De Facto Population." *Applied Demography* 7(2): 1–3.

Tapinos, G., A. Mason, and J. Bravo (Eds). 1997. *Demographic Responses to Economic Adjustment in Latin America*. Oxford: Clarendon Press.

United Nations. 1998. *Demographic Yearbook—1996*. New York: United Nations.

U.S. Bureau of the Census. 1983. *1980 Census of Population, Characteristics of the Population, Chapter A: Number of Inhabitants, Part 1: US Summary*, PC80-1-A1. Washington, DC: U.S. Government Printing Office.

U.S. Bureau of the Census. 1988. *The Coverage of Population in the 1980 Census*. Report PHC80-E4. Washington, DC: U.S. Government Printing Office.

U.S. Bureau of the Census. 1991. "Refined 1990 Census Coverage Estimates." Press release of 18 June, CB91-222. Washington, DC.

U.S. Bureau of the Census. 1993a. *1990 Census of Population and Housing Supplemental Reports: Urbanized Areas of the United States and Puerto Rico*, 1990 CPH-S-1-2. Washington, DC: U.S. Government Printing Office.

U.S. Bureau of the Census. 1993b. *1990 Census of Population: Social and Economic Characteristics, United States*, 1990 CP-2-1, Table 1. Washington, DC: U.S. Government Printing Office.

Wachter, K. W. 1991. "Elusive Cycles: Are There Dynamically Possible Lee-Easterlin Models for U.S. Births?" *Population Studies* 45: 109–135.

12

Mortality

MARY A. MCGEHEE

NATURE AND USES OF MORTALITY STATISTICS

Death is a principal "vital event" for which vital statistics are collected and compiled by the vital statistics registration system; the others are live births, fetal deaths, marriages, and divorces. Adoptions, legitimations, annulments, and legal separations also may be included. The vital statistics system includes the legal registration, statistical recording and reporting of the occurrence of vital events, and the collection, compilation, analysis, presentation, and distribution of vital statistics (United Nations, 1953, p. 4). The vital statistics system employs the registration method of collecting the data on vital events, which typically involves the reporting to government officials of events as they occur and the recording of the occurrence and the characteristics of these events.

Broadly speaking, death statistics are needed for demographic studies and for public health administration. The most important uses of death statistics include (1) the analysis of the present demographic status of the population as well as its potential growth; (2) filling the administrative and research needs of public health agencies in connection with the development, operation, and evaluation of public health programs; (3) the determination of administrative policy and action in connection with the programs of government agencies other than those concerned with public health; and (4) filling the need for information on population changes in relation to numerous professional and commercial activities. Death statistics are needed to make the analyses of past population changes that are required for making projections of population and their demographic characteristics. The latter are employed in developing plans for housing and educational facilities, managing the Social Security program, and producing and providing services and commodities for various groups in the population. The analysis of mortality statistics is essential to programs of disease control. Local health authorities use mortality statistics reports to determine the administrative action needed to improve public health in local areas. All these uses are in addition to the demands of individuals for documentary proof of death.

DEFINITION OF CONCEPTS: STATISTICAL LIFE AND DEATH

Adequate compilation and measurement of vital events require that the concepts of life and death be given formal definition, even though the meaning of these concepts may appear obvious, at least in a physical sense, to most persons. Recent developments in the medical field have gone a long way to blur even the clinical distinction between life and death. When does life begin and end for statistical purposes—that is, for the counting of births and deaths? In fact, vital statistics systems identify three basic, complementary, and mutually exclusive categories: live births, deaths, and fetal deaths (i.e., fetal losses).

The United Nations and the World Health Organization have proposed the following definition of death: "Death is the permanent disappearance of all evidence of life at any time after birth has taken place (post-natal cessation of vital functions without capability of resuscitation)" (United Nations, 1953, p. 6; World Health Organization, 1950, p. 17). A death can occur only after a live birth has occurred. The definition of a death can be understood, therefore, only in relation to the definition of a live birth (see Chapter 3 or Chapter 15). For one thing, it excludes the entire category of fetal mortality, or pregnancy losses that occur prior to the completion of the birth process.

Although the definition of a "death" excludes losses prior to (live) births, these events are commonly called fetal deaths. A fetal death is formally defined as "death (disappearance of life) prior to the complete expulsion or extraction from its mother of a product of conception irrespective of the duration of pregnancy; the death is indicated by the fact that after such separation the fetus does not breathe or show any other evidence of life, such as beating of the heart, pulsation of the umbilical cord, or definite movement of voluntary muscles" (WHO, 1950).

The term "fetal death" is employed in present demographic practice to embrace the events variously called stillbirths, miscarriages, and abortions in popular medical or legal usage. The term "stillbirth" is often used synonymously with late fetal deaths, say a fetal death of 28 or more completed weeks of gestation, although the term is sometimes employed to refer to all fetal deaths.

The term "miscarriage" is popularly employed to refer to spontaneous or accidental terminations of fetal life occurring early in pregnancy. The term "abortion" is defined as any termination of pregnancy before 28 weeks of gestation. There are two major categories of abortions: spontaneous and induced. Induced abortions are those initiated by deliberate action undertaken with the intention of terminating pregnancy; all other abortions are considered as spontaneous. The recommendation of the United Nations and the World Health Organization is to group all of these events, miscarriages and abortions as well as stillbirths, under the heading "fetal death" and to classify them as early, intermediate, and late according to the months of gestation.

SOURCES OF DATA FOR
MORTALITY STUDIES

The basic data on deaths for mortality studies, for the statistically developed areas, come from vital statistics registration systems and, less commonly, from national population registers, as noted. The analysis of the death statistics from the vital statistics registration system depends on the availability of appropriate population data from a census or survey, or population estimates, to be used as bases for computing rates of various kinds. Dependence on a second data collection system is not necessary where an adequate national population register system is in effect.

The vital statistics registration system is likely to be inadequate in the underdeveloped countries; for these areas, other sources of data for measuring mortality have to be considered. The principal alternative sources are (1) national censuses and (2) national sample surveys. National censuses and sample surveys may provide (1) data on age composition from which the level of recent mortality can be inferred and (2) direct data on mortality. The national sample surveys may also provide additional detailed data permitting a more complete analysis of mortality. A sample survey may be employed to follow up a sample of decedents reported in the registration system. The inference regarding the level of

mortality is easier and firmer where two censuses are available, but special techniques permit this inference with only one census in certain cases. Direct data on deaths are infrequently obtained in censuses, but in recent decades sample surveys have been used in a number of areas to measure mortality levels. The sample survey is not an acceptable substitute for the registration system with respect to the legal aspects of registrations, however, since every vital event should be registered for legal purposes.

Vital statistics from civil registers are infrequently available in Africa. The availability of vital statistics is only slightly greater for much of Asia and parts of Latin America. In these continents, coverage is uneven and the statistics generally incomplete and unreliable. Estimated death rates for these areas, however, are becoming increasingly available from sample surveys or from the analysis of census returns.

Mortality statistics are ordinarily presented in the statistical yearbooks of countries or in special volumes presenting vital statistics. In the United States, a volume on mortality statistics was published each year from 1900 (the year when the annual collection of mortality statistics for the death registration area began) to 1993 by the U.S. Census Bureau or the U.S. Public Health Service. In addition, provisional statistics as well as certain final data are published in brief reports in advance of the publication of the bound volumes. The United Nations' *Demographic Yearbooks* for 1957, 1961, 1966, 1967, 1974, 1980, and 1985 emphasized tabulations of mortality. Other special compilations of mortality data include *Annual Epidemiological and Vital Statistics*, published by the World Health Organization since 1962, and the *World Health Statistics Annual*, published by the World Health Organization since 1948.

QUALITY OF DEATH STATISTICS

We may consider the deficiencies of death statistics based on vital statistics registration systems under three headings: (1) accuracy of the definition of death applied, (2) completeness of registration, and (3) accuracy of allocation of deaths by place and time.

Application of Definition

Not all countries follow the definition of death recommended by the United Nations in obtaining a count of deaths. In some countries, infants who die within 24 hours after birth are classified not as deaths but as stillbirths or, failing provisions for this, are disregarded altogether (i.e., they are not classified as live births, deaths, or fetal deaths). In other countries (e.g., Algeria, Martinique, and Guadeloupe), infants who are born alive but who die before the end of the registration period, which may last a few months, are considered stillbirths or are excluded from all tabulations.

Completeness of Registration

Basis and Extent of Underregistration

The registration of deaths for a country may be incomplete because of either (1) failure to cover the entire geographic area of the country or all groups in the population or (2) failure to register all or nearly all of the vital events in the established registration area. Typically, both of these deficiencies apply if the first is true. Many less developed countries currently collect death statistics only in a designated registration area (e.g., Indonesia, Ghana, Turkey, Brazil, Myanmar) or try to secure complete registration only in designated sample registration areas (e.g., India) for a variety of reasons. The registration area may exclude parts of the country where good registration is a practical impossibility in view of the country's economic and social development and financial condition. Remote rural, mountainous, or desert areas in a country may not be serviced by registrars. The national government may not have complete administrative control over certain parts of the territory it claims as a result of civil disorder (e.g., former Burma) or a territorial dispute with another country (e.g., India. Pakistan). Nomadic and indigenous groups (e.g., nomadic Indians in Ecuador, jungle Indians in Venezuela, full-blooded aborigines in Australia), or particular ethnic or racial groups (Palestinian refugees in Syria, African population in former Bechuanaland, Bantus in South Africa) may be excluded or hardly covered. Commonly, in underdeveloped countries, babies who die before the end of the legal registration period are registered neither as births nor deaths. In Taiwan, for example, deaths must be registered within 5 days and births within 15 days. A sample test conducted about 1965 showed that a large proportion of babies who died within 15 days were not registered in any way at all.

The United Nations finds death registration to be substantially incomplete for most countries of the world, including nearly all of those considered underdeveloped. According to an analysis of data that the United Nations carried out for 1951–1955, only about 33% of the world's deaths were being registered: the percentage varied regionally from 7% for East Asia to 100% in North America and Europe. Generally, a registration system that records 60% or more of deaths is considered to be a useful source of mortality data. If completeness is below 60%, the value of the data may be affected by nonrepresentativeness (Preston, 1984). Carefully derived estimates of the completeness of registration are rarely, if ever, available. Several countries have provided estimates to the United Nations that are given in its *Demographic Yearbook*. These estimates are typically below 90%: even so, they probably overstate the actual extent of registration.

In the United States, the annual collection of mortality statistics began in 1900, when the registration area consisted of 10 states, the District of Columbia, and a number of cities, accounting for only 41% of the population of the United States. Complete geographic coverage of the United States was not achieved until 1933, when the last state joined the registration area. Currently, more than 99% of the deaths occurring in the United States are believed to be registered.

Reporting of fetal "deaths" in the United States is less complete. Even so, registration is believed to be relatively complete for fetal losses at 28 or more weeks of gestation. Statistical data on fetal losses include only those occurring at a stated or presumed gestation period of 20 or more weeks.

Measurement of Underregistration

Several approaches are used to measure the completeness of death registration, none of which is highly satisfactory. The results of studies of underregistration of births, including birth registration tests and estimates made by demographic analysis, have general implications for the completeness of death reporting. An appreciable underregistration of births suggests a substantial underregistration of deaths, even though the types of inducements to comply with the laws regarding registration differ for these events.

Chandra Sekar (now Chandrasekaran) and Deming have presented a mathematical theory that, when applied to a comparison (i.e., matching) of individual entries on a registrar's lists of deaths with the individual entries on the lists obtained in a house-to-house canvass, gives national unbiased estimates of the completeness of registration (Chandra Sekar and Deming, 1949). The basic procedure is to divide the area covered (either geographically or by a combination of characteristics) into subgroups, each of which is highly homogeneous. (A highly homogeneous population is defined as one in which each individual has an equal probability of being enumerated.) Within such subgroups, the correlation between unregistered and unenumerated events would be very low. The percentage of "enumerated" deaths registered in each subgroup is assumed, therefore, to apply to the unenumerated deaths that are registered in the subgroup to derive the total number of deaths that occurred in the subgroup. An estimate of the total number of deaths (registered and unregistered) in the area could then be derived by cumulating the total number of deaths corrected for underregistration for subgroups. Relating the figures for registered deaths to this total nationally would then give an unbiased estimate of the completeness of registration.

This procedure represents one of the more promising ways of evaluating the reported number of deaths or death rates, or of estimating them, particularly for the statistically underdeveloped areas. The various procedures for accomplishing this include, in addition to the combined use of registration data and survey data represented by "population-growth—estimation studies," the use of stable population models, repetitive and overlapping sample household surveys, the use of sample registration areas, and the analysis of statistics by age from successive censuses (Mauldin, 1965, pp. 642–647).

Accuracy of Allocation by Place and Time

Accuracy of Allocation by Place

Part of the difficulty in the geographic allocation of deaths is due to the utilization of hospitals in large cities by residents of the surrounding suburban and rural areas whose death in these hospitals results in an excessive allocation of deaths to the large cities. This bias is more likely to occur in the more industrialized countries where there is greater access to hospital facilities and a higher proportion of deaths occur in hospitals. However, many causes contribute to a patient's moving to some area other than his or her usual place of residence; it cannot be assumed that the movement is always from rural or suburban areas to large cities. Deficiencies in the geographic allocation of deaths may also result from fatal accidents or unexpected deaths that occur away from the usual place of residence. This is more likely to occur in the more industrialized areas where modern means of transportation have contributed to high population mobility. A special problem relates to the assignment of residence of decedents who have lived in an institution outside their area of origin for a considerable period of time. In the United States, all deaths that occur in institutions of all types are allocated to the place of residence before entry into the institution, regardless of the length of time the decedent spent in the institution. Because of difficulties in the allocation of deaths to the place of usual residence of the decedent, even death statistics tabulated on a usual-residence basis often have a pronounced "occurrence" bias, particularly for central cities of large metropolitan areas.

Deaths tabulated by place of occurrence and place of residence are useful for different purposes, although the United Nations recommends that tabulations for geographic areas within countries should be made according to place of usual residence. The occurrence data represent the "service load"; the residence data reflect the incidence of death in the population living in an area.

Accuracy of Allocation by Time

Most countries tabulate their death statistics in terms of the year the death occurred, reassigning the deaths from the year of registration. Some countries, including a number of underdeveloped ones, however, fail to make this reassignment. The death statistics published for these countries for any year relate to events that happened to be registered in that year. The United Nations has recommended that the principal tabulations of deaths should be on a year-of-occurrence basis rather than on a year-of-registration basis. Few countries have tabulated the data in both ways so as to establish the difference in the results. The death statistics for any year based on events registered in that year may be lower or higher than the number that actually occurred in the year because some events occurring in the year may not be registered until many years have passed and the events registered during the year may include events of many earlier years.

FACTORS IMPORTANT IN ANALYSIS

Mortality shows significant variations in relation to certain characteristics of the decedent and certain characteristics of the event. These characteristics of the event and the decedent define the principal characteristics that are important in the demographic analysis of mortality.

In view of the close relation between age and the risk of death, age may be considered the most important demographic variable in the analysis of mortality. No other general characteristic of the decedent or of the event offers so definite a clue as to the risk of mortality. (This is true only for the general population; for special population groups, other factors may be more important than age, e.g., duration of disability for disabled persons or cause of illness for the hospitalized population.) The other characteristics of the decedent of primary importance include sex and usual place of residence. Elements of primary importance characterizing the event are the cause of death, place of death, and date of occurrence and of registration of the death.

Other demographic characteristics of the decedent important in the analysis of mortality are marital status, socioeconomic status (e.g., occupation, literacy, educational attainment), and urban-rural (or size-of-locality) residence. The United Nations also includes in its second-priority list the age of the surviving spouse (for married persons), industry and class of worker (as employer, employee, etc.) of the decedent, marital status of the parents (for deceased infants), and number of children born (for females of childbearing age or older). The list can be extended to cover other factors that would permit analysis of the significant social and economic factors in mortality—for example, the race or other ethnic characteristic of the decedent, such as nativity, country of birth, religion, language, or citizenship.

Mortality also varies by community and the immediate physical environment. These characteristics include the climate, the altitude, the quality of health facilities, environmental conditions, such as the type of water supply, degree of air pollution, and the quantity and quality of food available. We also could include here those characteristics previously cited relating to the place of death or usual place of residence of the decedent, such as the specific geographic subdivision, urban-rural residence, or size of locality.

MEASURES BASED ON DEATH STATISTICS

Observed Rates

There are many measures of mortality based on death statistics. They vary in the aspect of mortality they describe, their degree of refinement or elaboration, whether they are summary measures or specific measures, and whether they are measures of mortality per se or merely mortality-related measures. We can distinguish among the measures of mortality so-called observed rates from so-called adjusted rates. The distinction is only approximate. The observed rates are typically the simpler rates and are computed directly from actual data in a single brief calculation. The adjusted rates are more complex both with respect to method of calculation and to interpretation. They are often hypothetical representations of the level of mortality for a given population group, involving the use of various assumptions to derive summary measures based on sets of specific death rates.

Crude Death Rate

The simplest and most common measure of mortality is the crude death rate. The crude death rate is defined as the number of deaths in a year per 1000 of the midyear population. That is,

$$\frac{D}{P} \times 1000 \qquad (12.1)$$

The crude death rate for Costa Rica in 1994, for example, is calculated by dividing the count of deaths in Costa Rica in 1994 by the estimated population of Costa Rica on July 1, 1994:

$$\frac{13,314}{3,266,000} \times 1000 = 4.1 \qquad (12.2)$$

The midyear population is employed as an approximation to the average population "exposed to risk" of death during the year. The midyear population may be approximated by combining data on births, deaths, and immigration for the period between the census date and the estimate date with the count from the previous census, as an arithmetic or geometric mean of the population estimated directly on the

basis of these components for two successive January 1 dates, and in other ways.

An array of crude death rates for a wide range of countries around 1995 described as having rather complete death registration shows Costa Rica to have the lowest rate at 4.1.

Country and year	Rate
Chile (1994)	5.4
China (1995)	5.0
Canada (1995)	7.1
Costa Rica (1994)	4.1
Cuba (1995)	7.1
Israel (1995)	7.4
Japan (1995)	7.4
Mexico (1995)	4.8
Puerto Rico (1994)	7.7
Sweden (1995)	11.0
United States (1995)	8.8
Yugoslavia (1995)	10.2

Source: United Nations, *Demographic Yearbook*, 1996, table 24.

Other countries may have had slightly higher or lower rates than those shown here. The range of historical variation has been much greater, however.

Crude death rates may be computed for any period, but typically they are computed for the calendar year or the "fiscal" year (i.e., the 12-month period from July 1 to June 30). In the latter case, the population figure should relate to January 1 of the fiscal year. Crude death rates are calculated for 12-month periods such as calendar years or fiscal years so as to eliminate the effect of seasonal or monthly variations on the comparability of the rates. In the calculation of the crude death rate, as well as of other measures of mortality, for the census year, the census counts of population are commonly employed, even though the census may have been taken as of some date in the year other than July 1.

Sometimes an annual average crude death rate covering data for two or three years is computed in order to represent the longer period with a single figure or to add stability to rates based on small numbers or intended for use in extensive comparative analysis. These annual average rates may be computed in several different ways. Formulas are given for 3-year averages. In one procedure, crude rates are computed for each year and averaged—that is,

$$\frac{1}{3}\left[\frac{D_1}{P_1} \times 1000 + \frac{D_2}{P_2} \times 1000 + \frac{D_3}{P_3} \times 1000\right] \qquad (12.3)$$

The average annual death rate for 1992–1994 for Mexico according to this formula is

$$\frac{1}{3}\left[\frac{409,814}{89,538,000} \times 1000 + \frac{416,335}{91,261,000} \times 1000 + \frac{419,074}{93,008,000} \times 1000\right] = \frac{1}{3}(4.58 + 4.56 + 4.51) = 4.6$$

This procedure gives equal weight to the rates for the 3 years.

In the second procedure, the average number of deaths is divided by the average population:

$$\frac{1/3(D_1 + D_2 + D_3)}{1/3(P_1 + P_2 + P_3)} \times 1000 \qquad (12.4)$$

The 1992–1994 rate for Mexico according to this formula is 4.5:

$$\frac{1/3(409,814 + 416,335 + 419,074)}{1/3(89,538,000 + 91,261,000 + 93,008,000)} \times 1000$$

$$= \frac{1/3(1,245,223)}{1/3(273,807,000)} \times 1000 = \frac{415,074}{91,269,000} \times 1000 = 4.5$$

This procedure in effect weights the three annual crude death rates in relation to the population in each year and, hence, may be viewed as more exact than the first procedure for measuring mortality in the period.

In a third procedure, the average number of deaths for the 3 years is divided by the midperiod population:

$$\frac{1/3(D_1 + D_2 + D_3)}{P_2} \times 1000 \qquad (12.5)$$

This is the most commonly used and most convenient procedure and, in effect, assumes that P_2 represents the average population exposed to risk of death in this period, or the average annual number of "person-years of life" lived in the period (Chapter 15). The assumption of an arithmetic progression in the population over the 3-year period is consistent with this general assumption. Normally, annual population figures are not available for small areas; there are only the census counts. According to this formula, the average annual death rate for 1992–1994 for Mexico is

$$\frac{1/3(409,814 + 416,335 + 419,074)}{91,261,000} \times 1000$$

$$= \frac{1/3(1,245,223)}{91,261,000} \times 1000 = \frac{415,074}{91,261,000} \times 1000 = 4.5$$

Note that all three formulas give essentially the same result to a single decimal in the present illustration. Similar results may be expected from the three procedures unless there are sharp fluctuations in the size of the population.

The "crude death rate" has a specific and a general meaning. In its specific meaning, it refers to the general death rate for the total population of an area, corresponding to the definition given earlier. More generally, however, it may be used to refer to the general death rate for any population group in an area, such as the male population, the native population, or the urban population. For example, the crude death rate for the rural population of Chile in 1992 is represented by

$$\frac{D_r}{P_r} \times 1000 = \frac{11,170}{2,207,996} \times 1000 = 5.1$$

The formula calls for dividing the deaths in rural areas during a year by the midyear population of rural areas. In this more general sense, the principal characteristic of a "crude" rate is that *all ages* are represented in the rate.

The crude death rate should be adjusted for underregistration of the deaths and for underenumeration of the population if satisfactory estimates of these errors are available, according to the following formula:

$$\frac{D \div C_d}{P \div C_p} \qquad (12.6)$$

where C_d represents the percent completeness of registration of deaths and C_p represents the percentage completeness of the census counts or population estimates (as decimals). Generally, in the underdeveloped countries or in the earlier stages of the development of a death registration system in a country, the extent of underreporting of deaths is much greater than the extent of underenumeration of the population in the census. In the statistically more developed situation, the registration of deaths has usually improved to the point where the completeness of death registration exceeds the completeness of census enumeration. It may be prudent to correct neither the deaths nor the population when the percentage of completeness is believed to be about the same for each. If only death corrections are available, it is advisable to apply them only if they are much larger than the presumed understatement of the population figures, and the same is true in the opposite situation.

Monthly Death Rate

There is an interest in examining variations in mortality over periods shorter than a year. Monthly death rates computed directly would not be comparable from month to month, however, because of differences in the number of days. Ordinarily, therefore, monthly figures on deaths are converted to an annual basis before rates are computed. Monthly deaths may be "annualized" by inflating the number of deaths for a given month (D_m) by the ratio of the total number of days in the year to the number in the particular month (n_m); the corresponding rate is then computed by dividing the annualized number of deaths by the population for the month:

$$\frac{\frac{365}{n_m} \times D_m}{P_m} \times 1000 \qquad (12.7)$$

The annualized death rate in the United States for January 1990 is obtained as follows:

$$\frac{\frac{365}{31} \times 216,654}{248,143,000} \times 1000 = \frac{2,550,926}{248,143,000} \times 1000 = 10.3$$

Monthly death rates are also affected by seasonal variation and excess mortality due to epidemics. It is desirable to remove these influences from monthly data if the underlying trend of the death rate is to be ascertained. Instead, substitute rates are calculated, serving as estimates of what might have been expected had epidemic conditions not intervened. A monthly death rate adjusted for epidemic excess may be further adjusted for seasonal variation by dividing the adjusted rate for the month by an appropriate seasonal adjustment factor for the month. The variations in the monthly crude death rate due to seasonality result largely from large differences in seasonality by cause of death (Rosenwaike, 1966). Several causes, such as certain diseases of early infancy and motor vehicle accidents, exhibit seasonal patterns unlike that of the overall crude rate. Seasonal patterns of mortality in countries other than the United States may vary according to their location and climactic conditions. Various procedures for calculating seasonal indexes are described in the standard statistical texts, and particular procedures that may be used for calculating seasonal indexes for deaths are described in various journal articles (Rosenberg, 1965, 1966; Rosenwaike, 1966; Sakamoto-Momigama, 1978). Note, in addition, that seasonal patterns may themselves have a trend.

Another procedure that permits analysis of changes on a monthly basis involves direct calculation of annual death rates. Rates are computed for successive 12-month periods ending in each successive month—that is, for example, from January 1996 to December 1996, from February 1996 to January 1997, from March 1996 to February 1977, and so on. The deaths for each 12-month period are divided by the population at the middle of the period to derive the death rates. In this way, the monthly "trend" of the death rate can be observed and analyzed on a current basis without distortion by seasonal variations and without need to apply seasonal adjustment factors. Rates of this kind based on provisional data are published monthly with a lag of less than 2 months following the close of a particular 12-month period by the U.S. National Center for Health Statistics for the United States.

Year-to-year percentage changes in the death rate on a current basis can also be measured by comparing the rates for the same month in successive years. Such rates do not require adjustment for the number of days in the month (except for February) or for seasonal variations. Annual relative changes can also be measured on a current basis by comparing cumulative rates covering all the months in a year to date with the corresponding period in the preceding year—that is, for example, January to May 1997, and January to May 1996; January to June 1998, and January to June 1997.

Specific Death Ratios and Rates

The crude death rate gives only a very general indication of the level of mortality and its changes. There is also a need for measures that describe the specific components of the overall number of deaths and the crude rate. Various types of specific death ratios and rates are of interest both in themselves and for their value in the analysis of the total number of deaths and the crude rate.

Specific death ratios and rates refer to specific categories of deaths and population. These categories may be subdivisions of the population or deaths according to sex, age, occupation, educational level, ethnic group, cause of death, and so forth. We have already described the general (all ages) death rates for certain very broad classes of the population as crude rates (e.g., crude rate for the male population, urban population, native population). These same general rates, however, may also be viewed as specific rates (e.g., sex-specific, urban-rural specific, nativity-specific, etc.). Except in the case of age, which always defines a rate as specific, there is, then, no clear dividing line between a crude rate and a specific rate. A rate is understood to be "crude" unless specifically indicated otherwise or unless it is specific with respect to age.

Age-Specific Death Rates

As we have stated, age is the most important variable in the analysis of mortality. Most tabulations of deaths require cross-classification with age if they are to be useful. The United Nations recommends tabulation of deaths by age, sex, and cause in the following age detail: Under 1, 1, 2, 3, 4, 5-year age groups to 80–84, 85 and over, and not stated (United Nations, 1953). The United Nations also recommends tabulations of infant deaths by age (under 28 days, under 1 year, not stated) and month of occurrence; of infant deaths by sex and detailed age (under 1 day, 1, 2, 3, 4, 5, 6 days; 7 to 13, 14 to 20, 21 to 27, 28 days to under 2 months; 2, 3, 4, . . . 11 months; not stated); and, as stated, of total infant deaths by cause of death.

The tabulations of deaths by age are subject to a number of deficiencies. The principal ones, evident where the deficiencies are pronounced, include (1) substantial and variable underregistration of deaths by age, (2) extensive misreporting of the age of the decedent, and (3) an excessive proportion of "age not stated." Reporting of age of decedents among the extreme aged (say, 5-year age groups 85 and over) is believed to be quite inaccurate in most countries. The exact or even approximate age of most decedents at these ages is not known to surviving relatives, friends, or neighbors, and their report tends to be a guess, with a tendency toward exaggeration of age. Because of serious errors in the population at these ages also, observed death rates among the extreme aged are highly unreliable.

A distribution of deaths by age typically shows a bimodal pattern, as illustrated in Figure 12.1 and Table 12.1 with recent data for several countries. The number and proportion of deaths are at a peak at age under 1 year; there are a trough at about ages 1 to 14 and a second peak at about ages

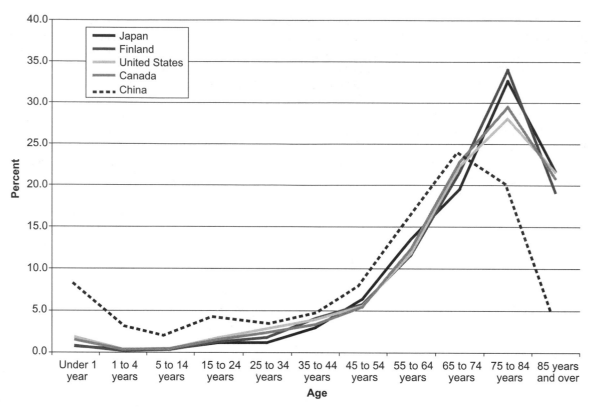

FIGURE 12.1   Percent Distribution of Deaths by Age, for Selected Countries: Around 1990

TABLE 12.1   Percentage Distribution of Deaths by Age, for Various Countries: Around 1990

Age (years)	Japan, 1990	Finland, 1990	United States, 1990	Canada, 1990	China,[1] 1989
Total	100.0	100.0	100.0	100.0	100.0
Under 1	0.7	0.7	1.8	1.4	8.0
1 to 4	0.3	0.1	0.3	0.3	3.0
5 to 14	0.3	0.3	0.4	0.4	2.0
15 to 24	1.1	1.2	1.7	1.5	4.3
25 to 34	1.1	1.7	2.8	2.3	3.9
35 to 44	2.9	4.0	3.9	3.3	5.0
45 to 54	6.3	5.7	5.5	5.4	7.9
55 to 64	13.4	11.6	11.8	12.3	16.1
65 to 74	19.5	21.5	22.2	22.8	24.2
75 to 84	32.6	34.0	28.0	29.4	20.1
85 and over	21.7	19.1	21.6	20.8	5.6

[1] Data from civil registers which are incomplete or of unknown completeness.

Sources: United Nations, *Demographic Yearbook*, 1995, Table 18; and U.S. National Center for Health Statistics, *Vital Statistics of the United States, 1990, Vol. II, Mortality, Part A*, 1994, Table 1.27.

65 to 74, after which the numbers fall off rapidly to the terminal ages of the life span.

The figures in Table 12.1 describe the relative importance of deaths at each age, allowing jointly for the effect of the distribution of the population by age and the variation in death rates from age to age. In the absence of counts or estimates of population by age, calculation of the percentage distribution of deaths by age serves as a simple way of analyzing the role of age as a factor in mortality. To the extent that deaths at each age have the same percentage net reporting error, proportions of deaths by age are relatively free of error and are valid for international comparisons.

The principal way of measuring the variation in mortality by age, however, is in terms of age-specific death rates.

TABLE 12.2   Calculation of Age-Specific Death Rates for Japan, 1990, and of Change in Rates, 1980 to 1990

| | | 1990 | | | Change in death rates | |
| | | Deaths | | 1980[1] | Amount[2] | Percentage[2] |
Age (years)	Population (thousands) (1)	Number (2)	Rate [(2) ÷ (1)] × 1000 = (3)	Death rate (4)	(3) − (4) = (5)	[(5) ÷ (4)] × 100 = (6)
Total	123,612	819,856	6.6	6.2	+0.5	+7.3
Under 1	1,217	5,616	4.6	7.5	−2.9	−38.6
1 to 4	5,293	2,367	0.4	0.6	−0.2	−29.9
5 to 14	16,037	2,619	0.2	0.2	−0.1	−29.5
15 to 24	18,856	9,148	0.5	0.6	−0.1	−12.5
25 to 34	15,901	9,315	0.6	0.8	−0.2	−22.7
35 to 44	19,714	23,862	1.2	1.6	−0.4	−23.1
45 to 54	17,151	51,986	3.0	4.0	−0.9	−23.3
55 to 64	14,508	110,269	7.6	8.6	−1.0	−11.6
65 to 74	8,946	159,744	17.9	24.9	−7.1	−28.4
75 and over	5,989	444,930	74.3	90.5	−16.2	−17.9

[1] Deaths for Japanese nationals in Japan only.
[2] Based on unrounded numbers.
Source: United Nations, *Demographic Yearbook*, 1991, Tables 7 and 13; 1980, Tables 7 and 13.

An age-specific death rate is defined conventionally as the number of deaths of persons of a given age during a year (D_a) per 1000 of the midyear population at that age (P_a)—that is,

$$M_a = \frac{D_a}{P_n} \times 1000 \qquad (12.8)$$

Age-specific death rates are usually computed for 5- or 10-year age groups; but, because of the relatively great magnitude of the death rates among infants, separate rates are usually shown for the age groups under 1 and 1 to 4. The calculation of a set or schedule of age-specific death rates is illustrated for Japan in 1990 in Table 12.2. The rate for the age group 75 and over is derived by dividing deaths at ages 75 and over by the population aged 75 and over:

$$\frac{444,930}{5,989,000} \times 1000 = 74.3$$

This is a type of central rate—that is, a rate relating events in a given category during a year to the average population of the year in the category. The average population is ordinarily taken as the midyear population but often the census counts are employed in the calculation of rates for the census year. (Note that 2- or 3-year average age-specific death rates may be computed in the same way as average crude death rates, using the midperiod population.)

Table 12.2 also illustrates the calculation of changes in age-specific death rates from one date to another. Absolute changes and percentage changes are shown. An increase is indicated by a plus (+) sign and a decrease by a minus (−) sign. In calculating the percentage change (col. 6), the absolute change (col. 5) is divided by the rate at the earlier date (col. 4). Because of the often very low level of death rates at the younger ages above earliest childhood, and the very high level of death rates at the older ages, absolute figures tend to "minimize" the indication of change at the younger ages and to "maximize" it at the older ages, whereas percentages tend to have the opposite effect.[1]

It is important to recognize the relation of a crude death rate to the underlying age-specific death rates. A crude rate may be viewed as the weighted average of a set of age-specific death rates, the weights being the proportions of the total population at each age—that is, it may be viewed as the cumulative product of a set of age-specific death rates and an age distribution for a given population:

$$\sum_{a=0}^{\infty}\left(\frac{D_a}{P_a}\right)\left(\frac{P_a}{P}\right) = \sum_{a=0}^{\infty}\frac{\frac{Da}{Pa} \times P_a}{P} = \frac{\sum_{a=0}^{\infty} D_a}{P} = \frac{D}{P} \quad (12.9)$$

where D and P represent total deaths and population, respectively, D_a and P_a deaths and population at each age, respectively, D_a/P_a an age-specific death rate, and P_a/P the proportion of the population in an age group. Similarly, the change in the crude death rate between two dates may be viewed as a joint result of changes in age-specific rates and changes in age composition. A crude death rate may have declined because age-specific death rates tended to fall or

[1] In computing the percentage differences between death rates, particularly by age, because the base is often small, special attention should be given to the number of significant digits to be shown in the result, taking account of the number of significant digits in the basic rates.

because the proportion of the population in childhood and the young adult ages, where age-specific death rates are low, increased.

Similarly, age-specific death rates may vary from country to country in a quite different degree from the corresponding crude death rates. The various age-specific death rates may generally be much higher in one country than in another, while the crude rates in the two countries may be nearly the same or have an opposite relation.

Death rates may be made specific for sex and for other characteristics in combination with age. An age-sex specific death rate is defined as the number of deaths of males or females in a particular age group per 1000 males or females in the age group:

$$\frac{D_a^m}{P_a^m} \times 1000, \frac{D_a^f}{P_a^f} \times 1000 \qquad (12.10)$$

Next to age, sex may be considered the most important variable in the analysis of mortality. In fact, age-specific death rates are almost always sex-specific also. A comparison of male and female death rates by age is given in the form of the percentage excess of the male rate over the female rate for a few countries in Table 12.3. Death rates of males show a marked excess over death rates for females in all or most age groups, particularly in areas of low mortality. The lower the general level of mortality, the greater the excess of male over female mortality tends to be. Thus, the gap between the rates for the sexes tends to be smaller in the less developed countries. It may even be completely erased (e.g., Bangladesh, Nepal, and Mali) or the female rates may be higher only in older childhood or the repro-

ductive ages (e.g., Sri Lanka, India, and Pakistan). Generally, too, the time trends in the differences between male and female age-specific death rates have followed the preceding patterns as mortality declined. A number of studies have considered the causes of the sex differences in mortality (Rogers *et al.*, 2000, Chapter 3; Wingard, 1982).

Death rates may be limited on the basis of other characteristics in addition to age and sex, for example, nativity, race, various socioeconomic characteristics, and cause of death. Other types of specific death rates are considered in the next sections.

Cause-Specific Death Ratios and Rates

An important aspect of the analysis of mortality relates to the classification by cause of death. The classification of deaths according to cause employed by national governments generally follows the International Classification of Diseases as promulgated by the World Health Organization (WHO). The classification has regularly gone through a decennial revision under the auspices of the WHO or its predecessor organizations in order that it may be consistent with the latest diagnostic practice and with medical advances. The Ninth Revision of the International Classification was adopted by the World Health Organization in 1975 and has been used for compiling mortality data in the United States since 1979 (World Health Organization, 1977). The Eighth Revision of the International Classification was adopted by the World Health Organization in 1965 and was first employed in modified form in the United States in 1968 (U.S. National Center for Health Statistics, 2001; WHO, 1967). The Seventh Revision

TABLE 12.3 Comparison of Male and Female Age-Specific Death Rates, for Various Countries: Around 1990

| Age (years) | United States, 1990 | | | El Salvador, 1992 | | | Korea, 1994 | | |
	Male (1)	Female (2)	Excess of male rate[1] (2) − (1) = (3)	Male (4)	Female (5)	Excess of male rate[1] (4) − (5) = (6)	Male (7)	Female (8)	Excess of male rate[1] (7) − (8) = (9)
All ages									
Under 5	2.8	2.2	0.6	6.4	5.3	1.1	1.4	1.1	0.2
Under 1	13.6	10.7	2.9	28.7	22.6	6.0	3.5	2.9	0.6
1 to 4	0.5	0.4	0.1	1.4	1.4	0.1	0.8	0.7	0.1
5 to 14	0.3	0.2	0.1	0.7	0.5	0.2	0.5	0.3	0.1
15 to 24	1.5	0.5	1.0	2.7	0.9	1.9	1.2	0.5	0.7
25 to 34	2.0	0.7	1.3	5.1	1.3	3.8	1.9	0.8	1.2
35 to 44	3.1	1.4	1.7	7.1	2.3	4.8	3.7	1.2	2.5
45 to 54	6.1	3.4	2.7	10.2	4.4	5.8	8.4	3.0	5.4
55 to 64	15.5	8.8	6.7	16.6	9.7	6.9	17.6	7.3	10.3
65 to 74	34.9	19.9	15.0	16.6	9.7	6.9	43.4	21.7	21.8
75 and over	98.8	74.0	24.7	78.0	66.2	11.7	203.0	178.3	24.7

[1] Based on unrounded numbers.

Source: U.S. National Center for Health Statistics, *Vital Statistics of the United States, 1993*, Vol. II, *Mortality*, Part A, Tables 1.27 and 1.4; and United Nations, *Demographic Yearbook*.

of the International Classification was adopted by the World Health Organization in 1955 and was used for compiling mortality data in the United States from 1958 to 1967 (WHO, 1957). The Sixth Revision was adopted by the World Health Organization in 1948 and was used for compiling mortality data in the United States from 1949 through 1957.

Comparability of cause-of-death statistics has been affected by each decennial revision of the International Classification. To promote flexibility, the manual for the Ninth Revision does not contain the special tabulation lists used in earlier revisions. A basic tabulation list was adopted instead with the intent of allowing each country or area to adapt the list to its own needs by constructing an appropriate list of categories. The U.S. National Center for Health Statistics has adapted the WHO lists in the form of five alternative lists for purposes of tabulation and publication in the volumes of *Vital Statistics in the United States* for 1968 and later years.

In the Ninth Revision of the International Classification, the causes of death are classified under 17 major headings, several of which represent the principal anatomical sites of diseases in the body (U.S. Department of Health and Human Services, 1990). Chapter XVII, injury and poisoning, was a major departure from the corresponding chapter in earlier revisions because of the change in the role of the E code for external causes. In the Sixth, Seventh, and Eighth Revisions, Chapter XVII (accidents, poisonings, and violence) had two alternative classifications, one for the nature of the injury (N code) and the other for the external cause (E cause). Chapter XVII of the Ninth Revision only has titles for nature of injury as part of the main classification. In 1987, the codes for HIV/AIDS (*042–*044) were added. These codes are not part of the Ninth Revision. The major classes with their code numbers are as follows:

    I Infectious and parasitic diseases (000–139)
   II Neoplasms (140–239)
  III Endocrine, nutritional, and metabolic diseases and immunity disorders (240–279)
   IV Diseases of the blood and blood-forming organs (280–289)
    V Mental disorders (290–319)
   VI Diseases of the nervous system and sense organs (320–389)
  VII Diseases of the circulatory system (390–459)
 VIII Diseases of the respiratory system (460–519)
   IX Diseases of the digestive system (520–579)
    X Diseases of the genitourinary system (580–629)
   XI Complications of pregnancy, childbirth, and the puerperium (630–676)
  XII Diseases of the skin and subcutaneous tissue (680–709)
 XIII Diseases of the musculoskeletal system and connective tissue (710–739)
  XIV Congenital anomalies (740–759)
   XV Certain conditions originating in the perinatal period (760–779)
  XVI Symptoms, signs, and ill-defined conditions (780–799)
 XVII Injury and poisoning (E800–E999)

A list of selected causes of deaths with code numbers, identification of the major class to which each listed cause belongs, and comparability ratios between the Ninth and Eighth Revisions for selected causes (based on U.S. data) are presented in Table 12.4 (U.S. National Center for Health Statistics, 1980).

Three special aspects of the quality of cause-of-death tabulations are worth special consideration. These relate to the determination of the cause to be tabulated when more than one cause of death is reported, the problems of historical and international comparability, and the use of the category, "symptoms, signs, and ill-defined conditions" (ICD-9 category numbers 780–799). The World Health Organization's specification of the form of medical certification and of the coding procedures to be used in processing death certificates deals with these problems. Since the Sixth Revision in 1948, the rule has been that the certification must make clear the train of morbid events leading to death and, when more than one cause of death is reported, the cause designated by the certifying medical attendant as the underlying cause of death is the cause tabulated (Střiteský, Šantruček, and Vacek, 1967). This is the cause that the medical examiner judges to be the one that started the train of events leading directly to death. The rule is important in affecting the tabulations of deaths because a large proportion of death certificates filed may report more than one condition as the cause of death, as is true in the United States (U.S. National Center for Health Statistics, 1984).

The comparability of the tabulations of deaths by cause, from area to area, depends on the skill of the certifying medical attendant in diagnosing the cause of death and in describing the cause on the death certificate, and, to a more limited extent, on the skill of the coder in classifying the cause on the basis of the information on the certificate. Several studies on the quality of medical certification have been undertaken. An extensive bibliography prepared by the U.S. National Center for Health Statistics indicated that no definitive conclusions had been reached regarding the quality of medical certification. No country has been able to develop a well-defined program for evaluating the quality of medical certifications reported on death certificates or for measuring the effects of errors on the levels and trends of cause-of-death statistics. The comparability of tabulations would vary with the cause of death. International comparability is also affected by the fact that the year a revision of the International Classification is put into actual use by the member nations varies from country to country. The comparability of cause-of-death tabulations over time is affected not only by revisions in the classification scheme but also

TABLE 12.4 Abbreviated List of Selected Causes of Death According to the Ninth (1979) Revision of the International Classification of Diseases, and Comparability Ratios between the Ninth and Eighth Revisions

Major Class	Cause of death	Detailed list number	Estimated comparability ratio[1]	Major class	Cause of death	Detailed list number	Estimated comparability ratio[1]
I	Shigellosis and amebiasis	004, 006	0.9818	VIII	Pneumonia	480–486	0.9199
					Influenza	487	0.9714
	Certain other intestinal Infections	007–009	0.1821		Bronchitis, chronic and unspecified	490–491	0.9383
	Tuberculosis	010–018	0.7668		Emphysema	492	0.9770
	Whooping cough	033	0.8571		Asthma	493	1.3544
	Streptococcal sore throat, scarlatina, and erysipelas	034–035	1.4286	IX	Ulcer of stomach and duodenum	531–533	1.1192
	Meningococcal infection	036	0.9788		Appendicitis	540–543	1.0080
	Septicema	038	0.8500		Hernia of abdominal cavity and intestinal obstruction without mention of hernia	550–553, 560	0.9432
	Acute poliomyelitis	045	0.5000				
	Measles	055	0.9167				
	Viral hepatitis	070	1.3986				
	Syphilis	090–097	1.0089	X	Chronic liver disease and cirrhosis	571	1.0110
	All other infectious and parasitic diseases	Remainder of 000–139	1.0321		Nephritis, nephrotic syndrome, and nephrosis	580–589	1.7397
II	Malignant neoplasms, including neoplasms of lymphatic and hematopoietic tissues	140–208	1.0026		Hyperplasia of prostate	600	1.0232
				XI	Pregnancy with abortive outcome	630–638	3.8125
	Benign neoplasms, carcinoma in situ, and neoplasms of uncertain behavior and of unspecified nature	210–239	1.2085	XIV	Other complications of pregnancy, childbirth, and the puerperium	640–676	0.9840
					Congenital anomalies	740–759	0.9984
				XV	Birth trauma, intrauterine hypoxia, birth asphyxia, and respiratory distress syndrome	767–769	0.7483
III	Diabetes mellitus	250	0.9991				
	Nutritional deficiencies	260–269	0.7167		Other conditions originating in the perinatal period	760–766, 770–779	1.4639
IV	Anemias	280–285	0.9296				
VI	Meningitis	320–322	0.9459	XVI	Signs, symptoms, and ill-defined conditions	780–799	0.9102
VII	Rheumatic fever and rheumatic heart disease	390–398	0.6648				
					All other diseases	Residual	0.7786
	Hypertensive heart disease	402	3.3022	XVII	Motor vehicle accidents	E810–E825	
	Hypertensive heart and renal disease	404	1.2119		All other accidents and adverse effects	E800–E807 E826–E949	0.9841
	Ischemic heart disease	410–414	0.8784		Suicide	E950–E959	1.0032
	All other forms of heart disease	415–423 425–429	2.5035		Homicide and legal intervention	E960-E978	1.0057
	Cerebrovascular diseases	430–438	1.0049		All other external causes	E980–E999	0.9675

[1] Ratio of deaths assigned according to the Ninth Revision to deaths assigned according to the Eighth Revision.

Source: U.S. National Center for Health Statistics. *Monthly Vital Statistics Report. Estimates of Selected Comparability Ratios Based on Dual Coding of 1976 Death Certificates by the Eighth and Ninth Revisions of the International Classification of Diseases.* By A.J. Klebba and J.H. Scott. 1980. DHEW Publication No. (PHS) 80-1120. Vol. 28., No. 11, Supplement. Washington, DC: U.S. Public Health Service.

by improved diagnosis and changing fashions in diagnosis. These last factors may account, in part, for the recent rise in mortality attributable to the chronic diseases of later life in the less developed countries.

Although some deaths are extremely difficult to classify, care in the certification of cause of death keeps the number of deaths of ill-defined or unknown cause to a minimum. The proportion of deaths assigned to "symptoms, senility, and ill-defined conditions" (Eighth Revision category numbers 780–796 and Ninth Revision category numbers 780–799) may be employed as one measure of the quality of reporting cause of death. For example, this category accounts for less than 1% of the deaths in Australia (1994), slightly more than 1% in the United States (1993), but for 21% in Egypt (1987) and 21% in South Africa (1993). Clearly, the cause-of-death tabulations for Egypt and South Africa should be used with caution.

Mortality by cause of death may be analyzed in terms of two observed measures: death ratios specific for cause and death rates specific for cause. The former measure requires simply a distribution of deaths by cause and hence can be computed for intercensal years even when population figures are lacking.

A *cause-specific death ratio* represents the percentage of all deaths due to a particular cause or group of causes. The death ratio for cause C is

$$\frac{D_c}{D} \times 100 \qquad (12.11)$$

where D_c, represents deaths from a particular cause or group of causes, and D represents all deaths. Death ratios by cause are shown for several countries in Table 12.5. A set of death ratios readily permits comparisons from country to country, or from one year to another for the same country, of the relative importance of a particular cause or group of causes of death. For example, the death ratio for cerebrovascular disease is considerably higher in Spain (13.0%) and Japan (14.9%) than in some other countries (e.g., 6.7% in the United States, 1990, and 4.5% in El Salvador, 1990). The death ratio for tuberculosis is much higher in Zimbabwe (4.3% in 1990) than in the other countries.

The population exposed to risk of death from a particular cause or group of causes may be directly taken account of, in rough terms, by calculating "crude" cause-of-death rates (Table 12.6). Separate death rates may be calculated for each cause or group of causes of death. A cause-specific death rate is conventionally defined as the number of deaths from a given cause or group of causes during a year per 100,000 of the midyear population.

$$\frac{D_c}{P} \times 100,000 \qquad (12.12)$$

A cause-specific death rate employs a larger constant, or k, factor than a crude death rate or an age-specific death rate because there are relatively few deaths from many of the causes.

It should be noted that a cause-specific death rate is unlike other types of death rates in one important respect—

TABLE 12.5 Deaths and Death Ratios Specific by Cause, for Various Countries: 1990 (Deaths are classified according to the Ninth (1979) Revision of the International Statistical Classification of Diseases, Injuries, and Causes of Death. Ratios are the number of deaths from each cause per 100 deaths from all causes.)

Cause of death[1]	United States		Zimbabwe[2]		El Salvador[3]		Spain		Japan[4]	
	Deaths	Ratios	Deaths	Ratios	Deaths	Ratios	Deaths	Ratios	Deaths	Ratios
All causes	2,148,463	100.0	34,829	100.0	28,224	100.0	333,142	100.0	820,305	100.0
Tuberculosis (010–018)	1,810	0.1	1,501	4.3	132	0.5	861	0.3	3,664	0.4
Malignant neoplasm of female breast (174)	43,391	2.0	100	0.3	38	0.1	5,398	1.6	5,848	0.7
Diabetes mellitus (250)	47,664	2.2	349	1.0	347	1.2	8,989	2.7	9,470	1.2
Cerebrovascular diseases (430–438)	144,088	6.7	1,175	3.4	1,256	4.5	43,263	13.0	121,944	14.9
Atherosclerosis (440)	18,047	0.8	45	0.1	11	z	9,626	2.9	2,118	0.3
Chronic liver disease and cirrhosis (571)	25,815	1.2	419	1.2	345	1.2	7,892	2.4	16,804	2.0
Nephritis, nephrotic syndrome, and nephrosis (580–589)	20,764	1.0	461	1.3	282	1.0	5,632	1.7	17,140	2.1
Congenital anomalies (740–759)	13,085	0.6	485	1.4	214	0.8	1,382	0.4	3,571	0.4
All other diseases	1,683,588	78.4	25,849	74.2	20,168	71.5	231,232	69.4	584,134	71.2
Accidents, suicides, and homicides (E810–E999)	150,211	7.0	4,445	12.8	5,431	19.2	18,867	5.7	55,612	6.8

z Less than 0.05.

[1] Numbers in parentheses represent the code numbers in the Ninth (1979) Revision of the International Classification.

[2] Data from incomplete registers.

[3] Includes deaths of foreigners temporarily in country.

[4] Japanese nationals only.

Source: United Nations, *Demographic Yearbook*, 1995, Table 20.

TABLE 12.6 Death Rates Specific by Cause, for Various Countries: 1990

Cause of death[1]	United States	Zimbabwe[2]	El Salvador	Spain	Japan	Sweden	Argentina
All causes	859.7	371.7	545.7	855.1	664.0	1111.6	789.0
Tuberculosis (010–018)	0.7	16.0	2.6	2.2	3.0	0.5	4.1
Malignant neoplasm of the female breast[3] (174)	42.8	z	z	33.5	11.3	41.0	37.0
	19.1	3.7	6.7	23.1	7.7	17.9	17.2
Diabetes mellitus (250)	57.7	12.5	24.3	111.0	98.7	120.3	79.3
Cerebrovascular diseases (430–438)	57.7	12.5	24.3	111.0	98.7	120.3	79.3
Atherosclerosis (440)	7.2	0.5	0.2	24.7	1.7	29.1	22.2
Chronic liver disease and cirrhosis (571)	10.3	4.5	6.7	20.3	13.6	7.6	9.6
Nephritis, nephrotic syndrome, and nephrosis (580–589)	8.3	4.9	5.5	14.5	13.9	5.2	14.7
Congenital anomalies (740–759)	5.2	5.2	4.1	3.5	2.9	4.8	9.3
All other diseases	673.7	277.0	389.9	593.5	472.8	850.6	568.4
Accidents, suicide, and homicide (E810–E999)	60.1	47.4	105.0	48.4	45.0	58.4	51.1
Population	249,911,000[4]	9,369,000	5,172,000	38,959,000	123,537,000	8,559,000	32,547,000

z Less than 0.05.

[1] Numbers in parentheses represent the code numbers in the Ninth Revision of the International Classification.

[2] Data from civil registers which are incomplete or of unknown completeness.

[3] Per 100,000 females 15 and over.

[4] Estimate.

Source: Table 12.5 and United Nations, *Demographic Yearbook*, various years.

that is, the base population cannot logically be limited to the class defined in the numerator (a particular cause). In an age-specific death rate, for example, the deaths at a given age are related to the population *at that age*. In a cause-specific rate, however, the general population cannot be classified by cause of death even though our interest is in defining the population at risk of death from the given cause. (The conventional "case-fatality rate," for example, indicates the risk of dying from a particular cause during a period among persons who have incurred the illness or injury during the period. Another type of case-fatality rate could be defined in relation to the entire population suffering from a particular illness, injury, or disability.) This limitation can be partly overcome, and the usefulness of cause-specific death rates greatly increased, by making them age-specific or age-sex specific also, especially because many causes of death are largely or wholly confined to a particular age or age-sex group in the population. For example, deaths due to scarlet fever, measles, whooping cough, and diphtheria are largely confined to childhood; infantile diarrhea and enteritis, congenital malformations, immaturity, and so forth are virtually confined to infancy; deaths due to diabetes, cerebrovascular diseases, nephritis, cirrhosis, and so on affect largely persons over 50. It may be argued that because certain causes have relevance only to a restricted part of the age distribution or to only one sex, general rates for these causes have no significance and only age-sex-cause-specific rates should be computed for them.

Cause-specific death rates have no particular advantage over death ratios in indicating the relative importance of the various causes of death for a particular area in a given year. Their advantage lies in comparisons from area to area of the relative frequency of a particular cause of death "adjusted for" the size of the population in each area. We can say, for example, that the death rate from cerebrovascular diseases in Sweden (120 per 100,000 population) is nearly five times the rate in El Salvador (24.3). (See Table 12.6.) The cause-specific death rates in a set covering all causes sum to the crude death rate (per 100,000).

In analyzing mortality in terms of cause of death, it is useful to distinguish two broad classes of deaths, designated as *endogenous* and *exogenous*, and to compute separate rates for these classes of deaths (Bourgeois-Pichat, 1952). There is no clear distinction between exogenous and endogenous mortality (Carnes and Olshansky, 1997); therefore, the causes of death assigned to these two categories may vary somewhat depending on the judgment of the person doing the research (Poston and Rogers, 1985; Sowards, 1997; Stockwell *et al.*, 1987). Generally, however, the former class of deaths is presumed to arise from the genetic makeup of the individual and from the circumstances of prenatal life and the birth process; and the latter class is presumed to arise from purely environmental or external causes. Endogenous mortality would include mortality from such causes as the chronic diseases of later life (e.g., heart disease, cancer, diabetes) and certain diseases peculiar to early infancy (e.g., immaturity, birth injuries, postnatal asphyxia). Exogenous mortality would include mortality mainly from infections and accidents. Endogenous mortality has a typically biological character and is resistant to treatment, control, and cure whereas exogenous mortality is viewed as relatively preventable and treatable.

The endogenous death rate is derived as follows:

$$\frac{D_{en}}{P} \times 1000 \qquad (12.13)$$

where D_{en} represents deaths due to endogenous causes and P represents midyear population. The exogenous death rate is derived as follows:

$$\frac{D_{ex}}{P} \times 1000 \qquad (12.14)$$

where D_{ex} represents deaths due to exogenous cases and P represents midyear population. Table 12.7 presents statistics on deaths and death rates for endogenous and exogenous causes (ill-defined conditions" and "all other diseases" of the B list being assigned in part to endogenous causes and in part to exogenous causes) for Brazil, the United States, and Canada. Data are shown separately for the total

population, infants, older persons, and persons of intermediate age. Generally now, endogenous causes dominate at most ages, but especially in infancy and the older ages. Exogenous causes dominate in adolescence and early adulthood but fall off with increasing age until there is a virtual "monopoly" of endogenous causes in older age. The lower the general level of mortality, the more pronounced is the relative role of endogenous causes.

Death Rates Specific for Social or Economic Characteristics

Important variations in mortality are or may be associated with a number of social and economic characteristics of the decedent, among them ethnic group, marital status, educational attainment, occupation, income, and socioeconomic class. Such variations have implications for understanding the physical and socioeconomic factors in health and for planning public health and other welfare programs. Because the specific subgroups of the population classified by a socioeconomic characteristic may have different age and sex distributions (e.g., the proportion 65–74 years in an occupational class), it is desirable to calculate the death rates for socioeconomic groups separately for age and sex groups. We will give direct consideration here to death rates for only

TABLE 12.7 Exogenous and Endogenous Deaths for Selected Countries, 1988 to 1991

Cause of death[1]	United States, 1990											
	All ages	Under 1	1–64	65–69	70–74	75–79	80–84	85–89	90–94	95–99	100+	Total 65+
Exogenous deaths												
001–139	55,612	840	33,596	2,953	3,425	4,035	4,157	3,487	2,176	773	170	21,176
320–322	1,017	197	485	70	76	67	61	36	20	5	—	335
323	—	—	—	—	—	—	—	—	—	—	—	—
460–465	264	33	78	18	14	20	24	27	22	24	4	153
466	633	75	111	44	46	72	85	92	67	34	7	447
480–486	77,415	627	8,217	4,015	6,404	10,372	14,381	15,174	11,640	5,310	1,275	68,571
487	2,098	7	177	87	159	238	386	475	353	176	40	1,914
500–508	9,108	20	860	572	910	1,400	1,776	1,780	1,241	451	98	8,228
771	875	875	—	—	—	—	—	—	—	—	—	—
800–999	150,211	1,315	114,782	6,276	6,168	6,818	6,231	4,749	2,711	978	183	34,114
Exogenous	297,233	3,989	158,306	14,035	17,202	23,022	27,101	25,820	18,230	7,751	1,777	134,938
All causes	2,148,463	38,351	567,619	217,333	260,616	301,114	300,325	244,882	148,118	57,765	12,340	1,542,493
Endogenous	1,851,230	34,362	409,313	203,298	243,414	278,092	273,224	219,062	129,888	50,014	10,563	1,407,555
% exogenous	13.8	10.4	27.9	6.5	6.6	7.6	9.0	10.5	12.3	13.4	14.4	8.7
% endogenous	86.2	89.6	72.1	93.5	93.4	92.4	91.0	89.5	87.7	86.6	85.6	91.3
SS&I[2]	22,829	6,409	7,945	1,185	1,337	1,499	1,643	1,314	921	441	135	8,475
exogenous	3,158	667	2,216	77	88	115	148	139	113	59	19	741
endogenous	19,671	5,742	5,729	1,108	1,249	1,384	1,495	1,175	808	382	116	7,734
Exogenous	300,391	4,656	160,522	14,112	17,290	23,137	27,249	25,959	18,343	7,810	1,796	135,679
Endogenous	1,848,072	33,695	407,097	203,221	243,326	277,977	273,076	218,923	129,775	49,955	10,544	1,406,814
Total	2,148,463	38,351	567,619	217,333	260,616	301,114	300,325	244,882	148,118	57,765	12,340	1,542,493
% Exogenous	14.0	12.1	28.3	6.5	6.6	7.7	9.1	10.6	12.4	13.5	14.6	8.8
% Endogenous	86.0	87.9	71.7	93.5	93.4	92.3	90.9	89.4	87.6	86.5	85.4	91.2

(continues)

TABLE 12.7 *(continued)*

Cause of death[1]	Brazil, 1988					
	All ages	Under 1	1–64	65–74	75+	65+
Exogenous deaths						
001–139	47,829	19,075	22,376	2,953	3,425	6,378
320–322	2,940	1,244	1,541	93	62	155
323	—	—	—	—	—	—
460–465	913	691	164	15	43	58
466	—	—	—	—	—	—
480–487	35,980	627	24,934	4,015	6,404	10,419
487	—	—	—	—	—	—
500–508	—	—	—	—	—	—
771	—	—	—	—	—	—
E47–E53	53,311	910	46,762	2,699	2,940	5,639
E54	4,492	0	4,024	281	187	468
E55	23,341	58	22,789	345	149	494
E56	14,939	124	13,913	513	389	902
Exogenous	183,745	22,729	136,503	10,914	13,599	24,513
All causes	833,369	119,792	378,453	136,834	198,290	335,124
Endogenous	649,624	97,063	241,950	125,920	184,691	310,611
% exogenous	22.0	19.0	36.1	8.0	6.9	7.3
% endogenous	78.0	81.0	63.9	92.0	93.1	92.7
SS&I[2]	157,812	26,406	56,290	25,178	49,938	75,116
exogenous	34,795	5,010	24,351.87	2,008	3,425	5,433
endogenous	123,017	21,396	31,938.13	23,170	46,513	69,683
Exogenous	218,540	27,739	160,855	12,922	17,024	29,946
Endogenous	614,829	92,053	217,598	123,912	181,266	305,178
Total	833,369	119,792	378,453	136,834	198,290	335,124
% Exogenous	26.2	23.2	42.5	9.4	8.6	8.9
% Endogenous	73.8	76.8	57.5	90.6	91.4	91.1

Cause of death[1]	Canada, 1991					
	All ages	Under 1	1–64	65–74	75+	65+
Exogenous deaths						
001–139	1,454	26	413	332	683	1,015
320–322	63	19	23	7	14	21
323	—	—	—	—	—	—
460–465	39	4	11	3	21	24
466	55	6	12	8	29	37
480–487	6,776	34	514	837	5,391	6,228
487	—	—	—	—	—	—
500–508	—	—	—	—	—	—
771	—	—	—	—	—	—
E47–E53	8,785	53	5,615	804	2,313	3,117
E54	3,593	—	3,146	277	170	447
E55	622	12	567	24	19	43
E56	237	6	194	22	15	37
Exogenous	21,624	160	10,495	2,314	8,655	10,969
All causes	195,568	2,571	48,513	44,217	100,267	144,484
Endogenous	173,944	2,411	38,018	41,903	91,612	133,515
			—			—
% exogenous	11.1	6.2	21.6	5.2	8.6	7.6
% endogenous	88.9	93.8	78.4	94.8	91.4	92.4
SS&I[2]	3,682	437	1,259	596	1,390	1,986
exogenous	407	27	272	31	120	151
endogenous	3,275	410	987	565	1,270	1,835
Exogenous	22,031	187	10,723.75	2,345	8,775	11,120.17
Endogenous	173,537	2,384	37,789.25	41,872	91,492	133,363.8
Total	195,568	2,571	48,513	44,217	100,267	144,484
% Exogenous	11.3	7.3	22.1	5.3	8.8	7.7
% Endogenous	88.7	92.7	77.9	94.7	91.2	92.3

—zero.

[1] Ninth Revision of the International Classification of Diseases.

[2] "Symptoms, Signs, and ill-defined conditions."

Source: WHO, *World Health Statistics Annual, 1993, 1994;* and *NCHS. 1990, Vital Statistics of the United States*, Table 1.27.

a few of the possible characteristics, particularly marital status, occupation, and socioeconomic status.

Death rates specific for marital status, age, and sex are useful not only for the analysis of mortality patterns but also for the study of the dissolution of marriage. To compute such rates, both death rates distributed by age, sex, and marital status and population rates distributed by these characteristics are needed.

Such rates are affected by differences in the errors in, and by the comparability of, the information on marital status on death certificates and in the census. These are general problems affecting vital rates for socioeconomic groupings of the population since the numerator of the rate comes from the vital statistics system and the denominator comes from the census.

Little data are available of a satisfactory quality on deaths for occupations and socioeconomic status. The principal tabulations of deaths for occupational categories have been made for the United States and the United Kingdom, although several other countries have compiled such data. National mortality data on occupations have appeared decennially from 1851 to-date for England and Wales, with the latest report covering the years 1979–1980 and 1982–1990. Canada also has produced a major report describing mortality on occupations in British Columbia with data covering 1950 through 1984 (Gallagher et al., 1989). The first report describing occupational mortality in the United States was published for scattered years beginning in 1890.

Death statistics and death rates for occupations are subject to a number of important types of errors. They are subject to the errors of death statistics in general and to errors in the reporting, coding, and classification of occupation. Whenever a high proportion of deaths is unclassified or not clearly classified by occupation, the quality of the statistics on deaths is in question. Like death rates for marital status, death rates for occupations are affected by differences in the nature and accuracy of the information returned on the death certificate as compared with that returned in the population census. The problem of disagreement between the reporting of occupations in the two sources can be sharply reduced by combining occupations into major groups.

In the United States, the lack of correspondence between numerator and denominator of the death rate is chiefly a result of the large proportion of decedents reported as "not in the labor force" or "retired" in the census (current activity) for whom a report of usual occupation is given on the death certificate. This problem can largely be eliminated by limiting the tabulations to the age range 20 to 59 or 20 to 64, although this excludes the majority of deaths.

In 1997, the United States published a study that described mortality by occupation, industry, and cause of death using data from 24 reporting states for the years 1984 to 1988 (U.S. NIOSH/Burnett, Maurer, and Dosemeci, 1997). The report included an analysis for all white and

black males and females aged 20 and older. Women listed in the census as "housewives, homemakers" were excluded from both the occupation and industry analysis. This was the first report of its kind since 1962 when a study describing the variation of mortality by occupation and industry among men 20 to 64 years of age in the United States in 1950 resulted in the publication of a number of study on this subject. In the 1962 report, for example, death rates (per 100,000 population) were presented for specific occupations, by age and color of decedent, and for specific industry groups, by age of decedent (U.S. NIOSH/Burnett et al., 1997). Standardized mortality ratios were presented for specific occupations by color, for major occupation groups by selected causes of death and color, and for specific occupations and industries by selected causes of death.

A *standardized mortality ratio* (SMR) for a particular occupation or industry among males compares the tabulated numbers of deaths in that occupation or industry with the number to be expected had the age-specific death rates for the total male population with work experience prevailed in that occupation or industry. The method of calculation used in the 1962 publication is illustrated with data on deaths from tuberculosis of white miners in the United States in 1950 (U.S. National Office of Vital Statistics, 1950b).

Age (years)	Number of white miners p_a	Death rate from tuberculosis, all working males M_a
20–24	74,598	.0001226
25–29	85,077	.0001612
30–34	80,845	.0002154
35–44	148,870	.0003396
45–54	102,649	.0005682
55–59	42,494	.0007523
60–64	30,037	.0008237
Total, 20–64	564,570	.0009565

[1] Expected deaths from tuberculosis for white miners = $\Sigma M_a p_a$ = Σ column (1) × column (2) = 206
[2] Tabulated deaths from tuberculosis for white miners = d = 540
[3] Standardized mortality ratio =

$$\frac{d}{\sum M_a p_a} \times 100 \quad \text{or} \quad \frac{\sum m_a p_a}{\sum M_a p_a} \times 100 = \frac{540}{206} \times 100 = 263$$

In this calculation, the age-specific death rates for all working males (col. 2) are assumed to apply to white miners (col. 1) in order to derive the expected number of deaths from tuberculosis for white miners. The standardized mortality ratio represents the ratio of the number of actual deaths from tuberculosis for white miners, 540, to the expected number, 206, expressed as an index (i.e., per 100). As later formulas show, the standardized mortality ratio is equivalent to the relative mortality of an occupation group computed by the method of "indirect standardization." Like all summary measures of this kind, the standardized ratios may mask differences found in the underlying age-specific rates (Silcock, 1959, pp. 183–192).

The 1997 report uses *age-standardized proportionate mortality ratios* (PMR) for the four race-sex groups, by age (age 20 and over, 20 to 64 years of age, and 65 and over), for 325 occupation categories and 235 industry categories and for selected causes of death (188 causes for females and 192 causes for males) as a measure of comparison. The proportionate mortality rate allows one to determine whether the proportion of deaths from a certain cause of death for a certain occupation is higher (greater than 100) or lower (less than 100) than the corresponding proportion for all occupations combined (U.S. NIOSH/Burnett *et al.*, 1997). A PMR greater than 100 is an indication of a higher relative risk of mortality. For example, a PMR of 156 for white male truck drivers aged 20 years and older (occupation code 804) who died as a result of a motor vehicle accident (E810–E825, E929.0) means that the proportion of deaths from this cause for white male truck drivers was 56% higher than that for all males in all occupations combined for this cause.

An advantage of the PMR is that it does not require the population data needed for population-based measures such as the SMR (U.S. National Center for Health Statistics/Rosenberg *et al.*, 1993). However, the PMR has certain limitations as an indicator of relative mortality risk. First, it is a ratio, not a death rate, because total deaths instead of the population at risk are used in its calculation (Dever, 1991). Second, PMRs can overstate the risk of mortality if the risk of death for all causes for an occupation or industry is low. Conversely, the PMR can understate mortality risk if the overall risk of death is high (Decoufle, Thomas, and Pickle, 1980). Third, abnormally high mortality in any of the major causes of death can distort the PMR. This is illustrated by the case of a low PMR resulting from a disproportionately or unusually high number of deaths from a major cause of death and vice versa. Finally, having a category of unreported occupations that are not distributed proportionately can affect the PMR (Zeighami and Morris, 1983). The formula given in the 1997 report for calculating age-adjusted proportionate mortality rates is as follows (U.S. NIOSH/Burnett *et al.*, 1997):

	Cause of death		
Occupation causes	*Cause X*	*Other causes*	*All*
Occupation Y	A_i	B_i	N_{1i}
Other occupations	C_i	D_i	N_{2i}
All occupations	M_{1i}	M_{2i}	T_i

$i = i^{th}$ age group (5-year age groups 20–24, 25–29, etc.)

A_i = observed number of deaths for a specific occupation (industry) and cause-of-death combination for the ith age group

$$E(A_i) = \frac{M_{1i} N_{1i}}{T_i}$$

where $E(A_i)$ = expected number of deaths for a specific occupation (industry) and cause-of-death combination for the ith age group.

$$PMR = \frac{\sum A_i}{\sum E(A_i)} \times 100 \qquad (12.15)$$

The association between causes of death and occupation and industry of a decedent may be explained by several factors, such as the level of health required for certain occupations (e.g., firefighter), the attraction of certain ethnic groups to particular types of occupations, and the socioeconomic status (income, educational attainment, etc.) of the decedent that encourages a lifestyle or behavior (e.g., smoking, alcohol consumption) that may be more strongly associated with mortality than the occupations themselves (U.S. National Center for Health Statistics/Rosenberg *et al.*, 1993).

In 1992, a rather comprehensive study of the effect of demographic, social, and economic factors on mortality was published by the U.S. National Institutes of Health/Rogot, Sorlie, Johnson, and Schmitt, 1992. Data for the study came from the 1979–1985 follow-up of the U.S. National Longitudinal Mortality Study (NLMS). The NLMS is a long-term prospective study of mortality that is used mainly to examine socioeconomic, demographic, and occupational mortality differentials in the United States. The results of the 1992 study were published in a book titled, *A Mortality Study of 1.3 Million Persons: By Demographic, Social, and Economic Factors: 1979–1985 Follow-up*, which was the second in a series of data books containing information from the NLMS. The first data book was published in 1988 and included data for 1979 to 1981. Standardized mortality ratios (SMRs) were calculated for 16 characteristics (e.g., nativity, education, income, marital status, employment status, etc.), by age, sex, and race, for the leading causes of death.

Adjusted Rates

Rates Adjusted to a Probability Basis

In general, the rates we have considered so far may be described as "central rates." Although they give a satisfactory indication of the relative frequency of the event of death, they do not describe precisely the risk of dying for any actual cohort (i.e., they are not true probabilities). Such probabilities express the chance that death will occur during a particular period to a person in a particular population group alive at the beginning of the period. When the probability is expressed as a ratio, the denominator represents the initial population "exposed to risk" and the numerator the frequency with which the event of death occurs in this particular population over the period. The most commonly computed probabilities of death are specific by age and relate to a 1-year period. An age-specific probability of dying might answer the question, for example, what is the chance that a newborn child will die before it reaches its first birthday? Such probabilities are referred to as "mortality rates" to distinguish them from the "central death rates" or "death rates" that we have previously described.

Conventional Infant Mortality Rate

Analysis of infant mortality has commonly been carried out in terms of the "infant mortality rate" rather than the infant death rate to approximate the probability of death among infants in a given year. The accuracy of the approximation varies from one situation to another but depends in general on the annual fluctuations in the number of births. We shall refer to this rate as the "conventional infant mortality rate" to distinguish it from certain other types of infant mortality rates, to be described, which are more akin to true probabilities. The conventional infant mortality rate is defined as the number of infant deaths per year per 1000 live births during the year:

$$\frac{D_o}{B} \times 1000 \qquad (12.16)$$

where D_o represents deaths of infants during a year and B represents live births during the same year.

Infant mortality rates vary in the following array for 1990 from 3.9 in Finland to 101.9 in Pakistan (United Nations, 1995).

Country	Rate	Country	Rate
Australia	5.7	Finland	3.9
Turkey	44.4	Portugal	7.5
Chile	11.1	Sweden	3.7
Costa Rica	13.2	India	74.0
Argentina	22.2	Thailand[1]	32.0
United Kingdom	6.2	France	4.6
Japan	4.3	United States	7.5
Pakistan[1]	101.9	Venezuela	21.0
Peru	81.0	Yugoslavia	16.4

[1] 1993.

Ordinarily, the conventional infant mortality rate gives a sufficiently close approximation to the chance of dying between birth and attainment of the first birthday for the year to which the basic data on deaths relate. It has been widely used as an indicator of the health conditions of a community and, hence, of its level of living, although it may not be particularly appropriate for this purpose in developed areas.

Because of the very high level of mortality in the first hours, days, and weeks of life and the difference in the causes accounting for infant deaths at the earlier and later ages of infancy, the conventional infant mortality rate may usefully be "broken up" into a rate covering the first month or so and a rate for the remainder of the year. The rate for the first period is called the neonatal mortality rate, and the rate for the second period is called the post-neonatal mortality rate. The neonatal mortality rate is defined as the number of deaths of infants under 4 weeks of age (28 days) or under 1 month of age during a year per 1000 live births during the year:

$$\text{Neonatal mortality rate} = \frac{D_{0-3weeks}}{B} \times 1000$$

$$\text{or} \quad \frac{D_{<1month}}{B} \times 1000 \qquad (12.17)$$

Because nearly all (over 95%) deaths of infants under 1 month of age occur to babies born in the same year, the resulting neonatal mortality rate is close to a probability of neonatal death. The post-neonatal mortality is defined as the number of infant deaths at 4 through 51 weeks of age or 1 through 11 months of age during a year per 1000 live births during the year:

$$\text{Post-neonatal mortality rate} = \frac{D_{4-51weeks}}{B} \times 1000$$

$$\text{or} \quad \frac{D_{1-11months}}{B} \times 1000 \qquad (12.18)$$

The formula for the post-neonatal mortality rate is quite far from expressing a true probability because more than a third of the infant deaths over 1 month of age in a year may occur to births of the previous year.

Adjusted Infant Mortality Rates

The conventional infant mortality rate is not a true probability, as has been noted. We can recognize this immediately by noting that not all of the infant deaths in a given year occurred to births in the same year; some occurred to births of the previous year. Consider, for example, the year of birth of the older infants (e.g., 10 months old) dying toward the beginning of the calendar year (e.g., February) as compared with the younger infants (e.g., 2 months old) dying toward the end of the year (e.g., October). If the number of births does not fluctuate much from year to year, the conventional infant mortality rate for a year will represent rather well the probability of an infant dying during the year. If there are sharp fluctuations in the number of births between years and within years, however, the conventional infant mortality rate will give a distorted indication of the level and trend of infant mortality (U.S. Bureau of the Census/Moriyama and Greville, 1944). It is desirable then to adjust the conventional rate to allow for the true population exposed to risk. Three alternative ways of calculating adjusted infant mortality rates are described next.

First, it is useful to consider the following diagram, which schematically shows the relationship among births in 3 successive years ($y - 1$, y, and $y + 1$), deaths under 1 in these

TABLE 12.8 Calculation of Conventional and Adjusted Infant Mortality Rates, for Japan: 1995–1997

Item	Symbols and fomulas	Year (y)			
		1994	1995	1996	1997
Births	B	1,238,328	1,187,064	1,206,555	1,191,665
Infant deaths					
D_y''	(X)	(X)	1,108	948	914
D_y'	(X)	(X)	3,946	3,598	3,489
Conventional infant mortality rate.	$\dfrac{D_y' + D_y''}{B_y} \times 1,000$	(X)	4.3	3.8	3.7
Adjusted Infant Mortality rates:					
A	$\dfrac{D_y' + D_{y+1}''}{B_y} \times 1,000$	(X)	4.1	3.7	(X)
B	$\left[\dfrac{D_y'}{B_y} + \dfrac{D_y''}{B_{y-1}}\right] \times 1,000$	(X)	4.2	3.8	3.7
C	$\dfrac{D_y}{f'B_y + (1-f')B_{y-1}}$	(X)	4.2	3.8	3.7

X: Not applicable.

[1] Separation factor $(f') = \dfrac{D_y'}{D_y' + D_y''}$. Factors: 1995, .7808; 1996, .7915; 1997, .7924.

Basic data from Japan, Ministry of Health and Welfare.

years, and the number of survivors reaching their first birthday in these years (l_1).

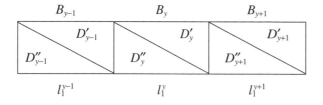

D_y' and D_y'' together make up infant deaths in year y; D_y' is the portion occurring to births in year y (B_y) and D_y'' is the portion occurring to births of the previous year (B_{y-1}). The cohort of births in year y (B_y) loses D_y' members through death in year y and D_{y+1}'' members through death in year $y + 1$ while moving toward its first birthday (l_1^{y+1}).

Table 12.8 illustrates the calculation of the adjusted infant mortality rate with data for Japan from 1995 to 1997 by several procedures. All the procedures allow for the fact that some of the infant deaths in a year occur to births of the same year and some occur to births of the previous year or, conversely, that some of the babies born in a given year who die before their first birthday die in the same year as the year of birth and some die in the following year. The separation of the deaths by birth cohort is readily possible in the case of Japan because the deaths are tabulated by year of birth. Normally, this is not the case, and *the separation factors for infant deaths*—that is, the proportions for dividing the

deaths according to birth cohort—must be estimated or, more commonly, assumed on the basis of statistics for other countries.

In the first procedure for calculating an "adjusted infant mortality rate" (Formula A in the table), the portion of deaths under 1 in year y and the portion of deaths under 1 in year $y + 1$ occurring to births in year y are combined and divided by the births in year y. Deaths in 1995 and 1996 are related to births in 1995 for Japan:

Formula A:

$$\frac{D_y' + D_{y+1}''}{B_y} \times 1000 \quad \text{or} \quad \frac{3946 + 948}{1,187,064} \times 1000 = 4.1 \quad (12.19)$$

In the next procedure (Formula B), each portion of the infant deaths occurring in a given year is related to the births in the appropriate year and cohort. The formula is illustrated with deaths in 1995 and births in 1995 and 1994 for Japan:

Formula B:

$$\left(\frac{D_y'}{B_y} + \frac{D_y''}{B_{y-1}}\right) \times 1000 \quad \text{or} \quad \left(\frac{3946}{1,187,064} + \frac{1108}{1,238,328}\right)$$
$$\times 1000 = (.00332 + .00089) \times 1000 = 4.2$$
$$(12.20)$$

In the third procedure for calculating an adjusted infant mortality rate for a particular year (Formula C), infant deaths in year y are divided by a weighted average of births in years y and $y - 1$. The weights may be taken as the same (separation) factors by which infant deaths in any year are divided into two parts according to birth cohort. Given statistics on deaths in a calendar year distributed by age and year of birth of the decedent, the separation factors for infant deaths are computed as follows:

$$f' = \frac{D'_y}{D'_y + D''_y} \quad \text{and} \quad f'' = 1 - f' \qquad (12.21)$$

Evaluating the formulas with data for Japan in 1995, we have

$$f' = \frac{3946}{5054} = .7808 \quad \text{and} \quad f'' = 1 - .7808 = .2192$$

The formula for the infant mortality rate, illustrated with figures on deaths for Japan in 1995, is as follows:

Formula C:

$$\frac{D_y}{f' B_y + f'' B_{y-1}} \times 1000 \qquad (12.22)$$

where f' and f'' are the weights or separation factors:

$$\frac{3946 + 1108}{(.7808)1,187,064 + (.2192)1,238,328} \times 1000$$

$$= \frac{5054}{926,860 + 271,441} \times 1000 = 4.2$$

The values of D'_y and D''_y in the present case were obtained directly by tabulation. In most cases, however, it is necessary to estimate or assume the factors. Accurate estimates of the factors can be made on the basis of tabulations of deaths by detailed age at death under 1 year (for example, days under 1 week, weeks under 1 month, months under 1 year). The procedure consists of (1) assuming that within each tabulation cell the deaths are rectangularly (evenly) distributed over time and age, (2) determining the proportions for separating deaths in each cell according to year of birth, (3) estimating the number in each cell that occurred to births of the previous year, (4) cumulating the numbers in step 3 over all tabulation cells, and (5) dividing the sum in step 4 by the total number of infant deaths in the year. The result is f'' and f' is obtained as the complement of f''.

One procedure for deriving separation factors from a tabulation by detailed age is illustrated in Table 12.9. This is the kind of tabulation recommended by the United Nations. Assuming a rectangular distribution over the calendar year and within each age, we can set down the proportion of deaths at each age that occurred to births of the previous year. Specifically, it was assumed that one-twelfth of the deaths in the year at any particular age occurred in a month, and 1/365 of the deaths in the year at any age occurred in a single day. Thus, of the deaths 11 months old in 1990, all from January through November and one-half of those in December were assumed to occur to the births

of 1989, since only the annual total is known for this age, we take 11.5/12 of the total. Proportions for separating deaths at each age under 1 into two birth cohorts are derived in the same general way. These proportions are then applied cumulatively to the total number of deaths at each age in the calendar year to derive the estimates of all infant deaths in the year belonging to the two birth cohorts. The resulting separation factors for deaths of female infants in the United States in 1990 are .8672 and .1328.

For most countries, tabulations of infant deaths by detailed age are lacking and it is necessary to estimate the separation factors for infant deaths from more limited data for the countries or even to assume them on the basis of information for other countries. Fortunately, the separation factors for infants vary only over a moderate range and small variations in the factors make little difference in the infant mortality rate. Separation factors may be observed to vary in relation to the general level of infant mortality. Hence, given a rough estimate of the infant mortality rate, appropriate separation factors may be determined. Separation factors corresponding approximately to various levels of the infant mortality rate are as follows:

	Separation factors			
	model life tables[2]		U.S. life tables[3]	
Infant mortality rate	f'	f''	f'	f''
200	.60	.40	.68	.32
150	.67	.33	.68	.32
100	.75	.25	.75	.25
50	.80	.20	.84	.16
25	.85	.15	.86	.14
15	.95	.05	.86	.14
10	NA	NA	.86	.14
5	NA	NA	.88	.12

In view of the limitations of the procedures for adjusting infant mortality rates, when annual figures are not required annual average rates based directly on infant deaths and births as reported for the years covered may serve adequately as adjusted measures for this period. The preferred formula for a 3-year annual average infant mortality rate is

$$\frac{D_0^{y-1} + D_0^y + D_0^{y+1}}{B_{y-1} + B_y + B_{y-1}} \times 1000 \qquad (12.23)$$

where the symbols identify infant deaths and births for 3 successive years. The influence of births in adjacent years on deaths of a given year is allowed for by this averaging

---

[2] Based on a regression analysis relating infant mortality rates and separation factors implicit in the series of model life tables shown in A. J. Coale and Demeny, *Regional Model Life Tables and Stable Populations*, Princeton, NJ, Princeton University Press, 1966.

[3] Based on the historical series of life tables for the United States published by the U.S. Census Bureau and the U.S. National Center for Health Statistics and made available in a personal memorandum from J. S. Siegel.

TABLE 12.9 Calculation of Separation Factors for Deaths of Female Infants on the Basis of Annual Data on Deaths by Detailed Age, for the United States: 1990 (One-twelfth of the annual total of deaths is assumed to occur in each month.)

Age at death	Assumed proportion born in previous year (1)	Infant deaths		
		Total (2)	Born in 1989 (1) × (2) = (3)	Born in 1990 (2) − (3) = (4)
Total	(X)	38,351	5,093	33,258
11 months	$\dfrac{11.5}{12}=.9583$	347	333	14
10 months	$\dfrac{10.5}{12}=.8750$	346	303	43
9 months	$\dfrac{9.5}{12}=.7916$	430	340	90
8 months	$\dfrac{8.5}{12}=.7083$	499	353	146
7 months	$\dfrac{7.5}{12}=.6250$	635	397	238
6 months	$\dfrac{6.5}{12}=.5417$	772	418	354
5 months	$\dfrac{5.5}{12}=.4583$	1,040	477	563
4 months	$\dfrac{4.5}{12}=.3750$	1,536	576	960
3 months	$\dfrac{3.5}{12}=.2917$	2,126	620	1506
2 months	$\dfrac{2.5}{12}=.2083$	2,910	606	2304
28 to 59 days[1]	$\dfrac{1.5}{12}=.1250$	3,401	425	2,976
21 to 27 days	$\dfrac{21}{365}+\dfrac{1}{2}\left(\dfrac{7}{365}\right)=\dfrac{49}{730}=.0671$	966	65	901
14 to 20 days	$\dfrac{14}{365}+\dfrac{1}{2}\left(\dfrac{7}{365}\right)=\dfrac{35}{730}=.0479$	1,308	63	1,245
7 to 13 days	$\dfrac{7}{365}+\dfrac{1}{2}\left(\dfrac{7}{365}\right)=\dfrac{21}{730}=.0288$	2,015	58	1,957
6 days	$\dfrac{6}{365}+\dfrac{1}{2}\left(\dfrac{1}{365}\right)=\dfrac{13}{730}=.0178$	376	7	369
5 days	$\dfrac{5}{365}+\dfrac{1}{2}\left(\dfrac{1}{365}\right)=\dfrac{11}{730}=.0151$	444	7	437
4 days	$\dfrac{4}{365}+\dfrac{1}{2}\left(\dfrac{1}{365}\right)=\dfrac{9}{730}=.0123$	574	7	567
3 days	$\dfrac{3}{365}+\dfrac{1}{2}\left(\dfrac{1}{365}\right)=\dfrac{7}{730}=.0096$	813	8	805
2 days	$\dfrac{2}{365}+\dfrac{1}{2}\left(\dfrac{1}{365}\right)=\dfrac{5}{730}=.0068$	1,340	9	1,331
1 day	$\dfrac{1}{365}+\dfrac{1}{2}\left(\dfrac{1}{365}\right)=\dfrac{3}{730}=.0041$	1,846	8	1,838
1 to 23 hours[2]	$\dfrac{1}{8,760}+\dfrac{1}{2}\left(\dfrac{23}{8,760}\right)=\dfrac{25}{17,520}=.0014$	10,265	14	10,251
Under 1 hour[2]	$\dfrac{1}{2}+\dfrac{1}{8,760}=\dfrac{1}{17,520}=.0007\cong 0$	4,362	—	4,362

Separation factors:

f′ $\dfrac{D'}{D'+D''}=\dfrac{33,258}{38,351}=.8672$

f″ $\dfrac{D''}{D'+D''}=\dfrac{5,093}{38,351}=.1328$

[1] Treated as deaths of one month of age. All of the January (or initial month) deaths and one-half of the February (or second-month) deaths of this age were assumed to occur to births of the previous calendar (or fiscal) year.

[2] 8760 represents the number of hours in the year.

Source: Basic data from U.S. National Center for Health Statistics, *Vital Statistics of the United States, 1990*, Vol. II, *Mortality*, Part A, 1994, Table 2.12.

formula except at the fringes of the period. The relative error from this formula is small unless there are extremely sharp changes in the annual numbers of births.

Mortality Rates at Ages above Infancy

Death rates at the ages above infancy can also be adjusted to a probability basis (i.e., expressed as mortality rates). Let us consider the problem first in terms of single ages. For those few countries (e.g., Japan, Venezuela) for which tabulations of deaths by single ages and years of birth are available, the task is simple. One can immediately adapt any of the formulas given for deriving infant mortality rates. Tables 12.10 and 12.11 indicate two ways of calculating mortality rates in single ages, allowing for the fact that deaths at a given age during a year belong to two dif-

ferent birth cohorts or, conversely, that a single birth cohort may experience deaths at two ages during a year. The data are for children under 10 years and persons 60 to 69 years in Japan in 1996, and mortality rates are calculated according to formulas of type A and B for the former and type B for the latter. (Other procedures, employed in the construction of life tables, are described in the Chapter 13.) Adapting Formula A or 12.19 for use with population figures, we have

$$\frac{D_a'' + D_{a+1}'}{P_a'} \times 1000 \qquad (12.24)$$

where D_a'' and D_{a+1}', represent deaths at age a and deaths at age a + 1 in a given year, respectively, to the population aged a at the beginning of the year, and P_a' represents the

TABLE 12.10 Calculation of Mortality Rates for the Population under 10 Years of Age by Formula A, for Japan: 1996

Age on January 1, 1996	Year of Birth	Age at death	Deaths 1996 D_a (1)	Population January 1, 1996[1] P_a' (2)	Mortality rate $\dfrac{D_a'' + D_{a+1}'}{P_a'} \times 1000$ [(1) ÷ (2)] × 1000 = (3)
Under 1 year	1995	Under 1 and 1	1345		
		Under 1	948	1,182,522	1.1
1 year	1994	1	397		
		1 and 2	585		
		1	375	1,187,421	0.5
2 years	1993	2	210		
		2 and 3	365		
		2	225	1,179,977	0.3
3 years	1992	3	140		
		3 and 4	273		
		3	156	1,193,449	0.2
4 years	1991	4	117		
		4 and 5	267		
		4	144	1,200,349	0.2
5 years	1990	5	123		
		5 and 6	187		
		5	103	1,216,619	0.2
6 years	1989	6	84		
		6 and 7	201		
		6	111	1,250,690	0.2
7 years	1988	7	90		
		7 and 8	202		
		7	115	1,291,536	0.2
8 years	1987	8	87		
		8 and 9	147		
		8	71	1,331,085	0.1
9 years	1986	9	76		
		9 and 10	152		
		9	74	1,362,403	0.1
		10	78		

[1] Equals three-fourths of the population estimate for October 1, 1995, plus one-fourth of the population estimate for October 1, 1996.

Source Basic data from Japan, Ministry of Health and Welfare, *Vital Statistics, 1996, Japan*, Vol. I, Table 5; and Japan, Statistics and Information Department, *Population Estimates by Age and Sex as of October 1, 1996*, Tables 1 and 4.

TABLE 12.11   Calculation of Separation Factors and Mortality Rates for Ages under 10 years and 60 to 69 Years by Formula B, for Japan: 1996

	Deaths			Separation factor[1]				
		Born in earlier of 2 possible years	Born in later of 2 possible years	f″ $\dfrac{D_a''}{D_a}$	f′ $\dfrac{D_a'}{D_a}$	Population, January 1, 1996[2]	Mortality rate	Central death rate
	Total							
	D_a	D_a''	D_a'	(2) ÷ (1) =	(3) ÷ (1) =	P_a'	$\left[\dfrac{D_a'}{P_{a-1}'}+\dfrac{D_a''}{P_a'}\right]\times 1{,}000$	$\dfrac{D_a}{P_a}\times 1{,}000$[3]
Age	(1)	(2)	(3)	(4)	(5)	(6)	(7)	(8)
Under 1 year	4,546	948	3,598	0.2085	0.7915	1,182,522	[4]3.8	3.8
1 year	772	375	397	0.4858	0.5142	1,187,421	0.7	0.7
2 years	435	225	210	0.5172	0.4828	1,179,977	0.4	0.4
3 years	296	156	140	0.5270	0.4730	1,193,449	0.2	0.2
4 years	261	144	117	0.5517	0.4483	1,200,349	0.2	0.2
5 years	226	103	123	0.4558	0.5442	1,216,619	0.2	0.2
6 years	195	111	84	0.5692	0.4308	1,250,690	0.2	0.2
7 years	205	115	90	0.5610	0.4390	1,291,536	0.2	0.2
8 years	158	71	87	0.4494	0.5506	1,331,085	0.1	0.1
9 years	150	74	76	0.4933	0.5067	1,362,403	0.1	0.1
60 years	11,467	5,561	5,906	0.4850	0.5150	1,573,466	7.2	7.2
61 years	12,311	5,632	6,679	0.4575	0.5425	1,504,305	8.0	8.1
62 years	13,179	6,350	6,826	0.4818	0.5182	1,494,323	8.8	8.9
63 years	14,479	6,931	7,548	0.4787	0.5213	1,474,103	9.8	9.8
64 years	15,299	7,044	8,255	0.4604	0.5396	1,434,525	10.5	10.6
65 years	16,164	7,620	8,544	0.4714	0.5286	1,370,319	11.5	11.7
66 years	16,760	7,812	8,948	0.4661	0.5339	1,327,249	12.4	12.6
67 years	17,762	8,194	9,568	0.4613	0.5387	1,284,155	13.6	13.8
68 years	18,183	8,330	9,853	0.4581	0.5419	1,236,849	14.4	14.6
69 years	19,341	9,049	10,292	0.4679	0.5321	1,194,184	15.9	16.1

[1] Implicit in tabulations of deaths by year of birth of decedent.

[2] Equals three-fourths of the population estimate for October 1, 1995, plus one-fourth of the population estimate for October 1, 1996.

[3] Based on July 1, 1996, population estimates (not shown).

[4] Formula B for infants (under 1 year) is $\dfrac{D_0'^y}{B^y}+\dfrac{D_0''^y}{B^{y-1}}$ Total births numbered 1,182,029 for 1995 and 1,184,000 for 1996.

Source: Basic data from Japan, Ministry of Health and Welfare, *Vital Statistics, 1996, Japan*, Vol. I, Table 5; and Japan, Statistics and Information Department, *Population Estimates by Age and Sex as of October 1, 1996*, Tables 1 and 4.

population aged a at the beginning of the year. The formula indicates the chance that the population at a given age a at the beginning of a year will die during the following year. The deaths included in the formula relate to two different ages. The 1-year mortality rate for the population aged 2 on January 1, 1996, in Japan is calculated as follows (Table 12.10):

$$\left(\frac{D_2''+D_3'}{P_2'}\right)\times 1000 = \left(\frac{225+140}{1{,}179{,}977}\right)\times 1000 = 0.3$$

Similarly, the 1-year mortality rate for the population aged 1 is 0.5.

Formula B provides somewhat different mortality rates from Formula A, and the results have a somewhat different interpretation. Adapting Formula B or 12.20 for use with population figures, we have

$$\left(\frac{D_a'}{P_{a-1}'}+\frac{D_a''}{P_a'}\right)\times 1000 \qquad (12.25)$$

where D_a' and D_a'' represent the portions of deaths at age a in a particular year associated with different birth cohorts and P_a and P_{a-1} the populations in the same age and the next younger age at the beginning of the year. Consider an example based on the data for Japan in Table 12.11:

$$\left(\frac{D_2'}{P_1'}+\frac{D_2''}{P_2'}\right)\times 1000$$

$$\left(\frac{210}{1,187,421} + \frac{225}{1,179,977}\right) \times 1000 = 0.4$$

Such a formula tells the chance of dying at age 2—that is, between one's second birthday and one's third birthday. The chance of dying at age 1—that is, between one's first birthday and one's second birthday—is represented by

$$\left(\frac{D_1'}{P_0'} + \frac{D_1''}{P_1'}\right) \times 1000$$

The mortality rate of 0.4 at age 2 compares with a central death rate at age 2 of 0.4 (Table 12.11). In general, however, central death rates tend to be higher than mortality rates because, barring net immigration and changes in numbers of births, the midyear population in an age cohort will be smaller than the population at the beginning of the year. This is suggested by the differences between the mortality rates and central death rates for ages 60 to 69 years shown in Table 12.11.

The rate of 0.5, obtained with Formula A as the mortality rate of the population initially 1 year of age, is intermediate to the mortality rates for ages 1 and 2 shown by Formula B, 0.7 and 0.4, respectively. In general, the results from Formula A fall between the results from Formula B for successive ages. This relationship corresponds to the ages of the deaths reflected in each formula.

The considerable deviation of the separation factors from .50–.50 in infancy reflects the fact that infant deaths tend to be concentrated at the earliest ages of infancy—that is, near the time of birth. This concentration results from the predominant role of the endogenous causes of mortality at this age. The greater risk of dying in the first part of an age would also be expected to apply to some of the ages above infancy, but the available data show that this phenomenon tends to disappear quite quickly and is hardly evident once the first year of life has passed. Table 12.11 presents the separation factors for deaths by single ages under 10 implied by the tabulations of deaths by age and year of birth for Japan in 1996. Although there are small fluctuations in the separation factors, they converge rapidly to about .50–.50. Even the separation factors for deaths at ages 1 and 2 are close to these values. At the higher ages of life also, where mortality rates are rising rapidly, the separation factors implied by the tabulated data for Japan approximate .50–.50 and show no particular trend with increasing age even though such a trend would be expected. Illustrative data for ages 60 to 69 for Japan in 1996 are shown in Table 12.11.

There are neither tabulations of death statistics by age and year of birth nor tabulations of deaths by subdivisions of single years of age above infancy for the United States. The separation factors needed to compute mortality rates for ages above infancy in the United States cannot be derived from these sources, therefore. The only study intended to establish the separation factors for ages above infancy in the United States was based on a 10% sample of deaths at ages 1 to 4 in 1944, 1945, and 1946 (U.S. National Office of Vital Statistics, 1950a). The tabulation of these deaths by year of birth indicated separation factors rather close to .50–.50 for each age. Since a moderate variation in the separation factor has only a slight effect on the mortality rate, it seems best to employ a separation factor of 0.50 for splitting deaths according to birth cohort at the ages above infancy and for calculating 1-year mortality rates at these ages.

The discussion so far has been confined to mortality rates for single ages in a single year. Mortality rates for longer periods of time and for age groups may also be calculated. Such rates may be constructed from observed data over a number of calendar years and represent a *real cohort*, or they may be constructed from observed data for a single calendar year and represent a *synthetic cohort*.

For example, it is possible to calculate the risk of dying for a 5-year old in a 5-year period from the appropriate probabilities for this 5-year period. The probabilities at successive ages in successive calendar years would be used. A synthetic probability of this kind could be derived by combining the appropriate single-year-of-age probabilities for a single calendar year. The formula would take the following form:

$$_5q_5' = 1 - (1 - q_5')(1 - q_6')(1 - q_7')(1 - q_8')(1 - q_9') \quad (12.26)$$

where q_5' represents the 1-year mortality rate between ages 5 and 6, and $_5q_5$ the risk of a 5-year old dying in the next 5 years. Ordinarily, single-year-of-age tabulations of death statistics are not available or are too inaccurate to serve as a basis for the calculation of death rates and mortality rates for single years of age. Adjusted estimates of deaths and death rates in single ages may be derived by various types of interpolation procedures from 5-year age data.

A rough estimate of the annual mortality rate for a 5-year age group may be derived as follows:

$$_{5}^{y+1}q_x^y = D_a \div \left(_5P_a + \frac{1}{2}\,_5D_a\right)$$

1. Set down total deaths in a given age group during the year.
2. Set down the population in this age group at the middle of the year.
3. Add one-half of the deaths in step 1 to the population in step 2. (This is the base population for the rate, i.e., the population at the beginning of the year that would be in this age group at the middle of the year.)
4. Divide the figure in step 1 by the result in step 3.

This procedure disregards the effect of net immigration on deaths and population during the year.

For the probability that a person aged 60 to 64 years of age would die within one year, according to experience in the United States in 1990, the corresponding figures are

1. Deaths = 154,831
2. Population on July 1, 1990 = 10,619,000
3. Base population 10,619,000 + ½(154,831) = 10,696,416
4. Rate = 154,831/10,696,416 = .01448 or 14.5 per 1000

Cause-Specific Mortality Rates

Measures giving the chance of dying from a particular cause at a particular age in a year or 5-year period, or of eventually dying from this cause, have been developed, principally in connection with the preparation of life tables by cause of death (Chapter 15). Cause-specific probabilities of death can be computed in a manner paralleling the calculation of general probabilities of dying. In the case of general cause-specific probabilities for single ages for single calendar years, the deaths from a particular cause or group of causes at a particular age (a) for a given calendar year may be divided by the population at age a at the middle of the year plus one-half of all deaths at age a during the year. (The base population may alternatively be estimated as the mean of the population at age a and the population at the next younger age $(a - 1)$ at the beginning of the year, or the mean of the population at age a at the middle of the year and age $a - 1$ at the middle of the previous year.) The required data on deaths would normally be obtained by interpolation from 5-year age data. As before, this procedure disregards the net migration occurring during the year of the estimate. A 1-year cause-of-death probability for a 5-year age group may be derived as follows:

1. Set down (a) total deaths in the given age group, (b) deaths from the particular cause in this age group during the year, and (c) the population in this age group at the middle of the year.
2. Add one-half of all deaths at these ages (item la) to the figure in item1c. (This is the base population for the rate—that is, the population at the beginning of the year that would be 60 to 64 at the middle of the year.)
3. Divide the figure in item 1b by the result in step 2.

For calculating the risk of death from heart disease in the United States at ages 60 to 64 in 1990, the corresponding figures are as follows:

1. All deaths, 154,831; deaths due to heart disease, 48,449; and population, July 1, 1990, 10,619,000
2. Base population = 10,619,000 + 1/2(154,831) = 10,696,416
3. Rate = 48,449 ÷ 10,696,416 = .004529 or 452.9 per 100,000

Cause-specific probabilities for 5-year time periods, whether for single ages or 5-year age groups, particularly those derived "synthetically" on the basis of data for a single calendar year, are, as suggested earlier, akin to the measures developed in connection with life tables (see Chapter 13).

The conventional infant mortality rate, previously described as an approximate measure of the risk of dying in infancy, may be viewed as the sum of a series of rates each of which represents the chance of dying in infancy from a particular cause. In analyzing differences in overall infant mortality rates, it is useful to separate the infant deaths by cause into the two broad classes, endogenous and exogenous, described earlier, and to compute separate rates. The formula for the *endogenous infant mortality rate* is

$$\frac{D_o^{en}}{B} \times 1000 \qquad (12.27)$$

and the formula for the *exogenous infant mortality rate* is

$$\frac{D_o^{ex}}{B} \times 1000 \qquad (12.28)$$

As suggested earlier, the endogenous set of causes is related to the genetic makeup of the infant, the circumstances of life *in utero*, and the conditions of labor. The exogenous set of causes is related to the contact of the infant with the external world. Endogenous infant mortality includes mainly mortality from congenital anomalies, immaturity, birth injuries, postnatal asphyxia, and so on (i.e., conditions that are difficult to prevent or treat in the present state of knowledge). Exogenous infant mortality includes mainly infections and post-natal accidents (i.e., conditions that are relatively preventable or treatable). The endogenous infant mortality rate is estimated at 18.3 in the United States in 1966 and at 14.4 in Norway in 1959. About one-quarter of the infant deaths in these countries are exogenous, whereas in Costa Rica over 60% are in this category (Table 12.7). As a result, in Costa Rica the exogenous infant mortality rate is well above the endogenous rate. This type of comparative international analysis of the infant mortality rate in terms of endogenous and exogenous causes is useful in determining the extent to which the rate can reasonably be reduced in the present state of knowledge.

The *maternal mortality rate* is a widely used type of cause-specific mortality rate representing approximately the risk of dying as a result of "complications of pregnancy, childbirth, and the puerperium" (ICD-9 category numbers 630–676). This rate is conventionally defined as the number of deaths due to puerperal causes per 10,000 or 100,000 births. With a constant of 100,000, the formula is

$$\frac{D^p}{B} \times 100,000 \qquad (12.29)$$

where D^p represents deaths due to puerperal causes. Maternal mortality rate vary widely around the world.

Some illustrature figures relating to the years around 1995 are 8 (per 100,000 births) for Israel 12 for Japan, 65 for Mexico, 260 for Brazil, 590 for Cambodia, and 830 for Nepal (Population Reference Bureau, 2002).

The figures suggest the range and variation in this measure for the countries of the world in recent years. In the formula the number of births is employed as an approximation to the number of women exposed to the risk of dying from puerperal causes.

Rates Adjusted for Population Composition

The level of an observed death rate, like that of other observed rates, is affected by the demographic composition of the population for which the rate is calculated. The age composition of the population, in particular, is a key factor affecting the level of the crude death rate. For purposes of comparing death rates over time or from area to area, it is useful to determine the difference between the rates on the assumption that there are no differences in age composition. It is particularly important to eliminate the effect of the differences in age structure of two populations being compared if one is trying to compare their health conditions. Crude death rates are especially unsatisfactory for this purpose. A crude death rate of a population may be relatively high merely because the population has a large proportion of persons in the older ages, where death rates are high; or it may be relatively low because the population has a large proportion of children and young adults, where death rates are low. The crude death rate of a country may actually rise even though death rates at each age remain stationary, if the population is getting older.

The procedure of adjustment of the crude rates to eliminate from them the effect of differences in population composition with respect to age and other variables is sometimes called standardization. Often, death rates are adjusted or standardized for both age and sex. Other variables for which death rates may be adjusted or standardized are racial composition, nativity composition, urban-rural composition, and so on. We shall confine our discussion largely to standardization for age since this is the most important and most common variable for which the standardization of death rates is carried out.

Age-adjusted rates can be interpreted as the hypothetical death rate that would have occurred if the observed age-specific rates were associated with a population whose age distribution equalled that of the standard population. However, it is important to recognize that age-adjusted or age-standardized rates have no direct meaning in themselves. They are meaningful only in comparison with other similarly computed rates. Since they are useful only for comparison, the commonest application of the procedure is to compute such rates for the areas or population groups whose mortality is to be compared and to calculate the relative differences of the resulting rates. The meaningful measure then is a ratio, index, or percentage difference between rates similarly adjusted.

A number of methods have been developed for adjusting death rates for age composition or for deriving indexes or relative measures of age-adjusted mortality. We shall consider four principal methods. The measures are the age-adjusted or age-standardized death rate calculated by the direct method, the age-adjusted or age-standardized death rate calculated by the indirect method, the comparative mortality index, and the life table death rate.

Direct Standardization

The simplest and most straightforward measure is the age-adjusted death rate derived by the direct method. For most comparisons, this is the preferred procedure and it provides the best basis for determining the relative difference between mortality in two areas or at two dates. In this method, a "standard" population is selected and employed in deriving all the age-adjusted rates in a set to be compared. If the same standard population is employed, as required, all the rates are directly comparable. The formula calls for computing the weighted average of the age-specific death rates in a given area, using as weights the age distribution of the standard population. The formula for direct standardization is

$$m_1 = \frac{\sum m_a P_a}{P} \times 1000 \quad \text{or} \quad \sum m_a \frac{P_a}{P} \times 1000 \quad (12.30)$$

where $m_a = \frac{d_a}{p_a}$ = age-specific death rate in the given area, P_a represents the standard population at each age, and P or ΣP_a represents the total of the standard population. (Capital letters are used here to identify the elements of the standard population, and lowercase letters are used to identify the elements of the populations under study.) Each age-specific rate is multiplied, in effect, by the proportion of the standard population in each age group. (In standardizing a death rate for age and sex jointly, each age-sex-specific death rate is multiplied by the proportion of the total standard population in that age-sex group.) The age-standardized death rate for the standard population is the same as its own crude death rate, since the age-specific death rates for the standard population would be weighted by its own population. The relative mortality of the given area is derived by dividing the age-standardized rate for the area by the crude death rate of the standard population.

$$RM_1 = \frac{\sum m_a P_a}{P} \div M = \frac{\sum m_a P_a}{\sum M_a P_a}$$

Illustrative calculations are shown for a group of countries around 1990 in Table 12.12. The population of the United States is employed as a standard population to calculate the age-standardized death rate for Czechoslavakia (1990), Ecuador (1990), Finland (1990), and Japan (1990). The steps in calculating the age-adjusted death rate by the direct method for Japan are as follows:

TABLE 12.12   Calculation of Age-Standardized Death Rates by the Direct Method, for Several Countries: 1990

Age	Standard population (in thousands) (P_a) United States, 1990	Age-specific death rates (m_a)			
		Czechoslovakia, 1990	Ecuador, 1990	Finland, 1990	Japan, 1990
Under 1 year	3,217	11.4	33.1	5.7	4.6
1 to 4 years	15,137	0.4	3.3	0.3	0.4
5 to 9 years	18,099	0.3	0.7	0.2	0.2
10 to 14 years	17,114	0.2	0.7	0.2	0.1
15 to 19 years	17,754	0.6	1.2	0.8	0.4
20 to 24 years	19,020	0.8	1.7	1.1	0.5
25 to 29 years	21,313	0.9	1.8	0.9	0.5
30 to 34 years	21,863	1.3	2.2	1.4	0.6
35 to 39 years	19,963	2.1	2.7	1.9	0.9
40 to 44 years	17,616	3.4	3.4	2.8	1.4
45 to 49 years	13,873	5.7	4.7	3.8	2.4
50 to 54 years	11,351	9.0	6.4	6.0	3.7
55 to 59 years	10,532	13.8	9.5	8.8	6.1
60 to 64 years	10,616	21.4	13.0	14.0	9.3
65 to 69 years	10,112	32.9	20.8	21.9	13.7
70 to 74 years	7,995	49.3	31.2	35.3	23.5
75 to 79 years	6,121	80.2	50.3	58.1	42.1
80 to 84 years	3,934	127.0	71.8	96.3	75.9
85 years and over	3,080	216.7	166.0	184.2	158.1
(1) Total standard population = ΣP_a = P	248,710	(X)	(X)	(X)	(X)
(2) Expected deaths = $\Sigma m_a P_a$	(X)	3,163,087	1,365,663	2367,408	1723,156
(3) Age-adjusted death rate = $\dfrac{\Sigma m_a P_a}{P} = \dfrac{(2)}{(1)}$	8.6	12.7	5.5	9.5	6.9
(4) Percentage difference from U.S. rate [(3) − 8.6] ÷ 8.6	(X)	+47.9	−36.2	+10.7	−19.4
(5) Crude death rate (CDR)	8.6	11.7	5.2	10.0	6.6
(6) Percentage difference or CDR from U.S. rate [(5) − 8.6] ÷ 8.6	(X)	+36.0	−39.5	+16.3	−23.3

X: Not applicable.

Sources: Basic data from United Nations, *Demographic Yearbook* (various dates).

1. Record the population in each age group for the United States (standard population).
2. Record the age-specific death rates for Czechoslovakia.
3. Compute the cumulative product of the population figures in step 1 and the death rates in step 2 (3,163,087).
4. Divide the result in step 3 (3,163,087) by the total population of the United States (248,710,000). The result is 12.7 per 1000.

The crude death rate in Czechoslovakia, 11.6 per 1000 population, is 36% greater than the crude death rate in the United States, 8.6 (Table 12.12). The adjustment of the crude rate in Czechoslovakia raised it to 12.7, reflecting the fact that the age composition of Czechoslovakia's population is more favorable for a low crude death rate than that of the United States. Equating the age distributions raises the relative excess of the Czechoslovakia rate to a relative excess of 48%. Note that (direct) standardization caused a

rise in the death rate for Ecuador and Japan also. Both the crude and adjusted death rates for Ecuador and Japan indicate that these countries have populations with lower mortality than that for the United States.

Two basic types of standard populations are used to compute the age-adjusted death rate by the direct method: internal and external. The internal standard selected may be the age distribution of one of the areas or dates (e.g., earliest, middle, or latest in a series) being compared, or the sum or average of the age distributions for the areas or dates being compared. The external standard is a real or theoretical distribution of some sort. Different results for the relative differences between adjusted rates will be obtained depending on the age distribution selected as a standard. In fact, the choice of standard may even affect the direction of the difference between the rates for the populations being compared. Hence, it is desirable to select the standard population carefully. The general rule is to select as a standard an age distribution that is similar to the age distributions of the various populations under study. If the mortality of two populations is being compared, this may best be achieved by using as a standard the (unweighted) average of the two distributions. Since this would apply to time series as well, use of the age distribution of the first year's (or last year's) population in a time series as the standard over a long period is to be avoided. It is not always possible to follow this rule closely since the populations being compared may have quite different age distributions. Yet the farther apart the age distributions are, the more important it is to make the comparison of their mortality on the basis of adjusted figures. In some cases, it may be desirable to forego comparisons of summary measures and compare the schedules of age-specific death rates.

The need for age adjustment is particularly great in connection with cause-specific death rates. Certain causes of death are concentrated in one or another part of the age distribution. Hence, the level of the observed death rate from these causes is particularly affected by the age distribution of the population. For example, a population with a relatively large proportion of older persons will tend to have a relatively high death rate from heart disease and a population with a relatively small proportion of older persons will tend to have a relatively low death rate from this cause. It is important to note that standardization is not considered to be appropriate when age-specific death rates in the populations being compared tend to change trends or become inconsistent over time. The calculation of an age-adjusted death rate for a specific cause by the direct method follows the same form as the calculation of a general age-adjusted death rate by the direct method except that age-cause specific rates are used for the areas under study.

Indirect Standardization

As we have seen, calculation of the age-adjusted death rate by the direct method requires age-specific death rates or deaths by age for the area under study. These may not be available, even though a count or estimate of the total number of deaths and an estimate of the crude death rate are at hand. In this case, if counts or estimates of the age distribution of the population are also available, it is possible to adjust the death rate by an indirect method. The formula for indirect standardization is

$$m_a = \left(\frac{d}{\sum M_a p_a} \right) M = \left(\frac{\sum m_a p_a}{\sum M_a p_a} \right) M \quad (12.31)$$

The relative mortality is, therefore, $RM_2 = \dfrac{\sum m_a P_a}{\sum M_a p_a}$

where, for the "standard" population, M_a represents age-specific death rates and M represents the crude death rate; and, for the population under study, d represents the total number of deaths and p_a represents the population at each

age. This formula calls for adjusting the crude death rate of the "standard" population by a factor representing the ratio of the recorded number of deaths to the number expected on the basis of the age-specific deaths rates of the "standard" population and the population by age in the area under study.

The steps in calculating the age-adjusted death rate by the indirect method for Czechoslovakia in 1990, using the population of the United States as the standard, are as follows (Table 12.13):

1. Set down the age-specific death rates for the United States in 1990 ("standard").
2. Set down the population by age for Czechoslovakia in 1990.
3. Compute the cumulative product of the death rates in step 1 and the population in step 2 (124,552). This is the number of deaths expected on the basis of the age-specific death rates in the United States in 1990 and population by age in Czechoslovakia in 1990.
4. Divide the result in step 3 (124,552) into the total number of deaths registered in Czechoslovakia in 1990 (183,785). The result is 1.4756.
5. Multiply the result in step 4 (1.4756) by the crude death rate of the United States (8.6) to derive the adjusted death rate.

The adjusted rate for Czechoslovakia using the indirect method is 12.7 and exceeds the rate in the United States by 48%, that is, by the factor computed in step 4, minus 1, per 100. In this particular case, the level of the rate and the relative excess of the rate over the U.S. rate are the same as the corresponding figures based on the direct method. The adjusted rates for Finland and Japan using the indirect method were very similar to those calculated using the direct method, but the age-adjusted rate for Ecuador using the indirect method was twice as large as that using the direct method (Table 12-12). In general, the range of variation in the relative mortality of various populations resulting from the use of the indirect method as compared with the direct method or from the use of different standards in the indirect method may be quite wide and, in fact, the indications of relative mortality may go in opposite directions (as for Ecuador).

We should expect the relative mortality of two areas measured by the direct and indirect methods to be different. Although the rates for the two areas being compared are, in effect, weighted by the same populations with in each method, the indirect method weights the age-specific death rates by the population of the area under study and the direct method weights the rates by the "standard" population. Accordingly, in indirect standardization, strictly only two populations can be compared at the same time. It should be apparent that the standardized mortality ratio described earlier is a simple application of indirect standardization.

TABLE 12.13   Calculation of Age-Standardized Death Rates by the Indirect Method, for Several Countries: 1990

Age	Age-specific death rates (M_a) United States, 1990	Population (in thousands) Czechoslovakia	Ecuador (p_a)	Finland	Japan[1]
All ages	8.6	15,660	9,649	4,998	123,612
Under 1 year	9.7	207	241	65	1217
1 to 4 years	0.5	856	1012	247	5,293
5 to 9 years	0.2	1,144	1,262	327	7,487
10 to 14 years	0.3	1,354	1,224	325	8,550
15 to 19 years	0.9	1,276	1,039	303	10,033
20 to 24 years	1.1	1,061	917	344	8,823
25 to 29 years	1.2	1,084	790	377	8,092
30 to 34 years	1.5	1,134	666	383	7,809
35 to 39 years	2.0	1,252	563	405	9,028
40 to 44 years	2.5	1,185	448	441	10,686
45 to 49 years	3.8	949	351	325	9,042
50 to 54 years	5.9	764	295	275	8,109
55 to 59 years	9.3	780	226	252	7,745
60 to 64 years	14.6	772	203	255	6,763
65 to 69 years	21.6	723	140	223	5,118
70 to 74 years	32.7	353	109	167	3,828
75 to 79 years	49.3	404	75	140	3,026
80 to 84 years	76.8	242	52	92	1,838
85 years and over	153.3	120	36	52	1125
(1) Expected deaths = $\Sigma M_a p_a$	(X)	124,552	37,538	45,648	1,054,925
(2) Registered deaths (d)	2,148,463	183,785	50,217	50,058	820,305
(3) Ratio, $\dfrac{\text{Registered deaths}}{\text{Expected deaths}} = \dfrac{d}{\sum M_a p_a} = \dfrac{(2)}{(1)}$	(X)	1.4756	1.3378	1.0966	0.7776
(4) Age-adjusted death rate = 8.6 x (3)	8.6	12.7	11.5	9.4	6.7
(5) Percent difference from U.S. rate[2] = [(4) − 8.6] ÷ 8.6	(X)	+47.6	+33.8	+9.7	−22.2

(X): Not applicable.

[1] Population with age not reported distributed on the basis of reported distribution.

[2] also = [1 − (3)] × 100.

Comparative Mortality Index

The comparative mortality index (CMI) is a measure of relative mortality, usually employed to indicate changes over time in the overall mortality of an area. It uses a shifting pattern of population weights, designated to overcome the problems of prolonged use of a single standard age distribution. The formula is

$$CMI = \frac{\sum w_a m_a}{\sum w_a M_a} \qquad (12.32)$$

where M_a represents the age-specific death rates in the standard or initial year, m_a, represents the age-specific death rates in later years, and

$$w_a = \frac{1}{2}\left(\frac{P_a}{P} + \frac{p_a}{p}\right)$$

where P_a and P are populations of the standard or initial year and p_a and p are populations of each later years being calculated.

The formula calls for taking a ratio of (1) the weighted sum of age-specific death rates in each year to (2) the similarly weighted sum of age-specific death rates of the initial year. The weights are the average of (1) the proportion of the total population in the age group in the initial year and (2) the corresponding proportion in each later year.

Life Table Death Rate

The life table death rate, the fourth type of age-adjusted rate considered here, is the most difficult one to derive, requiring the construction of a life table from the observed age-specific death rates for each population examined. It is also the most difficult to interpret. The subject of life tables is treated separately and in detail in the next chapter. We may note here that the assumption of a constant annual number of births and a constant set of age-specific death rates corresponding to the observed age-specific death rates of an area in a given year or period generates a population with an unchanging total size and age distribution, called the "life-table stationary population," which has its own crude birth and death rates. The crude death rate of this population is called the "life table death rate." In effect, the life table death rate may be viewed as an age-adjusted death rate resulting from the weighting of age-specific death rates by the life table stationary population.

Summary Note on Age-Adjustment

We have considered a number of ways of calculating age-adjusted death rates. This discussion suggests that there is no perfect method of removing the effects of age composition when the mortality experiences of different populations are being compared. The direct method of standardization employs a common standard population for all the areas or dates being compared, but the results are affected by the choice of standard population and the standard may be unreasonable for widely different populations or over long periods of time. In the indirect method of standardization and in the calculation of the comparative mortality index, the comparability of results is affected by the use of a different standard population for each area or date for which comparative measures are derived. The calculation of life table death rates avoids the problem of the arbitrary choice of a standard population, since life table death rates are generated entirely from the age schedules of age-specific death rates; in effect, however, each set of age-specific rates is weighted by a different population, derived from those very age-specific rates. For a complete analysis of mortality, it is desirable to examine the differences in the individual age-specific rates.

Measures of Pregnancy Losses

Much loss of potential life occurs as a result of fetal losses, and there is a close relationship between fetal and neonatal mortality.

Fetal Mortality

As we have seen, the definition of fetal "death" complements the definitions of live birth and death. In some countries, however, the definition employed differs from the international recommendations: live-born children dying early in life (e.g., before registration of birth or within 24 hours of birth) may be classed with fetal deaths. A more important problem is the incompleteness and irregularity of reporting of fetal deaths. This limitation applies to the data for most countries of the world. The duration of pregnancy required for registration varies widely. Reporting of early fetal deaths may be seriously incomplete even where required by law. When registration of all fetal deaths is not mandatory, countries differ as to what is to be registered as a late fetal death; 28 weeks is most frequently specified as the minimum period. As a result, international comparability is far greater for the late fetal deaths than for all fetal deaths taken together.

In view of this situation, the United Nations has recommended that fetal deaths be tabulated by period of gestation into four classes: under 20 completed weeks, 20 to 27 completed weeks, 28 to 36 completed weeks, and 37 completed weeks and over (and not stated). It has designated fetal deaths of at least 28 weeks of gestation, combined with fetal deaths of unknown gestational age, as "late" fetal deaths; fetal deaths under 20 weeks' gestation as "early" fetal deaths; and fetal deaths of 20 to 27 weeks' gestation as "intermediate" fetal deaths. Gestational age reported in months should be allocated to the corresponding intervals in weeks. The data on late fetal deaths are subject to substantial error introduced by incorrect reporting of gestational age. The determination of age is often difficult and comparability of the tabulations is affected by the differences in the skill of the medical attendant in making this determination.

The loss through fetal deaths may be measured by the fetal death ratio or the fetal death rate. The *fetal death ratio* is defined as the number of fetal deaths reported in a year per 1000 live births in the same year, or

$$\frac{D^f}{B} \times 1000$$

where D^f represents either all fetal losses or late fetal losses. Because of the variability in coverage of the early and intermediate fetal losses mentioned earlier, it is preferable from the point of view of international comparability to compute the fetal death ratio on the basis of late fetal losses only. The fetal death rate relates the fetal losses more closely to the population at risk than the fetal death ratio (i.e., it is more akin to a probability). The formula includes the fetal losses in the denominator as well as in the numerator:

$$\frac{D^f}{B + D^f} \times 1000$$

This rate should also be calculated with late fetal losses only.

In spite of the theoretical advantage of the fetal death rate, the fetal death ratio may be considered preferable for international comparisons. The registration of fetal losses is irregular, and the effect of this irregularity is compounded when fetal losses are included with the births in the base of the fetal death rate. Because of the likelihood that poor registration of fetal losses will occur in association with poor registration of births and hence that errors in each component will offset one another to some extent, fetal death ratios may sometimes be of satisfactory quality even where the basic data are questionable.

Specific fetal death ratios may be calculated in terms of period of gestation of the fetus or in terms of the age of the mother (requiring data on the age of mother for births and fetal deaths). Other characteristics of principal importance in the analysis of fetal losses are the marital status of the mother (legitimacy of the fetus), the sex of the fetus, the number of children previously born to the mother, and the type of birth (single or plural issue). Other factors include the cause of fetal death, hospitalization, age of father, date of marriage (for legitimate pregnancies), level of education of parents, and the occupational characteristics of the parents.

Perinatal Mortality

The causes of death in early infancy are believed to be so akin to those accounting for late fetal losses that various measures of mortality combining fetal losses and deaths of early infancy have been proposed. The combination of these deaths is also intended to eliminate the errors resulting from deliberate and inadvertent misclassification as between fetal losses, births, and neonatal deaths. The combined risk of dying during the period near parturition (i.e., just before, during, and just after birth) is measured by various so-called perinatal mortality ratios and rates. The formulas differ with respect to the age limits of the infant deaths and the gestational age of fetal losses to be included, and with respect to whether fetal losses are included in or excluded from the base of the ratios. Neonatal deaths, deaths under 1 week, or deaths under 3 days, in combination with all fetal losses or late fetal losses, are possible ways of operationally defining perinatal deaths. In view of the general lack of tabulated data on infant deaths under 3 days, this coverage is not very useful for international comparisons. The World Health Organization defines the perinatal period as extending from the 28th week of gestation to the seventh day of life. For computational purposes, the lower limit of viability is taken as 28 complete weeks of gestation and the early part of extra-uterine life is taken to be the first 7 days of life.

One formula for the *perinatal mortality ratio* is, then, the number of deaths under 1 week of age and late fetal losses per 1000 live births in a year:

$$\frac{D^z + D^f}{B} \times 1000$$

where D^z represents deaths under 1 week, D^f represents late fetal losses, and B represents births. Another formula is the number of neonatal and late fetal deaths per 1000 live births in a year:

$$\frac{D^n + D^f}{B + D^f} \times 1000$$

where D^n represents neonatal deaths.

The corresponding *perinatal mortality rate* differs by including late fetal losses in the denominator, thus approximating a probability more closely. It is considered the preferred measure because the denominator is more representative of the population at risk (Hoyert, 1994). The perinatal mortality rate can be defined as the number of perinatal deaths per 1000 live births and fetal losses as illustrated in the following formula:

$$\frac{D^z + D^f}{B + D^f} \times 1000 \quad \text{or} \quad \frac{D^n + D^f}{B + D^f} \times 1000$$

where the symbols have the same meaning as they did previously.

These various measures give essentially the same indications of international differences. The perinatal mortality rate has a small theoretical advantage over the perinatal mortality ratio, but the perinatal mortality ratio is probably more stable for international comparison. In the United States, there is little numerical difference between the perinatal ratios and rates, and the difference becomes smaller as perinatal mortality decreases (U.S. NCHS, 1989).

For a fuller discussion of these measures, with illustrations, see Chapter 14.

References

Bourgeois-Pichat, J. 1952, July–Sept. "Essai sur la mortalité 'biologique' de l'homme" [Essay on the "Biological" Mortality of Man]. *Population* (Paris) 7(3): 381–394.

Carnes, B. A., and S. J. Olshansky. 1997. "A Biologically Motivated Partitioning of Mortality." *Experimental Gerontology* 32: 615–631.

Chandra Sekar, C. C., and W. E. Deming. 1949. "On a Method of Estimating Birth and Death Rates and the Extent of Registration." *Journal of the American Statistical Association* 44: 101–115.

Decoufle, P., T. L. Thomas, and L. W. Pickle. 1980. "Comparison of the Proportionate Mortality Ratio and Standardized Mortality Ratio Risk Measures." *American Journal of Epidemiology* 111: 263–269.

Dever, G. E. A. 1991. *Community Health Analysis: Global Awareness at the Local Level.* 2nd ed. Gaithersburg, MD: Aspen.

Gallagher, R. P., W. J. Threlfall, P. R. Band, and J. J. Spinelli. 1989. *Occupational Mortality in British Columbia: 1950–1984.* Vancouver, BC: Cancer Control Agency of British Columbia.

Mauldin, W. P. 1965. "Estimating Rates of Population Growth." In *Family Planning and Population Programs: A Review of World Developments* (pp. 642–647). Proceedings of the International Conference of Family Planning Programs, Geneva. Chicago: University of Chicago Press.

NIOSH. 1997. *Mortality by Occupation, Industry, and Cause of Death: 24 Reporting States, 1984–1988.* By C. Burnett, J. Maurer, and M. Dosemeci. DHHS (NIOSH) publication 97–114.

Population Reference Bureau. 2002. *2000 Women of the World.* By Justine Sass and Lori Ashford. Wall Chant. Washington, DC: Population Reference Bureau.

Poston, Dudley L., and R. G. Rogers. 1985. "Toward a Reformulation of the Neonatal Mortality Rate." *Social Biology* 32: 1–12.

Preston, S. H. 1984. "Use of Direct and Indirect Techniques for Estimating the Completeness of Death Registration Systems." In *Data Bases for Mortality Measurement* (pp. 66–90). Papers of the Meeting of the United Nations/World Health Organization Working Group on Data Bases for Measurement of Levels, Trends and Differentials in Mortality, Bangkok, 20–23, October 1981. New York: United Nations.

Rogers, R. G., R. A. Hummer, and C. B. Narn. 2000. *Living and Dying in the U.S.A.* San Diego: Academic Press.

Rosenberg, H. M. 1966. "Recent Developments in Seasonally Adjusting Vital Statistics." *Demography* 3(2): 305–318.

Rosenwaike, I. 1966. "Seasonal Variation of Deaths in the United States, 1951–60." *Journal of the American Statistical Assocation* 61(315): 706–719.

Sakamoto-Momiyama, M. 1978. "Changes in the Seasonality of Human Mortality: A Medico-Geographical Study." *Social Science and Medicine* 12: 29–42.

Silcock, H. 1959, September. "The Comparison of Occupational Mortality Rates." *Population Studies* (London) 13(2): 183–192.

Sowards, K. A. 1997. "Premature Birth and the Changing Composition of Newborn Infectious Disease Mortality: Reconsidering 'Exogenous' Mortality." *Demography* 34: 399–409.

Stockwell, E. G., D. A. Swanson, and J. W. Wicks. 1987. "The Age-Cause Proxy Relationship in Infant Mortality." *Social Biology* 34: 249–253.

Střiteský, M. S., M. Šantruček, and M. Vacek. 1967. Summary of "The Train of Morbid Events Leading Directly to Death—A Practical and Methodological Problem." In United Nations, *Proceedings of the World Population Conference 1965* (Belgrade) (pp. 453–454). Vol. II. New York.

United Nations. 1953. *Principles for a Vital Statistics System*. Statistical Papers, Series M, No. 19.

United Nations. Various years. *Demographic Yearbook*.

U.S. Bureau of the Census. 1944. "Effect of Changing Birth Rates upon Infant Mortality Rates." By I. Moriyama and T. N. E. Greville. *Vital Statistics—Special Reports*, Vol. 19, No. 21. pp. 401–412.

U.S. Department of Health and Human Services. 1990. *International Classification of Diseases*, Vol. 1, 9th revision, 3rd ed. DHHS Publication 89-1260. Washington, DC: U.S. Government Printing Office.

U.S. National Center for Health Statistics (NCHS). 1980. *Monthly Vital Statistics Report*. "Estimates of Selected Comparability Ratios Based on Dual Coding of 1976 Death Certificates by the Eighth and Ninth Revisions of the International Classification of Diseases." By A. J. Klebba and J. H. Scott. DHEW Publication No. (PHS) 80-1120, Vol. 28, No. 11, Supplement. Rockville, MD: Public Health Service. .

U.S. National Center for Health Statistics. 1984. *Monthly Vital Statistics Report*. "Multiple Causes of Death in the United States," Vol. 32(10), Supplement(2). Washington, DC: U.S. Government Printing Office.

U.S. National Center for Health Statistics. 1989. *Monthly Vital Statistics Report* (Provisional Statistics), "Births, Marriages, Divorces, and Deaths for [month, year]. Washington, DC: Public Health Service.

U.S. National Center for Health Statistics. 1993. "Mortality by Occupation, Industry, and Cause of Death: 12 Reporting States, 1984." By H. M. Rosenberg, C. Burnett, J. Maurer, and R. Spirtas. *Monthly Vital Statistics Report* 42(4) Supplement. Hyattsville, MD: Public Health Service.

U.S. National Center for Health Statistics. 2001. "Comparability of Cause of Death between ICD-9 and ICD-10: Pretiminary Estimates." By R. N. Anderson, A. M. Miniño, D. L. Hoyert, and H. M. Rosenberg. *Monthly Vital Statistics Reports* 49(2).

U.S. National Institutes of Health. 1992. *A Mortality Study of 1.3 Million Persons; by Demographic, Social, and Economic Factors: 1979 1985 Follow-Up*. By E. Rogot, P. D. Sorlie, N. J. Johnson, and C. Schmitt. NIH Pub No. 92-3297.

U.S. National Institutes of Occupational Safety and Health (NIOSH). 1997. "Mortality by Occupation, Industry, and Cause of Death: 24 Reporting States, 1984–1988," by C. Burnett, J. Maurer, and M. Dosemeci. DHHS (NIOSH) publication 97–114.

U.S. National Office of Vital Statistics. 1950a. "Investigations of Separation Factors at Ages 1–4 Based on 10 Percent Mortality Sample." By T. N. E. Greville. In *Vital Statistics—Special Reports, Selected Studies*, Vol. 33, No. 7.

U.S. National Office of Vital Statistics. 1950b. *Vital Statistics-Special Reports*, Vol. 53(2).

U.S. Public Health Service. 1965. "Seasonal Adjustment of Vital Statistics by Electronic Computer." By H. M. Rosenberg (pp. 201–210). *Public Health Reports*, Vol. 80, No. 3.

Wingard, D. L. 1982. "The Sex Differential in Mortality Rates: Demographic and Behavioral Factors." *American Journal of Epidemiology* 115: 205–216.

World Health Organization. 1950, December. *Official Records of the World Health Organization*, No. 28, *Third World Health Assembly*, Geneva, 8 to 27 May 1950.

World Health Organization. 1957. *Manual of the International Statistical Classification of Diseases, Injuries, and Causes of Death*, 1965 Revision, Vol. I.

World Health Organization. 1967. *Manual of the International Statistical Classification of Diseases, Injuries, and Causes of Death*, 1965 Revision, Vols. I and II.

World Health Organization. 1977. *International Classification of Disease. Manual of the International Statistical Classification of Diseases, Injuries, and Causes of Death*. Based on the recommendations of the World Health Assembly. Volume 1, Geneva.

Zeighami, E. A., and M. D. Morris. 1983. "The Measurement and Interpretation of Proportionate Mortality." *American Journal of Epidemiology* 117: 90–97.

Suggested Readings

Bourgeois-Pichat, J. 1952, July–September. "Essai sur la mortalité 'biologique' de l'homme" (Essay on the "Biological" Mortality of Man). *Population* (Paris), 7(3): 381–394.

Chandra Sekar, C., and W. E. Deming. 1949, March. "On a Method of Estimating Birth and Death Rates and the Extent of Registration." *Journal of the American Statistical Association* 44(245): 101–115.

Comstock, G. W., and R. E. Markush. 1986. "Further Comments on Problems in Death Certification." *American Journal of Epidemiology* 124: 180–181.

Crimmins, E. M. 1981. "The Changing Pattern of American Mortality Decline, 1940–77, and Its Implications for the Future." *Population and Development Review* 7: 229–253.

Dever, G. E. A. 1991. *Community Health Analysis: Global Awareness at the Local Level*. 2nd ed. Gaitherberg, MD: Aspen.

Dorn, H. F. 1966. "Underlying and Contributory Causes of Death." In W. Haenszel (Ed.), U.S. Public Health Service, *Epidemiological Approaches to the Study of Cancer and Other Chronic Diseases* (pp. 421–430), National Cancer Institute Monograph 19.

Fletcher, B. 1988. "Occupation, Marriage and Disease-Specific Mortality Concordance." *Social Science and Medicine* 27(6): 615–622.

Forbes, D., and W. P. Frisbie. 1991. "Spanish Surname and Anglo Infant Mortality: Differentials over a Half Century." *Demography* 28: 639–660.

Frisbie, W. P., D. Forbes, and R. G. Rogers. 1992. "Neonatal and Post-neonatal Mortality as Proxies for Cause of Death: Evidence from Ethnic and Longitudinal Comparisons." *Social Science Quarterly* 73: 535–549.

Gregorio, D. I., S. J. Walsh, and D. Paturzo. 1997. "The Effects of Occupation-Based Social Position on Mortality in a Large American Cohort." *American Journal of Public Health* 87: 1472–1475.

Guest, A. M., G. Almgren, and J. M. Hussey. 1998. "The Ecology of Race and Socioeconomic Distress: Infant and Working-Age Mortality in Chicago." *Demography* 35: 23–34.

Hammond, E. I. 1965. July. "Studies in Fetal and Infant Mortality. I. A Methodological Approach to the Definition of Perinatal Mortality." *American Journal of Public Health* 55(7): 1012–1023.

Horiuchi, S., and J. R. Wilmoth. 1998. "Deceleration in the Age Pattern of Mortality at Older Ages." *Demography* 35: 391–412.

Hummer, R. A. 1996. "Black-White Differences in Health and Mortality: A Review and Conceptual Model." *Sociological Quarterly* 37: 105–125.

Kannisto, V. 1957. "The Value of Certain Refinements of the Infant Mortality Rate." *Bulletin of the World Health Organization* 16(4): 763–782.

Kaplan, G. A., E. R. Pamuk, J. W. Lynch, R. D. Cohen, and J. L. Balfour. 1996. "Inequality in Income and Mortality in the United States: Analysis of Mortality and Potential Pathways." *British Medical Journal* 312: 999–1003.

Kawachi, I., B. P. Kennedy, K. Lochner, and D. Prothrow-Smith. 1997. "Social Capital, Income Inequality, and Mortality." *American Journal of Public Health* 87: 1491–1498.

Kilpatrick, S. J. 1962, November. "Occupational Mortality Indices." *Population Studies* (London) 16(2): 175–187.

Kitigawa, E. M. 1966, September. "Theoretical Considerations in the Selection of a Mortality Index, and Some Empirical Comparisons." *Human Biology* 38(3): 293–308.

Kitigawa, E. M., and P. M. Hauser. 1973. *Differential Mortality in the United States: A Study of Socioeconomic Epidemiology*. Vital and Health Statistics Monographs. Cambridge, MA: Harvard University Press.

Kitigawa, E. M., and P. M. Hauser. 1977. "On Mortality." *Demography* 14: 381–389.

Koskinen, S., and T. Martelin. 1994. "Why Are Socioeconomic Mortality Differences Smaller Among Women than among Men?" *Social Science and Medicine* 38: 1385–1396.

Kpedekpo, G. M. K. 1968. "Evaluation and Adjustment of Vital Registration Data for the Compulsory Registration Areas of Ghana." *Demography* 5(1): 86–92.

Krueger, D. E. 1966, January. "New Numerators for Old Denominators—Multiple Causes of Death." In W. Haenszel (Ed.), U.S. Public Health Service, *Epidemiological Approaches to the Study of Cancer and Other Chronic Diseases* (pp. 431–442). National Cancer Institute Monograph 19.

Legaré, J. M. 1966, September–October. "Quelques considérations sur les tables de mortalité de génération. Application à l'Angleterre et au Pays de Galles" (Some Considerations Relating to Generation Life Tables. Application to England and Wales). *Population* (Paris) 21(5): 915–938.

Logan, W. P. D. 1953. "The Measurement of Infant Mortality." *Population Bulletin of the United Nations*, No. 3, pp. 30–67.

Lopez, A. D., G. Caselli, and T. Valkonen. 1995. *Adult Mortality in Developed Countries: From Description to Explanation*. Oxford: Clarendon Press.

Madigan, F. C. 1957, April. "Are Sex Mortality Differentials Biologically Caused?" *Milibank Memorial Fund Quarterly* 35(2): 202–223.

Manton, K. B. 1980. "Sex and Race Specific Mortality Differentials in Multiple Cause of Death Data." *Gerontologist* 20: 480–493.

Martin, W. J. 1951. "A Comparison of the Trends of Male and Female Mortality." *Journal of the Royal Statistical Society*. Series A (General), 114(3): 287–306.

Moriyama, I. M., and L. Guralnick. 1956. "Occupational and Social Class Differences in Mortality" (pp. 61–73). In *Trends and Differential in Mortality*. 1955 Annual Conference, Milibank Memorial Fund, New York.

Olshansky, S. J., and B. A. Carnes. 1994. "Demographic Perspectives on Human Senescence." *Population and Development Review* 20: 57–80.

Olshansky, S. J., and B. A. Carnes. 1997. "Ever Since Gompertz." *Demography* 34: 1–15.

Polednak, A. P. 1997. *Segregation, Poverty, and Mortality in Urban African Americans*. New York: Oxford University Press.

Poston, D. L., and R. G. Rogers. "Toward a Reformulation of the Neonatal Mortality Rate." *Social Biology* 32: 1–12.

Preston, S. H., and M. R. Haines. 1991. *Fatal Years: Child Mortality in Late Nineteenth-Century America*. Princeton, NJ: Princeton University Press.

Rogers, R. G., and R. Hackenberg. 1987. "Extending Epidemiologic Theory: A New Stage." *Social Biology* 34: 234–241.

Rogers, R. G., R. A. Hummer, and C. B. Narn. 2000. *Living and Dying in the U.S.A.* San Diego: Academic Press.

Rosenberg, H. M. 1966. "Recent Developments in Seasonally Adjusting Vital Statistics." *Demography* 3(2): 305–318.

Schofield, R., D. Reher, and A. Bideau. 1991. *The Decline of Mortality in Europe*. Oxford: Clarendon Press.

Silcock, H. 1959, November. "The Comparison of Occupational Mortality Rates." *Population Studies* (London) 13(2): 183–192.

Sorlie, P. D., E. Backlund, and J. B. Keller. 1995. "U.S. Mortality by Economic, Demographic, and Social Characteristics: The National Longitudinal Mortality Study." *American Journal of Public Health* 85: 949–956.

Sowards, K. A. 1997. "Premature Birth and the Changing Composition of Newborn Infectious Disease Mortality: Reconsidering 'Exogenous' Mortality." *Demography* 34: 399–409.

Sowder, W. T. 1954, September. "Why Is the Sex Difference in Mortality Increasing?" In U.S. Public Health Service Public Health Reports, Vol. 69, No. 9, pp. 860–864.

Spiegelman, M., and H. H. Marks. 1966, September. "Empirical Testing of Standards for the Age Adjustment of Death Rates by the Direct Method." *Human Biology* 38(3): 280–292.

U.S. National Center for Health Statistics. 1969. "Comparability of Marital Status, Race, Nativity, and Country of Origin on the Death Certificate and Matching Census Record, United States, May–Aug. 1960." *Vital and Health Statistics*, Series 2. No. 34.

U.S. National Center for Health Statistics. 1968. *Vital Statistics Rates in the United States, 1940–1960*. By Robert D. Grove and Alice M. Hetzel. PHS Pub. 1677, Chapter 2.

U.S. National Center for Health Statistics. 1968. "Comparability of Age on the Death Certificate and Matching Census Record, United States, May–Aug. 1960." *Vital Statistics Rates in the United States*, Series 2, No. 29.

U.S. National Center for Health Statistics. 1992. *International Collaborative Effort on Perinatal and Infant Mortality*. Proceedings. By R. Hartford. Hyattsville, MD: National Center for Health Statistics.

U.S. National Center for Health Statistics. 1994. "Effect on Mortality Rates of the 1989 Change in Tabulating Race." By D. L. Hoyert, *Vital Health Statistics* 20(25). Washington DC: U.S. Government Printing Office.

U.S. National Office of Vital Statistics. 1951. "Mortality, Occupation, and Socio-Economic Status." By Jean Daric. *Vital Statistics-Special Reports, Selected Studies*, Vol. 33, No. 10. pp. 175–187. Sept. 21, 1951. (Translation of "Mortalité, profession, et situation sociale," *Population* (Paris), 4(4): 672–694, Oct.–Dec. 1949.)

Vallin, J., S. D'Souza, and A. Palloni. 1990. *Measurement and Analysis of Mortality: New Approaches*. Oxford: Clarendon Press.

Wilkinson, R. G. 1989. "Class Mortality Differentials, Income Distribution, and Trends in Poverty 1921–1981." *Journal of Social Policy* 18: 307–335.

Williams, D. R., R. Lavizzo-Mourey, and R. C. Warren. 1994. "The Concept of Race and Health Status in America." *Public Health Reports* 109: 26–41.

Wingard, D. L. 1982. "The Sex Differential in Mortality Rates: Demographic and Behavioral Factors." *American Journal of Epidemiology* 115: 205–216.

Wolfenden, H. H. 1962, November. "On the Theoretical and Practical Considerations Underlying the Direct and Indirect Standardization of Death Rates." *Population Studies* (London), 16(2): 188–190.

World Health Organization. 1977. *Manual of Mortality Analysis*, Geneva: World Health Organization.

Yanagishita, M., and J. M. Guralnik. 1988. "Changing Mortality Patterns that Led Life Expectancy in Japan to Surpass Sweden's." *Demography* 25: 611–624.

Yerushalmy, J. 1951, August. "A Mortality Index for Use in Place of the Age-Adjusted Death Rate." *American Journal of Public Health* 41: 907–922.

Zenger, E. 1993. "Siblings' Neonatal Mortality Risks and Birth Spacing in Bangladesh." *Demography* 30: 477–488.

APPENDIX 12.A1. NOTES ON MAJOR RECENT DEVELOPMENTS IN U.S. MORTALITY STATISTICS*

Tenth Revision of International Classification of Diseases

The Tenth Revision (ICD-10) of the International Classification of Diseases was promulgated by the World Health Organization in 1992–1994 and implemented in the United States beginning with deaths in 1999. It replaces the Ninth Revision of the International Classification of Diseases (ICD-9), which was implemented in the United States with 1979 mortality data. ICD-

* Prepared by Jacob S. Siegel.

10 differs from ICD-9 in a number of ways. First, it is far more detailed than ICD-9; ICD-10 has 8000 categories while ICD-9 has 5000. Next, ICD-10 uses alphanumeric codes while ICD-9 uses only numeric codes. A further difference is that some additions and changes were made to the "chapters" of ICD-10; ICD-10 has 21 chapters as compared with 17 for ICD-9 (with two supplementary categories). Finally, some changes were made in the coding rules and rules for selecting the underlying cause of death. Some of these changes are evident from Table 12.A1, which displays the chapter titles and code ranges for the Tenth Revision of the International Classification of Diseases.

The changeover to the new classification system necessarily introduces certain discontinuities between the tabulations of deaths by cause between the years when the changeover occurs. Hence, some measure of the effect of the changeover is critical to the interpretation of mortality trends. Comparability ratios are intended to measure the discontinuities in cause-of-death tabulations in the year the new classification is introduced—1999 in the case of the United States. Comparability ratios simply represent the ratio of the number of deaths from a given cause classified according to ICD-10 and the number from this cause classified according to ICD-9. The ratios shown in Table 12.A2 are based on coding the same deaths occurring in 1996 by both the ninth and tenth revisions and measure the net effect of ICD-10 on the numbers counted in each cause-class. A comparability ratio of 1.00 denotes no net effect of ICD-10 on that cause.

2000 POPULATION STANDARD FOR AGE-ADJUSTING DEATH RATES

In 1999 the U.S. National Center for Health Statistics introduced a new population standard for deriving age-adjusted death rates. The new standard replaces the existing standard based on the 1940 population. The 1940 standard had been in use for over a half century so that, given the tremendous changes in the age structure of the U.S. population since 1940, age-adjusted death rates and the observed death rates for any recent year are far apart. The introduction of the new standard is intended not only to produce more realistic age-adjusted measures and comparisons, but also to reduce confusion among data users, who have had to deal with rates adjusted by alternative standard populations. The 2000 standard population is much older than the 1940 standard population; it has a higher mean age, a lower proportion of children, and a higher proportion of elderly persons. Inasmuch as such a population would give greater weight to the higher age-specific death rates of later life, use of the new standard produces adjusted rates that are much higher than the old standard. At the same time, rates adjusted by the 2000 standard population are much closer to the observed rates for current years than rates adjusted by the 1940 standard population.

All comparisons are affected by the introduction of the new standard, but usually not by very much because the same standard is being applied in each case. For example, the percentage decrease in the age-adjusted death rate

TABLE 12.A1   Chapter Titles and Code Ranges for the Tenth Revision of the International Classification of Diseases

Chapter Number	Chapter title	Code range
I	Certain infectious and parasitic diseases	A00-B99
II	Neoplasms	C00-D48
III	Diseases of the blood and blood-forming organs and certain disorders involving the immune mechanism	D50-D89
IV	Endocrine, nutritional, and metabolic diseases	E00-E90
V	Mental and behavioral disorders	F00-F99
VI	Diseases of the nervous system	G00-G99
VII	Diseases of the eye and adnexa	H00-H59
VIII	Diseases of the ear and mastoid process	H60-H95
IX	Diseases of the circulatory system	I00-I99
X	Diseases of the respiratory system	J00-J99
XI	Diseases of the digestive system	K00-K93
XII	Diseases of the skin and subcutaneous tissue	L00-L99
XIII	Diseases of the musculoskeletal system and the connective tissue	M00-M99
XIV	Diseases of the genitourinary system	N00-N99
XV	Pregnancy, childbirth, and the puerperium	O00-O99
XVI	Certain conditions originating in the perinatal period	P00-P96
XVII	Congenital malformations, deformations, and chromosomal abnormalities	Q00-Q99
XVIII	Symptoms, signs, and abnormal clinical and laboratory findings, not elsewhere classified	R00-R99
XIX	Injury, poisoning, and certain other consequences of external causes	S00-T98
XX	External causes of morbidity and mortality	V01-Y98
XXI	Factors influencing health status and contact with health services	Z00-Z99

Source: U.S. National Center for Health Statistics. 2001. "Comparability of Cause of Death between ICD-9 and ICD-10: Preliminary Estimates," by R. N. Anderson, A. M. Miniño, D. L. Hoyert, and H. M. Rosenberg. *National Vital Statistics Reports* 49(2), Table B.

TABLE 12.A2   Estimated Comparability Ratios for Selected Causes of Death in the United States: 1996 (Based on Ninth and Tenth Revisions of the International Classification of Diseases.)

List number	Cause of death	Estimated comparability ratio[1]
010	Septicemia	1.1949
016	Human immunodeficiency virus (HIV) disease	1.0637
019	Malignant neoplasms	1.0068
023	Colon, rectum, anus	0.9993
027	Trachea, bronchus, and lung	0.9837
029	Breast	1.0056
033	Prostate	1.0134
037	Lymphoid, hematopoietic, and related tissue	0.0042
046	Diabetes mellitus	1.0082
053	Major cardiovascular diseases	0.9981
054	Diseases of heart	0.9858
070	Cerebrovascular diseases	1.0588
071	Atherosclerosis	0.9637
076	Influenza and pneumonia	0.6982
082	Chronic lower respiratory diseases	1.0478
093	Chronic liver disease and cirrhosis	1.0367
097	Nephritis, nephrotic syndrome, and nephrosis	1.2320
108	Certain conditions originating in the prenatal period	1.0658
109	Congenital malformations, deformations, and chromosomal abnormalities	0.8470
112	Accidents (unintentional injuries)	1.0305
124	Intentional self-harm (suicide)	0.9962
127	Assault (homicide)	0.9983

[1] Comparability ratios subject to sampling error.

Source: U.S. National Center for Health Statistics. 2001. "Comparability of Cause of Death between ICD-9 and ICD-10: Preliminary Estimates," by R. N. Anderson, A. M. Miniño, D. L. Hoyert, and H. M. Rosenberg. *National Vital Statistics Reports* 49(2), Table 1.

between 1979 and 1995 based on the year 2000 standard is only moderately smaller than the decrease based on the 1940 standard—mostly as a result of the fact that the base for calculating the percentage is larger when the rate is adjusted by the 2000 population. The trends in age-adjusted rates for most leading causes of death are nearly parallel. The percent changes in the age-adjusted rates between 1979 and 1995 using the two standards for some of the leading causes are as follows:

	Standard population	
Cause of death*	1940	2000
All causes	−12.7	−9.2
Diseases of heart	−30.7	−26.2
Malignant neoplasms	−0.7	+3.8
Cerebrovascular diseases	−35.8	−34.3
Chronic obstructive pulmonary diseases	+42.8	+58.7
Accidents and adverse effects	−28.8	−24.8
Pneumona and influenza	+15.6	+29.4
Diabetes mellitus	+36.1	+33.8

*Ninth Revision, International Classification of Diseases (ICD-9).

A fuller explanation of the basis for the introduction of the new standard population and of the effect of introducing it on U.S. mortality trends and sex-race differences is given in the following reports of the U.S. National Center for Health Statistics: "Age Standardization of Death Rates: Implementation of the Year 2000 Standard," by R. N. Anderson and H. M. Rosenberg, *National Vital Statistics Reports*, Vol., 47, No. 3, 1998, and "Age-Adjusted Death Rates: Trend Data Based on the Year 2000 Standard Population," by D. L. Hoyert and R. N. Anderson, *National Vital Statistics Reports*, Vol. 49, No. 9, 2001.

REVISION OF U.S. STANDARD CERTIFICATES AND REPORTS

Finally, among the major recent developments in U.S. mortality statistics is the revision of the standard certificates for reporting and recording the events of birth, death, and fetal death. Standard certificates are developed to promote uniformity in data collection across registration areas. The NCHS designs the standard forms in cooperation with state vital statistics officials. The revision of the standard certificates is generally carried out every 10 to 15 years. The previous standard certificates were introduced in 1989 and the new standard certificates are gradually being adopted by the states beginning in 2003. So far only a few states have changed over to the new standard forms and it is expected that full implementation will be phased in over several years. The process involved in revising the content of the standard certificates and reports is described in the "Executive Summary" of the *Report of the Panel to Evaluate the U.S. Standard Certificates and Reports*, available at the web site of U.S. NCHS (www.cdc.gov/nchs). The draft certificates are also available at this web site.

NCHS has issued an updated version of its *Physicians' Handbook on Medical Certification of Death* (2003 Revision) and *Coroners' Handbook on Death Registration and Fetal Death Reporting* (2003 Revision).

13

The Life Table

HALLIE J. KINTNER

NATURE AND USE OF LIFE TABLES

Some of the measures of mortality discussed in Chapter 12 are associated with a statistical model known as a life table. A life table is designed essentially to measure mortality, but various specialists employ it in a variety of ways. Public health workers, demographers, actuaries, economists, and many others use life tables in studies of longevity, fertility, migration, and population growth, as well as in making projections of population size and characteristics and in studies of widowhood, orphanhood, length of married life, length of working life, and length of disability-free life. In its simplest form, an entire life table is generated from age-specific mortality rates, and the resulting values are used to measure mortality, survivorship, and life expectation. In other applications, the mortality rates in the life table are combined with other demographic data into a more complex model that measures the combined effect of mortality and changes in one or more socioeconomic characteristics (e.g., a table of working life, which combines mortality rates and labor force participation ratios and measures their combined effect on working life).

Life tables are, in essence, one form of combining mortality rates of a population at different ages into a single statistical model. They are principally used to measure the level of mortality of the population involved. One of their main advantages over other methods of measuring mortality is that they do not reflect the effects of the age distribution of an actual population and do not require the adoption of a standard population for acceptable comparisons of levels of mortality in different populations. Another is that a life table readily permits making mortality allowances for age cohorts, eliminating the burdensome task of compiling death statistics for age cohorts from annual death statistics by age, even when the latter are available.

TYPES OF LIFE TABLES

Life tables differ in several ways, including the reference year of the table, the age detail, and the number of factors comprehended by the table. We may distinguish two types of life tables according to the reference year of the table: the current or period life table and the generation or cohort life table. The first type of table is based on the experience over a short period of time, such as 1 year, 3 years, or an intercensal period, in which mortality has remained substantially the same. Commonly, the death statistics used for a current life table relate to a period of 1 to 3 years, and the population data used relate to the middle of that period (usually close to the date of a census). This type of table, therefore, represents the combined mortality experience by age of the population in a particular short period of time (treated synthetically or viewed cross-sectionally); it does not represent the mortality experience of an actual cohort. Instead, it assumes a hypothetical cohort that is subject to the age-specific death rates observed in the particular period. Therefore, a current life table may be viewed as a snapshot of current mortality. It is an excellent summary description of mortality in a year or a short period.

The second type of life table, the generation life table, is based on the mortality rates experienced by a particular birth cohort (e.g., all persons born in the year 1900). According to this type of table, the mortality experience of the persons in the cohort would be observed from their moment of birth through each consecutive age in successive calendar years until all of them die. Obviously, data over a long period of years are needed to complete a single table, and it is not possible wholly on the basis of actual data to construct generation tables for cohorts born in the 20th century. This type of table is useful for projections of mortality, for studies of mortality trends, and for the measurement of fertility and reproductivity. In general, unless otherwise specified, the term "life table" is used in this chapter to refer to a current life table.

Life tables are also classified into two types—complete (or unabridged) and abridged—according to the length of the age interval in which the data are presented. A complete life table contains data for every single year of age from birth to the last applicable age. An abridged life table contains data at intervals of 5 or 10 years of age for most of the age range. Demographers usually prepare the simpler abridged life table rather than the more elaborate complete life table. Tables with values for 5- or 10-year intervals are sufficiently detailed for most purposes, and the abridged table is less burdensome to prepare. Moreover, it is often more convenient to use. Tables 13.1 and 13.2 are illustrations of complete and abridged life tables, respectively. Occasionally, the basic values from a complete life table are presented only for every fifth age in order to economize on space.

We may also distinguish a conventional life table, which is concerned only with the general mortality experience of a cohort by age, from a multiple decrement table, which describes the separate and combined effects of more than one factor. Mortality is always involved. Multiple decrement tables are of several forms. The mortality factor may be applied in terms of component death rates (e.g., for causes of death), or mortality may be combined with changes in one or more socioeconomic characteristic(s) of the population. Multiple decrement tables describe the diminution of an original cohort through these factors (e.g., the attrition of the single population through mortality and marriage). Increment-decrement tables and multistate tables, elaborations of multiple decrement tables, describe the effect of accession to and withdrawal from the original cohort at various stages in its life history. Examples include a table of working life (which combines mortality rates and labor force participation ratios) and a nuptiality table (which combines mortality rates and data on the prevalence or incidence of marriage and divorce).

AVAILABILITY OF LIFE TABLES

The first recognized life table was published in 1693 by Halley. It was based on birth and death registration data for the city of Breslau during the years 1687 to 1691. The assumption adopted in the preparation of this table that the population of Breslau had remained stationary (i.e., that the total population and the numbers in each age and sex group did not change over many decades) was not entirely correct and, therefore, the resulting life table could not be regarded as being correct. Other life tables were prepared in the 17th and 18th centuries on the basis of limited data, but they were subject to necessary simplifying assumptions that rendered them inexact.

The first scientifically correct life table based on both population and death data classified by age was prepared by Milne and published in 1815. It was based on the mortality experience in two parishes of Carlisle, England, during the period 1779–1787. A large number of life tables have been published since then. In the early years, most of these pertained to European countries, particularly Scandinavian countries, but life tables are now available for most countries of the world and every continent is represented.

In the United States, official complete life tables have been prepared since 1900–1902 in connection with the decennial censuses of population. These tables are based on the registered deaths in the expanding death registration area (continental United States first being covered for the 1929–1931 table) in the 3-year period containing the census year. Hence, there is an unbroken decennial series of complete life tables covering the 20th century (U.S. Bureau of the Census, 1921, 1936, 1946; U.S. National Office of Vital Statistics, 1954; U.S. National Center for Health Statistics, 1964, 1975, 1985a, 1997a). There are some tables also for intercensal periods, as for 1901–1910, 1920–1929, and 1930–1939. An annual series of abridged life tables was started in 1945 and continued to the end of the 20th century. They are now published on a provisional basis for a given year just after the close of the year and on a revised basis in the annual volume on mortality statistics for the year or in current reports. These annual tables are based on the annual death registration and on postcensal estimates of population.

In addition to national tables, tables have been prepared from time to time for geographic areas varying in size from specific cities to geographic divisions and regions. Sets of life tables for all states have now been published in connection with the censuses of 1930 (whites only), 1940 (whites only), 1950 (nonwhite tables for states in the South region only), 1960 (race/ethnic group for selected states), 1970, 1980, and 1990 (U.S. National Office of Vital Statistics, 1948, 1956a; U.S. National Center for Health Statistics, 1966, 1977, 1990, 1998). Life tables for geographic divisions or regions corresponding to these state tables have also been published (U.S. National Office of Vital Statistics, 1956b; U.S. National Center for Health Statistics, 1965). For the first time, life tables for metropolitan and nonmetropolitan areas as a whole were published for 1959–1961 (U.S. National Center for Health Statistics, 1967). For some periods prior to 1940, separate tables were published for the urban and rural populations.

Special compilations of life tables or analytic studies of life tables were published in connection with the 1900, 1910, 1930, and 1940 censuses. The life tables included in these volumes covered the death registration states or the United States as a whole, specified individual states and cities, and the urban and rural parts of the death registration states in some cases. A general guide to the U.S. life tables for 1900 to 1959 has been published (U.S. National Center for Health Statistics, 1963).

TABLE 13.1 Complete Life Table for the Total Population of the United States: 1989–1991

Age Interval — Period of life between two exact ages (1) x to $x+1$ (years)	Proportion dying — Proportion of persons alive at beginning of age interval dying during interval (2) q_x	Of 100,000 born alive — Number living at beginning of age interval (3) l_x	Number dying during age interval (4) d_x	Stationary population — In the age interval (5) L_x	In this and all subsequent age intervals (6) T_x	Average remaining lifetime — Average number of years of life remaining at beginning of age interval (7) e_x
0–1	0.00936	100,000	936	99,258	7,536,614	75.37
1–2	0.00073	99,064	72	99,028	7,437,356	75.08
2–3	0.00048	98,992	48	98,968	7,338,328	74.13
3–4	0.00037	98,944	37	98,926	7,239,360	73.17
4–5	0.00030	98,907	30	98,892	7,140,434	72.19
5–6	0.00027	98,877	27	98,863	7,041,542	71.22
6–7	0.00025	98,850	25	98,838	6,942,634	70.23
7–8	0.00023	98,825	23	98,814	6,843,796	69.25
8–9	0.00020	98,802	20	98,792	6,744,983	68.27
9–10	0.00018	98,782	18	98,773	6,646,191	67.28
10–11	0.00016	98,764	16	98,756	6,547,418	66.29
11–12	0.00016	98,748	16	98,740	6,448,662	65.30
12–13	0.00022	98,732	22	98,721	6,349,922	64.31
13–14	0.00032	98,710	32	98,694	6,251,201	63.33
14–15	0.00047	98,678	46	98,655	6,152,507	62.35
15–16	0.00063	98,632	62	98,601	6,053,852	61.38
16–17	0.00077	98,570	76	98,532	5,955,251	60.42
17–18	0.00089	98,494	88	98,450	5,856,719	59.46
18–19	0.00096	98,406	94	98,359	5,758,269	58.52
19–20	0.00101	98,312	99	98,263	5,659,910	57.57
20–21	0.00104	98,213	102	98,162	5,561,647	56.63
21–22	0.00109	98,111	107	98,058	5,463,485	55.69
22–23	0.00112	98,004	110	97,949	5,365,428	54.75
23–24	0.00114	97,894	112	97,838	5,267,479	53.81
24–25	0.00116	97,782	113	97,726	5,169,641	52.87
25–26	0.00117	97,669	114	97,612	5,071,915	51.93
26–27	0.00119	97,555	116	97,497	4,974,303	50.99
27–28	0.00121	97,439	118	97,380	4,876,806	50.05
28–29	0.00126	97,321	123	97,260	4,779,426	49.11
29–30	0.00133	97,198	129	97,134	4,682,167	48.17
30–31	0.00140	97,069	136	97,001	4,585,033	47.23
31–32	0.00147	96,933	142	96,862	4,488,032	46.30
32–33	0.00154	96,791	149	96,717	4,391,170	45.37
33–34	0.00162	96,642	157	96,564	4,294,454	44.44
34–35	0.00170	96,485	164	96,403	4,197,890	43.51
35–36	0.00178	96,321	171	96,236	4,101,487	42.58
36–37	0.00188	96,150	181	96,060	4,005,252	41.66
37–38	0.00198	95,969	190	95,874	3,909,192	40.73
38–39	0.00207	95,779	198	95,680	3,813,318	39.81
39–40	0.00217	95,581	207	95,478	3,717,638	38.90
40–41	0.00228	95,374	217	95,266	3,622,161	37.98
41–42	0.00240	95,157	228	95,043	3,526,395	37.06
42–43	0.00254	94,929	241	94,809	3,431,852	36.15
43–44	0.00271	94,688	257	94,560	3,337,044	35.24
44–45	0.00292	94,431	276	94,293	3,242,484	34.34
45–46	0.00318	94,155	299	94,006	3,148,191	33.44
46–47	0.00348	93,856	327	93,693	3,054,186	32.54
47–48	0.00380	93,529	355	93,352	2,960,493	31.65
48–49	0.00414	93,174	386	92,981	2,867,142	30.77
49–50	0.00449	92,788	417	92,580	2,774,161	29.90
50–51	0.00490	92,371	453	92,145	2,681,581	29.03
51–52	0.00537	91,918	494	91,671	2,589,437	28.17
52–53	0.00590	91,424	539	91,155	2,497,766	27.32
53–54	0.00647	90,885	588	90,591	2,406,611	26.48
54–55	0.00708	90,297	639	89,978	2,316,020	25.65
55–56	0.00773	89,658	693	89,312	2,226,043	24.83

(continues)

TABLE 13.1 (continued)

Age Interval — Period of life between two exact ages (1) x to x+1 (years)	Proportion dying — Proportion of persons alive at beginning of age interval dying during interval (2) q_x	Of 100,000 born alive — Number living at beginning of age interval (3) l_x	Of 100,000 born alive — Number dying during age interval (4) d_x	Stationary population — In the age interval (5) L_x	Stationary population — In this and all subsequent age intervals (6) T_x	Average remaining lifetime — Average number of years of life remaining at beginning of age interval (7) e_x
56–57	0.00844	88,965	751	88,590	2,136,731	24.02
57–58	0.00926	88,214	817	87,806	2,048,142	23.22
58–59	0.01019	87,397	891	86,952	1,960,336	22.43
59–60	0.01120	86,506	969	86,022	1,873,385	21.66
60–61	0.01223	85,537	1,046	85,014	1,787,363	20.90
61–62	0.01328	84,491	1,122	83,930	1,702,349	20.15
62–63	0.01439	83,369	1,200	82,769	1,618,419	19.41
63–64	0.01560	82,169	1,282	81,528	1,535,650	18.69
64–65	0.01691	80,887	1,368	80,203	1,454,122	17.98
65–66	0.01827	79,519	1,453	78,793	1,373,919	17.28
66–67	0.01967	78,066	1,536	77,298	1,295,127	16.59
67–68	0.02121	76,530	1,623	75,719	1,217,829	15.91
68–69	0.02297	74,907	1,721	74,047	1,142,110	15.25
69–70	0.02499	73,186	1,829	72,272	1,068,064	14.59
70–71	0.02727	71,357	1,946	70,384	995,792	13.96
71–72	0.02979	69,411	2,068	68,377	925,408	13.33
72–73	0.03251	67,343	2,189	66,249	857,031	12.73
73–74	0.03534	65,154	2,303	64,003	790,783	12.14
74–75	0.03824	62,851	2,403	61,650	726,780	11.56
75–76	0.04126	60,448	2,494	59,201	665,131	11.00
76–77	0.04455	57,954	2,582	56,663	605,930	10.46
77–78	0.04819	55,372	2,668	54,038	549,267	9.92
78–79	0.05239	52,704	2,761	51,324	495,229	9.40
79–80	0.05723	49,943	2,858	48,514	443,905	8.89
80–81	0.06277	47,085	2,956	45,607	395,391	8.40
81–82	0.06885	44,129	3,038	42,610	349,784	7.93
82–83	0.07535	41,091	3,096	39,543	307,174	7.48
83–84	0.08207	37,995	3,118	36,436	267,631	7.04
84–85	0.08907	34,877	3,106	33,324	231,195	6.63
85–86	0.09705	31,771	3,083	30,230	197,871	6.23
86–87	0.10627	28,688	3,049	27,164	167,642	5.84
87–88	0.11625	25,639	2,981	24,149	140,478	5.48
88–89	0.12688	22,658	2,875	21,221	116,330	5.13
89–90	0.13834	19,783	2,737	18,415	95,109	4.81
90–91	0.15135	17,046	2,580	15,756	76,695	4.50
91–92	0.16591	14,466	2,400	13,266	60,939	4.21
92–93	0.18088	12,066	2,182	10,975	47,673	3.95
93–94	0.19552	9,884	1,933	8,918	36,698	3.71
94–95	0.21000	7,951	1,670	7,116	27,780	3.49
95–96	0.22502	6,281	1,413	5,575	20,664	3.29
96–97	0.24126	4,868	1,174	4,281	15,090	3.10
97–98	0.25689	3,694	949	3,220	10,809	2.93
98–99	0.27175	2,745	746	2,372	7,589	2.76
99–100	0.28751	1,999	575	1,712	5,217	2.61
100–101	0.30418	1,424	433	1,208	3,506	2.46
101–102	0.32182	991	319	832	2,298	2.32
102–103	0.34049	672	229	558	1,467	2.18
103–104	0.36024	443	160	363	909	2.05
104–105	0.38113	283	108	229	546	1.93
105–106	0.40324	175	71	140	317	1.81
106–107	0.42663	104	44	82	178	1.71
107–108	0.45137	60	27	47	96	1.59
108–109	0.47755	33	16	25	49	1.48
109–110	0.50525	17	9	9	24	1.39

Source: U.S. National Center for Health Statistics. 1997. *U.S. Decennial Life Tables for 1989–91.* Vol. 1, no. 1, pp. 6–7.

TABLE 13.2   Abridged Life Table for the Total Population of the United States: 1989–1991

Age interval	Proportion dying	Of 100,000 born alive		Stationary population		Average remaining lifetime
Period of life between two ages (1) x to x + n year	Proportion of persons alive at beginning of age interval dying during interval (2) $_nq_x$	Number living at beginning of age interval (3) l_x	Number dying during age interval (4) $_nd_x$	In the age interval (5) $_nL_x$	In this and all subsequent age intervals (6) T_x	Average number of years of life remaining at beginning of age interval (7) e_x
0–1	0.009360	100,000	936	99,258	7,536,614	75.37
1–5	0.001888	99,064	187	395,814	7,437,356	75.08
5–10	0.001143	98,877	113	494,080	7,041,542	71.21
10–15	0.001337	98,764	132	493,566	6,547,418	66.29
15–20	0.004248	98,632	419	492,205	6,053,852	61.38
20–25	0.005539	98,213	544	489,732	5,561,647	56.63
25–30	0.006143	97,669	600	486,882	5,071,915	51.93
30–35	0.007706	97,069	748	483,546	4,585,033	47.23
35–40	0.009832	96,321	947	479,326	4,101,487	42.58
40–45	0.012781	95,374	1,219	473,970	3,622,161	37.98
45–50	0.018947	94,155	1,784	466,610	3,148,191	33.44
50–55	0.029371	92,371	2,713	455,538	2,681,581	29.03
55–60	0.045964	89,658	4,121	438,680	2,226,043	24.83
60–65	0.070356	85,537	6,018	413,444	1,787,363	20.90
65–70	0.102642	79,519	8,162	378,127	1,373,919	17.28
70–75	0.152879	71,357	10,909	330,661	995,792	13.96
75–80	0.221066	60,448	13,363	269,740	665,131	11.00
80–85	0.325242	47,085	15,314	197,520	395,391	8.40
85–90	0.463473	31,771	14,725	121,176	197,871	6.23
90–95	0.631526	17,046	10,765	56,031	76,695	4.50
95–100	0.773285	6,281	4,857	17,158	20,664	3.29
100+	1.000000	1,424	1,424	3,506	3,506	2.46

Source: Based on Table 13-1.

The United Nations *Demographic Yearbook* for 1996 is the most recent *Yearbook* to contain a comprehensive collection of national life tables. Values of the expectation of life, (1-year) mortality rates, and survivors from the two latest official complete life tables, largely for years in the period 1979–1995, are included. These values are shown for single ages up to 5 years and at every fifth age thereafter to 85 years. Similar tables in the 1985, 1980, 1974, 1967, 1966, 1961, 1957, and 1953 *Yearbooks* carry the life tables back to 1900. In addition, the latest value of the expectation of life is published every year. In the 1996 collection, values for the expectation of life are shown for 229 countries, but the other two life table functions are shown only for about 135 countries.

A compilation of life tables for a large number of countries spanning a wide range of time has been published by Keyfitz and Flieger (1968, 1990). Life tables for males and females for each country and year included in the compilation were derived electronically from official data on births, deaths, and population classified by age and sex, where such data were considered to be of satisfactory quality. While the first citation concerned only 29% of the world's population,

the second citation refers to 152 countries. The later volume includes actual trends to 1985 and population projections to 2020. Sets of model life tables have been published by the United Nations (1982), Coale and Demeny (1966), and Coale, Demeny, and Vaughn (1983). These sets of tables correspond to values for life expectancy at birth varying generally by fixed intervals in years. The UN tables cover from 20 years to 73.9 years, mostly in intervals of 2.5 years. The Coale and Demeny tables relate to four different "regions" distinguished by the age pattern of mortality. The tables for females correspond to values for life expectancy at birth ranging from 20 to 80 years in intervals of 2.5 years; and the male tables are presented as companion tables. These tables are useful for estimating life table functions for countries for which not all the data necessary for the preparation of a life table are available. The World Health Organization annually publishes life expectancy by sex in the *World Health Statistics Annual*. The Population Reference Bureau frequently publishes life expectancy data in its *World Population Data Sheet*. Life tables for 229 countries are available from the U.S. Census Bureau's website.

ANATOMY OF THE LIFE TABLE

Life Table Functions

The basic life tables functions—$_nq_x$, l_x, $_nd_x$, $_nL_x$, T_x, and e_x—can be observed in Tables 13.1 and 13.2. These six columns are generally calculated and published for every life table. However, in some cases, because of limitations of space, columns may be omitted. (For example, the United Nations publishes only q_x, l_x, and e_x in the *Demographic Yearbook*.) This is done without a significant loss of information because the functions are interrelated and some can be directly calculated from the others. In general, the mortality rate ($_nq_x$) is the basic function in the table (i.e., the initial function from which all other life table functions are derived).

Alternative Interpretations

Life table functions are subject to two different interpretations depending on the interpretation given to the life table as a whole. In the more common interpretation, the life table is viewed as depicting the lifetime mortality experience of a single cohort of newborn babies, who are subject to the age-specific mortality rates on which the table is based. In the second interpretation, the life table is viewed as a stationary population resulting from the (unchanging) schedule of age-specific mortality rates shown and a constant annual number of births.

The Life Table as the Mortality Experience of a Cohort

Under the first interpretation, the life table model conceptually traces a cohort of newborn babies through their entire life under the assumption that they are subject to the current observed schedule of age-specific mortality rates. The cohort of newborn babies, called the radix of the table, is usually assumed to number 100,000. In this case, the interpretation of the life table functions in an abridged table would be as follows:

x to $x + n$ The period of life between two exact ages. For instance, "20–25" means the 5-year interval between the 20th and 25th birthdays.

$_nq_x$ The proportion of the persons in the cohort alive at the beginning of an indicated age interval (x) who will die before reaching the end of that age interval ($x + n$). For example, according to Table 13.2, the proportion dying in the age interval 20–25 is 0.005539—that is, out of every 100,000 persons alive and exactly 20 years old, 554 will die before reaching their 25th birthday. In other words, the $_nq_x$ values represent the probability that a person at his or her xth birthday will die before reaching his or her $x + n$th birthday.

l_x The number of persons living at the beginning of the indicated age interval (x) out of the total number of births assumed as the radix of the table. Again, according to Table 13.2, out of 100,000 newborn babies, 98,213 persons would survive to exact age 20.

$_nd_x$ The number of persons who would die within the indicated age interval (x to $x + n$) out of the total number of births assumed in the table. Thus, according to Table 13.2, there would be 544 deaths between exact ages 20 and 25 to the initial cohort of 100,000 newborn babies.

$_nL_x$ The number of person-years that would be lived within the indicated age interval (x to $x + n$) by the cohort of 100,000 births assumed. Thus, according to Table 13.2, the 100,000 newborn babies would live 489,732 person-years between exact ages 20 and 25. Of the 98,213 persons who reach age 20, the 97,669 who survive to age 25 would live 5 years each (97,669 × 5 = 488,345 person-years) and the 544 who die would each live varying periods of time less than 5 years, averaging about 2 1/2 years

$$544 \times 2.55 = 1387 \text{ person-years}$$

T_x The total number of person-years that would be lived after the beginning of the indicated age interval by the cohort of 100,000 births assumed. Thus, according to Table 13.2, the 100,000 newborn babies would live 5,561,647 person-years after their 20th birthday.

e_x The average remaining lifetime (in years) for a person who survives to the beginning of the indicated age interval. This function is also called the complete expectation of life or, simply, life expectancy. Thus, according to Table 13.2, a person who reaches his or her 20th birthday should expect to live 56.63 years more, on the average.

The interpretation of the functions in a complete life table is the same as in the abridged table except that the q_x, d_x, and L_x values relate to single-age intervals. The l_x, T_x, and e_x values have the same interpretation as in the abridged table because they are not "interval" values but pertain to exact age x.

The Life Table as a Stationary Population

An alternate interpretation of the life table is the one associated with the concept of a stationary population. A stationary population is defined as a population whose total number and distribution by age do not change with time. Such a hypothetical population would result if the number of births per year remained constant (usually assumed at 100,000) for a long period of time and each cohort of births experienced the current observed mortality rates throughout life. The annual number of deaths would thus equal 100,000 also, and there would be no change in the size of the population.

In this case, the interpretation of x to $x + n$, $_nq_x$ and e_x would be as previously indicated, but, given that births are constant at 100,000 per year and that the observed death rates at each age remain in effect for the life of the cohort, for the other life table functions, it would be as follows:

l_x The number of persons who reach the beginning of the age interval each year. According to Table 13.2, there would be 98,213 persons reaching exact age 20 every year.

$_nd_x$ The number of persons that die each year within the indicated age interval. According to Table 13.2, there would be 544 deaths between exact ages 20 and 25 every year.

$_nL_x$ The number of persons in the population who at any moment are living within the indicated age interval. According to Table 13.2, there would be 489,732 persons living between exact ages 20 and 25 in the population at any time.

T_x The number of persons in the population who at any moment are living within the indicated age interval and all higher age intervals. According to Table 13.2, there would be 5,561,647 persons over exact age 20 living in the population at any time.

Each interpretation has its particular applications. For example, the interpretation of the life table as the history of a cohort is applied in public health studies and mortality analysis, and in the calculation of survival rates for estimating population, net migration, fertility, and reproductivity. The interpretation of the life table as a stationary population is used in the comparative measurement of mortality and in studies of population structure.

Life Span and Life Expectancy

In measuring longevity, two concepts should be distinguished: *life span* and *life expectancy*. The first concept tries to establish numerically the age limit of human life (i.e., the age that human beings as a species could reach under optimum conditions). There is no known exact figure for the life span of human beings or any other species (Carey, 1997). However, by using the verified age of the longest lived individual, one operational definition of life span for a species can be constructed, namely, the maximum recorded age at death. Using this operational definition, the life span for humans appears to be just over 120 years (Olshansky, Carnes, and Cassel, 1990).

Life expectancy is the expected number of years to be lived, on the average, by a particular population at a particular time. Sufficiently accurate records have been available for some time for many countries from which estimates have been prepared. These estimates have generally come from a current life table, although in some instances they have been prepared from more limited data.

CONSTRUCTION OF CONVENTIONAL LIFE TABLES

General Considerations

The main concern in this section is with methods of constructing life tables where satisfactory data on births, deaths, and population are available. (Model life tables and indirect techniques of life table construction are often employed for statistically underdeveloped countries, as discussed in Chapter 22 and Appendix B.) Mathematical formulas and demographic procedures are discussed in detail, and techniques for manipulating the mortality data are presented. It should be observed that in every instance underlying these procedures, formulas, and techniques, there is an assumption that the data on births, deaths, and population are fully accurate. It is well known, however, that one of the most important aspects of the preparation of a life table is the testing of the data for possible biases and other errors. Most of the procedures used to check on the accuracy of the data have been discussed in previous chapters and will not be discussed again here. It suffices that the level of inaccuracy that can be tolerated depends mostly on the intended use of the life table.

One factor that is usually involved in the selection of the method to be used in the construction of a life table is the degree of adherence to the observed data that is desired. Full adherence to the observed values implies that the final life table functions will exhibit all the fluctuations in the observed data, whether these are due to real variations or to errors in the data. On the other hand, overgraduation (i.e., excessive "smoothing" of the data by mathematical methods) will eliminate or reduce true variations in the age pattern of mortality rates. Therefore, it must be decided whether the emphasis in the life table should be on its closeness to the actual data or on its presentation of the underlying mortality picture after fluctuations have been removed. In the statistically developed countries, as the quality and quantity of data have improved with the passage of time, fewer irregular fluctuations have been noticed in the observed mortality rates. Therefore, the tendency has been to place stronger emphasis on adherence to the data and less emphasis on eliminating or reducing the fluctuations.

The Complete Life Table

As was indicated before, a complete life table is a life table in which the values of the functions are shown for single years of age. This type of table either can be computed directly from the observed data or can be obtained by suitable interpolation of an abridged life table. In many instances, even when a complete life table is being constructed, the observed data are combined into age groups and then interpolated to obtain the single-year values. This pro-

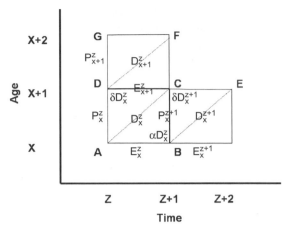

FIGURE 13.1 ••

cedure is generally used to smooth out artificial fluctuations in the data or to adjust for what are believed to be inconsistencies or errors in the data.

Basic Construction Problems

The construction of complete life tables can be considered in terms of three broad phases. First, the basic data on deaths, population, and births are checked for inconsistencies, biases, and other errors, and adjustments are made where necessary. Second, the death rates and mortality rates are computed and graduated (i.e., mathematically smoothed). Third, the remaining functions of the life table are calculated. As indicated previously, this chapter emphasizes the second and third steps.

Life tables are based on probabilities of dying, the probability that an individual alive at age x dies before reaching his or her next birthday (age $x + 1$). The Lexis diagram (Figure 13.1) shows the relation of the number attaining age x, the population in age x, and the deaths at age x. Individual lives move along diagonal lines from the origin up and to the right. In general, then,

D_x^z The number of deaths that occur during calendar year z among persons who have attained age x at last birthday (the area encompassed by points ABCD in Figure 13.1).

αD_x^z The number of persons who attained age x in the calendar year z and died before the end of the calendar year (the area encompassed by points ABC).

δD_x^z The number of persons alive at the beginning of calendar year z who were x years old last birthday and died before attaining age $x + 1$ (the area encompassed by points ADC).

P_x^z The number of persons alive at the beginning of calendar year z who are x years old last birthday (the line from point A to point D).

E_x^z The number of persons attaining age x in year z (the line from point A to point B).

Note that $\alpha D_x^z + \delta D_x^z = D_x^z$ and $E_{x+1}^z = P_x^z - \delta D_x^z$.

There are several alternative ways to compute mortality rates, q_x, from vital statistics and census data. One approach relates deaths in the parallelogram ABCE to lines connecting AB. Under the assumption of no migration, the mortality rate for ages above 1 would be

$$q_x = \frac{\alpha D_x^z + \delta D_x^{z+1}}{E_x^z} \qquad (13.1)$$

The corresponding mortality rate for the first year of life would replace the denominator with the number of births in year z. However, these formulas involve the partial mortality experience of 2 consecutive calendar years rather than the experience of a single calendar year.

Another approach concerns deaths in ABCD and relates αD_x^z to lines connecting AB and δD_x^z to lines connecting AD. For ages above 1

$$q_x = 1 - \left(1 - \frac{\alpha D_x^z}{E_x^z}\right)\left(1 - \frac{\delta D_x^z}{P_x^z}\right) \qquad (13.2)$$

The mortality rates could be based on the experience of a single calendar year if it is assumed that there is little change in mortality or in the seasonal birth pattern between the 2 years. In that case, the formulas for ages above 1 and for infants would be

$$q_x = 1 - \frac{P_x^{z+1}}{E_x^z} \cdot \frac{E_{x+1}^z}{P_x^z} \qquad (13.3)$$

$$q_0 = 1 - \frac{P_0^{z+1}}{B^z} \cdot \frac{E_1^z}{P_0^z} \qquad (13.4)$$

These formulas directly employ deaths in the single year z only, although deaths for prior years are required to determine the population at the beginning of the year at age under 1, or P_x^z in general.

It should be noted that these formulas require the registered deaths in every calendar year to be separated according to whether they occurred before or after the birthday anniversary in that year. When the death statistics are not available in this form, the usual approach is to estimate separation factors f_x from other sources or to assume that those observed in other populations apply in the present case.

Generally, separation factors above age 1 are assumed to be 0.5. Deaths under age 1 are concentrated at the beginning of the interval; about half of infant deaths in the United States occur in the first week of life and 65% happen within the first month. The average age at death for infants rises with increasing infant mortality levels. Preston, Keyfitz, and Schoen (1972) suggested the following approximation for the separation factor for those less than 1 year of age:

$$_1a_0 = 0.07 + 1.7 \cdot {_1m_0} \qquad (13.5)$$

Given the separation factors, to calculate the q_x the deaths would be estimated as follows:

$$\delta D_x^z = f_x'' D_x^z \tag{13.6}$$

$$\alpha D_x^z = (1 - f_x'') D_x^z = f' D_x^z \tag{13.7}$$

The separation factor f_x' represents the proportion of deaths at a given age in a given year that occurred after the birthday anniversary in that year. In the case of infant deaths, f_x' represents the proportion of all infant death in a year that occurred to babies born in the year. Small errors in the separation factors do not materially affect estimates.

In the computation and graduation of the mortality rates, three different age segments are recognized as having peculiar problems and are treated separately. The first is the youngest age segment, which generally includes ages under 5. Where the quality of data is sufficiently good and the level of mortality is low, the first segment can be limited to the first year of life. The second segment generally covers the bulk of the table, from age 5 to age 85, where the most reliable data are found. The third segment covers the oldest ages, 85 years and older, and usually contains the data of highest uncertainty. It should be observed that these are somewhat arbitrary divisions. It is entirely possible or even advisable in some cases, depending on the nature of the observed data, further to subdivide some of these segments. The number of segments and their age limits should be determined based on an analysis of the data available.

Mortality at Ages Under 5 Years

The methods used to compute mortality risks at ages less than 5 years must necessarily be adapted to the type and quality of data available. As the quality and quantity of data improve, it is feasible to extend to ages 1 to 4 years the methods used in the main body of the life table. Owing to the distinct peculiarities of mortality during the first year of life, however, special procedures must be used to compute the death rates at ages less than 1 year.

On many occasions, the census counts are particularly inaccurate at the younger ages. It may be desirable or necessary, then, to design formulas or procedures to obtain the mortality rates at ages under 5 years on the basis of recorded births rather than on population counts. The most frequently used procedure employs the registered birth and death statistics. For the United States 1989–1991 decennial life table, mortality rates for those under 2 years were based on registered births and deaths while the companion rates for those 2 years and over were based on registered deaths and population counts (U.S. National Center for Health Statistics, 1997b).

The calendar-year infant mortality rate is often used to represent the mortality risk for the first year of life. This procedure partially substitutes cohort for period data. The conventional infant mortality rate is the number of deaths in

infancy to a group of persons born in the same year. The calendar-year infant mortality rate is computed as the ratio of the number of deaths of those less than 1 year (in that year) to the number of live births in that year. So deaths in year $z + 1$ of infants born late in the year z are represented by deaths in year z to those born late in year $z - 1$.

If the vital statistics tabulations are sufficiently detailed, it is possible to use days, weeks, months, or quarter-years as units for constructing q_x for young ages. The United States 1989–1991 decennial life tables, for example, used 0 to 1 day, 1 to 7 days, 7 to 28 days, 28 to 365 days, and 1 to 2 years. The procedure assumes that births are uniformly distributed within these intervals.

It is not necessary to begin with mortality rates. At ages under 2 years, the United States decennial life tables did not begin with mortality rates but rather with observed and life table deaths. For each age interval 0 to 1 day, 1 to 7 days, 7 to 28 days, 28 to 365 days, and 1 to 2 years, the formula was

$$_t d_x = \frac{l_{0t} D_x}{_t E_x}$$

where $_t D_x$ denotes the number of deaths occurring in 1989–1991 between exact ages x and $x + t$, and $_t E_x$ is a weighted count of births during 1987–1991. The denominator assumes that births are uniformly distributed over the year. The values of $_t d_x$ were then used to calculate values of l_x up to age 2 years by successive application of the formula $l_{x+t} = l_x - d_x$.

For ages 1 to 4, other approximations of the mortality rates may be used when the census data are considered to be of acceptable accuracy and the death rates are low. A central death rate, m_x, is calculated from the observed deaths, D_x, and the census count, P_x, using the formula

$$m_x = \frac{D_x}{P_x} \tag{13.8}$$

In some instances, this formula is modified to improve its reliability by using an average population derived from the populations at three adjacent ages, as follows:

$$m_x = \frac{3 D_x}{P_{x-1} + P_x + P_{x+1}}$$

where D_x denotes the number of deaths to those aged x. The population at risk of dying at age x during the 3-year period includes mainly members of three adjacent annual birth cohorts; hence the denominator sums the populations aged $x - 1$, x, and $x + 1$. This approach was used for the United States 1989–1991 decennial life table for ages 2 to 4. For example, deaths at age 2 during 1989–1991 were divided by the sum of the populations at ages 1, 2, and 3.

The central death rates are then converted to the needed mortality rates, or probabilities, by means of the formula

$$q_x = \frac{2m_x}{2+m_x} \qquad (13.9)$$

This formula is based on the assumption that deaths between exact ages x and $x+1$ occur, on the average, at age $x+\frac{1}{2}$, as, for example, when deaths at age x in a given year are rectangularly distributed by age and time interval. The formula for q_x shown may be derived from the basic formula for m_x and expresses this assumption more explicitly:

$$m_x = \frac{D_x}{P_x} \quad \text{and} \quad q_x = \frac{D_x}{P_x + .5D_x} \qquad (13.10)$$

Then, dividing numerator and denominator by P_x,

$$q_x = \frac{m_x}{1+.5m_x} = \frac{2m_x}{2+m_x}$$

Mortality at Ages 5 to 84

The main segment of a life table is that covering ages 5 to 84. For this range we usually have the most accurate data on observed mortality. The goal is to obtain a smooth curve of death rates by age that joins age 5 with the previously computed rates for ages below 5. The death statistics and population data are combined into the conventional 5-year age groups: 5 to 9, 10 to 14, and so on. Grouping eliminates most of the problems associated with digit preference in age reporting and accomplishes part of the desired graduation, and this particular grouping has been found especially satisfactory. The death statistics employed would be the total of the deaths recorded in the observation period; usually 1, 2, or 3 years, and the population data would refer to the middle of the period.

There are two main approaches to obtaining mortality rates for single-year ages. One approach is to interpolate the population counts and registered deaths from the aggregated data to the corresponding single-year-of-age intervals. Then, q_x is calculated using

$$q_x = \frac{D_x}{P_x + .5 \cdot D_x} \qquad (13.11)$$

The U.S. decennial life table for 1989–1991 used this approach for ages 5 to 94 (U.S. National Center for Health Statistics, 1997b).

The other main approach is to obtain central age-specific death rates from the grouped data using Equation (13.11), test for data anomalies and adjust the rates if necessary, calculate, $_nq_x$, and then graduate them to obtain single-year rates. Any abrupt change in the mortality curve is regarded as reflecting a possible anomaly in the data. Each possible anomaly is investigated in detail and, if necessary, adjustment procedures are developed for the data. These adjustment procedures vary considerably in detail; they are not generally subject to broad generalization because each set of data has it own peculiarities.

Graduation of Mortality Rates

Once the data have been adjusted, the calculation of the mortality rates for single years of age becomes an exercise in graduation techniques. A large number of graduation methods have been used in the past, and new ones are constantly being devised. However, it is important that the analyst select the method most appropriate for the data involved, taking into account limitations in time, personnel, mathematical skill, and possible use of the final life table. The selection of the interpolation formula to be used depends mostly on the desired balance between smoothness and closeness of fit to the data. In general, an improvement in smoothness can only be made at the expense of closeness of fit. The analyst must judge, according to his or her experience, the relative importance that should be given to each of the two opposing considerations.

The three most commonly used interpolation techniques to compute single-year q_x values from grouped (interval) values are (1) Sprague multipliers, (2) Beers multipliers, and (3) Karup-King multipliers. All three of these techniques were designed so that the sum of the interpolated single-year values for "countable items" (e.g., deaths) is consistent with the total number of countable items for the group (interval) as a whole. The U.S. decennial life tables for 1989–1991 used Beers multipliers (U.S. National Center for Health Statistics, 1997b).

Mortality at Ages 85 and Over

Population and death data at the oldest ages have always been considered to be of low accuracy. In most life tables prepared in the past, the statistics at these ages have been disregarded because of the low credibility that most demographers and actuaries assign to the basic registration and census data. Because the quality of these data has been improving, however, the tendency now is to retain as much of them as possible for constructing the life table. This can be done either by basing the final rates partially on the recorded data or by extending the range of the main portion of the life table beyond age 84—say to age 89 or 94.

In practice, it has been found that, regardless of the total volume of data and their accuracy, there is some point at the older ages beyond which arbitrary methods must be applied. At those very old ages, the data become either too scanty to be statistically reliable or they are regarded as invalid because of errors in age reporting and coverage in the census or death statistics. For practical purposes, any reasonable method can be used because the effect of the choice of rates at these ages on the life table functions at the younger ages would be relatively minor. The method selected, however, should produce a smooth juncture with the mortality rates in the main portion of the life table. It should also produce mortality rates that increase smoothly with advancing age.

One method used is to assume that mortality rates increase at the oldest ages by about the same percentage as, or, more realistically, a decreasing percentage of that found at the end of the main portion of the life table. Empirically, in the low mortality countries, the percentage of increase at the later ages has been found to be about 10% per year of age. This means that every mortality rate at the oldest ages would be 10% higher than the rate at the next previous age or a declining function of 10%. A second method is to fit a third degree polynomial to the last three acceptable mortality rates and to an assumed rate of unity at a very high age chosen arbitrarily (e.g., age 110). A third method is to fit a Gompertz-Makeham curve to the end values of the main portion of the life table.

A fourth method is to adopt a series of rates, based on mortality experience in other populations, that are believed to be acceptably accurate. In the 1989–1991 United States decennial life tables, death rates at ages 85 and over were based, at least in part, on the experience of the Medicare program (U.S. National Center for Health Statistics, 1997b). Medicare data were considered more accurate than conventional death rates, already described as suffering from age misreporting among the extreme elderly. Medicare death rates at ages 85 to 94 were blended with those based on census populations and registered deaths; rates for older ages were based entirely on Medicare data. The Medicare rates were based directly on data on deaths and Medicare enrollments for ages 66 to 105. The rates were then smoothed or graduated (see Appendix C for a discussion of "smoothing"). Graduated rates at the oldest ages were replaced by rates obtained by a method of extrapolation set forth in the Annual Social Security Trustees Reports. In this method for each sex, a minimum percentage increase from q_{x-1} to q_x was required. The level of q_x for females was not allowed to rise to a level higher than that for males of the same age and race/ethnic group.

Derivation of Other Life Table Functions

The other life table functions are calculated using standard procedures, once the single-year q_x's have been determined. The first values to be computed are the series of l_x's or number of survivors for single years of age. These values are obtained using the formula

$$l_x = (1 - q_{x-1})l_{x-1} \qquad (13.12)$$

According to this formula, the number of survivors to a given age, l_x, equals the number reaching the previous age, l_{x-1}, times the probability of surviving from that age to the next, $(1-q_{x-1})$. The calculations for l_x can be "set in motion" by use of the radix of 100,000 for l_0. As examples, the calculations for Table 13.1 at ages 1, 2, and 37 would be as follows:

$$l_1 = (1 - q_0) \cdot l_0 = (1 - .00936) \cdot 100,000 = 99,064$$

$$l_2 = (1 - q_1) \cdot l_1 = (1 - .00073) \cdot 99,064 = 98,992$$

$$l_{37} = (1 - q_{36}) \cdot l_{36} = (1 - .00188) \cdot 96,150 = 95,969$$

The d_x's or deaths are the second series of values to be calculated. These follow the formula

$$d_x = l_x - l_{x+1} \qquad (13.13)$$

This means that the number of deaths at a given age equals the difference between the number surviving to that age and the number surviving to the subsequent age. The calculations for Table 13.1 at ages under 1, 1, and 36 would be as follows:

$$d_0 = l_0 - l_1 = 100,000 - 99,064 = 936$$

$$d_1 = l_1 - l_2 = 99,064 - 98,992 = 72$$

$$d_{36} = l_{36} - l_{37} = 96,150 - 95,969 = 181$$

The third series is the L_x's, the number of person-years lived by the cohort at a given age. These are computed using the approximation

$$L_x = f_x'' l_x + f_x' l_{x+1} = f_x'' l_x + (1 - f_x'') l_{x+1} \qquad (13.14)$$

With the exception of age under 1, the L_x's are the average of l_x and l_{x+1}. The calculations for Table 13.1 at ages under 1, 1, and 36 would be as follows:

$$L_0 = .207 l_0 + .793 l_1 = .207(100,000) + .793(99,064) = 99,258$$

$$L_1 = 0.5 l_1 + 0.5 l_2 = 0.5(99,064) + 0.5(98,992) = 99,028$$

$$L_{36} = 0.5 l_{36} + 0.5 l_{37} = 0.5(96,150) + 0.5(95,969) = 96,060$$

The fourth series of values, the T_x's, the total number of person-years lived by the cohort after reaching age x, is computed by summing the L_x's for ages x and over to the end of the life table. Algebraically, we have

$$T_x = \sum_{y=x}^{y=\omega} L_y \qquad (13.15)$$

where ω is the last age in the life table. For example, T_{85} is the sum of all the L_x's from L_{85} to L_{109} in the calculations for Table 13.1: $T_{85} = L_{85} + L_{86} + L_{87} + \ldots + L_{108} + L_{109} = 30,230 + 27,164 + 24,149 + \ldots + 25 + 9 = 197,871$. T_0 is the sum of the entire column of L_x's and represents the total number of person-years lived by the cohort in its lifetime.

The final series of values, e_x, expectation of future life, is computed using the formula

$$e_x = \frac{T_x}{l_x} \qquad (13.16)$$

The calculations for Table 13.1 at ages 0 and 36 would be as follows:

$$e_0 = \frac{T_0}{l_0} = \frac{7,536,614}{100,000} = 75.37$$

(Hence, expectation of life at birth can be determined by inspection of T_0, with a shift of the decimal.)

$$e_{36} = \frac{T_{36}}{l_{36}} = \frac{4,005,252}{96,150} = 41.66$$

The Abridged Life Table

Specific Short-Cut Methods

The most fundamental step in life table construction is to convert the observed age-specific death rates into their corresponding mortality rates, or probabilities of dying. As we have seen, in a complete life table, the basic formula for this transformation is

$$q_x = \frac{2m_x}{2 + m_x} \qquad (13.17)$$

where m_x is the observed death rate at a given age and q_x is the corresponding probability of dying. As stated earlier, this formula is based on the assumption that deaths between exact ages x and $x + 1$ are rectangularly distributed by age and time interval. One of the key features of the various shortcut methods described below is the procedure for making this basic transformation from $_nm_x$ to $_nq_x$ when the data are grouped. Another difference in the methods is in the way the stationary population is derived. We will describe four shortcut methods here: the Reed-Merrell method, the Greville method, the Keyfitz-Frauenthal method, and the method of reference to a standard table.

The Reed-Merrell Method

Although it has now largely been replaced by other methods, the Reed-Merrell (Reed and Merrell, 1939) method was for many years one of the most frequently used shortcut procedures for calculating an abridged life table. In this method the mortality rates are read off from a set of standard conversion tables showing the mortality rates associated with various observed central death rates. The standard tables for $_3m_2$, $_5m_x$, and $_{10}m_x$ were prepared on the assumption that the following exponential equation holds:

$$_nq_x = 1 - e^{-n \cdot _nm_x - an^3 \cdot _nm_x^2} \qquad (13.18)$$

where n is size of the age interval, $_nm_x$ is the central death rate, a is a constant, and e is the base of the system of natural logarithms. Reed and Merrell found that a value of $a = 0.008$ would produce acceptable results. The conversion of $_nm_x$'s to $_nq_x$'s by use of the Reed-Merrell tables is usually applied to 5-year or 10-year data, but special age groups are employed at both ends of the life table. At the younger ages the most frequently used groupings are (1) ages under 1, 1, and 2 to 4 or (2) ages under 1 and 1 to 4. Conversion tables for these ages or age groups, as well as for $_5m_x$ and $_{10}m_x$ were worked out by Reed and Merrell; they are reproduced in Appendix A.

For example, the death rate for the age group 55 to 59 ($_5m_{55}$) observed in the United States in 1991, .009263, would be converted to the 5-year mortality rate ($_5q_{55}$), .04534, by using the Reed-Merrell table of values of $_5q_x$ associated with $_5m_x$. We look up .009263 in the $_5m_x$ column, read off the cor-

responding $_5q_{55}$ value, interpolating as required. The conversion tables are used to derive $_5q_x$ from $_5m_x$ for all 5-year age groups from 5 to 9 on. At the higher ages, the mortality rate for the open-end group (e.g., 85 years old and over) is evidently equal to one because the life table ends at the age where there are no more survivors.

Once the mortality rates have been calculated, the construction of the abridged life table continues with the computation of each entry in the survivor column, l_x, and the death column, $_nd_x$, along standard lines, using the formulas

$$l_{x+n} = (1 - _nq_x)l_x \qquad (13.19)$$

$$_nd_x = l_x - l_{x+n} \qquad (13.20)$$

All three shortcut methods described in this section follow the same procedure in deriving l_x and $_nd_x$.

In the calculation of the next life table function, $_nL_x$, each of the three methods to be discussed follows a different procedure. In the Reed-Merrell method, T_x values are directly determined from the l_x's for ages 10 and over, or 5 and over, by use of the following equations:

$$T_x = -.20833l_{x-5} + 2.5l_x + .20833l_{x+5} + 5\sum_{\alpha=1}^{\infty} l_{x+5\alpha} \qquad (13.21)$$

if the age intervals in the table are 5-year intervals, and

$$T_x = 4.16667l_x + .8333l_{x+10} + 10\sum_{\alpha=1}^{\infty} l_{x+10\alpha} \qquad (13.22)$$

if the age intervals in the table are 10-year intervals. These equations are based on the assumption that the area under the l_x curve between any two ordinates is approximated by the area under a parabola through these two ordinates and the preceding and following ordinates (Formula 13.21) or the following ordinate only (Formula 13.22).

For the ages under 10, Reed and Merrell note that L_x may be determined directly from the following linear equations:

$$L_0 = .276l_0 + .724l_1 \qquad (13.23)$$

$$L_1 = .410l_1 + .590l_2 \qquad (13.24)$$

$$_4L_1 = .034l_0 + 1.184l_1 + 2.782l_5 \qquad (13.25)$$

$$_3L_2 = -.021l_0 + 1.384l_2 + 1.637l_5 \qquad (13.26)$$

$$_5L_5 = -.003l_0 + 2.242l_5 + 2.761l_{10} \qquad (13.27)$$

L_0 should be determined from l_o and l_1 by use of separation factors appropriate for each situation, however. $_nL_x$ for ages 10 and over may be derived by taking the differences between the T_x's, and e_x is computed as the ratio of T_x to l_x.

An illustration of the application of the Reed-Merrell method is given in Table 13.3, which shows the calculation

TABLE 13.3 Calculation of Abridged Life Table for Males in Urban Colombia, 1993,
by the Reed-Merrell Method

Age interval (exact ages, x to x + n)	$_nm_x$	$_nq_x$	$_nd_x$	l_x	$\sum_{\alpha=0}^{\infty} l_{x+5\alpha}$	T_x	$_nL_x$	e_x
0–1[2]	0.0275	0.025485	2,549	100,000	1	6,548,117	98,155[2]	65.5
1–5	0.0015	0.005848	570	97,451	1	6,449,962	388,305[3]	66.2
5–10	0.0006	0.002996	290	96,881	1	6,061,657	483,595[4]	62.6
10–15	0.0007	0.003494	338	96,591	1,163,934	5,578,062	482,418	57.7
15–20	0.0037	0.018343	1,766	96,253	1,067,343	5,095,644	477,352	52.9
20–25	0.0059	0.029103	2,750	94,487	971,090	4,615,292	465,721	48.9
25–30	0.0056	0.027642	2,536	91,737	876,603	4,152,571	452,249	45.3
30–35	0.0052	0.025691	2,292	89,201	784,866	3,700,322	440,239	41.5
35–40	0.0055	0.027155	2,360	86,909	695,665	3,260,083	428,637	37.5
40–45	0.0054	0.026667	2,255	84,549	608,756	2,831,446	417,181	33.5
45–50	0.0067	0.032988	2,715	82,294	524,207	2,414,265	404,928	29.3
50–55	0.0088	0.043120	3,431	79,579	441,913	2,009,337	389,820	25.2
55–60	0.0139	0.067320	5,126	76,148	362,334	1,619,517	368,711	21.3
60–65	0.0213	0.101433	7,204	71,022	286,186	1,250,806	338,112	17.6
65–70	0.0338	0.156455	9,985	63,818	215,164	412,694	295,191	14.3
70–75	0.0514	0.228672	12,310	53,833	151,346	617,503	239,142	11.5
75–80	0.0781	0.327397	13,594	41,523	97,513	378,361	173,617	9.1
80–85	0.1129	0.438558	12,248	27,929	55,990	204,744	106,307	7.3
85 and over	0.1593	1.000000	15,681	15,681	28,061[5]	98,437[6]	98,437	6.3

[1] Entries not required for the calculations desired.
[2] $_1L_0 = .276\, l_0 + .724\, l_1$
[3] $_4L_1 = .034\, l_0 + 1.184\, l_1 + 2.782\, l_5$
[4] $_5L_5 = -.003\, l_0 + 2.242\, l_5 + 2.761\, l_{10}$
[5] Includes an estimate for l_{90}, l_{95}, and l_{100} (=12,380)
[6] $T_{85} = {}_\infty L_{85} = l_x/{}_\infty m_x$ (= 15681/0.1593)
Source: Observed age-specific death rates from United Nations, *Demographic Yearbook*, 1996, Table 26.

of an abridged life table for urban Colombia in 5-year age intervals for 1993 from the observed central death rates from the United Nations' *Demographic Yearbook*. In this case, the conversion tables are employed to obtain $_nq_x$ at all ages and use is made of the tables for m_0, $_4m_1$, and $_5m_x$. The steps are as follows:

1. Read off $_nq_x$ values corresponding to $_nm_x$ values from the appropriate conversion table in Appendix A.
2. Derive the l_x and $_nd_x$ columns by the following steps:
   a. Multiply q_0 (.025485) by the radix l_0 (100,000) to obtain d_0 (2,549).
   b. Subtract d_0 from l_0 to get l_1 (97,451).
   c. Continue multiplying the successive values of l_x by the corresponding $_nq_x$ values to get $_nd_x$ and subtracting the successive values of $_nd_x$ from l_x to get l_{x+n}.
3. Sum the values of l_x from the end of life to age x.

$$\left(= \sum_{\alpha=0}^{\infty} l_{x+5\alpha}\right)$$

4. Substitute these sums and the indicated l_x values in equation (13.21) to get T_x. For example, T_{25} is obtained from Equation (13.21) as follows:

$T_{25} = -.20833(94,487) + 2.5(91,737) + .20833(89,201)$

$+ 5(784,866) = 4,152,571$

5. Derive $_nL_x$ for the ages under 10 years by use of Equations (13.23), (13.25), and (13.27). The separation factors given in Equation (13.23) have been used for convenience although 0.15 and 0.85 would have been more realistic choices.

Greville's Method

A method suggested by T. N. E. Greville (1943) converts the observed central death rates to the needed mortality rates by the use of the formula

$$_nq_x = \frac{_nm_x}{\dfrac{1}{n} + {}_nm_x\left[\dfrac{1}{2} + \dfrac{n}{12}\left({}_nm_x - \log_e c\right)\right]} \quad (13.28)$$

where c comes from an assumption that the $_nm_x$ values follow an exponential curve. $\log_e c$ could be assumed to be about 0.095. Using this method with the observed death rate of .009263 for $_5m_{55}$ (United States, 1991) cited in the preceding page, would also lead to a mortality rate of .045341 as follows:

TABLE 13.4   Calculation of Abridged Life Table for Males in Urban Colombia, 1993,
by the Keyfitz-Frauenthal Method

Age interval (exact ages, x to x + n)	n	$_nm_x$	$_nP_x$	$(_nP_{x-n} - {_nP_{x+n}})(_nm_{x+n} - {_nm_{x-n}})/48_nP_x$	$_nq_x$	l_x	$_nd_x$	$_nL_x$	T_x	e_x
0–1	1	0.0275	218,599		0.025485	100,000	2,549	98,155	6,560,686	65.6
1–5	4	0.0015	1,045,612		0.005848	97,451	570	388,305	6,452,425	66.2
5–10	5	0.0006	1,280,393		0.002996	96,881	290	483,892	6,064,156	62.6
10–15	5	0.0007	1,289,824	0.0000102	0.003545	96,591	342	482,410	5,580,531	57.8
15–20	5	0.0037	1,077,176	0.0000238	0.018447	96,249	1,775	477,311	5,198,121	52.0
20–25	5	0.0059	1,053,570	0.0000017	0.029077	94,474	2,747	465,653	4,620,810	48.9
25–30	5	0.0056	1,032,450	−0.0000012	0.027606	91,727	2,532	452,209	4,155,157	45.3
30–35	5	0.0052	967,247	−0.0000006	0.025662	89,195	2,289	440,219	3,702,948	41.5
35–40	5	0.0055	769,837	0.0000019	0.027134	86,906	2,358	428,625	3,262,729	37.5
40–45	5	0.0054	623,693	0.0000126	0.026700	84,548	2,257	417,176	2,834,104	33.5
45–50	5	0.0067	456,546	0.0000376	0.033127	82,291	2,726	404,889	2,414,928	29.4
50–55	5	0.0088	381,569	0.0000675	0.043369	79,565	3,451	389,718	2,012,039	25.3
55–60	5	0.0139	284,877	0.0001134	0.067669	76,114	5,151	368,499	1,622,321	21.3
60–65	5	0.0213	257,531	0.0001748	0.101810	70,963	7,225	337,824	1,253,822	17.7
65–70	5	0.0338	176,277	0.0004468	0.157376	63,738	10,031	294,734	915,998	14.4
70–75	5	0.0514	131,927	0.0006518	0.229148	53,707	12,307	238,616	621,264	11.6
75–80	5	0.0781	83,108	0.0012880	0.327626	41,400	13,564	173,041	382,648	9.2
80–85	5	0.1129	48,381	−0.0027950	0.423353	27,836	11,784	108,841	209,607	7.5
85 and over		0.1593			1.000000	16,052	16,052	100,766	100,766	6.3

Source: Observed age-specific death rates from United Nations, *Demographic Yearbook*, 1996, Table 26.

$$_5q_{55} = \frac{.009263}{\frac{1}{5} + .009263\left[\frac{1}{2} + \frac{5}{12}(.009263 - .095)\right]}$$

$$_5q_{55} = \frac{.009263}{.204300}$$

$$_5q_{55} = .04534$$

The derivation of $_5q_{55}$ by this method requires several columns in a manual calculation, but it may be programmed for direct calculation by computer on the basis of the $_5m_x$'s and the two constants, n and $\log_e c$. In Greville's method, the central death rates in the life table and in the observed population are assumed to be the same, and the desired value of $_nL_x$ is calculated by the use of

$$_nL_x = \frac{_nd_x}{_nm_x} \qquad (13.29)$$

For the last age interval, that is, the interval with the indefinite upper age limit, the usual approximation for $_\infty L_x$ is

$$_\infty L_x = \frac{l_x}{_\infty m_x} \qquad (13.30)$$

The Keyfitz-Frauenthal Method

Keyfitz and Frauenthal (1975) suggested the following procedure for converting the annual central age-specific death rate to the life table $_nq_x$:

$$_nq_x = 1 - \exp\left[-n\cdot\left(_nm_x + \frac{(_nP_{x-n} - {_nP_{x+n}})(_nm_{x+n} - {_nm_{x-n}})}{48_nP_x}\right)\right] \qquad (13.31)$$

where P is the observed population in the age interval. For example, the observed death rate for $_5m_{55}$ (U.S., 1991) cited in the preceding section would be converted to a mortality rate of .04553 as follows:

$$_5q_{55} = 1 - \exp\left[-5\cdot\left((.009263) + \frac{(14,093,824 - 10,423,513)\cdot(.014319 - .005758)}{48\cdot(11,644,495)}\right)\right]$$

The desired value of $_nL_x$ is calculated as

$$_nL_x = \frac{n(l_x - l_{x+n})}{\ln l_x - \ln l_{x+n}}\left[1 + \frac{n}{24}(_nm_{x+n} - {_nm_{x-n}})\right] \qquad (13.32)$$

An illustration of the application of the Keyfitz-Frauenthal method is given in Table 13.4, which shows the calculation of an abridged life table for urban Colombia in 5-year age intervals for 1993. The steps are as follows:

1. Set down n, the width of each age interval.
2. Calculate differences between alternate populations and between alternate death rates, and multiply them together, to obtain the numerator.
3. Calculate the denominator.
4. Obtain value of exponential term.
5. Calculate $_nq_x$ as 1 − (4).
6. Obtain $_nL_x$. Derive $_nL_x$ for the ages under 5 years by use of Equations (13.23) and (13.25). The separation factors given in Equation (13.23) have been used for

convenience although 0.85 and 0.13 would have been more realistic choices (see p. 285).

7. Calculate T_x and e_x in usual manner. Save $_\infty L_x$ by $l_x \div _\infty m_x$.

Method of Reference to a Standard Table

A fourth method that is used frequently in routine calculations bases the conversion of the observed $_n m_x$ to the life table $_n q_x$ on the relation that exists in a complete life table between the observed $_n m_x$ and the life table $_n q_x$ (U.S. National Office of Vital Statistics, 1947). Because this method obtains the new table by reference to a standard table, it should only be used when mortality in both tables is of a comparable level.

A simple application of this concept assumes that in each age interval the relation of $_n q_x$ to observed $_n m_x$ shown by the standard table applies to the table under construction. This relation was used in the construction of the annual U.S. abridged tables for 1946 to 1996. New standard tables were adopted and the factors employed were modified when new decennial life tables became available. The value $_n g_x$ is computed for the standard life table on the basis of the observed central death rate $(_n m_x)$ and the mortality rate $(_n q_x)$, using the formula

$$_n g_x = \frac{n}{_n q_x} - \frac{1}{_n m_x} \quad (13.33)$$

where $_n g_x$ represents the average number of years lived in the age group by those dying in the age group (Sirken, 1966). The index $_n g_x$ lies between 0 and n. This value is assumed to apply to the new life table at the same age. The required mortality rates in the new life table are computed using the formula

$$_n q_x = \frac{n \cdot _n m_x}{1 + _n g_x \cdot _n m_x} \quad (13.34)$$

where $_n m_x$ refers to the observed $_n m_x$ values applicable to the new table under construction. In the previous example, if the 1989–1991 U.S. life table was used as the standard, the value of $_5 g_{55}$ would be equal to 2.97741. The observed death rate of .009263 for ages 55 to 59 in the United States in 1991 would be converted to the mortality rate for 1991, .045392, as follows:

$$_5 q_{55} = \frac{5(.009263)}{1 + 2.195846(.009263)}$$

$$_5 q_{55} = \frac{.046315}{1.020340}$$

$$_5 q_{55} = .045392$$

For the calculation of $_n L_x$ in the abridged table, one may apply the simple relationship $_n L_x / (l_x + l_{x+n})$ from the standard table (U.S. National Office of Vital Statistics, 1947). The annual abridged U.S. tables made since 1954 employ another relationship between l_x and $_n L_x$, involving a factor we may designate as $_n G_x$ (Sirken, 1966). The value of $_n G_x$, representing the distribution of deaths in the interval x to $x + n$, is obtained from the standard table by the formula

$$_n G_x = \frac{n l_x - _n L_x}{_n d_x} \quad (13.35)$$

This value is assumed to apply to the new table, and it is used in the formula

$$_n L_x = n l_x - _n G_x \cdot _n d_x \quad (13.36)$$

to obtain the desired value of $_n L_x$ in the new table. The value for the open-ended interval, $_\infty L_x$, is determined by a special formula. A factor r_x is computed for the standard table as follows:

$$r_x = \frac{_\infty m_x \cdot _\infty L_x}{l_x} \quad (13.37)$$

where $_\infty m_x$ is the observed central death rate for the open-ended interval. This factor is applied in the new table by using the formula

$$_\infty L_x = \frac{l_x r_x}{_\infty m_x} \quad (13.38)$$

The method of reference to a standard table is particularly useful and convenient for constructing an annual series of life tables. The $_n g_x$ and $_n G_x$ factors can be calculated once from a complete life table in the initial year and used repeatedly for each year until a new complete table is prepared.

Comparison of Methods

A comparison of the mortality rates for the United States in 1991 derived by the four methods described is shown in Table 13.5. It may be observed that the results are very similar. Tables 13.3 and 13.4 may be compared for the difference in results when the Reed Merrell method and the Keyfitz-Frauenthal method are applied to urban Colombia in 1993. It should be noted that in Greville's method the central death rates in the life table $(_n m_x^l)$ are required to agree with the central death rates observed in the population $(_n m_x^p)$. This is not the case in the Reed-Merrell method or in the method of reference to a standard table, however. There is no generally agreed upon requirement that these two sets of central death rates should be equal in numerical value. In fact, it can be maintained that because the distribution of the life table population is different from the distribution of the actual population in any age interval, the two rates should be different. A method has been proposed by Keyfitz to compute a life table that would agree with the observed data after adjustment for the differences in the age distribution of the populations (Keyfitz, 1966; 1968). This method is complex and is beyond the scope of this book.

GENERATION LIFE TABLES

In previous sections of this chapter, various methods for preparing current life tables have been discussed. In every instance, the basic data for these methods involve a census

TABLE 13.5   Comparison of Mortality Rates for the Total United States Population, 1991, Computed by Four Different Abridged Life Table Methods

Age interval (exact ages, x to x + n)	$_ng_x$ Standard[1]	$_nm_x$ Observed[2]	Computed $_nq_x$			
			Reed- Merrell	Greville	Reference to standard table	Keyfitz-Frauenthal
1–5	422.203800	0.000474	0.001856	0.001894	0.001975	
5–10	−103.093000	0.000215	0.001074	0.001074	0.001099	
10–15	−45.045000	0.000258	0.001289	0.001289	0.001305	0.001293
15–20	8.575279	0.000890	0.004441	0.004441	0.004416	0.004432
20–25	3.345601	0.001101	0.005491	0.005491	0.005485	0.005483
25–30	4.249223	0.001230	0.006133	0.006133	0.006118	0.006125
30–35	−1.625560	0.001541	0.007678	0.007678	0.007724	0.007676
35–40	0.308471	0.001977	0.009840	0.009840	0.009879	0.009853
40–45	3.585178	0.002536	0.012606	0.012606	0.012566	0.012664
45–50	1.963739	0.003805	0.018859	0.018859	0.018884	0.019011
50–55	2.246376	0.005758	0.028412	0.028411	0.028422	0.028554
55–60	2.195846	0.009263	0.045341	0.045340	0.045392	0.045527
60–65	2.278723	0.014319	0.069283	0.069282	0.069333	0.069135
65–70	2.294695	0.021368	0.101741	0.101739	0.101846	0.101717
70–75	2.352904	0.032051	0.148948	0.148946	0.149017	0.149153
75–80	2.421006	0.048068	0.215454	0.215461	0.215286	0.216034
80–85	2.497600	0.075754	0.319215	0.319274	0.318507	0.320953

[1] Computed from the life table for the United States, 1981, total population, which is used as the standard table. The $_ng_x$ factors at ages below 50 seem irregular and would be expected to approximate 2.5. However, where death rates are low, the computed $_nq_x$ is relatively insensitive to large variations in $_ng_x$.
[2] Ratio of deaths to population observed in the United States in 1991.

of the population (or accurate estimates of the population distributed by age and sex), the deaths recorded in the year of the census or in a number of years around the census year, and the births in a few years just prior to the census year. Life tables prepared from these data portray the mortality experience of the population observed during the relatively short period to which the data on deaths apply.

Because life tables are mathematical models that trace a cohort of lives from birth to death according to an assumed series of mortality rates, it would be logical to try to base the life table on the mortality rates experienced by an actual birth cohort. For this purpose, it is necessary to have collected data on an annual basis for many years before a life table could be prepared. For example, a generation life table for the birth cohort of 1900 would employ the observed death or mortality rates for infancy in 1900, for age 1 in 1901, for age 2 in 1902, and so on until the latest available rates at the highest ages are obtained; the remaining rates would have to be obtained by projection. Table 13.6 presents selected values from a generation life table for the cohort of white females born in 1900 in the United States, prepared by Bell, Wade, and Goss (1992).

A sufficient period of time has elapsed since mortality data have been systematically recorded for a number of generation life tables to have been prepared. For example, Jacobson (1964) prepared life tables for white males and females born in the United States in 1840 and every 10th year

thereafter through 1960, on the basis of the mortality rates experienced in each year of the life of these cohorts and projected mortality rates. Earlier, Dublin and Spiegelman (1941), Dublin, Lotka, and Spiegelman (1949), and Spiegelman (1957) developed or described such tables. Generation life tables can be used to compute generation reproduction rates, to study life expectancy historically, to project mortality, and to make estimates of orphanhood (Gregory, 1965). A series of such tables could represent the development of mortality and life expectancy of real cohorts over time and improve the basis for analyzing the relation between the earlier mortality of a cohort and its later experience. In view of the general tendency for mortality to fall, the expectation of life at birth in a generation life table tends to be higher than in the current table for the starting year of the generation life table. A comparison of life expectations at birth in two such tables reflects the average improvement in mortality for the actual cohort over its lifetime. Conversely, current life tables typically understate the probable life expectancy to be observed in the future for persons at a given age because mortality is expected to continue declining. The generation life table for the cohort of U.S females born in 1900, for example, shows a life expectation at birth of 58.3 years (Bell *et al.*, 1992). In contrast, the current life table for 1900 shows a life expectation at birth of 49.0 years. The actual experience of the 1900 cohort added nearly 10 years to its life expectation at birth.

TABLE 13.6 Selected Values from the Generation Life Table for the Cohort of Females Born in the United States in 1900

Calendar year	Exact age (x)	Mortality rate (q_x)	Number surviving (l_x)	Average remaining lifetime (e_x)
1900	0	.11969	100,000	58.3
1901	1	.05470	88,031	65.2
1905	5	.00624	82,532	65.4
1910	10	.00172	81,108	61.5
1915	15	.00105	80,255	57.1
1920	20	.00221	78,484	53.4
1925	25	.00239	76,611	49.6
1930	30	.00234	74,814	45.7
1935	35	.00217	73,192	41.7
1940	40	.00231	71,500	37.6
1945	45	.00239	69,792	33.5
1950	50	.00283	67,819	29.4
1955	55	.00411	65,034	25.4
1960	60	.00439	62,177	21.6
1965	65	.00711	57,755	18.0
1970	70	.00987	52,055	14.7
1975	75	.14062	44,735	11.7
1980	80	.19618	35,959	8.9
1985	85	.29205	25,457	6.6
1990	90	.43457	14,394	4.7
1995	95	.60400	5,700	3.4
2000	100	.76175	1,358	2.5
2005	105	.87040	176	1.9
2010	110	.94318	10	1.4

Rates after 1985 are projected.

Source: F. C. Bell, A. Wade, S. Goss, *"Life Tables for the United States Social Security Area, 1900–2080" Actuarial Study* No. 107, Office of the Actuary, U.S. Social Security Administration. SSA Pub. No. 11-11536. August, 1992, pp. 54–55.

The analysis of cohort mortality could serve as an improved basis for projecting mortality. One approach used at present is to trace the mortality experience of a series of cohorts from a group of current life tables prepared in the past for as many years back as is considered reliable. The mortality curves for these cohorts are incomplete to various degrees, but once the cohorts have reached the older ages, the mortality curves can be projected over their remaining lifetime in various ways. Currently, the general practice, however, is to project mortality on an age-specific basis rather than on a cohort basis—that is, to analyze the series of rates for the same age group and to project the rates for each age group separately.

As stated earlier, the preparation of a generation life table requires compilation of data over a considerable period of time on an annual basis and also the projection of some or many incomplete cohorts. It is, therefore, a burdensome task to prepare many such tables "manually," but the use of a computer reduces this burden considerabley. (The basic "input" for an annual series of generation life tables, for example, is the matrix of observed central death rates by single ages and single calendar years.) The fact that the basic data for a single table pertain to many different calendar years means that the time reference of the generation life table is indefinite. The indefiniteness of the time reference is more pronounced for cohort life tables than it is for cohort measures of fertility, for example, which have a more concentrated incidence by age.

One characteristic of the generation life table may be viewed either as an advantage or as a disadvantage, depending on one's interest. A generation life table can involve the combination of mortality rates that are significantly different in nature, owing to the improvement in mortality over a long period of time. For example, the health conditions today at the turn of the 21st century are significantly different from those existing at the turn of the 20th century and the corresponding mortality patterns are dissimilar. On the other hand, this type of table does reflect the actual combination of changing health conditions and intracohort influences to which particular cohorts were subject. A current table reflects the influence of a more unitary set of health conditions and a single mortality pattern.

INTERRELATIONS, COMBINATION, AND MANIPULATION OF LIFE TABLE FUNCTIONS

Most demographers are only infrequently faced with the task of constructing a complete, or even an abridged, life table. Many do often have the task of manipulating in various ways available life tables or life table functions. This may involve the calculation of a missing function for a given table, the combination of functions from different tables, or the combination of entire tables.

Interrelations of Functions

The manipulation of life table functions is aided by a review of how these functions are interrelated. All the functions in a life table are dependent on other functions in the table, but usually the q_x function is regarded as being independent of all other functions. A particular q_x value is clearly independent of all other q_x values at either earlier or later ages. A particular l_x, d_x, or L_x value is dependent only on the values of q_x at age x and earlier ages. A particular T_x value is dependent on values of L_x at age x and later ages, and hence on the entire column of q_x values. A particular value of e_x is dependent, in effect, only on the values of q_x at age x and all later ages. Although e_x is computed from T_x and l_x, which are dependent on earlier values of q_x, the absolute values of the T_x's and l_x's are "washed out" in the calculation of e_x. Implicitly, in the derivation of e_x, the q_x's for age x and later ages are weighted by the percentage distribution of the L's that they generate. Because of the sharp drop from q_0 to q_1, e_1 is commonly higher than e_0; thereafter, e_x tends to fall steadily. At low levels of q_0, e_0 begins to exceed e_1.

In some cases, values are presented for only some of the life table functions. Some or all of the others may be desired. Let us consider the case where, as in the UN *Demographic Yearbook*, we are given 1-year values of q_x, l_x, and e_x at every fifth age and we want $_5L_x$ values for computing 5-year survival rates (ratios of $_5L_x$'s; see later). We apply the following relationships:

$$e_x = \frac{T_x}{l_x}$$

$$\therefore T_x = e_x l_x$$

$$\text{and } _5L_x = T_x - T_{x+5}$$

The $_5q_x$'s corresponding to the l_x values at every fifth age are calculated by $1 - \frac{l_{x+5}}{l_x}$ and the $_5d_x$'s corresponding to the l_x values are calculated by $l_x - l_{x+5}$.

Given the same basic information as just noted, we may wish to secure the values for the individual ages of some function. In that case, any of the standard interpolation formulas may be applied. We may interpolate q_x or l_x to single ages and obtain single values of d_x as a by-product. Or we may derive T_x at every fifth age as described in the preceding paragraph and then apply one of the interpolation formulas to secure T_x at single ages. Single values for e_x may be secured by direct interpolation or by interpolating the l_x function to single ages and completing the table. (Interpolation procedures are discussed more fully in Appendix C.)

Combination of Tables and Functions

First, let us consider the case where life tables for two populations are available and we should like to have a single life table for the combined population. Suppose, for example, we want to derive a single table for the general population from separate life tables for the male and female populations. This can be done by weighting the q_x's from the male and female tables in accordance with the distribution of the population by sex at each age. A new table may now be recomputed from the combined q_x's and an assumed radix of 100,000. If only one of the other functions is wanted, the values from the separate tables may be combined on the basis of population weights in only a few scattered ages because the shifts from age to age in the distribution of the population by sex could introduce unacceptable fluctuations by age in these functions for the combined population, and the resulting values for different functions may not be consistent with one another. (Note that these functions would not all receive the same population weights, e.g., l_x would be weighted by the population at age x, and T_x and e_x would be weighted by the population for ages x and over, the weights in each case reflecting the ages covered by the measure.) Only the use of a constant weighting factor over all ages can prevent fluctuations by age in the values of a function. If an entire column for a function is wanted, therefore, it is best to recompute the values for the function by starting with the weighted q_x's.

A different problem is represented by the need for separate male and female life tables whose values bear a realistic absolute relation to one another. The tables for males and females as originally computed do not bear a consistent "additive" relationship to one another because births of boys and girls do not occur in equal numbers, as is implied by the radixes of the separate life tables for males and females. To make the tables additive, it is necessary to inflate the l_x, d_x, L_x, and T_x values of the male life table by the sex ratio at birth in the actual population. Thus, the stationary male population at each age adjusted for absolute comparability with the female stationary population is derived by

$$\frac{B^m}{B^f} \cdot L_x^m \tag{13.39}$$

and the stationary male population of all ages, adjusted for combination with the total female stationary population, is obtained by

$$\frac{B^m}{B^f} \cdot T_0^m \tag{13.40}$$

The birthrate (and also the death rate) for the male and female life tables taken in combination is given by

$$\frac{\dfrac{B^m}{B^f} l_0 + l_0}{\dfrac{B^m}{B^f} T_0^m + T_0^f} \tag{13.41}$$

The ratio of children under 5 to women of childbearing age in the stationary population, a measure known as the replacement quota, is obtained by

$$\frac{\dfrac{B^m}{B^f} \cdot L_{0-4}^m + L_{0-4}^f}{L_{15-49}^f} \tag{13.42}$$

We have been describing the procedures by which we may arrive at life table values for a total population consistent in absolute level with the life table values for the separate component male and female populations. Even if the stationary populations are properly combined and reduced to the level of a single table with a radix of 100,000 by applying the factor

$$\frac{100,000}{\dfrac{B^m}{B^f} 100,000 + 100,000} \tag{13.43}$$

to the absolute functions in each table, the resulting d_x, l_x, L_x, and T_x would not agree exactly with the values derived directly from the weighted q_x's. Nor will the e_x or q_x values or the derived survival rates agree. Figures for e_0 consistent with the derivation of a combined table just described may be derived from the reciprocal of the formula given earlier for the birthrate:

$$\frac{\frac{B^m}{B^f} T_0^m + T_0^f}{\frac{B^m}{B^f} l_0 + l_0} \tag{13.44}$$

The q_x's can be obtained as the ratio of d_x to l_x:

$$\frac{\frac{B^m}{B^f} d_x^m + d_x^f}{\frac{B^m}{B^f} l_x^m + l_x^f} \tag{13.45}$$

The directly computed table takes account of the actual distribution of the population by sex at each age, while the method described links the two tables only by the sex ratio at birth. The differences between these two combined tables tend to be quite small, even inconsequential, however, because the proportions of the sexes approximate equality and have only a small variation over much of the age distribution. On the other hand, the two combined tables for the white and nonwhite populations of the United States would show more pronounced differences because the proportions of these groups in the population are quite different and vary more by age. To convert the basic tables for the white and nonwhite populations into additive form, the factor for adjusting the nonwhite table (B_N/B_T) is about .20; and to derive the combined table with a radix of 100,000, the factor is about 100,000 / 120,000, or .83.

STATISTICAL ANALYSIS OF LIFE TABLES

Frequently it is difficult to see whether the differences between two life tables are significant or merely reflect chance fluctuations. Sampling variation is especially important when the life tables are based on sample surveys or follow-up observational studies, but it also affects life tables based on vital rates from large populations, such as countries. In this case, deaths are viewed as a random sample of the superpopulation of deaths that have occurred over time and might occur. In recognition of this stochastic variation, the U.S. National Center for Health Statistics publishes standard errors for the probabilities of dying and life expectancies in decennial life tables.

Statistical tests are based on an interpretation of the count of deaths in a population as a random variable in the observed population. Chiang (1968) assumed that $_nD_x$, the count of actual deaths in an age-sex group, is a binomial random variable in $_nP_x$ persons (trials) with fixed probability of dying $_nq_x$. Based on this assumption, the expected number of deaths in a sample of persons is $_nP_x \cdot {_nq_x}$, The variance of the number of deaths is $Var(_nD_x) = {_nP_x} \cdot {_nq_x} \cdot {_np_x}$, where p is the probability of surviving or $1-q_x$.

This leads to an estimate for the variance of the age-specific probability of dying:

$$Var\ {_nq_x} = \frac{_nq_x^2(1-_nq_x)}{_nD_x} \tag{13.46}$$

The variance of life expectancy is

$$Var\ e_x = \frac{\sum_{a=x}^{\omega-n} l_a^2 [e_{a+n} + n - {_na_a}]^2 Var(_nP_a)}{l_x^2} \tag{13.47}$$

Statistical tests for differences in life expectancy at age x between two populations i and j is

$$Z = \frac{e_{x,i} - e_{x,j}}{\left[(Var(e_{x,i}) + Var(e_{x,j}))^{.5}\right]} \tag{13.48}$$

For example, Hummer, Rogers, Nam, and Ellison (1999) used nationally representative data from the National Health Interview Survey-Multiple Cause of Death linked file to examine the association of religious attendance and sociodemographic factors with overall mortality. They calculated life expectancy at age 20 for both sexes and all race/ethnic groups. They examined whether e_{20} differs significantly between those attending religious services once per week, whose e_{20} was 61.912 years, and those attending services more than once per week, whose e_{20} was 62.925 years. The statistical test for differences in e_{20} between the two groups is

$$Z = \frac{62.925 - 61.912}{\sqrt{(.0095524)^2 + (.0066757)^2}} = 86.92$$

The value of the test statistic exceeds the critical value of 1.96, so we can conclude that this difference is statistically different from zero. Therefore, persons who attend religious services more than once per week have significantly different life expectancy from those who attend only once per week.

Because life tables for the United States and the states are based on a large number of deaths, the standard errors are rather small. Stochastic variation is not the only source of error for life table functions, and it is generally thought to be smaller than measurement errors, such as age misreporting.

APPLICATIONS OF LIFE TABLES IN POPULATION STUDIES

Inasmuch as the measurement of mortality is involved in many types of demographic studies, the life table model and life table techniques as special tools for measuring mortality can be applied in a wide variety of population studies. The life table is a tool in the analysis of fertility, reproductivity, migration, and population structure; in the estimation and projection of population size, structure, and change; and in the analysis of various social and economic characteristics of the population, such as marital status, labor force status, family status, and educational status. In many of these cases, the standard life table functions are combined with probabilities for other types of contingent events (e.g., first-marriage rates, rates of entry into the labor force) in order to obtain new measures.

Mortality Analysis

It is impractical to discuss here all of the many types of analyses of mortality that could be performed on the basis of life table values. The most frequently used procedures involve comparisons between populations of life expectancy at birth and at various ages, of proportions surviving to various ages, and of mortality rates at various ages.

Measurement of the Level of Mortality, Survivorship, and Life Expectancy

The most common general use of a life table is to measure the level of mortality of a given population. As such, it offers some new measures that eliminate some of the problems involved in the use of existing standard measures. For example, the difference in the crude death rates of two populations, as was indicated in the previous chapter, is affected by the difference in the age composition of the populations. However, standardized rates have the disadvantage of depending on the particular selection of a standard population. Life tables have the advantage that the overall death rate of the life table (m^l) represents the result of the weighting of the age-specific life table death rates (m_x^l) by a population (L_x) generated by the series of observed death rates themselves. However, because the weighting scheme involves a variable population distribution from table to table, there is still an issue of comparability between the overall life table death rates. As will be described later, the life table also has the special advantage of providing measures of mortality that automatically are structured in cohort form. Hence, it eliminates the usually laborious task of compiling death statistics according to birth cohorts, even where this is possible. Often, insufficient basic data are available for doing this for a particular country and a life table is the only means of making a necessary allowance for the mortality of age cohorts.

The *expectation of life at birth* is the life table function most frequently used as an index of the level of mortality. It also represents a summarization of the whole series of mortality rates for all ages combined, as weighted by the life

table stationary population. In fact, the reciprocal of the expectation of life, $1/e_0$, is equivalent to the "crude" death rate, m^l, of the life table population, as can be seen from the following derivation:

$$m^1 = \text{Total number of deaths/Total population}$$

$$= \frac{l_0}{T_0} = \frac{1}{\dfrac{T_0}{l_0}} = \frac{1}{e_0} \qquad (13.49)$$

For example, the death rate in the 1989–1991 U.S. life table is calculated from Table 13.1 as follows:

$$m^1 = \frac{l_0}{T_0} = \frac{100,000}{7,536,614} = .01327, \text{ or} \qquad (13.50)$$

$$m^1 = \frac{1}{e_x} = \frac{1}{75.37} = .01327 \qquad (13.51)$$

The same formulas give the "crude" birthrate, f^l, of the life table population, and the growth rate of this population (r^l) is, of course, zero:

$$f^l = \frac{l_0}{T_0} = \frac{1}{e_0} = m^l \qquad (13.52)$$

$$\therefore r^l = f^l - m^l = 0 \qquad (13.53)$$

Because the infant mortality rate strongly affects the expectation of life at birth, the *expectation of life at age 1* has been suggested as a comparative measure of the general level of mortality of a population, perhaps in conjunction with the infant mortality rate. Another life table function frequently used is the *expectation of life at age 65*. This value measures mortality at the older ages, the ages where most of the deaths in the developed countries currently occur. (Much of the measured change here may reflect inadequacies in the underlying data.) Other life table values used to measure mortality are the *probability of surviving from birth to the 65th birthday*.

$$_{65}p_0 = \frac{l_{65}}{l_0} \qquad (13.54)$$

and the age to which half of the cohort survives—that is, the *median age at death* of the initial cohort assumed in the life table. The median age at death is the age corresponding to l_x value 50,000 in a life table with a radix of 100,000.

Illustrative changes in the mortality record of white males in the United States during the 20th century, as measured by life table values, are shown in Table 13.7. It suggests that significant improvement has been recorded during the first year of life. The variation in these measures is suggested by the figures for several countries, which are shown in Table 13.8.

Measures based on the life table have been used in the intensive analysis of vital statistics. Naturally, the type of vital statistics most frequently analyzed with life table

TABLE 13.7 Change in the Mortality of White Males in the United States According to Various Life Table Measures: 1900 to 1996 [Life tables for periods before 1929–31 relate to the Death Registration States]

Period	Expectation of life at birth	Expectation of life at age 1	Expectation of life at age 65	Probability of surviving from birth to age 65	Median age at death of initial cohort
1900–02	48.23	54.61	11.51	.392	57.2
1909–11	50.23	56.26	11.25	.409	59.3
1919–21	56.34	60.24	12.21	.507	65.4
1929–31	59.12	62.04	11.77	.530	66.4
1939–41	62.81	64.98	12.07	.583	68.7
1949–51	66.31	67.41	12.75	.635	70.7
1959–61	67.55	68.34	12.97	.658	71.4
1969–71	67.94	68.33	13.02	.663	71.5
1979–81	70.82	70.70	14.26	.724	74.2
1989–91	72.72	72.35	15.24	.760	76.1
1996	73.90	73.40	15.80	.779	77.2
Increase, 1900–2 to 1996	25.67	18.79	4.29	.387	20.0
Increase, 1949–51 to 1996	7.59	5.99	3.05	.144	6.5

Source: Various official United States life tables.

TABLE 13.8 Mortality of Females According to Various Life Table Measures, for Selected Countries: Around 1990

Country and year	Expectation of life at- Birth	Age 1	Age 65	Probability of surviving from birth to age 65	Median age at death of initial cohort
Argentina, 1990–2	75.59	76.30	17.26	.826	80.3
Bangladesh, 1988	55.97	61.50	11.98	.566	68.6
Canada, 1992	80.89	80.36	19.88	.886	83.8
China, 1990	70.49	71.92	14.74	.756	75.8
Egypt, 1991	66.39	58.65	12.87	.702	72.6
India, 1986–90	58.90	62.60	12.90	.572	68.6
Japan, 1994	82.98	82.29	20.97	.919	>85
Moldova, 1994	69.79	70.18	13.19	.717	73.6
Peru, 1990–95	66.55	70.65	14.59	.727	77.3
Philippines, 1991	66.70	68.70	13.70	.692	73.6
Russian Federation, 1994	71.18	71.29	14.58	.741	75.4
Zimbabwe, 1990	62.00	65.10	13.30	.613	70.7

Source: United Nations *Demographic Yearbook, 1996*, Tables 32 and 33.

TABLE 13.9 Mortality Rate of White Females as Percent of the Mortality Rates of White Males in the United States for Selected Ages, as shown by various life tables: 1900 to 1996 [Life tables for periods before 1929–31 relate to the Death Registration States]

Period	Exact age 0	1	10	20	30	40	50	60	70	80
1900–02	83	90	90	93	97	88	87	88	91	91
1909–11	83	92	87	86	91	79	81	84	91	93
1919–21	80	90	85	101	105	90	91	88	92	95
1929–31	80	89	77	87	91	78	75	78	84	90
1939–41	79	89	70	68	79	72	66	67	78	87
1949–51	77	89	67	45	63	62	55	56	68	82
1959–61	76	88	67	35	54	57	50	48	58	77
1969–71	76	87	73	34	49	57	52	45	51	68
1979–81	78	84	89	32	39	55	53	50	50	61
1989–91	77	89	88	36	35	45	57	56	56	61
1996	82	77	66	33	41	49	59	60	63	72

Note: Ratios of q_x per 100.
Source: Various official United States life tables.

measures is mortality because these measures were originally designed for precisely that application, and that application is usually the simplest. The analysis of mortality could cover variations in time and between population groups by age, sex, ethnic group, race, marital status, geographic residence, and other demographic characteristics that may be regarded as being associated with the overall level of mortality. Table 13.9 shows, for example, the vari-

ation in time, by age, of the relative mortality of white males and females in the United States in terms of life table mortality rates. Although mortality of white males has improved tremendously during the 20th century in the United States (Table 13.7), the improvement has been greater for white females (Table 13.9).

Model life tables may be used to evaluate the quality of mortality data for statistically underdeveloped populations and to establish the validity of recorded differences in the patterns of mortality of these populations. The mortality data for a country in earlier historical periods or for some segment of the current population may appear to be so defective as to raise a question whether the corresponding life tables provide an accurate representation of the patterns of mortality actually experienced. Zelnik (1969), for example, compared the age patterns of mortality in official U.S. life tables for whites and blacks from 1900–1902 to 1959–1961 with Coale-Demeny model life tables to examine the quality of the U.S. official life tables for blacks (see Chapter 22).

Analysis of Fertility, Reproductivity, and Age Structure

Life table measures and techniques have also been used to analyze other vital phenomena in addition to mortality. The procedures usually involve the combination of mortality with the specific vital rates that are being analyzed. These procedures have particular application in studies of fertility and reproductivity. For example, age-specific fertility rates are combined with survival rates from life tables to calculate the net reproduction rate (Chapter 17). The mean length of a generation, which is simply the average age of mothers at the birth of their daughters, is another measure based on both fertility rates and life table survival rates.

The life table is an important instrument for the analysis of population dynamics and age structure. Studies of the relation of growth rates, birthrates, and death rates to age structure depend heavily on the use of life tables, particularly to indicate the effects on age structure of various levels of mortality and to develop the "stable" age distributions corresponding to various levels of fertility (Chapter 23). The stationary population distributions of life tables correspond to given levels of mortality and a zero growth rate.

Calculation of Life Table Survival Rates

Survival rates are defined in terms of two ages, and hence two time references, the initial age and date and the terminal age and date. Both age references are equally applicable, but survival rates are more commonly identified symbolically in terms of the initial ages than in terms of the terminal ages. Survival rates express survival from a younger age to an older age, but they can be used to restore deaths to a population. Survival rates used to reduce a population for deaths are multiplied against the initial population; survival rates used to restore deaths are divided into the terminal population in a reverse calculation:

$$\text{Forward survival: } {}_5P_x^t \cdot {}_5s_x^5 = {}_5E_{x+5}^{t+5} \tag{13.55}$$

$$\text{Reverse survival: } \frac{{}_5P_x^t}{{}_5s_x^5} = {}_5E_{x-5}^{t-5} \tag{13.56}$$

where the elements represent the initial or terminal populations, the 5-year survival rate, and the expected later or

earlier populations. Normally, "revival" rates, which directly express "revival" from an older to a younger age, are not used.

The most common form of survival rate employed in population studies is for a 5-year age group and a 5-year time period. The general formula is

$$_5s_x^5 = \frac{{}_5L_{x+5}}{{}_5L_x} \tag{13.57}$$

According to the 1989–1991 U.S. life table (Table 13.2), the proportion of the population 45 to 49 years old that will survive 5 years is calculated as follows:

$$_5s_{45}^5 = \frac{455{,}538}{466{,}610} = .97627$$

The proportion of the population 75 years and over that will live another 10 years is

$$_\infty s_{75}^{10} = \frac{{}_\infty L_{85}}{{}_\infty L_{75}} \quad \text{or} \quad \frac{T_{85}}{T_{75}}$$
$$= \frac{197{,}871}{665{,}131} = .29749 \tag{13.58}$$

Survival rates for population age groups are computed from the L_x values of the life table, using the L_x value for the initial age group as the denominator and the L_x value for the terminal age group as the numerator.

A complete life table readily permits calculation of survival rates for single ages for 1 year or any other time period. A 1-year survival rate for a single age is represented by $s_x = \frac{L_{x+1}}{L_x}$. The proportion of the population 64 years of age on a given date that will survive to the same date in the following year, on the basis of the 1989–1991 complete U.S. life table (Table 13.1), is

$$s_{64} = \frac{L_{65}}{L_{64}} = \frac{78{,}793}{80{,}203} = .98242$$

The proportion of 65-year-olds who are expected to live another 10 years is

$$s_{65}^{10} = \frac{L_{75}}{L_{65}} = \frac{59{,}201}{78{,}793} = .75135$$

Survival rates involving birthdays are computed using the l_x values. The proportion of newborn babies who will reach their fifth birthday is

$$\frac{l_5}{l_0} = \frac{98{,}877}{100{,}000} = .98877$$

The proportion of 60-year-olds that will reach their 65th birthday is

$$\frac{l_{65}}{l_{60}} = \frac{79{,}519}{85{,}014} = .93536$$

The proportion of infants born in a year who will survive to the end of that year (when the cohort is under 1 year of age) is

$$\frac{L_0}{l_0} = \frac{99,258}{100,000} = .99258$$

while the proportion of the newborn infants who will reach their first birthday is

$$\frac{l_1}{l_0} = \frac{99,064}{100,000} = .99064$$

If survival from birth to a given age interval is wanted, then the survival rate is $\frac{_nL_x}{nl_0}$ or, for a 5-year age group, $\frac{_5L_x}{5l_0}$. Here n, or 5, cohorts of 100,000 births are at risk. For survival from birth to age interval 30 to 34, we have

$$\frac{483,546}{500,000} = .96709$$

Survival rates involving 5-year age groups may also be computed using values of L_x or l_x for the midpoint age. The survival rate from birth to age interval 30 to 34 may be approximated by

$$\frac{l_{32.5}}{l_0} = \frac{L_{32}}{l_0} = \frac{96,717}{100,000} = .96717$$

This approximation has little effect on the survival rate, particularly in the ages up through young adulthood.

Survival rates for parts of a calendar year may be calculated by interpolating between the L_x's. A $\frac{3}{4}$-year survival rate from a complete life table is computed as follows (except at age under 1):

$$\frac{\frac{1}{4}L_x + \frac{3}{4}L_{x+1}}{L_x} \qquad (13.59)$$

For age 45,

$$\frac{\frac{1}{4}(94,006) + \frac{3}{4}(93,693)}{94,006} = .9975$$

For ages under 1, life tables giving L_x values by months of age or other subdivisions of age under 1 should be used. Alternatively, special factors may be derived from statistics for infant deaths in a manner similar to the way the separation factors for all infant deaths were derived.

Use of Life Table Survival Rates

In the use of life table survival rates in population studies, decisions have to be made regarding the selection of the life table and life table survival rates most appropriate for a particular problem. Where a life table is not available for the particular year or period, but for prior and subsequent years or for the initial and terminal years of the period, special survival rates may have to be computed on the basis of the available life tables. Commonly, for example, life tables are available for the census years, but we are interested in measuring population changes or net migration for the intercensal period. Survival rates appropriate for this purpose may be derived by (1) calculating the required survival rates from each of the two tables and (2) averaging them. This assumes that mortality changes occurred evenly over the intercensal period. We should also consider whether they were sufficiently great to justify the additional calculations.

In other cases, there may be a question of adjusting rates for various geographic, racial, ethnic, or other socioeconomic categories. Differences in age-specific death rates for various geographic, ethnic, or socioeconomic categories should be examined, when they can be computed, to determine whether life table survival rates for the general population should be adjusted for these differences. For example, the convergence of state mortality for each sex-race in the United States group to the national level has been so pronounced over the past several decades that, for most purposes, it is not necessary to employ separate life tables for each state in making population projections for states. National life tables for each sex-race group are adequate.

Survival rates for the general population can be adjusted directly for geographic or socioeconomic variations by use of observed central death rates for the various categories, as follows: (1) take the complement of the general survival rate; (2) calculate an adjustment factor for the particular geographic or socioeconomic category in terms of central death rates, (3) multiply the adjustment factor by the complement of the general survival rate, and (4) take the complement of the result in step 3. For example, if $_5s_x^5$ is a 5-year survival rate for ages x to x + 4 and $_5m_x$ is a central death rate at ages x to x + 4 for the general population, we may develop survival rates for the single population as follows:

(1) $1 - {_5s_x^5}$ (a type of 5-year mortality rate)
(2) $(_5m_x + {_5m_{x+5}})$ for the single population ÷ $(_5m_x + {_5m_{x+5}})$ for the general population
(3) $= (1) \cdot (2)$
(4) $= (1) - (3)$

Sometimes the evidence will not justify making this type of adjustment in the general rates or suggest that it is unnecessary.

Migration may be a troublesome element in making a correct estimate of deaths by means of life table survival rates for populations that are not closed (i.e., affected by migration). Application of survival rates to the initial population tends to understate deaths for a population with net in-migration and to overstate deaths for a population with net out-migration. A reverse procedure for applying the survival rates has the opposite effect (Chapters 18 and 19).

In many cases, official life tables are available but they are based on seriously incomplete statistics on deaths and are not satisfactory for most uses. In these cases, and in others where life tables are not available for the country, one may have to decide whether to construct a life table, "borrow" a life table from another country, or employ a model life table. Commonly, the countries that lack life tables simply do not have adequate death statistics for constructing such tables. In some cases, one may construct a table by use of population census data and "stable population techniques," but it is more practical and convenient to "borrow" another country's table or, preferably, to adopt a model table appropriate to the population under study. The selection of a model table and use of stable population techniques are discussed in Chapter 22 and Appendix B.

The estimates of survivors will differ depending on the age interval employed in computing the survival rates. (We consider this question apart from the age detail required in the estimates of survivors.) With few exceptions, 5-year survival rates are sufficiently detailed to take account of the important variations in the estimates of survivors. For most calculations, 10-year age intervals will be adequate, however. The use of survival rates with a given age interval implies that the actual population has the same distribution by age as the life table population in this interval. For this reason, survival rates for very broad age spans should be avoided except in rough calculations. Hence, the terminal open-ended interval should relate to a relatively limited age span containing only a small percentage of the total population. Terminal group 65 and over is to be avoided except for very "young" populations (e.g., Syria, Guatemala). On the other hand, for countries with relatively old populations (e.g., France, Great Britain), a terminal group of 75 and over may be unsatisfactory.

While life table survival rates represent the ratio of l_x or L_x values to one another, the actual level of survival rates is affected only by the q_x's in the age range to which the survival rates apply. Hence, life table survival rates for various populations may properly be combined on the basis of the population distribution at these ages. For example, 5-year survival rates with initial ages 40 to 44, for the white and nonwhite populations of the United States, would be combined on the basis of the distribution of the population in these race groups at ages 40 to 44 in order to obtain a survival rate for both populations combined.

National Census Survival Rates

Another means of allowing for mortality, national census survival rates, employs life table concepts but does not involve the actual use of life tables. National census survival rates are particularly applicable in the measurement of internal net migration, but they are also used in measuring or evaluating the level of mortality and in constructing life tables, especially for countries lacking adequate vital statistics. National census survival rates essentially represent the ratio of the population in a given age group in one census to the population in the same birth cohort at the previous census. Normally, then, census survival rates pertaining to the children born in the decade are not computed. An illustration of the method of computation of census survival rates for several countries and a comparison with life table survival rates are presented in Table 13.10. National census survival rates measure mortality essentially, but they are affected by the relative accuracy of the two census counts employed in deriving them. Underlying their use are certain basic assumptions. They are that the population is a closed one (i.e., that there was no migration during the intercensal period) and that there has been no abnormal influence on mortality (e.g., war). Census survival rates may be rather irregular, often fluctuating up and down throughout the age scale and exceeding unity in some ages. Note particularly the rates for Botswana in Table 13.11. The more inconsistent in accuracy are the data from the two censuses, the more erratic the census survival rates are.

In the use of national census survival rates to measure internal net migration for geographic subdivisions of countries, the fact that the rates incorporate both the effect of mortality and relative net census error is considered an advantage. The reasoning is that because net migration is obtained as a residual and the census survival rates "incorporate" the effect of the relative accuracy of the census counts in addition to mortality, the estimates of net migration are unaffected by the errors in the census data. National census survival rates for the United States have been used both in the estimation of net migration of age, sex, and race groups, for states and counties in historical studies, and in the evaluation of the levels of mortality shown in the official life tables.

LIFE TABLES WITH MULTIPLE DECREMENTS

Conventional life tables represent the reduction of the life table cohort by mortality alone. Life tables with multiple decrements describe how attrition from more than one factor reduces the life table cohort. A double decrement table is a type of multiple decrement life table in which there are two forms of exit from the initial cohort, one of which is mortality and the other is some change in social or economic status. One example is a nuptiality (marriage formation) table, which follows a cohort of never-married persons as they are exposed to marriage rates and death rates. Another example of a double decrement table is one that follows a cohort of first

TABLE 13.10   National Census Survival Rates for Males for Botswana, Ireland, Turkey, and Uruguay, 1980–1990

Age (years)		Census survival rate, 1980–1990						Life table rate, survival Uruguay 1984–1986
		Botswana						
		Population		Rate.				
		1980	1990	(2) ÷ (1) =	Ireland	Turkey	Uruguay	
At first census	At second census	(1)	(2)	(3)	(4)	(5)	(6)	(7)
0–4	10–14	86,069	88,615	1.029581	0.988389	1.178368	0.949638	0.962900
5–9	15–19	74,301	71,704	0.965048	0.957009	1.041048	0.975587	0.995636
10–14	20–24	58,709	53,038	0.903405	0.778674	0.905234	1.137193	0.993229
15–19	25–29	42,972	44,203	1.028647	0.723915	0.971136	1.041833	0.989527
20–24	30–34	32,646	35,568	1.089506	0.876978	0.953246	1.000395	0.987296
25–29	35–39	26,498	29,592	1.116764	0.954542	1.022280	1.147528	0.985492
30–34	40–44	20,327	22,412	1.102573	0.962540	0.996185	1.16505	0.980693
35–39	45–49	16,826	17,813	1.058659	0.961294	0.944353	1.103631	0.970599
40–44	50–54	15,600	15,529	0.995449	0.936017	0.896453	1.006115	0.952333
45–49	55–59	13,575	12,231	0.900994	0.921369	0.896584	0.932286	0.919222
50–54	60–64	11,424	10,008	0.876050	0.870831	0.840947	0.904868	0.873166
55–59	65–69	10,090	8,297	0.822299	0.831721	0.759667	1.068891	0.815967
60–64	70–74	8,477	6,537	0.771145	0.723513	0.641406	1.203539	0.734393
65 and over	75 and over	21,220	13,070	0.615928	0.384943	0.402123	1.147139	0.625499

Source: Basic data from United Nations, *Demographic Yearbook*, 1996, Table 34; 1994, Table 7; 1993, Table 26; 1988, Tables 7, 26; 1983, Table 7.

marriages as they as exposed to divorce and mortality. Multiple decrement tables allow for several decremental factors (including death). An example of a multiple decrement table is a cause-of-death life table, which subdivides the conventional life table into component tables for the causes of death. This type of table provides information about the population eventually dying of each cause and their average age at death as well as the probability that a person will eventually die from that cause.

Anatomy of Multiple Decrement Tables

The basic features of multiple decrement tables can be observed in Table 13.11. Cause-of-death life tables consist of one or more (component) conditional tables relating to those ultimately dying from a particular cause of interest (or from a set of such causes) and another table relating to those dying from all other causes (those not of interest). Table 13.11 consists of two conditional tables, one for malignant neoplasms and the other for all other causes of death. This set of tables divides the basic life table functions that were shown in the abridged life table for the United States in Table 13.2. The basic life table functions—$_nq_x$, l_x, $_nd_x$, $_nL_x$, T_x, and e_x—can be observed in each conditional table. For cause-of-death life tables, the conditional life tables are mutually exclusive and additive. Each death is represented in only one d_x column. The sum of life table deaths across all ages and conditional tables represents the life table deaths attributed to all causes combined. The two tables display the most salient aspect of cause-specific mortality.

The multiple decrement table conceptually traces a cohort of newborn babies through their entire life under the assumption that they are subject to the current observed schedule of age-specific mortality rates from different causes of death. The radix (cohort of newborn babies) is split among the component tables according to the cause of death. Panel A of Table 13.11 includes only 22,024 babies who eventually die from malignant neoplasms. Panel B of Table 13.11 begins with only the 77,973 babies who eventually die from other causes. The panels of the multiple decrement life table are linked in that together they represent what happens to the initial cohort. Therefore, the 22,024 who ultimately die from malignant neoplasms and the 77,973 who eventually die from other causes sum to the 100,000 radix of the conventional life table.

The interpretation of the life table functions in these abridged tables is as follows:

x to x + n The period of life between two exact ages. For instance, "20–25" means the 5-year interval between the 20th and 25th birthdays.

$_nq_x$ The proportion of the persons in the cohort alive at the beginning of an indicated age interval (x) who will die from a particular cause before reaching the end of that age interval (x + n). For example, according to Table

TABLE 13.11   Multiple Decrement Life Table for Malignant Neoplasms and Other Causes,
United States 1989–91

| Period between two exact ages, x to x+n (years) | Proportion of persons alive at beginning of age interval dying during interval from cause c | Of 100,000 born alive | | Stationary population | | Average number of years of life remaining at beginning of age interval for those who will eventually die from cause c | Of 100,000 born alive who eventually die from cause c |
| | | Number living at beginning of age interval who eventually die from cause c | Number dying during age interval from cause c | Population in this age interval who will eventclly die from cause | In this and all subsequent age intervals | | Number living at beginning of age interval |

A. Malignant Neoplasms

	$nq_{x,neoplasms}$	$l_{x, neoplasms}$	$nd_{x,neoplasms}$	$nL_{x,neoplasms}$	$nT_{x, neoplasms}$	$e_{x,neoplasms}$	$l^*_{x,neoplasms}$
0–1	0.00002	22,024	2	22,022	1,587,922	72.10	100,000
1–5	0.00014	22,021	13	88,053	1,565,900	71.11	99,990
5–10	0.00017	22,008	16	109,999	1,477,847	67.15	99,929
10–15	0.00016	21,992	15	109,919	1,367,849	62.20	99,854
15–20	0.00021	21,976	20	109,830	1,257,929	57.24	99,785
20–25	0.00028	21,956	28	109,710	1,148,099	52.29	99,692
25–30	0.00043	21,928	42	109,534	1,038,389	47.35	99,566
30–35	0.00080	21,886	77	109,235	928,855	42.44	99,374
35–40	0.00152	21,808	146	108,677	819,620	37.58	99,022
40–45	0.00291	21,662	277	107,618	710,943	32.82	98,360
45–50	0.00572	21,385	539	105,578	603,325	28.21	97,100
50–55	0.01046	20,846	966	101,816	497,748	23.88	94,654
55–60	0.01732	19,880	1,553	95,519	395,932	19.92	90,267
60–65	0.02628	18,327	2,248	86,017	300,413	16.39	83,217
65–70	0.03600	16,079	2,863	73,239	214,397	13.33	73,009
70–75	0.04728	13,217	3,374	57,648	141,157	10.68	60,011
75–80	0.05613	9,843	3,393	40,731	83,510	8.48	44,691
80–85	0.06310	6,450	2,971	24,822	42,778	6.63	29,286
85–90	0.06504	3,479	2,066	12,228	17,957	5.16	15,796
90–95	0.06054	1,412	1,032	4,482	5,729	4.06	6,413
95–100	0.05107	380	321	1,100	1,247	3.28	1,727
100+	1.00000	60	60	147	147	2.46	271

B. Other Causes

	$nq_{x,other}$	$l_{x, other}$	$nd_{x,other}$	$nL_{x,other}$	$nT_{x, other}$	$e_{x,other}$	$l^*_{x,other}$
0–1	0.0093400	77,973	934	77,156	5,947,292	76.27	100,000
1–5	0.0017400	77,039	174	307,738	5,870,136	76.20	98,802
5–10	0.0009700	76,865	97	384,083	5,562,398	72.37	98,579
10–15	0.0011700	76,768	117	383,548	5,178,315	67.45	98,455
15–20	0.0039900	76,651	399	382,258	4,794,768	62.55	98,305
20–25	0.0051600	76,252	516	379,970	4,412,510	57.87	97,793
25–30	0.0055800	75,736	558	377,285	4,032,540	53.24	97,131
30–35	0.0067100	75,178	671	374,213	3,655,255	48.62	96,415
35–40	0.0080100	74,507	801	370,533	3,281,043	44.04	95,555
40–45	0.0094100	73,706	941	366,178	2,910,510	39.49	94,528
45–50	0.0124500	72,765	1,245	360,713	2,544,333	34.97	93,321
50–55	0.0174700	71,520	1,747	353,233	2,183,620	30.53	91,724
55–60	0.0256800	69,773	2,568	342,445	1,830,388	26.23	89,484
60–65	0.0376900	67,205	3,769	326,603	1,487,943	22.14	86,190
65–70	0.0529900	63,436	5,299	303,933	1,161,340	18.31	81,356
70–75	0.0753400	58,137	7,534	271,850	857,408	14.75	74,560
75–80	0.0997000	50,603	9,970	228,090	585,558	11.57	64,898
80–85	0.1234200	40,633	12,342	172,310	357,468	8.80	52,112
85–90	0.1265800	28,291	12,658	109,810	185,158	6.54	36,283
90–95	0.0973300	15,633	9,733	53,833	75,348	4.82	20,049
95–100	0.0453600	5,900	4,536	18,160	21,515	3.65	7,567
100+	1.0000000	1,364	1,364	3,355	3,355	2.46	1,749

Source: U.S. National Center for Health Statistics, 1999.

TABLE 13.12   Actual Deaths and Life Table Deaths for Malignant Neoplasms and Other Causes,
United States: 1989–1991

Exact ages	Actual deaths			Life table deaths		
	Total $_nD_x$	Neoplasms $_nD_{x,\,neoplasms}$	All other causes $_nD_{x,other}$	Total $_nd_x$	Neoplasms $_nd_{x,\,neoplasms}$	All other causes $_nd_{x,other}$
0–1	114,810	274	114,536	936	2	934
1–5	21,444	1,545	19,899	187	13	174
5–10	12,238	1,774	10,463	113	16	97
10–15	13,599	1,581	12,018	132	15	117
15–20	46,609	2,258	44,351	419	20	399
20–25	63,099	3,226	59,873	544	28	516
25–30	79,018	5,578	73,440	600	42	558
30–35	101,279	10,482	90,797	748	77	671
35–40	117,550	18,118	99,432	947	146	801
40–45	135,123	30,758	104,364	1,219	277	942
45–50	156,378	47,214	109,164	1,784	539	1,245
50–55	201,256	71,674	129,582	2,713	966	1,747
55–60	295,958	111,499	184,459	4,121	1,553	2,568
60–65	465,044	173,739	291,305	6,018	2,248	3,770
65–70	651,048	228,339	422,709	8,162	2,863	5,299
70–75	787,101	243,437	543,664	10,909	3,374	7,535
75–80	904,394	229,612	674,782	13,363	3,393	9,970
80–85	904,222	175,431	728,791	15,314	2,971	12,343
85–90	737,820	103,545	634,276	14,725	2,066	12,659
90–95	447,208	42,868	404,340	10,765	1,032	9,733
95–100	175,745	11,607	164,138	4,857	321	4,536
100+	37,506	1,571	35,935	1,424	60	1,364
Total, all ages				100,000	22,024	77,976

Source: Published and unpublished data from the U.S. National Center for Health Statistics.

13.11 panel A, the proportion dying from malignant neoplasms in the age interval 20 to 25 is 0.00028. That is, out of every 100,000 persons alive and exactly 20 years old, 28 will die from malignant neoplasms before reaching their 25th birthday. In other words, the $_nq_x$ values represent the probability that a person at his xth birthday will die from malignant neoplasms before reaching his or her $x + n$th birthday.

l_x The number of persons living at the beginning of the indicated age interval (x) out of the total number of births assumed as the radix of the table who will ultimately die from a particular cause. Again, according to Table 13.11, out of 22,024 newborn babies who eventually die from malignant neoplasms, 21,956 persons would survive to exact age 20.

$_nd_x$ The number of persons who would die from a particular cause within the indicated age interval (x to x + n) out of the 100,000 births assumed in the combined tables. Thus, according to Table 13.11, there would be 28 deaths from malignant neoplasms between exact ages 20 and 25 to the initial cohort of 100,000 newborn babies.

$_nL_x$ The number of person-years that would be lived within the indicated age interval (x to x + n) by the cohort who

will ultimately die from malignant neoplasms. Thus, according to Table 13.11, the 100,000 newborn babies would live 109,710 person-years between exact ages 20 and 25. Of the 21,956 persons who reach age 20 before eventually dying from malignant neoplasms, the 21,928 who survive to age 25 would live 5 years each (21,928 × 5 = 109,640 person-years) and the 28 who die would each live varying periods of time less than 5 years, averaging about $2\frac{1}{2}$ years (28 × 2.5 = 70 person-years)

T_x The total number of person-years that would be lived after the beginning of the indicated age interval by the cohort of those who eventually die from malignant neoplasms. Thus, according to Table 13.11, the 22,024 newborn babies who ultimately die from malignant neoplasms would live 1,148,099 person-years after their 20th birthday.

e_x The average remaining lifetime (in years) for a person who survives to the beginning of the indicated age interval for those ultimately dying from a particular cause. Thus, according to Table 13.11, persons who reach their 20th birthday and who eventually die from malignant neoplasms should expect to live 52.29 years more, on the average.

The multiple decrement table is a way to partition the conventional life tables into conditional tables for each cause of death. The conditional tables are linked to the conventional life table by several relationships. At all ages, the number of survivors and person-years in the conventional life table is the respective sum over the conditional tables. That is,

$$l_x = \sum_c l_{x,c} \quad \text{and} \quad {}_nL_x = \sum_c {}_nL_{x,c}$$

Furthermore, the life expectancy for a population is the average of the multiple decrement life expectancies for the separate causes of death, weighted by the proportions dying of each cause:

$$e_x = \sum \frac{(l_{x,c}e_{x,c})}{l_x}$$

For example, life expectancy at birth in Table 13.2 is 75.37, which is the weighted sum of life expectancy at birth for those who eventually die from malignant neoplasms (72.10) and those who eventually die from other causes (76.27), where the weights are the proportions of the 100,000 births who eventually die from each cause. So

$$e_0 = \left(\frac{22,024}{100,000}\right) \cdot 72.10 + \left(\frac{77,976}{100,000}\right) \cdot 76.27$$

Table 13.11 shows life table deaths for malignant neoplasms and other causes for the United States in 1989–1991, using the life table deaths by cause (${}_nd_{x,c}$) series of Table 13.12. We have added the column l_x^*, which rescales the l_x series to the radix 100,000. The rescaling is not necessary but simplifies comparison of rates of population attrition for each cause.

Construction of Multiple Decrement Tables

Double-decrement and multiple-decrement tables may be constructed either on the basis of age-specific probabilities of the occurrence of the events (occurrence/exposure rates) or on the basis of prevalence ratios, obtained usually from censuses or surveys. When prevalence ratios are used, the life table stationary population is distributed into different statuses according to the prevalence of those statuses in the actual observed population.

The construction of multiple decrement tables is described in terms of cause-of-death life tables. As mentioned, multiple decrement cause-of-death life tables subdivide total life table deaths into the different causes or groups of causes of death. In constructing a multiple decrement table, one first constructs a conventional life table using age-specific probabilities of dying for all causes combined. Then, from the counts of actual deaths by cause, the proportion of deaths due to each cause is computed. Next, ${}_nd_x$, life table deaths between ages x and x + n, are separated into c cause-of-death subcategories ${}_nd_{x,1}, {}_nd_{x,2}, \dots {}_nd_{x,c}$. This sub-

division of life table deaths by cause is made on the basis of the actual distribution of deaths by cause at each age:

$$_nd_{x,c} = {}_nd_x\left(\frac{{}_nD_{x,c}}{{}_nD_x}\right) \tag{13.60}$$

Table 13.12 shows the actual deaths and life table deaths for the 1989–1991 U.S. life table. Total deaths have been divided into two subcategories, malignant neoplasms and other causes. The actual deaths are the averages from 1989 to 1991. The column for total life table deaths comes from Table 13.2. Beginning at age under 1 year, we allocate total life table deaths into life table deaths by cause proportionally based on the actual deaths:

$$d_{0,neoplasms} = d_0 \cdot \frac{D_{0,neoplasms}}{D_0} = 936 \cdot \left(\frac{274}{114,810}\right) = 2$$

$$d_{0,other} = d_0 \cdot \frac{D_{0,other}}{D_0} = 936 \cdot \left(\frac{114,536}{114,810}\right) = 934$$

All life table deaths are included in the allocation. For example, the life table deaths at age under 1 by cause sum to the total life table deaths for age under 1 (934 + 2 = 936).

The life table deaths partitioned by cause are used to construct life tables conditional on dying from that cause. The ${}_nd_{x,c}$ series can be used to construct the conditional life table showing the survival distribution for individuals who eventually die of one cause by defining the initial population $l_{0,c}$ to be

$$l_{0,c} = {}_\omega d_{0,c} = \sum_{x=0}^{\omega-n} {}_nd_{x,c} \tag{13.61}$$

The sum of the ${}_nd_{x,c}$ terms across all ages represents all life table deaths for the cth cause. Table 13.11 indicates that the sum of all life table deaths from malignant neoplasms is 22,024; this becomes the radix for the conditional life table for malignant neoplasms.

Table 13.12 shows the summations of the ${}_nd_{x,c}$ terms, which yield the totals, $l_{0,neoplasms} = 22,024$ and $l_{0,other} = 77,976$. The reader can confirm that ${}_\omega d_0 = l_0 = 100,000 = $ sum of $l_{0,c}$. The $l_{0,c}$ estimates tell us that, of 100,000 persons born, 22% would eventually die from malignant neoplasms and 78% would die from other causes, at the 1989–1991 survival probabilities.

We estimate the number of survivors for the cause at subsequent ages, $l_{x,c}$, by subtraction of the ${}_nd_{x,c}$ terms. That is,

$$l_{x+n,c} = l_{x,c} - {}_nd_{x,c} \tag{13.62}$$

The $l_{x,c}$ series is exactly the l_x series of the conventional life table, except that it describes the survival experience of persons eventually dying of a particular cause c.

The life table deaths for each cause and age group are used to calculate the cause-specific probability of dying. These are also called probabilities of death from specified causes and represent the probability that an individual will die of cause c after surviving to age x but before reaching age x + n.

$$_nq_{x,c} = \frac{_nd_{x,c}}{l_x} \qquad (13.63)$$

For example, the probability that an individual aged 20 will die from malignant neoplasms before age 25 is

$$_5q_{20,neoplasms} = \frac{28}{98,213} = .000285$$

The sum of the life table deaths for cause c is the number who eventually die of cause c from among the births that begin the life table (l_0). The probability that an individual eventually dies of the cth cause is

$$_\omega q_{0,c} = \sum_{a=0}^{\omega-n} \frac{_nd_{a,c}}{l_0} = \frac{_\omega d_{0,c}}{l_0} \qquad (13.64)$$

Life expectancy for each conditional table is constructed according to the formulas for constructing abridged life tables with the substitution of the conditional terms $_nl_{x,c}$ and $_nL_{x,c}$ for the conventional life table quantities $_nl_x$ and $_nL_x$.

Cause-Elimination Life Tables

Life tables have been computed under the assumption that a specific decrement (for instance, a cause of death or group of causes of death) is eliminated, that is, that it is impossible to die from the eliminated cause (Greville, 1948; U.S. National Center for Health Statistics, 1968, 1985b, 1999). Such cause-elimination life tables describe the hypothetical situation that a cause of decrement has been eliminated. This is the same as assuming that the probability of dying from that cause is zero (or the probability of surviving form it is 1.0). Note that while deaths from a cause are assumed to disappear, the disease itself is not assumed to go away.

Two important cautions must be observed in interpreting cause-elimination life tables. First, they provide no information about future longevity even though they can be useful in formulating assumptions about future longevity. They simply give us additional insight into the current cause pattern of mortality. Second, they are theoretical constructs in that they hypothesize shifts in mortality that do not occur independently and hence do not realistically represent the actual gains from eliminating a cause. It is likely that the gains from eliminating a cause would, in actual experience, be much smaller than shown in the table, as explained below.

Cause-elimination life tables are usually based on the assumption that eliminating one cause of death has no effect on the risk of dying from the remaining causes. The potential gain in life expectation as measured by cause-elimination life tables is constrained by the fact that indi-

viduals saved would be immediately subject to the death rates from other causes, usually major causes in later life. This phenomenon is called "competing risks." Because death from the cause eliminated would often have occurred at the older ages, few additional years would be added if the individual survived and died shortly after from another cause. The various causes of decrement are assumed to act independently of each other in the present case. If the causes are assumed not to be independent, it is still possible to develop a cause-eliminated life table if the interconnectedness can be modeled explicitly (Manton and Stallard, 1984).

Anatomy of Cause-Elimination Life Tables

Table 13.13 presents an abridged life table for the total population of the United States in 1989–1991, prepared on the assumption that malignant neoplasms (cancer) are eliminated as a cause of death. A series of such life tables, considered in comparison with a life table for all causes combined, provides various measures of the relative importance of the different causes of death. The cause-elimination life table includes the basic life table functions—$_nq_x$, l_x, $_nd_x$, $_nL_x$, T_x, and e_x, as well as three additional functions.

The interpretation of the life table functions in an abridged life table would be as follows:

x to $x + n$ The period of life between two exact ages

$_nq_x^{(-i)}$ The proportion of the persons in the cohort alive at the beginning of an indicated age interval (x) who will die before reaching the end of that age interval (x + n) assuming that malignant neoplasms have been eliminated as a cause of death. Comparison of Tables 13.13 and 13.2 indicates that when malignant neoplasms have been eliminated as a cause of death, the proportion dying in the age interval 20 to 25 falls from .00554 to .00526.

$l_x^{(-i)}$ The number of persons living at the beginning of the indicated age interval (x) out of the total number of births posited as the radix of the table, assuming that malignant neoplasms have been eliminated. According to Table 13.13, out of 100,000 newborn babies, 98,282 persons would survive to exact age 20 assuming that malignant neoplasms have been eliminated. Note that the number of survivors to age 20 is higher in Table 13.13 (which assumes that no one dies from malignant neoplasms), than in Table 13.2, (which assumes that no causes of death have been eliminated).

$_nd_x^{(-i)}$ The number of persons who would die within the indicated age interval (x to x + n) out of the 100,000 births, assuming no deaths from neoplasms. Of the 98,282 survivors to age 20, 517 are expected to die before age 25. Again comparing Tables 13.2 and 13.13, the number of deaths between exact ages 20 and 25 to the initial cohort of 100,000 newborn babies would fall from 544 to 517 if malignant neoplasms were eliminated.

TABLE 13.13 Abridged Life Table Eliminating Malignant Neoplasms as a Cause of Death, for the Total Population of the United States: 1989–1991

Age interval — Period of life between two exact ages stated in years	Proportion dying — Proportion of persons alive at beginning of age interval dying during interval	Of 100,000 born alive — Number living at beginning of age interval	Of 100,000 born alive — Number dying during age interval	Stationary population — In this age interval	Stationary population — In this and all subsequent age intervals	Average remaining lifetime — Average number of years of life remaining at beginning of age interval	Average remaining lifetime — Probability of eventually dying of specified cause	Average remaining lifetime — Gain in life expectancy eliminating specified cause	Average remaining lifetime — Gain in life expectancy for those who would have died
x to x + n	$_nq_x^{(-i)}$	$l_x^{(-i)}$	$d_x^{(-i)}$	$_nL_x^{(-i)}$	$T_x^{(-i)}$	$e_x^{(-i)}$	ψ_x^i	$g_x^{(-i)}$	$\gamma_x^{(-i)}$
0–1	0.00934	100,000	934	99,260	7,872,401	78.72	0.22023	3.36	15.25
1–5	0.00175	99,066	174	395,855	7,773,142	78.46	0.22229	3.39	15.24
5–10	0.00096	98,893	95	494,206	7,377,287	74.60	0.22257	3.38	15.20
10–15	0.00117	98,798	116	493,766	6,883,081	69.67	0.22266	3.38	15.16
15–20	0.00405	98,682	400	492,499	6,389,315	64.75	0.22280	3.37	15.13
20–25	0.00526	98,282	517	490,144	5,896,816	60.00	0.22355	3.37	15.08
25–30	0.00572	97,765	559	487,464	5,406,672	55.30	0.22451	3.37	15.03
30–35	0.00691	97,206	672	484,413	4,919,208	50.61	0.22546	3.37	14.95
35–40	0.00834	96,534	805	480,736	4,434,795	45.94	0.22641	3.36	14.84
40–45	0.00989	95,729	946	476,396	3,954,059	41.30	0.22713	3.33	14.64
45–50	0.01327	94,783	1,257	470,980	3,477,663	36.69	0.22712	3.25	14.33
50–55	0.01900	93,526	1,777	463,492	3,006,684	32.15	0.22568	3.12	13.81
55–60	0.02890	91,748	2,652	452,556	2,543,192	27.72	0.22173	2.89	13.04
60–65	0.04467	89,097	3,980	436,062	2,090,636	23.46	0.21426	2.57	11.99
65–70	0.06790	85,117	5,780	411,798	1,654,573	19.44	0.20221	2.16	10.69
70–75	0.10827	79,337	8,590	376,115	1,242,775	15.66	0.18522	1.71	9.23
75–80	0.17008	70,747	12,033	324,472	866,659	12.25	0.16283	1.25	7.66
80–85	0.27173	58,714	15,954	254,085	542,187	9.23	0.13699	0.84	6.11
85–90	0.41446	42,760	17,722	168,451	288,102	6.74	0.10950	0.51	4.65
90–95	0.59446	25,037	14,884	84,814	119,651	4.78	0.08285	0.28	3.37
95–100	0.74997	10,154	7,615	28,428	34,836	3.43	0.06057	0.14	2.33
100+	1.00000	2,539	2,539	6,408	6,408	2.52	0.04189	0.06	1.45

Source: U.S. National Center for Health Statistics. R. N. Anderson, 1999. "United States Life Tables Eliminating Certain Causes of Death." *U.S. Decennial Life Tables for 1989–91*, vol. 1, no. 4. Hyattsville, MD: U.S. National Center for Health Statistics.

$_nL_x^{(-i)}$ The number of person-years that would be lived within the indicated age interval (x to x + n) by the cohort. Thus, according to Table 13.13, the 100,000 newborn babies would live 490,144 person years between exact ages 20 and 25.

$T_x^{(-i)}$ The total number of person-years lived after the beginning of the indicated age interval. Thus, according to Table 13.13, the 100,000 newborn babies would live 5,896,816 person-years after their 20th birthday.

$e_x^{(-i)}$ The average remaining lifetime (in years) for a person who survives to the beginning of the indicated age interval, assuming that malignant neoplasm has been eliminated as a cause of death. Thus, according to Table 13.13, a person who reaches his or her 20th birthday should expect to live, on average, 60 more years.

Ψ^i The probability of eventually dying of the specific cause, malignant neoplasms in this case. According to Table 13.13, 22% of live births would die from malignant neoplasms. Note that this type of probability was discussed previously with multiple decrement life tables.

$g^{(-i)}$ The gain in life expectancy from eliminating a specified cause. If malignant neoplasms were eliminated as a cause of death, then 3.36 years would be added to life expectancy at birth for the total U.S. population in 1989–1991. This column represents the difference in e_0 between Tables 13.13 and 13.2.

$\gamma^{(-i)}$ The gain in life expectancy for those who would have died if the cause not been hypothetically eliminated. According to Table 13.13, those who would have died from malignant neoplasms can expect to live, on average, 15.25 additional years at birth.

Construction of Cause-Eliminated Life Table

Cause-elimination life tables are usually constructed in association with cause-of-death tables. They also use information about the actual distribution of deaths by cause at each age. The first step is the calculation of the probabilities of survival with the ith cause eliminated, $_np_x^{(-i)}$ by the exponential formula (Chiang, 1968; Greville, 1948).

$$_np_x^{(-i)} =_n p_x^{\left(1-\frac{nD_{x,c}}{nD_x}\right)} \qquad (13.65)$$

This formula employs the probability of surviving ($_np_x$) from the corresponding life table for all causes combined and the actual distribution of deaths by cause at each age.

Then the age-specific probabilities of death if the ith cause of death is eliminated are calculated as

$$_nq_x^{(-i)} = 1 -_n p_x^{(-i)} \qquad (13.66)$$

The number of survivors at each age assuming that the ith cause is eliminated $l_x^{(-i)}$ are calculated successively starting with $l_0^{(-i)} = 100{,}000$ by the formula

$$l_{x+n}^{(-i)} =_n p_x^{(-i)} l_x^{(-i)} \qquad (13.67)$$

The number of persons living in the stationary population in the age interval x to x + n assuming elimination of the ith cause is estimated using

$$_nL_x^{(-i)} = (n -_n f_x) \cdot l_n^{(-i)} +_n f_x \cdot l_{x+n}^{(-i)} \qquad (13.68)$$

with $_nf_x$ computed from the life table for all causes combined as

$$_nf_x = \frac{nl_x -_n L_x}{l_x - l_{x+n}} \qquad (13.69)$$

This procedure assumes that the average number of years lived by those who die within the age interval is the same in the life table eliminating the ith cause as in the life table for all causes combined.

The number of persons in the stationary population in the oldest age group, $L_\omega^{(-i)}$ is estimated by

$$L_\omega^{(-i)} = T_\omega^{(-i)} = \frac{e_\omega \cdot l_\omega^{(-i)}}{1 -_n r_{\omega-n}^i} \qquad (13.70)$$

where e_ω comes from the life table for all causes combined and $_nr_{\omega-n}^i$ denotes the proportion of deaths observed in the last age interval attributable to the ith cause of death.

With the value of $T_\omega^{(-i)}$ available, values of $T_x^{(-i)}$ for successively younger ages were calculated by

$$T_x^{(-i)} = T_{x+n}^{(-i)} +_n L_x^{(-i)} \qquad (13.71)$$

Finally, life expectancy at each age assuming the ith cause is eliminated is obtained by

$$e_x^{(-i)} = \frac{T_x^{(-i)}}{l_x^{(-i)}} \qquad (13.72)$$

The probability that an individual eventually dies of the cth cause is

$$_\omega q_{x,c} = \sum_{a=x}^{\omega-n} \frac{_nd_{a,c}}{l_x} = \frac{_\omega d_{x,c}}{l_x} = \psi_x^i \qquad (13.73)$$

For any age, the gain in life expectancy from eliminating a specific cause of death is the difference in life expectancy from two life tables—the cause-elimination life table and the life table for all causes combined:

$$g_x^{(-i)} = e_x^{(-i)} - e_x \qquad (13.74)$$

For the gain in life expectancy for those who would have died from the ith cause of death,

$$\gamma_x^{(-i)} = \frac{e_x^{(-i)} - e_x}{\psi_x^i} \qquad (13.75)$$

Increment-Decrement Tables

Increment-decrement tables are a type of multiple decrement table that allows for both increments and decrements in the initial cohort, such as labor force entry and exit, school enrollment and withdrawal, and marriage, divorce, and widowhood. When data and computer facilities are limited, they are typically constructed from age-specific prevalence ratios.

While conventional increment-decrement tables allow both entries and exits in the table, these appear as net entries and net exits for age intervals over broad age bands in the table. For example, tables of working life constructed by this method assume a unimodal curve of labor force participation, reaching a maximum in young adulthood and then falling to zero in older ages. The table may show only net entries into the labor force until about age 35 and only net exits from the labor force thereafter.

Increment-decrement life tables are constructed by disaggregating a conventional life table into those in the "state" (e.g., in the labor force) and those "not in the state" (e.g., not in the labor force). To achieve this, observed prevalence ratios (e.g., labor force participation ratios) are applied to the stationary population ($_nL_x$) of the basic life table. The occurrence/exposure rates of net entry or net exit at each age have to be derived indirectly. Various techniques may be employed in developing them. Application of prevalence ratios in single years of age to the stationary population yields the stationary population in the state (e.g., in the labor force) in single years. The survivors at each age in the state ^1l_x and not in the state ^0l_x can be calculated by interpolation of the stationary population. The implicit rates of labor force entry and exit can be derived after removing the effect of mortality. An increment-decrement table may also be constructed by employing occurrence/exposure rates. These rates may be derived from census reports or from surveys on current status and status at an earlier date. Cross-sectional data from a single census measuring the changes in the proportions over single ages can also be used to derive the rates.

Increment-decrement tables provide some types of information not available from conventional tables and double-decrement tables. Using tables of working life as illustration, we can obtain such measures as the proportion of the cohort ever entering the labor force, the average remaining years of active life, the rate of accessions to the labor force and retirements at each age, and the mean ages of entry into the labor force and retirement.

Increment-decrement tables are limited because they cannot model all possible transitions between the states under consideration. For this reason, multistate tables have largely replaced increment-decrement tables. Unlike increment-decrement tables, multistate tables of working life are not limited to a unimodal curve of labor force participation and can handle those individuals who enter the labor the force, exit, and then reenter it.

MULTISTATE LIFE TABLES

Multistate life tables are a major extension of life tables. Both conventional life tables and multiple decrement life tables model departures, over time, from a cohort of live births. Conventional life tables concern two states—life and death—while multiple decrement models allow for more than two states—life and various causes of death, for example. Multistate models, in contrast, allow not only for movements between life (an active state) and death (an absorbing state) but also for all possible movements among various types of active states. For example, a multistate nuptiality model allows individuals to move from being unmarried to married, from married to divorced, from divorced to remarried, and from remarried to divorced. Because of this flexibility, multistate models have had a broad range of applications, including marital status, labor force behavior, interregional migration, and health status.

Multistate models relate to "states", which typically include death and various categories for the living. States are mutually exclusive and discrete. There are several types of states. Absorbing states (like death) only permit entries. Transient states allow both entries and exits. In addition, some states (like never married) permit only exits. Together, the states are the elements of the "state space."

Mathematically, multistate models are a type of Markov process. Markov processes assume that transition probabilities depend only on age (or duration in state) and current state. Furthermore, the probabilities are assumed independent of the previous state.

Anatomy of Multistate Models

Unlike conventional tables or multiple decrement tables, multistate models do not have a standard table format with a small set of measures shown in every analysis. Instead, measures are selectively presented according to the requirements of the analysis. Many measures have counterparts in conventional and multiple decrement life tables. Output measures include lifetime transition probabilities, proportion of the population dying while in each state, expected duration of stay in each state (e.g., marriage), and number of transitions to each state per person.

Construction of Multistate Models

Multistate life tables are constructed from transition probabilities between the states analyzed in the table. There are different ways of deriving the basic transition probabilities. They may be obtained from a survey with a retrospective question on the previous year's status. Alternatively, the appropriate transitions, including deaths, may be secured from a longitudinal (panel) survey. The panel data for two dates can be used both to validate retrospective data from a single survey and to provide the matrix of required transition data. The appropriate transitions can also be calculated from census population counts and vital statistics. The construction of a multistate table is illustrated in this chapter with a table of working life.

Working-Life Tables

Working-life tables model the worklife history of a hypothetical cohort assumed to experience currently prevailing labor force ratios. Multistate models of working life describe labor force attachment as a dynamic process. Members of the population are viewed as entering and leaving the labor market repeatedly during their lifetimes, with nearly all participating for some period during their lives. Tables of working life are useful in understanding the mechanisms and implications of changes in the labor force. These tables provide an indication of the average number of working years to be expected after a given age by all persons or by persons in the labor force attaining that age. In addition, the tables provide information on age-specific rates of accession to, and separation from, the labor force. These measures are used in legal proceedings to estimate work years lost and earnings foregone by individuals whose careers have been truncated by death. They are often used by governments for estimating manpower replacement needs for industry and assessing the economic implications of changes in economic activity ratios and the age-structure of the population.

The construction of a working-life table for U.S. males in 1979–1980, developed by Smith (1982, 1986), is shown as Table 13.14. The major source of data for constructing this table is the Current Population Survey (CPS), the nationwide monthly household survey sponsored by the U.S. Bureau of Labor Statistics. Because individuals are interviewed during each of four successive months and

State at time 1, age x	State at time 2, age x+1			
	Total	In labor force	Not in labor force	Dead
In labor force	Group A	Actives	Exits	Deaths of actives
Not in labor force	Group B	Entrants	Inactives	Deaths of inactives

FIGURE 13.2 Labor force flows for the 1979–1980 Tables of Working Life

again in the same 4 months of the following year, CPS records can be matched so that each person's status at the beginning and end of a 12-month interval can be compared. To construct the table of working life shown as Table 13.14, individuals' labor force status in a given month of 1979 was matched to that information in the same month of 1980. If labor force status changed between the two reference dates, then labor force transitions were registered. Surviving respondents were classified as "active" or "inactive" if their status was identical at both dates, and as "entrants" or "exits" if their status changed. The state space of this multistate model consists of three states: two labor force states (active and inactive) and death. Four transitions among the states are possible, two between the labor force statuses and two between each of these and death. Life table calculations are carried out on single-year-of-age data. Life table calculations are based on exact ages, but the survey data have a slightly different age reference. In the survey, when the average person claims to have a certain age x, that person's age is actually halfway between exact age x and exact age x + 1. Therefore, the survey data have to be recentered to exact ages before developing the life table functions. Mortality rates were assumed to be identical for all persons of a given age, regardless of labor force status. The number of persons expected to die between interviews was estimated using a standard mortality schedule.

As an example of the process involved in constructing a working life table, we first calculate a transition matrix for each age by setting up a 2 × 2 contingency table of labor force status in 1980 by labor force status in 1979, as shown in Figure 13.2. Age-specific transition probabilities (p_x, shown in columns 2 to 6 in Table 13.14) indicate the likelihood that an individual of a given exact age and labor force status will be in each of three possible states (active, inactive, or dead) 1 year later. For each age and labor force status, the transition probabilities sum to 1. For example, at age 16,

$$p_x^d + {}^i p_x^i + {}^i p_x^a = .00130 + .70257 + .29613 = 1.00000$$

For each combination of age and labor force status, the transition probabilities are computed as row percentages from tables, such as is shown in Figure 13.2. For example, the probability of exiting the labor force beginning at age x is

$${}^a p_x^i = \frac{Exits_x}{Group\ A_x} \tag{13.76}$$

where p is the transition probability, the prefixed superscript a refers to the state at time 1, the suffixed superscript i refers to the state at time 2, and Group A_x refers to the row total from Figure 13.2.

Age-specific rates of transfer between statuses m_x (columns 7 to 9 in Table 13.14) are the number of transfers from state 1 to state 2 between exact ages x and x + 1 per thousand cohort members age x in the stationary population. These transfer rates allow for multiple status changes by individuals during the year. Transfer rates are computed from transition probabilities as follows:

$${}^a m_x^i = \frac{4 \cdot {}^a p_x^i}{\left(1 + {}^a p_x^a\right)\left(1 + {}^i p_x^i\right) - \left({}^a p_x^i \cdot {}^i p_x^a\right)} \tag{13.77}$$

For example, the rate of separation from the labor force at age 17 is

$$
\begin{aligned}
{}^a m_x^i &= \frac{4 \cdot {}^a p_x^i}{\left(1 + {}^a p_x^a\right)\left(1 + {}^i p_x^i\right) - \left({}^a p_x^i \cdot {}^i p_x^a\right)} \\
&= \frac{4 \cdot .22043}{(1 + .77808) \cdot (1 + .61255) - (.22043 \cdot .38597)} = .31692
\end{aligned}
$$

The probability of moving into and out of the labor force is relatively high at some ages, such as 16 and 17, when many start their careers with temporary summer jobs. Although some individuals will make changes repeatedly during the year, only their final transition is included in the year-to-year comparisons. Their other changes are lost.

The survivors from an initial cohort of 100,000 births, l_x, are in column 10 of Table 13.14. They are calculated from the survivors in the preceding age x − 1 and the probability of surviving from age x + 1 to age x:

TABLE 13.14   Working-Life Table for Men, United States: 1979–1980

Exact age (1)	Probability of transition between specific states during age interval x to x + 1					Age-specific rates of transfer per 1000 persons in initial status during age interval x to x + 1		
	Living to dead p_x^d (2)	Inactive to Inactive $^ip_x^i$ (3)	Inactive to Active $^ip_x^a$ (4)	Active to Inactive $^ap_x^i$ (5)	Active to active $^ap_x^a$ (6)	Mortality m_x^d (7)	Labor force accession $^im_x^a$ (8)	Voluntary labor force separation $^am_x^i$ (9)
16	.00130	.70257	.29613	.26233	.73637	.00126	.61967	.36095
17	.00148	.61255	.38597	.22043	.77808	.00149	.55491	.31692
18	.00165	.58417	.41418	.17233	.82602	.00165	.58722	.24433
19	.00177	.55755	.44068	.14453	.85370	.00177	.62430	.20475
20	.00189	.53996	.45815	.12034	.87777	.00189	.64607	.16970
21	.00200	.52949	.45851	.09781	.90019	.00200	.85514	.13678
22	.00206	.51802	.47991	.08162	.91632	.00207	.66891	.11376
23	.00208	.50424	.49369	.07061	.92731	.00208	.68945	.09861
24	.00205	.49676	.49919	.05970	.93825	.00205	.69448	.06305
25	.00202	.49823	.49976	.05036	.94763	.00202	.69103	.06963
26	.00197	.49443	.50360	.04307	.95496	.00197	.69456	.05942
⋮								
65	.02820	.90426	.06754	.24122	.73058	.02860	.08239	.29425
66	.03043	.90424	.06533	.24690	.72267	.03090	.08005	.30255
67	.03293	.90565	.06142	.25232	.71475	.03348	.07554	.31033
68	.03577	.90603	.05820	.25232	.71191	.03642	.07167	.31072
69	.03893	.90693	.05414	.25343	.70764	.03970	.06679	.31262
70	.04238	.90671	.04891	.25038	.69724	.04330	.06062	.32276
71	.04603	.90957	.04440	.25865	.69532	.04711	.05505	.32073
72	.04979	.90948	.04073	.26201	.68820	.05106	.050570	.32619
73	.05359	.90651	.03990	.27557	.67084	.05507	.05028	.34723
74	.05750	.90943	.03307	.27980	.66270	.05920	.04179	.35356
75	.06161	.91349	.02478	.22977	.70850	.06357	.03037	.28162

Exact age	Survivors in each status to exact age x per 100,000 persons born			Number of status transfers within surviving population during age interval x to x + 1		Deaths by labor force status		
	Labor force status			Labor force entries $^it_x^a$ (13)	Voluntary labor force exits $^at_x^i$ (14)	Total t_x^d (15)	Active $^at_x^d$ (16)	Inactive $^it_x^d$ (17)
	Total l_x (10)	Active ^al_x (11)	Inactive ^il_x (12)					
16	97,823	46,923	50,900	28,496	18,694	123	65	58
17	97,700	56,660	41,040	21,827	18,474	145	87	58
18	97,555	59,926	37,629	20,534	15,272	161	103	58
19	97,394	65,085	32,309	18,645	13,809	172	119	53
20	97,222	69,801	27,421	16,354	12,188	183	136	48
21	97,039	73,833	23,206	13,992	10,338	194	151	43
22	96,845	77,335	19,510	12,016	8,962	200	163	37
23	96,644	80,226	16,418	10,466	8,023	201	169	32
24	96,443	82,499	13,944	8,967	6,930	198	171	26
25	96,246	84,366	11,880	7,618	5,927	194	172	22
26	96,052	85,885	10,167	6,562	5,140	189	171	19
⋮								
65	70,376	24,686	45,690	3,830	6,739	1,965	655	1,330
66	68,391	21,121	47,270	3,812	5,971	2,081	610	1,471
67	66,310	18,351	47,959	3,627	5,340	2,184	576	1,607
68	64,126	16,062	48,064	3,428	4,707	2,294	552	1,742
69	61,833	14,232	47,801	3,152	4,202	2,407	534	1,874
70	59,426	12,649	46,777	2,806	3,834	2,518	514	2,004
71	56,908	11,107	45,801	2,486	3,346	2,619	491	2,128
72	54,288	9,756	44,532	2,220	2,982	2,703	467	2,236
73	51,585	8,528	43,057	2,123	2,772	2,764	440	2,325
74	48,821	7,439	41,382	1,695	2,426	2,807	407	2,400
75	46,013	6,298	39,715	1,176	1,654	2,835	373	2,462

(continues)

TABLE 13.14   (continued)

| | Person years lived in each status during age x | | | Person years lived in each status beyond exact age x | | |
Age	Total L_x (18)	Active L_x^a (19)	Inactive L_x^i (20)	Total T_x (21)	Active T_x^a (22)	Inactive T_x^i (23)
16	97,762	51,792	45,970	5,430,730	3,820,429	1,610,301
17	97,628	58,293	39,335	5,332,968	3,768,638	1,564,330
18	97,475	62,506	34,969	5,235,340	3,710,345	1,524,995
19	97,308	67,443	29,865	5,137,865	3,647,839	1,490,026
20	97,130	71,817	25,313	5,040,557	3,580,395	1,460,162
21	96,941	75,583	21,358	4,943,427	3,508,578	1,434,849
22	96,744	78,780	17,964	4,848,486	3,432,995	1,413,491
23	96,544	81,363	15,181	4,749,742	3,354,215	1,395,527
24	96,345	83,433	12,912	4,653,196	3,272,852	1,380,348
25	96,149	85,125	11,024	4,556,853	3,189,419	1,367,434
⋮						
65	69,384	22,903	46,481	1,002,062	180,527	841,535
66	67,351	19,736	47,615	832,678	137,624	795,054
67	65,218	17,207	48,011	865,327	117,887	747,440
68	62,960	15,147	47,833	800,109	100,681	699,428
69	60,629	13,440	47,189	737,129	85,533	851,596
70	58,166	11,878	46,288	676,500	72,093	604,407
71	55,597	10,431	45,166	618,334	60,216	558,118
72	52,936	9,142	43,794	562,737	49,784	512,953
73	50,203	7,963	42,220	509,801	40,642	169,159
74	47,417	6,869	40,548	459,596	32,659	426,939
75	44,596	5,873	38,723	412,181	25,791	385,390

Expectation of active and inactive life by current labor force status

| | Total population | | | Currently active in labor force | | Currently inactive in labor force | |
Exact age	Life expectancy e_x (24)	Active years remaining e_x^a (25)	Inactive years remaining e_x^i (26)	Active years remaining $^a e_x^a$ (27)	Inactive years remaining $^a e_x^i$ (28)	Active years remaining $^i e_x^a$ (29)	Inactive years remaining $^i e_x^i$ (30)
16	55.5	39.1	16.5	39.8	15.7	38.3	17.2
17	54.6	38.6	16.0	39.3	15.3	37.7	16.9
18	53.7	38.0	15.6	38.7	15.0	37.1	16.6
19	52.8	37.5	15.3	38.1	14.7	36.4	16.3
20	51.8	36.8	15.0	37.4	14.5	35.7	16.1
21	50.9	36.2	14.8	36.7	14.3	35.0	16.0
22	50.0	35.4	14.6	35.9	14.1	34.2	15.8
23	49.1	34.7	14.4	35.1	14.0	33.4	15.7
24	48.2	33.9	14.3	34.3	13.9	32.6	15.6
25	47.3	33.1	14.2	33.5	13.8	31.8	15.6
26	46.4	32.3	14.1	32.7	13.8	30.9	15.5
⋮							
65	14.2	2.3	12.0	4.1	10.1	1.2	13.1
66	13.6	2.0	11.6	3.9	9.7	1.0	12.6
67	13.0	1.8	11.3	3.8	9.3	0.8	12.2
68	12.5	1.6	10.9	3.6	8.9	0.7	11.8
69	11.9	1.4	10.5	3.4	8.5	0.5	11.4
70	11.4	1.2	10.2	3.2	8.1	0.4	11.0
71	10.9	1.1	9.8	3.1	7.8	0.3	10.5
72	10.4	0.9	9.4	2.8	7.5	0.2	10.1
73	9.9	0.8	9.1	2.6	7.3	0.1	9.7
74	9.4	0.7	8.7	2.2	7.2	0.1	9.3
75	9.0	0.6	8.4	1.7	7.2	0.0	8.9

Source: S. J. Smith, 1986, February. *Worklife Estimates: Effects of Race and Education.* Bulletin 2254, U.S. Bureau of Labor Statistics.

$$l_x = l_{x-1} \cdot (1 - p_{x-1}^d) \qquad (13.78)$$

Columns 11 and 12 in Table 13.14 represent the number of survivors from the initial cohort remaining in a labor force status for each age. Survivors are allocated between states using the transfer rates. The number of survivors in each state at age x is the number in that state at the previous age $x - 1$ plus persons entering that state minus those exiting that state and those who died while in the state of interest. For example, the number of inactives at age x is

$$^i l_x = {}^i l_{x-1} + \left({}^a L_{x-1} \cdot {}^a m_{x-1}^i \right) - \left({}^i L_{x-1} \cdot {}^i m_{x-1}^a \right) - \left({}^i L_{x-1} \cdot {}^i m_{x-1}^d \right) \quad (13.79)$$

The number of survivors in each state at age x can be restated in terms of the number of survivors from the previous age and the number of transfers among states, shown in columns 13 through 17 in Table 13.14. Continuing with the example of the number of inactives at age x,

$$^i l_x = {}^i l_{x-1} + {}^a t_{x-1}^i - {}^i t_{x-1}^a - {}^i t_{x-1}^d \qquad (13.80)$$

For example, the number of inactives at age 20 is

$$\begin{aligned} ^i l_{20} &= {}^i l_{19} + {}^a l_{19}^i - {}^i l_{19}^a - {}^i l_{19}^d \\ &= 32{,}309 + 13{,}809 - 18{,}645 - 53 = 27{,}421 \end{aligned}$$

Assuming that deaths and labor force entries and exits are evenly distributed throughout the year, the total number in the stationary population alive at midyear is half of the sum of the stationary population at the beginning and end of that interval:

$$L_x = \frac{l_x + l_{x+1}}{2}, \ L_x^i = \frac{{}^i l_x + {}^i l_{x+1}}{2}, \ \text{or} \ L_x^a = \frac{{}^a l_x + {}^a l_{x+1}}{2}$$

The number in each state at midyear, computed in this way, is shown in columns 18 through 20 of Table 13.14. This figure is also known as the number of person-years lived by the group in any state as it passes through a given age.

Columns 21 through 23 in Table 13.14 are the sum of the person years (of total life, active life, inactive life) from age x to the end of the table. For example, the sum of the person-years lived in inactive status from age x to the end of the table is

$$T_x^i = \sum_{x=x}^{x=\omega} L_x^i$$

Columns 24 through 30 of Table 13.14 show many measures of the expectation of life for the total population. The population-based expectancy of working life is the average number of years to be spent in the labor force above exact age x for each person reaching that age. This is an overall measure for the total cohort and can be derived for every age. The average working life expectancy for the total population at age x is

$$e_x^a = \frac{T_x^a}{l_x}$$

For example, the average working life expectancy for the total population at age 66 is

$$e_{66}^a = \frac{T_{66}^a}{l_{66}} = \frac{137{,}624}{68{,}391} = 2.0$$

Other life expectancies also can be calculated, but Table 13.14 does not present all the information that is required. The labor force-based expectancy of working life refers to the average number of years to be spent in the labor force above a given exact age for each person in the labor force at that age. It is the ratio of total number of years in the labor force from age x onward to the number of survivors in the labor force at age x. For example, the average working life expectancy for those currently working is

$$^a e_x^a = \frac{{}^a T_x^a}{{}^a l_x}$$

However, $^a T_x^a$ is not shown in Table 13.14, which follows a cohort of individuals through a lifetime of labor force entries and exits to estimate average remaining working life for all persons in the cohort. It is possible to follow other, more specific cohorts through their lifetime using the same general procedure. First, a cohort is identified, such as those who entered the labor force at a specific age. Then, survivors of the original cohort are subjected to the transfer rates appropriate to their current age and status to derive the survivors at each age over the lifetime. This set of survivors by age is converted into person-years of activity and inactivity in the labor force for that group during the age interval. The person-years are then summed across all ages and then averaged over persons alive and in the given status at the initial age. Figure 13.3 demonstrates some of these calculations by following a cohort of men at initial age 16.

Because of the high variances of the transition probabilities, resulting mainly from the detailed cross-classification of the sample data, and because of the problems of heterogeneity and age dependency, multivariate analysis may be used to improve the stability and other qualities of the data (i.e., regression analysis with covariates may be applied to the original rates).

THE LIFE TABLE IN CONTINUOUS NOTATION

Up to this point, this chapter has presented life tables using discrete notation, both because it is easier for most people to grasp and because it facilitates applications. This section introduces the life table in continuous notation because much of demographic theory rests on the use of this notation in life table analysis.

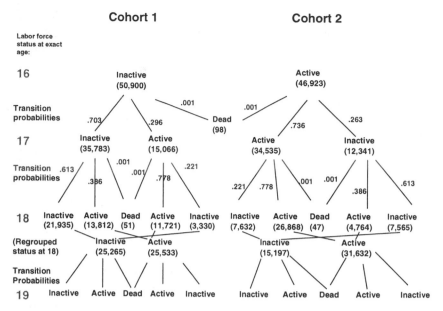

FIGURE 13.3   Selected portion of the labor force status-specific markov chain for men, initial age 16

In this formulation, age is viewed as a continuous variable rather than a discrete variable. The notation for the basic life table functions changes. In the discrete formulation, the basic life table functions were indexed with age shown as a subscript. When continuous notation is used, they are indexed with age shown in parentheses to indicate the value at which the function is evaluated. For example, the number of survivors at age x is l_x in the discrete formulation but $l(x)$ in continuous notation.

In the discrete formulation, time was indexed in terms of years, but with continuous notation, time can be broken into smaller increments. For example, the number of survivors in a 5-year age interval can be viewed as the sum of the number of survivors in 5 single-year age groups or 10 half-year age groups. As the age group interval becomes narrower, eventually the difference between an interval and a point disappears. So continuous notation uses an integral ($\int$) rather than a summation sign (Σ) to represent sums.

For example, the number of person-years lived in the age interval x to $x + n$ is

$$_nL_x = \lim_{k \to 0} \sum_{a=x}^{x+n-k} {}_kL_a = \int_{a=x}^{x+n} l(a)da \qquad (13.81)$$

In continuous notation, life expectancy is

$$e_x = \frac{\int_{a=x}^{\omega} l(a)da}{l_x} \qquad (13.82)$$

The hazard rate or the force of mortality (or instantaneous death rate) is defined as

$$h(t) = \mu(x) = -\frac{l'(x)}{l(x)} = -\frac{d}{dx}\ln l(x) \qquad (13.83)$$

Increasing the hazard rate corresponds to decreasing survival time.

The number of survivors at each age can be defined as the integral of its hazard function,

$$l(x) = \exp\left[-\int_0^x \mu(a)da\right] \qquad (13.84)$$

where $l(0)$ is set to 1.

It is possible to estimate the force of mortality from life table survivors at age x. For example, Jordan (1967, p. 18) uses the following approximation:

$$\mu(x) = -\frac{1}{l(x)}\frac{d}{dx}l(x) \approx \frac{(d_{x-1}+d_x)}{2lx} = \frac{(l_{x-1}-l_{x+1})}{2lx}$$

Another approach is to define a cumulative force of mortality for the age interval from x to $x + n$:

$$_nh_x = \int_x^{x+n} \mu(a)da$$

Manton and Stallard (1984) have suggested adding a column for the cumulative force of mortality to the life table by using

$$_nh_x = -\ln(1 - {}_nq_x) = -\ln {}_np_x$$

This column can also be calculated for multiple decrement life tables.

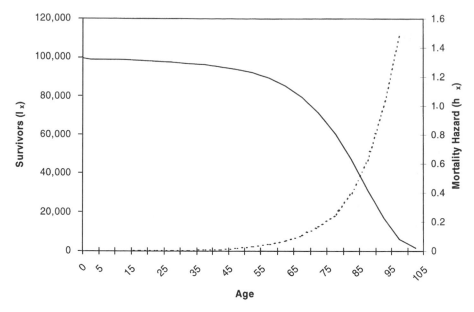

FIGURE 13.4   Survivors of 100,000 births and force of mortality by age in life table for total United States, 1989–91

Figure 13.4 compares the survival function l_x to the hazard function h_x for the U.S. abridged life table shown in Table 13.2. The number of survivors falls with increasing age, while the mortality hazard increases with age. Note that this graph uses the approximation $\mu\left(x+\dfrac{1}{2}\right) = h_x$.

References

Bell, F., A. Wade, and S. Goss. 1992. *Life Tables for the United States Social Security Area 1900–2080.* Actuarial Study, No. 107. Office of the Actuary, U.S. Social Security Administration. SSA Pub. No. 11-11536.

Carey, J. R. 1997. "What Demographers Can Learn from Fruit Fly Actuarial Models and Biology." *Demography* 34: 17–50.

Chiang, C. L. 1968. *Introduction to Stochastic Processes in Biostatistics.* New York: John Wiley and Sons.

Coale, A., and P. Demeny. 1966. *Regional Model Life Tables and Stable Populations.* Princeton, NJ: Princeton University Press.

Coale, A., P. Demeny, and B. Vaughn. 1983. *Regional Model Life Tables and Stable Populations.* New York: Academic Press.

Dublin, L. I., A. J. Lotka, and M. Spiegelman. 1949. *Length of Life.* Rev. ed. New York: Ronald Press.

Dublin, L. I., and M. Spiegelman. 1941. "Current Versus Generation Life Tables, *Human Biology*, 13: 439–458.

Gregory, I. 1965. "Retrospective Estimates of Orphanhood from Generation Life Tables." *Milbank Memorial Fund Quarterly* 43(3): 323–348.

Greville, T. N. E. 1943. "Short Methods of Constructing Abridged Life Tables," *Record of the American Institute of Actuaries*, 32(65): 29–42.

Greville, T. N. E. 1948. "Mortality Tables Analyzed by Cause of Death." *The Record*, American Institute of Actuaries, Vol. 37, Part II, No. 76.

Hummer, R., R. Rogers, C. B. Nam, and C. G. Ellison. 1999. "Religious Involvement and U.S. Adult Mortality." *Demography* 36: 273–285.

Jacobson, P. H. 1964. "Cohort Survival for Generations Since 1840." *Milbank Memorial Fund Quarterly* 42(3): 36–51.

Jordan, C. W. 1967. *Life Contingencies.* Chicago: Society of Actuaries.

Keyfitz, N. 1966. "A Life Table That Agrees with the Data." *Journal of the American Statistical Association* 61(314): 305–311.

Keyfitz, N. 1968. "A Life Table That Agrees with the Data: II." *Journal of the American Statistical Association* 63(324): 1253–1268.

Keyfitz, N., and W. Flieger. 1968. *World Population: An Analysis of Vital Data.* Chicago: University of Chicago Press.

Keyfitz, N., and W. Flieger. 1990. *World Population Growth and Aging: Demographic Trends in the Late 20th Century.* Chicago: University of Chicago Press.

Keyfitz, N., and J. Frauenthal. 1975. "An Improved Life Table Method." *Biometrics*, 31: 889–899.

Manton, K., and E. Stallard. 1984. *Recent Trends in Mortality Analysis.* Orlando, FL: Academic Press.

Olshansky, J., B. Carnes, and C. Cassell. 1990. "In Search of Methuselah: Estimating the Upper Limits to Human Longevity." *Science* 250: 634–640.

Preston, S., N. Keyfitz, and R. Schoen. 1972. *Causes of Death: Life Tables for National Populations.* New York: Seminar Press.

Reed, L. J., and M. Merrell. 1939. "A Short Method for Constructing an Abridged Life Table." *American Journal of Hygiene* 30(2): 33–62.

Sirken, M. G. 1966. "Comparison of Two Methods of Constructing Abridged Life Tables by Reference to a 'Standard' Table" (pp. 1–11). U.S. National Center for Health Statistics. *Vital and Health Statistics*, Series 2, No. 4 Revised.

Smith, S. 1982. *Tables of Working Life: The Increment-Decrement Model.* U.S. Bureau of Labor Statistics, Bulletin 2135.

Smith, S. 1986. *Worklife Estimates: Effects of Race and Education.* U.S. Bureau of Labor Statistics, Bulletin 2254.

Spiegelman. M. 1957. "The Versatility of the Life Table," *American Journal of Public Health* 47(3): 297–304.

United Nations. 1982. *Model Life Tables for Developing Countries.* ST/ESA/SerA/77. New York: United Nations.

U.S. Bureau of the Census. 1921. *United States Life Tables, 1890, 1901, 1910, and 1901–10.* Washington, DC: Government Printing Office.

U.S. Bureau of the Census. 1936. *United States Life Tables, 1930.*

U.S. Bureau of the Census. 1946. *United States Life Tables and Actuarial Tables, 1939–41*.

U.S. National Center for Health Statistics. 1963. *Guide to United States Life Tables, 1900–59*.

U.S. National Center for Health Statistics. 1964. *U.S. Life Tables: 1959–61*, vol. 1, no. 1.

U.S. National Center for Health Statistics. 1965. *Life Tables: 1959–61*, vol. 1, no. 3, "Life Tables for the Geographic Divisions of the United States, 1959–61."

U.S. National Center for Health Statistics. 1966. *U.S. Life Tables: 1959-61*, vol. 2, nos. 1–51, State Life Tables. Hyattsville, MD: National Center for Health Statistics.

U.S. National Center for Health Statistics. 1967. *U.S. Life Tables: 1959–61*, vol. 1, no. 5. "Life Tables for Metropolitan and Nonmetropolitan Areas of the United States: 1959–6l."

U.S. National Center for Health Statistics. 1968. *U.S. Life Tables: 1959–61*, vol. 1, no. 6, "United States Life Tables by Causes of Death, 1959–6l."

U.S. National Center for Health Statistics. 1975. *U. S. Decennial Life Tables for 1969–71*, vol. 1, no. 1, U.S. Decennial Life Tables. DHEW Pub. No. HRA 75-1150.

U.S. National Center for Health Statistics. 1977. *U.S. Decennial Life Tables for 1969–71*, vol. 2, nos. 1–51, State Life Tables. Hyattsville, MD: National Center for Health Statistics.

U.S. National Center for Health Statistics. 1985a. *U.S. Decennial Life Tables for 1979–81*, vol. 1, no. 1, U.S. Decennial Life Tables. DHHS Pub. No. PHS 85-1150-1. Washington, DC: U.S. Government Printing Office.

U.S. National Center for Health Statistics. 1985b. *U.S. Decennial Life Tables for 1979–81*, vol. 1, no. 2, "U.S. Life Tables Eliminating Certain Causes of Death". By L. Curtin and R. Armstrong. DHHS Pub. No. PHS 86-1150-2. Washington, DC: U.S. Government Printing Office.

U.S. National Center for Health Statistics. 1990. *U.S. Decennial Life Tables for 1979–81*, vol. 2, nos. 1–51, "State Life Tables." Hyattsville, MD: National Center for Health Statistics.

U.S. National Center for Health Statistics. 1997a. *United States Decennial Life Tables for 1989–91*, vol. 1, no. 1. "U.S. Life Tables." DHHS Pub. No. PHS-98-1150-1. Hyattsville, MD.

U.S. National Center for Health Statistics. 1997b. *United States Decennial Life Tables for 1989–91*, vol. 1, no. 2. "Methodology of the National and State Life Tables." DHHS Pub. No. PHS-98-1150-2. Hyattsville, MD.

U.S. National Center for Health Statistics. 1998. *U.S. Decennial Life Tables for 1989–91*, vol. 2, nos. 1–51, "State Life Tables." Hyattsville, MD: National Center for Health Statistics.

U.S. National Center for Health Statistics. 1999. *U.S. Decennial Life Tables for 1989–91*, vol. 1, no. 4, "U.S. Life Tables Eliminating Certain Causes of Death." Hyattsville, MD: National Center for Health Statistics.

U.S. National Office of Vital Statistics, 1947. *Vital Statistics-Special Reports, Selected Studies*, vol. 23, no. 11, "U.S. Abridged Life Tables, 1945."

U.S. National Office of Vital Statistics. 1948. *State and Regional Life Tables, 1939–41*.

U.S. National Office of Vital Statistics, 1954. *Vital Statistics-Special Reports, Life Tables for 1949–51*, vol. 41, no. 1, "United States Life Tables, 1949–51."

U.S. National Office of Vital Statistics, 1956a. *Vital Statistics-Special Reports*, vol. 41, Supplement, *State Life Tables*: 1949–51.

U.S. National Office of Vital Statistics. 1956b. *Vital Statistics-Special Reports, Life Tables for 1949–51*, vol. 41, no. 4, "Life Tables for the Geographic Divisions of the United States. 1949–51."

Zelnik, M. 1969. "Age Patterns of Mortality of American Negroes: 1900–02 to 1959–61," *Journal of the American Statistical Association* 64(326): 433–434.

Suggested Readings

Part A   Theory and Construction of Life Tables

Armstrong, R. J. 1998. "Methodology of the National and State Life Tables: 1989–1991." *U.S. Decennial Life Tables for 1989–1991*, vol. 1, no. 2. National Center for Health Statistics. Hyattsville, MD. DHHS Pub. PHS-98-1150-2.

Batten, R. W. 1978. *Mortality Table Construction*. Englewood Cliffs, NJ: Prentice-Hall.

Chiang, C. L. 1968. *Introduction to Stochastic Processes in Biostatistics* (Chapters 9–12). New York: John Wiley and Sons.

Chiang, C. L. 1984. *The Life Table and Its Applications*. Malabar, FL: Krieger.

Jacobson, P. H. 1964. "Cohort Survival for Generations Since 1840." *Milbank Memorial Fund Quarterly* 42(3): 36–51.

Jordan, C. W. 1967. *Life Contingencies*. (Chapters 14 and 15). Chicago, IL: Society of Actuaries.

Keyfitz, N. 1966. "A Life Table That Agrees with the Data." *Journal of the American Statistical Association* 61(314): 305, 311.

Keyfitz, N. 1977. *Introduction to the Mathematics of Population with Revisions*. Part 1, "The Life Table." Reading, MA: Addison-Wesley.

Keyfitz, N. 1968. "A Life Table That Agrees with the Data: II." *Journal of the American Statistical Association* 63(324): 1253–1268.

Keyfitz, N. 1985. *Applied Mathematical Demography*, 2nd ed. New York: Springer Verlag.

Namboodiri, N. K., and C. M. Suchindran. 1987. *Life Table Techniques and Their Applications*. Orlando, FL: Academic Press.

Preston, S., N. Keyfitz, and R. Schoen. 1972. *Causes of Death: Life Tables for National Populations* (Chapter 2). New York: Seminar Press.

Schoen, R. 1978. "Calculating Life Tables by Estimating Chiang's a from Observed Rates." *Demography* 15: 625–635.

Sirken, M.G. 1966. "Comparison of Two Methods of Constructing Abridged Life Tables by Reference to a 'Standard' Table." U.S. National Center for Health Statistics. *Vital and Health Statistics* (pp. 1–11), Series 2, No. 4 Revised.

Part B   Applications, Multiple Decrement Tables, Cause-Elimination Tables, and Multistate Tables

Arriaga, E. E. 1984. "Measuring and Explaining the Change in Life Expectancies." *Demography* 21: 83–96.

Bongaarts, J. 1987. "The Projection of Family Composition over the Life Course with Family Status Life Tables. In J. Bongaarts, T. Burch, and K. Wachter (Eds.), *Family Demography: Methods and Their Application* (pp. 189–212). New York: Oxford University Press.

Hayward, M., W. R. Grady, and S. D. McLaughlin. 1988. "Recent Changes in Mortality and Labor Force Behavior among Older Americans: Consequences for Nonworking Life Expectancy." *Journal of Gerontology: Social Sciences* 43: S194–S199.

Hoem, J. 1978. "A Markov Chain Model of Working Life Tables," *Scandinavian Actuarial Journal*: 1: 1–20.

Ishikawa, A. 1994. "Abridged Working Life Tables for Japanese Men and Women: 1990." *Jinko Mondai Kenkyu/Journal of Population Problems* 49: 57–70.

Keyfitz, N. 1977. "What Difference Would It Make If Cancer Were Eradicated? An Examination of the Taeuber Paradox." *Demography*, 14: 411–418.

Kochanek, K. D., J. D. Maurer, and H. M. Rosenberg. 1994. "Causes of Death Contributing to Changes in Life Expectancy: United States, 1984–1989," *Vital and Health Statistics* 20(23). Hyattsville, MD: U.S. National Center for Health Statistics.

Land, K., J. Guralnik, and D. Blazer. 1994. "Estimating Increment-Decrement Life Tables with Multiple Covariates from Panel Data: The Case of Active Life Expectancy." *Demography* 31: 297–319.

Land, K., G. Hough, and M. McMillen. 1986. "Voting Status Life Tables of the United States, 1968–1980." *Demography*, 23: 381–402.

Lee, E. S., and G. K. Bowles. 1954. "Selection and Use of Survival Ratios in Population Studies." *Agricultural Economics Research* 6(4): 120–125.

Long, L. H. 1973. "New Estimates of Migration Expectancy in the United States." *Journal of the American Statistical Association* 68(341): 37–43.

Manton, K., and E. Stallard, 1984. *Recent Trends in Mortality Analysis.* Orlando, FL: Academic Press.

Namboodiri, N. K., and C. M. Suchindran. 1987. *Life Table Techniques and Their Applications* (Chapters 6–9). Orlando, FL: Academic Press.

Pollard, J. H. 1988. "On the Decomposition of Changes in Expectation of Life and Differentials in Life Expectancy." *Demography* 25: 265–276.

Rogers, A. 1995. *Multiregional Demography: Principles, Methods and Extensions.* New York: J. Wiley and Sons.

Rogers, R., A. Rogers, and A. Belanger. 1989. "Active Life among the Elderly in the United States: Multistate Life table Estimates and Population Projections." *The Milbank Quarterly* 67: 370–411.

Schmertmann, C. P., A. Amankwaa, and R. Long. 1998. "Three Strikes and You're Out: Demographic Analysis of Mandatory Prison Sentencing." *Demography* 35: 445–463.

Siegel, J. S. 2002. *Applied Demography: Applications to Business, Government, Law, and Public Policy* (Chapters 7, 8, and 13). San Diego: Academic Press.

Stockwell, E. G., and C. B. Nam. 1963. "Illustrative Tables of School Life." *Journal of the American Statistical Association* 58(304): 1113–1124.

Willekens, F. 1987. "The Marital Status Life Table." In J. Bongaarts, T. Burch, and K. Wachter (Eds.), *Family Demography: Methods and Their Application*, (pp. 125–149). New York: Oxford University Press.

Wolf, D. A. 1988. "The Multi-State Life Table with Duration Dependence. *Mathematical Population Studies*, 1: 217–245.

Wood, J., D. Holman, A. Yashin, R. Peterson, M. Weinstein, and M. Chang. 1994. "A Multi-state Model of Fecundability and Sterility." *Demography* 31: 403–426.

Yashin, A., I. Iachine, K. Andreev, and U. Larsen. 1998. "Multistate Models of Postpartum Infecundity, Fecundability and Sterility by Age and Parity: Methodological Issues." *Mathematical Population Studies*, 7: 51–78, 109–110.

14

Health Demography

VICKI L. LAMB AND JACOB S. SIEGEL

NATURE AND USES OF HEALTH STATISTICS

Health is a leading characteristic of the members of a population, akin to other demographic and socioeconomic characteristics. It is an important correlate of other demographic and socioeconomic characteristics as well. For example, health statistics are often used in interpreting trends in mortality and in designing assumptions for making projections of mortality. Moreover, health has often been the subject of inquiry in population surveys and censuses.

In recent decades, the conceptualization of population health has extended beyond measures of mortality (e.g., life expectancy, infant mortality) to include specific health measures such as the incidence or prevalence of morbid conditions, or summary measures of health such as healthy life expectancy and health-related quality of life. This extension of population health is due in part to secular trends of increased life expectancy, which has shifted the focus of population health from the *quantity* of life to the *quality* of life, defined in a number of different ways. The World Health Organization (WHO) and various research organizations have worked to develop and promote summary measures of population health that combine measures of mortality and measures of health conditions to represent the state of a population's health in a single number. Summary measures of population health are important because of the various types of potential applications, as enumerated by Murray, Salomon, and Mathers (1999, pp. 3–4):

1. Comparing the health of one population with the health of another population
2. Comparing the health of the same population at different points in time
3. Identifying and quantifying health inequalities within populations

4. Providing appropriate and balanced attention to the effects of nonfatal health conditions on overall population health
5. Informing debates on priorities for health service delivery and planning
6. Informing debates on priorities for research and development in the health sector
7. Improving professional training curricula in public health
8. Analyzing the benefits of health interventions for use in cost-effectiveness analyses

In addition, the WHO has initiated a new global health policy that aims to meet the major health problems and issues in the new century. The health policy initiative, "Health for All in the 21st Century" (HFA), was established to improve global health and reduce health inequities within and between countries through the development of health priorities and targets for the first two decades of the 21st century. Member countries have been encouraged to set their own goals in relation to the HFA goals. In the United States, "Healthy People 2010" has been launched to meet two overarching goals: to increase the quality of the years lived and years of healthy life, and to eliminate health disparities (U.S. Department of Health and Human Services, 2000a, p. 2).

U.S. goals target leading health indicators, including those for morbid conditions, lifestyle habits, and access to health care. The measurement of the incidence and prevalence of morbid conditions, particularly chronic/degenerative diseases, age at onset, case-fatality rates, and the physical and emotional effects of health conditions have become increasingly important concerns in understanding population health. Thus, there is a need for a broader array of health statistics to represent the occurrence and distribution of health conditions to characterize population health.

DEFINITION OF CONCEPTS

Health

It is difficult to define health in operational terms because health is multidimensional and, in part, socially defined. The World Health Organization gave health a positive definition in its Constitution in 1946: "Health is a state of complete physical, mental, and social well-being and not merely the absence of disease or infirmity." The definition of health has been both broadened (Mahler, 1981) and sharply narrowed (Dubos, 1968, Chapter 4). The latter defined health as "a modus vivendi enabling imperfect men to achieve a rewarding and not too painful existence while they cope with an imperfect world." In spite of efforts to quantify health status, for the most part health is measured in terms of its converse, such as disease, disability, and death.

Health Conditions

Several general terms are employed to indicate a lack of good health, such as disease, illness, health condition, and morbid condition, and the definitions overlap. *Disease* refers to the biophysical state of ill health, whereas *illness* is the social experience of being sick or diseased. *Morbidity* is a broad term for any health condition. As such, morbidity encompasses diseases, injuries, and impairments. More specifically, morbidity encompasses *acute conditions* (including acute illnesses and injuries) and *chronic conditions* (including chronic illnesses and impairments). The terms acute and chronic do not have precise definitions but are distinguished on the basis of the duration and the type of health condition considered. An acute condition typically has a rapid onset, has a relatively short duration, and usually ends with either recovery or death. A chronic condition usually involves a lengthy period of evolution and progression, has a long duration, and is considered relatively intractable to treatment. Infectious diseases, for example, are usually classified as acute, while cardiovascular diseases are classified as chronic. *Impairments* are chronic conditions involving abnormalities of body structure and appearance, the most common being chronic sensory and musculoskeletal conditions. *Comorbidity* is a term referring to multiple chronic conditions in one individual.

The classification of morbid conditions used by national governments follows the same classifications recommended about every 10 to 20 years by the World Health Organization for the classification of causes of death. The tenth revision of the *International Statistical Classification of Diseases and Related Problems* (*ICD-10*) was published by the WHO in 1992–1994. The ninth revision remained generally in effect in 1998, however. The United States shifted to the new classification beginning in 1999. Major changes between *ICD-9* and *ICD-10* are that *ICD-10* (1) includes more detailed categories (8000 versus 5000), (2) uses alphanumeric rather than numeric codes, and (3) changes some of the rules for coding and for the classification of underlying cause of death (U.S. National Center for Health Statistics/Anderson *et al.*, 2001a).

The ICD includes classifications for mental illnesses as well as physical illnesses. Chapter V of *ICD-10*, "Mental and Behavioral Disorders," provides clinical descriptions in addition to diagnostic guidelines. In the United States a separate publication, *The Diagnostic and Statistical Manual of Mental Disorders* (*DSM-IV*, American Psychiatric Association, 1994), also gives a classification of mental illnesses. The codes and terms provided in *DSM-IV* are fully compatible with *ICD-10*. According to Mausner and Kramer (1985, p. 25), in the system of classification of mental disorders, the clinician assigns a category on the basis of observations relating to clinical syndromes, personal disorders, physical disorders and conditions, severity of psychosocial stressors, and highest level of adaptive functioning during the previous year.

A *disability* refers to an acute or chronic condition that affects an individual's ability to function and carry out his or her activities. The U.S. National Health Interview Survey defines disability as "any temporary or long-term reduction of a person's activity as a result of an acute or chronic condition." It refers, therefore, to the consequences of health conditions. It is useful to distinguish those disabilities that can be managed in part or on the whole by technological devices and structural changes in the community and those that cannot. Such a distinction can aid in defining degrees of disability, from slight to moderate to severe.

In 1980 the World Health Organization issued the *International Classification of Impairments, Disabilities, and Handicaps* (ICIDH). It was developed to model and standardize concepts in the disablement process. Because disability is viewed as a consequence of disease, and the identification of a disease does not adequately portray the full consequences of the condition, the ICIDH was to be an extension of the ICD scheme. In the ICIDH scheme, an impairment refers to a loss or abnormality of psychological function or physiological or anatomical structure or function; a disability is a restriction or inability to perform an activity in the range considered normal for a person; and a *handicap* is a limitation or inability to perform one's social role(s) due to an impairment or disability (World Health Organization, 1980).

The current ICIDH scheme has been difficult to use for a number of reasons: (1) the overlaps between the various concepts, especially between disability and handicap, (2) the lack of clarity about the specific meanings associated with the categories, (3) the difficulty in applying the classification scheme to various theories and models of disablement, (4) the difficulty in adapting currently collected health data to conform with the ICIDH framework, and (5) the failure of the ICIDH scheme to encompass the possibility for reversals, reductions in severity, or recovery.

Since 1995 there have been efforts to revise the ICIDH framework and definitions. A new version of the ICIDH, renamed the *International Classification of Functioning, Disability and Health* (WHO, 2001), has been published. The new ICF is restructured to capture both the positive and negative aspects of functioning and focuses on (1) body functions and body structures, (2) activities performed by an individual, and (3) participation in, and classification of, the areas of life in which an individual is involved. In addition, environmental factors are also part of the new classification scheme. "Environmental factors" is broadly defined and encompasses "assistive" products and technologies, the natural environment and human changes to the environment, support and relationships provided by people and animals, attitudes and beliefs, and formal services, governmental systems, and policies that affect the disabled.

SOURCES OF DATA FOR HEALTH STUDIES AND QUALITY OF HEALTH STATISTICS

Health data can be obtained both from the general sources for demographic data, such as censuses, vital statistics registrations, and general sample surveys, and from specialized sources, such as sample surveys on health, administrative records on health (e.g., disease registries), epidemiological studies, and clinical trials. These sources all provide quantitative data on health. We consider each of these in turn and then comment briefly on qualitative sources of information on health. The U.S. Department of Health and Human Services periodically publishes an *International Health Data Reference Guide* (e.g., U.S. Department of Health and Human Services, 2000b), which presents an overview of international health data from vital statistics, hospital statistics, health personnel statistics, and population-based surveys. The purpose of the guide is to provide information about sources of health data around the world useful for supporting international studies and comparisons of population health.

Censuses

Periodically, population censuses have obtained information regarding conditions that we now term sensory, physical, and mental impairments. The 1830 U.S. census was the first U.S. census to contain questions intended to determine the number of persons who were "deaf, dumb, or blind." The 1840 U.S. census added the category of "insanity." Recent censuses of the United States (1980, 1990, and 2000) have had questions on activity limitations with respect to work, use of transportation, or personal care. The

2000 U.S. census, for example, asked the following yes/no questions:

Does this person have any of the following long-lasting conditions:
  a. Blindness, deafness, or a severe vision or hearing impairment?
  b. A condition that substantially limits one or more basic physical activities such as walking, climbing stairs, reaching, lifting, or carrying?
Because of a physical, mental, or emotional condition lasting 6 months or more, does this person have any difficulty in doing any of the following activities:
  a. Learning, remembering, or concentrating?
  b. Dressing, bathing, or getting around inside the home?
  c. (Answer if this person is 16 years old or over.) Going outside the home alone to shop or visit a doctor's office?
  d. (Answer if this person is 16 years old or over.) Working at a job or business?

Demographers have used both historic (Costa, 2000; Elman and Myers, 1997, 1999) and recent (Geronimus *et al.*, 2001; Hayward and Heron, 1999) U.S. census data to examine trends in health and health expectancy in the United States.

Vital Statistics and Administrative Records

The various registration systems constituting the total vital registration system for a country produce several sets of data directly or indirectly related to health, including data on births and deaths, and possibly fetal losses, induced terminations of pregnancy, the health conditions associated with these events, marriages, and divorces.

Administrative records may be maintained as a surveillance device for health conditions or use of health care services. Such records include *disease registries* and *health care utilization records*. State and provincial health departments, and public and private research organizations, often maintain files on communicable diseases and selected chronic conditions. For example, the U.S. National Cancer Institute supports a cancer registry, and the U.S. National Heart, Lung, and Blood Institute supports a pediatric cardiomyopathy registry. The latter is a national registry of children with different forms of cardiomyopathy and is designed to measure the relative frequency of the disease, to describe the survival experience of the patients, to advance knowledge of its causes, and to identify new diagnostic and therapeutic procedures (New England Research Institute, 1996).

Health care utilization records are usually maintained by the agencies that administer health programs. The Centers for Medicare and Medicaid Services (formerly the Health Care Financing Administration) in the United States maintains complete records of conditions reported for Medicare claims and State Departments of Health maintain records for Medicaid claims. The former is the program of national health insurance for the elderly, and the latter is the program of public medical care for the indigent.

General Sample Surveys and National Health Surveys

General sample surveys not specifically designed as health surveys, such as the Current Population Survey and the Survey of Income and Program Participation in the United States, occasionally carry questions on health, such as on work disability or functional status, to accompany the principal questions on labor force participation and income.

An increasing number of countries conduct periodic surveys specifically devoted to health. Examples of population-based health surveys are the National Health Interview Survey of the United States, the National Health Interview Survey in the Netherlands, the Göteborg Study in Sweden, and the Health Survey for England. These surveys secure their data by interviewing the general population, conducting actual physical tests, or reviewing medical records.

The U.S. Agency for International Development has funded a set of Demographic and Health Surveys (DHS) in less developed countries. ORC Macro conducts these surveys. Since 1985, more than 100 surveys have been conducted in Africa, Asia, the Near East, Latin America, and the Caribbean (see Table 14.1). Typically, a DHS is a nationally representative sample of between 5000 and 30,000 households, with a focus on women between the ages of 15 and 49. These surveys deal with subjects such as contraceptive practices, breast-feeding, lifetime reproductive behavior, HIV/AIDS and other sexually transmitted diseases (STDs), health characteristics of children (e.g., height, weight, immunization, diarrhea, fever), women's work history, and background information about the husband. These data are used to provide information and analyses of the state of health of women and children in less developed countries.

The World Health Organization, the United Nations, and U.S. National Institutes of Health have sponsored numerous health surveys in less developed countries. These surveys are cross-sectional, secure data by self-reports, and usually relate to specific diseases and the elderly.

Epidemiological Studies

Epidemiological studies are concerned with the distribution of diseases, injuries, and impairments in human populations and the possible risk factors associated with them. The goal is to identify the determinants of the diseases and to devise programs of disease prevention and control. Epidemiological studies are a principal tool of *community*

TABLE 14.1 Demographic and Health Surveys Conducted by Macro International, Inc., and National Agencies with Support of the U.S. Agency for International Development: 1985 to 2001

Continent and region	Number of countries	Number of surveys
All areas	66	118
Africa	35	60
Western Africa	12[1]	22
Middle Africa	4	5
Eastern Africa	14	24
Southern Africa	2	2
North Africa	3	7
Asia	18	30
West Asia	4	7
Central Asia	4	5
South Asia	5	9
Southeast Asia	5	9
Latin America and Caribbean	13	28
Caribbean	3	6
Central America[2]	4	6
South America[3]	6	16

[1] One from Ondo State, 1986.
[2] Includes Mexico, 1987.
[3] Includes Northeast Region of Brazil, 1991.
Source: ORC Macro, 2002.

or *population medicine*, which has the community as its primary object of concern.

There are several different types of epidemiological studies, each with many variants. In *case-control studies*, a group of patients with a disease under study is matched by a group of healthy persons (the controls) on the basis of a variety of criteria including age, sex, race, and socioeconomic characteristics. Such studies try to identify other characteristics that distinguish the two groups. In *longitudinal studies*, a group that does not have the particular disease is selected for the study of the disease; base data on demographic, socioeconomic, and health characteristics are secured; and the group is followed up to see who develops the disease being studied and to ascertain their distinguishing characteristics. When the same individuals are canvassed over time, the study is designated a *panel* study. When the same population is canvassed, the study is designated a *cohort* study. Some studies mix features of case-control studies and longitudinal studies.

In community studies, random samples of a population or population groups may be studied alone or as paired units (one being a control). Schools or even cities may be the population units sampled. The sample in one city may be subjected to the health program being tested, while the sample in another city is not. A sample of schools in a city may be divided into schools subject to the treatment program and those used as controls. Alternatively, all schools in a city may be included in a study, with a sample of students in each school subject to the program and another sample in that school carried as controls. In another variation, a single sample of the population may be followed longitudinally and examined before and after a health program is put into effect. In designing health surveys, the investigator should plan to inquire about a basic set of descriptive variables, such as age, sex, race, and socioeconomic status, and a more specialized set of variables relevant to the specific study.

Clinical Trials

The purpose of *clinical trials* is to evaluate the efficacy of a treatment protocol for humans compared with no treatment or an alternative treatment. Clinical trials accompany the practice of *clinical medicine*, which deals with the medical care of individuals. Clinical medicine contrasts with basic research in a laboratory on animals, and with community medicine, which as noted earlier, oversees the health of communities.

A clinical trial must be carefully controlled for the results to be valid. The method normally uses *double-blind randomized samples* to compare medical treatments. In this design, called *randomized clinical trials*, one experimental group receives the treatment being tested and another control group receives a placebo or dummy treatment, and neither the subjects nor the researchers know who is in the experimental group and who is in the control group.

One type of clinical trial, called an interventional trial with sequential design, in which the responses have a binary outcome, uses data for pairs of patients, each receiving one of the two treatments (e.g., drugs) being compared. Discordant pairs, where the treatment effect differs for the members of the pair, provide the basis for preferring one treatment to the other. In this methodology, a relatively small number of examinations of the data are made during the course of the trial and repeated significance testing is carried out. The investigator may discontinue the trial use of the treatment (i.e., a drug) or give it to all subjects if a sufficiently large difference is observed during the course of the trial.

Qualitative Sources

Quantitative methods provide most of the data and analytic information about health, but qualitative methods are used in a variety of ways to support quantitative research. Specifically, *qualitative methods* may be used to plan quantitative studies, either to develop the questionnaire or to develop hypotheses about the relevant factors, and to interpret the results of the quantitative analysis. Case studies and focus-group discussions represent two widely used qualitative methods employed in health studies.

Ethnographic research, another qualitative method, can be used to construct models of "regional" (i.e., geographic, ethnic, class) illnesses, including their symptoms and etiology, by gathering data about the terminology used for different conditions and about folk methods of prevention, diagnosis, and treatment. Measures of self-assessed health can be greatly improved by developing questionnaires and instructional material that take into account regional views as to good health, by educating health providers in the most accurate ways of reporting illness, and by educating individuals in the community about health matters (Obermeyer, 1996).

PROBLEMS WITH HEALTH DATA SOURCES

Census and Survey Data, Vital Statistics, and Administrative Records

Census data, as is true of all survey data, are subject to errors of coverage and errors of classification. The undercounting of certain groups, such as particular age groups, some racial minorities, economically disadvantaged persons, and certain types of households particularly affect census data. Similarly, vital statistics and administrative records may sometimes be seriously incomplete and inadequate in other ways, particularly in less developed countries. In deference to using inadequate records, other sources of data should be employed to measure health outcomes and services, or the sources should be adjusted, to the extent possible, to allow for statistical deficiencies.

Information gathered via survey methods, whether they are general, health, or epidemiological surveys, share a number of problems. The health-related information is gathered via self-reports, and the data may be biased for a number of reasons. These biases may vary for gender, race, education, social status, and the availability of health insurance. In addition, the data on health conditions are typically obtained via probes for the specific conditions, and some conditions may not be documented.

Another aspect of unreliable reporting by respondents, particularly persons with little education, is that they may give overly favorable reports of their current health status or may not recall previous health conditions accurately. More education is associated with greater awareness of health problems, higher utilization of health services, and, as a result, possibly higher reporting of morbidity. A problem common to all morbidity studies is the discrepancy between objective indicators of health and subjective reports. If a disease is not life threatening, it may be considered of little importance from a medical point of view but considered quite disabling by the individual in a self-assessment of health. Moreover, respondents tend to interpret their health status in relation to their own view of normal health and well-being. The respondent may be too accepting of pain and dysfunction, or the opposite.

These problems are particularly evident in the area of reproductive morbidity (discussed more fully later in this chapter). The problem of consistency between objective indicators and subjective reporting of health is aggravated by the gap between the understanding of illnesses in some non-Western countries and the biomedical categories of diseases. It is not uncommon for views of an illness in these countries and the biomedical categories for the illness to be at odds.

Missing reports present another problem in that such reports are not well represented by the actual reports received. Persons who do not report their health status are more likely to be suffering from a health condition, or a more severe health condition, than those who do report their condition, or to be disabled, or more severely disabled, than those who do report their condition. It is better, therefore, to use methods of imputing the missing data on the basis of sample follow-up studies and other data than to assume that the missing data are randomly distributed or distributed like the reported cases.

Multicollinearity (i.e., correlation of risk factors) may confound the results of analyses. If a factor is being tested and it is correlated with another factor that may truly be exerting a cause-effect influence, the effect may erroneously be attributed to the factor being tested. A study may be interpreted to show that eating green vegetables reduces the risk of heart disease, but people who eat green vegetables may also exercise regularly and be more health conscious. Hence, the cause of the reduction in heart disease may be eating green vegetables, exercising frequently, being health conscious, or all in combination.

Epidemiological Studies and Clinical Trials

Epidemiological studies have important limitations or potential limitations. They cannot definitively prove a cause-effect relation between so-called risk factors and the disease; at best, they show a probable cause-effect relation. Risk assessment in epidemiological studies is more likely to be valid if the association is strong (e.g., smoking and lung cancer) than when it is weak. Moreover, the sample may be biased and not representative of the universe from which it was drawn (e.g., based only on listed telephone subscribers) or may not represent the larger population (e.g., based only on adult white males).

The problem of *censoring* is usually present in epidemiological studies. It arises from the fact that the actual date of the onset of a health condition cannot be known, only the prior examination date and the date when the health condition was identified. For example, an epidemiological study may seek to identify risk factors for infection and the progression from infection to clinical disease. In HIV, the exact time of infection is not known, but it could be set as falling in the interval between the last negative blood test and the first positive blood test. The data for this period are described as interval censored, and the data for the infection time are described as left censored. Some subjects who will get the disease (AIDS) would not have been diagnosed with it at the time it occurred or at the time of the study; the data for them are right censored. Similarly, the period between the actual time of infection and the actual time of onset of disease, the latency period, cannot be fixed closely because neither the first date nor the last date is known. Data for the latency period are censored both on the left and the right, or doubly censored. It is often the case that a study does not run long enough to reveal the full effects of a factor on all participants (e.g., the effect of low consumption of calcium in the diet on osteoporosis).

Clinical trials have their limitations or potential limitations. In clinical trials, as in epidemiological studies, the sample is often limited to a particular segment of the population (e.g., middle-aged white males, nurses), and under these conditions, the results cannot safely be generalized to the whole population.

MEASURES OF HEALTH STATUS, FUNCTIONING, AND USE OF HEALTH SERVICES

Measures of Health Status

Measures of health may be based on either subjective information on health conditions or objective information. For example, the percentage of respondents assessing their health as poor, fair, good, or excellent is a commonly used subjective measure. However, many health measures are based on respondents' self-reports of actual health conditions, after a diagnosis by a health professional.

Prevalence Ratios and Incidence Rates

The measures differ also as to whether they refer to the health status of a population group at some date or to health events occurring to an exposed population over a year or similar period. The former are called measures of *prevalence*, and the latter are called measures of *incidence*.

When data are available, we can compute prevalence ratios for acute illnesses, chronic illnesses, injuries, or impairments, or these conditions can be incorporated into a general *prevalence ratio for acute conditions* (acute illnesses and injuries) and a general *prevalence ratio for chronic conditions* (chronic conditions and impairments). The prevalence ratio for an acute disease is the percentage of persons with the acute disease at a specific date. Table 14.2 shows prevalence ratios for two acute childhood conditions for most countries of sub-Saharan Africa for various years from 1991 to 2000. In addition to measures for the total population, measures for the noninstitutional population and the institutional population are often computed separately because of the difference in the sources of the data and the notably different levels of the measures.

Incidence rates for specific conditions may be computed as the number of persons incurring a particular health condition during a year, or the number of particular health conditions incurred during a year, per 100,000 persons. Incidence measures roughly parallel the various types of prevalence measures. The most common measures are the *incidence rate for acute illnesses*, either the number of persons incurring an acute illness during a year or the number of acute illnesses incurred during a year, per 100,000 persons, and the *incidence rate for chronic illnesses*, either the number of persons incurring a chronic illness during a year or the number of chronic illnesses incurred during a year, per 100,000 persons. Separate rates can be computed for acute illness, injury, chronic illness, and impairments. For example, we may compute the number of persons incurring an injury during a year, or the number of injuries in a year, per 100,000 persons. The latter measure is also labeled the number of episodes of injuries during a year per 100,000 persons. The incidence rate for an acute or chronic condition is calculated simply by

$$IR_C = (I_C \div P) * 100,000 \qquad (14.1)$$

where I_c represents the number of acute or chronic conditions occurring during the year and P the number of persons in the population. Table 14.3 shows incidence rates for several types of cancers for six countries in East Asia for 2000.

The *average duration of illness* refers to the period of time that a condition lasts. The relation between an incidence rate and a prevalence ratio for a given year may be represented roughly by

Prevalence ratio
$$\approx \text{incidence rate} * \text{average duration of illness} \qquad (14.2a)$$

Average duration of illness
$$\approx \text{prevalence ratio/incidence rate} \qquad (14.2b)$$

For example, if the incidence rate of an illness is 200 per 100,000 population and the prevalence ratio equals 1000 per 100,000 population, then the average duration of the illness is roughly 5 years. The precise relation is affected by the annual fluctuations in the incidence rate and by the survival rate of those who have incurred the condition—the case-fatality rate (explained below)—in the several years prior to the year of reference.

Age-Specific and Cause-Specific Prevalence Ratios and Incidence Rates

A type of cause-specific measure, the *case-fatality rate*, determines, on a cross-sectional basis, what proportion of persons having a disease or injury die from it during a year. It is the ratio per 100 of the deaths from the disease or injury during the year to the persons who have the disease or injury at the middle of the year:

TABLE 14.2 Prevalence Ratios for Two Infectious Conditions of Children Under Age 5 in Most Countries of Sub-Saharan Africa: Selected Years, 1991 to 2000 (Percentage of children under age 5 reported as having the health condition at the time of the survey.)

Country and year	Acute respiratory tract infection	Diarrhea
Benin, 1996	15.7	26.1
Botswana, 2000	38.5	6.5
Burkina Faso, 1999	13.5	20.0[1]
Cameroon, 2000	7.0	18.9[2]
Central African Republic, 1995	28.2	26.5[1]
Chad, 2000	12.5	31.2
Comoros, 2000	10.1	18.3
Cote d'Ivoire, 2000	3.7	20.1
Eritrea, 1995	23.0	23.6
Ethiopia, 2000	24.4	23.6
Gambia, 2000	7.7	21.5
Ghana, 1998	13.8	17.9
Guinea Bissau, 2000	10.1	31.5
Guinea, 1999	15.9	21.2
Kenya, 1998	20.1	17.1
Madagascar, 2000	10.5	12.8
Malawi, 1996	12.3	16.1
Mali, 1996	15.3	25.3
Mauritania, 1991	12.0	28.6[1]
Mozambique, 1997	11.8	20.7
Namibia, 1992	18.0	20.6
Niger, 2000	11.8	40.0
Nigeria, 1999	11.3	15.3
Rwanda, 1992	32.6	21.8
Senegal, 2000	6.6	21.3[1]
Sierra Leone, 2000	8.7	25.3
Tanzania, 1999	13.9	12.4
Togo, 1998	20.2	31.1
Uganda, 1995	27.1	23.5
Zambia, 1996	12.7	23.5
Zimbabwe, 1999	15.8	13.9

[1] For 1996.
[2] For 1998.

Note: The prevalence of acute respiratory tract infection and diarrhea often varies by season. Country surveys were administered at different times and, hence, the prevalence data are not fully comparable across countries.

Source: UNICEF, 2001.

TABLE 14.3 Incidence Rates for Specified Types of Cancer, by Sex, for Eastern Asian Countries:
2000 (Incidence rates represent the number of new cases of the health condition reported during
the year per 100,000 persons.)

Country and sex	Melanoma	Colon/Rectal	Stomach	Lung	Leukemia
Males					
China, People's Republic of	0.21	12.24	33.25	35.06	4.07
China, Hong Kong	1.16	43.01	23.95	91.62	6.80
Japan	0.63	77.74	124.63	76.78	7.75
Korea, Democratic People's Republic of	0.28	10.23	48.25	31.08	4.66
Korea, Republic of	0.33	13.01	61.09	40.32	4.92
Mongolia	0.45	2.47	22.54	16.63	3.16
Females					
China, People's Republic of	0.17	10.12	17.90	16.04	3.17
China, Hong Kong	1.06	39.48	14.16	46.07	5.16
Japan	0.49	54.06	58.66	27.17	5.20
Korea, Democratic People's Republic of	0.23	9.34	24.17	11.36	3.42
Korea, Republic of	0.26	11.48	29.33	13.91	3.56
Mongolia	0.38	2.11	15.30	7.16	3.27

Source: Ferlay *et al.*, 2001.

$$CFR = (D_c \div P_c) * 100 \qquad (14.3)$$

where D_c represents the number of deaths from the cause and P_c is the number of persons having the same health condition. A study of the "Global Burden of Tuberculosis" (Dye *et al.*, 1999) estimated the global case-fatality rate for tuberculosis as 23. However, the case-fatality rate exceeded 50 in African countries with high rates of HIV infection. This measure can be restructured in cohort form as the proportion of persons having a disease or injury at the beginning of a year who die from that disease or injury during the subsequent year. A reduction in the case-fatality rate of a disease or injury would tend to increase the prevalence of the disease, and this effect would also occur if there was an increase in the average duration of the condition. Such relations have important implications for the analysis of the relative costs of death and illness and hence the costs of a disease-prevention program.

All of these measures can be calculated for the entire population or a particular segment of it, such as an age group. Hence, we can calculate *age-cause-specific prevalence ratios* and *age-cause-specific incidence rates*:

$$_{cr}IR_{sa} = (_{cr}I_{sa} \div P_{sa}) * 100,000 \qquad (14.4)$$

where *IR* represents the incidence rate, *cr* is respiratory cancer, *sa* is the sex-age group, and *P* is the population. For example, the incidence rate for cancer of the respiratory system in 1999, for U.S. males aged 60 to 64, was 291.4 per 100,000 (NAACCR, 2001). Thus,

$$_{cr}IR_{m,60-64} = \{(7685 \div 2,637,268)\} * 100,000 = 291.4$$

Age-Adjusted Measures and Probabilities

Just as there are age-adjusted or age-standardized measures of mortality, there are *age-adjusted measures of*

morbidity. These are summary measures representing the weighted combination of age-specific ratios or rates of illness, injury, and impairment, employing common age distributions as weights for the populations being compared. We can calculate morbidity ratios and morbidity rates adjusted for age following the procedures given in Chapter 12.

Central age-specific rates may be converted to *probabilities of incurring an illness*, injury, or impairment during a year. For single ages,

$$_cIR_a^p = \{_cI_a \div (P_a + \tfrac{1}{2}D_a)\} * 100 \qquad (14.5a)$$

or, more exactly,

$$\{_cI_a \div (_{nc}P_a + \tfrac{1}{2}{}_{nc}D_a + \tfrac{1}{2}{}_cI_a)\} * 100 \qquad (14.5b)$$

where *c* and *nc* refer, respectively, to persons having the health condition and those not having it. Central age-specific measures may also be converted to *transition probabilities* for use in constructing tables of healthy life (see the discussion that follows). Such probabilities represent the proportion of the population in each health status at a given date that will be located in the same or another health status at some subsequent date (e.g., a year later) or die during the period.

Measures of Functioning

There are numerous measures of health that focus on what one cannot do or has difficulty doing because of health conditions. As noted previously, a health condition that limits functioning is termed a *disability*. Early measures of disability were based on questions about limitations in performing one's "major activity" due to health reasons in surveys such as the U.S. National Health Interview Survey and the Canadian Health Survey of 1978–1979. Such questions on activity limitation were used to determine long-term disability.

Numerous other measures of limitations are based on the concept of restricted activity or comorbidities. A selected list, with only limited explication, is given here:

- Number of days of restricted activity associated with acute conditions per 100 persons per year
- Average number of days of restricted activity per episode of acute condition in a year
- Number of days of restricted activity associated with chronic conditions per 100 persons with chronic conditions per year
- Average number of days of restricted activity associated with chronic conditions per chronic condition in a year

Other, more specific, measures of restricted activity are defined in terms of days of work-loss or school-loss and bed-disability days. A work-loss day or a school-loss day is a day on which one would have worked or attended school but did not do so for a whole day because of an illness or injury. A bed-disability day is one on which a person stays in bed for all or most of the day. Here are some measures based on these concepts:

- Days of bed disability associated with acute illness per 100 persons per year
- Days of bed disability associated with injury per 100 persons per year
- Days of bed disability associated with acute conditions (illnesses plus injuries) per 100 persons per year
- Days of work loss associated with acute conditions per 100 currently employed persons per year (restricted to persons 18 years and over)
- Days of bed disability associated with chronic conditions per 100 persons per year
- Days of work loss associated with chronic conditions per 100 currently employed persons per year (restricted to persons 18 years and over)

Multiple Measures of Functional Limitations

There has been a general shift away from measuring disability based on such general assessments of activity limitations. Clearly these questions are unsuitable for portions of the population that do not engage in a "major activity" such as an occupation (e.g., the unemployed, persons who have retired). More recent research has utilized specific *activities of daily living (ADLs)*, based on the work of Katz *et al.* (1983). The ADL items typically ask about the inability to carry out certain personal-care routines, such as eating, dressing, toileting, grooming, transferring into and out of bed, and bathing. Disability measures or scales may also include certain more complex routines associated with independent living, designated *instrumental activities of daily*

living (IADLs), such as using the telephone, going shopping, and handling one's own money. Sometimes, the level of disability is defined in terms of the number of ADLs and IADLs that an individual is unable to perform. Many other scales and measures of disability are found in the public health and gerontological literature (see, e.g., Kane and Kane, 2000; McDowell and McDowell, 1996; U.S. National Center for Health Statistics/Erickson *et al.*, 1995).

Disability Prevalence Ratios and Disability Incidence Rates

Distinguishing prevalence measures from incidence measures, we can compute *age-specific disability prevalence ratios* and *age-specific disability incidence rates*. The former are calculated as the percentage of the population in an age group with a disability. One type of such a measure is an *age-cause-specific disability prevalence ratio*, for example, the percentage of the population in an age group with a chronic disease (such as arthritis) that limits functioning. *Cause-specific disability prevalence ratios* may also be presented as age-adjusted ratios, as shown in Table 14.4.

The number of persons that incurred a disability in a year as a percentage of the midyear total population, or as a percentage of the midyear nondisabled population, is a *central disability incidence rate*, and is usually based on a first-time diagnosis of a specific condition that limits activity. The central rate for some age can be converted to a cohort rate or probability based on an assumption of rectangularity in the distribution of disablements during the year and within the age according to the formula:

TABLE 14.4 Age-Adjusted Prevalence Ratios of Activity Limitations Due to Chronic Conditions, for the United States: 1997 and 1998 (Percentage for age range indicated)

Chronic condition and sex	1997	1998
Arthritis (ages 18 years and older)		
Total	27	26
Female	31	30
Male	22	20
Chronic back conditions (ages 18 years and older)		
Total	32	30
Female	33	30
Male	31	29
Chronic lung and breathing problems (ages 45 years and older)		
Total	2.5	2.5
Female	2.4	2.3
Male	2.7	2.7

Note: Standard population = U.S. age distribution, 2000.
Source: U.S. National Center for Health Statistics, 2001b.

$$DiR^p = Di \div \left(P + \tfrac{1}{2} D\right) \qquad (14.6a)$$

or, more exactly,

$$Di \div \left(P_{nd} + \tfrac{1}{2} D_{nd} + \tfrac{1}{2} Di\right) \qquad (14.6b)$$

where all elements refer to specific age x, DiR^p represents the probability of incurring a disability during the year, Di disablements during the year, P_{nd} the midyear nondisabled population, and D_{nd} deaths of nondisabled persons during the year. The formula expresses the probability of a nondisabled person at exact age x becoming disabled between exact age x and exact age x+1 during a year.

Other Health-Related Measures

The concepts of *dependence* and *long-term care* relate to physical dependence on others for care. Long-term care is generally defined as the provision of health, personal care, and social services over time to individuals who have functional limitations. It encompasses home care, community services, and institutional care. Most persons in long-term care settings in the United States reside in nursing homes, although the rate of nursing home residency has been declining. Both prevalence and incidence measures can be calculated for these dependent statuses. For example, note the very different values for the "stock" (prevalence) and "flow" (incidence) measures of residence in nursing homes at ages 65 and over in the United States: At any given time, about 5% of the population 65 and over resides in nursing homes; in the course of a year, some 8% of the elderly population enter nursing homes; and over the course of their lives, 33 to 50% of the elderly will enter a nursing home.

Measures of Use of Health Services and Availability of Support

There are several commonly used measures of the use of health services that provide formal support to ill persons and of kinship networks that provide informal support to them:

- Number of physician visits per 100 persons in a year
- Number of dental visits per 100 persons in a year
- Number of hospital stays (discharges) per 100 persons in a year
- Percentage of persons aged 65 years and over who have living children
- Percentage of persons aged 50 years and over who have living parents 65 years and over
- Number of days of care delivered per week by caregivers per 100 dependent persons
- Average number of days of care delivered per week by each caregiver

MEASUREMENT OF REPRODUCTIVE HEALTH

Definition and Sources of Data

In the United Nations 1994 World Plan of Action, *reproductive health* is defined as "a state of complete physical, mental, and social well-being . . . in all matters relating to the reproductive system and to its functions and processes" (United Nations, 1994). Accordingly, reproductive health is concerned with the health correlates of reproductive events (i.e., conception, pregnancy, birth, and the postpartum period) and the ability to bear healthy children and avoid pregnancy loss, to regulate fertility, and to engage in satisfying sexual behavior without fear of disease or unwanted pregnancy. This definition goes well beyond the provision of family planning services. For example, it encompasses the measurement of sexuality, including the study of patterns of sexual behavior. These patterns are important in affecting the exposure to sexually transmitted diseases and reproductive tract infections, the choice of contraceptive methods, and other health aspects of reproductive events.

The organizations that have provided information about reproductive health include the World Health Organization (e.g., maternal mortality, social factors in contraceptive use), Family Health International (e.g., maternal mortality, reproductive morbidity, and sexually transmitted diseases), the International Women's Health Coalition (e.g., reproductive tract infections), ORC Macro (e.g., demographic and health surveys, obstetric morbidity in the Philippines), the London Maternal and Child Epidemiology Unit (e.g., various projects in less developed countries), and the Population Council (e.g., numerous community studies relating to reproductive health). The U.S. Agency for International Development funds some of these organizations in whole or in part.

Measuring reproductive health presents special problems because of the possible inconsistency between the results of different measures, the fact that many conditions can be asymptomatic or result from clandestine behavior, and the often frivolous view of reproductive conditions taken by the community and physicians (Obermeyer, 1996; Stewart *et al.*, 1996; WHO, 1989). The discrepancy between objective and subjective information is especially problematic for reproductive health.

Reproductive health is measured by a combination of self-reports, clinical examinations, and laboratory analyses. Respondents' perceptions of what is healthy and unhealthy affect the nature and consistency of the measures when a condition is reported. In fact, a "culture of silence" heavily influences the reporting of reproductive morbidity because women's problems are not viewed with much seriousness in many countries. Many of these conditions are not considered serious from a medical point of view, and women tolerate them as part of reproductive functioning. This is true even though these conditions do affect a woman's general functioning and can be measured by functional criteria. Because access to medical services is limited in many less developed countries (LDCs), many women are unaware that they really have a definite illness. For example, in many Islamic and Hindu communities, the practice of Purdah forbids women from being seen in a hospital or clinic unless the husband's permission is obtained.

Studies of reproductive morbidity can be hospital based or community based. However, most of the available studies on maternal mortality are hospital based, not community based, even though such studies do not give a representative description of the extent of maternal mortality in the community. Studies of reproductive morbidity in the community are almost rare in LDCs (Zurayk *et al.*, 1993).

Reproductive morbidity studies can deal with specific morbid conditions or a wide range of such conditions. Because of the special difficulties of interpreting the results of morbidity research, the research method and scope of each morbidity study need to be fully described in the analyst's report. This requirement is not usually met (WHO, 1989). The validation of indicators, such as by clinical examination, is rare although some studies do compare self-reports of health conditions and actual medical diagnoses (Zurayk *et al.*, 1993). The geographic focus is uneven, as is the focus on particular morbid conditions. Only a handful of countries have received attention (e.g., Nigeria, Ghana, Gambia, India, Singapore, and Bangladesh).

Morbidity studies involving interviews pose difficult problems of (1) how to design studies, (2) how to access the women respondents, (3) how to ask the appropriate questions, and (4) how to interpret the responses. For example, the role of the interviewer is critical. Whether the interviewer is a male or female, of the same or different social class, a physician or not, or a stranger or not can affect the quality of the data collected. Recall bias is a serious problem as well.

The risk factors for reproductive health include both proximate and contextual variables (Obermeyer, 1996). Some variables, such as age, parity, pregnancy history, use of health services, and medical history can be measured quantitatively with some precision. Other variables, such as the use of contraceptive methods, sexual practices, and practices relating to personal hygiene, are also quantifiable but are difficult to measure. Still others deal with perceptions, motivations, attitudes, and psychological contextual factors, such as religiosity, feelings of control, and interpretations of morbid conditions.

Maternal Health

Measures

Maternal mortality is conventionally measured by the maternal mortality ratio, representing the risk of a woman's dying from complications of pregnancy, childbirth, or the puerperium. According to the Tenth International Classification of Diseases, *maternal death* is the death of a woman "while pregnant, or within 42 days of termination of pregnancy, irrespective of the duration and the site of the pregnancy, from any cause related to or aggravated by the pregnancy or its management, but not from accidental or incidental causes" (*ICD-10*, Class XV, codes O00–O99). According to the ninth revision, maternal deaths are the sum of deaths due to abortion (code AM 42), direct obstetric causes (code AM 43), and indirect obstetric causes (code AM 44).

The WHO defines two other concepts related to maternal deaths, namely late maternal deaths and pregnancy-related deaths. As suggested, the WHO also distinguishes direct obstetric deaths from indirect obstetric deaths. A *late maternal death* is a death more than 42 days and less than 1 year after termination of pregnancy from any cause related to or aggravated by the pregnancy. *Direct obstetric deaths* result from obstetric complications of the pregnant state (pregnancy, labor, and puerperium), from interventions, omissions, incorrect treatment, or from a chain of events resulting from any of these causes. *Indirect obstetric deaths* are those resulting from previously existing disease or disease that develops during pregnancy, and are not due to direct obstetric causes but were aggravated by the physiological effect of pregnancy. A *pregnancy-related death* is a death of a woman while pregnant or within 42 days of the termination of pregnancy irrespective of the cause of death.

The *maternal mortality ratio* is now generally defined as the number of deaths due to puerperal causes per 100,000 births. The formula is

$$MMR_1 = (D^p \div B) * 100,000 \qquad (14.7)$$

where D^p represents deaths due to puerperal causes. Formerly, when maternal deaths were more numerous, a constant multiplier of 10,000 was commonly used, and it may be reasonably used today for groups of countries with relatively high maternal mortality.

The maternal mortality ratio varies widely. The WHO with UNICEF (WHO, 1996) published country-by-country estimates of maternal mortality ratios for 1990. The global estimate was 430 deaths per 100,000 births. The highest rates occurred primarily in the less developed regions. In terms of world regions, maternal deaths ranged from 11 per 100,000 births for North America to 1060 per 100,000 births in East Africa in 1990.

In the formula for estimating the maternal mortality ratio, the number of births is employed as an approximation to the number of women exposed to the risk of dying from puerperal causes. A refinement of the maternal mortality ratio, the *maternal mortality rate*, broadens the denominator to include late fetal losses and induced terminations of pregnancy:

$$MMR_2 = \{D^p \div (B + L^{lf} + A)\} * 100,000 \qquad (14.8)$$

where L^{lf} represents late fetal losses and A (induced) abortions.

Another measure, which reflects both the risk of death per pregnancy and the number of pregnancies, is the *lifetime risk of maternal death*. It is calculated by the formula

$$LRMD = 1 - (1 - MMR)^{1.2 TFR} \qquad (14.9)$$

where *MMR* is the maternal mortality ratio, which is expressed as a decimal, *TFR* is the total fertility rate (see Chapter 15), and *1.2* is a multiplier to adjust for pregnancies not ending in live births (Tinker and Koblinsky, 1993). As shown in Table 14.5, in 1988 the lifetime risk of maternal death for women in the more developed countries is about 1 in 150 whereas the risk for women in the less developed countries is about 1 in 50.

Among the factors important in the analysis of maternal mortality are the woman's age and parity. Rates are higher for very young women, high-parity women, older women, and women with short birth intervals. Underlying these demographic phenomena are such conditions as chronic disease and malnutrition, poverty, unwanted

TABLE 14.5   Lifetime Risk of Maternal Death, by Region and Subregion: 1988

Continent and region	Maternity mortality ratio, 1988 (1)	Total fertility rate, 1991 (2)	Lifetime risk 1 − [1 − (1)]^{1.2*(2)} = (3)
World	0.0037	3.4	0.015
More developed countries	0.0003	1.9	0.007
Less developed countries	0.0042	3.9	0.020
Africa	0.0063	6.1	0.045
North	0.0036	5.0	0.021
East	0.0068	6.8	0.054
Middle	0.0071	6.0	0.050
West	0.0076	6.4	0.057
South	0.0027	4.6	0.015
Asia	0.0038	3.9	0.018
East	0.0012	2.2	0.003
Southeast	0.0034	3.4	0.014
South	0.0057	4.4	0.030
West	0.0028	4.9	0.016
South America	0.0022	3.3	0.009
North America	0.0001	2.6	—
Europe	0.0002	1.7	—
Oceania	0.0060	2.6	0.019

Note: — Rounds to zero.

Source: Tinker and Koblinsky, 1993, Table 1.1. © 1993, The World Bank. Reprinted by permission.

pregnancies, inadequate prenatal and obstetric care, and lack of access to a hospital. In addition, there are the direct causes of maternal deaths—obstetric complications and unsafe abortions.

Measures of Pregnancy Losses

Much loss of potential life occurs because of losses during pregnancy, so-called *fetal mortality*. There is a close relation between fetal losses and neonatal mortality. Hence, we cover fetal losses and *perinatal mortality* (i.e., the combination of late fetal losses and early infant mortality) together in this section. According to the WHO (1992), as we may recall from Chapter 12, *neonatal deaths* are deaths among live births during the first 28 completed days of life. Those neonatal deaths occurring during the first seven completed days of life are designated *early neonatal deaths*; deaths during the remainder of the period (from the 8th day through the 28th day) are designated *late neonatal deaths*.

Pregnancy Losses and Fetal Losses

The WHO-recommended definition of fetal "death" complements the definition of (live) birth and death. In 1950 the World Health Organization recommended the following definition of fetal "death" for international use: "Death prior to the complete expulsion or extraction from its mother of a product of conception, irrespective of the duration of pregnancy; the death is indicated by the fact that after such separation, the fetus does not breathe or show any other evidence of life such as beating of the heart, pulsation of the umbilical cord, or definite movement of involuntary muscles" (U.S. National Office of Vital Statistics, 1950). The WHO maintained this recommendation in the tenth revision in 1992.

In some countries, however, the definition employed differs from the international recommendation: Live-born children dying early in life (e.g., before registration of birth or within 24 hours of birth) may be classed with fetal deaths. A more important problem is the incompleteness and irregularity of reporting of fetal deaths. This limitation applies to the data for most countries of the world. The duration of pregnancy required for registration varies widely. Reporting of early fetal deaths may be seriously incomplete even where required by law. When registration of only late fetal deaths (rather than all fetal deaths) is mandatory, countries differ as to what is to be registered as a late fetal death: 28 weeks of gestation is most frequently specified as the minimum period. On balance, international comparability is far greater for late fetal deaths than for all fetal deaths taken together (Casterline, 1989).

The World Health Organization has recommended the term *fetal deaths* as the generic term for all pregnancy losses. Accordingly, fetal deaths encompass those pregnancy losses known by other names, such as miscarriages, abortions, and stillbirths. Granting that there is an advantage in a general term for this class of events for statistical purposes, a preferred term is *pregnancy losses* rather than fetal deaths. A term is also needed for pregnancy losses excluding induced terminations of pregnancy—that is, for spontaneous terminations of pregnancy—and for this the term *fetal losses* is suggested. This is the usage of the U.S. National Center for Health Statistics. The term *abortion* may be used in its restricted sense for induced terminations of pregnancy. The main reason for replacing the term fetal deaths with the terms pregnancy losses and fetal losses is that in the UN statistical system, "death" can occur only after a live birth. In addition, a general term is needed for all losses during pregnancy, and a restricted term is needed for losses that exclude (induced) abortions.

The WHO also recommended that "fetal deaths" should be distinguished by length of gestation period as early (less than 20 completed weeks of gestation), intermediate (20 completed weeks but less than 28), and late (28 completed weeks and over). Gestational ages reported in months should be allocated to the corresponding interval in weeks. The determination of age is often difficult, and comparability of the tabulations is affected by the difference in the skill of the medical attendant in making this determination. Even the data on late fetal losses are subject to substantial error introduced by incorrect reporting of gestational age. In view of the very poor reporting of early fetal losses and the variation from one reporting jurisdiction to another of the minimum period for which fetal loss reporting is required, fetal loss rates in official sources are normally limited to fetal losses with 20 weeks or more, or 28 weeks or more, of gestation. Where the gestation period is not stated, as is often the case, some assumption has to be made regarding the period of gestation. The World Health Organization classifies these "unstated" cases in a fourth class.

In the United States, a separate U.S. Standard Report of Stillbirth (later Fetal Death) was introduced in 1939, although state vital statistics laws dictate the exact form and content of the certificates used for each state. Reporting is required for fetal losses of 20 weeks or more in all reporting areas (with some variation by birth weight) but several states require reporting of all fetal losses. Where reporting is required only for fetal losses of 20 weeks or more, the U.S. National Center for Health Statistics assigns "unstated" cases to the period 20 weeks or more (U.S. National Center for Health Statistics, 1991, pp. 14–15).

Fetal losses may be measured by the fetal loss ratio or the fetal loss rate. The *fetal loss ratio* is defined as the number of fetal losses reported in a year per 1000 live births in the same year, or

$$FLR = \left(L^{lf} \div B\right) * 1000 \qquad (14.10)$$

where L^{lf} represents all fetal losses or late fetal losses. Because of the variability of coverage of the early and intermediate fetal losses mentioned earlier, it is preferable from the point of international comparability to compute the fetal loss ratio on the basis of late fetal losses only. The same data required to compute the fetal loss ratio can be used to compute the more precise *fetal loss rate*. The fetal loss rate relates fetal losses more closely to the population at risk than the fetal loss ratio. The formula includes the fetal losses in the denominator as well as in the numerator:

$$FLR^p = \left\{L^{lf} \div \left(B + L^{lf}\right)\right\} * 1000 \qquad (14.11)$$

For the reason stated, this measure also should best be calculated with late fetal losses only. In this case, the denominator represents pregnancies carried to term or nearly carried to term. Late fetal loss ratios and late fetal loss rates for a number of countries are presented in Table 14.6.

In spite of the theoretical advantage of the fetal loss rate, the fetal loss ratio may be considered preferable for international comparisons. The registration of fetal losses is irregular, and the effect of this irregularity is compounded when fetal losses are included with the births in the base of the fetal loss rate. Because of the likelihood that poor registration of fetal losses will occur in association with poor registration of births and, hence, that the errors in each component will offset one another to some extent, fetal loss ratios may sometimes be of satisfactory quality even where the basic data are questionable.

Specific fetal loss ratios and fetal loss rates may be calculated in terms of the period of gestation of the fetus or in terms of the age of mother (requiring data on the date of termination of pregnancy for fetal losses and on the age of mother for births, respectively). Other characteristics of importance in the analysis of fetal losses are marital status of mother (distinguishing marital from nonmarital pregnancies), sex of the fetus, total birth order (counting live births

TABLE 14.6 Fetal Loss Ratios and Fetal Loss Rates, for Selected Countries: 1991

Country	Fetal losses (1)	Births (2)	Ratio [(1) / (2)] × 1000 = (3)	Rate [(1) / [(2) + (1)]] × 1000 = (4)
Cuba	1,891	173,896	10.87	10.76
Chile	1,754	299,456	5.86	5.82
Italy	2,887	562,787	5.13	5.10
Japan	4,376	1,223,245	3.58	3.56
Australia	1,150	257,247	4.47	4.45
Tunisia	2,116	207,455	10.20	10.10
Spain	1,564	395,989	3.95	3.93

Source: United Nations, 1995, Tables 9 and 12.

plus fetal losses and abortions), birth weight, and plurality of fetus. Other factors include the cause of fetal loss, hospitalization, age of father, date of marriage (for marital pregnancies), level of education of parents, and the occupational characteristics of the parents.

Pregnancy losses include so-called *abortions*. The latter term is not commonly used in international statistical compilations because it tends to have legal, programmatic, and ethical implications that are not desirable in a statistical concept. In theory, the term encompasses both *spontaneous* and *induced terminations of pregnancy*. Spontaneous abortions, or spontaneous terminations of pregnancy, correspond roughly to what in popular usage are designated as miscarriages. Stillbirth is another popular as well as legal term for spontaneous abortions, usually those with longer periods of gestation. Its legal definition varies according to the particular political jurisdiction. Spontaneous abortions are far more common than induced abortions (James, 1970). Induced abortions may be legal or illegal depending on the laws of the particular jurisdiction. In practice, the term "abortion" is usually limited to induced abortions, which may be defined as induced terminations of pregnancy before the fetus has became capable of surviving, with appropriate support, to the neonatal period and eventually maintaining an independent life outside the uterus of the mother (WHO, 1970).

Information on abortions comes from the official statistics of countries where abortion has been made legal although the data may be compiled by private organizations, as in the United States. The data may come from hospital records or survey responses. In 1970, the U.S. National Center for Health Statistics began to separate reports of (induced) abortions from other fetal losses. To improve comparability of data on (induced) abortions, they have to be purged of reports of spontaneous abortions. There are no reliable statistics on illegal abortions.

There are several measures of abortions (i.e., legal induced terminations of pregnancy) in common use. They parallel those for fetal losses defined in the narrower sense given here. The *general abortion rate* can be defined as the number of legal, induced pregnancy terminations in a calendar year per 1000 women 15 to 44 or 15 to 49 at midyear. The age range of the women may be selected to allow for their ages at the time of the pregnancy termination.

The *abortion ratio* is the number of legal, induced pregnancy terminations in a year per 1000 births, or alternatively, terminations in a calendar year per 1000 births in the year from July 1 of the year to June 30 of the following year. The *abortion rate* (approximating a probability of abortion) is the number of legal, induced pregnancy terminations in a year per 1000 births, late fetal losses, and legal, induced pregnancy terminations. The births are taken from July 1 of the year to June 30 of the following year to match the time of conception with the time of abortion. The restriction to

legal, induced abortions and late fetal losses is intended to lend stability and comparability to the measures by excluding the inadequately recorded illegal abortions and early and intermediate fetal losses. Analysis of these measures employs such variables as the woman's age, total number of prior births, and the marital status of the woman.

With appropriate adjustments in the data, it is possible to develop an estimate of the pregnancies exposed to the risk of abortion during a year. Total pregnancies may be represented by the sum of births, abortions, and fetal losses. A *general pregnancy rate*, and a set of consistent, albeit approximate, rates for these components may be calculated as the number for each of them in a year per 1000 women 15–44 years of age at the middle of the year. For example, in the United States in 1997, the general pregnancy rate was 103.7, the general fertility rate was 65.0, the general abortion rate was 22.2, and the general fetal loss rate was 16.5 (U.S. National Center for Health Statistics/Ventura *et al.*, 2001c). A more exact general pregnancy rate for a given year may be calculated by employing births from July 1 of the year to July 1 of the following year. The number of pregnant women at a particular date can be estimated by summing births in the following 9 months, abortions in the next 6 months, and fetal losses of 20 weeks or more in the next 20 weeks.

Perinatal Mortality

The causes of death in early infancy are believed to be so akin to those accounting for fetal losses that various measures combining fetal losses and deaths of early infancy have been devised. The combination of these events is also intended to eliminate the errors resulting from deliberate and inadvertent misclassification among fetal losses, births, and neonatal deaths. The combined risk of dying during the period near parturition (i.e., just before, during, and after birth) is measured by various so-called perinatal death ratios and perinatal mortality rates. The formulas differ with respect to the age limits of the infant deaths and the gestational age of fetal losses to be included, and with respect to whether fetal losses are included in or excluded from the base of the measures. Neonatal deaths, deaths under 1 week, and deaths under 3 days, in combination with intermediate and late fetal losses, or with late fetal losses only, are possible ways of operationally defining perinatal deaths. In view of the general lack of tabulated data on infant deaths under 3 days, the use of this period is not very useful for international comparisons.

The World Health Organization defines the *perinatal period* as the period of prenatal existence after viability of the fetus is reached, the duration of labor, and the early part of extra-uterine life. The WHO recommends in *ICD-9* that "countries should present, solely for international comparisons, 'standard perinatal statistics' in which the numerator

TABLE 14.7 Perinatal Death Ratios and Perinatal Death Rates, for Selected Countries: Various
Years: 1991 to 1994

Country, year	Late fetal losses[1] (1)	Deaths under 1 week (2)	Births (3)	Ratio $PDR_a = \{[(1) + (2)] / (3)\} \times 1000 =$ (4)	Rate $PDR_a^p = \{[(1) + (2)] / [(3) + (1)]\} \times 1000 =$ (5)
Cuba, 1991	1,891	811	173,896	15.54	15.37
Chile, 1994	1,321	1,496	288,175	9.78	9.73
Italy, 1992	2,546	2,350	567,841	8.62	8.58
Japan, 1994	4,048	2,086	1,238,328	4.95	4.94
Australia, 1994	898	830	258,051	6.70	6.67
Spain, 1991	1,564	1,314	395,989	7.27	7.24

[1] Fetal losses of 28 weeks or more of gestational age.
Source: United Nations, 1995, Tables 9 and 12.

and denominator of all rates are restricted to fetuses and infants weighing 1000 grams or more or, where birth weight is unavailable, [having] the corresponding gestational age (28 weeks) or body length (35 cm crown-heel)" (United Nations, 1994, p. 27; WHO, 1992). According to the tenth revision, the perinatal period commences at 22 completed weeks (154 days) of gestation (the time when birth weight is normally 500 grams) and ends at seven completed days after birth.

Because birth weight and gestational age are not recorded on the death certificate in the United States, the National Center for Health Statistics was unable to adopt these definitions. The NCHS uses three definitions, designated I, II, and III. In definition I, the one generally used for international comparisons, the lower "age" limit of fetal loss is taken as 28 completed weeks of gestation and the early part of extra-uterine life is taken to be the first 7 days of life. The corresponding formula for the *perinatal death ratio* is, then, the number of deaths under 1 week of age and late fetal losses per 1000 live births in a year:

$$PDR_a = \{(D^z + L^{lf}) \div B\} * 1000 \qquad (14.12)$$

where D^z represents deaths less than 1 week, L^{lf} represents late fetal losses, and B represents births. The formula under definition III is the number of infant deaths under 1 week and fetal losses of 20 weeks' gestation or more per 1000 live births in a year:

$$PDR_b = \{(D^z + L^{lf}) \div B\} * 1000 \qquad (14.13)$$

where L^{lf} represents fetal losses of 20 weeks gestation or more.

The corresponding *perinatal mortality rate* differs by including late fetal losses, or intermediate and late fetal losses, in the base of the ratio, thus approximating a probability more closely. Specifically, the perinatal mortality rate is defined as

$$PDR_a^p = \{(D^z + L^{lf}) \div (B + L^{lf})\} * 1000 \qquad (14.14)$$

or

$$PDR_b^p = \{(D^z + L^{lf}) \div (B + L^{lf})\} * 1000 \qquad (14.15)$$

where the symbols have the same meaning as in formulas PDR_a and PDR_b in the previous equations. These two measures give essentially the same indications of international differences, as can be noted in Table 14.7. The perinatal mortality rate has a small theoretical advantage over the perinatal death ratio, but the perinatal death ratio is probably more stable for international comparisons.

Other measures of perinatal mortality have been proposed. The *feto-infant mortality rate* is one such measure and it was proposed by the International Collaborative Effort on Perinatal and Infant Mortality. It extends the concept of perinatal mortality to include the entire infant period and includes fetal losses of 28 or more weeks of gestation in both the numerator and denominator of the rate. The feto-infant mortality rate has two advantages over the traditional infant mortality rates. First, it eliminates the problem of having to make the distinction between a fetal "death" and a birth, a problem that has made international comparisons difficult. Second, it is a more encompassing measure of pregnancy performance (U.S. National Center for Health Statistics/ Hartford, 1992).

Contraception

Effectiveness of contraception may be considered in three dimensions: clinical effectiveness, use effectiveness, and demographic effectiveness. *Clinical effectiveness* refers to the effectiveness of a contraceptive method under ideal conditions (i.e., when the method is used consistently and as instructed). *Use effectiveness* refers to the actual experience of couples using a method in terms of periods of protection provided. *Demographic effectiveness* refers to the effect on population growth of the use of the method in terms of births averted. Demographic effectiveness is more difficult to measure than use effectiveness. A contraceptive averts births by delaying conception when a woman is in a

TABLE 14.8   Prevalence Ratios of Contraceptive Use for Women of Reproductive
Age, by Age, for Selected Countries of Sub-Saharan Africa: Various Years:
1986 to 1999 (Percentage of women in age group)

Country, year	Age groups (years)						
	15–19	20–24	25–29	30–34	35–39	40–44	45–49
Benin, 1996	9.4	18.6	16.8	17.1	19.0	16.7	10.9
Botswana, 1988	17.2	25.8	37.1	35.6	38.3	36.1	16.7
Burkina Faso, 1998–1999	0.9	12.9	12.6	15.4	13.6	10.0	5.1
Cote d'Ivoire, 1998–1999	10.7	13.9	18.4	15.6	13.1	21.5	8.3
Ghana, 1998	19.7	21.0	22.3	24.8	26.6	19.4	15.9
Guinea, 1992	0.7	0.8	1.5	2.3	3.3	1.8	1.0
Kenya, 1998	18.0	31.2	40.1	45.6	47.2	44.3	31.1
Madagascar, 1997	5.6	16.0	19.3	21.7	22.9	19.7	12.6
Malawi, 1996	10.7	22.7	18.1	26.0	28.4	24.2	20.9
Mali, 1995–1996	4.6	5.9	6.1	9.1	8.2	8.1	3.3
Mozambique, 1997	0.7	4.3	5.4	6.2	9.4	7.9	7.6
Niger, 1998	6.1	9.8	9.4	10.3	9.0	6.3	2.4
Nigeria, 1990	1.3	5.1	6.0	6.5	8.7	8.4	4.6
Senegal, 1997	5.5	9.1	13.0	15.4	17.3	16.5	9.5
Tanzania, 1999	8.8	26.7	25.9	25.0	27.2	29.6	16.4
Togo, 1998	15.0	23.6	24.3	26.4	22.2	27.2	17.7
Uganda, 1995	9.9	12.2	13.4	20.7	18.6	17.6	16.0
Zambia, 1996	16.9	24.6	28.3	27.9	31.2	30.0	17.8
Zimbabwe, 1999	42.1	53.7	60.9	58.2	56.8	46.4	39.4

Source: U.S. Bureau of the Census, 2001.

fecundable condition. Basically, fecundability refers to the ability to conceive. Some fecundable women are infecund and, therefore, infertile; they are able to conceive but physiologically cannot complete a pregnancy. The term *fecundability* has adopted a specific meaning, however, as the probability of conceiving during a month for cohabiting women who are not pregnant, sterile, or infecundable.

Measures of Contraceptive Practice

Both measures of prevalence and measures of incidence figure among the many measures of contraceptive practice. The more commonly used measures are noted, and then we call attention to the use of multiple-decrement life tables for this purpose. Several measures of prevalence are based on the number of patients served annually by the national family planning program (i.e., covering all family planning clinics in a country). The percentage of women of reproductive age (15 to 44) practicing contraception is one such measure. It is often calculated for specific groups such as age groups or marital groups. For example, data on the age-specific prevalence of current contraceptive use by women in selected sub-Saharan African countries for various years from 1986 to 1999 are given in Table 14.8, using data from the Demographic and Health Surveys. For women aged 15 to 19 years, several countries show a current

use of 1% or less and only 8 of 20 countries show a figure of 10% or more.

A related group of measures gives the percentage of women of reproductive age (15 to 44) using various contraceptive methods. Table 14.9 shows the prevalence of contraceptive use according to method for selected Latin American countries for various years from 1991 to 1999. Measures of contraceptive use classified by type are often also made specific for age and marital groups. More specific measures may distinguish the potential demand for contraception, the demand that is satisfied, and the unmet need (Goliber, 1997; Westoff and Bankole, 1995).

Contraceptive acceptance rates and contraceptive termination rates are types of incidence rates. These are the basic rates needed for the construction of multiple-decrement life tables designed to measure use effectiveness and demographic effectiveness of contraception. The life tables yield, among other measures, continuation ratios—that is, the proportion of acceptors who continue to use a contraceptive method for a given period after acceptance. A multiple-decrement table designed to measure the effectiveness of intrauterine devices would be constructed on the basis of rates of devices lost (from pregnancies, expulsions, and removals) by months since insertion. The table would provide figures for the cumulative proportions retaining the devices.

TABLE 14.9 Prevalence Ratios of Contraceptive Use by Women of Reproductive Age, 15 to 49 Years, by Method for Selected Latin American Countries: Various Years: 1991 to 1999 (Percentage of women 15–49 years of age)

Country, year	No method	Any method[1]	Pill	IUD	Sterilization		Condom	Other modern	Traditional
					Total	Female			
Belize, 1991	53.3	46.7	14.9	1.9	NA	18.7	1.9	6.7	2.5
Bolivia, 1998	51.7	48.3	3.8	11.1	NA	6.5	2.6	1.1	23.1
Brazil, 1996	23.3	76.7	20.7	1.1	42.7	40.1	4.4	1.3	6.4
Columbia, 1995	27.8	72.2	12.9	11.1	26.4	25.7	4.3	4.6	12.9
Costa Rica, 1992–1993	25.0	75.0	18.0	9.0	21.0	20.0	16.0	1.0	10.0
Ecuador, 1994	43.2	56.8	10.2	11.8	NA	19.8	2.6	1.6	10.8
El Salvador, 1998	40.2	59.8	8.1	1.5	NA	32.5	2.6	9.6	5.6
Guatemala, 1998–1999	61.8	38.2	5.0	2.2	17.5	16.7	2.3	3.9	7.3
Honduras, 1987	59.4	40.6	13.4	4.3	12.8	12.6	1.8	0.6	7.6
Mexico, 1995	33.0	67.0	8.0	15.0	27.0	NA	4.0	4.0	9.0
Nicaragua, 1998	39.7	60.3	13.9	9.1	26.6	26.1	2.6	5.2	2.5
Paraguay, 1998	37.7	62.1	13.1	11.1	NA	8.0	7.3	8.0	14.6
Peru, 1996	35.8	64.2	6.2	12.0	9.7	9.5	4.4	9.0	22.9

Note: NA: Not available.
[1] Excludes percentage for female sterilization where figures are given for both sexes.
Source: U.S. Bureau of the Census, 2001.

MEASURES LINKING MORTALITY AND MORBIDITY

The Relation between Changes in Mortality and Changes in Morbidity

After the turn of the 20th century in the more developed countries, and after World War II in the less developed countries, there has been a pronounced shift in the pattern of the causes of morbidity, as with the causes of mortality, from a predominance of acute, infectious, and parasitic diseases to a predominance of chronic, endogenous, accident-related, and self-imposed conditions (Olshansky *et al.*, 1997). The category *endogenous diseases* includes such diseases as cardiovascular diseases, cancer, diabetes, kidney diseases, arthritis and rheumatism, emphysema, and certain diseases of early infancy. However, the exact scope of endogenous diseases is arbitrary, particularly with respect to the inclusion or exclusion of respiratory illnesses.

The change in the pattern of morbidity has been termed the *epidemiologic transition* (Omran, 1971, 1977). Epidemiologic transition theory has directed attention to the shifts in disease patterns and causes of mortality, and the resulting impacts on life expectation and population growth. A major premise of epidemiologic transition theory is that mortality is the fundamental factor in population dynamics.

Measurement of the relation between changes in morbidity and changes in mortality is complex, partly because the relation varies over the age scale, over time, and between birth cohorts. The initial assumptions regarding mortality and morbidity trends have been that the two were closely related and therefore followed close trajectories over time.

Thus, if mortality declines, then morbidity also declines. Alter and Riley (1989; Riley and Alter, 1996) have demonstrated, using historical data sources, that morbidity levels tended to rise after mortality declines, rather than the reverse. This does not reflect increases in incidence, but rather improvements in case fatality rates and rising prevalence levels.

As countries progress through the later stages of the epidemiologic transition, the traditional indicators of population health, based on mortality rates alone, are expected to change little. Therefore, the incidence, prevalence, and duration of morbid conditions, case-fatality rates, and the disabling effects of morbid conditions are increasingly important concerns in the examination of population health. Various scholars, including some at the World Health Organization, have graphically modeled the relation between mortality, disability, and morbidity survival curves. A generalized diagram of these relations over the age scale is shown in Figure 14.1 (WHO, 1984). Much of the analysis of the relation between mortality and disability or morbidity in recent years has been carried out in terms of tables of active or healthy life. We turn next to a discussion of this measurement tool.

Measurement of Active (Healthy, Independent) Life Expectancy

Tables of *active (healthy, independent) life* can be constructed to elucidate the relation between morbidity and mortality quantitatively. A method for estimating active life expectancy was outlined by Sullivan (1971). The so-called Sullivan method employs age-specific prevalence ratios of

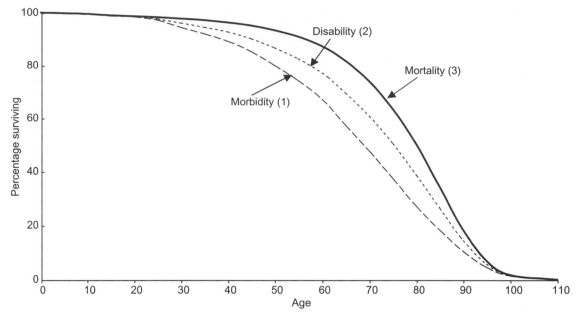

FIGURE 14.1 Stylized Representation of the Relation between the Age Curves for Morbidity, Disability, and Mortality (Percentage of the initial birth cohort who survive to the indicated ages (1) without a (chronic) disease or (major) disability, (2) without a (major) disability but with at least one (chronic) disease, or (3) with at least one (major) disability resulting from at least one (chronic) disease at the higher ages.)

disability (i.e., the percentages of persons in each age interval who are disabled) and current basic life tables to produce estimates of active life expectancy. In most cases, the age-specific disability ratios are derived from sample surveys.

The disability prevalence ratios are used to calculate the person-years of life lived in health (i.e., nondisabled condition) for the age intervals using the L_x life table function (see Chapter 13 for a more detailed explanation of the life table functions):

$$L_{x(hs)} = (1 - DPR) * L_x \qquad (14.16)$$

where healthy status is denoted by hs and DPR is the age-specific disability prevalence ratio. The person-years of health for each age interval ($L_{x(hs)}$) are summed from age x forward to the end of the table to obtain the total person-years that are healthy, or active (i.e., nondisabled), life:

$$T_{x(hs)} = {}^{\infty}\sum_{x=a} L_{[x(hs)=a]} \qquad (14.17)$$

The healthy, or active, life expectancy values are obtained by dividing total healthy person-years at each age by the l_x value at that age from the basic life table:

$$e_{x(hs)} = T_{x(hs)} \div l_x \qquad (14.18)$$

The prevalence-ratio method of life table construction has serious limitations. In particular, it does not allow for a transition from disabled status to nondisabled status. The prevalence-ratio method may be considered as following the model of double-decrement tables in that two factors operate to reduce the original cohort, death and dependency, but the probabilities of becoming dependent and of dying are only

implicit or derivable indirectly. Thus, the estimates are only a rough reflection of the health levels of a population at a particular time (Crimmins, Saito, and Hayward, 1993).

Multistate Method

With the availability of several sample health surveys providing longitudinal data on changes in health status and the development of new techniques of life table construction, analysts began to employ the multiple-decrement method and its logical extension, the increment-decrement method, and the multistate method. Tables constructed by the first method explicitly measure the shift from independence to dependence and from these states to death, but they fail to make an explicit allowance for returns to independence (Katz *et al.*, 1983). Tables constructed by the second method have the advantage that the model explicitly measures the shift from dependence to independence as well as from independence to dependence, but the disadvantage is that this can be done only on a net basis within each age group. That is to say, shifts in both directions cannot be measured for the same age span.

Further advances in mathematical demography led to the application of the more flexible multistate life table model to measure changes in health status (Rogers, Rogers, and Branch, 1989; Rogers, Rogers, and Belanger, 1989, 1990). The multistate model permits two or more radices (i.e., multiple starting states—e.g., the initially independent population and the initially dependent population) and follows these populations as they age, shift to a dependent status, return to an independent status, and die. The multistate model can be used to analyze changes in degrees of health (e.g., no functioning problems, some functioning problems, unable to manage independent living, and unable to manage personal care) within each age group and over the age scale (see, e.g., Crimmins, Hayward, and Saito, 1994, 1996; Land, Guralnik, and Blazer, 1994; Rogers, Rogers, and Balanger, 1989). Thus, the multistate model can deal with multiple exits from and entries to the same state within each age interval. Moreover, it can handle the use of separate age schedules of mortality for each health status rather than a single average level of mortality.

The results on expectation of healthy years from prevalence-ratio tables, multiple increment-decrement tables, and multistate tables are not comparable because of differences in the data, methods, and assumptions employed (Rogers *et al.*, 1990). While the results from the multistate tables are viewed as more realistic and valid, the data on mortality and health transitions may be unstable because of the smaller number of incidence cases than prevalence cases and the greater disaggregation of the data. Hence, even the estimates of healthy life expectancy at particular dates from multistate tables should be viewed with caution.

The basic data for the construction of a table of active, healthy, or disability-free life come from longitudinal (panel) health surveys providing observations of the health status of a person at two or more points in time (e.g., a year apart). A single health survey inquiring about current and prior health status could provide the data, but the retrospective reports would patently be less accurate than current reports. In the United States, the list of recent national health surveys include the Longitudinal Study of Aging (LSOA), the National Long Term Care Survey (NLTCS), the Health and Retirement Study (HRS), and the Established Populations for Epidemiologic Studies of the Elderly (EPESE). In addition to providing the health data, these surveys provide the basis for measuring differential mortality according to health status. Inasmuch as the sample sizes may be quite small for some groups, the observed mortality rates may be quite irregular and considerable smoothing of the rates may be necessary before constructing life tables. The results must also be evaluated for the possible effect of losses to the sample between waves that differ according to health status.

Multistate tables of disability-free or healthy life can be constructed in several ways. Only a few approaches are mentioned here, without attempting a full exposition of this complex subject. A more detailed presentation of a method for developing a multistate life table is given in Chapter 13, "The Life Table." The order and form of the computations given here may differ somewhat from those described in Chapter 13. Because of the number and complexity of the calculations, the construction of multistate life tables is normally carried out with matrix operations by computer.

A basic step in the construction of a multistate table of active life is the determination of the health transitions according to age between survey dates, such as from an independent state to a dependent state or from a dependent state to an independent state. The observed transition rates from state i to state j in the age interval x to $x+n$ can be in the form of central transfer rates (M_x) (i.e., the ratio of transfers to the midperiod population). Because of irregularities in their age pattern, the rates may require smoothing. A log-linear regression equation may be used for this purpose (Crimmins, Hayward, and Saito, 1994; Rogers, Rogers, and Belanger, 1990):

$$M_x = e^{(\alpha + \beta x)} \qquad (14.19)$$

This model assumes that the transition process depends only on age, but if the transition rates do not vary by age, a different equation may have to be used for smoothing. If there are only two origin states and two destination states (excluding death), two regression equations have to be solved for two sets of coefficients. With three origin and destination states (excluding death), four regression equations have to be solved for four sets of coefficients.

The smoothed central transfer rates, represented in matrix form by $\mathbf{M}(x,n)$, next have to be converted to a transition probability matrix, $\mathbf{P}(x,n)$. The elements in this matrix, $^iP_x^j$, represent the probability that a person at exact age x and in state i at the beginning of an interval will be in state j at the end of the interval (e.g., 1 year later) at exact age $x + n$. The following numerical approximation has been proposed for this conversion (Crimmins *et al.*, 1994; Rogers and Ledent, 1976; Schoen, 1988, P. 70; Willikens *et al.*, 1982):

$$\mathbf{P}(x,n) = [\mathbf{I} + n/2\, \mathbf{M}(x,n)]^{-1} [\mathbf{I} - n/2\, \mathbf{M}(x,n)] \qquad (14.20)$$

where $\mathbf{P}(x,n)$ is the transition-probability matrix, $\mathbf{M}(x,n)$ is the matrix of transition rates, and $\mathbf{I}$ is the identity matrix.

In the simplest situation relating to the multistate analysis of health status, there are two origin states and three destination states, including death, representing three states, four possible transitions across states, and six transitions in total, including "transitions" from a state to the same state, as indicated by the following paradigm:

Transition probabilities

State of origin, exact age x	State of destination, exact age x+1			
	Independent life (a)	Dependent life (i)	Death (d)	Total
Independent life (a)	X	X	X	1.000
Dependent life (i)	X	X	X	1.000

The survivors at exact age x and the person-years lived between exact age x and exact age $x + 1$ (or $x + n$), in each health state, may be calculated by the matrix formulas:

$$\mathbf{l}(x+n) = \mathbf{l}(x) * \mathbf{P}(x, n) \qquad (14.21)$$

$$L(x, n) = n/2 \left[l(x) + l(x + n) \right] \qquad (14.22)$$

The second equation assumes that $l(x)$ changes linearly within the interval and that the transfers are distributed rectangularly in the interval. An element in the matrix $l(x+n)$ is ${}^{ij}l(x+n)$ and an element in the matrix $L(x,n)$ is $L^j(x, x+n)$.

We can obtain the absolute number of life table transfers between health states of each type, $D(x,n)$, by the formula

$$D(x, n) = L(x, n) * M(x, n) \qquad (14.23)$$

Finally, the expectation of life for each health state at each exact age may be derived by the usual formulas. For example,

$$e^i(x) = T^i(x) \div l(x) \qquad (14.24)$$

$$\text{or} \quad {}^i e^i(x) = T^i(x) \div {}^i l(x) \qquad (14.25)$$

$$\text{or} \quad {}^a e^i(x) = T^i(x) \div {}^a l(x) \qquad (14.26)$$

where T^i_x is the number of person-years lived in state i beyond age x, derived by summing the L^i_x values in a given state, and l_x is the number of survivors to age x. The first formula, the so-called population-based value, gives the average years of dependent life of *all* survivors at exact age x, while the second and third formulas, the so-called status-based values, give the average years of dependent life at age x of survivors in the *dependent* state and survivors in the *independent* state. Corresponding formulas can be used to derive the life expectancy values for the independent state. To estimate these measures, separate survival populations according to health state must be carried forward. One possibility is to disaggregate the radix of the life table, at some age above birth, according to the observed prevalence in each of the health states in the actual population.

Alternatively, the change between $l(x)$ and $l(x+1)$ may be derived from the formulas:

$$l(x + 1) = l(x) - L(x) M(x) \qquad (14.27)$$

$$\begin{aligned} {}^i l(x + 1) = {}^i l(x) &+ \left[L^a(x) * {}^a m^i(x) \right] \\ &- \left[L^i(x) * {}^i m^a(x) \right] - \left[L^i(x) * {}^i m^d(x) \right] \end{aligned} \qquad (14.28)$$

$${}^i l(x + 1) = {}^i l(x) + {}^a t^i(x) - {}^i t^a(x) - {}^i t^d(x) \qquad (14.29)$$

$M(x)$, representing the ratio of transfers $D(x)$ to the life table stationary population $L(x)$, is known from the observed population, but we do not know $L(x)$ at this point because we do not know the $l(x)$s. We can estimate $l(x)$, $L(x)$, and $d(x)$ by successive approximation through an iterative technique: First, the changes in $l(x)$—that is, $d(x)$—are approximated as the product of $l(x)$ and $M(x)$. Next, we use these estimates of $d(x)$ to derive first estimates of $l(x+1)$ and $L(x)$. Now we multiply $M(x)$ by these first estimates of $L(x)$ to derive second estimates of $l(x+1)$, $d(x)$, and $L(x)$. This process can be repeated if necessary.

In a different approach, the number of survivors at the beginning of an age interval may be derived from the number of survivors at the beginning of the previous age interval with transition probabilities calculated directly from the survey. For example, the number of independent persons dying and the number transferring from the independent population to the dependent population are subtracted from the independent population, and those transferring from the dependent population to the independent population are added to the latter:

$$l_{x+1} = l_x * \left(1 - p^d_x \right) \qquad (14.30)$$

$${}^a l_{x+1} = {}^a l_x - \left({}^a l_x * {}^a p^d_x \right) - \left({}^a l_x * {}^a p^i_x \right) + \left({}^i l_x * {}^i p^a_x \right) \qquad (14.31)$$

where a, i, and d represent independence, dependence, and death, respectively. Similarly, for the dependent population:

$${}^i l_{x+1} = {}^i l_x - \left({}^i l_x * {}^i p^d_x \right) - \left({}^i l_x * {}^i p^a_x \right) + \left({}^a l_x * {}^a p^i_x \right) \qquad (14.32)$$

As we saw in Chapter 13, the $m(x)$, the central transfer rates, can then be derived from the transition probabilities (Formula 13.77).

Tables of healthy (disability-free) life by the multistate method have been calculated for only a few countries, including United States, Canada, Japan, the Netherlands, and France, but more than two dozen countries, including several in Africa and Asia, have prepared tables of disability-free life by the simpler methods. An illustration of the results from applying multistate life table methods to measure life expectancy according to health status is presented in Table 14.10. This table shows, for example, that while women at age 70 in the United States have a substantially greater total life expectancy than men, the independent active life expectancy of the two sexes is much closer.

Most tables constructed so far have tended to define active or healthy life, or to conceptualize morbidity, in terms of dependency (i.e., having ADL and/or IADL limitations). They can then be used to measure the lifetime chances of becoming dependent, expectancies of independent and dependent life at each age, the shares of the remaining life that will be independent and dependent at each age, average duration of dependency before recovery and before death, the probability of dying in independent and dependent states, and the mean age of dependent persons. Combinations of tables of disability-free life for the sexes and for a succession of years can answer such questions as the following: Are the extra years of life expectancy of women over those of men years of dependent life or independent life? What is the comparative proportion of life spent free of disability for men and women? Has health status improved among the elderly? Has health status improved in tandem with life expectancy? By simulation, these questions can be answered: What is the relative effect of shifts in mor-

TABLE 14.10 Years of Expected Life by Functioning Status for U.S. Females and Males at Ages 70, 80, and 90: 1984–1990

Age and sex	Total expected life	Expected active life			Expected inactive life			Percentage inactive
		Total	No functioning problems	Some functioning problems	Total	Unable to manage independent living	Unable to manage personal care	
Female								
70 years	13.9	11.1	4.3	6.8	2.8	1.0	1.8	20.1
80 years	8.4	5.5	1.6	3.9	2.9	1.0	1.9	34.5
90 years	4.8	1.8	0.3	1.5	2.9	0.9	2.0	60.4
Male								
70 years	10.3	8.9	4.1	4.8	1.4	0.6	0.8	13.6
80 years	6.0	4.4	1.6	2.8	1.6	0.7	0.9	26.7
90 years	3.3	1.6	0.4	1.2	1.8	0.7	1.1	54.5

Source: Crimmins, Hayward, and Saito, 1996, Table 3. © 1996 Gerontological Society of America. Reprinted by permission.

tality and morbidity on the size and life expectation of the dependent population? What is the effect of a change of age at onset of dependency on the size and life expectation of the dependent population?

Tables measuring life expectancy of persons who have incurred certain chronic illnesses (e.g., diabetes, arthritis) can also be constructed. For this purpose, one needs information on age-specific rates of occurrence, rates of "recovery," and differences in death rates of those with the chronic disease and those without it. Such tables are especially useful in elucidating the impact on health of various interventions. They can answer such questions as the following: What is the expectation of life spent free of the disease? What is the proportion of life spent free of the disease? Has the age of onset of the disease been changing? Has the age of disability changed, assuming a fixed age of onset of the disease? What is the effect of a change in the age at onset of the disease on the period of disability?

Measures of Overall Health Status

Relative Index of Overall Physical Health

Many proposals have been made for constructing a health index. To derive a relative index of overall physical health, one may consider calculating the average of a variety of physiological biomarkers and measures of performance at each age and then deriving an index of health at each age by comparing these summary measures with the corresponding value for some band of young ages, such as 25 to 34, taken as standard. Because of the great variability in the biomarkers and in the performance of individuals at given ages, this approach has been considered futile. It should be useful, however, in showing the general shift in health over the age scale, even if it cannot serve as a standard for individuals.

Quality-Adjusted Life Years and Disability-Adjusted Life Years

The so-called *quality-adjusted life year* (QALY) is a measure that combines the impact of premature death and disability into a single measure. There are many variants of the measure. To implement it, a single currency—that is, measurement unit—is required. Time can serve this purpose, and the measure can take the form of the sum of the years lost to premature death and the years lived with a disability.

An internationally standardized measure is needed that incorporates health conditions, not just mortality, into assessments of health status; evaluates the burden of particular health conditions in a demographically plausible way; and measures the burden of disease and injury in a measurement unit that can also be used to measure the cost-effectiveness of interventions (i.e., the cost per unit of disease burden averted). The measure, known as the *disability-adjusted life year* (DALY), an internationally standardized form of the QALY, is designed to meet these requirements. In brief, one DALY is 1 lost year of healthy life. The measure was developed in connection with the WHO project on the Global Burden of Disease (GBD, see Murray and Lopez, 1996).

The DALY combines years of life lost to premature death and years of healthy life lost to disability of a specified severity and duration. A premature death as defined here is a death that occurs before the age to which the decedent would have been expected to live on the basis of his or her age and sex and the current life table for Japan, the table with the highest current life expectation (82.5 years for women and 80.0 years for men). DALYs are calculated for each health condition in a population and then summed over all conditions. To calculate the DALYs for a particular condition, estimates are made for years of life lost and years lived with a disability of specified severity and duration for the condition.

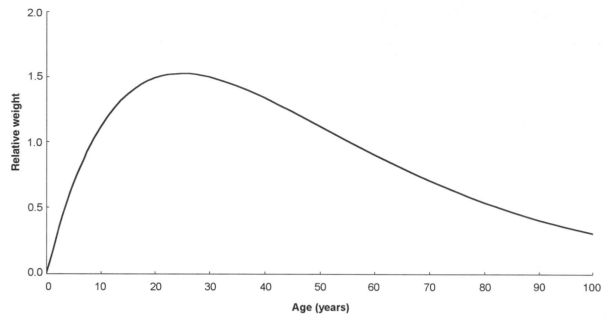

FIGURE 14.2   Relative Value of a Year of Life Lived at Different Ages, as Incorporated into DALYs.
Source: Murray and Lopez, 1996.

Relative values of a year of life lived at different ages are incorporated in the DALYs. For example, the DALYs are computed on the assumption that the relative value of a year of life rises rapidly from zero at birth to a peak in the early twenties, after which it steadily declines (Figure 14.2). Disabling conditions are assigned "severity" weights between 0 (perfect health) and 1 (equivalent to death) and then grouped into seven classes according to their severity. The GBD researchers also decided to discount future life years by 3% per year on the ground that a year of healthy life now is worth more to society than a year of healthy life at some future time. As an example of results obtained, noncommuncable diseases, which affect mainly older people, accounted for only 31% of years of life lost in the world in 1990, but they accounted for 56% of all deaths. On the other hand, injuries, which affect mainly young people, accounted for only 10% of deaths, but for 15% of years of life lost.

The number of years lived with a disability is calculated from information on the incidence of the disability, its age of onset, its estimated duration, and its severity. To calculate the years lived with a disability in a population, the years lived with a disability in each incident, adjusted for severity, are multiplied by the number of cases in the population. The GBD findings show the importance of disability in evaluating the health status of the world's population and, in particular, the importance of encompassing mental health conditions in this evaluation because their incidence has been grossly underestimated.

Figure 14.3 depicts the variation in 1990 of the DALYs among the regions of the world and the contribution to the total DALYs of the regions resulting from years of life lost

(YLL) and years lost to disability (YLD). The rates of premature death varied sharply among the regions; for example, the rate was seven times higher in sub-Sahara Africa (SSA) than in the established market economies (EME). On the other hand, there was relatively little variation in rates of disability, the SSA-to-EME ratio being about 2 to 1.

Measures of Health-Related Quality of Life

There have also been efforts to develop measures of the *health-related quality of life*, using more inclusive definitions of health. Such measures focus more on the quality of life than on formal indications of ill health and use of health services, even though the latter do reflect the "health-related quality of life." These measures may include such aspects of health as mental health, cognitive functioning, social functioning, intimacy, and productivity, as well as physical health, contacts with health providers, and self-assessed health. They also may incorporate some of the measures described earlier, particularly a measure on self-perceived health. They also may take into account many marginally pathological conditions. These include such activity-limiting (even if not severely limiting), time-consuming, discomforting, and health-compromising conditions as poor sleep, backache, fatigue, poor vision, poor hearing, headaches, allergies, dental problems, and elimination problems.

The U.S. Centers for Disease Control and Prevention (CDC) has developed a set of measures to track population health status and health-related quality of life (U.S. Centers for Disease Control and Prevention, 2000). The assessment consists of four core questions about "healthy days" that include self-assessed health, and days spent with

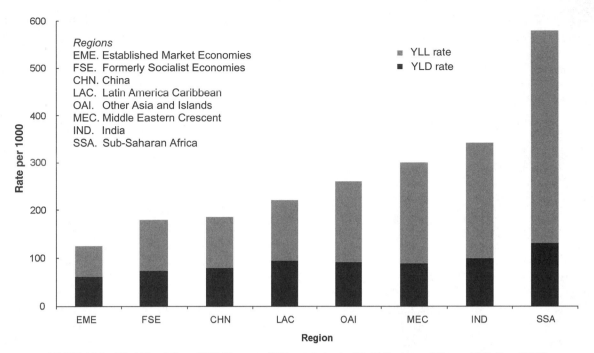

FIGURE 14.3   Disability-Adjusted Life Years per 1000 population by World Region and Years of Life Lost (YLL)
and Years Lost to Disability (YLD): 1990
Source: Murray and Lopez, 1996, Figure 12. © 1996. World Health Organization; reprinted with permission.

physical illness, mental problems, or the inability to pursue one's usual activities. These four items are used to create a summary index of unhealthy days within the past 30 days. An additional ten questions can be included with the four core questions to ascertain more detailed information about healthy days. These additional questions ask about any activity limitations, or days with pain, depression, anxiety, sleeplessness, or lack of vitality (U.S. Centers for Disease Control and Prevention, 2000).

Other efforts to measure health and quality of life include the Medical Outcomes Study Short Forms (SF-12 and SF-36), which also include self-assessments of general health and questions about activities and functional limitations, physical and emotional problems, and pain (e.g., Ware, Kosinski, and Dewey, 2000). Additional measures have been proposed. (See, e.g., U.S. National Center for Health Statistics/Erickson *et al.*, 1995.) Thus, the definition and measurement of the health quality of life continue to be areas of debate among the experts.

GENERAL ANALYTIC DEVICES AND HEALTH PROJECTION MODELS

General Analytic Devices

We consider next several analytical techniques that are widely used in research on health demography. They are ecological analysis, cohort analysis, multivariate logistic regression models, proportional hazards models, and grade of membership analysis. We briefly mention also the ran-

domized response technique and meta-analysis, which the reader may occasionally encounter in studies on health research.

Ecological Analysis

Numerous epidemiological studies have used ecological analysis as a method of demonstrating a relation between a health characteristic and certain explanatory variables. In *ecological analysis*, the units of observation are small geographic areas composing the total area under consideration rather than individuals. The correlation between the measures of health characteristics and the explanatory variables, both calculated for these small geographic units, is typically interpreted to represent the correlation between the variables for individuals. The "area" method rather than the "individual" method may be employed both for reasons of convenience and necessity; the data to be managed may be vastly reduced or they may be unavailable for individual respondents.

Because of this extension of the conclusions from areas to individuals, the validity of ecological correlation has been questioned. To the extent that the areas are small, numerous, and internally homogenous in the relevant characteristics, the extension should be more valid. Further improvement would result if the area data were weighted according to the size of the population in the geographic areas.

Cohort Analysis

Cohort analysis has been widely applied in health studies to reflect the changes over the life course in health conditions and to obviate the possible misinterpretation of the explanatory factors in health outcomes that could result from cross-sectional analysis. The changes in a specific type of health experience over the age scale for a birth cohort may not be reflected accurately in the record of health experience over the age scale in a particular year or short span of years.

Cohorts differ in their health experiences and potential for longevity mainly because of the differing influences of genetic and environmental factors, particularly the latter. Environmental factors, broadly conceived, include all influences that are not genetic, such as lifestyle, behavior, occupation, education, income, and access to health care, as well as the demographic characteristics of the person and the characteristics of the physical environment. A third factor, stochastic influences, or chance, also contributes to variation among cohorts. The composition of cohorts, especially their social and economic characteristics, may change in unique ways from cohort to cohort, with the result that considerable complexity is introduced into the analysis of cohort trends. There are pronounced cohort differences in the prevalence of specific chronic diseases such as heart disease, lung cancer, or stomach cancer. In the United States, cohorts born in the 1920s and 1930s have high levels of risk for lung and stomach cancer. Cohorts born in later decades have decreasing levels of risk for these conditions because of decreasing levels of cigarette use (Manton and Myers, 1987; Manton and Stallard, 1982; Patrick *et al.*, 1982).

Cohort analysis also allows for the measurement of the shifting influence of *unobserved heterogeneity* of risk and exposure in each cohort. Each cohort includes individuals of differing health and survival potential, so that the composition of the cohort with respect to its health potential changes as the cohort ages. Weaker individuals drop out of the cohort while the stronger members remain, with the result that the average health status and mortality potential of the cohort continually change (Keyfitz and Litman, 1979; Manton and Stallard, 1984).

Multivariate Logistic Regression

In regression analysis the dependent variable may be either an unrestricted absolute variable or a polytomous (usually dichotomous) variable that may be related to one or more independent variables. In health studies, the dependent variable is often expressed as a dichotomous variable—that is, as the probability of the occurrence of an event. If we let $P(t)$ be the probability that an individual experiences an event at time t, given that the individual is at risk of experiencing the event at time t, and if we let x_1 and x_2 be two explanatory variables, in a first approximation we can express $P(t)$ as a linear function of the explanatory variables,

$$P(t) = a + b_1 x_1 + b_2 x_2 \qquad (14.33)$$

For example, $P(t)$ could be the probability of entering a hospital at time $t = 1, 2, 3, 4$, and so forth, x_1 could be age, and x_2 could be the number of chronic health conditions among a specified list. This equation has the limitation that $P(t)$ can in fact take on values only between 0 and 1, while the equation can produce any real number for $P(t)$. To deal with this problem, we can make a logit transformation of $P(t)$,

$$\ln[P(t)/1 - P(t)] = a + b_1 x_1 + b_2 x_2 \qquad (14.34)$$

A *logit transformation* takes the natural logarithm of the ratio of a proportion to the complement of the proportion. It expresses the *odds ratio* in terms of the natural logarithms rather than the natural numbers. Because $P(t)$ varies between 0 and 1, logit $P(t)$ varies between minus infinity and plus infinity (see Appendix C for further explanation; also see Halli and Rao, 1992, pp. 103–104.

The *multivariate logistic regression* equation presented as (14.34) is one in which the natural logarithm of the odds of the dependent variable is predicted by a linear function of the independent variables. The regression coefficients b_1 and b_2 give the change in the logit, or "log odds," for each unit increase in x_1 and x_2, respectively, holding the other factor constant. The logistic equation can be generalized to include k explanatory variables:

$$\ln[P(t)/1 - P(t)] = a + b_1 x_1 + b_2 x_2 + \ldots + b_k x_k \qquad (14.35)$$

or in exponential form

$$P(t)/[1 - P(t)] = \exp(a + b_1 x_1 + b_2 x_2 + \ldots + b_k x_k) \qquad (14.36)$$

Proportional Hazards Models

Many mathematical functions have been applied to describe the age variations of chronic disease and the relation between a disease and other variables. We consider here a selected group of these functions. We define $P(t, t + s)$ as the probability that an individual experiences an event in the interval from t to $t + s$, given that the individual is at risk of experiencing the event at time t. This is called the *discrete time hazard rate*. In relating the hazard rate to one or more explanatory variables, it is conventional to calculate the natural logarithm of the hazard rate. Three multivariate models—the exponential, Weibull, and Gompertz—are commonly used for this purpose (Allison, 1984).

In the exponential function, with two explanatory variables, the natural logarithm of $h(t)$ is set equal to a linear function of the explanatory variables,

$$\ln h(t) = a + b_1 x_1 + b_2 x_2 \qquad (14.37)$$

where a, b_1, and b_2 are constants to be estimated. In this case the hazard function is constant over time. Such a model is useful for relating health characteristics to explanatory variables at some particular instance in time. It is unrealistic, however, for analyzing morbidity over time or over the age scale because the hazard rate would change with time or age.

If the logarithm of the hazard rate increases or decreases linearly with the logarithm of time, we can express this relation in a regression equation based on the Weibull model:

$$\ln h(t) = a + b_1 x_1 + b_2 x_2 + c \ln t \qquad (14.38)$$

where c is a constant greater than -1. Another function that allows the hazard rate to change with time (or age) is the Gompertz function. The regression equation is

$$\ln h(t) = a + b_1 x_1 + b_2 x_2 + ct \qquad (14.39)$$

where c is a constant that may be either positive or negative. The exponential model is a special case of the Gompertz and Weibull models. These models are solved by maximum likelihood procedures.

Proportional hazards models are ways of applying regression analysis to time-dependent variables. The exponential, Gompertz, and Weibull models are forms of proportional hazards models. The proportional hazards model describing two time-constant variables, may be written as

$$\ln h(t) = a(t) + b_1 x_1 + b_2 x_2 \qquad (14.40)$$

where $h(t)$ is the hazard rate and $a(t)$ is any function of time. This model is called the proportional hazards model because for any two individuals at any particular time the ratio of their hazard rates is a constant, although it may vary for the explanatory variables. That is,

$$h(t)_i / h(t)_j = c \qquad (14.41)$$

where i and j refer to different individuals and c does not depend on time but may depend on the explanatory variable. Although the hazard rates are no longer proportional when time-varying explanatory variables are introduced, the model is still called proportional hazards.

Cox (1972) proposed the method of partial likelihood as a way of solving the model. Partial likelihood solves for the coefficients b_1 and b_2, discarding the information about the function a(t) and treating the information about b_1 and b_2 as if the model was an ordinary likelihood function. The Cox method is widely applied in estimating regression models with continuous time data (Allison, 1984).

Grade of Membership Analysis

Grade of membership (GoM) procedures are multivariate classification techniques based on "fuzzy" data sets. Fuzzy data sets are groupings of data based on criteria that are partly ambiguous or incomplete. An example of a fuzzy classification is the classification of persons according to race in the United States. Many individuals are of mixed race, but they choose to assign themselves (in self-enumeration) to a single racial category or are assigned to a

single racial category by the enumerator or investigator. Disability is another characteristic of individuals that is associated with or composed of several fuzzy data sets. In grade of membership analysis the individual is "split up" into several classes, with weights or scores, based on the "components" of the fuzzy data set (e.g., races in the mixture or types of disability). The scores for each individual range from 0 to 1 and sum to 1. Such scores or proportions are the grades of membership. A grade of membership is, therefore, a measure of the degree to which an individual is a member of a particular fuzzy set. The grade of membership procedure determines, at the same time, both the identity of the fuzzy subgroups in the population and the profile of attributes that defines the subgroups.

The method calls for a number of grade of membership runs. For each run, the number of pure types (K) is predetermined by the analyst. The procedure is applied iteratively until the model converges. The parameters of the grade of membership function are estimated by maximizing a multinomial likelihood function. The choice of K, $K + 1$, or $K - 1$ groups is based on the goal of minimizing the heterogeneity, and maximizing the homogeneity, within groups. At convergence the solution for the values of the variables represents the maximization of the within-group homogeneity and the minimization of the between-group homogeneity.

Woodbury and Clive (1974) introduced the grade of membership procedure as a way to study symptoms of clinical conditions. Portrait, Lindeboom, and Deeg (2001), applying this method to the concept of health status, conclude that underlying health status can be described by six health dimensions ("pure types"). They used estimates of the dimensions of health derived by the GoM method to apportion total life expectancy at selected older ages into components denoted as "health expectancies," similar to active life expectancies discussed previously in this chapter. The results indicate that at age 65, males are expected to live another 14.95 years, whereas females are expected to live 20.29 years. Of the total life expectancy, each sex is expected to live about 7 healthy years, and the additional years females "enjoy" are very likely to be unhealthy years. In Manton and Stallard (1991), the GoM method is used to develop multidimensional distinctions among disability levels and to decompose life expectancy at the older ages into eight disability types.

Randomized Response Technique

In research on population health involving surveys, it is often necessary to secure information on sensitive subjects, such as having had an abortion, using illegal drugs, or driving while intoxicated. In such cases, it may not be wise to ask a direct question, even if self-enumeration is the method of data collection. The randomized response technique is designed to secure more complete and accurate responses on sensitive subjects. The technique has more than one variation. Commonly, the sensitive question is asked in conjunction with another innocuous question, and the respondent determines which question he or she answers, using some probability device under his or her control. For example, if the probability device is the toss of a coin, heads could mean that the respondent should answer the sensitive question. The enumerator would not know the choice in the individual case, but the probability of picking the sensitive or the innocuous question over all respondents is known. Finally, the reader is cautioned that, in less developed countries particularly, this device for obtaining sensitive information may have no advantage over simpler and more direct methods (Mensch, Hewitt, and Erulkar, 2003).[1]

Meta-Analysis

Meta-analysis is the statistical analysis of the results of a group of studies, all designed to test a given hypothesis or treatment, for the purpose of arriving at an integrated conclusion. In meta-analysis, each study is a unit of observation. Combined analysis of the primary results adds to the power of the findings (e.g., the ability to identify the statistical significance of the differences) and aims to interpret or reconcile conflicting conclusions, even when the primary results do not permit firm conclusions. For example, the New England Research Institute (1994) conducted a meta-analysis of the protective effects of hormone replacement against coronary heart disease in women and found an insignificant association between estrogen therapy and heart disease mortality/morbidity, once major methodological differences in the various studies were controlled. Meta-analysis cannot overcome the defects of poorly designed studies or eliminate response bias, and if the individual studies show marginally significant results, meta-analysis will not necessarily provide statistically significant results.

Health Projection Models

In preparing projections of health status, demographic factors are usually treated as exogenous, while health conditions are generally treated as endogenous. Because health is most commonly compromised and most costly at the older ages, it is important to carry out the computations in considerable age detail and cover a wide range of ages. Figures at least up to ages 85 years and over are necessary. Another guideline is applicable, *especially* because we are dealing

with projections. It is desirable to compute some type of measure(s) of uncertainty. This could be done by deriving alternative reasonable series with different assumptions for basic components, modeling the effect of different independent factors or methods, or possibly measuring confidence limits stochastically.

There are a variety of models of projection procedures, not always distinguishable. Manton, Singer, and Suzman (1993) enumerated the following types: (1) actuarial models, (2) demographic forecasts, (3) economic forecasts, (4) epidemiological forecasts, and (5) health and functional forecasts. The actuarial model and the demographic model are rather similar. They are typically based on life tables, and assumptions regarding health conditions are imposed on population projections disaggregated by age and sex. This is an application of the ratio method, given basic population projections derived by the cohort-survival method. The actuarial models tend to project selected populations (e.g., those to be insured), whereas demographic projections tend to be general-purpose projections. Both the actuarial model and the demographic model assess the statistical uncertainty of the projections by presenting alternative series with varying assumptions on the components. Both actuarial and demographic projections have been criticized because they do not assess the statistical uncertainty of the series by the most instructive methods (Manton *et al.*, 1993; Preston, 1993; Tolley, Hickman, and Lew, 1993).

In the econometric model, a system of simultaneous linear equations links health changes and relevant factors, and a least-squares solution is used to establish the relationship and project health changes. Epidemiological forecasts use prevalence ratios for diseases and data from epidemiological investigations to estimate the population impact of a disease or health condition. Forecasts are based on longitudinal data on the physiological status of individuals. In the health process model, the projections of health states are antecedent to and determine the projections of mortality. Disease risks are described as a multivariate stochastic process of physiological change (Manton and Stallard, 1992; Woodbury and Manton, 1983). This approach contrasts with the first four methods, which are discrete-state and discrete-time models of projections.

References

Allison, P. 1984. *Event History Analysis: Regression for Longitudinal Event Data*. Beverly Hills, CA: Sage.

Alter, G. C., and J. Riley. 1989. "Frailty, Sickness and Death: Models of Morbidity and Mortality in Historical Populations." *Population Studies* 43: 25–45.

American Psychiatric Association. 1994. *Diagnostic and Statistical Manual of Mental Disorders*, DSM-IV. Washington, DC: American Psychiatric Association.

Casterline, J. B. 1989. "Collecting Data on Pregnancy Loss: A Review of Evidence from the World Fertility Survey." *Studies in Family Planning* 20: 81–95.

---

[1] It is pertinent to mention here a very different survey device, namely multiplicity (or network) sampling in which the respondent households provide information not only about themselves but also about close relatives (e.g., parents, children, siblings) not in the households. By stretching the size of the sample in effect, this device is particularly applicable for surveying the prevalence of rare diseases.

Costa, D. 2000. "Understanding the Twentieth-Century Decline in Chronic Conditions Among Older Men." *Demography* 37: 53–72.

Cox, D. R. 1972. "Regression Models and Life Tables." *Journal of the Royal Statistical Society*, Series B34: 187–202.

Crimmins, E. M., M. D. Hayward, and Y. Saito. 1994. "Changing Mortality and Morbidity Rates and the Health Status and Life Expectancy of the Older Population." *Demography* 31: 150–175.

Crimmins, E. M., M. D. Hayward, and Y. Saito. 1996. "Differentials in Active Life Expectancy in the Older Population of the United States." *Journal of Gerontology: Social Sciences* 51B: S111–S120.

Crimmins, E. M., Y. Saito, and M. D. Hayward. 1993. "Sullivan and Multistate Methods of Estimating Active Life Expectancy: Two Methods, Two Answers." In J. M. Robine, C. D. Mathers, M. R. Bone, and I. Romieu, *Calculation of Health Expectancies: Harmonization, Consensus Achieved and Future Perspectives* (pp. 155–160). Montrouge: John Libbey Eurotext.

Dubos, R. 1968. *Man, Medicine and Environment.* New York: Frederick A. Praeger.

Dye, C., S. Scheele, P. Dolin, V. Pathania, and M. C. Raviglione. 1999. "Global Burden of Tuberculosis: Estimated Incidence, Prevalence, and Mortality by Country." *Journal of the American Medical Association* 282: 677–686.

Elman, C., and G. C. Myers. 1997. "Age and Sex-Differentials in Morbidity at the Start of an Epidemiological Transition: Returns from the 1880 U.S. Census." *Social Science & Medicine* 45: 943–956.

Elman, C., and G. C. Myers. 1999. "Geographic Morbidity Differentials in the Late Nineteenth-Century United States." *Demography* 36: 429–443.

Ferlay, J., F. Bray, P. Pisani, and D. M. Parkin. 2001. GLOBOCAN 2000: Cancer Incidence, Mortality and Prevalence Worldwide, Version 1.0. IARC [International Association of Cancer Registries] CancerBase No. 5. Lyon, France: IARCPress. Limited version available online at www-dep.iarc.fr/globocan/globocan.htm.

Geronimus, A. T., J. Bound, T. A. Waidmann, C. G. Colen, and D. Steffick. 2001. "Inequalities in Life Expectancy, Functional Status, and Active Life Expectancy Across Selected Black and White Populations in the United States." *Demography* 38: 227–251.

Goliber, T. J. 1997. "Population and Reproductive Health in Sub-Saharan Africa." *Population Bulletin* 52(4): 1–44. Washington, DC: Population Reference Bureau.

Halli, S. S., and K. V. Rao. 1992. *Advanced Techniques of Population Analysis.* New York: Plenum.

Hayward, M. D., and M. Heron. 1999. "Racial Inequality in Active Life Among Adult Americans." *Demography* 36: 77–91.

James, W. H. 1970. "The Incidence of Spontaneous Abortion." *Population Studies* 24: 241–245.

Kane, R. L., and R. A. Kane (Eds.). 2000. *Assessing Older Persons: Measures, Meaning, and Practical Applications.* New York: Oxford University Press.

Katz, S., L. G. Branch, M. H. Branson, J. A. Papsidero, J. C. Beck, and D. S. Greer. 1983. "Active Life Expectancy." *New England Journal of Medicine* 309: 1218–1223.

Keyfitz, N., and G. Litman. 1979. "Mortality in a Heterogeneous Population." *Population Studies* 33: 333–343.

Land, K. C., J. M. Guralnik, and D. G. Blazer. 1994. "Estimating Increment-Decrement Life Tables with Multiple Covariates from Panel Data: The Case of Active Life Expectancy." *Demography* 31: 297–319.

Mahler, H. 1981, February/March. "Health for All by the Year 2000." *World Health Statistics.*

Manton, K. G., and G. C. Myers. 1987. "Recent Trends in Multiple-Caused Mortality 1968 to 1982: Age and Cohort Components." *Population Research and Policy Review* 6: 161–176.

Manton, K. G., B. H. Singer, and R. M. Suzman. 1993. "The Scientific and Policy Needs for Improved Health Forecasting Models for Elderly Populations." In K. G. Manton, B. H. Singer, and R. M. Suzman (Eds.),

Forecasting the Health of Elderly Populations (pp. 3–35). New York: Springer-Verlag.

Manton, K. G., and E. Stallard. 1982. "A Cohort Analysis of U. S. Stomach Cancer Mortality: 1950 to 1977." *International Journal of Epidemiology* 11: 49–61.

Manton, K. G., and E. Stallard. 1984. "Heterogeneity and Its Effect on Mortality Measurement." *Proceedings, Seminar on Methodology and Data Collection in Mortality Studies, July 7–10, 1981.* Dakar, Senegal: International Union for the Scientific Study of Population.

Manton, K. G., and E. Stallard. 1991. "Cross-Sectional Estimates of Active Life Expectancy for the U.S. Elderly and the Oldest-Old Populations." *Journal of Gerontology: Social Sciences* 46: 170–182.

Manton, K. G., and E. Stallard. 1992. "Projecting the Future Size and Health Status of the U.S. Elderly Population." *International Journal of Forecasting* 8: 433–458.

Mausner, J. S., and S. Kramer. 1985. *Epidemiology: An Introductory Text.* Philadelphia: W. B. Saunders.

McDowell, I., and C. McDowell. 1996. *Measuring Health: A Guide to Rating Scales and Questionnaires.* New York: Oxford University Press.

Mensch, B. S., P. C. Hewitt, and A. S. Erulkar. 2003. "The Reporting of Sensitive Behavior by Adolescents: A Methodological Experiment in Konya." *Demography* 40(2): 247–268.

Murray, C. J. L., and A. D. Lopez (Eds.). 1996. *The Global Burden of Disease: A Comprehensive Assessment of Mortality and Disability from Diseases, Injuries, and Risk Factors in 1990 and Projected to 2020. Summary.* Cambridge, MA: Harvard University Press.

Murray, C. J. L., J. Salomon, and C. Mathers. 1999. "A Critical Examination of Summary Measures of Population Health." *WHO Global Programme on Evidence for Health Policy, Discussion Paper No. 2.* Geneva: World Health Organization.

New England Research Institute. 1994, Summer/Fall. *Network.*

New England Research Institute. 1996, Spring/Summer. *Network.*

North American Association of Central Cancer Registries (NAACCR). 2001. *CiNA+* [Cancer in North America]. Available online at www.naaccr.org/cinap/index.htm.

Obermeyer, C. M. 1996, January. "A Research Agenda for Reproductive Health." *IUSSP Newsletter* 54: 10–19.

Olshansky, S. J., B. Carnes, R. G. Rogers, and L. Smith. 1997. "Infectious Diseases: New and Ancient Threats to World Health." *Population Bulletin* 52(2). Washington, DC: Population Reference Bureau.

Omran, A. R. 1971. "The Epidemiologic Transition: A Theory of the Epidemiology of Population Change." *Milbank Memorial Fund Quarterly* 49: 509–538.

Omran, A. R. 1977. "Epidemiologic Transition in the United States: The Health Factor in Population Change." *Population Bulletin* 32(2). Washington, DC: Population Reference Bureau.

ORC Macro. 2002. www.measuredhs.com.

Patrick, C. H., Y. Y. Palesch, M. Feinleib, and J. A. Brody. 1982. "Sex-Differences in Declining Cohort Death Rates from Heart Disease." *American Journal of Public Health* 72: 161–166.

Portrait, F., M. Lindeboom, and D. Deeg. 2001. "Life Expectancies in Specific Health States: Results from a Joint Model of Health Status and Mortality of Older Persons." *Demography* 38: 525–536.

Preston, S. H. 1993. "Demographic Change in the United States, 1970–2050." In K. G. Manton, B. H. Singer, and R. M. Suzman (Eds.), *Forecasting the Health of Elderly Populations* (pp. 51–77). New York: Springer-Verlag.

Riley, J. C., and G. Alter. 1996. "The Sick and the Well: Adult Health in Britain During the Health Transition." *Health Transition Review* 6: 19–44.

Rogers, A., and J. Ledent 1976. "Increment-Decrement Life Tables: A Commont." *Demography* 13: 287–290.

Rogers, A., R. G. Rogers, and A. Belanger. 1990. "Longer Life but Worsening Health? Measurement and Dynamics." *Gerontologist* 30: 640–649.

Rogers, A., R. G. Rogers, and L. Branch. 1989. "A Multistate Analysis of Active Life Expectancy." *Public Health Reports* 104: 222–226.

Rogers, R., A. Rogers, and A. Belanger. 1989. "Active Life Among the Elderly in the United States: Multistate Life Table Estimates and Population Projections." *Milbank Memorial Fund Quarterly* 67: 370–411.

Schoen, R. 1988. *Modeling Multigroup Populations*. New York: Plenum Press.

Stewart, M. K., C. K. Stanton, M. Festin, and N. Jacobson. 1996. "Issues in Measuring Maternal Morbidity: Lessons from the Philippines Safe Motherhood Survey Project." *Studies in Family Planning* 27: 29–36.

Sullivan, D. F. 1971. "A Single Index of Mortality and Morbidity." *Health Reports* 86: 347–354.

Tinker, A., and M. A. Kolinsky, 1993. "Making Motherhood Safe." *World Bank Discussion Papers No, 202*. Washington, DC: The World Bank.

Tolley, H. D., J. C. Hickman, and E. A. Lew. 1993. "Actuarial and Demographic Forecasting Methods." In K. G. Manton, B. H. Singer, and R. M. Suzman (Eds.), *Forecasting the Health of Elderly Populations* (pp. 39–49). New York: Springer-Verlag.

UNICEF. 2001. *The State of the World's Children 2000*. Geneva: UNICEF. Available online at www.unicef.org.

United Nations. 1994. *World Plan of Action Conference Document*. International Conference for Population and Development. Cairo, Egypt: United Nations.

United Nations. 1995. *Demographic Yearbook*. New York: United Nations.

U.S. Bureau of the Census. 2001. *International Database*. Available online at www.census.gov/ipc/www/idbnew.html.

U.S. Centers for Disease Control and Prevention. 2000. *Measuring Healthy Days*. Atlanta, GA: Centers for Disease Control and Prevention.

U.S. Department of Health and Human Services. 2000a. *Healthy People 2010: Understanding and Improving Health*, 2nd ed. Washington, DC: U.S. Government Printing Office.

U.S. Department of Health and Human Services. 2000b. *International Health Data Reference Guide, 1999*. DHHS Publication No. (PHS) 2000-1007.

U.S. National Center for Health Statistics. 1991. *Vital Statistics of the United States:* Vol. II, *Mortality*, Part A. Washington, DC: U.S. Government Printing Office.

U.S. National Center for Health Statistics. 1992. *International Collaborative Effort on Perinatal and Infant Mortality. Proceedings*. By R. Hartford. Hyattsville, MD: National Center for Health Statistics.

U.S. National Center for Health Statistics. 1995. "Years of Healthy Life," by P. Erickson, R. Wilson, and I. Shannon. *Healthy People 2000: Statistical Notes*, No. 7.

U.S. National Center for Health Statistics. 2001a. "Comparability of Cause of Death Between ICD-9 and ICD-10: Preliminary Estimates," by R. N. Anderson, A. M. Miniño, D. A. Hoyart, and H. M. Rosenberg. *National Vital Statistics Reports* 49(2).

U.S. National Center for Health Statistics. 2001b. *DATA2010: The Healthy People 2010 Database*. Available online at WONDER.CDC.GOV/DATA2010.

U.S. National Center for Health Statistics. 2001c. "Trends in Pregnancy Rates for the United States, 1976–97: An Update," by S. J. Ventura, W. D. Mosher, S. C. Curtin, J. C. Abma, and S. Henshaw. *National Vital Statistics Reports* 49(4).

U.S. National Office of Vital Statistics. 1950. "International Recommendations on Definitions of Live Birth and Fetal Death." Washington, DC: U.S. Public Health Service.

Ware, J. E., M. Kosinski, and J. E. Dewey. 2000. *How to Score Version 2 of SF-36® Health Survey*. Lincoln, RI: QualityMetric.

Westoff, C. F., and A. Bankole. 1995. *Unmet Need: 1990–1994*. DHS Comparative Studies, No. 16. Calverton, MD: ORC Macro.

Willekens, F. J., I. Shah, J. M. Shah, and P. Ramachandran. 1982. "Multistate Analysis of Marital Status Life Tables: Theory and Application." *Population Studies* 36: 129–144.

Woodbury, M. A., and J. Clive. 1974. "Clinical Pure Types as a Fuzzy Partition." *Journal of Cybernetics* 4: 111–121.

Woodbury, M. A., and K. G. Manton. 1983. "A New Procedure for Analysis of Medical Classification." *Methods of Information in Medicine* 21: 210–220.

World Health Organization. 1970. "Spontaneous and Induced Abortion." *Technical Report Series* No. 461.

World Health Organization. 1980. *International Classification of Impairments, Disabilities, and Handicaps: A Manual of Classification Relating to the Consequences of Disease*. Geneva: World Health Organization.

World Health Organization. 1984. *The Uses of Epidemiology in the Study of the Elderly: Report of a Scientific Group on the Epidemiology of Aging*, Technical Report Series 706. Geneva: World Health Organization.

World Health Organization. 1989. *Measuring Reproductive Morbidity*, Report of a Technical Working Group, Geneva, August 30–September 1.

World Health Organization. 1992, 1993, 1994. *International Statistical Classification of Diseases and Related Problems. Volume I: ICD-10, Tabular List*. (1992); *Volume II: Instructional Manual*. (1993); *Volume III: Alphabetical Index*. (1994). Geneva: World Health Organization.

World Health Organization. 1996. *Revised 1990 Estimates of Maternal Mortality: A New Approach by WHO and UNICEF*. Geneva: World Health Organization.

World Health Organization. 2001. *International Classification of Functioning, Disability, and Health*. Geneva: World Health Organization.

Zurayk, H., H. Khattab, N. Younis, M. El Mouelhy, and M. Faddle. 1993. "Concepts and Measures of Reproductive Morbidity." *Health Transition Review* 3: 17–40.

Suggested Readings

General Methods of Analysis

Allison, P. D. 1984. *Event History Analysis: Regression for Longitudinal Event Data*. Quantitative Applications in the Social Sciences. Paper No. 07-046. Beverly Hills, CA: Sage.

Armstrong, B. K., E. White, and R. Saracci. 1992. *Principles of Exposure Measurement in Epidemiology*. New York: Oxford University Press.

Dever, G. E. A. 1991. *Community Health Analysis: Global Awareness at the Local Level*. 2nd ed. Gaithersburg, MD: Aspen.

Manton, K. G., and E. Stallard. 1992. "Demographics (1950–1987) of Breast Cancer in Birth Cohorts of Older Women." *Journals of Gerontology* 47: 32–42.

Manton, K. G., M. A. Woodbury, and H. D. Tolley. 1994. *Statistical Applications Using Fuzzy Sets*. New York: John Wiley & Sons.

Omran, A. 1977. "Epidemiologic Transition in the United States: The Health Factor in Population Change." *Population Bulletin* 32(2). Washington, DC: Population Reference Bureau.

Pol, L. G., and R. K. Thomas. 2001. *The Demography of Health and Health Care*, 2nd ed. New York: Plenum.

Rockett, I. 1994. "Population and Health: An Introduction to Epidemiology." *Population Bulletin* 49(3). Washington, DC: Population Reference Bureau.

Susser, M. 1987. "Epidemiology in the United States after World War II: The Evolution of Technique." *Epidemiologic Review* 7: 147–177.

Wallace, R., and A. Herzog. 1995. "Overview of the Health Measures in the Health and Retirement Study: Background and Overview." *Journal of Human Resources* 30 (Supp.): S84–107.

World Health Organization, Regional Office for Europe. 1996. *Health Interview Surveys: Toward International Harmonization of Methods and Instruments*. Edited by A. de Bruim, H. S. J. Pivacet, and A. Nossikov. WHO Regional Publications, European Series, No. 58.

Williams, D. R., R. Lavizzo-Mourey, and R. C. Warren. 1994. "The Concept of Race and Health Status in America." *Public Health Reports* 109: 26–41.

Health and Mortality

Cohen, J., 1984. "Demography and Morbidity: A Survey of Some Interactions." In Nathan Keyfitz (Ed.), *Population and Biology: Bridge between Disciplines* (pp. 199–220). Proceedings of a Conference. Liège, Belgium: Ordina Editions.

Freedman, V. L., and B. J. Soldo (Eds.). 1994. *Trends in Disability at Older Ages: Summary of a Workshop.* Washington, DC: National Academy Press.

Fries, J. 1980. "Aging, Natural Death, and the Compression of Morbidity." *New England Journal of Medicine* 303: 130–135.

Gribble, J., and S. Preston (Eds.). 1993. *The Epidemiological Transition: Policy and Planning Implications for Developing Countries.* Washington, DC: National Academy Press.

Hummer, R. A. 1996. "Black-White Differences in Health and Mortality: A Review and Conceptual Model." *Sociological Quarterly* 37: 105–125.

Ingram, D., S. Stoll, and G. Baker. 1995. "Is Attempting to Assess Biological Age Worth the Effort?" *Gerontologist* 35(5): 707.

Johansson, S. 1991. "The Health Transition: The Cultural Inflation of Morbidity during the Decline of Mortality." *Health Transition Review* 1(1): 39–68.

Nusselder, W. J. 1998. *Compression or Expansion of Morbidity? A Life Table Approach.* Amsterdam: Thesis Publications.

Olshansky, S. J., and B. Carnes. 1994. "Demographic Perspectives on Human Senescence." *Population and Development Review* 20(1): 57–80.

Olshansky, S. J., B. Carnes, R. G. Rogers, and L. Smith. 1997. "Infectious Diseases: New and Ancient Threats to World Health." *Population Bulletin* 52(2). Washington, DC: Population Reference Bureau.

Riley, J. 1990. "The Risk of Being Sick: Morbidity Trends in Four Countries." *Population and Development Review* 16(3): 403–431.

Riley, J. 1992. "From a High Mortality Regime to a High Morbidity Regime: Is Culture Everything in Sickness?" *Health Transition Review* 2(1): 71–78.

Schneider, E., and J. Brody. 1983. "Aging, Natural Death, and the Compression of Morbidity: Another View." *New England Journal of Medicine* 309: 854–856.

Verbrugge, L., and A. Jette. 1994. "The Diablement Process." *Social Science and Medicine* 38(1): 1–14.

Wolinsky, F., and R. Johnson. 1992. "Perceived Health Status and Mortality among Older Men and Women." *Journal of Gerontology: Social Sciences* 47(6): S304–S312.

Tables of Healthy Life

Crimmins, E., M. Hayward, and Y. Saito. 1994. "Changing Mortality and Morbidity Rates and the Health Status and Life Expectancy of the Older Population." *Demography* 31(1): 159–175.

Crimmins, E., Y. Saito, and D. Ingegneri. 1989. "Changes in Life Expectancy and Disability-Free Life Expectancy in the United States." *Population and Development Review* 15(2): 235–267.

Manton, K., and E. Stallard. 1991. "Cross-Sectional Estimates of Active Life Expectancy for the U.S. Elderly and Oldest-Old Population." *Journal of Gerontology: Social Sciences* 46(3): S170–S182.

Manton, K., E. Stallard, and L. Corder. 1995. "Changes in Morbidity and Chronic Disability in the U.S. Elderly Population: Evidence from the 1982, 1984, and 1989 National Long-Term Survey." *Journal of Gerontology: Social Sciences* 50B(4): S194–S204.

Mathers, C. D., J. McCallum, and J-M. Robine (eds). 1994. *Advances in Health Expectancies.* Canberra: Australian Institute of Health and Welfare.

Robine, J-M., C. D. Mathers, M. R. Bone, and I. Romieu. 1992. *Calculation of Health Expectancies: Harmonization, Consensus Achieved, and Future Perspectives.* Montrouge, France: John Libbey Eurotext.

Robine, J-M., and K. Ritchie. 1991. "Healthy Life Expectancy: Evaluation of a New Global Indicator for Change in Population Health." *British Medical Journal* 302: 457–460.

Rogers, A., R. Rogers, and A. Belanger. 1989. "Active Life among the Elderly in the United States: Multistate Life Table Estimates and Projections." *Milbank Memorial Fund Quarterly* 67(3–4): 370–411.

Wilkins, R., and Adams, O. 1983. *Healthfulness of Life: A Unified View of Mortality, Institutionalization, and Non-Institutionalized Disability in Canada, 1978.* Montréal: Institute for Research on Public Policy.

Reproductive Health

AbouZahr, C., and E. Royston, 1991. *Maternal Mortality: A Global Fact Book.* Geneva: World Health Organization.

Anderson, B., K. Katus, A. Puur, and B. Silver. 1994. "The Validity of Survey Responses on Abortion: Evidence from Estonia." *Demography* 31(1): 115–132.

Casterline, J. B. 1989. "Collecting Data on Pregnancy Loss: A Review of Evidence from the World Fertility Survey." *Studies in Family Planning* 20(2): 81–85.

Coeytaux, F., A. Leonard, and E. Royston (Eds.). 1989. *Methodological Issues in Abortion Research.* New York: The Population Council.

Fathalla, M. 1988. "Reproductive Health: A Global Overview." *Annals of the New York Academy of Sciences* 626: 1–10.

Goliber, T. J. 1997. "Population and Reproductive Health." *Population Bulletin* 52(4) Washington, DC: Population Reference Bureau.

Graham, W., and O. Campbell. 1990. *Measuring Maternal Health: Defining the Issues.* London: Maternal and Child Epidemiology Unit, London School of Hygiene and Tropical Medicine.

Hammond, E. I. 1965. "Studies in Fetal and Infant Mortality. I. A Methodological Approach to the Definition of Perinatal Mortality," *American Journal of Public Health* 55(7): 1012–1023.

Henshaw, S. K., and J. Van Vort (Eds.). 1992. *Abortion Handbook: Readings, Trends, and State and Local Data to 1988.* 1992 Edition. New York: The Alan Guttmacher Institute.

IUSSP. 1975. *Measuring the Effect of Family Planning Programs on Fertility.* Liège, Belgium: Ordina Editions.

IUSSP. 1984. *Survey Analysis for the Guidance of Family Planning Programs.* Liège, Belgium: Ordina Editions.

IUSSP. 1992. *Measurement of Maternal and Child Mortality, Morbidity and Health Care: Interdisciplinary Approaches.* Liège, Belgium: Ordina Editions.

Obermeyer, C. 1996. "A Research Agenda for Reproductive Health." *Newsletter* 54. International Union for the Scientific Study of Population.

Potter, R. 1967. "The Multiple Decrement Life Table as an Approach to the Measurement of the Use-Effectiveness and Demographic Effectiveness of Contraception." *Proceedings of the Conference of the International Union for the Scientific Study of Population*, Sydney, Australia.

Singh, S., and D. Wulf. 1994. "Estimated Levels of Induced Abortion in Six Latin American Countries." *International Family Planning Perspectives* 20(1): 4–13.

Stecklov, G. 1995. "Maternal Mortality Estimation: Separating Pregnancy-Related and Non-Pregnancy-Related Risks." *Studies in Family Planning* 26(1): 33–38.

Stewart, M. K., C. K. Stanton, M. Festin, and N. Jacobson. 1996. "Issues in Measuring Maternal Morbidity: Lessons from the Philippines Safe Motherhood Survey Project." *Studies in Family Planning* 27(1): 29–36.

World Health Organization. 1990. *Measuring Reproductive Morbidity.* Report of a Technical Working Group, Geneva, August 30–September 1, 1989. WHO/MCH/90.4.

Younis, N., H. Khattab, H. Zurayk, M. El-Mouelhy, M. F. Amin, and A. F. Farag. 1993. "A Community Study of Gynecological and Related Morbidities in Rural Egypt." *Studies in Family Planning* 24(3): 175–186.

Zurayk, H., H. Khattab, N. Younis, M. El-Mouelhy, and M. Fadle Amin. 1993. "Concepts and Measures of Reproductive Morbidity." *Health Transition Review* 3(1): 17–40.

Projections of Health Status

Kunkel, S., and R. Applebaum. 1992. "Estimating Prevalence of Long-Term Disability for an Aging Society." *Journal of Gerontology: Social Sciences* 47(5): S273–S260.

Manton, K. G. 1984. "The Application of Disease-Specific Models for Health Trend Projections." *World Health Statistics Quarterly*, No. 3.

Manton, K. G., B. Singer, and R. Suzman (Eds.). 1993. *Forecasting the Health of Elderly Populations*. New York: Springer-Verlag.

Manton, K. G., and E. Stallard. 1993. "Projecting Morbidity and Mortality in Developing Countries during Adulthood." In J. Gribble and S. Preston (Eds.), *The Epidemiological Transition: Policy and Planning Implications for Developing Countries* (pp. 101–125). Washington, DC: National Academy Press.

Manton, K. G., E. Stallard, and B. Singer. 1992. "Projecting the Future Size and Health Status of the U.S. Elderly Population." *International Journal of Forecasting*. Special Issue 8(3): 433–458.

Stoto, M., and J. Durch. 1993. "Forecasting Survival, Health, and Disability: Report of a Workshop." *Population and Development Review* 19(3): 556–581.

15

Natality

Measures Based on Vital Statistics

SHARON ESTEE

CONCEPTS

We employ "natality" here as a general term representing the role of births in population change and human reproduction. There are also the terms "fertility" and "births." The three terms have alternative and overlapping meanings, and convention has, in fact, often established a particular choice of term to be used in a particular context. In one sense, the term "fertility" is synonymous with natality in referring to the birth factor in population change in the broadest sense. Accordingly, we may speak either of natality statistics, measures, studies, and so forth, or of fertility statistics, measures, studies, and so forth. In a more restricted sense and more commonly, the term "fertility" refers to the more refined analysis of natality and to certain more or less refined measures of natality. It is because this usage of the term "fertility" is so common that we have preferred to use the less committed term "natality" to identify the subjects treated in this and the next chapter.

"Birth statistics" and "birthrates" tend to have a more narrow reference than "natality statistics" and "natality rates" because the former commonly refer to birth statistics per se from the registration system and generally exclude those types of natality statistics that are derived from censuses and surveys. Typically, "fertility statistics" come from either source. In this chapter and the next two chapters, we have tried to maintain the distinction between birthrates and fertility rates in terms of the source of the data and the complexity of the measures. At the same time, we have tried to recognize the conventions in terminology that have already been established.

"Fertility" refers to actual birth performance, as compared with "fecundity," which refers to the physiological capacity to reproduce (International Union for the Scientific Study of Population 1982, pp. 78–79).[1] One's fertility is limited by one's fecundity and is usually far below it. Infecund persons are also described as sterile. The term fecundibility refers to a special aspect of fecundity, namely the probability of conceiving measured on a monthly basis.

The terms "natality," "fertility," and "births" may relate to total births, including live births and "stillbirths," but they have come increasingly to refer to live births only. We will use the word "births" to mean "live births" only, unless otherwise specified. We cite again, as given in Chapter 3, the statistical definition of a live birth that is recommended by the World Health Organization (1950, p. 17) and the United Nations (1991a, p. 17):

> Live birth is the complete expulsion or extraction from its mother of a product of conception, irrespective of the duration of pregnancy, which, after such separation, breathes or shows any other evidence of life such as beating of the heart, pulsation of the umbilical cord, or definite movement of voluntary muscles, whether or not the umbilical cord has been cut or the placenta is attached; each product of such a birth is considered live-born.

According to this definition, the period of gestation, or the state of life or death at the time of registration, is not relevant. The U.S. standard contains this definition plus a statement recommended by the American College of Obstetricians and Gynecologists to assist in the determination of what should be considered a live birth: "Heartbeats are to be distinguished from transient cardiac contractions; respirations are to be

[1] In the Romance languages, the cognate words have opposite meanings. For example, *fécondité* in French means *fertility* in English. The terms should be paired in terms of their meanings as follows:

English	French	Spanish
Fertility	Fécondité	Fecundidad
Fecundity	Fertilité	Fertilidad

distinguished from fleeting respiratory efforts or gasps" (U.S. National Center for Health Statistics, 1997a, p. 2). The definition of death, also given in Chapter 3, complements that of live birth, because death is "the permanent disappearance of all evidence of life at any time after live birth has taken place." "Fetal deaths" are excluded from both "live births" and "deaths," because fetal death refers to the disappearance of life prior to the expulsion or extraction from its mother of a product of conception. Stillbirths, miscarriages, and abortions are types of fetal deaths and, hence, are excluded from live births (United Nations, 1991a, p. 17).

BASIC DATA FOR NATALITY STUDIES

The basic data for natality studies come from (1) the vital statistics registration system, (2) national censuses, and (3) national sample surveys. In several countries in which the vital statistics registration system has been incorporated into a national population register system, the latter is then the source of natality data. The first source, the registration system, provides birth statistics principally. The second source, national censuses, provides (1) data on the age composition of the population from which the level of recent fertility can be inferred, (2) direct data on births and fertility, (3) statistics on children by the family status of their parents, (4) population data on fertility-related variables, and (5) population bases for calculating various types of fertility rates. The national sample surveys may provide (1) the same types of data as a census (national data) and (2) additional detailed data permitting a more complete analysis of fertility, including data on special aspects of fertility not amenable to collection in a census and data on the number and timing of marriages, pregnancies, and births.

The types of data and the analytic measures based principally on the birth registration system are sufficiently different from those derived from censuses or surveys to suggest separate detailed treatment of these topics. Therefore, two chapters are devoted to natality in this volume, distinguished in terms of the collection system furnishing the data. This, the first, relates to natality as measured by birth statistics from a registration system, and the second (Chapter 16) examines natality as measured by censuses and surveys. A final note on natality data and measures based on national population registers is included in this chapter because the population register system is viewed as closely akin to and as an extension of the registration system.

QUALITY OF BIRTH STATISTICS

Birth statistics suffer from a number of deficiencies similar to those characteristic of death statistics. We can consider the types of deficiencies under five headings: (1)

accuracy of the definition employed and of its application, (2) completeness of registration, (3) accuracy of allocation by place, (4) accuracy of allocation by time, and (5) accuracy of the classification of the births in terms of demographic, socioeconomic, and medical characteristics. For the more developed countries, the deficiencies in (1), (2), and (4) have largely been overcome and the concern is primarily with the problems in (3) and (5). For the statistically underdeveloped areas, all of these deficiencies are important, but the problem in (2) looms largest.

Application of Definition

To meet the requirements of the definition recommended by the United Nations, the count of births must include all live-born products of pregnancy and exclude pregnancies not terminating in a live birth, (i.e., fetal losses). One common problem is the failure to register the birth of a child who dies very shortly after birth or who dies before the parents have registered the birth. Depending on national laws and practices, the registration period may vary from a few days to a few years following the date of birth (United Nations, 1985, pp. 26–27). In some cases (e.g., Zaire, Poland) newborn infants who die within 24 hours after birth are excluded from the tabulations of live births (United Nations, 1985, pp. 66 and 71). In others (e.g., Algeria, French Guiana, and Malaysia), registration of the birth of the infant is not required if the infant dies before the established registration period ends (United Nations, 1998a). The countries that were formerly part of the Union of Soviet Socialist Republics (e.g., Azerbaijan, Belarus, Kazakhstan, the Russian Federation) exclude infants which die within 7 days of birth if gestation is less than 28 weeks, birthweight is less than 1000 grams, and length is less than 35 centimeters (United Nations, 1998a).

Completeness of Registration

As in the discussion of mortality in Chapter 12, to which reference should be made, we may distinguish two aspects of the incompleteness of registration of birth statistics: (1) the failure to cover the entire geographic area of a country or all groups in the population and (2) the failure to register all the vital events in the established registration area. In the past, some less developed countries registered births only in designated registration areas (e.g., Nigeria, Indonesia, Ghana).[2] Nomadic and indigenous groups (e.g., nomadic Indians in Ecuador; jungle Indians in Brazil, Peru, or Venezuela) or particular ethnic or racial groups (Vietnamese

---

[2] According to a report on the progress of civil registration and vital statistics, those efforts that focused on the development of civil registration systems in demonstration areas usually have failed to produce the desired result of nationwide systems (United Nations, 1991b, p. 8).

refugees in Hong Kong) may be excluded from the groups covered. Special groups (e.g., alien armed forces, nonresident foreigners, all foreigners) may be excluded in some cases (United Nations, 1999, p. 301). Sample registration schemes are used in some countries (e.g., India, Pakistan, and Bangladesh) to produce fertility measures and population growth rates, but these schemes do not provide adequate civil registration systems for legal, administrative, and other statistical purposes (United Nations 1991b, p. 9).

The United Nations finds birth registration to be substantially incomplete for many countries of the world, particularly those considered underdeveloped. Nearly one-third of all births, about 40 million infants, fail to be registered each year according to estimates by UNICEF (1998). The United Nations classifies a country's registration of births as being relatively complete if at least 90% of the births are registered. Fifty-two percent of 217 countries listed in the *1997 Demographic Yearbook* (United Nations, 1999) met this criterion. The highest proportion of countries achieving this level of coverage occurs in Europe (44 out of 47 countries) and the lowest in Africa (8 out of 57).

Measurement by Match Studies

The United Nations (1991a) recommends that civil registration systems should be evaluated regularly regarding completeness of coverage and accuracy of reporting. Direct methods for assessing the degree of coverage involve matching birth records to such independent data sources as government and private administrative systems (e.g., infant death certificates, school enrollment records, hospital records) and lists generated from population censuses and surveys. A dual-record system in which information on births is collected from two independent sources—a civil registration system, sometimes in specified sample registration areas, and a survey—has been used to determine the apparent coverage of the registration system and to estimate the number of vital events. A number of countries (e.g., India, Pakistan, Ghana, Iraq, Indonesia) have adopted this approach since the 1970s to assess the coverage of their registration systems (United Nations, 1991a, pp. 49–50). Birth registration is often found to vary sharply between regions of a country. For example, in Pakistan's Punjab Province 88% of all births are registered compared to 46% in its North-West Frontier Province; in Turkey's western region, 84% are registered compared to 54% in its eastern region (UNICEF, 1998).

In the United States, when the birth registration area was initially established in 1915, it covered the District of Columbia and 10 Northeastern and North Central states and encompassed only 31% of the population. Complete geographic coverage of the United States was not achieved until 1933, when the last state joined the registration area. Even so, registration of births in the U.S. birth registration area

was not complete. In fact, only 90% completeness of registration in a state was a condition for joining the registration area, and the testing procedure was quite crude (Shapiro, 1950).

Three systematic national tests of the completeness of birth registration in the United States have been conducted, one in 1940, a second in 1950, and a third in 1969–1970. The 1969–1970 test was based on a match of listings of children under 5, made over a 9-month period in the National Health Survey-Health Interview Survey sample and in part of the Current Population Survey sample, with birth certificates on file. No attempt was made to determine whether certificates were filed for children who died. The study was intended to provide only national estimates of the completeness of birth registration, by color, in the period 1964–1968. The tests of 1940 and 1950 had similar methodological designs; all children under 3 or 4 months of age enumerated in the 1940 and 1950 censuses, respectively, were matched with births registered during the 3 or 4 months preceding the censuses. A special enumeration form was completed for each infant to secure the information needed to locate the birth certificate and to carry out an analysis of the extent of underregistration. The matching study of 1950 was conducted by the U.S. National Office of Vital Statistics, and that of 1969–1970 was conducted by the U.S. Bureau of the Census in cooperation with the U.S. National Center for Health Statistics.

The overall test results indicated a completeness of birth registration of 92.5% in 1940, 97.9% in 1950, and 99.2% in 1964–1968. The most impressive differences in each year were found between whites and nonwhites and between births in hospitals and births outside hospitals (Schachter, 1962; U.S. National Center for Health Statistics, 1997b).

Measurement by Aggregate Methods

Given the amount of time and resources required to match birth records to other data sources and to implement dual-record systems, aggregate methods are also recommended by the United Nations (1991a) to assess the completeness and accuracy of birth registration systems. Fertility statistics derived from a census or a survey can be compared to measures derived from a country's registration system. Each of these sources of fertility measurement is subject to different types of errors that must be taken into account when making these comparisons. In all three systems, births of children who are no longer living tend to be underreported, but surveys and censuses are more prone to errors caused by the difficulty, especially among older women, in recalling the timing of births or ages of children. Disentangling these possible sources of error and determining their effects on estimated fertility trends and measures of current and completed fertility is not an easy matter, as shown in an evaluation of the birth history data collected in a national fertility survey in India (Bhat, 1995). In this instance, birth statistics from the country's Sample Registration System, its 1981 census, and several surveys were used to help assess the accuracy of statistics derived from birth histories gathered in a recent National Family Health Survey.

Accuracy of Characteristics of Births

The tabulations of births may suffer from inaccuracies or deficiencies with respect to the geographic allocation of the birth, the allocation to the year of occurrence, and specific demographic and social characteristics of the births, the infants, and the parents (age of mother or father, order of birth of child, education of mother or father, etc.). Of the many possible characteristics that may be useful for preparing birth statistics, the United Nations (1973, pp. 20–22) recommends that priority be placed on gathering the following 12 items: attendant at birth, date of occurrence, date of registration, place of occurrence, type of birth (i.e., single or multiple issue), legitimacy status,[3] sex, weight at birth, age (or date of birth) of mother, date (or duration) of marriage for married parents, number of children born alive to the mother, and the usual place of residence of the mother. The United Nations lists an additional 25 items that are also desirable, including gestational age of infant; the nationality, ethnicity, education, occupation, and place of birth of both parents; the usual place of residence of the father; and information about prior births and fetal deaths for the mother. In a survey of national practices, the United Nations (1985, pp. 36–37) found that all 88 countries that replied to the survey collected the date of birth and sex of the infant and % or more gathered date and place of birth, date of registration, the age (or date of birth) of the mother, the usual place of residence of the mother, and the occupation of the father.

The United States Standard Certificate of Live Birth contains the items recommended by the United Nations plus other medical, social, and behavioral items identified by a national committee as important for examining maternal and child health. Each state, in turn, adopts all or part of the national standard and may add items of its own. Since the early 1900s, when the first U.S. standard for births was developed, it has been revised periodically (U.S. National Center for Health Statistics, 1996, technical appendix, p. 2). The revision adopted in 1989 required the collection of more extensive medical information than previously gathered, including more details on the woman's pregnancy history,

prenatal care, method of delivery, obstetric practices, medical risks, and birth outcomes (e.g., congenital anomalies). The expanded content was made possible by the use of check boxes in place of open-ended questions and by the extensive use of automation in many states. By 1995, nearly 70% of all births in the United States were registered via electronic birth certificate systems (U.S. National Center for Health Statistics, 1997b).

Accuracy of Allocation by Place

Deficiencies in the geographic allocation of births usually take the form of excessive allocation of births to cities at the expense of the surrounding unincorporated suburban and rural areas. In the United States, this appears to result from the classification of city of residence from postal information. Although the question "Inside city limits?" is posed on the U.S. Standard Certificate of Live Births in an effort to differentiate between mothers who live within city boundaries and those who do not, it appears that this question is inappropriately answered as yes by many mothers or by hospital staff who do not bother to confirm the residence of the mother. One means to avoid this erroneous allocation of births would be to assign municipal location based on the mother's actual address using available computer software. Not only would the allocation of births according to political units such as county and city be improved by using this method, but the allocation to many other types of geographic units (e.g., school districts, census tracts) would be possible as well.

The United Nations recommends that the principal tabulations of birth statistics for geographic areas within countries be made according to place of usual residence rather than according to place of occurrence (United Nations, 1991a, p. 47). Both types of figures are useful for different purposes. The occurrence data represent the true "service" load (i.e., requirements for maternity services). The residence data are more appropriate for measuring the fertility of the resident population and the relation of the social and economic characteristics of the population to the level of fertility. When the population data from the census are in terms of usual residence, the birth statistics should preferably be tabulated on the same basis, so that the two series will be comparable. Even if a census has been taken on a *de facto* basis, birth statistics by residence are probably more useful than birth statistics by occurrence (e.g., in the measurement of net migration).

On a national level, the United Nations recommends that birth statistics be tabulated on a *de facto* or present-in-area basis (United Nations, 1991a, p. 47). These statistics are customarily treated as a good approximation of births to residents for most countries because the national difference between the *de facto* and the *de jure* (resident) populations tends to be negligible.

---

[3] A group of experts convened in New York by the United Nations Statistics Division in November 1998 to revise the Draft Principles and Recommendations for a Vital Statistics System recommended that the term "legitimacy" should not appear in birth records for individuals to help eliminate stigma that may be associated with the term. The concept of legitimacy, however, is considered technically accurate and may be used in statistical reports on the incidence of marital and nonmarital fertility (Gonzolez, 1998).

Accuracy of Allocation by Time

About three out of four countries tabulate their birth statistics in terms of the year of occurrence of the birth, reassigning the births from the year of registration, as recommended by the United Nations (1991a, pp. 46–47). Most of those that fail to make the reassignment to date of occurrence are generally less developed (e.g., Seychelles, Nicaragua) (United Nations 1985, pp. 76–78). The birth statistics published for these countries for any year relate to events that were registered in that year. Inasmuch as the laws requiring early registration are often not observed and are rarely enforced, and the social pressures to register a birth may be few and weak or apply at some late date (e.g., on entering school), many births are not registered for some time, even years, after the birth has occurred (UNICEF, 1998). The differences between birth statistics tabulated by year of occurrence and year of registration are minimal in the more developed areas because of the strict requirements for early registration and the general compliance with them. In Belgium and the Netherlands, for example, birth certificates must be filed within 3 days of the birth; in the United States, state requirements vary, but all states require filing within 3 to 10 days of the birth; birth certificates have to be filed within 14 days in Japan and within 4 weeks in Norway (United Nations, 1985, pp. 60–63). Even so, in these countries the births are allocated to the actual year and month of occurrence. However, the consistent lag tends to reduce the extent of the problem. Because of the considerable delays in registration and the failure to reallocate the births in many countries, the net overstatement or understatement of births in any year may be substantial. Because of the greater pressures to register a death promptly, the difference between the numbers of births on the two bases is likely to be much greater than between the numbers of deaths.

There may also be some error in regard to the year for which a birth is reported if a specific year is regarded as favorable or unfavorable. For example, when the year of the horse starts a new cycle in the Oriental countries, it tends to show low birthrates, apparently because of an effort to avoid registration as of that year insofar as possible (Azumi, 1968).

Accuracy of Classification by Demographic, Socioeconomic, and Medical Characteristics

Errors may occur in the tabulations of the demographic and social characteristics of births and in the corresponding tabulations of the population employed to calculate birth and fertility rates. These errors may take the form of differential underregistration of births in certain categories, biases in reporting the characteristics of the births or of the parents of the newborn children, and errors of these kinds in the corresponding populations. To evaluate the degree of error, information from birth certificates has been compared to information gathered from independent sources such as surveys of recent mothers (Fingerhut and Kleinman, 1985) or from the related medical records of hospitals and clinics (e.g., in Brazil; see Jorge et al., 1993; in the United States, see Piper et al., 1993). Basic demographic characteristics such as the age of the mother tend to be more accurately reported than social traits such as education. Information about the mother is more accurate and complete than that for the father; and medical information about the birth or the newborn appears to be the least adequately reported of all.

GENERAL ASPECTS OF THE ANALYSIS OF NATALITY STATISTICS

Problems in Analysis of Natality Statistics

The analysis of natality is, in several ways, more complicated than the analysis of mortality. Even the statistical definition of birth is more problematic than the definition of death. The differences in the complexity of measurement of natality result from the special and, to some extent, unique characteristics of natality and of the factors affecting childbearing. These special characteristics give rise to a variety of measures, which may be quite different and which may give inconsistent results.

We may enumerate six such characteristics. First, the entire population is not subject to the risk of having a child. Motherhood is largely restricted to women of childbearing age, while fatherhood, even though less constrained by a man's physiology, usually occurs within a somewhat limited range of ages. Second, natality may be measured in relation to fathers as well as mothers, or even couples. Two parents, with different demographic, socioeconomic, and other characteristics, are involved in each birth. Third, the event of birth in a sense occurs to both a child and a parent (or parents) and, in measuring natality, the characteristics of both the child and the parent have to be considered jointly. Death, however, occurs to an individual only. Fourth, the same adult can have more than one birth in a lifetime and may be more or less continuously exposed to the risk of parenthood even after having a child. In fact, parenthood may occur twice to the same individual in a single year and, even, in the form of multiple births, twice or more to the same individual at the same hour. Death can occur but once, however, just as birth can occur but once to the newborn child.

Fifth, the time period of reference in relation to the population at risk is quite important because of the possibility of large annual fluctuations in fertility and large differences between annual levels of fertility and the levels of fertility performance of individuals and couples over a lifetime. Furthermore, changes in fertility over time as represented by period measures may reflect not only changes in the quantity (or quantum) of births but also shifts in the timing (or tempo) of births. Although it is well established that changes in the timing of first and subsequent births can cause annual fluctuations in the number of births (Hajnal, 1947; Ryder, 1956, 1980), those shifts in timing often occur simultaneously for women of many cohorts, suggesting that the shifts may be due to events unique to the period rather than to events peculiar to given cohorts (Ní Bhrolcháin, 1992). The challenge is to create accurate period and cohort measures of fertility and to interpret them appropriately in terms of causes of temporal shifts and consequences for population growth. To improve the accuracy of period measures and conclusions that may be drawn from these measures, refinements have been suggested based on age, parity (defined below), birth order, and length of time since last birth (Bongaarts and Feeney, 1998; Ní Bhrolcháin, 1992).

Finally, changes in fertility are strongly affected by personal attitudes, preferences, and motivations of women and their partners as shaped by the social and economic contexts within which they live. Shifts in childbearing have taken place in some highly industrialized countries like the United States and Sweden within the context of even more profound changes in the way in which individuals form relationships and establish families. It is no longer sufficient to analyze fertility within the bounds of traditional marriages; in many countries, it is necessary to explore the growing tendency to have children in nonmarital unions or independently of either legal or nonmarital unions. Such complexity requires the collection of extensive data, care in measurement, and the development of often elaborate theoretical frameworks.

In certain respects, the handling of birth statistics is somewhat simpler than the handling of death statistics. For instance, the analysis of births does not present the complexities faced in classifying deaths by cause. Furthermore, as a component of change in the estimation of age distributions, births during any period affect only the initial ages of the distribution and, by their nature, define particular "births cohorts" to which deaths and migrants must be assigned. Deaths during the period affect the entire age distribution and, as ordinarily tabulated, must be redistributed by age to correspond to the distribution of the population by birth cohorts at the particular date and with the population born during the period.

Factors Important in Analysis

The special characteristics of births and birth statistics just described suggest many of the variables that are important or useful in the measurement and analysis of natality. The variables of prime importance are the age of the child's mother and father and the age-sex distribution of the population. For many years, marriage was nearly as important as was one's age in ascertaining the risk of childbearing. The increase in the proportion of births outside of marriage in

countries throughout the world, however, has contributed to an increased complexity in analyzing natality relative to marital status. The complexity includes difficulties in acquiring information about fathers who are not legally tied to the child in vital registration systems, lack of information on the formation or duration of nonmarital unions, and a failure to understand how childbearing patterns may change in the future in the increasingly diverse process of family formation. Although it is still necessary to examine variables associated with childbearing within marriage such as age at marriage, interval since marriage, and duration of marriage, it is also important to try to examine similar characteristics of extramarital relationships.

Other variables of considerable theoretical importance that reflect sharp differences in fertility are parity of mother (that is, the number of children born to the woman), order of birth of the child, and interval since previous birth, marriage, or formation of a nonmarital union; but there are few data on these subjects from the vital statistics tabulations that can be related to population data from a census or survey. Furthermore, although there is considerable interest in examining these characteristics for fathers as well as for mothers, such information is generally not gathered for fathers in vital registration systems. Some characteristics of interest in the analysis of natality relate essentially to the births, such as sex, month of occurrence, and place of occurrence in terms of urban-rural residence, metropolitan-nonmetropolitan residence, or size of place. Others relate to the ethnic or socioeconomic characteristics or status of the parents, such as color, race, or ethnic affiliation, occupation, educational attainment, religion, and income. Data on these topics provide information on variations in fertility with respect to the demographic and socioeconomic characteristics of the parents, but here too, few data are available on many of them from registration sources.

MEASURES BASED ON BIRTH STATISTICS

A great number of measures of natality are based on birth statistics. These vary with the aspect of fertility that they are describing, their degree of refinement or elaboration, whether they are summary measures or specific measures, and whether they are measures of fertility per se or merely fertility-related measures. As in the case of measures of mortality, our outline of measures of fertility distinguishes, first, observed rates from adjusted rates. The distinction is only approximate. The observed rates tend to be the simpler rates and to be computed directly from actual data (i.e., they measure the phenomenon described, without assumption of hypothetical conditions), whereas the adjusted rates are more complex both with respect to method of calculation and to interpretation. The latter are often hypothetical representations of the fertility level for a given population group, serving as summary measures based on a set of specific fertility rates and various procedures for combining them.

Observed Rates

Crude Birthrate

The simplest and most common measure of natality is the crude birthrate. The crude birthrate is defined as the number of births in a year per 1000 midyear population—that is,

$$\frac{B}{P} * 1000 \qquad (15.1)$$

The issues in the choice of a base population are the same as for the crude death rate. As was noted in Chapter 12, the midyear population is employed as an approximation of the average population "exposed to risk" during the year or of the number of person-years lived during the year.

An array of crude birthrates based on complete or nearly complete vital statistics registration for a wide range of countries around 1995 (Table 15.1) indicates a low of 9.2 for the Russian Federation (1995) and a high of 33.1 for Tajikistan (1993). Rates vary somewhat by region of the world, with the lowest rates in western and eastern Europe and North America and the highest in sub-Saharan Africa (McDevitt, 1996, p. 31). In fact, estimated birthrates for many countries in sub-Saharan Africa, based in most cases on sample surveys and censuses rather than vital statistics, are about twice as high as the rate for the world, estimated to be roughly 23 births per 1000 people around 1996 (McDevitt, 1996, A-11-12). The rates for Mali, Niger, and Ethiopia, for example, are 51, 54, and 46, respectively.

TABLE 15.1 Crude Birthrates, General Fertility Rates, and Total Fertility Rates, for Various Countries: Around 1995

| Country and year | Crude birthrate | General fertility rate | Total fertility rate | Percentage difference from the United States[1] | | |
				Crude birthrate	General fertility rate	Total fertility rate
Egypt (1992)	27.1	126.4	3,854	84.4	93.6	90.1
El Salvador (1992)[2]	30.1	127.4	3,518	104.8	95.1	73.6
Germany (1996)	9.7	46.6	1,323	−34.0	−28.6	−34.7
Hungary (1996)	10.3	47.7	1,459	−29.9	−27.0	−28.0
Iran, Islamic Republic of (1994)[2]	21.9	99.1	2,940	49.0	51.8	45.0
Ireland (1996)[3]	13.9	61.9	1,914	−5.4	−5.2	−5.6
Israel (1995)[4]	21.1	94.7	2,882	43.5	45.0	42.2
Japan (1996)	9.6	47.3	1,396	−34.7	−27.6	−31.1
Panama (1995)	23.5	98.6	2,718	59.9	51.0	34.1
Poland (1996)	11.1	49.4	1,580	−24.5	−24.3	−22.1
Puerto Rico (1996)	16.8	72.0	2,064	14.3	10.3	1.8
Russian Federation (1995)[5]	9.2	41.0	1,333	−37.4	−37.2	−34.2
Sri Lanka (1995)[3]	19.0	80.4	2,336	29.3	23.1	15.2
Sweden (1996)	10.8	55.7	1,610	−26.5	−14.7	−20.6
Tajikistan (1993)[5]	33.1	153.2	4,236	125.2	134.6	109.0
Tunisia (1995)	20.8	88.2	2,667	41.5	35.1	31.6
United Kingdom (1996)	12.5	60.1	1,726	−15.0	−8.0	−14.8
United States (1996)	14.7	65.3	2,027	(X)	(X)	(X)
Venezuela (1996)[6]	22.3	95.1	2,684	51.7	45.6	32.4
Yugoslavia (1995)	13.3	62.4	1,896	−9.5	−4.4	−6.5
Average percentage difference	(X)	(X)	(X)	20.4	21.5	14.6

Note: Crude birthrates are live births per 1000 population. General fertility rates are live births per 1000 women aged 15 to 44 years. Total fertility rates equal the sum of the age-specific birthrates for women in 5-year age groups from 15 to 49 years times 5.

X: Not applicable.

[1] Plus signs have been omitted.

[2] Based on civil registers, which are incomplete or of unknown completeness.

[3] Data tabulated by year of registration rather than year of occurrence.

[4] Including data for East Jerusalem and Israeli residents in certain territories under occupation by Israeli military forces since June 1967.

[5] Excluding infants born alive after less than 28 weeks of gestation, of less than 1000 grams in weight, and less than 35 centimeters in length, who die within 7 days of birth.

[6] Excluding Indian jungle population.

Source: United Nations, 1999, Tables 7, 9, and 11; United Nations, 1998; U.S. National Center for Health Statistics, 1998b, Table 2 and Appendix Table II.

Current geographic variation may also encompass reasonably well the range of historical variation. For example, the crude birthrate in the United States appears to have approximated 50 around 1800 (Grabill, Kiser, and Whelpton 1958, p. 5), and it declined to 15 in 1996. Natural fertility, or fertility uncontrolled in any way, would be higher than has actually been experienced by any country's population. On the basis of an analysis made by Henry (1961) of fertility in a number of populations where little or no fertility control is practiced, we may estimate a crude birthrate of about 60 as corresponding to conditions of natural fertility.

In computing the crude birthrate for geographic subdivisions of countries, it is preferable to employ births allocated by place of usual residence, particularly if the population data are distributed in terms of place of usual residence. Satisfactory birthrates by residence may often be computed, however, on the basis of population data tabulated on a *de facto* basis. The use of residence data for births is more important for the smaller geographic units than for the larger ones, because the smaller the area, the more likely the rate is to be affected by the movement of mothers to hospitals to have their babies. Rates by residence more truly reflect the propensity of the population living in an area to have births than rates by occurrence. In computing rates with births by occurrence, some freedom in the choice of type of population is often possible, although use of *de facto* population figures is preferable.

As with the crude death rate, sometimes an annual average crude birthrate covering data for 2 or 3 years is computed in order to describe the longer period or to add stability to the rates. As was noted in Chapter 12, these annual average rates may be computed in a number of ways, all of which give essentially the same results. The crude rates may be computed for each year and averaged, the annual average number of births may be divided by the annual average population, or the average number of births for the 3 years may be divided by the midperiod population. The last

$$\frac{1/3(B_1 + B_2 + B_3)}{P_2} * 1000 \qquad (15.2)$$

is the most commonly used procedure.

Like the term "crude death rate," the term "crude birthrate" when unqualified means the crude birthrate for the total population of an area, but one may also speak of the crude birthrate of a particular population group in the area, such as a race, nativity, residence, or occupation group. For example, the crude birthrate for the black population of the United States in 1996 is represented by

$$\frac{B_b}{P_b} * 1000 = \frac{594,781}{33,503,435} * 1000 = 17.8$$

In this more general sense the principal characteristic of a "crude" birthrate is that all ages and both sexes are represented in the rate.

The birthrate should be adjusted for underregistration of the births and for underenumeration of the population if satisfactory estimates of these errors are available, according to the following formula:

$$\frac{B \div C_b}{P \div C_p} * 1000 \qquad (15.3)$$

where C_b represents the percentage completeness of registration of births and C_p represents the percentage completeness of the census counts or population estimates.

Official national birthrates for the United States are now based on the uncorrected figures. The U.S. National Center for Health Statistics has followed this practice since 1959, on the ground that the underregistration of births is rather small and has presumably become smaller than the understatement of the population. It has published an official series of birthrates for the years 1909 to 1959 employing births adjusted for underregistration; during all or most of this period, births were presumed to be less completely reported than the census population.

Monthly Birthrate

For births, as for deaths, there is an interest in examining variations over periods shorter than a year. We note only very briefly here the measures of the monthly variation in the birthrate, corresponding to those described for the death rate in Chapter 12. The monthly birth rate may be "annualized" by inflating the number of births for a given month by the ratio of the total number of days in the year to the number in the particular month and then dividing by the population for the month. The annualized birthrate in the United States for November 1997, adjusted for underregistration, is obtained as follows:

$$\frac{\dfrac{365}{30} * B_{\text{November 1997}}}{P_{\text{November 1997}}} = \frac{\dfrac{365}{30} * 302,000}{268,592,000} * 1000$$

$$= \frac{3,674,333}{268,592,000} * 1000 = 13.7$$

For births, as for deaths, analysis of monthly changes may be carried out on the basis of rates computed for successive 12-month periods ending in each successive month. Rates of this kind for the United States, based on provisional data, are published with a lag of about 6 months by the U.S. National Center for Health Statistics (1998a). Year-to-year changes in the birthrate on a current basis can also be measured by comparing the rates for the same month in successive years. The rates in this comparison do not require adjustment for the number of days in the month or for seasonal variations (except for February in leap year). Annual relative changes can also be measured on a current basis by comparing cumulative rates covering all the months in a year to date with the corresponding period in the preceding year—that is, for example, January to May 1999 and January to May 1998.

General Fertility Rate

Although the crude birthrate is a valuable measure of natality, particularly in indicating directly the contribution of natality to the growth rate, its analytic utility is extremely limited. This is because it is affected by many factors, particularly the specific composition of a population with respect to age, sex, and related characteristics. Because the age and sex composition of a population has such a strong influence on the level of its crude birthrate, measures of natality that are less affected by differences in age-sex composition from one population group to another are more useful analytically for interarea and intergroup comparisons. A number of such measures have been developed and are variously referred to as specific, general, adjusted, or standardized, and as birthrates, fertility rates, or reproduction rates, depending generally on their degree of complexity or on their particular significance.

The simplest overall age-limited measure is the general fertility rate, defined as the number of births per 1000 women of childbearing age. It may be represented by

$$\frac{B}{P^f_{15-44}} * 1000 \qquad (15.4)$$

The total number of births, regardless of age of mother, is employed in the numerator and the female population 15 to 44 years of age is employed in the denominator.

Applying the formula to the data for Panama in 1995 (Table 15.2), we have

$$\frac{61,939}{628,160} * 1000 = 98.6$$

This figure may be compared with the corresponding figure for the United States in 1996, 65.3. On the basis of this comparison, we can say that fertility in Panama is about one and a half times as great as fertility in the United States. The general fertility rate is sometimes defined in relation to the number of women 15 to 49 years of age but, as noted below, women aged 45 to 49 contribute relatively few births to the total number. It is preferable, therefore, to avoid dilution of the denominator of the rate with this group when the risk is so low, by excluding it from the population of childbearing age used in the rate. General fertility rates for various countries around 1995 are shown in Table 15.1.

Age-Specific Birthrates

A set or "schedule" of age-specific birthrates for a given date and population group serves as a basis for a detailed comparison, with corresponding rates for other population groups, that is unaffected by differences between the groups in age-sex composition. A set of rates may consist of the rates for 5-year age groups from 10–14 to 45–49, 15–19 to 45–49, or 15–19 to 40–44. The age classification recommended by the United Nations has 10 categories, under 15 years, quinquennial groups 15–19 to 45–49, a terminal group 50 and over, and a group of "unknown" age (United Nations, 1973, p. 82); but rates are shown in the

TABLE 15.2 Calculation of General Fertility Rate and Age-Specific Birthrates, for Panama: 1995

Age of mother	Births Reported (1)	Not reported distributed[1] (1) × factor[2] = (2)	Female population (3)	Rates [(2) ÷ (3)] × 1000 = (4)
15 to 19 years	11,720[3]	11,886	127,068	93.5
20 to 24 years	18,638	18,903	126,010	150.0
25 to 29 years	15,309	15,526	116,325	133.5
30 to 34 years	10,123	10,267	101,959	100.7
35 to 39 years	4,101	4,159	85,917	48.4
40 to 44 years	1,028	1,043	70,881	14.7
45 to 49 years	153[4]	155	57,899	2.7
Not reported	867	(X)	(X)	(X)
15 to 44 years	61,939	61,939	628,160	98.6

X: Not applicable.

[1] Births to mothers of age not reported are distributed proportionately among births to mothers of reported age.

[2] $\dfrac{\text{Total births}}{\text{Births to mothers of reported age}} = \dfrac{61,939}{61,072} = 1.014196$

[3] Includes births to mothers under age 15.

[4] Includes births to mothers 50 and over.

Source: United Nations, 1998.

TABLE 15.3   Age-Specific Birthrates and Median Age of Mother, for Various Countries:
Around 1995 (Birthrates are live births per 1000 women in specified group.)

Country and year	Birthrates by age of woman							Median age of mother
	15 to 19 years[1]	20 to 24 years	25 to 29 years	30 to 34 years	35 to 39 years	40 to 44 years	45 to 49 years[2]	
Egypt (1992)	13.3	150.9	252.9	180.4	120.5	39.2	13.6	28.4
El Salvador (1992)	108.7	192.3	166.1	116.8	75.4	33.8	10.5	26.5
Germany (1996)	9.6	55.4	90.2	75.8	28.4	4.9	0.2	28.7
Hungary (1996)	29.9	92.6	100.0	48.9	16.9	3.4	0.1	26.2
Iran (1994)	46.2	147.0	151.7	113.4	74.6	36.4	18.7	28.3
Ireland (1996)[3]	16.1	52.2	108.0	129.4	64.2	12.2	0.6	30.6
Israel (1995)	18.2	121.8	188.3	150.6	78.2	17.9	1.5	28.9
Japan (1996)	3.9	39.7	109.9	95.4	27.4	2.9	0.1	29.4
Mexico (1995)	85.2	172.1	166.1	123.7	70.9	26.6	7.6	27.1
Panama (1995)	93.5	150.0	133.5	100.7	48.4	14.7	2.7	26.1
Russian Federation (1995)	44.7	112.8	66.7	29.5	10.6	2.2	0.1	23.9
Sri Lanka (1995)[3]	29.6	95.1	132.5	113.0	72.7	21.8	2.6	29.1
Sweden (1996)	7.8	59.2	116.4	92.3	38.9	7.0	0.3	29.0
Tajikistan (1993)	53.9	271.9	225.5	159.6	93.6	35.7	6.9	27.2
Tunisia (1995)	13.6	93.0	151.6	144.2	89.7	33.5	7.7	30.3
United Kingdom (1996)	29.7	76.2	106.8	88.6	36.9	6.8	0.3	28.1
United States (1996)	55.6	110.4	113.1	83.9	35.3	6.8	0.3	26.6
Venezuela (1996)	88.1	147.8	130.0	93.1	54.6	19.0	4.0	26.2
Yugoslavia (1995)	32.6	126.6	121.6	69.1	24.1	4.7	0.5	26.3

[1] Includes births to women under age 15. Base is the female population 15 to 19 years of age.

[2] Includes births to women age 50 and over. Base is the female population 45 to 49 years of age.

[3] Data tabulated by year of registration rather than year of occurrence.

Source: Based on United Nations, 1999, Table 11; U.S. National Center for Health Statistics 1998b, Table 3.

Demographic Yearbook for the group under 20, and a terminal group 45 and over (United Nations, 1999, Table 11).

An age-specific birthrate is defined as the number of births to women of a given age group per 1000 women in that age group:

$$f_a = \frac{B_a}{P_a^f} * 1000 \qquad (15.5)$$

The formula for the birthrate at ages 20 to 24 is

$$f_{20-24} = \frac{B_{20-24}}{P_{20-24}^f} * 1000 \qquad (15.6)$$

Age-specific birthrates as here defined are a type of "central" rate, in somewhat the same sense that age-specific death rates are central rates. The corresponding probabilities are discussed later. The rate for women 20 to 24 years old in Panama (1995) is, therefore (Table 15.2),

$$\frac{18,903}{126,010} * 1000 = 150.0$$

Table 15.3 presents schedules of age-specific birthrates for a number of countries around 1995, and Figure 15.1 displays these rates graphically. The lines approximate normal curves moderately skewed to the right. Despite the general similarity of these curves from one country to another, there are interesting differences as well. For example, birthrates peak for women in their early twenties (20 to 24 age group) in several countries (e.g., Tajikistan, El Salvador), while, in other countries (e.g., Iran, United States), the rates are high and nearly equal in the two 5-year age groups for women in their twenties. Birth rates for women 15 to 19 years of age vary considerably from a low of 4 per 1000 in Japan to a high of 109 per 1000 in El Salvador. The relative magnitudes of the age-specific birth rates are more evident when the schedules of rates are converted into percent distributions, as is shown in Table 15.4. The rates for ages 45 to 49 are of little absolute or relative importance, and the rates for ages 40 to 44 usually fall below those for ages 15 to 19. Most births—from 94 to 99% depending on the country—occur to women between 15 and 39 years of age. Births in the peak childbearing years, those between ages 20 and 29, account for a low of 42% of births in Ireland to a high of 67% of births in Russia.

Differences in the age pattern of childbearing may also be measured in terms of the median age of childbearing (*median age of mother*) or the mean age of childbearing (*mean age of mother*). Both measures are used but under different circumstances. Calculating these measures on the basis of age-specific birthrates rather than numbers of births

Births per 1,000 women

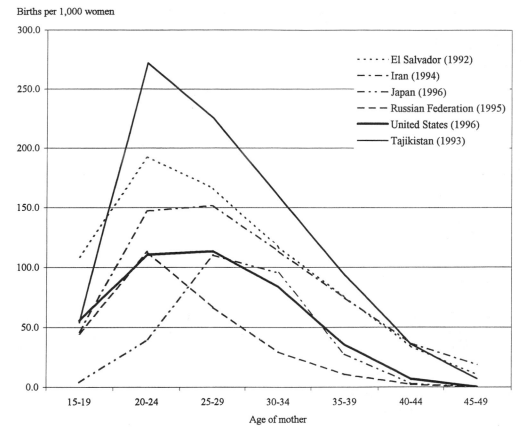

FIGURE 15.1   Age-Specific Birthrates for Various Countries: Around 1995
Note: Points are plotted at midpoint of age intervals.
Source: Table 15.3

TABLE 15.4   Percentage Distribution of Age-Specific Birthrates by Age of Mother, for Various
Countries: Around 1995

Country and year	All ages	15 to 19 years[1]	20 to 24 years	25 to 29 years	30 to 34 years	35 to 39 years	40 to 44 years	45 to 49 years[2]
Egypt (1992)	100.0	1.7	19.6	32.8	23.4	15.6	5.1	1.8
El Salvador (1992)	100.0	15.4	27.3	23.6	16.6	10.7	4.8	1.5
Germany (1996)	100.0	3.6	20.9	34.1	28.7	10.7	1.9	0.1
Hungary (1996)	100.0	10.3	31.7	34.3	16.8	5.8	1.1	0.0
Iran (1994)	100.0	7.9	25.0	25.8	19.3	12.7	6.2	3.2
Ireland (1996)[3]	100.0	4.2	13.6	28.2	33.8	16.8	3.2	0.2
Israel (1995)	100.0	3.2	21.1	32.7	26.1	13.6	3.1	0.3
Japan (1996)	100.0	1.4	14.2	39.3	34.2	9.8	1.0	0.0
Mexico (1995)	100.0	13.1	26.4	25.5	19.0	10.9	4.1	1.2
Panama (1995)	100.0	17.2	27.6	24.6	18.5	8.9	2.7	0.5
Russian Federation (1995)	100.0	16.8	42.3	25.0	11.1	4.0	0.8	0.0
Sri Lanka (1995)[3]	100.0	6.3	20.3	28.4	24.2	15.6	4.7	0.6
Sweden (1996)	100.0	2.4	18.4	36.2	28.7	12.1	2.2	0.1
Tunisia (1995)	100.0	2.6	17.4	28.4	27.0	16.8	6.3	1.4
United Kingdom (1996)	100.0	8.6	22.1	30.9	25.7	10.7	2.0	0.1
United States (1996)	100.0	13.7	27.2	27.9	20.7	8.7	1.7	0.1
Venezuela (1996)	100.0	16.4	27.5	24.2	17.3	10.2	3.5	0.7
Yugoslavia (1995)	100.0	8.6	33.4	32.1	18.2	6.4	1.2	0.1

[1] Includes births to women under age 15. Base is the female population 15 to 19 years of age.
[2] Includes births to women aged 50 and over. Base is the female population 45 to 49 years of age.
[3] Data tabulated by year of registration rather than year of occurrence.
Source: United Nations, 1999, Table 11; U.S. National Center for Health Statistics, 1998b, Table 3.

eliminates the effect of differences in the age-sex composition of the populations being compared. They may be interpreted then as describing the age pattern of childbearing of a synthetic cohort of women—that is, a hypothetical group of women who are viewed as having in their lifetime the (fertility) experience recorded in a single calendar year.

Both the median age and the mean age are ordinarily computed from data compiled for 5-year age groups. The mean age of a distribution of birthrates is computed according to the following formula:

$$\bar{a} = \frac{\sum_a a f_a}{\sum_a f_a} \qquad (15.7)$$

where a represents the midpoint of each age interval (17.5, 22.5, etc.) and f_a represents an age-specific birthrate for a 5-year age group. (The formula follows the form of a weighted average of ages, the weights being the age-specific birthrates.)

The considerable similarity of the age distributions of birth rates suggests that the median age would vary only little. For the array of countries shown in Table 15.3, the highest and lowest median ages vary by 6.7 years out of a range of about 35 years of reproductive life, but if the two extreme cases of the Russian Federation (23.9) and Ireland (30.6) are excluded, the difference falls to only 4.2 years. These differences tend to distinguish populations that have their children relatively early in the childbearing period and those that have them relatively late. On this basis, childbearing occurs relatively early in the Russian Federation and relatively late in Ireland. These differences may be accounted for in terms of the differences in the median age at first birth and in the median interval between births. To the extent that marriage is a precursor of childbearing, the age at marriage and the interval between marriage and the first birth may also account for these differences.

Fertility Rates Specific for Order of Birth

Another dimension for analyzing fertility, in addition to the age of the mother, is the order of birth of the child. Order of birth refers to the number or sequence of the child among the live births of the mother, including the present child. The simplest way of analyzing births classified by order of birth consists of calculating the proportional distribution of the births by order. Such a percentage distribution of births by order is much less affected by underregistration of births than are rates and can be computed without use of population data; but at the same time, the percentages are affected by such factors as the distribution of the female population by age. As illustrated by data for several countries, those with the lowest levels of fertility have proportionately more

births of first or second order than those with higher levels of fertility:

Birth order	Egypt, 1992	Japan, 1996	Panama, 1995	United States, 1996
Total	100.0	100.0	100.0	100.0
First	34.7	47.6	34.1	40.8
Second	22.9	36.8	25.3	32.2
Third	16.1	12.8	16.2	16.1
Fourth	10.9	2.2	8.8	6.2
Fifth	6.9	0.4	5.2	2.3
Sixth	4.3	0.1	3.3	1.0
Seventh	2.3	—	2.3	0.4
Eighth and over	2.0	—	3.7	0.5
Not reported	—	—	1.1	0.6

—: Zero or rounds to zero.

General fertility rates may be computed for each order of birth without reference to age of the mother. A *general order-specific fertility rate* is defined as the number of births of a given order per 1000 women of childbearing age:

$$\frac{B_i}{P^f_{15-44}} * 1000 \qquad (15.8)$$

where B_i represents births of a given order and P^f_{15-44} the number of women 15 to 44 years of age. Thus, the general second-order fertility rate is

$$\frac{B_2}{P^f_{15-44}} * 1000 \qquad (15.9)$$

where B_2 refers to births of the second order. This formula is evaluated for Panama in 1995 as follows (Table 15.5):

$$\frac{15,698}{628,160} * 1000 = 25.0$$

Note that the sum of the general order-specific rates over all orders equals the general fertility rate, that is

$$\sum_{i=1}^{\infty} \frac{B_i}{P^f_{15-44}} = \frac{B}{P^f_{15-44}} \qquad (15.10)$$

Usually, there is a category of births of order not reported. This category may be treated separately or distributed over the births of reported order *pro rata*.

Variations in order-specific birthrates by age may be analyzed in terms of *age-order-specific rates*. A rate of this type is represented by the formula:

$$f_a^i = \frac{B_a^i}{P_a^f} * 1000 \qquad (15.11)$$

where B_a^i represents births of a given order to women of a given age group and P_a^f relates to all the women in a particular age group, without regard to the number of children

TABLE 15.5 Calculation of General Order-Specific Birthrates and Order-Specific Birthrates for Women 20 to 24 Years of Age, for Panama: 1995

Birth order	Births			Ages 20 to 24 including age not reported[1]	Rates	
	All ages (1)	Ages 20 to 24 reported (2)	Age not reported (3)	$\frac{(1)}{(1)-(3)}*(2)=$ (4)	All ages (1) ÷ female pop. 15 to 44[2] = (5)	Ages 20 to 24 (4) ÷ female pop. 20 to 24[3] = (6)
All orders	61,939	18,638	867	18,873[4]	98.6	149.8[4]
First	21,101	7,368	128	7,413	33.6	58.8
Second	15,698	5,934	108	5,975	25.0	47.4
Third	10,051	3,419	85	3,448	16.0	27.4
Fourth	5,468	1,337	47	1,349	8.7	10.7
Fifth	3,211	382	33	386	5.1	3.1
Sixth	2,072	88	28	89	3.3	0.7
Seventh	1,407	18	21	18	2.2	0.1
Eighth and over	2,262	13	39	13	3.6	0.1
Not reported	669	79	378	182	1.1	1.4
Median order of birth	(X)	(X)	(X)	(X)	2.1	1.8

X: Not applicable.

[1] Births to mothers with age not reported are distributed proportionately among births to mothers with age reported.

[2] Female population 15 to 44 years of age = 628,160.

[3] Female population 20 to 24 years of age = 126,010.

[4] Number of births obtained by summation of figures for each order; numbers and rates differ from figures obtained by distributing ages not reported without regard to order of birth (18,903 and 150.0).

Source: United Nations Statistics Division, 1998.

they have had. This is a type of central rate, as we have defined it. For example, the second-order birthrate for women 20 to 24 years old in Panama (1995) is (Table 15.5):

$$\frac{B_{20-24}^2}{P_{20-24}^f}*1000 = \frac{5,975}{126,010}*1000 = 47.4$$

The sum of age-order-specific rates over *all orders* for a particular age group equals the general age-specific birthrate for that age group (the rates being additive because the denominators are the same)—that is,

$$\sum_{i=1}^{\infty}\frac{B_a^i}{P_a^f}*1000 = \frac{B_a}{P_a^f}*1000 \qquad (15.12)$$

The age-order-specific rates cannot be added for a particular order over *all ages* to derive the general fertility rate for that order, however, because the denominators of the rates are all different.

In the calculation of age-order-specific birthrates, it is desirable to dispose both of births of "unknown" age and of births of "unknown" order, both of which ordinarily appear in the basic tabulations. This can be done satisfactorily by (1) prorating the "unknown ages" for each order among the "known ages" for each order and then (2) prorating the "unknown orders" for each age group among the "known orders" for each age group, or vice versa.

Median ages of childbearing may be computed for each order of birth from age-order-specific birthrates, as shown in Table 15.6. These values give an indication of the "typical" age at which mothers have their first, second, or later child. Differences between values for consecutive orders give a rough idea of the spacing intervals between births. The median age for first births suggests the typical age of starting families, and by determining the average number of children per woman by other methods, we can identify by interpolation the typical age of completing families. For example, the typical age of starting families in Panama in 1995 is estimated at 21.6 years, the median age of first births. The annual "total fertility rate," discussed later, of 2.7 children corresponds in Table 15.6 to a median age of about 27 years, which may be taken as the typical age of completing families in Panama. Each child tends to follow the previous child after an interval of about 2.5 to 3.3 years, with a total average interval of about 6 years from the birth of the first child to the birth of the third, and normally last, child. For women who have more than three children in Panama, the average time between each successive later birth tends to be about 1.5 to 2.5 years.

Marital and Nonmarital Fertility Rates

Observed fertility rates may be further refined by taking marital status into account in classifying births and defining

TABLE 15.6 Age-Order-Specific Birthrates, for the United States, 1996, and Panama, 1995

Country, year, and order of birth	General fertility rate[2]	Age of mother[1]							Median age of mother
		15 to 19 years[3]	20 to 24 years	25 to 29 years	30 to 34 years	35 to 39 years	40 to 44 years	45 to 49 years[4]	
United States (1996)									
All orders[5]	65.3	55.6	110.4	113.1	83.9	35.3	6.8	0.3	26.5
First	26.8	43.7	52.0	42.7	23.4	7.8	1.4	0.1	24.0
Second	21.1	9.9	37.4	39.5	30.5	11.4	1.9	0.1	27.3
Third	10.5	1.7	14.8	19.7	17.8	8.2	1.4	0.1	28.9
Fourth	4.1	0.2	4.5	7.2	7.2	4.1	0.9	—	30.1
Fifth	1.5	—	1.2	2.5	2.8	1.8	0.5	—	31.2
Sixth	0.6	—	0.3	0.9	1.2	0.9	0.3	—	32.5
Seventh	0.3	—	0.1	0.4	0.6	0.5	0.2	—	33.3
Eighth and over	0.3	—	—	0.2	0.5	0.6	0.3	—	35.8
Median order of birth	1.8	1.1	1.6	1.9	2.1	2.4	2.6	3.0	(X)
Panama (1995)									
All orders[5]	98.6	93.0	149.8	133.7	101.0	48.7	14.8	2.7	26.1
First	34.0	68.1	59.4	29.8	12.8	3.4	1.1	0.1	21.6
Second	25.3	20.6	47.9	36.9	21.9	7.0	1.1	0.2	24.9
Third	16.2	3.9	27.6	28.1	20.6	8.4	1.3	0.1	27.4
Fourth	8.8	0.4	10.8	18.1	14.2	5.7	1.0	0.2	28.9
Fifth	5.2	0.1	3.1	11.5	9.9	4.9	1.0	0.3	30.4
Sixth	3.3	—	0.7	5.8	8.2	4.6	1.3	0.1	31.4
Seventh	2.3	—	0.1	2.3	6.4	4.3	1.6	0.2	33.9
Eighth and over	3.6	—	0.1	1.2	7.0	10.3	6.4	1.5	36.8
Median order of birth	2.1	1.2	1.8	2.5	3.3	4.5	6.9	7.6	(X)

—: Represents zero or rounds to zero.

X: Not applicable.

[1] Births to mothers of age not reported are distributed proportionately among births to mothers of reported age.

[2] General fertility rates are live births per 1000 women aged 15 to 44 years.

[3] Includes births to mothers under 15 years of age.

[4] Includes births to mothers 50 years of age and over.

[5] Births of order not reported are distributed proportionately among births of reported birth order.

Source: United Nations Statistics Division, 1998; U.S. National Center for Health Statistics, 1998b, Tables 2 and 3.

the base population. In many countries, births still occur primarily within marriage, but in a number of countries, the proportion of births occurring outside marital unions has become significant (United Nations, 1998b, pp. 54–55). In the past, marital fertility measures have used labels derived from the concept of the legitimacy status of the child at birth. The United Nations defines legitimate live births as those that occur to parents who are married at the time of birth according to the prevailing civil laws of the area. Births occurring within nonmarital unions have usually been classified as illegitimate. To avoid stigmatizing a child, the use of such labels on a child's birth certificate is no longer recommended, even though the concept of legitimacy may continue to be used for technical and statistical purposes by the United Nations and some countries (see footnote 3). We have chosen to use the terms "marital" and "nonmarital" in place of "legitimate" and "illegitimate" in labeling various fertility measures, thereby classifying the birth in terms of the marital status of the parents rather than the apparent legal

status of the child. Except as noted later, this change merely affects the label of the measure and not the way in which it is calculated.

General and Age-Specific Marital and Nonmarital Fertility Rates

The general marital fertility rate and the general non-marital fertility rate relate live births to married women and live births to unmarried women, respectively. The *general marital fertility rate* (formerly, general legitimate fertility rate) is defined as the number of live births occurring to married women in a year per 1000 married women 15 to 44 years of age at the middle of the year:

$$\frac{B^m}{P^{fm}_{15-44}} * 1000 \qquad (15.13)$$

where B^m represents live births to women who were legally married at the time of birth and P^{fm}_{15-44} represents married women (including those who are separated but not yet

TABLE 15.7 General Marital and Nonmarital Fertility Rates and Age-Specific Birthrates by Marital Status, for Various Countries: Around 1995

Marital status, country, and year	General marital or nonmarital fertility rate	Age-specific birthrates by marital status						
		15 to 19 years[1]	20 to 24 years	25 to 29 years	30 to 34 years	35 to 39 years	40 to 44 years	45 to 49 years[2]
Married[3]								
Australia (1994)	90.9	162.8	179.7	186.4	126.8	44.9	6.7	0.3
Chile (1992)	102.7	230.3	198.1	150.6	98.3	49.0	12.5	1.0
Hungary (1996)	68.7	394.4	214.7	128.1	52.6	16.8	3.2	0.1
Ireland (1996)[4,5]	110.4	376.8	266.7	216.3	171.6	77.9	13.7	0.7
Poland (1996)	73.9	601.7	254.8	131.0	61.8	25.0	5.7	0.3
Sweden (1996)	75.2	304.3	249.6	193.0	109.8	39.3	6.6	0.3
United States (1996)	83.7	346.3	209.1	157.0	102.4	41.1	8.0	(X)
Unmarried[6]								
Australia (1994)	33.3	18.6	40.7	52.1	49.5	28.8	6.9	0.2
Chile (1992)	65.6	47.4	82.5	87.8	83.3	62.6	20.1	1.6
Hungary (1996)	23.3	16.9	30.3	42.6	37.5	17.0	3.7	0.1
Ireland (1996)[4,7]	26.0	15.5	37.8	33.7	32.5	19.1	5.6	0.3
Poland (1996)	12.6	7.8	17.2	21.0	22.0	15.8	4.5	0.2
Sweden (1996)	45.6	6.4	45.0	88.3	77.5	38.5	7.8	0.3
United States (1996)	44.8	44.1	70.7	56.8	41.1	20.1	4.8	(X)

Note: General marital or nonmarital fertility rates are total live births to women in a given marital status per 1000 women 15 to 44 years of age in the same marital status. Age-specific birthrates by marital status are live births to women of a given marital status and age group per 1000 women in the specified group.

X: Not available

[1] Includes births to women under age 15; the base is women 15 to 19 years of age.
[2] Includes births to women age 50 and over; the base is women 45 to 49 years of age.
[3] Includes births to women who are separated.
[4] Data tabulated by year of registration rather than year of occurrence.
[5] Includes births to women who are "consensually" married but not for those who are separated.
[6] Includes births to women who are single, "consensually" married, widowed, or divorced.
[7] Includes births to women who are separated but not for those who are "consensually" married.

Source: United Nations, 1998c; U.S. National Center for Health Statistics, 1998b, Tables 1, 17 and supplementary table, "Female Population by Marital Status, Age, Race and Hispanic Origin: United States, 1996."

divorced) who are 15 to 44 years of age.[4] An array of general marital fertility rates for years around 1995 is shown in Table 15.7. The rates given here range from 68.7 for Hungary to 110.4 for Ireland. The *general nonmarital fertility rate* (formerly, the illegitimacy rate) is defined as the number of live births to unmarried women in a year, regardless of the age of the mother, per 1000 unmarried women 15 to 44 years old at the middle of the year:

$$\frac{B^u}{P^{fu}_{15-44}} * 1000 \tag{15.14}$$

[4] The term "general marital fertility rate" was formerly used to represent the total number of live births in a year, regardless of the age and marital status of the mother, per 1000 married women 15 to 44 year of age at the middle of the year (Shryock, Siegel, and Stockwell, 1976, p. 281). This particular measurement of all births relative to only married women is no longer as useful as it once was, given the increasing number of births to women who are unmarried. As a result, this measure is not included here and the term "general marital fertility rate" is reserved for births to married women per 1000 married women 15 to 44 years of age.

where B^u represents live births to women who were not legally married at the time of birth and P^u_{15-44} represents unmarried women (i.e., single, widowed, divorced, or cohabiting partner) who are 15 to 44 years of age. An array of general nonmarital fertility rates for years around 1995 is shown in Table 15.7. The rates given here range from 12.6 for Poland to 65.6 for Chile, a country in which nearly 7% of the women of childbearing ages are living in consensual unions (United Nations, 1998).

Age-specific marital birthrates and age-specific nonmarital birthrates may also be computed for women in specific age categories—that is,

$$\frac{B^m_a}{P^{fm}_a} * 1000 \tag{15.15}$$

and

$$\frac{B^u_a}{P^{fu}_a} * 1000 \tag{15.16}$$

The *nonmarital birth ratio* (formerly, the illegitimacy ratio) is defined as the number of live births to unmarried women per 1000 total live births:

$$\frac{B^u}{B} * 1000 \qquad (15.17)$$

where B^u represents births to unmarried women and B total births. This ratio may be subject to considerable understatement because extramarital births are more likely to go unregistered than births occurring within marriage and because unmarried parents may report themselves as married to avoid social stigma for their child. The nonmarital birth ratio has an extremely wide range depending on the situation in a given area: it may vary from nearly 0 to more than 500 per 1000 live births:

Country and year	Nonmarital birth ratio
Australia (1994)	256.1
Chile (1992)	368.1
Costa Rica (1995)	465.9
Cyprus (1996)	14.9
France (1994)	361.0
Japan (1996)	12.8
Kazakhstan (1996)	176.0
Poland (1996)	101.7
Spain (1995)	110.9
Sri Lanka (1995)	15.4
Sweden (1996)	538.9
United States (1996)	323.9

The nonmarital birth ratio is strongly affected by the relative frequency of nonmarital unions. The rise in cohabitation in many developed countries, particularly in Western Europe, the United States, and Australia, has resulted in ratios between 250 and 550. The highest ratio, 539 in Sweden, indicates that over half of the births are to women who are not married at the time of the birth even though they are likely to be living with the father of the child. Latin American countries, with long-standing traditions of consensual unions, exhibit nonmarital birth ratios between 350 and 500, as exemplified by the ratios for Chile and Costa Rica, which equal 368 and 466, respectively. In countries where nonmarital unions are uncommon, the nonmarital birth ratio tends to be rather low, as occurs in Asian and Southern European countries. In Japan, for example, only 13 out of 1000 live births occur to unmarried women.

Duration-Specific Marital Fertility Rates

For those births occurring to married couples, fertility varies as sharply with the duration of the marriage as with the age of the parents. Tabulations of births by duration of marriage are rendered more useful for analysis if they are cross-tabulated by age of mother and order of birth. With the increase in the number of births occurring outside marriage, information about nonmarital unions including their duration would be useful. Vital records systems usually document a mother's marital status but rarely gathers information about the duration of the marriage and never about the length of nonmarital unions. Population registers tend to be a good source of information about the duration of marriages but, like vital records, do not gather comparable data on "consensual" living arrangements. As a result, information about the duration of either marital or nonmarital unions is generally obtained from surveys or censuses.

The simplest measure, the *duration-specific marital birth ratio*, is merely the percentage distribution of births to married women by duration of married life. In most countries, the highest proportion of births to married women tends to occur in the first 5 years of marriage, as seen in Table 15.8. The concentration of births within the first 12 months of marriage is noticeably high in Japan and Panama, two rather different countries; the first has a much higher proportion of births occurring within marriage than the latter. Ireland exemplifies the other extreme with relatively few births to married women occurring within the first 12 months of marriage.

Availability of the number of married women distributed by duration of married life makes it possible to compute duration-specific marital fertility rates. A *duration-specific marital fertility rate* is defined as the number of live births to women married for a specific number of years per 1000 women 15 to 44 (or 15 to 49) years of age married for this number of years—that is,

$$\frac{B_t^m}{P_{15-44t}^{fm}} * 1000 \qquad (15.18)$$

where B_t^m represents live births to women married t years and P_{15-44t}^{fm} represents women 15 to 44 years of age married t years. Unfortunately, reliable estimates of the distribution of the female population by marital duration suitable for use in computing fertility rates have become increasingly difficult to obtain. European countries that calculated these rates in the past no longer do so. As a result, duration-specific marital fertility rates are shown for only one country, Sweden. The usefulness of these rates is limited because slightly less than half of the births in Sweden occur to women who are married at the time of the birth.

For classifying the births, duration of married life is the number of completed years elapsed between the date of marriage and date of birth of the child. In the absence of information on the exact date of marriage, duration may be based on the difference between the *year* of marriage and the *year* of the birth. This procedure introduces an upward bias in the frequencies for all durations except the category under-

TABLE 15.8 Percentage Distribution of Births to Married Women, and Marital Fertility Rates, by Duration of Mother's Married Life, for Selected Countries: 1996

Duration of marriage	Percentage distribution of births to married women[1]						Marital fertility rate
	Australia (1996)	France (1994)	Ireland[2] (1996)	Japan (1996)	Panama (1994)	Sweden (1997)	Sweden[3] (1997)
All durations	100.0	100.0	100.0	100.0	100.0	100.0	54.1
Under 1 year	8.7	11.7	1.5	19.1	19.0	15.1	203.2
1 year	11.8	14.8	8.5	17.0	13.3	16.0	201.0
2 years	11.4	11.8	10.1	14.0	9.3	13.1	165.9
3 years	11.4	11.3	10.2	13.0	7.9	11.9	153.8
4 years	10.6	10.1	10.0	10.5	7.2	9.8	127.2
5 years	9.6	8.3	9.1	7.8	6.1	7.6	98.2
6 years	8.2	6.4	8.9	5.6	4.8	6.2	81.0
7 years	6.7	5.0	7.5	4.1	4.2	6.0	47.0
8 years	5.4	4.0	6.7	2.7	3.9	3.5	24.4
9 years	4.1	3.3	4.6	1.8	3.0	2.6	34.6
10 to 14 years	9.6	9.3	13.1	3.6	8.2	6.0	19.2
15 to 19 years	2.0	3.1	5.6	0.4	2.2	1.5	5.8
20 years and over	0.3	0.9	1.5	—	0.6	0.4	0.9
Not reported	—	—	2.6	0.3	10.3	0.3	211.3
Median years[4]	4.6	4.0	5.9	3.0	3.4	3.5	3.4[5]

—: Represents zero or rounds to zero.

[1] Age of married women may equal 10 to 49, 15 to 49, or 15 to 44 years of age depending on the country.

[2] Percentages for 9 years and 10 to 14 years of duration were estimated using births in 1994 by year of marriage obtained from the Central Statistics Office, Ireland.

[3] Rates are live births to women married for specified periods of time per 1000 married women aged 15 to 49 years with married life of corresponding durations.

[4] In calculating the median, ages not reported were excluded from the total.

[5] The total for calculating the median marital fertility rate was obtained by adding the rates for durations under 1 year to 9 years, and 5 times the rates for durations 10 to 14, 15 to 19, and 20 and over (assumed to represent 20 to 24).

Source: Sweden, Statistics Sweden, 1998a; 1998b, Table 3.10; United Nations, 1998c.

1-year.[5] On the other hand, the category under-1-year is inflated by births conceived prior to marriage.

Period Adjusted Rates

We have been discussing observed measures of natality—that is, those measures that are derived directly from tabulations of births in a given year or brief period of years and estimates of midyear or midperiod population. We want to extend the discussion to consider two classes of adjusted rates relating to a given year or brief period of years. The first class of adjusted rates includes various types of summary rates that are adjusted for the demographic composition of the population, particularly its age-sex composition. Comparative fertility analysis often requires other more refined overall measures of the fertility of a population than

the crude birthrate, the general fertility rate, and the general marital or nonmarital fertility rate. The second class covers various types of annual rates that have a meaning or structure akin to that of a cohort (i.e., birth probabilities specific for such characteristics of the women as her age, parity, or duration of married life). They are analogous to the mortality rates discussed in Chapters 12 and 13. Because an understanding of the calculation of birth probabilities requires an understanding of cohort fertility measures, however, the discussion of birth probabilities will be postponed until after cohort fertility has been considered.

Rates Adjusted for Age-Sex Composition

As stated earlier, as an overall measure, the crude birthrate in particular is subject to important limitations for analytic studies. Like the crude death rate, it is affected by variations in the demographic composition of the population, particularly its age and sex composition. The analysis of time trends and of group fertility differences is enhanced by eliminating as completely as possible the effect of differences in the age-sex composition of the populations being compared. This is only partially accomplished by computa-

[5] The category under-1-year is seriously understated because births that occurred within 12 months after marriage but in the next calendar year are classed with the duration 1 year rather than in the group under-1-year. The upward bias for all higher categories is important when the number of births is changing rapidly and the duration categories are in single years; otherwise it is negligible.

tion of the general fertility rate. Both the crude birthrate and the general fertility rate may be adjusted (or standardized) for variations in age-sex composition. In addition, other types of age-sex adjusted measures of fertility, particularly the total fertility rate, may be calculated. As with death rates, birth or fertility rates may be adjusted (or standardized) by either the direct or indirect method. Even though the basic methods of standardization were described in Chapter 12, because age-adjustment of birth and fertility rates may differ in detail from age-adjustment of death rates and because rates of a different design may be involved, we consider the calculation of age-adjusted birth and fertility rates separately here. In addition, we discuss the decomposition of differences in crude rates between two populations to establish the relative contribution of age structure and age-specific rates. Also, brief attention is given to the adjustment of fertility rates for variables other than age and sex.

Age-Sex Adjusted Birthrate

We turn first to the calculation of the age-sex adjusted ("crude") birthrate by the direct method. The formula is as follows:

$$\frac{\sum f_a P_a^f}{P} * 1000, \text{ or } \sum f_a\left(\frac{P_a^f}{P}\right) * 1000 \quad (15.19)$$

where f_a equals the age-specific (maternal) birthrates in a particular population, P_a^f equals the female age distribution in the standard population, and P equals the total of the standard population (all ages, both sexes). As may be seen from the right side of formula 15.19, the age-specific birthrates are weighted by the proportions that females of a given age make up of the total population. The use of the overall total population rather than the female population of childbearing age or the total female population is intended to provide an adjusted rate of the approximate magnitude of the crude birthrate.

The calculation of the age-sex adjusted birthrate by this method is shown in Table 15.9 for several countries around 1995, using the population of the United States in 1996 as a standard. Taking Panama as an example, we find that the cumulative product of the age-specific birth rates for Panama and the female population of the United States by age is 5,199,800. Dividing this figure by the total population of the United States, 265,284,000, gives the age-sex adjusted birth rate for Panama, 19.6. This rate may be compared with the age-sex adjusted rate (i.e., the crude birthrate) for the United States in 1996 (14.7) to measure the difference between the two countries in the "underlying" level of fertility. We see that the adjustment decreased the percentage difference in fertility between the two countries; the difference was 33% of the U.S. rate when based on adjusted

TABLE 15.9   Calculation of Age-Sex Adjusted Birthrates by the Direct Method, for Various Countries: Around 1995

| Age of mother | Standard population (thousands) (P_a^f) United States (1996) | Age-specific birthrates, f_a | | | | |
		El Salvador (1992)	Hungary (1996)	Japan (1996)	Panama (1995)	Tunisia (1995)
15 to 19 years[1]	9,043	108.7	29.9	3.9	93.5	13.6
20 to 24 years	8,561	192.3	92.6	39.7	150.0	93.0
25 to 29 years	9,469	166.1	100.0	109.9	133.5	151.6
30 to 34 years	10,708	116.8	48.9	95.4	100.7	144.2
35 to 39 years	11,318	75.4	16.9	27.4	48.4	89.7
40 to 44 years	10,506	33.8	3.4	2.9	14.7	33.5
45 to 49 years[2]	9,376	10.5	0.1	0.1	2.7	7.7
(1) $\Sigma P_a^f f_a$ = expected births	3,891,494	6,759,763	2,761,298	2,777,981	5,199,800	5,338,123
(2) Age-sex adjusted birthrate (ASABR) = [(1)/265,284,000] * 1000[3]	14.7	25.5	10.4	10.5	19.6	20.1
(3) Percentage difference ASABR from U.S.[4] = {[(2)/(14.7)] − 1.0} * 100	(X)	+73.5	−29.3	−28.6	+33.3	+36.7
(4) Crude birthrate (CBR)	14.7	30.1	10.3	9.6	23.5	20.8
(5) Percent difference of CBR from U.S.[4] = {[(4)/(14.7)] − 1.0} * 100	(X)	+104.8	−29.9	−34.7	+59.9	+41.5

X: Not applicable.

[1] Includes births to women under 15 years of age.

[2] Includes births to women 50 years of age and over.

[3] Total U.S. population in 1996 = 265,284,000.

[4] U.S. crude birthrate = 14.7.

Source: United Nations, 1999; United Nations, 1998c, Table 11; U.S. National Center for Health Statistics, 1998b, Table 1 and Appendix Table II.

rates but 60% when based on crude rates. It is implied that the age-sex composition of Panama's population is more favorable for a high level of fertility than that of the United States. Subtracting the difference in age-adjusted fertility rates (4.9) from the total difference between the crude rates (8.8) yields an estimate of the effect of the difference in age composition (3.9) on the difference between the crude rates. Because these results are affected by the choice of the population used as a standard, we consider this decomposition of the difference in the crude rates preliminary and consider the more refined calculation that follows.

The general fertility rate may also be further adjusted for age-sex composition by the direct method by applying the following formula:

$$\frac{\sum f_a P_a^f}{\sum P_a^f} * 1000 \qquad (15.20)$$

This formula is like the formula for the age-sex adjusted birthrate, except that the divisor here is the female population of childbearing age rather than the total population. Hence, age-sex adjusted general fertility rates are of the same order of magnitude as unadjusted general fertility rates. Relative variations in age-sex adjusted general fertility rates are the same as those in age-sex adjusted "crude" birthrates; hence, the former type of rate is infrequently used.

The crude birthrate may also be adjusted for age-sex composition by the indirect method when age-specific birthrates for the particular population are lacking or defective. The conventional calculation by this method follows the formula:

$$\frac{b}{\sum F_a p_a^f} * F * 1000 \qquad (15.21)$$

where the symbols have the following meaning:

For the particular population:
  b = total births
  p_a^f = female population by age
For the "standard" population:
  F_a = age-specific birthrates
  F = crude birthrate

Note that this formula may be restated as

$$\frac{\sum f_a p_a^f}{\sum F_a p_a^f} * F * 1000 \qquad (15.22)$$

that is to say, the relative difference in adjusted fertility between the two areas is equivalent to *direct* standardization in which the population distribution of the *particular* population under study is the standard population. In effect, then, in "indirect standardization" the age-specific *pattern* of fertility is borrowed for the population under study and the standard population is the age-sex distribution of the study population.

The calculation of age-sex adjusted rates using the indirect method is illustrated in Table 15.10 for several countries using the age-specific birthrates of the United States in 1996 as the pattern for fertility and the population of Panama as the standard population. For example, for Panama in 1995, we proceed as follows: First, we compute the cumulative product of the age-specific rates for the United States (the standard weights) and the number of women in Panama in each age group. The result, 46,186, represents the number of births that Panama would have had in 1995 if its age-specific birthrates were equal to those of the United States in 1996. The ratio of the actual number of births in Panama in 1995, 61,939, to the expected number equals 1.3411. Multiplying this ratio times the crude birthrate of the United States (14.7) gives a sex-age adjusted birthrate per 1000 population of 19.7 for Panama. Before the adjustment of the crude birthrate, fertility in Panama appeared to be 60% greater than in the United States (23.5/14.7), as shown in Table 15.9; following the adjustment, the difference appeared to be only 34% (19.7/14.7). The result suggests that a difference in age-sex composition accounts for a considerable part of the difference in crude birthrates.

The age-sex adjusted birthrates derived from indirect standardization were similar to those produced through direct standardization for all of the countries considered here except Tunisia, as illustrated by the following summary of rates and percentage differences from the crude birthrate of the United States:

Country and year	Crude birthrate	Adjusted birthrate		Percentage difference from U.S. rate		
		Direct[a]	Indirect[b]	Crude	Direct[a]	Indirect[b]
El Salvador (1992)	30.1	25.5	25.2	+104.8	+73.5	+71.4
Hungary (1996)	10.3	10.4	10.7	−29.9	−29.3	−27.2
Japan (1996)	9.6	10.5	10.0	−34.7	−28.6	−32.0
Panama (1995)	23.5	19.6	19.7	+59.9	+33.3	+34.0
Tunisia (1995)	20.8	20.1	17.6	+41.5	+36.7	+19.7
United States (1996)	14.7	14.7	14.7	(X)	(X)	(X)

X: Not applicable

[a] The standard population is the U.S. population in 1996.

[b] The pattern of age-specific birthrates for the United States in 1996 is assumed to apply to each country, but the standard population implied for each country's calculation is the population of that country.

TABLE 15.10   Calculation of Age-Sex Adjusted Birthrates by the Indirect Method,
for Various Countries: Around 1995

Age of mother	Age-specific birthrates (F_a) United States (1996)	Female population (thousands), p_a^f				
		El Salvador (1992)	Hungary (1996)	Japan (1996)	Panama (1995)	Tunisia (1995)
15 to 19 years[1]	55.6	301	386	4,016	127	469
20 to 24 years	110.4	260	403	4,804	126	414
25 to 29 years	113.1	212	344	4,593	116	388
30 to 34 years	83.9	173	299	3,955	102	337
35 to 39 years	35.3	142	347	3,848	86	284
40 to 44 years	6.8	120	428	4,274	71	222
45 to 49 years[2]	0.3	97	376	5,576	58	160
(1) $\Sigma F_a p_a^f$ = expected births	(X)	89,792	145,227	1,771,653	46,186	155,526
(2) Actual births	3,891,494	154,014	105,272	1,206,555	61,939	186,416
(3) Ratio, actual births/expected births = (2)/(1)	(X)	1.7152	0.7249	0.6810	1.3411	1.1986
(4) Age-adjusted birthrate = (3) $* 14.7$[3]	14.7	25.2	10.7	10.0	19.7	17.6
(5) Percentage difference from the United States, 1996 = {[(4)/ (14.7)] − 1.0} $* 100$	(X)	+71.4	−27.2	−32.0	+34.0	+19.7

X: Not applicable.

[1] Includes births to women under 15 years of age.

[2] Includes births to women 50 years of age and over.

[3] U.S. crude birthrate = 14.7.

Source: United Nations, 1999, Tables 7 and 9; United Nations, 1998c; U.S. National Center for Health Statistics, 1998b, Tables 2 and 3.

As suggested by the discussion of age-adjustment of death rates in Chapter 12, the magnitude of the discrepancy between the age-adjusted rates obtained from these two methods can be related to the general magnitude of the difference in the age composition of the countries being compared. Moreover, the rates adjusted by the indirect method for different countries are, in effect, based on different population weighting schemes. Because of the more limited comparability of a set of rates calculated by the indirect method of age-adjustment and its use of borrowed patterns of age-specific fertility, the direct method is the preferred method of calculation.

The age-sex adjustment using the indirect approach is particularly applicable to some statistically underdeveloped countries because only data on the total number of births and the population distribution by age and sex are required for the calculation. This may be the case in a country such as Tunisia, where the age-specific birthrates used in the direct method of standardization included 26,453 births (14.2% of the total) for which the mother's age had not been recorded on the birth certificate. To the extent that these births may not be distributed proportionately to those in which the mother's age is reported (the assumption used in allocating the births with unreported age of mother), the age-specific rates may be distorted and could produce less reliable age-adjusted rates in the direct method.

Decomposition of Difference between Rates

It is of interest to measure precisely the degree to which the difference between the crude birthrates of two populations can be attributed to differences in age-specific rates relative to the age-sex structures of the two populations. The method of decomposition used for this purpose relies on direct standardization and can be used to determine the relative contribution of a number of different factors that comprise a rate change. To demonstrate the usefulness of this method, we will consider the relatively simple example of the crude birthrate expressed as the product of age-specific birthrates and the proportion of women in specific age categories relative to the total population, as shown in the following equation:

$$\frac{B}{P} * 1000 = \sum_a \frac{B_a * 1000}{P_a^f} * \frac{P_a^f}{P} \qquad (15.23)$$

where B equals total births, B_a represents births to women of a given age group, P_a^f equals the female population in age groups, and P is the total population. As described earlier, by using standardization, one may first determine what the difference in the crude birthrates of two populations would be if the age-specific birthrates of the two populations differed but the population structures were the same. The resulting birthrates for each population would be adjusted for the difference in age-sex structure, and the difference between the age-sex adjusted rates would provide a measure of the effect due to the age-specific rates, called the rate effect. Next, to determine the effect of the differences in the age-sex structures, called the compositional effect, one would produce adjusted birthrates in which the age-specific rates were held constant and the proportion of women in each age group was allowed to vary.

In a more refined calculation, when computing the rate and compositional effects that account for observed differences in crude birthrates between two populations, the standards to be used for the age-sex structure and age-specific rates, respectively, should be the average for each of these factors in the two populations (Kitagawa, 1995). By using the average as the standard, one may eliminate an interaction effect that may occur when one uses other standards. The interaction effect results from the fact that the rate effect depends on the choice of population standard and the compositional effect depends on the choice of rates used in the calculations.

For example, the first step in calculating the rate effect for two populations, labeled populations 1 and 2, would be to compute the age-sex adjusted birthrate in each population. The equation for population 1 would be

$$\sum \frac{B_{1a}}{p_{1a}^f} * \left(\frac{\dfrac{p_{2a}^f}{P_2} + \dfrac{p_{1a}^f}{P_1}}{2} \right) \qquad (15.24)$$

where the symbols have the following meaning for population 1:

p_{1a}^f = females by age group
P_1 = total population
B_{1a} = births to females by age group

with corresponding terms for population 2. This equation may also be written as

$$\frac{\sum \dfrac{p_{2a}^f}{P_2} * \dfrac{B_{1a}}{p_{1a}^f} + \sum \dfrac{p_{1a}^f}{P_1} * \dfrac{B_{1a}}{p_{1a}^f}}{2} \qquad (15.25)$$

in which the age-sex adjusted rate for population 1 using the structure of population 2 as a standard is added to the crude birthrate of population 1 and the resulting sum is divided by 2. The results of such calculations can be seen in Table 15.11, in which the United States (1996) is shown as population 1 and Panama (1995) as population 2. For the United States, the age-sex adjusted birthrate equals 16.12, which is one-half of the sum (32.24) of the United States' crude birthrate (14.67) and its adjusted rate (17.57) when Panama's population structure serves as a standard. Using similar calculations, Panama's age-sex adjusted rate equals

21.57. The rate effect, which is the difference between the age-sex standardized rates of the two populations, equals 21.57 − 16.12, or 5.45. The compositional effect (the difference between the age-specific-rate-standardized "crude" rates) equals 3.42. The overall difference between the crude birthrates of Panama and the United States (8.87) equals the sum of the rate effect (5.45) and the compositional effect (3.42). Calculating the percentage of each of these effects relative to the total, we see that the difference in the age-specific rates of the two countries (the rate effect) accounts for 61.5%, while the difference in their age-sex structures (the compositional effect) accounts for 38.5% of the overall difference in the crude birthrates of Panama and the United States. This process can be extended to more variables and to more complex functional relations among the variables that comprise a rate, as shown in detail in Das Gupta (1993).

Total Fertility Rate

The total fertility rate (TFR) is another age-sex adjusted measure of fertility that takes account of age detail within the childbearing ages, but it is of a quite different order of magnitude. Once again we begin, in the direct method of computation, with a set of age-specific maternal birthrates for the population under study. In theory, the total fertility rate represents simply the sum of the age-specific birthrates over all ages of the childbearing period. Hence, the age-specific rates are given equal weight and the resulting measure of fertility is of the approximate magnitude of "completed family size"— that is, the total number of children 1000 women will bear in their lifetime (see the following and Chapter 17). If the actual rates are for single years of age, then they each receive a weight of 1; if the actual rates are for 5-year age groups, as is the usual case, then they each receive a weight of 5. In the latter case, the calculation is simply carried out by summing the rates and multiplying the total by 5:

$$5 \sum_{a=15-19}^{a=45-49} f_a * 1000 \qquad (15.26)$$

An array of total fertility rates based on data for 5-year groups was given in Table 15.1. The rate for El Salvador, for example, was obtained by summing the age-specific birthrates (per 1000) shown in Table 15.3 and multiplying by 5:

$$5(f_{15-19} + f_{20-24} + f_{25-29} + f_{30-34} + f_{35-39} + f_{40-44} + f_{45-49})$$
$$= 5(108.7 + 192.3 + 166.1 + 116.8 + 75.4 + 33.8 + 10.5)$$
$$= 5(703.6) = 3,518$$

The rate for ages 15 to 19 includes the few births to women under 15. The total fertility rates shown in Table 15.1 vary from 1323 for Germany, 1996, to 4236 for Tajikistan, 1993; that is, the highest fertility shown is over three times as great as the lowest fertility shown.

The total fertility rate is recommended as an easy-to-compute and effective measure of age-sex adjusted fertility

TABLE 15.11 Standardization and Decomposition of Crude Birthrates as a Function of
Age-Specific Birthrates and Age Composition of the Female Population, for the United States
1996 and Panama 1995

Age groups (a)	Age-specific birthrates $\frac{B_a}{P_a^f} * 1000$		Proportion of females in the population by age group $\frac{P_a^f}{P}$	
	United States (1996) Population 1 (f_{1a})	Panama (1995) Population 2 (f_{2a})	United States (1996) Population 1 (p_{1a}/P_1)	Panama (1995) Population 2 (p_{2a}/P_2)
15 to 19[1]	55.6	93.5	0.034088	0.048296
20 to 24	110.4	150.0	0.032271	0.047894
25 to 29	113.1	133.5	0.035693	0.044213
30 to 34	83.9	100.7	0.040365	0.038753
35 to 39	35.3	48.4	0.042665	0.032655
40 to 44	6.8	14.7	0.039604	0.026941
45 to 49[2]	0.3	2.7	0.035343	0.022006
Crude birthrate (CBR) = $\frac{B}{P} * 1000$	14.67	23.54	(X)	(X)

Birthrates	Standardization		Decomposition	
	Panama (1995) Population 2	United States (1996) Population 1	Difference (effects)	Percent distribution of effects
Age-sex-population-standardized crude birthrates	21.57	16.12	Rate effect: 5.45	61.5
Age-specific-rate-standardized crude birthrates	20.56	17.14	Compositional effect: 3.42	38.5
Crude birthrate (CBR)	23.54	14.67	Total effect: 8.87	100.0

X: Not applicable.

[1] Includes births to women under 15 years of age.

[2] Includes births to women 50 years of age and over.

Source: United Nations, 1999, Tables 7 and 11; United Nations, 1998c; U.S. National Center for Health Statistics, 1998b, Table 3 and Appendix Table II.

for year-to-year or area-to-area comparisons. Because the weighting pattern of the age-specific birthrates is always the same in computing total fertility rates by the direct method and the weighting pattern is a generally reasonable one, there is little question regarding the comparability of a set of total fertility rates computed in this way. The relative level of fertility between two populations, measured by comparing total fertility rates, will be very similar to that shown by age-sex adjusted birthrates (direct method) because there are roughly the same numbers of women in each of the childbearing ages.

Because the total fertility rate combines the birth rates over all childbearing ages in a given year, it may also be viewed as representing the completed fertility of a synthetic cohort of women. For example, the total fertility rate of 3518 for El Salvador in 1992 may be interpreted to mean that a cohort of 1000 women would have 3518 children in their lifetime on the average, assuming that they bear children at each age at the rates prevailing in El Salvador in 1992 and that none of the women die before reaching the end of the

childbearing period. Under corresponding assumptions, 1000 women living in Germany would have only 1323 children in their lifetime, fewer than the number required to replace their parents.

When only a count of total births is available and a tabulation of births by age of mother is lacking, the indirect method of deriving the total fertility rate may be used. The formula is

$$\frac{b}{\sum F_a p_a^f} * 5 \sum F_a * 1000 \qquad (15.27)$$

where F_a refers to the "standard" set of age-specific birthrates and, hence, $5\sum F_a$ represents the total fertility rate corresponding to this standard set of rates; b and p_a refer to total births and the population by age for the area or group under study, respectively. In this formula, the total fertility rate based on the standard set of age-specific birthrates ($5\sum F_a$) is adjusted upward or downward by the ratio of reported total births for the particular population (b) to the number of births expected in the particular population on the basis of the standard set of age-specific birthrates ($\Sigma F_a p_a^f$). It will be noted that this formula parallels that for the calculation of the age-sex adjusted ("crude") birthrate by the indirect method:

$$\frac{b}{\sum F_a p_a^f} * F * 1000 \tag{15.28}$$

The application of this procedure is illustrated in the following tabular display, where the total fertility rate for Egypt in 1996 is obtained from a set of age-specific rates for 1992, estimates of the female population by age in 1996, and an estimate of total births in 1996 (McDevitt, 1996, Table A.5; United Nations, 1998c):

Age (years)	Age-specific birthrates, 1992 (F_a) (1)	Female population, 1996 (p_a^f) (2)
15 to 19	13.3	3,042,000
20 to 24	150.9	2,651,000
25 to 29	252.9	2,312,000
30 to 34	180.4	2,001,000
35 to 39	120.5	1,726,000
40 to 44	39.2	1,481,000
45 to 49	13.6	1,257,000

(1) Expected births, 1996 = $\Sigma F_a p_a^f$	1,669,503
(2) Reported births, 1996 = b	1,792,000
(3) Factor = (2) ÷ (1)	1.07337
(4) TFR, 1992 = $5\Sigma F_a$	3,854
(5) TFR, 1996 = TFR, 1992 * Factor = (4)*(3)	4,137

First, the age-specific birthrates in Egypt in 1992 from ages 15 to 19 to 45 to 49 are set down (col. 1). The rate for ages 15 to 19 includes the few births to women under 15, and the rate for ages 45 to 49 includes the few births to women 50 and over—that is,

$$\frac{B_{<20}}{P_{15-19}^f} \quad \text{and} \quad \frac{B_{45+}}{P_{45-49}^f} \tag{15.29}$$

Next, the total fertility rate for Egypt in 1992 (standard TFR) is calculated as five times the sum of the age-specific birthrates in 1992—that is, $5 \times 770.8 = 3854$. The "expected" number of births is obtained as the cumulative product of the rates (on a unit basis) in column 1 and the female population by age for Egypt in 1996 in column 2. This product is 1,669,503. The estimated number of births in 1996 for Egypt is 1,792,000. Dividing the estimated number of births (1,792,000) by the expected number (1,669,503) gives the factor (1.07337) for adjusting the standard total fertility rate. Accordingly, the estimated total fertility rate for 1996 is 1.07337 × 3854, or 4137.

This procedure is particularly applicable for providing estimates when tabulations of births by age of mother are not readily available. Thus, in the case of Egypt, the United Nations database contains births by age of mother for 1992 and estimates of the female population for 1992 and 1996. Using an estimate of the total number of births in Egypt for 1996 prepared by the U.S. Bureau of the Census (McDevitt, 1996, Table A.5), this method provided a means for estimating Egypt's total fertility rate for the more recent year. The technique is also useful for updating a time series of total fertility rates when the total number of births is known for a given year, but births have not yet been tabulated by age of mother. An early estimate of the total fertility rate may be obtained by using the age-specific birthrates of the preceding year.

Separate total fertility rates may readily be derived for significant categories of the population or of births. Two types of examples may be given. The total fertility rate may be calculated for geographic, residence, race or ethnic groups, or other subdivisions of the population of a country. In these calculations, the births and the women both relate to the same geographic, residence, or race or ethnic group. The resulting figures for various categories of a classification (e.g., Hispanic, non-Hispanic) are independent and cannot be combined. The total fertility rate for each birth order may be obtained by summing the (5-year) age-specific rates for each order over all ages of childbearing and multiplying by 5. Thus, the rate for first births may be obtained by summing first birthrates over all ages ($5\Sigma f_a^1$), the rate for second births may be obtained by summing second birthrates over all ages ($5\Sigma f_a^2$), and so on. The sum of order-specific total fertility rates over all orders equals the overall total fertility rate.

Rates Adjusted for Marital Status

Birth and fertility rates may be adjusted or standardized for other population characteristics in addition to age and sex, such as urban-rural residence, race or ethnic group, marital status, and duration of marriage. Standardization for marital status, age, and sex, for example, goes beyond the refinement in general marital or nonmarital fertility rates by taking account of marital and nonmarital fertility by age within the childbearing period. Crude birthrates and general fertility rates may be adjusted for age, sex, and marital status by an extension of the procedures for direct standardization described earlier. Age-specific marital fertility rates (births to married women per 1000 married women) and age-specific nonmarital fertility rates (births to single, widowed, or divorced women per 1000 unmarried women) are combined on the basis of a standard distribution by age, sex, and marital status. If the expected births are divided by the total population, an age-sex-marital-status adjusted (crude) birthrate is derived:

$$\frac{\sum_a f_a^m P_a^{fm} + \sum_a f_a^u P_a^{fu}}{P} \tag{15.30}$$

where f_a^m and f_a^u represent the age-specific fertility rates of married and unmarried women, respectively, P represents the total population, and P_a^{fm} and P_a^{fu} represent the number of females by age in the standard population who are married and unmarried, respectively. If the expected number is divided by the number of women of childbearing age, we obtain the general fertility rate adjusted for these factors:

$$\frac{\sum_a f_a^m P_a^{fm} + \sum_a f_a^u P_a^{fu}}{P_{15-44}^f} \quad (15.31)$$

A change in the crude birthrate, the general fertility rate, and the general marital fertility rate may be considered as resulting jointly from changes in the proportions of married (or unmarried) women at each age and from changes in age-sex-specific marital (and nonmarital) fertility. Comparison of the unadjusted rates and the adjusted rates is useful in identifying the separate contribution of each of these factors to the total change in the unadjusted rates.

Cohort Fertility Measures

We have already considered the calculation and interpretation of schedules of age-specific central birthrates and of total fertility rates for a particular year. As we have noted, such schedules of birthrates and their sums can be considered as applying to a synthetic cohort. Rates for different calendar years may be combined to derive various measures describing the fertility of true birth or marriage cohorts of women.

Fertility of Birth Cohorts

Consider an array of age-specific central birthrates, for a current year and a series of earlier years, for each age 14 to 49 identified in terms of year of birth of the mother. Table 15.12 shows a portion of such an array (i.e., age-specific rates for ages 14 to 18 from 1992 to 1996 for the United States). The age-specific birthrates for successive single ages from age 14 on, in successive years, may now be combined to derive cumulative fertility rates (per 1000 women) to any given age to any given year for any particular cohort. For example, the cumulative fertility rate for the birth cohort of 1977–1978 to exact age 19 on January 1, 1997, is derived as the sum of the following age-specific birthrates:[6]

[6] The cohorts of mothers are defined in terms of July 1-to-June 30 years of birth. A group of persons born in July 1-to-June 30 12-month periods would have conventional completed ages on July 1 and assumed to have exact ages on January 1 in subsequent years. Cumulative fertility up to a given exact age on a January 1 date combines the rates for all prior ages and calendar years in the cohort's experience. For example, the cohort of women born in 1977–1978 (July 1 to June 30) was under 1 (0) years of age (in completed years) on July 1, 1978, and 18 years of age on July 1, 1996 (=1996–1978). It is assumed to be of exact age 19 on January 1, 1997. The cohort's cumulative fertility on January 1, 1997, when it was of exact age 19, combines birthrates for ages 14, 15, 16, 17, and 18 through 1996.

$$f_{14}^{1992} + f_{15}^{1993} + f_{16}^{1994} + f_{17}^{1995} + f_{18}^{1996} \quad (15.32)$$

Using the data for the United States given in Table 15.12, we have (per 1000 women)

$$7.9 + 20.8 + 38.5 + 58.9 + 78.3 = 204.4$$

The rates pertaining to any particular cohort fall along diagonal cells in the array. The cumulative fertility rate for the birth cohort of 1978–1979 to exact age 18 on January 1, 1997, is derived as the sum of the following age-specific birthrates:

$$f_{14}^{1993} + f_{15}^{1994} + f_{16}^{1995} + f_{17}^{1996} \quad (15.33)$$

The U.S. figures are

$$8.0 + 20.7 + 37.1 + 55.7 = 121.5$$

Cumulative and Completed Fertility Rates

By deriving a set of cumulative fertility rates showing fertility up to each successive age, one can follow the fertility progress of a birth cohort through the childbearing ages. The fertility history of the 1946–1947 birth cohort, illustrated with data for the United States, is described as follows:

Age covered	Cumulative fertility rate		Reference date (Jan.1)	Age-specific birthrates cumulated through-	
	Rate per 1000 women	Percent of completed rate		Age	Calendar year
Up to age 20	346.5	16.0	1967	19	1966
Up to age 25	1,136.5	52.4	1972	24	1971
Up to age 30	1,734.5	80.0	1977	29	1976
Up to age 35	2,031.1	93.7	1982	34	1981
Up to age 40	2,143.2	98.8	1987	39	1986
Up to age 45	2,167.3	100.0	1992	44	1991
Up to age 50	2,168.3	100.0	1997	49	1996

If central birthrates over all ages of childbearing for a given birth cohort are combined in the manner described, then the *completed fertility rate* for this cohort is obtained:

$$f_{14}^y + f_{15}^{y+1} + f_{16}^{y+2} \cdots + f_{47}^{y+33} + f_{48}^{y+34} + f_{49}^{y+36} \quad (15.34)$$

where y refers to the calendar year when the cohort is 14 years of age. For example, the completed fertility rate for the cohort born in 1946–1947 (exact age of 50 on January 1, 1997) is computed as follows:

$$f_{14}^{1961} + f_{15}^{1962} + f_{16}^{1963} \cdots + f_{47}^{1994} + f_{48}^{1995} + f_{49}^{1996} \quad (15.35)$$

TABLE 15.12 Central Birthrates, 1992 to 1996, and Cumulative Fertility Rates, 1993 to 1997, by Age of Mother, for Each Birth Cohort from 1973–1974 to 1981–1982, for the United States

Age	1992	1993	1994	1995	1996	Birth cohort
Current age:	Central rates					
14 years	7.9	8.0	8.0	7.6	7.0	
15 years	20.9	20.8	20.7	19.8	18.4	1981–82
16 years	38.8	38.8	38.5	37.1	34.7	1980–81
17 years	61.7	61.1	60.8	58.9	55.7	1979–80
18 years	85.6	84.4	83.8	81.6	78.3	1978–79
	1973–74	1974–75	1975–76	1976–77	1977–78	

Age	1993	1994	1995	1996	1997	Birth cohort
Exact age:	Cumulative rates					
15 years	7.9	8.0	8.0	7.6	7.0	
16 years	(¹)	28.7	28.7	27.8	26.0	1981–82
17 years	(¹)	(¹)	67.2	65.8	62.5	1980–81
18 years	(¹)	(¹)	(¹)	126.1	121.5	1979–80
19 year	(¹)	(¹)	(¹)	(¹)	204.4	1978–79
	1973–74	1974–75	1975–76	1976–77		1977–78

Note: Birth cohort is identified by years shown in margins between the diagonal lines. Central birthrates relate to calendar years indicated. Cumulative rates relate to January 1 of years indicated. Rates are per 1000 women.

[1]Cumulative rates cannot be derived on the basis of the annual rates given.

Source: U.S. National Center for Health Statistics, 1996, Tables 1-19 and 1-20; 1998c, Tables 201-202.

TABLE 15.13 Cumulative Fertility Rates, by Exact Age of Mother and Birth Order, for Women in Each Birth Cohort from 1971–1972 to 1980–1981, January 1, 1996, and for Women in Each Birth Cohort from 1971–1972 to 1976–1977, January 1, 1997, for the United States (Rates are per 1000 women.)

Birth cohort[1]	Age of woman	Total	Birth order								
			1	2	3	4	5	6	7	8 and over
Cumulative fertility rate by exact age, January 1, 1996											
1980–81	15 years	7.6	7.6	—	—	—	—	—	—	—
1979–80	16 years	27.8	26.3	1.4	0.1	—	—	—	—	—
1978–79	17 years	65.8	59.6	5.7	0.5	—	—	—	—	—
1977–78	18 years	126.1	108.7	15.4	1.9	0.1	—	—	—	—
1976–77	19 years	210.1	170.7	33.3	5.4	0.7	—	—	—	—
1975–76	20 years	310.9	237.2	59.7	12.0	2.0	—	—	—	—
1974–75	21 years	422.9	301.0	93.7	22.8	4.8	0.5	0.1	—	—
1973–74	22 years	537.9	357.9	132.0	37.2	8.9	1.6	0.3	—	—
1972–73	23 years	648.1	405.3	171.0	53.8	14.2	3.1	0.6	0.1	—
1971–72	24 years	753.1	446.9	208.4	71.2	20.2	5.0	1.2	0.2	—
Central birthrates by current age, calendar year 1996											
1976–77	19 years	95.8	64.2	24.6	5.9	1.1	—	—	—	—
1975–76	20 years	106.6	62.8	31.7	9.4	2.2	0.4	0.1	—	—
1974–75	21 years	110.8	56.7	36.6	12.9	3.5	0.9	0.2	—	—
1973–74	22 years	112.5	51.2	39.0	15.8	4.8	1.3	0.3	0.1	—
1972–73	23 years	112.5	47.2	39.6	17.6	5.8	1.7	0.5	0.1	—
1971–72	24 years	112.0	45.0	39.2	18.5	6.4	2.0	0.6	0.2	0.1
Cumulative fertility rate by exact age, January 1, 1997											
1976–77	20 years	305.9	234.9	57.9	11.3	1.8	—	—	—	—
1975–76	21 years	417.5	300.0	91.4	21.4	4.2	0.4	0.1	—	—
1974–75	22 years	533.7	357.7	130.3	35.7	8.3	1.4	0.3	—	—
1973–74	23 years	650.4	409.1	171.0	53.0	13.7	2.9	0.6	0.1	—
1972–73	24 years	760.6	452.5	210.6	71.4	20.0	4.8	1.1	0.2	—
1971–72	25 years	865.1	491.9	247.6	89.7	26.6	7.0	1.8	0.4	0.1

—: Represents zero or rounds to zero.
[1] Period from July 1 of initial year to June 30 of terminal year.
Source: U.S. National Center for Health Statistics, 1998c, Tables 201 and 202 for 1995 and 1996.

The completed fertility rate is attained by some age in the late forties. As is suggested by a comparison of the cumulative rates from age 45 on, very little change occurs after the cohort reaches age 45. The cumulation can, in fact, be terminated with the age-specific birthrate at age 44, or continued to higher ages up through the rate for age 49 if the necessary data are available.

We have illustrated the procedure for deriving cumulative fertility rates to each age of childbearing for a current or a past year. Cumulative fertility rates for births of a particular order (first, second, etc.) may be derived in a similar manner from an array of age-order-specific rates, except that the rates for first births only, second births only, and so on for each birth cohort, are combined. These rates state the total number of first births, second births, and later births that 1000 women have had by the age and date indicated. Table 15.13 illustrates cumulative rates to exact ages 15 to 24 as of January 1, 1996 (corresponding to the birth cohorts of 1971–1972 to 1980–1981) for individual birth orders, for

the United States. For example, by this date, the cohort born in 1972–1973 and of exact age 23 years, has had 405.3 first births, 171.0 second births, 53.8 third births, and so on (per 1000 women).

The updating of these cumulative rates to January 1, 1997, is achieved by combining them with the central birthrates, by age and birth order, for 1996. Central birthrates for ages 19 to 24 and cumulative rates by birth order as of January 1, 1997, for exact ages 20 to 25 are shown in Table 15.13. For example, the cohort of 1972–1973, which had 405.3 first births (per 1000 women) by January 1, 1996, when it was at exact age 23, had 47.2 additional first births in 1996, when it was 23 years of age, and hence a cumulative rate of 452.5 first births by January 1, 1997, when it was at exact age 24.

The cumulative or completed fertility rates for several consecutive birth cohorts or ages for a given date may be averaged to represent the cumulative or completed fertility rate for these birth cohorts or ages as a group. The cumulative

TABLE 15.14 Cumulative Fertility Rates, by Exact Age of Mother and Birth Order, for Women in Groups of Birth Cohorts from 1942–1947 to 1977–1982, for the United States: January 1, 1997
(Rates are averages of the rates per 1000 women for single cohorts.)

Birth cohorts[1]	Exact age of mother on January 1, 1997	Total	Birth order								
			1	2	3	4	5	6	7	8 and over
1977–82	15 to 19 years	84.3	72.2	10.6	1.4	0.1	—	—	—	—
1972–77	20 to 24 years	533.6	350.8	132.2	38.6	9.6	1.9	0.4	0.1	—
1967–72	25 to 29 years	1,068.0	565.0	319.4	126.3	40.2	12.0	3.7	1.0	0.4
1962–67	30 to 34 years	1,576.0	738.4	504.8	219.0	74.9	24.7	8.9	3.3	2.0
1957–62	35 to 39 years	1,878.7	815.7	618.1	284.3	101.2	35.2	13.8	5.7	4.7
1952–57	40 to 44 years	1,969.8	834.3	649.8	301.8	111.2	40.8	17.0	7.5	7.4
1947–52	45 to 49 years	2,047.7	851.1	672.7	316.3	122.1	46.6	20.0	9.2	9.7
1942–47	50 to 54 years	2,302.6	875.3	723.8	388.9	174.3	74.7	33.9	15.8	15.9

—: Represents zero or rounds to zero.

[1] Period from July 1 of initial year to June 30 of terminal year.

Source: U.S. National Center for Health Statistics, 1998c, Table 202, 1997.

rates for exact ages 20 to 24 as of January 1, 1997, shown in Table 15.14 were derived by averaging the cumulative rates for ages 20 to 24, respectively, shown in Table 15.13.

It should be evident that, because childbearing is spread over more than 30 years of life, the completed fertility rate for any given cohort cannot be assigned to any particular calendar year as a measure of fertility in that year. The rate certainly does not reflect fertility in the year of birth of the cohort, and it tells us little or nothing about fertility in the year the cohort reached childbearing age (age 14, say) or in the year the cohort completed childbearing (age 45, say). Inasmuch as fertility is concentrated at the ages 20 to 29, the completed fertility rate for a particular cohort may be assigned roughly to the decade when the cohort moved through the ages 20 to 29. To simplify our historical analysis, we may choose to assign it arbitrarily to the single calendar year when the cohort was at the mean age of childbearing. Inasmuch as the mean age of childbearing varies from birth cohort to birth cohort for a given population and from population to population, when we are dealing with many cohorts, we may make a rough general assignment of the completed fertility rate to the year when the cohorts were 25 years of age.

Timing of Childbearing for Cohorts

Measures of "timing" or "spacing" of births for actual birth cohorts give a more realistic indication of the timing or spacing of births than those calculated from births in a single calendar year. The measures include the mean age of mother (mean age of childbearing), median age of mother, cumulative fertility in percentages, and mean and median intervals between births.[7] The median age of mother indi-

cates whether a cohort tends to have its children relatively early or relatively late in the childbearing period, particularly in comparison with earlier or later cohorts. For births occurring within marriage, it is affected both by the timing of marriage, as measured, say, by the median age at first marriage and by spacing of births within marriage. Other events such as completion of schooling, obtaining a job, or getting a promotion may also affect the timing of births, regardless of the marital status of the woman. The basic data for the calculation consist of a distribution of age-specific birthrates for single ages and single calendar years, for a single birth cohort of women, or of age-specific birthrates for 5-year age groups at 5-year time intervals, for a 5-year group of birth cohorts. That is, the median is based on

$$f_{14}^y, f_{15}^{y+1}, f_{16}^{y+2} \dots, f_{47}^{y+33}, f_{48}^{y+34}, f_{49}^{y+36} \qquad (15.36)$$

$$f_{15-19}^y, f_{20-24}^{y+5}, f_{25-29}^{y+10}, f_{30-34}^{y+15}, f_{35-39}^{y+20}, f_{40-44}^{y+25} \qquad (15.37)$$

where y represents the calendar year when the cohort was 14 or the cohorts were 15 to 19 and where the rates for ages 15 to 19 and 40 to 44 include any births for the ages under 15 and over 44, respectively. The resulting median age is identified as the median age of births for this particular birth cohort or group of birth cohorts. The terms "median age of births," "median age of childbearing," and median age of mother" are used interchangeably in this context.

Another general indication of the spacing of a cohort's births is obtained by converting the set of cumulative

---

[7] Cohort fertility measures are typically derived for women, but comparable measures for men could be created if information were available

for a sufficient number of fathers. Vital registration systems, however, typically gather information about the mother's pregnancy and childbearing history and not about the father's. With an increase in marital dissolution and nonmarital childbearing, information about the father's history is even less likely to be acquired through vital statistics than ever before.

TABLE 15.15 Percentage Distribution of Women by Parity, by Exact Age, in Groups of Birth Cohorts from 1947–1952 to 1977–1982, for the United States: January 1, 1997

Birth cohorts[1]	Exact age of women on January 1, 1997	Total	Birth order							
			0	1	2	3	4	5	6	7 and over
1977–82	15 to 19 years	100.0	92.8	6.2	0.9	0.1	—	—	—	—
1972–77	20 to 24 years	100.0	64.9	21.9	9.4	2.9	0.8	0.2	—	—
1967–72	25 to 29 years	100.0	43.5	24.6	19.3	8.6	2.8	0.8	0.3	0.1
1962–67	30 to 34 years	100.0	26.2	23.4	28.6	14.4	5.0	1.6	0.6	0.3
1957–62	35 to 39 years	100.0	18.4	19.8	33.4	18.3	6.6	2.1	0.8	0.6
1952–57	40 to 44 years	100.0	16.6	18.5	34.8	19.1	7.0	2.4	1.0	0.8
1947–52	45 to 49 years	100.0	14.9	17.8	35.6	19.4	7.6	2.7	1.1	0.9

—: Represents zero or rounds to zero.

[1] Period from July 1 of initial year to June 30 of terminal year.

Source: Table 15.14.

fertility rates to each successive age for the cohort into percents of the completed fertility rate. An illustration was given in the tabular display at the beginning of this section. A more specific indication of spacing, relating to particular birth intervals, may be obtained from an analysis of order-specific rates for birth cohorts. This type of analysis is parallel to that described earlier in connection with calendar year data. The median age for first births occurring to the cohort reflects the typical age of initiating childbearing. As before, birth intervals may be approximated by taking the difference between the median ages for successive orders.

Parity Distribution of Women

Cumulative fertility rates by live birth order and exact age of mother, for women in single-year birth cohorts or groups of birth cohorts, at a particular date, provide the basis for deriving the distribution of all women by parity at a particular age or age range (corresponding also to a particular birth cohort or cohorts) at this date. *Parity* refers to the number of children previously born alive to a woman. Zero-parity women are women who have never had a child, 1-parity women are women who have had only one child, and so forth. A parity distribution of women can be computed for each age and date (i.e., each birth cohort observed on a particular date) for which cumulative fertility rates have been developed.

Note, first, that the cumulative rate for first births per 1000 women to any date and age represents the number of women who have had one or more children. These women are all different because no woman could have had more than one first birth; but it includes women who have had two, three, four, or more children. The percentage of zero-parity or childless women is obtained, therefore, by subtracting the cumulative first birthrate from 1000 (yielding the number of zero-parity women per 1000 women) and dividing by 10 (yielding the percentage of zero-parity women). For example, the percentage of zero-parity women

aged 40 to 44 on January 1, 1997 (birth cohorts of 1952–1953 to 1956–1957) in the United States (16.6% in Table 15.15) is derived as follows from the data in Table 15.14:

$$\frac{1000 - 834.3}{10} = \frac{165.7}{10} = 16.6\%$$

The proportions of women at individual parities one and over can be obtained by taking the difference between cumulative fertility rates for successive orders (yielding the number of n-parity women per 1000) and dividing by 10 (yielding the percentage of n-parity women):

$$\text{Percent at parity } n = \frac{\left(\begin{array}{c} \text{Cumulative rate, order } n - \\ \text{Cumulative rate, order } n+1 \end{array} \right)}{10}$$

(15.38)

For example, the percentage of second-parity women aged 40 to 44 on January 1, 1997 (birth cohorts of 1952–1953 to 1956–1957) given in Table 15.15 is calculated on the basis of data in Table 15.14 as follows:

$$\frac{649.8 - 301.8}{10} = \frac{348.0}{10} = 34.8\%$$

The percentage of women in a terminal (open-ended) parity group is found by dividing the cumulative rate for the lowest parity included in the terminal group by 10. For example, the percentage of 40 to 44-year-old women in 1997 at seventh and higher parity is found by dividing the cumulative rate for seventh-order births by 10:

$$\frac{7.5}{10} = 0.8\%$$

The percentage of zero-parity women at ages 45 to 49 (15% in Table 15.15) reflects approximately the extent to which the women in a population have been remaining childless, both outside marriage and within marriage (from infecundity or voluntary choice). This percentage is different for each new cohort completing the childbearing period and may be higher or lower for cohorts completing childbearing in the future. It represents the maximum estimate of the extent of infecundity for a given cohort. If we subtract from the proportion of zero-parity women at ages 45 to 49 the proportion of women at these ages who have never married and have never had a child, as shown by the census or national sample surveys (about 6% for U.S. women in 1995),[8] we obtain an estimate of the proportion of ever-married women who are childless. Where voluntary childlessness is small, this adjusted percentage (9%) serves as a rough estimate of the extent of infecundity of married women.

Birth Probabilities

Birth probabilities represent the probability that a birth will occur over some time period to a woman with a given set of demographic characteristics, such as age, parity, age-parity, parity-birth interval, or duration of marriage, and so on, at the beginning of the period. The probabilities are usually expressed as the number of births in a year per 1000 women in the class at the beginning of the year.

Birth probabilities specific by age indicate the chance that a woman of a given exact age at the beginning of the year will have a birth during the year. An age-specific probability may be represented by $\bar{p}_a$. A value of $\bar{p}_a$ may be approximated by f_a, the central birthrate at age a during the year. For example, the 1-year birth probability for a cohort of women of exact age 20 on January 1, 1996, in the United States is 107 per 1000 (Table 15.13).[9] A similar relation between $\bar{p}_a$ and f_a may be assumed for grouped data—that is, $_n\bar{p}_a$, the probability that a cohort of women of exact ages a to $a + n$ at the beginning of a year will have a birth during the year—may be approximated by $_nf_a$ the central birthrate for ages a to $a + n$, or $_n\bar{p}_a \doteq {_nf_a}$. For example, the 1-year birth probability for cohorts of women of exact ages 20 to 24 on January 1, 1996, in the United States is represented

---

[8] According to the 1995 Current Population Survey (Bachu, 1997), 65.9% of the 992,000 never-married women ages 40 to 44 had never had a child. This suggests that 654,000, or 6.4%, of the estimated 10,244,000 women in their early 40s were never married and at zero parity.

[9] Equating the age-specific birth probability for age a and the central birth rate for age a implies that no deaths occur to the women in the half year between the beginning and middle of the year, or between exact age a and completed age a—that is,

$$\bar{p}_a = \frac{B_a}{p_a^f + \frac{1}{2}D_a^f} \doteq \frac{B_a}{P_a^f} = f_a$$

Mortality over a half year tends to be rather low for women in the childbearing ages, especially in countries where mortality is generally low, so that the assumption has only negligible effect.

simply by the central birthrate for women 20 to 24 years of age in 1996, 110.9 births per 1000 women (computed from Table 15.13).

Birth probabilities specific by parity indicate the chances that a woman of a given parity at the beginning of the year will have a child during the year (and attain the next parity). Such rates would only be meaningful for women of childbearing age, so that normally the probabilities are made specific with respect to both age and parity. *Age-parity-specific birth probabilities* indicate the chances that a woman of a given parity and exact age at the beginning of a year will have a child during the year (i.e., will attain the next parity before her next birthday). In general, an age-parity-specific birth probability is calculated from central birthrates and cumulative fertility rates by order. The general formula for an age-parity-specific birth probability is

$$_n\bar{p}_a^i = \frac{_nf_a^{i+1}}{\sum_{\omega_1}^{a+n} {_nf_a^i} - \sum_{\omega_1}^{a+n} {_nf_a^{i+1}}} * 1000 \qquad (15.39)$$

where $_n\bar{p}_a^i$ represents the probability that a cohort of women of exact ages a to $a + n$ and of parity i at the beginning of a year will have an $i + 1$th child during the calendar year, and

$_nf_a^{i+1} = i + 1$th order birth rate for women of completed age a to $a + n$ years in the calendar year

$\sum_{\omega_1}^{a+n} {_nf_a^i} =$ cumulative fertility rate of order i to beginning of year for a cohort of women of exact ages a to $a+n$

$\sum_{\omega_1}^{a+n} {_nf_a^{i+1}} =$ cumulative fertility rate of order $i+1$ to beginning of next year for a cohort of exact ages a to $a+n$

For example, the birth probability of first-parity women aged 20 to 24 in 1996 in the United States is calculated from the second-order birthrate in 1996 for the cohort aged 20 to 24 in 1996 (37.2), the cumulative fertility rate for the first-order births to this cohort by the beginning of 1996 (349.7), and the cumulative rate for second-order births by the beginning of 1996 (133.0). Each of these values is derived from Table 15.13 by averaging the corresponding rates for the single ages 20 to 24. Each of the cumulative rates includes some women who also had higher-order births. The difference between the cumulative rates represents the rate for women who have had births of first order only. Thus, the birth probability of first-parity women aged 20 to 24 in 1996 in the United States is calculated as follows:

$$\frac{37.2}{349.7 - 133.0} * 1000 = 172$$

The birth probability of zero-parity women aged 20 to 24 in 1996 is calculated from the first-order birthrate in 1996 for the cohort 20 to 24 in 1996 (52.6) and the cumulative fertility rate for first-order births to this cohort by the beginning of 1996 (349.7):

$$\frac{52.6}{1000 - 349.7} * 1000 = 81$$

The calculation for the terminal (open-ended) parity group may be illustrated with the calculation of the probability that seventh-and-higher parity women of exact age 25 to 29 on January 1, 1996, will have another (eighth-and-higher order) child during 1996 (data not shown in tables). The central birthrate for eighth-and-over births in 1996, 0.2, is divided by the cumulative rate to January 1, 1996, for women of exact age 25 to 29 who have had 7 children—that is, the difference between the cumulative rate for 7 or more (1.1) and the cumulative rate for 8 or more (0.5):

$$\frac{0.2}{1.1 - 0.5} * 1000 = \frac{0.2}{0.6} * 1000 = 333$$

Parity-specific probabilities can also be calculated to refer only to married women. One procedure is to develop probabilities of first marriage among all women by age first, then the probability of first births among zero-parity married women, then the probability of second births among 1-parity women, and so on. A substitute for, or addition to, the usual detail by age would be duration of married life or birth interval. Further refinements would, therefore, develop the probabilities separately by the interval in months between marriage and first births, and between births of successive orders. The age variable may be included only in terms of age at marriage in the first marriage probabilities or it may be included throughout the whole set of figures.

Parity-Progression Ratios

Parity-progression ratios (*probabilité d'agrandissement*) developed by Henry may be computed as an extension of the study of birth histories (Henry, 1953; Wunsch and Termote, 1978, Chap. 5). In general, they represent the probability, on a retrospective basis, of having an $n + 1$th child among those that have had an nth child. Parity-progression ratios may be defined in several ways depending on the data available and the degree of refinement sought. They may be based on birth statistics or survey/census data on fertility, and on birth cohorts, marriage cohorts, the married population within birth cohorts, or the corresponding period data.

In their simplest form, parity-progression ratios may be computed as ratios of the number of births of adjacent orders in a current year. The formula may then be given simply as follows:

$$a_i = \frac{B_{i+1}}{B_i} \tag{15.40}$$

where B_i represents births of a given order in some year and B_{i+1} are births of the next higher order in the same year. In

a more refined form, parity progression ratios may be computed for birth cohorts and may make allowances for marriage and the different intervals between the births of different parities. In another form, the rates are based on the proportions of married women who have had children of a particular order and above. The parity-progression ratio a_i would then be defined as follows:

$$a_0 = m_{1+} \tag{15.41}$$

$$a_1 = \frac{m_{2+}}{m_{1+}} \tag{15.42}$$

$$a_i = \frac{m_{i+1+}}{m_{i+}} \tag{15.43}$$

where $m_{1+}, m_{2+}, \ldots, m_{i+}$ are the percents of married women in a given year who have had 1 or more, 2 or more, ... $i + 1$ or more children and where $a_0, a_1, \ldots, a_i$ are the "probabilités d'agrandissement" of the families with 0 (without children), 1 child, ..., i children, or, in general, the probabilities that a family will be enlarged by an additional child each year. These probabilities are calculated only for cohorts of women who have reached the end of the childbearing period.

Fertility of Marriage Cohorts

Women who marry in a certain year (i.e., a marriage cohort) share a common experience in relation to the political, social, and economic conditions at the time of marriage and at successive years of married life. This experience may encompass such specific aspects of living as housing conditions, life style, and tastes. Insofar as these factors influence fertility behavior, it is of interest to study the fertility of marriage cohorts. We have already made reference to the relation of marriage duration to fertility (see the earlier section, "Duration-Specific Marital Fertility Rates").

A central marital birthrate specific for duration of marriage for a given calendar year has been defined, in effect, as the number of births occurring to women of a given marriage duration (i.e., a given marriage cohort) in the year per 1000 married women of that "duration" (i.e., marriage cohort) at the middle of the year:

$$\frac{B_{y,t}^{fm}}{P_{y,t}^{fm}} * 1000 \tag{15.44}$$

where y defines the calendar year, t the number of years since marriage, and B^{fm} and P^{fm} represent births to married women and the number of married women, respectively. To derive cohort fertility tables for marriage cohorts, we need such rates annually. However, annual estimates of the size of a given marriage cohort, which constitute the denominators of the rates, are rarely computed, because census data on marital status by years since marriage (or age at first marriage), and data on death, divorces, immigration, and emigration by marital status and year of marriage are rarely available. For this reason, the denominator used in computing rates for marriage cohorts is usually the original size of each marriage cohort.[10] Computed in this way, however, duration-specific birthrates tend to be increasingly understated as the duration of marriage grows, because the denominator tends progressively to overstate the current size of the marriage cohort. The usefulness of such measures for understanding natality within a population as a whole is further weakened as more and more births occur outside of marriage, and comparable information about the formation of nonmarital unions is not gathered in vital registration systems or censuses and may be available only through surveys.

Paternal Rates

As stated earlier, fertility measures are commonly computed with reference to the female population, but they may equally well be computed with reference to the male population. The historical tendency to study fertility almost exclusively in terms of women's attitudes, behaviors, and characteristics without adequate reference to the corresponding attributes of men has been challenged (e.g., Bianchi, 1998; Goldscheider and Kaufman, 1996). Research based largely on survey data has demonstrated the importance of investigating the role of men in reproductive planning, their use of contraceptives, and the degree of agreement between partners about childbearing goals (e.g., Dodoo, 1998; Thomson, 1997).

Investigation of paternal fertility using vital records is sometimes hampered by the absence of information about the biological father, particularly for births occurring outside marriage. For example, the age of the father was not stated on over 15% of the birth certificates for the United States in 1996 (U.S. National Center for Health Statistics, 1998b). Tabulations of births by such basic characteristics as father's age requires the allocation of "unknowns." The United Nations recommends that births for which the father's age is not reported should be distributed proportionately to those for which the age is reported (United Nations, 1988). The National Center for Health Statistics recommends a further refinement of this allocation such that the mother's age is taken into account as well because the records on which the father's age are not stated are more likely to be those of younger women, particularly teenagers (U.S. National Center for Health Statistics, 1998b).

The general paternal fertility rate is defined as the number of births, regardless of age of father, per 1000 males 15 to 54 years of age; that is[11]

$$GFR_m = \frac{B}{P^m_{15-54}} * 1000 \qquad (15.45)$$

For Poland in 1996, we have

$$\frac{428,203}{11,098,941} * 1000 = 38.6$$

The different choice of ages for males from that for females results from the longer span of the reproductive years for males.

An age-specific paternal birthrate is defined as the number of births to men of a given age group per 1000 men in that age group:

$$f^m_a = \frac{B^m_a}{P^m_a} * 1000 \qquad (15.46)$$

As in the general fertility rate, age-specific birthrates for men are defined for a broader range of age categories than for women, with the upper interval typically encompassing births to men of ages 55 years or more relative to men 55 to 59 years of age or 55 to 64 years of age. The age-specific paternal birthrates shown in Table 15.16 depict a considerable degree of diversity between countries. In some countries, notably Egypt and several countries in Latin America, relatively high age-specific rates are shown for men in their fifties. The United Nations (1988, p. 99) cautions that international comparability may be affected by national registration practices and specifically notes that the birthrates for men at ages 55 or more may be affected by the delay in registration until a certificate is needed for acquiring specific benefits for the child. As a result principally of the generally higher age of marriage of males than females and the greater length of the male reproductive age span, the characteristic age span of male fertility is different from that of females. Furthermore, the median age of fathers tends to be a few years higher than the median age of mothers. When the age-specific rates for men are compared with those for women shown in Table 15.3, a general pattern observed is that the age-specific maternal birthrates tend to be somewhat higher at the younger ages while the reverse is true at the higher ages.

Because of the use of a broader age group of the population in the base, the general fertility rate for men tends to

[10] The marriages corresponding to births in a calendar year should properly be the marriages for 12-month periods, July 1 to June 30. For example, marriages of 1990–1991 correspond to women married 5 years on July 1, 1996 and to births in 1996 occurring to women married 5 years.

[11] In calculating the general paternal fertility rate, the United Nations (1988, p. 99) uses males aged 15 to 64 years as the base, but it acknowledges in its technical notes that the upper limit, 64, is higher than the more commonly used limits of 54 or 59. The age range, 15 to 54, was adopted here for consistency with practices of the U.S. National Center for Health Statistics and because of the relatively low frequency of births reported for men aged 55 or over in most countries.

TABLE 15.16   Age-Specific Paternal Birthrates, for Various Countries: Around 1995
(Birthrates are live births per 1000 men in specified group.)

	Birthrates by age of father[1]								
Country and year	15–19 years[2]	20–24 years	25–29 years	30–34 years	35–39 years	40–44 years	45–49 years	50–54 years	55 and over[3]
Cuba (1995)	11.7	65.1	83.2	66.7	38.8	17.8	8.2	3.3	3.0
Egypt (1992)	1.1	31.2	168.0	238.5	194.1	114.3	61.5	32.9	37.7
Hungary (1996)[4]	4.9	51.9	111.4	75.4	32.1	12.7	3.9	1.3	0.6
Israel (1995)	1.4	50.0	163.0	186.2	125.2	56.0	16.2	6.8	5.3
Panama (1995)	20.6	111.7	142.4	128.5	87.1	57.6	34.1	18.1	15.0
Poland (1996)	3.8	63.6	113.4	75.1	35.8	14.0	4.2	1.2	0.5
Puerto Rico (1996)	32.1	108.1	124.4	93.7	51.0	24.3	11.0	5.9	4.8
United States (1996)[4,5]	23.0	84.4	107.7	94.3	51.5	20.4	6.9	2.5	0.3
Venezuela (1996)	23.9	110.6	137.8	117.1	88.0	55.1	31.0	19.3[6]	
Yugoslavia (1995)[4]	3.1	57.7	127.5	107.2	52.7	17.4	5.4	1.4[6]	

[1] Births with unreported fathers' ages are distributed in proportion to births of reported fathers' ages regardless of age of mother unless otherwise noted.
[2] Includes births to men under age 15. Base is the male population 15 to 19 years of age.
[3] Includes births to men aged 55 and over. Base is the male population 55 to 59 years of age.
[4] Rates based on age distributions in which births to fathers of age unreported exceeded 10% of total.
[5] Births with unreported father's age are distributed in proportion to births of reported father's age within each 5-year age category of the mother.
[6] Includes births to men aged 50 and over. Base is the male population 50 to 59 years of age.
Source: United Nations Statistics Division, 1998; U.S. National Center for Health Statistics 1998b, Table 20.

TABLE 15.17   Comparison of Paternal and Maternal Fertility Measures, for Various Countries: Around 1995

		Ratio, paternal to maternal rate	
Country and year	Excess of paternal median age (years)	General fertility rate	Total fertility rate
Cuba (1995)	4.5	0.811	1.002
Egypt (1992)	5.6	0.813	1.141
Hungary (1996)	2.9	0.758	1.008
Israel (1995)	3.5	0.822	1.059
Panama (1995)	5.2	0.843	1.132
Poland (1996)	2.5	0.781	0.986
Puerto Rico (1996)	3.2	0.862	1.103
United States (1996)	2.5	0.783	0.964
Venezuela (1996)	4.6	0.840	1.122
Yugoslavia (1995)	3.7	0.770	0.986
Average	3.8	0.808	1.050

Note: General paternal fertility rates are live births per 1000 men aged 15 to 54 years. General maternal fertility rates are live births per 1000 women aged 15 to 44 years. Total fertility rates equal 5 times the sum of the age-specific birthrates in 5-year intervals ranging from 15 to 49 for women and from 15 to 59 for men.
Source: Tables 15.1, 15.3, and 15.16; United Nations, 1998c.

run somewhat lower than the general fertility rate for women (Table 15.17). Unlike the general fertility rate, the total fertility rate for males tends to run somewhat higher than the corresponding rate for females (Table 15.17). This is primarily because of the greater length of the reproductive period, the higher age of fathers, and the less stringent physiological limitations on the number of children born to men. The proportions of the sexes have an indirect effect on maternal and paternal total fertility rates, because this factor affects the proportions who form marital or nonmarital unions. Births typically occur at older ages for fathers than for mothers and, therefore, at ages with fewer persons. At these higher ages there is typically a smaller proportion of men than women, and, as a result, a higher proportion of men in marriages or cohabiting living arrangements.

Whether the measure is the general fertility rate or the total fertility rate, paternal and maternal rates give about the same indications of changes over time for a given area or of differences from area to area. For the 10 countries listed in Table 15.17, the male and female total fertility rates have the extremely high correlation coefficient of .99. Paternal fertility rates are generally considered less satisfactory than maternal rates, however, because of the longer and less clearly defined reproductive period and the greater deficiency in the reporting of the characteristics of the father on the birth certificate.

Measures Based on Population Registers

In Chapter 2, we considered the population register as a general source of population data comprehending within its scope the functions of both a registration system for births and deaths and a registration system for international and internal migration. In the system as it operates in Sweden, for example, a personal record is created at birth on the basis of notification of the birth to the local registrar, and of the events subsequently affecting the individual (i.e., marriage, divorce, change of residence, and death) are entered into an automated information system (Andersson, 1997). The resulting database contains detailed information about the parents and the birth that is useful for examining fertility. As in vital registration systems, however, population registers contain details about the father only if the parents are married to one another. Using data from the population register of Finland during the mid-1980s, for example, Lutz (1989) was able to examine the relationship between several demographic dimensions of fertility, including age, parity, duration of marriage, and time span between births for nearly all mothers and all but about 6% of the fathers.

Because the population register system calls for the notification of government authorities by householders, on the occasion of a birth, rather than periodic reporting of births occurring over a particular past period, this basis of collection is more akin to the registration method than to the census or survey method. We consider here, then, the special problems and potentialities of analysis of natality statistics derived from population registers.

Population registers constitute an extremely valuable source of data for natality analysis. As a self-contained system, the population register system theoretically provides both the births on a residence basis for any period and the resident population at any required date, both nationally and for geographic subdivisions. As operated in some countries, the system ensures correct allocation of births to the municipality of residence of the mother. Where the population register system is fully developed, registration of births is believed by national authorities to be virtually 100% complete.

The system permits calculation of birthrates for small geographic units in a country on a regular monthly and annual basis with extremely short time lags. Births by marital status of the mother and the father provided by the system can be related to national estimates of population by age, sex, and marital status. In some cases, the register may provide data on other socioeconomic characteristics of the population (e.g., occupation), albeit not regularly updated, which may be employed in the calculation of fertility rates for the corresponding socioeconomic groups. Annual age-parity-specific birth probabilities, cumulative fertility rates by order of birth, and parity distributions of women and men may be developed wholly from the system after it has been operating for a number of years.

The registers may provide data on the mothers or fathers of the newborn children supplementing the information on the individual forms for births. The population registers readily permit the selection of a sample of births or of their parents in a given period. The provincial and local governments can utilize the population registers for the analysis of the local fertility situation; and, if the data are insufficient,

they can be extended by field surveys in the area, using the entries in the register as the sampling frame. Finally, the register data may be supplemented by the results of a census or national sample survey that provides information on the socioeconomic characteristics of the population for use in the calculation of the corresponding types of vital rates.

References

Andersson, G. 1997. "Childbearing Trends in Sweden 1961–1995." *Stockholm Research Reports in Demography* No. 117. Stockholm University, Demography Unit.

Azumi, K. 1968. "The Mysterious Drop in Japan's Birthrate." *Transaction* 5(6): 46–48.

Bachu, A. 1997. "Fertility of American Women: June 1995 (Update)." *Current Population Reports* Series P20-499, www.census.gov/prod/3/97pubs/p20–499.pdf.

Bhat, M. 1995. "On the Quality of Birth History Data Collected in National Family Health Survey, 1992–92." *Demography India* 24(2): 245–258.

Bianchi, S. M. (Ed.) 1998. "Special Issue: Men in Families." *Demography* 35(2): 133–258.

Bongaarts, J., and G. Feeney. 1998. "On the Quantum and Tempo of Fertility." *Population and Development Review* 24(2): 271–291.

Das Gupta, P. 1993. *Standardization and Decomposition of Rates: A User's Manual.* U.S. Bureau of the Census. *Current Population Reports*, Series P23-186. Washington, DC: U.S. Government Printing Office.

Dodoo, F. N. 1998. "Men Matter: Additive and Interactive Gendered Preferences and Reproductive Behavior in Kenya." *Demography* 35(2): 229–242.

Fingerhut, L. A., and J. C. Kleinman. 1985. "Comparability of Reporting between the Birth Certificate and the 1980 National Natality Survey." *Vital and Health Statistics.* Series 2, No. 99. U.S. National Center for Health Statistics.

Goldscheider, F. K., and G. Kaufman. 1996. "Fertility and Commitment: Bringing Men Back In." In J. B. Casterline, R. D. Lee, and K. A. Foote (Eds.), *Fertility in the United States: New Patterns, New Theories* (pp. 87–99). *Population and Development Review* 22 Supp.

Gonzolez, V. 1998. United Nations, Statistics Division. Personal communication.

Grabill, W. H., C. V. Kiser, and P. K. Whelpton. 1958. *The Fertility of American Women.* New York: John Wiley & Sons.

Hajnal, J. 1947. "The Analysis of Birth Statistics in the Light of the Recent International Recovery of the Birth Rate." *Population Studies* I(2): 137–164.

Henry, L. 1953. Fécondité des Mariages: Nouvelle Méthode de Mesure (Fertility of Marriages: A New Method of Measurement). Travaux et Documents, Cahier No. 16. Institut National d'Études Démographiques. Paris: Presses Universitaires de France. English translation: UN/ESCAP Population Translation Series No. 3 (1980).

Henry, L. 1961. "La fécondité naturelle. Observation, théorie, résultats." *Population* 16(4): 625–636.

International Union for the Scientific Study of Population (IUSSP). 1982. *Multilingual Demographic Dictionary*, 2nd ed., English Section. Adapted by Etienne van de Walle from the French Section by Louis Henry. Liège, Belgium: Ordina Editions.

Jorge, M. H. P. de Mello, S. L. D. Gotlieb, M. L. M. S. Soboll, M. F. de Almeida, and M. do R. D. O. Latorre. 1993. "Evaluation of the Information System on Live Births and of the Use of Its Data in Epidemiology and Health Statistics" ["Avaliação do Sistema de Informação Sobre Nascidos Vivos e o Uso de Seus Dados em Epidemiologia e Estatísticas de Saúde"]. *Revista de Saúde Pública* 27(6 Supp.): 2–46.

Kitagawa, E. M. 1995. "Components of a Difference between Two Rates." *Journal of the American Statistical Association* 50(272): 1168–1194.

Lutz, W. 1989. *Distributional Aspects of Human Fertility: A Global Comparative Study.* A volume in the series *Studies in Population.* H. H. Winsborough (Ed.). London: Academic Press.

McDevitt, T. M. 1996. *World Population Profile: 1996.* U.S. Bureau of the Census, Report WP/96. Washington, DC: U.S. Government Printing Office.

Ní Bhrolcháin, M. 1992. "Period Paramount? A Critique of the Cohort Approach to Fertility." *Population and Development Review* 18(4): 599–629.

Piper, J. M., E. F. Mitchel, Jr., M. Snowden, C. Hall, M. Adams, and P. Taylor. 1993. "Validation of 1989 Tennessee Birth Certificates using Maternal and Newborn Hospital Records." *American Journal of Epidemiology* 137(7): 758–768.

Ryder, N. B. 1956. "Problems of Trend Determination During a Transition in Fertility." *Milbank Memorial Fund Quarterly* 34(1): 5–21.

Ryder, N. B. 1980. "Components of Temporal Variations in American Fertility." In R. W. Hiorns (Ed.), *Demographic Patterns in Developed Societies* (pp. 15–54). London: Taylor and Francis.

Schachter, J. 1962. "Matched Record Comparison of Birth Certificate and Census Information: United States, 1950." *Vital Statistics—Special Reports* 47(12). U.S. National Vital Statistics Division, Public Health Service.

Shapiro, S. 1950. "Development of Birth Registration and Birth Statistics in the United States." *Population Studies* 4(1): 86–111.

Shryock, H. S., J. S. Siegel, and E. G. Stockwell. 1976. *The Methods and Materials of Demography.* Condensed edition. San Diego, CA: Academic Press.

Sweden, Statistics Sweden. 1998a. "Married Women by Year of Marriage." Unpublished table.

Sweden, Statistics Sweden. 1998b. "Vital Statistics." *Population Statistics, 1997.* Part 4.

Thomson, E. 1997. "Couple Childbearing Desires, Intentions, and Births." *Demography* 34(3): 343–354.

UNICEF. 1998. "Civil Rights League Table: Birth Registration." *Progress of Nations, 1998.*

United Nations. 1973. *Principles and Recommendations for a Vital Statistics System.* Statistical Papers, Series M, No. 19, Rev. 1.

United Nations. 1985. *Handbook of Vital Statistics Systems and Methods,* Vol. II, *Review of National Practices.* Studies in Methods, Series F, No. 35.

United Nations. 1988. *Demographic Yearbook, 1986.*

United Nations. 1991a. *Handbook of Vital Statistics Systems and Methods,* Vol. I, *Legal, Organizational and Technical Aspects.* Studies in Methods, Series F, No. 35.

United Nations. 1991b. *Progress Report on Civil Registration and Vital Statistics, Report of the Secretary-General.* Economic and Social Council, January 2.

United Nations. 1998a. "Data Available as of 1 July 1998." *Population and Vital Statistics Report.* Statistical Papers, Series A, Vol. L, No. 3.

United Nations. 1998b. *World Population Monitoring: Selected Aspects of Reproductive Rights and Reproductive Health.*

United Nations. 1998c. United Nations Economic and Social Information System, *Demographic Yearbook Database.*

United Nations. 1999. *Demographic Yearbook, 1997.*

U.S. National Center for Health Statistics. 1996. *Vital Statistics of the United States, 1992,* Vol. I, *Natality.*

U.S. National Center for Health Statistics. 1997a. *State Definitions and Reporting Requirements for Live Births, Fetal Deaths, and Induced Terminations of Pregnancies, 1997 Revision.*

U.S. National Center for Health Statistics. 1997b. *U.S. Vital Statistics System: Major Activities and Developments, 1950–95.*

U.S. National Center for Health Statistics. 1998a. "Births, Marriages, Divorces, and Death for November 1997." *Monthly Vital Statistics Report* 46(11).

U.S. National Center for Health Statistics. 1998b. "Report of Final Natality Statistics, 1996." *Monthly Vital Statistics Report* 46(11) Supplement.

U.S. National Center for Health Statistics. 1998c. *Vital Statistics of the United States.* Unpublished tables by year, 1993 through 1997.

World Health Organization. 1950. *Official Records of the World Health Organization.* No. 28. *Third World Health Assembly,* Geneva, 8 to 27 May 1950.

Wunsch, G. G., and M. G. Termote. 1978. *Introduction to Demographic Analysis: Principles and Methods.* New York: Plenum Press.

Suggested Readings

Barkalov, N. B., and J. Dorbritz. 1996. "Measuring Period Parity-Progression Ratios with Competing Techniques: An Application to East Germany." *Zeitschrift für Bevölkerungswissenschaft* 21(4): 459–505.

Brass, W. 1990. "Cohort and Time Period Measures of Quantum Fertility: Concepts and Methodology." In H. A. Becker (Ed.), *Life Histories and Generations* (Vol. II, pp. 455–476). Utrecht: University of Utrecht, ISOR.

Bulatao, R. A., and R. D. Lee (Eds.). 1983. *Determinants of Fertility in Developing Countries.* 2 vols. New York: Academic Press.

Calot, G. 1993. "Relationships between Cohort and Period Demographic Indicators: The Translation Problem Revisited." *Population* 5: 183–221.

Casterline, J. B., R. D. Lee, and K. A. Foote (Eds.). 1996. *Fertility in the United States: New Patterns, New Theories. Population and Development Review* 22 Supp.

Chandra Sekar, C., and E. W. Deming. 1949. "On a Method of Estimating Birth and Death Rates and the Extent of Registration." *Journal of the American Statistical Association* 44(245): 101–115.

Chen, R., and S. P. Morgan. 1991. "Recent Trends in the Timing of First Births in the United States." *Demography* 28(4): 513–533.

Coale, A. J., and M. Zelnik. 1963. *New Estimates of Fertility and Population in the United States.* Princeton, NJ: Princeton University Press.

Davis, K., M. S. Bernstam, R. Ricardo-Campbell (Eds.). 1996. *Below-Replacement Fertility in Industrial Societies: Causes, Consequences, Policies. Population and Development Review* 12 Supp.

Easterlin, R. A. 1975. "An Economic Framework for Fertility Analysis." *Studies in Family Planning* 6: 54–63.

Ewbank, D. 1993. "Coarse and Refined Methods for Studying the Fertility Transition in Historical Populations." In D. S. Reher and R. Schofield (Eds.), *Old and New Methods in Historical Demography* (pp. 345–360). Oxford: Clarendon Press.

Feeney, G. 1983. "Population Dynamics Based on Birth Intervals and Parity Progression." *Population Studies* 37: 75–89.

Feeney, G. 1991. "Fertility Decline in Taiwan: A Study Using Parity Progression Ratios." *Demography* 28(3): 467–479.

Foster, A. 1990. "Cohort Analysis and Demographic Translation: A Comparative Study of Recent Trends in Age-Specific Fertility Rates from Europe and North America." *Population Studies* 44: 287–315.

Hajnal, J. 1950. "Births, Marriages, and Reproductivity, England and Wales, 1938–47." *Reports and Selected Papers of the Statistics Committee,* Vol. 2. United Kingdom, Royal Commission on Population. London: H. M. Stationary Office.

Henry, L. 1961. "Some Data on Natural Fertility." *Eugenics Quarterly* 8(2): 81–91.

Henry, L. 1972. *On the Measurement of Human Fertility: Selected Writings,* translated and edited by M. C. Sheps and E. Lapierre-Adamcyk. Amsterdam: Elsevier Publishing Company.

Heuser, R. L. 1976. *Fertility Tables for Birth Cohorts by Color: United States, 1917–73.* U.S. National Center for Health Statistics.

Hobcraft, J. 1996. "Fertility in England and Wales: A Fifty-Year Perspective." *Population Studies* 50: 485–524.

Hobcraft, J., J. Menken, and S. Preston. 1982. "Age, Period and Cohort Effects in Demography: A Review." *Population Index* 48(1): 4–43.

Knudsen, L. B. 1993. *Fertility Trends in Denmark in the 1980s: A Register Based Socio-Demographic Analysis of Fertility Trends*. No. 44. Danmarks Statistik.

Kuczynski, R. R. 1932. *Fertility and Reproduction: Methods of Measuring the Balance of Births and Deaths*. New York: Falcon Press.

Leete, R., and A. Iqbal (Eds.). 1993. *The Revolution in Asian Fertility: Dimensions, Causes, and Implications*. Oxford: Clarendon Press.

Lewis, R. A., and R. H. Rowland. 1995. "Regional Trends in Crude Birth, Death, and Natural Increase Rates in Russia and the USSR: 1897–1989." *Post-Soviet Geography* 36(10): 617–643.

Luke, B., and L.G. Keith. 1991. "The United States Standard Certificate of Live Birth: A Critical Commentary." *Journal of Reproductive Medicine* 36(8): 587–591.

Lutz, W., S. Scherbov, and A. Volkov (Eds.). 1994. *Demographic Trends and Patterns in the Soviet Union Before 1991*. London and New York: Routledge. Laxenburg, Austria: International Institute for Applied Systems Analysis [IIASA].

Morgan, S., and Renbao Chen. 1992. "Predicting Childlessness for Recent Cohorts of American Women." *International Journal of Forecasting* 8: 477–493.

Namboodiri, N. K. 1981. "On Factors Affecting Fertility at Different Stages in the Reproductive History: An Exercise in Cohort Analysis." *Social Forces* 59: 1114–1129.

Ní Bhrolcháin, M. 1987. "Period Parity Progression Ratios and Births Intervals in England and Wales, 1941–1971." *Population Studies* 41: 103–125.

Pandey, A., and C. M. Suchindran. 1997. "Estimation of Birth Intervals and Parity Progression Ratios from Vital Rates." *Sankhya: Indian Journal of Statistics*, Series B, 59(1): 108–122.

Potter, R. G., Jr. 1963. "Birth Intervals: Structure and Change." *Population Studies* (London) 17(2): 155–166.

Pullum, T. W. 1980. "Separating Age, Period and Cohort Effects in White US Fertility: 1920–1970." *Social Science Research* 9: 225–244.

Rallu, Jean-Louis, and L. Toulemon. 1994. "Period Fertility Measures: The Construction of Different Indices and their Application to France, 1946–89." *Population*. English Selection. 6: 59–130.

Rindfuss, R. R., S. P. Morgan, and K. Offutt. 1996. "Education and the Changing Pattern of American Fertility." *Demography* 33: 277–290.

Rindfuss, R. R., S. P. Morgan, and G. Swicegood. 1988. *First Births in America: Changes in the Timing of Parenthood*. Berkeley, CA: University of California Press.

Rindfuss, R. R., and A. M. Parnell. 1989. "The Varying Connection Between Marital Status and Childbearing in the United States." *Population and Development Review* 15: 447–470.

Ryder, N. B. 1986. "Observations on the History of Cohort Fertility in the United States." *Population and Development Review* 12: 617–643.

Ryder, N. B. 1990. "What Is Going to Happen to American Fertility?" *Population and Development Review* 16: 433–454.

Smith, H. L., S. P. Morgan, and T. Koropeckyj-Cox. 1996. "A Decomposition of Trends in the Nonmarital Fertility Ratios of Blacks and Whites in the United States, 1960–1992." *Demography* 33(2): 141–151.

Zakharov, S. V., and E. I. Ivanova. 1996. "Fertility Decline and Recent Changes in Russia: On the Threshold of the Second Demographic Transition." In J. Davanzo (Ed.), *Russia's Demographic "Crisis"* (pp. 36–83). Rand Conference Proceedings. Santa Monica, CA: Rand Center For Russian and Eurasian Studies.

Zhu, J. 1994. "A Model of the Age Patterns of Births by Parity in Natural Fertility Populations." *Mathematical Population Studies* 4(3): 153–173.

Natality

Measures Based on Censuses and Surveys

THOMAS W. PULLUM

The previous chapter discussed the use of vital statistics to measure natality, especially for areas with established and relatively complete vital registration systems. This chapter continues the discussion of natality, but by use of census and sample survey data. Methods and issues particularly relevant to the measurement of natality in statistically less developed areas will be the subject of Chapter 22. Reproductivity, in which survivorship is combined with fertility, is the topic of Chapter 17. Some measures are discussed in more than one of these chapters because they can be estimated from various sources or are conceptually closely related. This chapter focuses on how to obtain fertility measures from a census or survey data, even if the measures can also be calculated from vital statistics data. When useful, comparisons will be made with a wider range of measures.

Some examples will illustrate the nature of the overlap among these chapters. The classical estimate of the crude birthrate (CBR) uses vital statistics data for the numerator and census data for the denominator, combining generic types of data from both Chapters 15 and 4. As we will see, it is also possible to estimate the CBR entirely from a fertility survey if it includes a household roster. Thus, there is some discussion of the CBR here, as well as in Chapter 15. The total fertility rate (TFR) can be calculated completely with survey data and is similar to the gross reproduction rate (GRR) and the net reproduction rate (NRR), measures of reproductivity discussed in Chapter 17.

Most of the measures in Chapters 15, 16, and 17 can be classified into three types, according to their numerators and denominators. *Birthrates* have both male and female births in the numerators and both males and females in the denominator. The crude birth rate (CBR) is an example of a birthrate; indeed, it is the only measure of natality consistently labeled a birth rate. By contrast, *fertility* rates have both male and female births in the numerators, but just one sex in the denominator, usually females because fertility has

traditionally been considered to be an attribute of women, and most data sources for births provide more information about the mother than about the father. The general fertility rate (GFR) and TFR are the most common examples of fertility rates. Third, a *reproduction* rate is limited to female births in the numerator as well as females in the denominator, and describes the replacement of females by females (or males by males). The GRR and NRR are the best known examples of reproduction rates.[1]

The distinction between birth, fertility, and reproduction rates is didactically useful and the computational relations between them can be seen as simple. For example, the GFR can be calculated by dividing the CBR by the proportion of the total population who are women aged 15 to 44. The GRR can be calculated by multiplying the TFR by the proportion of all births that are girls (assuming that the proportion of births that are girls does not greatly depend on the age of the mother).

Recent decades have seen a major transformation in the kinds of data available for demographic estimation, particularly related to natality. When this book originally appeared, it made only limited reference to fertility surveys and the birth rosters they contain. Most examples in the original chapter were based on census data. Since that time, there has been a complete reversal in the relative importance of censuses and surveys for measuring fertility. In the United States, the National Center for Health Statistics has conducted several rounds of the National Survey of Family Growth (often referred to as "NSFG"). Internationally, with primary sponsorship by the U.S. Agency for International Development, nearly two hundred fertility surveys have been conducted by the World Fertility Survey (WFS, 1973–1984) and the Demographic and Health Surveys

[1] This classification differs from common usage and the terminology of the IUSSP's *Multilingual Demographic Dictionary*, which uses "birth" and "fertility" interchangeably for some natality measures, particularity age-specific and order-specific rates and probabilities.

(DHS, since 1985). Many other surveys have been carried out with support from the U.S. Centers for Disease Control and Prevention (CDC) or under other auspices.

Along with this revolution in data availability, recent decades have seen a shift from aggregates to individuals as the units of analysis, and the corresponding adaptation of statistical tools to the analysis of demographic data. Statistical methods themselves have expanded enormously in recent decades because of a contemporaneous growth of computing capacity. Thirty years ago, for example, Poisson regression, logit regression, and hazard models, all of which are particularly appropriate for demographic analysis, were unavailable. For these reasons, this revised chapter differs dramatically from the original version.

We will present the measurement of fertility as fundamentally a description of an individual-level process. When at all possible, fertility measures are now generated with individual-level data—a fertility survey or a public-use sample from a census—rather than the tabulated information in a full census. The most useful measures of fertility, and indeed most of the traditional measures, can be interpreted in one or the other of the following two ways: (1) as the average or expected number (in the statistical sense) of births that a woman has in an interval of time, "controlling" for such characteristics as her age, marital duration, and parity, or (2) as the probability that a woman has a birth in an interval of time, controlling for such characteristics as her age, marital duration, and parity.

Otherwise, these measures differ from one another only in terms of the reference interval of time, what they "control" for, how they control for it, and whether they are cohort or synthetic cohort measures. When calculated from a sample, each measure has a standard error (sometimes difficult to estimate) that can be used to construct confidence intervals or test hypotheses. Most have the potential to be included in some form of multivariate analysis.

TYPES OF DATA AVAILABLE IN A CENSUS OR SURVEY

Census Data

Censuses have long been effectively employed in the more developed countries in the measurement and analysis of fertility, especially in the "dimensions of time and space." Census data on children ever born and the age-sex distribution have been used to track and analyze historical changes in fertility, including the years before vital registration was initiated or adequately developed for demographic applications. For example, the U.S. census data on children ever born, as reported for elderly women, have been employed to analyze the historical shifts in the familial support available to them. In addition, censuses have been used to describe and analyze geographic variations in fertility within

countries, both currently and historically. Censuses providing retrospective data on fertility, released as public use microdata samples, permit manipulation of individual-level data that can be linked to other demographic and socioeconomic variables for current and historical fertility analysis. For a further discussion of measures of fertility based on aggregated census data, refer to Chapter 22 of this volume (statistically less developed areas) and to Chapter 17 of the first edition of this book (H. S. Shryock, J. S. Siegel, and E. G. Stockwell, 1976) (more developed areas).

As described elsewhere (see, for example, Chapter 2), many countries of the world conduct a census every 10 years, and some do so every 5 years. Prior to the 1970s, a census typically provided the best available data for estimating fertility, particularly in a less developed country. Vital registration systems were (and often continue to be) seriously incomplete, and only a few countries had conducted large-scale fertility surveys. This data deficiency led to creative ways to estimate fertility indirectly using one census or, even better, two successive censuses.

Some censuses include information on the number of children ever born (CEB). For example, this was a standard item for U.S. censuses from 1900 through 1990, but it is no longer collected in the U.S. census. This item is useful but says nothing about the timing of the births, apart from inferences based on the woman's age or the ages of children in the household.

Prior to the widespread use of fertility surveys, the inadequacy of vital registration systems in less developed countries led to the inclusion of fertility-related questions on census forms. This occurred notably in Africa, where William Brass of the London School of Hygiene and Tropical Medicine advised several central statistical offices, but also in Latin America and Asia. Such questions may ask whether a child was born in the last year (or another reference period), the number of children born in the previous 5 years (or another reference period), or the length of time since the most recent birth. The value of such data depends on a correct interpretation of reference periods and time intervals.

As a minimum, every census produces an age distribution. This contains information about fertility because the people observed to be age a at last birthday are the survivors of persons born exactly a to $a + 1$ years before the census. For example, infants, who are under one year of age (aged zero) at last birthday, are the survivors of the births during the previous elapsed year (not calendar year). The number of surviving children is less than the number of births (assuming no net immigration), so it is necessary in estimating the number of births with such data to use a reverse survival method, requiring assumptions about mortality. Many censuses in East and Southeast Asia include information to identify the children who were born to a specific woman in the household. With a plausible life table that spans the ages of the children, and also the mothers, it is possible to use the "own-children" method to estimate age-specific fertility rates during the 15 or so years before the census. This method falls within the rubric of indirect estimation, which is discussed elsewhere, including Chapter 22 and Appendix C.

The original version of this chapter devoted substantial space to the child-woman ratio (CWR), that is, the ratio of the number of children aged 0 to 4 to the number of women aged 15 to 49 reported in a census. The CWR is calculated from an age-sex distribution. If mortality is ignored, it is approximately five times the general fertility rate (discussion follows). In view of the current availability of more appropriate data, we have less need for the CWR as a measure of fertility and will discuss it only briefly.

In summary, census data alone are not as well suited for fertility measurement and analysis as survey data and now are infrequently used for this purpose, apart from the own-children method. Censuses provide population counts, or are the basis for intercensal and postcensal estimates of population, that can serve as the denominators of some rates; but they generally provide useful information about numbers of births only if supplemented with estimates of survivorship.

Survey Data

Special surveys on fertility, contraceptive use, and related topics are now the primary source of data for fertility analysis. Prior to the early 1970s, when the World Fertility Survey (WFS) began, most surveys of this genre were oriented primarily around the estimation of contraceptive prevalence. When WFS was launched, there was considerable skepticism that reliable retrospective birth histories could be collected in the less developed countries. Many experts believed that the reported birth histories would be incomplete because respondents would omit children who had died or were born long ago, and birth dates would often be unknown or erroneously reported. The WFS surveys soon demonstrated that reliable birth histories could indeed be collected.

In a typical fertility survey, a female respondent is first asked how many children she ever had, and how many are still alive, and then she is asked a series of questions (mainly date, sex, and survivorship) about each birth, beginning with the most recent one and working backward. (Some surveys begin with the earliest birth and work toward the present.) In addition, fertility surveys include the woman's own date of birth and a marriage history, giving dates of marriage and of marital dissolution. The definition of marriage is generally flexible and includes cohabitation. Many of the early surveys defined eligible respondents to be ever-married women aged 15 to 49, but it is now more common to include all women 15 to 49 (occasionally 15 to 44), regardless of marital status. Most surveys include a household roster that lists all persons in the household (with some characteristics, such as age, sex, and relation to head),

including households that have no eligible respondents. This roster is especially important for calculating all-women fertility rates if the eligible respondents are limited to ever-married women.

The information in the birth history is coded onto a computer record, or set of records, for each case. To facilitate calculations, dates consisting of a month field and year field are typically converted into century month codes (cmc's), which begin with cmc = 1 for January 1900. Thus, for example, the cmc for August 1999 would be $8 + 99 * 12 = 1196$, because August is the eighth month of the year and a year contains 12 months. It seems likely that cmc's will continue to originate with January 1900 well into the 21st century. The date of interview is also converted to a century month code. This date will vary over the interval of data collection, usually several months. Care must be taken with the calculation of rates that extend into these months, because respondents provide incomplete information about the interval of data collection. Days of the month are ignored; in calculations it is necessary to make some arbitrary but consistent assumptions, for example, that events always occur on the first day of a month.

A birth history, sometimes requiring reference to the woman's birth date, marriage history, and date of interview, thus provides the following kinds of information for each respondent:

Children ever born and children still living (forced to match the responses to the direct questions on these totals)

Number of births in a window (interval) of age, calendar time, time since survey, or marital duration (elapsed time since first marriage), or an intersection of such windows

A classification of these numbers of births into whether they were marital, premaritally conceived, or premaritally born, using either the "ever-married" or "currently married" criterion for marital status

Length of intervals between births, including the interval from first marriage to first birth (closed intervals) and from first marriage (if no birth has occurred) or latest birth to date of interview (the "open" interval)

Exposure to risk of an event, as described in the next section

The respondents can also be classified according to other covariates for which data may be available, such as education. With this information it is possible to calculate rates within subgroups or to use a multivariate method.

This chapter includes examples from a specific Demographic and Health Survey, the 1998 National Demographic and Health Survey of the Philippines, the main results of which were published in January 1999 (Philippines National Statistics Office and Department of Health, and Macro International, 1999). It is subsequently referred to as "Philippines

NDHS Report, 1999". The fieldwork for this survey was conducted from early March through early May 1998 and included interviews with 13,983 women. The rates given here differ somewhat from those in that report, mainly because we simplify the illustrative calculations by not using weights. A substantive analysis of this survey should use weights, as in the published report.

MEASURES OF FERTILITY IN AN INTERVAL OF AGE OR MARITAL DURATION

This section discusses the most common of the specific fertility rates and birth probabilities. All calculations are based on individual-level data from a survey.

Terminology

In fertility analysis, as in the analysis of mortality, migration, or other demographic events, *exposure to risk* is a key concept. This term refers to the time during which a person is at risk of experiencing an event, whether or not the event actually occurred. For example, the age-period-specific fertility rate for ages 20 to 24 in 1990–1994 is estimated from women who were in at least part of the age interval 20 to 24 during at least part of the time interval 1990–1994. A particular woman's exposure to risk is the amount of time that she was in this state.

When aggregated data are used to calculate rates, exposure to risk is approximated with a midpoint count (or estimate) of the number of persons at risk. Thus, the definitions of fertility rates in Chapter 15 gave counts or estimates of women for the denominators. Individual-level data allow the calculation of exposure to risk on a case-by-case basis.

An *interval of age* has a clear meaning and is generally either a single year or a standard 5-year interval. An *interval of time*, or a *period*, can have two possible interpretations. The first is calendar time. A rate that is calculated for a calendar year, such as 1998, or a 5-year interval, such as 1995–1999, is easily compared with rates from other data sources.

Another possibility is to interpret time as elapsed time before the interview—for example, the year (12 months) prior to the month of interview (perhaps ignoring the actual month of interview, because it has incomplete exposure). An advantage of this interpretation of time is that there is complete exposure for every case, regardless of the date of interview. A disadvantage is that comparisons with other sources are blurred, because the start and end dates of intervals are linked to the dates of fieldwork.

An interval of *marital duration* refers to the length of time since the date of first marriage. Like age, it is generally given in single completed years, beginning with duration zero, or in standard 5-year intervals. For example, marital duration 10 to 14 years begins exactly 10 years after

the date of first marriage and ends exactly 15 years after the date of first marriage. It is customary not to re-initialize marital duration if a woman is widowed or divorced or remarries. It is also customary not to make any deductions for time between marriages or to label births between marriages as nonmarital. Such elaborations are possible, if a marital history can be consulted, but are rarely worth the trouble unless there is a specific interest in the measurement of fertility outside of marriage.

The term "window" will refer to an interval of time, stated in century month codes, extending from the beginning to the ending month. A window may be restricted by the requirement that a woman have a specific age or marital duration (in which case it can be thought of as an interval of age or marital duration). A window may be truncated on the left by the date of first marriage, or it may be truncated on the right by the month of interview.

Assume that we know the following for each woman, by calendar month and year:

Her date of birth (needed for the calculation of age)
Her date of first marriage (needed for the calculation of marital duration)
The dates of birth of all her live births
The date of interview

The following kinds of measures are commonly calculated from such data:[2]

Age-period-specific fertility rates
Age-period-specific marital fertility rates
Marital duration-period-specific marital fertility rates
Order-period-specific fertility rates
Period-specific-birth probabilities

All such measures are specific for a time period, typically 5-year intervals of calendar years or of years before the interview month. Our examples will assume 5-year intervals of calendar years, as well as 5-year intervals of age and marital duration. The measures designated as rates in this list fall in the class of "central" rates when calculated from aggregrate data.

To calculate fertility measures from survey data, it is desirable to have a survey that includes all women, not just ever-married women. We shall assume that the data include all women, but will describe the modifications to estimate rates using only ever-married women.

Period Rates

Age-Specific Fertility Rates

We now turn to the most common kinds of specific fertility rates. These rates all have the form of the average or

---

[2] Conventionally, the names of these measures do not incorporate a reference to the fact that they are period-specific, but this is done here to describe them more fully and to elucidate the method of derivation.

expected number of births to a woman, controlling variously for time period, age, marital status, marital duration, or the order of the birth.

The age-period-specific fertility rate was introduced in the preceding chapter, in which it was calculated with vital statistics data in the numerator and census data (or intercensal or postcensal estimates) on numbers of women in the denominator. Here we calculate it entirely from survey data.

If a refers to an age interval and t to a time interval or period, then the rate for this age and period is calculated as

$$f(a,t) = b(a,t)/e(a,t) \qquad (16.1)$$

where $b(a,t)$ is the total number of births observed at time t to women aged a at time of birth and $e(a,t)$ is the total woman-years of exposure to risk at age a during time t. Such rates are sometimes defined to include a factor of 1000, but we shall omit such a factor.

For example, the numerator of the age-period-specific fertility rate for age 20 to 24 in period 1990–1994 consists of the number of births that occurred in 1990–1994 to women who were aged 20 to 24 at the time of the birth. The denominator consists of the total time that the women in the survey were exposed to ages 20 to 24 in 1990–1994. The computational strategy is to examine each woman in the file and locate the window when (if ever) she satisfied the age and period requirements for the rate. The woman's exposure to risk will then be the length of this window. Her relevant births (if any) will be those that occurred within this window. Births and exposures are accumulated for all women in the survey, and then the accumulated births are divided by the accumulated exposures.

We shall illustrate the strategy in detail, continuing with an age-period-specific rate for ages 20 to 24 in 1990–1994. January 1990 converts to cmc = $1 + 90*12 = 1081$ and December 1994 converts to $12 + 94*12 = 1140$. (Because December 1994 is 1 month less than 5 years after January 1990, the last month can also be calculated as $1081 + 59 = 1140$.) Therefore the window for 1990–1994 is expressed as (1081 to 1140).

The window of time when a woman was aged 20 to 24 must be calculated separately for every woman in the survey. If the cmc of the woman's birth is called B, then she turned 20 in month $B + 20*12$, and 60 months later, she turned 25. The month before this was the final month in her window for ages 20 to 24. Therefore, the window of time when she was aged 20 to 24 is (B + 240 to B + 299).

Most women will have no exposure to ages 20 to 24 during 1990–1994, or to any other specific combination of age and period. A woman will have exposure to this combination of age and period only if her 20th birthday occurred in or before December 1994 *and* her 25th birthday occurred in or after January 1990. For any other woman, the period window (1081 to 1140) and the age window (B + 240 to B + 299) will not intersect. Most women who have any such exposure will have fewer than 60 months; 60 months (5

years) is the maximum possible. (Calculations of exposure will be in months, with subsequent division by 12 to convert to years.)

To repeat, a woman will have some exposure if $B + 240 \leq 1140$ *and* $1081 \leq B + 299$. This condition is equivalent to $B \leq 900$ *and* $782 \leq B$ and can be stated in terms of a range for B as $782 \leq B \leq 900$. Suppose, for example, that the woman was born in December 1972, so $B = 12 + 72*12 = 876$. Her window for ages 20 to 24 is (1116 to 1175), and the intersection of this variable window for ages 20 to 24 with the fixed window for period 1990–1994 will be (1116 to 1140). This particular woman's exposure to risk is the length of this window, including the first and the last months: $1140 - 1116 + 1 = 25$ months. Her contribution to the numerator of this fertility rate will consist of any births that she had from cmc 1116 to cmc 1140, inclusive. The number of such births is obtained by reviewing the dates in the woman's birth history.

It is efficient to determine each woman's contribution to the numerators and denominators of a full array of rates, not just a single rate. Table 16.1 shows the windows of exposure for the woman in the preceding example, assuming that the interview was conducted in April 1998 (cmc 1180). The window for each relevant age interval is given in the last column of the table, and the window for each relevant time period is given in the bottom row of the table. The intersection of the age and period windows is given inside the table.

Now suppose that this woman had had three births, given in her birth history with these dates: August 1990, March 1994, and January 1998. These dates convert to century month codes $8 + 90*12 = 1088$, $3 + 94*12 = 1131$, and $1 + 98*12 = 1177$, respectively. The number of births in the intervals in the age-by-period array that include these dates is incremented by one; this leads to the contributions to the birth array shown in Table 16.2. A zero in a cell indicates that the woman had exposure to that cell, but no births.

Table 16.3 converts the windows of risk into the contributions this woman would make to the cells of the exposure array, expressed in months. For equal intervals of age and period (e.g., 5 years), a specific woman's contribu-

TABLE 16.1 Windows of Age-by-Period Exposure for an Illustrative Woman Born in December 1972 and Interviewed in April 1998

| Age | Period | | | Window for age |
	1985–1989	1990–1994	1995–1999	
15–19	1056–1080	1081–1115	—	1056–1115
20–24	—	1116–1140	1141–1175	1116–1175
25–29	—	—	1176–1180	1176–1180
Window for period	1021–1080	1081–1140	1141–1180	

Source: See text for explanation.

tion to the arrays of exposures (and births) will always be located on two adjacent diagonals going from the upper left to the lower right. We give half a month of exposure to the month of interview (and include any births reported in that month).

Three rows and three columns are shown for this respondent's age-by-period array, but they are extracted from a larger array that would extend to ages 45 to 49 and to periods going back as far as desired, up to 35 years (if the age range of eligible respondents is 50 − 15 = 35 years). In practice this kind of array is often taken back no more than 10 years. The further back it goes, the greater the chance of reporting error. If maternal mortality is high, there is omission of the higher-fertility women who have died, along with their births, so that the more remote rates are biased downward. A comparison of the more remote rates with those obtained

from an earlier survey can help to identify patterns of reporting error and selectivity.

These steps are repeated for every woman in the survey, until a full array of exposures and a corresponding full array of rates are obtained. Exposures are converted to years by dividing the months of exposure by 12, and the total births are divided by total exposure, cell by cell, to give the age-period specific fertility rates.

Because there is a cutoff age in a fertility survey (usually age 49), the array of rates will be empty in the lower left of the table. If we go back more than five years, we have no information about women aged 45 and over; if we go back more than 10 years, we have no information about women aged 40 and over; and so on.

Tables 16.4 through 16.6 give the numbers of births, months of exposure, and age-period-specific fertility rates for the 1998 NDHS of the Philippines. The last time interval is labeled "1995–1999", but the data for that interval should be understood to extend only to the fieldwork in 1998. In these and later tables, cells with zeros or dashes should be interpreted to be outside the time and age (or duration) range of the survey.

How would these rates be estimated if the survey was limited to ever-married women? The answer is relatively simple if there is an accompanying household roster that indicates which women were selected for the interviews, and if there is a negligible amount of childbearing by never-married women. Assume that these two conditions are true.

The birth array would be calculated exactly as shown earlier, but would necessarily be limited to the birth histories of the ever-married women. The exposure array, however, would be calculated from all the women in the household roster who were in the age range of the eligible respondents at the time of the survey, usually 15 to 49, and would not be limited to the ever-married women in the survey. The rates would again be calculated by dividing the birth array by the exposure array, cell by cell.

If the researcher wishes to calculate age-period-specific rates within socioeconomic categories, using a survey

TABLE 16.2   Contributions of the Illustrative Woman to the Numerators of Age-Period-Specific Fertility Rates

	Period		
Age	1985–1989	1990–1994	1995–1999
15–19	0	1	—
20–24	—	1	0
25–29	—	—	1

Source: See text for explanation.

TABLE 16.3   Months of Age-by-Period Exposure for the Illustrative Woman

	Period		
Age	1985–1989	1990–1994	1995–1999
15–19	25 months	35 months	0 months
20–24	0 months	25 months	35 months
25–29	0 months	0 months	4.5 months

Source: See text for explanation.

TABLE 16.4   Numerators of Age-Period-Specific Fertility Rates (numbers of births):
Philippines, 1998

Age	1965–1969	1970–1974	1975–1979	1980–1984	1985–1989	1990–1994	1995–1999
15–19	309	572	732	765	745	710	463
20–24	75	1104	1709	2101	2231	2186	1342
25–29	0	82	1338	1791	2173	2370	1495
30–34	0	0	107	1062	1395	1754	1098
35–39	0	0	0	67	689	882	676
40–44	0	0	0	0	32	315	211
45–49	0	0	0	0	0	5	24

Source: Based on the 1998 National Demographic and Health Survey (NDHS) of the Philippines (Philippines National Statistics Office, Department of Health, and Macro International, 1999).

TABLE 16.5   Denominators of Age-Period-Specific Fertility Rates (years of exposure):
Philippines, 1998

Age	1965–1969	1970–1974	1975–1979	1980–1984	1985–1989	1990–1994	1995–1999
15–19	4,789.58	7,184.83	9,040.25	10,204.92	10,753.75	11,145.50	8,717.04
20–24	364.58	4,789.58	7,184.83	9,040.25	10,204.92	10,753.75	7,091.21
25–29	0	364.58	4,789.58	7,184.83	9,040.25	10,204.92	6,926.50
30–34	0	0	364.58	4,789.58	7,184.83	9,040.25	6,589.42
35–39	0	0	0	364.58	4,789.58	7,184.83	5,646.67
40–44	0	0	0	0	364.58	4,789.58	4,469.67
45–49	0	0	0	0	0	364.58	2,626.13

Source: Based on the 1998 NDHS of the Philippines (Philippines National Statistics Office, Department of Health, and Macro International, 1999).

TABLE 16.6   Age-Period-Specific Fertility Rates (births per year); Philippines, 1998

Age	1965–1969	1970–1974	1975–1979	1980–1984	1985–1989	1990–1994	1995–1999
15–19	.0645	.0796	.0810	.0750	.0693	.0637	.0531
20–24	.2057	.2305	.2379	.2324	.2186	.2033	.1892
25–29	—	.2249	.2794	.2493	.2404	.2322	.2158
30–34	—	—	.2935	.2217	.1942	.1940	.1666
35–39	—	—	—	.1838	.1439	.1228	.1197
40–44	—	—	—	—	.0878	.0658	.0472
45–49	—	—	—	—	—	.0137	.0091

Source: Tables 16.4 and 16.5.

limited to ever-married women, this will be possible only for categories specified for the women in the household survey. Region, type of residence, and education are usually available in the household survey, but not much more. In an all-women survey, rates can be made specific for any characteristics of the respondents. Rates that are defined only for ever-married women, such as the marital fertility rates to be discussed next, are obviously unaffected by the restriction of eligibility to ever-married women.

Age-Specific Marital Fertility Rates

Marital fertility rates are restricted according to marital status, but otherwise they are calculated in the same way as rates that do not refer to marital status. The marital fertility rate for age a and period t is

$$mf(a,t) = mb(a,t)/me(a,t) \qquad (16.2)$$

where $mb(a,t)$ is the total marital births observed at time t to women aged a at time of birth and $me(a,t)$ is the total woman-years of marital exposure to risk at age a at time t.

This type of rate is limited to births and exposure that occur after first marriage. As stated earlier, the marriage history is typically not consulted for any dates other than the date of first marriage (or when the couple first lived together as "married"). If M is the month of first marriage, then any

TABLE 16.7   Windows of Age-by-Period Marital Exposure
for the Illustrative Woman

Age	Period		Window for Age
	1990–1994	1995–1999	
15–19	—	—	1056–1115
20–24	1118–1140	1141–1175	1116–1175
25–29	—	1176–1180	1176–1180
Window for period	1081–1140	1141–1180	

Source: See text for explanation.

window will omit exposure and births prior to M. For example, if the respondent in the previous example was married in February 1993 (i.e., $M = 2 + 93 * 12 = 1118$), then the window (1116–1140) will be reduced to (1118–1140); this will be the respondent's window of exposure to marital fertility while at ages 20 to 24 in period 1990–1994; the exposure to risk will be $1140 - 1118 + 1 = 23$ months. Births prior to month 1118 will be ignored, leaving two marital births, in months 1131 and 1171. After the window in which the first marriage occurred, there will be no difference between a woman's contributions to the numerator and denominator of the marital rate and the overall rate. The windows of risk, marital births, and marital exposure for the illustrative woman are given in Tables 16.7 through 16.9.

TABLE 16.8   Marital Births for the Illustrative Woman

Age	Period	
	1990–1994	1995–1999
15–19	0	—
20–24	1	0
25–29	—	1

Source: See text for explanation.

TABLE 16.9   Months of Age-by-Period Marital Exposure for the Illustrative Woman

Age	Period	
	1990–1994	1995–1999
15–19	0 months	0 months
20–24	23 months	35 months
25–29	0 months	4.5 months

Source: See text for explanation.

TABLE 16.10   Numerators of Marital-Age-Period-Specific Fertility Rates (births): Philippines, 1998

Age	1965–1969	1970–1974	1975–1979	1980–1984	1985–1989	1990–1994	1995–1999
15–19	299	544	698	727	707	681	432
20–24	73	1081	1681	2069	2194	2142	1312
25–29	0	79	1317	1782	2155	2342	1481
30–34	0	0	105	1058	1391	1749	1097
35–39	0	0	0	67	685	880	674
40–44	0	0	0	0	31	315	211
45–49	0	0	0	0	0	5	24

Source: Based on 1998 NDHS of the Philippines (Philippines National Statistics Office, Department of Health, and Macro International, 1999).

TABLE 16.11   Denominators of Marital-Age-Period-Specific Fertility Rates (years of exposure): Philippines, 1998

Age	1965–1969	1970–1974	1975–1979	1980–1984	1985–1989	1990–1994	1995–1999
15–19	747.75	1374.92	1655.92	1756.83	1710.50	1625.83	965.38
20–24	153.00	2601.42	4229.58	5170.42	5625.50	5649.92	3511.42
25–29	0	253.58	3809.92	5945.92	7223.08	8134.33	5472.13
30–34	0	0	314.58	4316.83	6498.42	8101.58	5954.83
35–39	0	0	0	329.75	4446.33	6682.25	5250.63
40–44	0	0	0	0	336.42	4498.42	4240.17
45–49	0	0	0	0	0	338	2507.29

Source: Based on 1998 NDHS of the Philippines (Philippines National Statistics Office, Department of Health, and Macro International, 1999).

Working from a data file, each respondent's contributions to the arrays for marital births and marital exposures are calculated; months of marital exposure are converted to years; and the rates are calculated by dividing births by exposure, cell by cell. Tables 16.10 through 16.12 give the numbers of marital births, months of marital exposure, and age-period-specific marital fertility rates for the 1998 NDHS of the Philippines.

Marital Duration-Specific Marital Fertility Rates

Marital fertility can be referenced by the woman's date of marriage rather than her date of birth. The marital fertility rate for duration d and period t is

$$mf(d,t) = mb(d,t)/me(d,t) \qquad (16.3)$$

where $mb(d,t)$ is the total marital births observed at time t to women with duration d at time of birth and $me(d,t)$ is the total woman-years of marital exposure to risk at duration d at time t.

For example, if the illustrative woman was married in month $M = 1118$, then she had marital duration 0 to 4 years in the window (M to $M + 59$)—that is, (1118 to 1177), and so on. Her windows of exposure, marital births, and months of exposure for the marital duration rates are given in Tables 16.13 through 16.15.

The marital duration-period-specific rates are calculated, as shown earlier, by dividing the accumulated array of births by the accumulated array of exposures (converted to years). Tables 16.16 through 16.18 give the numbers of marital births, the months of marital exposure, and marital duration-

TABLE 16.12 Marital-Age-Period-Specific Fertility Rates (births per year): Philippines, 1998

Age	1965–1969	1970–1974	1975–1979	1980–1984	1985–1989	1990–1994	1995–1999
15–19	.3999	.3957	.4215	.4138	.4133	.4189	.4475
20–24	.4771	.4155	.3974	.4002	.3900	.3791	.3736
25–29	—	.3115	.3457	.2997	.2983	.2879	.2706
30–34	—	—	.3338	.2451	.2141	.2159	.1842
35–39	—	—	—	.2032	.1541	.1317	.1284
40–44	—	—	—	—	.0921	.0700	.0498
45–49	—	—	—	—	—	.0148	.0096

Source: Tables 16.10 and 16.11.

TABLE 16.13 Windows of Marital Duration-by-Period Exposure for the Illustrative Woman

		Period		Window
		1990–1994	1995–1999	for duration
Marital	0–4	1118–1140	1141–1177	1118–1177
duration	5–9	—	1178–1180	1178–1180
Window for period			1081–1140	1141–1180

Source: See text for explanation.

TABLE 16.15 Months of Marital Duration-by-Period Exposure for the Illustrative Woman

		Period	
		1990–1994	1995–1999
Marital	0–4	23 months	37 months
duration	5–9	0 months	2.5 months

Source: See text for explanation.

TABLE 16.14 Marital Births for the Illustrative Woman

		Period	
		1990–1994	1995–1999
Marital	0–4	1	1
duration	5–9	—	0

Source: See text for explanation.

period-specific marital fertility rates for the 1998 NDHS of the Philippines.

Age-Period-Cohort Relationships

Each of the arrays of fertility rates described can be examined from any of three perspectives or directions. One of these perspectives is the woman's life course, indicated by her age (in the case of age-period-specific fertility rates and age-period-specific marital fertility rates) or by her marital duration (in the case of duration-period-specific marital fertility rates), as shown in the columns of Tables 16.6, 16.12, and 16.18. The second perspective is across time periods, as shown in the rows of these tables.

A third perspective, perhaps less obvious, is across birth cohorts (in the case of the first two kinds of rates) or across marriage cohorts (in the case of the third kind of rates), as shown by the diagonals extending from the upper left to the lower right of these tables. Recall that a birth cohort consists of persons born in the same time interval and a marriage cohort consists of persons married in the same time interval.

In an array of age-period-specific rates, for example, rates in the same row, referring to the same age interval, can be compared across columns or periods, to identify patterns of change over time. They can also be compared across diagonals, to identify patterns of change across birth cohorts.

Rates calculated for the typical 5-year interval of age/duration and 5-year interval of time will draw from a 10-year (rather than 5-year) cohort of births. For example, women who are aged 25 to 29 in any part of the time interval 1995–1999 could have been born as early as 1995 − 30 = 1965 and as late as 1999 − 25 = 1974 (i.e., anytime during the 10 years between January 1, 1965 and December 31, 1974). This feature of the widths of intervals carries over to a larger class of rates. We have not described age-cohort-specific rates, for example, although the procedures for calculating them are very similar to those described for age-period-specific rates. If such rates were calculated for 5-year age groups and 5-year birth cohorts, then the period intervals would be spread over 10 years. In general, if the intervals for the first two dimensions are $w1$ and $w2$ years, then an interval for the third dimension will be $w3 = w1 + w2$ years. The wider intervals will overlap one another. For

TABLE 16.16   Numerators of Marital Duration-Period-Specific Fertility Rates (births):
Philippines, 1998

Age	1965–1969	1970–1974	1975–1979	1980–1984	1985–1989	1990–1994	1995–1999
0–4	348	1372	2374	3065	3346	3511	2334
5–9	24	319	1126	1649	1982	2148	1292
10–14	0	13	283	783	1170	1306	808
15–19	0	0	18	187	530	766	505
20–24	0	0	0	19	130	346	235
25–29	0	0	0	0	5	36	56
30–34	0	0	0	0	0	1	1

Source: Based on 1998 NDHS of the Philippines (Philippines National Statistics Office, Department of Health, and Macro International, 1999).

TABLE 16.17   Denominators of Marital Duration-Period-Specific Fertility Rates
(years of exposure): Philippines, 1998

Age	1965–1969	1970–1974	1975–1979	1980–1984	1985–1989	1990–1994	1995–1999
0–4	838.17	3272.25	5700.58	7432.00	8218.42	9116.92	6200.21
5–9	62.58	895.08	3347.92	5778.33	7531.58	8290.67	5862.58
10–14	0	62.58	898.92	3347.92	5780.83	7532.50	5260.29
15–19	0	0	62.58	898.92	3347.92	5780.83	4802.75
20–24	0	0	0	62.58	898.92	3347.92	3500.96
25–29	0	0	0	0	62.58	898.92	1870.42
30–34	0	0	0	0	0	62.58	389.88

Source: Based on 1998 NDHS of the Philippines (Philippines National Statistics Office, Department of Health, and Macro International, 1999).

TABLE 16.18   Marital Duration-Period-Specific Fertility Rates (births per year): Philippines, 1998

Age	1965–1969	1970–1974	1975–1979	1980–1984	1985–1989	1990–1994	1995–1999
0–4	.4152	.4193	.4164	.4124	.4071	.3851	.3764
5–9	.3835	.3564	.3363	.2854	.2632	.2591	.2204
10–14	—	.2077	.3148	.2339	.2024	.1734	.1536
15–19	—	—	.2876	.2080	.1583	.1325	.1051
20–24	—	—	—	.3036	.1446	.1033	.0671
25–29	—	—	—	—	.0799	.0400	.0299
30–34	—	—	—	—	—	.0160	.0026

Source: Tables 16.16 and 16.17.

example, cohorts described with the diagonals of the usual age-period-specific rates will refer to birth dates such as 1950–1959, 1955–1964, 1960–1969, 1965–1974, and so on. This blurring in the third dimension, so to speak, has the effect of suppressing some of the variation in that dimension in the same way that a moving average does. The linkages between age/duration, period, and cohort are relevant to all demographic and socioecnomic variables that have an age dimension (e.g., mortality, labor force).

Order-Specific Fertility Rates

As may be recalled from Chapter 15, a woman's parity is the number of live births that she has had. Any of the pre-

ceding rates can also be made specific for the parity of the mother or, equivalently, the birth order of the latest child. Such rates are sometimes called parity-specific, with reference to the mother, and sometimes called order-specific, with reference to the child; we shall describe them as order-specific. These rates were introduced in Chapter 15, but their construction will be briefly reviewed in the present context.

It is easiest to clarify the labeling with an example. An age-period-order-specific rate is specific for order two if it measures the rate of childbearing of second births for women in each combination of age and period. When a second birth occurs, the woman moves from parity one to parity two. Thus the rate is indexed by the birth that closes the interval.

By convention, the denominators of these rates *do not* depend on the woman's parity. They do not reflect the fact that, say, a woman who has had no births at all has no immediate risk of having a second birth, or that, say, a woman who has had one or more births is no longer at risk of having a first birth. Only the woman's contribution to the numerator depends on her parity. That contribution will be one birth if she has a birth of the specified order in the age-period window. Thus, the numerators of the three-way rates are formed by disaggregating the numerators of the two-way rates. As a result, when the age-period-order-specific rates are added up across all birth orders, the sum will be simply the age-period-specific rate.

The order-specific rate for births of order j, for age a at time t, is given by

$$f_j(a,t) = b_j(a,t)/e(a,t) \qquad (16.4)$$

where $b_j(a,t)$ is the number of births *of order j* and $f(a,t) = \sum_j f_j(a,t)$.

Consider again the illustrative woman who was born in December 1972 and had births in century months 1088, 1131, and 1177. This respondent's windows of age and period were given earlier, and her months of exposure to risk were given in Table 16.3. These will be her contributions to the denominator of *every* order-specific rate within the combinations of age and period. We now wish to identify her contributions to fertility rates that are specific for age, period, and order.

The woman's three births were classified by age and period in Table 16.2. We now repeat that table, with "first," "second," and "third" inserted in the table to identify birth order, as shown in Table 16.19.

The first birth will contribute only to the numerator of the age-period-order-specific rate for ages 15 to 19, period 1990–1994, order 1. The second birth will contribute only to the numerator of the age-period-order specific rate for ages 20 to 24, period 1990–1994, order 2. The third birth will contribute only to the numerator of the age-period-order-specific rate for ages 25 to 29, period 1995–1995, order 3. The woman contributes nothing to the numerators of any other age-period-order-specific rates.

It would be possible also to disaggregate the woman's exposure to risk in order to describe the months of exposure to risk of a first birth, second birth, and so on, within each cell of the exposure (denominator) array and to calculate order-specific rates that controlled for parity in the same way as for age and period, but we emphasize that the conventional order-specific rates do not do this.

If desired, any of the other rates that are specific for possible combinations, i.e., of age, period, cohort, marital status, or marital duration, can also be made specific for birth order.

Tables 16.20 and 16.21 give the arrays of births by age, period, and birth order, for birth orders one and two, from the 1998 NDHS of the Philippines. Tables 16.22 and 16.23 give the corresponding age-period-order-specific rates, obtained by dividing the successive panels of births by the exposures in Table 16.5.

Birth Probabilities

A fertility rate is essentially an average or expected *number of births* that occur in an interval. A birth probability, by contrast, is the (estimated) *probability that one or more births* will occur within that interval. A retrospective

TABLE 16.19 Contributions of the Illustrative Woman to the Numerators of Order-Age-Period-Specific Fertility Rates

Age	Period		
	1985–1989	1990–1994	1995–1999
15–19	0	1 (first)	—
20–24	—	1 (second)	0
25–29	—	—	1 (third)

Source: See text for explanation.

TABLE 16.20 Numerators of Order-Age-Period-Specific Fertility Rates for Order 1: Philippines, 1998

Age	1965–1969	1970–1974	1975–1979	1980–1984	1985–1989	1990–1994	1995–1999
15–19	208	399	478	519	509	482	336
20–24	32	389	546	696	791	788	543
25–29	0	14	195	246	321	392	289
30–34	0	0	12	73	86	123	90
35–39	0	0	0	2	12	31	32
40–44	0	0	0	0	3	9	2
45–49	0	0	0	0	0	0	0

Source: Based on 1998 NDHS of the Philippines (Philippines National Statistics Office, Department of Health, and Macro International, 1999).

TABLE 16.21   Numerators of Order-Age-Period-Specific Fertility Rates for Order 2:
Philippines, 1998

Age	1965–1969	1970–1974	1975–1979	1980–1984	1985–1989	1990–1994	1995–1999
15–19	79	145	191	195	183	176	107
20–24	30	354	563	678	730	713	436
25–29	0	11	241	363	422	499	326
30–34	0	0	15	115	133	196	150
35–39	0	0	0	6	34	34	39
40–44	0	0	0	0	0	6	5
45–49	0	0	0	0	0	0	1

Source: Based on 1998 NDHS of the Philippines (Philippines National Statistics Office, Department of Health, and Macro International, 1999).

TABLE 16.22   Order-Age-Period-Specific Fertility Rates for Order 1: Philippines, 1998

Age	1965–1969	1970–1974	1975–1979	1980–1984	1985–1989	1990–1994	1995–1999
15–19	.0434	.0555	.0529	.0509	.0473	.0432	.0385
20–24	.0878	.0812	.0760	.0770	.0775	.0733	.0766
25–29	—	.0384	.0407	.0342	.0355	.0384	.0417
30–34	—	—	.0329	.0152	.0120	.0136	.0137
35–39	—	—	—	.0055	.0025	.0043	.0057
40–44	—	—	—	—	.0082	.0019	.0004
45–49	—	—	—	—	—	—	.0000

Source: Tables 16.20 and 16.5.

TABLE 16.23   Order-Age-Period-Specific Fertility Rates for Order 2: Philippines, 1998

Age	1965–1969	1970–1974	1975–1979	1980–1984	1985–1989	1990–1994	1995–1999
15–19	.0165	.0202	.0211	.0191	.0170	.0158	.0123
20–24	.0823	.0739	.0784	.0750	.0715	.0663	.0615
25–29	—	.0302	.0503	.0505	.0467	.0489	.0471
30–34	—	—	.0411	.0240	.0185	.0217	.0228
35–39	—	—	—	.0165	.0071	.0047	.0069
40–44	—	—	—	—	—	.0013	.0011
45–49	—	—	—	—	—	—	.0004

Source: Tables 16.21 and 16.5.

survey is actually the only data format (other than a prospective survey, which is only rarely available) that allows the direct calculation of birth probabilities. We will briefly show how this may be done, staying with 5-year intervals of age and time.

In the context of rates, we described the construction of a numerator array of births and a denominator array of exposures. Each woman made contributions (often zero) to the cells of the numerator and denominator arrays. For each woman, each cell was expressed in terms of a window of century months, within which births and exposure may have occurred. The rates were subsequently calculated from a cell-by-cell division of the accumulated contributions to the numerator and denominator arrays. In a typical situation where exposure is calculated in months but we want a single-year rate, at some point (most easily after all observations have been accumulated) the exposure must be divided by 12.

The approach for probabilities is similar, but the arrays of births and exposures are calculated slightly differently. For probabilities, an individual woman's contribution to a numerator cell of births can only be zero if she had no births in the window, or one if she had one *or more* births in the window. An algorithm for calculating her contribution to the numerator of a rate needs only to be altered by recoding any positive number of births into just one birth. A woman's contribution to the corresponding denominator cell of exposure will depend in part on whether she actually had a birth during the window of observation. This may seem counterintuitive and calls for some justification.

Consider the probability that a woman will have a birth while aged 20 to 24, which is to be estimated with births and exposure observed within that age interval during 1990–1994. The outcome is binary: Either a birth occurs, in which case a code of 1 is assigned, or no birth occurs, in which case a code of 0 is assigned.

The classical example of a trial with a binary outcome is the toss of a coin. We toss a coin once, and assign code 1 to a success, say a head, and code 0 to a failure, a tail. The numerator or outcome can be 0 or 1, interpreted as the (possible) number of heads or successes when the number of trials—the denominator—is 1. If we tossed n independent but identical coins, the number of successes could be any integer k between 0 and n, inclusive, and k would have a binomial distribution with denominator n.

This familiar model may clarify the requirement that if the outcome takes the values 0 or 1, then the denominator, or degree of risk associated with the outcome, must never be less than the value of the numerator. If the denominator could be less than 1 when the numerator is 1, we would have the potential to produce an estimated probability greater than 1, which is not allowed.

The relevant data in a window of age and time are generally censored on either the left or the right, and sometimes (if the interview occurred within the time interval) on both the left and the right. There are three possibilities.

If the observation is not censored, and the woman had a full 60 months of exposure to the window, then her contribution to the denominator will be 1 (the number of months in the window divided by 60).

If the observation is censored, *and no birth occurred in the window*, then her contribution to the denominator will be the *fraction* of the full 5-year or 60-month interval for which she was observed—that is, the number of months in the window divided by 60. This fraction indicates that the observation is only partial.

The remaining possibility is that the observation is censored but a birth does occur. This is where the coin-tossing analogy becomes relevant. *If a birth occurred*, then *it does not matter* that there was less than full observation of the woman, and we credit the case with a contribution of 1 to the denominator. Indeed, we *must* credit her with 1 to avoid having a contribution to the denominator that is less than the contribution to the numerator.

To summarize,

• If there was *no censoring* within the cell, then exposure for the probability equals the exposure for the rate.

• If there was *censoring* and *no birth*, then exposure for the probability equals the exposure for the rate.

• If there was *censoring* and *a birth* (one or more), then exposure must be augmented to reach the length it would have had in the absence of censoring (e.g., 60 months).

• After the exposure in a cell has been accumulated across all respondents, the sum must be normalized to a maximum of one unit per woman (e.g., by dividing the total months by 60).

These rules are consistent with an assumption that the probability of having a birth is uniform within the interval of age and time (or intervals of other dimensions, depending on the specific rate). If this assumption is not plausible, then (as with a rate) the researcher may choose to adopt shorter intervals, within which the assumption is safer.

Reconsider the illustrative woman born in December 1972, with births in century-months 1088, 1131, and 1177. We described in detail the calculation of this woman's contributions to the numerator and denominator arrays of age-period-specific fertility rates. How would these contributions differ for age-period-specific birth probabilities?

First consider the numerator array. Cells with no births will continue to make a contribution of zero. Because the woman's births occurred in different cells of the age-by-period array, the three cells with a contribution of one birth to the numerator of a rate also contribute one birth to the numerator of a probability. The numerator array will thus be exactly the same as Table 16.3 and need not be repeated.

The contributions to the denominator array will remain unchanged for those cells in which no births occurred. In the three cells in which a birth occurred, the months of exposure must be increased to 60. After the accumulation of all exposures, we emphasize that the total in each cell must be normalized by dividing by 60 months, rather than 12 months, and that the probability extends across a 5-year range, whereas the rate is interpreted in terms of a single year. The denominator contributions are given in Table 16.24, prior to the division by 60.

Tables 16.25 through 16.27 give the births, exposures, and age-period-specific birth probabilities for the 1998

TABLE 16.24 The Illustrative Woman's Contributions to Risk for the Age-Period-Specific Birth Probabilities

Age	Period		
	1985–1989	1990–1994	1995–1999
15–19	25 months	60 months	0 months
20–24	0 months	60 months	35 months
25–29	0 months	0 months	60 months

Source: See text for explanation.

TABLE 16.25   Numerators of Age-Period-Specific Birth Probabilities (births): Philippines: 1998

Age	1965–1969	1970–1974	1975–1979	1980–1984	1985–1989	1990–1994	1995–1999
15–19	391	450	568	599	588	558	401
20–24	72	732	1213	1458	1613	1566	1097
25–29	0	79	920	1327	1622	1785	1255
30–34	0	0	104	777	1079	1336	945
35–39	0	0	0	65	536	715	587
40–44	0	0	0	0	32	276	197
45–49	0	0	0	0	0	5	24

Source: Based on 1998 NDHS of the Philippines (Philippines National Statistics Office, Department of Health, and Macro International, 1999).

TABLE 16.26   Denominators of Age-Period-Specific Birth Probabilities (years of risk):
Philippines, 1998

Age	1965–1969	1970–1974	1975–1979	1980–1984	1985–1989	1990–1994	1995–1999
15–19	5,041.75	7,989.92	10,129.08	11,276.92	11,820.58	12,157.92	9,723.63
20–24	643.42	5,932.33	9,438.33	11,715.92	13,163.58	13,546.17	9,868.00
25–29	0	670.50	6,237.83	9,693.83	12,006.67	13,511.42	10,091.54
30–34	0	0	773.33	6,021.58	9,189.33	11,454.58	8,929.33
35–39	0	0	0	613.00	5,616.83	8,521.17	7,096.38
40–44	0	0	0	0	486.67	5,224.08	4,968.38
45–49	0	0	0	0	0	383.25	2,694.38

Source: Based on 1998 NDHS of the Philippines (Philippines National Statistics Office, Department of Health, and Macro International, 1999).

TABLE 16.27   Age-Period-Specific Birth Probabilities (probability of a birth in 5 years):
Philippines, 1998

Age	1965–1969	1970–1974	1975–1979	1980–1984	1985–1989	1990–1994	1995–1999
15–19	.3878	.2816	.2804	.2656	.2487	.2295	.2062
20–24	.5595	.6170	.6426	.6222	.6127	.5780	.5558
25–29	—	.5891	.7374	.6845	.6755	.6606	.6218
30–34	—	—	.6724	.6452	.5871	.5832	.5292
35–39	—	—	—	.5302	.4771	.4195	.4136
40–44	—	—	—	—	.3288	.2642	.1983
45–49	—	—	—	—	—	.0652	.0445

Source: Tables 16.25 and 16.26. Calculation: (Cell in Table 16.25 ÷ Cell in Table 16.25) × 5.

NDHS of the Philippines. Because these probabilities refer to 5-year intervals of age, they are much larger than the corresponding annual rates given in Table 16.6.

Standard Errors and Sample Design

Standard Errors

When sample data are used to calculate fertility rates or birth probabilities, it should be clearly understood that these are *estimates* of the rates and probabilities for the population from which the sample is drawn. We have followed demographic practice in referring to the preceding quantities as birth probabilities, but they are actually only estimates of birth probabilities. They are subject to sampling error, therefore, measured in terms of standard errors. A standard error can be interpreted as the average deviation (ignoring direction) of an estimate from the true (population) value across all possible random samples of the same size. It can be used for constructing interval estimates (confidence intervals) and for testing hypotheses about the rates and probabilities in the population. Fortunately, it is fairly easy to produce good estimates of the standard errors of specific rates.

The generic form for a specific rate is $r = b/e$, where r is the rate (ignoring any multipliers such as 1000), b is a count or frequency of births, and e is a measure of exposure in woman-years. Let $s.e.(r)$ denote the estimated standard error of the rate.

As a good first approximation, for a fixed amount of exposure, the number of births has a Poisson distribution. A useful property of a Poisson distribution is that its mean and variance are equal. The observed number of births will be the maximum likelihood estimate of both the mean and the variance of the distribution. Therefore,

$$s.e.(r) = \sqrt{b}/e = \sqrt{r}/e = r/\sqrt{b}. \qquad (16.5)$$

Any of the three forms on the right-hand side of this equation can be used. Suppose, for example, that an age-specific rate for ages 30 to 34 is .100 births per woman per year, and the numerator of this rate included 400 births. Then the estimated standard error of the rate would be

$$s.e.(r) = r/\sqrt{b} = .100/\sqrt{400} = .005$$

Another useful property of a Poisson sampling distribution for a birth count is that it is well approximated by a normal distribution having the same mean and standard deviation, especially for large samples. Adapting the usual formulas for confidence intervals for parameters whose estimates have asymptotically normal sampling distributions, a 95% confidence interval for the underlying true rate will be $r \pm 1.96r/\sqrt{b}$. The 95% confidence interval for the rate estimated in the preceding paragraph would thus range from .090 to .110.

Suppose there are two independent estimates r_1 and r_2 of the true rates for two subpopulations (or two time periods, two age groups, etc.). Then the test statistic for a null hypothesis that the underlying rates are equal will be

$$z = (r_1 - r_2)/\sqrt{(r_1^2/b_1) + (r_2^2/b_2)}. \qquad (16.6)$$

For example, a two-sided null hypothesis will be rejected at the .05 level if the calculated test statistic is greater than 1.96 or less than −1.96.

The standard error for an estimated birth probability is estimated by drawing on statistical theory for a binomial distribution. Say that the estimated probability is $p = b/e$, where both b and e are different from the preceding discussion of rates; here b is the total relevant birth count limited to 0's and 1's, and e is the total exposure, scaled to be 1 if a birth occurred or there was no censoring, or the appropriate fraction if no birth occurred and there was censoring. Then the standard error of p is estimated to be

$$s.e.(p) = \sqrt{p(1-p)/e} = (p/\sqrt{b})(\sqrt{1-p}). \qquad (16.7)$$

The standard error of p is similar to the standard error of r, particularly when p (or r) is small. Formulas for con-fidence intervals and test statistics using estimated proba-bilities and standard errors can be found in statistics texts.

Sample Design

In a simple random sample, every case in the population has the same probability of appearing in the sample and this probability is independent of whether another case appears. Statistical theory is based on such a model, but virtually no fertility survey follows these criteria. Most surveys have a stratified cluster design, in which relatively small subpopu-lations are oversampled and relatively large subpopulations are undersampled. Census enumeration districts or other such administrative areas comprise the primary sampling units, within which households and individuals are selected. These departures from the model of a simple random sample have two important implications.

First there is the issue of sampling weights, which com-pensate for oversampling and undersampling. Such weights are inversely proportional to the probability that a case in the sample would have been selected from the population. If a case was oversampled, for example, the weight would be relatively small, and if it was undersampled, the weight would be relatively large. If needed, weights are calculated by the survey organization and included on each computer record, generally near the case identification codes. They are generally constructed so that (if the decimal point is prop-erly located) the average value of the weights is 1.0, and the total of the weights, across the entire sample, is equal to the number of cases in the sample.

If weights are provided, we recommend that they be used in the calculation of the descriptive measures given in this chapter (even though we did not follow that practice for the illustrations with data from the Philippines). Otherwise, the measures will be biased toward the oversampled subpopu-lations. The weights compensate for this bias. Statistical computer packages generally have a weight option. The researcher simply invokes that option and identifies the weight variable. If x_i is the value of a variable for case i, and w_i is the weight for case i, then the main effect of the weight option is to replace x_i by $w_i x_i$, to replace x_i^2 by $w_i x_i^2$, and so on. In the calculation of mean CEB, for example, if x_i is the CEB for woman i, the mean CEB would be $\sum_i w_i x_i / \sum_i w_i$. The weight w_i appears in the denominator in place of an implied count of 1 for case i. An unweighted estimate has a slightly smaller standard error than a weighted estimate—which is one reason why some researchers do not use weights.

There is uniform agreement that *for the calculation of standard errors*, every real case in the sample should be given equal importance. This practice means that parallel computer runs are often required: one with weights for estimation and one without weights to get standard errors for the construction of confidence intervals or tests of hypotheses.

Thus, the recommended practice with respect to weights is as follows:

- Use sampling weights when unbiased descriptive estimates are desired.
- Use sampling weights in multivariate models unless the model includes all the stratifying variables or you are confident that the model is fully specified.
- Omit sampling weights for the estimation of standard errors *or* use software that gives "robust" weighted estimates.

The second issue for the analysis of complex sampling designs comes from the use of sample clusters. The cases in these clusters are not independent, but overlap in the information they provide. The degree of overlap is reflected in the intraclass correlation. This is not easily calculated and varies from one variable to another. The lack of independence will not alter the estimates of summary statistics, rates, probabilities, and coefficients, but it will affect standard errors. If the clustering is not taken into account, the estimated standard errors will tend to be too small, and as a result, the *p*-values in hypothesis tests will be understated and confidence intervals will be too narrow. If possible, the magnitude of these effects should be assessed with a computer package.

MEASURES OF OVERALL FERTILITY

Overall fertility refers to the total number of births relative to the total number of persons or women in the population. Age and marital duration are ignored, except where women are restricted to the range of the childbearing ages. These measures are described after the specific rates, rather than before them, because they involve some concepts introduced in connection with the specific rates.

Crude Birthrate

The crude birthrate (CBR) was defined in Chapter 15 to be the number of births in a fixed reference period, generally a year, divided by the (total) population at the midpoint of the reference period, multiplied by 1000. Typically, the numerator comes from vital statistics and the denominator comes from a census or is estimated from census data.

It is possible to estimate the CBR entirely from survey data if the survey includes a roster for all the sample households, including the households that had no eligible respondents. The household sample then represents the general population at the time of data collection. The birth histories provide a count of the number of births during a recent time interval for the sample, giving the numerator of the CBR. The total household count can serve as the denominator of the CBR for recent time periods. Because of the general interest in the CBR, we will go into some detail on the issues raised when it is estimated with such data.

The fieldwork for the 1998 NDHS of the Philippines was conducted entirely in 1998, so the survey could be used to estimate the CBR in 1997. The numerator would consist of all births observed in the birth histories for 1997, namely 1586 births (Philippines NDHS Report, 1999, Table C4). An approximation for the denominator would be the total number of persons in the household survey, namely 60,349 persons (Philippines NDHS Report, 1999, Table C1). The ratio, multiplied by 1000, is $(1586/60,349) \times 1000 = 26.3$. In this illustration, the numerator and denominator are unweighted. The weighted estimate of the CBR for the 36 months before the survey is 28.0 (Philippines NDHS Report, 1999, Table 3.1).

The standard error of the unweighted estimate of the CBR for 1997 is $(\sqrt{1586}/60,349) \times 1000 = .66$, so that a 95% confidence interval for the estimated rate (unweighted) would range from 25.0 to 27.6 (= 26.3 ± 1.96 times .66). Following the practice of ignoring weights for the calculation of standard errors, we could also use .66 to construct a confidence interval for the *weighted* CBR, so that a 95% confidence interval for the weighted estimate would range from 26.7 to 29.3 (= 28.0 ± 1.96 times .66).

The median date of the 1998 NDHS fieldwork was approximately April 1, 1998; the midpoint of 1997 was July 1, 1997. One might argue that a denominator at the time of the survey is too large and could be improved by projecting the household population back nine months, or .75 of a year, using the Philippines' estimated annual growth rate of 2.0%. We would not advocate such an adjustment because it ignores an inherent linkage between the numerator and denominator data. If we deflated the denominator population, then to be consistent we should also deflate the number of women who produced the births, and this in turn would deflate the number of births. The same adjustments would be made to both the numerator and the denominator and they would cancel out (assuming no change in the birth rate in this period).

Another way to improve the denominator would be to use the household survey to calculate person-years lived by all household members during 1997. Although this step would be an improvement, such a denominator would ignore anyone who had died between the beginning of 1997 and the date of the survey, and would be somewhat too *small*. Whatever adjustments to the denominator one might make for a recent time interval, they are unlikely to be outside the range of sampling error.

Compared with the traditional definition, the numerator described earlier omits births to women who had a birth during the reference window of time but died between the birth and the interview. Such women and their births are omitted from the survey. This effect is small unless adult female mortality is extremely high. The numerator also omits births to women who were near the end of the eligible age range at the beginning of the window and "aged out" by the date of interview (e.g. who turned 50 between these two dates). This effect is also negligible (unless the window is backdated several years before the interviews) because women near the upper end of eligibility have very low fertility. Because of the biases in the numerator and denominator, it is safest to limit the survey estimate of the CBR to a recent time interval, but in order to gain statistical stability, an interval longer than 1 year is desirable. DHS reports typically include an estimate of the CBR for 1 to 36 months before the interview. A 3-year estimate will have a smaller standard error, by a factor of approximately $1/\sqrt{3} = .58$.

Child-Woman Ratio and General Fertility Rate

Another measure from a census or household survey is the child-woman ratio (CWR), the number of children under 5 divided by the number of women of childbearing age, multiplied by 1000. After division by five (because the numerator represents 5 years of births, rather than 1 year), the CWR can be interpreted as an estimate of the general fertility rate 2½ years earlier, but with a downward bias because it omits children who died prior to the census or survey. It also slightly understates the number of women of childbearing age at the reference date because it omits women who died. If it pertains to a geographic subdivision of a country, it is affected by migration of mothers between the reference date and the survey date. The CWR is an indirect or substitute measure of fertility; variations in the CWR will correspond closely to variations in the direct measures of fertility.

The general fertility rate (GFR) is the number of births (in an interval of time) to women aged 15 to 49 (sometimes 15 to 44), divided by the total number of women aged 15 to 49 (or 15 to 44). Using woman-years, rather than numbers of women, a survey estimate of the GFR is simply the sum of the numerators of the age-specific rates, divided by the sum of the denominators of the age-specific rates:

$$GFR(t) = \frac{\sum_a b(a,t)}{\sum_a e(a,t)} \qquad (16.8)$$

Using the 1998 NDHS of the Philippines, we estimate the GFR for 1990–1994 to be (710 + 2186 + 2370 + 1754 + 882 + 315 + 5)/(11,145.50 + 10,753.75 + 10,204.92 + 9040.25 + 7184.83 + 4789.58 + 364.58) = 8222/43,803.41 = 0.1877. The estimate for 1995–1999 would be (463 + 1342 + 1495 + 1098 + 676 + 211 + 24)/(8717.04 + 7091.21 + 6926.50 + 6589.42 + 5646.67 + 4469.67 + 2626.13) = 5309/42,066.64 = 0.1262. The numerators and denominators come from the last two columns of Tables 16.4 and 16.5, respectively.

Measures of Cohort Cumulative and Completed Fertility

Cumulative fertility refers to the number of children, or average number of children, born prior to some age or marital duration. Total or completed fertility refers to cumulative fertility up to the final age or marital duration in which any fertility occurs. This section will describe "true" cohort measures of cumulative fertility, "synthetic" cohort measures of cumulative fertility, and various linkages between these measures and the specific rates.

True Cohort Cumulative and Completed Fertility

Perhaps the simplest measure of cumulative fertility is the mean number of children ever born, or mean CEB. A question on CEB is included in every fertility or contraceptive prevalence survey, in many surveys that are conducted for entirely different purposes, and in many censuses.

The mean CEB for women within an age interval can be interpreted as the true cumulative fertility of a birth cohort. For example, the 1998 NDHS of the Philippines was conducted almost entirely during the months of March and April 1998, and the mean completed fertility of women aged 30 to 34 (at the date of interview) was found to be 2.69 children (Philippines NDHS Report, 1999, Table 3.6; weighted estimate). These women were born between the beginning of April 1963 and the end of April 1968. Making a coarse assumption of a uniform age distribution within the age interval 30 to 34, these women had an average exact age of 32.5 years at the date of interview. Thus, the figure of 2.69 is interpreted as the mean number of children born prior to age 32.5 by women who were themselves born from April 1963 through April 1968 and who survived to the date of interview. The cohorts represented by successive age intervals will slightly overlap because the field work is spread over an interval of time.

The women aged 35 to 39 in the same survey had a mean CEB of 3.47 children. It is not necessarily the case that 3.47 − 2.69 = 0.78 is the average number of children born between ages 32.5 and 37.5 for any real cohort, because the means 2.69 and 3.47 refer to different (even if slightly overlapping) birth cohorts. If fertility is increasing from one cohort to the next, as happened during the U.S. "baby boom," an older cohort may have lower cumulative fertility than a younger cohort, even at a later age.

To estimate the "current" (i.e., at the time of the survey) CEB for women at exact age 35, a researcher would typically average the means for ages 30 to 34 and 35 to 39, obtaining (2.69 + 3.47)/2 = 3.08. An alternative might be to calculate the mean for women in an age interval centered on exact age 35 (e.g., ages 32 years and 7 months through 37 years and 6 months of age) at the date of interview. For cohort comparisons, a more direct approach is possible with survey data. For the cohort born during 1960–1964, for example, exact age 35 was reached before the 1998 survey described earlier; so the birth histories could be used to calculate each woman's CEB at the beginning of the month when she had her 35th birthday. The average of these CEBs would be the average CEB at exact age 35 for this birth cohort. Birth cohorts above exact age 35 (at the survey date) could be compared in terms of the mean number of children they had had by exact age 35.

The CEB can be interpreted as *completed* fertility for women aged 45 to 49 or greater, but may actually underestimate completed fertility because of underreporting of the fertility of older cohorts. Women may omit children who were born long ago and died while young. Moreover, women who have had numerous children have a higher risk of dying from maternal or related causes. After the first birth, which is the most hazardous, the risk of maternal mortality is roughly proportional to the number of children. Women who died from such causes will be omitted from a census or survey, with the result that the mean CEB is biased downward. Thus, it is common in a less developed country for the mean CEB to reach a maximum for women aged about 45 to 49 and to decline steadily for older women, contrary to historical information about fertility trends.

An overall mean CEB calculated for women 15 to 49 will be sensitive to the age distribution within that age range. Many observed age distributions, particularly in the less developed countries, have more women in their twenties than in their thirties, and more in their thirties than in their forties. A mean will thus be weighted toward younger women, particularly if the population was growing rapidly when these women were born. A mean CEB calculated for a very broad age interval, or an overall mean CEB, is largely descriptive and has serious limitations for comparisons across groups or time periods. Direct standardization on some standard age distribution will slightly improve the usefulness of the CEB for making comparisons. In the absence of an obvious standard, a uniform age distribution can be used; in this case the standardized mean CEB will simply be the unweighted average of the mean CEBs in all the age intervals.

Synthetic Cumulative and Total Fertility

As a generalization, synthetic measures are constructed by interpreting period data as if they referred to a cohort. The best-known example is in the context of mortality (see, for example, Chapter 13), in which period data on the mortality of persons aged 0, 1–4, 5–9, . . . , 85+ are used to prepare an abridged life table. The survivorship column of the life table is interpreted as a description of a hypothetical or synthetic birth cohort as it passes from birth to exact ages 1, 5, 10, . . . , 85, even though the data for these age intervals actually come from different birth cohorts. The survivorship column of the life table provides a synthetic

answer to a hypothetical "what if" question, namely "What is the chance of surviving to each exact age *a* if a cohort of women experiences throughout their lives the mortality observed in a recent interval of time?"

The concept of a synthetic cohort is easily extended to the measurement of fertility. (See, for example, Chapter 15.) Corresponding to the three period-specific fertility rates described earlier, for 5-year intervals of time and either age or marital duration, there are three cumulative totals for time period t, given as follows:

- $CFR(x,t)$ is five times the sum of the age-period-specific rates up to exact age x.
- $CMFR(x,t)$ is five times the sum of the age-period-specific marital rates up to exact age x.
- $CMDFR(x,t)$ is five times the sum of the marriage-duration-period-specific rates up to exact duration x

Thus,

$$CFR(x,t) = 5\sum_{a<x} f(a,t) \qquad (16.9)$$

This cumulative fertility rate at time t can be interpreted as the number of children that a woman would be expected to have (i.e., would have on average) if she experienced the time t rate for ages 15 to 19 for 5 years, the time t rate for ages 20 to 24 for 5 years, and so on, up to the age interval that extended from exact age x-5 to exact age x. In short, it is the expected number of births prior to age x, based on the fertility observed for different age intervals during time interval t. It is implicit that the woman survives to age x; possible mortality is ignored.

Similarly,

$$CMFR(x,t) = 5\sum_{a<x} mf(a,t) \qquad (16.10)$$

is the cumulative *marital* fertility up to age x, with the additional assumption that the woman is married from the earliest age in the summation, usually age 15. This cumulative rate can be very high because age-specific marital fertility rates are higher than age-specific fertility rates, especially in the younger ages where fewer women are married. It is preferable to apply a synthetic cohort interpretation to the *duration*-period-specific marital rates, in which case the cohorts are indexed by marital duration, rather than age. Thus, the cumulative marital duration fertility rate,

$$CMDFR(x,t) = 5\sum_{d<x} mf(d,t) \qquad (16.11)$$

gives the expected (or average) number of births in the first x years of marriage, without any reference, implicit or explicit, to age at marriage.

As described earlier, retrospective rates produced by a survey will be right-censored for earlier time periods, so that the full range of ages and marital durations will usually be available only for the most recent 5-year time period. For that time period, at least, the age-specific rates can be calculated out to ages 45 to 49 and the duration-specific rates out to duration 30 to 34. The cumulative fertility rate out to exact age 50 is the well-known total fertility rate, or *TFR*—that is,

$$TFR(t) = 5 \sum_{a<50} f(a,t) \qquad (16.12)$$

and the cumulative marital duration fertility rate out to exact duration 35 is known as the total marital duration fertility rate or *TMDFR*—that is,

$$TMDFR(t) = 5 \sum_{d<35} mf(d,t) \qquad (16.13)$$

There is no need to duplicate here the discussion of these rates and their interpretation given in Chapter 15. Also see Chapter 17 for modifications to limit the births to daughters and to take account of survivorship, leading to the gross reproduction rate and the net reproduction rate. Our purpose here is simply to indicate how the cumulative fertility rates, total fertility rates, and reproduction rates can be built up from specific rates derived from survey data.

Adding up the rates in the final columns of Tables 16.6 and 16.18, respectively, and multiplying by 5, we obtain an unweighted TFR for the Philippines in 1995–1999 of $(0.0531 + 0.1892 + 0.2158 + 0.1666 + 0.1197 + 0.0472 + 0.0091) \times 5 = 4.00$. This number can be interpreted as the mean number of children that a woman would eventually have if she survived to the end of the childbearing ages and experienced the age-specific fertility rates observed during 1995–1999. The TMDFR for 1995–1999 is $(0.3764 + 0.2204 + 0.1536 + 0.1051 + 0.0671 + 0.0299 + 0.0026) \times 5 = 4.78$. This number can be interpreted as the mean number of children that a woman would eventually have *if she ever married*, survived to the end of the childbearing ages, and experienced the observed *duration*-specific *marital* fertility rates.

The total marital fertility rate (TMFR) for 1995–1999, calculated from the final column of Table 16.12, would be $(0.4475 + 0.3736 + 0.2706 + 0.1842 + 0.1284 + 0.0498 + 0.0096) \times 5 = 7.32$. This number can be interpreted as the mean number of children that a woman would eventually have if she married at age 15, survived to the end of the childbearing period, and experienced the observed age-specific marital fertility rates. The TMFR is required for the Bongaarts decomposition procedure (see Chapter 22). It should be interpreted cautiously because of its sensitivity to the high fertility of the early age intervals, even if very few women of those ages are actually married.

It is also possible to cumulate order-specific rates to obtain a total fertility rate TFR_j for each birth order j. For example, if the age-order-specific rates for order 1 are added across age (and multiplied by five if the age intervals are 5 years wide), we obtain TFR_1, which can be interpreted as the proportion of women who will ever have a first birth in a

synthetic cohort subject to the observed period rates. It is possible for such a sum to exceed 1.0 if, say, the real cohorts tended to time their first births to occur during the observed period. For a real cohort followed over time, it would of course be impossible for the proportion to exceed one, so the interpretation must be modified if this happens to the synthetic measure. Similarly for higher birth orders. As noted earlier, if the age-order-specific rates are added across birth orders, we get the age-specific rates. Therefore, the sum of the order-specific total fertility rates, across birth orders j, will be the overall *TFR*—that is,

$$TFR_j(t) = 5 \sum_{x<50} f_j(x,t) \qquad (16.14)$$

and

$$TFR(t) = \sum_j TFR_j(t) \qquad (16.15)$$

For 1995–1999, the order-specific rates for the illustrative data set are obtained from the last column of Tables 16.22 and 16.23 by adding the order-specific rates and multiplying the sums by five. They are as follows, for birth orders 1 to 4: $TFR_1 = 0.88$, $TFR_2 = 0.61$, $TFR_3 = 0.62$, and $TFR_4 = 0.47$. (Tables 16.22 and 16.23 give the order-specific rates for orders 1 and 2 only.) Calculated as a residual, $TFR_{5+} = 4.00 - 0.88 - 0.61 - 0.62 - 0.47 = 1.42$. For a synthetic cohort interpretation, about 88% of women would eventually have a first birth, about 61% would eventually have a second birth, about 62% would eventually have a third birth, and about 47% would eventually have a fourth birth. This kind of interpretation could be extended to individual birth orders five, six, and so forth, but not to an aggregation such as five or more.

Parity-Progression Ratios

Chapter 15 defined parity-progression ratios and showed how they can be calculated with vital statistics data. The birth histories in a fertility survey are a much more direct source of information about parity progression. The progression from parity j to parity $j + 1$ is the closure of a birth interval, and birth histories contain information about both the beginnings and ends of birth intervals. The probability of making such a transition, given that parity j was reached (i.e., the parity-progression ratio) will be labeled PPR_j.

There are some important distinctions between order-specific fertility rates and parity-progression ratios, in terms of data requirements and interpretation, despite a superficial similarity in their names. Parity-progression ratios are indexed by the order of the birth that *begins* a birth interval (with a woman beginning at zero), whereas order-specific rates are indexed by the order of the birth that *closes* a birth interval. As another distinction, order-specific rates are typically calculated for specific ages (or marital durations) and periods; parity-progression ratios are typically calculated for cohorts or periods, but not for specific ages (or durations). Most important, parity-progression ratios are actually (estimated) conditional probabilities, rather than (central) rates, limited to the subpopulation at risk of making each successive transition to a higher parity.

True-Parity Progression Ratios

The following discussion draws on Hinde (1998, Chapter 9). If we follow a real cohort of women (that is, look retrospectively at the completed birth histories of the survivors of a real cohort), the probability that a woman who reached order j would go on to parity $j + 1$ could be readily estimated by dividing the number of women who ever reached parity $j + 1$ by the number of women who ever reached parity j. If n_k is the number of women who eventually had exactly k births, then

$$PPR_j = \left(\sum_{k>j} n_k \right) \bigg/ \left(\sum_{k \geq j} n_k \right) \qquad (16.16)$$

Such an estimate can be seriously deficient if the cohort has not yet reached the end of the childbearing ages, because of two possible sources of bias. The first problem may be described as right-censoring. Some of the women who have reached parity j will eventually go on to parity $j + 1$, but they have not been observed long enough for this to be witnessed. Right-censoring always produces an *under*estimate of the cohort's eventual parity progression ratio. The second problem is left-censoring: some women have not yet even reached parity j, so the estimate will be biased toward women who reached parity j earlier, rather than later, in the life course. Women who reach a given parity early will tend to have larger completed families, so left-censoring tends to produce an *over*estimate of the cohort's eventual parity progression ratio.

Instead of regarding the parity-progression ratio as a characteristic of a birth cohort, with the attendant difficulty

of making estimates before the cohort has completed its childbearing, we can shift to a period-specific definition from the birth-cohort definition, and try to estimate the probability of making a transition from parity j to parity $j + 1$, for all birth cohorts or age groups pooled, within an interval of time.

Suppose, for example, that we used the 1998 survey to estimate the progression from parity one to parity two. Pooling all age groups, we could identify women who had a first birth in 1990, say, and determine the proportion of them who had a second birth in 1990 or later. (It is possible to have two births in the same year, and we include the possibility of twins or other multiple births.) Then these women would have had nine calendar years (1990 to 1998; 1998 is only partially observed) in which to have a second birth. Since very few completed intervals are longer than this, the estimated PPR_1 could be interpreted as only a slight underestimate of the true probability that a woman who had a first birth in 1990 would eventually have a second birth.

Continuing to think of the transition from parity one to parity two, in order to keep the notation as simple as possible, let N_{1990} be the number of women who had a first birth in 1990, and *of those women*, let n_t be the number of women who had a second birth in $t = 1990, \ldots, 1997$. Then

$$PPR_1 = \left(\sum_{k=0}^{8} n_{1990+k} \right) \bigg/ N_{1990} \qquad (16.17)$$

The number of years following the reference year (in this case the reference year is 1990) is arbitrary, so long as it includes "virtually all" of the next-order births. To keep the right-censoring effect the same for a series of estimates, one could use 1980 through 1990, for example, as the reference years for the first birth and a 9-year interval (including the reference years) as the interval in which the second birth could have occurred.

Tables 16.28 and 16.29, from the 1998 NDHS of the Philippines, illustrate the necessary intermediate calculations. Table 16.28 shows that 337 women had a first birth in 1990. Table 16.29 gives the number of women who had a

TABLE 16.28   Births by Order and Calendar Year, 1990 to 1998: Philippines, 1998

Order	1990	1991	1992	1993	1994	1995	1996	1997	1998
1	337	366	402	331	389	385	406	416	85
2	327	323	341	339	294	301	346	339	78
3	268	270	268	292	259	263	237	273	68
4	221	214	212	216	191	202	187	186	42
5	173	133	157	156	154	147	133	144	36
6	108	99	124	108	105	111	94	118	25
7	80	68	75	57	80	82	76	65	23
8	59	58	56	37	50	52	50	54	11

Source: Based on 1998 NDHS of the Philippines (Philippines National Statistics Office, Department of Health, and Macro International, 1999).

TABLE 16.29 Number of Women With a Birth of Order 1 in Row Year and a Birth of Order 2 in Column Year, 1990 to 1998: Philippines, 1998

Year of order 1 birth	Year of order 2 birth								
	1990	1991	1992	1993	1994	1995	1996	1997	1998
1990	0	79	126	55	20	9	10	8	1
1991	0	0	101	121	40	25	18	12	1
1992	0	0	2	102	127	56	20	20	3
1993	0	0	0	7	65	107	50	22	8
1994	0	0	0	0	2	87	134	51	6
1995	0	0	0	0	0	1	93	119	17
1996	0	0	0	0	0	0	4	90	35
1997	0	0	0	0	0	0	0	5	5
1998	0	0	0	0	0	0	0	0	1

Source: Based on 1998 NDHS of the Philippines (Philippines National Statistics Office, Department of Health, and Macro International, 1999).

first birth in 1990 (or other calendar years) and had a second birth in a later year. The number of women shown for a second birth in years 1990 through 1998 is 0 + 79 + 126 + 55 + 20 + 9 + 10 + 8 + 1 = 308. Therefore the estimate of PPR_1 for reference year 1990 is 308/337 = 0.91. (This is probably an underestimate, since for earlier years we observe some longer gaps between first and second births.) Tables analogous to Table 16.29, describing transitions from a second to a third birth, from a third to a fourth birth, and so on, are also possible but are not presented here.

There is progressive left-censoring (omission of women who never had a first birth) in the estimates just described. It increases as we push the starting year backward in time because a fertility survey omits women over age 49 at the time of the survey. The 1990 estimate given earlier, for example, omits women who were over age 49 in 1998 (i.e., over age 41 in 1990) so the denominator of PPR_1 for 1990 is limited to women who had their first birth by age 41. The synthetic measures discussed here will reduce that problem.

Continuing to think of the transition from parity one to parity two, and retaining the previous notation for reference year 1990, the "true" probability of progressing from parity one to parity two,

$$PPR_1 = \left(\sum_{k=0}^{8} n_{1990+k} \right) \Big/ N_{1990}$$

is algebraically equivalent to

$$PPR_1 = 1 - (1-a_0)(1-a_1)\dots(1-a_8) \qquad (16.18)$$

where

$a_0 = n_{1990}/N_{1990}$
$a_1 = n_{1991}/(N_{1990} - n_{1990})$
$a_2 = n_{1992}/(N_{1990} - n_{1990} - n_{1991})$ and so on, and in general

$$a_j = n_{1990+j} \Big/ \left(N_{1990} - \sum_{k=0}^{j} n_{1990+k} \right)$$

Here a_j is analogous to q_x in the construction of a life table. It is the estimated probability of changing state (parity, rather than survivorship status) in an interval of time or age.

In words, the probability of *not* going on to a second birth (within 9 years of 1990, inclusive) is the probability of not going on to a second birth in the same year, times the probability of not doing so a year later (given that the woman did not already go on), times the probability of not doing so a year after that (given that the woman did not already go on), and so on, until "virtually all" transitions have occurred. Repeating the calculation of PPR_1 for reference year 1990, just described, this procedure would require the following intermediate steps:

$a_0 = 0/337, 1 - a_0 = 337/337$
$a_1 = 79/(337 - 0) = 79/337, 1 - a_1 = 258/337$
$a_2 = 126/(337 - 79) = 126/258, 1 - a_2 = 132/258$
$a_3 = 55/(258 - 126) = 55/132, 1 - a_3 = 77/132$
$a_4 = 20/(132 - 55) = 20/77, 1 - a_4 = 57/77$
$a_5 = 9/(77 - 20) = 9/57, 1 - a_5 = 48/57$
$a_6 = 10/(57 - 9) = 10/48, 1 - a_6 = 38/48$
$a_7 = 8/(48 - 10) = 8/38, 1 - a_7 = 30/38$
$a_8 = 1/(38 - 8) = 1/30, 1 - a_8 = 29/30$

and

$$PPR_1 = 1 - (337/337)(258/337)(132/258)$$
$$(77/132)(57/77)(48/57)(38/48)(30/38)(29/30)$$
$$= 1 - (29/337) = 308/337 = 0.91$$

Note that this result is identical to the one obtained earlier.

Synthetic Parity-Progression Ratios

To construct a synthetic analog, we will index the measure by the year in which the *second* birth occurred and borrow the successive year-specific a_j measures from successive cohorts (indexed by the second birth) rather than from the same cohort (indexed by the first birth). As before, let N_t be the number of first births in year t. Expand the previous notation by replacing n_t with $n_{t1,t2}$, where $t1$ is the year when the first birth occurred and $t2$ is the year when the second birth occurred. Thus, the previous symbol n_{1991}, for example, would become $n_{1990,1991}$. The synthetic measure for 1997, the year of the *second* birth, would be

$$PPR_1^* = 1 - (1 - a_0^*)(1 - a_1^*) \ldots (1 - a_8^*) \quad (16.19)$$

where again we cover a span of 9 years, inclusive, and

$a_0^* = n_{1997,1997}/N_{1997},$

$a_1^* = n_{1996,1997}/(N_{1996} - n_{1996,1996})$

$a_2^* = n_{1995,1997}/(N_{1995} - n_{1995,1995} - n_{1995,1996})$ and so on, and in general

$$a_j^* = n_{1997-j,1997} \left/ \left(N_{1997-j} - \sum_{k=0}^{j} n_{1997-j,1997-j+i} \right) \right.$$

Tables 16.28 and 16.29 also include the necessary data from the Philippines' 1998 NDHS to estimate PPR_1^* for 1997 (indexed by the year in which the second birth occurred, rather than first). It requires these intermediate steps:

$a_0^* = 5/416 = 0.0120$

$a_1^* = 90/(406 - 4) = 0.2239$

$a_2^* = 119/(385 - 1 - 93) = 0.4089$

$a_3^* = 51/(389 - 2 - 87 - 134) = 0.3072$

$a_4^* = 22/(331 - 7 - 65 - 107 - 50) = 0.2157$

$a_5^* = 20/(402 - 2 - 102 - 127 - 56 - 20) = 0.2105$

$a_6^* = 12/(366 - 101 - 121 - 40 - 25 - 18) = 0.1967$

$a_7^* = 8/(337 - 79 - 126 - 55 - 20 - 9 - 10) = 0.2105$

$a_8^* = 1/(373 - 1 - 96 - 130 - 52 - 26 - 23 - 3 - 5)$
$\quad = 0.0270$

$PPR_1 = 1 - (1 - 0.0120)(1 - 0.2239)(1 - 0.4089)(1 - 0.3072)$
$\quad (1 - 0.2157)(1 - 0.2105)(1 - 0.1967)(1 - 0.2105)$
$\quad = 0.88$

This synthetic analog of the cohort estimate of PPR_1 is also biased downward somewhat because a few of the second births in 1997 were preceded by birth intervals longer than 8 years. Nevertheless, it is close to the true cohort estimate for first births in 1990, which was 0.91.

FINAL NOTE

The main goal of this chapter has been to describe in detail the manner in which a wide range of fertility measures can be calculated from survey microdata data. Nearly all of these measures were developed prior to the availability of fertility surveys and were originally defined in terms of vital statistics data for numerators and census data for denominators, as described in Chapter 15. The original definitions were appropriate for the available data sources, but—apart from limitations of sample size—retrospective surveys can be a superior source. When individual-level data are available, it is natural to see fertility as a stochastic characteristic of individuals (rather than as a deterministic characteristic of aggregates) to be expressed in terms of estimated expected values and estimated probabilities, conditional on a range of other characteristics. The essential ingredients are whether a birth (or a number of births) occurred in an interval, together with a measure of exposure to risk, such as the length of the interval or the amount of the interval spent in a given state (such as an age or marital status). Retrospective surveys fall short of a continuous population register, but they are much closer to the process than the traditional sources of data.

The individual-level components can be cumulated into numerators and denominators and manipulated to describe an aggregate, as in this chapter. They can also be used in multivariate statistical analyses that involve a wide range of risk factors, partitioning according to proximate determinants, and related variables and models. Poisson regression, logit regression, and hazard modeling are possible with the individual-level components, but these do not fall within the scope of this chapter.

References

Hinde, A. 1998. *Demographic Methods* (Chapters 8–11). London: Arnold.

International Union for the Scientific Study of Population (IUSSP). 1982. *Multilingual Domographic Dictionary*, English Setion. Second edition adapted by Etienne van de Walle. Liège, Belgium, Ordina Editions.

Philippines National Statistics Office (NSO) and Department of Health (DOH), and Macro International, Inc. (MI). 1999. *National Demographic and Health Survey 1998*. Manila: NSO and MI.

Shryock, H. S., J. S. Siegel, and E. G. Stockwell, 1976. *The Methods and Materials of Demography*. Condensed Edition. New York: Academic Press.

Suggested Readings

Bulatao, Rudolfo, A., and J. B. Casterling. (eds.). 2001. *Global Fertility Transition*. A Supplement to Vol. 27, 2001, *Population and Development Review*. New York: The Population Council.

Casterline, J. B., R. D. Lee, and K. A. Foote (Eds.). 1996. *Fertility in the United States: New Patterns, New Theories*. A Supplement to Vol. 22, 1996, *Population and Development Review*. New York: Population Council.

Cleland, J., and C. Scott (Eds.). 1987. *The World Fertility Survey: An Assessment of Its Contribution*. London: Oxford University Press.

Kiser, C. V., W. H. Grabill, and A. A. Campbell. 1968. *Trends and Variations in Fertility in the United States*. Cambridge, MA: Harvard University Press. Esp. pp. 297–310.

Whelpton, P. K., A. A. Campbell, and J. E. Patterson. 1966. *Fertility and Family Planning in the United States*. Princeton, NJ: Princeton University Press. Esp. pp. 1–31, 416–419.

Reproductivity

A. DHARMALINGAM

The study of reproductivity is concerned with the extent to which a group is replacing its own numbers by natural processes. Measures of reproductivity or population replacement are thus essentially measures of natural increase expressed in terms of a generation rather than a year or other brief period of time. The group may be a true or a synthetic birth cohort, or a true or a synthetic marriage cohort. The analysis of reproductivity has led mathematical demographers to the concept of the stable population and of its vital measures. Originally viewed as indicating the intrinsic or ultimate results of current fertility and mortality, these concepts have been found to have much wider applications in the estimation of current vital measures and population structure and in many types of demographic analysis.

Certain measures describing annual, instead of generational experience, are sometimes considered simple measures of reproductivity. Among these are the crude rate of natural increase and the vital index. Natural increase was defined in Chapter 11 as the difference between the number of births and the number of deaths. The crude rate of natural increase is thus the (algebraic) excess of births over deaths per 1000 of the population, or the difference between the crude birthrate and the crude death rate. This rate can be expressed as

$$r_n = \frac{B - D}{P} \times 1000 \qquad (17.1)$$

$$= b - d \qquad (17.2)$$

where r_n = rate of natural increase, B = births during a calendar year, D = deaths during a calendar year, P = midyear population, b = the birthrate, and d = the death rate.

The vital index (VI) is the ratio of the number of births in a year to the number of deaths in the year, times 100. In other words,

$$VI = \frac{B}{D} \times 100 \qquad (17.3)$$

One of the few virtues of this index is that it can be computed for an area for which postcensal population estimates are not available. It indicates crudely the extent to which the force of natality exceeds that of mortality in a given year.

The rate of natural increase is the most direct indication of how rapidly a given population actually grew during a given year as the result of vital processes. If births exceed deaths, there is growth and the rate is positive. If deaths outnumber births, the population fails to increase during the year, and the rate is negative. The crude rate of natural increase, like its two components, is influenced by the current age structure. If, for example, a relatively large proportion of a population is in adolescence and early adulthood, the population tends to have a relatively high birthrate and a relatively low death rate; these result in a high crude rate of natural increase. If, however, a relatively small proportion of the population is within these ages, its rate of natural increase tends to be relatively low. For example, after a devastating war, the sex ratio of the population in the reproductive ages may be abnormally low so that the crude rate of natural increase will be depressed for some years thereafter. Because the age and sex composition of a population at a given time is determined by the previous trend of its birth and death rates and by its migration history during the same time span, any measure of reproductivity that fails to take account of the actual age and sex composition of the population is an inadequate measure of the long-term replacement tendencies in that population.

The actual experience of a generation may be observed over a period of some 30 years, or the experience may be synthesized from current data. For many years, reproduction rates were computed only from current vital statistics because it was thought that the fertility of women in, say, 30 successive years of age in the childbearing period in a single calendar year could be combined to approximate the fertility and reproductivity of an actual cohort of women passing through the childbearing period. In the late 1940s, demographers started to realize that these synthetic rates were frequently unreliable measures of actual reproductivity and began to observe and analyze real cohorts as well.

CONVENTIONAL REPRODUCTION RATES

Conventional reproduction rates are measures of reproductivity over a generation that are based on the experience of a single year or other short period; that is, they are synthetic measures of lifetime reproductivity. Reproductivity reflects the net force of fertility and mortality, and the net reproduction rate is the basic measure of this force. We also have to consider, however, two related measures that represent limiting cases in which mortality is assumed to be nil until the end of the childbearing period. These are the gross reproduction rate and the total fertility rate.

Total Fertility Rate

As the reader may recall from Chapters 15 and 16, the total fertility rate (TFR) is the sum of the age-specific birthrates of women over their reproductive span, as observed in a given year. It is expressed as

$$TFR = \sum_{\omega 1}^{\omega 2} \frac{B_x}{P_x} \times 1000 \qquad (17.4)$$

where B_x is the number of live births registered during the year to mothers of age x, x represents an interval of one year of age, and P_x is the midyear female population of the same age. The age-specific fertility rates are cumulated from $x = \omega_1$ to $x = \omega_2$, where ω_1 to ω_2 may be ages 10 to 54, ages 15 to 44, or whatever age range is available and appropriate.

In usual practice, the total fertility rate is calculated by a shorter method. The specific birthrates are calculated for 5-year age groups and thus the subscript i represents 5-year age intervals such as 15 to 19, 20 to 24, . . . 40 to 44, and 45 to 49 years. The expression for total fertility, using these seven 5-year age groups is then

$$TFR = 5 \sum_{i=1}^{7} \frac{B_i}{P_i} \times 1000 \qquad (17.5)$$

where B_i is the number of live births registered during the year to mothers of age group i, i is an interval of 5 years, and P_i is the midyear female population of the same age. The main purpose of the factor 5 in Formula (17.5) is to apply the average rate for the age group, given in the formula, to five successive single years, so that the sum of the age-specific rates will be commensurate with that in (17.4).

When, for convenience, we use seven 5-year age groups in our calculations, the age limits will not encompass the full

TABLE 17.1 Computation of Total Fertility Rate for New Zealand: 1996

Age (years)	Number of women (1)	Number of births (2)	Births per 1000 women $[(2) \div (1)] \times 1000 =$ (3)
15–19	132,400	4,371[1]	33.0
20–24	140,650	11,296	80.3
25–29	145,850	17,247	118.3
30–34	154,310	16,054	104.0
35–39	150,170	6,612	44.1
40–44	133,480	1,055	7.9
45–49	124,080	51[2]	0.4
Sum		56,686	388.0
Total fertility rate = $5 \times \Sigma$ col. (3)			1940.0

[1] Includes births to women under 15 years of age.
[2] Includes births to women 50 years of age and over.
Source: New Zealand, Statistics New Zealand, 1998.

childbearing range. Births to younger women should then be allocated to the youngest age group shown and those to older women to the oldest age group shown. For example, any births registered for women aged 52 would be allocated to age 49, or to the age group 45 to 49. Likewise, births for which the age of mother was not reported should be allocated among the childbearing ages.

The total fertility rate states the number of births 1000 women would have if they experienced a given set of age-specific birthrates throughout their reproductive span. A rate of 1940 for New Zealand in 1996 (see Table 17.1), for example, means that if a hypothetical group of 1000 women were to have the same birthrates at each single year of age as were observed in New Zealand in 1996, they would have a total of 1940 children by the time they reached the end of the reproductive period, taken as 49 years old, assuming all of them survived to that age. The total fertility rate is sometimes expressed per woman rather than per 1000 women. Thus, alternatively, the TFR can be described as the number of live births a woman would have in her lifetime if she followed a given schedule of age-specific birthrates. The procedure for computing the total fertility rate is shown in the table.

Reproduction Rates

The conventional reproduction rate (called *taux classique de reproduction* by French demographers) measures the replacement of the female population only, whereas the total fertility rate involves births of both sexes. The net reproduction rate was devised by the German statistician, Richard Böckh in 1884 (Böckh, 1884, 1890). It was vigorously advocated by his pupil, Robert R. Kuczynski, in many publications, his most definitive statement being given in *The Measurement of Population Growth* (Kuczynski, 1936). Kuczynski himself computed many such reproduction rates and compiled those that had been computed by others. As will be described later, we are indebted to Alfred J. Lotka for the first rigorous mathematical analysis of these rates as measures of reproductivity and of their place in a whole set of measures relating to "intrinsic" population change and the stable population (Dublin and Lotka, 1925).

Gross Reproduction Rate

The gross reproduction rate (GRR) is a special case of the total fertility rate. Whereas the total fertility rate measures the total number of children a cohort of women will have, the gross reproduction rate measures the number of daughters it will have. Thus, a total fertility rate can be converted to a gross reproduction rate simply by multiplying it by the proportion of the total births that were female births in the calendar year or years for which it is computed. This conversion is not exact, but it is a close approximation to the gross reproduction rate we would obtain if female births at each age of woman were employed in the calculations. There is a slight variation of the sex ratio at birth with the age of the mother. The gross reproduction rate also assumes that all females survive to the end of the childbearing period. The formula for the gross reproduction rate is

$$GRR = \frac{B^f}{B^t} \sum_{\omega 1}^{\omega 2} \frac{B_x}{P_x} \cdot k \qquad (17.6)$$

where B_x is the number of infants born to mothers of age x, P_x is the number of women at age x at midyear, ω_1 and ω_2 are, respectively, the lower and upper limits of the childbearing period, the fraction B^f/B^t is the proportion of total births that are female, and k is a constant equal to unity (1), 100, or 1000.

If data are available on the number of *female* births according to age of mother, the GRR can be calculated directly without the B^f/B^t adjustment as follows:

$$GRR = \sum_{\omega 1}^{\omega 2} \frac{B_x^f}{P_x} \cdot k \qquad (17.6a)$$

where Bx is the number of *female* infants born to mothers of age x.

If the computation uses 5-year age groups, (17.6) becomes

$$GRR = 5 \frac{B^f}{B^t} \sum_{i=1}^{7} \frac{B_i}{P_i} \cdot k \qquad (17.7)$$

The gross reproduction rate may be viewed and defined in several ways, namely, as (1) an age-standardized fertility rate for female births with the rate of each age being given equal weight; (2) the average number of daughters that a group of females starting life together would bear if all members of the initial group of females survived through the childbearing period; (3) the ratio between the number of females in one generation at, say, age 15 and the number of their daughters at the same age, if there were no mortality during the childbearing period; or (4) the ratio between the number of female births in two successive generations assuming no deaths before the end of the childbearing period. The last three definitions are phrased as if the measure applied to a real cohort or pair of cohorts; but any of these interpretations can be used regardless of whether the GRR is computed from synthetic cohort data (i.e., data over a "lifetime" for a single calendar year) or data compiled over the lifetime of a real cohort.

Our initial definition of reproductivity stated that it is the natural increase of a population over a generation and hence implied that it is the resultant of mortality and fertility over this period. The gross reproduction rate thus represents a limiting case of this concept, the case where mortality through the end of the childbearing period is zero.

Net Reproduction Rate

The net reproduction rate (NRR) is a measure of the number of daughters that a cohort of newborn girl babies will bear during their lifetime assuming a fixed schedule of age-specific fertility rates and a fixed schedule of age-specific mortality rates. Thus, the net reproduction rate is a measure of the extent to which a cohort of newly born girls will replace themselves under given schedules of age-specific fertility and mortality. Some girls will die before attaining the age of reproduction, others will die during the reproductive span, and others will live to complete the reproductive ages. Expressed in symbols we have

$$NRR = \frac{B^f}{B^t} \sum_{\omega 1}^{\omega 2} \frac{B_x}{P_x} \cdot \frac{L_x}{l_o} \qquad (17.8)$$

where $B_x/P_x = f_x$, the age-specific fertility rate at age x, and Lx/l_o is a life-table survival rate, with l_0 being the radix of the life table, or 100,000. Again, when 5-year age groups are used, we have

$$NRR = 5 \frac{B^f}{B^t} \sum_{i=1}^{7} \frac{B_i}{P_i} \cdot \frac{{}_5 L_x}{{}_5 l_o} \qquad (17.9)$$

$$= \frac{B^f}{B^t} \sum_{i=1}^{7} \frac{B_i}{P_i} \cdot \frac{{}_5 L_x}{100,000} \qquad (17.9a)$$

If the survivors in each age interval are assumed to bear daughters as specified by a current schedule of age-specific birthrates, then to obtain the net reproduction rate, multiply each ${}_nL_x$ value by the corresponding age-specific birthrate for baby girls, sum the cross-products, and divide by 100,000.

A rate of 1.00 (or 100 or 1000, depending on the value of k) means exact replacement, a rate above unity indicates that the population is more than replacing itself, and a rate below unity means that the population is not replacing itself. The interpretations corresponding to those given for the gross rate are (1) an age-standardized "mortality-adjusted" fertility rate with each age being given an equal weight; (2) the average number of daughters born to a group of females starting life together, (3) the ratio between the number of females in one generation at, say, age 15, and the number of their daughters at the same age, and (4) the ratio between female births in two successive generations. All these interpretations include allowance for mortality up through the childbearing period. As previously indicated, the net reproduction rate is frequently abbreviated NRR, but the usual symbol in mathematical demography is Lotka's R_0. The rationale of R_0 is made clear in the next section.

The procedure for computing the gross and net reproduction rates is shown in Table 17.2. From statistics on births and population, we have computed age-specific birthrates for New Zealand in 1996. For convenience, the age-specific rates are computed from births of both sexes, so we use the symbol $_5f_x^T$. The transition to female births only is made later, in a single step, by applying the proportion of all births that are female. Also for convenience, we have grouped our data in 5-year age groups. In this form the figures in column 2 do not look like survival rates because the survival rates have been cumulated over 5 years. We

could have used instead the female survival rate to the midpoint of each age interval $\frac{l_{17.5}}{l_0}$, $\frac{l_{22.5}}{l_0}$, and so on. For example, the survival rate to age 17.5 is $\frac{98,904}{100,000} = 0.98904$. In this approach, the sum of column 3 would need to be multiplied by 5 to produce the net reproduction rate. From the female life table for 1996, we read off, or sum, the values of $_5L_x$ for x taken successively at ages 15, 20, 25, ... 45. Because these are for 100,000 women, we divide them by 100,000 to obtain values per woman (the 4.94560 years for the age group 15 to 19 is equivalent to 494,560 years lived by a cohort of females who number 100,000 at birth).

The specific steps are as follows:

Step 1. Compute the age-specific birthrate per female, and enter it in column 1.

Step 2. From an appropriate life table, find the number of years lived by females in the stationary population for each interval of age. In an abridged life table, $_5L_x$ will be given directly. (In a life table with single years of age, $_5L_x$ can be obtained by summing five successive values of L_x or by subtracting T_{x+5} from T_5.)

Step 3. Divide $_5L_x$ by 100,000, and enter the result in column 2.

Step 4. Multiply each entry of column 2 by the corresponding entry of column 1 and enter the result in column 3.

Step 5. To obtain the gross reproduction rate, multiply the sum of the entries in column 1 by the proportion of births that are female (.48551) and then by the factor 5.

Step 6. To obtain the net reproduction rate, apply the factor .48551 to the sum of column 3.

These rates are expressed per woman, but they could also have been expressed per 100 women or per 1000 women. It is important to note that in the conventional reproduction rates, the age-specific fertility and mortality rates all refer to the same fixed period of time, say a given calendar year or the average of a few years. Moreover, if a life table is not available for exactly the same year as that of the fertility schedule, approximate reproduction rates for that year may be obtained by using a life table for an adjacent year or years. In general, it is more important for the fertility data to relate to the reference year than the mortality data, which are not likely to vary much over a few years and would have less effect than the fertility rates on the level of reproductivity.

These reproduction rates are defined in terms of the female population, but analogous rates can also be computed for both sexes combined or for the male population only. (See the section on "Reproduction of the Male Population" presented later in this chapter.) Reproductivity is usually studied in terms of mothers and daughters because the fecund period for females is shorter than it is for males and

TABLE 17.2 Computation of Gross and Net Reproduction Rates for New Zealand: 1996

Age of mother (years)	Age-specific birth rate per female $_5f_x^T$ (1)	Survival rate[1] $\frac{_5L_x^F}{\ell_0^F}$ (2)	Number of births $_5f_x^T \cdot \frac{_5L_x^F}{\ell_0^F}$ (1) × (2) = (3)
15–19	0.03301	4.94560	0.16327
20–24	0.08031	4.93198	0.39610
25–29	0.11825	4.91951	0.58174
30–34	0.10404	4.90505	0.51031
35–39	0.04403	4.88659	0.21516
40–44	0.00790	4.86117	0.03842
45–49	0.00041	4.81951	0.00198
Sum	0.38796	X	1.90698

$$GRR = 5\frac{B^F}{B^T}\sum {_5f_x^T} = 5(.48551)(0.38796) = 0.94179$$

$$NRR, \text{ or } R_0 = 5\frac{B^F}{B^T}\sum {_5f_x^T} \cdot \frac{_5L_x^F}{5 \cdot \ell_0^F}$$

$$= \frac{B^F}{B^T} \cdot \sum {_5f_x^T} \cdot \frac{_5L_x^F}{\ell_0^F}$$

$$= (.48551)(1.90698) = 0.92586$$

X Not applicable.

[1] Also allows for 5-year grouping of ages.

Source: Based on Table 17.1. The life tables used here were taken from Cheung, 1999.

because demographic and other characteristics (age, marital status, and so on) are much more likely to be known for mothers than for fathers, especially in the case of non-marital births.

The ratio of the net reproduction rate to the gross reproduction rate is called the *reproduction-survival ratio*. It is the proportion of potential reproductivity that survives the effects of mortality.

THE STABLE POPULATION: ITS VITAL RATES AND OTHER CHARACTERISTICS

The assumption of the constancy of age-specific birthrates and death rates for a generation, which is made in the calculation of the gross reproduction rate and the net reproduction rate, defines the basic conditions of a general theoretical model. Lotka developed a model that described the age composition implied by the given sets of vital rates and expressed reproductivity on an annual as well as on a generation basis. This model is designated the "stable population" model. Lotka demonstrated in 1907 that if a population is subject to a fixed schedule of age-specific fertility rates and a fixed schedule of age-specific mortality rates for an indefinite period of time and if meanwhile there is no migration, ultimately the age composition of the population would assume a fixed characteristic distribution (Lotka, 1907). Coale (1968) has investigated the time required for a population with a given age structure and given age-specific fertility and mortality schedules to approach its ultimate stable form.

In 1925, Lotka proved that a closed population (i.e., a population without immigration) with constant age-specific fertility and mortality schedules would eventually have a constant rate of natural increase (Dublin and Lotka, 1925). Lotka called this rate the *true rate of natural increase*. It has also been called the *intrinsic rate of natural increase*. (The *life table stationary population* can be viewed as a stable population with a zero rate of natural increase.)

Intrinsic Rate of Natural Increase

Lotka computed the true rate of natural increase by solving the integral equation

$$\int_0^\infty e^{-rx} f(x) p(x) dx = 1 \qquad (17.10)$$

where $p(x)$ is the probability of surviving from birth to age x, r is the intrinsic rate of increase per person per year, and $f(x)$ is the number of live female births per year to each woman of age x. Note that $p(x)$ is the L_x of the life table divided by l_o. Because $f(x)$ is zero outside the childbearing period, we could substitute the limits ω_1 and ω_2, or approximately 15 to 49, as the limits of the definite integral.

In practice, a very close approximation to the real root of Equation (17.10) is given by the quadratic equation

$$\frac{1}{2}\beta r^2 + \alpha r - \ln R_0 = 0 \qquad (17.11)$$

where

$$\alpha = \frac{R_1}{R_o} \qquad (17.12)$$

$$\beta = \alpha^2 - \frac{R_2}{R_o} = \left(\frac{R_1}{R_o}\right)^2 - \frac{R_2}{R_o} \qquad (17.13)$$

where ln represents a logarithm to the base e, R_0 is the net reproduction rate, and R_1 and R_2 are the first and second moments of the curve representing the age schedule of net reproductivity. The general equation for these moments is given by

$$R_n = \int_o^\infty x^n f(x) p(x) dx \qquad (17.14)$$

The intrinsic measures that are presented here as relatively exact employ at most the second moments. Fortunately, the terms involving the higher moments converge quite rapidly toward zero.

Solving the quadratic Equation (17.11) for r, we obtain, for the positive radical, which corresponds to the real root:

$$r = \frac{-\alpha + \sqrt{\alpha^2 + 2\beta \ln R_o}}{\beta} \qquad (17.15)$$

and substituting for α and β in terms of R_0, R_1, and R_2, we obtain, as given by Kuczynski (1932, p. 59)

$$r = \frac{\frac{R_1}{R_o} - \sqrt{\left(\frac{R_1}{R_o}\right)^2 - 2\left[\frac{R_2}{R_o} - \left(\frac{R_1}{R_o}\right)^2\right] \ln R_o}}{\frac{R_2}{R_o} - \left(\frac{R_1}{R_o}\right)^2} \qquad (17.16)$$

As we see from the computations for Table 17.3, this form enables us to evaluate r, because R_0 was derived in Table 17.2, and R_1 and R_2 can also be derived from the same basic statistics.

Mean Length of Generation

The mean length of generation is defined as the mean age of mothers at the birth of their daughters. Because the stable population is growing at the annual rate r, compounded continuously, and the net reproduction rate, R_0, is its rate of growth in one generation, T years, we may write in an approximate formulation

$$R_0 = e^{rT} \qquad (17.17)$$

TABLE 17.3   Calculation of Intrinsic Rate of Increase (r), New Zealand: 1996

Age of mother x to x + 4 (years)	Annual births of daughters per female $_5F_x$ (1)	Pivotal (midpoint) age $(x + 2\frac{1}{2})$ (2)	$\frac{_5L_x^F}{\ell_0}$ (3)	Products Zero moment (R_0) $(1) \times (3) =$ (4)	Products First moment (R_1) $(2) \times (4) =$ (5)	Products Second moment (R_2) $(2) \times (5) =$ (6)
15–19	.01603	17.5	4.94560	.07927	1.38723	24.27650
20–24	.03899	22.5	4.93198	.19231	4.32700	97.35751
25–29	.05741	27.5	4.91951	.28244	7.76712	213.5957
30–34	.05051	32.5	4.90505	.24776	8.05219	261.6963
35–39	.02138	37.5	4.88659	.10446	3.91728	146.8981
40–44	.00384	42.5	4.86117	.01865	0.79280	33.69404
45–49	.00020	47.5	4.81951	.00096	0.04568	2.16999
Sum	.18836	(X)	(X)	.92586	26.28931	779.6882

$GRR = 5\sum \text{col. (1)} = 5 \times .18836 = 0.94179$

$NRR = R_0 = \sum \text{col. (4)} = 0.92586$

$R_1 = \sum \text{col. (5)} = 26.28931$

$R_2 = \sum \text{col. (6)} = 779.6882$

$\alpha = \dfrac{R_1}{R_0} = 28.39451$

$\beta = \alpha^2 - \dfrac{R_2}{R_0} = -35.8761$

$\log_e R_0 = -.07703$

Substituting the values for R_0, R_1, and R_2 in equation (17.16), we obtain

$r = -.00271$

X: Not applicable.

Source: Table 17.2.

Note: Inconsequential discrepancies from the handling of decimals may be disregarded.

Note the similarity to the formula for population growth, $P_t/P_0 = e^{rt}$.

$$T = \frac{1}{r} \ln R_o \qquad (17.18)$$

Because from (17.11),

$$\ln R_o = \frac{1}{2}\beta r^2 + \alpha r \qquad (17.19)$$

$$T = \alpha + \frac{1}{2}\beta r \qquad (17.20)$$

Because every year the stable population is $(1 + r)$ times larger than the year before, at the end of a generation, it will be larger by a factor equal to the net reproduction rate. Of course, if r is negative, R_0 will be less than one.

Intrinsic Birthrate

The true or intrinsic birthrate is the birthrate that would eventually be reached in a population subject to fixed fertility and mortality schedules. Thus, it is the birthrate of the stable population. The intrinsic birthrate may be expressed by the equation

$$b = \frac{1}{\int_o^\infty e^{-rx} p(x)dx} \qquad (17.21)$$

where b is the birthrate per person per year and the integral represents the total female stable population. This transcendental equation can be solved directly for b in a manner similar to that used for solving (17.10) for r; or, if we first determine the arithmetic value of r, we can substitute it in (17.21) and evaluate the definite integral.

A satisfactory approximation to Equation (17.21) may be obtained from

$$b = \frac{1}{\int_o^\infty e^{-r(x+1/2)} \cdot \dfrac{L_x}{l_o}} \qquad (17.22)$$

Intrinsic Death Rate

The true, or intrinsic, death rate is the death rate that would eventually be reached in a population subject to fixed fertility and mortality schedules, or the death rate of the stable population. The intrinsic death rate is then equal to the difference between the intrinsic birthrate and the intrinsic rate of increase:

$$d = b - r \qquad (17.23)$$

Stable Age Distribution

The proportion of females within the age interval x to $x \pm dx$ may be expressed by

$$c(x) = be^{-rx}p(x) \qquad (17.24)$$

We see that $c(x)$ can be found when b and r have been determined.

Ordinarily these computations will have been performed for the female population only. We may also desire to know the corresponding vital measures of the stable male population or of the population of both sexes combined. We need first to know the sex ratio at birth, which fortunately is very nearly constant from year to year. According to Lotka, the sex ratio of the stable population of all ages is

$$\frac{N_m}{N_f} = \frac{B_m}{B_f} \cdot \frac{\overline{L}_m + rL'_m}{\overline{L}_f + rL'_f} \qquad (17.25)$$

where B_m/B_f is the sex ratio at birth, $\overline{L}$ is the mean length of life in the life table, and L' the first moment of the function L_x. The subscript denotes the sex. The birthrate of both sexes combined then becomes

$$b_{m+f} = \frac{b_f \cdot \left(1 + \dfrac{B_m}{B_f}\right)}{\dfrac{N_m + N_f}{N_f}} \qquad (17.26)$$

Lotka stated that the rate of natural increase, r, must be the same for both males and females. R_0 is not the same for males and females in actual populations, however, because T is greater for males than for females. The greater male mean length of generation in turn stems from later average age at marriage and a longer fecund period. Hence, in the human species, there have probably been more female generations than male generations. Mathematical demographers have not yet been able to arrive at a complete system of logical relationships between the measures for males and females.

Computation of Measures

Intrinsic Rate of Natural Increase

Let us now illustrate how r, the intrinsic rate of natural increase, can be computed from (17.16). We do so in Table 17.3 using the statistics from the New Zealand census of 1996, previously applied in Tables 17.1 and 17.2.

Step 1. Compute age-specific birthrates per woman and multiply each age-specific birthrate by .48551 (the proportion of all births that are female) to obtain birthrates of daughters (col. 1). In this particular case, we can begin with the rates in column 3 of Table 17.1 and multiply them by .48551 and divide by 1000.

Step 2. Enter the pivotal (midpoint) values of each of the age intervals (col. 2).

Step 3. From the appropriate life table, record the number of years lived by females in the stationary population for each 5-year age interval and divide by 100,000 (col. 3).

Step 4. Multiply each entry of column 1 by the corresponding entry of column 3. The result shows the expected female births to the female stationary population (col. 4).

Step 5. Multiply each entry of column 2 by the corresponding entry of column 4 and enter the result in column 5.

Step 6. Multiply each entry of column 2 by the corresponding entry of column 5 and enter the result in column 6.

Step 7. Sum columns 1, 4, 5, and 6. (Note that the gross reproduction rate is equal to the sum of col. 1 multiplied by 5 and that the net reproduction rate is equal to the sum of col. 4.)

Step 8. Obtain R_0, R_1, and R_2 as the sums of columns 4, 5, and 6, respectively.

Step 9. Compute α and β from the expressions

$$\alpha = \frac{R_1}{R_0} \quad \text{and} \quad \beta = \alpha^2 - \frac{R_2}{R_0}$$

Step 10. Compute r from Formula (17.16).

With the natural logarithm of 0.92586 equal to -0.07703, this equation reduces to $r = -0.00271$.

Mean Length of Generation

We have from (17.20), $T = \alpha + \frac{1}{2}\beta r$. Using the values previously computed from the 1996 census of New Zealand:

$$T = 28.39451 + \frac{1}{2}(-35.8761 \times -.00271)$$

$$= 28.39451 + \frac{1}{2}(.09722) = 28.44312$$

Intrinsic Birth and Death Rates and Stable Age Distribution

Having calculated the intrinsic rate of natural increase (see Table 17.3), we can proceed to compute the intrinsic birthrate, the intrinsic death rate, and the stable age

TABLE 17.4 Computation of the Intrinsic Birth and Death Rates, and the Age Distribution, of the Stable Population, for New Zealand: 1996

Age interval (x to x + 4, in years)	Midpoint (x + 2.5) (1)	$r(x + 2.5)$ or $-.00271(x + 2.5)$ $-.00271 \times (1) =$ (2)	$e^{-r(x+2.5)}$ or $\dfrac{1}{e^{r(x+2.5)}}$ (3)	$\dfrac{_5L_x^F}{\ell_0^F}$ (4)	Female stable population derivative $(3) \times (4) =$ (5)	$\dfrac{_5L_x^M}{\ell_0^m}$ (Sex ratio at birth, 1.05969) (6)	Male stable population derivative $(3) \times (6) =$ (7)	Female $(5) \times \dfrac{100,000}{\sum(5)+\sum(7)}$ (8)	Male $(7) \times \dfrac{100,000}{\sum(5)+\sum(7)}$ (9)
0–4	2.5	−.00677	1.00679	4.96599	4.99972	5.25703	5.29274	2,827	2,992
5–9	7.5	−.02031	1.02052	4.95905	5.06080	5.24730	5.35496	2,861	3,027
10–14	12.5	−.03385	1.03443	4.95513	5.12573	5.24128	5.42173	2,898	3,065
15–19	17.5	−.04739	1.04853	4.94560	5.18561	5.22453	5.47808	2,932	3,097
20–24	22.5	−.06093	1.06282	4.93198	5.24183	5.18664	5.51249	2,963	3,116
25–29	27.5	−.07447	1.07731	4.91951	5.29985	5.14570	5.54353	2,996	3,134
30–34	32.5	−.08801	1.09200	4.90505	5.35631	5.10912	5.57915	3,028	3,154
35–39	37.5	−.10155	1.10689	4.88659	5.40889	5.07400	5.61634	3,058	3,175
40–44	42.5	−.11509	1.12197	4.86117	5.45411	5.03314	5.64705	3,083	3,193
45–49	47.5	−.12863	1.13727	4.81951	5.48108	4.97399	5.65677	3,099	3,198
50–54	52.5	−.14217	1.15277	4.74775	5.47308	4.87195	5.61625	3,094	3,175
55–59	57.5	−.15571	1.16849	4.63715	5.41845	4.70608	5.49899	3,063	3,109
60–64	62.5	−.16925	1.18442	4.47209	5.29682	4.44116	5.26018	2,995	2,974
65–69	67.5	−.18279	1.20056	4.22438	5.07163	4.02992	4.83817	2,867	2,735
70–74	72.5	−.19633	1.21693	3.85871	4.69577	3.44902	4.19721	2,655	2,373
75–79	77.5	−.20987	1.23352	3.33681	4.11601	2.67425	3.29873	2,327	1,865
80–84	82.5	−.22341	1.25033	2.58634	3.23379	1.75868	2.19894	1,828	1,243
85–89	87.5	−.23695	1.26738	1.64461	2.08434	0.89992	1.14054	1,178	645
90 and over	95.0	−.25726	1.29338	0.95634	1.23691	0.37955	0.49090	699	278
Sum					89.24075	(X)	87.64277	50,452	49,548

$b_F = .01121$ $d_F = .01392$ $b_M = .01209$ $d_M = .01480$

$b_T = .01164$ $d_T = .01435$ $r = -.00271$

Source: Table 17.3 and Cheung, 1999.

distributions of the female and male populations. The computations are set forth in Table 17.4.

Step 1. Set down the midpoint of the age intervals (col. 1).

Step 2. Multiply each midpoint of column 1 by −0.00271, the value of r. Enter the result in column 2.

Step 3. Compute the value $\dfrac{1}{e^{r(x+2.5)}}$. Since r is negative, the entries in column 3 all exceed 1.000. If r were positive, they would all fall between zero and one.

Step 4. From the female life table, record the average number of years one woman would live during each age interval. This is obtained by dividing $_5L_x$ for the appropriate interval of the female stationary population by 100,000. Record the results in column 4.

Step 5. Multiply each entry in column 4 by the corresponding entry in column 3. Record the products in column 5. Sum these entries and record the result at the bottom of column 5.

Step 6. From the corresponding male life table, multiply the average number of years each male would live during each age interval by the sex ratio at birth and record the product in column 6.

Step 7. Multiply each entry in column 6 by the corresponding entry in column 3, and record the products in column 7. Sum these entries, and record the result at the bottom of column 7.

Step 8. Compute the intrinsic birth and death rates. The total number of female person-years is the total of column 5, or 89.24075. There is 1 female birth. (The radix of the female life table is 100,000 births, but we have changed it to 1 in the calculations shown in Table 17.4.) Therefore, to obtain the female birthrate per person, we use the fraction $\dfrac{1}{89.24075}$, which is 0.01121. The intrinsic birthrate per 1000 of the female population—the conventional form—is, therefore, 11.21. The birthrate for the entire stable population (both sexes) is

$$\frac{1+1.05969}{89.24075+87.64277} = \frac{2.05969}{176.88352} = .01164$$

or 11.64 per 1000. The intrinsic death rate equals the intrinsic birthrate minus the intrinsic rate of natural increase, or $11.64 - (-2.71)$, which equals 14.35 per 1000.
Step 9. To compute the distribution of the stable population by age and sex, we add the sums of columns 5 and 7, obtaining 176.88352, which is the total stable population derivative of both sexes. To express the distribution per 100,000 of the total population, divide 100,000 by this total and multiply each value in columns 5 and 7 by this constant factor. Post the results in columns 8 and 9, respectively.

Formula (17.24) gives the age distribution per unit for a given sex. Because the number of female births is 1, then the female birthrate is, as in formulas (17.21)

$$\frac{1}{\sum e^{-rx} p(x)}$$

or, in our table, the reciprocal of the total of the entries in column 5 as in Formula (17.22). In the actual computations in our worksheet, the value of b does not appear explicitly.

The results obtained give a stable population consisting of 100,000 persons with the appropriate numbers of males and females in accordance with the sex ratio at birth. Often the distribution is wanted for the female (or male) population only. Then we use the sum of column 5—or column 7—alone rather than the total of the two sums. For example, for females under 5 years old, the percentage is:

$$\frac{4.99972}{89.24075} \times 100 = 5.603\%$$

Some Approximations

The amount of calculation required for some of these measures can be reduced appreciably by using shortcut formulas described by Coale. These appear in two separate articles. We will describe first his earlier proposal for approximating the intrinsic rate of natural increase (Coale, 1955). Coale's calculations involve two relationships:

$$NRR = e^{rT} \tag{17.27}$$

$$\frac{NRR}{GRR} \approx \frac{l_T}{l_o} \tag{17.28}$$

where NRR is the net reproduction rate, GRR is the gross reproduction rate, r is the intrinsic rate of natural increase, T is the mean length of a female generation, and $\dfrac{l_T}{l_0}$ is the probability of a female's surviving to age T.

The intrinsic rate of natural increase can be estimated by determining T from the approximate relationship (17.27), Thus

$$l_T \cong l_o \frac{NRR}{GRR} \tag{17.29}$$

and calculating r from (17.27), using natural logarithms (ln), we obtain

$$r = \frac{\ln NRR}{T} \tag{17.30}$$

Because r and T are reciprocally related, the percentage error in estimating r varies inversely with that in estimating T. Coale tested the accuracy of the approximation by comparing the results it yields with the results of exact computations of T for 17 different countries. The root mean square error was about 1.8% of the average value of T. Coale (1955, p. 96) also gave an approximation, first suggested by Lotka, for b, the intrinsic birthrate.)

Let us use this approximation to estimate r and compare the result with the closer estimate of Table 17.3. We take the values of NRR and GRR from that table:

$$l_T = \frac{0.92586}{0.94179} \times 100,000 = 98,308$$

Consulting the New Zealand life table for 1996 and interpolating, we find that this value of l_T corresponds to a T of 29.02 years. Substituting in (17.31) we have

$$r = \frac{\ln 0.92586}{29.02} = \frac{-.07703}{29.02} = -0.00265$$

which compares well with the $-.00271$ found by the more exact method.

The shortcut method is very close. There are other possible approximations, however. Because $T = \alpha + \frac{1}{2}\beta r$, it can be seen that the second term can be ignored when r is small. Then

$$T \cong \alpha = \frac{R_1}{R_o} \tag{17.31}$$

From Table 17.3, $T = \dfrac{26.28931}{0.92586} = 28.394$ years:

$$\frac{R_1}{R_0} = \frac{\sum xf(x)p(x)}{\sum f(x)p(x)} \tag{17.32}$$

$f(x)$ being the fertility rate at age x and $p(x)$ the survival rate to age x. This can be seen as a weighted age (x) in which the weights are the rates of age-specific survivors of births.

We may then substitute this new estimate of T in the equation $R_0 = e^{rT}$, obtaining

$$r = \frac{-0.07703}{28.394} = -.00271$$

This is the same as that obtained through the exact method illustrated earlier.

In a later article, Coale gave still another way of approximating r. This method (Coale, 1957) involves using 29 years as an estimate of T and getting r_1, as a first approximation to the value of r, which is then adjusted according to the extent to which

$$\int_{\omega_1}^{\omega_2} e^{-r_1 x} f(x) p(x) dx \text{ fails to equal 1.} \qquad (17.33)$$

The excess of the estimate from 1 is designated δ and the adjusted value of r becomes

$$r_1 + \frac{\delta}{29 - \dfrac{\delta}{r_1}} \qquad (17.33a)$$

Coale regarded this approximation as better than that based on (17.28).

Relation between Actual and Intrinsic Rates of Increase

Preston and Coale (1982) demonstrated that there is a necessary link between the actual rate of increase of a population and the intrinsic rate of increase of the corresponding stable population. Specifically, Preston (1986) showed that the mean age-specific growth rate up to age T, the mean length of generation, is a close approximation to Lotka's intrinsic rate of increase. In other words,

$$r \approx \bar{r} = \frac{1}{T} \int_0^T r(x) dx \qquad (17.34)$$

where r is the intrinsic rate of increase, T the mean length of generation, and $r(x)$ the age-specific growth rates. T is usually close to the mean age of childbearing, say, A^*. Thus, alternatively, one can derive $\bar{r}(A^*)$—the mean growth rate of the population segment below the mean age at childbearing. However, it is found that the intrinsic rate of increase is better approximated by $\bar{r}(T)$ than by $\bar{r}(A^*)$.

The preceding relation between the rate of increase of a population below age T and the intrinsic rate of increase has important implications for population momentum. If an intrinsic growth rate of zero (i.e., $R_0 = 1$) is attained and maintained in a population, then the population below age T will remain approximately constant in size from the time at which it is attained. But we know from the experiences of the more developed and some less developed countries that a population continues to grow in size even after attaining replacement-level fertility. It thus follows that the growth momentum must occur above age T. "The momentum results from projecting into higher ages the larger cohorts of persons already born, and not from projecting growth into the reproductive [or young adult] ages of the births still to occur" (Preston, 1986, p. 350).

REPRODUCTIVITY ESTIMATED FROM CENSUS STATISTICS

In the absence of adequate birth statistics, attempts have been made to compute measures of reproductivity wholly from census statistics or from census statistics and life tables. The methods described in this section are applicable to many countries with good age-sex statistics from censuses but with inadequate birth statistics, including many less developed countries. It is often desirable, however, to make some kind of correction for undercounting young children, or otherwise to adjust the age-sex distribution, when measuring reproductivity from census data.[1]

Measures Based on Age-Sex Distributions: The Replacement Index

The *replacement index* is computed on the basis of the age distribution of the actual female population and a female life table for the same period. The calculation involves dividing the ratio of children under five years of age to females in the reproductive ages in the actual population, by the corresponding ratio in the life table stationary population. Thus defined, this measure relates to reproductivity in the 5 years preceding the reference date of the observed age distribution. We may exercise a choice in the age groups for children and women employed in the measures, just as we do in the case of the general fertility ratio.

In his 1920 census monograph, Thompson (1931) devised several types of measures that he called replacement indexes. Of these, his *permanent replacement index* corresponded to the index just described. (Net replacement indexes similar to those defined by Thompson were computed for many countries of the world as part of the computer program devised by Keyfitz and Flieger (1968).)

Subsequently Lotka gave a generalized mathematical treatment of replacement indexes and showed how a replacement index is related to the intrinsic rate of natural increase (Lotka, 1936). He defined the index J in the same way as Thompson's permanent replacement index, namely, as the quotient of two ratios, the numerator, the ratio of children under a given age to women in the childbearing ages

---

[1] The general approach is similar to that in estimating fertility measures from survey data described in Chapter 16. In the United States, reproduction rates, like other fertility measures, were first based on census data, for several reasons: (a) the failure of the Birth Registration Area to cover the entire United States until 1933; (b) the lack of national statistics on resident births until 1937; and (c) the fact that fertility data on some characteristics (such as farm-nonfarm residence) are available from the census but not from the registration system. The last of these reasons is still an important one. On the other hand, we must recognize that undercounting of young children in the United States has become more serious than underregistration of births but that we have little information on current geographic variation of either of these types of errors.

in the actual population and, the denominator, the same ratio in the life table population. Thus, in integral notation,

$$J = \frac{\int_p^q c(a)da}{\int_u^v c(a)da} \div \frac{b_o \int_p^q p(a)da}{b_o \int_u^v p(a)da} \qquad (17.35)$$

where $c(a)$ is a segment of the age distribution in the actual population and $p(a)$ is the probability at birth of surviving to age a; p and q are the lower and upper limits, respectively, of the younger age group of both sexes, and u and v are the lower and upper limits, respectively, of the age groups of women in the reproductive ages. The symbol b_0 denotes the birthrate per person in the life table population in which

$$c(a) = b_0 p(a) \qquad (17.36)$$

In the more conventional demographic notation, this is

$$J = \frac{P_{0-4}}{P_{15-49}^f} \div \frac{L_{0-4}^f + \frac{B_m}{B_f} L_{0-4}^m}{L_{15-49}^f} \qquad (17.37)$$

Note that in deriving the total number of children in the life table population, it is necessary to combine the number of boys and girls from their respective life tables, inflating the number of boys by the sex ratio of births.

The replacement index, then, gives us a method for approximating the net reproduction rate in the absence of vital statistics. Table 17.5 illustrates the computation of the J index with 1996 statistics for New Zealand consistent with those used in Tables 17.3 and 17.4. We have used the simpler statistical notation instead of Lotka's integral equation:

$$r' = \frac{\ln J}{\alpha_2 - \alpha_1} \qquad (17.38)$$

where ln represents a natural logarithm and α_2 and α_1 are defined in Table 17.5.

The value of $J(0.98179)$ greatly exceeds the value of $R_0(.92586)$ in Table 17.3, and the value of $r(-.00062)$ is considerably less than that of $r(-.00271)$ in Table 17.3. This could arise from the extent to which the 1996 population of New Zealand was not of stable form, the use of very different data systems, and the difference in the reference date and sexes (of children) of the two calculations.

Reproduction Rate Estimated from Women's Own Children Under 5

Up to this point in our discussion of the use of census data to approximate net reproductivity, we have dealt only with the data obtainable from age-sex distributions. Because it was not until the 1940 census of the United States that data were tabulated and published on the distribution of

TABLE 17.5 Computation of Replacement Index (J) and Substitute Intrinsic Rate of Natural Increase for New Zealand: 1996

Steps	Calculation
1. Ratio, children 0–4 to women 15–49 years: census population	
a. P_{0-4}^T	279,606
b. P_{15-49}^F	954,675
c. Ratio (a) ÷ (b)	.29288
2. Ratio, children 0–4 to women 15–49 years: life table population	
a. L_{0-4}^M	496,091
b. L_{0-4}^F	496,599
c. L_{15-49}^F	3,426,941
d. $\dfrac{1.05969(a)+(b)}{(c)}$	.29831
3. Replacement Index (J) = (1,c) ÷ (2,d)	.98179
4. Rate of Increase $r' = \dfrac{\ln J}{\alpha_2 - \alpha_1}$	
a. $\ln J$	−.01838
b. α_1 = Mean age of children 0–4 in life table population[1]	2.69
c. α_2 = Mean age of women 15–49 in life table population[2]	32.42
d. $\alpha_2 - \alpha_1$	29.73
e. r' = (a) ÷ (d)	−.00062

[1] The mean age for each sex was based on values for L_0 and L_{1-4} in the abridged life table for New Zealand, and midpoints of 0.5 and 3.0, respectively, were assumed for these age groups. The resulting mean ages for males and females were then weighted in proportion to the assumed distributions of births by sex in New Zealand.

[2] Computed on the basis of the life table population in 5-year age groups and the midpoints of these age intervals.

Source: Statistics New Zealand, 1998.

women by the number of their own children under 5 years old in the household, it is not surprising that no attention was paid by demographers to the computation of reproduction rates from such data. In 1942, Grabill developed a method for calculating gross and net reproduction rates from data on own children under 5 years, of women of childbearing age, which was most completely described in an article by Grabill and Cho (1965).

They began by estimating the age-specific birthrates corresponding to the ratios of own children to women by age. Let B_x^f denote the number of daughters born to women of age x and P_x^f the number of women of age x; then

$$F_x = \frac{B_x^f}{P_x^f} \qquad (17.39)$$

is the age-specific birthrate.

Let s_x be the life table probability of survival from birth to age x, or the probability that daughters will live to their mother's age. Thus, using life table probabilities, one can expect that a census or survey taken i years after the birth of the daughters will show $B_x^f S_i$ surviving daughters of age i. Similarly, the survivorship among women "x" to age "$x + i$" would be $P_x^f \left(\dfrac{S_{x+i}}{S_x} \right)$. The ratio of surviving daughters born to surviving women would be

$$R_{x+i} = \frac{B_x^f s_i}{P_x^f \left(\dfrac{S_{x+i}}{S_x} \right)} \qquad (17.40)$$

Given $F_x = \dfrac{B_x^f}{P_x^f}$, $B_x^f = F_x P_x^f$. Substituting $F_x P_x^f$ for B_x^f in (17.40), we get

$$R_{x+i} = \frac{F_x s_x s_i}{S_{x+i}} \qquad (17.41)$$

and

$$F_x = R_{x+i} \left[\frac{s_{x+i}}{s_x s_i} \right] \qquad (17.42)$$

Replacing the F_x values in the conventional formulas for gross and net reproduction rates with the mathematically identical values $R_{x+i} \left[\dfrac{S_{x+i}}{S_x S_i} \right]$ yields

$$GRR = \sum R_{x+i} \cdot \frac{s_{x+i}}{s_x s_i} = \frac{1}{s_i} \sum R_{x+i} \cdot \frac{s_{x+i}}{s_x} \qquad (17.43)$$

because s_i is a constant

$$NRR = \left[\sum R_{x+i} \left(\frac{s_{x+i}}{s_x s_i} \right) \cdot s_x \right] = \frac{1}{s_i} \sum R_{x+i} \cdot s_{x+i} \qquad (17.44)$$

The summation in (17.43) and (17.44) is to be taken over all ages for which $R_{x+i} > 0$.

Using a life table notation and daughters under 5 years old, we may write

$$NRR = \frac{1}{\displaystyle\sum_0^4 L_x} \cdot \sum R_A^{0-4} \cdot L_A \qquad (17.45)$$

where $\displaystyle\sum_0^4 L_x$ is the female life table stationary population under 5 years old expressed on a unit-radix basis, A is the age of women at the census date, R_A^{0-4} is the ratio of daughters under 5 years old to women aged A, and L_A is the female life table stationary population age A, expressed on a unit-radix basis. Using a specific survival-rate notation, $_5 s_A$, or $_5 s_x'$ if we understand x to cover the childbearing ages, we have

$$NRR = \frac{1}{_5 s_0} \sum {}_5 R_x \cdot {}_5 s_x' \qquad (17.46)$$

Similarly, the gross reproduction rate is

$$GRR = \frac{500{,}000}{\displaystyle\sum_0^4 L_x} \sum R_A^{0-4} \cdot \frac{L_A}{L_{A-2.5}} \qquad (17.47)$$

It is assumed in expression (17.47) that women age A at the census date were, on the average, $2\frac{1}{2}$ years younger at the time their daughters under 5 years old were born. This assumption is not very reasonable for females near the beginning or end of the childbearing period, but the errors tend to cancel so that the overall effect on the GRR is slight.

Again, in our survival rate notation, we have

$$GRR = \frac{1}{s_{0-4}} \sum \frac{{}_5 R_x \cdot {}_5 s_x'}{{}_5 s_x''} \qquad (17.48)$$

where $_5 s_x'$ is the survival rate of women from birth to exact ages x to $x + 5$, and $_5 s_x''$ is the survival rate to exact ages $x - 2.5$ to $x + 2.5$.

One important consideration in the use of age-specific ratios of own children to compute reproduction rates has not yet been brought out, however—namely, that "own children" fail to account for all children under 5 years (or under 1, etc.). The obvious remedy is to make a correction on the basis of the total number of children in the population. This can be an overall correction, not taking account of variations with age of mother because these do not have much effect on a reproduction rate, which is a sum over all ages.

Our illustration comes from The Gambia. The method has also been applied to several other less developed countries (e.g., Sri Lanka, Korea).

In Table 17.6, we have translated the L_A's and L_x's into survival rates for convenience of manipulation. In summing columns 4 and 6, we would ordinarily multiply by 5 because we are dealing with 5-year age groups of women, and the rates are averages for the 5 years. On the other hand, the children under 5 in the numerator of column 1 are survivors of births over a 5-year period, and they need to be reduced to annual births. Hence, the 5's cancel.

This method can be applied as well to geographic subdivision of countries, including the more developed countries, for which vital statistics may not be available, such as type-of-residence areas (e.g., rural-form population, urbanized areas). This method can be applied also to a country for which there are no census or survey data on own children by age of mother. The application requires a form of indirect standardization to estimate the schedule of age-specific ratios of children to women.[2] Grabill and Cho (1965, p. 59)

---

[2] Inasmuch as we know the total number of girls under age 5 and the number of women according to age, we use the schedule of age-specific ratios of own female children under 5 per 1000 women for another country for which such ratios are available ("the standard"), to derive the "expected" number of children under 5 in the country of interest. We then divide this number into the total number of girls under 5 to obtain an adjustment factor. The factor is then applied to the standard schedule of ratios to obtain an estimated schedule of ratios for the country of interest. The remaining steps would then be the same as before with the use of an appropriate life table.

TABLE 17.6 Computation of Net and Gross Reproduction Rates from Ratios of Own Children to Women for The Gambia: 1990

Age of women (years)	Own children under 5 per 1000 women $_5R_x$ (1)	Adjusted ratio[1] $_5R'_x$ col. (1) × factor = (2)	Survival rate $_5L_x \div 500{,}000 = {}_5s'_x$ (3)	$_5R'_x \bullet$ $_5s'_x$ (2) × (3) = (4)	Survival rate $_5L_{x-2.5} \div 500{,}000 = 5s''_x$ (5)	$_5R'_x \bullet$ $\frac{_5s'_x}{_5s''_x}$ (4) ÷ (5) = (6)
15–19	327	169	.8512	144	.8572	168
20–24	993	514	.8404	432	.8458	511
25–29	1219	631	.8290	523	.8347	627
30–34	973	504	.8166	412	.8228	501
35–39	823	426	.8022	342	.8094	422
40–44	484	251	.7824	196	.7923	247
45–49	250	129	.7592	98	.7708	127
Sum				2147		2603

Survival rate for children (from life table) $= \dfrac{_5L_0}{5 \cdot \ell_0} = \dfrac{454{,}600}{500{,}000} = 0.9086$

$\text{NRR} = \dfrac{2147}{.9086} = 2632 \text{ or } 2.632 \text{ per woman}$

$\text{GRR} = \dfrac{2603}{.9086} = 2864 \text{ or } 2.864 \text{ per woman}$

[1] $\text{Adjustment factor} = \dfrac{\text{Total female children under 5}}{\text{Own children under 5 of women 15 to 49}} = \dfrac{1004}{1939} = .51779$

Source: Survival rates derived from an abridged life table for 1992 given in The Gambia, Central Statistics Department, 1998, pp. 43–45. Data on own children and women were extracted from the *Gambian Contraceptive Prevalence and Fertility Determinants Survey, 1990*. Alieu Sarr of the Central Statistics Department, Banjul, The Gambia, provided the data. For survey details see Pacqué-Margolis *et al.*, 1993.

illustrated this procedure using two states, one of which is assumed to lack statistics on own children. A worksheet like Table 17.6 does not yield estimates of annual age-specific birthrates as a by-product. Grabill and Cho (1965, pp. 58–69) gave two procedures for making such estimates, however.

With the aid of life table survival rates, age-specific ratios of children under 5 to women can be adjusted to restore deaths among children and women. The figures thus adjusted become equivalent to birthrates cumulated over a 5-year period for women aged $2\frac{1}{2}$ years younger than at the end of the period. To derive birthrates for conventional 5-year age groups, one has to apply some type of interpolation formula, such as Sprague's. The reader is referred to the article for the details of the procedures and for a table of multipliers that can be used for this purpose.

Although the own-children method was first developed in the early 1940s, the basic principles of the method have remained the same to date. However, it has been refined and extended. The extensions allow us to estimate birthrates by duration since first marriage for ever-married women (Retherford, Cho, and Kim, 1984), age-specific birthrates for currently married women (Ratnayake, Retherford, and Sivasubramaniam, 1984), age-parity-specific birthrates (Retherford and Cho, 1978), and age-specific birthrates for men (Retherford and Sewell, 1986).

Children Ever Born

From the observed or estimated sex ratio at birth and the number of children ever born, one may compute the number of daughters ever born to a given group of women. Such an approach is directly applicable to the more developed countries or other areas where the basic data are adequate. For women who have completed the childbearing period, say those 50 years old and over, the average number of daughters ever born represents an estimate of the generation gross reproduction rate for these cohorts of women. It is an upwardly biased estimate, however, because those women who died before attaining the given age certainly averaged fewer children than those who survived. This measure is a measure of generational reproductivity and is discussed further in the section on "New and Improved Measures of Reproductivity."

The analyst faces a different situation in the statistically less developed countries where the data on children ever born and vital statistics are deficient. Several techniques of measuring reproductivity use data on children ever born collected in a census or survey, to adjust the age-specific fertility pattern obtained from vital registration or derived from information on births in the prior 12 months, disaggregated by age of mother, in a census or survey. The two most widely used such techniques are the P/F ratio technique, originally developed by Brass, and the Arriaga technique. A major difference between these two techniques relates to the assumption about past fertility. While Brass's technique is based on the assumption that fertility has been constant during a certain period, say the past 10 or 15 years, the Arriaga technique requires no such assumption. As the fertility transition has been under way in almost all less developed countries, the potential for the application of the Brass technique has become limited. Readers interested in Brass's P/F technique and in the Arriaga technique are referred to the standard source for indirect estimation techniques (United Nations, 1983) and to Chapter 22.

MISINTERPRETATIONS AND SHORTCOMINGS OF CONVENTIONAL MEASURES

Interpretation of Conventional Rates

During the 1920s and 1930s, Dublin, Lotka, Lorimer, Osborn, Notestein, and other prominent demographers stated explicitly that the net reproduction rate and other measures of the stable population merely described what would happen if the fertility and mortality schedules of a given period continued unchanged sufficiently long in a closed population. These measures did not represent a description of what was happening or forecasts of what would eventually happen to the given population. It was recognized that both fertility and mortality were indeed changing in many of the populations studied.

Because the general trend in fertility had been downward for many decades, however, the reproduction rates came to be regarded as conservative indicators of how far reproductivity would eventually fall. It was frequently stated that the current levels of the crude rate of natural increase were due to transitory favorable age distributions (resulting from past births, deaths, and migration) and could not be maintained. When the net reproduction rate of the United States fell below unity in the 1930s, some demographers wrote that our population was no longer replacing itself.

Then, after the end of World War II, a sudden, very fundamental change took place. The sharp upturn of age-specific fertility rates led some demographers to challenge the inevitability of a decline in the population, and at the same time the interpretation of the classical reproduction rates was profoundly modified and their utility was seen to be much less than had been thought (Dorn, 1950). Since the end of the "baby boom" in the mid-1960s, most Western countries have been experiencing below-replacement-level fertility. This has again raised concerns about possible population decline in these countries (Bongaarts and Feeney, 1998; Lesthaghe and Willems, 1999). The situation has also suggested, however, the possible relevance of the classical

reproduction rates to Western populations that were approaching or approximating a stationary condition, that is, a stable condition with a zero rate of increase.

Let us try to see how the misinterpretation of the earlier reproduction rates came about. One of the ingredients in reproduction rates is a schedule of age-specific fertility rates for a given year or other short period of time. This schedule is treated as if it represented the performance of a cohort of women as they pass through the successive ages of the childbearing period. Likewise, the mortality schedule is treated as if it could be used to describe the proportion of women in a given cohort who survive from birth to successive ages of the childbearing period. The conventional life table is the same kind of "synthetic" cohort. The usefulness of these "synthetic" measures depends, in large degree, on the extent to which they describe the fertility, mortality, or reproductivity of some past or future period, or, from another viewpoint, on whether actual cohorts have had this experience or could have had this experience.

It is obvious that the conventional rates assume that the fertility rate at one age is independent of the rates at earlier ages for the same group of women. Suppose in a given year, t, women aged 25 had a fertility rate f_{25}^t and those aged 35 had a fertility rate f_{35}^t. Then, 10 years later would f_{25}^{t+10} for the younger cohort be likely to equal f_{35}^t for the older cohort, if at prior ages they had had very different fertility rates? One cohort may have lived through ages 20 to 24 in a depression, the other in prosperity (or one in wartime, the other in peacetime). Their distribution by age at marriage may have been very different. The proportions marrying by different ages may also have been different, perhaps because there was a great shortage of marriageable men arising from war losses. Marriages and births are believed to be postponed or advanced because of the prevailing economic and sociopsychological conditions. In the 1930s and 1940s, most of the reproduction rates that were available to demographers were for the interwar period for countries that were belligerents in World War I and had suffered from the Great Depression of the 1930s. In fact, relatively few reproduction rates then available applied to populations that had spent their reproductive lives in periods of stability or gradual social change. More generally, there was a tendency to extrapolate short-run conditions into long-run consequences.

Other Limitations of Conventional Reproduction Rates

The conventional reproduction rates may also imply impossible values by order of birth, and corresponding male and female rates may be very different. Some of the shortcomings have been remedied by refinements that are described in the next major section.

Impossible Reproduction Rates by Order of Birth

Reproduction rates can be computed separately for each order of birth. Working with American fertility data for the years during World War II, Whelpton (1946) noticed some logical absurdities. When he added the first birthrates over all ages from 15 through 49 for native white women in 1942, he obtained a rate of 1084. In other words, it was implied that 1000 women living through the childbearing period would have 1084 first births! In view of the existence of some involuntary sterility and spinsterhood, even 1000 first births would be impossible for a real cohort.

The explanation of this paradox lies in the facts that many women in their thirties had their first child in 1942 after postponing marriage and childbearing during the depression and many younger women were marrying and beginning childbearing relatively early as the result of the psychology of the prosperous wartime period. This combination of events could not occur in the lifetime of a real cohort of women. This analysis brings out clearly the fact that the changes in the timing of childbearing make fertility at one age not independent of fertility at earlier ages. In the Western more developed countries, indicators of period fertility have shown substantial declines since the mid-1960s. It is argued that part of the decline was due to postponement of childbearing to later ages. It is possible that a stop to postponement could lead to a substantial increase in period total fertility rates.

Inconsistent Male and Female Reproduction Rates

Although reproduction rates are usually computed only for the female population, rates for the male population can also be computed. The calculation of reproduction rates for males and females has shown that they are not compatible, however.

Kuczynski (1932), for example, calculated a net reproduction rate of only 977 per 1000 French females in 1920–1923 but one of 1194 per 1000 French males. He attributed the inconsistency to a lack of balance between the sexes in the reproductive ages, arising from deaths of men in World War I. A lack of balance could also arise in some countries from the greater international migration of men than of women. In monogamous societies, persons of the sex in short supply in the reproductive ages would be expected to have the higher reproduction rate because a greater proportion of them would be able to find marital partners. *Apparent* values of the conventional reproduction rates are affected by underenumeration and misstatements of age in the population, underregistration of births, and errors in coverage and age-reporting of deaths. Differences in the calculated rates for the two sexes are affected only by the sex *differences* in the quality of the basic data and in population composition, however.

Differences between male and female reproduction rates may lead to different conclusions regarding population replacement. Could the female sub-replacement net reproduction rates, especially prevalent in Western Europe during the 1930s, validly have been interpreted as foreshadowing failure of the population to reproduce itself when corresponding male reproduction rates were well above unity? Part of the rise in German fertility during the early years of rule under National Socialism (1920s) may have reflected an increasingly favorable balance of the sexes as men too young to have fought in World War I attained marriageable age. Hence, some of the increase in female reproduction rates appeared to represent the passing of a temporary shortage of husbands rather than any fundamental change in the fertility of married couples. On the other hand, war losses of men in World War I were not the only cause of declining reproduction rates during the interwar period. This is suggested by the fact that reproductivity also declined in the neutral Scandinavian countries.

Thorough analyses of the theoretical relationships between male and female reproduction rates were made independently but about the same time by Vincent (1946) and Karmel (1948a and 1948b).

We have discussed the problem of the consistency at male and female reproduction rates in the context of the conventional (period or synthetic) reproduction rates. It is necessary, however, to point out that these inconsistencies do not disappear when the improvements to be discussed in the next section—including rates for real cohorts—are introduced. (Reproduction rates for the male population are discussed in a separate section of the chapter.)

NEW AND IMPROVED MEASURES OF REPRODUCTIVITY

Adjusted Period Rates

Whelpton's Adjustment

Much of the criticism of the conventional reproduction rates that has just been summarized is mingled with suggestions for improving them. In the United States, the attempts at improvement first took the form of continuing to use period data but taking account of additional demographic factors.

Such an approach was taken by Whelpton shortly after the end of World War II. As mentioned in the preceding section of this chapter, Whelpton (1946) showed that the conventional reproduction rates could lead to absurd results when dissected into their components with respect to order of birth. This conclusion led him to develop a "life table" procedure for the computation of age and parity-specific rates.

Birth statistics disaggregated by order of birth and by age of mother were readily available for the United States; and there were also population data giving the distribution of women by age and parity for selected periods. Whelpton used the distributions for 1940 and 1910 published in the 1940 census reports. To obtain such distributions for intermediate and later years, a large amount of computation and some fairly broad assumptions were obviously required.

Starting with a hypothetical cohort of women, Whelpton allowed for mortality and parity by subtracting deaths and successive numbers who bore a first child, second child, and so on. His allowance for fecundity and marriage represents an attempt to confine the specific rates to women at risk in the actuarial sense. On the basis of the meager evidence then available, Whelpton assumed that 10% of women were "sterile" (i.e., involuntarily childless) and that an additional 10% would not marry before the end of the child-bearing period. This method of allowing for marital status is more limited than the computation of nuptial reproduction rates, which introduces marital status as another specific characteristic in the rates.

For the years from 1920 to 1944, Whelpton found that net reproduction rates adjusted for age-parity-marriage-fecundity were lower than the conventional reproduction rates for every year except 1921, for which the rates were the same. The differences, however, were not large. Although the "life table" procedure used by Whelpton to "standardize" the total fertility rate (TFR) for parity did produce meaningful results, it did not deal directly with distortions created by timing changes. Changes in the *numbers* of birth during a period due to delay or recovery in childbearing affect not only ordinary age-specific rates and the total fertility rate but also life table rates (i.e., rates adjusted for parity, marriage, and fecundity).

Ryder's Translation Equation

In a 1956 article, Norman Ryder proposed a *translation* equation to adjust the period measures of fertility for changes in the tempo or timing of childbearing. In a number of articles, Ryder showed how the TFR was influenced by changes in the timing of childbearing among cohorts of women in the United States (e.g., Ryder, 1956, 1959, 1964, 1986). In Ryder's equation, the TFR is linked to the completed fertility rate (CFR) of a cohort and changes in the mean age at childbearing per cohort, say (c years):

$$TFR = CFR \times (1 - c) \qquad (17.49)$$

If there was no change in mean age at childbearing from one cohort to the next, then Equation (17.49) becomes $TFR = CFR$. If the mean age at childbearing increases by, say, 0.05 year per cohort (e.g., from 29.00 years for one cohort to 29.05 for the next, etc.), then substitution in Equation

(17.60) gives $TFR = CFR \times (1 - 0.05)$. That is, an increase of 0.05 year in the mean age at childbearing per cohort would result in a TFR that is 5% less than the corresponding CFR. Similarly, if the mean age at childbearing decreases by, say, 05 year for successive cohorts, then the TFR would be greater than the corresponding CFR by 10%.

Despite being simple and responsive to the changes in timing on the TFR, Ryder's equation has not been widely applied in empirical studies. This is due to two main reasons (Bongaarts and Feeney, 1998): (1) Ryder assumes that changes in period fertility are due to changes in the tempo and quantum of cohort fertility; however, the writings on this issue do not seem to support this assumption (e.g., Brass, 1974; Ní Bhrolcháin, 1992; Pullum, 1980); and (2) changes in mean age at childbearing of aggregate cohorts may not necessarily result from changes in tempo or timing. In other words, mean age at childbearing for all births could change as a result of declines in higher order births while the timing of individual births may not change. Although Ryder noted that this problem could be solved by applying the translation formula to each birth order separately, he did not follow this idea up in his later work.

Bongaarts-Feeney Method

As mentioned earlier, changes in the TFR can arise as a result of changes in its quantum component or in its tempo or timing component or as a result of changes in both components. To overcome the problems inherent in the methods of Welpton, Ryder, and others, Bongaarts and Feeney (1998) developed a method to adjust the TFR for changes in tempo of childbearing. Application of this method gives a tempo-adjusted TFR.

The principle behind the method is simple, and the derivation of the formula is straightforward. If the mean age of mothers at childbearing of any birth order i changes by an amount r per annum (r_i), then the observed number of births of order i ($B_{i,obs}$) may be expressed as $1 - r_i$ times the number of births had there been no change in their timing ($B_{i,adjs}$). In other words,

$$B_{i,adj} = \frac{B_{i,obs}}{(1 - r_i)} \qquad (17.50)$$

Extending the preceding formula for birth-order-specific total fertility rates, we get

$$TFR_{i,adj} = \frac{TFR_{i,obs}}{(1 - r_i)} \qquad (17.51)$$

where $TFR_{i,obs}$ is the observed total fertility rate for order i, $TFR_{i,adj}$ is the total fertility rate for order i if there had been no changes in the timing of i-order births, and r_i is the annual change in the mean age at childbearing for order i. Summing over i, we get the adjusted total fertility rate:

$$TFR_{adj} = \sum_{i=1}^{n} TFR_{i,adj} \qquad (17.52)$$

Application of this method depends on the availability of age-order-specific fertility rates for at least two points of time, say, t and $t - n$. Using the age-order-specific fertility rates, order-specific total fertility rates (TFR$_i$s) and order-specific mean ages at childbearing (MAC$_i$s) can be derived. The annual change in mean age at childbearing for birth order i is obtained as

$$r_i = \frac{MAC_{i,t} - MAC_{i,t-n}}{n} \qquad (17.53)$$

where $MAC_{i,t}$ is the mean age at childbearing for birth order i for the end period t, $MAC_{i,t-n}$ is the mean age of childbearing for birth order i for the initial period $t-n$, and n is the number of years between the initial and end periods.

An illustrative calculation and results from an application of the Bongaarts-Feeney method to Italy, Belgium, and France are given in Table 17.7. As the figures in the last column indicate, tempo-adjusted total fertility rates for all three countries for calendar years 1988–1990 are greater than the observed TFRs. Bongaarts and Feeney (1998) applied their method to the United States and Taiwan, and they concluded that tempo-adjusted fertility measures are preferable to unadjusted period measures to reflect changes in real cohort fertility. A comparison of (1) completed cohort fertility rates for U.S. women born in 1904 through 1941 with weighted averages of (2) adjusted TFRs and (3) observed TFRs, over the years during which the cohorts in (1) were in the main childbearing ages, showed that com-

pleted cohort fertility rates estimated from adjusted TFRs provided a far closer approximation to the corresponding observed cohort fertility rates than those estimated from unadjusted TFRs.

Reproduction rates for cohorts born in a given year should be compared with the conventional (i.e., synthetic) rates 28 or so years later (i.e., at the time when the cohort was near its average age of childbearing). Females born in a given year or period were not at the beginning of their childbearing period until about 15 years later, at the average age of childbearing until about 25 to 30 years later, and at the end thereof until about 50 years later. Any of these lags are more reasonable than a comparison in the year of birth of the cohort. As was said in Chapter 16, however, there is no one-to-one correspondence between the fertility of a birth cohort and that of any particular year or short period. In any case, note that the fluctuations in the period rates are much greater than those in the generation rates. Generations that exhibited fertility well below average in some periods made up the deficit by fertility well above average in other periods.

Generation Reproduction Rates

So far, the improved measures of reproductivity that we have described have simply been annual, or period, reproduction rates computed from fertility rates specific for other demographic variables in addition to age. In considering generation reproduction rates, we are moving to measures of reproductivity that are based on the fertility and mortality experience of an actual cohort of women during its reproductive years and not on the experience of one calendar year or

TABLE 17.7 Birth-Order-Specific Period Total Fertility Rates (TFR$_i$), Birth-Order-Specific Mean Ages at Childbearing (MAC$_i$), Observed Period Total Fertility Rates (TFR$_{obs}$), and Period Total Fertility Rates Adjusted for Tempo Shifts (TFR$_{adj}$): Italy, Belgium, and France, 1980 and ca. 1989

Country (year)	Birth order 1		Birth order 2		Birth order 3		Birth order 4+		TFR$_{obs}$ (all orders)	TFR$_{adj}$ (all orders)
	TFR$_1$	MAC$_1$	TFR$_2$	MAC$_2$	TFR$_3$	MAC$_3$	TFR$_{4+}$	MAC$_{4+}$		
Italy										
1980	.771	24.6	.581	27.6	.210	30.2	.080	34.0	1.64	1.64[1]
1990	.628	26.4	.466	29.3	.160	31.8	.080	34.7	1.33	1.60[2]
r_i(1980–1990)		+.18		+.17		+.16		+.07	−.31	−.04
Belgium										
1980	.80	24.8	.54	27.1	.21	29.4	.12	31.8	1.67	1.67[1]
1988	.74	26.2	.51	28.1	.21	30.1	.11	30.6	1.57	1.81
r_i(1980–1988)		+.175		+.125		+.088		−.15	−.10	+.14
France										
1980	.82	24.6	.68	27.2	.31	29.2	.14	32.4	1.95	1.95[1]
1989	.77	26.2	.59	28.5	.30	30.4	.13	33.3	1.79	2.01
r_i(1980–1989)		+.178		+.144		+.133		+.10	−.16	+.06

[1] Adjusted TFR set equal to Observed TFR in initial years.

[2] Illustrative calculation: $1.60 = \frac{.628}{(1-.18)} + \frac{.466}{(1-.17)} + \frac{.160}{(1-.16)} + \frac{.080}{(1-.07)}$

Source: Adapted from Lesthaeghe and Willems, 1999, p. 214.

other short period cumulated over all the reproductive ages. With this very important difference, the generation gross and net reproduction rates are defined just as they are in the case of the conventional, or "classical," reproduction rates.

Generation rates can be derived in several ways. We will consider, first, generation rates that can be obtained from vital statistics and then rates that can be obtained from census or survey statistics on children ever born.

Generation Rates from Vital Statistics

A direct method of computing a generation net reproduction rate would be to start with female births of a given year, say 1950. The female births to native women of the same cohort would be added throughout its childbearing period. Thus, we would add the births in 1965 to girls 15 years old, the births in 1966 to girls 16 years old, the births in 1967 to girls 17 years old, and so on through the births in 1999 to women 49 years old. Mortality of the mothers (earlier generation) is introduced at each successive age so that no survival rates are required. The sum of these successive female births divided by the initial size of the cohort of mothers is the net reproduction rate for the cohort of 1950. This method would not be appropriate for countries of heavy immigration or emigration. Earlier in the chapter, we discussed approximate methods of computing conventional rates from census data in the absence of adequate birth statistics. We now have shown that, given adequate vital statistics, it is possible to compute generation reproduction rates without population data from censuses.

Generation reproduction rates were first computed by Pierre Depoid (1941) for France. The first American generation rates were computed by Thomas Woofter (1947).

Depoid's Method

Depoid (1941) calculated the conventional age-specific fertility rates (15 to 19 through 45 to 49 years) for 5-year cohorts beginning with 1826 to 1830 and ending with 1900 to 1905. Multiplying the sum of these fertility rates (daughters only) for a cohort by 5 gives the gross reproduction rate. For the same cohorts, he computed the probability of survival from birth to various ages up to 50 for females. The summed products of the fertility rates and the survival rates gave the generation net reproduction rate. All reproduction rates were for women who had completed their childbearing period.

Woofter's Method

To obtain generation reproduction rates, Woofter (1947) computed the number of daughters surviving to the exact ages of mothers at the time when their daughters were born. More precisely, the age-specific fertility rates used were those of the calendar years when the cohort of women attained specific ages. Woofter originally named the cohorts according to the calendar year when they were 15, not according to the calendar years of their birth. Thus, they were identified by the year when they entered the childbearing period. For his "1915" cohort, for example, he cumulated the age-specific fertility rate of 15-year-old females in 1915, the rate of 16-year-olds in 1916, and so on through the rate of 44-year-olds in 1944. The sum is his generation gross reproduction rate. Applying to each cohort of daughters the mortality rates appropriate to the calendar years through which they must survive and summing the products of the appropriate fertility and survival rates, Woofter obtained the generation net reproduction rate.

Woofter's method of computing generation reproduction rates mixes two generations. In other words, the mortality used for the computation of his generation reproduction rate is not that to which a single generation of women has been exposed but is made up, in varying proportions, of the mortality to which the mothers have been exposed and the mortality to which their daughters have been exposed. This method requires the projection of mortality rates into future years even when we are concerned with fertility that was completed in the recent past (Lotka, 1949).

Whelpton's Method

The preparation of cumulative and completed fertility rates for cohorts was discussed in Chapter 15. When such completed fertility rates are multiplied by the proportion of births that are female, we have generation gross reproduction rates. In the United States, Whelpton (1954) had done pioneering work on assembly of the vital statistics data and their adjustment and on the methodology of calculating the measures. This work was extended by Whelpton and Campbell (1960) for the U.S. National Office of Vital Statistics (predecessor to the National Center for Health Statistics).

Most of the complications in the methodology stem from inadequacies in the underlying vital statistics and population statistics, particularly for earlier years. Generation gross reproduction rates for more recent years can be readily computed from completed fertility rates for annual birth cohorts of women by current age of woman and live birth order.

Ideally, one would develop a generation life table for the same cohort of females or, what amounts to the same thing, apply an annual survival rate for each year that comes from the life table of that year. This procedure would involve a great deal of work but probably less than is devoted to estimating cumulative fertility. A shortcut would be to use a life table applying to the date at which the cohort had completed roughly half of its childbearing. This age tends to be fairly constant.

Whelpton (1954) paid some attention to this problem in the mid-fifties. In the European context, Pressat (1966) devoted some space in his text to methods of computing both net and gross reproduction rates for actual cohorts.

Generation Rates from Children Ever Born

It has already been mentioned that the derivation of the gross reproduction rate from data on children ever born to women of completed fertility is quite direct. For example, the number of children ever born per 1000 women 45 to 49 years old as reported in Chile in 1960 was 3621. Multiplying this rate by the proportion of female births in 1960, 0.49166, gives 1780. This is a generation gross reproduction rate, albeit one that has been affected by any selective mortality and net immigration among the women of this cohort. To approximate the generation net reproduction rate, we multiply by the survival rate $\frac{L_{27}}{l_0}$ from a Chilean life table for 1940, when this cohort was roughly at its average age of childbearing. Numerically, 1780 times 0.63623 gives 1115, or NRR = 1.115.

Another approximate method was utilized in a report based on statistics for 1964 from the Current Population Survey (U.S. Bureau of the Census, 1966). This approximation is based on a "replacement quota." This quota is computed as follows:

1. From the sex ratio at birth, compute the total number of births corresponding to 1000 female births (e.g., for a sex ratio of 1050, this would be 2050). This is the number of births required for a cohort of 1000 women to replace itself if all of them survived through the childbearing period.
2. Divide this "gross" quota by the survival rate of women to the average age of childbearing. The quotient is the replacement quota. In the report cited, the average age of childbearing was taken as 27 and the survival rate as .963, so that the replacement quota is 2130 (= .2050 ÷ .963) births.

The survival rate used was based on a current life table; and again, as a refinement, a life table corresponding to the year when the cohort was 27 years old could be used instead. This would be about 20 years earlier, or 1944. The number of children ever born reported by women 45-to-49-years old in 1964 was 2437. This is 1.144 times the quota, indicating an approximate generation net reproduction rate of 1.144 for these women. An alternative calculation is 2437 (CEB) * .4878 (proportion female) * .963 (survival rate) = 1144, or 1.144 per woman.

OTHER TYPES OF REPRODUCTIVITY MEASURES

Incomplete Reproductivity of Cohorts

Very little of recent fertility is reflected in the reproductivity of cohorts that have completely passed through the childbearing age. It is usually this recent fertility that is of greatest interest, however, because we wish to get some clue concerning the effect of recent events upon the eventual size of completed families. Much can be learned by comparing the cumulative reproductivity of cohorts still in the midst of the childbearing period with that of earlier cohorts when these latter were at the same age.

We may then want to extrapolate, by some method or other, the net reproductivity of the cohort to the end of its childbearing period. Shortly after they began studying cohort reproductivity, both Woofter (1949) and Whelpton (1946) addressed this problem. Since that time, demographers have studied the problem of extrapolating the incomplete fertility of cohorts; but they have paid very little attention to adjusting the cumulative fertility to take account of future changes in mortality. This situation may reflect the fact that, in the United States and other Western countries, survival rates are high and fairly stable at the ages concerned. Moreover, in making population projections, demographers customarily treat future fertility and future mortality separately and are not explicitly concerned with reproductivity.

Nuptial Reproduction Rates

To the analysis of the possibilities latent in constant age-specific fertility and mortality rates Wicksell (1931), Charles (1938–1939), and other demographers have added constant age-specific first-marriage rates. The results are called the nuptial gross reproduction rate and the nuptial net reproduction rate. The nuptial gross reproduction rate is obtained by applying current marital fertility rates to the proportions of married women at each age that would result from current marriage rates. Charles (1938–1939, p. 681) defined this rate as "the number of girls who would be born on the average to each woman passing though the childbearing period if the specific fertility rates of single and married women and the marriage rate at each age for a given year were all to remain constant." The nuptial net reproduction rate is the number of girls who would be born on the average to a birth cohort of females if, in their lifetime, they were subject at each age to the specific fertility rates of single and ever-married women, the marriage rate, and the mortality for a given year.

An age-specific fertility rate may be viewed as a weighted average of rates specific for additional demographic variables such as duration of marriage and parity (Stolnitz and Ryder, 1949). The conventional reproduction rates are then implicitly a function of the existing composition by marital status, marital duration, parity, and other variables. Consequently, conventional net reproduction rates do not effectively remove the influence of the current population's demographic history. However, net rates adjusted for duration of marriage, parity, and so on may be strikingly different from unadjusted ones.

Spiegelman (1968, p. 286) expressed the nuptial net reproduction rate by the formula

$$R_o'' = \frac{1}{fl_o} \sum_{\omega 1}^{\omega 2} fi_x' \, fn_x \, fl_x + \frac{1}{fl_0} \sum_{\omega 1}^{\omega 2} fi_x'(1 - fn_x) fl_x \quad (17.54)$$

where $f \, l_x$ is the survival rate of women to age x, $f \, n_x$ is the corresponding age-specific proportion of married women in the current population, and fi_x' and fi_x'' are the fertility rates of married and unmarried women, respectively, at age x. The two terms represent marital and nonmarital reproductivity, respectively. In this formulation, the conventional net reproduction rate has simply been divided into these two components without any effect on the total.

A nuptial reproduction rate may also be computed by the use of a hypothetical standard population of women disaggregated by marital status, age, and duration of marriage. The standard population is developed by life table techniques ("multiple decrement" procedure) from an initial group of 100,000 single women who are then reduced by death rates, marriage rates, and rates of dissolution of marriage in a given period. The standard population gives the number of women at each age who are unmarried and, further, the number of married women at each age distributed by duration. We apply age-specific birthrates of unmarried women to the unmarried women of the standard population and birthrates of married women at each age and marriage duration to the married women of the standard population. The resulting cumulative product represents the total number of births that would be born to a cohort of women with the fertility rates of the country and year under examination and the marriage and mortality rates of the standard population.

Reproductivity of Marriage Cohorts

Another approach to reproductivity is to deal with cohorts of marriages (i.e., with the subsequent fertility and mortality of couples marrying in a given year). If this analysis is to be brought to bear on population replacement, however, one must go on to consider the proportion of each sex that eventually marries, age at marriage, dissolution of marriage by death or divorce, remarriage, and nonmarital fertility. Most of the computations of reproductivity for marriage cohorts have been confined to gross reproduction rates and have not been extended to net reproduction rates.

Using data collected in the 1946 Family Census in Great Britain, Glass and Grebenik (1954, pp. 136–137) estimated the net fertility of specific marriage cohorts as follows:

1. They constructed generation life tables for males and females.
2. For three marriage periods, they distributed marriages jointly by age of bride and by age of groom, using 5- and 10-year age groups, respectively.
3. For these joint age groups, they computed joint survival rates from the generation life tables.

4. The joint survival rates were applied to the corresponding duration-specific fertility rates from the family census tabulations.
5. These results were weighted by the age distribution of marriages for the corresponding cohort, so as to obtain the overall net fertility of that marriage cohort.

These calculations were regarded as a sort of exercise by Glass and Grebenik; they regarded their estimates of generation replacement rates based on birth cohorts as being more useful. "To go beyond these estimates of net marital fertility and to apply the concept of replacement means introducing the missing factors into the calculations—in this case, premarital mortality, the probability of first marriage, the chances of dissolution of marriage by divorce as well as death, the likelihood of remarriage, and the contribution of illegitimacy" (Glass and Grebenik, 1954, p. 278). Even though Glass and Grebenik did not then undertake these further calculations, their work called for very detailed tabulations, exceedingly complex calculations, and many assumptions. This major reliance on date of marriage rather than on the mother's date of birth arose, in part, from the fact that the latter item was not included on the birth certificate in England and Wales until 1938. Nonetheless, taking account of these factors regarding marriage has enriched the analysis of fertility trends and may have provided a better basis for projecting fertility into the future.

The use of marriage cohorts is one way of avoiding inconsistent male and female reproduction rates. These inconsistencies were discussed earlier, and the next section returns to this issue in dealing explicitly with male reproductivity.

Reproduction of the Male Population

Although both a mother and a father are involved in every birth, it has been customary to disregard this biological fact, and to measure fertility and reproduction primarily for females and only secondarily for males and the total population. Paternal rates could be used as easily as maternal rates, however, if adequate data were collected; and, in fact, reproduction rates have been calculated directly for males (Hopkin and Hajnal, 1947; Kuczynski, 1932; Tietze, 1939). A male reproduction rate, in terms of the number of sons sired by a "synthetic cohort" of males starting life together, was first published by Kuczynski (1932, pp. 36–38). The first male reproduction rates based on American data were published by Myers (1941).

Paternal reproduction rates are particularly useful in measuring the replacement of various social and economic groups defined by a characteristic of the father, such as occupation. To obtain the necessary fertility data for such characteristics of the father, census or survey data on men distributed by the number of their children are usually needed.

A previous section discussed the conventional replacement indexes, using all children and women. The numerator in Formula (17.37) could have been restricted to girls. Here we will illustrate formulas for replacement indexes for males and for both sexes combined. For males, then, the formula may be written

$$RI_m = \frac{P_{0-4}^m}{P_{15-54}^m} \div \frac{L_{0-4}^m}{L_{15-54}^m} \qquad (17.55)$$

where the two ratios are for the actual and life table male populations, respectively. Similarly, for both sexes, we may write

$$RI_t = \frac{P_{0-4}^t}{P_{15-54}^t} \div \frac{L_{0-4}^t}{L_{15-54}^t} \qquad (17.56)$$

These indexes are easy to compute because they call only for the age distribution and a life table; they are especially useful for countries where adequate birth registration does not exist. If only separate-sex life tables are available, the life table elements will have to be combined by weighting with sex ratios of births, when calculating the measure for both sexes.

The reproduction rate for men can also be computed using an extension of the own-children method presented in a previous section. The extension of the method requires matching children to fathers instead of mothers. The results, however, tend to be less precise than those for mothers, for two reasons. First, censuses normally do not ask men for the number of children they have fathered and the number still living. As this information is used for matching children to parent, the absence of it for fathers can increase the matching errors. Second, when a union is dissolved, children generally accompany the mother rather than the father. The own-children methodology can match such children to the mother but not to the (correct) father. This results in a larger volume of unmatched children. For these reasons, the own-children method produces fertility estimates that are less accurate for men than for women (Cho, Retherford, and Choe, 1986; Retherford and Sewell, 1986).

The procedure and equations for computing fertility estimates for men are the same as those for women given in Equations (17.45) to (17.48). However, men are substituted for women in the equations and the reproductive age range is extended by 5 years to age 54.

RELATIONSHIPS BETWEEN VITAL RATES AND AGE STRUCTURE IN ACTUAL AND STABLE POPULATIONS

The stable population model has been used (1) to assist in analyzing implications of vital rates, (2) to show the manner in which population would grow over time under specified conditions, (3) to estimate vital rates of populations of statistically underdeveloped countries, and (4) to evaluate, estimate, or correct age distributions of such countries. The first two uses of the stable population model are connected with its use in projections of populations for the more developed countries and also with studies of past trends designed to measure the relative contribution of the components of population growth to total growth, especially for age groups.

A fundamental kind of demographic analysis is the analysis of the relationship between changes in the components of population change and changes in age-sex structure. The types of analysis undertaken have been both historical and theoretical. The empirical, historical analysis has reached some surprising conclusions, upsetting, for example, intuitive beliefs concerning the relative importance of fertility and mortality in the aging of Western populations since the start of the 20th century. The basic approach, designed to isolate the contribution of each component to changes in age structure, is to "hold constant" one component at a time and to use the actual historical values of the other components.

First, demographic and mathematical analysis (Coale, 1956; Hermalin, 1966; Siegel, 1993; pp. 330–334) has shown, as Hermalin stated (pp. 451–452), that

1. The measure of mortality that [directly] determines the effect of changes in mortality on age composition and growth is the relative change in survival rates, rather than the relative change in the corresponding mortality rates.
2. Improvements in mortality can be made that have no effect at all on the age distribution. Specifically, a proportional increase in the probability of surviving a fixed number of years, which was the same at all ages, would leave the age distribution unaffected though it would increase the growth rate.
3. The effect of mortality improvement on the growth rate varies with the initial level of mortality as well as the magnitude of the change. A change in expectation of life at birth from 30 to 40 years, for example, will produce a higher growth rate than a change from 60 to 70 years, for a given level of fertility.

An analysis of changes in the American population by Hermalin (1966) reached conclusions that seem to apply to many other Western countries. He extended and refined the work of Valaoras (1950) and Lorimer (1951). Hermalin found that, for the first six decades of the 20th century in the United States,

1. Immigration had little effect on age composition and this effect was to make the population younger.
2. Changes in fertility have been the dominant influence in the age composition of the population, leading to a marked aging of the population.
3. Whether declining mortality rates have served to "age" or "young" the population depends on the measure one wishes to employ. On balance, however, declining mortality led to a somewhat younger population.

Coale (1956) had shown earlier that the reason why declining mortality had had so little effect on age structure lay in the U-shaped or J-shaped age pattern of historical improvements in survival rates. The reduction of mortality has had a considerable effect on population growth, however; the 1960 population of the United States is estimated to have been about one-third larger as the result of improvements in survival rates since 1900. Further improvements in mortality have had a smaller effect on overall population growth after 1960, and fertility and immigration have been the chief determinants of population growth. However, the effect of mortality on the *aging* of the population appears to have exceeded that of fertility in this later period (Preston, Himes, and Eggers, 1989).

Hornseth (1953) examined the contributions of these factors to the increase of the population 65 years old and over in the United States. He was interested in the absolute size of the elderly population rather than in the proportion of elderly persons in the total population. Hornseth concluded that the most important element in the sharp increase in the aged population during the *first* 50 years of the 20th century had been the rapid increase in births in the last half of the 19th century, and that the large immigration in the first quarter of the 20th century and the reduction in mortality ranked much lower and in that order. The role of these factors in the growth of the elderly population in the *second* half of the century appears to have been reversed.

Keyfitz (1968) made a number of important theoretical contribution in this area. We recall that Coale (1956) had shown that the effect of declines in mortality rates on age structure depends on the age-pattern of these declines. According to Keyfitz "a *neutral* change in mortality may be defined as one that is either constant at all ages or, without being constant, has an incidence such that the age distribution of the population, or at least its mean age, is unaffected. If the incidence of improved mortality is, on balance, at younger ages, then the age distribution becomes younger, and vice versa" (Keyfitz, 1968, p. 237). He derived an index, or set of weights, that tells us whether the change is neutral, and, if not, whether it falls on the younger or the older side of neutrality. Keyfitz also gave expressions for decomposing changes in the intrinsic rate of natural increase and the net reproduction rate into component factors. (e.g., intrinsic birth and death rates).

Although the stable population model has been valuable in understanding the long-term changes in the age structure, Preston, Himes, and Eggers (1989) have demonstrated that the stable model has only limited practical utility for figuring out what specific demographic conditions contribute to a population's growing older or younger at a particular time. Preston *et al.* studied aging in the United States and Sweden during 1980–1985 by using an alternative accounting system that views aging as a function of age-specific growth rates. Their analysis showed that declining mortality was the principal source of aging in both Sweden and the United States during 1980–1985. Migration has also played an important role in both countries. Recent trends in fertility have made a relatively small contribution to current trends in aging. Preston *et al.* (1989, p. 699) inferred that "the United States is currently an aging population not mainly because fertility has fallen from its historic levels . . . but because mortality has declined in the course of the 20th century in such a way as to increase the growth rate of the older population."

Preston and Coale (1982) and Preston (1986) also made some further important theoretical contributions. They have demonstrated that the equations that describe the relationships among demographic parameters in a stable population are a special case of a set of similar equations that applies to a closed population (Preston and Coale, 1982). Building on the earlier related works (Bennett and Horiuchi, 1981; Hoppensteadt, 1975; Langhaar, 1972; Trucco, 1965; Von Foerster 1959), Preston and Coale pointed out that there is a necessary relation in a closed population between a population's age structure at time *t*, its age-specific force of mortality at time *t*, and its set of age-specific growth rates at time *t*. The value of the new synthesis seems to lie in its power to illuminate the specific demographic conditions responsible for population aging (Preston *et al.*, 1989) and the legacy of past population dynamics (Horiuchi, 1995; Horiuchi and Preston, 1988). As indicated in a previous section, Preston used the new synthesis to show also that the intrinsic growth rate of a population is closely approximated by the average of age-specific growth rates below the age represented by *T*, the mean length of generation (Preston, 1986). An implication of the relation between the actual and intrinsic growth rates is that any disparity between the two must be primarily due to an unusual population growth pattern at ages above *T*.

Finally, some analysts have shown that the "no migration" assumption that restricts the application of stable/ stationary population theory is not necessary (Espenshade, Bouvier, and Arthur, 1982). Under certain conditions of net immigration and fertility, the theory can incorporate migration. As long as fertility is below replacement, conclude Espenshade *et al.*, a constant number and age distribution of immigrants (with fixed fertility and mortality schedules) lead to a stationary population. Neither the level of the net reproduction rate nor the size of the annual immigration affect the emergence of a stationary population.

FINAL NOTE

We round out the involved discussion on reproductivity in this chapter with some general observations.

1. The conventional reproduction rates may be easily and readily computed if the necessary statistics are available, but they must be interpreted with considerable caution

since they are hypothetical constructs involving many assumptions.

2. In areas of fertility decline or increase, statistics for real cohorts are required to answer the question whether the population is actually reproducing itself.

3. Stable population concepts have been found to have many useful applications. For example, in the less developed countries with an actual population that is roughly stable (constant fertility and mortality) or quasi-stable (constant fertility but moderately declining mortality), the model can be used to approximate the age structure and its basic demographic parameters. For the more developed countries, expecially those with little or no immigration/emigration, the stable population model, particularly in its stationary form, provides a useful generalized model of age structure of such a population and its basic demographic parameters.

4. Analysis of reproductivity now includes not only the computation and interpretation of the conventional measures, but measures adjusted for a variety of demographic factors, disaggregation of the rates for marital status, duration of marriage, order of birth, and other factors, measures for real birth cohorts and marriage cohorts, and measures of paternal reproductivity.

5. The electronic computer has opened up new possibilities for processing detailed input data on reproductivity and for deriving a wide variety of measures relating to replacement and to the stable population.

6. If the appropriate data on fertility are collected in a census or sample survey and public-use microdata files are prepared, whether for a more developed or less developed country, the methods of Chapter 16 may be applied to derive the measures of reproductivity described in this chapter. Measures based on aggregate data may also be derived from either the census or sample survey, as explained in this chapter.

References

Bennett, N. G., and S. Horiuchi. 1981. "Estimating the Completeness of Death Registration in a Closed Population." *Population Index* 42: 207–221.

Bongaarts, J., and G. Feeney. 1998. "On the Quantum and Tempo of Fertility." *Population and Development Review* 24: 271–291.

Böckh, R. 1884. *Statistisches Jahrbuch der Stadt Berlin.* (pp. 30–34).

Böckh, R. 1890. "Die Statistische Messung der Ehelichen Fruchtbarkeit." *Bulletin de l'Institut International de Statistique.* Volume V, First Section, pp. 165–166.

Brass, W. 1974. "Perspectives in Population Prediction: Illustrated by the Statistics of England and Wales." *Journal of the Royal Statistical Society A* 137: 55–72.

Charles, E. 1938–1939. "Differential Fertility in Scotland, 1911–1931." *Transactions of the Royal Society of Edinburgh* 59: 673–686.

Cheung, M-J. 1999. *Mortality, Morbidity and Population Health Dynamics.* Unpublished PhD thesis, Population Studies Centre, University of Waikato, Hamilton, NZ.

Cho, L-J., R. D. Retherford, and M. K. Choe. 1986. *The Own-Children Method of Fertility Estimation.* Honolulu: East-West Center.

Coale, A.J. 1955. "The Calculation of Approximate Intrinsic Rates." *Population Index* 21(2): 94–97.

Coale, A. J. 1956. "The Effect of Declines in Mortality on Age Distribution" (pp. 125–132). In *Trends and Differentials in Mortality.* New York: Milbank Memorial Fund.

Coale, A. J. 1957. "A New Method for Calculating Lotka's *r*—The Intrinsic Rate of Growth in a Stable Population." *Population Studies* 1: 92–94.

Coale, A. J. 1968. "Convergence of a Human Population to Stable Form." *Journal of the American Statistical Association* 63: 395–435.

Depoid, P. 1941. "Reproduction nette en Europe depuis l'origine de statistiques de l'état civile." *Etudes démographiques*, No. 1. Statistique générale de la France, Imprimerie nationale.

Dorn, H. F. 1950. "Pitfalls in Population Forecasts and Projections." *Journal of the American Statistical Association*, 45: 320–322.

Dublin, L. I., and A. J. Lotka. 1925. "On the True Rate of Natural Increase." *Journal of the American Statistical Association.* 20: 305–339.

Espenshade, T. J., L. F. Bouvier, and W. B. Arthur. 1982. "Immigration and the Stable Population Model." *Demography* 19(1): 125–134.

Gambia, Central Statistics Department. 1998. *Population and Housing Census 1993. Mortality Analysis and Evaluation. Volume 3,* Department of State for Finance and Economic Affairs. Banjul, The Gambia.

Glass, D. V., and E. Grebenik. 1954. "The Trend and Pattern of Fertility in Great Britain." In *Papers of the Royal Commission on Population,* Vol. VI, Part I, *Report.* Appendix 2 to Chapter 6, pp. 136–137.

Grabill, W. H., and L. J. Cho. 1965. "Methodology for the Measurement of Current Fertility from Population Data on Young Children." *Demography* 2: 50–73.

Hermalin, A. I. 1966. "The Effect of Changes in Mortality Rates on Population Growth and Age Distribution in the United States." *Milbank Memorial Fund Quarterly,* 44: 451–469.

Hopkin, W. A. B., and J. Hajnal. 1947. "Analysis of the Births in England and Wales, 1939, by Father's Occupation." (2 parts) *Population Studies* 1(2): 187–203, and l(3): 275–300.

Hoppensteadt, F. 1975. *Mathematical Theories of Populations: Demographics, Genetics, and Epidemics.* Philadelphia: Society for Industrial and Applied Mathematics.

Horiuchi, S. 1995. "The Cohort Approach to Population Growth: A Retrospective Decomposition of Growth Rates for Sweden." *Population Studies* 49: 147–163.

Horiuchi, S., and S. H. Preston. 1988. "Age-Specific Growth Rates: The Legacy of Past Population Dynamics." *Demography* 25: 429–442.

Hornseth, R. A. 1953. "Factors on the Size of the Population 65 Years and Older." Unpublished paper summarised in *Population Index* 19: 181–182.

Karmel, P. H. 1948a. "An Analysis of the Sources and Magnitudes of Inconsistencies Between Male and Female Net Reproduction Rates in Actual Populations." *Population Studies* 2: 240–273.

Karmel, P. H. 1948b. "The Relations between Male and Female Nuptiality in a Stable Population." *Population Studies* 1: 353–387.

Keyfitz, N. 1968. "Changing Vital Rates and Age Distributions." *Population Studies* 22: 235–251.

Keyfitz, N., and W. Flieger. 1968. *World Population: An Analysis of Vital Data.* Chicago: University of Chicago Press.

Kuczynski, R. R. 1932. *Fertility and Reproduction.* New York: Falcon Press.

Kuczynski, R. R. 1936. *The Measurement of Population Growth.* New York: Oxford University Press.

Langhaar, H. L. 1992. "General Population Theory in the Age-Time Continuum." *Journal of the Franklin Institute* 293: 199–214.

Lesthaeghe, R., and P. Willems. 1999. "Is Low Fertility a Temporary Phenomenon in the European Union?" *Population and Development Review* 25: 211–228.

Lorimer, F. 1951. "Dynamics of Age Structure in a Population with Initially High Fertility and Mortality." In United Nations, *Population Bulletin*, No. 1, pp. 31–41.

Lotka, A. J. 1907. "Relation between Birth Rates and Death Rates." *Science* (New Series) 26(653): 21–22.

Lotka, A. J. 1936. "The Geographic Distribution of Intrinsic Natural Increase in the United States, and an Examination of the Relation between Several Measures of Net Reproductivity." *Journal of the American Statistical Association* 31: 273–294.

Lotka, A. J. 1949. "Critique de certains indices de reproductivité. "Unpublished paper presented at the International Union for the Scientific Study of Population, Geneva.

Myers, R. J. 1941. "The Validity and Significance of Male Net Reproduction Rates." *Journal of the American Statistical Association* 36: 275–282.

New Zealand, Statistics New Zealand. 1998. *Demographic Trends 1997*. Wellington: Statistics New Zealand.

Ní Bhrolcháin, M. 1992. "Period Paramount? A Critique of the Cohort Approach to Fertility." *Population and Development Review* 18: 599–629.

Pacqué-Margollis, S., M. Guèye, M. George, and M. Thomé. 1993. *Gambian Contraceptive Prevalence and Fertility Determinants Survey*. Center for Applied Research on Population and Development, Sahel Institute, Bamako, Mali; Medical and Health Services Department and National Population Commission, Banjul, The Gambia; The Population Council, Bamao, Mali.

Pressat, R. 1966. *Principes d'analyse: cours d'analyse démographique de l'Institut démographie de l'Université de Paris*. Editions de l'Institut national d'études démographiques, Paris (pp. 51–59 and 113–123).

Preston, S. H. 1986. "The Relation between Actual and Intrinsic Growth Rates." *Population Studies* 40: 343–351.

Preston, S. H., and A. J. Coale. 1982. "Age Structure Growth, Attrition, and Accession: A New Synthesis." *Population Index* 48: 215–259.

Preston, S. H., C. Himes, and M. Eggers. 1989. "Demographic Conditions Responsible for Population Aging." *Demography* 26: 691–704.

Pullum, T. W. 1980. "Separating Age, Period and Cohort Effects in White U.S. Fertility, 1920–70." *Social Science Research* 9: 225–244.

Ratnayake, K., R. D. Retherford, and S. Sivasubramaniam. 1984. *Fertility Estimates for Sri Lanka Derived from the 1981 Census*. Matara, Sri Lanka: Department of Geography, Ruhuna University; Honolulu: East-West Population Institute, East-West Center.

Retherford, R. D., and L-J. Cho. 1978. "Age-Parity-Specific Birth Rates and Birth Probabilities from Census or Survey Data on Own Children." *Population Studies* 32: 567–81.

Retherford, R. D., L-J. Cho, and N. Kim. 1984. "Census-Derived Estimates of Fertility by Duration Since First Marriage in the Republic of Korea." *Demography* 38: 537–74.

Retherford, R. D., and W. H. Sewell. 1986. "Intelligence and Family Size Reconsidered." Paper presented at the Annual Meeting of the Population Association of America, San Francisco.

Ryder, N. 1956. "Problems of Trend Determination during a Transition in Fertility." *Milbank Memorial Fund Quarterly* 34: 5–21.

Ryder, N. 1959. "An Appraisal of Fertility Trends in the United States." In *Thirty Years of Research in Human Fertility: Retrospect and Prospect* (pp. 38–49). New York: Milbank Memorial Fund.

Ryder, N. 1964. "The Process of Demographic Translation." *Demography* 1: 74–82.

Ryder, N. 1986. "Observations on the History of Cohort Fertility in the United States." *Population and Development Review* 12: 617–643.

Siegel, J. S. 1993. *A Generation of Change: A Profile of America's Older Population*. New York: Russell Sage Foundation.

Spiegelman, M. 1968. *Introduction to Demography*, Rev. ed. (pp. 283–292). Cambridge, MA.: Harvard University Press.

Stolnitz, G. J., and N. B. Ryder. 1949. "Recent Discussion of the Net Reproduction Rate." *Population Index* 15: 114–128.

Thompson, W. S. 1931. *Ratio of Children to Women: 1920*. Census Monograph XI (pp. 157–174). Washington, DC: U.S. Bureau of the Census.

Tietze, C. 1939. "Differential Reproduction in England." *Milbank Memorial Fund Quarterly* 17: 288–293.

Trucco, E. 1965. "Mathematical Models for Cellular Systems; The von Foerster Equation." Parts I and II. *Bulletin of Mathematical Biophysics* 27: 285–304 and 449–470.

United Kingdom. 1949. Royal Commission on Population. *Report* (pp. 60–63 and 241–258). London: H. M. Stationery Office.

United Nations. 1983. *Indirect Techniques for Demographic Estimation. Manual X.* Population Studies No. 81, Department of International Economic and Social Affairs. New York: United Nations.

U.S. Bureau of the Census. 1966. "Fertility of the Population: June 1964 and March 1962." *Current Population Reports*. Series P-20, No. 147.

Valaoras, V. G. 1950. "Patterns of Aging of Human Populations." *The Social and Biological Challenge of Our Aging Population. Proceedings of the Eastern States Health Education Conference, March 31-April 1, 1949* (pp. 67–85). New York: Columbia University Press.

Vincent, P. 1946. "De la mesure du taux intrinsèque d'accroissement naturel dans les populations monogames." *Population* (Paris) 1: 699–712.

von Foerster, H. 1959. "Some Remarks on Changing Populations." Pp. 382–407 in F. Stohlman (Ed.), *The Kinetics of Cellular Proliferation*. New York: Green and Stratton.

Whelpton, P. K. 1946. "Reproduction Rates Adjusted for Age, Parity, Fecundity, and Marriage." *Journal of the American Statistical Association*. 41: 501–516.

Whelpton, P. K. 1954. *Cohort Fertility: Native White Women in the United States* (pp. 480–492). Princeton, NJ: Princeton University Press.

Whelpton, P. K., and A. A. Campbell. 1960. Fertility Tables for Birth Cohorts of American Women. In *Vital Statistics Special Reports. Selected Studies*. Vol. 51, Part I, U.S. National Office of Vital Statistics.

Wicksell, S. D. 1931. "Nuptiality, Fertility, and Reproductivity." *Scandinavisk Aktuarietidskrift*. 14: 125–157.

Woofter, T. J. 1947. "Completed Generation Reproduction Rates." *Human Biology* 19(3): 133–153.

Woofter, T. J. 1949. "The Relation of the Net Reproduction Rate to Other Fertility Measures." *Journal of the American Statistical Association* 44: 501–517.

Suggested Readings

Arthur, W. B., and J. W. Vaupel. 1984. "Some General Relationships in Population Dynamics." *Population Index* 50: 214–226.

Coale, A. J. 1957. "How the Age Distribution of a Human Population Is Determined." *Cold Spring Harbor Symposia on Quantitative Biology* 22: 83–89.

Coale, A. J. 1972. *The Growth and Structure of Human Populations*, Princeton, NJ: Princeton University Press.

Coale, A. J. 1985. "An Extension and Simplification of a New Synthesis of Age Structure and Growth." *Asian and Pacific Census Forum* 12: 5–8.

Espenshade, T. J., L. Bouvier, and W. B. Arthur. 1982. "Immigration and the Stable Population Model." *Demography* 19(1): 125–134.

Foster, A. 1990. "Cohort Analysis and Demographic Translation: A Comparative Study of Recent Trends in Age-Specific Fertility Rates from Europe and North America." *Population Studies* 44: 287–315.

Glass, D. V. 1940. *Population Policies and Movements* (pp. 383–415). New York: Oxford University Press.

Grabill, W. H., and L. J. Cho. 1965. "Methodology for the Measurement of Current Fertility from Population Data on Young Children." *Demography* 2: 50–73.

Hajnal, J. 1947. "The Analysis of Birth Statistics in the Light of the Recent International Recovery of the Birth-Rate." *Population Studies* 1(2): 137–164.

Hajnal, J. 1950. "Births, Marriages, and Reproductivity, England and Wales, 1938–1947." In *Papers of the Royal Commission on Population*, Vol. II, *Reports and Selected Papers of the Statistics Committee* (pp. 303–400). London, H. M. Stationery Office.

Hajnal, J, 1959. "The Study of Fertility and Reproductivity: A Survey of Thirty Years." pp. 11–37 in *Thirty Years of Research in Human Fertility: Retrospect and Prospect*. Papers presented at the 1958 Annual Conference, October 22–23, 1958, Part II. New York: Milbank Memorial Fund.

Hermalin, A. I. 1966. "The Effect of Changes in Mortality Rates on Population Growth and Age distribution in the United States." *Milbank Memorial Fund Quarterly* 44(4): 451–469, Part I.

Horiuchi, S. 1995. "The Cohort Approach to Population Growth: A Retrospective Decomposition of Growth Rates for Sweden." *Population Studies* 49: 147–163.

Hyrenius, H. 1948. "La mesure de la reproduction et de la accroissement naturel." Population (Paris)3: 271–292.

Karmel, P. H. 1947. "The Relations between Male and Female Reproduction Rates." *Population Studies* 1: 249–274.

Lam, D. 1984. "The Variance of Population Characteristics in Stable Populations, with Applications to the Distribution of Income." *Population Studies* 38: 117–127.

Lotka, A. J. 1936. "The Geographic Distribution of Intrinsic Natural Increase in the United States, and an Examination of the Relation Between Several Measures of Net Reproductivity." *Journal of the American Statistical Association* 31(194): 273–294.

Ní Bhrolcháin, M. 1987. "Period Parity Progression Ratios and Birth Intervals in England and Wales, 1941–1971: A Synthetic Life Table Analysis." *Population Studies* 41: 103–125.

Preston, S. H., C. Himes, and M. Eggers. 1989. "Demographic Conditions Responsible for Population Aging." *Demography* 26: 696–704.

United Nations. 1954. "The Cause of the Aging of Populations: Declining Mortality or Declining Fertility?" *Population Bulletin,* No. 4, pp. 30–38.

U. S. Bureau of the Census. 1944. *Sixteenth Census of the United States: 1940. Population. Differential Fertility: 1940 and 1910. Standardized Fertility Rates and Reproduction Rates.* Pp. 3–5; 39–40.

Wachter, K. W. 1988. "Age Group Growth Rates and Population Momentum." *Population Studies* 42: 487–494.

Whelpton, P. K. 1946. "Reproduction Rates Adjusted for Age, Parity, Fecundity, and Marriage." *Journal of the American Statistical Association* 41(236): 501–516.

Woofter, T. J. 1947. "Completed Generation Reproduction Rates." *Human Biology* 19(3): 133–153.

18

International Migration

BARRY EDMONSTON AND MARGARET MICHALOWSKI

Migration is the third basic factor affecting change in the population of an area; the other two factors, births and deaths, have been treated in earlier chapters. The importance of migration in affecting the growth and decline of populations and in modifying the demographic characteristics of the areas of origin and the areas of destination has long been recognized.

In particular, migration is an important element in the growth of the population and the labor force of an area. Knowledge of the number and characteristics of persons entering or leaving an area is required, together with census data on population size and vital statistics, to analyze the changes in the structure of the population and labor force of an area. The measurement and analysis of migration are important in the preparation of population estimates and projections for a nation or parts of a nation. Data on such factors as the sex, age, citizenship, mother tongue, duration of residence, occupation, and education of the immigrant facilitate an understanding of the nature and magnitude of the problem of social and cultural integration that occurs in areas affected by heavy immigration.

The sociologist is concerned with the social and psychological effects of migration on the migrant and on the populations of the receiving and sending areas and the acculturation and adjustment of migrant populations. The economist is interested in the relation of migration to the business cycle, the supply of skilled and unskilled labor, the growth of industry, and the occupational and employment status of the migrant. The legislator and political scientist are concerned with the formulation of policies and laws regarding immigration and, to a lesser extent, internal migration, and the enfranchisement and voting behavior of migrants.

CONCEPTS AND DEFINITIONS

Migration is a form of geographic or spatial mobility involving a change of usual residence between clearly defined geographic units. Some changes of residence, however, are temporary or short term, and do not involve changes in usual residence; these are usually excluded from the statistics on migration. They include brief excursions for visiting, vacation, or business, even across national boundaries. Other changes in residence, although permanent, are short-distance movements and, hence, are also excluded from the data on migration. In practice, such short-distance movements affect the scope of internal but not international migration. Thus, the term "migration" has in general usage been restricted to relatively permanent changes in residence between specifically designated political or statistical areas or between type-of-residence areas (for example, rural-to-urban movement).

For demographic purposes, two broad types of migration are identified: international migration and internal migration. The former refers to movement across national boundaries. It is designated as emigration from the standpoint of the nation from which the movement occurs and as immigration from that of the receiving nation. The term "internal migration" refers to migration within the boundaries of a given country.

The distinction between international and internal migration is not always clear because non-self-governing territories have some but not all of the characteristics of independent states. Depending on the purpose of the statistics and on the time of the migration and the characteristics of the migrant, such movements as those between the former occupied zones of postwar Germany, between Puerto Rico and the United States, or between France and the former

455

Algeria might be classified as either internal or international migration. A historical series for a country may include an area for part of the series that later becomes independent, and it may not be possible to reconstruct the figures from internal to international migration. For example, the migration statistics of the United Kingdom include the Irish Republic prior to April 1, 1923, and immigration statistics for Canada do not include Newfoundland prior to its confederation with Canada on March 31, 1949.[1]

The sources of data, the types of data available, and the techniques of estimation and analysis are sufficiently different for international and internal migration, however, to warrant separate treatment of these two types of migration. Therefore, two chapters are devoted to migration in this volume, the first to international migration and the second to internal migration.

Recognizing the importance of international migration and the need for statistics that would be comparable across countries, the United Nations developed a set of recommendations for the collection of such data.[2] A recommended general definition is that an *international migrant* is a person who changes his or her country of abode. A person's country of abode is "the country where that person spends most of his or her daily night rest over a period of a year." To facilitate the use of this definition in organizing national statistics, the United Nations also developed a taxonomy of international inflows and outflows of people. (See the section on data collection systems.)

Refugees represent a special class of immigrants who are admitted under special dispensation of the host country, ostensibly because they are victims of political persecution in their home country. Economic distress in the country of origin is not usually viewed as an acceptable basis of refugee status, although this and cultural pressures have been recognized at times. The 1967 United Nations Protocol on Refugees defined a *refugee* as any person who is outside the country of his or her nationality, is unable or unwilling to return to that country because of persecution or a well-founded fear of persecution, and is unable or unwilling to avail himself or herself of the protection of his or her own government. Claims of persecution may be based on the person's race, religion, nationality, or political opinion.

Other governmental entities and nongovernmental organizations may use the same definition, a more restrictive definition, or a broader definition. The U.S. definition of refugees set forth in the Refugee Act of 1980 conforms to the UN definition. The U.S. Committee for Refugees, which publishes an annual refugee survey, excludes persons as refugees who have opportunities for permanent settlement in their countries of asylum or elsewhere, even if they cannot return to their homelands because of continued fear of persecution. This describes the large groups of "refugees" who have settled in the United States, Canada, Western Europe, and Australia. In practice, because of the many instances of famine and civil war, the United Nations employs a more inclusive definition of refugee status than set forth in the 1967 protocol, one which does not require location outside the home country and a "well-founded fear of persecution." The United Nations, as well as many other organizations, refer to the large numbers of persons who have been uprooted but who remain within the borders of their own country as refugees, although they are more properly labeled *internally displaced persons*. The widening of the application of refugee status to include economic hardship, however, has tended to confound the concept and make it extremely difficult to assign numbers to this group. The more developed countries tend to combine refugees and *asylees*, the latter being those who are already in the host country and whose claim to refugee status has not yet been adjudicated.

Many countries are reluctant hosts (and a few are willing hosts) to a large number of *illegal immigrants* (also called illegal aliens and undocumented immigrants). The principal causes for their entry into the host country relate generally to more favorable economic and social conditions in the country of destination than in the country of origin. Some illegal immigrants have entered the host country by illegal entry (illegal border crossings that involve entrance without inspection). In the United States, these persons are referred to as EWIs (*entrants without inspection*). Others have entered with proper documents as visitors (e.g., tourists, students, and other temporary visitors) but stay beyond the approved period or otherwise violate the terms of their admission; these are referred to as *visa overstayers* in the United States. Finally, still other illegal immigrants, *entrants with false documents*, have entered with counterfeit, altered, or borrowed immigration documents. The members of the first group do not appear in any reports of the immigration service unless they are apprehended. Members of the second group are listed in the records of the immigration service; hence, it is possible to estimate their numbers approximately, if a nation's international statistics can provide an estimate of the number of temporary visitors who exit the country. Generally, it should be possible to make more accurate estimates for the second group than for the first group. The third group is similar to the first in being essentially absent from official records.

---

[1] Great Britain, *The Registrar General's Statistical Review of England and Wales, the Year 1963*, Part 11. Tables, Population, 1965. p. vi and table S. Canada, Statistics Canada, "Population Growth in Canada", by M. V. George, *1971 Census of Canada Profile Studies*, Catalogue 99–701, Ottawa: Statistics Canada.

[2] United Nations, *Recommendations on Statistics of International Migration. Revision 1. ST/ESA/STAT/SER.M/58/REV.1., 1998;* United Nations. *Recommendations on Statistics of International Migration.* Statistical Papers, Series M, No. 58, 1980.

The illegal border crossers and visa overstayers have accounted for most illegal immigrants in the United States in recent decades. Illegal border crossers make up about 60% of the total illegal immigrant population; visa overstayers contribute the remaining 40%.[3] Illegal immigration has figured prominently as a public issue in some Western countries in recent decades (Bean *et al.*, 1990), particularly the United States, France, and Germany. Hence, estimating their numbers and annual flows has also become an important task for the formulation of public policy relating to immigration into these countries. Estimates are also required for the purpose of preparing postcensal estimates and projections of each affected country and for the purpose of evaluating the completeness of census coverage. Governments also need to know the number of illegal immigrants in order to measure their economic effects and to administer various public programs in which they participate.

Temporary international migration has become a more important topic in recent years. Although temporary from the legal point of view, the movement plays an important role in international business and education. First, temporary migration is gaining importance as international or global business evolves. Managers increasingly look to a global labor market for persons with many of the skills and qualifications needed for their firms to compete successfully in the current business environment. Second, temporary migration is frequently of substantial duration, resembling more permanent migration, especially for migrants who stay longer than a "typical" period of time (i.e., 1 year for workers and a period of several years for students). In some cases, while living in a country, migrants are permitted to adjust their temporary status to a permanent one and then take up citizenship in their new country of residence. In the 1995–1996 fiscal year in the United States, 255,000 formerly temporary migrants became permanent residents— 28% of the 916,000 who became permanent residents.[4]

The major contributing factors that have influenced the development of temporary flows between Canada and the United States are the provision with 1989 Free Trade Agreement (FTA) for facilitating the migration of technical and managerial personnel in connection with cross-border investment and a long tradition of post-secondary education exchanges. An expansion of this agreement to include Mexico and the creation in 1994 of the new trade zone based on the North American Free Trade Agreement (NAFTA) further spurred labor migration among North American countries. NAFTA permits movement of people between the three countries to participate in business, trade, and investment activities and to provide professional services and expertise.

Following the official terminology of particular countries, people participating in this type of migration are called *nonimmigrants* (in the United States), *nonpermanent residents* (in Canada), and *temporary residents* (in Australia).

U.S. nonimmigrants are aliens admitted to the country for a specified purpose and temporary period but not for permanent stay. Tourists, who visit from a few days to several months, are the most numerous group of nonimmigrants to the United States. Second in volume are business persons coming to the United States to engage in commercial transactions. Other categories, much smaller in size, are foreign students and temporary workers.

Canadian nonpermanent residents are aliens with work or student permits and those who were admitted into the country on the basis of a special Minister of Citizenship and Immigration permit, which is issued for humanitarian reasons. The category also includes asylum seekers in Canada. Their share of the total group of nonpermanent residents ranged between 30 and 40% in the mid-1990s.[5] Although they have a different legal status, many asylum seekers in Canada are part of the foreign student population and labor force.

Australian temporary residents are people approved for nonpermanent stay in Australia for specific purposes that result in some benefit to Australia.[6] This definition directly relates entry of temporary migrants to benefits gained by Australia. The focus of approval is based on needs for skilled employment, the social and cultural situation, and international relations. This category includes top managers, executives, specialists, and technical workers, as well as diplomats and other personnel of foreign governments, longstay temporary business entrants, temporary workers who can remain with one employer up to 3 months and a total of up to 1 year ("working holiday makers"). These employed foreigners are generally sponsored by an Australian business or other organization to work in Australia as a skilled, paid employee. Australia has a separate category for students who are admitted into the country to undertake formal or informal study. In 1998, foreign students were slightly more numerous than temporary residents.

Later in this chapter, we provide some numerical evidence of the importance of temporary migrants in selected countries. We limit here the concept of temporary migrant to those foreigners who are in a country legally on a temporary basis but who have limited rights to work or study.

[3] U.S. Immigration and Naturalization Service, *Statistical Yearbook of the Immigration and Naturalization Service, 1997*. Washington, DC: U.S. Government Printing Office, 1999, p. 199.

[4] U.S. Immigration and Naturalization Service. *Statistical Yearbook of the Immigration and Naturalization Service, 1996*. Washington, DC: U.S. Government Printing Office, 1997.

[5] Canada, Statistics Canada, Demography Division, unpublished estimates.

[6] Australia, Department of Immigration and Multicultural Affairs. *Statistical Report: Temporary Entrants, 1997–1998*. Australia, 1999.

TYPES OF INTERNATIONAL MIGRATION

International migratory movements may be variously classified as temporary or permanent movements, movements of individuals and families or movements of whole nations or tribes, movements of citizens or aliens, voluntary or forced movements, peaceful or nonpeaceful movements, movements of civilians or military personnel, and movements for work, study, or other purposes.[7] A common basis of classification of immigration statistics, important because of its relation to the collection systems often employed, is the mode of travel or type of entry or departure point (i.e., sea, air, or land).

More permanent movements are generally made as a result of racial, ethnic, religious, political, or economic pressures, or a combination of these, in the area of emigration, and corresponding attractive influences in the area of immigration. Of the persons who enter or leave any country in a given period, only a portion may be permanent immigrants or emigrants. At the present time, much of the international mobility of labor, although of economic significance, is of a temporary nature. This movement would not properly be included in the statistics of (permanent) migration but in those of temporary movements: yet as noted previously, there is strong interest in such figures. This is particularly true on the European continent, where daily, weekly, or seasonal movements over national boundaries occur on a considerable scale. On the American continent, a similar case may be seen in the seasonal traffic across the border between Mexico and the United States and the daily commuting between Canada and the United States (e.g., between Detroit and Windsor) from home to factory or office.

Conquest, invasion, colonization, forced population transfers, and refugee movements represent types of mass movements. Conquest and invasion illustrate types of nonpeaceful mass movements of a tribe or nation (e.g., the invasion of Poland by the Germans in 1939, the invasion of Kuwait by the Iraqis in 1990). The racial and nationalistic ideologies of countries have been major factors in forced migrations of ethnic groups, tribes, or nations (e.g., the importation of black slaves into the Western Hemisphere during the 18th century and the transfer of millions of Jews to concentration camps in German-occupied territories during World War II). War and other political upheavals have resulted in numerous forced population transfers and refugee movements (e.g., the exchange of millions of persons between India and Pakistan after the partition of India in 1947, the exchange of population between Greece

and Turkey in the early 1920s, and the movement of Palestinian refugees to Jordan and the West Bank after the establishment of the state of Israel in 1948). The shipment of troops under military orders may be considered a type of forced migration.

Colonization is a movement of a tribe or nation, or of individuals and families for the purpose of settling in a relatively uninhabited area discovered or conquered by the "mother" country (e.g., the movement to the Western Hemisphere by Europeans during the colonial period and the movement to Australia by the British in the early part of the 20th century). Historically, another important type of international movement associated with colonization was the movement related to the coolie contract system, which was theoretically voluntary and often led to permanent settlement. It flourished in the 19th century on the initiative of the colonial powers, especially Great Britain, France, and the United States. For example, Britain recruited Asian Indians for labor on plantations and in mines in Burma, Ceylon, Fiji, East Africa, and various Caribbean Islands. France recruited Indochinese for New Caledonia. The United States recruited Chinese, Japanese, Filipinos, and other Asian nationals for work in Hawaii and continental United States, and Mexicans for work in the southwestern states.

COLLECTION SYSTEMS

Data on international migration may be derived from a variety of sources.[8] We distinguish five classes of migration data corresponding to these several sources:

1. Statistics collected on the occasion of the movement of people across international borders, mostly as by-products of the administrative operations of border control, and "passenger statistics" obtained from lists of passengers on sea or air transport manifests.
2. Statistics of passports and of applications for passports, visas, work permits, and other documents for international migration.
3. Statistics obtained in connection with population registers.
4. Statistics obtained in censuses or periodic national population surveys through inquiries regarding previous residence, place of birth, nationality, or citizenship.
5. Statistics collected in special or periodic inquiries regarding migration, such as a registration of aliens or a count of citizens overseas.

In addition, estimates of total net migration or net migration of particular groups (foreign born, aliens, civilian

---

[7] For a general typology of migration, see William Petersen, *Population*, 2nd ed., Collier-MacMillan Limited. Toronto, 1969, pp. 289–300; and William Petersen, "A General Typology of Migration," in Charles B. Nam (Ed.), *Population and Society*, Houghton-Mifflin, pp. 288–297.

[8] We are concerned here principally with sources of data relating to the volume of immigration and emigration. Vital statistics provide some information on international migration through questions on country of birth and citizenship asked of parents of newborn infants and for decadents.

citizens, armed forces) for particular past periods may be made on the basis of these or other statistics. For example, estimates of net migration of citizens of the country, including armed forces, may be made in some cases on the basis of counts or estimates of the citizens overseas. The various ways of estimating net migration by indirect methods will be treated in a subsequent section. In this section we treat the direct sources of migration statistics, describe the kinds of statistics provided, and consider their relation to one another.

The data collection systems listed do not usually provide adequate data for four special categories of inter-national migrants—temporary immigrants, refugees, emigrants, and illegal immigrants. In the final part of this section, we consider the availability of data for two of these migrant groups. Problems of estimating emigration and illegal immigration and are discussed in a later section.

Border Control Data and Administrative Data Sources

We consider here the first two of the sources of migration statistics listed earlier. Border control data are the most important source for the direct measurement of migration, if not the most frequently available of the various sources, and hence, this source is given most detailed consideration in this chapter. Statistics from the operations of border control relate to any of several systems of collecting migration statistics at the point of actual movement across international borders. These collection systems may distinguish "land border control statistics," which relate particularly to movement across land borders, from "port control statistics," which relate particularly to movement into and out of a country via its airports and seaports. The collection of information at land borders is much more difficult than at ports. This is due in large part to the heavier traffic, with only a small proportion of all travelers being classified as migrants. Declaration forms are not commonly used at land borders and, hence, types of travelers are not distinguished. Some national systems employ coupons detachable at points of departure and arrival from special identity documents issued to migrants by their own governments. They cover both land and port movement.

Collection of migration statistics on the basis of travel documents or special forms requires that the agency responsible for the operation have agents at the border points who are authorized to request the desired statistical information from international travelers. Passports and work permits carried by travelers crossing the borders may be used to facilitate obtaining data on some classes of travelers.

Normally a distinction is made between permanent and temporary migrants, on the one hand, and border traffic, on the other. Persons residing in border areas may make frequent moves across the border and employ special sim-plified travel documents (border crossing cards). Border traffic is then usually omitted from the principal tabulations on migration.

The types of administrative organization for collecting and compiling immigration statistics vary from that where the data are collected and published by a single immigration agency to that where several administrative agencies are involved in the collection of the migration data, with publication by each of them, one of them, or a central statistical office. The organization adopted varies with the situation in each country. Questionnaires may be required from travelers and migrants by such departments as immigration, police, customs, exchange control, or public health. The information obtained on these forms by the various authorities participating in border control activities may or may not be used for statistical purposes. It is still a major problem in many countries to eliminate duplication between the items of information collected and published by the different agencies and to ensure that these items cover the field without leaving serious gaps.

Instead of or in addition to statistics based on various travel documents or special report forms, the country may collect "passenger statistics," or "statistics of sea and transport manifests." Tabulations of "passenger statistics" are based on counts of names on copies of passenger lists furnished by steamship companies and airlines, or statistical returns compiled from them by the transportation companies. Migrants cannot usually be distinguished from other travelers (unless the ship or plane on which they are traveling is specifically an "emigrant transport"), and the classification of passengers in terms of previous country of usual residence or intended country of usual residence is not precise. Emigrants do not necessarily embark from their country of last usual residence or disembark at their country of intended usual residence. Often, transport manifests are checked in the border control operations against the identity papers of the travelers. This type of collection system is not applicable to land border movement.

Availability of Data

Statistics of international migration are now available for many immigration-receiving countries. For the most part, those countries collecting such data normally collect only the data they need for their own administrative purposes. For many countries, detailed statistics on migration are scattered through the publications of several national agencies. To facilitate use of these data, the United Nations assembled and published a bibliography of statistics on international travelers and migrants covering 24 selected countries over the 1925–1950 period.[9] Statistics for the

---

[9] United Nations, *Analytical Bibliography of Statistics on International Migration, 1925–1950*, Population Studies, Series A, No. 24, 1955.

period 1918–1947 are available in another United Nations publication.[10]

International compilations of migration data for the post–World War II period are available in various issues of the United Nations' *Demographic Yearbook* beginning with its 1949/1950 volume, the current frequency being biennial (even years). During the 1950-to-1970 period, the *Yearbook* occasionally presented national data on international arrivals and departures classified by major categories, long-term immigrants and emigrants according to age and sex, and country/area of intended residence, together with extensive explanations for the lack of comparability. Since 1970, the United Nations has compiled only national data on long-term immigrants and emigrants classified by age and sex. In addition, the United Nations recommends that it would be preferable for each country to present its migration statistics in a single, easily available publication. Publications of the Organisation for Economic Co-operation and Development (OECD) in Paris, particularly its annual *Trends in International Migration*, are useful sources of comparative information for its industrialized member countries.[11]

Collection of Border Control Data in the United States

Immigration data for the United States are available or may be developed from several sources. As indicated in Chapter 2, the principal source of data on immigration for the United States is the tabulations of the Immigration and Naturalization Service, resulting from the administrative operations of border control. One collection system secures tabulations of aliens on the basis of visas or other documents surrendered at ports of entry; these cover legal or "documented" movements. The Immigration and Naturalization Service also compiles data on passengers on air and seagoing vessels, "border-crossers," and crewmen. Several other federal agencies compile statistics of incidental use in the measurement of international movements (e.g., U.S. Census Bureau statistics on the volume of immigration reported in decennial censuses and Current Population Surveys). Finally, limited comparative or supplementary data for the United States may be obtained from the reports on immigration of various foreign countries.

History of Collection of Migration Data

Official records of immigration to the United States have been kept by a federal agency since 1820; official records of emigration have been kept only since 1908 and were dis-

continued in 1957. The Department of State, the Department of Labor, and other departments compiled the statistics before this work was shifted from the Department of Labor to the Justice Department in 1944, where it is now located.

The immigration office has issued a report on immigration each year since it was established in 1820, except for the years from 1933 to 1942, when the report appeared only in abbreviated form or was not published at all. Although these reports have been designed primarily to describe the administrative operations of the immigration office, an extensive body of statistical data on immigration has been included in them. The immigration statistics of the Immigration and Naturalization Service are now published in the annual *Statistical Yearbook of the Immigration and Naturalization Service*—replacing the earlier *Annual Report of the Immigration and Naturalization Service* and the *I and N Reporter* (a monthly or quarterly report). The yearbook is published with a lag of approximately 2 years following the close of the fiscal year (beginning October 1 and ending the following September 30) to which the figures relate; the yearbook is also available on the Immigration and Naturalization Service's website.

Since 1820, the official immigration statistics have changed considerably in completeness and in the basis of reporting. Reports for Pacific ports were not included until 1850. Entries of Canadians and Mexicans over the land borders first began to be reported in 1906. Until 1904 only third-class passengers were counted as immigrants; first- and second-class passengers were omitted. The current series on "immigrant aliens admitted" (i.e., aliens admitted for permanent residence in the United States) began in 1892 (except during 1895 to 1897); earlier, the figures related to "immigrant aliens arrived" or "alien passengers." Historical U.S. immigration statistics also include varying reports for aliens "admitted" (i.e., immigrants receiving permission to immigrate, although not necessarily arriving in the United States) and aliens "arrived" (i.e., immigrants actually disembarking in the United States).

Principal Collection Systems

The data on migration of the Immigration and Naturalization Service do not fit any simple classification scheme and, in fact, because of the complexity and variety of the data, more than one classification scheme is required to present them. We may identify two principal collection systems and a few subsidiary and supplementary ones. The first is confined to aliens and is based on visa forms surrendered by aliens at ports of entry and visas issued to aliens adjusting their status in the country to permanent residence. We will refer to the resulting data as "admission statistics." This system covers only a small part of the movement across the United States borders. The second principal collection system is more inclusive than the first and, in general, covers

---

[10] United Nations, *Sex and Age of International Migrants for Selected Countries, 1918–1947*, Population Studies, Series A, No. 11, 1953.

[11] Organisation for Economic Co-operation and Development, *Trends in International Migration—1999 Edition*, Paris: Organisation for Economic Co-operation and Development, 1999.

all persons arriving at and departing from U.S. ports of entry. We shall refer to these data as "arrival statistics." From a demographic point of view, however, these data have serious limitations not shared by the first classification, including lack of the more detailed information collected in admission statistics. This system covers three subsidiary groups: passengers arriving or departing principally by sea or air, land border crossers, and crewmen. The types of statistics compiled and their precise definitions vary from one period to another. The description given generally applies to the situation since World War II.

In general, "admission statistics" covers four classes: (1) aliens admitted to the United States as "immigrant aliens admitted," (2) aliens departing from the United States as "emigrant aliens departed," (3) aliens admitted as "nonimmigrant aliens admitted," and (4) aliens departing as "nonemigrant aliens departed." Immigrant aliens are nonresident aliens admitted to the United States for permanent residence (or with the declared intention of residing here permanently) or persons residing in the United States as nonimmigrants, refugees, or "parolees" who acquired permanent residence through adjustment of their status.

Table 18.1 provides an example of migration data derived from admission statistics (using data on "immigrant aliens admitted") for flows between Canada and the United States for the 1910-to-1997 period. The annual average migration from Canada to the United States for the overall period (36,500) exceeds the average flow from the United States to Canada (18,900) by about 17,600. This difference implies

that, overall, the migration to the United States from Canada has greatly exceeded the migration to Canada from the United States. The net migration from Canada to the United States was particularly large in the early decades of the 1900s. In recent years the net migration has been at lower levels, less than 10,000 per year, and in the 1970–1979 period, there was a net migration from the United States to Canada.

Emigrant aliens are resident aliens departing from the United States for a permanent residence abroad (or with the declared intention of residing permanently abroad). As stated, statistics on emigrant aliens were discontinued as of July 1, 1957, when persons departing were no longer inspected.

The first two classes, which are considered as the basic classes of alien migrants, are supplemented by two additional classes of alien admissions or departures—nonimmigrant aliens admitted and nonemigrant aliens departed. In general, nonimmigrant aliens are nonresident aliens admitted to the United States for a temporary period[12] or resident aliens returning to an established residence in the United States after a temporary stay abroad (i.e., an absence of more than 12 months). On the basis of recent experience, numerically the most important group of nonimmigrant aliens is the group, temporary visitors for pleasure. Other numerically important groups are returning residents, temporary visitors for business, transit aliens, temporary workers and industrial trainees, and students. Also included among nonimmigrant aliens are foreign government officials, exchange aliens, and members of international organizations.

"Nonemigrant aliens departed" are nonresident aliens departing after a temporary stay in the United States or resident aliens departing for a temporary stay abroad (i.e., for less than 12 months). Data on nonemigrant aliens were tabulated up to July 1, 1956; such figures are not available since that date. The classes of arrival and the classes of departure do not correspond to each other completely because the intended length of stay as declared does not always correspond to the actual length of stay. Thus, persons who are admitted as nonimmigrant aliens for a temporary stay but remain longer than a year are classified as emigrant aliens on departure, and aliens who are admitted for permanent residence but decide to depart within a year are classified as nonemigrant aliens on departure.

The second collection system provides "arrival" and "departure" statistics and, as stated, may be viewed as having three distinct components. The first component covers principally arrivals and departures by sea and air, the second covers "border crossers" (i.e., persons who cross frequently to or from Canada or Mexico), and the third covers crewmen. The statistics are classified by citizenship. The first component may also be designated as "passenger" statistics: the

TABLE 18.1 Migration between Canada and the United States, by Country of Last Permanent Residence: 1910 to 1997

Period	Canada to United States[1]		United States to Canada[2]	
	Numbers	Annual average	Numbers	Annual average
Total, 1910–1997	3,211,512	36,500	1,666,686	18,900
1910–1919	708,715	70,900	694,059	69,400
1920–1929	949,286	94,900	238,632	23,900
1930–1939	162,703	16,300	96,311	9,600
1940–1949	160,911	16,100	70,164	7,000
1950–1959	353,169	35,300	97,687	9,800
1960–1969	433,128	43,300	153,609	15,400
1970–1979	179,585	18,000	193,111	19,300
1980–1989	148,035	14,800	72,586	7,300
1990–1997	115,980	14,500	50,527	6,300

[1] U.S. Immigration and Naturalization Service, *Statistical Yearbooks.*
[2] Canada, Citizenship and Immigration Canada, Annual Reports.
Source: U.S. Bureau of the Census and Statistics Canada, *Current Population Reports*, Series P-23, No. 161, *"Migration between the United States and Canada,"* (for the period 1910–1988). Washington, DC: U.S. Census Bureau, 1992.

[12] More than 3 days if a Mexican resident is applying for admission and more than 6 months if a Canadian resident is applying for admission.

count is derived from lists of names on passenger manifests prepared by the airlines and steamship companies.

The second component, border crossers, represents principally a count, made by immigration inspectors at established points of entry, of persons entering the United States over its land borders with Canada and Mexico. It is a count of crossings; hence, the same persons may be counted more than once.

As mentioned earlier, in addition to the two basic classes of international migrants (immigrants or "new permanent arrivals" and emigrants departing or "permanent resident departures"), some statistical information is secured for several other groups of persons who cross the borders of the United States. Some account should be taken of these other groups in any assessment of the impact of immigration on the population, especially the *de facto* population: Particular attention should be given to the following categories:

1. *Nonimmigrant aliens.* Most nonimmigrants are tourists whose visits range from a few days to a few months. A large number of other nonimmigrants are business persons who stay typically for less than a few weeks. Nonimmigrants, however, also include several groups who usually stay in the United States for several months or more. Among them are government officials, students, and temporary workers as well as their spouses and children. In recent years, about 1 million nonimmigrants entered the United States annually.[13]

2. *Aliens paroled into the United States.* From time to time, special legislation allows political refugees to enter and remain in the United States outside the requirements of the Immigration Act. Refugees from Hungary after the supression of the revolution in 1956, refugees from the Communist regime in Cuba in the 1960s, and El Salvadorian refugees after the civil war in the 1990s were granted asylum by special legislation.

3. *Arrivals from and departures to the outlying areas of the United States.* In the basic tabulations on admissions, the United States and its outlying areas are treated as a unit. Data on movement between the United States and Puerto Rico are currently available, however, in the form of passenger statistics compiled by Puerto Rican authorities.

4. *U.S. government employees and dependents.* Direct data are not available for military personnel, but their number may be estimated from data on the number of U.S. military personnel overseas given in census reports and reports of the U.S. Department of Defense. Estimates for other Federal employees and their dependents may be made by a similar method using data from the Office of Personnel Management.

5. *Illegal entrants and unrecorded departures.*

6. *Aliens deported from the United States or departing voluntarily under deportation proceedings.* During 1997, 1,537,000 deportable aliens were located. Almost all deportees had entered the United States without inspection and were removed under conditions of voluntary departure.

Except for daily commuting, all of the movement across a country's borders, however temporary, should be considered demographically significant in relation to a *de facto* count of the population. The groups of migrants who would be considered consistent with a *de jure* count of the population would be much more restricted. In the case of the United States, these include members of the armed forces who are transferred into and out of the United States, all "immigrant aliens admitted" and "emigrant aliens departed," certain classes of "nonimmigrant aliens admitted" and "nonemigrant aliens departed" (such as students, resident aliens arriving and departing, some temporary visitors for business, and temporary workers and industrial trainees), "refugees" and "parolees" who enter under special legislation and may later have their status adjusted to that of permanent residents, and citizens who change their usual residence (i.e., move to or from outlying areas and foreign countries). The discontinuance of data collection for certain of these categories (emigrant and nonemigrant aliens departed) and the volatility of the figures for passenger movement (citizens arriving and departing, aliens departing) present a challenge in estimation of additions through immigration to both the *de jure* and the *de facto* populations. Procedures used currently by the U.S. Census Bureau are described further in the section on estimation of net migration.[14]

Quality of Statistics

The quality of data on international migration based on frontier control operations is generally much poorer than that of census counts or birth and death statistics. Such data tend to suffer from serious problems of completeness and international comparability. There are several reasons for the poor quality of the data. First, there are many forms of international movement, and they are not easy to define or classify. Second, the classification based on duration of stay or

---

[13] B. L. Lowell (Ed.), *Temporary migrants in the United States*, U.S. Commission on Immigration Reform, Washington, DC, 1996.

[14] For other discussions of U.S. immigration statistics and population estimates, see U.S. Immigration and Naturalization Service and U.S. Bureau of International Labor Affairs, 1999, *The Triennial Comprehensive Report on Immigration*; B. Edmonston (Ed.), 1996, *Statistics on U.S. Immigration: An Assessment of Data Needs for Future Research.* Washington, DC: National Academy Press; U.S. Census Bureau, "National and State Population Estimates: 1990 to 1994," by E. Byerly and K. Deardoff. 1995, *Current Population Reports*, P25–1127. Washington, DC: U.S. Census Bureau.

purpose of migration depends on statements of intentions, and the actual movements may not correspond to these statements of intentions. Next, the mere counting of persons on the move is extremely difficult, especially when a country has a very long boundary that is poorly patrolled. It is certain that many international migrants enter or leave a country unrecorded under these conditions. Controls over departures are usually less strict than over arrivals so that statistics of emigration are more difficult to collect and less accurate than statistics of immigration. This type of problem is illustrated by unrecorded movement over the Mexican border to the United States. Between 1990 and 1997, 9.8 million aliens were apprehended for being in the United States illegally: more than 90% of these were Mexicans who were apprehended by district offices along the Mexican border. Most of those apprehended, however, had been in the United States for less than a few weeks.[15]

The complexity and diversity of definitions and classification systems used in different countries also seriously impede international comparability of migration statistics. In the recent review of different data collection systems, the United Nations concluded that, where available, data from population registers are most satisfactory for the measurement of international migration.[16] Border collection data, which have been traditionally considered a major source of information on migration flows and which in the past formed a base model for the United Nations recommendations on international migration statistics, are judged rarely to provide the best measures of international migration flows. Nevertheless, the United Nations advises that this source should be explored by individual countries inasmuch as various data sources present different opportunities for the implementation of the definitions of long-term and short-term migrants that the United Nations recommends.

Data from Population Registers

A fully developed system of national population accounting would cover movement into and out of a country as well as births, deaths, and internal movements. Under this system, international movement, including arrivals into the country and departures from it, is simply a special type of change of residence that must be reported to the local registrar. Reporting of change of residence is generally exempted from declaration if the duration of absence is short. At present, this is a relatively uncommon source of migration statistics. Few countries in the world, mainly countries of western and northern Europe, have a system of continuous population registration from which it is possible

to derive satisfactory immigration and emigration statistics. These include Austria, Belgium, Denmark, Finland, Germany, Iceland, Israel, Italy, Japan, Liechtenstein, Luxembourg, the Netherlands, Norway, Spain, Sweden, Switzerland, and Taiwan.[17] In addition, Eastern and Central European countries as well as those of the Commonwealth of Independent States (the successor states of the former Union of Soviet Socialist Republics) are reviewing their population registers with the goal of improving the possibilities of collecting adequate statistics on international migration through that data source.

Census or Survey Data

Censuses and national surveys offer useful data on a variety of important aspects of international migration. In the United States, the decennial census and the Current Population Survey contain limited direct information on the volume of immigration. Combined with other data, this information, serves as a basis for making estimates of net immigration for intercensal periods.[18] Limited data for the United States may also be obtained from the censuses of various foreign countries. We consider, first, data on prior residence and nativity, giving attention to data on the year of arrival for the foreign-born population.

Residence Abroad at a Previous Date

Censuses or national sample surveys may, in effect, provide information on immigration during a fixed period prior to the census or survey date. From a theoretical point of view, the type of immigration data obtained in a census or survey differs in several respects from data compiled in connection with the administrative operations of border control. The latter represent counts of arrivals and departures during a given period. The former represent a classification of the population living in the country at a particular date according to residence inside or outside the country at some previous specified date. The census data on migration cover only persons who were alive both at the census date and at the previous specified date. Hence, the number of "immigrants" reported in the census or survey is deficient. A count of immigrants during the period between the previous date

---

[15] Pages 164–165, Table 61, in U.S. Immigration and Naturalization Service, *Statistical Yearbook of the Immigration and Naturalization Service, 1997*, Washington, DC: U.S. Government Printing Office 1999.

[16] See footnote 2.

[17] R. E. Bilsborrow, G. Hugo, A. S. Oberai, and H. Zlotnik, *International Migration Statistics: Guidelines for Improving Data Collection Systems*, Geneva, Switzerland; International Labour Office, 1997; Michel Poulain, "Confrontation des statistiques de migrations intra-européenes: vers plus d'harmonisation," *European Journal of Population* 9:353-3.

[18] A description of the census concepts and definitions and selected decennial census data on the foreign-born population of the United States can be found in C. Gibson and E. Lennon, "Historical Census Statistics on the Foreign-Born Population of the United States: 1850 to 1990," *Population Division Working Paper* No. 29, Washington, DC: U.S. Bureau of the Census, 1999. www.census.gov.

TABLE 18.2   Number of Persons 5 Years of Age and Older Abroad 5 Years Prior to the Census,
as Reported in the Censuses of Population for Canada and the United States:
Around 1980 and 1990

Country	Date of census	Number abroad	Total population[1]	Percentage abroad	Reported immigration during period[2]
Canada[3]					
	May 14, 1996	928,700	28,846,800	3.2	1,176,100
	June 4, 1991	913,300	27,296,900	3.3	873,800
	June 3, 1986	463,900	25,309,300	1.8	499,800
	June 3, 1981	556,200	24,343,200	2.3	590,400
United States					
	April 1, 1990	4,821,100	230,445,800	2.1	2,927,000
	April 1, 1980	3,931,800	210,232,300	1.9	2,496,000

[1] Population 5 years of age and older.
[2] Reported immigration for 5-year period preceding the census.
[3] Total population data collected on a 100% basis.

Source: Canada: Statistics Canada, "Interprovincial and International Migration in Canada" (91-208); "Mobility Status and Interprovincial Migration," *Census 1986* (93-108); "Mobility and Migration," *Census 1991* (93–322); www.statcan.ca/english/census96/apr14/mobil.htm. United States: Immigration and Naturalization Service, *Immigration and Naturalization Service Yearbook*, 1975 to 1990, Washington, DC: INS. Bureau of the Census, *1980 Census of Population*, Volume 1, *Characteristics of the Population*, PC 80-1-C1., *U.S. Summary*, Table 80, Washington, DC: Bureau of the Census, 1981. Bureau of the Census, *1990 Census of Population, Social and Economic Characteristics, United States*, 1990 CP-2-1, Table 18, Washington, DC: Bureau of the Census, 1993.

and the census date does not include the number of children born abroad during this period who immigrated into the country, immigrants who died (in the country of immigration), or immigrants who departed during the period (e.g., returned to the country of origin). Even though the census or survey figures exclude the departures of those who arrived during the migration found, they cannot properly be viewed as estimates of net immigration because they fail to allow for the departure of persons who were living in the country prior to the migration period. For example, U.S. census data usually represent immigration for the 5 years prior to the census; hence they relate only to "survivors" 5 years old and over at the census date. Censuses or surveys cannot readily provide any separate information on emigration for a country.

Data on prior residence abroad are available only for the brief periods before each census or survey in which a question on "previous residence" is asked. On the other hand, the census or survey data on immigration are likely to provide comprehensive information for certain types of migrants (e.g., aliens and citizens, civilians and military personnel). In addition, certain demographic characteristics of the "immigrants" (especially age, sex, and marital status) and their socioeconomic characteristics may be readily tabulated.

In spite of the simplicity of the question and its value in providing data on the volume of immigration and the characteristics of immigrants, these types of data are available for few countries. These data are illustrated in Table 18.2, using Canada and the United States as examples. Data relating to the volume of immigration and the characteristics of immigrants, based on a question relating to previous residence, are given in the reports on internal migration derived from the census. A category of "persons abroad" is shown in the published tables as one of three major categories of migration status (namely, nonmigrant, internal migrant, and immigrant). This category refers to persons living in the country at the census date who reported that their place of residence at a specified previous date was in a foreign country (or in an outlying area for the United States).

Nativity

Census data on nativity, particularly on the foreign born, serve both as direct indicators of the volume and characteristics of immigrants and as a basis for estimating them. Data on the foreign born are especially valuable for measuring migration when "border control" data on migration are lacking, are of poor or questionable quality, or are irregularly compiled. Some important kinds of classifications may not be available in the regular immigration tabulations, but may appear in the census data. Hence, measurement of the volume of immigration of certain groups or of certain characteristics of immigrants may be possible only from census data. Where similar material is available from both sources, the census data may aid in validating the indications of the "regular" immigration data. For most countries, including the United States, the body of census information relating to the foreign-born population is more extensive and detailed than the immigration data collected at time of arrival.

A classification of the U.S. population by nativity has been made since 1850 in connection with the census question on "State or country of birth." The number of schedule inquiries relating to the foreign-born population increased with each succeeding census after 1850 until the peak in 1920, when there were questions, among others, on country of birth, mother tongue, and year of immigration. In each year since 1850, the foreign born were tabulated at least by age and sex.

Volume of Immigration

Census tabulations of the foreign-born population provide information on "net lifetime immigration" of the foreign-born (i.e., net immigration over the lifetime of the present population). Census data on the foreign born do not provide an indication of the volume of immigration during any particular past period of time. Moreover, even if the data are tabulated by year or period of immigration, foreign-born persons who returned to live abroad or who died prior to the census date are excluded. At the older ages, both of these factors may have an important impact in reducing the numbers of foreign born far below the numbers of immigrants who may have originally entered the country. Surviving immigrants are counted only once, even though they may have moved to the country in question more than once in a lifetime.

In sum, the census figures provide information specifically on the balance of immigration and emigration of foreign-born persons during the last century, diminished by the number of deaths of immigrants in the country prior to the census date. Thus,

$$P_F = (I_F - E_F) - D_F \qquad (18.1)$$

$$(I_F - E_F) = P_F + D_F \qquad (18.2)$$

where P_F refers to the foreign-born population, I_F and E_F refer to immigrants and emigrants born abroad, respectively, and D_F refers to deaths of foreign-born persons in the country. It should be particularly noted that the quantity $I_F - E_F$ does not represent net migration in the usual sense, because the emigrants here consist solely of former immigrants ("return migrants"), and movement of native persons is entirely excluded.

Characteristics of Immigrants

Much information regarding the geographic and residence distribution and the demographic, social, and economic characteristics of immigrants can be obtained from census data on the nativity of the population. The characteristics of the surviving immigrants are reflected in the current composition of the foreign-born population with respect to such variables as age, sex, country of birth, mother tongue, occupation, and educational attainment. Some of these characteristics (e.g., place of residence or occupation)

undergo changes after the date of arrival, others (e.g., country of birth, year of immigration, or mother tongue) should not change at all, and still others change in measurable ways (age) or may change little or not at all (educational attainment for adults). However, the distributions are affected by differences in the emigration and mortality of immigrants in different categories as well as errors of reporting and coverage. Hence, the adequacy of the foreign-born data in reflecting the characteristics of immigrants varies with the characteristic.

The distinctive geographic distribution of immigrants and the influence of immigration on the geographic distribution of the general population may be inferred from a comparison of the geographic distribution of the native, foreign-born, and total populations of a country.

Differences in the fertility level of immigrants and the nonimmigrant population may be ascertained from differences between the foreign-born and the native populations in the general fertility rate or in the average number of children ever born.

For studies of the impact of immigration on a country's social and economic structure, census data on the foreign born are particularly valuable. Census data giving detailed tabulations of the foreign-born population by area of present residence and country of birth permit the calculation of indexes of the relative concentration of various ethnic groups among the immigrants in various parts of a country.[19] Census data on the detailed occupation and country of birth of the foreign born provide the basis for measuring the tendency of various ethnic groups among the immigrants to concentrate in certain lines of work. Census data on the proportion of foreign born in the labor force, classified by occupation and industry, are also useful in measuring the minimal impact of immigration on a country's labor force and economy over a broad period of time.[20]

Studies of the changes in the social and economic status of immigrants and of the cultural assimilation of immigrants involve comparisons of the characteristics of the immigrants and the general population and observation of changes in the immigrants over time. The use of census data is necessary or preferable in such studies over the use of border control statistics. Census data must also be employed where the immigrants are to be classified according to their status with respect to characteristics that necessarily change or that may change after immigration (e.g., citizenship, employment status, occupation, language spoken), or where the immigration data are not tabulated in terms of the characteristic (e.g., educational attainment). Greater comparability

[19] See Table 14 in E. P. Hutchinson, *Immigrants and Their Children, 1850–1950*, 1950 Census Monograph, New York. John Wiley & Sons, 1956.

[20] J. P. Smith and B. Edmonston (Eds.), *The New Americans: Economic, Demographic, and Fiscal Effects of Immigration*, Washington, DC: National Academy Press, Chapters 4 and 5, 1997.

in the classification is probably achieved by use of census data, even where these conditions do not apply.[21]

Timing of Immigration

There is specific interest in the timing of immigration. Knowledge solely of the number and characteristics of immigrants over the indeterminate past is of limited practical value in migration analysis. How long the immigrant has been in the host country is relevant to the immigrant's assimilation, including the immigrant's opportunities for acquiring citizenship there or learning the language of the host country. We should like to know the number and characteristics of immigrants at least for intercensal periods. Inferences regarding intercensal trends in the volume of migration or the characteristics of migrants cannot safely be made directly from a series of census figures for the total number of foreign-born persons or from a series of derived measures based on statistics for the foreign born.

Tabulations by year of immigration would indicate directly the volume of immigration (for surviving immigrants who had not emigrated) for particular past periods. Such statistics are useful in refining migration analyses based on date or place of birth. Each immigrant would be asked the date of arrival in the country of present residence or the date of departure from the country of birth. This method requires an additional question relating to date of migration on the questionnaire. The data may be tabulated in terms of year or *period of immigration* or *duration of residence* in the country of immigration.

A question on year of immigration or number of years of residence of the foreign-born population was asked in the decennial censuses of the United States from 1890 to 1930, omitted from the censuses of 1940 to 1960, and then restored to the questionnaire in 1970.[22]

Miscellaneous Other Sources

Other sources of immigration data are given brief treatment here because they are relatively uncommon. These include special surveys, registrations of aliens, tabulations of permits for work abroad, and tabulations of passports and visas issued.

The occasional special surveys may involve inquiries relating to the nativity, previous residence, or citizenship of the resident population. Surveys may be taken of the country's citizens living abroad. The figures obtained from such a survey would represent net lifetime emigration of a country's citizens including the natural increase of these emigrants but excluding former citizens who had become naturalized in the countries of emigration.

Occasional, periodic, or continuous special registrations of aliens may be carried out. In several countries (e.g., the United States until 1981, Japan, and New Zealand), aliens are required to register annually. The count of alien registrants in a single registration may be interpreted as representing lifetime net surviving alien immigrants, that is, total immigration of aliens, less deaths, emigration, and naturalizations of aliens prior to the record date. Obviously, such data tell us nothing about the timing of migration without tabulations by year of entry (or duration of residence) or age. Typically, country of nationality is obtained rather than country of last permanent residence. A registration of aliens was conducted in the United States in 1940 by the Immigration and Naturalization Service in accordance with the requirements of the Alien Registration Act of 1940, and an annual registration was conducted between 1951 and 1981 in accordance with the requirements of the Internal Security Act of 1950 and the Immigration and Nationality Act of 1952.[23]

Foreign workers may have the obligation to secure a work permit, as in most European countries, the United States, Canada, and Australia. As measures of immigration, the data are compromised by emigration and by the fact that not all permits are used. Moreover, the procedure followed in renewing permits may be ill adapted to the recording of international movements. The statistics of alien identity cards also have this defect.

Counts of passports and visas issued by a particular country relate to citizens and aliens, respectively. There is no way of knowing exactly what percentages of passports and visas are actually used, or if used, when the traveler departs or returns and how many trips the traveler makes. Tabulation of the number of travelers listed on a passport or visa is required to determine the possible number of travel-

---

[21] Examples of the use of census tabulations on the foreign born in the study of cultural and ethnic assimilation of immigrants are given in: R. D. Alba, J. R. Logan, B. J. Stults, G. Marzan, and W. Zhang, "Immigration Groups in the Suburbs: a Reexamination of Suburbanization and Spatial Assimilation," *American Sociological Review* 64(3): 446–460, June 1999; J. E. Coughlan, D. J. McNamara, *Asians in Australia: Patterns of Migration and Settlement,* South Melbourne, Australia: MacMillan Education, 1997; S. M. Lee, "Do Foreign Birth and Asian Minority Status Lower Canadian Women's earnings," *Canadian Studies in Population* 26(2): 159–182, 1999; D. Myers and S. W. Lee, "Immigration Cohorts and Residential Overcrowding in Southern California," *Demography* 33(1): 51–65, February 1996; and E. Ng and F. Nault, "Fertility among Recent Immigrant Women to Canada, 1991: an Examination of the Disruption Hypothesis," *International Migration Review* 35(4): 559–578, 1999.

[22] In the 1890 and 1900 censuses, the question was the number of years of residence of the foreign born in the United States. The tabulation in 1890 was limited to alien males 21 years old and over.

[23] Each alien, regardless of date of immigration or length of stay, was required to register in January of each year and provide information regarding his or her address, sex, date of birth, country of birth, citizenship, date of entry into the United States, permanent or temporary status, and current occupation. Tabulations of aliens who reported under the Alien Address Program were shown in the *Annual Report of the Immigration and Naturalization Service* and the *I and N Reporter.* They distinguished permanent residents from nonpermanent residents and showed numbers of aliens by nationality and state of current residence.

TABLE 18.3 Temporary Immigrants in Australia, Canada, and the United States for Various Years

Country	Temporary immigrants	Foreign-born population	Total population	Percentage of	
				Foreign-born population	Total population
Australia					
June 1998	196,700[1]	4,322,600[2]	18,532,200[2]	4.6	1.1
Canada					
June 1991	223,400	4,566,300	26,994,000	4.9	0.8
May 1996	166,700	5,137,800	28,528,100	3.2	0.6
United States					
April 1990	537,900	19,767,300	248,709,900	2.7	0.2

[1] Total includes 93,986 foreigners in Australia for temporary work-related stay and 102,689 foreign students.
[2] Estimated as of June 1997.
Source: United States: Bureau of Census, unpublished data. Gibson, C. J. and E. Lennon, "Historical Census Statistics on the Foreign-born Population of the United States: 1850 to 1990," *Population Division Working Paper*, No. 29. Washington, DC: U.S. Bureau of the Census, 1999. Statistics Canada, "Immigration and Citizenship," Ottawa: Supply and Services Canada, 1992, *1991 Census of Canada*, Catalogue number 95-316.; and unpublished data. Department of Immigration and Multicultural Affairs, *Statistical Report: Temporary Entrants*, 1997–1998, 1999. Australian Bureau of Statistics, *Estimated Resident Population by Country of Birth, Age and Sex, Australia*, Catalogue 3221.0.

ers involved. Although passports and visas have severe limitations for measuring the actual volume of international migration, they may be useful in evaluating data or estimates from other sources.

Special Categories of International Migrants

We consider next mainly two types of international migrants—temporary immigrants and refugees—that were not fully described in the data collection systems discussed earlier.

Temporary Immigrants

Census data on the foreign born should not be perceived as information on immigration flows into the country. The foreign-born population in the census includes a variety of categories of international migrants such as persons who do not have a legal status (e.g., illegal, undocumented, or irregular-status immigrants), legal permanent residents, humanitarian admissions (e.g., refugees and asylees), and persons who have a right to residence for a limited period only (e.g., temporary immigrants). The 1990 census data for the United States show that there were 19.7 million foreign-born persons in the country (8% of the total population). The census does not provide data on the different categories of immigrants. However, estimates produced using the census data demonstrate that the great majority of them, 17.8 million or over 85%, were living in the country legally.[24] Among legal residents, 38% were naturalized citizens, and 45% were permanent resident aliens. The remaining 1.9 million were persons admitted to the country on a

humanitarian basis (who can, after 1 year, adjust their status to permanent residence) or as temporary immigrants (e.g., students, business persons, teachers, and other workers). Depending on the category, foreign-born persons have different access to labor markets. Access to employment can range from unrestricted to limited-to-nongovernment jobs only (e.g., noncitizens), and from permission to be with a designated employer (e.g., some temporary immigrants) to lack of right to employment (e.g., spouses of some temporary immigrants). Foreign-born persons also have different access to services in the area of health and social assistance. For these reasons, conclusions drawn from the research based on the census data on the foreign born require attention to the internal diversity of this population.

In the United States, it is estimated that the number of temporary immigrants exceeded one-half million in 1990 (see Table 18.3). They represented almost 3% of the foreign-born population and 0.2% of the total population. In comparison, in Canada, the temporary immigrant population was only half the size of the U.S. temporary immigrant population but relatively more important, representing almost 5% of Canada's foreign-born population. Canada's temporary immigrants as a share of the foreign-born population decreased to just over 3% in 1996. In Australia, the temporary immigrant population was about 200,000 in 1998, accounting for nearly 5% of Australia's foreign-born population.

Apart from being a selective population in terms of skills, temporary immigrants are also different from recent "traditional" (i.e., permanent) immigrants in their geographical origins. Census data from the United States and Canada

[24] M. Fix and J. S. Passel, 1994, *Immigration and Immigrants: Setting the Record Straight*. Washington, DC: The Urban Institute.

TABLE 18.4   Top 10 Countries of Temporary Immigrants and Recent Permanent Immigrants
to the United States and Canada: 1990 and 1991

United States:

	Temporary immigrants[1]				Recent permanent and illegal immigrants 1987–1991		
Rank	Place of birth	Number	Percentage	Rank	Place of birth	Number	Percentage
1	Japan	62,800	12.2	1	Mexico	729,400	31.8
2	People's Republic of China	31,600	6.1	2	Philippines	113,700	5.0
3	Korea	27,800	5.4	3	El Salvador	89,800	3.9
4	India	24,900	4.8	4	Korea	76,900	3.4
5	Taiwan	23,400	4.6	5	People's Republic of China	74,200	3.2
6	Canada	22,400	4.4	6	Viet Nam	70,600	3.1
7	U.S.S.R.	21,500	4.2	7	U.S.S.R.	67,900	3.0
8	United Kingdom	19,300	3.8	8	India	59,600	2.6
9	Philippines	17,100	3.3	9	Dominican Republic	54,100	2.4
10	Mexico	16,800	3.3	10	Nicaragua	52,100	2.3
	Subtotal (10 countries)	267,600	52.0		Subtotal (10 countries)	1,388,300	60.6
	Other countries	246,600	48.0		Other countries	902,600	39.4
	Total	514,200	100.0		*Total*	2,290,900	100.0

Canada:

	Temporary immigrants				Recent permanent immigrants 1988–1991		
Rank	Place of birth	Number	Percentage	Rank	Place of birth	Number	Percentage
1	United States	18,200	8.1	1	Hong Kong	60,900	10.3
2	Philippines	15,100	6.8	2	Poland	41,200	6.9
3	Sri Lanka	12,700	5.7	3	People's Republic of China	38,600	6.5
4	Hong Kong	11,000	4.9	4	Philippines	35,400	6.0
5	People's Republic of China	10,900	4.9	5	India	31,700	5.3
6	United Kingdom	9,300	4.2	6	Lebanon	23,900	4.0
7	Iran	8,200	3.7	7	Viet Nam	22,700	3.8
8	Trinidad and Tobago	7,000	3.1	8	United Kingdom	22,700	3.8
9	Japan	6,800	3.0	9	Portugal	18,400	3.1
10	India	5,800	2.6	10	United States	18,300	3.1
	Subtotal (10 countries)	105,000	47.0		Subtotal (10 countries)	313,800	52.9
	Other countries	118,400	53.0		Other countries	279,200	47.1
	Total	223,400	100.0		*Total*	593,000	100.0

[1] Persons who "came to stay" in the United States in 1987 or later.

Source: Statistics Canada, 1991 Canadian Census of Population unpublished data; United States Bureau of Census estimates based on the 1990 U.S. Census of Population and unpublished data.

provide evidence of these differences (see Table 18.4). More than half of the 500,000 temporary immigrants in the United States were born in 10 countries. Recent permanent and illegal immigrants (i.e., those who came to stay during the 3-year period prior to the census) are even more concentrated in terms of their origins. Over 60% were born in the 10 top countries of birth. The same countries are major countries of origin for temporary, permanent, and illegal immigrants. Their relative numerical importance, however, within the top 10 countries differs. Mexico ranks tenth among the countries of origin for temporary immigrants and ranks first among permanent and illegal immigrants. Philippines is the

ninth country among the 10 top origins for temporary immigrants but the second for permanent and illegal immigrants. The other difference between geographical origins of the two immigrant categories is the importance of the "more developed" countries as their origins. There were four such countries among the major countries of origin for temporary immigrants to the United States—Japan, Taiwan, Canada, and United Kingdom—but none are among the top 10 for the permanent or illegal immigrants.

Canada's temporary immigrants are more diversified than those in the United States. Less than 50% of Canada's temporary immigrants are from the 10 top countries of birth. The 10 top source countries for temporary immigrants and permanent immigrants also differ in Canada. Nevertheless, as for the United States, temporary immigrants are distinctive when compared with permanent residents. Data on temporary immigrants show the importance for Canada of the mutual migratory flows with the United States. Persons born in the United States were the most numerous group of temporary immigrants in Canada, representing 8% of the total. In the United States, Canadians, although comparable in numbers, were ranked as the sixth group among temporary immigrants, constituting only 4% of the total.[25]

Refugees and Aslyees

Refugees are viewed as temporary immigrants because the first priority for the United Nations is to repatriate refugees and, when that is not practical, to provide a safe haven for the refugees in neighboring countries until they can return to their homeland. Humanitarian values of the host country have been the basis of accepting refugees, rather than the political, economic, and cultural reasons that underlie the admission of permanent immigrants.

The United Nations High Commission for Refugees (UNHCR) recognizes a broad group of *persons of concern*—that is, all those persons who benefit from the organization's protection and assistance, including refugees, returnees, and internally displaced persons, as well as some other groups in the resident population. Table 18.5 presents data compiled by UNHCR (2000) for 1999 for refugees and other persons of concern to UNHCR. It shows a total of 22 million refugees and other persons of concern, including 12 million refugees, mostly in Asia, Africa, and Europe; 1 million asylum seekers, mainly in North America and Europe; 3 million returnees, mainly in Europe, Africa, and Asia; 4 million internally displaced persons, nearly all in Asia and Europe; and 3 million other persons of concern, mostly in Europe and Africa. These data were obtained from the host countries, except where UNHCR had to substitute a more reasonable figure on the basis of its own evaluation.

Several factors make it difficult to measure the number of refugees and asylees with any precision. First is the different interpretations given to the concept "refugee," as explained earlier. The inconsistent application of the concepts "refugee" and "internally displaced person" clouds the statistical picture, producing multiple and contradictory estimates of the size of the affected populations. Next

---

[25] Starting with the 1991 census, Canada made statistics on temporary immigrants available directly from the census. In addition, estimates independent from census sources, using information on admissions of foreigners from Citizenship and Immigration Canada, are produced by Statistics Canada on an annual basis for years between censuses (see Statistics Canada, *Annual Demographic Statistics, 1998*, catalogue no. 91-213-XPB), 1999.

TABLE 18.5 Refugees and Other Persons of Concern to the United Nations High Commissioner for Refugees (UNHCR): End–1999

Type and region	Estimate (in 1000s)	Type and region	Estimate (in 1000s)
ALL TYPES, TOTAL	22,258	*Returned refugees*	2510
Africa	6,251	Africa	934
Asia	7,309	Asia	618
Europe	7,285	Europe	952
Latin America	90	Latin America	6
Northern America	1,242	Northern America	—
Oceania	81	Oceania	—
Refugees	11,675	*Internally displaced persons*	3969
Africa	3,523	Africa	641
Asia	4,782	Asia	1725
Europe	2,608	Europe	1603
Latin America	61	Latin America	—
Northern America	636	Northern America	—
Oceania	65	Oceania	—
Asylum-Seekers	1,182	*Others of concern*	2922
Africa	61	Africa	1092
Asia	24	Asia	160
Europe	473	Europe	1649
Latin America	2	Latin America	21
Northern America	606	Northern America	—
Oceania	16	Oceania	—

— Less then 500.

Source: United Nations High Commissioner for Refugees, *Refugees and Others of Concern to UNHCR: 1999 Statistical Overview*. Geneva, Switzerland: UNHCR, July 2000.

are the serious practical problems of securing counts of refugees, given their tremendous numbers, the large areas involved, and the often remote and hostile places where they are located. Once the refugees have been settled in concentrated areas and programs of assistance have been set up, it becomes much more practicable to compile demographic data. Even so, problems remain if the refugees settle among persons of similar ethnicity, move about in the country of asylum or even across international borders, register more than once, or try to frustrate counting efforts. Moreover, a refugee population, like any population, is dynamic, with members dying, getting married, having children, and moving from place to place; hence, any demographic data on refugees quickly become outdated. Another problem is that the record system for demographic events may be inadequate and employ substandard practices. The data on asylees from countries of origin will usually be inconsistent with data on returnees from countries of destination, and the data on refugees and asylees, even for the more developed countries, will not be comparable because of differences in definitions, format, time interval, and detail. Some host governments announce inflated estimates of the number of refugees, asylees, or returnees on their territory with the hope of securing additional funds; others do so with the hope of winning public support for reducing the number of refugees and asylees admitted. As a result, the barriers to the compilation of good refugee statistics are considerable and the quality of the data varies greatly.

Estimates of the number of refugees have been based on visual assessment, extrapolations of health surveys, and special registration systems. If resources are adequate, conditions of stability prevail, and there is support from the host government, UNHCR can secure detailed information of good quality about refugees. Under conditions of stability, a registration or census (or sample survey of the total population) can be attempted in such camp settlements. An important parameter critical for evaluating refugee conditions is an estimate of mortality. Retrospective surveys of surviving family members are a possible tool for measuring population size and mortality, but are subject to recall bias. The major limitation for the measurement of mortality with retrospective surveys in refugee populations, however, is the selective mortality of whole villages and families, leaving no members behind to report on the deaths that occurred. Even surveys that attempt to collect mortality data for relatives, however, may fail to uncover mortality to distant relatives or villages if there are no surviving members.

Many notable refugee movements have occurred in the past few centuries, some being massive exoduses to neighboring countries as a result of wars. We note in particular the vast refugee movements associated with and following World War II; and the large displacements of tribal populations in sub-Saharan Africa in the 1990s, particularly from Rwanda to Zaire; the forced movements of Serbs, Croats, and Bosnians within former Yugoslavia and from it to several other European countries such as Italy, Sweden, and Germany; and of Afghans to Pakistan and Iran. Secessionist movements, insurgencies, civil wars, and domestic unrest were widespread in the last decade of the 20th century. Many nations (e.g., France, Canada, United Kingdom, Spain, Sri Lanka, Sudan, Burundi, Turkey, and Iraq) contain ethnic or religious groups seeking independence, and some citizens have already left these countries claiming refugee status. It is extremely difficult to quantify most of these population movements.

The United States admits persons as refugees under numerical ceilings for specific regions of origin, set by law and administrative regulations, with the possibility for the refugees to secure adjustment to permanent resident status after 1 year. The United States covers most refugee admissions by separate legislation. Since World War II, large groups of refugees have been admitted to the United States from Hungary and other former Soviet bloc countries, Cuba, the former Soviet Union, Vietnam and other countries of Indochina, Iraq, and Bosnia. The admission ceiling for 1997, set by President Clinton in consultation with the Congress, was 78,000. In fiscal year 1996–1997, about 69,000 refugees arrived in the United States and, in addition, about 10,000 persons were granted asylum. A small additional group was admitted as *parolees*, temporary admissions whose entry is deemed to be in the public interest or justified on humanitarian groups although they may appear to be inadmissible.

COMBINATION, EVALUATION, AND ESTIMATION OF INTERNATIONAL MIGRATION STATISTICS

As we have suggested, adequate data on immigration, emigration, or net migration are often not available for a country, even though a number of direct sources of data bearing on international migration for that country may exist. One method of expanding the quantity of information on migration for a given country is to refer to the migration statistics for other countries furnishing or receiving migrants from the country under study. This approach depends on the fact that any international movement involves two countries—the country of immigration and the country of emigration—and therefore may be reported by two countries. Because overlapping as well as complementary information may be available, this approach also serves as a basis of evaluation of migration data. Let us imagine two arrays presenting statistics of migration between all the pairs of countries in the world. One such array would give the statistics reported by the country of immigration, and the second would give the statistics reported by the country of emigration. If immigration and emigration were completely and consistently reported for all the countries of the world, the two arrays would agree or nearly agree. For example, the total immigration reported for a given country would coincide with the emigration reported by all the other countries that furnish emigrants to the country in question. Likewise, the total emigration reported for a given country would coincide with the immigration received by all other countries from the country under consideration.

In practice, of course, migration statistics are lacking for many countries and the statistics available are often incomplete and inconsistent. The lack of comparability of the migration statistics from one country to another is a major problem. The types of movement counted as migration and the categories of persons classed as migrants will differ from country to country, partly because there are many different ways of defining a migrant and the categories of migration and because there are many different systems for collecting the data. A small part of the difference in the counts of migrants reported by different countries for a given year may result from the fact that there is a gap in time between departure from one country and arrival in another. Some travelers may change their destination or not be admitted to a country; moreover, births and deaths may occur during the moves. There is also a problem in the statistical identification of the country of origin as well as destination. Although the statistics usually relate to country of last permanent residence, in some cases they relate to country of birth, country of last previous residence, or country of citizenship and these may differ from one another.

In spite of the limitations mentioned, the binational reporting of international migration provides a useful, if not always fully adequate, basis for evaluating the accuracy of migration data for a country or for filling in missing data, particularly on emigration.

The possibility of combining and comparing statistics from different countries applies to census statistics as well as to statistics of border control. Suppose we are trying to estimate the net total movement to or from a country or a particular stream and its counterstream. We can approximate the true "net lifetime immigration" for a country somewhat more closely, for example, if we try to "balance" the census count of the foreign-born population in the country with the census count of persons in other countries who had been born in the country in question. In practice, it is usually possible to identify at least those few countries that are principal destinations of the emigrants of some country or that are the principal origins of the immigrants of that country. Many national censuses identify a long list of countries of origin for their foreign born. If the principal movement from a country is to one or two countries only, examination of the census reports of only these few countries is required to measure net migration for the country of emigration. For example, 744,830 persons living in the United States in 1990 were born in Canada, and 249,080 persons living in Canada in 1991 were born in the United States; these figures indicate a "net surviving emigration" of approximately 496,000 persons from Canada to the United States up to 1990. With census statistics as with regular immigration statistics, there may be a serious problem of comparability resulting from differences in the nature of the census questions, the type of census (*de facto* or *de jure*), and the dates of the two censuses.

Estimation and Evaluation of Net Migration

In view of the lack of adequate statistics on migration for many countries and many periods, it is often necessary to estimate the volume of migration. Although there is interest in separate figures on immigration and emigration, the available methods do not permit making adequate estimates of immigration or emigration separately; only the balance of migration can be satisfactorily estimated by these methods. For the most part, the same methods are useful in evaluating the reported migration data as for deriving alternative estimates of net migration. Accordingly, we treat the procedures for the estimation and evaluation of net migration jointly in the present section.

Intercensal Component Method for the Total Population

Approximate estimates of net immigration can often be derived for intercensal periods by use of census data on the total population. The general formula for estimating the total volume of net immigration in an intercensal period involves a rearrangement of the elements of the standard intercensal component equation:

$$(I - E) = (P_1 - P_0) - (B - D) \tag{18.3}$$

Net immigration is derived as a residual; as previously stated, estimates of immigration and emigration cannot be obtained separately. The method simply involves subtracting an estimate of natural increase ($B - D$) during the period from the net change in population during the period ($P_1 - P_0$). If the data used to arrive at the estimate are exact, an exact estimate of the balance of all in-movements and out-movements is obtained. Because, however, the census counts and vital statistics as recorded are subject to unknown degrees of error, the residual estimates of net immigration may be in substantial error. In addition, the relative error of net immigration may be considerable when the amount of migration is small.

Estimates of intercensal net migration for Canada and the United States derived by the residual method are shown in Table 18.6. For the United States during the 1980–1990 period, population increase amounted to 22,164,000 (i.e., 248,710,000 minus 226,546,000) and natural increase amounted to 17,205,000; hence, the estimated net migration was 4,959,000 (i.e., 22,164,000 minus 17,205,000). For Canada during the 1981-to-1991 period, population increase amounted to 3,220,100 (i.e., 28,120,100 minus 24,900,000) and natural increase amounted to 1,975,000; hence, the estimated net migration was 1,245,000 (i.e., 3,220,000 minus 1,975,000). Estimated net migration into either Canada or the United States is less than recorded arrivals because of emigration.[26]

Intercensal Cohort-Component Method

The cohort-component method is applicable to the estimation of net migration, for age (birth) cohorts, for the total population and for segments of the population that are fixed over time (e.g., sex, race, and country of birth) or relatively fixed over time (e.g., mother tongue and religion). This procedure involves the calculation of estimates for age cohorts on the basis of separate allowances for the components of population change (deaths only for all age groups born by

---

[26] In the United States, recorded arrivals are inflated in the 1980–1990 period by IRCA legalizations: some are recorded as new permanent residents in the period although they may have entered the United States prior to 1980 and, therefore, may have been counted in the 1980 census.

TABLE 18.6 Calculation of the Estimated Intercensal Net Migration by the Residual Method, for Selected Countries: About 1980 to 1990

Item	Canada[1]	United States
(1) First census date	July 1, 1981	April 1, 1980
(2) First census population	24,900,000	226,546,000
(3) Second census date	July 1, 1991	April 1, 1990
(4) Second census population	28,120,000	248,710,000
(5) Net change, (4)-(2)	3,220,000	22,164,000
(6) Births	3,806,000	38,032,000
(7) Deaths	1,831,000	20,827,000
(8) Natural increase, (6)-(7)	1,975,000	17,205,000
Estimated net migration:		
(9) Residual method, (5)-(8)	1,245,000	4,959,000
Recorded migration		
(10) Gross arrivals based on migration records	1,381,000	5,808,000

[1] The July 1 population is a population estimate using the census count of population adjusted to July 1 and for net census undercoverage.

Source: Canada: Statistics Canada, *Annual Demographic Statistics, 1994*, Ottawa: Statistics Canada, 1995, Tables 1.1, 3.3, 3.4, and 4.1.

United States: U.S. Census Bureau, "U.S. Population Estimates by Age, Sex, Race, and Hispanic Origin: 1980 to 1991," *Current Population Reports*, P25-1095, Tables 1 and 2, Washington, DC: U.S. Government Printing Office, 1993. Immigration and Naturalization Service, *Statistical Yearbook of the Immigration and Naturalization Service*, annual reports from 1980 to 1990, Washington, DC: Immigration and Naturalization Service, 1982 to 1993.

the starting date and births and deaths for the newborn cohorts). The compilation of death statistics for birth cohorts to allow for the mortality component is so laborious, however, even where the basic statistics on death are available, that survival rates are normally used instead. The survival rates may be life-table survival rates or so-called national census survival rates. (Census survival rates are discussed in Chapters 13 and 19).

One formula for this purpose covering age (birth) cohorts other than those born during the intercensal period is

$$(I_a - E_a) = P_a^1 - sP_{a-t}^0 \qquad (18.4)$$

where I_a and E_a represent immigrants and emigrants in a cohort defined by age a at the end of the period, P_a^1 the population at this age in the second census, P_{a-t}^0 the population t years younger at the first census, and s the survival rate for this age cohort for an intercensal period of t years. That is, s is a simplified representation of $_nS_{a-t}^t$ for the cohort aged a to $a + n$ years at the end of period t. For the newborn cohorts, the formula is

$$(I_a - E_a) = P_a^1 - sB \qquad (18.5)$$

where B represents the births that occurred in the intercensal period.

Table 18.7 illustrates the procedure for estimating the intercensal net migration of males between 1980 and 1990 for age cohorts for the United States by use of life-table survival rates. Ten-year survival rates for 5-year age groups are first computed from the 1985 U.S. life table by the formula:

$$_5S_x^{10} = \frac{_5L_{x+10}}{_5L_x} \qquad (18.6)$$

where $_5S_x^{10}$ represents the probability of survival from age x to x + 5 for a 10-year period. These rates (col. 3) are applied to the population at the first census (col. 1) to derive an estimate of the expected survivors 10 years older at the later census date. The difference (col. 4) between the population at the second census (col. 2) and the expected population (col. 1 × col. 3) is an estimate of net migration.

These calculations represent an application of the conventional survival-rate procedure. One defect of this method is that it has a tendency to understate or overstate the number of (implied) deaths during the intercensal period. In an "emigration" country, the initial population in an age cohort overstates the average population exposed to risk during the following intercensal period, and the terminal population understates the average population exposed to risk, because some persons emigrate. A more satisfactory estimate of (implied) deaths and net migration may be made by adjusting for the mortality of migrants during the reference period. This adjustment is carried out in two ways in Table 18.7. In the first method, we proceed by (1) "surviving" the initial population to the date of the second census (col. 1 × col. 3), (2) calculating the corresponding "forward" estimate of net migration (col. 4 = col. 2 − (col. 1 × col. 3)), (3) "reverse surviving" or "younging" the population at the second census to the data of the first census by dividing it by the survival rate (col. 2 / col. 3), (4) calculating the corresponding "reverse" estimate of net migration from the "younged" population (col. 5 = col. 2 / col. 3 − col. 1), and (5) averaging the two estimates of net migration in cols. 4 and 5.[27] The formulas are

Forward estimate: $M_1 = (I_a - E_a)_1 = P_a^1 - sP_{a-t}^0$ (18.7a)

Reverse estimate: $M_2 = (I_a - E_a)_2 = \dfrac{P_a^1}{s} - P_{a-t}^0$ (18.7b)

Average estimate: $M_3 = \dfrac{M_1 + M_2}{2}$ (18.7c)

[27] The bias in the estimates of net migration derived by the life-table survival-rate method was first described by J. S. Siegel and C. H. Hamilton, who proposed averaging the forward and reverse methods as a solution for the problem. See their paper "Some Considerations in the Use of the Residual Method of Estimating Net Migration," *Journal of the American Statistical Association* 47(259): 475–500, Sept. 1952.

TABLE 18.7 Calculation of Estimates of Net Migration of Males for Age (Birth) Cohorts, by the Life-Table Survival Method, for the United States: 1980–1990

Age (years) 1980	Age (years) 1990	Census, April 1, 1980[1] (1)	Census, April 1, 1990[1] (2)	10-Year life-table survival rate[2] (3)	Estimated net immigration Forward estimate[3] (2) − [(1) × (3)] = (4)	Reverse method[4] [(2) ÷ (3)] − (1) = (5)	Average method[5] [(4) + (5)] ÷ 2 = (6)	Refined method[6] Square root of survival rate √(3) = (7)	Refined method[6] Net immigration (4) ÷ (7) or (5) × (7) = (8)
All ages	All ages	127,122,329[7]	121,239,418	(X)	5,044,505	5,356,991	5,200,748		5,165,165
Births, 1985–1990	0–4	8,505,711	9,392,409	0.987316	994,584	1,007,362	1,000,973	.993638	1,000,952
Births, 1980–1985	5–9	8,563,457	9,262,527	0.985016	827,385	839,971	833,678	.99248	833,654
0–4	10–14	8,362,009	8,767,167	0.996402	435,241	436,813	436,027	.998199	436,026
5–9	15–19	8,539,080	9,102,698	0.995094	605,506	608,491	606,999	.997544	606,997
10–14	20–24	9,316,221	9,675,596	0.989227	459,738	464,744	462,241	.994599	462,235
15–19	25–29	10,755,409	10,695,936	0.984499	107,248	108,937	108,093	.992219	108,089
20–24	30–34	10,663,231	10,876,933	0.982889	396,162	403,059	399,611	.991408	399,595
25–29	35–39	9,705,107	9,902,243	0.980941	382,108	389,532	385,820	.990425	385,802
30–34	40–44	8,676,796	8,691,984	0.975887	224,408	229,952	227,180	.987870	227,163
35–39	45–49	6,861,509	6,810,597	0.965825	183,580	190,076	186,828	.982764	186,800
40–44	50–54	5,708,210	5,514,738	0.947425	106,636	112,554	109,595	.973358	109,555
45–49	55–59	5,388,249	5,034,370	0.916806	94,391	102,957	98,674	.957500	98,581
50–54	60–64	5,620,670	4,947,047	0.871444	48,950	56,172	52,561	.933512	52,436
55–59	65–69	5,481,863	4,532,307	0.809704	93,622	115,625	104,623	.899836	104,043
60–64	70–74	4,669,892	3,409,306	0.725970	19,105	26,316	22,710	.852039	22,423
65–69	75–79	3,902,955	2,399,768	0.614085	3,020	4,918	3,969	.783636	3,854
70–74	80–84	2,853,547	1,366,094	0.475989	7,837	16,465	12,151	.489920	11,359
75+	85+	3,548,413	857,698	0.226218	54,982	243,047	149,014	.475624	115,601

[1] U.S. Bureau of the Census, *1980 Census of Population*, Vol, I, *Characteristics of the Population*, chapt. B. PC 80-1-B1, Table 43, *1990 Census of Population*, 1990 CPH-2.

[2] Calculated from U.S. official life tables for 1985.

[3] Formula 18.7a

[4] Formula 18.7b

[5] Formula 18.7c

[6] Formulas 18.9a or 18.9b.

[7] Total includes births, 1980 to 1990.

X: Not applicable.

The calculation of deaths to the cohorts born during the period requires special treatment. Exposure is less than the full intercensal period (10 years in Table 18.7). The survival rate for the cohort under 5 years of age at the end of the decade is 0.987316, and the survival rate for the cohort 5 to 9 is 0.985016. The forward and reverse survival procedures are then applied in the same way as for the older cohorts, the births in the two 5-year periods being taken as the initial population for the first two age groups. The estimation of deaths for cohorts born during the decade (i.e., under 5 and 5 to 9 years of age of age in this example) are calculated from the midperiod life-table survival rates on the basis of the following formulas:

$$\frac{L_{0-4}}{5l_0} \quad \text{and} \quad \frac{L_{5-9}}{5l_0} \qquad (18.8)$$

As we stated, the averaging of the forward method (equation 18.7a) and the reverse method (18.7b) is designed to adjust for the bias in the implied estimates of deaths of immigrants and emigrants that characterize each method. The averaging process produces improved estimates of net migration as compared with the conventional forward method, especially at the ages above 60, where survival rates are lower and the forward and reverse estimates tend to differ most. This method too has its limitations, however, in that two separate estimates must first be computed and the weighting of the two estimates is arbitrary.

The second method of estimating net migration deals with these limitations. A single equation will be used to derive the estimates, and for this the forward equation and the reverse equation are equally satisfactory. The method involves an adjustment of either the forward or the reverse estimates by the square root of the survival rate, representing survival for approximately one half the period.[28]

$$M_F = (I_a - E_a)_F = \frac{P_a^1 - sP_{a-t}^0}{\sqrt{s}} \qquad (18.9a)$$

$$M_R = (I_a - E_a)_R = [(P_a^1 \div s) - P_{a-t}^0] \times \sqrt{s} \qquad (18.9b)$$

$$M_F = M_R = I_a - E_a \qquad (18.9c)$$

Table 18.7 shows the calculation of estimates of net immigration to the United States, for birth cohorts of males between 1980 and 1990 by this method. They can be derived either by dividing the forward estimate (col. 4), or by multiplying the reverse estimate (col. 5), by the square root of the survival rate (col. 7). For this population, the average estimates and the refined estimates are very close over much of the age span but begin to diverge at the older ages where the survival rates are relatively low.

Intercensal Component Method for the Foreign-Born Population

Intercensal changes in the volume of immigration are obscured in a historical series on the number of foreign-born persons. Combined use of such data at successive censuses in some form may serve as a basis for estimating intercensal net immigration.

The intercensal change in the foreign-born population understates the net immigration of foreign-born persons during an intercensal period by the number of deaths of foreign-born persons in the area during the period. Thus, solving the intercensal component equation for the foreign-born population for $I_F - E_F$, we have

$$P_F^1 = P_F^0 + I_F - E_F - D_F \qquad (18.10)$$

$$(I_F - E_F) = P_F^1 - P_F^0 + D_F \qquad (18.11)$$

where P_F^0 and P_F^1 represent the foreign-born population at the first and second censuses, respectively, I_F and E_F represent persons born abroad entering and leaving the area during the intercensal period, respectively, and D_F represents the

number of deaths of foreign-born persons in the area during the intercensal period. The factor of births does not figure among the components of change of the foreign-born population. As suggested earlier, total (gross) immigration (or emigration) of the foreign born cannot be estimated by this residual procedure, only the net numbers of foreign-born persons arriving (or departing).

The number of deaths may be quite large and have a considerable effect on the estimate of net immigration, particularly if large numbers of immigrants arrived in preceding decades and are now of advanced age. The difference in the number of foreign-born persons may even suggest net emigration when net immigration actually occurred. For example, the figure for the United States for the 1950–1960 decade (−693,000) suggests a substantial net emigration, whereas frontier control data show a substantial net immigration of aliens during this period (2,238,000). When Formula (18.11) is used to estimate net migration to the United States, 1950–1960 (i.e., when an allowance for the deaths of the foreign born is made), the resulting figures show a substantial net immigration of foreign-born persons:

Central age-specific death rates applied to midperiod population	1,736,000
Life table survival-rate method	1,805,000
Census survival-rate method	1,450,000

The estimates of net immigration vary between 1.4 and 1.8 million. Each of the estimates, however, is much higher than the estimate of −693,000 that ignores deaths to the foreign-born population.

The allowance for the deaths of the foreign-born population during the intercensal period can be made by use of statistics of deaths or by estimating deaths on the basis of death rates or survival rates. Illustrations will be given here of several procedures. The calculations are quite simple when only an estimate of total net immigration is wanted and both population and deaths are tabulated by nativity. As Formula (18.11) shows, it is merely necessary to take the difference between the counts of the foreign-born population in the two censuses and add the number of deaths of the foreign-born. (This method corresponds to the "vital statistics" method of estimating net migration described in Chapter 19.)

In the event that statistics of deaths of foreign-born persons are lacking, as is the common situation, the number may be estimated by applying appropriate central age-specific death rates to the midperiod foreign-born population. This procedure has been worked out for the foreign-born population of the United States for 1980–1990. The specific steps consist of (1) cumulatively multiplying central age-sex specific death rates for the general population by the estimated foreign-born population distributed by age and sex for 1985 (i.e., an average of the foreign-born populations in 1980 and 1990), to determine the average annual number of deaths of foreign-born persons, and (2)

---

[28] J. S. Siegel developed this refined method of adjusting for the bias in the estimate of deaths to migrants. See J. S. Siegel, *Applied Demography: Applications to Business, Government, Law, and Public Policy*, San Diego: Academic Press, 2002, pp. 22–23. It was originally applied in the estimation of retirements by the life-table residual method. See M. Gendell and J. S. Siegel, "Trends in Retirement Age by Sex, 1950–2005, *Monthly Labor Review* 115(7): 22–29, July 1992.

TABLE 18.8 Calculation of Estimates of Net Immigration of Foreign-Born Females, for Age (Births) Cohorts, by the Life-Table Survival Method, for the United States: 1980–1990

Age (years) 1980	1990	Census, April 1, 1980[1] (1)	Census, April 1, 1990[2] (2)	10-Year life-table survival rate[3] (3)	Forward estimate[4] $(2)-[(1)\times(3)]=$ (4)	Reverse method[5] $[(2)+(3)]-(1)=$ (5)	Average[6] $[(4)+(5)]\div2=$ (6)	Square root of survival rate $\sqrt{(3)}=$ (7)	Net immigration $(4)+(7)$ or $(5)\times(7)=$ (8)
All ages	All ages	7,468,812	10,096,455	(X)	3,339,877	3,790,893	3,749,627		3,744,486
(X)	0–4	(X)	126,999	0.990090[8]	(X)	128,270	128,270	.990090[8]	128,270[8]
(X)	5–9	(X)	237,416	0.988348[8]	(X)	240,215	240,215	.988348[8]	240,215[8]
0–4	10–14	109,544	355,894	0.997321	246,643	247,306	246,975	.998660	246,975
5–9	15–19	211,271	533,506	0.997420	322,780	323,615	323,198	.998710	323,198
10–14	20–24	287,573	800,346	0.995813	513,977	516,138	515,057	.997904	515,056
15–19	25–29	414,470	1,040,868	0.994666	628,609	631,979	630,294	.997329	630,291
20–24	30–34	571,126	1,093,950	0.993796	526,367	529,653	528,010	.996893	528,008
25–29	35–39	648,142	992,072	0.991984	349,126	351,947	350,536	.995984	350,534
30–34	40–44	688,804	898,465	0.988424	217,635	220,183	218,909	.994195	218,906
35–39	45–49	587,044	726,979	0.981871	150,578	153,358	151,968	.990894	151,962
40–44	50–54	536,528	631,462	0.970665	110,673	114,017	112,345	.985223	112,333
45–49	55–59	460,333	520,005	0.953435	81,108	85,069	83,088	.976440	83,065
50–54	60–64	463,910	495,958	0.928130	65,389	70,452	67,921	.963395	67,874
55–59	65–69	440,186	455,531	0.891873	62,941	70,572	66,757	.944390	66,647
60–64	70–74	323,925	304,427	0.840124	32,290	38,434	35,362	.916583	35,229
65–69	75–79	385,923	311,617	0.763504	16,963	22,218	19,590	.873787	19,413
70–74	80–84	410,826	265,576	0.646634	−78	−121	−100	.804236	−97
75+	85+	929,207	305,384	0.312639	14,877	47,587	31,232	.559041	26,607

X: Not applicable.

A minus sign denotes net emigration.

Source: [1]U.S. Bureau of the Census, *1980 Census of Population*, Vol. I, *Characteristics of the Population*. Ch. D., Part 1, Sect. 1, PC80-1-D1-A, Table 253.

[2]U.S. Bureau of the Census, *1990 Census of Population, Foreign-Born Population in the United States*, 1990 CP-3-1. Table 1

[3]Calculated from U.S. official abridged life tables for 1985.

[4]Formula 18.7a

[5]Formula 18.7b

[6]Formula 18.7c

[7]Formula 18.9a or 18.9b

[8]Reduced-period survival rate not requiring adjustment for $\sqrt{5}$ in col. 7. Entries in col. 8 equal col. 2 ÷ col. 3, same as for col. 5.

multiplying the result by 10, the number of years in the period. The estimate of total deaths of the foreign-born population of the United States between 1980 and 1990 obtained in this way is 2,171,000. The resulting estimate of net immigration of foreign-born persons during the decade following Formula (18.11) is

$$(19,767,000-14,080,000)+2,171,000=7,858,000$$

Estimates of net immigration of the foreign born for age (birth) cohorts are obtained by use of a survival-rate procedure. Either life-table survival rates or census survival rates may be employed. The life-table survival-rate procedure is illustrated in Table 18.8, which develops estimates of net immigration of the foreign-born female population of the United States by age from 1980 to 1990. The steps are

similar to those described earlier when the estimates of net immigration were derived for the total male population (Table 18.7). The foreign-born female population in 1980 (col. 1) is aged 10 years by appropriate survival rates (col. 3) to 1990. (The survival rates used are midperiod averages of 10-year survival rates for white females from the U.S. life tables for 1985.) The survivors 10 years old and over are then subtracted from the foreign-born population 10 years old and over in 1990 (col. 2) to obtain the "forward" estimate of net immigration in column 4.

The procedure just described is the conventional forward procedure, but it does not provide an estimate of net immigration for the newborn children. A reverse survival-rate procedure provides an alternate estimate for ages 10 and over (col. 5) in which allowance is made for deaths to the population during the decade, and makes possible the calculation of estimates of net immigration of children born during the intercensal period. The two sets of estimates of net immigration are then averaged (col. 6) to derive "Conventional" average estimates of net immigration of foreign-born females to the United States, 1980–1990 ([(col. 4) + (col. 5)] / 2). To reduce the calculations, estimates for the children born during the period derived by the reverse method may be combined with estimates for the other age groups derived by the forward method. The result in this case is 3,708,000 as compared with the 3,750,000 obtained by the average method. Once again the calculations relate to age cohorts, so that age groups 10 years apart are paired in the two censuses; all the calculations for the same age cohorts are shown on the same line of the table.

Here again, it is desirable to adjust the results to allow more precisely for the bias in the estimates of deaths and net immigrants. Table 18.8 shows the adjusted results, obtained by dividing the forward estimates of net migration by the square root of the survival rate (col. 8 = col. 4 ÷ col. 7).

The estimation of deaths for the cohorts born abroad in the intercensal period (i.e., under 5 and 5 to 9 years of age at end of period) requires special treatment because these groups are exposed to the risk of death in the United States for much less than 10 years as a result both of recent birth abroad and of the staggered timing of immigration. For example, the population under 5 years old in 1990 has been at risk for only 1.25 years on the average (2.5×0.5 years), and the population 5 to 9 years old in 1990 has been at risk for only 3.75 years on the average (7.5×0.5 years). The first factors (i.e., 2.5 and 7.5) represent the average period of time between birth and the 1990 census, and the second factor (i.e., 0.5) reflects the fact that the migrants entered the country or departed at various times during the period between birth and the census, with an assumed average residence in the area of one-half the period. Therefore, the survival rates for the two age groups, under 5 and 5 to 9, respectively, in *exact* ages, are as follows:

$$\frac{L_{0-5}}{1.25 l_0 + L_{0-3.75}} \quad \text{and} \quad \frac{L_{5-10}}{L_{1.25-6.25}}$$

As was stated earlier, alternative estimates of net immigration of the foreign-born population employing the survival-rate procedure may be derived by use of national census survival rates instead of life-table survival rates. It may be recalled from Chapter 13 that census survival rates represent the ratios of the population in a given age at one census to the population in the same age cohort at an earlier census and are usually computed for the native population to exclude the effects of international migration from the rates. They are intended to represent the combined effect of mortality and the relative change from one census to the next in the percent (net) error in census coverage for a given age cohort. Their presumed advantage is that the estimates of net migration resulting from their use may be more accurate than when life-table survival rates are used, because errors in census enumeration are incorporated in the census survival rates rather than in the (residual) estimates of net migration, as in the case when life-table survival rates are used. In both instances, for the census survival-rate method and the life-table survival-rate method, the assumption is made that the mortality levels of the foreign-born and the total populations are the same.

The steps are the same as with life-table survival rates, once the census survival rates have been calculated. The cohorts born during the intercensal period once again require special treatment. For the computations relating to the U.S. foreign-born population, as before, the populations under 5 and 5 to 9 years old in 1990 have to be "younged" to the estimated date of arrival in the United States, not to the date of birth; and only a reverse estimate of net migration is possible.

The general procedure just described may be extended to derive estimates of net immigration, by age and sex, according to race, country of birth, mother tongue, or other "ascribed" or fixed demographic characteristic, or combination of them. Table 18.9 presents the calculation of estimates of the net migration of males and females, born in the Philippines, to the United States between 1980 and 1990, based on U.S. census statistics on country of birth. A (forward) estimate of net immigration to the United States of males and females born in the Philippines is made by carrying the population of the United States born in the Philippines, for 1980, forward to 1990, by the use of 10-year census survival rates and 10-year life-table survival rates, and comparing the survivors with the corresponding 1990 census figures. Reverse estimates of net immigration of children under 10 are prepared by "younging" the 1990 census figures back to the average date of immigration. The overall estimate of net immigration of Filipinos to the United States, for males (239,000) and females (311,000) combined, derived by the census survival-rate method, is 550,000. By the life-table survival-rate method, the combined estimate of net immigration for both sexes is 530,000. This estimate may be compared with the estimate of 516,000 Philippine-born immigrants coming to the United States during the decade and surviving to 1990, based on visa data and survival calculations. The percentage differences between the census and life-table survival-rate methods are small for most ages but become rather large among some adult ages, especially for males aged 35 to 44 years. Table 18.9 also shows a comparison of estimates of the net migration of the foreign born based on the census survival-rate method and estimates of immigration based on visa data. The differences are quite large for most adult ages. It is apparent that the U.S. censuses and the visa data reflect quite different levels of immigration.

TABLE 18.9. Comparison of Estimates of Net Migration of the Philippine-Born Population, for Sex and Age (Birth) Cohorts, by the Census and Life-Table Survival-Rate Methods, for the United States: 1980–1990

Age in 1990 (years)	Estimates of net immigration						Percentage difference from census survival-rate method			
	Census survival-rate method		Life-table survival-rate method		Visa data		Life-table survival-rate method		Visa data	
	Male (1)	Female (2)	Male (3)	Female (4)	Male (5)	Female (6)	Male 100x{(3) − (1)}/ (1) = (7)	Female 100x{(4) − (2)}/ (2) = (8)	Male 100x{(5) − (1)}/ (1) = (9)	Female 100x{(6) − (2)}/ (2) = (10)
All ages	239,372	310,692	230,621	300,464	202,399	314,051	−3.7	−3.3	−15.4	+1.1
Under 5	3,190	2,369	3,110	2,306	2,789	2,793	−2.5	−2.6	−12.6	+17.9
5–14	24,156	24,653	24,155	24,741	27,182	26,821	—	+0.4	+12.5	+8.8
15–24	28,453	30,252	28,465	30,299	45,694	50,534	—	+0.2	+60.6	+67.0
25–34	36,984	39,308	34,847	37,417	33,717	75,911	−5.8	−4.8	−8.8	+93.1
35–44	42,097	57,213	37,751	53,160	38,420	68,668	−10.3	−7.1	−8.7	+20.0
45–54	46,087	77,236	43,289	74,430	22,907	33,333	−6.1	−3.6	−50.3	−56.8
55–64	41,898	72,141	41,382	71,168	15,452	26,619	−1.2	−1.3	−63.1	−63.1
65 and over	16,507	7,521	17,622	6,943	16,237	29,371	+6.8	−7.7	−1.6	+290.5

Notes: Visa data are numbers of legal immigrants, by age and sex, "survived" from the year of entry to 1990, using life-table survival rates. The survival-rate estimates are based on the forward method.
—Less than 0.05 percent.

TABLE 18.10 Calculation of Estimates of Net Immigration of Females from Hong Kong to Canada, by Age (Birth) Cohorts, by the Life-Table Survival-Rate Method: 1991–1996

Age (years) 1991	1996	Canadian females born in Hong Kong		5-year life-table survival rate (3)	Survivors $(1) \times (3) =$ (4)	Net migration	
		Census, June 1, 1991 (1)	Census, May 14, 1996 (2)			Forward estimate $(2) - (4) =$ (5)	Adjusted estimate $(4) + \sqrt{(3)} =$ (6)
All ages	All ages	77,325	124,315	(X)	77,792	47,766	47,963
(X)	Under 5	X	1,240	0.9987	1,242[1]	1,242[1]	1,242[1]
Under 5	5–9	1,470	4,245	0.9989	1,468	2,777	2,779
5–9	10–14	3,700	7,590	0.9993	3,697	3,893	3,894
10–14	15–19	4,590	10,400	0.9988	4,585	5,815	5,818
15–19	20–24	5,860	10,705	0.9984	5,850	4,855	4,859
20–24	25–29	5,955	9,765	0.9983	5,945	3,820	3,823
25–29	30–34	9,140	15,060	0.9978	9,120	5,940	5,947
30–34	35–39	13,480	19,330	0.9968	13,437	5,893	5,902
35–39	40–44	13,090	17,975	0.9949	13,023	4,952	4,965
40–44	45–49	9,385	12,795	0.9922	9,311	3,484	3,498
45–49	50–54	2,890	3,910	0.9880	2,855	1,055	1,061
50–54	55–59	2,715	3,865	0.9804	2,662	1,203	1,215
55–59	60–64	1,730	2,985	0.9691	1,677	1,308	1,329
60–64	65–69	1,210	1,810	0.9516	1,151	659	676
65–69	70–74	880	1,400	0.9232	812	588	612
70–74	75–79	735	725	0.8759	644	81	87
75+	80+	495	515	0.6309	312	203	256

X: Not applicable.

[1] Reverse estimate.

Source: 1991 and 1996 Canadian Census of Population unpublished data; 1996 Abridged Life Tables, Statistics Canada unpublished data.

Table 18.10 illustrates the calculation of estimates of the net movement of population between two areas on the basis of place-of-birth data from the census of the destination country. The illustration relates to the movement of the female population between Hong Kong and Canada in the 1991–1996 period. The basic procedure is the same as in the illustration in Table 18.8, but here account is taken of the movements over a 5-year period. The net movement of Hong Kong–born females is estimated by "surviving" the Canadian female population born in Hong Kong (col. 1) forward to 1996 (col. 4), by use of 5-year life-table survival rates (based on 1996 life tables), shown in col. 3. The estimated survivors are subtracted from the 1996 female population of Canada born in Hong Kong (col. 2) to obtain the preliminary estimates of net migration from Hong Kong to Canada for females for age cohorts during the 1991-to-1996 period (col. 5). Then the final estimates (col. 6) are obtained by dividing the estimates in col. 5 by $\sqrt{s}$ (i.e., square root of col. 3).

Changes in Alien Population

The same types of procedures as described in the previous section may be employed in connection with census counts of aliens, where available. The change in the number of aliens between two dates is affected by naturalizations as well as by net immigration and deaths:

$$P_A^1 = P_A^0 + I_A - E_A - D_A - N \qquad (18.12)$$

$$(I_A - E_A) = P_A^1 - P_A^0 + D_A + N \qquad (18.13)$$

where A refers to aliens and N refers to naturalizations. Hence the net immigration of aliens is estimated as the sum of the net change in the number of aliens, deaths of aliens, and naturalizations.

Data on Nationals Abroad

Estimates of the net migration of nationals or a particular segment of them (e.g., employees of the national government and their dependents, armed forces) during some period, complementing the estimates for the foreign born or aliens, may be derived by a similar method from statistics or estimates of these groups living outside the country at the beginning and end of the period. The formula may be arrived at by solving the component equation relating to this special population for the net migration component:

$$M_0 = (O_1 - O_0) - (B_0 - D_0) \qquad (18.14)$$

where O_0 and O_1 represent the country's overseas population at the initial and terminal date in the period, respectively, B_0 represents births to the country's overseas population, D_0 represents deaths to the country's overseas population, and M_0 represents net movement overseas. The sign of the result is then changed so that it will refer to movement vis-à-vis the country in question, not the country's population abroad. Net movement into the country of its nationals from overseas equals $-M_0$, therefore.

United States Procedure of Estimating Net Migration

The estimates of net civilian immigration to the United States currently employed by the U.S. Census Bureau in its population estimates illustrate the composite use of several of the sources and methods that have been described. The statistics of net civilian immigration for the United States in recent decades cover the following categories:

1. Immigrant aliens
2. Refugee aliens
3. Permanent emigration of legal residents
4. Net migration of illegal immigrants
5. Net migration of nonrefugee temporary residents (mainly foreign students and temporary workers)
6. Net migration from Puerto Rico and other outlying areas under U.S. jurisdiction
7. Net movement of civilian citizens affiliated with the U.S. government (federal government employees and dependents, including military dependents)

Categories 1, 2, and 5, represent "frontier control" statistics compiled by the U.S. Immigration and Naturalization Service. Categories 3 and 4 are numerically substantial but lack reliable data; they are estimates prepared by the U.S. Census Bureau. Category 6 is based on passenger statistics compiled by the Planning Board of the Commonwealth of Puerto Rico. Category 7 represents estimates prepared by the U.S. Census Bureau, and derived from data on the overseas population provided by the U.S. Department of Defense and the U.S. Office of Personnel Management.

Estimating Illegal Immigration

It is impossible to estimate the number of illegal immigrants in a country with a small relative error. This is so because illegal movements are clandestine and the status of illegal immigrants is not a matter of public record, or readily or accurately ascertained by direct enquiry. If illegal immigrants constitute several million in a population of a few hundred million, however, as appears to be the case for the United States, we should be able to detect their presence by manipulating available demographic data, including censuses, large national surveys, vital statistics, and immigra-

tion data. We should be able to measure the number of illegal immigrants with less than a 50% relative error, if not by less than a 25% relative error, by demographic analyses and a combination of data from several record systems.

The data to be used in measuring illegal immigration include census data, sample survey data, Social Security and other administrative data, and immigration data. The immigration records could include records of persons listed in alien registrations, records of immigrant aliens admitted legally, records of visitors and other short-term "nonimmigrants," and records of aliens held for deportation (including illegal immigrants apprehended at the border). Although a great variety of methods as well as data can be employed to estimate illegal immigrants, none are robust and all require broad and sometimes extensive assumptions. In practice, these methods are combined and different methods may be applied in estimating the different types of illegal immigrants. Moreover, it is useful to analyze the data in terms of the principal countries of origin. Among the general types of studies are the following:

1. A special household survey of foreign-born persons covering selected subnational areas where foreign-born persons are concentrated
2. Comparative analysis of aggregate administrative data and census and/or national sample survey data (e.g., employment data from Social Security or other administrative records and from census records)
3. Demographic analysis of census and survey data (e.g., analysis of the regional variation or trend of death rates or sex ratios, component analysis of changes in successive national sample surveys or censuses, and comparative analysis of census data on population and the labor force in paired principal countries of origin and destination)
4. Case-by-case matching of two or more, preferably independent, collection systems (e.g., census, post-enumeration surveys, or Social Security records, tax files, or other administrative records)
5. Historical analysis of the records of border apprehensions and year-to-year matching of these records in order to measure those entering without inspection
6. Matching of visas of arriving temporary visitors with visas of departing temporary visitors in subsequent years in order to measure visa overstayers
7. Intensive checks at selected official border crossing points in order to measure persons attempting to enter with fraudulent documents

Matching border apprehensions and Social Security files should provide useful information on the socioeconomic characteristics of illegal entrants who have been apprehended.

Some more specific methods of measuring illegal immigration are described in the following sections.

Use of Immigrant Records Only

An analysis of historical data on border apprehensions and the characteristics of those apprehended could provide a basis for rough estimates of the number of illegal entrants, especially if multiple apprehensions are identified by record matching. This might involve imputing ratios of illegal entrants to apprehensions for sections of the national border. Alternatively, the records of temporary aliens admitted and the records of temporary aliens departing within a specified period could be matched to identify those who had failed to leave the country within a reasonable time of their required departure date.[29]

Demographic Analysis

In one application of demographic analysis, we can compare the trend of death rates according to age and sex over a series of years for a particular part of the country in which aliens are concentrated with the trends of death rates in the balance of the country. For this purpose, the assumptions are made that only a small portion of the illegal population is enumerated in the censuses or is included in the postcensal population estimates on which the death rates are based but that all or nearly all of the deaths of illegal immigrants are included in the death statistics. If the illegal population has increased greatly over the observation period in the designated geographic area, then the death rates at the young adult ages in this area would show substantially larger increases or substantially smaller decreases than in the balance of the country at these ages during the period.[30]

One of the common observations made about illegal immigration is that young adult males predominate in the movement. A substantial drop in the sex ratio of an age cohort over a decade for a country of origin and a substantial rise in the sex ratio for the country of destination during the same period for the same cohort might indicate that many more males than females emigrated from the first country to the second country during the period. The question still arises whether this shift is more extreme than could be accounted for by reported migration of the sexes from the country of origin to the country of destination.[31]

Demographic Analysis Linking Survey and Immigration Data

Net illegal immigration can be estimated as a residual by decomposing the change in the foreign-born population or the population born in one or more of the countries of principal origin of immigrants on the basis of census counts or survey estimates of the foreign-born population at two dates and data on the components of change. For this purpose, census or sample survey data on the total foreign-born population at one date are combined with data on legal immigration and estimates of deaths and emigration of legal immigrants, and then compared with data on the total foreign-born population at a later date.[32]

When data on country of origin are available in censuses or surveys, they can be used to prepare separate estimates of illegal immigration.[33] For analysis of illegal immigration for specific countries of origin, the data should preferably be tabulated by age and sex because allowance has to be made for mortality by use of life tables. Analysis by country of origin requires data on legal immigration and emigration of legal immigrants. In the United States data on legal immigration can be obtained from the U.S. Immigration and Naturalization Service. Different life tables and different allowances for emigration of legal immigrants can be used to provide alternative estimates. A complementary type of study can be carried out using two consecutive censuses of the country of emigration (e.g., Mexico) and again making alternative allowances for mortality and emigration of legal immigrants.

Estimates of the number of illegal immigrants residing in a country, for different countries of origin, can be made by comparing the number of legally resident immigrants from an alien registration and a census count of the total number of foreign born.[34] This approach can be extended to make

---

[29] For an example of studies using immigrant records, see R. Warren, "Annual Estimates of Nonimmigrant Overstays in the United States: 1985 to 1988," in F. D. Bean, B. Edmonston, and J. S. Passel (Eds.), *Undocumented Migration to the United States: IRCA and the Experience of the 1980s*, Washington, DC: Urban Institute Press, 1990.

[30] The use of this method is illustrated in J. G. Robinson, "Estimating the Approximate Size of the Illegal Alien Population in the United States by the Comparative Trend Analysis of Age-Specific Death Rates," *Demography* 17: 159–176, 1980.

[31] For an illustration of the use of this method to estimate the flow of illegal immigrants from Mexico to the United States, see F. D. Bean, A. G. King, and J. S. Passel, "The Number of Illegal Migrants of Mexican Origin in the United States: Sex-Ratio Based Estimates for 1980. *Demography* 20(1): 99–106, 1983.

[32] An example of the application of this approach is given in K. Woodrow and J. S. Passel, "Post-IRCA Undocumented Immigration to the United States: An Assessment Based on the June 1988 Current Population Survey," Chapter 2 in F. D. Bean, B. Edmonston, and J. S. Passel (Eds.), *Undocumented Migration to the United States: IRCA and the Experience of the 1980s*, Washington, DC: Urban Institute Press, 1990.

[33] For country-of-origin estimates, for example, estimates of the Mexican-born population of the United States, J. S. Passel and K. Woodrow analyzed the Current Population Surveys conducted in 1979 and 1983 in order to estimate illegal immigration from Mexico to the United States between these years. See their paper, "Change in the Undocumented Alien Population in the United States, 1979–1983, *International Migration Review* 21(4): 303–334, 1987.

[34] Minimal estimates of illegally present immigrants in 1980 in the United States, for selected countries of birth, were derived by R. Warren and J. S. Passel by subtracting the number of legally resident immigrants based on an alien registration from the census count of immigrants (modified to account for deficiencies in the data). See their paper, "A Count of the Uncountable: Estimates of the Undocumented Aliens Counted in the United Stated Census," *Demography* 24: 375–393, August 1987.

separate estimates of the illegal immigrant population for subnational areas.[35]

Comparison of Aggregate Administrative Records

Comparison of two data series, one of which is likely to include all or most illegal immigrants in a country and the other of which is likely to exclude all or most of them, represents another possible avenue of estimation. Two general illustrations may be given. The first compares two national data series on employment in the United States over a decade or so, one based on household reporting of employment status and the other based on establishment reporting of the numbers of employees. Any sharp change in the number of illegal immigrants over the observation period should be evident from a comparison of changes in the differences between these two series. A second comparison can be carried out between census figures on school enrollment for states and administrative data on enrollment for states. The differences between the two sets of data would be attributed to illegal residents of school age. We are assuming that the latter series includes many, if not most, illegal residents while the former includes few or none of them. At best such comparisons can provide minimal estimates of employed illegal residents or of school-age children of illegal immigrants.

Dual Systems Analysis

A potentially more productive, but also more costly, approach is to match individual records in various censuses, surveys, and administrative record files such as Social Security records and national income tax returns. For example, in 1977 the U.S. Social Security Administration developed an estimate of the number of illegal residents aged 18 to 44 years in the United States in 1973 on the basis of a match of the Current Population Survey, Social Security records, and federal income tax returns. The estimate obtained was 3.9 million, with a subjective 68% confidence interval ranging from 2.9 to 5.7 million.[36]

Sample Survey

It is theoretically possible to obtain an estimate of the number of illegal residents and their demographic and socioeconomic characteristics by direct inquiry in a survey.

The survey could be framed as a sample survey of the foreign-born population and can be restricted to the areas in a country where the foreign-born population is concentrated. Intensive probing could be used to determine the circumstances of entry and the residence of the survey respondents and the members of their households. Such a survey, however, presents great difficulties because of the illegal status of the respondents or their household members. It would generally be seen as threatening to the respondents, once they learn the purpose of the survey. At best, such a survey would yield a minimal estimate of the number of illegal immigrants.

Estimating Emigration

Earlier we mentioned that few countries collect data specifically on emigrants. Relatively fewer countries collect comprehensive emigration statistics that cover all groups of emigrants. Countries where emigration is measured on a regular basis, usually by a central statistical agency, employ a combination of different data sources and methods. The United States, Canada, and Australia are good examples of varied approaches taken by different countries.

Because, as noted previously, the collection of statistics on emigration for the United States was discontinued in 1957 and no direct measure of emigration has been available since then, estimates have had to be prepared. The U.S. Census Bureau estimates emigration of foreign-born and the U.S.-born legal, permanent residents separately. These statistics exclude emigration of citizens affiliated with the federal government (civilians and members of armed forces and their dependents). No attempt is made to estimate emigration of other groups of residents in the country that are included in the international migration component of population change: i.e., Puerto Ricans, non-refugee temporary residents, and illegal residents in addition to federally affiliated citizens. Only data on net migration are available for those groups.

Estimates of emigration of the U.S. born and foreign-born permanent residents are developed by demographic analysis using a variety of administrative sources and the census. Since 1997, for the foreign born, an assumption is made that the trend in emigration follows the trend in the size of the foreign-born population according to country of birth. Ahmed and Robinson applied crude rates of emigration for countries, in a residual technique with the cohort survival method, to the 1980 and 1990 census data on the foreign born tabulated by detailed demographic characteristics (sex, age, period of immigration, and country of birth).[37] For emigration of the U.S.-born population, the U.S. Census Bureau makes an annual allowance of 48,000, based on

[35] Extensions of the country-of-birth approach have been made by Passel and Woodrow to illustrate the use of the method for making estimates of the illegal immigrants for states of the United States. See J. S. Passel and K. Woodrow, "Geographic Distribution of Undocumented Immigrants: Estimates of Undocumented Aliens Counted in the 1980 Census by State," *International Migration Review* 18: 642–671, Fall 1984.

[36] Social Security Administration, unpublished paper, "Estimates of the Illegal Immigrant Population of the United States," Washington, DC: Social Security Administration, 1977.

[37] For more details, see B. Ahmed and J. G. Robinson, "Estimates of the Foreign-Born Population: 1980–1990," *Population Division Working Paper* No. 9, U.S. Bureau of Census, 1994, www.\\ccnsus.gov.

research by Fernandez.[38] This estimate is composed of two elements. The first component is calculated by applying the cohort-survival method to the census data of selected foreign countries on the U.S.-born persons living in these countries. The second component is based on the U.S. State Department data on registrations of U.S. citizens living abroad. It covers countries for which foreign-country census data on U.S.-born persons are not available or are of poor quality.

Since 1999, Canada's statistical agency, Statistics Canada, measures total emigration through three components: emigration of Canadian citizens and alien permanent residents, return of emigrants, and net emigration of Canadian residents temporarily abroad.[39] Although published data reflect total emigration, data on the individual components are provided on request. Aliens with temporary status in Canada (nonpermanent residents) are also included as a component of international migration, but only their net migration is measured.

The first two components are estimated using a model based on administrative data. These data are extracted by the Canada Customs and Revenue Agency from the federally administered Child Tax Benefit program and provide information only on children whose families are entitled to the benefit (the entitlement is established by the presence of children under age 18 and the prescribed family income). In addition, the estimate of emigration uses data collected by the U.S. Immigration and Naturalization Service on Canadian residents admitted to the United States for permanent residence. The model accounts for the different propensity to emigrate and return, respectively, between those receiving and not receiving the benefit.[40] The third component, Canadians temporarily abroad, is measured from the estimated trend in the size of the Canadian population residing temporarily outside the country. The trend is estimated on the basis of the results of the Reverse Record Check conducted in 1991 and 1996, which is the major survey for estimation of the coverage error in the Canadian census.[41]

In Australia, all international arrival and departure statistics are derived from a combination of "100%" border control statistics and sampling at the borders. All permanent movement (arrivals and departures) and all temporary movements with a duration of stay in the country or abroad of 1 year or more are fully registered. Measurement of temporary movements with a duration of stay of less than 1 year are based on a sample of these movements. Passenger cards are the source of these statistics, with the addition of information on passport and visa data. Australia distinguishes between movements of Australian residents, settlers (foreigners who hold immigrant visas and New Zealand citizens who indicate intention to settle), and visitors.

Currently, the Australian Bureau of Statistics calculates net international migration as the difference between permanent and long-term arrivals and permanent and long-term departures. There is also a special component of "category jumping." This component is a measure of the net effect of changes in travel intentions from short term to permanent/long term or vice versa.[42] In Australian practice, therefore, emigration includes departures of Australian residents (citizens and aliens with permanent residence status) who on departure state that they are departing permanently or intend to stay abroad for more than 12 months, and departures of visitors who had stayed in Australia for 12 months or more. Although not used for preparing population estimates, the data on short-term departure of Australian residents and overseas visitors are also published.

The preceding discussion demonstrates that for estimating emigration, the United States relies primarily on census data, Canada uses administrative data other than border control data predominately, and Australia employs border control data, with an explicit reference to permanent and temporary movement as measured by the duration of residence.

So far the direct method of measuring emigration known *as multiplicity* or *network sampling* has not been considered. This method involves inquiring of members of the original sample households in a survey and members of households of close relatives (within a specified degree of consanguinity, e.g., siblings, parents, and children) about members of the households who have gone "abroad" to live during a specified past period. There are issues here of the omission of single-person or even family households all of whose members have moved "overseas" and of the sample weighting. No country has made a serious effort to fully exploit this method, but it remains a serious possibility.

[38] For more details, see E. W. Fernandez, "Estimation of the Annual Emigration of U.S. Born Persons by Using Foreign Censuses and Selected Administrative Data: Circa 1980," *Population Division Working Paper*, No. 10, U.S. Bureau of Census, 1995. www.census.gov.

[39] For the data and a brief description of the methodology, see Statistics Canada, "*Annual Demographic Statistics, 1999*," Ottawa, Ontario: Statistics Canada, 2000.

[40] For more details on the research leading to development of the method, see D. Morissette, "Estimation of Emigration," Demography Division, Ottawa, Ontario: Statistics Canada, 1999; and D. Morissette, "Estimation of Returning Canadians," Demography Division, Ottawa: Statistics Canada, 1999, www.dissemination.statcan.ca/english/concepts/demog/index.htm.

[41] For more details on the research leading to development of the method, see M. Michalowski, "Canadians Residing Temporarily Abroad: Numbers, Characteristics and Estimation Methods," Demography Division, Ottawa: Statistics Canada, 1999, www.dissemination.statcan.ca/english/concepts/demog/index.htm.

[42] For a description of the categories and procedures, see Australian Bureau of Statistics, "Australian Demographic Statistics, December 1994," 1995; and Australian Bureau of Statistics, "Statistical Concepts Library," catalogue 3228.0, www.abs.gov.au/websitedbs.

TECHNIQUES OF ANALYSIS

Few specialized demographic techniques have been devised for the analysis of international migration. Many of the techniques of analysis used in other demographic fields, especially for internal migration, apply equally to international migration. We will, accordingly, touch on this subject only briefly in this chapter, leaving the more complete discussion to the chapter on internal migration.

General Aspects of Migration Analysis and Demographic Factors Important in Analysis

Analysis of international migration presents certain complexities arising from the special characteristics that distinguish it from, say, mortality analysis and natality analysis. The conceptual difficulties in defining a migrant are much greater than in defining a birth or a death. These difficulties are associated with the variety of definitions in a given country and between countries and with the variety of collection systems, and they result in serious problems of international comparability. Unlike the events of birth or death, migration necessarily involves two areas: the area of origin and the area of destination. This fact leads to interest in particular migration streams and counterstreams as well as in total migration to an area; to the need to analyze immigration, emigration, and net migration jointly; and to difficulties in formulating measures of analysis, particularly rates. Formulation of migration rates involves practical and theoretical problems. Immigration cannot be viewed as a risk to which the members of the receiving population are subject in the same sense that this population is subject to the risk of death or bearing children, because the migrants come from outside the population. On the other hand, one can view emigration as a risk associated with the population of the area of origin. Analysis in terms of net migration, which is often necessary because of the lack of adequate statistics on immigration and emigration, presents special arithmetic and logical problems because net migration may be a positive or negative quantity and may differ considerably in magnitude from the gross volume of movement into or out of the country.

Unlike death, but like bearing a child, the event of migration may occur repeatedly to the same person or may not occur at all to an individual in his or her lifetime. Hence, there is need to differentiate migration (i.e., number of moves) from migrants (i.e., number of persons who have moved) and to specify precisely the geographic areas and the time period for which migration status (e.g., migrant, nonmigrant) is defined. The time period must be chosen carefully because it introduces one of the main complications in defining migration rates.

Analysis of international migration involves some of the same factors found to be important in other fields of demographic analysis as well as other factors especially pertinent to this subject. Analysis of international migration streams calls for data on country of last permanent residence of immigrants and country of next permanent residence of emigrants. Country of birth or citizenship may serve as a substitute for previous permanent residence or as a supplement to it. For both administrative and demographic uses, it is important to have data on citizenship, type of migration (e.g., permanent, temporary, and "commuters" or "border crossers"), and the legal basis of entry of aliens.

Tabulations on type of migration and legal basis of entry may also provide general or detailed information on causes of migration—that is, whether the migrant intends to settle permanently, study, tour, or work temporarily. There is interest in the demographic, social, and economic characteristics of migrants. In recommending a program to improve international migration statistics, the U N Population Commission at its third Session in May 1958 urged the "provision of statistics most relevant to the study of demographic trends and their relation to economic and social factors, including statistics on age, sex, marital condition, family size, occupation and wages of migrants."[43] The variation of rates of migration by age and sex may be quite pronounced and is important for its effect on the composition of the population of the sending and receiving countries. It is also of value to have data on major occupation groups and industrial classes, particularly in connection with an analysis of the impact of migration on the sending and receiving countries' economies. Data on the mother tongue, ethnic origin or race, education, marital status, and family composition of the immigrants are useful in the analysis of the assimilation of immigrants. Tabulations on state or province of intended future residence for immigrants and on state of last permanent residence for emigrants are useful for making current estimates of population for such subdivisions.

Some analysts of international migration also take into account various nondemographic factors, such as changes in legislation regarding immigration and emigration, programs to assist immigrants, modes and costs of travel, and economic and social conditions at origin and destination, including wars, sociolegal status of minorities, business cycles, adequacy of harvests, and many other social and economic factors that are not necessarily measured by the population census or immigration statistics.

Net Migration, Gross Migration, and Migration Ratios

Movement into a country, previously referred to as immigration, may also be referred to as *gross immigration*. Similarly, movement out of a country, previously referred to as

---

[43] United Nations, *Problems of Migration Statistics*, Series A, Population Studies 5: 2, 1958.

emigration, may also be referred to as *gross emigration*. The balance of gross immigration and gross emigration for a given country is referred to as *net immigration* or *net emigration*, depending on whether immigration or emigration is larger. A series of figures on gross immigration or emigration for several countries constituting some broader geographic area, say a continent, cannot be combined by addition to obtain the corresponding figures on gross immigration or emigration for the broader area, because some of the movement may have occurred between the constituent countries and hence would balance out in the measurement of immigration to or emigration from the area as a whole.

Net migration figures, however, can be added together to obtain totals for broader areas or subtracted from one another to obtain figures for constituent areas. The latter relation may be seen either by an algebraic or a graphic presentation. If we consider the movement affecting two countries, then we may diagram this movement as follows:

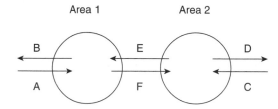

Thus, we have the following relationships:

(1) = Immigration to areas 1 and 2 as a unit, excluding movement between areas 1 and 2 = A + C.
(2) = Emigration from areas 1 and 2 as a unit, excluding movement between areas 1 and 2 = B + D.
(3) = (1) − (2) = net immigration to areas 1 and 2 as a unit, calculated directly = (A + C) − (B + D).
(4) = Net immigration, area 1, taken separately = (A + E) − (B + F).
(5) = Net immigration, area 2, taken separately = (C + F) − (D + E).
(6) = (4) + (5) = Net immigration, areas 1 and 2 as a unit, calculated by summing net migration for the component areas = (A + C) − (B + D).

Note that the results in (3) and (6) are the same. They can be extended to cover *n* areas, in fact, the entire world. At the global level, we know that only births and deaths affect population growth. If comparable international migration data were available for every country for the same period, a purely hypothetical situation at present, the sum of the net immigration or net emigration figures for the various countries would therefore have to be zero.

It should be evident that any one of many very different amounts of immigration and emigration may underlie any given net figure. A net figure of zero may represent the balance of two equally large migration currents or

the absence of all movement. There is interest, then, in the basic immigration and emigration figures even when the net movement is known. In analyzing the differences between the total movement and the net movement, a useful concept is that of *gross migration*, the sum of immigration and emigration. This figure may also be called *migration turnover*. It is intended to represent the total movement across the borders of an area during a period. For example, the net immigration of 949,700 into Canada during the 1991–1996 period represents the balance of an immigration of 1,178,800 and an emigration of 229,100. In total, 1,407,900 (i.e., 1,178,800 plus 229,100) moves occurred across the Canadian borders during that period (Table 18.11).

Various types of ratios may be computed to indicate the relative magnitude of immigration (I), emigration (E), net migration (I − E, or M), and gross migration (I + E), to or from a country:

$$\frac{\text{Emigration}}{\text{Immigration}} = \frac{E}{I} \tag{18.15}$$

$$\frac{\text{Net immigration}}{\text{Immigration}} = \frac{I - E}{I} \text{ where } I > E \tag{18.16}$$

$$\frac{\text{Net emigration}}{\text{Immigration}} = \frac{E - I}{E} \text{ where } E > I \tag{18.17}$$

$$\frac{\text{Immigration}}{\text{Gross migration}} = \frac{I}{I + E} \tag{18.18}$$

$$\frac{\text{Emigration}}{\text{Gross migration}} = \frac{E}{I + E} \tag{18.19}$$

$$\frac{\text{Net migration}}{\text{Gross migration}} = \frac{I - E}{I + E} \tag{18.20}$$

The ratio to be selected for some particular analytic study depends on the type of analysis being made and the migration characteristics of the area under study. For an area characterized by immigration, the ratio of net immigration to gross immigration may be used to measure the proportion of (gross) immigration that is effectively added to the population (i.e., the proportion that is uncompensated by emigration). Similarly, for an area characterized by emigration, the ratio of net emigration to (gross) emigration may be used to measure the proportion of the (gross) emigration that is effectively lost (i.e., the proportion that is uncompensated by immigration). Table 18.11 illustrates the computation of these measures on the basis of data for Canada for the 10-year periods from 1861–1871 to 1891–1901, for the 5-year periods from 1976–1981 to 1991–1996, and for the 1996–1999 period. At the end of the 19th century, Canada was a country of large-scale immigration and emigration, with an overall net emigration. In the mid-1970s to the mid-1980s, the volume of emigration was approximately 50% of

TABLE 18.11   Amounts and Ratios of Net and Gross Migration, for Canada, 1861 to 1901 and 1976 to 1999

Period[1]	Immigration[2] (1)	Emigration[3] (2)	Net migration (1) − (2) = (3)	Gross migration (1) + (2) = (4)	Ratio, net migration to immigration or emigration[4] (3) ÷ (1) or (3) ÷ (2) = (5)	Ratio, net migration to gross migration (3) ÷ (4) = (6)
1861–1871	260,000	410,000	−150,000	670,000	−0.3659	−0.2239
1871–1881	350,000	404,000	−54,000	754,000	−0.1337	−0.0716
1881–1891	680,000	826,000	−146,000	1,506,000	−0.1768	−0.0969
1891–1901	250,000	380,000	−130,000	630,000	−0.3421	−0.2063
1976–1981	587,000	278,200	308,800	865,200	0.5261	0.3569
1981–1986	497,000	277,600	219,400	774,600	0.4414	0.2832
1986–1991	883,600	212,500	671,100	1,096,100	0.7595	0.6123
1991–1996	1,178,800	229,100	949,700	1,407,900	0.8056	0.6746
1996–1999	592,300	164,100	428,200	756,400	0.7229	0.5661

[1] Periods based on census years, which refer to the periods beginning July 1 and ending June 30.
[2] Citizenship and Immigration Canada data.
[3] Demography Division, Statistics Canada estimates.
[4] Ratio is based on emigration when net migration is negative and on immigration when net migration is positive.
Source: Statistics Canada, *Profile Studies*, Cat. 99–701 vol. v, Part. 1, 1976. Demography Division, Statistics Canada (for the 1976 to 1999 period).

the volume of immigration, with net immigration ranging from 44 to 53% of the level of immigration. Since then, immigration has increased and emigration has decreased, so that the current level of net immigration is a still higher proportion of the level of immigration. At the beginning of the 1990s, 80% of Canadian immigration was effectively added to the growth to the country's population.

Another measure, the ratio of net migration to gross migration, or net migration to migration turnover (Formula 18.20), is a measure of migration effectiveness. It measures the relative difference between the effective addition or loss through migration and the overall gross movement. The ratio varies from negative one to positive one, the higher (or lower) the ratio from zero, the fewer the moves required to produce a given net gain (or loss) in population for a particular country.

The logic of the interpretation of migration ratios, where negative values appear in the numerator or where the numerator or denominator is very small, should be considered. A negative sign may simply be taken to indicate that emigration exceeds immigration. Extremely large ratios resulting from very small denominators must ordinarily be interpreted with special care. Extremely small ratios resulting from very small numerators simply indicate that the effective addition or loss is small in relation to gross migration or migration turnover.

Migration Rates

Only limited use has been made of migration rates in the analysis of international migration or national population growth. In fact, no particular set of rates has yet become standard. Theoretically, the analogues of some of the types of rates used in natality or mortality analysis could be employed here. The logical difficulties of determining the form of migration rates and of interpreting them are probably greater for the reasons suggested earlier. The analytic measures used could also follow the form of those used in internal migration analysis because many of the problems of analysis are the same (Chapter 19).

Several crude rates may be constructed on the basis of separate figures on immigration and emigration. These rates represent the amount of immigration, emigration, net migration, or gross migration per 1000 of the midyear population of a country and may be symbolized as follows:

$$\text{Crude immigration rate} = \frac{I}{P} \times 1000 \qquad (18.21)$$

$$\text{Crude emigration rate} = \frac{E}{P} \times 1000 \qquad (18.22)$$

$$\text{Crude net migration (i.e., net immigration or net emigration) rate} = \frac{I - E}{P} \times 1000 \qquad (18.23)$$

$$\text{Crude gross migration rate} = \frac{I + E}{P} \times 1000 \qquad (18.24)$$

We illustrate the application of the various formulas by computing the rates for the United Kingdom in 1995. The number of immigrants during 1995 was 245,452, the number of emigrants during that year was 191,570, and the estimated population on July 1, 1995 was 58,606,000. Substituting the first and third values in the formula for the crude immigration rate, we have (245,452/58,606,000) × 1000, or 4.2. The crude emigration rate is (191,570/58,606,000) × 1000 or 3.3. The difference between the crude immigration rate and the crude emigration rate equals the crude net immigration rate (0.9), and the sum of the two rates equals the crude gross migration rate (7.5). The net migration rate may be either a crude net immigration rate or a crude net emigration rate. The gross migration rate is a measure of the relative magnitude of migration turnover and the population that it affects. Additional illustrative computations are given in Table 18.12.

Various kinds of specific rates may also be computed. The rates may be specific for age, sex, race, or other characteristics of the migrants. An age-specific net migration rate is computed as the amount of net migration (net immigration or net emigration) at a given age per 1000 of the midyear population at this age:

$$\frac{I_a - E_a}{P_a} \times 1000 \qquad (18.25)$$

where I_a and E_a represent immigration and emigration at age a, respectively, and P_a represents the midyear population at age a.

The most appropriate general base for the calculation of rates describing the relative frequency of migration for a country during a period is the population of that area at the middle of the period. This is particularly the case where the migration data are frontier control data, or visa data, which cover all movements into and out of the country during the period. The midperiod population represents here the average population "at risk" of sending out emigrants or receiving immigrants during the migration period. The midperiod population can serve as a common base for the calculation of rates of immigration, emigration, net immigration, and net emigration.

When the migration data come from a census or survey, they are ordinarily restricted to the cohorts of persons living both at the beginning and at the end of the migration period (i.e., excluding immigrants who were born, died, or emigrated during the period). In this case, use of a midperiod population may be less appropriate and less convenient, particularly for migration periods of more than 1 year, and usually practical substitutes are used. Because population data corresponding to these immigration data are readily available in the census or survey, it is common to use the census population as a base. Census or survey data on the number of persons resident in the country who are living abroad at a particular previous date (e.g., t years earlier) are typically expressed as a percentage of the census or survey population t years old and over. These rates may loosely be interpreted as the rates of immigration for the area during the period or, more exactly, the proportion of immigrants in the population at the census or survey date (since the numbers of immigrants are diminished by deaths and emigrants between the date of arrival and the census date).

The current census population may also be used as a base where rates of net immigration are computed from census data on nativity. As may be recalled, data on the foreign born represent lifetime immigration excluding immigrants who subsequently died or emigrated. For example, the rate of lifetime net immigration may be computed from the data on nativity in a single census as the percentage (or per thousand) that the population living in the country, but born outside the country, constitutes of the total population living in the country.

The various types of rates we have been discussing can all be computed on an age-specific basis provided the migration data and the population data have been tabulated by age. Some are central rates in the same sense as crude death rates and age-specific death rates, others are "reverse cohort" rates, as when the terminal population in the same cohort as the migrants is used as a base. They are not "true" rates or probabilities of migration—that is, they do not represent the chance that a person observed at some date will migrate into or out of an area during a specified subsequent period.

Normally, probabilities are expressed for relatively restricted categories of the population, such as an age group, but we can extend the term loosely here to relate to general populations. If probabilities of migration are to be computed, it is not always apparent what population should be used in the denominator. The population in a country at the beginning of the specified migration period (plus one-half the immigrants and one-half the births during the period) represent the approximate population exposed to the risk of losing members through emigration during the subsequent period. In an age-specific rate for a 1-year period, this population can be approximated by the midperiod population at some age plus one-half the deaths and emigrants at that age during the year. An annual age-specific probability of emigration between exact ages a and $a + 1$ is

$$\varepsilon_a = \frac{E_a}{P_a + \frac{1}{2}D_a + \frac{1}{2}E_a} \qquad (18.26)$$

where E_a represents emigrants at a given age during the year, P_a represents the midyear population at age a, and D_a represents deaths during the year at age a. The immigrants at age a who arrive during the year and who are at risk of emigration during the year are already included in the midperiod population figure (P_a).

Probabilities of immigration cannot be based on the initial population of an area. Immigration to an area during a period is not a risk to which the population of the area at

TABLE 18.12 Various Rates of Migration for Selected Countries, around 1995

Country and year (1995 unless noted otherwise)	Immigration[1] (1)	Emigration[1] (2)	Population[2] (in thousands) (3)	Immigration rate (1) ÷ (3) × 1,000 = (4)	Emigration rate (2) ÷ (3) × 1,000 = (5)	Net migration rate [(1) − (2)] ÷ (3) × 1,000 = (6)	Gross migration rate [(1) + (2)] ÷ (3) × 1,000 = (7)
Africa							
South Africa	5,064	8,725	41,244	0.1	0.2	−0.1	0.3
Zimbabwe	2,901	3,282	11,526	0.3	0.3	—	0.5
North America							
Canada	300,313	165,725	29,615	10.1	5.6	+4.5	15.7
Dominican Republic, 1994	984,557	1,044,806	7,769	126.7	134.5	−7.8	261.2
United States[3]	878,288	263,232	262,765	3.3	1.0	+2.3	4.3
South America							
Ecuador, 1994	471,961	348,845	11,221	42.1	31.1	+11.0	73.1
Venezuela, 1991	62,482	77,388	19,787	3.2	3.9	−0.8	7.1
Asia							
Indonesia	218,952	57,096	194,755	1.1	0.3	+0.8	1.4
Israel, 1990	197,533	14,191	4,660	42.4	3.0	+39.3	45.4
Japan	87,822	72,377	125,197	0.7	0.6	+0.1	1.3
Kazakhstan, 1994	400,925	811,312	16,740	24.0	48.5	−24.5	72.4
Republic of Korea	101,612	403,522	45,093	2.3	8.9	−6.7	11.2
Europe							
Belarus	206,839	207,044	10,281	20.1	20.1	—	40.3
Belgium	62,950	36,044	10,137	6.2	3.6	+2.7	9.8
Czech Republic, 1994	10,207	265	10,336	1.0	0.0	+1.0	1.0
Finland	12,222	8,957	5,108	2.4	1.8	+0.6	4.1
Germany	1,096,048	698,113	81,661	13.4	8.5	+4.9	22.0
Iceland	2,867	4,285	267	10.7	16.0	−5.3	26.8
Italy, 1994	99,105	65,548	57,204	1.7	1.1	+0.6	2.9
Latvia, 1994	3,046	21,856	2,548	1.2	8.6	−7.4	9.8
Netherlands	96,099	63,321	15,459	6.2	4.1	+2.1	10.3
Norway	26,678	19,311	4,360	6.1	4.4	+1.7	10.5
Poland, 1994	6,907	25,904	38,544	0.2	0.7	−0.5	0.9
Russian Federation, 1994	1,146,735	337,121	147,968	7.7	2.3	+5.5	10.0
Sweden	45,887	33,984	8,831	5.2	3.8	+1.3	9.0
Switzerland	90,957	69,357	7,041	12.9	9.9	+3.1	22.8
United Kingdom	245,452	191,570	58,606	4.2	3.3	+0.9	7.5
Oceania							
Australia	253,940	149,360	18,049	14.1	8.3	+5.8	22.3

—Less than 0.05.

[1] Long-term immigrants: Nonresidents, or persons who have not continuously lived in the country for more than 1 year, arriving for a length of stay of more than 1 year.

Long-term emigrants: Residents, or persons who have resided continuously in the country for more than 1 year, who are departing to take up residence abroad for more than 1 year.

[2] Estimated midperiod population.

[3] U.S. Bureau of Census estimate: Immigration includes refugees and illegal entrants as well as legal permanent residents; emigration includes departures of legal foreign-born and native residents.

Source: United Nations, *Demographic Yearbook*, 1996, Tables 5, 35, and 36.

the beginning of the period is subject because the immigrants are not a part of this initial population. The number of immigrants entering a country is logically related to the population at the beginning of the period in all the other countries of the world, or at least those countries where the immigrants originate. An immigration rate computed on this base would have only theoretical interest and would be of little or no practical value in analyzing population growth in a particular country. Inasmuch as probabilities of immigration cannot be computed, the substitute procedure of computing the "probability" that an area will receive immigrants is employed; this "probability" is based on the population of the area at the end of the migration period.

We can consider computing probabilities of net immigration or net emigration by employing the fiction that they are gross immigration or gross emigration rates, respectively. Net emigration can reasonably be related to the population at the beginning of the migration period, but, again, there is no simple, logical base for computing a net immigration rate. It would also be confusing to have a different base for different rates in a time series or in an array of rates for various countries. Under these circumstances, we must abandon our effort to compute actual probabilities of net migration, and accept the midpoint population as the best compromise. When this choice is inconvenient, as is often the case, we would fall back on the census or survey population, which is normally the terminal population.

Immigration and Population Growth

We next consider certain aspects of the measurement of immigration in relation to the other components of population growth and to overall population growth.

Immigration as a Component of Population Growth

It may be desired to express the relative importance of migration as a component of national population growth during a period in terms of the percentage that each component of population change contributes to the total increase or decrease during the period. For this purpose, because some components are positive (births and immigration) and others negative (deaths and emigration), it is best to combine them so that logically related items in the distribution have a common sign for the calculation of the percentages. We can compute the percentages that net immigration (+) and natural increase (+) constitute of the total increase, or net emigration (−) and natural decrease (−) constitute of the total decrease, but not the percentages that the individual components constitute of total increase or total decrease.

The importance of net immigration or net emigration in relation to population growth for a country may be more sensitively measured by the ratio of net immigration (M) or net emigration to natural increase (births minus deaths, or B − D) during the period. These ratios express the amount of net migration as a "percentage" of the amount of natural increase:

$$\frac{M}{B-D} \times 100 \qquad (18.27)$$

Other measures of the relation of migration to population change may be developed on the basis of the concepts of migration turnover (i.e., the sum of immigration and emigration), natural turnover (i.e., births plus deaths), and population turnover (i.e., the sum of the four components). These values may be related to one another and to the total population in order to measure the magnitude of the basic demographic changes that a population experiences and has to deal with over a year or longer period.

Total Contribution of Migration to Population Change

It is sometimes desirable to measure not simply net immigration or emigration during a period for a country but the total effective contribution of immigration or emigration to the country's population growth or loss during the period. Estimation of the "net population change attributable to migration" involves adjusting net immigration or emigration, as reported, to allow for the natural increase of the migrants, or involves estimating net migration in a special way so as to incorporate its own natural increase. In general, net immigration or net emigration during a period must be reduced for the deaths of the migrants and increased for the births occurring to them during the period. The estimate of population loss attributable to emigration must include the natural increase of the emigrants after emigration because this natural increase as well as the emigrants themselves was lost to the population. Inasmuch as all the descendants of the migrants during a period represent gains or losses due to migration during the period, births occurring to the (native) children of the migrants will also have to be taken into account in a long period of observation. All of these adjustments must be estimated because statistics on the deaths of migrants and on births to migrant women are not normally available.

An estimate of the net population gain due to net immigration or net loss due to net emigration for one or more intercensal periods may be derived by (1) aging to a later census date the initial census population and estimated births occurring to the initial population during the intercensal period and (2) subtracting the resulting estimates of expected survivors from the later census counts. The aging of the population may be accomplished by means of life-table survival rates or national census survival rates. Death statistics should not be used because deaths occurring to the initial population are required, not deaths occurring to the average resident population. The procedure for estimating net gain or loss due to migration is illustrated by the material in Table 18.13 relating to age cohorts of the male and female populations of Canada for the period 1986–1991.

For the cohorts already born by the initial date, simpler calculations can be employed than when one is estimating net immigration or emigration for birth cohorts as a residual. It is necessary neither to compile death statistics for these cohorts nor to estimate their deaths with survival rates

Total net gain

(1)	Population, July 1, 1986	26,203,800
(2)	Births to initial population	1,888,560
(3)	Survivors, July 1, 1991, assuming no net immigration	27,157,603
(4)	Population, July 1, 1991	28,120,100
(5)	Estimated net gain due to net immigration	961,669
(6)	Reported net immigration	671,075

Components of estimate of total net gain due to net immigration

(1)	Net immigration estimated as a residual, (1b) − (1a) − (1c) + (1d) =	928,976
	(a) Population, July 1, 1986	26,203,800
	(b) Population, July 1, 1991	28,120,100
	(c) Births as reported	1,933,293
	(d) Deaths as reported	945,969
(2)	Births to net migrants, (2a) − (2b) =	44,733
	(a) Births as reported	1,933,293
	(b) Births to initial population	1,888,560
(3)	Deaths to net migrants, (3a) − (3b) − 3(c) =	12,040
	(a) Deaths as reported	945,969
	(b) Deaths to initial population	880,505
	(c) Deaths to initial population's births	53,424
(4)	Net gain due to net immigration, (1) + (2) − (3) =	961,669
(5)	Net population gain, (1b) − (1a) =	1,916,300
(6)	Proportion of net population gain due to net immigration, (4)/(5) =	0.5018
(7)	Reported net immigration, (7a) − (7b) =	671,075
	(a) Reported immigration	883,607
	(b) Reported emigration	212,532

by a special procedure as before. The conventional forward survival procedure usually suffices. On the other hand, the calculation of births occurring to the initial population presents a special problem. In the present case, this was done by (1) computing age-specific fertility rates for the 1986–1991 period for the general population and (2) applying these rates to the survivors of the initial female population for each year. In step 1, annual intercensal estimates of the population by age and sex are required. For Canada, the official estimates for July 1, 1986, adjusted for census undercoverage, were employed. In step 2, annual figures for the expected female survivors 15 to 44 years of age were derived by "aging" the 1986 census-based population estimates from 1986 to 1991 by use of life-table survival rates and then interpolating the figures for 1986 and 1991 linearly to individual years. The fertility rates were then applied.

The resulting births were then "aged" to 1991, like the initial population, using life-table survival rates. The estimated net gain due to net immigration is then obtained as the difference between the observed 1991 population and the surviving population.

The top panel of Table 18.13 shows the calculation for total net gain due to net immigration (row 5) as the difference between the observed population and the expected

1991 population (row 4–row 3). The expected 1991 population assumes no net immigration and is the sum of the 1991 survivors of the initial 1986 population and the survivors of the births to the initial population (row 2).

The lower panel of Table 18.13 displays the components of the estimate of total net gain due to net immigration. Step 1 shows the calculation of net immigration during 1986–1991 as a residual, obtained by subtracting births (1c) from and adding deaths (1d) to net population change (1b − 1a). Net immigration for the 1986–1991 period in Canada is estimated as 928,000. Step 2 involves the calculation of births to net immigrants as the difference between births reported for the 1986–1991 period (2a) and births estimated as occurring to the initial 1986 population (2b, taking survivorship into account), or 45,000 births. Step 3 is the calculation of deaths to net immigrants as the difference between deaths reported for the 1986–1991 period (3a) and the sum of deaths to the initial population (3b) and deaths to the initial population's births (3c), or 12,000 deaths. Step 4 presents the calculation of net population gain due to net immigration as net immigration (1), plus births to net immigrants (2), minus deaths to net immigrants (3), or 962,000. Canada's total population gain for the 1986–1991 period was 1,916,300, so that its net gain due to immigration accounted for more than 50% (6) of net population gain.

The reported net immigration for the period was 671,000 (7); but this figure represents the balance between legal immigration and emigration. The estimated net gain due to net immigration includes the effect of births and deaths to net migrants, as well as the combined effects of population change due to immigration, emigration, net international flows of Canadian residents, net international flows of nonpermanent residents, and miscellaneous categories of persons moving in and out of Canada from July 1, 1986 to June 30, 1991.

Births to net migrants are obtained as the difference between (1) births as reported and (2) births as estimated for the initial population. Deaths of net migrants may be derived as the difference between (1) the reported deaths and (2) the deaths occurring to the initial population and its births. The latter figure is the difference between (1) the initial population and its births and (2) their survivors.

Another procedure for estimating the net gain or loss in population due to international migration consists of applying life-table survival rates to the reported net migration figures, distributed by age and sex, for a period (e.g., 5 or 10 years) to obtain estimates of surviving "net migrants" at the end of the period and then of applying general fertility rates, age-adjusted birthrates, or age-specific birthrates to "net migrant" women in age groups (estimated for the middate of the period) to obtain estimates of births for the whole period. In each case, the required rates must ordinarily be borrowed, possibly from the general population.

TABLE 18.14   Calculation of Total Population Change through the Hypothetical Elimination of
Immigration, for the United States: 1900–1990 (Figures in thousands)

Initial year	Ending year	Total population, July 1, 1990 (1)	If no immigration in the period		If no immigration in the period and after		Estimated Net immigration[1] (6)
			Estimated population, July 1, 1990 (2)	Difference in population (1) − (2) = (3)	Estimated population, July, 1, 1990 (4)	Difference in population (1) − (4) = (5)	
1980	1990	248,712	238,133	10,579	238,133	10,579	8,200
1970	1980	248,712	239,194	9,518	228,614	20,098	6,866
1960	1970	248,712	243,498	5,214	223,400	25,312	2,684
1950	1960	248,712	243,440	5,272	218,128	30,584	2,352
1940	1950	248,712	245,122	3,590	214,539	34,173	1,790
1930	1940	248,712	247,273	1,439	213,100	35,612	−132
1920	1930	248,712	239,407	9,305	203,795	44,917	2,790
1910	1920	248,712	234,225	14,487	189,309	59,403	2,530
1900	1910	248,712	231,426	17,286	174,145	74,567	4,920

[1] Total is 32,000,000.

Source: Estimates derived from a reconstruction of U.S. population by age, sex, and race, from 1850 to 1990 by Passel and Edmonston (1994). See footnote 46 and text.

Because the migrants enter or leave at various dates in the estimate period, it may be assumed that exposure to death or birth is for one-half of the period—that is, the migrants are "aged" for only one-half of the estimate period and the births to women entering in the estimate period occur at one-half the rate of the general population. The births are then aged to the end of the estimate period and added to the survivors of the net migrants.

The "net gain attributable to immigration" is of special interest in connection with the analysis of past and projected population changes. Projections of population changes due to immigration are often helpful for the development of population policy, particularly immigration policy.[44]

The proportion of total projected population growth attributable to immigration may be derived as the difference between a series of projections assuming no immigration for a particular period and a second series allowing for net immigration during the period.[45] Edmonston and Passel have proposed a population projection model using immigrant generations (i.e., foreign born, sons and daughters of the foreign born, and subsequent generations) that provides a framework for making alternative assumptions about net immigration.[46] For example, Table 18.14 shows estimates of the cumulative effects on the population of the United States of net immigration between 1900 and 1990, illustrating the effect of periods of 10-year immigration on population growth to 1990.

These cumulative additions to the U.S. population resulting from net immigration were derived as follows. A series of projections were created, beginning with the initial 1900 population distributed by immigration generation, sex, and age. One set of projections assumed no net immigration during each successive 10-year period (col. 2.). A second set of projections assumed no net immigration after a particular decennial census date (col. 4.). Finally, a third set of projections was constructed that assumed the historical level of net immigration between 1900 and 1990, reproducing the observed population change. The differences between the population in 1990 (from the third series) and the first projection series, and the differences between the population in 1990 and the second projection series, indicate the net gains attributable to net immigration under the specified assumptions.

For example, if there were no net immigration between 1900 and 1910, the 1990 U.S. population would have been

[44] J. P. Smith and B. Edmonston (Eds.), *The New Americans: Demographic, Economic, and Fiscal Effects of Immigration*, Washington, DC: National Academy Press, Chapter 3, 1997.

[45] For example, population projections assuming no net immigration were published in U.S. Bureau of the Census (December 1967), *Current Population Reports*, Series P-25, No. 381. "Projections of the Population of the United States, by Age, Sex, and Color to 1990, with Extensions of Population by Age and Sex to 2015." See also Chapter 3 in J. P. Smith and B. Edmonston (Eds.), *The New Americans: Demographic, Economic, and Fiscal Effects of Immigration*, Washington, DC: National Academy Press, 1997.

[46] See B. Edmonston and J. S. Passel, "Immigration and Immigration Generations in Population Projections," *International Journal of Forecasting* 8(3): 459–476, Nov. 1992; B. Edmonston and J. S. Passel, "Immigration and Ethnicity in National Population Projections," pp. 277–299 in *Proceedings of the International Population Conference, Montreal, 1993*, Vol. 2, Liège, Belgium: International Union for the Scientific Study of Population. See also J. S. Passel and B. Edmonston, "Immigration and Race: Recent Trends in Immigration to the United States," in B. Edmonston and J. S. Passel (Eds.), *Immigration and Ethnicity: The Integration of America's Newest Arrivals*, Washington, DC: The Urban Institute, 1994.

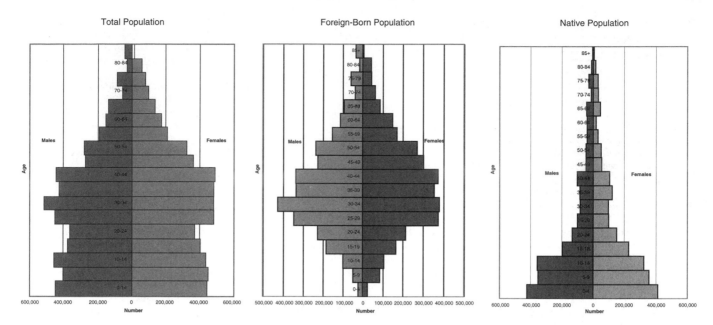

FIGURE 18.1   Population Pyramids for the Asian-American Population, by Nativity, for the United States, March, 1996–1998.
Source: March 1996–1998 Current Population Surveys, U.S. Bureau of the Census.

231,426,000, or 17,286,000 less than observed in 1990. The estimated net immigration for the 1900–1910 period was 4,920,000, so that 12,366,000 (i.e., 17,286,000–4,920,000) represents the additional population growth due to the descendants of the original immigrants. Alternatively, if there were no net immigration after 1900, the 1990 population would have been 174,145,000, or 74,567,000 less than observed in 1990, and the additional population growth due to the descendants of the immigrants would have been 42,567,000 (i.e., 74,567,000–32,000,000).

Graphic Techniques

In addition to the standard types of charts, including various types of maps, a few special graphic techniques can be employed in the description and analysis of international migration. One technique, for example, would be to use maps containing arrows of varying width to indicate the volume and direction of migration between areas. On such maps or charts, the width of each arrow would be directly proportional to the volume of migration; and the length and position of the arrows would identify the areas of origin and destination.

A somewhat different type of chart, the population pyramid, described in detail in Chapter 7, has a special application to immigration analysis. A pyramid may serve to depict, albeit roughly, the historical sequence of the various waves of immigration into an area and their relative numerical importance. Heavy immigration at some era in a popu-

lation's history will often be reflected prominently in the contour of the pyramid. A protrusion of the bars at the upper ages suggests immigration many decades earlier, because international migration tends to occur in the ages of youth. The ethnic identity of the migration waves may be reflected in the pyramids if the various ethnic groups are shown separately or if separate pyramids are drawn for each group.

Pyramids for the total Asian-American population of the United States, and for first (i.e., foreign-born) and second and higher (i.e., native, post-immigrant) generations, in 1996–1998 (using average data from 3 years of the Current Population Survey) make evident the succession of the waves of foreign immigration to the United States from Asia over the last three-quarters of a century and their distinctive age composition according to generation, as Figure 18.1 illustrates.

The population pyramid for the total Asian-American population, shown at the left, fails to display the distinctive differences in age and sex composition shown by the nativity groups. The foreign-born population, shown in the middle pyramid, includes primarily young and middle-aged adults, ranging in age from about 25 to 54 years; there are relatively few foreign-born Asian-Americans who are children or youth, or elderly. The native Asian-American population, shown in the right pyramid, is composed principally of children and youth. Native Asian-Americans who are in the adult years are the children of the relatively few Asian-Americans who resided in the United States before about 1960. There are very few elderly Asian Americans; they are either the children or grandchildren of Asian immigrants who came to the United States prior to World War II.

Suggested Readings

Akers, D. S. 1967. "Immigration Data and National Population Estimates for the United States." *Demography* 4(l): 262–272.

Badets, J., and T. Chui. 1994. "Canada's Changing Immigrant Population" *Focus on Canada* series. Ottawa, Ontario: Statistics Canada.

Battistella, G., and A. Paganoni (Eds.). 1996. *Asian Women in Migration.* Manilla, Philippines: Scalabrini Migration Center.

Bean, F., T. J. Espenshade, M. J. White, and R. F. Dymowski. 1990. "Post-IRCA Changes in the Volume and Composition of Undocumented Migration to the United States: An Assessment Based on Apprehensions Data." In F. D. Bean, B. Edmonston, and J. S. Passel (Eds.), *Undocumented Migration to the United States: IRCA and the Experience of the 1980s* (pp. 111–158). Washington, DC: The Urban Institute.

Bilsborrow, R. E., G. Hugo, A. S. Oberai, and H. Zlotnik. 1997. *International Migration Statistics: Guidelines for Improving Data Collection Systems.* Geneva, Switzerland: International Labour Office.

Borjas, G. J., and R. B. Freeman (Eds.). 1996. *Immigrants and the Work Force.* Chicago: University of Chicago Press.

Bouvier, L. F., and D. Simcox. 1995. "Foreign-Born Professionals in the United States." *Population and Environment* 16(5): 429–444.

Boyd, M., and M. Vickers. 2000. "100 Years of Immigration in Canada." *Canadian Social Trends* 58: 2–12. Ottawa, Ontario: Statistics Canada.

Bratsberg, B., and D. Terrell. 1996. "Where Do Americans Live Abroad?" *International Migration Review* 30(3): 788-8-2.

Chiswick, B. R. (Ed.). 1992. *Immigration, Language, and Ethnicity.* Washington, DC: AEI Press.

Cornelius W. A., P. L. Martin, and J. F. Hollifield (Eds.). 1994. *Controlling Immigration. A Global Perspective.* Palo Alto, CA: Stanford University Press.

Edmonston, B. (Ed.). 1996. *Statistics on U.S. Immigration: An Assessment of Data Needs for Future Research.* Washington, DC: National Academy Press.

Ellis, M., and R. Wright. 1998. "When Immigrants Are Not Migrants: Counting Arrivals of Foreign-Born Using the U.S. Census." *International Migration Review* 32(1): 127–144.

Espenshade, T. J. 1990. "Undocumented Migration to the United States: Evidence from a Repeated Trials Model." In F. D. Bean, B. Edmonston, and J. S. Passel (Eds.), *Undocumented Migration to the United States: IRCA and the Experience of the 1980s* (pp. 159–182). Washington, DC: The Urban Institute.

Fix, M., and J. S. Passel. 1994. *Immigration and Immigrants. Setting the Record Straight.* Washington, DC: The Urban Institute.

Gibson, C. J., and E. Lennon. 1999. *Historical Census Statistics on the Foreign-Born Population of the United States: 1850 to 1990. Population Division Working Paper* No. 29. Washington, DC: U.S. Bureau of the Census.

Halli, S. S., and L. Driedger (Eds.). 1999. *Immigrant Canada: Demographic, Economic and Social Challenges.* Toronto, Ontario: University of Toronto Press.

Hill, K. 1985. "Indirect Approaches to Assessing Stocks and Flows of Migrants." In D. B. Levine, K. Hill, and R. Warren (Eds.), *Immigration Statistics: A Story of Neglect* (pp. 205–224). Washington, DC: National Academy Press.

Jasso, G., and M. Rosenzweig. 1990. *The Chosen People: Immigrants in the United States.* New York: Russell Sage Foundation.

Kritz, M. M., L. L. Lim, and H. Zlotnik. 1992. "International Migration System—A Global Approach." Oxford, UK: Oxford University Press.

Lee, S. M. 1998. "Asian-Americans: Diverse and Growing." *Population Bulletin* 53(2), June. Washington, DC: Population Reference Bureau.

Lowell, B. L. (Ed.). 1996. *Temporary Migrants in the United States.* Washington, DC: U.S Commission on Immigration Reform.

Martin, P. L., and E. Midgley. 1999. "Immigration to the United States," *Population Bulletin* 54(2), June. Washington, DC: Population Reference Bureau.

Massey, D., D. Arango, G. Hugo, A. Kouaouci, A. Pellegrino, and J. E. Toylor. 1993. "Theories of International Migration: A Review and Appraisal." *Population and Development Review* 19(3): 431–465.

Michalowski, M. 1992. "The Dynamics of Recent South-North Flows of Temporary Workers: A Canadian Case Study." In *Peopling of the Americas* (vol. 2, pp. 255–277). IUSSP, Vera Cruz, Mexico.

Michalowski, M. 1996. "Visitors and Visa Workers: Old Wine in New Bottles?" In A. B. Simmons (Ed.), *International Migration, Refugee Flows and Human Rights in North America—The Impact of Trade and Restructuring.* New York: Center for Migration Studies.

Organisation for Economic Co-operation and Development. 1997. *Trends in International Migration: Continuous Reporting System on Migration, Annual Report 1996.* Paris: OECD.

Portes, A. 1997. "Immigration Theory for a New Century: Some Problems and Opportunities." *International Migration Review* 31(4): 799–825.

Rudolph, C. W. 1999. (Ed.). "Reconsidering Immigration in an Integrating World." *Journal of International Law and Foreign Affairs* 3(2).

Sloan, J., and S. Kennedy. 1992. *Temporary Movements of People to and from Australia.* Canberra, Australia: Bureau of Immigration Research.

Simmons, A. B. (Ed.). 1996. *International Migration, Refugee Flows and Human Rights in North America: The Impact of Free Trade and Restructuring.* New York: Center for Migration Studies.

United Nations. 1998. *Population Distribution and Migration.* ST/ESA/SER.R/133. New York: United Nations.

United Nations. 1998. *Recommendations on Statistics of International Migration.* Revision 1, ST/ESA/STAT/SER.M/58/REV.1. New York: United Nations.

United Nations. 1998. *World Population Monitoring 1997. International Migration and Development.* Population Division (ST/ESA/SER.A/169). New York: United Nations.

United Nations High Commission for Refugees (UNHCR). 2000. *The State of the World's Refugees.* London: Oxford University Press.

U.S. Bureau of the Census and Statistics Canada. 1992. "Migration between the United States and Canada." *Current Population Reports*, P-23, No. 161. Washington, DC: U.S. Bureau of the Census.

U.S. Immigration and Naturalization Service. 2000. *Statistical Yearbook of the Immigration and Naturalization Service, 1998.* Washington, DC: U.S. Government Printing Office.

U.S. Immigration and Naturalization Service and U.S. Department of Labor. 1999. *The Triennial Comprehensive Report on Immigration.* Washington, DC: U.S. Government Printing Office.

Woodrow, K., and J. S. Passel. 1987. "Preliminary Estimates of the Undocumented Immigration to the United States, 1980–1986: Analysis of the June 1986 Current Population Survey." *Proceedings of the Social Statistics Section*, American Statistical Association, San Francisco, CA.

Zlotnik, H. 1996. "Migration to and from Developing Countries: A Review of Past Trends." In W. Lutz (Ed.), *The Future Population of the World: What Can We Assume Today?* (pp. 229–335). Laxenburg, Austria: IIASA.

19

Internal Migration and Short-Distance Mobility[1]

PETER A. MORRISON, THOMAS M. BRYAN, AND DAVID A. SWANSON

Population movement—migratory or local—usually is deliberate. That makes the presence (or absence) of movers in a place a matter of choice, not chance. The voluntary movement of people selects distinct types of individuals from their origins. Consequently, migration and mobility typically affect more than just total numbers of inhabitants. Over time, a population may be changed or transformed as people realize their intentions to enter or leave an area. A population's composition may be altered with respect to age, sex, race, ethnicity, income, education, and other socioeconomic characteristics. In California, for example, non-Hispanic whites constituted nearly 80% of the population in 1970 but only 50% by 2000, as Hispanics and nonwhites migrated in. Primarily through foreign immigration, the Hispanic population rose from 12% of the total population of the state in 1970 to 31% by 2000; the Asian population rose from 3% to 12% (see, for example, Gober, 1993). In Florida, persons 65 years and older rose from 8.6% of the total population in 1950 to 17.6% in 2000, principally through an ongoing influx of retirees into the state (Smith, Tayman, and Swanson, 2001, p. 135). Sustained out-movement—migration or local residential mobility—can drain away the more youthful, educated, and skilled members of the population and leave behind older, undereducated, and unskilled adults in an entire subregion like the Mississippi Delta or a particular city like St. Louis.

Now as in the past, people continue to migrate for reasons that are connected with the workings of national economic and social systems. A characteristic of modern economies is the quick exploitation of newly developed resources or

knowledge, a process that requires the abandonment of old enterprises along with the development of new ones. Such economies depend on migration to alter the labor forces of localities more quickly than could be accomplished through natural increase alone.

Within a nation, mobility rates and migration patterns can vary widely among areas. Wide differences in mobility rates and migration patterns, and their potential for rapid change, underscore the importance of measuring migration accurately and understanding its operation. Data limitations, though, make this a daunting task. The populations of some areas remain stable for long periods, while those of others change dramatically. Some places look much as they did a generation ago, while others have apartment complexes springing up seemingly overnight in what once were strawberry fields.

CONCEPTS OF MOBILITY AND MIGRATION

The demographic concept of "mobility" refers to spatial, physical, or geographic movement (as distinct from the sociological concept, which refers to a change in status, e.g., of occupation). This chapter deals with geographic forms of mobility, not "social mobility." The term "migration," as used by demographers, refers to mobility across a relevant political or administrative boundary—a region, state, or county, for example—distinguishing it from the more local form of mobility (often termed "residential mobility") within a particular community. The intended distinction here is one of both distance and type: Migration refers to moves from one "community" to another or, more broadly, long-distance (instead of short-distance) moves (Long, Tucker, and Urton, 1988b).

Although conceptually distinct, migration and local mobility are imperfectly distinguished empirically. "Local

[1] This chapter contains adaptations of material from Morrison (1975, 1977, and 1980), Morrison and Wheeler (1976), and Smith, Tayman, and Swanson (2001), as well as from Shryock, Siegel, and Stockwell (1976). Additional materials were provided by Michael Greenwood and Larry Long.

community" has no precise definition (Zax, 1994). Operationally, moves across state or county lines are almost universally deemed to be migratory, although they may cover very short distances for people living near those lines. Intracounty moves are even more difficult to classify. If a person moves from one town to another within the same county, or from one neighborhood to another within the same town, does that move reflect migration or local mobility? The decision may be made on practical statistical grounds or be arbitrary. Distinctions between migration and local mobility are critical for some types of analyses, but not for others (Zax, 1994). If, for example, one is developing migration data for use in a set of population projections, then all moves into or out of the geographic areas to be projected would be defined as migration, regardless of the distance moved, the degree of change in the living environment, or the size of the area.

In the United States, a change in one's usual place of residence must involve crossing a county boundary to qualify as migration. Alternatives such as commuting, or the diurnal movement between home and workplace, or between home and school and so on do not qualify as migration. Further, a distinction between international migration and internal migration is made, as was explained in Chapter 18.

Place of Residence

As noted by Smith *et al.* (2001, p. 98), the simple question, "Where do you live?" defies an equally simple answer. In the United States, for example, many retirees are seasonal residents of several places; itinerant farm workers follow the harvest seasonally from place to place. Further complicating matters, a dual-career couple may consider themselves a single family but they are really two households if the spouses live and work in different cities, joining each other only on weekends. Children of divorced couples may spend alternating weeks or months with each parent. College students whose parental home is, say, Chicago may reside for most of the school year in Boston, living "away from home." Itinerant professional baseball players spend much of the year "moving" from city to city. Where, can we say, do these people live? Moreover, for the places involved (be they a seasonal resort community or a college town), how many inhabitants are there?

The answers here are consequential because mobility and migration typically refer to changes in a person's place of usual residence (Smith *et al.*, 2001, pp. 99–100). Because of this focus on changes in usual residence, traditional measures of geographic mobility and migration miss common types of temporary population movements such as daily commuting to work, movements between weekday homes and weekend homes, seasonal migration, business trips, vacations, and the sometimes itinerant life on the road of retired couples in recreational vehicles. Such nonpermanent moves are numerous but may go uncounted, despite sub-

stantial impacts on both the sending and receiving regions (Behr and Gober, 1982; McHugh, Hogan, and Happel, 1995; Smith, 1989). Because the focus here is on changes in one's place of usual residence, temporary and seasonal mobility, although important, lies beyond the scope of this chapter.

Alternatively, some minimum-distance threshold might define those moves to be classified as "migration," but other difficulties may then arise. Respondents may err in reporting the distance of their moves; or the distance assigned to a move may require information on longitudes and latitudes. In any case, distance alone is an imperfect metric for distinguishing migratory moves. Permanently migrating 60 miles from one community in Rhode Island to another community in Massachusetts may differ altogether from daily commuting 60 miles each way from home to work within Los Angeles County, California.

As a practical matter, the migrant is defined operationally as a mover who changes her or his administrative area of usual residence. The area may be the primary, secondary, or even tertiary division in a country. The name of the specific administrative area of prior residence usually is recorded as well. With this information, migrants can be characterized according to whether or not the move was also between higher levels of administrative (or statistical) areas. For example, if migrants in India are defined as movers between different districts, interstate migrants and interregional migrants can also be distinguished (the latter being defined as migrants between two natural regions).

Defining a migrant as a mover between two administrative areas honors the concept of a change in environment or milieu, albeit crudely. One administrative area or region may differ culturally from another, as in India, where states are distinguished primarily by the different languages their inhabitants speak.

Length of Migration Interval

Given the basic definition of a migrant as a person whose current place of residence is different from an earlier place of residence, some choice has to be made as to the length of the time interval for which the change in residence is reported. National statistical offices traditionally use either 1- or 5-year intervals for developing migration statistics (U. S. Census Bureau/Long and Boertlein, 1990a). Migration data covering different intervals simply reflect different aspects of the migration process and the actual sequences of moves people undertake (elaborated in DaVanzo and Morrison, 1981, 1982; DaVanzo, 1983). Consider a 1995 resident of Dallas, Texas, who moved to Houston in 1996, then to Boston in 1998, then back to Houston in 1999. With annual surveys, a succession of short (e.g., annual) migration intervals would discern all three moves. However, the response to the retrospective question, "Where did you live five years ago?" asked in 2000 in Houston would discern just one move (from Dallas to Houston). Lengthy multiyear intervals cancel out the repetitive moves of chronic and temporary movers; for the latter, though, multiyear intervals may provide a superior measure of long-term population mobility. Still, multiyear intervals obscure multiple moves within the time interval and introduce measurement errors on the part of respondents who cannot accurately recall the timing or location of earlier moves. Furthermore, longer intervals may miss individuals who die after moving (e.g., an ailing elderly person who has moved to a retirement community). For any particular inquiry, the purpose may favor a certain time interval, but availability of data typically imposes limitations. In general, 1-year data provide truer estimates of the number of moves, whereas 5-year data provide truer estimates of the number of permanent movers.

Because of the impact of multiple moves and births and deaths of migrants, migration data based on different intervals (e.g., 5- and 1-year intervals) are not directly comparable. Lack of comparability has important implications for many uses of migration data. Whereas birth and death data can be converted easily into intervals of different lengths, the corresponding conversion of migration data is a complex and somewhat capricious undertaking.

In sum, the definition of a migrant is necessarily arbitrary. Inevitably, some movers within an administrative area conform more closely to the theoretical conception of migration; conversely, other movers cross area boundaries but remain within the same "community." A classification problem crops up when either minimum distances or arbitrary areas are used. A definition of "migrant" in terms of a minimal distance moved would also be arbitrary unless there was some natural break in the continuous distribution of moves. Indeed, it has been suggested that a migrant be defined as a mover within a labor market area, with the minimum distance set at the point where commuting to work becomes so time-consuming and expensive as to require a change of residence (Lansing and Mueller, 1967).

Political or administrative units are rarely delineated in terms of a grid that yields uniform and equal areas. The effect of the size and shape of political units on the measurement of migration has been discussed by Lee *et al.* (1957), among others. Countries, and even regions within them, differ geographically in size and shape; this makes it difficult to develop meaningful international comparisons of migration rates. Long (1991) argued that the only really comparable mobility rates are those including all changes of usual residence (address) in the numerator, since these are independent of the country's geographic subdivisions.

In measuring mobility or distinguishing movers from nonmovers, the time period may be either variable or fixed and must also be specified. Examples of variable periods are the period since birth (which yields lifetime mobility) and the period since the last move. Examples of fixed periods

are 1 year, 5 years, and 10 years. If the mobility period coincides with the last intercensal period, the resulting migration statistics may be useful in measuring the components of population change or in studying the consistency of population size and the components of change. Too long a period degrades the quality of reporting (through nonresponse and reporting errors) and omits a substantial proportion of the population (namely, those born and those dying during the mobility period) from the mobility statistics. In addition to the date of the last census, mobility questions have also referred to dates of historic significance, such as the beginning or end of a war or a political coup.

Classification of Population by Mobility Status

Mobility data are usually obtained from questions that compare current residence with residence at a prior date, with those persons reporting a specified type of change in residence being classified as "migrants." These data yield a classification of the population by mobility status. An example of such a classification based on "1-year" data from the March 2000 Current Population Survey for the United States (U.S. Census Bureau/ Schachter, 2001b) is as follows:

Total population[1]	100.0
Same house (nonmover)	83.9
Different house in the same county (intracounty movers)	9.0
Migrants (intercounty movers)	
Different county, same state (intrastate migrants)	3.3
Interstate migrants	3.1
Movers from abroad	0.6

Only those persons whose residences differ at the beginning and the end of the period are counted as movers. Movers who died during the period are omitted from the classification altogether, and movers who returned by the end of the period to their initial residence are classified as nonmovers. Furthermore, only one move per person is counted during the period.

In principle, survey questions that directly ask respondents about mobility histories can detect all moves made during a specified period, but again, information is obtained only for persons who survive to the end of the period. A count of all moves, including those of decedents, requires data from a continuous population register or from surrogate respondents still alive to report on persons no longer in the household.

Lifetime and Recent Migration

One of the oldest ways of measuring internal migration is with questions on place of birth, with place usually including country and large internal subdivisions, such as states, provinces, or regions, and less often including smaller subdivisions, such as counties, municipalities, or other types of

---

[1] Population 1 year old and over.

localities. Such questions were originally asked in censuses but sometimes are included in surveys. They are said to offer measures of "lifetime" mobility because they enable the analyst to determine the difference between the place where people were born and the place where they lived at the time of the census or survey. Since the questions usually refer to large geographical areas, the resulting data reflect moves that cover considerable distances.

Surveys often focus on more recent moves, asking "Did you live at this street address on this date 1 year ago?" (or 5 years ago or some other interval). Those answering no are asked whether the move crossed some significant boundary (e.g., a county or state line) or to name the locality of residence 1 year earlier. Although survey sample sizes are rarely large enough to show gross flows for any but the most populous geographical units, knowing locality of residence at the survey date and 1 year earlier can reveal the distance moved or the type of move (e.g., rural to urban, metropolitan to nonmetropolitan, central city to suburbs).

Table 19.1 illustrates both types of data, as derived from the Census 2000 Supplementary Survey for the United States. Column 1 shows the percentage of the population of each state living in their state of birth. The percentage not living in their state of birth includes people born in another U.S. state or the District of Columbia, or born outside the 50 states and the District of Columbia. Column 2 from the same survey shows the percentage of each state's population living in a different residence at the time of the survey than 1 year earlier. The illustration in column 2 of recent, mostly local, moves contrasts with the measure in column 1 of "lifetime" moves from one state to another—usually, but not always, over significant distances.

States vary more on the born-in-state-of-residence measure than on the residential mobility rate. The percentage of the population not living in their state of birth varied by a factor greater than three and a half (from a high of 77.0% in Nevada to a low of 21.6% in Louisiana). One-year residential mobility rates varied by a factor of just over 2 (from 23.7% in Nevada to 11.1% in New York). Moving from one dwelling to another in a year's time occurs routinely everywhere, whereas departing from one's state of birth may vary widely across states. Lifetime interstate migration, measured in this way, represents a longer and more difficult move than simply changing residence locally, although some interstate moves, especially when a metropolitan area overlaps state boundaries, cover short distances and in reality constitute "residential mobility."

The percentage of a state's population that was born in that state reflects the proclivity of natives of the state to leave it and the propensity of non-natives of the state to move into it. States like Louisiana and Pennsylvania, a high percentage of whose residents live in their state of birth, typically have experienced significant outmigration of youth and "aging in place" of the population that remained. By

TABLE 19.1 U.S. States Ranked by Percentage of Population Living in State of Birth, and Percentage Not Living in Same Residence as 12 Months Earlier: 2000

State	Percentage of population living in state of birth	Percentage (aged 1+) who changed residence in past 12 months
Louisiana	78.4	16.1
Pennsylvania	78.3	11.6
Michigan	74.6	14.7
Mississippi	74.3	15.9
Ohio	74.2	14.4
Iowa	74.0	15.6
Alabama	73.9	15.1
West Virginia	73.7	12.8
Kentucky	73.5	15.3
North Dakota	72.6	16.0
Indiana	71.7	16.2
Wisconsin	71.6	15.6
Minnesota	69.9	13.4
Maine	67.8	12.8
Nebraska	67.4	17.8
South Dakota	66.6	15.9
Missouri	66.2	17.9
Illinois	65.8	15.5
New York	65.6	11.1
Massachusetts	65.5	13.1
North Carolina	63.5	16.7
Utah	63.3	18.2
Tennessee	63.0	17.6
Rhode Island	62.6	12.9
Oklahoma	62.3	18.3
Arkansas	61.4	17.8
Kansas	61.3	17.0
Texas	61.3	18.7
South Carolina	59.2	15.7
Georgia	58.9	17.8
Connecticut	57.1	13.7
Montana	56.8	15.9
Hawaii	56.6	16.8
Vermont	55.3	14.3
New Jersey	52.9	12.1
New Mexico	51.3	17.5
Virginia	50.8	14.3
California	50.6	16.6
Delaware	50.0	15.2
Idaho	49.9	17.5
Maryland	49.0	15.0
Washington	47.5	20.1
Oregon	45.8	20.9
Dist. Of Columbia	43.5	17.6
New Hampshire	43.4	14.9
Wyoming	41.4	19.5
Colorado	41.1	21.1
Alaska	37.6	22.1
Arizona	33.9	21.3
Nevada	23.0	23.7

Source: U.S. Census Bureau, Census 2000 Supplementary Survey, available at www.census.gov.

contrast, states like Nevada, Arizona, and Alaska, with low percentages of the resident population born in the state, typically have experienced considerable inmigration. That influx often consists of younger people leaving their state of birth but may also include retirees attracted by a favorable climate or other amenities.

States also vary considerably according to the other measure—the percentage who move from one dwelling unit to another in the 12 months prior to answering the questionnaire. We mentioned above the 2-to-1 ratio of Nevada's 12-month residential mobility rate to New York's rate. In general, the states with the lowest percentage of population living in its state of birth exhibited high rates of residential mobility (i.e., moves in the preceding 12 months), so that some association exists between the two measures on the state level. The association is not perfect, however. New York State, the state with the lowest rate of residential mobility, ranked 19th according to the percentage living in state of birth. Louisiana, the state with the highest percentage of residents born in the state, had a residential mobility rate that exceeded the rates in many other states.

The two measures in the table illustrate "long term" and "recent" conceptualizations of internal migration. When both measures are derived from the same data set (e.g., a particular census), their utility can be expanded by combining them to show recent flows that represent people (1) leaving their state of birth, (2) returning to their state of birth, and (3) making repeat (or onward) moves, as represented by people who moved from one state to another in the most recent period but were neither moving to nor from their state of birth. This approach has most often been applied with census data on state or province of birth and state or province of residence 5 years previously, but on occasion 1-year data have been used as well (Newbold, 1997).

International Comparisons of Spatial Mobility

Analyses of most demographic subjects have featured international comparisons, and sustained efforts have been made to achieve greater international comparability in measures of analysis. In contrast, comparisons of countries in terms of "mobility propensity" have been rare. Measuring movement across spatial units of different sizes creates insurmountable problems of translating one country's migration-defining geographic units into another's—for example, U.S. counties into Swiss cantons or Japanese prefectures.

An alternative to developing such a conversion algorithm is to focus on the second measure shown in Table 19.1, the measure of residential mobility. The percentage of the population that changes usual residence in 1 year is insensitive to the spatial differences in migration-defining units and thus can provide a measure of total mobility that is internationally comparable, as is shown in Table 19.2.

TABLE 19.2 Percentage of the Population Changing Usual Residence in 1 Year, for Selected Countries: Around 1981

Country	Percentage who moved
Ireland	6.1
Belgium	7.3
Austria	7.6
Netherlands	7.7
France	9.4
Japan	9.5
Sweden	9.5
Great Britain	9.6
Israel	11.3
Switzerland	13.7
Hong Kong	14.6
Australia	17.0
United States	17.5
Canada	18.0

Source: Official documents identified in Long (1991).

Table 19.2 reveals considerable variability in residential mobility rates among the 14 countries shown, ranging from annual rates of 6.1% in Ireland to 17 to 18% in Australia, the United States, and Canada. These differences tend to prevail among large geographic areas within each of the countries (Long, 1991). That is, the differences cannot be attributed to very rapidly growing areas with high population turnover. (See the rates for Nevada in Table 19.1.)

Nor can the differences be attributed to varying age composition. Because mobility rates are high among young adults, countries with older populations might be expected to have lower rates of moving (U.S. Census Bureau/ Schachter, 2001a). The differences revealed in Table 19.2 tend to persist across age groups, although differences are somewhat greater at young-adult ages and less at the oldest age categories (Long, 1992). The diminished differences in residential mobility of the very old reflects the fact that at these age groups increasing frailty and moves to children's homes or group homes account for considerable mobility and are fairly uniform forces among the developed countries shown in Table 19.2.

The greater differences among countries in the residential mobility rates of young adults presumably reflect greater variability in the life cycle events that typically govern the timing of leaving home, progress in school attainment or training beyond the compulsory ages, and opportunities to enter the labor force and set up independent households. Different rates of moving at other age groups may reflect the liquidity and fluidity in labor and housing markets and other country-specific conditions. The differences shown in Table 19.2 appear to reflect national policies, practices, and perhaps customs that constitute pervasive influences on the overall rates of moving. Data for earlier years suggest strong persistence of differences among countries in rates of residential mobility (Long, 1991). Other evidence, too, suggests relative stability of annual rates of residential mobility, with only limited sensitivity to relatively modest business-cycle changes (Long, 1988).

The residential mobility concept lumps internal migration with short-distance mobility. There is no direct way of separating the two in a way that permits international comparisons except by measuring distance moved. This can be accomplished by asking people how far they move or by measuring the distance from very small areas like postal delivery zones. The United States has used the former approach, finding relatively modest rounding of distances moved. Britain has used the latter approach, and a few other countries have calculated distance moved for movers between localities by employing centroids of locality of origin and locality of destination. There is some evidence that differences among countries are greater among "local movers" than at longer distances (Long, Tucker, and Urton, 1988a).

Gross and Net Migration

Gross migration is the movement of people into and out of an area; net migration is the difference between the two. For a nation as a whole, disregarding immigration, inmigration equals outmigration, so net internal migration is zero. The distinction between gross and net migration has increasing analytic and practical significance at more local levels, for several reasons.

First, there are no "net migrants," only people who move. To understand, for example, New York's level of net outmigration between 1985 and 1990 of 0.8 million means accounting for the decisions behind the moves of 2.3 million people coming to or moving away from that state during this period (U.S. Census Bureau, 1995). Sometimes, the volume of net migration is deceptively small, as with metropolitan Albuquerque, New Mexico, during the 1960s. This metropolitan area's 1970 population of about a third of a million included a gain of just 22 "net migrants" since 1960. This net figure reveals little or nothing of what went on in Albuquerque: In a typical year throughout the decade, some 44 thousand people—more than one-sixth of the population— moved to the metropolitan area, replacing about the same number who left for other areas (Morrison and Wheeler, 1976).

Second, whatever level of net migration an area registers, the larger gross migratory exchange of individuals involved may well reshape the composition of its resident population. At one extreme, for example, is the 1970s genre of energy boom towns in the Rocky Mountain and Northern Great Plains states (e.g., Gillette, Wyoming, or Colstrip, Montana). Such "instant cities" typically attracted a largely male population motivated by personal gain to sites possessing few of the standard prerequisites for urban greatness (Morrison, 1977).

As another example, in the early 1990s, data on California's driver's license-address-change program suggested an increasing migratory exodus from the state and a declining influx of newcomers, making California a net exporter of population to other states. These gross comings and goings signaled, however, that a fundamental, perhaps necessary, generational change was under way that was reshaping the state's workforce. Nearly one of every two adults moving to California from another state was under age 30, whereas one of every four adults moving out of state was over age 45. These contrasting age profiles of arriving and departing migrants are no accident. They reveal in part a rebalancing of labor supply with demand, as aerospace manufacturing waned and the state adapted to a changing future tied partly to its Pacific Rim access. They may also reflect the effect of "white flight" as many white native Californians decided to abandon their homes before the "invasion" by foreign migrants.

Third, the distinction between gross and net migration has important practical implications, especially in newly growing areas. Nineteenth-century Oregonians were said to offer an occasional prayer: "We thank the goodness and the grace / That brought us to this lovely place/And now with all our hearts we pray/ That other folks will stay away." A century later, affected communities sought to impose local population "ceilings" or enact other measures to control migratory influx. In attempting to control its growth, does a community abridge the freedom of outsiders to move in if, indeed, a continuing procession of people come and go? It may be argued that zero net migration, even if deliberately induced, does not necessarily abridge the right of access to a community so long as residents continually depart (Morrison, 1977).

Table 19.3 shows in-, out-, and net migration for every state and the District of Columbia between 1985 and 1990. These numbers refer strictly to internal migrants, or people moving from one state to another within the United States. Although the decennial census also collects data on immigration from abroad, it does not collect data on emigration to foreign countries. This precludes the possibility of calculating overall net migration estimates for states (or any other regions), reflecting both internal and international migration, on the basis of decennial census data only.

International and Internal Migration

As noted in Chapter 18, it is useful to distinguish international (or foreign) and internal (or domestic) migration. International migration refers to moves from one country to another, whereas internal migration refers to moves from one place to another within a particular country. The data shown in Table 19.3 refer solely to internal migrants. Although internal migration typically is the more dominant of the two types of movement in subnational population

TABLE 19.3 In-, Out-, and Net Migration for States:
1985–1990

Interstate migrants only, excluding international migration

State and region	In-Migrants	Out-Migrants	Net Migrants[1]
Northeast			
Connecticut	291,140	342,983	−51,843
Maine	132,006	98,688	33,318
Massachusetts	444,040	540,772	−96,732
New Hampshire	191,130	129,070	62,060
New Jersey	569,590	763,123	−193,533
New York	727,621	1,548,507	−820,886
Pennsylvania	694,020	771,709	−77,689
Rhode Island	105,917	93,649	12,268
Vermont	74,955	57,970	16,985
Midwest			
Illinois	667,778	1,009,922	−342,144
Indiana	433,678	430,550	3,128
Iowa	194,298	288,670	−94,372
Kansas	272,213	295,663	−23,450
Michigan	473,473	606,472	−132,999
Minnesota	320,725	316,363	4,362
Missouri	448,280	420,223	28,057
Nebraska	141,712	181,662	−39,950
North Dakota	56,071	107,018	−50,947
Ohio	622,446	763,625	−141,179
South Dakota	69,036	91,479	−22,443
Wisconsin	307,168	343,022	−35,854
South			
Alabama	328,120	292,251	35,869
Arkansas	240,497	216,250	24,247
Delaware	94,129	68,248	25,881
District of Columbia	109,107	163,518	−54,411
Florida	2,130,613	1,058,931	1,071,682
Georgia	804,566	501,969	302,597
Kentucky	278,273	298,397	−20,124
Louisiana	225,352	476,006	−250,654
Maryland	531,803	430,913	100,890
Mississippi	193,148	220,278	−27,130
North Carolina	748,767	467,885	280,882
Oklahoma	279,889	407,649	−127,760
South Carolina	398,448	289,107	109,341
Tennessee	500,006	368,544	131,462
Texas	1,164,106	1,495,475	−331,369
Virginia	863,567	635,695	227,872
West Virginia	123,978	197,633	−73,655
West			
Alaska	105,605	154,090	−48,485
Arizona	649,821	433,644	216,177
California	1,974,833	1,801,247	173,586
Colorado	465,714	543,712	−77,998
Hawaii	166,953	187,209	−20,256
Idaho	137,542	157,121	−19,579
Montana	84,523	137,127	−52,604
Nevada	326,919	154,067	172,852
New Mexico	192,761	204,218	−11,457
Oregon	363,447	280,875	82,572
Utah	177,071	213,233	−36,162
Washington	626,156	409,886	216,270
Wyoming	62,286	118,979	−56,693

[1] A minus sign (−) denotes net outmigration; otherwise, net inmigration.
Source: U.S. Bureau of the Census, *1990 Census Special Tabulations, County-to-County Migration Flows,* SP 312, 1993.

growth, international migration has grown increasingly important in the United States and other Western countries and has a substantial impact on demographic change in certain countries and certain parts of countries.

Several categories of international migrants have been defined for the United States, among them immigrant aliens admitted, refugees, asylees, and parolees, nonimmigrant aliens admitted, and illegal immigrants (Martin and Midgley, 1999; for exact definitions, see U.S. Immigration and Naturalization Service, 2000). Legal immigration to the United States (including refugees and asylees but excluding nonimmigrant aliens) has averaged about 800,000 per year in recent years (U.S. Immigration and Naturalization Service, 1999). Neither the U.S. Immigration and Naturalization Service (INS) nor the U.S. Census Bureau collects data on the emigration of U.S. residents to foreign countries. The number of emigrants is currently estimated to be around 200,000 per year. See Chapter 18 for a detailed discussion of international immigration.

ISSUES OF MIGRATION MEASUREMENT

As we have seen, migration is conceptually complex. However measured, migration is arbitrarily defined with reference to distance, time intervals, geographic boundaries, permanence of moves, and notions of usual place of residence. In addition, conventional measures may understate the true extent of migration and mobility and distort their character because of inadequacies in the data (Zelinsky, 1980).

Definitions

Given this general discussion of concepts, a number of basic terms require definition. It should be emphasized, however, that although the present definitions are supported by most users, terminology in the field of population mobility is not yet as standardized as that in natality or mortality. The terms given here are of general applicability. For example, they are mostly applicable to both variable-period and fixed-period mobility; but in using them, one should indicate the time period unless that is clear from the context.

Mobility/migration period/interval. The period to which the question on previous residence applies or the period over which mobility or migration may have occurred.
Mobility status. A classification of the population into major categories of mobility on the basis of a comparison of residences at two dates.

Mover. A person who moved from one address (house or apartment) to another.

Short-distance or local mover. A person who moved only within a specified political or administrative area.

Migrant. A person who moved from one specified political or administrative area to another.

Mover from abroad. An "immigrant" or other type of mover from outside the country into the country.

Area of origin (departure). The area from which a migrant moves.

Area of destination (arrival). The area to which a migrant moves. (With some sources of migration data, there are intervening residences that are not recorded as origins or destinations.)

Inmigrant. A person who moves to a migration-defining area from some place outside the area, but within the same country.

Outmigrant. A person who moves from a migration-defining area to a place outside it, but within the same country.

Nonmigrant. A person who has remained a resident of a migration-defining area but who may have changed residence within this area. The number of nonmigrants is equal to the number of nonmovers plus the number of short-distance movers.

Net inmigration. The calculated balance between inmigration and outmigration.

Immigrant. A migrant to the area from a place outside the country.

Emigrant. A migrant from the area to a place in another country.

Every move is an outmigration with respect to the area of origin and an inmigration with respect to the area of destination. Every migrant is an outmigrant with respect to the area of departure and an inmigrant with respect to the area of arrival. As is the case with international migrants, the number of inmigrants (or outmigrants) is not additive when a set of secondary divisions of a country is combined into a set of primary divisions. According to the direction of the balance of migration to an area, it may be characterized as net inmigration or net outmigration. In a column of net migration figures, the net flow is indicated by a plus (+) or minus (−) sign, depending in whether it is in or out.

Gross migration. Either inmigration or outmigration. The sum of both is sometimes also referred to as gross migration or the migration turnover for an area.

Lifetime migration. Migration that has occurred between birth and the time of the census or survey. A lifetime migrant is one whose current area of residence and area of birth differ, regardless of intervening migrations. Lifetime migration for an area may be either gross or net migration. The terms "lifetime inmigrant" and "lifetime outmigrant" are also used.

Migration stream. A group of migrants sharing a common origin and destination within a given migration period. Although strictly speaking a "stream" refers to movement between two actual areas, the term may refer also to movement between two type-of-residence areas (e.g., a nonmetropolitan-to-metropolitan migration stream), where neither the origin nor the destination represents an actual place. The movement in the opposite direction to a stream is called its counterstream. Thus, if a migration stream is from area A to area B during a period, the counterstream is from area B to area A during the same period. The concepts of stream and counterstream were used first by E. G. Ravenstein (1889) for describing rather heavily unidirectional flows, like those between rural areas and towns in the 19th century. In a general sense, a counterstream can be thought of as the lesser of the two movements. The two are often of nearly equal size and indeed may exchange rankings from time to time. Eldridge (1965) referred to the stream in the prevailing direction as the "dominant stream" and to the counterstream as the "reverse stream." The difference between a stream and its counterstream between two areas is the net stream, or net interchange between the areas. Similarly, the sum of the stream and the counterstream is called the gross interchange between the two areas.

Return migrant. A person who moves back to an area of former residence. Not all return migration is identified in the usual sources of migration data; identification requires knowing an individual's origin and destination for at least two moves (see DaVanzo and Morrison, 1981).

Migration Rates and Their Bases

Common to population-based mobility rates derived from various sources is the question of the proper base to use, an issue discussed at some length by Hamilton (1965), Thomlinson (1962), and *UN Manual VI* (United Nations, 1970). The appropriate base for calculating any rate is the population at risk of the occurrence of the event under consideration. For mortality and fertility, the choice is clear: The population at risk of dying in an area is the population of that area, and the population at risk of giving birth consists of all females of childbearing age. In calculating rates of migration, though, the choice is less obvious. Most studies addressing this question focus on whether the initial, terminal, or midpoint population (i.e, the origin or destination population, or some average of the two) should be used to calculate migration rates and what adjustments for births, deaths, and migration during the time period should be made to estimate the total number of person-years lived (Bogue, Hinze, and White, 1982; Hamilton, 1965). For the most part, measures of mobility that involve population bases and rates are discussed in the subsection on "Measures Used in Analysis."

A measure of the rate of mobility, or the ratio of the number of movers in an interval of time to the population at risk during that interval, is

$$m = (M/P)*k \qquad (19.1)$$

where

m = the mobility rate
M = the number of movers
P = the population at risk
k = a constant, such as 100 or 1000

For mobility and movers, the more specific terms "migration" and "migrants" may be substituted.

For the country as a whole, this rate measures the overall level of mobility or migration. In the case of migration, three analogous rates are those of inmigration, outmigration, and net migration, which are given respectively by

$$m_i = (I/P)*k \qquad (19.2)$$

$$m_o = (O/P)*k \qquad (19.3)$$

$$m_n = ((I-O)/P)*k \qquad (19.4)$$

where I and O are the numbers of inmigrants and outmigrants, respectively. If the migration interval is short, say a year or less, the initial, final, or average populations all yield about the same rates. For a 5-year period, there can be considerable difference.

The next choice concerns the area to be used as a base. For outmigration from an area, the population at risk is clearly that of the area itself. For inmigration, however, the population at risk is that of the balance of the country. This base is rarely used, but see Shryock (1964) for illustrations. Mainly as a practical matter, inmigration rates and outmigration rates are both based on the destination population. Net migration rates preferably should be the difference between in- and outmigration rates that have the same population base. This goal can be achieved also by use of an average of the origin and destination populations, where this is practical, or as suggested later, where lifetime migration is concerned, by an average of the population born in the state and the population resident in the state.

SOURCES OF DATA AND STATISTICS

Whereas birth and death data are readily available for the more developed countries lacking a continuous population register, the same cannot be said for migration data. The ideal migration data set for an area would include data on at least the following (U.S. Census Bureau/Wetrogan and Long, 1990b):

Origins and destinations of migrants
Data available in 1-year age groups and sex
Data available on an annual basis for a variety of time periods
Data available for a number of geographic levels
Data consistent with the relevant population base for calculating migration rates

Ideally, these data would be available for states, counties, and a variety of subcounty areas (Smith *et al.*, 2001, p. 112). Unfortunately, no single data set even comes close to meeting all of these criteria. In fact, no federal agency in the United States directly tracks population movements, although various European countries with population registers do.

Population Registers

A continuous population register system requires every person to transfer his or her record from one local registry office to another when moving. Migration statistics are compiled from these changes of residence. Such statistics have been published for many years by the Nordic countries and a few other western European countries, and more recently by eastern European and Asian countries as well. Among such countries are Belgium, Denmark, Finland, Hungary, Iceland, Israel, Italy, Japan, Netherlands, Norway, Poland, Singapore, Spain, and Sweden.

Censuses and Surveys

Mobility data derived from censuses and surveys are of two broad types. The first type consists of those tabulated from direct questions about mobility or about prior residence—place of birth, place of residence at a fixed past date, duration of residence, last prior residence, mobility history, number of moves, and so on. The second type consists of estimates of net migration derived from (1) counts of total population or population disaggregated by age and sex, at two censuses, and (2) natural increase (births minus deaths) or intercensal survival rates, which are derived in turn from (a) life tables or (b) comparison of the age distributions of countries not experiencing immigration or emigration in successive censuses. The difference between the total change in population during an intercensal period and the change due to natural increase is imputed to net migration. Usually, however, this difference also includes net immigration from abroad. These estimates are derived by a residual method and hence are called residual estimates.

Censuses

The most common source of migration data is a regular census. Fixed-period-migration data have been collected in every U.S. decennial census since 1940, and lifetime-migration data in every U.S. decennial census since 1850. The former data are based on responses to a question asking place of residence 5 years earlier (except for the 1950 census, which asked place of residence 1 year earlier). The U.S. Census Bureau tabulates in- and outmigration data disaggregated by age, sex, and race for all states and counties.

Numerous problems plague migration data from the U.S. decennial census, as described by Smith *et al.* (2001, p. 113). First, the data cannot gauge the effects of multiple moves during the 5-year period. For example, a person may have lived in an apartment in Chicago in 1995, moved to a house in the suburbs in 1996, been transferred to a job in Atlanta in 1998, and retired to Sarasota in January 2000. Census migration data would show only the move from Chicago to Sarasota, completely missing the other moves. Data from the decennial census substantially understate the full extent of mobility and migration during a 5-year period (see DaVanzo and Morrison, 1981; U.S. Census Bureau/Long and Boertlein, 1990a).

A second problem is that the question regarding residence 5 years earlier is included only in the long form of the U.S. census questionnaire, which was sent to 15 to 25% of households in the United States (with the proportion varying from one census to another). This creates problems of data reliability, especially for small places and for detailed categories such as age, sex, and race/ethnicity groups (Isserman, Plane, and McMillen, 1982). Reliability of the data is also affected by the respondent's lack of knowledge regarding geographic boundaries or inability to remember accurately his or her place of residence 5 years earlier (U.S. Census Bureau/Wetrogan and Long, 1990b).

A third problem with migration data from the census is that data covering both in- and outmigration are not available below the county level. Outmigration data present an even greater problem than inmigration data, because they must be compiled from questionnaires filled out by ex-residents throughout the country.

Other problems noted by Smith *et al.* (2001, p. 114) include (1) the inevitable failure of the U.S. decennial census to cover emigration to foreign countries, (2) census undercount problems, and (3) problems of assigning dates to any moves.

Sample Surveys

Considering only sample surveys, the most common source of U.S. migration data is the Current Population Survey (CPS). The reader is already familiar with the fact that this survey is conducted by the Census Bureau, covers some 50,000 households, and is designed primarily to obtain labor force information. Every March, supplementary questions are asked that include migration. The survey collects data on geographic mobility for the United States and its regions, including data on the characteristics of migrants.

Other federally sponsored surveys that have been used to study mobility and migration include the American Housing Survey (AHS), the Survey of Income and Program Participation (SIPP), and the National Longitudinal Surveys (NLS). These surveys provide data that are useful for many types of migration analyses, but generally do not serve as a sufficient basis for measuring and analyzing state and local migration because of small sample sizes and the sample designs.

As the reader may also recall, the American Community Survey collects monthly data from a large rolling sample of households. Initiated in 1996, as now envisioned it eventually will cover every place in the United States, providing usable data for small places over a 5-year period. Migration data in this survey are based on place of residence 1 year earlier rather than 5 years earlier, with the effect of complicating comparisons with migration data from the decennial census.

Migration Histories

Almost all specialized types of questions for gathering mobility data have been limited to surveys. The most common type is the mobility or migration history—a roster of previous usual residences with the dates of moves. Such a history may be accompanied by a similar listing of all jobs for persons of working age. From such histories it is possible to summarize the number of lifetime moves or the number of moves in a given period. Such data are sometimes obtained by a simple, direct question, however. Likewise, instead of determining occupation, employment status, marital status, and so on, at a fixed past date from a more-or-less complete history, a direct question referring to the past date that is central to the study may be employed. Other topics include permanence of migration, number of household members who moved together, month of migration, reasons for moving, migration plans or intentions, and cost of moving.

Migration histories are not limited to national sample surveys but may come from surveys of specific areas. Since a relatively small proportion of the population moves frequently and repeatedly, the surveys do not usually attempt to record all former residences (or all moves) but only the last "k" residences and perhaps also the residence at birth. Furthermore, the exact address is usually not recorded but only the area of residence, and there may be other restrictions on the information recorded.

Such histories are typically easier to trace in countries with population registration systems, such as the Netherlands. The population statistics of the Netherlands are based on automated municipal population registers and are compiled by Statistics Netherlands. Each inhabitant has a unique identification number and is registered in the municipality where he or she lives. When a person dies or emigrates, the data about them are kept by the municipality of last residence. No data are erased from the system. For example, if a person moves, the new address is added to the information already available. The old address is kept as well, but in a historic portion of the personal file (Netherlands, Statistics Netherlands, 1998). This procedure is followed in other population registration systems as well.

Status at Prior Date

To obtain a person's current characteristics, the researcher may make use of questions that are a regular part of a general purpose survey. To obtain the characteristics at a past date (i.e., retrospectively), such surveys increasingly include additional questions to elicit that information (DaVanzo, 1982). Recording the respondent's status prior to migration provides a basis for measuring differential propensities to migrate and for describing temporal sequences. Pinning down the temporal sequence of events can clarify causal relationships and help to answer such questions as, did the unemployment of a given worker precede (hence possibly cause) a recorded move? Or, did a previously employed worker end up jobless after migrating?

One weakness of such retrospective data is the inevitability of response error. Respondents never recollect events and their timing with perfect accuracy, and recall accuracy diminishes as elapsed time increases. Recent tests in the United States indicate that the number of changes in status as measured by retrospective questions is considerably underestimated. Comparisons of current survey reports with reports of matched persons secured in a decennial census 6 years later indicated that the number of shifts in occupation reported in the census was considerably understated. As a corollary, the retrospective description of jobs 6 years earlier must have been subject to considerable response error. Presumably, errors of recall would be fewer for a 1-year period, however. With the advent of large-scale continuous measurement devices, such as the American Community Survey, these errors should be reduced and more timely information on migration patterns produced.

Other facets of mobility covered in surveys include respondents' expectations, intentions, or desires to move. Questions on these attitudinal facets of behavior may be evaluated by checking at the end of the reference period to determine whether or not the respondent who expressed an expectation, intention, or desire to move in fact did so (i.e., actually left the former address). In the case of migration (as opposed to merely moving), it would also be necessary to ascertain whether the person had also left the county, municipality, and so on. Securing this additional information (by interviewing other members of the household or neighbors, obtaining postal change-of-address files, etc.) may be feasible but costly.

Residual Estimates

As shown in Table 19.3, estimates of net migration can be derived from gross migration data by subtracting the number of outmigrants from the number of inmigrants. However, gross migration data are not always available. In such cases, net migration can be estimated indirectly "differenary" them as a residual by comparing an area's population at two dates, them "differenary", and removing, allowing for the change due to natural increase. The residual is attributed to net migration. This approach is known as the indirect or residual method.

Residual estimates require no special questions and may be computed from population counts disaggregated by age and sex, or even from population totals. The indirect methods to be discussed in this section are (1) the national growth-rate method and (2) the residual method comprising (a) the vital statistics method and (b) the survival-rate method. The use of place-of-birth statistics is sometimes considered an indirect method, but since it requires a special question and since there are some direct measures derivable from the data, it will be treated separately in the next major section.

National Growth-Rate Method

This is a crude method in which the estimated migration rate, m_i, for area i is given by

$$m_i = \left\{ \left[(P_i^1 - P_i^0)/P_i^0 \right] - \left[(P_t^1 - P_t^0)/P_t^0 \right] \right\} * k \quad (19.5a)$$

where P_t^1 and P_t^0 represent the national population at the beginning and end of the intercensal period, respectively, P_i^0 represents the populations of the geographic subdivisions at the beginning of the period, and P_i^1 represents their populations at the end of the period.

This rate is customarily multiplied by a constant, such as 100 or 1000. Thus, for a geographic division, a rate of growth greater than the national average is interpreted as net inmigration and a rate less than the national average as net outmigration. The same procedure can be applied to specific age-sex groups to derive estimates of net migration for birth cohorts. This method yields an estimate of the rate of internal migration for geographic subdivisions on the assumption that rates of natural increase and of net immigration from abroad are the same for all parts of the country. It requires no vital statistics.

Vital Statistics Method

A simple variant of the preceding method may be used to obtain a rough indication of the extent of net migration for geographic subdivisions by comparing the rate of growth of each area with the rate of natural increase of the nation. This method assumes that the rate of natural increase is the same throughout the country.

$$m_i = \{[(P_i^1 - P_i^0)/P_i^0] - [(B_t - D_t)/P_t^0]\} * k \qquad (19.5b)$$

where P_i^1 represents the populations of the geographic subdivisions at the end of the intercensal period, P_i^0 is the populations of the geographic subdivisions at the beginning of the period, B_t is the number of births nationally during the intercensal period, and D_t is the number of deaths nationally during the intercensal period, so that $[(B_t - D_t)/P_t^0]$ equals the national natural rate of increase during the intercensal period.

This formula yields an estimate of the total rate of net migration, including international migration, rather than the net internal migration rate. Where net immigration is negligible, Formulas (19.5a) and (19.5b) yield the same results (provided the census counts and the vital statistics are consistent).

If a country has reasonably complete vital statistics and if the two successive censuses are about equally complete, then a more refined application of the vital statistics method is possible. Then the vital statistics method is almost always used to estimate net migration for the total population (i.e., all age-sex groups combined) of an area within a country. As before, the intercensal component equation is the means of estimating net migration as a residual with vital statistics for each area.

$$M_i = (P_i^1 - P_i^0) - (B_i - D_i) \qquad (19.6)$$

where M_i represents the amount of net migration for area i and the other symbols also refer to area i.

The result is the difference between the total number of persons moving into an area during a given intercensal period and the number moving out. This estimate of net migration reflects both the inmigrants and outmigrants who died before the second census (Siegel and Hamilton, 1952). The net migration obtained for a given area is that with respect to all other areas and thus represents net international migration combined with net internal migration. This method may be used to estimate net migration for a sex, race, nativity group, or any other group defined by a characteristic that is invariant over time, provided that the population and vital statistics are available for the characteristic. The main issue concerning the method is not the theoretical validity of Equation (19.6), which represents what Siegel and Hamilton (1952) call "exact net migration," but rather the effect of errors in the terms on the right-hand side of the equation upon the accuracy of the estimate. A further issue is the accuracy of this method as applied to actual statistics in comparison with that of other methods, such as the survival-rate method (Hamilton, 1966; Siegel and Hamilton, 1952; Stone, 1967).

Changes in Area Boundaries

One possible source of error in residual estimates of net migration is a change in the boundaries of the geographic area or areas in question. Unless the population figures and those on natural increase can be adjusted to represent a constant area (ordinarily the present rather than the original area), the estimates will reflect the population in the transferred territory as well as net migration. If the territory transferred is an entire administrative unit of some sort (for example, a municipality that is transferred from one province to another), the requisite statistics will usually be readily available. Often, however, the transferred territory does not follow any previous legal boundaries. In that case, rough estimates will have to be made, for example, on the basis of new and old maps, using the land areas involved as a rough indicator of the proportions of an old administrative unit's population and vital events that are to be attributed to the new units. The transfer will usually occur during the intercensal period. Vital events for the years after the transfer will often be on the new geographic basis and will require no adjustment. There may be a lag in the geographic assignment of vital events, however. In any case, if the transfer occurred during a year and the vital statistics are available for whole years only, a special proration must be made for the year of transfer.

Exclusion of International Migration

As previously mentioned, any variant of the residual method includes in its estimate of net migration the net immigration from abroad (unless a specific effort is made to remove that component). One approach is to confine the computations to the native population. In the case of the vital statistics method, this approach requires that the native population be available separately from the two censuses and that deaths also be tabulated by nativity. The inputs and method of this approach for calculating net internal migration for a state may be described as follows:

(1) Native population of state at second census
(2) Native population of state at first census
(3) Total births in intercensal period
(4) Deaths of natives in intercensal period

Estimated net migration of the native population to the state from other states is given by (1) − (2) − (3) + (4). As explained in Chapter 8, "native" means born in the country, not just born in the state. Births are all native by definition, and babies born during the intercensal period are included in the native population counted at the end of the period (unless they emigrated or died).

The other approach to estimating net internal migration is to allow directly for net immigration from abroad (by subtraction). For this purpose, of course, one must know not only the total immigration but also the area (state, province, etc.) of intended residence of the immigrants and the area of last residence of the emigrants. One must assume that immigrants went to their announced area of destination and that emigrants departed for abroad from their reported area of last residence. Note that direct data on emigration are not available for the United States and its states and this component must be estimated.

Other Issues

Because the estimates of net migration represent a residual obtained by subtraction, relatively moderate errors in population counts or in statistics of births or deaths produce much larger percentage errors in the migration estimates. Fortunately, these errors sometimes offset one another to some degree. For example, the population counts at the two successive censuses may represent about the same amount of net underenumeration. For the same percentage error, errors in the population statistics have more effect on the estimates of net migration than do errors in the vital statistics.

Although the vital statistics method is adaptable to making estimates of net migration for age groups, it is rarely used for this purpose, mainly because of the effort involved in both data compilation and calculations. The advent of computer-intensive methods now makes it much more feasible to produce estimates in this detail. A detailed account and evaluation of this method is provided by Hamilton (1967).

Survival-Rate Method

The survival-rate method is the favored variant for statistically less developed countries because it does not require accurate vital statistics, which are usually unavailable in these countries. It is commonly used elsewhere as well, since it is easily implemented and yields estimates of net migration for age and sex groups without the use of deaths statistics in this detail. Equation (19.7) provides the basic formula for estimating net migration ($M_x^{x+t'}$) using the survival-rate method.

$$M_x^{x+t'} = \left(P_{x+t}^t - sP_x^0\right) \div \sqrt{s} \qquad (19.7)$$

where P_x^0 and P_{x+t}^t represents the population figures at the beginning and end of the period, respectively, for the cohort, s the survival rate for the cohort, and $\sqrt{s}$ (the square root of the survival rate) an adjustment for deaths of migrants during the period (Siegel, 2002, p. 22).

Two main types of survival rates are used, those from life tables and those from censuses. The former are derived from a life table, if possible for the same geographic area and time period to which the estimate of net migration applies. Usually, however, for a county or city without an appropriate life table, one could use a recent life table for its province, its region, or the national population, making the choice on

the basis of available information as to comparative mortality. For a city, for example, the life table for a group of highly urbanized states might be most appropriate. The census survival rate represents the ratio of the numbers in the same national cohort at successive censuses. The objective in structuring this rate is to approximate a closed population. This method requires no life table and no vital statistics and has the advantage of eliminating the effects of some of the errors in the population statistics from the migration estimates.

Like the vital statistics method, the life-table variants of the survival-rate method are designed to measure net migration exactly, assuming that there are no errors in the underlying population and vital statistics and that population and migrants have the same level of mortality. To close the theoretical gap between the vital statistics method and the life-table survival-rate method, an allowance has to be made, in the equation for the latter method, for the deaths of migrants in the area during the period (deaths of inmigrants after immigration and deaths of "outmigrants" before possible outmigration). In other words, an adjustment is necessary to make the number of deaths to residents of a given area during a given period from the survival method approximately equivalent to the number of "recorded" deaths—that is, deaths to "nonmigrants" plus deaths to inmigrants. That is the function of the element $\sqrt{s}$ in the equation.

There are two ways of applying life-table survival rates. In one method, called the forward survival-rate method, the estimate of net migration is obtained as in Equation (19.7). Another way, called the reverse survival-rate method, carries out the calculations in reverse. Here the survival rate is divided into the number in the age group at the end of the intercensal period. Thus,

$$M_x^{x+t''} = \left\{\left(P_{x+t}^t \div s\right) - P_x^0\right\} \sqrt{s} \qquad (19.8)$$

where the symbols have the same meaning as for the forward equation (Siegel, 2002, p. 22). It can be shown that the two methods give identical results and that the distinction between the two methods is unnecessary—that is, $M' = M''$:

$$\begin{aligned}
&\left(P_{x+t}^t - sP_x^0\right) \div \sqrt{s} \\
&= \left\{\left(P_{x+t}^t \div s\right) - (s \div s)P_x^0\right\} \div \left(\sqrt{s} \div s\right) \qquad (19.9) \\
&= \left\{\left(P_{x+t}^t \div s\right) - P_x^0\right\}\sqrt{s}
\end{aligned}$$

In practice, the analyst can simply apply the forward formula (Siegel, 2001, p. 22).

In an earlier design of the survival-rate formulas (i.e., excluding the element $\sqrt{s}$), the forward formula and the reverse formula gave different results because they did not allow exactly for the deaths of migrants during the period, either including deaths of inmigrants over the whole period or deaths of outmigrants over the whole period (Siegel and Hamilton, 1952). It was considered expedient under these circumstances to average the results of the two formulas.

The amount of difference between the migration estimates from the forward and reverse methods applied in this way depends on the amount of net migration and on the level of the survival rate. The percentage difference is a function of only the survival rate. Generally, when the term "survival-rate method" is used without qualification, it refers to the forward method. As we saw, under the revised design of the calculations, the forward method and the reverse method yield the same results.

Life-Table Survival-Rate Method

A more specific expression may be substituted at this point for the survival rate, s. If the survival rate is expressed for a 5-year age group and a 10-year period in life table notation, namely,

$$S_x = (_5L_{x+10})/(_5L_x) \qquad (19.10)$$

Equations (19.8) and (19.9) may be adapted accordingly. As an example,

$$M_{10-14}^{20-24} = \left\{ P_{20-24}^{10} - \left\{ (_5L_{20}/_5L_{10}) * (P_{10-14}^0) \right\} \right\} \div \sqrt{_5L_{20}/_5L_{10}}$$

If there is an open-end interval, say 85 years and over, in the census age distribution, then the 5-year survival rate for $s_{80+} = T_{85} \div T_{80}$, and the 10-year survival rate for $s_{75+} = T_{85} \div T_{75}$.

In using actual life tables, the demographer would prefer to have one covering the full intercensal period. If, instead, only tables centering on the two census dates are available, survival rates can be computed from both life tables and the results averaged so as to give a better representation of the conditions prevailing over the decade.

When the intercensal period is not 5 or 10 years, complications arise. The survival rates will have to be calculated for the number of years in the intercensal period, and this calculation will require additional work if only an abridged life table is available. Furthermore, the survivors will appear in unconventional 5-year age groups. They should be redistributed into conventional 5-year age groups so that they may be compared with the age groups of the second census. Estimates of net migration obtained by subtraction of the survivors from the second census will then be in terms of conventional age groups.

Even if there is no external migration, estimated net migration over all the geographic subdivisions could not be expected to add to zero at each age group. There are errors of coverage and age reporting in the input data, and the life table will only approximate deaths to persons in each birth cohort. As a final step, then, the net migration figures for each age-sex group (i.e., birth cohort) should be adjusted to add to zero (or to the net external migration). Moreover, as with the vital statistics method, it will often be desirable to smooth the reported age distribution in the census and to make corrections for other types of gross errors.

Applications of the survival-rate method frequently omit the cohorts born during the intercensal period, even when adequate statistics on registered births are available. The more comprehensive figures are recommended, however, in the interests of a more nearly complete estimate of net migration and of greater comparability with the vital statistics method. As described in Chapter 13, the survival rates for children born during the intercensal period are of a different form from those for the older ages. Babies born during the first quinquennium of a 10-year intercensal period will be 5 to 9 years old at the end of the period, and those born during the second quinquennium will be under 5 years old. Births can be represented by the radix, l_0, of the life table so that

$$S_B^{5-9} = {}_5L_5/5l_0 \text{ and } S_B^{0-4} = {}_5L_0/5l_0 \qquad (19.11)$$

Census Survival-Rate Method

In the other form of the survival-rate method, the census survival rate is computed as the ratio of the population aged $x + n$ at the second census to the population aged x at the first census, where the censuses are taken n years apart (in the absence of net immigration or after adjusting the survival rates to exclude net immigration). Thus,

$$S_x^{x+n} = (P_{x+n}^{t+n}/P_x^t) \qquad (19.12)$$

Here t is the date of the first census.

A rate that reflects mortality but not migration is desired. Hence, census survival rates have to be based on national population statistics; and, if there is appreciable external migration, it is preferable to base them on the native population as counted in the two national censuses. Once survival rates based on a closed population are secured, however, it is permissible to apply them to the total population figures for local areas so as to include the net migration of the former immigrants in the estimates. (In so doing, it is assumed that the level of mortality of the foreign-born is the same as that of the native population.) The census survival rates are intended to measure mortality plus relative coverage and reporting errors in the two censuses. The confounding of the two effects is actually an advantage. Inasmuch as the disturbing influence of the errors in the population data are reflected in the census survival rates, it is unnecessary to correct for them and, hence, these errors are, in effect, largely excluded from the estimates of net migration. There are two very important assumptions with this method. They are (1) that the survival rates are the same for the geographic subdivisions as for the nation and (2) that the pattern of relative errors in the census age data is the same from area to area.

The first assumption is commonly employed; for example; it is also made when a model life table or a life table for a larger area containing the area in question is used. The second assumption specifically means that the relative change in the percentage completeness of coverage for a particular age (i.e., birth) cohort between the two censuses is the same for the country as a whole and for each area for which net migration is being estimated.

Because of coverage and age reporting errors in the censuses, or because of net immigration from abroad, a national census survival rate will sometimes exceed unity. This is an impossible value, of course, as far as survival itself is concerned; but, for the purpose of estimating net migration, this is the value of the rate that should be used. This fact has to be allowed for when estimating the expected population 10-to-14-years old over a 10-year intercensal period. *UN Manual VI* (United Nations, 1970) treats the problem of estimating net migration of children born during the intercensal period when adequate birth statistics are not available. It uses area-specific child-woman ratios derived from the second census. If the ratios of children aged 0 to 4 to women aged 15 to 44 and of children aged 5 to 9 to women aged 20 to 49 are denoted by CWR_0 and CWR_5, respectively, then estimates of net migration for the age groups 0 to 4 (denoted by net $_5M_{0,i}$) and 5–9 (denoted by net $_5M_{5,i}$) are given by

$$Net_5M_{0,i} = (1/4)[(CWR_0)*(Net_{30}M^{(f)}{}_{15,i})] \quad (19.13)$$

$$Net_5M_{5,i} = (3/4)[(CWR_5)*(Net_{30}M^{(f)}{}_{20,i})] \quad (19.14)$$

where net $_{30}M_{15,i}{}^{(f)}$ and net $_{30}M_{20,i}{}^{(f)}$ are the area estimates of net migration for females aged 15 to 44 and 20 to 49 respectively. If the flow of migration was even and constant fertility ratios are assumed, then one-fourth of the younger and three-fourths of the older children would have been born before their mothers migrated. These proportions are derived as follows: the children under 5 years old at the census were born, on the average, 2.5 years earlier; only one-fourth of their mothers' migration occurred after that date. The children 5 to 9 years old at the census were born, on the average, 7.5 years earlier; three-fourths of their mothers' migration occurred after that date.

Considerable methodological discussion of intercensal survival rates with tables for the United States are contained in a report by the U.S. Census Bureau (1965). This publication also contains a fairly complete bibliography on the subject. Rates are based on both the total population and the native population. The report notes that, if we add the estimates at a given age for all subnational areas, we obtain totals approximating zero. This is always the case whatever the nature of error in the age data or in the survival rates and is one of the features that distinguishes the census survival rate (CSR) method from the life table survival rate (LTSR) method.

The census survival rates computed from national statistics for the *total* population reflect both mortality and net immigration from abroad. Hence, the estimates of net migration represent internal migration plus any excess or deficit of the area's rate of net immigration relative to the national rate. Furthermore, the estimates summed over all areas must balance to zero for any age-sex group so as to represent net internal migration only.

The assumption that mortality, or survival, levels are nearly equal throughout the various geographic areas of the country deserves scrutiny, particularly in countries where mortality is high. Where mortality is high, where there is known to be much regional variation in mortality, or where net migration rates are low, some adjustment for differences in survival rates is necessary. Available information on mortality differences between the geographic subdivisions and the nation may be used to adjust the census survival rates. External evidence on mortality from vital statistics or sample surveys is best for this purpose. The methodology of making adjustments is described at length in *UN Manual VI* (United Nations, 1970). In brief, the ratio of the regional life-table survival rate to the corresponding national life-table survival rate must be computed and applied to the national census survival rates as an adjustment factor.

Estimates calculated by the survival-rate methods, like those calculated by the vital statistics method, are affected by changes in area boundaries and reflect international migration to some extent unless specific allowances are made for these phenomena. As has been shown, the effects of errors in the components of the population estimating equation are somewhat different, however. In the vital statistics variant of the residual method, it is the relative size of the net census errors in the population figures at the two censuses for the area in question that concerns us. (If the error for an age-sex group at the first census is different from that at the second census, the difference will be included in the estimated net migration.) In the survival-rate variant, on the other hand, it is the applicability to the given geographic area of the relative national coverage ratios at the two censuses that is in question. Similarly, in the first case, the completeness of death registration and perhaps also the accuracy of reported ages at death are of concern; whereas, in the second case, the applicability of the survival rates used to the area in question is of concern. The sources of error in the survival-rate methods are discussed by Hamilton (1966), Price (1955), and Stone (1967), and in *UN Manual VI* (1970).

Comparative Results from Different Methods

Estimates of net migration for age-sex groups made by the survival-rate method are sometimes adjusted to add to an estimate of net migration for all ages combined made by the vital statistics (VS) method. As noted earlier, Siegel and Hamilton (1952) demonstrated that the latter method gives a theoretically exact measure of net migration whereas the former method can only approximate the true estimate. Which method gives more accurate estimates in an actual situation depends on a host of empirical considerations and has been debated for particular situations (Hamilton, 1967; Tarver, 1962; United Nations, 1970). On the basis of U.S.

data, Hamilton (1967) and Tarver (1962) found that the forward census survival-rate method tends to give (algebraically) lower estimates of net migration than the vital statistics method. The authors of *UN Manual VI* (1970) stated that "Since the number of deaths is likely to be larger in the larger of the two components of net migration (inmigration and outmigration), CSR estimates obtained by the forward method will generally be smaller than those obtained by the VS method." They concluded, however, that it is difficult to make a general statement regarding the relative accuracy of the two methods for the net migration of all ages combined. No research has been reported comparing the vital statistics method and the survival-rate method applied according to the new design described here (i.e., adjusting by $\sqrt{s}$ for the bias in the measurement of deaths and net migration).

Uses and Limitations

In summary, the residual method cannot be used to estimate gross inmigration or outmigration or migration streams. The migration period must be the intercensal or similar period. In any of its variations, this method can be used to estimate net migration for a fixed area, for a group defined by an unchanging characteristic (e.g., sex, race, nativity), or for a group defined by a characteristic that changes in a fixed way with time (age).

The residual method cannot ordinarily be used for social and economic groups, mainly because the corresponding characteristics (e.g., marital status, occupation, income) change frequently and unpredictably during the intercensal period. In most countries, educational level changes so seldom for adults, however, that net migration according to educational attainment could probably be estimated fairly well for the adult population.

Rural-urban migration is such an important element in internal migration, particularly in the less developed countries, that there is great interest in measuring it by some means. This may be accomplished, but as with other methods, the residual method has many pitfalls in this application. Other things being equal, the method works best when the urban and rural areas are defined in terms of whole administrative units and changes in classification are rarely made. Here one may obtain constant territories over the intercensal period by reassigning whole localities that have been shifted from the rural to the urban classification or vice versa. When, however, the reclassification of territory involves annexations and retrocessions or a radically different set of boundaries for the units in question, there are serious problems in adjusting the statistics and these may be insurmountable. The *UN Manual VI* (1970) describes some of the devices that can be used to handle these difficulties.

As previously stated, normally census errors in classification as well as in coverage will be reflected as errors in the estimated net migration. Furthermore, death statistics are not available separately for all the areas or groups in question, and life tables for larger populations will be inappropriate in varying degrees.

The major advantage of indirect methods of estimating net migration is that they can be applied when no direct data on in- and outmigration are available. Consequently, they are particularly useful for small areas. However, the accuracy of these estimates depends heavily on the accuracy of the underlying population estimates (or counts) and the vital statistics or survival rates. Vital statistics and the associated survival-rates in the United States are generally quite accurate, but the accuracy of population estimates and census counts varies over time and from place to place. In particular, since net migration is often estimated for decades, changes in the coverage from one census to another may cause estimates of net migration to be too high or too low. Changes in geographic boundaries over time may also affect net migration estimates. This generally is not a problem for states and counties, but may be significant for cities, census tracts, zip code areas, and other subcounty areas.

Estimates of net migration disaggregated by age, sex, and race for states in the United States were produced for each decade from 1870 to 1950 (Lee *et al.*, 1957) and were extended to counties in the 1950s, 1960s, and 1970s (White, Meuser, and Tierney, 1987). Estimates of total net migration for states and counties for the 1980s and 1990s have been produced by the Census Bureau and are available on the Internet. To our knowledge, however, no further disaggregation of these estimates by age, sex, and race have been produced for all states and counties in the United States. Analysts choosing to use data on net migration may have to produce the data themselves.

Miscellaneous Sources

In many countries, administrative records gathered for purposes other than measuring internal spatial movements have been adapted to measure place-to-place flows of people. The records most commonly used for migration estimates on a continuing basis in the United States come from the Internal Revenue Service (IRS), the federal agency responsible for collecting taxes. Income tax returns are to be filed as of April 15 each year, and the Census Bureau matches the returns from year to year according to the taxpayer's Social Security number. Each tax return used for this purpose includes the number of "dependents" (other family members) and the street address from which the form is filed. Year-to-year matches provide annual estimates of gross flows for states and counties that are available on the IRS's website (*www.irs.gov*). No information on individuals or individual households is released—just gross flows.

As explained in Chapters 2 and 18, the Immigration and Naturalization Service (INS) within the U.S. Department of Justice is the major source of international migration statistics in the United States. The INS produces annual statistics on the number of legal immigrants according to type, country of origin, state of intended residence, age, sex, marital status, occupation, and several other characteristics. See Chapters 2 and 18 and Immigration and Naturalization Service (1999, 2000) for further information regarding the INS data.

In other countries, similar tracking systems can provide information on spatial movements. A system of national health care can record an individual's successive movements, at least insofar as these involve seeking health care. A rich source of statistics on internal movements is a fully developed national information system that involves noting the changing locations where individuals receive government services of varying types.

Some of the partial population registers (i.e., registers of a population subgroup) have been, or could be, used to estimate the migration of particular population subgroups. By various assumptions, migration rates for a subgroup could be extended to the general population; or the data may simply be used to describe and analyze migration differentials among classes within the subgroup. Several illustrations follow.

In the United States, the national social insurance scheme that provides pensions to retired workers and their surviving dependents, the Old Age and Survivors Insurance system operated by the U.S. Social Security Administration, is the basis for a 1% continuous work history sample. The sample gives the age, sex, and place of employment of workers covered by the program. Migration can be approximated by comparing successive places of employment of individual workers at yearly intervals. The chief shortcomings of the procedure include (1) a lack of correspondence between area of employment and area of residence, (2) incompleteness of coverage (for example, in the past some industries have not been covered), and (3) sampling error. These data are best suited, therefore, for making estimates for large areas like states. A pioneering study with this material for two states was carried out by Bogue (1952), who tried to measure job mobility as well as geographic mobility. An example of a subsequent study using this source and exploring its applicability is provided by Morrison and Relles (1975).

Another source involving use of administrative records to gauge migration flows and patterns is files of drivers' license address changes (DLAC). One such application has been made by the state of California in preparing its annual official population estimates for counties. California reports changes in interstate driver's license addresses annually. When a person with a driver's license from another state applies for a California driver's license, that person is required to relinquish the license from his or her previous state of residence. The information is recorded and the driver's license is returned to the previous state of residence. Similarly, other states return California drivers' licenses to

the California authorities when former California drivers apply there for new licenses. The DLAC data provide an annual measure of the volume and directions of gross migration of the adults licensed to drive, for the counties of California. These estimates, in turn, can be extended to the entire population, based on the further estimate that one change of a driver's license address corresponds to 1.5 actual moves. Despite important limitations, the DLAC data have proven sufficiently useful to be incorporated into the methodology by which the state prepares its official population estimates (Johnson and Lovelady, 1995).

In Canada, the Family Allowance System provides estimates of both monthly and annual flows; place-to-place migration data are available for sex and age groups as well as socioeconomic characteristics. Croze (1956) estimated the net migration in France for the period 1950–1952 for departments, using electoral lists. Registers of electors (voters) are maintained and updated locally, and changes in registrations for each community are reported annually. Comparisons of a sample of the names in the alphabetical listings of successive city directories, with allowances for death and the attainment of adulthood (usually age 18 in the directories), identify persons who have entered or left the area. Goldstein (1958) made the classic study of this type for Norristown, Pennsylvania. It gives a detailed account of the validity of this type of data and methodology.

ANALYSIS OF DIRECT DATA

Place of Birth

Uses and Limitations

The traditional item that represents a direct question relating to migration is place of birth. This item has long been included in national censuses, and it is occasionally found in sample surveys. The first national census to contain such an item was that of England and Wales in 1841. As explained in Chapters 8 and 18, two kinds of specificity are usually called for: (1) in the case of the foreign born, the country of birth; and (2) in the case of the native population, the primary geographic subdivision (i.e., state, province, etc.) or, often also, the secondary subdivision, such as the district in India or Pakistan. "Native" may be defined sometimes to include persons born in the outlying territories of the country and not covered by the census in question. Usually those natives are separately identified, however.

Several examples will be given of the treatment of data on internal migration from the question on birthplace in national population censuses. The most detailed and basic statistics, from which various summary statistics are derived, are given in the cross-classification of residence at birth by residence at the time of the census. Some countries show such cross-classifications, or consolidations thereof, for secondary divisions (Taeuber, 1958). Changes of residence in these cross-classified statistics may be viewed as representing migration streams between the time of birth and the time of enumeration.

Frequently the statistics of streams are consolidated into categories like "living in given state, born in different state" and "born in given state, living in different state." These data may be viewed as representing lifetime inmigrants and lifetime outmigrants for each state, respectively.

Characteristics (e.g., age and socioeconomic characteristics) of lifetime migrants are usually shown in terms of these consolidated categories (e.g., whether or not born in area of enumeration), because the full detail would be voluminous; but they are sometimes shown for migration streams.

In the United States, data on the state of birth of the native population have been collected at every census from 1850 onward. A cross-classification of each state of residence at the time of the census with each state, territory, and possession at time of birth has been shown in full detail. In addition, the state of birth has been shown in some reports for the urban, rural-nonfarm, and rural-farm parts of states and for individual cities of varying minimal size. The census inquiry does not provide information on urban-rural residence, or city of residence, at birth.

The accuracy or quality of the statistics on place of birth of the native population is not of concern here except insofar as they pertain to internal migration. On the assumption that the statistics are accurate, what would they actually measure, and how useful are these measures to the demographer?

Unlike the estimates of migration derived by the residual method, which are limited to net movements, place-of-birth data can represent inmigrants, outmigrants, and specific streams. The statistics often reveal nothing about intrastate migration, and even when secondary subdivisions are specified in the recording of birthplace, intra-area mobility (short-distance movement) is not covered. Moreover, the statistics do not take account of intermediate movements between the time of birth and the time of the census, and persons who have returned to live in their area of birth appear as nonmigrants. In sum, these statistics do not indicate the total number of persons who have moved from the area in which they were born to other areas, or to any specific area, during any given period of time.

The question of time reference deserves particular attention. Unless the statistics from one census were tabulated by age, they tell us nothing about when the move occurred. With a tabulation by age, the only specification is that given by age itself; for example, a migrant 35 years old must have moved within the 35 years preceding the census. Thus, the older the migrant, the less is known about the date of the move and the greater the likelihood of intervening moves between other areas of the same class. Even statistics tabulated by age for two successive censuses are not fully adequate for measuring migration in an intercensal period,

although they do greatly enhance the value of the data. Also, inasmuch as the statistics on state, province, and so on of birth are limited to the native population of the country, the internal migration of the foreign-born population subsequent to its immigration is not included.

There is little quantitative evidence of the accuracy with which birthplace is reported. The fact that birthplace is a constant in a person's life should strengthen recall. Since, however, for everybody except young children, it relates to a more remote date than does the migration question regarding residence at a fixed past date, recall on the part of respondents will likely fade over time and the responses will be less accurate for persons about whom the information is provided by others.

Statistics on place of birth are subject to the types of errors of reporting and data processing that affect the generality of demographic characteristics; in addition, they have some sources of error that are *sui generis*. These include uncertainties about area boundaries at the time of birth and about the reporting of birthplace for babies who were not born at the usual residence of their parents. There have been several attempts to measure the gross and net effects of these sources of error by such methods as re-interviews or matching studies of a sample of the original records. For the 1980 and 1990 U.S. censuses, there was, overall, little inconsistency between the census responses on place of birth and the reinterview responses (U.S. Census Bureau, 1995, p. 19). Thus, it appears that the census responses accurately reflect the actual state or foreign country of birth. The introduction of automated coding in 1990 contributed to the consistency of the data.

From the standpoint of measuring internal migration, it would be ideal if birthplace were reported in terms of present boundaries. (Otherwise, a person who lived in a part of state A that was transferred to state B is automatically classified as a migrant whether he moved or not.) Rarely, however, are instructions provided in the census on this point. This is a problem with other migration questions as well, but the chances are greater that a boundary change occurred if lifetimes are being considered. In the United States, West Virginia was detached from Virginia and became a separate state in 1863. It is evident from the subsequent statistics for many decades thereafter that some respondents born in West Virginia before 1863 gave Virginia as their birthplace whereas others gave West Virginia. In adapting to this situation, the analysts at the University of Pennsylvania combined these two states as one birthplace for 1870 in their monumental study of population redistribution in the United States from 1870 to 1950 (Lee *et al.*, 1957).

In statistically developed countries, a very high proportion of births take place at hospitals rather than in the home. The two places may be located in different areas; thus, some ambiguity is introduced in the question on birthplace. From what was said earlier about the desirability of measuring changes in usual residence rather than de facto residence, it is clear that our preference is for the location of the parents' usual residence, rather than that of the hospital. Because most hospitals are located in urban areas, a bias would be introduced toward urban birthplaces unless the parents' usual residence was reported. When the home and hospital are located within the same tabulation area, the birthplace statistics are not affected, of course.

The UN (1970) pointed out a related problem in certain countries where births occur under more traditional auspices. In India, for example, it is customary for a woman to return to her father's household to bear the first child and often the second and subsequent children. This custom gives rise to some spurious migration as measured from place-of-birth statistics.

Previously, we discussed the appropriate bases of migration rates. In the case of place-of-birth statistics, there are appropriate situations for using either the population at origin or the population at destination. In either case, however, the population at the time of the census tends to be used. This decision is made on the ground that the population at risk does not have a fixed birth date. One practical way of handling the fact that different populations are at risk for inmigration and outmigration is to average the population born in the state and the population resident in the state. Both of these populations are available from the census tabulations of the place-of-birth responses. The resident population is the most practical, if not the most appropriate, base for inmigrants. The population born in the state is the most appropriate base for outmigrants. An average of these two numbers could serve as a representative common population at risk of migration for the state in the computation of immigration, outmigration and net migration rates. An illustration of the calculation of measures of net lifetime migration is given for the regions of Hungary in 1931 in Table 19.4 (see page 518).

Measures Used in Analysis

Among the wide range of migration rates based on place-of-birth data that can be computed, we shall discuss the interregional migration rate, the inmigration rate for a region, the outmigration rate for a region, the net migration rate for a region, and the turnover rate.

1. *Interregional migration rate of the native population*

$$m_r = \left[\left(\sum N_{ij} - \sum N_{i=j} \right) / N \right] * 100 \quad (19.15)$$

where N represents the total native population, subscript i the region of enumeration and subscript j the region of birth, N_{ij} the number of natives living in region i and born in region j, including those living in the region of birth (i = j) and $\sum N_{i=j}$ the number of natives living in the region of birth. Thus, $\sum N_{ij} = N$.

This leads us to an alternative expression of the rate:

$$m_r = \left[\left(\sum N_{i \neq j} \right) / N \right] * 100 = \left[\left(\sum M_{ij} \right) / N \right] * 100 \quad (19.16)$$

where $N_{i \neq j}$ represents an interregional migration stream, which may be called M_{ij}.

2. *Inmigration rate for a region*

$$im_1 = \left[\sum_j M_{1j} / N_1 \right] * 100 \quad (19.17)$$

where M_{1j} refers to the migrants living in region 1 who were born in region j; and N_1 is the native population enumerated in region 1. Note that $\Sigma_j M_{1j} = \Sigma_j N_{1j} - N_{11} = N_1 - N_{11}$

3. *Outmigration rate for a region*

$$om_1 = \left[\sum_j M_{i1} / N_1 \right] * 100 \quad (19.18)$$

where $\Sigma_j M_{i1}$ refers to the migrants from region 1 to the ith region and N_1 represents the total population born in region 1. Again,

$$\sum_j M_{i1} = \sum_j N_{i1} - N_{11} = N_1 - N_{11}$$

4. *Net migration rate for a region*

$$nm_1 = \left[\left(\sum_j M_{1j} - \sum_i M_{i1} \right) / N_i \right] * 100 \quad (19.19)$$

If the outmigration rate is computed using the native population living in the region as the base, the outmigration rate can be subtracted from the inmigration rate.

5. *Turnover rate*

$$m_1^T = \left[\left(\sum M_{1j} + \sum M_{i1} \right) / N_1 \right] * 100 = m_1^I + m_1^0 \quad (19.20)$$

The turnover rate does not carry a sign. The difference between the rate computed directly and the same rate computed by adding the in- and outmigration rates is due to rounding

Birth-Residence Index

This index is simply the net gain or loss for an area through inter-area migration. In other words, it is the net effect of lifetime migration upon the surviving population. The formula for area 1 may be written as

$$BR_1 = \sum_j M_{1j} - \sum_i M_{i1} = I_1 - O_1 \ldots \quad (19.21)$$

Note that this formula (Equation 19.21) is the numerator of the net migration rate (Equation 19.19). Thus, the sum of the birth-residence indexes taken over all areas of the country must be equal to zero, or

$$\sum BR_i = 0 \quad (19.22)$$

As Shryock (1964) noted, a particular net gain or loss may result from qualitatively different patterns of inmigration and outmigration over time. For example, a zero balance may have arisen from (1) zero balances at every decade in the past, (2) net inmigration in recent decades balanced by heavier net outmigration in earlier decades, (3) net outmigration in recent decades balanced by heavier net inmigration in earlier decades, or (4) more complex patterns. A migration of a given size in a recent decade has the effect ordinarily of a migration of larger size at an earlier decade because of the different proportion of survivors from migrants of the two decades, but the analysis is further complicated by differences in the age distributions of the migrants in the two decades and by changing mortality conditions.

Intercensal Change in the Birth-Residence Index

This measure is defined as the difference in the birth-residence indices of two consecutive census years for a given state (or group of states) and is intended to approximate the net migration during the intervening intercensal period. This measure is thus designed to relate state-of-birth data to a fixed period as opposed to the many different lifetimes represented by a surviving population.

How accurate is this approximation? Because the basic data are confined to the native population, changes in the birth residence index are produced only by internal migration and deaths, aside from errors in the census data themselves (Shryock, 1964). It is important to note, however, that a birth-residence surplus in one state and the coincidental birth-residence deficit in another state may both be reduced by the deaths of people who migrated into the first state from the second. It is probable that, when a large birth-residence surplus in a state begins to shrink, the shrinkage is due at least in part to deaths of the earlier inmigrants, and the shrinkage of some of the large deficits may likewise be attributed to the same cause. Shryock (1964) pointed out, however, that it does not follow that the decennial change in the birth residence index is always reduced arithmetically by mortality. The decennial approximation is to net migration, and mortality may have more effect upon the smaller gross component (say, inmigration) than upon the larger gross component (say, outmigration).

More detailed discussion of the failure of the index to measure intercensal migration accurately is given by Shryock (1964). Note that the defect in the measure arises not primarily from errors in the census data, but rather from the limited validity of the measure. In other words, place-of-birth statistics are not suited to measure migration in a fixed period of time regardless how they are manipulated; at best they yield only approximations to what is sought, and the direction of the bias can only be inferred.

The measure we have just defined is

$$BR_2 - BR_1 = (I_2 - I_1) - (O_2 - O_1) \qquad (19.23)$$

where the subscripts 1 and 2 indicate the first and second censuses, respectively.

Gross Intercensal Interchange of Population

The sum of the absolute values of the change during an intercensal period in the number of nonresident natives of an area (outmigrants) and the change in the number of resident natives of other states in the area (inmigrants) has been termed the "gross intercensal interchange of population." This may be viewed as a measure of gross interstate migration, or of population turnover, for a given state. This measure will almost certainly be too low because the "error" terms for both inmigrants and outmigrants are errors of omission (Shryock, 1964). The formula may be written as

$$GIIP = |I_2 - I_1| + |O_2 - O_1| \qquad (19.24)$$

The formula has not been complicated by introducing a second type of subscript ($I_{i,\ t}$, etc.), but it is to be understood as applying to a particular state or province.

Refined Measurement of Intercensal Migration

Since statistics on place of birth are often the only available statistics relating to gross internal migration and migration streams in a country, it is important to consider how, despite their shortcomings, they may be refined to serve the demographer's interests. When we turn from examining the data on lifetime migration from a single census to estimates made by differencing figures from successive censuses, we are moving from direct to indirect measurement of migration. First, it should be pointed out that biased estimates can be obtained of intercensal inmigration, outmigration, or a migration stream and not just of net migration (i.e., the intercensal change in the birth-residence index). The first step, as before, is to subtract the figure for the earlier census from the corresponding figure from the later census. This, however, produces a biased estimate because no allowance has been made for intercensal changes to the "net migrants." All the adjustments proposed for removing the bias are allowances for intercensal mortality. No adjustments have been proposed to allow for return migration or onward migration. Migration of these types during the intercensal period are not included in the Change Index (United Nations, 1970).

To allow for intercensal mortality, Equation (19.23) may be modified as follows:

$$BR_2 - BR_1 = (I_2 - S^I I_1) - (O_2 - S^O O_1) \qquad (19.25)$$

where S^I and S^O are the intercensal survival rates for the lifetime inmigrants and outmigrants as counted at the earlier census, respectively. The two terms of (19.25) give net migration among persons born outside the area and persons born inside the area, respectively. (Any of the formulas in this section may be taken to apply to a birth cohort as well as to the total native population.) The most obvious type of survival rate to use is an intercensal survival rate, and this requires that the place-of-birth data be tabulated by age at both censuses.

UN Manual VI (United Nations, 1970) gives procedures for three situations, namely, where place of birth has been tabulated by age for neither of two successive censuses, for one but not the other, and for both. In the first situation, it is possible to use only an overall life-table survival rate (e.g., T_{10}/T_0), thus assuming that migrants had the age distributions and age-specific mortality rates of the life-table population. Unrealistic as this assumption is, this adjustment is better than not allowing for mortality at all.

When age is cross-tabulated at only one census, that census is very likely to be the later one. This circumstance is preferred because the intercensal survival rate for a period of k years can then be computed as the ratio of the population k years old and over at the second census to the population of all ages at the first census. Because the population born in a given state or province is a closed population just like the total native population of the country (neglecting return immigration of natives and emigration of natives abroad), a forward intercensal survival rate can be calculated for any tabulated area of birth ($N_{j,\,a+k}^{t+k} \div N_{j,a}^t$).

The third procedure—that applicable where state of birth is tabulated by age for two censuses—is similar in its strategy to the second, but the computations are much more detailed. The computations are carried out separately for each age (birth) cohort.

Residence at a Fixed Past Date

Fixed-period migration can be obtained by a question of the form, "Where did you live on [date]" or "Where did you live 5 years ago?" Often, however, the question is in several parts, with the parts specifying the levels of area detail required. In many ways, this is the best single item on population mobility. It counts the migrants over a definite past period of time associated with the current population and provides gross as well as net migration statistics. These gross statistics do not, however, include all of the moves during the period or even all of the persons who have moved during the period. So-called gross migration from the fixed-period question is partly a net measure because circular migrants during the migration period are counted only once, and migrants who died during the migration period and children born after the reference date are not included in the statistics. With regard to the last of these categories, the convention of assigning the residence of the mother to the children born during the migration period was employed in a few Current Population Surveys in the United States. Like other migration questions in censuses, this question is not very well suited to a *de facto* census. In spite of these limitations, a wide range of useful measures can be derived from

the absolute figures, and useful analyses of geographic patterns, time series, differentials, and so forth can be based on these measures.

The United States census of 1940 was the first to include a question of this type, relating to a 5-year period. Such a 5-year question has been included in each decennial census (except 1950) since that year. The census 2000 question was essentially the same as that of 1940. The inclusion of a fixed-period migration question in national sample surveys has also become more prevalent. United States is one of the countries that includes a fixed-period migration question on a regular basis. After experimenting with a variety of migration intervals, the U.S. Census Bureau settled on a 1-year interval for its survey of April 1948 and with a few exceptions has continued with a 1-year interval to the present.

Choice of Mobility Period

In choosing the reference date for the mobility question, considerations of usefulness and of accuracy may conflict to an extent. From the standpoint of demographic analysis, the date of the previous census has many advantages, since the components of population change can then readily be studied for the intercensal period. If the intercensal period is 10 years rather than 5 years, however, errors of memory and lack of knowledge may be excessive in reporting prior residence. Anthropologists have found that other events are remembered relatively well if they are tied in with some event of historical significance, such as the outbreak of a war or the achievement of national independence; but the irregular time intervals thus defined do not lend themselves very well to time series or to demographic analysis in general.

The longer the migration interval, the greater the number of children that will be omitted from the coverage of the question, and the less will characteristics such as age and marital status recorded in the census correspond to those at the time of the move. On the other hand, a very short period (i.e., 1 year or less) may not yield enough migrants for detailed analysis of migration streams. Furthermore, one must consider the representativeness of the 1-year period or, to a lesser extent, any period shorter than the intercensal period. The U.S. Census Bureau (concurring with many experts in the field) judges a 5-year mobility period, on balance, to be optimal for a census, even though a 1-year period may be highly useful in an annual sample survey.

Average Annual Movers

Another problem arises in the computation of average annual numbers or rates. If the number of moves has been compiled from a population register over a period of years, it is quite appropriate to obtain such averages by dividing the number of moves by the number of years. When, however, the number of movers is defined by the number of persons whose residence at the beginning of a fixed period is different from that at the census or survey date, then the calculation produces an estimate with a downward bias and the longer the interval the greater the bias.

The reasons for this bias are as follows:

1. A larger proportion of movers will have died over the longer period than over the shorter period. Emigration from the country has the same directional bias in its effect on the migration statistics as deaths.
2. A mover has a greater opportunity to return to his or her original residence over a longer period than over a shorter period. Hence, the number of persons per year appearing to be movers will be smaller for the longer period.
3. Since a mover is counted as such only once, regardless of the number of times he or she moves, the proportion of movers in any one of five 1-year periods is expected to be larger than one-fifth the proportion over a 5-year period—given a constant proportion of movers per year.
4. When children born after the base date are not covered by the mobility questions, fewer movers are counted for the longer period. Children born during the mobility interval are then excluded from the base population. The effect on the overall rate also depends on the age-specific mobility rates. Young children tend to be more mobile than the average for the population of all ages (U.S. Census Bureau/Schachter, 2001b).

Nonetheless, averages computed for periods of unequal length can be used with appropriate caution in the analysis. If the apparent average was greater for the longer period than for the shorter period, then the true difference was in the same direction and at least as large. This bias also affects annual estimates computed from the "intercensal change in the birth-residence index" and estimates of net migration made by the survival-rate method.

Quality of the Data and Statistics

The data obtained by the question on residence at a fixed past date are subject to essentially the same types of errors of reporting and tabulation in censuses and surveys as are other demographic, social, and economic characteristics. In addition, the reporting of this item is affected by the types of errors that are peculiar to reporting past events and their placement in time.

Data secured from a sample survey are, of course, subject to sampling error as well as nonsampling error. The Content Reinterview Surveys of the 1980 and 1990 U.S. censuses did not secure information on the accuracy of reporting residence 5 years prior to the census. The share of persons for whom prior residence was allocated in the 1990 census was 6.4%; the percentage not reporting prior residence in cen-

suses has been rising. Among persons in households interviewed in the Current Population Survey, the proportion failing to answer the question on residence 1 year earlier is quite low—on the order of a fraction of 1%. These omissions are now filled by computerized allocations. Of households eligible for interview, however, about 4 to 5% are not interviewed at all in an average month. The members of these households are also nonrespondents on the migration questions, of course. Inflating the sample data to "control" totals (that is, independent estimates of total population disaggregated by age, sex, race, and Hispanic origin) gives these nonrespondents the same characteristics as those persons in the specific age-sex-race-Hispanic-origin group that reported, although actually they may have had a somewhat different distribution on such a characteristic as mobility. This weighting partially corrects for bias due to undercoverage. Because of the allocations and adjustments, the published statistics do not show any cases "not reported" on migration.

A recurring difficulty in both censuses and sample surveys of the United States has been the biased reports of the urban or rural origin of movers. This difficulty arises partly from the rather complex urban-rural definition now in use and partly from a strong tendency for persons living outside a city but in its suburbs to give the city as their residence. This tendency leads to an overstatement of outmigration from urban areas and an understatement of that from rural areas. As a result, the United States has had to discontinue the direct measurement of rural-urban migration. In countries where the areas classified as urban have relatively permanent boundaries, this problem may be less acute.

Measures Used in Analysis

Many of the measures used in analyzing fixed-period mobility are identical or similar to those used with the kinds of mobility data that were discussed previously. There are also similar problems regarding the choice of population base, annual averages, and so on.

Mobility or Migration Status

To analyze mobility or migration status, the simplest type of derived figures is the percentage distribution by mobility status. For some purposes (e.g., comparisons of two states in the same country), it would be better to base the percentage distribution on the total excluding the "not reported" cases. For some countries, the "unknowns" shown are only partial unknowns since the nonresponses had been partly allocated. The percentages for various types of mobility can also be regarded as mobility rates per 100 of the resident population.

In a distribution for a particular geographic subdivision, some of the figures also represent inmigration rates, for example, the category "different county" in the distribution by mobility status for a county. Of necessity, such a distribution excludes outmigrants. Such "status rates" include inmigrants to the area during the "migration" period, but exclude outmigrants during the migration period. (The elements in the percent distribution of the population by migration are being called "status rates," although this name is quite clearly a demographic oxymoron. "Rates" measure change over a period, and "status" refers to the condition at a particular date. Here, the participation of the surviving population in the event of mobility over a prior 1-year or 5-year period is ascertained at a particular time.) In the case of fixed-period migration, the population at the beginning of the period rather than the end of the period (i.e., the population at the end plus a portion of the outmigrants during the period minus a portion of the inmigrants during the period) more nearly represents the population "at risk" of outmigration (disregarding births and deaths during the period). This population is usually available or can be estimated.

The choice of a population base for the rates is significant not so much for its effect on the size of the base as for its effect on the number of migrants. Persons who are excluded or included (preferably in part) to approximate the population at the beginning of the period have a 100% migration rate, and their number must be deducted from or added to the number of migrants as well as the base. If a migration rate is to be based on the initial population, the inmigrants from outside the region should be removed from the resident migrants in each region and the outmigrants to other regions should be restored in order to include just those migrants who lived in the region earlier.

In-, Out-, and Net Migration Rates

In-, out-, and net migration rates may be expressed by formulas analogous to those shown earlier for place-of-birth statistics. Again, it is possible to base the rate on the population at the beginning or end of the period or on the mid-period population.

A *partial migration rate* is defined as the number of migrants to an area from a particular origin, or from an area to a particular destination, per 1000 or per 100 of the population at either origin or destination. The *partial outmigration rate* can be expressed as

$$m_{ji}^0 = (M_{ji}/P_i)*1000 \qquad (19.26)$$

where M_{ji} is the stream from area i to area j. For the stream from j to i, the partial outmigration rate is

$$m_{ij}^I = (M_{ij}/P_i)*1000 \qquad (19.27)$$

The *gross rate of population interchange* may be defined as

$$GRI_{i \leftrightarrow j} = [(M_{ij}+M_{ji})/(P_i+P_j)]*1000 \qquad (19.28)$$

The net rate of population interchange is then

$$NRI_{i \leftrightarrow j} = [(M_{ij}-M_{ji})/(P_i+P_j)]*1000 \qquad (19.29)$$

The "effectiveness" of internal migration may be measured by the ratio of net migration to turnover—a measure proposed by Shryock (1959). The higher the ratios for a set of areas, the fewer the moves that are required to effect a given amount of population redistribution among them. There are patently other important aspects of the effectiveness of migration that are not comprehended in this measure. This ratio ranges from 0 to 100. The effectiveness of a stream and its counterstream may also be measured in this fashion. Often the counterstream is as large as the stream, so that there is little net migration and a low ratio of effectiveness.

Migration Preference Index

The Migration Preference Index is another measure of fixed-period mobility. This measure, first suggested by Bachi (1957), is defined as the ratio (times a constant) of the actual to the expected number of migrants in a stream when the expected number is directly proportionate to both the population at origin and the population at destination.

> This measure indicates, then, whether streams are greater or smaller than would be expected from considerations of population size alone. It does not include any assumption about the expected effect of distance, but we can compare measures for different streams in the light of our knowledge of contiguity and of mileage and, in fact, in the light of knowledge that we may have about the relative attractiveness of the areas. (Shryock, 1964)

This index can be computed in several ways. The most useful one, however, relates to interarea migrants only—that is, the Preference Index for a state relates to interstate migration only. To compute the index, interstate migrants are assumed to be distributed proportionately to the population at origin and the population at destination. Take the national rate of interarea (interprovincial, interregional, etc.) migration. Assume that it is uniformly the outmigration rate for all areas of the given class. Compute the expected total number of outmigrants from a given area to all destinations. Distribute these among the other areas in proportion to their population, to obtain the expected number of migrants in each stream. The Preference Index is then given by

$$P.I. = [M_{OD}(\textstyle\sum P_i - P_0)/(mP_0P_D)]*100 \qquad (19.30)$$

where M_{OD} = actual number of migrants from 0 to D
$\quad P_0$ = population at origin 0
$\quad P_D$ = population at destination D
$\quad \sum P_i$ = national population
$\quad m$ = proportion of interarea migrants in the national population

This index may vary from 0 to ∞. The total number of expected inmigrants can be obtained by summing the expected numbers in all the inmigration streams, but the indices themselves are not additive (Shryock, 1964). For an illustration of the computation of the migration preference index, see Tables 21.12 and 21.13 in Shryock, Siegel, and Stockwell (1976).

Distance of Move

A very different way of reducing the data is to compute the distance (in kilometers or miles) between the points of origin and destination. Actually, instead of points (i.e., addresses), it would be practical to start with statistics on origin and destination grouped in tabulation areas, and estimate the distance between the centers of the areas of origin and destination.

Duration of Residence and Last Prior Residence

The typical question on duration of residence has the form, "How long has subject person been living in this area?" (i.e., the area of usual residence). The logical companion question, and that recommended by the United Nations, is one concerning the name of the previous area of residence; but in national censuses most countries asking the question on duration of residence have been content to ask only for place of birth. There are two ways of defining a migrant from such data:

1. A person who had moved into the area at any time in the past and was still resident there. This category would include primary, secondary (or progressive), and return migrants. By this definition, the number of migrants would exceed that of lifetime migrants.
2. A person who had moved into the area since a given date—1 year ago, 2 years ago, and so forth. Again this might be a person who had migrated only once since his or her birth, a secondary migrant, or a return migrant. The areas referred to earlier are those areas, such as municipalities, counties, and so on, that are "migration-defining" for the particular country.

The item on duration of residence in national censuses has been especially popular in the Americas, and a number of countries have also asked for previous area of residence. In the United States, a question on year moved to present residence was included in the census of 2000 and several earlier censuses. Since, however, the year of the move into the county of residence has not been determined, this item has not yielded any migration statistics for the United States. It was a part of the Housing Census in each case and demographers have made little use of the data.

If only the last previous place of residence has been obtained or tabulated, the resulting statistics, like those from the item on place of birth, have an indefinite time reference. However, these statistics describe direct moves whereas the place-of-birth statistics may conceal intervening moves.

The chief virtue of the question on duration of residence (or on year of last move) is that it gives the distribution of lifetime movers by date of latest move. If the previous place of residence has also been ascertained, then the time is also fixed for streams of migration. Such statistics describe the inmigrants now living in an area, but they do not produce a very useful time series. Since only the latest move is recorded, the number of moves in the earlier years will be seriously understated because of multiple moves and deaths. Origin-destination tabulations for the most recent migration interval will yield data approximating those from the fixed-period item for the same interval; the shorter the interval, the closer the approximation. Furthermore, percentage distributions by duration of residence enable us to distinguish those parts of the country to which migrants have gone in relatively recent years.

A number of countries have cross-tabulated duration of residence in a place by place of birth or by place of last previous residence. From such statistics on migration streams, the volume of in-, out-, and net migration, and median duration of residence can be computed, as well as the corresponding rates using the current population as the base. For an illustration of the calculation of median duration of residence from data on duration of residence of inmigrants to a state cross-classified by state of last residence, see Table 21.15 in Shryock, Siegel, and Stockwell (1976). As with statistics on place of birth, it is not possible to compute "propensity" rates (using as a base the origin population at a fixed past date), however.

The statistics on duration of residence and area of previous residence are subject to the usual types of reporting errors that have been discussed for other migration questions. In addition, there is the likelihood of preferences for round numbers in the reporting of duration in years.

Few additional measures have been proposed for this subject. In addition to the percentage distribution by duration of residence and the median duration of residence, a measure of dispersion, like the interquartile range, could also be computed. There is a high positive correlation between duration of residence and age, and tables giving a cross-classification by age are a prerequisite for adequate analysis. When the same tabulation is available for successive censuses, there are opportunities for more complex methods and measures. The *UN Manual VI* (United Nations, 1970, Table B.15) carries a dummy table illustrating the computation for an intercensal period.

Measures Derived from Microdata

The increasing availability of microdata, especially longitudinal microdata, since the 1970s has fostered significant advances in measuring people's mobility and, as a consequence, refined conceptualizations of the process itself. The Public Use Microdata Sample (PUMS) from the U.S. decennial census is one such source. Although cross-sectional, it affords considerable latitude in tailoring the definition of particular population segments for which census migration measures are calculated—for example, persons classified by multiple variables simultaneously, such as current area of residence, household or family type, occupation, race, and so forth.

More significant, perhaps, has been the proliferation of longitudinal microdata sources, which have greatly expanded the frontiers of migration research during the 1980s and 1990s. These data sets afforded researchers new and more exact approaches to defining and studying the migration sequences formed by individual moves (see DaVanzo and Morrison, 1981, 1982). Noteworthy data sources used for migration research include the University of Michigan's Panel Study of Income Dynamics (PSID), the National Longitudinal Surveys (NLS), and High School and Beyond (HS&B).

The wealth of new data on migration, and the sequences of moves that became discernible, demanded new conceptualizations and measures. The act of migration came to be seen as more than an isolated once-and-for-all event. Using longitudinal microdata, researchers demonstrated that the majority of moves that people make are not first moves, but repeat moves that form sequences of migration. The possibility of delineating those sequences empirically invited new measures of the types of migration sequences that arose, new theoretical conceptualizations for explaining such sequences, and new insights into the consequences such sequences may have for the populations at origin and destination.

Multistate Life Tables of Interregional Transfers

In earlier chapters we noted the application of multistate methods to life tables. Such an extension of life table methods has led to the development of tables of working life, nuptiality tables, tables of healthy life, and so on, which provide measures of average years of working life, single life, and healthy life, respectively, and other related measures. These methods may also be applied to the measurement of interregional migration (Willekens and Rogers, 1978), but a full explanation of the construction and use of tables of interregional transference is beyond the scope of this chapter. Here we only present a brief outline and refer the reader to Namboodiri (1993), who provided an empirical example using Yugoslavia and Slovenia. The four general steps in the derivation of a multistate table for interregional migration are as follows:

1. Calculate central age-specific migration rates and death rates.

2. Use the central rates in step 1 as estimates of the corresponding transition intensities.
3. Convert the transition intensities in step 2 into transition probabilities.
4. Use the transition probabilities in step 3, in combination with an assumed radix for the number of births in each region to construct the table.

The population distribution at the end of a given period is derived as a matrix product of the initial matrix and the transition probabilities for the period. The results correspond to the l_x function and the $_nd_x$ function of the conventional life table. From such a table we can provide information on the proportion of persons ever moving between the two regions, the time that will be spent in each region in any year or in a lifetime, the numbers dying in each region, and related measures.

A table of migration expectancy, without reference to origin and destination, that provides estimates of average moves per person may be calculated by a more conventional method—that is, a double-decrement table based on the probability of dying and the probability of moving in each year, or only the probability of moving, omitting the allowance for mortality (Long, 1973).

DETERMINANTS AND CONSEQUENCES OF MIGRATION

What causes change in an area's migration patterns over time? Here we can only touch on the major themes that stand out from the immense research literature that has addressed the question over the decades. More extensive discussions on the determinants of migration may be found in DaVanzo and Morrison (1981), Greenwood (1997); Long (1988); Mohlo (1986), Morrison (1975), U.S. Census Bureau/Schachter (2001b), and Zelinsky (1980).

Sample Survey Data

Questions on reasons for moving are among the more popular items in sample surveys on internal migration. These questions represent an attempt to determine motivation by asking movers why they moved. This approach is quite different from trying to draw inferences on causes of migration from data on migration differentials or on the comparative characteristics of sending and receiving areas. In the survey approach, there are no attempts to establish a "control group" of nonmigrants by seeking to measure the prevalence among them of the conditions cited by movers as reasons for moving. Thus, we cannot say, for example, whether unsatisfactory housing conditions are more prevalent among migrants in a given period than among those who did not migrate. "Push-pull" theories are seldom tested explicitly, for example by asking the respondent to compare his or her attitudes toward the areas of origin and destination. On the other hand, studies that ask reasons for moving probably do measure the subjective importance of the conditions cited as a reason for leaving.

The main problems of measurement for this topic seem to be the choice of a reasonable number of predesignated reasons that are mutually exclusive and the choice of analytically relevant classifications of reasons. There has been little standardization of categories or reasons among the various surveys that have investigated this topic. The respondent is often allowed to give more than one reason so that the sum of reasons given may exceed the number of persons reporting.

There is frequently an attempt, either in the questions themselves or in the tabular classification of the replies, to distinguish job-related from personal or social reasons. The survey results support this distinction because job-related reasons are relatively much more frequent among the migrants than among the short-distance movers. In the March 2000 Current Population Survey of the United States, for example, only 5.6% of the intracounty movers gave work-related reasons, while 31% of the intercounty movers gave such reasons (Table 19.5). Most moves are for housing-related reasons; they accounted for 52% of all the moves and 65% of the intracounty moves.

General Theory of Migration

In the highly industrialized countries, the population of almost every region and locale is continuously recomposed over time by a gradual procession of migrants coming and going, for the most part by choice. The purposefulness of migration makes it a largely autonomous process and one that is indicative of opportunity seeking. The view that personal success is as readily achievable beyond as within one's native region is a distinctive and deeply ingrained element of the cultures of industrialized societies. It is the product of the persistent pull of economic opportunities in other places that enables individuals alert to opportunity to exploit newly developed resources or knowledge quickly.

The national and regional economies benefit from people's readiness to migrate and from the resulting economic and social realignments, as a freely-mobile population rearranges itself in space to answer the changing needs of the economy. The economies of rapidly growing regions, like huge parabolic mirrors, gather migrants extensively from many origins and direct them to locales of expanding employment growth. Without a tradition of migration, which moves people from areas where jobs are dwindling to places where workers are needed, national economic development would be more sluggish and less efficient than is actually the case.

TABLE 19.4   Calculation of Net Lifetime Migration Rates for the Regions of Hungary: 1931
(Figures relate to the Trianon area of Hungary. Numbers in thousands.)

Item	Hungary	Transdanubia	Great Plain[1]	Budapest	North
Born in specified region					
(1) Total	8072[2]	2819	3560	550	1128
(2) Living in other regions	896	327	267	170	132
(3) = (2)/(1) Rate of outmigration[3]	11.1	11.6	7.5	30.9	11.7
Living in specified region					
(4) Total	8072[2]	2600	3611	793	1064
(5) Born in other regions	896	91	325	414	66
(6) = (5)/(4) Rate of inmigration[4]	11.1	3.5	9.0	52.2	6.2
Net gain (+) or loss (−) of survivors through interregional migration					
(7) = (5) − (2) Net migration	—	−236	+58	+244	−66
(8) = [(2) + (5)]/2 Average of populations born in region and living in region	8072[2]	2710	3586	672	1096
(9) = (7)/(8) Net migration rate[5]	—	−8.7	+1.6	+36.3	−6.0
(10) = Rate with variable base[6]	—	−8.4	+1.6	+30.8	−5.9

[1] Excludes Budapest.
[2] Discrepancy between figure for total Hungary and sum of figures for the four regions is a result of rounding.
[3] Percent of population born in specified region.
[4] Percent of population living in specified region.
[5] Percent of the average of the populations born in the region and living in the region.
[6] Base varies depending on direction of net migration.
Source: Based on Siegel (1958), Table IV-H.

TABLE 19.5 Percentage Distribution of Movers within the United States
by Main Reason for Moving and Type of Move: March 1999 to March 2000
(movers aged 1 and over)

Reason for moving	Total	Intracounty	Intercounty
Total movers (in 1000s)	41,642	24,399	17,243
Percentage	**100.0**	**100.0**	**100.0**
Family-related reasons	**26.3**	**25.9**	**26.9**
Change in marital status	6.2	6.2	6.2
To establish own household	7.4	9.3	4.7
Other family reasons	12.7	10.4	16.0
Work-related reasons	**16.2**	**5.6**	**31.1**
New job/job transfer	9.7	1.4	21.6
To look for work/lost job	1.3	0.5	2.4
Closer to work/easier commute	3.5	3.0	4.2
Retired	0.4	0.1	0.9
Other job-related reason	1.2	0.6	2.0
Housing-related reasons	**51.6**	**65.4**	**31.9**
Wanted to own home/not rent	11.5	14.3	7.5
New/better house/apartment	18.5	24.2	10.3
Better neighborhood/less crime	4.4	4.8	3.9
Cheaper housing	5.5	7.5	2.8
Other housing reason	11.7	14.7	7.4
Other reasons	**6.0**	**3.0**	**10.1**
Attend/leave college	2.3	0.7	4.4
Change of climate	0.7	0.2	1.6
Health reasons	1.1	0.8	1.6
Other reason	1.8	1.3	2.5

Source: U.S. Census Bureau/Schachter (2001a). Primary source is the Current Population Survey, March 2000.

In the final analysis, migration is a process whose consequences flow from the inherent selectivity of the act itself and from the resulting growth or decline bestowed on regions and places. Accordingly, migration tends to select distinct types of individuals according to an array of characteristics (Morrison and DaVanzo, 1986; see also Blau and Duncan, 1967). For example, migrants tend to be more youthful, more educated, and more trained or experienced in professional lines of work, than their counterparts who do not migrate. Those who migrate are also inclined to migrate repeatedly. Beyond such readily observable attributes, the element of deliberate choice in most moves sharply differentiates persons by motive. Owing to its selectivity, migration is noteworthy as a sorting mechanism, filtering and sifting the population as some of its members move about while others stay put. A place that grows by net migration of 1000 has gained 1000 people who are there essentially because they want to be there. Natural increase does not contribute deliberate residents; it only adds to population numbers by the lottery of birth and death.

The influx of self-selected persons has repercussions for places. For example, heavy migration had left a powerful demographic legacy in metropolitan San Jose, California, by 1970. Its population became both youthful and noticeably hypermobile (that is, prone to further onward migration). About 21 migrants per 100 residents entered the population and 17 per 100 residents departed each year. Conversely, the city of St. Louis illustrates how heavy and prolonged out-migration from a place can alter the age structure of the remaining population, drawing away potential parents and leaving behind an elderly population that no longer can replace itself. Natural decrease results, that is, the number of people dying exceeds the number being born, and population decline acquires its own dynamic (Morrison, 1974).

References

Bachi, R. 1957. "Statistical Analysis of Demographic Series." *Bulletin de l'institut international de statistique* 36(2): 234–235. Proceedings of the 30th meeting of the Institute. Stockholm.

Behr, M., and P. Gober. 1982. "When a Residence Is Not a House: Examining Residence-Based Migration Definitions." *Professional Geographer* 34: 178–184.

Blau, P., and O. D. Duncan. 1967. *The American Occupational Structure.* New York: John Wiley & Sons.

Bogue, D. 1952. *A Methodological Study of Migration and Labor Mobility in Michigan and Ohio in 1947.* Scripps Foundation Studies in Population Distribution, No. 4. Miami, OH: Scripps Foundation for Research in Population Problems.

Bogue, D., K. Hinze, and M. White. 1982. *Techniques for Estimating Net Migration*. Chicago: University of Chicago Press.

Croze, M. 1956. Un instrument d'étude des migrations intérieures: Les migrations d'électeurs (An instrument for studying internal migration: the migration of electors). *Population* 11(2): 235–260.

DaVanzo, J. 1982. "Techniques for Analysis of Migration-History Data." RAND N-1842-AID/NICHD. Santa Monica, CA: RAND Corporation.

DaVanzo, J. 1983. "Repeat Migration in the United States: Who Moves Back and Who Moves On?" *Review of Economics and Statistics* 65: 552–559.

DaVanzo, J., and P. Morrison. 1981. "Return and Other Sequences of Migration in the United States." *Demography* 18: 85–101.

DaVanzo, J., and P. Morrison. 1982. "Migration Sequences: Who Moves Back and Who Moves On?" RAND R-2548-NICHD. Santa Monica, CA: RAND Corporation.

Eldridge, H. T. 1965. "Primary, Secondary, and Return Migration in the United States, 1955–60." *Demography* 2: 445.

Gober, P. 1993. "Americans on the Move." *Population Bulletin* 48(3). Washington, DC: Population Reference Bureau.

Goldstein, S. 1958. *Patterns of Mobility, 1910–1950: The Norristown Study*. Philadelphia, PA: University of Pennsylvania Press.

Greenwood, M. 1997. "Internal Migration in Developed Countries. In M. Rosenzweig and O. Stark (Eds.), *Handbook of Population and Family Economics* (pp. 647–720). Amsterdam, Holland: Elsevier Science.

Hamilton, C. H. 1965. "Practical and Mathematical Considerations in the Formulation and Selection of Migration Rates." *Demography* 2: 429–443.

Hamilton, C. H. 1966. "Effect of Census Errors on the Measurement of Net Migration." *Demography* 3: 393–415.

Hamilton, C. H. 1967. "The Vital Statistics Method of Estimating Net Migration by Age Cohorts." *Demography* 4: 464–478.

Isserman, A., D. Plane, and D. McMillen. 1982. "Internal Migration in the United States: An Evaluation of Federal Data." *Review of Public Data Use* 10: 285–311.

Johnson, H., and R. Lovelady. 1995. *Migration between California and Other States: 1985–1994*. Sacramento, CA: Demographic Research Unit, California Department of Finance.

Lansing, J. B., and E. Mueller. 1967. *The Geographic Mobility of Labor*. Ann Arbor, MI: Survey Research Center, University of Michigan.

Lee, E., A. Miller, C. Brainerd, and R. Easterlin. 1957. "Methodological Considerations and Reference Tables." In S. Kuznets and D. Thomas (Eds.), *Population Redistribution and Economic Growth: United States, 1870–1950* (pp. 15–56). Philadelphia: The American Philosophical Society.

Long, L. 1973. "New Estimates of Migration Expectancy in the United States." *Journal of the American Statistical Association* 68(341): 37–43.

Long, L. 1988. *Migration and Residential Mobility in the United States*. New York: Russell Sage Foundation.

Long, L. 1991. "Residential Mobility Differences among Developed Countries." *International Regional Science Review* 14: 133–147.

Long, L. 1992. "Changing Residence: Comparative Perspectives on Its Relationship to Age, Sex, and Marital Status." *Population Studies* 46: 141–158.

Long, L., C. Tucker, and W. Urton. 1988a. "Measuring Migration Distances: Self-Reporting and Indirect Methods." *Journal of the American Statistical Association* 83: 674–678.

Long, L., C. Tucker, and W. Urton. 1988b. "Migration Distances: An International Comparison." *Demography* 25: 633–640.

Martin, P., and E. Midgley. 1999. "Immigration to the United States." *Population Bulletin* 54. Washington, DC: Population Reference Bureau.

McHugh, K., T. Hogan, and S. Happel. 1995. "Multiple Residence and Cyclical Migration: A Life Course Perspective." *Professional Geographer* 47: 251–267.

Mohlo, I. 1986. "Theories of Migration: A Review." *Scottish Journal of Political Economy* 33: 396–419.

Morrison, P. 1974. "Urban Growth and Decline: San Jose and St. Louis in the 1960s." *Science* 185: 757–762.

Morrison, P. 1975. "Toward a Policy Planner's View of the Urban Settlement System." RAND P-5357. Santa Monica, CA: RAND Corporation.

Morrison, P. 1977. "Migration and Rights of Access: New Public Concerns of the 1970s." RAND P-5785. Santa Monica, CA: RAND Corporation.

Morrison, P. 1980. "Current Demographic Change in Regions of the United States." In V. Arnold (Ed.), *Alternatives to Confrontation: A National Policy Toward Regional Change* (pp. 63–94). Lexington, MA: D.C. Heath & Co.

Morrison, P., and J. DaVanzo. 1986. "The Prism of Migration: Dissimilarities between Return and Onward Movers. *Social Science Quarterly* 67: 504–516.

Morrison, P., and D. Relles. 1975. "Recent Research Insights into Local Migration Flows." RAND P-5379. Santa Monica, CA: RAND Corporation.

Morrison, P., and J. Wheeler. 1976. "The Image of Elsewhere in the American Tradition of Migration. RAND Document P-5729. Santa Monica: RAND Corporation.

Namboodiri, K. 1993. *Demographic Analysis: A Stochastic Approach*. San Diego, CA: Academic Press.

Netherlands, Statistics Netherlands. 1998. "Statistics of the Population with a Foreign Background, Based on Population Register Data." Working Paper 6, ECE Work Session on Migration Statistics at the Conference of European Statisticians Geneva, March 25–27, 1998.

Newbold, K. 1997. "Race and Primary, Return and Onward Interstate Migration." *Professional Geographer* 49: 1–14.

Price, D. 1955. "Examination of Two Sources of Error in the Estimation of Net Internal Migration." *Journal of the American Statistical Association* 50: 689–700.

Ravenstein, E. 1889. "The Laws of Migration." *The Journal of the Royal Statistical Society*, LII, 241–301.

Shryock, H. S. 1959. "The Efficiency of Internal Migration in the United States." *International Population Conference, Vienna, 1959*. Vienna: The Working Committee of the Conference.

Shryock, H. S. 1964. *Population Mobility within the United States*. Chicago: Community and Family Study Center, University of Chicago.

Shryock, H. S., J. S. Siegel, and E. G. Stockwell. 1976. *The Methods and Materials of Demography*, condensed ed. San Diego, CA: Academic Press.

Siegel, J. S. 1958. *The Population of Hungary*, International Population Statistics Reports, Series P-90, No. 9. Washington, DC: U.S. Bureau of the Census.

Siegel, J. S. 2001. *Applied Demography: Applications to Business, Government, Law, and Public Policy*. San Diego, CA: Academic Press.

Siegel, J., and C. H. Hamilton. 1952. "Some Considerations in the Use of the Residual Method of Estimating Net Migration." *Journal of the American Statistical Association* 47: 480–481.

Smith, S. 1989. "Toward a Methodology for Estimating Temporary Residents." *Journal of the American Statistical Association* 84: 430–436.

Smith, S. K., J. Tayman, and D. A. Swanson. 2001. *State and Local Population Projections: Methodology and Analysis*. New York: Plenum Press/Kluwer Academic.

Stone, L. 1967. "Evaluating the Relative Accuracy and Significance of Net Migration Estimates." *Demography* 4: 310–330.

Taeuber, I. 1958. *The Population of Japan*. Princeton, NJ: Princeton University Press.

Tarver, J. 1962. "Evaluation of Census Survival Rates in Estimating Intercensal State Net Migration." *Journal of the American Statistical Association* 57: 841–862.

Thomlinson, R. 1962. "The Determination of a Base Population for Computing Migration Rates." *Milbank Memorial Fund Quarterly* 40: 356–366.

United Nations, 1970. *Methods of Measuring Internal Migration.* Manual VI, *Methods of Estimating Population.* New York: United Nations.

U.S. Census Bureau. 1965. "National Census Survival Rates, by Color and Sex, for 1950 to 1960." By D. S. Akers and J. S. Siegel. *Current Population Reports*, Series P-23, No. 15.

U.S. Census Bureau. 1990a. "Comparing Migration Measures Having Different Intervals." By L. Long and C. Boertlein. *Current Population Reports*, P-23, No. 166.

U.S. Census Bureau. 1990b. "Creating Annual State-to-State Migration Flows with Demographic Data." By S. Wetrogan and J. Long. *Current Population Reports*, P-23, No. 166.

U.S. Census Bureau. 1995. "Selected Place of Birth and Migration Statistics: 1990." CPH-L-121.

U.S. Census Bureau. 2001a. "Geographic Mobility: March 1999 to March 2000." By J. Schachter. *Current Population Reports* P20-538.

U.S. Census Bureau. 2001b. "Why People Move: Exploring the March 2000 Current Population Survey. By J. Schachter. *Current Population Reports* P23-204.

U.S. Immigration and Naturalization Service. 1999. *Statistical Yearbook of the Immigration and Naturalization Service: 1997.*

U.S. Immigration and Naturalization Service. 2000. *Statistical Yearbook of the Immigration and Naturalization Service.* Online at *www.ins.usdoj.gov/graphics/aboutins/statistics/Immigs.htm.*

White, M., P. Meuser, and J. Tierney. 1987. "Net Migration of the Population of the United States by Age, Race, and Sex: 1970–1980." Ann Arbor, MI: Inter-University Consortium for Political and Social Research.

Willekens, F., and A. Rogers. 1978. *Spatial Population Analysis: Methods and Computer Programs.* Laxenburg, Austria: International Institute for Applied Systems Analysis.

Zax, J. 1994. "When Is a Move a Migration?" *Regional Science and Urban Economics* 24: 341–360.

Zelinsky, W. 1980. "The Impasse in Migration Theory: A Sketch Map for Potential Escapees." In P. Morrison (Ed.), *Population Movements: Their Forms and Functions in Urbanization and Development* (pp. 19–46). Liège, France: Orlina Editions.

Suggested Readings

Clark, D., and W. Hunter. 1992. "The Impact of Economic Opportunity, Amenities and Fiscal Factors on Age-Specific Migration Rates." *Journal of Regional Science* 32: 349–365.

Clark, D., T. Knapp, and N. White. 1996. "Personal and Location-Specific Characteristics and Elderly Interstate Migration." *Growth and Change* 27: 327–351.

Clark, W. A. V. 1986. *Human Migration.* Volume 7, Scientific Geography Series. Beverly Hills, CA: Sage.

DaVanzo, J. 1978. "Does Unemployment Affect Migration? Evidence from Micro-data." *Review of Economics and Statistics* 60: 504–514.

Engels, R., and M. Healy. 1981. "Measuring Interstate Migration Flows: An Origin-Destination Network Based on Internal Revenue Service Records." *Environment and Planning* A 13: 1345–1360.

Fischer, M., and P. Nijkamp (Eds.). 1987. *Regional Labour Markets: Analytical Contributions and Cross-national Comparisons.* Amsterdam: North-Holland.

Goldscheider, C. 1987. "Migration and Social Structure: Analytic Issues and Comparative Perspectives in Developing Nations." *Sociological Forum* 2: 674–696.

Goldscheider, C., and F. Goldscheider. 1994. "Leaving and Returning Home in 20th Century America." *Population Bulletin* 48(4). Washington, DC: Population Reference Bureau.

Graves, P., and P. Linneman. 1979. "Household Migration: Theoretical and Empirical Results." *Journal of Urban Economics* 6: 383–404.

Greenwood, M. 1981. *Migration and Economic Growth in the United States: National, Regional and Metropolitan Perspectives.* New York: Academic Press.

Greenwood, M. 1985. "Human Migration: Theory, Models, and Empirical Studies." *Journal of Regional Science* 25: 521–544.

Greenwood, M., G. Hunt, and J. McDowell. 1986. "Migration and Employment Change: Empirical Evidence on the Spatial and Temporal Dimensions of the Linkages." *Journal of Regional Science* 26: 223–234.

Greenwood, M., G. Hunt, D. Rickman, and G. Treyz. 1991. "Migration, Regional Equilibrium, and the Estimation of Compensating Differentials." *American Economic Review* 81: 1382–1390.

Kintner, H., and D. Swanson. 1993. "Towards Measuring Uncertainty in Estimates of Intercensal Net Migration." *Canadian Studies in Population* 20: 153–191.

Kulkarni, M., and L. Pol. 1994. "Migration Expectancy Revisited: Results for the 1970s, 1980s and 1990s." *Population Research and Policy Review* 13: 195–202.

McHugh, K. 1985. "Reasons for Migrating or Not." *Sociology and Social Research* 69: 585–588.

Meuser, P., and M. White. 1989. "Explaining the Association between Rates of In-migration and Out-migration." *Papers of the Regional Science Association* 67: 121–134.

Morrison, P. 1971. "Chronic Movers and the Future Redistribution of Population: A Longitudinal Analysis." *Demography* 8: 171–184.

Morrison, P., and J. DaVanzo. 1986. "The Prism of Migration: Dissimilarities between Return and Onward Movers. *Social Science Quarterly* 67: 504–516.

Nam, C., W. Serow, and D. Sly (Eds.). 1990. *International Handbook on Internal Migration.* New York: Greenwood Press.

Plane, D. 1993. "Demographic Influences on Migration." *Demography* 27: 375–383.

Rees, P. 1977. "The Measurement of Migration from Census Data and Other Sources." *Environment and Planning* A 9: 247–272.

Rogers, A. (Ed.). 1984. *Migration, Urbanization and Spatial Population Dynamics.* Boulder, CO: Westview Press.

Rogers, A. 1990. "Requiem for the Net Migrant." *Geographical Analysis* 22: 283–300.

Smith, S., and D. A. Swanson. 1998. "In Defense of the Net Migrant." *Journal of Economic and Social Measurement* 24: 249–264.

Zachariah, K. C. 1962. "Method of Estimating Net Migration." *Journal of the American Statistical Association* 57: 175–183.

20

Population Estimates

THOMAS BRYAN

THE NATURE AND USE OF POPULATION ESTIMATES

Currently, the most complete and reliable source of information on the population of countries and their geographic subdivisions is a census based on house-to-house enumeration. However, populations change constantly and sometimes quite rapidly, making census statistics for every tenth year, even every fifth year, inadequate for most purposes. Although state, provincial, and even local governments sometimes conduct special censuses, these sparse data rarely meet all public needs. Moreover, the method of complete enumeration is expensive, laborious, and time-consuming, and it is not applicable to past and future dates. Population estimates are used by government officials, market research analysts, public and private planners, and others for determining national and subnational allocations of funds (Martin & Serow, 1979), calculating denominators for vital rates and per capita time series, establishing survey "controls", guiding administrative planning, developing market indicators, and preparing descriptive and analytical studies (Long, 1993).

To meet the need for up-to-date population figures, a wide variety of estimating techniques, including the use of sample surveys, have been developed. Like a census, sample surveys are rather expensive and cannot provide data for past or future dates. However, nonsurvey or analytic techniques involving the use of vital statistics, immigration, and other data symptomatic of population change, as well as mathematical methods, are relatively inexpensive to apply and can be used to prepare estimates for past and future dates as well as for current dates.

TYPES OF POPULATION ESTIMATES

Estimates can be broadly divided into three types on the basis of their time reference and method of derivation. These types, which pose different methodological problems and are associated with different levels of reliability, are (1) *intercensal estimates*, which relate to a date intermediate to two censuses and take the results of these censuses into account; (2) *postcensal estimates*, which relate to a past or current date following a census and take that census and possibly earlier censuses into account, but not later censuses; and (3) *projections*, which are conditional "estimates" of population at future dates (Davis 1995).[1] Both postcensal estimates and projections can be regarded as extrapolations, and intercensal estimates as interpolations. Though extrapolative techniques may be used in making both population estimates and projections, estimates are most commonly made with the addition of "symptomatic" data, and projections encompass many considerations not encountered in making estimates. Therefore, detailed coverage of population projections is left entirely to the following chapter. It should also be noted that estimates must frequently be made for areas that have never had an accurate census; hence there may be no base on which to extrapolate or interpolate estimates and they must be generated from alternate data sources and by alternate techniques.

Estimates vary in several other respects: the geographic areas of reference, the segments of the population they distinguish, and whether they refer to people physically present (e.g., daytime or nighttime population) or usual residents. Areas may be a whole country, the major geographic subdivisions of a country, or broad classes of areas within the country (e.g., urban and rural areas, city-size classes). Estimates may be made of the total population of an area or of particular classes of the population, such as age, sex, race, nativity, family and marital status, educational attainment,

---

[1] The term "estimate" is generally used by demographers to refer to approximations of population size for current or past dates white "projection" refers to approximations for a future date.

employment status, and so forth. An important aspect of the type of population estimates to be made relates to the definition of population employed for the estimate. Estimates, like census counts, vary as to whether they refer to the de jure (usual resident) population or the de facto (physically present) population. Countries tend to employ the same type of population in their estimates as in their previous censuses. Another dimension of the problem of definition relates to coverage of armed forces, both at home and abroad, and coverage of nationals abroad.

INTERNATIONAL AND NATIONAL PROGRAMS OF POPULATION ESTIMATES

In planning a national population estimates program, the responsible agency in the national government determines which estimates it will make according to the demand or need for various kinds of figures, the availability and quality of basic data, the effort necessary to produce the estimates, and the resources (i.e., funds, personnel, and time) available. On this basis, it is likely to recommend that estimates of the total population and of the population classified according to age and sex, for a nation, are most important, followed by estimates for the nation's primary political subdivisions, first of the total population, then of age, sex, and other characteristics. Estimates of total population for secondary geographic subdivisions (e.g., counties in the United States) would be of next importance in a national program.

Estimates of the total population, age, race, sex, and ethnicity are generally obtained with analytic techniques. Estimates encompassing further population detail, such as marital status, educational attainment, literacy, employment status, broad occupation and industry groups, are important, but normally are best obtained from continuing or periodic national sample surveys. These characteristics present special problems of estimation because they may change during the lifetime of individuals (e.g., a change from married to divorced) and the requisite data on the components of change are frequently unavailable or cannot be estimated satisfactorily.

The best sources for the national population data are typically the national governments themselves. The figures characteristically appear in national statistical yearbooks and also in special reports, both of which are commonly printed but are increasingly found in electronic format and on the Internet (see Chapter 2). National estimates usually fail to include adjustments for deficits in census coverage or other census errors and may lack comparability with estimates from other countries because of differences in the categories of the population represented. The scope of national population estimates programs varies enormously with respect to the resources devoted to it, the frequency and

detail of the estimates, as well as the type of publication. The extent to which the methodology is explained and the results are analyzed also varies substantially. The discussion of the methodology will show wide differences in the methods employed and the quality of the results, depending on the resources and data available.

United Nations Program

The United Nations conducts the most comprehensive international population estimates and publication program in the world. Its publication *Demographic Yearbook* (see Chapter 2) presents for each country of the world, sovereign and nonsovereign, estimates of population with about a 2-year lag (United Nations, 1999). Currently, 229 "countries" are reported. Other estimates published regularly in the *Yearbook* include an annual table showing aggregates of population for the world, continents, and regions, both at decennial intervals and for the current year; estimates for the total population by age and sex for selected countries; and estimates of the total population of capital cities and of each city that had 100,000 or more inhabitants according to the latest available data. Data on population components, such as mortality and natality, are generally reported for the 5 most recent years.

Generally, the estimates displayed in the *Yearbook* are official figures that are consistent with the results of national censuses or sample surveys taken in the period. Thus, they have been revised by the national government or by the United Nations on the basis of a census or survey where discontinuities appeared to exist, so as to form a consistent series. They refer to July 1 of the estimate year, but may have been computed by the United Nations as the mean of two year-end official estimates. When an acceptable official estimate of population is not available for a given year, the United Nations prepares its own estimate. These estimates may take into account available information on the reliability of census and survey results and data on natural increase and net migration, so as to produce estimates for various postcensal and intercensal years comparable to one another and to the figures for the census date. The methodology and quality of the estimates are indicated by a type-of-estimate code accompanying each estimate. The code is composed of four parts, identifying the nature of the basic data, their recency, the nature of the adjustment since the base date, and the quality of this adjustment.

United States

The official population estimates for the United States prepared by the U.S. Census Bureau relate to the population on a *de jure* basis (usual residence) rather than the *de facto* (actually present) population, just as with the decennial census. This agency regularly publishes a wide variety of population estimates for the nation as a whole as well as states, counties, places and other county subdivisions, and metropolitan areas. Four types of population estimates are regularly prepared for the United States as a whole: (1) the total population residing in the United States (that is, the population as usually defined in the decennial census), (2) the total population including armed forces overseas (that is, the total population resident in the United States plus armed forces of the United States stationed overseas), (3) the civilian population (that is, the total resident population minus armed forces stationed in the United States), and (4) the civilian noninstitutional population (that is, civilian population minus persons residing in institutional group quarters).[2] The civilian noninstitutional population is important, as it represents the universe for many demographic surveys, including the U.S. Census Bureau's Current Population Survey (CPS). Because in previous decennial censuses individuals were assigned geographically according to their usual place of residence and because the armed forces overseas were not allocated to a residence in the United States, only the first and third types of population estimates have been prepared for subdivisions of the United States.

Monthly estimates for the period April 1, 2000, and forward are postcensal estimates, based primarily on the 2000 decennial census enumeration and estimates of the population change from the census date to the reference dates of the estimates. Estimates of the United States resident population include persons resident in the 50 states and the District of Columbia. They exclude residents of the commonwealth of Puerto Rico and residents of the outlying areas under United States sovereignty or jurisdiction, who are estimated separately. The definition of residence conforms to the criterion used in the 2000 census, which defines a resident of a specified area as a person "usually resident" in that area.

For the United States as a whole, postcensal and intercensal estimates are released in five broad tables and may be found on the Internet (census.gov/population/www/ estimates/uspop.html). Therein, can be found present total monthly population estimates statistics for the resident population, resident population plus armed forces overseas, civilian population, and civilian noninstitutional population. Also presented are annual population estimates for age groups and sex, with totals, medians, means, and 5-year age group summaries by sex, annual population estimates by sex, race, and Hispanic origin, selected years, with totals, median, and mean ages. Additional details may be found on this site on monthly postcensal resident population, resident population plus armed forces overseas, civilian population, and civilian noninstitutional population, for single years of age, sex, race, and Hispanic origin, quarterly estimates of monthly postcensal resident population, resident population plus armed forces overseas, civilian population, and civilian noninstitutional population.

For states, postcensal and intercensal estimates of total population are published for each midyear date and may also be found on the Internet (census.gov/population/www/ estimates/statepop.html). The Census Bureau produces total population, estimates by age and sex, and estimates by race and Hispanic origin. Tables released include total state population estimates and demographic components of change, annual time series of state population estimates by age and sex, and annual time series of state population estimates by race and Hispanic origin.

The U.S. Census Bureau is also responsible for generating subcounty estimates for general purpose governmental units, which are those that have elected officials who can provide services and raise revenue. These include all incorporated places and functioning minor civil divisions (MCDs). Subcounty population totals are produced annually and may be found on the Internet (census.gov/population/ www/estimates/popest.html). Estimates of metropolitan areas (MAs) based on subcounty estimates may also be found on the Internet (census.gov/population/www/ estimates/metropop.html).

The Census Bureau works closely with state representatives in the Federal State Cooperative for Population Estimates (FSCPE) to create these estimates. Informal cooperation between the U.S. federal government and the states in the area of local population estimates existed as early as 1953. In 1966, the National Governor's Conference, in cooperation with the Council of State Governments, initiated and sponsored the First National Conference on Comparative Statistics held in Washington, D.C. This conference gave national recognition to the increasing demand for subnational population estimates. Between 1967 and 1973, a group of Census Bureau and state employees, charged with developing annual subnational population estimates, formally established the Federal State Cooperative Program for Population Estimates (census.gov/population/www/ coop/history.html).

In addition to the release of actual estimates, the Census Bureau's program of population estimates includes the occa-

---

[2] Institutionalized persons include persons under formally authorized, supervised care or custody in institutions. Such persons are classified as "patients" or "inmates" of an institution regardless of the availability of nursing or medical care, length of stay, or the number of persons in the institution. Generally, institutionalized persons are restricted to the institutional buildings and grounds and thus have limited interaction with the surrounding community. These institutions include correctional facilities, nursing homes, mental hospitals, and juvenile institutions. Noninstitutionalized persons include all persons who live in group quarters other than institutions and in households. Persons living in the following places are classified as "other persons in group quarters" when there are 10 or more unrelated persons living in the unit: rooming houses, group homes, religious group quarters, college quarters, agricultural and other workers' dormitories, emergency shelters, and hospital dormitories. Otherwise, these living quarters are classified as housing units (U.S. Census Bureau, 1990b).

sional publication of reports explicating methods of making state or county population estimates for use by local technicians. Population estimates for states, counties, and cities are also published by many state and local government agencies and by private organizations. Population estimates for a state and its counties may appear in the reports of the state health department, a state planning agency, the business or social research bureau at the state university, or the budget office or equivalent (Illinois Department of Public Health, 1999). The reports of many local planning commissions contain current estimates for local areas.

METHODOLOGY

General Considerations

Choice of Data and Method

The most important factor determining the choice of the method to be used in preparing a population estimate is the type and quality of data available for this purpose. If, for example, an estimate of the total population of an area is wanted and the only relevant information at hand is the total size of the population at two or more census dates, then a purely mathematical or graphic approach may have to be used. The level of accuracy required and the amount of time, funds, and trained personnel available are other important considerations in determining the choice of method.

The data on which a population estimate may be based can be divided roughly into two categories: (1) "direct" data and (2) "indirect" symptomatic data, which apply to the base date and data for the period between the base date and the estimate date. The classification depends on the specific kind of data and their use in a given method. Direct data are those obtained from censuses, population registers, and special compulsory or quasi-compulsory registrations as well as recorded data on the components of population change (i.e., statistics on births, deaths, and migration) when these data are used to measure these phenomena themselves.

Indirect data, on the other hand, are those that are used to produce estimates of certain parameters on the basis of information that is only indirectly related to or "symptomatic" of its actual value. Examples of indirect data are school enrollment and school census data, income tax returns, statistics on gas and electric meter installations, employment statistics, statistics on voter registrations, birth and death statistics (when used to reflect total population change directly rather than to measure natural increase), and statistics on housing construction, conversion, and demolition. Most often, estimation techniques utilizing indirect data are used when direct data are unavailable or partially complete.

It should be apparent that data of a given type may be direct for one kind of estimate and indirect for another and that there is no rigid dividing line between the two classes of data. Data on registrations for military service represent indirect data if they are being employed symptomatically to estimate the total male population as such and direct data if they are being employed to estimate the male population of registration age directly. Both direct and indirect data may be used in combination in preparing a given population estimate. To complete an estimate, the available direct and indirect data may have to be manipulated on the basis of hypotheses or assumptions. These hypotheses or assumptions may involve the use of a mathematical formula or its equivalent, such as a graph. Estimation by use of assumptions or a mathematical formula is required to make effective use of indirect data. If the analyst lacks reliable data of both the direct and indirect types, mathematical models are required (i.e., some assumptions must be made as to the trend of population change following the base date and expressed in terms of some mathematical formula or graphic device).

The usefulness of indirect data for population estimation depends on the extent to which factors other than population size and distribution influence them. Changes in the number of children attending school may result from changes in the laws relating to attendance and in their enforcement and in the availability of school facilities, as well as from changes in the number of children of school age. In addition, the prevalence of private schools and home schooling in an area may confound enrollment data collection. Employment, housing construction, and the number of public utility customers change with economic conditions as well as with population and households. The number of deaths varies not only with the size of the population but with the "force of mortality," which sometimes shows sharp fluctuations, for example as the result of an epidemic. It is apparent that the usefulness of indirect data as symptomatic indicators of population change will vary with the particular situation and that many of them will be of little or no value in preparing estimates for the less developed areas.

In general, the data to be used should be carefully evaluated according to the requirements set forth in previous chapters. The coverage of the latest census is especially important. A detailed understanding of definitions and collection procedures may be important in a particular case. The method used in collecting the data may give important indications as to the consistency of a series and the likelihood of over- or undercounting.

Some Estimating Principles

Some principles of population estimation may serve as rough guides (with numerous exceptions) of the assumptions and decisions made in an official estimates program:

1. Greater accuracy can generally be achieved for an entire country than for its geographic subdivisions. The national population is much more likely to be a closed population than is that of a subdivision of the country. Moreover, when there is immigration, it is likely to be registered for administrative reasons while internal migration will go unrecorded. In general, more direct data, data of better quality, and more information on how to adjust these data for deficiencies are available for the larger areas, particularly for entire countries, than for the smaller areas. Furthermore, the size of small populations may fluctuate widely, with the result that accurate estimation is extremely difficult or impossible. Depressed economic opportunities in one region of a country would have little discernible effect on the size of the population of the country but a particular state or province in this region might be sharply affected. A single factory closing would have little or no effect on the size of the population of a state, but it might cause the population of a small county in the state to be reduced sharply. It is usually advisable, therefore, to consider the sum of all geographic subareas (when available) in relation to an independently estimated area total to help determine relative accuracy and the potential need for adjustment. For example, the sum of estimates for provinces should be compared to the national total.

2. More accurate estimates can generally be made for the total population than for the demographic characteristics of the population of the area. Fewer data and data of poorer quality are usually available for making estimates of the population of a given area classified by age, race, sex, and other characteristics than of the total population of the area. It is usually advisable, therefore, to adjust estimates for such classes to the area total for the characteristic (e.g., estimates for age classes in the population of a province should be adjusted to the estimated total of all ages for the province).

3. In general, assuming that the available data are of good quality, direct data are to be preferred to indirect data. The more nearly the basic data approximate an exact count of the population being estimated or reflect actual change in that population since some base date (when the population figure is closely known), and the less adjustment or manipulation of the data required, the smaller the error to be expected in the resulting estimate. In actual practice, allowing that the direct or indirect data may in fact be defective, the choice may be determined by the accuracy, completeness, internal consistency, and recency of the data. In measuring population change, use of data that reflect actual population change (i.e., direct data, such as births, and deaths, etc.) and of methods whose steps parallel actual demographic processes (e.g., aging) may be expected, on the average, to produce more accurate estimates than the use of data and methods that are indirect. Again assuming that the available data are of good quality, this principle suggests, first, the use of direct data before use of indirect data in the

preparation of a particular estimate and the use of both direct and indirect data before mathematical methods are resorted to as a main procedure. The principle suggests, second, the desirability of employing a "cohort" approach, where possible, because such procedures by their very nature follow actual demographic changes. The most common application of a cohort approach is in the preparation of estimates of age groups.

4. An estimate may be cross-checked against another estimate derived by an equally accurate, or more accurate, method using different data and assumptions. Two or more independent estimates based in whole or part on different data or different methods, each considered highly accurate, can sometimes be worked out. If the estimates differ considerably from one another, doubt is cast on both; if they are quite similar, one may have greater confidence in each.

5. The quality of the base data, the quality of the data used to allow for change since the base date, and the period of time that has elapsed since the base date all have a major effect on the accuracy of the final estimate. It is reasonable to assume that the poorer the quality of the data and the longer the estimating period, the less reliable resulting population estimates will be.

6. The averaging of methods *may* be employed as a basis for improving the accuracy of population estimates. The methods to be averaged should employ different indicators or essentially different procedures and assumptions. Averaging may affect the accuracy of population estimates in two ways. It may reduce the risk of an extreme error and it may partly offset opposite biases characteristic of the two types of estimates being averaged. The methods to be averaged may be selected subjectively or on the basis of various quantitative indications given by studies of the accuracy of the methods (discussed later). For example, two methods that have relatively low average errors but that have opposite biases may be considered good candidates for averaging. The existence of opposite biases is indicated by a negative correlation between the percentage errors for the geographic units in a distribution (e.g., states) according to the two methods. The methods to be averaged may be given the same weights or different weights, which may be determined subjectively or quantitatively on the basis of evaluation studies. However, it is important to note that the assumptions on which any weights are assigned must be well specified, as the optimal weights for one place or time period may *not* be appropriate for another place or time period.

In developing population estimates, four broad categories of procedures may be used (Siegel, 2002, p. 404):

1. Mathematical extrapolation   (e.g. exponential trends; linear interpolation)

2. Censal-ratio methods   (e.g., housing-unit method to vital-rates method)

3. Component methods   (e.g., component methods I and II)

4. Statistical methods   (e.g., ratio-correlation)

Each of these procedures may be applied more or less successfully based on the principles defined, as well as the geographic level being estimated and quality of data available.

NATIONAL ESTIMATES

Three decisions must be made before devising national population estimates: (1) the methodology, (2) the data sources, and (3) a program of evaluation. The type of estimates being made then determines in large part the frequency, the extent of revision, and the need for adjustment. Typically, total population estimates are made with greater frequency than estimates of components of population change or estimates at subnational geographic levels. Usually, a set of estimates is released in preliminary, intermediate, and final stages. Oftentimes, these stages are necessitated by the slow process of collecting the supporting data and evaluating them. Finally, estimates are typically adjusted periodically so that they agree with the census or a population register.

In consideration of these decisions and determinations, this discussion is structured to consider estimates of national population first and then estimates of the geographic subdivisions of countries. Under each of these headings, postcensal estimates will first be considered for the total population, then for the two most basic demographic characteristics, age and sex—which are the most easily measured. Naturally, other characteristics of the population (such as race or ethnicity) are possible with these techniques if supporting data are available. However, estimates of these "subgroup" variables are subject to considerable error as their definitions often vary or the classification may in fact be self-reported. Both the national and subnational sections and the total and "subgroup" sections will be concluded with a discussion of intercensal adjustment. In presenting the techniques that are applicable for a given area, techniques using direct data will be described first, then techniques depending on both direct and indirect data or on indirect data only, then those involving principally mathematical assumptions.

National Population, Postcensal

Several methods are available for making postcensal estimates of a nation's population, each applicable under different circumstances. It is preferable, when possible, to prepare postcensal estimates on the basis of census counts and direct data on postcensal changes from registration systems or administrative records. From time to time, a special national registration may be taken that may serve as a basis for an estimate of national population or for evaluating an estimate of national population derived by other methods. The nature and function of population registers have been described in previous chapters. The data from the register may be employed to update the count from the previous census, rather than to provide the current estimates directly. The register may differ slightly from the census insofar as it may use different definitions and geographic boundaries. Typically the information from the register at the census date is evaluated, on the basis of the census returns, and the register is adjusted to agree with the census. Adequate postcensal estimates may also be derived by updating the results of a national sample survey or a national registration to the estimate date, on the basis of the balance of births, deaths, and migration.

Another important consideration in making national estimates is the universe to be estimated. In certain instances, estimates are desired simply for the national resident population, while other programs stipulate additional information on the population overseas, armed forces personnel, and institutionalized populations. Each of these characteristics requires additional data and methodological refinements.

While most planning and national reporting requirements continue to involve only estimates of total population, a growing number are beginning to require estimates for various population subgroups, such as age, sex, race, and sex. While the demand for more and greater detail on characteristics in population estimates is clearly growing, the supply of high-quality detailed estimates has been slow to expand (Rives and Serow, 1984, p. 64). This has been due to both the dramatically greater resources required by such a program, as well as the reduced accuracy that inevitably characterizes estimates of subgroups.

As with estimating the total national population, it is important to consider what the most appropriate "base" population is. In most methods, a decennial census number or sequential combinations thereof are used as part of the process. Oftentimes, the results of decennial censuses are adjusted or differ in the results on the basis of whether sample or 100% data are used. In general, as errors or undercounts may usually be attributable to a particular component of the total population, it is advised that the 100% data be used (where possible) and that the most recent count resolutions and undercount adjustments be utilized.

Component Methods

A simple component method may be used for estimating the total national population when a satisfactory census count and satisfactory administrative records on births, deaths, and migration are available. The method consists essentially of adding natural increase and net immigration for the period since the previous census to the latest census count or the latest previous estimate. The basic estimating equation is as follows:

$$P_t = P_0 + B - D + I - E \qquad (20.1)$$

where P_t represents the current population, P_0 represents the base resident population, B represents births to resident women, D represents deaths of residents, I represents immigrants, and E represents emigrants. A fictitious example is as follows:

Estimated population, July 1, 1998:	P_0	**47,566,235**
Events for July 1, 1998, to June 30, 1999		
Live births	B	+932,476
Deaths	D	−455,238
Natural increase		+477,238
Entries	I	+396,876
Exits	E	−377,895
Entries minus exits		+18,981
Net population increase		+496,219
Estimated population, July 1, 1999	P_1	**48,062,454**

If an estimate including the country's armed forces overseas is required, P_0 should include the armed forces overseas and D should include the military deaths overseas. If an estimate of the resident population of a country is required, one procedure is to carry the resident population at the census date forward by adding resident births, subtracting resident deaths (only), and adding net immigration including movements of the armed forces into and out of the country. Table 20.1 presents an example. Another possibility is to subtract the armed forces overseas on the estimate date from an estimate of population including armed forces overseas.

TABLE 20.1 Calculation of Annual Intercensal Estimates of the Resident Population of the United States: April 1, 1980, to April 1, 1990

Date	Postcensal population estimate (1)	Intercensal adjustment (2)	Intercensal population estimates (1) + (2) =
April 1, 1980	226,545,805	—	226,545,805
July 1, 1980	227,048,628	−33,926	227,014,702
July 1, 1981	229,419,923	−171,724	229,248,199
July 1, 1982	231,765,518	−312,233	231,453,285
July 1, 1983	234,042,411	−455,328	233,587,083
July 1, 1984	236,224,876	−601,209	235,623,667
July 1, 1985	238,469,164	−749,441	237,719,723
July 1, 1986	240,829,869	−900,696	239,929,173
July 1, 1987	243,143,690	−1,054,465	242,089,225
July 1, 1988	245,494,110	−1,211,588	244,282,522
July 1, 1989	247,961,185	−1,371,675	246,589,510
April 1, 1990	250,204,514	−1,494,641	248,709,873

Source: Internal U.S. Census Bureau document.

The data used to implement the component method are generally found in national administrative records. Birth and death data are collected regularly in most nations. Data on immigration and (less commonly) emigration are also generally collected, though they are often confounded by illegal migration, failure of migrants to officially report their entry and exit, and errors in migration records. See Chapters 2 and 18 for further information on national data sources regarding immigration and emigration.

Cohort-Component Method

The component method may be modified for use in estimating components of the population. Typically, the modified component method is used for estimating age and sex and is known as the "cohort-component" method. The basic estimating equation for the cohort-component method is similar to that for the component method as applied to the total population, except that the component equation must be evaluated for each age group and the birth component is included only at the very youngest ages. While births are typically easily derived at the national level, a special problem in making age estimates relates to the determination of the number of deaths and migrants that belong to a particular cohort. Addressing this problem ordinarily involves subdividing both the reported data on deaths and net migrants into age (birth) cohorts using separation factors. For example, at age 0, the distribution of deaths within the year of age is sufficiently uneven to require the use of special separation factors. To subdivide the deaths by cohorts, proportions may be derived from tabulations of deaths by year of birth (see Chapter 13).

Any separation factor may be derived on the basis of expert opinion or local area evidence of specific mortality levels. Generally in the more developed countries a separation factor of approximately .9 for deaths of infants and approximately .6 for those 1 year of age is obtained. Hence, the number of deaths corresponding to the cohort under 1 on the beginning estimate date is .90 D_0 (where D_0 represents infant deaths between the beginning and ending estimate dates), and to the cohort aged 1, .60 D_0 + .40 D_1. Henceforth, all cohorts would receive a "rectangular" separation factor, which is expressed as .50 D_1 +.50 D_2 and so on. It should be noted that a rectangular assumption disregards any available information regarding monthly variations in the number of deaths.

Another approach may be illustrated with estimates for single ages in Canada, as shown in Table 20.2. Rather than using separation factors, Statistics Canada attributes events of a given age directly to the population of that age on July 1, 1998. This is because the age is calculated not as of the event but as of July 1, 1998. Suppose that estimates for single years of age on July 1, 1999, are desired, given esti-

TABLE 20.2   Estimation of the Permanent Male Population of Canada, for Selected Ages: 1999

All ages	Population July 1, 1998 (1)	Deaths July 1, 1998–1999 (2)	Immigrants July 1, 1998–1999 (3)	Emigrants[1] July 1, 1998–1999 (4)	Population July 1, 1999 (5)
Total	30,011,435[2]	222,425	173,011	58,787	30,244,125
Births[3]	340,891	1,817	591	80	
0	344,500	297	2,853	195	339,585
1	358,510	150	2,320	463	346,861
2	385,712	97	2,381	611	360,217
3	390,091	88	2,419	734	387,385
4	393,430	67	2,573	828	391,688
0–4	**1,872,243**	**699**	**12,546**	**2,831**	**1,825,736**
5	401,526	59	2,605	898	395,108
6	412,364	68	2,604	946	403,174
7	416,686	50	2,581	977	413,954
8	418,373	55	2,820	990	418,240
9	404,160	62	2,862	979	420,148
5–9	**2,053,109**	**294**	**13,472**	**4,790**	**2,050,624**
⋮					
85	69,137	6,550	43	19	72,666
86	58,313	6,156	21	15	62,611
87	49,835	5,838	18	14	52,163
88	41,967	5,332	18	14	44,001
89	34,795	4,998	16	12	36,639
85–89	**254,047**	**28,874**	**116**	**74**	**268,080**
90+	121,093	24,015	43	69	126,853

[1] Emigrants represent the emigrants net of returning Canadians who emigrated from Canada but subsequently returned.
[2] Total excludes births during the period.
[3] The events for the births (age "−1") are events that relate to births July 1, 1998–1999.
Source: Estimates Branch, Statistics Canada.

mates of this kind for July 1, 1998. The basic equations, representing estimates for single years of age over a 1-year period are

For the population under 1:
$$P_0^{t+1} = B - D_{-1} + I_{-1} - E_{-1} \qquad (20.2)$$

For the population aged 1 and higher:
$$P_{a+1}^{t+1} = P_a^t - D_a + I_a - E_a \qquad (20.3)$$

where P = the estimated population
B = births
D = deaths
E = number of emigrants
I = number of immigrants
o = infants
a = the age of the event as of July 1, 1998.

1. First, the base population must be set down in single years of age according to ages on July 1, 1998 (col. 1).
2. Births during the 12-month period July 1, 1998, to July 1, 1999, are set down at the head of column 1. The events for the age "−1" are events that relate to the births between July 1, 1998 and July 1, 1999. Hence, to derive the population aged 0 in 1999, the events to the population aged "−1" are added to or subtracted from the births.

3. Next, an estimate of the number of deaths occurring to each age during July 1, 1998, to July 1, 1999 (distributed by age as of July 1, 1998) is needed. These are shown in column 2.
4. The immigration (col. 3) and emigration (col. 4) components require recording of age as of July 1, 1998. If single-year-of-age data are not available, the reader may refer to techniques in described in Appendix C.
5. The final estimates (col. 5) for the following age are obtained by subtracting the difference between deaths and net international migrants, from the initial population (col. 1). For 5-year groups, for example, the cumulation on line 0–4 yields the estimate for ages 1–5.

A set of annual midyear postcensal estimates by age normally has to be built up from the census counts in single years of age, which may require adjustment for various types of reporting errors, such as underenumeration and age misreporting, particularly age heaping. The census figures would usually also have to be carried forward to the middate of the first postcensal year.

As mentioned earlier, the base population on which postcensal estimates of population change are built is very important. Oftentimes, in a census, problems may arise from underenumeration, and occasionally overenumeration, but also from age misreporting. Official adjustments for under-enumeration and age misreporting are often made after a census is completed, and a number of courses can be taken with these adjustments with respect to the estimates. The unchanged census counts may be employed on the putative ground that the postcensal estimates by age should be comparable with the official census counts or that the correction factors are subject to too much error to be used with confidence. The corrections may simply be applied and carried forward. Alternatively, one may "inflate" the census counts, carry these corrected figures forward by age cohorts to an older age, then "deflate" the results to census level by use of the corrections at the last census applicable at the older age group. Note in the following formula that the "deflation" factor (c_{a+5}) differs from the "inflation" factor (c_a) because a different age group is involved at the different dates, P represents the population, D represents deaths, and M represents migration:

$$_5P_{a+5} = \frac{(c_a *_5 P_a) - D + M}{c_{a+5}} \quad (20.4)$$

The resulting estimates are at a level comparable to the official census counts and should be related to these in measuring changes by age in the postcensal period. Often annual estimates of the population in the conventional 5-year age groups are all that is desired. Even so, it is probably more efficient to carry out most of the calculations in single years of age because of the changing identity of the cohorts in the estimate for any 5-year age group.

Limited Cohort-Component Method

The cohort-component method may be applied in a more limited way than described here—that is, in less detailed or precise form, at less frequent intervals, or in combination with mathematical or other procedures not employing components. One variation, described later, is particularly applicable to a country that has reliable birth statistics by year, death statistics by age, and a negligible volume of net immigration. The method consists simply of carrying forward the population by 5-year age groups, as enumerated at the previous census, for 5 years by the use of life-table survival rates. Annual estimates of population by age may then be secured by interpolating to each calendar year between the census counts and the estimates 5 years later by age. This interpolation may be applied to the absolute numbers or the percentage distributions by age, but in each case the interpolated figures should be tied in with the preestablished total population figure.

This method of deriving estimates at quinquennial and annual intervals is illustrated with data for the Republic of Slovenia in Table 20.3. Census counts by age and sex for March 31, 1991, as enumerated (cols. 1 and 2) are carried forward to March 31, 1996 (col. 5) by use of survival rates

from a current life table (cols. 3 and 4). The survival rates used are derived from the Abridged Life Table by Sex, Republic of Slovenia, 1991–1992. The survival calculations are carried out separately for males and females because the survival rates come separately for each sex, but only the survivors for both sexes combined need to be recorded.

Table 20.3 goes on to illustrate the calculation of estimates of population for ages for July 1, 1993. Having established the age distribution in 1996 by a cohort method, relatively simple mathematical procedures will give a close approximation to consistent age estimates for prior dates. First approximations are obtained by linear interpolation of the absolute numbers for each age group in 1991 and 1996:

$$P_a^t = m_0 P_a^0 + m_1 P_a^1 \quad (20.5)$$

where m_0 and m_1 represent the interpolation multipliers. In this example, the interpolation multipliers are based on the following fractions:

March 31, 1991–July 1 1993 = 824 days/1828 days = .451

March 31, 1991–March 31, 1996

July 1, 1993–March 31, 1996 = 1004 days/1828 days = .549

March 31, 1991–March 31, 1996

These multipliers are the proportions of the (5-year) intercensal period before (.451) and after (.549) the estimate date, and they are applied in reverse order.

$$P_a^{1993} = .549 P_a^{1991} + .451 P_a^{1996} \quad (20.6)$$

The resulting initial total for July 1, 1993 (1,883,629) is derived on the basis of the assumption of a linear growth "rate" between 1986 and 1991. The assumption of a linear growth "rate" is oftentimes tenuous, as it does not directly consider current events that could move the population higher or lower, or perhaps even in the opposite direction of this type of estimate. These considerations aside, the linear growth rate over short periods of time is conservative and simple, and is justifiable particularly when used for interpolation between established figures.

Interpolation of age groups to single calendar years by cohorts would be undesirable for several reasons. Cohort interpolation of 5- or 10-year age groups to some intermediate date within a 5-year time period would initially produce estimates in "odd" 5-year age groups that would then require redistribution into the conventional ages. Such calculations would be more numerous, and not necessarily more exact or consistent with the initial figures, than the calculations for linear interpolation at the same ages. Under these circumstances, it is preferable to interpolate between figures for the same 5- or 10-year age groups; this procedure does not require the redistribution of the interpolated figures by age.

Mathematical Extrapolation

For countries lacking current administrative records on the components of population changes—and this includes

TABLE 20.3   Estimation of the Population of the Republic of Slovenia, by Age, for 1996 and 1993, by the Survival-Rate Method

Age (years)		Census population, March 31, 1991[1]		Survival rate		Survivors (both sexes) March 31, 1996 $[(1)*(3)]$ $+ [(2)*(4)] = (5)$[3]	Estimated population July 1, 1993[2]	
1991	1996	Male[2] (1)	Female[2] (2)	Male (3)	Female (4)		Initial[4] (6)	Adjusted (6) * 1.06775[5] (7)
All ages	All ages	892,499[6]	954,505[6]	X	X	1,928,214[6]	1,883,629[6]	2,011,241[6]
Births, 1991–1996	Under 5	68,538	65,176	0.990	0.993	132,572	X	X
Under 5	5 to 9	77,788	73,331	0.998	0.999	150,893	142,754	152,425
5 to 9	10 to 14	75,752	71,846	0.999	0.999	147,462	149,084	159,184
10 to 14	15 to 19	72,173	70,197	0.999	0.999	142,219	144,667	154,467
15 to 19	20 to 24	76,148	76,919	0.995	0.998	152,573	148,175	158,213
20 to 24	25 to 29	79,962	79,612	0.991	0.998	158,735	156,416	167,013
25 to 29	30 to 34	87,769	82,190	0.993	0.998	169,128	164,897	176,068
30 to 34	35 to 39	79,730	74,363	0.990	0.997	153,116	160,874	171,773
35 to 39	40 to 44	61,587	58,887	0.985	0.995	119,235	135,196	144,355
40 to 44	45 to 49	62,593	60,436	0.980	0.992	121,267	121,318	129,537
45 to 49	50 to 54	58,968	61,663	0.969	0.985	117,856	120,918	129,110
50 to 54	55 to 59	52,420	61,335	0.952	0.978	109,902	115,604	123,436
55 to 59	60 to 64	35,845	56,301	0.920	0.969	87,536	100,154	106,939
60 to 64	65 to 69	20,491	32,768	0.877	0.950	49,113	68,718	73,373
65 to 69	70 to 74	22,312	35,867	0.830	0.923	51,605	54,090	57,755
70 to 74	75 to 79	17,270	30,891	0.764	0.864	39,900	49,714	53,082
75 to 79	80 to 84	8,134	18,072	0.645	0.759	18,968	32,382	34,576
80 to 84	85 to 89	2,883	7,572	0.498	0.620	6,134	14,295	15,263
85 to 89	90 to 94	674	2,255	0.370	0.504	1,386[7]	4,375[8]	4,671[8]

X: Not applicable.

[1] Source: Slovenia, Statistical Office of the Republic of Slovenia, *Results of Surveys, 1994*, Tables 3.1 and 10.29.

[2] Ages of 1991.

[3] Ages of 1996.

[4] Obtained by linear interpolation: $.549P_{1991} + .451P_{1996}$.

[5] Factor obtained by dividing the independent estimate (2,011,241) by the initial estimate resulting from linear interpolation (1,883,629).

[6] Ages under 90 years.

[7] Ages 90 to 94 years.

[8] Ages 85–89 years.

many countries in the world—the figure for the base year is typically updated by use of an assumed rate of population increase. When making estimates, geometric extrapolation (reflecting exponential increase), linear, and quadratic functions are all possible. The application of mathematical extrapolation is undertaken in a four-step procedure: (1) observations are plotted on a graph, (2) all extrapolative functions are graphed for comparison, (3) the extrapolative function that conforms to the most general judgment regarding the most likely future behavior of the series and lowest potential error is selected, and (4) the value of the selected function is calculated for the projection date (Davis, 1995, p. 31).

The rate of change assumed for the postcensal period may take several forms, including the average annual rate of change in the previous intercensal period, an extrapolation of the rates for the two previous intercensal periods, or a rate assumed when only one or no census was taken. The method of updating the latest census figure or other base figure implies, of course, that the population has been changing at

a more or less constant rate since the base date. The specific steps for projecting a population by use of an exponential rate of increase may be illustrated with data for Latvia (Lativia, Central Statistical Bureau, 1999).

If the average annual growth rate between July 1, 1980, and July 1, 1990 (i.e., the last intercensal period), is assumed to continue to 1998, the estimated population of Latvia on July 1, 1998, may be determined as follows: From the general formula for population growth:

$$\frac{P_t}{P_0} = e^{rt} \tag{20.7}$$

(or $P_t = P_0 e^{rt}$ where P_t represents the current year population, P_0 represents the base year population, r represents the exponential rate, and t represents years). Thus:

Solving for r: $\frac{1}{t}\ln(P_t/P_0)$

$$r = \frac{1}{10}\ln\left(\frac{2,671,709}{2,525,189}\right) = .00564$$

To estimate the population 8 years from base, r (.00564) is multiplied by 8 to get $e^{rt} = 1.04512$. This factor is then multiplied by the 1990 population of 2,671,709 to get a 1998 population of 2,792,000. If annual population estimates are required, the extrapolated rate can be determined for each year of the period. This extrapolation also can be easily performed using many of today's spreadsheet programs. As mentioned, other forms are possible, affording the analyst a range of choices of mathematical functions to use. As described in the "Evaluation" section of this chapter, when data are available, one of the best guides for selecting a function is to fit the curves to observed growth patterns and compare results with a census in an "ex-post" style of test (Davis, 1995, pp. 29–30).

It should also be noted that most projections using exponential growth functions trace growth paths without any known upper limits. Obviously, exponential growth cannot occur indefinitely. In recognizing this, a modified exponential equation may be considered. This differs from the exponential equation in that there is an established upper and lower bound to the rate of population change. Over time, the population is assumed to approach this bound asymptotically. This may be the case when population estimates are being made for an area with administrative boundaries, which, when reached, significantly constrain further population growth. The modified exponential may be written as

$$y = ab^x + c \qquad (20.8)$$

This Equation (20.8) basically resembles the form of the exponential equation, except for the addition of the constant c (Davis, 1995, p. 25).

Extrapolative techniques may also be used in preparing postcensal estimates of population components. However, these procedures give relatively crude results and are to be used only when lack of suitable information on births, deaths, and migration make it impractical to use some type of cohort-component method.

Two types of mathematical procedures, both employing a single independently determined estimate of the current total population, are illustrated in Table 20.4. In this example, estimates have been made for broad age groups for the Philippines on July 1, 1998, by (1) linear extrapolation of the absolute census counts by age for 1980 and 1990 and (2) linear extrapolation of the percentage of the population in each age group at the two censuses. In both instances, the population is "controlled" to a national total. This "control" total may be derived from conventional geometric extrapolation, another type of extrapolation, or by other

TABLE 20.4 Estimation of the Population of the Philippines by Age, for July 1, 1998, by Linear Extrapolation of Numbers and Percentages

| Age (years) | Census population | | Linear extrapolation of numbers, July 1, 1998 | | Census percentage distribution | | Linear extrapolation of percentages, July 1, 1998 | |
	May 1, 1980 (1)	May 1, 1990 (2)	Initial estimates (3)	Adjusted estimates (4)	May 1, 1980 (5)	May 1, 1990 (6)	Percentages (7)	Population estimates (8)
All ages	48,098,460	60,559,116	70,783,719	73,097,125[1]	100.00	100.00	100.00	73,097,125[1]
Under 5	7,666,197	8,466,973	9,072,175	9,368,678	15.94	13.98	12.38	9,051,367
5 to 9	6,605,446	8,061,008	9,261,847	9,564,549	13.73	13.31	12.97	9,477,856
10 to 14	5,949,904	7,465,732	8,716,290	9,001,162	12.37	12.33	12.29	8,986,191
15 to 19	5,255,641	6,640,651	7,783,284	8,037,663	10.93	10.97	11.00	8,038,639
20 to 24	4,588,224	5,768,325	6,741,908	6,962,252	9.54	9.53	9.51	6,954,155
25 to 29	3,854,164	4,945,251	5,845,398	6,036,441	8.01	8.17	8.29	6,060,406
30 to 34	2,998,581	4,201,026	5,193,043	5,362,766	6.23	6.94	7.51	5,490,421
35 to 39	2,419,171	3,501,621	4,394,642	4,538,271	5.03	5.78	6.40	4,675,899
40 to 44	2,077,506	2,753,843	3,311,821	3,420,060	4.32	4.55	4.73	3,460,174
45 to 49	1,660,486	2,221,488	2,684,315	2,772,045	3.45	3.67	3.84	2,810,405
50 to 54	1,386,743	1,905,828	2,334,073	2,410,357	2.88	3.15	3.36	2,457,984
55 to 59	1,094,560	1,439,403	1,723,898	1,780,240	2.28	2.38	2.46	1,797,831
60 to 64	905,496	1,127,881	1,311,349	1,354,207	1.88	1.86	1.85	1,349,369
65 to 69	718,336	807,620	881,279	910,082	1.49	1.33	1.20	879,378
70 to 74	440,304	565,339	668,493	690,341	0.92	0.93	0.95	693,198
75 to 79	283,810	385,644	469,657	485,007	0.59	0.64	0.67	493,397
80+	193,891	301,483	390,246	403,001	0.40	0.50	0.58	420,455

Source: Republic of the Philippines *1980 Census of Population and Housing*, Volume 2, National Summary.
Republic of the Philippines *1990 Census of Population and Housing*, Report No. 3, Socio-Economic and Demographic Characteristics.
Republic of the Philippines 1991 *Philippine Statistical Yearbook*.
[1] Independent estimate, derived by geometric extrapolation.

methods, such as a national estimate based on population registers.

The preliminary estimates are derived at each age by linear extrapolation. Given an all-ages control, they receive a further proportional adjustment to the assigned figure for the total population. In this instance, the independent national population estimate 73,097,125 (col. 4) was made by geometric extrapolation. The resulting adjustment is approximately 3.3%.

In the second procedure, the estimates are calculated by the linear extrapolation of the percentage distribution. First, the percentage distributions by age in 1980 and 1990 are computed (cols. 5 and 6). Second, estimates of this distribution on July 1, 1998, are again derived by linear extrapolation, employing the same multipliers as for linear extrapolation of the absolute census counts (col. 7). The extrapolated percentages will automatically add to 100%. The extrapolated percentages are then multiplied by the independent estimate for the total population for July 1, 1998 (73,097,125), to secure the population estimates for age groups on that date.

Other Methods

Most nations are statistically well developed enough to utilize either component methods or extrapolative techniques for making population estimates. However, in many statistically underdeveloped countries, the data necessary for utilizing these methods are frequently limited. In these situations, an effective estimates system must be developed from a known base population at a specific date, then adjusted on the basis of ratios to what *is* known about the nation's rate of growth or other data symptomatic of change. In statistically undeveloped countries, there are potential hindrances to both determining a base population, as well as to the collection of numerator data for ratios and other symptomatic data necessary for developing estimates (see Chapter 22).

There are several types of situations for which the base population for estimates must be derived from extremely limited data, such as when there is an incomplete or poor census or censuses or when only one census has been taken. Estimates based on incomplete censuses include estimates based on censuses covering a minority of the population or conducted over an extended period of time. This category also includes estimates based on partial sample surveys and estimates based on counts of selected groups in the population, such as those covered in agricultural, school, or other censuses, and those listed in various types of special registers, such as lists of taxpayers or voters. With a partial census, sample survey, or registration of individuals, the error in the total population figure is compounded by errors in the partial count. Poorly conducted censuses suffer primarily from two shortcomings: the failure to enumerate the

relevant population (nearly always with differential coverage) and poor age reporting by the population canvassed. This leads to a population base on which it is very difficult to calculate rates and ratios, which again compound errors in population estimates and components.

Even estimates based on one census are difficult to prepare; however, the estimating situation is vastly improved from having no census at all. Standard mathematical formulas are not directly usable, and estimates can only be made under these circumstances by the use of rather arbitrary assumptions. The most common principle is the "estimating ratio," which is the relation of the total population to the unit of measurement or the "indicator" data. As compared with a partial or incomplete census, or no census whatsoever, one has a firm base to which an estimate of postcensal change can be added; or it allows for the computation of a firm estimating ratio by which the total population can be estimated from the indicator data.

If there is a base population upon which to develop current estimates (though perhaps not totally reliable), there may be an ongoing population register or survey that will make possible rough estimates of the current population and its demographic characteristics. More commonly, there are no direct measures of the demographic parameters and they must be estimated indirectly. There are two main types of indirect estimation techniques. The first type includes methods for adjusting data that have been collected by the traditional systems (such as a method designed to estimate a death rate from vital-registration data of uncertain accuracy). The second includes methods based on questions that can be answered with reasonable accuracy and that provide data that permit indirect estimation (such as using information on the incidence of orphanhood to estimate adult mortality). The reliance on special questions has led the second method to be most commonly associated with special sample surveys or censuses (United Nations, 1983, pp. 2–3).

Where the whole population or an important part of it has not been counted, and there is no possibility of estimating demographic parameters, population estimates have to be based on "conjectures." A conjectural estimate is one based on numerical data not relating to the population itself. Conjectural procedures vary from guessing to conversions of data on inhabited land area, tax revenues, or total production or consumption of a staple commodity, to a population estimate by applying a factor representing the ratio of population to the unit of measurement. Conjectural estimates are commonly subject to a very wide margin of error.

The need to evaluate and correct the basic data for population estimates is all the more important in the case of those statistically underdeveloped countries that have little experience in census taking or systematic collection of vital statistics (e.g., countries with only one census or none).

An evaluation of such data, and their correction where necessary, are essential steps in making reliable population estimates and in determining the confidence limits of the estimates made. Refer to Chapter 22 (Methods for Statistically Undeveloped Areas) for a detailed discussion of these methods. For a detailed discussion of mathematical techniques for making population estimates based on limited data, refer to the United Nations publication *Manual X: Indirect Techniques for Population Estimation* (1983). Further information on estimating demographic components may be found in Brass (1975) and Arriaga *et al.* (1994).

National Population, Intercensal

Intercensal and postcensal procedures serve different purposes with respect to the validation of estimates results. If the aim is to optimize estimates of total population in series longer than an intercensal period, intercensal estimates are of value because census enumerations act as a "hedge" against cumulative error in the measurement of change (U.S. Census Bureau, 1992, p. xiv). Intercensal estimates are produced following each census in order to reconcile postcensal estimates with census counts, thus ensuring the internal consistency of the estimates system (Statistics Canada, 1987, p. 35).

While providing necessary adjustments for consistency, intercensal estimates present the additional problem of allowing for the difference between the "expected" number at the later census date (P_1') and the number enumerated (P_1), the so-called error of closure. This difference represents the balance of errors in the elements of the estimating equation (including the population counts from the earlier and later censuses). The error of closure can be accounted for by three sources: (1) in estimating the postcensal change in population during the decade, faulty or incomplete data or discrepancies between the universe of the base population and the universe to which each of the components applies; (2) differential completeness of coverage in the two censuses, producing error in the estimate of intercensal change; and (3) for population subgroups, misclassification among the first census, the second census, and the various sources for the measurement of change (U.S. Census Bureau, 1992, p. xv). The use of "adjusted" or "unadjusted" census results must be considered as well. If and when intercensal national estimates are made, it is important to maintain consistency between the initial and second censuses.

Assuming that the census counts between which the intercensal estimates are to be made are maintained without change, there are several methods to allocate the total error to each respective intercensal year. One simple arithmetic device assumes that the adjustment for the error of closure is purely a function of time elapsed since the first census; hence, the correction for each year is derived by interpolat-

ing between zero at the earlier census date and the error of closure assigned to the later census date. These interpolated corrections may then be combined with the original postcensal population estimates. More sophisticated techniques distribute the error of closure over the intercensal period in proportion to the postcensal population, total population change, or one or more of the components of change. Less refined methods are satisfactory for the calculation of intercensal estimates, but as noted, to make full use of the available data, the special problem of the error of closure must be dealt with.

Making intercensal estimates by components of population change is confounded by the need to adjust for the error of closure by age and other segments. Not all of the difference between the census count for age and the count for the same cohort at the later census can be accounted for by errors in the available estimates of net change due to deaths and net migration (and births for youngest age groups). Part of the discrepancy may be a consequence of the difference between the net undercounts in the two censuses for the age groups in the same cohort. This irregularity cannot reasonably be attributed entirely to errors in the independent estimates of net change. Several alternative procedures for handling the error of closure in connection with adjusting postcensal estimates by age made by the cohort-survival method may be considered first. In addition, input data may need to be adjusted to conform to changes in definitions—not only in the data themselves but in census definitions as well. These methods produce estimates that are in one way or another comparable with the census counts.

Deriving total national intercensal estimates is a relatively easy affair, typically arrived at by associating each estimated annual change with a portion of the adjustment necessary for the estimate and the second census to agree. An illustration of the adjustment for error of closure in the total United States population estimates between 1980 and 1990 is shown in Table 20.5.

The intercensal estimates between 1980 and 1990 are derived as follows:

$$P_t = Q_t \frac{[(10-t)Q_{10} + tP_{10}]}{10Q_{10}} \tag{20.9}$$

where t is expressed in years since the first census, P_t is the intercensal estimate at time t, Q_t is the postcensal estimate at time t, P_{10} is the April 1, 1990, census count, Q_{10} is the April 1, 1990, postcensal estimate, and Q_0 is the April 1, 1980, census count. This equation takes into account both the length of time from the previous census and the size of the postcensal population estimates (U.S. Census Bureau, 1987). Note that t may be fractional if the estimate date is not April 1. For example, t would equal .25 for July 1, 1980. Numerous other linear and exponential methods are avail-

TABLE 20.5   Calculation of Annual Intercensal Estimates of the Resident Population of the United States: July 1, 1980 to July 1, 1989

Date	Postcensal population estimate (1)	Intercensal adjustment (2)	Intercensal population estimates (1) + (2) = (3)
April 1, 1980	226,545,805	—	226,545,805
July 1, 1980	227,048,628	−33,926	227,014,702
July 1, 1981	229,419,923	−171,724	229,248,199
July 1, 1982	231,765,518	−312,233	231,453,285
July 1, 1983	234,042,411	−455,328	233,587,083
July 1, 1984	236,224,876	−601,209	235,623,667
July 1, 1985	238,469,164	−749,441	237,719,723
July 1, 1986	240,829,869	−900,696	239,929,173
July 1, 1987	243,143,690	−1,054,465	242,089,225
July 1, 1988	245,494,110	−1,211,588	244,282,522
July 1, 1989	247,961,185	−1,371,675	246,589,510
April 1, 1990	250,204,514	−1,494,641	248,709,873

Source: Internal U.S. Census Bureau document.

able for generating intercensal estimates, but they frequently generate very similar results unless there has been a very dramatic shift in population in a very short period of time.

As discussed, attributing intercensal adjustments to components of the population is a considerably more difficult task. Derivations of the extrapolative technique and component technique may be used most effectively to make estimates of the components of the national population.

Component Methods

When the cohort-component method is used to develop postcensal national population estimates, distortions may occur that become magnified over the length of the postcensal period. Typically, these distortions are caused by reporting errors and undercounts in the census population from which the estimates are developed. This distortion is compounded by the possibility that the net undercount rate may change significantly over time from one age group to another. Furthermore, the growth rate of a cohort from the census date to the estimate date may be significantly different from the corresponding growth rate based on populations adjusted for net undercounts (U.S. Census Bureau/Das Gupta and Passel, 1987).

To counter these distortions, the U.S. Census Bureau has used the "inflation-deflation method" since the 1970 census. The inflation-deflation procedure combines the use of postcensal estimates by the cohort-component method, cohort adjustment for the error of closure in single ages, and allowance for net census undercounts (U.S. Census Bureau, 1992, pp. xvii–xviii).

The cohort method ideally requires a base free of net undercounts. It is desirable to have a set of estimates by age on the initial census date that have been corrected for net undercounts. To these the estimates of net cohort change are added. For example, the April 1, 1980, U.S. census population, including armed forces overseas, is "inflated" for estimated net census undercounts by age, sex, and race. The resulting estimates are carried forward by age to July 1 of each subsequent year by adding births, subtracting deaths, and adding net migration. The net estimates are then "deflated" to reflect estimated percentage net census undercounts by age, sex and race. A pro rata adjustment is then made to bring the estimates into agreement with the total population in each sex-age group obtained by carrying forward the census population with information on subsequent births, deaths, and immigration without regard to age. This calculation provides "true" intercensal estimates by age and, when continued to April 1, 1990, provides a "true" population in each year from 1980 to 1990. The difference between the "true" population in 1980 and 1990 and the census counts represents tentative estimates of net undercounts by age in these years.

Mathematical Extrapolation

An intercensal estimate generated by this technique is technically defined as *interpolation*. Interpolation considers what is known at a base date (initial census) as well as at a later date (second census) and makes assumptions, possibly taking other information into account, to determine what is known about intermediate dates. Numerous methods, ranging from very simplistic to extremely complex ones, are available for interpolation, though it should be noted that complexity is not always correlated with accuracy. In fact, many of the most complex interpolative functions will generate results that are nearly identical to simple ones, in making intercensal estimates. This often minimizes the debate about which method to use, whether a simple or complex method, rather than about which exact method. Further consideration must be made as to whether to interpolate by age group (e.g., 20 to 24 in 1990 and 20 to 24 in 2000) or by cohort (e.g., 20 to 24 in 1990 and 30 to 34 in 2000). In interpolating by age group, the assumption is that mortality is accounted for by the difference between the initial and second census values by age group. In interpolating by cohort, survival rates for each cohort must be considered. The most simplistic method may be classified as a linear model, which may be applied either by interpolating a population (or proportion of the population) to dates intermediate beween two censuses or by the forward-reverse survival-rate procedure.

TABLE 20.6 Calculation of Intercensal Estimates of the Population of the Philippines by Age, for July 1, 1988, by Linear Interpolation of Numbers and Percentages

| Age (years) | Census population | | Linear interpolation of numbers, July 1, 1988 | | Census percentage distribution | | Linear interpolation of percentages July 1, 1988 | |
	May 1, 1980 (1)	May 1, 1990 (2)	Initial estimates[1] (3)	Adjusted estimates (4)	May 1, 1980 (5)	May 1, 1990 (6)	Percents (7)	Population estimates (8)
All ages	48,098,460	60,559,116	58,278,816	58,057,316[2]	100.00	100.00	100.00	58,057,316[1]
Under 5	7,666,197	8,466,973	8,320,431	8,288,808	15.94	13.98	14.34	8,325,132
5 to 9	6,605,446	8,061,008	7,794,640	7,765,015	13.73	13.31	13.39	7,772,851
10 to 14	5,949,904	7,465,732	7,188,335	7,161,015	12.37	12.33	12.34	7,161,799
15 to 19	5,255,641	6,640,651	6,387,194	6,362,918	10.93	10.97	10.96	6,362,200
20 to 24	4,588,224	5,768,325	5,552,367	5,531,264	9.54	9.53	9.53	5,531,526
25 to 29	3,854,164	4,945,251	4,745,582	4,727,546	8.01	8.17	8.14	4,724,708
30 to 34	2,998,581	4,201,026	3,980,979	3,965,848	6.23	6.94	6.81	3,952,804
35 to 39	2,419,171	3,501,621	3,303,533	3,290,977	5.03	5.78	5.64	3,277,011
40 to 44	2,077,506	2,753,843	2,630,073	2,620,077	4.32	4.55	4.51	2,615,844
45 to 49	1,660,486	2,221,488	2,118,825	2,110,772	3.45	3.67	3.63	2,106,762
50 to 54	1,386,743	1,905,828	1,810,835	1,803,953	2.88	3.15	3.10	1,799,055
55 to 59	1,094,560	1,439,403	1,376,297	1,371,066	2.28	2.38	2.36	1,369,188
60 to 64	905,496	1,127,881	1,087,185	1,083,052	1.88	1.86	1.87	1,083,426
65 to 69	718,336	807,620	791,281	788,274	1.49	1.33	1.36	791,241
70 to 74	440,304	565,339	542,458	540,396	0.92	0.93	0.93	540,060
75 to 79	283,810	385,644	367,008	365,613	0.59	0.64	0.63	364,746
80+	193,891	301,483	281,794	280,723	0.40	0.50	0.48	278,965

Source: Republic of the Philippines *1980 Census of Population and Housing*, Volume 2, *National Summary*.
Republic of the Philippines *1990 Census of Population and Housing*, Report No. 3, *Socio-Economic and Demographic Characteristics*.
Republic of the Philippines *1991 Philippine Statistical Yearbook*.
[1] Interpolation factors are .183 and .817.
[2] Independent estimate derived by geometric interpolation.

Two examples of linear interpolation by age group are illustrated in Table 20.6. Estimates have been made for broad age groups for the Philippines on July 1, 1988, on the basis of the 1980 and 1990 census counts by (1) linear interpolation of the absolute census counts and (2) linear interpolation of the percentages of the population in each age group at the two censuses.

In the first procedure, the preliminary estimates must be adjusted *pro rata* to the assigned total population (which in this instance is obtained by geometric interpolation). In the second procedure, the interpolated percentages will automatically add to 100% for all ages. The specific steps in the calculation of estimates by the method of linear interpolation are as follows. First, the linear interpolation is calculated:

May 1, 1980–July 1, 1988: 2984 days/3653 days = .817
July 1, 1988–May 1, 1990: 669 days/3653 days = .183

These multipliers are the proportions of the (10-year) intercensal period before (.817) and after (.183) the estimate date, and are applied in reverse order. Substituting as follows:

$$P_a^{7/1/1988} = .183 P_a^{5/1/1980} + .817 P_a^{5/1/1990} \qquad (20.10)$$

The initial estimates are then "controlled" to the independent total population for July 1, 1988 (58,057,316), obtained by geometric interpolation of the census counts, as shown here:

$$X^{7/1/1988} = X^{5/1/1980} * \left(\frac{X^{5/1/1990}}{X^{5/1/1980}} \right)^{\frac{2984}{3653}} \qquad (20.11)$$

This results in an adjustment of about −0.4%. Final estimates based on census percentage distributions are then calculated by applying the interpolated percentage to the independent national estimate (58,057,316).

The forward-reverse survival-rate procedure "survives" cohorts forward and backward to interpolate population estimates. An example is illustrated for the Philippines on February 1, 1985 (Table 20.7). The procedure involves the calculation of two preliminary estimates, one by aging the first census (cols. 1 to 6) forward in time and the second by "younging" the second census (cols. 7 to 12) backward in time; and then averaging the two estimates (cols. 13 to 14). First, the May 1, 1980, census population was aged to May 1, 1985, by use of the UN model life tables (United Nations,

1982, pp. 266–267). The tables used correspond to the South Asia Pattern and were selected on the basis of Philippine male and female life expectancy (Philippines, National Statistical Coordination Board, 1991) in 1980 (for the forward portion) and 1990 (for the reverse portion). It was assumed that net immigration equaled or approximated zero (though this assumption is often incorrect and must be considered seriously). The "forward" estimates of the population for February 1, 1985 (col. 6), were derived by linear interpolation, at each age, between the census counts for May 1, 1980, and the survivors on May 1, 1985. The equation employed for this purpose, expressing the calculations in terms of multipliers, is

$$P_a^{2/1/1985} = .049 P_a^{5/1/1980} + .951 P_a^{5/1/1985} \qquad (20.12)$$

The multipliers are the proportions of the (5-year) intercensal period before (.951) and after (.049) the estimate date, and are applied in reverse order:

(May 1, 1980–February 1, 1985) ÷ (May 1, 1980–
May 1, 1985) = 1738 days/1827 days = .951
(February 1, 1985–May 1, 1985) ÷ (May 1, 1980–
May 1, 1985) = 89 days/1827 days = .049

A second set of preliminary estimates for February 1, 1985, was prepared by the "reverse" procedure. The May 1, 1990, census counts were "younged" to May 1, 1985, by use of the UN model life tables. Estimates of population for February 1, 1985, were then made by interpolating between these estimates for May 1, 1985, and the census counts for 1980 at each age. The equation expressing the latter calculation in terms of multipliers is identical to that given earlier in connection with the forward estimates of the population for May 1, 1985.

The differences between the forward and reverse estimates are principally a reflection of differences in census net undercounts for a given cohort at the two censuses, but they also reflect any net immigration during the intercensal period. The final estimates are derived by averaging the forward and reverse estimates, with weights in reverse relation to the time lapse from the census dates (col. 13), as follows:

(May 1, 1980–February 1, 1985) ÷ (May 1, 1980–
May 1, 1990) = 1738 days/3653 days = .475
(February 1, 1985–May 1, 1990) ÷ (May 1, 1980–
May 1, 1990) = 1915 days/3653 days = .525

These multipliers are the proportions of the (10-year) intercensal period before (.475) and after (.525) the estimate date and are applied in reverse order. Substituting as follows:

$$P_a^{2/1/1985} = .525 P_a^{5/1/1980} + .475 P_a^{5/1/1990} \qquad (20.13)$$

The preliminary estimates for 1985 are thus averaged with weights of .525 for the forward estimate and .475 for

the reverse estimate. These results are then adjusted *pro rata* to the independent estimate of the total population on February 1, 1985, derived by geometric interpolation of the census counts for 1980 and 1990 (col. 14). The independent estimate is derived by the following equation:

$$X^{2/1/1988} = X^{5/1/1980} * \left(\frac{X^{5/1/1990}}{X^{5/1/1980}} \right)^{\frac{1738}{3653}} \qquad (20.14)$$

where 1738 equals the number of days from May 1, 1980, to the estimate date of February 1, 1985. The factor for adjusting the weighted estimates to the independently derived estimate of the total for February 1, 1985, is (53,669,990 / 53,373,706) or 1.00555.

The difficulty with linear interpolation, especially when populations are rapidly changing, is that there are often significant deviations in values where two interpolation curves meet. Various methods have been employed to effect a smooth junction of the interpolations made for one range of data with the interpolations made for the next (adjacent) range. Osculatory interpolation is a method that accomplishes that purpose. It involves combining two overlapping polynomials into one equation. Although osculatory interpolation encompasses a wide variety of possible equations, only a few are used for interpolating population estimates. These include Sprague's fifth-difference equation, Karup-King's third-difference equation, and Beer's six-term ordinary and modified formula. These techniques are discussed in detail in Appendix C.

Final Considerations

It is important to note, especially for estimates of the components of a national population, that it is the total household and nonhousehold population that is being considered. Generally, no special adjustments are necessary at this geographic level to account for nonhousehold or "group quarters" population. Consideration must be made for this population, however, if it constitutes an unusually large portion of the total population or if the number or proportion has changed significantly since the most recent census (Land and Hough, 1986). In this situation, it is necessary to obtain group-quarters figures in the same level of demographic detail as the household population used in the selected estimation procedure (Rives and Serow, 1984, 74).

SUBNATIONAL ESTIMATES

Subnational Population, Postcensal

Estimating the population of geographic subdivisions of a country, such as states, provinces, counties, and cities, generally requires a somewhat different approach than

TABLE 20.7 Calculation of the Intercensal Estimates of the Population of the Philippines by Age, for July 1, 1985, by the Forward-Reverse Survival-Rate Method

Age 1980	Age 1985	Census population, May 1, 1980 Male (1)	Female (2)	Survival rate Male (3)	Female (4)	Survivors (both sexes) May 1, 1985 [(1)*(3)+[(2)*(4)] = (5)	Preliminary population estimate, February 1, 1985[1] (6)	Weighted population estimates, February 1, 1985 prel.[1] Initial (13)
All ages	All ages	24,128,755	23,969,705	X	X	53,397,044[2]	53,137,413[2]	53,373,706[2]
Births, 1980–1985	Under 5 years	3,831,113	3,544,100	0.8945	0.9037	6,629,734	6,680,520	7,346,698
Under 5	5 to 9	3,932,770	3,733,427	0.9669	0.9702	7,424,766	7,384,619	7,415,674
5 to 9	10 to 14	3,396,682	3,208,764	0.9924	0.9936	6,559,095	6,529,245	6,580,100
10 to 14	15 to 19	3,036,022	2,913,882	0.9949	0.9955	5,921,308	5,888,690	5,834,251
15 to 19	20 to 24	2,566,848	2,688,793	0.9938	0.9942	5,224,132	5,192,972	5,082,395
20 to 24	25 to 29	2,210,308	2,377,916	0.9924	0.9932	4,555,256	4,520,902	4,378,134
25 to 29	30 to 34	1,918,288	1,935,876	0.9907	0.9919	3,820,643	3,780,362	3,657,123
30 to 34	35 to 39	1,521,082	1,477,499	0.9877	0.9897	2,964,653	2,937,925	2,867,693
35 to 39	40 to 44	1,227,966	1,191,205	0.9819	0.9862	2,380,506	2,365,659	2,326,577
40 to 44	45 to 49	1,046,208	1,031,298	0.9724	0.9807	2,028,727	2,010,683	2,001,586
45 to 49	50 to 54	825,018	835,468	0.9563	0.9702	1,599,536	1,589,109	1,575,183
50 to 54	55 to 59	682,996	703,747	0.9320	0.9514	1,306,097	1,295,732	1,290,563
55 to 59	60 to 64	528,491	566,069	0.8950	0.9207	989,834	989,834	992,827
60 to 64	65 to 69	441,026	464,470	0.8418	0.8746	777,481	774,583	777,812
65 to 69	70 to 74	349,270	369,066	0.7716	0.8082	567,776	584,937	610,379
70+	75+	445,780	472,225	0.6845	0.7158	643,155	611,640	636,711

Age 1990	Age 1985	Census population, May 1, 1990 Male (7)	Female (8)	Survival rate Male (9)	Female (10)	"Younged" population, May 1, 1985 (both sexes) [(7)÷(9)]+[(8)÷(10)] = (11)	Preliminary population estimate, February 1, 1985[1] (12)	Weighted population estimates, February 1, 1985 final (53,669,990/53,373,706) * (13) = 1.00555 * (13) = (14)
All ages	X	30,443,187	30,115,929	X	X	53,920,133[2]	53,634,871[2]	53,669,990[3]
Under 5	Under 5	4,342,516	4,124,457	0.9747	0.9776	X	X	X
5 to 9	5 to 9	4,125,409	3,935,599	0.9941	0.9952	8,104,474	8,082,999	7,387,480
10 to 14	10 to 14	3,799,408	3,666,324	0.9959	0.9967	7,493,513	7,449,997	7,456,839
15 to 19	15 to 19	3,320,861	3,319,790	0.9950	0.9957	6,671,675	6,636,309	6,616,627
20 to 24	20 to 24	2,866,207	2,902,118	0.9939	0.9949	5,800,793	5,774,080	5,866,637
25 to 29	25 to 29	2,459,263	2,485,988	0.9925	0.9938	4,979,344	4,960,179	5,110,608
30 to 34	30 to 34	2,110,791	2,090,235	0.9900	0.9920	4,239,204	4,220,337	4,402,437
35 to 39	35 to 39	1,768,532	1,733,089	0.9851	0.9889	3,547,824	3,520,911	3,677,424
40 to 44	40 to 44	1,389,855	1,363,988	0.9767	0.9840	2,809,178	2,790,067	2,883,611
45 to 49	45 to 49	1,113,345	1,108,143	0.9622	0.9747	2,293,989	2,283,382	2,339,493
50 to 54	50 to 54	944,837	960,991	0.9397	0.9580	2,008,589	1,991,532	2,012,697
55 to 59	55 to 59	705,646	733,757	0.9048	0.9302	1,568,708	1,559,792	1,583,927
60 to 64	60 to 64	547,008	580,873	0.8545	0.8875	1,294,655	1,284,850	1,297,727
65 to 69	65 to 69	376,777	430,843	0.7874	0.8249	1,000,805	996,135	998,338
70 to 74	70 to 74	264,981	300,358	0.7026	0.7371	784,630	781,381	782,130
75 to 79	75 to 79	176,680	208,964	0.6083	0.6263	624,097	638,499	613,767
80+		131,071	170,412	0.4403	0.4250	698,655	664,421	640,246

Source: Republic of the Philippines 1980 Census of Population and Housing, Volume 2, National Summary.
Republic of the Philippines 1990 Census of Population and Housing, Report No. 3, Socio-Economic and Demographic Characteristics.
Republic of the Philippines 1991 Philippine Statistical Yearbook.
United Nations, 1982. Model Life Tables for Developing Countries, Population Studies Series A, No. 77. South Asia Pattern, Males, p. 266, Females p. 267.
X Not applicable. [1]Obtained by linear interpolation or weighting factors. See text for explanation. [2]Obtained by summation. [3]Independent estimate derived by geometric interpolation.

estimating the total population for a nation. There are usually fewer data, and these are generally of poorer quality, than data available for a nation as a whole. When data from a population register are available, they may be used for estimates, though they may be subject to intercensal revision following censuses. In considering the requirements of a traditional component method, births and deaths for subnational areas are available for many countries on a regular basis. When direct information on the volume of immigration and emigration (as well as the movement of domestic in- and out-movers) is not available, net migration must be estimated indirectly to apply traditional component methods. Regression-based techniques are possible depending on the level and availability of input data. One of the most commonly used methods of making subnational population estimates is the housing unit method; it is based on the number of housing units, the occupancy rate, and the average number of occupants in each housing unit in the area being estimated. Finally, a composite method may be used when the same data are not available or the same methods cannot be used for a set of subnational estimates at a given geographic level.

Data from population registers, registration data, and city directories may be used to develop population estimates for small geographic areas for occasional dates or on a regular basis. The registration must be compulsory (e.g., a military registration) or quasi-compulsory (i.e., voluntary but supported by strong pressures to participate, as, for example, registration for food ration books) to ensure reasonably complete coverage of the population. Registration data may have to be adjusted to include certain segments of the population not required to register and to exclude others required to register but not encompassed in the population for which estimates are being prepared. Military registration data are of limited usefulness for making population estimates, primarily because they usually cover only a narrow range of the age distribution and are likely to be incompatible with census data.

Delayed registrations obviously create a special problem. Because they may be numerous, it is desirable to include registrations for a short period following the initial registration date. On the other hand, it is hazardous to use a count of registrants for a date far removed from the date of the initial registration because the registration lists may not be adjusted to exclude persons who died or left the area after the initial registration date or to include persons who migrated into the area during this period.

Component Methods

As with national programs, estimates of regional and local population may be prepared for current dates by a component method if satisfactory data on births, deaths, and migration are available. For statistically developed countries, the required birth and death statistics or estimates are generally available with only a brief time lag. Subnational migration data, however, present a special problem. Not only must immigration and emigration be considered, but also in- and out-movers. Further, adequate data on migration for local areas for current years, particularly on a continuing basis, are rare. Migration data may be secured for geographic subdivisions of a country on a current basis from continuing national sample surveys, surveys on internal migration, population registers or registrations, special tabulations from appropriate administrative records such as tax returns and records of a family allowance system or social security system. Typically, the migration data from sample surveys fail to include those migrants who died during the reference period. The deaths of in-migrants must be included in the data on in-migrants just as they are included in the reported death statistics.

The inclusion of a migration question (i.e., residence at fixed previous date) on the census schedule makes possible the preparation of estimates for a specific precensal date by a component method involving direct measurement of migration. The general equations are

$$P^{t-x} = P^t + D^x - B^x - M^x \qquad (20.15)$$

or

$$P^{t-x} = P_c^t + D_c^x - M_c^x \qquad (20.16)$$

where P^{t-x} is the estimated total population at a particular date x years before the census (i.e., 1 year, 5 years, etc.), P^t is the census population, D^x is the number of deaths in the period of x years between the estimate date and the census date, B^x is the number of births during the period, and M^x is the number of (net) migrants during the period. The formula may take two forms. The elements may relate to (a) all ages or (b) the cohorts x years of age and over at the census date. In the former case, P^t and P^{t-x} relate to the total population at the census date and the estimate date, respectively, and D^x, B^x, and M^x relate to total deaths, births, and (net) migrants, respectively. In the latter case, P^{t-x} is the estimated total population at the estimate date, P_c^t is the census population aged x and over (1 and over, 5 and over, etc.), D_c^x is the number of deaths to the cohorts aged x and over on the census date, and M_c^x is the number of (net) migrants affecting these cohorts.

In the absence of actual data on internal migration, this component may be estimated with "symptomatic" data. To serve this purpose, the symptomatic data on internal migration must be available on a continuing current basis, must relate to a substantial segment of the population, must be internally comparable from year to year, and must fluctuate principally in response to changes in population. Many series of administrative data may be considered for this purpose, such as the population covered by tax returns or data on school enrollment. The derivation of migration data from these systems for the principal and secondary political units of a country as a set may be quite complex and involve modifications of the basic reporting form, the need for special tabulations, difficult problems of assigning residence, and other such concerns.

The results of component techniques may be further disaggregated to include age and sex detail. The "component" estimates may be based either on actual statistics on the age-sex composition of migrants or on symptomatic data for migrants. In Canada, considerable use is made of data on interprovincial migration by age and sex from the Family Allowance System, which maintains records on the movements of families in receipt of family allowances and the ages and sex of persons moving. Additionally, the characteristics of migrants may be derived from population registers for countries that have population registers.

A data source on which to base estimates of migration are tax-return records, such as is used by the U.S. Census Bureau for making state and county population estimates. In the tax-return method (formerly called the administrative records method), the U.S. Census Bureau uses tabulations of births and deaths, then estimates internal migration by deriving migration rates from annual federal tax returns. It is important to note that at the subnational geographic level, distinctions are often required between major age groups and household/nonhousehold populations. These components are added to derive total populations and should not generally be taken on their own as independent estimates. A detailed explanation follows.

The U.S. Census Bureau treats states as "tabulation geography" rather than "estimates geography." This means that the "county estimates" methodology is actually applied only to the counties, and the state population estimates are derived merely by summing the county estimates to the state level. The District of Columbia is treated as a county equivalent for estimation purposes. For the population residing in households the components of change are births, deaths, and net migration, including net immigration from abroad. For the nonhousehold population, change is represented by net change in that population (i.e., nonhousehold or group quarters population). Each of these components are listed in Tables 22.8, 22.9, and 22.10 and are covered in the following text. Table 20.8 shows the derivation of a July 1 population estimate for a hypothetical county in an estimate year.

Except for the net-migration component, the components of change are calculated for a July 1 county estimate from data items that are extrapolated. Extrapolation is necessary because data needed for the current estimate year are not always available. When some county data are not available for the current estimate year, an estimate is developed through simple assumptions. In the simplest case, it is assumed there is no change in the data between the current estimate year and the prior estimate year. In other cases, it is assumed that the distribution of data by county did not change from the prior year. The county distribution is then applied to the current total for the state data to estimate current year data for counties. In the discussions that follow, line numbers refer to a hypothetical county population estimate for a typical estimate year. The estimate of the

TABLE 20.8   Derivation of 1996 Under-65 Population Estimate for a Hypothetical County

	Value	Derivation or source
Base populations		
1. Base population	93,401	Revised estimate from prior year
2. Base group-quarters population under age 65	5,660	See text for detailed source
3. Base population aged 65 years and over	4,021	See text for detailed source
4. Household base population under age 65 years	83,705	$(4) = (1) - (2) - (3) - [(.00362) \times (3)]$
Estimated components of change for the household population under age 65		
5. Resident births: 7/1 (prior year) to 6/30 (estimate year)	1,924	See text for detailed source
6. Resident deaths to the household population under age 65 years	157	See text for detailed source
7. Immigration 7/1 (prior year) to 6/30 (estimate year)	164	See text for detailed source
8. Migration base	84,671	$(8) = (4) + 0.5 \times [(5) - (6) + (7)]$
9. Migration rate	−0.00943	See text for detailed source
10. Net migration	−798	$(10) = (8) \times (9)$
Estimated population under age 65		
11. Household population under age 65	84,838	$(11) = (4) + (5) - (6) + (7) + (10)$
12. Group quarters population under age 65	5,660	See text for detailed source
13. Total population under age 65	90,498	$(13) = (11) + (12)$

TABLE 20.9   Derivation of 1996 65-and-Over Population Estimate for a Hypothetical County

	Value	Derivation or source
Base populations		
1. Base total population aged 65 and over	4021	7/93 population estimate
2. Base group quarters population aged 65 and over	642	See text for detailed source
3. Estimated population reaching 65 in current year	225	See text for detailed source
4. Household base population aged 65 and over	3604	(4) = (1) − (2) + (3)
Estimated components of change for the household population aged 65 and over		
5. Resident deaths to the household population aged 65 and over	168	See text for detailed source
6. Foreign immigration 7/1/95 to 6/30/96	21	See text for detailed source
7. Migration base	3531	(7) = (4) + 0.5 × [(6) − (5)]
8. Migration rate	0.0317236	See text for detailed source
9. Net migration	112	(9) = (7) × (8)
Estimated population aged 65 and over		
10. Household population aged 65 and over	3569	(10) = (4) − (5) + (6) + (9)
11. 1994 group quarters population	586	See text for detailed source
12. Total population aged 65 and over	4155	(12) = (11) + (10)

TABLE 20.10   Final Estimate for a Hypothetical County

	Value	Derivation or source
1. Estimated total population under 65	90,498	Line 13 from Table 22.8
2. Adjustment factor for the population under 65	1.000435	See text for explanation
3. Final estimate for the population under 65	90,537	(3) = (2) × (1)
4. Estimated total population aged 65 and over	4,155	Line 12 from Table 22.9
5. Adjustment factor for the population aged 65 and over	1.001034	See text for explanation
6. Final estimate for the population aged 65 and over	4,159	(6) = (4) × (5)
7. Final population estimate	94,696	(7) = (3) + (6)

population under age 65 is calculated in Table 20.8, and is explained here.

The base total population is shown on line 1, which is the revised county estimate for the prior estimate year. Each year, the population estimate represents the population change from the prior year. The only year in which this is not true is the year of the decennial census. In the decennial year, an estimate is prepared that represents population change between the census date and July 1 of that year. For official population estimates, the decennial population is not adjusted for undercount.

The base group quarters population under age 65 is shown on line 2. This component is primarily a combination of military personnel living in barracks, college students living in dormitories, and persons residing in institutions. Inmates of correctional facilities, persons in health care facilities, and persons in Job Corps centers are also included in this category. These data are collected from state and other administrative records. Persons aged 65 and over residing in nursing homes and other facilities are excluded from this category because they are implicitly included in the estimate of the 65-and-over population. The base group quarters pop-

ulation for the current estimate year is the revised group quarters population from the prior estimate year. In the first estimate year following the decennial census, the base group quarters population is the group quarters population as enumerated in the decennial census.

The base total population aged 65 years and over is shown on line 3. This component is the revised estimate of the population aged 65 years and older from the prior estimate year.

The household base population under age 65 is shown on line 4. The group quarters populations (line 2) and the population aged 65 and over (line 3) are subtracted from the base population (line 1) to derive the under-65 household population. The household population under age 65 is also reduced by those persons aged 64 and over who will turn 65 (expressed as a factor) during the estimates cycle.

The estimated resident births, 7/1 (prior year) to 6/30 (estimate year) are shown on line 5. Resident births are recorded by residence of mother, regardless of where the birth occurred; hence, a county need not have a hospital to have resident births. If birth data are not available by county for a state for the estimate year when the county estimates are produced, then prior-year county birth data are used to approximate estimate-year births.

Estimated resident deaths to the household population under 65, 7/1 (prior year) to 6/30 (estimate year), are shown on line 6. Death data are tabulated by the most recent residence of the decedent, not by the place where death occurred. Deaths of the population under 65 years are tabulated by race and "controlled" to state tabulations. The estimated deaths are then adjusted to national death totals by race. If estimate-year death data are not available by county for a state when the county estimates are produced, the past year's death data are used.

The estimated net movement from abroad (immigration), 7/1 (prior year) to 6/30 (estimate year), is shown on line 7. Estimates of foreign immigrants are based on the national estimate of foreign migration developed by the Census Bureau. The estimate includes emigration from the United States and the immigration of refugees, legal immigrants, illegal immigrants, net movement from Puerto Rico, and federal and civilian citizen movement from abroad. The national estimate of the illegal immigrants is allocated to states and counties by using the distribution of the foreign-born population that arrived between 1985 and 1990 and was enumerated as residents in the 1990 census. Legal immigrants and refugees are distributed to counties on the basis of county of intended residence as reported to the Immigration and Naturalization Service.

The estimated migration base is shown on line 8. The migration base is developed by adding one-half of the following elements to the household base population under 65 years (line 4): estimated resident births (line 5), minus estimated resident deaths under 65 years (line 6), plus estimated net immigration (line 7). Only half of the additions/deletions to the population would have taken place by the midpoint of the 12 months; thus an "exposure factor" of one-half must be entered into the equation. The population at risk of migrating is usually considered the population at the midpoint of the period because the population at the beginning of the estimate period has not yet experienced the births and deaths that are reflected in the population at the end of the period. The population at the end of the period includes inmigrants and excludes outmigrants; thus the best tactic devised is to take the population at the midpoint of the period. Estimated resident births, estimated deaths to persons under age 65, and net immigration from abroad are assumed to have been evenly distributed throughout the estimate interval and, therefore, exposed to the risk of migration, on average, for one-half of the period.

The estimated migration rate is shown on line 9. This is the essential part of the tax return method. Changes in addresses for individual federal income tax returns are used to reflect the internal migration of the population under 65 years of age. Matching the returns for successive years for that age group furnishes a measure of that migration. The

status of the filer is determined by noting the address, used as a proxy for place of residence, on tax returns filed in the prior year and in the estimate year. The filers are then categorized for each county as (1) inmigrants, (2) outmigrants, and (3) nonmigrants. A net migration rate is then derived for each county, based on the difference between the inmigration and outmigration of the tax filers and their dependents. It should be noted that the original data delivered by the U.S. Internal Revenue Service to the U.S. Census Bureau are strictly confidential. Therefore, replication of this component is not possible.

The estimated net internal migration is shown on line 10. Net migration is the product of the migration base (line 8) and the net migration rate (line 9). If this figure is preceded by a minus sign (−), then if indicates net outmigration; otherwise, the figure represents net inmigration.

The estimated household population under age 65 is shown on line 11. The household base population under age 65 (line 4) is combined with the estimated components of change for the household population under age 65 to arrive at the estimated household population under age 65 in the estimate year.

The estimated group quarters population under age 65 is shown on line 12. Military personnel living off base and those living on base in family quarters are assumed to be included in the components of change of the household population, described earlier. Military barracks population figures and crews of naval vessels are obtained from an annual Department of Defense (DOD) survey of on-base housing facilities for unaccompanied personnel. College students living in dormitories, inmates of correctional and juvenile facilities, and persons in health care facilities, nursing homes, and Job Corps centers are also included in this estimate. Persons aged 65 and over residing in nursing homes and persons in homes for the aged are excluded from this estimate because they are implicitly included in the separate estimate of the 65-and-over population. Data on college dormitory populations relate generally to the fall of the preceding year. If no data are available for any component of the group quarters population, it is assumed that no change has occurred.

The estimated total population under age 65 is shown on line 13. The estimated total population under age 65 is the estimated household population under age 65 (line 11) and the estimated group-quarters population under 65 (line 12).

The estimate of the population aged 65 and over is calculated in Table 20.9, and is explained here.

The base total population aged 65 and over is shown on line 1. The base population for the estimate of the population aged 65 and over is the revised estimate of the household population 65 and over for the prior estimate year. The county-level tabulations of the number of Medicare enrollees are obtained from the Health Care Financing Administration (HCFA). The availability of these data allows for a separate estimate of change in the population over age 64. If the Medicare enrollment data are not available, the change from the prior estimate year is used.

The base group-quarters population aged 65 and over is shown on line 2. This component is an estimate of the population aged 65 and over residing in nursing homes, prisons, and other group quarters facilities.

The estimated population reaching age 65 in the current year is shown on line 3. This component is an estimate of the population who reached their 65th birthday during the estimate year. They are, in a sense, the number of people "born" into the 65-and-older age group.

The household base population aged 65 and over is shown on line 4. This component is calculated by subtracting the group quarters population (line 2) and adding the population turning age 65 in the current year (line 3).

The estimated resident deaths to the household population aged 65 and over, 7/1 (prior year) to 6/30 (estimate year), is shown on line 5 and is explained further in the paragraph on "deaths under 65" given earlier.

The estimated net inmigration 65 and over, 7/1 (prior year) to 6/30 (estimate year), is shown on line 6. The same type of calculation is used as for persons under age 65 (Table 20.8, line 7).

The estimated migration base 65 and over is shown on line 7. The same type of calculation as for the under-65 migration base (Table 20.8, line 8) is used.

Estimated migration rate 65 and over is shown on line 8, which is obtained by

$$MIGRO = \{MED_t - [MED_{t-1} + ((AGE_t - DEA0_t) * MCOV)]\}/MED_{t-1}$$

where MED is Medicare enrollees, AGE is the population turning 65 in the current year, DEAO is the period deaths to the population 65 and over, and MCOV is the Medicare coverage (Medicare coverage is defined as Medicare enrollees aged 65 and over in 1990 divided by the census population aged 65 and over).

The estimated net migration 65 and over shown on line 9 represents the same type of calculation as under-65 net migration (Table 20.8, line 10).

The estimated household population aged 65 and over is shown on line 10. The household base population aged 65 and over (line 4) is combined with the estimated components of change for the household population aged 65 and over to arrive at the estimated household population aged 65 and over in the estimate year.

The estimated group quarters population aged 65 and over is shown on line 11; these are persons aged 65 and over residing in nursing homes, correctional facilities, and other group quarters. See the calculation for the group quaters under-65 population for more details.

The estimated total population aged 65 and over is shown on line 12; this is the sum of the estimated household

population aged 65 and over (line 10) and the estimated group quarters population 65 and over (line 11).

The final total population estimate is calculated in Table 20.10 and is explained here.

The estimated total population under 65 is shown on line 1, as copied from Table 20.8, line 13.

The adjustment factor for the population under age 65 (line 2) is shown on line 2. This factor is used to ensure consistency between county estimates and independent estimates for the entire population of the United States. The factor is the national estimate of the total population under age 65 divided by the sum of the estimated total population under age 65 for all counties in the nation.

The final estimate of the under-age-65 population is shown on line 3, which is the estimated total population multiplied by the adjustment factor.

The estimated total population aged 65 and over is shown on line 4, as copied from Table 20.9, line 12.

The adjustment factor for the population aged 65 and over is shown on line 5. This factor is used to ensure consistency between county estimates and independent estimates for the entire population of the United States. The factor is the national estimate of the total population aged 65 and over divided by the sum of the estimated total population aged 65 and over for all counties in the nation.

The final estimate for the population aged 65 and over is shown on line 6; this is the estimated total population multiplied by the adjustment factor.

The final total population estimate is shown on line 7; this is the sum of the under-65 estimate and the 65-and-over estimate.

The final estimates of the components of change for states result from summing the under-and over-65 age segments for each (except births) county/state component.

The net internal migration shown also includes changes in group quarters for both the under-and over-65 population. The residual shown is the effect of the national proration procedure. It is the difference between the implementation of the national estimates model and the subnational model.

In addition to the tax-return method, there are many applications of other administrative-record data for making population estimates. Some of the most widely used are school enrollment and school census data. School enrollment is the actual number of students enrolled in an education system at some date, usually the first week of the academic year. A school census is a census of all households within a school district, generally for purposes of planning and development. School data, from whatever source, with carefully defined age limits are very useful for estimating purposes. School enrollment data, even if only by grade, are generally more dependable than school census data for measuring year-to-year population changes. Because the school series serves to measure changes in the population of school age, its coverage must be restricted to those ages where attendance is virtually complete (i.e., the compulsory school ages, or to the grades attended, for the most part, by children of compulsory school age). If grade data alone are available, only the elementary grades (excluding kindergarten but including any special and ungraded classes on the elementary level) should be included; high school enrollment data are unsatisfactory because many children drop out of high school and the dropout rates vary from year to year. The age or grade coverage must be the same from year to year, and the figures must relate to the same date in the school year. The school census, on the other hand, typically has better coverage of households. Information from school censuses may be used to calculate the proportion of school-age children enrolled in public schools and hence to indicate the coverage of school enrollment data.

Two U.S. Census Bureau methods that employ school enrollment data to estimate the civilian population under 65 are described in general terms here. Known as component methods I and II, each method takes direct account of natural increase and the net loss to the armed forces (inductions and enlistments less separations) and employs school enrollment data to estimate net migration. Component method I rests on the basic assumption that the migration rate of school-age children of a local area may be estimated as the difference between the percentage change in the population of school age in the area and the corresponding figure for the United States; the latter figure is presumed to represent for each area the effect of change due to all factors except internal migration. The migration rate of the total population of the local area is then assumed to be the same as the migration rate of the school-age population and is applied to the total population of the area at the census date plus one-half of the births in the postcensal period to derive the estimate of net migration.

The assumption in component method I that the trend of fertility in the local area during the postcensal period is the same as that in the country as a whole is subject to question. Changes in fertility vary notably from area to area, even in the short run; for example, the percentage change in the number of births between 1976–1983 and 1984–1991 (corresponding to the cohorts 6 to 13 years of age in January 1990 and 1998) differs substantially in a number of states from the corresponding figure for the United States. The other major assumption, the equivalence of the rate of net migration of school-age children and the total population, is only a rough rule to follow, as areas vary greatly in the age pattern of migration. Because of the more realistic nature of its assumptions and its more logical approach in measuring migration, component method II is expected to yield more accurate results.

Component method II first calls for estimating net migration of the cohorts of school-age children by comparing a current estimate of school-age children with the expected number (excluding migration) derived from the last census, next converting the number to a migration rate, and then converting this rate to a rate for the whole population. More specifically, the net migration component is estimated as follows: (1) enrollment in elementary grades 2 to 8 at the estimate date is adjusted to approximate the population of elementary school age (7.5 ↔ 15.5 years) on the basis of the relative size of these two groups at the last census (relating local school enrollment data to census counts in each case); (2) the "expected" population (assuming no net migration) of elementary school age on the estimate date is computed by "surviving" the population in the same cohorts at the time of the previous census (including, if necessary, births following the census) to this date; (3) net migration of children of school age is estimated as the difference between the "actual" population of school age and the "expected" population of school age; (4) net migration of school-age children is converted into a migration rate by dividing it by the population in the same age cohorts at the time of the last census (including, if necessary, one-half the natural increase during the postcensal period); (5) the migration rate of school-age children is adjusted to represent the migration rate of the total population on the basis of national gross migration experience (for example, as may be estimated from the Current Population Survey for the same postcensal period); and (6) total net migration is obtained by applying the migration rate (obtained in step 5) to the total population under age 65 at the last census plus one-half the natural increase during the subsequent postcensal period. As stated, the ratio of the migration rate for the total population to the rate for the school-age children is derived from national data on interstate or intercounty migration. Because migration rates change, though slightly, from year to year, and the ages of "migration exposure" over the postcensal period for the school-age cohort are determined by the length of the estimating period, the ratio of migration rates changes also as the estimating period increases.

Component method II rests on two important assumptions: (1) that there has been no change since the previous census in the ratio of the population of elementary school age to the number enrolled in the elementary grades and (2) that the ratio of the net migration rate of the total population to the migration rate of the school-age population for a given postcensal period, for a given local area, corresponds to that for gross interstate or intercounty migrants in the United States for the same period. The validity of both of these assumptions can be examined on the basis of census data or intercensal estimates. Change in the ratio of the population of elementary-school age to enrollment in grades 2 to 8 can be examined for several preceding censuses, but in view of the very high proportion of children attending school, this assumption would give rise to relatively little error. Moreover, the error is, in general, reduced by a *pro rata* adjustment of the initial estimates of school-age population for a set of local areas (e.g., states) to the independent estimate for the parent area (e.g., United States). The variation from area to area in the ratio of the school-age migration rate to the migration rate of the total population may be examined on the basis of state data on internal migration from the preceding census.

Numerous other variations in the use of school data in connection with a component method of estimating the population of geographic subdivisions of countries may be considered. Two of these are explained here to illustrate the variety of possibilities. In the grade-progression method, annual net migration of school-age children is determined by comparing the number of children enrolled in, say, grades 2 to 7 in one year with the number enrolled in grades 3 to 8 in the following year. In the age-progression method, the number of children enrolled in school aged, say, 7 to 13 years is compared with the number aged 8 to 14 in the following year to measure annual net migration of school-age children. Factors other than migration play only a small part in this year-to-year change, but allowance may be made for them. The other steps in the school-progression methods are modeled along the lines of component method II.

In the United States, estimates of age-sex detail are made for states using a version of component method II (U.S. Census Bureau, 1995). The estimates are produced for each single year of age by sex up to age 65. This method is chronologically cumulative, where the estimate period is from the date of the last census to the estimate date. The steps used in estimating single years of age (0 to 64) for the civilian population are as follows: (1) the resident population by single year of age is developed by carrying forward the April 1, 1990, census count (for each age) by cohort to the July 1 estimate date, (2) births for each new cohort for the period between April 1, 1990, and the July 1 estimate date are added where appropriate, (3) an estimate of the armed forces population for each age 17 to 64 on the estimate date is subtracted from the resident population to derive the civilian population, (4) an estimate of the net civilian migration for the postcensal period is added, and (5) an estimate of the net entries in to the civilian population from the armed forces during the estimate period is added.

These five steps result in unadjusted civilian age estimates without sex detail. Sex detail is developed by the following steps: (1) the 1990 census ratios of male-to-female civilian population is calculated for each year of age by state, (2) national sex ratios for single years of age are calculated for both the 1990 census civilian population and each estimate year, (3) the change in the national sex ratios between the census base year and the estimate year are used to update the 1990 state ratios, and (4) these are applied to the state single-year civilian population estimates for both sexes to obtain civilian sex detail by age. The final steps in the component method for age are to adjust each age-sex cell (0 to 64) to an independent national civilian population estimate for that age-sex cell. Then each age-sex cell is adjusted within a state to the civilian state population total. Finally, estimates of armed forces by age and sex are added to the civilian population to produce the resident population.

The vital statistics used in these age estimates are from the same sources used in the tax-return method described earlier. The net migration component revolves around elementary school enrollment and school-age migration. It is developed in two age stages. First, state school-age net migration for the estimate period is used to formulate an amount of net migration for each age under age 17. Then, each state's school-age migration rate is converted to net migration rates for single years 17 through 64 and applied to the appropriate base (cohort for that age minus one-half the deaths to the cohort) in order to derive net migration amounts. It is also possible to derive even more detailed estimates by race and ethnicity at lower geographic levels once estimates have been developed, using the ratio method.

Once preliminary estimates are developed using the component method it is important to adjust the estimates to a national total. If only segments of a nation are being estimated and controls cannot be applied, the estimates must be viewed as subject to great error. An important part of evaluating this technique, as explained further in the evaluation section, is the examination of the degree to which subnational estimates need to be adjusted in order to meet national totals.

Trend Extrapolation

One of the simplest methods for making population estimates is the so-called shift-share method. Recall the principles of extrapolating shares of population components (e.g., ages) when making national estimates. Similarly, trends in the "shares" of a national or regional population may be evaluated. Typically, the share of a national or regional population that an area constitutes may be measured at two past dates, and this "share" may be extrapolated to a later date (Smith & Sincich, 1988). Note that when making an estimate of this type, the technique should be used for all coordinate areas so as to make possible adjustment to a national or regional total. If measurements at two past dates in the nation or region are not available, extrapolations may be made from one date by assuming particular rates of growth (or decline) again assuming the rates of growth (or decline) lead to a total for each place that can be adjusted to a national or regional total.

Censal Ratio Method: Vital Rates Method

A more advanced application of "ratio extrapolation" is not based on shares of a national or regional total but rather on ratios of symptomatic data to the total population. The censal ratio method is among the earliest of these methods that were developed and may even be classified as a precursor to regression methods. The method may be traced to Whelpton as early as 1938, but was more fully developed by Bogue (1950). The method consists more specifically of (1) computing the ratio of symptomatic data to the total population at the census date, (2) extrapolating the ratio to the estimate date, and (3) dividing the estimated ratio into the value from the symptomatic series for the estimate date. In some cases the ratio is multiplied against the symptomatic series; see the housing-unit method later in the chapter. These steps are symbolically represented as follows:

$$r_0 = \frac{S_0}{P_0} \tag{20.17}$$

$$r_t = \ell r_0 = \ell \left(\frac{S_0}{P_0} \right) = \left(\frac{S}{P} \right)_t \tag{20.18}$$

$$S_t \div \left(\frac{S}{P} \right)_t = S_t \times \left(\frac{P}{S} \right)_t = P_t \tag{20.19}$$

where $\frac{S_0}{P_0}$ is the ratio at the census date, computed from the separate figures for the symptomatic series (S_0) and the population (P_0), ℓ is the factor by which r_0 is extrapolated to the estimate date, $\left(\frac{S}{P} \right)_t$ is the extrapolated ratio for the estimate date, and S_t is the reported current level of the symptomatic series. Obviously, the goal is to find the best extrapolated value for ℓ. Any number of techniques of mathematical extrapolation, including linear, geometric, logarithmic, and the like, as described earlier, may be selected to develop potential values for ℓ. As situations vary dramatically in small area estimates, depending on the demographic variable and the specific geographic area being estimated, a "good" value of ℓ in one situation may not be "good" in another. It should be noted that a single censal ratio is not always used to estimate the total population of an area; rather, averages of ratios based on appropriate symptomatic data may be used.

If the symptomatic data are to be useful, accurate and comparable data must be available at frequent intervals, including the census date, and the annual number of cases of the "event" should be high in relation to population size. It is also necessary for the ratio to be fairly stable or to change in a regular fashion if it is to be accurately projected from the census date to the estimate date. The necessity for great predictability and accuracy in the ratio must be stressed because a given percentage error in the ratio will result in a corresponding percentage error in the population estimate.

As with regression-based techniques, many series of data have been considered useful as symptomatic series. In the industrialized countries, the list includes school enrollment or school census data, number of electric, gas, or water meter installations or customers, volume of bank receipts, volume of retail trade, number of building permits issued, number of residential postal "drops" (residential units where mail is deposited), voting registration, welfare recipients, auto registration, birth statistics, death statistics, and tax returns. The types of symptomatic data available in nonindustrialized countries are relatively few and exclude most of those just mentioned. Such countries may have current data on school enrollment, poll taxes, or commodities distributed or monitored by the state.

Notably, some series are clearly *not* well adapted to the direct measurement of population change, though they may be useful as ingredients in other methods (e.g., ratio correlation methods) or in evaluating estimates prepared with other data. This is particularly true of the economic indexes such as volume of bank receipts and volume of retail trade. Changes in the buying power of the population and limitations on the availability of goods and services preclude a very high correlation between population change and economic change, and thus preclude the possibility of measuring one accurately in terms of the other. These series may fluctuate sharply in response to factors other than population change.

Bogue (1950) described in detail a censal ratio procedure for estimating the population in postcensal years employing both crude birth and death rates, which he called the vital rates method. This method extends the design of the simple censal ratio method by computing two intermediate estimates—one based on birthrates, the other based on death rates—which are then averaged to derive a single composite estimate. Bogue's suggested procedure for estimating the birth and death rates at current dates takes account of the postcensal changes in these rates in some broader area for which the current rates are known or readily ascertainable. It should be noted that if a small area has a large proportion of military personnel or group quarters, these should be excluded before the calculations are made, and then added back again at the estimate date. An example of the vital rates method for Multnomah County, Oregon, is presented in Table 20.11.

It is important to note that the reliability of this method depends principally on the correctness of the assumption that the birthrates and death rates of local areas vary in the same general manner as the rates of the larger areas that contain them. Additionally, the resulting estimates are extremely sensitive to the birth and death data employed. In the example of Multnomah County, the first assumption is violated to a certain degree, and the latter is clearly observed. By July 1, 1997, the official population estimate for Multnomah County had grown to 628,023 (U.S. Census Bureau, 1999) rather than having fallen to 570,202, as this method indicates.

TABLE 20.11 July 1 Estimate of Multnomah County, Oregon, Using the Vital Rates Method

1	Total resident population of Multnomah County, April 1 1990	**583,887**
2	Estimated births for county, April 1, 1989– April 1 1990	9,165
3	Birthrate per 1000 for county, 1989–1990 (line 2/line 1)	15.7
4	Birthrate for state, 1989–1990	19.9
5	Birthrate for state, 1997	20.2
6	Estimated county birthrate, 1997 (line 3/line 4 * line 5)	15.9
7	Births for county, 1997	9,007
8	Estimated "birth-based" county population 1997	**565,299**
9	Deaths for county, 1989–1990	5,715
10	Death rate for county, 1989–1990 (line 9/line 1)	9.8
11	Death rate for state, 1989–1990	8.8
12	Death rate for state, 1997	8.9
13	Estimated county death rate, 1997 (line 10/line 11 * line 12)	9.9
14	Deaths for county, 1997	5,693
15	Estimated "death-based" county population, 1997	**575,104**
16	Average of "birth-based" (step 8) and "death-based" (step 15) estimates = Total population July 1, 1997	**570,202**

Data source: Oregon State Data Center.

Although national and regional changes in fertility and mortality are generally reflected in states and smaller areas, extreme deviations from the broader pattern of change sometimes occur, particularly for the birthrate. The averaging process may partly offset opposite biases characteristic of the birthrate estimate and the death-rate estimate. If one population estimate is too low as a result of an overestimate of the birthrate, the other estimate is likely to be too high as a result of an underestimate of the death rate, because an age distribution that favors a high birthrate also generally favors a low death rate. One of the objections occasionally given to use of the vital rates method of making population estimates is that the resulting estimates cannot properly be used to compute birth and death rates. Because both the birthrate and the death rate are used in combination and the population estimate is different from a figure based on a single rate, this objection would appear to be only partially valid.

Regression-Based Methods

Regression-based methods, as they apply to subnational populations, rest on the premise that the statistical relationship between symptomatic data and the corresponding population remains unchanged over time. Three versions of such methods may be noted: ratio-correlation, difference-correlation, and "average" regression methods.

The most common regression-based approach to estimating the total population of an area is the ratio-correlation method. Introduced by Schmitt and Crosetti (1954), this method involves mathematically relating changes in several indicator series to population changes (expressed in the form of ratios to totals for geographic areas), by a multiple regression equation. More specifically, a multiple regression equation is derived to express the relationship between (1) the change over the previous intercensal period in an area's share of the total for the parent area for several symptomatic series and (2) the change in an area's share of the population of the parent area. The types of symptomatic data that have been used for this purpose are births, deaths, school enrollment, tax returns, motor vehicle registrations, employment, voter registration or votes cast, bank deposits, and sales taxes.

The method can be employed to make estimates for either the primary or secondary political, administrative, and statistical divisions of a country. In the United States, this method was used, in part, to prepare county population estimates during the 1980s. The results of the method were averaged with the results of other methods (most commonly administrative records tax returns method and component method II), and then "controlled" to state totals. The variables selected differed from state to state. Often, because of the small number of counties in some states, certain states were combined and estimated by one regression equation. An example of this method for preparing estimates of the population of counties for 1988, based on the relationship between the 1970 and 1980 census, is presented for the counties of Alabama and California. The dependent variable (Y_c) in the regression equation represents the ratio of a county's share of the state total population in 1980 to its share in 1970—that is,

$$Y_c = \frac{\text{Percentage of total state population in county i, 1980}}{\text{Percentage of total state population in county i, 1970}}$$

$$= \frac{\left(\dfrac{P_C}{P_{St}}\right)^{1980}}{\left(\dfrac{P_C}{P_{St}}\right)^{1970}} \qquad (20.20)$$

The independent variables (X_1, X_2, etc.)—for example, births—are expressed in a corresponding manner:

$$X_1 = \frac{\text{Percentage of total state births in county i, 1980}}{\text{Percentage of total state births in county i, 1970}}$$

$$= \frac{\left(\dfrac{P_C}{P_{St}}\right)^{1980}}{\left(\dfrac{P_C}{P_{St}}\right)^{1970}} \qquad (20.20)$$

The data for all variables are transformed by calculating ratios of percentage shares in the later year to corresponding percentage shares in the earlier year. These transformations cause the resulting coefficients to add approximately to 1.0 (U.S. Census Bureau, 1987c). The variables and regression equations for the two states are as follows:

Alabama variable	Symbol
Medicare enrollment	X_1
Automobile registrations	X_2
Resident births	X_3
Resident deaths	X_4

The regression equation is:

$$Y_c = -.238 + .383(X_1) + .412(X_2) + .325(X_3) + .126(X_4)$$

California variable	Symbol
Federal individual income tax returns	X_1
School enrollment Grades 1 to 8	X_2
Resident births	X_3
Automobile registrations	X_4
Registered voters	X_5
Dummy variable for counties with <10,000 population	X_6

The regression equation is:

$$Y_c = .042 + .134(X_1) + .370(X_2) + .056(X_3) + .337(X_4)$$
$$+ .062(X_5) + .016(X_6)$$

Estimates for 1988 (July) are prepared by substituting in the equation appropriate data for the 1980–1988 period. For example, the value X_3 for Alabama in 1988 would be computed as

$$X_3 = \frac{\text{Percentage of total state births in county i, 1988}}{\text{Percentage of total state births in county i, 1980}}$$

$$= \frac{\left(\dfrac{P_C}{P_{St}}\right)^{1988}}{\left(\dfrac{P_C}{P_{St}}\right)^{1980}} \quad (20.22)$$

Values for other independent variables would be derived in similar fashion. When the equation is solved, the results represent estimates of the following form:

$$\frac{\text{Percentage of total state population in county i, 1988}}{\text{Percentage of total state population in county i, 1980}}$$

$$= \frac{\left(\dfrac{P_C}{P_{St}}\right)^{1988}}{\left(\dfrac{P_C}{P_{St}}\right)^{1980}} \quad (20.23)$$

The ratio is applied to each county's percentage of the state population in 1980, as shown by the 1980 census, to arrive at its estimated percentage of the state population

share in 1988. The 1988 percentages for all counties are summed and adjusted to add to 100%. These percentages are then applied to the estimated resident population for the state for July 1, 1988, yielding an estimate of the resident population of each county on July 1, 1988.

Other variants of the regression method are possible and are used occasionally. One is the difference-correlation method. Similar in principle to the ratio-correlation method, difference-correlation differs in its construction of the variables that are used to reflect change over time. Rather than making ratios out of the two proportions at two dates, the difference-correlation method employs the *differences* between proportions (O'Hare, 1976; Schmitt and Grier, 1966; Swanson, 1978).

Another alternative was proposed by Namboodiri (1971). Known as the "average" regression technique, it is an unweighted average of the estimates provided by a number of simple regression equations, each of which relates the population ratio to *one* symptomatic ratio. Swanson (1980) tested a method for modifying regression coefficients to account for structural change and found that it increased accuracy for counties in Washington. Prevost and Swanson (1985) demonstrated that the ratio-correlation model can be interpreted as a set of weighted censal-ratio estimates, with the regression coefficients serving as the weights.

The accuracy of the regression-based techniques depends on the validity of the central underlying assumption that the observed statistical relationship between the independent and dependent variables in the past intercensal period will persist in the current postcensal period. The adequacy of this assumption is dependent on the size of the multiple correlation, among other factors (Mandell and Tayman, 1982; McKibben and Swanson, 1997; Swanson, 1980). Judgment is also important, as the analyst must take into account the reliability and consistency of coverage of each variable. The increasing availability of administrative data allows many possible combinations of variables. High correlation coefficients for two past intercensal periods would *suggest* that the degree of association of the variables is not changing very rapidly. In such a case, the regression based on the last intercensal period should be applicable to the current postcensal period. Furthermore, it is assumed that deficiencies in coverage in the basic data series will remain constant, or change very little, in the present period.

The shortcoming of regression-based methods are three-fold. First, the use of multiple and differing variables (oftentimes depending on the area being estimated), and in some instances averaging the results of multiple estimates, make it very difficult to decompose the error. Second, this process compromises the comparability of estimates between different subnational areas. Third, there are often substantial time lags in obtaining the symptomatic indicators for producing a current population estimate.

Regression-based methods have very limited application in the preparation of postcensal estimates of age-sex groups for small geographic areas. It is possible, of course, to apply the age distribution at the prior census date to a preassigned current total for the area, or to extrapolate the last two census age distributions to the current date and apply the extrapolated distribution to the current total. The resulting estimates are subject to such large errors, however, that these methods are viewed as having little value.

Census Ratio Methods: Housing-Unit Method

The housing unit method is one of the most widely used methods for preparing subnational population estimates. The method largely rests on the assumptions that everyone in the household population of an area can be associated with some sort of identifiable, conventional shelter and that changes in the number of occupied housing units essentially reflect changes in population. The equation for the housing-unit method is

$$P_t = [(H_t * O_t * PPH_t)] + GQ_t \qquad (20.24)$$

where

P_t = population at time t,
H_t = number of housing units at time t,
O_t = housing-unit occupancy rate at time t,
PPH_t = persons per household at time t,
and GQ_t = group quarters population at time t

Each of these variables must be compiled from administrative records or estimated indirectly. Data on the number of housing units may often be found in tax assessors' offices. If the number of housing units needs to be estimated for an area, building permits issued by local governments (for new construction, demolitions, and alterations) may be added to the past census figure. Other indicators of housing stock may include the number of electric, gas, or water utility connections or customers, residential postal delivery "drops," "certificates of occupancy," and so on (Smith and Lewis, 1980, 1983).

As they are essentially multipliers of the number of housing units in the housing-unit method, accurate estimates of the average number of persons occupying a housing unit and of vacancy rates are very important. Good sources of information on changes in average household size and in vacancy rates in the United States are the Current Population Survey and the American Housing Survey (Murdock and Ellis, 1991, pp. 186–187). These provide information on postcensal changes at the national level, which may be used to develop censal-ratio estimates of these variables for subnational areas. If these data are lacking, it is possible to project them from known past values using extrapolative and other techniques (Bryan, 1996; Roe *et al.*, 1992).

Finally, the size of the population living in group quarters (e.g., correctional facilities, rooming houses, college dormitories, institutions, etc.) must be considered. Most often, these data are collected in administrative records, either by the group-quarters facilities themselves or by the local governmental unit within which the group-quarters facility exists.

It should be apparent that once the data components of the housing-unit method are known, an exact determination of the population is possible; that is, the formula precisely specifies the relationships between the variables. Any "error" is due to inaccuracies in calculations or the components, not to an inherent flaw in the method itself. These inaccuracies, however, are especially problematic for the very small areas for which the housing-unit method is used. Therefore, it is again emphasized that the method be applied to all coordinate small areas within a state or county area (or corresponding region or province).

Composite Method

In general, a characteristic of the various methods of population estimation described is that they are single methods, not combinations of methods, which measure change in the total population of an area "directly." Uncertainties in projecting censal ratios including vital rates and average size of household, resulting in part from changes in the age and sex composition of the population, suggest the desirability of an alternative approach. The composite method is a "portfolio" of separate methods, each tailored to particular segments of the population. The results are combined to yield the "true" total population estimate. These results then may be adjusted to sum to the estimate for the larger area.

Many alternative "portfolios" are possible. For example, the number of deaths of persons 45 years and over distributed by age may be used to estimate the population in this age range. Likewise, the number of births may be used to estimate the number of females in the childbearing ages (18 to 44 years), which, in turn, may be used to estimate the number of males in this age range. School enrollment data may be used to estimate the population of school ages (5 through 17 years); while the number of births in the previous 5-year period, in conjunction with school enrollment data, may be used to estimate the population under 5 years of age. The ratio method, the component method, or mathematical interpolation may be used to subdivide the populations into single-year age groups as necessary. The principal steps in applying this version of the composite method are as follows:

1. Population 45 years and over:

a. Compute age-sex-race specific death rates by 10-year age groups for the census year on the basis of the census population, starting with the population 45 to 54 years and ending with 85 and over, for the country and each area.

b. Compute the corresponding death rates for the country for the 12-month period centered on the estimate date.

c. Prepare estimates of the age-sex-race specific death rates for each area for the 12-month period centered on the estimate date, on the assumption that the change in the death rate for each area from the census year was the same as for the country as a whole.

d. Compute the estimated population for each area on the estimate date in each age-sex group by dividing the number of deaths for each group in the year centered on the estimate date by its current specific death rate as obtained earlier. In the smaller areas, when deaths are distributed by age and sex, the numbers of deaths in some categories may be extremely small. The thinness of these data makes their use as a base for estimates very questionable. Consequently, in very small areas the procedure may be modified so that estimates are prepared for the age group 45 and over as a whole.

2. Population 18 to 44 years of age: Estimates of the number of females 18 to 44 years are first developed by the censal-ratio method in a manner corresponding to steps *a* through *d* using data on the number of births and the number of females 18 to 44 years of age. As with the death rate 45 and over, this method assumes that the change in age-specific birthrates for the local area was the same as for the country (or other large administrative area) as a whole. Then, the ratio of the number of civilian males to females at the last census in each area in this age range, adjusted for the change in this ratio for the country as a whole between the census date and the estimate date, is used to arrive at an estimate of the number of civilian males in the area. The number of civilian males, an estimate of military personnel, and the number of females are summed to yield an estimate of the total population 18 to 44 years of age.

3. Population under 18 years of age: The estimated population in this age group may be developed by a component procedure similar to that described for component method II:

a. Obtain the census population in the cohort that would be under 18 years on the estimate date.

b. Add births for the postcensal period.

c. Subtract deaths for the cohort for the same period.

d. Add an estimate of net migration.

The calculations may be carried out for two age groups separately, under 5 and 5 to 17 years. Estimates of net migration for the group under 18 years of age are obtained from the migration rate of the school-age population derived earlier as part of component method II. The factor used to convert the migration rate for the school-age population to the rate for the population under 18 years of age may be based on national ratios of interstate or intercounty migrants under 18 years of age to interstate or intercounty migrants in the school ages for the postcensal period.

The details of the composite method may be varied depending on the kind and quality of data available. The procedures of component method II may be applied to ages 18 to 44 as well as ages under 5 and 5 to 17. On the other hand, ages under 5 and 5 to 17 may be estimated by a censal-ratio procedure, using births and school enrollment as symptomatic data.

Total Subnational Population, Intercensal

As with national postcensal estimates, subnational postcensal estimates must be adjusted to account for the problem of error of closure in deriving intercensal estimates. The problem is typically greater for subnational areas than national areas as less information is usually available with which to make the necessary adjustments. In addition, the intercensal estimates of change due to each component, population change as a whole, or the population itself for all subarea in each year must be adjusted to agree with the corresponding intercensal figures established for the whole country. The error of closure for each subarea may be distributed over the intercensal period in proportion to one of the components of change for the subarea (e.g., net migration), the total population change, or the population itself.

Component Methods

Annual intercensal population estimates for geographic subdivisions may be prepared by the component method if satisfactory data on births, deaths, and migration are available.

Even if a country has the required birth and death statistics for making intercensal estimates for geographic subdivisions, it often lacks the required migration data or even data symptomatic of migratory changes. If this is the case, intercensal estimates of population for such geographic subdivisions may be developed on the basis of analytically derived estimates of net migration using these estimates to distribute the error of closure over the intercensal period. This procedure involves, first, estimating intercensal net migration (including the error of closure) for each geographic unit as a residual by the vital statistics method. Second, equal portions of the intercensal net migration may be allocated to each year of the intercensal period. Finally, the preliminary estimates of net migration or population are adjusted to the independently established estimates of net immigration or population (adjusted for error of closure) for the entire country in each year of the intercensal period.

As with previous methods for intercensal estimates of geographic subdivisions, preliminary estimates of population for such areas should be adjusted to agree with the independently established intercensal estimates of the national population (or other large administrative area). One method of effecting this task is to adjust the geographic distribution of each component, particularly net migration, to agree with the established national estimate for that component (e.g., net immigration). A simpler method is to adjust the preliminary estimates of the population of the subareas to the established estimates of the national population without reference to the individual components.

Intercensal estimates of age groups involve an adjustment for the intercensal error of closure at each age and for inconsistencies with annual estimates of the total population for each area by age. In a cohort-component method, the annual preliminary estimates of population by age and sex would be computed for each geographic unit. Then, it is necessary to determine the error of closure using previously mentioned techniques for each age cohort and distribute the error of closure over the expected population by age cohorts (or the same age groups). Then, the age-sex figures need to be "controlled" to area totals over all ages and to the national estimates for each age-sex group. Another procedure involves calculation of the expected population by use of life tables or death statistics and then allowing for net migration by cohorts as part of the adjustment for the error of closure.

Mathematical Interpolation and Extrapolation

As with national estimates, so for subnational estimates, mathematical extrapolation alone should only be used when direct information on births, deaths, and migration are lacking. The mathematical curves most commonly employed for this purpose are straight lines and geometric and exponential growth curves (see, e.g., Chapter 11). However, a great variety of other forms may be employed (e.g., higher degree polynomials, reverse geometric curves, and more complex exponentials such as the logistic). Geometric extrapolation is more logical than linear extrapolation in making population estimates, especially in undeveloped nations, where birthrates may remain nearly constant at a high level and death rates are constant or declining. Linear extrapolation may be more appropriate for some of the geographic subdivisions of these same countries because growth rates may be falling as a result of outmigration. The subareas of the same country could reasonably be treated differently, therefore, taking account of information identifying the areas of in- and outmigration. The extrapolation process may be applied to percentages representing the proportion that the population of an area constitutes of the population of some more inclusive area for which annual totals are available. The process of extrapolation is exactly as in Table 20.4, except that geographic units are extrapolated rather than age groups. In principle, mathematical methods involve adjustment to independent estimates for the parent area; in practice, no adjustment is necessary if linear extrapolation is used for both the parent area and its subdivisions and no adjustment is made if a satisfactory independent estimate is not available.

Another primarily mathematical method of estimating subnational population that also takes limited account of current data is the apportionment method. This method essentially involves distributing the postcensal *increase* in population in the parent area (e.g., a country) among the component parts of that area (e.g., states) in accordance with the distribution of the intercensal increase in the parent area among the component parts. If a subarea lost population in the intercensal period, its population in the latest census is assumed to remain unchanged. Except for the special treatment of areas that lost population, the apportionment method is approximately equivalent to arithmetic extrapolation when the results by the latter method are adjusted *pro rata* to the independent estimate of the total population of the parent area. Like the other mathematical methods, this method requires a current total for the parent area.

In general, these mathematical methods may prove less accurate than the various component methods and other methods using symptomatic data for the simple reason that they have no connection, direct or symptomatic, with the postcensal universe they are estimating. These methods usually employ the assumption that population change in the postcensal period is in the same direction and at the same pace as in the preceding intercensal period or periods. While this is often not the case, mathematical methods have certain advantages. Primarily, they are easy to apply, insofar as they take relatively little time and require only readily available data, and are simple enough in principle for the layman to understand. As the evaluation studies show, the mathematical methods are not very reliable for making postcensal population estimates for geographic subdivisions of countries, although they may be necessary in the absence of symptomatic data for the postcensal period. However, their reliability is quite different when they are used to prepare intercensal estimates.

As explained earlier in the section on national intercensal estimates, mathematical interpolation is a convenient and simple method of making intercensal estimates, given annual estimates of the total population of each area to which the estimates for subgroups (e.g., age groups) may be adjusted. Alternatively, the percentage of the total population of the area in each subgroup (e.g., age group) may be interpolated and applied to the estimates of the total population of the area at the estimate date.

EVALUATION OF METHODS

Design of Evaluation Studies

A variety of methods for making population estimates of nations and their geographic subdivisions, by age and sex, have been discussed with relatively little concern for their accuracy. A population estimation system in fact involves three elements: (1) the necessary data, (2) a sound statistical procedure to generate the estimates, and, (3) a system of evaluation on to ensure that the estimates are reasonable. A sound evaluation procedure is imperative for any estimates program, as it informs both the producers and the users of the estimates about the strengths and limitations of the estimators, or estimation formulas (National Academy of Sciences, 1980, p. 47). The motivation for evaluation comes both from statistical concerns as well as the implications in programs and applications based on the estimates.

An evaluation program may specifically assist in identifying statistical measures of error (or differences) that permit refinement of methods and improved techniques of producing estimates. Recall the most common applications of population estimates in funds allocation, denominators for vital rates and per capita time series, survey controls, administrative planning, marketing guidance, and descriptive and analytical studies. Evaluating the accuracy of methodology necessarily raises questions about the equity of allocation of resources among units of government (Swanson, 1981, pp. 12–22). Further, accurately monitoring the pace of demographic change is imperative for determining the need and demand for public services such as health care as well recreational and educational services, for establishing political boundaries, and for providing a host of publicly and privately furnished goods and services that are sensitive to changes in the size and composition of the resident populations.

Murdock and Ellis (1991, p. 242) identify five potential approaches to reviewing estimates: (1) examine the (estimates) in comparison with historical patterns of population change and of the components of population change, (2) evaluate the estimates relative to other estimates that have been made for the estimation area or areas similar to estimation area, (3) submit them to selected knowledgeable persons in the estimation areas for their assessment of the validity of the assumptions and of the estimated populations, (4) conduct sensitivity analysis of the effects of alterations in assumptions about key parameter, and (5) conduct historical simulations in which the accuracy of the estimation model in estimating population in past periods is evaluated.

In any of these approaches, statistical measures need to be used to perform the evaluation desired. Furthermore, standards need to be developed to assess whether the estimates meet standards of "accuracy." Any consideration of the accuracy of methods depends on the availability of adequate standards against which to judge the methods and the establishment of criteria of accuracy. Any definition of accuracy is tenuous at best, as different standards are applicable in almost any estimating situation.

Statistical Measures

The most common statistical measures used to evaluate estimates and measure differences are as follows:

Mean absolute error (MAE): $\dfrac{\sum_{t=1}^{h}|E_t - A_t|}{h}$ (20.25)

Total error: $\sum_{t=1}^{h}(E_t - A_t)$ (20.26)

Mean absolute percent error (MAPE):

$$\frac{\sum_{t=1}^{h}\left|\frac{(E_t - A_t)}{A_t}\right|}{h}*[100] \quad (20.27)$$

Root mean square error (RMSE): $\left[\dfrac{\sum_{t=1}^{h}\left(\dfrac{E_t - A_t}{A_t}\right)}{h}\right]^{1/2}$ (20.28)

Mean algebraic percent error(MALPE): $\dfrac{\sum_{t=1}^{h}\dfrac{(E_t - A_t)}{A_t}*100}{h}$ (20.29)

where
A is the actual population
E is the estimated population
t is the geographic area estimated
h is the number of geographic areas in a set
(Siegel, 2002, pp. 423–424)

The mean absolute error (MAE) is the average absolute amount of error in each estimate, total error is the total amount of error over all areas with signs regarded, mean absolute percent error (MAPE) is a measure of accuracy, root mean square error (RMSE) is a measure of accuracy giving more weight to large errors than to small errors, and mean algebraic percent error (MALPE) is essentially a measure of bias.

The rationale for using these measures is to detect change and identify individual problematic estimates or estimate series. It has been argued, however, that measures such as MAPE are invalid for evaluating error in that they may be strongly affected by the right skewness of the distribution of error (Swanson, Tayman, and Barr, 2000) and that they cannot effectively evaluate data series with wide ranges of population values. These shortcomings suggest that these evaluation tools have been pushed to the limit of their usefulness and that new tools should be examined. Several measures, some new and some old, have been developed to help address these shortcomings. One is known as a "loss function," which is designed to combine a weighted percentage and weighted numeric difference to create a highly sensitive index of relative error (Bryan, 1996). A recent proposal is the transformed MAPE (Swanson, Tayman, and Barr, 2000). The MAPE measure is inherently based on a right-skewed, asymmetrical distribution of absolute percent errors (APEs), and like any arithmetic average taken over such a set, it is prone to being pulled upward. The transformed MAPE addresses this issue by transforming the shape of the distribution of absolute percent errors (APEs) to produce an average that more accurately reflects the error represented by most of the observations.

For now, however, MAPE is the tool most commonly relied on for evaluating estimates. Note that the tools developed for performing evaluations of estimates are designed to detect the extent of error in the total population or the change in the population. Errors in estimates may be imperceptible because no apparent change has taken place when in fact substantial change has occurred in an estimate series. It is in these situations that submitting estimates series to experts in local data review and performing sensitivity analysis may be especially useful.

Although postcensal population estimates provide valuable information, only a single value for the number being estimated is usually presented. An issue frequently raised concerning population estimates (and more frequently projections) is the amount of confidence estimators have in these single values. One may point to a history of results with different methods in different situations and determine that one method may be superior to another. However, this history in and of itself does not *predict* the amount of error one may expect in estimates nor does it establish any degree of confidence in an untested estimate. Theoretically, an ideal environment is one that affords analysts the opportunity to measure confidence intervals surrounding estimates. Unfortunately, under the formal definition, confidence intervals cannot be constructed for postcensal estimates because the probability distribution of errors is unknown. If assumptions are made about the characteristics of the probability distribution of error in a set of estimates, then empirical confidence intervals may be constructed.

A logical assumption is that the distribution of estimate errors remains stable over time. This assumption was tested in series of state population forecasts from 1920–1980 by Smith and Sincich (1988). The critical assumption that the probability distribution of errors remains the same over time was reasonably well satisfied. Smith and Sincich (1988) also created empirical confidence intervals using a technique from Williams and Goodman (1971) that accommodates any error distribution (including asymmetric and truncated distributions) and additionally permits assessment of the confidence limits (by comparing the actual number of errors falling inside the limits with the expected number). Further research has also been done on developing confidence intervals. Swanson and Beck (1994) studied the distribution of errors of the ratio-correlation method at the county level over time using Washington State as a case study. They examined estimates made for 1970, 1980, and 1990 against corresponding census counts and demonstrated that 67%

"prediction intervals" generated for the estimates provided a reasonable view of accuracy: (1) the 67% interval contained the 1970 census count in 30 of 39 counties (77%), (2) the 1980 census counts in 24 counties (62%), and (3) the 1990 census counts in 31 counties (79%).

Without historical information on which to base assumptions of stability (or amount of error), one may still create tenuous empirical confidence intervals by assuming a unimodal, symmetric normal distribution (Blachman and Machol, 1987) or by relaxing the percentage confidence intervals.

National Estimates Evaluation

Perhaps the most convenient and accurate way to evaluate a national population estimate is to compare it with the results of an official census. Most often, estimates may be evaluated in an "ex-post"-style test whereby the selected estimate method is used to derive an estimate on the census date, and the results are then compared using selected statistical comparisons. When a national postcensal estimate of the total population is evaluated by comparison with the census count, the difference between the postcensal estimate and the later census count, i.e., the error of closure, and the ratio of the error of closure to the census count may be taken to reflect the amount and percent of error, respectively, in the postcensal estimate, measured over a whole intercensal period. The errors of closure (e.g., total, age, sex) can be examined to judge the accuracy of the postcensal estimates in relation to their census counts. It is important to note that not only should the official estimate be subjected to evaluation but also the results of competing methods, so that potential improvements or revisions in the methods used for the official estimates process may be considered.

The errors in postcensal estimates by age, as measured by the errors of closure, tend to be considerably greater than the error in the total for an area, particularly because of the effect of errors in reporting age in the two censuses. The errors in postcensal estimates represent in part the effect of carrying reporting errors at one age in the first census forward to a later age at the second census. The structuring of the calculations by age cohorts results in good comparability of age estimates with the previous census figures for the same birth cohorts but poor comparability with figures for the same age groups in either the first or second census.

The estimates of national population based on some population registers are viewed as being as accurate as a census count. Estimates from population registers are, in fact, closely akin to the estimates prepared by the component method. Commonly, at a census date the register is reviewed and corrected on the basis of the census results, and then the national total from the register, validated by the previous census, is kept up to date by use of the component data from the register. The discrepancies between census counts and totals from population registers are quite small in most countries having registers.

For the statistically less developed countries, the data on components are often inadequate to serve as a firm basis for preparing postcensal estimates. Where such data are used, the postcensal estimates are subject to considerable error. Whether this method or mathematical extrapolation is employed, it is probable also that in these countries the census counts are fairly incomplete and less comparable in coverage with one another. However, some less developed areas have relatively good censuses but poor vital statistics.

In a program of estimate evaluation, the values from the census or population register are generally regarded as the "truth," rendering any difference between it and an estimate wholly attributable to the estimate. For evaluative purposes, however, one should recognize that a population estimate may actually be more accurate for a specific area than a census or population register. In this context, a population estimate may offer the basis for use of demographic analysis to evaluate the quality of the census results themselves. Countries may use different types and even combinations of methods of demographic analysis to evaluate census results. (see Chapters 4, 7, and 22).

Subnational Estimates, Evaluation

As with national estimates, a census provides the most convenient and accurate base for evaluating of subnational estimates. In this regard, several important matters must considered before estimates are compared with census values. There is often a tendency to assume that the earlier and later censuses are completely consistent, but such consistency cannot be taken for granted. Subnational areas often differ in land areas and populations covered, and census definitions may change as well. If an estimate is based on a past census that differs from the more recent census in any significant way, an accurate evaluation is compromised. When estimates comparable to the last census are sought, the same methods of estimation may be employed as in the previous intercensal period, but the standard for evaluating the estimates is less evident, particularly for estimates of age groups. Alternative representations of a "true" population may be made with a special registration or a population register, which may provide more correct figures than the census. In addition, comparisons may be made with official estimates developed by local authorities.

There are several approaches to evaluation when the exact amount of error in the current census is not known. The first is simply to compare the census results with the estimates. While this comparison is affected by the error of closure, it illustrates how the estimates compare with the accepted standards in the census. Second, the net undercount for the past census may be added to the current estimate for each subnational area. This approach may produce more accurate postcensal estimates, but these estimates may now be less comparable with the later census and produce biased estimates of error. Third, the estimated proportion of population that each subnational area is of the national (or other parent area) total may be computed. This allows a test of the estimating procedure to determine how well it "predicts" the distribution of the national population, compensating for the large national error of closure (U.S. Census Bureau/ Starsinic, 1983, p. 3).

A large and growing number of studies have been carried out, particularly in the United States and the Great Britain, designed to evaluate various methods of preparing subnational population estimates. The U.S. Census Bureau has carried out an extensive program of evaluating postcensal estimates for states and local areas over the past several decades, and several important studies have been conducted by investigators in other settings. These studies typically employ census counts as the standard by which the estimates are judged.

First, the evaluation of major geographic subdivisions (states in the case of the United States) may be considered. The U.S. Census Bureau has made systematic comparisons between census counts for states and the corresponding estimates derived by several different basic methods and selected averages of these basic methods (U.S. Census Bureau/Starsinic, 1983; Zitter and Shryock, 1964). It is important that these comparisons against the census be considered "measures of difference" rather than "measures of error" as it is impossible to determine precisely the degree to which error in the census and error in the estimate contribute to the overall difference. Among other measures, the primary indicator of error was the average absolute percentage difference.

It is important to note that a direct "method-to-method" comparison is rarely possible when attempting to evaluate population estimates. Often it may not be practicable to test the most accurate method because of excessive time, cost, and resources. Other hindrances to doing this may include the unavailability or inconsistency of necessary data. Furthermore, as will be seen, certain methods are better suited to particularly large or particularly small geographic areas. While one method may generate good results at a national level, it may be wholly inadequate for a province or township. Thus, the amount of resources available and the geographic level, as well as the historical accuracy of each method, must always be considered.

U.S. System

U.S. Census Bureau Programs

We describe now the program for evaluating subnational estimates at the U.S. Census Bureau, as it is one of the most productive in the world and then look briefly at evaluation studies applicable to spesific methods in specific estimate areas.

The U.S. Census Bureau is responsible for generating state, county, and subcounty population estimates, and it has published numerous studies reporting the relative success and failure at each of these geographic levels.

State Estimates

The U.S. Census Bureau/Starsinic (1983) published the results for several estimate methods for states, as well as averages thereof, and made comparisons using "raw" data, data adjusted, for not census undersounts and data adjusted to the national census total. The official method for making state estimates by the late 1970s was a combination of component method II, the ratio-correlation method, and the administrative records method. Despite more promising expectations, it was found that the average of these three methods resulted in an average absolute difference of 2.48%, which was the highest state difference recorded (except for 1950). The errors had significant negative bias, with 19 states having differences in excess of −3% and five states showing differences in excess of −5%. Also, significant regional disparities were revealed in the evaluation. By adjusting for undercount in the 1970 census, the sum of the state estimates was brought to within 0.1% of the expected national total, the average absolute difference was reduced to 1.46%, and, perhaps more important, the negative bias was significantly reduced. Finally, by prorating the state estimates to the national census total, all state totals were automatically raised. This also reduced the average absolute difference (to 1.78%) and eliminated the negative bias (U.S. Census Bureau/Starsinic, 1983).

County Estimates

In evaluating county-level population estimates, tests have indicated that the accuracy of any particular estimate method varies considerably from county to county (and from state to state) over an extremely wide range. Test results also indicate a tendency for the percentage error to vary inversely with population size. Moreover, errors are typically larger for the more rapidly growing areas than they are for the less rapidly growing areas, and areas with population losses had the highest average errors. Smaller areas generally are subject to greater estimation error by almost any measure.

The most recent U.S. Census Bureau evaluation of county-level estimates was performed by Davis (1994). Numerous measures were used to evaluate the county estimates against the 1990 census, including the Index of Dissimilarity, MALPE, MAPE, and RMSE, though MAPE was the primary indicator. During the 1980s, different methods were used for counties in each state, as the members of the Federal State Cooperative Program for Population Estimates provided different types of data for producing the test estimates to the U.S. Census Bureau. The results of the evaluation are striking. Of the 3141 counties evaluated in 1990, the mean absolute percentage difference was 3.6%, a figure clearly better than the 4.2% recorded in 1980. It was observed that, as with the state estimates, there was a strong negative correlation between the size of the county and the percentage error obtained. Furthermore, counties that exhibited the fastest growth or decline during the decade had higher errors than those that had very slow growth (U.S. Census Bureau/Davis, 1994, p. 6).

Subcounty Estimates

Evaluation of estimates below the county level has proven very difficult. Census errors as well as estimate errors tend to be highest in the smallest geographic units. Furthermore, subcounty geography areas in the United States are extaemaly numerous, numbering nearly 40,000. This fact combined with the fact that subcounty areas vary widely in population size (ranging from one in some rural places to millions in major metropolitan areas), makes practical comparisons very difficult. It is also possible, that multiple estimates have to be prepared and then "controlled" to independent totals, as when places lie in multiple counties or when places exist (either dependent or independent) within minor civil divisions (MCDs), (Healy, 1982).

A U.S. Census Bureau evaluation (1985) of subcounty estimates generated by the administrative records method during the 1970s showed great variability in the errors of the estimates. Several conclusions about estimates evaluation at higher geographic levels can be reiterated for this study, although to a greater degree. The average absolute percentage error for all 35,644 subcounty areas was 15.2%. The percentage errors ranged from an average of 3.9% for areas over 100,000 to 35.1% for areas with population less than 100. Of the 35,644 areas, 23.6% had extreme errors of 20% or more. One-third of the 20,123 areas with populations of fewer than 1000 had extreme errors of 20% or more. The amount of error was also strongly correlated with the area's rate of change between 1970 and 1980. Areas that grew by 50% or more or declined by 15% or more had an average error of 29.2%, compared with 11.6% for the remaining areas. Bias in the estimates were negligible (U.S. Census Bureau/Galdi, 1985, p. 2).

Evaluation of Individual Methods

Component Methods

While component techniques are often used, they have several limitations of which users should be aware. The first is the assumption of the continuation of historical patterns in symptomatic data in measuring migration. The second is that the method is one of the most resource-intense procedures possible. Third, component methods are not appropriate for areas with substantial "special" population (Rives et al., 1989, pp. 30–31). The major advantage is that they effectively represent the processes that directly affect population change.

While the component method is a conceptually sound one, certain facts must be considered when using it to generate age detail. The use of the method may lead to distorted and unacceptable results when the undercount rates in the census differ greatly by age groups, particularly those that are adjacent. The problem is exacerbated by the possibility that the net undercount rate may change significantly over time. Further, the recorded growth rate in an age group from the census date to the estimate date may be significantly different from the corresponding growth rate based on populations adjusted for net undercounts (U.S. Census Bureau/Das Gupta and Passel, 1987a). For these reasons, component methods have not always fared well without a special adjustment, such as that represented by the inflation-deflation procedure.

Administrative Records

A major disadvantage of the administrative records method for general use lies in the inaccessibility of federal income tax records, even in summary form, to the general public. However, the Internal Revenue Service *does* make available data on county-to-county migration flows (Rives *et al.*, 1989, p. 79). Further, the estimates are subject to error because of the inaccuracy of the preceding census, boundary problems, residency problems, and coverage problems, though the method is flexible in estimating changes in geographic boundaries.

Trend Extrapolation

A comparison of intercensal changes for counties and even states in the United States for 1970–1980 and for 1980–1990 reveal numerous cases inconsistent with the assumption of trend extrapolation and emphasize the need for using symptomatic data for subnational estimates. In the case of the apportionment method, the assumption that the postcensal growth in local areas is fixed to the earlier growth in the area, as indicated by the change in the parent area, may readily be challenged with census data. The method is logically inapplicable if the postcensal change in the parent area moves in a different direction from the intercensal change in that area. Although there is usually a high correlation between growth trends for a given area in two successive intercensal periods and between the growth trends of broader areas and their geographic subdivisions, the assumption of similarity in these cases is tenuous.

Housing-Unit Method

While the components of most estimation methods rely on data symptomatic of change, few rely so directly as the housing-unit method. The results of other estimation methods based on symptomatic data are included in the discussions of the component method and regression method. Because of the ease of use, flexibility, and relative accuracy of the housing-unit method, it is heavily relied on by state and local agencies to estimate populations. As of 1990 (U.S. Census Bureau, 1990a, p. 4), 234 out of 336 state and local agencies relied on this method alone for subnational estimates. While no comprehensive ex-post tests have been performed of the housing unit method against a decennial census, numerous tests have been performed for limited geographic areas.

Early tests of the housing-unit method can be found in the research of Starsinic and Zitter (1968), who employed a variety of data sources and techniques to see which combination generated the best results. They compared their results with data gathered in special censuses in 47 cities with populations of greater than 50,000. They found (1) the method tends to generate estimates on the high side (of the 47 cities for which building permit data are available and used for making the estimates, the deviations were positive in about 30 cases); (2) the use of utility data rather than building-permit data generally reduces the errors, although here too there are substantially more positive than negative deviations and thus with utility data the positive bias of the method continues, although at somewhat a lower level; (3) smaller deviations result when average size of household is extrapolated than when the 1960 values are held constant; and (4) the average error in the estimate of the number of households when either building-permit or utility data are used is also quite high.

Smith and Lewis (1980) performed further tests when they completed the first comprehensive intercensal test of the housing-unit method using several combinations of techniques for estimating the number of households and persons-per-household (PPH) ratios. Using special census data for 22 places in Florida, Lewis and Smith began by estimating the number of housing units by four different techniques: two based on residential building permits and two based on the number of electric customers. They then used three different techniques to estimate PPH values. The first simply used the PPH of the most recent census, in this case, 1970. The second used a linear extrapolation of the trend between the 1960 and 1970 censuses. The third used a ratio of the PPH in a local area to the PPH in the United States times the proportional change in PPH for the United States since the most recent census.

Their study shows that the different techniques provide dramatically different results and that the electric-utility ratio method generated the most accurate estimate of housing units, with an error of 7.5% (MAPE). This was followed by the "absolute number" electric utility method at 10.4% (MAPE), the disaggregated building-permit method at 11.2% (MAPE), and the aggregated building permit method at 11.5% (MAPE). The results of using the three different PPH methods show that using PPH values unchanged from the previous census provides generally poor PPH estimates, yielding an error of 11.5% (MAPE). Simple extrapolation of PPH provided significantly improved results, with an error of 6.8% (MAPE), but was bettered by the shift-share method, which recorded an error of only 5.9% (MAPE).

In generating overall population estimates, Smith and Lewis used five different combinations of PPH estimates and housing-unit estimates. Of these combinations, the one joining the ratio PPH method with the electric-utility ratio method generated the best results with a total average absolute error of 12.3%. The benefits of these tests are that researchers could now see a clear pattern of combining variables in the framework of the housing-unit method so as to achieve more accurate population estimates.

Regression-Based Methods

The regression-based methods are perhaps the most extensively studied and evaluated methods of generating population estimates. Simple regressions and numerous variations have been studied and applied in an effort to estimate populations with a minimum of error. Most commonly, several techniques are compared in a particular case study. The results of this research have usually shown that the "best" method often depends on the situation in which it is applied and the quality of the data employed in the regression.

An instructive evaluation was performed by O'Hare (1976), who estimated the population of counties in Michigan in 1970. Comparing the difference-correlation technique to the ratio-correlation method, as well as the composite method, component method II, and vital rates method, O'Hare derived favorable results for the difference-correlation technique, as shown in Table 20.12.

It should be noted that while the difference-correlation method provided the best results in this evaluation, all of the methods performed well with small average errors and standard deviations. Mandell and Tayman (1982) evaluated the difference-correlation and ratio-correlation techniques further in the context of the strength of the correlation and the temporal stability of the coefficients in estimates for the 67 counties in Florida in 1970. They showed that while the difference-correlation technique consistently achieved higher R^2 values, it exhibited less temporal stability of the coefficients of the variables and consequently greater average errors.

To evaluate the "average" regression technique, Namboodiri compared its percentage errors with those of the ratio-correlation technique for estimating the population of North Carolina counties in 1960 (Namboodiri, 1971). Using 1950/1940 ratios, Namboodiri discovered in his study that the mean percentage of error provided by the average regression method was sharply less than the ratio-correlation

TABLE 20.12   The Mean and Standard Deviation of Absolute Percentage Errors for County Population Estimates Produced by Five Different Methods

Method	MAPE	Standard deviation of APE
Difference-correlation method	4.5	3.7
Ratio-correlation method	4.7	3.9
Composite method	4.9	3.8
Component method II	6.1	5.5
Vital rates method	6.3	4.2

method (5.8 against 9.5%) and that the ratio method had a much greater tendency to underestimate populations and to produce estimates with errors greater than 10%.

The conclusion that may be drawn from this mix of results is that no regression method uniformly or routinely outperforms another (O'Hare, 1980). While a high correlation may be indicative of a strong model, the temporal stability of the regression coefficients must be considered, given the nature of the assumption that they will remain constant over the estimation period, as Namboodiri (1972) and others (e.g., McCullagh and Zidek, 1987; Verma and Basavarajappa, 1987) have noted. Swanson (1980) and Swanson and Tedrow (1984) developed methods both for evaluating the stability of these coefficients and for making adjustments to them as necessary, while McKibben and Swanson (1997) examined theoretical and substantive issues underlying the changes in the coefficients.

FINAL NOTE

Future developments in the uses, scope, and methodology of population estimates are being guided by the astonishing gains in computing power and software developments. Conventional methods, as well as new ideas about estimating population, may be fully developed and tested with a timeliness and efficiency never before achievable. Improvements in geographic information systems in particular are making the production of very small area estimates and data presentation, such as the demographic and economic mapping system (DEMS) of the San Diego Association of Governments (sandag.cog.ca.us), vastly easier and more useful. Similarly, improvements in satellite imagery are providing the opportunity to develop population estimates using remote sensing (Wicks et al., 1999). Yet these increasingly sophisticated measures often come with a price of compromised privacy (whether perceived or real) of those being estimated. Further, while pursuing elaborate measures, the analyst should not forget that simple, naïve methods will sometimes yield more accurate estimates than elaborate, presumably sophisticated methods (Lee and Goldsmith, 1982, p. 203).

References

Arriaga, E., P. Johnson, and E. Jamison. 1994. *Population Analysis with Microcomputers*. Washington, DC: U.S. Census Bureau.

Blachman, N. M., and R. E. Machol. 1987. "Confidence Intervals Based on One or More Intervals." *Institute of Electrical and Electronic Engineers Transactions on Information Theory*, (IT-33): 373–382.

Bogue, D. J. 1950. "A Technique for Making Extensive Population Estimates." *Journal of the American Statistical Association* (45): 191–199.

Brass, W. 1975. *Methods for Estimating Fertility and Mortality from Limited and Defective Data*. Laboratories for Population Statistics. Chapel Hill, NC: University of North Carolina.

Bryan, T. 1996. "Linear and Logarithmic Population Forecasting Techniques." Paper presented at the Federal State Cooperative for Population Estimates Meetings, New Orleans, LA.

Canada, Statistics Canada. 1987. *Population Estimation Methods, Canada*. Catalogue 91-528E.

Davis, H. C. 1995. *Demographic Projection Techniques for Regions and Smaller Areas*. Vancouver, BC: University of British Columbia Press.

Goldberg, D., A. Feldt, and J. W. Smit. 1960. *Michigan Population Studies*, No. 1, "Estimates of Population Change in Michigan: 1950–60." Ann Arbor, MI: University of Michigan.

Healy, M. K. 1982. "Introduction to Basic Procedures." In *Population Estimates: Methods for Small Area Analysis*. Beverly Hills, CA: Sage.

Illinois Department of Public Health. 1999. *Survey of States on Population Estimates*. Springfield, IL.

Lativia, Central Statistical Bureau of Latvia. 1999. Courtesy CSB Statistician Ieva Kamenpusa, October 15, 1999.

Lee, E. S., and H. F. Goldsmith. 1982. *Population Estimates: Methods for Small Area Analysis*. Beverly Hills, CA: Sage.

Land, K. C., and G. C. Hough, Jr. 1986. "Improving the Accuracy of Intercensal Estimates and Postcensal Projections of the Civilian Noninstitutional Population: A Parameterization of Institutional Prevalence Rates." *Journal of the American Statistical Association* 81(393): 62–74.

Long, J. 1993. *Postcensal Population Estimates: States, Counties and Places*. Technical Working Paper No. 3. Washington, DC: U.S. Bureau of the Census.

Mandell, M., and J. Tayman. 1982. "Measuring Temporal Stability in Regression Models of Population Estimation." *Demography* 19(1): 135–146.

Martin, J. H., and W. Serow. 1979. "Conflict and Cooperation in Producing Population Estimates." *State Government* 52(4): 182–186.

McCullagh, P., and J. V. Zidek. 1987. "Regression Methods and Performance Criteria for Small Area Population Estimation." In R. Platek, J. N. K. Rao, C. E. Särndal and M. P. Singh (Eds.), *Small Area Statistics: An International Symposium* (pp. 62–72). New York: John Wiley and Sons.

McKibben, J., and D. A. Swanson. 1997. "Linking Substance and Practice: A Case Study of the Relationship Between Socio-Economic Structure and Population Estimation." *Journal of Economic & Social Measurement* 24: 135–147.

Murdock, S., and D. Ellis. 1991. *Applied Demography*. Boulder, CO: Westview Press.

Namboodiri, N. K. 1971. "The Average of Several Multiple Regression Estimates as an Alternative to the Multiple Regression Estimate in Postcensal and Intercensal Population Estimation." *Rural Sociology* 36(2).

Namboodiri, N. K. 1972. "On the Ratio-Correlation and Related Methods of Subnational Population Estimation." *Demography* 9: 443–453.

National Academy of Sciences. 1980. Panel on Small-Area Estimates of Population and Income. *Estimating Population and Income of Small Areas*. Washington, DC: National Academy Press.

O'Hare, W. 1976. "Report on a Multiple Regression Method for Making Population Estimates." *Demography* 13(3): 369–379.

O'Hare, W. 1980. "A Note on the Use of Regression Methods for Making Population Estimates." *Demography* 17(3): 341–343.

Philippines National Statistical Coordination Board. 1991. *1991 Philippine Statistical Yearbook*.

Prevost, R., and D. Swanson. 1985. "A New Technique for Assessing Error in Ratio-Correlation Estimates of Population: A Preliminary Note." *Applied Demography Interest Group Newsletter* 1(November): 1–4.

Rives, N. W., W. J. Serow, A. S. Lee, and H. F. Goldsmith. 1989. *Small Area Analysis: Estimating Total Population*. Rockville, MD: U.S. Department of Health and Human Services.

Roe, L., J. Carlson, and D. A. Swanson. 1992. A Variation of the Housing Unit Method for Estimating the Population of Small, Rural Areas: A Case Study of the Local Expert Procedure." *Survey Methodology* 18(1): 155–163.

Schmitt, R. C., and A. H. Crosetti. 1954. "Accuracy of Ratio-Correlation Method for Estimating Postcensal Population." *Land Economics* 30(3): 279–280.

Schmitt, R. C., and J. M. Grier. 1966. "A Method of Estimating the Population of Minor Civil Divisions. *Rural Sociology* 31: 355–361.

Siegel, J. S. 2002. *Applied Demography: Applications to Business, Government, Law, and Public Policy*. San Diego: Academic Press.

Smith, S., and B. Lewis. 1980. "Some New Techniques for Applying the Housing Unit Method of Local Population Estimation." *Demography* 17(3): 323–339.

Smith, S., and B. Lewis. 1983. "Some New Techniques for Applying the Housing Unit Method of Local Population Estimation: Further Evidence." *Demography* 20(3): 407–413.

Smith, S., and T. Sincich. 1988. "Stability over Time in the Distribution of Population Forecast Errors." *Demography* 25(3): 461–474.

Starsinic, D. E., and M. Zitter. 1968. "Accuracy of the Housing Unit Method in Preparing Population Estimates for Cities." *Demography* 5(1): 475–484.

Swanson, D. A. 1978. "An Evaluation of Ratio and Difference regression Methods for Estimating Small, Highly Concentrated Populations: The Case of Ethnic Groups." *Review of Public Data Use* 6: 18–27.

Swanson, D. A. 1980. "Improving Accuracy in Multiple Regression Estimates of Population Using Principles From Causal Modeling." *Demography* 17: 413–427.

Swanson, D. A. 1981. "Allocation Accuracy in Population Estimates: An Overlooked Criterion with Fiscal Implications." In *Small Area Population Estimates—Methods and Their Accuracy*. Washington, DC: U.S. Census Bureau (Small-Area Statistics Papers, Series GE-41, no. 7).

Swanson, D. A., and D. Beck. 1994. "A New Short-Term County Population Projection Method." *Journal of Economic and Social Measurement* 20: 25–50.

Swanson, D. A., J. Tayman, and C. Barr. 2000. "A Note on the Measurement of Accuracy for Subnational Demographic Estimates." *Demography* 37: 193–291.

Swanson, D. A., and L. M. Tedrow. 1984. "Improving the Measurement of Temporal Change in Regression Models for County Population Estimates." *Demography* 21: 373–381.

United Nations. 1982. Model Life Tables for Developing Countries, Population Studies No. 77. Series A. South Asia Pattern, Five-Year Life Table Survival Ratios.

United Nations. 1983. Manual X *Indirect Techniques for Demographic Estimation*. ST/ESA/SER.A/81 New York: United Nations.

United Nations. 1999. *1997 Demographic Yearbook*. New York: United Nations.

U.S. Census Bureau. 1983. "Evaluation of Population Estimate Procedures for States, 1980: An Interim Report." By D. Starsinic. *Current Population Reports*, P25-933. Washington, DC: U.S. Census Bureau.

U.S. Census Bureau. 1985. "Evaluation of 1980 Subcounty Population Estimates." By D. Galdi. *Current Population Reports*, P25-963. Washington, DC: U.S. Census Bureau.

U.S. Census Bureau.1987a. "A Critical Review of the Census Bureau's Inflation-Deflation Method." By Das Gupta P. and J. S. Passel. U.S. Census Bureau internal document.

U.S. Census Bureau. 1987b. "State Population and Household Estimates to 1985, with Age and Components of Change." *Current Population Reports*, P25-998. Washington, DC: U.S. Census Bureau.

U.S. Census Bureau. 1987c. *Current Population Reports* Series P26, No. 85-CA-C.

U.S. Census Bureau. 1990a. "State and Local Agencies Preparing Population and Housing Estimates." *Current Population Reports*, Series P-25, No. 1063. Washington, DC: U.S. Census Bureau.

U.S. Census Bureau. 1990b. "Summary Tape File 1A Technical Documentation". Washington, DC: U.S. Census Bureau.

U.S. Census Bureau. 1992. "U.S. Population Estimates, by Age, Sex, Race, and Hispanic Origin: 1980 to 1991." *Current Population Reports*, P25-1095. Washington, DC: U.S. Census Bureau.

U.S. Census Bureau. 1994. "Evaluation Postcensal Courty Estimates for the 1980s." By S. Davis. Population Division Working Paper, No. 5. Washington, DC: U.S. Census Bureau.

U.S. Census Bureau. 1995. "National and State Population Estimates, 1990–1994." *Current Population Reports*, P25-1127. Washington, DC: U.S. Census Bureau.

U.S. Census Bureau. 1999. Official County Population Estimates, 1999 Series.

Verma, R. B. P., and K. G. Basavarajappa. 1987. "Recent Developments in the Regression Method for Estimation of Population for Small Areas in Canada." In R. Platek, J. N. K. Rao, C. E. Särndal, and M. P. Singh (Eds.), *Small Area Statistics: An International Symposium* (pp. 46–61). New York: John Wiley and Sons.

Wicks, J., R. Vincent, J. DeAlmeida, and D. Swanson, 1999. "Population Estimates from Remotely Sensed Data: A Discussion of Recent Technological Developments and Future Plans." Paper presented at the Annual meeting of the Canadian Population Society, Lennoxville, Quebec, Canada.

Williams, W. H., and M. Goodman, 1971. "A Simple Method for the Construction of Empirical Confidence Limits for Economic Forecasts." *Journal of the American Statistical Association* 66: 752–754.

Zitter, M., and H. S. Shryock, Jr. 1964. "Accuracy of Methods of Preparing Postcensal Population Estimates for States and Local Areas." *Demography* 1(1): 227–241.

Suggested Readings

Espenshade, T. J., and J. M. Tayman. 1982. "Confidence Intevals for Postcensal State Population Estimates." *Demography* 19(2).

Harvey, J. 2000. "Small Area Population Estimation Using Satellite Imagery." *Statistics in Transition* 4(4).

Lee, E. S., and H. F. Goldsmith, 1982. *Population Estimates: Methods for Small Area Analysis.* Beverly Hills, CA: Sage.

Morrison, P. A., and D. A. Relles. 1975. "A Method for Monitoring Small-Area Population Change in Cities." *Public Data Use* 3(2).

Murdock, S. H., and D. R. Ellis. 1991. *Applied Demography: An Introduction to Basic Concepts, Methods and Data.* Boulder, CO: Westview Press.

National Academy of Sciences. Panel on Small-Area Estimates of Population and Income. 1980. *Estimating Population and Income of Small Areas.* Washington, DC: National Academy Press.

Platek, R., J. N. K. Rao, C. E. Särndal, and M. P. Singh (Eds.). 1987. *Small Area Statistics: An International Symposium.* New York: John Wiley and Sons.

Raymondo, J. 1992. *Population Estimation and Projection.* New York: Greenwood.

Rives, N. W., W. J. Serow, E. S. Lee, H. F. Goldsmith, and P. Voss, 1995. *Basic Methods for Preparing Small-Area Population Estimates.* Madison, WI: Applied Population Laboratory, University of Wisconsin.

Siegel, J. S. 2002. *Applied Demography: Applications to Business, Government, Law, and Public Policy.* San Diego: Academic Press.

21

Population Projections[1]

M. V. GEORGE, STANLEY K. SMITH, DAVID A. SWANSON, AND JEFF TAYMAN

ESTIMATES, PROJECTIONS, AND FORECASTS

Demographers are frequently called on to produce population information when census and related data are not available. Information about a present or past population not based on a census or population register is called an *estimate*. As discussed in the previous chapter, there are many ways to make population estimates. Some methods update information from the most recent census using censal ratio, regression, or component methods. They often use data from sample surveys or administrative records. Others use various techniques of interpolation to develop estimates for dates between censuses. Some methods provide estimates only for the total population, whereas others provide estimates for age, sex, race, and a variety of other demographic and socioeconomic characteristics.

Demographers typically refer to information about the future as either a *projection* or a *forecast*. Although these two terms are often used interchangeably, they can be differentiated according to the expected likelihood of their outcomes. A *projection* may be defined as the numerical outcome of a particular set of assumptions regarding the future population. It is a conditional calculation showing what the future population would be if a particular set of assumptions were to hold true. Because a projection does not attempt to predict whether those assumptions actually will hold true, it can be incorrect only if a mathematical error

is made in its calculation. Although a given projection can be judged by the merits of its assumptions in relation to the use to which it may be put, it can never be proven right or wrong by future events.

A *forecast* may be defined as the projection that is selected as the one most likely to provide an accurate prediction of the population. As such, it represents a specific viewpoint regarding the validity of the underlying data and assumptions. A forecast reflects a judgment, and it can be proven right or wrong by future events (or, more realistically, it can be found to have a relatively small or large error). *Projection* is a more inclusive term than *forecast*: All forecasts are projections but not all projections are forecasts. Projections and forecasts sometimes refer solely to total population, but often include information on age, sex, race, and other characteristics as well.

Distinctions among the terms *estimate*, *projection*, and *forecast* are not always clear-cut. When the data needed for population estimates are not available, techniques ordinarily used for population projections are sometimes used for calculations of current and past populations. A government statistical agency may view its calculations of future population as projections, but data users may interpret them as forecasts. In this chapter we use the term *estimate* to refer to a present or past population and *projection* to refer to a future population, regardless of their intended uses or the methodology employed. We use the term *forecast* for particular projections when discussing their accuracy.

USES OF POPULATION PROJECTIONS

Population projections can be used for a number of purposes. They provide a tool for analyzing the components of growth and the sensitivity of underlying assumptions.

---

[1] Like most chapters in this book, this chapter extends the original chapter on the title subject in Shryock and Siegel (1973). For this purpose it uses material adapted from George (1999, 2001), Smith *et al.* (2001), Statistics Canada (2001), and a variety of other sources.

Projections can raise our understanding of the determinants of population change. For example, what impact would a 20% decline in birthrates have on a country's population size and age structure in 50 years? How would eliminating all deaths due to a particular cause affect the population growth rate? How many people would move into a local area if a new factory employing 1000 people were opened?

Projections also can be used to provide information on possible future scenarios. Because we cannot "see" into the future, it is helpful to consider a range of scenarios based on different but reasonable assumptions. Alternative scenarios provide an indication of potential variations in future demographic trends, which facilitates planning for worst-case outcomes. Specific outcomes can be used to sound warnings about the perceived negative implications of particular trends and to call for actions directed toward preventing those outcomes from occurring.

Perhaps the most important use of population projections is in the role they can play as a rational basis for decision making. Changes in population size and composition have many social, economic, environmental, and political implications; for this reason, population projections often serve as a basis for producing other projections (e.g., households, families, school enrollment, income, and labor force). Population projections help decision makers in both the public and private sectors make informed choices.

National population projections, for example, can be used to plan for future Social Security and Medicare obligations (Lee and Tuljapurkar, 1997; Miller, 2001). State projections can be used to determine future water demands (Texas Water Development Board, 1997) and need for welfare expenditures (Opitz and Nelson, 1996). Local projections can be used to determine the need for new public schools (Swanson et al., 1998) and to select sites for fire stations (Tayman, Parrott, and Carnevale, 1994). Business enterprises use forecasts to predict demands for their products (Thomas, 1994) and to anticipate the health care costs of current and retired employees (Kintner and Swanson, 1994). Population projections can be used to forecast the demand for housing (Mason, 1996), the number of people with disabilities (Michaud, George, and Loh, 1996), and the number of sentenced criminals (Oregon Office of Economic Analysis, 2000).

Population projections take advantage of the two strong points of demography described in Chapter 1: the accurate recording of demographic processes over a period of years and the momentum that links demographic processes for one time period with those for another. Because the future is intimately tied to the past, projections based on past trends and relationships raise our understanding of the dynamics of population growth and often serve as forecasts of population change that are sufficiently accurate to support good decision making. The diverse and increasingly influential roles played by population projections make them an important part of modern demographic analysis.

POPULATION PROJECTION METHODS

Population projections may be prepared using either subjective or objective methods. Subjective methods are those in which data, techniques, and assumptions are not clearly identified; consequently, other analysts cannot replicate them exactly. Objective methods are those for which data, techniques, and assumptions are clearly identified, such that other analysts can replicate them exactly. We do not cover subjective methods in this chapter, but it is important to note that even objective methods require choices regarding variables, data sources, projection techniques, and so forth. At some level, every projection method requires the application of judgment.

Following Smith et al. (2001), we classify objective methods into three broad categories: (1) trend extrapolation, (2) cohort-component methods, and (3) structural models. Trend extrapolation methods are based on the continuation of observable historical trends. For methods of this type, future values of a variable are determined solely by its historical values. The cohort-component method divides the population into age-sex groups or birth cohorts and accounts for the fertility, mortality, and migration behavior of each cohort. A variety of techniques can be used to project each of the three components of population growth. Structural models rely on observed relationships between demographic and other variables (e.g., land uses, employment) and base population changes on projected changes in those other variables. The relationships in structural models are typically developed using regression analysis and variants thereof. In actual application, methods in these three categories are not always mutually exclusive. For example, applications of the cohort-component method often incorporate trend extrapolations of one type or another, and structural models are often used in conjunction with the cohort-component method.

DATA SOURCES

Population projections are influenced not only by the methods and assumptions used in their production, but also by the historical data series on which they are based. Census counts and postcensal estimates typically serve as the empirical foundation for the population on which projections are based, while vital statistics and immigration data serve as the empirical foundation for births, deaths, and immigration. Other data used as a basis for population and related projections include Social Security records, school enrollment, employment files, voter registration lists, change-of-address records, and property tax records. Data from sample surveys are sometimes used as well. Accurate and comprehensive data are essential for the production of useful projections.

ALTERNATIVE SERIES

The magnitude, distribution, and composition of future populations are far from certain. To reflect this uncertainty, the producers of population projections often publish a number of alternative series rather than a single series. The production of alternative series based on different assumptions is common in "official" population projections throughout the world (Australian Bureau of Statistics, 2000; Bongaarts and Bulatao, 2000; George, 2001; and Mosert and van Tonder, 1987). Alternative series are sometimes based on different projection methods, but a more common approach is to apply different combinations of assumptions using a single method. In the cohort-component method, for example, alternative series are frequently based on different combinations of assumptions concerning mortality, fertility, and migration. The number of alternative series can vary considerably; recent applications by the U. S. Census Bureau have had as many as 30 (Spencer, 1989) and as few as 2 (Campbell, 1996). According to a 1988 survey on methodological issues of national projections in 31 countries, 23 computed more than one variant (Keilman, 1991). The most common practice is to produce two, three, or four alternative series.

Several interpretations can be given to the alternative series in a set of projections. One is that each gives a reasonable view of future population change and that no one series is preferable to any other. The U.S. Census Bureau gave this interpretation to its projections of state populations between the 1950s and early 1990s. Not only did the Census Bureau decline to designate a "most likely" series, but also it explicitly stated that *none* of the projections was intended as a forecast (Wetrogan, 1990). Another interpretation is that, although each alternative series is reasonable, one is preferable to all the others. This is the interpretation the Census Bureau gave its set of state projections in the mid-1990s (Campbell, 1996). Both interpretations are common, but the current tendency among the producers of population projections seems to be to designate one particular series as the most likely (i.e., as the forecast). However, the production of alternative series is not the only way to deal with uncertainty.

GEOGRAPHIC AREAS

Population projections may be prepared for the world as a whole, for major regions of the world, for nations, and for a variety of subnational areas such as states, provinces, departments, cities, counties, census tracts, enumeration districts, postal areas, school districts, and individual blocks. Although many of the factors affecting the methodology and analysis of population projections are the same for all geographic areas, there are important differences as well. First, data are more readily available and more reliable for nations than for subnational areas and for large subnational areas than small subnational areas. Second, migration typically plays a greater role in population growth for subnational areas than for nations and for small subnational areas than for large subnational areas. Third, population growth rates are generally more variable for subnational areas than for nations and for small subnational areas than large subnational areas. Consequently, choices regarding data, techniques, and assumptions may be different for projections at one geographic level than for projections at another.

Much of the research on the methodology and analysis of population projections has focused on projections at the national, regional, and global levels (Bongaarts and Bulatao, 2000; Lutz, Vaupel, and Ahlburg, 1999; O'Neill *et al.*, 2001). However, some studies have dealt specifically with projections for subnational areas (Davis, 1995; Pittenger, 1976; Smith *et al.*, 2001). Many of the issues we discuss in this chapter are common to all population projections, but several relate primarily to small areas.

ORGANIZATION OF THIS CHAPTER

We start by discussing the major producers of international, national, and subnational projections. Next, we provide a description of the methods and materials used in preparing three basic types of population projections: (1) trend extrapolation, (2) the cohort-component method, and (3) structural modeling. We briefly discuss methods for preparing related projections on such topics as school enrollment, employment, and households. We follow this with a review of issues that we believe should be considered when preparing or evaluating population projections, including a discussion of forecast accuracy. We close with several conclusions regarding the nature and utility of population projections.

Before proceeding, it is useful to define six terms that are frequently used in describing population projections. Although not universal, these terms are generally understood by those working in the field. They are (1) base year, (2) launch year, (3) target year, (4) base period, (5) projection horizon, and (6) projection interval. The *base year* is the year of the earliest data used to make a projection, the *launch year* is the year of the most recent data used to make a projection, and the *target year* is the year for which the population is projected. The *base period* is the number of years between the base year and launch year, while the *projection horizon* is the number of years between the launch year and target year. The *projection interval* is the time increment for which projections are made (e.g., annually or every 5 years).

PRODUCERS OF POPULATION PROJECTIONS

International Producers

Three major agencies produce population projections for the entire world, its major regions, and virtually all countries. These are (1) the United Nations (UN), (2) the World Bank, and (3) the U.S. Census Bureau. These projections incorporate information from the latest round of censuses in each country and use the latest vital statistics and international migration data. The UN published its first comprehensive set of national, regional, and global population projections in 1958. It published its second set in 1966 and has published a new set every 2 years since 1978 (O'Neill *et al.*, 2001, p. 207). UN (1998) projections provide information on the age and sex structure of the population and include several variants based on different combinations of assumptions.

The World Bank began producing national, regional, and global population projections in 1978 and has produced a new set every few years since that time. Some sets have included several alternative series, others only a single series. Until the mid-1990s these projections were published in various issues of the *World Development Report*. Since then, they have been produced only for internal use (O'Neill *et al.*, 2001, p. 208).

The U.S. Census Bureau began producing national, regional, and global projections in 1985 and publishes updates approximately every other year (O'Neill *et al.*, 2001, p. 208). These projections are available online in its "International Data Base," which covers 227 countries and the major regions of the world (U.S. Census Bureau, 2001). Currently, projections of total population are available in 10-year intervals through 2050 and projections by age and sex are available for 2000 and 2025.

Several other agencies also produce international projections. The Population Reference Bureau publishes projections for all countries of the world, using a combination of projections produced by other agencies and those produced internally. The International Institute for Applied Systems Analysis (IIASA) produced several sets of projections for the world and 13 of its regions during the 1990s. With the assistance of Statistics Netherlands, the Statistical Office of the European Communities (EUROSTAT) produces national population projections by age and sex (generally three scenarios) for the countries of the European Union and the countries of the European Free Trade Association every 3 to 5 years (Cruijsen, 1994; EUROSTAT, 1998). Academic demographic centers (e.g., Australian National University), private-sector entities (e.g., The Futures Group), and other specialized institutions (e.g., U.S. National Research Council) also conduct research on population projections.

National Producers

Many agencies produce national-level projections for a single country. Typically, these agencies are parts of the national governments of the countries involved. The projections vary tremendously in terms of methodology, assumptions, quality of input data, frequency of production, length of projection horizon, and amount of detail provided.

The U.S. Census Bureau began producing projections of the U.S. population in the 1940s and has published updated projections a few times each decade ever since. Although there have been numerous changes in assumptions, techniques applied, demographic detail, alternative series, and projection horizons, the Census Bureau has used some form of the cohort-component method for every set of its national projections (Long and McMillen, 1987). A recent set included nine principal alternative series of projections through 2050, each with detail by single year of age, sex, race, and Hispanic origin (Day, 1996). The alternative series were based on combinations of different assumptions regarding fertility rates, mortality rates, and levels of net immigration. The most recent set of national projections, released in 2000, provide, for the first time, projections of population by nativity and extend the time horizon to 100 years (Hollmann, Mulder, and Kallan, 2000).

Subnational Producers

A variety of government agencies, research institutes, and private businesses produce subnational population projections. In the United States, for example, the U.S. Census Bureau makes projections for states; most state governments (or their designees) make projections for counties in their states (and for the state as a whole); and many local and regional governments make projections for cities, census tracts, block groups, and other small areas. Private businesses make (or compile from other sources) projections for states, counties, subcounty areas, and a variety of customized geographic areas (and demographic subgroups). Subnational projections have become increasingly common over the past few decades, especially for small areas. Similar trends have occurred in other countries, including Australia (Australian Bureau of Statistics, 2000), Canada (George, 2001), India (Indian Office of the Registrar General, 2001), Israel (Israeli Central Bureau of Statistics, 1987), New Zealand (Statistics New Zealand, 2000), and virtually all countries in Europe (Kupiszewski and Rees, 1999).

METHODS

Trend Extrapolation: Simple Methods

Trend extrapolation involves fitting mathematical models to historical data and using these models to project population values. Relatively low costs and small data require-

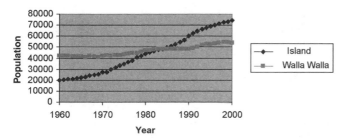

FIGURE 21.1 Population change in Island and Walla Counties, Washington, 1960–2000.

TABLE 21.1 Total Annual Population for the State of Washington, Island County and Walla Walla County: 1960 to 2000

Year	Time	State	Island	Walla Walla
1960	1	2,853,214	19,638	42,195
1961	2	2,897,000	20,300	42,000
1962	3	2,948,000	20,900	42,200
1963	4	2,972,000	21,100	41,600
1964	5	3,008,000	21,700	41,500
1965	6	3,065,000	22,400	41,400
1966	7	3,125,000	23,100	41,200
1967	8	3,229,000	24,200	42,000
1968	9	3,336,000	25,000	41,300
1969	10	3,397,000	25,700	41,000
1970	11	3,413,250	27,011	42,176
1971	12	3,436,300	27,400	42,600
1972	13	3,430,300	29,500	42,100
1973	14	3,444,300	31,600	42,600
1974	15	3,508,700	33,200	42,800
1975	16	3,567,890	34,700	43,500
1976	17	3,634,891	36,300	43,800
1977	18	3,715,375	37,528	44,400
1978	19	3,836,200	41,200	44,900
1979	20	3,979,200	42,200	46,100
1980	21	4,132,353	44,048	47,435
1981	22	4,229,278	45,443	47,134
1982	23	4,276,549	46,559	47,712
1983	24	4,307,247	47,551	48,248
1984	25	4,354,067	48,225	48,345
1985	26	4,415,785	49,661	48,287
1986	27	4,462,212	51,024	48,163
1987	28	4,527,098	52,436	48,170
1988	29	4,616,886	54,370	48,085
1989	30	4,728,077	56,523	48,277
1990	31	4,866,663	60,195	48,439
1991	32	5,000,371	62,700	49,300
1992	33	5,116,671	64,800	50,500
1993	34	5,240,900	66,500	51,800
1994	35	5,334,400	67,900	52,600
1995	36	5,429,900	68,900	52,700
1996	37	5,516,800	70,300	53,400
1997	38	5,606,800	71,600	54,000
1998	39	5,685,300	72,500	54,600
1999	40	5,757,400	73,300	54,600
2000	41	5,803,400	74,200	54,200

Source: Washington State Office of Financial Management (2000).

ments make trend extrapolation useful, not only in demography, but in other fields as well (Armstrong, 2001). Although there are many different methods by which historical values can be modeled, it is convenient to organize these methods into three categories: (1) *simple extrapolation methods*, which require data for only two dates and for which we discuss three approaches: linear change, geometric change, and exponential change; (2) *complex extrapolation methods*, which require data for a number of dates and for which we discuss four approaches: linear trend, polynomial curve, logistic curve, and ARIMA time series; and (3) *ratio extrapolation methods*, in which the population of a smaller area is expressed as a proportion of the population of its larger, "parent" area, and for which we discuss three approaches: constant share, shift share, and share of growth.

Although there are exceptions, trend extrapolation methods are used much more frequently for projections of total population than for projections of population subgroups (e.g., race or ethnic groups). We illustrate these methods using annual total population data for two counties, Island and Walla Walla, in the U.S. state of Washington, for the period 1960 to 2000 (Washington State Office of Financial Management, 2000). This constitutes a longer base period than the 10 to 20 years that are generally sufficient for applying trend extrapolation methods; we employ this data set simply as a heuristic device.

The Washington data are shown in Table 21.1, while projections for 2005, 2010, and 2015 are shown in Table 21.2. Figure 21.1 shows the population change in both Island and Walla Walla counties from 1960 to 2000. Note that during this period, Island County grew rapidly while Walla Walla County grew very slowly. We return to this fact in our summary comments on trend extrapolation methods.

Linear Change

This method assumes that in the future a population will change by the same amount over a given period (e.g., a year) as occurred during the base period. Average absolute change during the base period can be computed as

$$\Delta = (P_l - P_b)/(y) \qquad (21.1)$$

where Δ is the average absolute change, P_l is the population in the launch year, P_b is the population in the base year, and y is the number of years in the base period (i.e., the number of years between the base year, b, and the launch year, l). A projection using this method can be computed as

$$P_t = P_l + (z)(\Delta) \qquad (21.2)$$

where P_t is the population in the target year, P_l is the population in the launch year, and z is the number of years in the projection horizon (i.e., the number of years between the target year, t, and the launch year, l), and Δ is the average absolute change computed for the base period.

TABLE 21.2   Projection Results for Island and Walla Walla Counties Using Different
Extrapolation Methods: 2005–2015

	Island county				Walla Walla county			
Method/year	2000	2005	2010	2015	2000	2005	2010	2015
Simple								
Linear	74,200	81,020	87,841	94,661	54,200	55,701	57,201	58,702
Geometric	74,200	87,617	103,459	122,166	54,200	55,929	57,713	59,554
Exponential	74,200	87,599	103,416	122,091	54,200	55,934	57,724	59,572
Complex								
Linear	74,200	81,837	89,358	96,879	54,200	55,472	57,263	59,053
Quadratic	74,200	87,949	98,936	110,936	54,200	58,664	62,264	66,194
Logistic	74,200	83,749	90,437	96,172	54,200	56,302	58,542	60,872
ARIMA	74,200	77,287	78,889	79,719	54,200	53,870	53,863	53,863
Ratio								
Constant share	74,200	78,430	83,692	89,337	54,200	57,319	61,133	65,257
Shift share	74,200	82,999	93,352	104,803	54,200	53,139	52,216	50,978
Share of growth	74,200	80,371	87,930	96,095	54,200	55,559	57,221	59,017
Range								
Absolute	N/A	10,662	24,565	42,447	N/A	5,525	10,048	15,216
Percent[1]	N/A	12.65	26.94	42.05	N/A	9.88	17.55	25.97

[1] Base is mean of highest and lowest estimates.

For Island County, a model expressing its average absolute change between 1960 and 2000 is computed as $\Delta = 1364.05 = (74,200 - 19,638)/(40)$, and a projection for 2010 is computed as 87,840 (where $87,840 \approx 74,200 + [(10)(1364.05)]$). For Walla Walla County, a model expressing average absolute change over the same 40-year period is computed as $\Delta = 300.13 = (54,200 - 43,195)/(40)$, and a projection for 2010 as 57,201 (where $57,201 \approx 54,200 + [(10)(300.13)]$). Projections for both counties in 2005 and 2015 are found in Table 21.2.

Geometric Change

This method assumes that a population will change by the same percentage rate over a given increment of time in the future as during the base period. The average geometric rate of population change during the base period can be computed as

$$r = \left[\left(P_l / P_b \right)^{(1/y)} \right] - 1 \qquad (21.3)$$

where r is the average annual geometric rate of change, P_l is the population in the launch year, P_b is the population in the base year, and y is the number of years in the base period. A projection using this method can be computed as

$$P_t = (P_l)(1 + r)^z \qquad (21.4)$$

where P_t is the population in the target year, P_l is the population in the launch year, r is the average annual geometric rate of change, and z is the number of years in the projection horizon.

For Island County, the annual rate of geometric change between 1960 and 2000 is computed as $r = 0.0338 =$

$[(74,200/19,638)^{(1/40)}] - 1$, and a projection for 2010 as $103,459 \approx [(74,200)(1 + 0.0338)^{10}]$. For Walla Walla County, its annual rate of geometric change for the same 40-year period is computed as $0.0063 = [(54,200/42,195)^{(1/40)}] - 1$, and a projection for 2010 as $57,713 \approx [(54,200)(1 + 0.0063)^{10}]$. Projections for both counties in 2005 and 2015 using these models are provided in Table 21.2.

Exponential Change

The model for exponential change is closely related to the geometric one, but it views change as occurring continuously rather than at discrete intervals. The exponential rate of population change during the base period can be computed as

$$r = [ln(P_l / P_b)]/(y) \qquad (21.5)$$

where r is the average annual exponential rate of change, ln represents the natural logarithm, P_l is the population in the launch year, P_b is the population in the base year, and y is the number of years in the base period. A population projection using this method can be computed as

$$P_t = (P_l)(e^{rz}) \qquad (21.6)$$

where P_t is the population in the target year, P_l is the population in the launch year, e is the base of the system of natural logarithms (approximately 2.71828), r is the average annual exponential rate of change computed for the base period, and z is the number of years in the projection horizon.

For Island County, the annual rate of exponential change from 1960 to 2000 is computed as $0.0332 = [ln(74,200/19,638)]/(40)$, and a projection for 2010 as

$103,416 \approx (74,200)(e^{0.03332*10})$. For Walla Walla County, its annual rate of exponential change for the same 40-year period is computed as $0.0063 = [\ln(54,200/42,195)]/(40)$, and a projection for 2010 as $57,724 \approx (54,200)(e^{00.0063*10})$. Projections for both counties in 2005 and 2015 using these models are provided in Table 21.2.

Complex Extrapolation Methods

Unlike simple methods, complex extrapolation methods are constructed using base-period data for more than two dates. Accordingly, they can deal better with nonlinear population change. They also offer a quantitative basis for constructing measures of forecast uncertainty because statistical algorithms are used to estimate model parameters (Swanson and Beck, 1994). However, these features do not guarantee that complex extrapolation methods provide more accurate forecasts than simple extrapolation methods.

Typically, three basic steps are followed when applying complex extrapolation methods. The first is to assemble historical population data for different dates during the base period. For a model to be valid, the data must be based on consistently defined geographic boundaries for each date. The second step is to estimate the parameters of the model selected to generate the projection. Typically, graphs and statistical measures are used to determine how well a given model fits the data for the base period while the choice of a particular model reflects judgment about the nature of future population change. The final step is to generate projections using the model(s) selected.

A critical issue in the use of complex extrapolation methods is the selection of time units. This is important because time can be measured in several different ways and the one selected for a given problem affects the scale of certain parameters estimated by the curve-fitting process. Using the data in Table 21.1 as an example, consider two linear trend models, one using the original units for time (i.e., 1960 through 2000) and one using a logically equivalent alternative (i.e., 1 through 41, where 1 corresponds to 1960 and 41 corresponds to 2000). Both models will have the same fit with the historical data (e.g., the r^2 values will be the same), but the intercept will be different. Consistent time units must be used when estimating complex models and using them to project population values.

Linear Models

Linear models are the simplest of the complex extrapolation methods. They assume that a population will change by the same numerical amount in the future as in the past. This assumption is identical to that underlying the simple linear method discussed earlier, but the model is computed differently:

$$Y_i = a + b(X_i) \tag{21.7}$$

where Y_i is a set of i observations of values of a "dependent variable," X_i is a set of i observations of an "independent variable," a is the constant term, and b is the slope of the line describing the "best fitting linear" relationship between X and Y, as found by, for example, the method of least squares (NCSS Inc., 1995, pp. 1309–1310). In using this approach for purposes of developing a population projection model, it is convenient to recast X and Y as time and population, respectively. That is, as

$$P_i = a + b(T_i) \tag{21.8}$$

where P_i is the population for a set of time points (e.g., years) over the period $i = b$ to l (b = base year and l = launch year); a and b are the estimated intercept and slope, respectively, and T_i is time over the period $i = b$ to l.

For Island County, a linear trend model using the NCSS "linear trend growth model" routine (NCSS Inc., 1995, pp. 1371–1388) was estimated as $P_i = 12,639.64 + [(1,504.282)(T_i)]$, with an r^2 value of 0.986. The slope value implies that the population of Island County increased on average by 1054 persons each year of the base period. With this model, a projected population for Island County in 2010 is $89,358 \approx 12,639.64 + [1504.282)(51)]$. For Walla Walla County, the linear trend model was estimated as $P_i = 39,002.14 + [(358.0467)(T_i)]$, with an r^2 value of 0.928. With this same model, a projected 2010 population for Walla Walla County is $57,263 \approx 39,002.14 + [358.0467)(51)]$. Projections for both counties in 2005 and 2015 are shown in Table 21.2.

Polynomial Models

Polynomial models can be used for projections in which change is not constrained to be linear. The general formula for a polynomial curve is

$$Y_i = a + b_1(X_i) + b_2(X_i^2) + b_3(X_i^3) + \ldots + b_n(X_i^n) \tag{21.9}$$

where Y_i is a set of i observations of values of a dependent variable, X_i is a set of i observations of an independent variable, a represents the constant term, and b_j the slope of the line describing the "best-fitting" relationship between X_i^j and Y, holding constant the effects of X_i^k, (where $k \neq j$). Recasting X and Y as time and population, respectively, we have

$$P_i = a + b_1(T_i) + b_2(T_i^2) + b_3(T_i^3) + \ldots + b_n(T_i^n) \tag{21.10}$$

where P_i is the population for a set of time points over the period $i = b$ to l (b = base year and l = launch year), a is the estimated intercept term, b_i are the estimated partial slope coefficients, and T_i is time over the period $i = b$ to l.

In contrast to linear trend models, polynomial models have more than one term reflecting the independent variable (time). Consequently, there are more parameters to estimate. The coefficients of a polynomial curve (a, b_1, b_2, $\ldots b_n$) can be estimated using OLS regression techniques (NCSS Inc., 1995, pp. 1309–1310). These coefficients include both a measure of the linear trend (b_1) and measures of the nonlinear patterns ($b_2, b_3, \ldots, b_n$).

To illustrate the use of a polynomial curve for population projections, we use a second-degree polynomial (sometimes called a *quadratic function*). This function includes time (the linear term) and time squared (also called the *parabolic term*) on the right-hand side of the equation:

$$P_i = a + b_1(T_i) + b_2(T_i^2) \qquad (21.11)$$

where b_1 is the slope for the linear trend and b_2 is the slope for the nonlinear (parabolic) trend. A quadratic curve can produce a variety of growth scenarios, such as a population growing at an increasing rate, a population growing at a decreasing rate, a population declining at an increasing rate, or a population declining at a decreasing rate. Projections based on a quadratic curve can lead to very high (or low) projections for places that were growing (or declining) rapidly during the base period. Although a polynomial of any degree can be used, polynomials higher than second or at most third degree are seldom used for population projections. Nonlinear trends in the historical data also can be projected using curves based on logarithmic or other transformations of the base data.

For Island County, a quadratic model using the NCSS "multiple regression" routine (NCSS Inc., 1995, pp. 155–188) was estimated as $P_i = 16,432.8 + (974.998)(T_i) + (12.602)(T_i^2)$, with $r^2 = 0.993$. With this same model, a projected population for Island County in 2010 is $98,936 \approx 16,432.8 + (974.998)(51) + (12.602)(51^2)$. For Walla Walla County, the quadratic model was estimated as $P_i = 40,983.2 + (81.618)(T_i) + (6.5816)(T_i^2)$, with $r^2 = 0.963$. With this model, a projected population for Walla Walla County in 2010 is $62,264 \approx 40,983.2 + (81.618)(51) + (6.5816)(51^2)$. Projections for both counties in 2005 and 2015 are shown in Table 21.2.

Logistic Models

Unlike the extrapolation methods considered so far, the logistic approach explicitly allows one to place an upper limit on the ultimate size of the population for a given area. It is designed to yield an S-shaped pattern representing an initial period of slow growth rates, followed by a period of increasing growth rates, and finally a period of declining growth rates that approach zero as a population approaches its upper limit. The logistic model is consistent with Malthusian and other theories of constrained population growth.

Keyfitz (1968, p. 215) provides the following formula for a three-parameter logistic curve:

$$Y = a / [1 + b(e^{-cX})] \qquad (21.12)$$

where Y is the population, X is the time period, a reflects the upper asymptote, b and c are parameters that define the

shape of the logistic curve, and e is the base of the natural logarithm. Note that other formulas are available, some including more than three parameters (NCSS Inc., 1995, p. 1375; Pielou, 1969, pp. 19–32).

In using the logistic curve, one must sometimes determine the magnitude of the upper asymptote and the time required to reach it. Algorithms are available that estimate these parameters within the context of the model, but like parameters in an ordinary regression model (e.g., the intercept term), the estimated parameters may not be consistent with a substantive interpretation (e.g., a may not represent an actual upper population limit).

For our purposes, Keyfitz's formula is rewritten as

$$P_t = (a) / [1 + (b)(e^{-ct})] \qquad (21.13)$$

where P_t is the population in the target year, a, b, and c are the estimated parameters, and t is time. This model is useful because it can be generated by the NCSS package without the user having to provide predetermined population limits; rather, the NCSS algorithm uses the available historical information to generate the needed parameters.

For Island County, a logistic model using the NCSS "three-parameter logistic model" routine (NCSS Inc., 1995, p. 1375) was estimated as $P_t = (118,272.7)/[1 + (6.061401)(e^{-0.05843697t})]$ after 11 iterations, with $r^2 = 0.995293$. With this model, the projected population for Island County in 2010 is $90,437 \approx (118,272.7)/[1 + (6.061401)(e^{-0.05843697*51})]$. For Walla Walla County, the logistic model was estimated as $P_t = (41,712,310.00)/[1 + (1,059.927)(e^{-0.007814847t})]$ after 235 iterations, with $r^2 = 0.940$. With this model, the projected population for Walla Walla County in 2010 is $58,542 \approx (41,712,310.00)/[1 + (1,059.927)(e^{-0.007814847*51})]$. Projections for both counties in 2005 and 2015 using these models, respectively, are provided in Table 21.2.

ARIMA Time Series Models

ARIMA ("Autoregressive Integrated Moving Average") models have occasionally been used in the analysis and projection of populations as a whole and of their demographic attributes (Alho and Spencer, 1997; Carter and Lee, 1986; de Beer, 1993; Lee, 1993; and Pflaumer, 1992). The procedures used in ARIMA models are complicated, making them difficult to implement and explain to data users. We suggest consulting standard texts before attempting to apply this method (Box and Jenkins, 1976; Hanke *et al.*, 2001; Yaffee, 2000). It also may be useful to review the method of "moving averages," which forms part of the foundation of ARIMA (Hanke *et al.*, 2001, pp. 101–123). ARIMA models attempt to uncover the stochastic mechanisms that generate historical data series and use this information as a basis for developing projections. Three processes can describe the stochastic mechanism: (1) autoregressive, (2) differencing, and (3) a moving average. The autoregressive process has a memory in the sense that it is based on the correlation of each value of a variable with all preceding values. The impact of earlier values is assumed to diminish exponentially over time. The number of preceding values incorporated into the model determines its "order." For example, in a first-order autoregressive process, the current value is explicitly a function only of the immediately preceding value. However, the immediately preceding value is a function of the one before it, which is a function of the one before it, and so forth. Consequently, all preceding values influence current values, albeit with a declining impact. In a second-order autoregressive process, the current value is explicitly a function of the two immediately preceding values; again, all preceding values have an indirect impact.

A stationary time series is very important for the construction of a given ARIMA model. The differencing process is used to create a stationary time series (i.e., one with constant differences over time). When a time series is nonstationary, it can often be converted into a stationary time series by calculating differences between values. First differences are usually sufficient, but second differences are occasionally required (i.e., differences between differences). Logarithmic and square-root transformations can also be used to convert nonstationary to stationary time series. The moving average is used to represent any event that has a substantial but short-lived impact on a time series pattern. The order of the moving average process defines the number of time periods affected by a given event.

The ARIMA method is usually written as ARIMA (p,d,q), where p is the order of the autoregression, d is the degree of differencing, and q is the order of the moving average. (An ARIMA model based on time intervals of less than 1 year may also require a seasonal component.) The first and most subjective step in developing an ARIMA model is to identify the values of p, d, and q. The d-value is determined first because a stationary series is required to properly identify the autoregressive and moving average processes. The value of d is usually 0 or 1, but occasionally 2. Like the d-value, the p- and q-values are also relatively small (0, 1, or—at most—2). The patterns of the autocorrelation function (ACF) and the partial autocorrelation function (PACF) and their standard errors are used to find the correct values for p and q (Box and Jenkins, 1976; Yaffee, 2000). For example, a first-order autoregressive model (ARIMA (1,0,0)) is characterized by an ACF that declines exponentially and quickly along with a PACF that has a statistically significant spike only at the first lag. Once p, d, and q are determined, maximum likelihood procedures are used to estimate the parameters of a given ARIMA model.

The final step involves assessing the suitability of a given model. An adequate ARIMA model will have random residuals, no significant values in the ACF and PACF, and the smallest possible values for p, d, or q. Only after an ARIMA model has passed this assessment should it be used.

It is not unusual to repeat this sequence of steps several times before a suitable ARIMA model is found. In this process, it is best to start simple (e.g., ARIMA (0,1,0)), check the results, and then add additional changes in a systematic and incremental manner (e.g., ARIMA(1,1,0) if the model is not found to be suitable. If a suitable model is not found by the time one reaches, say, ARIMA (2,1,2), it is probably wise to abandon this approach.

One characteristic of an autoregressive model is that projections will eventually reach and maintain a constant numeric difference similar in value to the mean of the historical series (McCleary and Hay, 1980, p. 218). Consequently, population projections using ARIMA will often be similar to projections based on linear extrapolation methods (Pflaumer, 1992; Voss and Kale, 1985). The formulas used in computing projections from an ARIMA model depend on the specification of the values of p, d, and q, each of which is most easily determined using a computer package designed for estimating them.

Using the 1960-through-2000 population figures shown in Table 21.1, the NCSS (1995, pp. 1427–1436) ARIMA routine was used to develop models for Island and Walla Walla counties. Because the NCSS algorithm does not use ordinary least squares, it employs "pseudo-r^2" as a measure of fit rather than "r^2."

For Island County, a first-order autoregressive model with one degree of differencing and no moving average (ARIMA(1,1,0)) was found to be sufficient after 21 iterations and estimated as $P_{t+1} = [(0.876942)(P_t - P_{t-1}) + P_t]$, with "pseudo-$r^2$" = 0.9982. With this same model, a projected population for Island County in 2010 is $78,889 \approx [(0.876942)(78,646.5 - 78,370.4) + 78,646.5]$. For Walla Walla County, a first-order autoregressive model with one degree of differencing and no moving average (ARIMA(1,1,0)) also was found to be sufficient after three iterations, with a "pseudo-r^2" of 0.98505. In the case of Walla Walla County, it was estimated as $P_{t+1} = [(0.4573916)(P_t - P_{t-1}) + P_t]$. With this same model, a projected population for Walla Walla County in 2010 is $53,863 \approx [(0.4573916)(53,863 - 53,863) + 53,863]$. Projections for both counties in 2005 and 2015 are shown in Table 21.2.

There are three important points to bear in mind when using ARIMA models. First, because a given ARIMA model can have a number of alternative configurations, those that have values higher than 1 for p, d, and q, can be difficult to operationalize manually. That is, it may be difficult to manually recreate projection results created by a given software package using the parameters shown. This may be of particular concern for some users because it is not easy to explain how the projections are calculated. Second, during the base period "projected values" from a given ARIMA model are generated using the actual historical values. However, once beyond the scope of the historical data, projected values themselves are used to generate subsequent projected values. There may be a period subsequent to the launch date when a combination of actual and projected data may be used depending on the order and degree of differencing. Third, ARIMA (as well as the other complex extrapolation techniques covered here) can be used to place probabilistic confidence intervals around their forecasts.

Ratio Extrapolation Methods

Ratio extrapolation methods may be used where an area containing the population to be projected is part of a larger ("parent") area for which projections are available. They are often used where areas exist in a perfect hierarchical structure—that is, where geographic units at each level are mutually exclusive and exhaustive and can be aggregated to higher levels, culminating in one all-inclusive unit. As an example, consider census blocks in the United States, which can be aggregated successively into block groups, census tracts, counties, states, and finally the country as a whole. Ratio methods also can be used where there is not a perfect hierarchy—for example, in a city that is part of a county in which the geographic area (population) covered by all cities is less than the total area (population) of the county as a whole. In this case, the parent area is not the county but the area represented by all of the cities. Ratio methods can be applied in situations where the area (population) of interest is linked to the "parent" area (population) through considerations other than geography (this is akin to the "targeting" approach described later in regard to projecting mortality and fertility) and, in addition, ratios can be formed via lagged relationships.

We discuss three commonly used ratio methods: (1) the constant-share, (2) the shift-share, and (3) the share-of-growth approaches. As noted, all three require projections of a "parent" area in which the area of interest is located. We use Washington State as the "parent" area for applying these methods to Island and Walla Walla counties. Projections for Washington State are 6,137,403, 6,545,786, and 6,987,273, for the years 2005, 2010, and 2015, respectively (Washington State Office of Financial Management, 2001).

Constant-Share Method

In this method, the smaller area's share of the larger area's population is held constant at a level observed during the base period. Typically it is the share observed in the launch year. This *constant-share* method is expressed as

$$P_{it} = (P_{il}/P_{jl})(P_{jt}) \qquad (21.14)$$

where P_{it} is the population projection for smaller area (i) in the target year, P_{il} is the population of the smaller area in the launch year, P_{jl} is the population of the parent area (j) in the launch year, and P_{jt} is the projection of the parent area in the target year.

The constant-share method requires historical data for only one date; consequently, it is particularly useful for areas where changing geographic boundaries or poor records make it difficult or impossible to construct a reliable historical data series. Another requirement of this method is that projections for all of the smaller areas add exactly to the projection for the parent area. The main drawback of this method is that it assumes that all the smaller areas will grow at the same rate as the parent area. In many instances, this will not be a reasonable assumption.

Using the 2000 population figures shown in Table 21.1 for Island County and Washington State, a constant-share model yielded a projected 2010 population for Island County of 83,692 ≈ (74,200/5,803,400)(6,545,786). Using the 2000 population figures shown in Table 21.1 for Walla Walla County and Washington State, a constant share model yielded a projected 2010 population for Walla Walla County of 61,133 ≈ (54,200/5,803,400)(6,545,786). Projections for 2005 and 2015 using these models, respectively, are shown in Table 21.2.

Shift-Share Method

Unlike the constant-share method, the *shift-share* method is designed to deal with changes in population shares. Here, we describe one of several methods in which population shares are extrapolated linearly over time. This *shift-share* method is expressed as

$$P_{it} = (P_{jt})[(P_{il}/P_{jl}) + (z/y)((P_{il}/P_{jl}) - (P_{ib}/P_{jb}))] \qquad (21.15)$$

where the smaller area is denoted by i, the parent area by j, z is the number of years in the projection horizon, y is the number of years in the base period, and b, l, and t refer to the base, launch, and target years, respectively.

There is a problem inherent in the shift-share method: it can lead to substantial population losses in areas that grew very slowly (or declined) during the base period, especially when the projections cover long-range horizons (e.g., 20 or 30 years). In fact, this method can even lead to negative numbers. This problem can be dealt with by incorporating constraints on projected population shares or on the projected rates of change in those shares. The method also can lead to absurdly high projections for areas that have been growing very rapidly. As with many extrapolation methods, the shift-share approach must be used very cautiously for long-range projections, especially for places whose population shares have been declining (or increasing) rapidly.

Using the 1960 and 2000 population figures shown in Table 21.1, a shift-share model yielded a projected 2010 population for Island County of 93,352 ≈ (6,545,786)[(74,200/5,803,400) + (10/40)((74,200/5,803,400) − (19,638/2,853,214))]. For Walla Walla County, a shift-share model yielded a projected 2010 population of 52,216 ≈ (6,545,786)[(54,200/5,803,400) + (10/40)((54,200/

5,803,400) – (42,195/2,853,214))]. Projections for 2005 and 2015 are shown in Table 21.2.

Share-of-Growth Method

The third ratio method deals with shares of population *change* rather than population *size*. In this method, it is assumed that the smaller area's share of population change in the parent area will be the same over the projection horizon as it was during the base period. This *share-of-growth* method can be expressed as

$$P_{it} = P_{il} + [((P_{il} - P_{ib})/(P_{jl} - P_{jb}))(P_{jt} - P_{jl})] \quad (21.16)$$

where the components are defined as those in the shift-share method.

In many instances, the share-of-growth method seems to provide more reasonable projections than either the constant- or shift-share methods. However, it runs into problems when a growth rate in a smaller area has the opposite sign than that for the parent area. This can be dealt with using the "plus-minus" method described in Appendix C or by setting the share to zero and not letting it change.

Using the 1960 and 2000 population figures shown in Table 21.1, a shift-share model yielded a projected 2010 population for Island County of 87,930 ≈ 74,200 + [((74,200 − 19,638)/(5,803,400 − 2,853,214))(6,545,786 − 5,903,400)]. For Walla Walla County, a shift-share model yielded a projected 2010 population of 57,221 ≈ 54,200 + [((54,200 − 42,195)/(5,803,400 − 2,853,214))(6,545,786 − 5,803,400)]. Projections for 2005 and 2015 are shown in Table 21.2.

Summary Comments on Extrapolation Methods

Both simple and complex trend extrapolation methods suffer from several shortcomings. They do not account for differences in demographic composition or for differences in the components of growth. They provide little or no information on the projected demographic characteristics of the population. Because they have no theoretical content, they cannot be related to theories of population growth, except perhaps the logistic model, which is consistent with a Malthusian view of population dynamics. Consequently, they have limited usefulness for analyzing the determinants of population growth or for simulating the effects of changes in particular variables or assumptions. In addition, they can lead to unrealistic or even absurd results, even over relatively short horizons. In spite of their shortcomings, trend extrapolation methods have a number of advantages over other projection methods. They have few data requirements and, with the exception of the ARIMA and polynomial models, are quick and easy to apply. They are particularly useful when data series are incomplete, time and budgets are highly constrained, and information on population characteristics is not needed. Perhaps most important, they often provide reasonably accurate forecasts over short and even long projection horizons. There is no empirical evidence showing that more complex or sophisticated methods consistently produce more accurate forecasts than trend extrapolation methods.

As shown in Table 21.2, different methods sometimes produce dramatically different results. Island County, for example, grew rapidly between 1960 to 2000. Thus, it is not surprising that the range of projections is quite large, extending from 79,719 (logistic) to 122,166 (geometric) in 2015. The case is quite different for Walla Walla County, which experienced a much smaller population increase between 1960 and 2000. Here, the range is much smaller than that for Island County: the largest projection for 2015 is provided by the quadratic method (66,194) and the smallest (50,978) by the shift-share method. If trend extrapolation methods are to be used, which one(s) should be chosen for these two counties? Alternatively, should an average of projections from several methods be calculated? Should the same methods be used in both counties? The use of trend extrapolation methods does not remove the need to exercise judgment. We return to this issue toward the end of this chapter.

COHORT-COMPONENT METHOD

The cohort-component method was introduced by Cannan (1895), subsequently used by Bowley (1924), and later rediscovered independently by Whelpton (1928). It is the most widely used method for producing national-level population projections. Although current applications are more detailed and sophisticated than the earliest applications, the basic framework of the method has changed little since the pioneering work by these three men.

The cohort-component method divides the launch-year population into age-sex groups (i.e., birth cohorts) and accounts separately for the fertility, mortality, and migration behavior of each cohort as it passes through the projection horizon. It is a flexible and powerful method that can be used to implement theoretical models or serve as an atheoretical accounting procedure. It can provide in-depth knowledge on population dynamics. Also the cohort-component method can accommodate a wide range of assumptions and can be used at any geographic level—from the world as a whole down to nations, states/provinces, counties, and subcounty areas.

For purposes of population projection, the division of the population into age groups was an important methodological advance (de Gans, 1999). It allows one to account for the differences in mortality, fertility, and migration rates among different age groups at a particular time and to consider how rates change over time for individual cohorts.

Cohort-component models typically use either single years or 5-year groups. The oldest age group is virtually always "open-ended," usually 75+, 85+, or 90+. Age groups are typically divided by sex and are sometimes further subdivided by race, ethnicity, and other characteristics (where considered officially useful). Our discussion and examples focus on populations divided by age and sex, but the procedures we describe would be basically the same if the population were further subdivided by race, ethnicity, and other characteristics.

In the application of the method as originally developed, the first step in the projection process is to establish the launch-year population and calculate the number of persons in it who survive to the end of the projection interval (e.g., one year). This is done by applying age-sex-specific survival rates to each age-sex group in the launch-year population. The second step is to calculate migration during the projection interval for each age-sex group. The application of migration rates provides a projection of the number of persons in each age-sex group moving into or out of an area during the projection interval (or, for models using net migration rates, the net migration). The third step is to calculate the number of births occurring during the projection interval. This is accomplished by applying age-specific birthrates to the female population in each age group. The final step in the process is to add the number of births (separating male and female births) to the rest of the population.

These calculations provide a projection of the population by age and sex at the end of the projection interval. This population then serves as the starting point for the following interval (e.g., next year). The process is repeated until the final target year is reached. Figure 21.2 illustrates the steps in this process. Figure 21.2 is meant to be illustrative. Not each and every application of the cohort-component method follows the steps as shown. Illustrating this point, in the examples for national and subnational projections provided later for Canada, there are adjustments made to the basic steps shown in Figure 21.2 to deal with the effect of migration on births and deaths.

Projecting Mortality

The mortality rates (or their functional equivalents) used in cohort-component projections can be projected in a number of ways. The simplest is to assume that age-specific rates will remain unchanged at current levels. For short horizons, this will often be a reasonable assumption. For longer horizons, however, this assumption may not be valid and methods that incorporate changing rates then become necessary. Such methods include a variety of extrapolation techniques, techniques tying mortality rates in one area or population to those in another, and structural models that base changes in mortality rates on changes in socioeconomic variables.

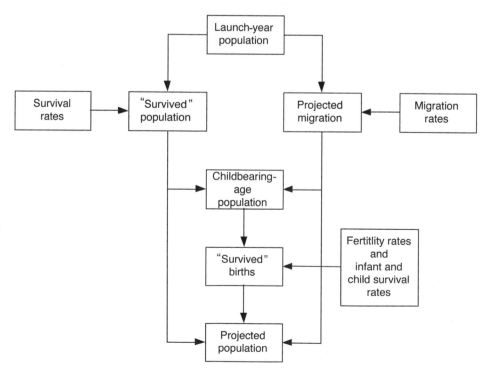

FIGURE 21.2   Overview of the cohort-component method for a projection interval.
Source: Smith *et al.* (2001, p. 47).

The use of extrapolation techniques assumes that the future will mirror the past in certain important ways. Although this is not always a valid assumption, it has often led to reasonably accurate forecasts. Extrapolation techniques have been widely used for mortality projections, sometimes following fairly simple procedures and other times applying more sophisticated procedures such as ARIMA time series models (Lee and Carter, 1992).

Extrapolation techniques are particularly appropriate when mortality trends are following a stable path. The critical question is whether trends will remain stable in the future. The answer to this question depends on one's views regarding the determinants of mortality trends (e.g., Ahlburg and Vaupel, 1990; Fries, 1989; Manton, Stallard, and Tolley, 1991; Olshansky, 1988).

A number of techniques tie mortality rates in one population to those in another. For example, the "targeting" approach is based on the idea that mortality rates in a given population will converge toward those observed in another population (i.e., the target). A target population is chosen that provides a set of mortality rates believed to be realistic for the population to be projected. This choice is based on similarities in socioeconomic, cultural, and behavioral characteristics; levels of medical technology; and primary causes of death (Olshansky, 1988, p. 500). It could be implemented using a "ratio" approach, as described earlier in this chapter in the section "Trend Extrapolation."

One form of targeting is called "cause-delay." In this approach, the target population is a younger cohort in the same population rather than the same cohort in a different population. Cause-delay models focus on the implications of delaying (or completely eliminating) the occurrence of one or more causes of death (Manton, Patrick, and Stallard, 1980; Olshansky, 1987). The basic premise behind this approach is that changes in lifestyle and medical technology have delayed the occurrence of various types of deaths until progressively older ages. Consequently, as time goes by, each cohort faces lower mortality risks at each age than did the previous cohort. Another form of targeting is to link changes in rates for the area in question to changes projected for a different area through the use of ratios.

Life tables are readily available for most areas of the world and can be used as a base for mortality projections. As the reader may recall, life tables are prepared both by the United Nations and by the vital statistics agencies in most countries. In the United States, for example, national life tables are published annually by the National Center for Health Statistics and a few times each decade by the Social Security Administration (Bell et al., 1992; U.S. National Center for Health Statistics, 1997). State life tables are typically constructed once every 10 years in the United States, when decennial census data become available to serve as denominators for the mortality rates.

Projecting Fertility

In projecting births, one can use a period perspective, a cohort perspective, or a combination of the two. The period perspective focuses on births to women at the same age over a series of years. The cohort perspective is longitudinal, focusing on the fertility patterns of a cohort of women as they pass through their childbearing years.

Although the cohort perspective is superior for some analytical purposes, it is difficult to implement when constructing population projections. Data on completed cohort fertility do not become available until after a cohort has passed through its childbearing years; for women under age 50, only partial data are available. Birth histories of past cohorts and the fertility expectations of current cohorts may be used as proxies for the missing data, but they do not necessarily provide reliable fertility forecasts for current and future cohorts. In addition, projections for subnational areas are complicated by the lack of relevant data and by the effects of migration, which may have a significant impact on the composition of an area's population and its fertility behavior. Because of these problems and the complexity of the method, we believe that most practitioners will be better served by using a period perspective for the production of fertility projections.

Several approaches may be used when applying the period fertility perspective. One is to hold current age specific birthrates (ASBRs) constant throughout the projection horizon (Day, 1996; Treadway, 1997). These rates are often based on data for the most recent year, but can also be based on an average of data for several recent years. Holding rates constant can be justified not only by the expectation that they will not change, but also by the belief that increases in current rates are as likely as declines. Another approach is to extrapolate historical trends. This approach is particularly useful for countries in the midst of the demographic transition from high to low fertility rates, but can lead to problems for countries in which the transition has already been completed. If no long-run trends are clearly discernible, recent changes in fertility rates may simply reflect short-run fluctuations and extrapolating those changes into the future may create large forecast errors. Time series techniques are frequently used to develop nonlinear models for projecting ASBRs (Carter and Lee, 1992; Land, 1986; Lee, 1993; Lee and Tuljapurkar, 1994).

The "targeting" approach described earlier is another technique that can be used to project fertility rates (U.S. Bureau of the Census, 1979). Before applying this technique, however, one must decide whether the convergence of one set of rates toward another is a realistic assumption. Projected ASBRs also can be derived by forming ratios of birthrates in one area to those in another and applying those ratios to the birthrates previously projected for the area of interest. Finally, structural models can be developed. Such models have occasionally been used for projecting fertility rates at the national level (e.g., Ahlburg, 1999; Sanderson, 1999), but have seldom been used at the subnational level (Isserman, 1985).

Even given our argument in favor of the period perspective, it is nonetheless important to keep the cohort perspective in mind when formulating assumptions about future fertility rates. For example, if recent changes have occurred in ASBRs, the cohort perspective may offer clues as to whether those changes reflect a shift in the long-run trend in ASBRs or simply a short-run change in the timing of births. It is in this sense that a combination of the period and cohort perspective may be useful. In addition, it is useful to note that there is increased use of the cohort approach in the European Economic Area, a development partially attributed to the availability of a long series of historical data (Cruijsen, 1994).

Fertility is often the most problematic part of national population projections (Keyfitz, 1982; Ryder, 1990). Long (1989) found that differences in fertility assumptions accounted for more of the variation in long-run projections of the U.S. population than did differences in either mortality or immigration assumptions. However, immigration was considered the most problematic component for the 1993 round of Canadian population projections (George, Loh, and Verma, 1997). For subnational areas in many countries, fertility may be less important than migration in explaining differences in rates of population growth (Congdon, 1992; Smith and Ahmed, 1990).

Projecting Migration

Migration often has a substantial impact on population growth at the national and subnational levels. For projection purposes, we may view migration in two ways: (1) gross migration and (2) net migration. As explained in Chapter 19, gross migration refers to the movement of people into and out of a given area; net migration refers to the difference between the two—that is, inmigration minus outmigration. For projecting population flows, each has its strengths and weaknesses. Gross migration models are "cleaner" from a theoretical and computational standpoint, but they require more data and are more complicated to apply than net migration models (Smith and Swanson, 1998). Both approaches are widely used for population projections.

We discuss two basic techniques for projecting gross migration. The first is based on the application of outmigration rates and inmigration proportions for each area to be projected. (U.S. Census Bureau, 1966, 1972, 1979). We describe this technique using states as the unit of reference and migration data based on 5-year time and age intervals. The same technique could be used for other geographic

areas and different lengths of migration intervals, if the data are available. Under this technique, outmigration rates by age and sex are calculated for each state using outmigration data from the decennial census as the numerators and state populations by age and sex (5 years before the census) as the denominators. These rates are then applied to the launch year population to provide a projection of the total "pool" of interstate outmigrants for all states. Migrants in this pool are allocated to each state according to the proportion of interstate migrants each state received during the base period (by age and sex).

The second technique for projecting gross migration uses "multiregional models" (Rogers, 1985, 1995). In these models, migration is viewed as part of an integrated system of mortality, fertility, and origin-destination-specific population streams by age and sex (and sometimes by other characteristics as well). For example, interstate migration in a multiregional model of the United States could be represented by a 51-by-51 matrix showing the number of people moving from each state to every other state (including the District of Columbia), by age and sex. Migration rates are calculated by dividing destination-specific gross migration streams by the population of each state of origin, giving each state 50 sets of age-sex-specific outmigration rates, one for each other state in the nation. Because these rates are based on the population at risk of migration, they reflect the probabilities of moving from one state to another during a given time period. A multiregional approach has been used by Statistics Canada and is illustrated in the example provided later (see, e. g., Table 21.5).

Migration also can be projected using net rather than gross migration. Net migration can be projected using two approaches, either alone or in combination: (1) "top-down" and (2) "bottom-up." The top-down approach distinguishes between the components of population growth (i.e., natural increase and net migration), but it focuses on estimates of total net migration rather than separate estimates for each age-sex cohort. It requires two steps. First, projections of total net migration are made, based on recent levels, historical trends, structural models, or some other design. Second, these projections are disaggregated by age-sex categories, on the base of distributions observed in the past. We call this a top-down approach because projections for broad demographic categories are made first and subcategories are derived from them; here, individual age-sex groups are derived from projections of total net migration. This was the approach taken in the earliest sets of cohort-component projections made for states and regions in the United States (Thompson and Whelpton, 1933; U.S. Bureau of the Census, 1957). It is currently used for the international migration component of national population projections in the United States. Projections of the level of total net foreign immigration are based on historical data and expectations regarding future levels; they are made for age, sex, and race/ethnicity categories according to the distributions observed in recent historical data (Day, 1996).

The second approach to projecting net migration focuses on the development of separate net migration rates for each age-sex cohort in the population. Projections are based on the application of age-sex-specific net migration rates to the base population in this same detail. We call this a bottom-up approach because figures for the broad categories are derived from those for the subcategories; here, the total volume of net migration projected for an area is the sum of the individual values projected for each age-sex group.

Net migration models generally combine international and internal migration. When net migration is calculated as a residual, this is the simplest approach. Separate projections of immigration could be made, however, by subtracting immigration from total net migration in the base data, and developing separate assumptions regarding future net flows of foreign and domestic migrants.

One drawback of net migration models is that they do not base migration rates on the population at risk. As a consequence, they create inconsistencies in projections for a group of areas. Consider population projections for states. The application of constant net migration rates to states with rapidly growing populations leads to steadily increasing levels of net inmigration over time, but the application of constant rates to states with slowly growing (or declining) populations leads to slowly growing (or declining) levels of net outmigration. Because net internal migration must sum to zero over all states (that is, the total number of interstate inmigrants must equal the total number of interstate outmigrants), this creates an internal inconsistency within the set of state population projections. It can also lead to bias, as projections based on net migration rates tend to be too high for rapidly growing places and too low for slowly growing or declining places.

Some of the problems associated with net migration models can be reduced by changing the denominators used in constructing the migration rates. Net migration rates for rapidly growing areas can be based on the population of a larger geographic unit rather than of the area itself. For example, rates for rapidly growing states can be based on the national population rather than the state population. This change has been found to reduce projected rates of increase for rapidly growing states greatly (Smith, 1986). Alternatively, projections of net migration (or population) can be constrained or controlled in various ways to prevent unreasonably large increases or declines (Smith and Shahidullah, 1995).

Calculations for net migration and mortality can be combined to create a simplified version of the cohort-component method (Hamilton and Perry, 1962). In this method, cohort-change ratios (CCR) covering the time interval between the two most recent censuses are calculated for each age-sex

cohort in the population. They are similar to national *census survival rates* in structure and are expressed as

$$_nCCR_x = {_nP_{x+y}}/{_nP_x} \qquad (21.17)$$

where $_nP_{x+y}$ is the population aged $x + y$ to $x + y + n$ in the year of the most recent census, $_nP_x$ is the population aged x to $x + n$ in the second most recent census, and y is the number of years between these two successive censuses. Cohort-change ratios also can be calculated for different race/ethnic groups. Projections can then be made by multiplying these ratios by the launch-year population in each age-sex group:

$$_nP_{x+y,t=y} = {_nCCR_x}({_nP_{x,l}}) \qquad (21.18)$$

where $_nP_{x+y,t}$ is the population aged $x + y$ to $x + y + n$ in year target year t, y years after l.

In many circumstances, especially for small areas, unique events and special populations must be taken into account when developing migration assumptions. Unique events are those having a substantial but short-lived impact on an area's volume and patterns of migration; for example, an economic boom or bust may have occurred during the base period. In such cases, one needs to decide if these conditions are likely to continue into the future and, if not, how to make appropriate adjustments. Special populations are groups of people who are in an area because of an administrative or legislative action. These include refugees, college students, prison inmates, and military personnel. Changes in special populations result from a different set of factors than those affecting the rest of the population. If changes in special populations are substantial, it is important to account for them separately when implementing the cohort-component method (Smith *et al.*, 2001, pp. 239–277). Migration is considerably more responsive than either fertility or mortality to changes in economic conditions, employment opportunities, housing patterns, transportation conditions, and neighborhood characteristics. Social and cultural conflicts, natural disasters, and government policies typically have more impact on migration rates than on mortality and fertility rates. Consequently, migration is generally more difficult to forecast accurately than either mortality or fertility, especially for small areas. In general, the smaller the subnational area, the greater the difficulty in developing accurate migration forecasts.

Implementing the Cohort-Component Method

Several issues must be considered when implementing the cohort-component method. To preserve the integrity of age cohorts as they progress through time, it is helpful to follow a basic principle: The number of years in the projection interval should be equal to the number of years in the age-groups or a multiple thereof. For example, 5-year age groups are well suited for making projections in 5- or 10-year intervals, but are not well suited for making projections in 1-year intervals. The logic is simple: the survivors of people aged 10 to 14 in 2005 will be 15 to 19 in 2010, but making projections of persons who will be 11 to 15 in 2006 is more complicated and the results less precise. Typically, the model is applied separately for each demographic subgroup. These strata are then combined to create other categories. The female stratum is typically projected first because a projection of females is needed to determine the projection of births. The procedures for applying the rates for compo-nents of change are the same for each subgroup. Cohort-component models are often constructed for 5-year age groups, starting with 0 to 4 and ending with 75+ or 85+. The use of 5-year age groups is common because projections of 5-year groups in 5-year intervals satisfy the needs of a wide range of data users and, in addition, can be readily interpolated both into single years of age and into individual years within a 5-year projection interval (using procedures described in Appendix C).

Single-year cohort-component models also are widely used, especially at the national level. Some county-level projections use this more detailed age breakdown. Cohort-component models with single years of age automatically provide annual projections and offer an obvious advantage over models built from more aggregated age groupings. They make it easier to provide projections for customized age groups (e.g., 5 to 17) required by data users in fields such as education, health care, and the criminal justice system. In addition, single-year models provide a more precise reflection of population aging; by focusing on single-year cohorts as they move through time, they pick up subtleties missed by 5-year models.

Single-year models are considerably more time consuming and costly to construct and maintain than 5-year models. A single-year model with 100+ as the terminal age group has 202 age-sex categories. In contrast, a 5-year model with 85+ as the terminal age category has only 36 age-sex categories. For a 20-year projection horizon, a single-year model requires the application of 202 separate birth, death, and migration rates for each of 20 distinct time periods. A 5-year model requires only 36 birth, death, and migration rates for four time periods. In spite of the widespread use of powerful microcomputers, issues of data management for single-year models are still imposing, especially when three or four race/ethnic groups are added to the task.

In some circumstances migration data are available only in 10-year intervals for 5-year age groups (e.g., between two decennial censuses). Strictly speaking, this would dictate the use of 10-year migration rates and 10-year projection intervals. However, one can transform 10-year migration rates into 5-year rates by taking the square roots of 1 plus the migration rates, averaging the results for two adjacent birth cohorts, and subtracting 1. Note that a given 5-year cohort appears in two 10-year cohorts, but in different 5-year time periods. Another approach is to use census data on migration in the 5-year period preceding the census, or to combine the two "estimates."

A final consideration before implementing the cohort-component method is the impact of data errors and data consistency. Data problems tend to increase as the level of demographic detail increases and as population size declines. It is important to review historical population data and, if necessary, to adjust the basic demographic rates before running the projection model. In some cases, it may be necessary to adjust for census enumeration and other forms of error as well.

Example of a National Projection

We illustrate the cohort-component method for national population projections using as an example Statistics Canada's "medium scenario" projection of the female population (Statistics Canada, 2001). Statistics Canada has been preparing population projections on a regular basis since 1969. They are given for single years of age and sex, each year, with a horizon of 25 years for the provinces and territories, and 50 years for Canada as a whole. Long-term projections are generally revised every 5 years, following the national census. The projections employ a regional cohort-component method. (The term "region" represents Canada's 10 provinces and three territories.) The input data for the projections (population by age and sex, fertility, mortality, immigration, emigration, nonpermanent residents, and internal migration) come from official population estimates published in Statistics Canada's, *Annual Demographic Statistics*.

In order to produce consistent and comparable projections for Canada and its provinces simultaneously, a "hybrid bottom-up" projection model is used. In this model, assumptions on fertility, mortality, immigration, emigration, and nonpermanent residents are developed at the national level and consistent provincial assumptions, incorporating internal migration assumptions, are derived from them. The model allows separate projections of each component at the provincial/territorial level, thereby taking into account regional differences (George and Loh, 2000). It has been the general practice to include several alternate assumptions for fertility, mortality, and migration in preparing the projections. The combination of assumptions yields numerous projections from which a set of projections representing plausible maximum, medium, and minimum population growth is selected for publication purposes.

Other special features of the projection model include (1) an adjustment of the base population for net census undercoverage; (2) the use of component parameters—fertility, mortality, emigration, and internal migration—based on population estimates that also are adjusted for net census undercoverage; (3) the use of the "Pearson Type III curve" for projecting age-specific fertility rates; (4) the projection of mortality using the Lee-Carter model (Lee and Carter, 1992); (5) the use of age-specific emigration rates to project emigration; (6) the use of the Rogers-Castro multiregional model (Rogers and Castro, 1978) to project interregional age-specific outmigration rates; and (7) taking the indirect effects of migration (internal and international) on births and deaths into account by "surviving" the population adjusted for migration, rather than the launch population, as is generally done in cohort-component projections.

The launch population in our example is the official set of estimates of Canada's female population by age on July 1, 2000 (first column of Table 21.3). Life expectancy at birth (e_o), used to represent the mortality component, is based on (1) the trend of life expectancy at birth in Canada, (2) the observed and projected mortality trends and patterns in other

industrialized countries, and (3) consideration of medical progress and health-related factors that are expected to affect future mortality. Three assumptions are developed in regard to future mortality; they incorporate a greater increase in male life expectancy than female life expectancy and, hence, reductions in the gap between male and female life expectancy at birth. (These assumptions are summarized later in Figure 21.4.)

The Lee-Carter model used to distribute the projected gains in e_o by age (in the form of age-specific death rates) involves the following equation:

$$\ln(m_x) = a_x + b_x k_t \qquad (21.19)$$

where $\ln(m_x)$ represents the logarithm of the central death rates at age x, a_x and b_x represent age-specific constants, and k_t represents time.

Table 21.3 Example of the Calculation of Projected Births, Canada: 2000–2001

| Age of mother | Calendar year 2000 | | | Calendar year 2001 | | | Projected births, July 1, 2000, to June 30, 2001 |
	Female population July[1] (1)	Fertility rates (2)	Births, (3) = (1) × (2)	Female population July[1] (4)	Fertility rates (5)	Births, (6) = (4) × (5)	(7) = {(3) + (6)}/2
15	200,341	0.00548	1,098	200,725	0.00535	1,074	1,086
16	200,917	0.00861	1,730	202,053	0.00842	1,701	1,716
17	200,783	0.01302	2,614	202,684	0.01276	2,586	2,600
18	201,164	0.01894	3,810	202,440	0.01861	3,767	3,789
19	204,943	0.02656	5,443	203,345	0.02613	5,313	5,378
20	204,680	0.03587	7,342	206,800	0.03536	7,312	7,327
21	202,626	0.04670	9,463	206,939	0.04613	9,546	9,505
22	200,593	0.05863	11,761	204,380	0.05802	11,858	11,810
23	203,550	0.07101	14,454	202,822	0.07039	14,277	14,366
24	205,067	0.08299	17,019	205,567	0.08241	16,941	16,980
25	205,918	0.09364	19,282	207,255	0.09314	19,304	19,293
26	201,925	0.10203	20,602	208,037	0.10166	21,149	20,876
27	204,162	0.10740	21,927	204,000	0.10720	21,869	21,898
28	208,697	0.10926	22,802	206,089	0.10925	22,515	22,659
29	218,615	0.10746	23,492	210,782	0.10763	22,686	23,089
30	219,846	0.10222	22,473	220,496	0.10255	22,612	22,543
31	219,208	0.09406	20,619	221,512	0.09452	20,937	20,778
32	220,974	0.08377	18,511	220,918	0.08431	18,626	18,569
33	226,851	0.07222	16,383	222,732	0.07281	16,217	16,300
34	239,975	0.06030	14,470	228,403	0.06088	13,905	14,188
35	257,817	0.04877	12,574	241,593	0.04932	11,915	12,245
36	266,928	0.03822	10,202	258,987	0.03872	10,028	10,115
37	271,402	0.02904	7,882	267,849	0.02946	7,891	7,887
38	267,494	0.02139	5,722	272,404	0.02173	5,919	5,821
39	271,218	0.01528	4,144	268,253	0.01555	4,171	4,158
40	269,080	0.01059	2,850	271,947	0.01080	2,937	2,894
41	264,843	0.00713	1,888	269,641	0.00727	1,960	1,924
42	262,199	0.00465	1,219	265,334	0.00476	1,263	1,241
43	257,968	0.00295	761	262,484	0.00302	793	777
44	250,841	0.00182	457	258,151	0.00186	480	469
Total	6,830,625	1.48002	322,995	6,824,622	1.48001	321,552	322,274

Source: Statistics Canada (2001).

To ensure a smooth transition from the last observation year to the first projection year, a_x is set equal to the logarithm of the 1996 age-specific death rates (m_x) for each sex, so that when k_t equals 0, the equation produces the 1996 central death rates at each age. The b_x series determines the rate of mortality change at each age. It is set to distribute the projected gains in e_o by age, according to the age-specific rates of change observed over the 1971–1990 period for both sexes at the national level. The k_t values are calculated to yield the exact e_o values assumed for each sex. Life table values at ages above "zero" are calculated from projected age-specific death rates. The required schedule of projected survivorship probabilities at different ages for each sex (e.g., S_x values for females in col. 7 of Table 21.4) is calculated from the L_x values of the life tables for Canada. The projected survival ratios by age for females are applied to the corresponding female population adjusted for migration in col. 6 of Table 21.4 to obtain the annual number of survivors. The survivors of the births (155,990 in the table) are obtained by multiplying the total number of female births during 2000 to 2001 (156,690) by the survival ratio from birth to age "under 1 year." The female births in this table are obtained by multiplying total births (322,274) in Table 21.3 by the proportion of female births (0.4862).

For projecting *fertility*, a Pearson Type III curve was applied to the TFRs shown in Figure 21.4 to derive projected age-specific fertility rates. This required four parameters: (1) the total fertility rate (TFR), (2) the mean age of fertility, (3) the variance of the age-specific fertility rates, and (4) the skewness of the age-specific fertility rates. The first parameter provides the level of fertility, while the other three provide a measure of the timing of births or age pattern of childbearing. The application of the model rests on an analysis of each of these four parameters and the formulation of assumptions on their future course over the projection period (Verma, *et al.*, 1994). A comparison of actual age-specific fertility rates for Canada in 1991 and those obtained from the Pearson Type III curve is shown in Figure 21.3.

As described in Figure 21.4, three assumptions are developed for the first parameter (TFR). Three assumptions are also developed for the mean age of fertility, and one assumption is developed for the variance and skewness of the age-specific fertility rates. Given their small impact, values for the latter two parameters are assumed to be constant over the projection period at the level of the 3-year average for 1995, 1996, and 1997.

In generating the age-specific fertility rates using the parametric model, the low fertility assumption is combined with a high value for mean age of fertility, which is assumed to increase from 28.5 in 1997 to 31.0 by 2026; and the high fertility assumption is combined with a low value for mean age of fertility, which is assumed to increase from 28.5 in 1997 to 29.0 by 2026. For the medium fertility assumption, the mean age of fertility is assumed to increase from 28.5 in 1997 to 30.0 by 2026.

Table 21.3 shows the derivation of projected births for 2000–2001. Births at each age are calculated by multiplying the female population of each childbearing age (15 to 44) by the corresponding fertility rates. Total births are derived by summing the values for each age so obtained. Because the projected population refers to July 1, an adjustment is required to convert calendar year births to "census year" births (i.e., July 1 of year t to June 30 of year $t + 1$). This adjustment is done by adding half of the births of year

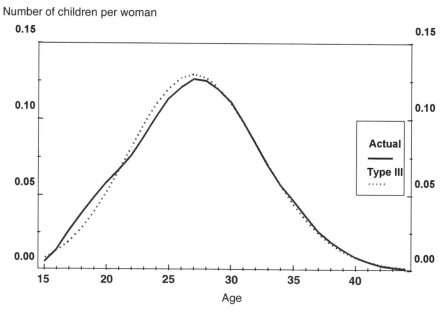

FIGURE 21.3 Comparison of actual and Pearson type III distributions of age-specific fertility rates, Canada, 1991.
Source: Statistics Canada (2001)

TABLE 21.4 A Cohort-Component Example for Population Projections of the Female Population of Canada, 2000–2001 (medium projections)

Age	Pop. at t (2000): "Launch Year" (1)	Immigrants (2)	Emigrants (3)	Net International Migration (4) = (2) − (3)	Non-Permanent Residents (NPR) (5)	Pop. adjusted for migration (6) = (1) + (4) − (5)	Sx (Survival ratio) (7)	Survivors at t + 1 (8) = (6) × (7)	Pop. at t + 1 (2001): First year of Projection (9) = (8) + (5)
−1	156,690	0	0	0	0	156,690	0.995536	155,990	156,056
0	158,410	1,947	169	1,778	66	160,122	0.999294	160,009	160,239
1	167,170	1,513	206	1,307	230	168,247	0.999673	168,192	168,563
2	170,843	1,476	245	1,231	371	171,703	0.999767	171,663	172,066
3	176,343	1,500	290	1,210	403	177,150	0.999814		
⋮									
14	199,459	1,593	437	1,156	1,145	199,470	0.999769	199,424	200,724
15	200,341	1,588	406	1,182	1,300	200,223	0.999740	200,171	202,049
16	200,917	1,520	378	1,142	1,878	200,181	0.999710	200,123	202,680
17	200,783	1,496	332	1,164	2,557	199,390	0.999684	199,327	202,436
18	201,164	1,715	266	1,449	3,109	199,504	0.999659		
⋮									
49	217,997	686	378	308	464	217,841	0.997645	217,328	217,709
50	213,697	634	334	300	381	213,616	0.997411	213,063	213,448
51	210,634	568	301	267	385	210,516	0.997150	209,916	210,215
52	210,510	514	270	244	299	210,455	0.996873	209,797	210,071
53	210,399	513	234	279	274	210,404	0.996545		
⋮									
95	7,165	1	0	1	2	7,164	0.826354	5,920	5,921
96	5,535	2	0	2	1	5,536	0.810513	4,487	4,487
97	3,871	1	0	1	0	3,872	0.793388	3,072	3,072
98	2,655	0	0	0	0	2,655	0.774765	2,057	2,057
99	1,832	1	0	1	0	1,832	0.697146		
100+	3,317	0	0	0	0	3,317	0.620460	3,335	3,335
Total	15,522,683	110,128	32,679	77,449	98,890	15,501,242		15,553,417	15,652,307.2

Note: The female population aged 0 at time t + 1 is obtained by first applying the proportion of female births (0.4862) to the total births (322,274), then applying the female survival ratio from birth to age 0.

Component	No. of Assumptions	Assumptions		
1. Fertility	3 TFR by 2026	High 1.80	Medium 1.48	Low 1.30
2. Mortality	3 M/F e₀ by 2026	High 81.5/85.0	Medium 80.0/84.0	Low 78.5/83.0
3. Immigration	3 levels by 2026	High 270,000	Medium 225,000	Low 180,000
4. Total emigration	1	2-year average of age-sex specific emigration rates (1997–1998 and 1998–1999)		
5. Nonpermanent residents	1	Constant number at 240,000		

FIGURE 21.4   Assumptions for national population projections, Canada.
Source: Statistics Canada (2001)

t and half those of year $t + 1$ (see Table 21.3). The adjusted births between July 1 and June 30, 2001, are then distributed by sex using a sex ratio at birth of 105.68 boys to 100.00 girls. Total births are multiplied by 0.4862 to obtain female births. Table 21.3 shows these calculations.

Statistics Canada deals with migration at the national level by projecting immigrants and emigrants as separate components. Net immigration accounted for 76% of the total population growth in Canada in 1999–2000. The impact of this component on growth is expected to increase substantially in the coming years, even if the current below-replacement fertility level remains constant.

Two approaches have been used for projecting immigration by Statistics Canada in the past. In the first, migration assumptions were formulated on the basis of the analysis of past trends, focusing on recent periods. The second approach was based on annual immigration government planning levels. The method chosen in the projection example presented here is a combination of these two approaches (George and Perreault, 1992). Given the increasing importance of this component and the wide fluctuations in immigration (e. g., 84,000 to 250,000 immigrants per year between 1985 and 1993), three assumptions (high, medium, and low) were formulated (see Figure 21.4). The age-sex composition of the projected numbers of immigrants was derived using an assumed age-sex distribution based on the average of "stock" (census) and "flow" (immigration) data (Verma and George, 1993).

Statistics Canada decomposes emigration into three elements: emigrants, net variation in persons temporarily abroad, and returning emigrants. The total numbers of emigrants are thus obtained by subtracting returning emigrants from the sum of emigrants and the net variation in persons temporarily abroad. Total emigration is projected by applying age-sex specific emigration rates to the projected population for each year. The required emigration rates were developed by calculating annual age-sex specific rates for

the years 1997–1998 and 1998–1999 and averaging them. In the single emigration assumption, these rates are kept constant from 2000 onward, as shown in Figure 21.4.

The nonpermanent resident population (NPR) is a group that forms part of the initial population in year t. It consists of the following persons and their dependants: (1) student authorization holders, (2) employment authorization holders, (3) ministers' permit holders, and (4) refugee status claimants. The size of the NPR population is expected to remain fairly stable. It is subject to natural increase but not to migration. Hence, the effect of NPRs in year t only on fertility and mortality (natural increase) is taken into account for projection purposes without actually "projecting" them to year $t + 1$. The following steps allow for this component. First, before the $t + 1$ year's projected population is produced, the number of NPRs disaggregated by age and sex is subtracted from equivalent age and sex groups in the total population (col. 1 of Table 21.4) in year t. Second, births and deaths of NPRs are then calculated separately for each year and are included in the totals for these components. Third, the stock of NPRs separated from the launch year population in year t is then added to the surviving permanent population in year $t + 1$. The process is continued for each year until the end of the projection period. A single assumption in terms of absolute numbers is developed for this component, as is shown in Figure 21.4. The projected NPR numbers are disaggregated by age and sex using an assumed distribution.

Table 21.4 presents the various steps involved in projecting the female population of Canada from 2000 to 2001 by the cohort-component method. As stated earlier, it includes refinements that distinguish it from the illustrative procedure shown for the cohort-component method in Figure 21.2. As an example of these refinements, births are calculated from "centered" birth rates, as shown in Table 21.3. The "under 1 year" population in col. 1 of Table 21.4 is based on female births derived from the calculation of total births, as shown in Table 21.3. The same procedure, as shown in Table 21.4, is used to produce the projected population for males in P_{t+1}. The sum of female and male populations gives the total population for both sexes together in year $t + 1$. The same process is continued for projecting the male, female, and total populations for each year until the end of the projection period (2026).

Example of a Subnational Projection

In the cohort-component method, the main difference between national and subnational projections is the addition of the component of internal migration. Although an assumption that future international migration will be negligible can be justified for many countries, internal migration plays a significant role in almost every country, and at the subnational level it is often the most important and complex component of population change. The example provided here is for the province of Ontario. The basic methodology used is the same as that used at the national level. As stated earlier, provincial projections of mortality, fertility, immigration, and emigration are tied to the national projections of these components.

The provincial assumptions of life expectancy at birth (e_o) are derived from the three national assumptions (Figure 21.4) by applying the 1995-and-1996-average provincial/national e_o ratios. The differences in e_o from one province to another are assumed to continue during the projection period. For example, the female provincial/national e_o ratio for Ontario was 1.00. This ratio was applied to the projected life expectancy value for Canada in 2026 to obtain 84.0, the life expectancy at birth projected for Ontario in 2026. The same approach with provincial/national ratios is used for other components to derive the corresponding provincial values from the values at the national level. The rest of the calculations involved in deriving the survival ratios shown in Table 21.5 are the same as for mortality projections at the national level.

The assumptions of fertility for Ontario are derived from the national assumptions as shown in Figure 21.4. In using the ratio method (as illustrated for mortality), average provincial/national ratios were calculated for the three most recent years and consideration was given to the extent to which Ontario (and each of the other regions) was "catching up" with the national fertility level. The calculation of fertility rates and births is made using the parametric approach described for Canada as a whole and as illustrated in Table 21.3.

With respect to immigration for provinces, the three assumed numbers at the national level were first distributed by province on the basis of the average distribution of immigrants for each province for the most recent years (1997–1999). The provincial totals were then distributed by age and sex on the basis of an assumed age-sex distribution.

Emigration was projected by applying age-specific emigration rates to the projected population at risk for each province. The provincial emigration rates were derived from the single assumption of emigration at the national level. With regard to the nonpermanent residents (NPR), the assumed number at the national level was distributed by province according to an average province/Canada ratio based on the distribution for the most recent years (see col. 6 of Table 21.5).

The projections of internal migration for provinces are based on a multiregional migration model (as illustrated in Table 21.5). The application of this model at the provincial level requires detailed migration data as follows: (1) origin-destination-specific migration streams disaggregated by age and sex for each province at 1-year migration intervals for a substantial time reaved and (2) the corresponding base population to compute outmigration rates. Statistics Canada produces estimates of interprovincial migration using administrative data files from three sources: Revenue Canada income tax files, Family Allowance files before 1993, and Child Tax Benefit Program files (which replaced Family Allowance files) since 1993 (Statistics Canada, 2002). The migration estimates are available (with age and sex detail) on an annual basis for each year since 1966–1967.

The application of a multiregional migration model requires projected age-sex specific outmigration rates and origin-destination proportions. The method has four basic steps. First, projected crude outmigration rates and origin-destination proportions are developed according to a selected migration scenario. Second, corresponding age-sex specific rates are derived from the extrapolated crude outmigration rates using the Rogers-Castro parametric model (Rogers and Castro, 1978; Bélanger, 1992). Third, these age-specific outmigration rates are applied to the corresponding provincial population to yield outmigrants by age and sex. Fourth, these outmigrants are distributed as inmigrants to other provincial destinations using the projected origin-destination proportions. (In this last step, it is assumed that the destination proportions do not vary by age or sex.) The assumed rates and proportions are then assessed in terms of the reasonableness and acceptability of the resulting levels of net migration, taking account of local expertise and expert judgment.

The notation and the various steps in the calculation of migrants (outmigrants, inmigrants and net migration) using the multiregional model are as follows (for details, see Verma and George, 2002):

Notation

M_1 = Total interregional migrants (using age-specific rates); OM = outmigrants;

MD = migrants for a specific origin-destination combination; IM = inmigrants; and NM = net migration;

x = age; s = sex; r = region; o = origin; d = destination; and t = year.

TABLE 21.5 A Cohort-Component Example for Population Projections of the Female Population
of Ontario, 2000–2001 (medium projections)

Age	Pop. at t (2000): "Launch Year" (1)	Immigrants (2)	Emigrants (3)	Net International Migration (4) = (2) − (3)	Net Internal Migration (5)	Non-Permanent Residents (NPR) (6)	Pop. adjusted for migration (7) = (1) + (4) + (5) − (6)	Sx (Survival ratio) (8)	Survivors at t + 1 (9) = (7) × (8)	Pop. at t + 1 (2001): First year of Projection (10) = (9) + (6)
−1	61,330	0	0	0	0	0	61,330	0.99567		
0	61,525	886	88	798	219	31	62,511	0.99935	61,065	61,096
1	65,168	798	107	691	202	121	65,940	0.99972	62,470	62,591
2	66,361	804	127	677	185	184	67,039	0.99980	65,922	66,106
3	68,452	813	150	663	169	209	69,075	0.99984	67,026	67,235
⋮										
14	75,848	844	220	624	123	571	76,024	0.99980	76,009	76,581
15	75,750	857	204	653	159	572	75,990	0.99978	75,973	76,727
16	74,834	827	188	639	207	754	74,926	0.99976	74,908	75,961
17	74,561	820	166	654	249	1,053	74,411	0.99974	74,392	75,639
18	73,734	929	134	795	296	1,247	73,578	0.99973		
⋮										
49	80,975	343	188	155	82	232	80,980	0.99775	80,798	80,972
50	79,518	342	167	175	76	174	79,595	0.99752	79,398	79,592
51	78,365	308	150	158	74	194	78,403	0.99726	78,188	78,327
52	79,434	269	137	132	67	139	79,494	0.99698	79,254	79,395
53	80,595	275	121	154	62	141	80,670	0.99666		
⋮										
95	2,660	1	0	1	1	2	2,660	0.81887	2,178	2,179
96	2,054	1	0	1	1	1	2,055	0.80265	1,649	1,649
97	1,435	0	0	0	0	0	1,435	0.78516	1,127	1,127
98	984	0	0	0	0	0	984	0.76634	754	754
99	679	0	0	0	1	0	680	0.74612	1,327	1,327
100+	1,235	0	0	0	0	0	1,236	0.66318		
Total	5,912,532	59,240	16,717	42,523	9,941	42,071	5,922,925		5,944,513	5,986,584

Note: The female population aged 0 at time t + 1 is obtained by first applying the proportion of female births (0.4862) to the total births (126,142), then applying the female survival ratio from birth to age 0.

Multiply age-sex outmigration rates by the corresponding population (P) to obtain outmigrants by age, sex, region:

$$OM_{x,s,r,t,t+1} = M_{x,s,r,t,t+1} * P_{x,s,r,t}. \qquad (21.20)$$

Sum to obtain total outmigrants by region (M_1):

$$M_{1\ r,t,t+1} = \text{sum } OM_{x,s,r,t,t+1} \text{ over } a \text{ and } s. \qquad (21.21)$$

Distribute outmigrants by destination using origin-destination (OD) proportions:

$$MD_{x,s,o,d,t,t+1} = OM_{x,s,r,t,t+1} * OD_{o,d,t,t+1}. \qquad (21.22)$$

For each destination, aggregate by origin to obtain inmigrants by age and sex:

$$IM_{x,s,d,t,t+1} = \text{sum } MD_{x,s,o,d,t,t+1} \text{ over } x,s,o. \qquad (21.23)$$

Subtract outmigrants from inmigrants to get net migration:

$$NM_{x,s,r,t,t+1} = IM_{x,s,r,t,t+1} - OM_{x,s,r,t,t+1} \qquad (21.24)$$

Three scenarios (assumptions) are developed to provide a range of net migration for each province: "West," "Central," and "Medium." The "West" scenario is based on the migrant data for the years 1992–1993; the "Central" scenario is based on the migrant data for the years 1984–1987; and the "Medium" scenario is the average of the "West" and "Central" scenarios. The West scenario is considered relatively favorable for a certain group of provinces, while the Central scenario is relatively favorable for the remaining provinces. The net-migration figures for Ontario presented in column 5 of Table 21.5 are taken from the Medium scenario.

The multiregional model described here is a sophisticated (and complex) method for projecting internal migration by age and sex (for further details, see Statistics Canada, 2001). Apart from the complexity of the method in terms of the data required and the projection process involved, the most cumbersome step is to obtain projected net-migration figures consistent with provincial inputs based on local knowledge or expert judement. One way to simplify the process may be to automate the implementation of the net-migration targets. This could hasten the crucial adjustment process required to improve the quality and acceptability of projection results.

Table 21.5 illustrates the various operations involved in projecting the female population of Ontario according to the "medium" assumption for 1 year, 2000–2001. The steps followed are the same as shown in Table 21.4, the only difference being the additional column of net internal migration (col. 5). The same process is continued for each year to 2026.

Summary Comments on the Cohort-Component Method

The cohort-component method is widely used, relatively easy to explain, and practical. It permits the use of already available data and existing theoretical knowledge on the dynamics of population growth, and it takes into account causal factors, at least at the level of basic components and compositional factors. It has the capability to produce consistent and comparable national and subnational projections that are easy to update on a regular basis. Much of the work required to use this method lies in the in-depth analysis and development of assumptions for each of the components of change. The cohort-component method also has its shortcomings and limitations. One is that it does not explicitly incorporate socioeconomic determinants of population change. For dealing with this issue, we now turn to a discussion of structural modeling.

STRUCTURAL MODELS

Demographers and others often face questions that cannot be answered using projection methods solely involving demographic factors—the demographic consequences of the closing of a large manufacturing plant, for example. Structural models come into play here because population projections developed by this method can account for factors such as the economy, environment, land use, housing, and the transportation system. We describe two general categories of structural models: economic-demographic models and urban systems models. Economic-demographic models are typically used to project population and economic activities for larger geographic areas such as counties, labor market areas, states, and nations. Urban systems models focus on small geographic areas such as census tracts and blocks and typically include projections of population, economic activities, land use, and transportation patterns. In addition to their differences in geographic scale, these two types of models often provide alternative explanations of the causes and consequences of population change. Some structural models contain only a few equations and variables (Mills and Lubuele, 1995), while others contain huge systems of simultaneous equations with many variables and parameters (Data Resources Incorporated, 1998; Waddell, 2000). Our objective is to provide a general introduction and overview of the use of structural models for population projection. We do not provide details for building or implementing these kinds of models; such details can be found in Putman (1991), San Diego Association of Governments (1998, 1999), and Treyz (1993).

Economic-Demographic Models

Economic-demographic models sometimes focus on the total population, but most often they deal with one or more of the components of population change. Only a few applications have dealt with fertility and mortality; typically, these applications have focused on the entire area of nations or regions where fertility and mortality are the most important contributors to population growth (Ahlburg, 1999). Fertility and mortality models have also been proposed for subnational areas, but have rarely been implemented (Isserman, 1985). For population projections, internal migration has been the predominant concern of economic-demographic models; consequently, we confine our discussion to models for migration and total population of subnational areas.

Virtually all economic-demographic models of migration are based on a premise, set forth more than a century ago, that people move principally "to 'better' themselves in material respects" (Ravenstein, 1889, p. 286). Economic factors such as job change, unemployment, and wages or income are therefore used to project migration or population. The empirical evidence clearly shows that the strongest links are found with job change rather than other economic factors (Isserman et al., 1985). The fact that jobs attract people and people create jobs underlies most economic-demographic models in use today. Migration and population change are also influenced by noneconomic factors such as climate, coastal location, life-cycle changes, personal characteristics, and social networks (Astone and McLanahan, 1994; DaVanzo and Morrison, 1978; Fuguitt and Brown, 1990; Massey et al., 1987). A complete migration model including both economic and noneconomic factors, however, is problematic for projecting migration or population because the independent variables themselves must be projected. Projections of these noneconomic variables are rarely available, while projections of economic variables can be obtained from national, state, or county-level economic models.

We describe three general approaches for designing and implementing economic-demographic models: (1) econometric models, which use regression methods to project migration as a statistical function of the economy; (2) balancing models, which project migration as the difference between the projected supply and demand for labor; and (3) ratio-based models, which typically derive population projections directly from employment projections.

Econometric Models

The econometric approach uses equations that determine migration from one or more economic variables. Parameters for these equations are estimated from historical data using regression techniques. Projections are then made by solving the equation(s) using the projected values of the independent variable(s). The migration equation(s) are typically integrated into a large economic model that also provides projections of the economic factors.

The most widely used econometric models of migration are "recursive," whereby migration is influenced by the economy but does not itself influence the economy. Recursive models cannot reflect the full range of interactions between migration and the economy, but nonetheless they have proven successful for projecting migration (Clark and Hunter, 1992; Greenwood, 1975; Greenwood and Hunt, 1991; San Diego Association of Governments, 1999; Tabuchi, 1985). Recursive relationships have also been implemented in multiregional migration models (Campbell, 1996; Foot and Milne, 1989; Isserman et al., 1985; Rogers and Williams, 1986). Nonrecursive models attempt to capture the joint impacts of migration and the economy on each other. Although they are more complicated and require larger resources than recursive models, "nonrecursive" models for projecting migration have been occasionally employed (Conway, 1990; Mills and Lubuele, 1995; Treyz et al., 1993).

Equilibrium Model

The concept behind the equilibrium model is simple. If labor supply exceeds labor demand, workers migrate out of the area; if labor demand exceeds labor supply, workers migrate into the area. Equilibrium models are typically less costly to implement and easier to use than econometric models because they do not require large-scale systems of equations, huge amounts of data, or the use of formal statistical procedures. However, they do require numerous computations and assumptions (see Murdock and Ellis, 1991, for an example). Labor demand is often represented by a measure of job opportunities typically projected using export-base models, input-output models, and extrapolation techniques (Greenberg et al., 1978; Murdock et al., 1984). Labor supply is determined by applying labor force participation ratios to a projected population derived from a cohort-component model that assumes zero net migration. The migration of workers is determined by the difference between projected labor supply and projected labor demand. As a final step, the migration of workers is converted into a projection of all economic migrants, including other family members, through assumptions related to characteristics such as marital status and family size.

Population/Employment Ratio

The population/ employment (P/E) model projects total population directly; it does not consider any single component of change. Despite some drawbacks, the P/E model is the easiest and least expensive way to incorporate economic factors into a population projection. The simplest P/E model uses a single ratio representing the relation of total population to total employment, holds the ratio constant at its current value, and applies the ratio to a projection of employment. This approach is no longer used very often because P/E ratios are known to change over time and vary according to demographic subgroup (Murdock and Ellis, 1991).

For many years, the "OBERS" model, developed by the U.S. Bureau of Economic Analysis (BEA) in the mid-1960s, was arguably the most widely used P/E model. Population, employment, and earnings projections for states and metropolitan areas were developed from this model until the mid-1990s (U.S. Bureau of Economic Analysis, 1995), when budget cutbacks forced the BEA to stop preparing projections. The approach taken in OBERS divides the population into three age groups: pre–labor pool (less than 18), labor pool (18 to 64), and post–labor pool (65+). Projections of the labor pool population are directly related to changes in employment and the pre–labor pool population projections are tied directly to the projections of the labor pool population. Post–labor pool projections are independent of economic changes. A numerical example of the OBERS approach is found in Smith *et al.* (2001).

Urban Systems Models

Urban systems models are used throughout the world to project the distribution of residential and nonresidential activities within urban or metropolitan areas. They differ in several important ways from economic-demographic models. First, they are designed to be used for much smaller geographic areas. Second, they use different independent variables. Along with economic factors such as jobs and income, urban systems models include land use characteristics (e.g., zoning, environmental constraints, land value, and land supply) and characteristics of the transportation system (e.g., travel times, cost, and distances). Third, they use geographic information system (GIS) technology, which plays an important, perhaps an essential, role in urban systems models (for a general discussion of GIS, see Appendix D). Fourth, urban systems models require considerably more information, time, and resources to implement than economic-demographic models. Finally, urban systems models address many issues (e.g., air quality, traffic congestion, loss of open space, and public transportation) that cannot be considered in most economic-demographic models.

Urban systems models vary considerably in their theoretical approaches, mathematical design, data requirements, and ease of implementation, but they typically consist of three major components—regional projections, land use and activity, and transportation (see Figure 21.5). They are usually applied using 5-year time intervals. Population and economic projections are required for the region covered by the model (e.g., metropolitan or labor market area). These regional projections are often produced using the economic-demographic models previously discussed. The land use and activity component consists of a complex set of procedures for distributing the regional projections into zones within the region. Applications typically involve between 150 and 300 zones. These zones often comprise one or more census tracts, but land use and activity models have been developed for smaller geographic areas such as census blocks, grid cells, and assessors' parcels (San Diego Association of Governments, 1998; and Waddell, 2000). The transportation component projects characteristics of the transportation system such as traffic volumes and speeds on roadways and on public transportation lines.

A fundamental characteristic of urban systems models is the iterative and explicit relationships between land use characteristics, activity location, and the transportation system as shown in Figure 21.5. The distribution of population in virtually all such models relies on the link between

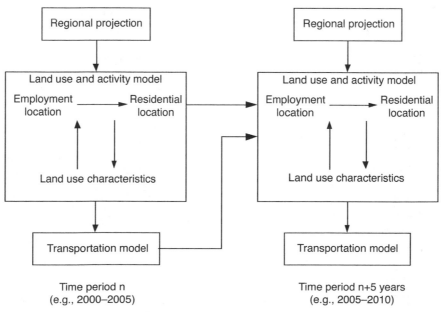

FIGURE 21.5 Components of an urban systems model.
Source: Smith *et al.* (2001, p. 219).

home (residential location) and workplace (employment location). These links are represented by travel probabilities between zones based on time, distance, or cost and commuting patterns (Putman, 1991). Residential location influences the spatial distribution of employment, particularly employment that serves a local population such as retail trade and services. As Figure 21.5 indicates, this relationship is implemented by assuming a lag between residential location and location of employment.

The transportation system both influences and is determined by land use and land use characteristics play an important role in determining the location of population and other activities. Urban system models contain procedures to reconcile the demand for land with its available supply (San Diego Association of Governments, 1998; and Waddell, 2000).

Comments on Structural Models

Structural models—especially urban systems models—require more resources and are more difficult to implement than the other models discussed in this chapter. They often require extensive base data, sophisticated modeling skills, and complex statistical procedures and computer programs. Therefore, they are accessible only to a relatively narrow range of practitioners, although the Transportation, Economic, and Land Use System (TELUS) may help reduce the barriers to implementing this system (Pignataro and Epling, 2000). In addition, there is no evidence to suggest that structural models provide more accurate population forecasts than other methods and, given their small geographic scale, their forecast accuracy is not likely to be high in many applications. Yet structural models are used more frequently today than ever before because of their ability to investigate and analyze a wide range of theoretical, planning, and policy questions (Boyce, 1988; Tayman, 1996b; Treyz, 1995). Decision making and planning often require the analysis of many interrelated factors for different geographic areas. For example, planners and policy makers may be required to meet the challenges posed by increasing traffic congestion, housing shortages, and deteriorating infrastructure. Structural models can make important contributions to the planning and decision-making process; they can, for example, provide warnings when proposed actions might lead to unintended or undesirable consequences (Schmidt, Barr, and Swanson, 1997; Tayman, 1996b). In some circumstances, preparing simulations and scenarios is more valuable than any specific projection or forecast.

RELATED PROJECTIONS

Projections of households, school enrollment, poverty, employment, health, and other population-related characteristics are needed for many types of planning, budgeting, and

analysis. For simplicity, we refer to these as *socioeconomic* projections. Because of the demand for socioeconomic projections and their close link to projections of basic demographic characteristics, it is not surprising that the former are often made on the basis of the latter and that public and private-sector organizations around the world are involved in the production of socioeconomic projections (CACI Inc., 2000; Fullerton, 1999; Kintner *et al.*, 1994; Siegel, 2002, pp. 508–510; Tayman, 1996b).

Much of the previous discussion of population projections can be applied to socioeconomic projections as well— terminology, data sources, methods, and evaluation criteria. The projection of socioeconomic characteristics, however, has two important features that distinguish it from strictly demographic projections.

The first is that some socioeconomic characteristics are directly affected by policy decisions (Opitz and Nelson, 1996). For example, projections of university enrollment are affected by changes in university entrance requirements, projections of prison populations are affected by changes in sentencing guidelines, and projections of housing demand are affected by changes in eligibility requirements for home mortgages. In some instances, then, knowledge regarding the details of public policy is essential to the production of projections of socioeconomic characteristics.

The second is that projections of socioeconomic characteristics involve *achieved* characteristics—those that can change over one's lifetime, such as marital status, income, educational attainment, occupation. As a result, projections of socioeconomic characteristics involve a variety of assumptions in addition to those for projections of strictly demographic characteristics. At high levels of aggregation, achieved characteristics are often related to ascribed characteristics (those that are set at birth, such as age and sex) in clearly identified patterns. For example, school enrollment is closely linked to the age structure of the population. These patterns form a basis for projecting socioeconomic characteristics.

Two fundamental approaches are frequently used to prepare such projections. The first approach is the "participation ratio method" (also known as the "participation rate method," "prevalence ratio method," and "incidence rate method"). In this approach, socioeconomic characteristics are related to demographic characteristics through the use of ratios (Siegel, 2002, pp. 509–511; Swanson and Klopfenstein, 1987; United Nations, 1999). Once such ratios are established, they can be projected in a number of ways, such as holding them constant at recent levels, extrapolating recent trends, tying them to ratios found in other areas, or developing structural models that forecast changes in them. The second approach is the cohort-progression method. In this approach, projections are developed by "surviving" people with particular socioeconomic characteristics. The Hamilton-Perry Method discussed earlier in this chapter is an example of this approach. Because these two approaches are used so frequently for projections of socioeconomic characteristics, we discuss them in some detail.

It should be noted that virtually all socioeconomic projections can be handled using structural models. In particular, many structural models are designed to deal with economic activity, including employment according to industry and occupation, income, and other variables (Data Resources Incorporated, 1998; Treyz, 1993, 1995). In the case of the "REMI" model, detailed user manuals show how one can "call" for particular projection outputs such as the total employed according to age and sex. It is worth noting that many structural models such as "REMI" explicitly accommodate user judgment in the development of the projections (Treyz, 1995).

Participation-Ratio Method

In this approach, current and historical data are used to construct participation ratios—that is, proportions of the population (stratified by age, sex, and perhaps other demographic characteristics) that have the socioeconomic characteristic of interest. These ratios are projected into the future using one or more of the techniques described previously. The projected ratios are then applied to population projections (stratified by age, sex, and other characteristics) for the geographic area(s) under consideration to obtain a set of socioeconomic projections. The population projection must have sufficient demographic detail to match up conceptually and empirically with the denominator originally used to construct the participation ratio of interest.

The steps used in this approach can be summarized as follows:

1. Launch year participation ratio = P^c_{dt}/P_{dt}
2. Projected participation ratio = (P^c_{dt+i}/P_{dt+i})
3. Independently projected population = P_{dt+i}
4. Projected population with the characteristic = $P^c_{dt+i} = (P^c_{dt+i}/P_{dt+i}) * (P_{dt+i})$

where

P = population
c = socioeconomic characteristic (e.g., number employed)
d = demographic data (e.g., age-sex)
t = launch date
$t + i$ = target date

As an example of this method, we show part of the results from a projection of "days of hospital care," prepared in the late 1980s by Kintner and Swanson (1994, p. 285), of male retirees of the General Motors Corporation. The projected number of male retirees aged 75 to 79 for 1990 was 5719 (using the cohort-component approach). Multiplying this number by 4263.7 "days of care" per 1000 males in this age group (a value taken from the 1987 National Hospital Discharge Survey), Kintner and Swanson obtained a projected value of 24,384 days of care for this group (24,384 ≈ 5719 * 4.2637).

Cohort-Progression Method

In this approach, the numbers with the socioeconomic characteristic or the corresponding participation ratios are projected on a cohort basis using information on changes in the numbers or participation ratios between two previous dates. The conventional form of this method uses ratios of the number of persons aged a with a particular socioeconomic characteristic in year t to the number of persons aged $a - y$ with that characteristic in year $t - y$. The initial projections are made by applying these ratios to the number of persons with the characteristic of interest in the launch year. This method can be represented as follows:

1. Initial cohort progression ratio = $P^c_{a,t}/P^c_{a-y,t-y}$
2. Projected cohort = $P^c_{a+y,t+y} = (P^c_{a,t}/P^c_{a-y,t-y}) * (P^c_{a-y,t})$

where the symbols generally have the same meaning that they had earlier, except that a has replaced d and y has replaced i.

The cohort progression method is applied recursively, as is done in any survivorship exercise. It is important to remember that cohort, progression ratios represent net cohort change rather than gross change. This distinction is important because fundamental patterns may be masked without knowing the numbers "entering and exiting" a population (Fullerton, 1999). The cohort-progression method in the form of participation ratios is used less often than the version of the method that employs absolute numbers. As an example of this method, consider a projection for 2003 of the number of persons aged 14 who are expected to be enrolled in school in Fredonia. In 2001, 40,437 of the children aged 13 were enrolled, and 41,073 of this same cohort (now 14 years of age) were enrolled in 2002. The ratio of 2002 to 2001 is 1.01573 = 41,073/40,437. Multiplying this ratio by the number of 13-year-olds enrolled in school in 2002 (40,200) yields a projection for 2003 of 40,832 children aged 14 who are expected to be enrolled (40,832 ≈ 1.01573 * 40,200).

Projecting Households and Families

Projections of households and families are required for many uses, particularly those that depend on information regarding future numbers of consumer units. For many goods and services, households and families are more effective units of demand than the individual because they are the basic units into which people are organized for purposes of consumption. In addition to demographic factors, the number of households depends on the supply and cost of housing, family income, and cultural norms regarding, among other things, the number of generations living together. Thus, procedures for projecting the number of households and families may vary according to whether they represent (1) extensions of past trends or (2) embodiments of various norms relating to the size and composition of households and assumptions regarding the supply and cost of housing, family income, and other such factors. Short of developing a structural model, assessment of potential changes in nondemographic factors over time will be important in choosing the assumptions for future participation ratios or cohort-progression ratios.

Participation-Ratio Method

A refined participation ratio would take into account demographic characteristics associated with household "headship." The general procedure consists of applying to the population, projected by age and sex, various estimating ratios that are related to marital, household, and family status, such as the proportion of the population in each marital category and the proportion of each age denominated as "household heads" ("headship ratios"). This method is often referred to as the "headship rate" method. In it, the total number of households is derived by summing the number of heads obtained by age and sex.

In a still more elaborate form of the participation ratio method, data on marital status, by age and sex, and data on various categories of family and household status, by age and sex of head, are combined, and the pertinent age-specific proportions and ratios are projected or held constant, as seems appropriate, to provide projections of married couples and of households and families by type. Depending on the data available and the procedure employed, one could obtain, for example, the number of households by age and sex of head; the number of households headed by families, by type of family (e.g., husband-wife, male head, female head); the number of households headed by individuals, by sex; the number of (secondary) families who live with other (primary) families in the same household; or the number of married couples and nuclear families, by whether they are living in their own households or in the households of others. In sum a very useful way to project households is to combine the projections of participation ratios with the results of a fully elaborated cohort-component population-projection model. This takes into account both changes in headship ratios and population composition.

Because of its operational simplicity, both in terms of the input required and the design of the model, and perhaps its reasonably good performance, the "headship ratio" approach has been adopted by the United Nations and several countries since it was first used in the United States as early as 1938 (United Nations, 1973, p. 31). It can take into account the latest population projections as its base, specifically, the projected adult population disaggregated by age and sex.

Cohort-Progression Method

We have already alluded to the use of the cohort approach in projecting the percentages in each socioeconomic category (e.g., marital status) when making projections of numbers in each category. The cohort approach may be extended to include the projection of the percentages of heads when data on heads of households by age are available for a series of dates. This general procedure is directly applicable to series like percentage married or percentage heads, which are essentially cumulative by age.

Projecting School Enrollment

Projections of the number of children who will be enrolled in school are needed to formulate educational policies and plan educational programs and, specifically, to plan for needed schools, classrooms, and teachers. Because almost all children in the compulsory-attendance ages for elementary school attend school, projections of the total population of elementary school age, in relation to the number expected to attend, are also useful in determining needs. In addition, projections of school enrollment ratios can be used in preparing projections of labor force participation ratios because the two sets of ratios are inversely related, especially at certain ages.

Projections of the educational attainment of a population are also needed for national planning. The present and prospective educational attainment of a population influences its development. Social and economic relationships in a population change in many ways as its educational level changes.

As was the case with the earlier discussion on household projections, this discussion covers the two principal methods, the participation-ratio method and the cohort-progression method. A simple component method can also be employed (i.e., allowing for new entrants, dropouts, deaths) but is not usually practical.

Participation-Ratio Method

One way to project enrollment is to develop age-specific enrollment ratios (i.e., proportions of the population enrolled in school at each age) in combination with the projected population by age (Swanson et al., 1998). The assumption relating to future age-specific enrollment ratios may be quite simple. One may assume, for example, that current age-specific enrollment ratios will continue into the future. One could also use one of the extrapolation techniques to project age-specific enrollment ratios. Past trends in the ratios may be assumed to continue as observed or to continue in a modified fashion. In those instances where the enrollment ratios approach 100% and extrapolation using a growth rate could cause these enrollment ratios to exceed 100, the complements of the enrollment ratios may be projected instead. Legal requirements and practices with respect to the ages or grades of school attendance have ordinarily been incorporated into projections of school-age population and school enrollment. The possibility of developing projections of enrollment that incorporate new norms representing more inclusive age and grade spans, and even hypothetical enrollment ratios for the base year, needs to be considered if provision is to be made in the future for upgrading the current level of school services.

When projections of school enrollment are made by the participation-ratio method, they rarely contain detail on grade or school level. To obtain such figures, one procedure is to prepare projections by age first, and then to distribute the projected total enrollment at each age by grade or school level on the basis of recent census, survey, or administrative data (holding the distribution constant or extrapolating it). Alternatively, projections of enrollment for broad school levels at each age may be calculated by the use of age-level enrollment ratios (i.e., in relation to total population at each age) and total enrollment at each age may then be derived by summation.

Cohort-Progression Method

This method is particularly useful for providing separate information on entries into and withdrawals from school by age. Here, one begins with a distribution of persons enrolled by age and carries this population forward by use of age-specific rates of net school accession and net school withdrawal. A set of net accession rates and net withdrawal rates may be derived by taking the relative difference between enrollment ratios at successive ages given in a census. A net accession rate is obtained for the ages where enrollment ratios are increasing, and a net withdrawal rate is obtained where enrollment ratios are decreasing. Rates of net accession are applied to the population not enrolled to derive new enrollees, who are added to the enrolled population, and rates of net withdrawal are applied to the enrolled population to derive dropouts and deaths, who are removed from the enrolled population.

The cohort-progression method may also be used to develop enrollment projections for grades. In this procedure, the number of enrolled persons classified by grade is carried forward to each subsequent calendar year by use of projected grade-retention rates or grade-progression rates, representing the proportion of children in a given grade who will advance to the next grade in the course of a year. A historical series of grade-retention rates may be developed on the basis of survey data or data from the administrative records of the school system and then projected forward on an annual basis.

As with age-specific enrollment ratios, in projecting grade-retention rates, the regular methods of extrapolation can be used, but if the rates are very high (i.e., near 100%) and the trend is one of rapid increase, conventional methods can produce values in excess of 100%. In this case, an asymptotic equation that prevents getting a projected value of 100% or more can be used, or the complements of the grade retention rates (i.e., grade-dropout rates) can be extrapolated on a geometric basis.

Projecting the Labor Force

Labor force projections are needed to indicate the number of jobs that the economy must make available and as a point of departure in making projections both of the economy as a whole (Fullerton, 1999) and of regional economies (Treyz, 1993, 1995). Labor force projections must be matched by projections of human resource requirements for effective national economic planning, however (Thompson, 1999). It is worth noting that some labor force projections have tended to assume that labor force participation ratios are independent of the general state of the economy, although, in fact, the number of persons seeking work does depend on the demand for labor, the availability of jobs, and the need for a job within the family (Rosenthal, 1999).

Participation Ratio Method

A simple age-specific ratio method may be employed: proportions of the population in the labor force by age and sex (i.e., labor force participation ratios or economic activity ratios) are assumed for future dates and applied to projections of the population of working age (e.g., 14 years and over) disaggregated by age and sex. In the simplest form of the method, these participation ratios are held constant at the level observed in the previous census or some recent survey. Such projections take account only of expected shifts in the future size, age, and sex composition of the population. For many ages of males, say from 25 to 54, the best assumption may be to use current participation ratios because nearly all males are in the labor force and likely to remain so. The projections may, however, allow explicitly for expected changes in participation ratios. The difficult problem is to determine how the ratios might change for males at the fringe ages of economic activity, for females, and for race and ethnic groups that historically have lagged in their labor force participation. Accordingly, it is useful to take into account the relationship between worker ratios and various socioeconomic variables affecting labor force participation. Because the variables of marital status and the presence or absence of young children define quite different levels of economic activity for female workers, it is especially useful to consider ratios specific for these variables separately in developing projections for women. Average age at marriage and the number of children previously born may also be taken into account directly or indirectly. Consideration may be given to the availability of public services and facilities, such as day care centers and nurseries, which could affect the participation ratios for women with children.

Cohort-Progression Method

A typical form of the cohort-progression method consists of carrying forward the economically active population by age and sex to future dates by use of probabilities of net entry and probabilities of net withdrawal through death or retirement. The probabilities of net entry are applied to the inactive population to determine accessions for the first year, and the probabilities of net withdrawal, separately for retirement and death if possible, are applied to the active population to determine separations for the year. The estimated new entrants are then subtracted from the inactive population and added to the active population. Similarly, separations due to retirement are subtracted from the active population and added to the inactive population (see, e.g., Kintner and Swanson, 1994). Rates of net entry and of net withdrawal due to retirement may be derived from the relative change in activity rates at consecutive ages as given by census data. In the current data for the United States, until about age 35, these changes are positive and the rates are considered rates of net entry. At the older ages, the changes are negative and the rates are considered rates of net withdrawal. The rates can then be adjusted to exclude the effect of mortality. This variation of the cohort method has the virtue of providing, as valuable by-products, the annual number of net entrants into, and net withdrawals from, the labor force, disaggregated by age. Such information is of specific use in national economic planning, both for the utilization of new workers and for management of retirement and other programs for older ages.

Projecting Health Characteristics

Health and health care issues represent a major budget and planning issue for many organizations (Kintner, 1989; Kintner and Swanson, 1994, 1996; Pol and Thomas, 2001). It has been estimated, for example, that General Motors Corporation spends 30% of its annual budget on health care for its employees and their dependents (Kintner and Swanson, 1996). With huge amounts of resources at stake, it is little wonder that the projection of health characteristics is of wide interest. However, health characteristics are also of interest because of issues beyond budgets and planning. For example, by 2015, it has been projected that the population of 29 African countries will be 8.1% smaller as a result of the impact of HIV/AIDS (United Nations, 1998, p. 31).

Participation-Ratio Method

As described in the beginning of this section, Kintner and Swanson (1994) used this approach in combination with the cohort-component method in projecting hospitalization levels for a retiree cohort. In the first step, hospital utilization ratios according to age and sex were developed from national surveys in the United States. These ratios were kept constant over the projection horizon, but they could have been modified by using one of the trend extrapolation methods described earlier this chapter. Next, the numbers of retirees was found by age and sex using a cohort-component approach. In the final step, the projected numbers in each age-sex group were multiplied by the corresponding hospital utilization ratios, and specific "cohort utilization levels" were found annually by taking a weighted sum of the products, where the weights are the number of surviving retirees in a given age-sex group for a given year.

Cohort-Progression Method

The projection of HIV/AIDS cases by the UN represents a variation on the cohort-progression method (United Nations, 1998). In the first step, models are used to estimate the annual incidence of new infections. Second, estimates of deaths due to AIDS are estimated using assumptions about the progression from HIV infection to AIDS and from AIDS to death. Third, these deaths are added to deaths expected in the absence of AIDS and revised life tables are calculated. Finally, the revised life tables are used in a cohort-component projection.

ADDITIONAL CONSIDERATIONS

The preceding sections of this chapter covered the nuts and bolts of producing population projections. Knowledge of these methods and materials is essential to the projection process but does not resolve all the issues related to constructing and evaluating population projections and using them for planning and analysis. To maximize the usefulness of population and related projections, a number of additional issues must be considered. Among the most important are the following.

Providing necessary detail refers to customizing projections made for a specific use or data user, so as to fit exactly the purposes for which they will be used (e.g., annual projections covering a 10-year horizon of the number of children living in a school district, by single years of age). In many instances, however, projections are made without reference to a particular use or data user. For these "general purpose" projections, it is much more difficult to determine which geographic areas, target years, and characteristics to include.

The needs of the largest number of data users can be met by making projections for a wide variety of geographic areas, characteristics, and target years. Using these building blocks, data users can put together projections that cover the specific areas, characteristics, and time periods they need.

The greater the amount of detail produced, however, the greater the amount of time and resources needed to construct the projections. Consequently, the producers of population and related projections typically provide only a limited amount of detail.

National government agencies generally make projections at the national level and for major subnational units such as states, provinces, or departments, often classified by age and sex. Related projections may include households, the labor force, and educational level. National projections often extend 50 or even 100 years into the future, while projections for subnational areas typically cover shorter horizons (e.g., 20 to 30 years). The level of detail included in national projections is often determined by the statistical needs of national government agencies.

Subnational (e.g., state, provincial, municipal) governmental agencies (or their designees) often make projections for states/provinces and smaller geographic areas (e.g., counties, cities, census tracts). The amount of socioeconomic and demographic detail included in these projections varies tremendously from one area to another; again, it is frequently determined by the statistical needs of governmental agencies. Some private companies make highly detailed projections for very small areas (e.g., block groups), but they typically cover very short horizons (e.g., 5 years).

Face validity is the extent to which a projection is based on appropriate methods, incorporates high-quality data, uses reasonable assumptions, and accounts for relevant factors. The appropriateness of a method depends primarily on the purposes for which a projection will be used and the type of data available. Many methods are appropriate for projections of total population, but projections of age groups usually require some type of cohort approach and projections of economic-demographic interactions require a structural model. Other types of projections require data and techniques specific to the nature of those projections (e.g., labor force participation ratios, school enrollment ratios). Data quality is determined by the length of the data series as well as its completeness, reliability, and timeliness.

Although "reasonableness" (of assumptions) is a subjective concept, assumptions can be judged according to the extent to which they fit current conditions, relevant theory, and changes in factors composing on affecting population change. These factors include population structure, mortality, fertility, and migration and socioeconomic characteristics. For small areas, other factors may play an important role as well: the size of the area, constraints on growth (e.g., flood plains, environmentally protected areas), location (e.g., distances from major employers and shopping centers), transportation characteristics (e.g., access to highways and railways), land-use policies (e.g., zoning and regulatory restrictions), and special populations, such as persons residing in prisons, college dormitories, and military barracks (Murdock *et al.*, 1991). Information on factors like these has been called "domain knowledge" (Ahlburg, 2001; Armstrong, 2001, p. 778).

Plausibility is the extent to which a projection is consistent with historical trends, the assumptions inherent in the model, and projections for other areas. Plausibility is closely related to face validity but focuses on the outcomes of the projection process rather than the inputs. If a projection is not based on valid data, appropriate methods, and reasonable assumptions, it is not likely to provide plausible results.

Like face validity, plausibility is a subjective concept but can be tested using a variety of internal and external evaluations. Internal evaluations address questions like: Are the projected trends consistent with those observed in the past, prevailing demographic conditions, and demographic theories? Consistency tests may be conducted by examining selected age groups (e.g., less than 1 year, ages of school attendance, labor force, retirement ages) and comparing projected demographic indices (e.g., growth rates, survival rates, birthrates) with those observed over the past few years. External evaluations compare projections with those produced for similar areas or those produced in other countries at a similar stage of development.

Production cost is an important consideration. Labor is the primary factor of production for most types of projections, so that the cost of labor is the primary cost of production. A great deal of time must be spent considering assumptions and relevant details; collecting, verifying, correcting, and adjusting input data; putting together projection models; and evaluating the plausibility of projection results. Other costs (e.g., computer hardware and software, purchases of proprietary data) are typically small in comparison. Costs increase with the level of methodological complexity and analytical sophistication required, the amount of socioeconomic and demographic detail included, the number of geographic units covered, and the extent to which domain knowledge is incorporated in the methodology. In many instances, tradeoffs will have to be made between the scope of projections and cost.

Timeliness has several dimensions. One refers to the release of input data. Some data are available only once per decade; others are available annually or even monthly. Some are available shortly after their reference dates; others only after a lag of several years. The more frequently and quickly data become available, the greater their usefulness for producing projections. Another dimension is the amount of time needed to construct a set of projections. Other things being equal, the more quickly projections become available to the data user, the greater their potential usefulness. A third dimension of timeliness is the frequency with which projections are updated. Because shifting trends often reflect short-run deviations rather than fundamental long-run changes, the availability of recent projections may be more important when dealing with short horizons than long horizons. There is no uniform practice among national agencies: Some update their projections annually, some every other year, and some at irregular intervals. A survey of 30 industrialized countries in 1988 showed that 15 countries updated their population projections only at intervals of 4 years or longer (Cruijsen and Keilman, 1992, p. 23). In the United States, national projections are updated roughly once every 4 years; in the United Kingdom, every 2 years; and in Australia, every 4 years. Statistics Canada revises long-run projections for Canada and its provinces and territories following every quinquennial census and prepares short-run (5-year) updates every year (George, 2001).

Ease of application is determined by the amount of time and the level of expertise needed to collect, verify, and adjust input data, develop a projection model, and generate the desired projections. This issue is particularly important for those with limited training or expertise in constructing projections or who face severe time or budget constraints. Several computer software packages are available for applying the cohort-component method at the national level (Bongaarts and Bulatao, 2000, Appendix A), but few, if any, software packages incorporate a variety of methods and account for the unique features of population growth and demographic change in small areas. This concept also refers to the extent to which data sources, assumptions, and projection techniques can be described clearly to data users. Some data users are interested only in the projections themselves, not in how they were produced; for them, this issue is irrelevant. Others, however, can truly evaluate and properly use a set of projections only if they understand precisely how they were made. For them, a clearer and more comprehensive description of the methodology adds considerable value to the projections.

Political considerations refer to the context in which projections are made. All projections are influenced by the context in which they are produced and by the perspectives of those who produce them—that is, all projections are judgmental in the sense that they reflect a variety of choices made during their preparation. The outcomes of cohort-component models are determined by assumptions regarding future mortality, fertility, and migration rates; structural models are affected by choices of variables and functional forms; labor force and school enrollment projections are influenced by assumptions as to trends in labor force participation and school enrollment ratios. Even projections made by simple trend extrapolation are affected by choices of data, techniques, and length of the base period. Judgment is sometimes influenced by political (i.e., nontechnical) considerations. As Moen (1984) noted, population growth is deeply embedded in politics. A national government may want to show that the elderly population is growing rapidly in order to support its initiative to overhaul the current retirement system. A state government may want to show that poverty rates are declining to illustrate the effectiveness of its economic policies. A business group may want to show the need for additional public investment in infrastructure.

If such political concerns outweigh technical considerations, the credibility of the projections may be compromised.

Data users must become aware of the political context in which projections were made. Who made the projections? Did they have a personal stake in the results? What roles were the projections expected to play? What data, techniques, and assumptions were applied? Political considerations do not uniformly compromise the objectivity of projections; in some instances, in fact, they may substantially improve their quality (Tayman, 1996a). Learning the answers to questions like these, however, will help data users evaluate projection results.

Forecast accuracy is, for many analysts and data users, the most important issue (Carbone and Armstrong, 1982; Mentzer and Kahn, 1995; Yokum and Armstrong, 1995). Without such information, the usefulness of projections for many purposes is limited. Fortunately, a substantial amount of information on forecast accuracy is available. Forecast error can be defined as the difference between a projected number and an "actual" number (Smith *et al.*, 2001, p. 302). For evaluating population projections, census counts are typically used as proxies for actual numbers; population estimates are sometimes used as well. Although it is widely recognized that census counts and population estimates also contain errors, such errors have relatively little impact on the accuracy of long-range projections and are seldom accounted for in evaluations of forecast accuracy.

Many measures of forecast accuracy can be used as suggested by the discussion in Chapter 20. The most common are the mean absolute percent error (MAPE), mean (algebraic) percent error (MPE or MALPE), median (or median absolute) percent error, root mean squared error, root mean squared percent error, and various transformations of these measures or their underlying data (Ahlburg, 2001; Siegel, 2002, pp. 471–484; Smith *et al.*, 2001). Some measures (e.g., MAPE) refer to precision, or how close a projection is to an actual value; others (e.g., MPE) refer to bias, or the tendency for projections to be too high or too low. For selected formulas, refer to Chapter 20.

Some generalizations on forecast accuracy are as follows.

1. Precision tends to increase as population size increases (Bongaarts and Bulatao, 2000; Isserman, 1977; Murdock *et al.*, 1984; White, 1954). Large "places" typically have smaller MAPEs than small "places," but once a certain population size has been reached, further increases in size generally do not lead to further increases in precision (Smith, 1987; Tayman, 1996b). Bias appears to have no consistent relationship with population size, as the tendency for projections to be too high or too low is about the same for small places as large places.

2. Precision tends to be greatest for places with positive but moderate population growth rates and to deteriorate as growth rates deviate in either direction from these levels (Isserman, 1977; Murdock *et al.*, 1984; Smith, 1987;

Tayman, 1996b). MAPEs are particularly large for places that have been either growing or declining rapidly. Bias is also affected by growth rates, as projections for places that have been losing population tend to be too low and projections for places that have been growing rapidly tend to be too high (Smith, 1987; Smith and Shahidullah, 1995).

3. Precision tends to decline as the length of the projection horizon increases. This result has been found not only for population projections (Bongaarts and Bulatao, 2000; Keilman, 1990; Keyfitz, 1981; Stoto, 1983), but for forecasts in other fields as well (Ascher, 1981; Batchelor and Dua, 1990; Schnaars, 1986). MAPEs have often been found to grow about linearly with the projection horizon, at least for several decades (Ascher, 1981; Schmitt and Crosetti, 1951; Smith and Sincich, 1991). The length of the projection horizon, however, appears to have no impact on the tendency for projections to be too high or too low (Smith and Sincich, 1991).

4. Forecast accuracy is not the same for all launch years (Keilman, 1990; Keyfitz, 1982; Long, 1995). Although measures of precision often show some degree of stability over time, measures of bias vary dramatically from one launch year to another (Isserman, 1977; Kale et al., 1981; Smith and Sincich, 1988). The study of past forecast errors may therefore tell us something about the likely level of precision of current projections, but it can tell us little or nothing about whether those projections are likely to be too high or too low.

5. The choice of projection method has no consistent impact on forecast accuracy. No single method uniformly produces more accurate population projections than all other methods. In particular, complex methods are no more likely to provide accurate forecasts of total population than simpler methods (Long, 1995; Pflaumer, 1992; Smith and Sincich, 1992; Stoto, 1983; White, 1954). Similar results have been found for other types of forecasts as well (Mahmoud, 1984; Pant and Starbuck, 1990; Schnaars, 1986). Causal models have been found to provide more accurate population forecasts than noncausal models in a few instances (Sanderson, 1999), but most studies have found no consistent differences between causal and noncausal models (Kale et al., 1981; Murdock et al., 1984; Smith and Sincich, 1992).

6. Averaging projections based on different methods, data sets, or combinations of assumptions often leads to greater forecast accuracy than can be achieved by individual projections. This result has been found for forecasts of variables as diverse as gross national product, corporate earnings, stock prices, electricity demand, psychiatric conditions, rainfall, and sunspot cycles (Clemen, 1989; Mahmoud, 1984; Schnaars, 1986). Raising the number of projections in the combination generally improves forecast accuracy, but by diminishing increments. Combining projections can be accomplished by using simple averages or various types of weighted averages. It improves forecast-

ing performance because each individual projection provides unique information and the errors tend to offset each other to some degree. Combining projections reduces the risk of making large errors. Although this device has seldom been used for population projections, there is some evidence that its use may now be increasing (Ahlburg, 1999; Smith and Shahidullah, 1995).

Accounting for uncertainty has been the subject of many studies conducted over the past 50 years. They have found roughly similar results regarding the precision of population forecasts. Table 21.6 shows "typical" MAPEs for a variety of projection horizons and geographic levels. (These hypothetical errors are based on the assumption that there are no errors in the launch-year populations.) Although errors for individual places will vary—with some having much larger errors and others much smaller errors than those shown here—this table provides rough but reasonable estimates of the average levels of precision that might be expected for current forecasts of states, counties, and census tracts. Errors for nations vary according to population size, with MAPEs for large countries generally being smaller than those shown here for states and MAPEs for small countries generally falling somewhere between those shown for states and counties (Bongaarts and Bulatao, 2000, pp. 38–44).

Given the widespread use of population projections for decision making in both the public and private sectors—and the high stakes often associated with those decisions—it is essential that data users have some understanding of the uncertainty inherent in population projections. Summaries of previous forecast errors are helpful, but they do not provide information regarding the uncertainty of a specific current set of projections. Such information can be provided in several ways. One approach is to construct several alternative series based on different methods or different specifications of a particular method. The most common practice is to produce several sets of cohort-component projections based on different combinations of assumptions (Campbell, 1996; Day, 1996; Statistics Canada, 2001). The primary benefit of producing alternative series is that they show the

TABLE 21.6 "Typical" Mean Absolute Percentage Errors, by Geographic Level and Length of Horizon

Geographic Level	Length of horizon (years)					
	5	10	15	20	25	30
State	3	6	9	12	15	18
County	6	12	18	24	30	36
Census tract	9	18	27	36	45	54

Source: Smith et al. (2001, Table 13.7).

populations stemming from different but reasonable models, techniques, and combinations of assumptions. The primary limitation is that they do not provide an explicit measure of uncertainty. The question, "How likely is it that the future population will fall within the range suggested by two alternative series?" cannot be answered using this approach.

Another approach is to construct prediction intervals to accompany a particular population forecast. Prediction intervals can be based on specific models of population growth (e.g., time series models), empirical analyses of past forecast errors, or the subjective judgment of population experts (Bongaarts and Bulatao, 2000, pp. 200–204; Smith *et al.*, 2001, pp. 334–339). The primary advantage of this approach is that it provides an explicit probability statement to accompany a particular population forecast. Disadvantages include: (1) model-based prediction intervals are data-intensive, difficult to produce, and subject to a variety of specification errors; (2) empirically based prediction intervals require the collection of a large amount of historical data and are dependent on the assumption that future error distributions will be similar to past error distributions; and (3) experts are often overconfident and tend to underestimate the uncertainty inherent in their forecasts (Bongaarts and Bulatao, 2000, p. 203). Alternative series and prediction intervals both provide useful information regarding the uncertainty of future population growth. Data users can incorporate this information into their deliberations and make better decisions than would be possible if they had no knowledge of the likely range of future errors. Using formal or informal "loss functions," they can assess the gains or losses associated with different forecast errors (Bongaarts and Bulatao, 2000, p. 188). In some instances (e.g., when it is more costly to anticipate too little growth than too much growth), the best choice may be to base decisions on high or low projections rather than the ones deemed most likely to provide an accurate forecast of future growth.

CONCLUDING NOTE

The production of population and related projections involves many choices regarding data, techniques, and assumptions. Making the best choices requires taking account of the purposes for which the projections will be used and the constraints under which they are produced. Simple methods require less time, data, and expertise than more complex methods, but they provide less demographic and socioeconomic detail and offer fewer opportunities to analyze the determinants and consequences of population growth. Investigating input-data series and correcting errors can improve data quality but are time consuming. Evaluating the consistency of projections with historical trends can uncover data and modeling errors but delays the release of projection results. Adjusting for special populations or unique events can improve forecast accuracy but requires specialized "domain knowledge." Providing a range of projections increases the amount of information available to data users but requires more production time and may open the door to political misuse of the results (e.g., choosing the scenario that favors a particular political position regardless of its technical merits). Only after balancing the costs and benefits of all aspects of the projection process can the analyst make optimal choices for any particular project.

These choices require the application of professional judgment. No matter how objective and rigorous the projection methodology, many subjective elements remain. Consequently, it is imperative that the analyst provide a clear, comprehensive explanation of the projection methodology. Otherwise, data users cannot truly evaluate projection validity and plausibility.

We believe that it is generally best to employ the simplest method(s) consistent with the purposes for which the projections will be used. This allows scarce resources to be directed toward activities that often have a substantial positive impact on the quality of the projections (e.g., evaluating and correcting input data, accounting for domain knowledge) rather than activities that have little or no impact (e.g., establishing an extensive database or developing a complicated model). Devoting resources to the collection of domain knowledge is particularly important for small-area projections, where unique events and special circumstances often play a major role in population change. In many instances, averages based on a variety of methods or sets of assumptions are preferable to projections based on a single model.

All forecasts are subject to error. Given the errors shown in Table 21.6, why should the analyst even bother making population and related projections? Why should data users pay any attention to them? There are several reasons for doing so. First, the projection process itself is educational, teaching a great deal about the components of population growth and the determinants of changes in related variables. Second, projections are helpful in analyzing the impact of alternative scenarios or combinations of assumptions on population growth and demographic change, regardless of the accuracy of specific forecasts. Finally, there is really no alternative to making projections: Ignoring potential change is generally not the best way to plan for the future.

Accuracy is an important characteristic, but it is not the only criterion on which projections can or should be judged. In the final analysis, projections can best be judged according to their "utility," or the improvements they bring to the quality of information used in decision making (Tayman and

Swanson, 1996). If these benefits are greater than the costs of production, then projections are worthwhile. Despite their shortcomings as forecasts, population and related projections can play an extremely important role in many types of planning and analysis.

References

Ahlburg, D. 1999. "Using Economic Information and Combining to Improve Forecast Accuracy in Demography." Unpublished paper. Rochester, MN: Industrial Relations Center, University of Minnesota.

Ahlburg, D. 2001. "Population Forecasting." In J. S. Armstrong, *Principles of Forecasting: A Handbook for Researchers and Practitioners* (pp. 557–575). Norwell, MA: Kluwer Academic Publishers.

Ahlburg, D., and W. Lutz. 1998. "Introduction: The Need to Rethink Approaches to Population Forecasts." *Population Development Review* 24: 1–14.

Ahlburg, D., and J. Vaupel. 1990. "Alternative Projections of the U. S. Population." *Demography* 27: 639–652.

Alho, J., and B. Spencer. 1997. "The Practical Specification of the Expected Error of Population Forecasts." *Journal of Official Statistics* 13: 203–225.

Armstrong, J. 2001. *"Principles of Forecasting: A Handbook for Researchers and Practitioners.* Norwell, MA: Kluwer Academic Publishers.

Ascher, W. 1981. "The Forecasting Potential of Complex Models." *Policy Sciences* 13: 247–267.

Astone, N., and S. McLanahan. 1994. "Family Structure, Residential Mobility and School Report: A Research Note." *Demography* 31: 575–584.

Australian Bureau of Statistics. 2000. *Population Projections, Australia, 1999 to 2101.* Canberra, Australia: Australian Bureau of Statistics.

Batchelor, R., and P. Dua. 1990. "Forecaster Ideology, Forecasting Technique, and the Accuracy of Economic Forecasts." *International Journal of Forecasting* 6: 3–10.

Bélanger, A. 1992. "Estimating Parameterized Migration Age Schedules for Canada and Provinces." Document de travail, Section des projections démographiques, Division de la démographie, Statistique Canada, Ottawa, Canada.

Bell, F., A. Wade, and S. Goss. 1992. *Life Tables for the United States Social Security Area 1900–2080.* Washington, DC: Social Security Administration.

Bongaarts, J., and R. Bulatao (Eds.). 2000. *Beyond Six Billion: Forecasting the World's Population.* Washington, DC: National Academy Press.

Bowley, A. 1924. "Births and Population in Great Britain." *The Economic Journal* 334: 188–192.

Boyce, D. 1988. "Renaissance of Large Scale Models." *Papers of the Regional Science Association* 65: 1–10.

Box, G., and G. Jenkins. 1976. *Time Series Analysis: Forecasting and Control.* San Francisco: Holden-Day.

CACI Inc. 2000. *Sourcebook for Zip Code Demographics.* Chantilly, VA: CACI Inc.

Campbell, P. 1996. "Population Projections for States by Age, Sex, Race, and Hispanic Origin: 1995 to 2050." Report PPL-47. Washington, DC: U. S. Bureau of the Census.

Cannan, E. 1895. "The Probability of a Cessation of the Growth of Population in England and Wales during the Next Century." *The Economic Journal* 5: 506–515.

Carbone, R., and J. Armstrong. 1982. "Evaluation of Extrapolative Forecasting Methods: Results of a Survey of Academicians and Practitioners." *Journal of Forecasting* 1: 215–217.

Carter, L., and R. Lee. 1986. "Joint Forecasts of U. S. Marital Fertility, Nuptiality, Births, and Marriages Using Time Series Models." *Journal of the American Statistical Association* 81: 902–911.

Carter, L., and R. Lee. 1992. "Modeling and Forecasting U. S. Sex Differentials in Mortality." *International Journal of Forecasting* 8: 393–411.

Clark, D., and W. Hunter. 1992. "The Impact of Economic Opportunity, Amenities and Fiscal Factors on Age-Specific Migration Rates." *Journal of Regional Science* 32: 349–365.

Clemen, R. 1989. "Combining Forecasts: A Review and Annotated Bibliography." *International Journal of Forecasting* 5: 559–583.

Congdon, P. 1992. "Multiregional Demographic Projections in Practice: A Metropolitan Example." *Regional Studies* 26: 177–191.

Conway, R. 1990. "The Washington Projection and Simulation Model." *International Regional Science Review* 13: 141–165.

Cruijsen, H. 1994. "National Population Projections in the European Economic Area—A Field in Motion." Joint ECE-Eurostat Work session on Demographic Projections, Luxembourg, (May). ECE Working Paper No. 4. Geneva, Switzerland: UN Economic Commission for Europe.

Cruijsen, H., and N. Keilman. 1992. "A Comparative Analysis of the Forecasting Process. In N. Keilman and H. Cruijsen (Eds.), *National Population Forecasting in Industrialized Countries* (pp. 3–25). Amsterdam: Swets and Zeitliinger.

Data Resources Incorporated. 1998. *Review of the U. S. Economy: Long-Range Focus, Winter 97–98.* Lexington, MA: Data Resources Incorporated.

DaVanzo, J., and P. Morrison. 1978. *Dynamics of Return Migration: Descriptive Findings From a Longitudinal Study. Report P-5913.* Santa Monica, CA: The Rand Corporation.

Davis, H. 1995. *Demographic Projection Techniques for Regions and Smaller Areas.* Vancouver, Canada: UBC Press.

Day, J. 1996. "Population Projections of the United States by Age, Sex, Race, and Hispanic origin: 1995 to 2050." *Current Population Reports*, P25, No. 1130. Washington, DC: U. S. Bureau of the Census.

de Beer, J. 1993. "Forecast Intervals of Net Migration: The Case of the Netherlands." *Journal of Forecasting* 12: 585–599.

de Gans, H. A. 1999. *Population Forecasting 1895–1945: The Transition to Modernity.* Dordecht: Kluwer Academic Publishers.

EUROSTAT. 1998. "Long-Term Mortality Scenarios for the Countries of the European Economic Area." By W. Van Hoorn and J. De Beer. EUROSTAT Working Papers, E. no.8.

Foot, D., and W. Milne. 1989. "Multiregional Estimation of Gross Internal Migration Flows." *International Regional Science Review* 12: 29–43.

Fries, J. 1989. "The Compression of Morbidity: Near or Far?" *The Milbank Quarterly* 67: 208–232.

Fuguitt, G., and D. Brown. 1990. "Residential Preferences and Population Redistribution." *Demography* 27: 589–600.

Fullerton, H. 1999. "Labor Force projections to 2008: Steady Growth and Changing Composition." *Monthly Labor Review* 122: 19–32.

George, M. V. 1999. "On the Use and Users of Demographic Projections in Canada." Joint ECE-Eurostat work session on demographic projections, Perugia, Italy (May). ECE Working Paper no. 15. Geneva, Switzerland: UN Economic Commission for Europe.

George, M. V. 2001. "Population Forecasting in Canada: Conceptual and Methodological Development." *Canadian Studies in Population* 28: 111–154.

George, M. V., and S. Loh. 2000. "Top Down versus Bottom Up: Statistics Canada's Hybrid Bottom-Up Case of National and Provincial Population Projections." Paper presented at the annual meeting of the Population Association of America, Los Angeles, CA.

George, M. V., S. Loh, and R. B. P. Verma. 1997. "Impact of Varying the Component Assumptions on Projected Total Population and

Age Structure in Canada." *Canadian Population Studies* 24: 67–86.

George, M. V., and J. Perreault. 1992. "Methods of External Migration Projections and Forecasts." In N. Keilman and H. Cruijsen (Eds.) *National Population Forecasting in Industrialized Countries* (pp. 87–103). Amsterdam: Swets and Zeitlinger.

Greenberg, M., D. Krueckeberg, and C. Michaelson. 1978. *Local Population and Employment Projection Techniques*. New Brunswick, NJ: Rutgers University, Center for Urban Policy and Research.

Greenwood, M. 1975. "Simultaneity Bias in Migration Models: An Empirical Investigation." *Demography* 12: 519–536.

Greenwood, M., and G. Hunt. 1991. "Forecasting State and Local Population Growth with Limited Data: The Use of Employment Migration Relationships and Trends in Vital Rates." *Environment and Planning A* 23: 987–1005.

Hamilton, C., and J. Perry. 1962. "A Short Method for Projecting Population by Age from One Decennial Census to Another." *Social Forces* 41: 163–170.

Hanke, J. A., G. Reitsch, and D. Wichern. 2001. *Business Forecasting*, 7th ed. Saddle River, NJ: Prentice Hall.

Hollmann, F. W., T. J. Mulder, and J. E. Kallan. 2000. "Methodology and Assumptions for the Population Projections of the United States: 1999–2100." *Population Division Working Paper*, No. 38. U. S. Census Bureau, Washington, DC.

Indian Office of the Registrar General. 2001. Chapter 4, "Population Projections, Provisional Population Totals," *Census of India 2001, Series 1*. Dehli: Indian Office of the Registrar General.

Israeli Central Bureau of Statistics. 1987. *Projections of Population in Judea, Samaria, and the Gaza Area up to 2002, Based on the Population in 1982*. Jerusalem, Israel: Israeli Central Bureau of Statistics.

Isserman, A. 1977. "The Accuracy of Population Projections for Subcounty Areas." *Journal of the American Institute of Planners* 43: 247–259.

Isserman, A. 1985. "Economic-Demographic Modeling with Endogenously Determined Birth and Migration Rates: Theory and Prospects." *Environment and Planning A* 17: 25–45.

Isserman, A., D. Plane, P. Rogerson, and P. Beaumont. 1985. "Forecasting Interstate Migration with Limited Data: A Demographic-Economic Approach." *Journal of the American Statistical Association* 80: 277–285.

Kale, B., P. Voss, C. Palit, and H. Krebs. 1981. "On the Question of Errors in Population Projections." Paper presented at the meeting of the Population Association of America, Washington, DC.

Keilman, N. 1990. *Uncertainty in National Population Forecasting: Issues, Backgrounds, Analysis, Recommendations*. Amsterdam: Swets and Zeitlinger.

Keilman, N. 1991. "National Projection Methods in Developed Countries." In W. Lutz (Ed.), *Future Demographic Trends in Europe and North America: What Can We Assume Today?* (pp. 465–486). San Diego, CA: Academic Press.

Keyfitz, N. 1968. *An Introduction to the Mathematics of Population*. Reading, MA: Addison-Wesley.

Keyfitz, N. 1981. "The Limits of Population Forecasting." *Population and Development Review* 7: 579–593.

Keyfitz, N. 1982. "Can Knowledge Improve Forecasts?" *Population and Development Review* 8: 729–751.

Kintner, H. 1989. "Demographic Change in a Corporate Health Benefits Population." *American Journal of Public Health* 79: 1655–1656.

Kintner, H., T. Merrick, P. Morrison, and P. Voss (Eds.). 1994. "*Demographics: A Casebook for Business and Government*." Boulder, CO: Westview Press.

Kintner, H., and D. A. Swanson. 1994. "Estimating Vital Rates from Corporate Databases: How Long Will GM's Salaried Retirees Live?" In H. Kintner, T. Merrick, P. Morrison, and P. Voss (Eds.), *Demo-graphics: A Casebook for Business and Government* (pp. 265–295). Boulder, CO: Westview Press.

Kintner, H., and D. A. Swanson. 1996. "Ties That Bind: A Case Study of the Link between Employers, Families, and Health Benefits." *Population Research and Policy Review* 15: 509–526.

Kupiszewski, M., and P. Rees. 1999. *Lessons for the Projection of Internal Migration from Studies in Ten European Countries*. Working Paper No. 40. Conference of European Statisticians, Joint ECE-EUROSTAT Work Session on Demographic Projections, Perugia, Italy, May.

Lee, R. 1993. "Modeling and Forecasting the Time Series of U.S. Fertility: Age Distribution, Range, and Ultimate Level." *International Journal of Forecasting* 9: 187–212.

Lee, R., and L. Carter. 1992. "Modeling and Forecasting U.S. Mortality." *Journal of the American Statistical Association* 87: 659–675.

Lee, R., and S. Tuljapurkar. 1994. "Stochastic Population Forecasts for the United States: Beyond High, Medium, and Low." *Journal of the American Statistical Association* 89: 1175–1189.

Lee, R., and S. Tuljapurkar. 1997. "Death and Taxes: Longer Life, Consumption and Social Security." *Demography* 34: 67–81.

Long, J. 1989. The Relative Effects of Fertility, Mortality, and Immigration on Projected Population Age Structure." Paper presented at the meeting of the Population Association of America. Baltimore, MD.

Long, J. 1995. "Complexity, Accuracy, and Utility of Official Population Projections." *Mathematical Population Studies* 5: 203–216.

Long, J., and D. McMillen. 1987. "A Survey of Census Bureau Projection Methods." *Climatic Change* 11: 141–177.

Lutz, W., J. W. Vaupel, and D. A. Ahlburg (eds.). 1999. *Frontiers of Population Forecasting*. New York: The Population Council (a supplement to *Population and Development Review* 24, 1998).

Mahmoud, E. 1984. "Accuracy in Forecasting: A Survey." *Journal of Forecasting* 3: 139–159.

Manton, K., C. Patrick, and E. Stallard. 1980. "Mortality Model Based on Delays in Progression of Chronic Diseases: Alternative to Cause Elimination Model." *Public Health Reports* 95: 580–588.

Manton, K., E. Stallard, and H. Tolley. 1991. "Limits to Human Life Expectancy: Evidence Prospects, and Implications." *Population and Development Review* 17: 603–637.

Mason, A. 1996. "Population and Housing" *Population Research and Policy Review* 15(5–6): 419–435.

Massey, D., R. Alarcon, J. Durand, and H. Gonzalez. 1987. *Return to Aztlan: The Social Process of International Migration from Western Mexico*. Berkeley, CA: University of California Press.

McCleary, R., and R. Hay. 1980. *Applied Time Series Analysis for the Social Sciences*. Beverly Hills, CA: Sage.

Mentzer, J., and K. Kahn. 1995. "Forecasting Technique Familiarity, Satisfaction, Wage, and Application." *Journal of Forecasting* 14: 465–476.

Michaud, J., M. V. George, and S. Loh. 1996. *Projections of Persons with Disabilities (Limited at Work/Perception); Canada, Provinces, and Territories, 1993–2016*. Ottawa, Canada: Statistics Canada.

Miller, T. 2001. "Increasing Longevity and Medicare Expenditures." *Demography* 38: 215–226.

Mills, E., and L. Lubuele. 1995. "Projecting Growth in Metropolitan Areas." *Journal of Urban Economics* 37: 344–360.

Moen, E. 1984. "Voodoo Forecasting: Technical, Political and Ethical Issues Regarding the Projection of Local Population Growth." *Population Research and Policy Review* 3: 1–25.

Mosert, W., and J. van Tonder. 1987. *Projections of the South African Population*. Pretoria, South Africa: Institute for Sociological and Demographic Research, Human Sciences Research Council.

Murdock, S., and D. Ellis. 1991. *Applied Demography: An Introduction of Basic, Concepts, Methods, and Data*. Boulder, CO: Westview Press.

Murdock, S., R. Hamm, P. Voss, D. Fannin, and B. Pecotte. 1991. "Evaluating Small Area Population Projections." *Journal of the American Planning Association* 57: 432–443.

Murdock, S., F. Leistritz, R. Hamm, S. Hwang, and B. Parpia. 1984. "An Assessment of the Accuracy of a Regional Economic-Demographic Projection Model." *Demography* 21: 383–404.

NCSS Inc. 1995. *NCSS 6.0 Users' Guide.* Kaysville, UT: NCSS.

Olshansky, S. 1987. "Simultaneous/Multiple Cause-Delay (SIMCAD): An Epidemiological Approach to Projecting Mortality." *Journal of Gerontology* 42: 358–365.

Olshansky, S. 1988. "On Forecasting Mortality." *Milbank Quarterly* 66: 482–530.

O'Neill, B., D. Balk, M. Brickman, and M. Ezra. 2001. "A Guide to Global Population Projections." *Demographic Research* 4(8): 204–288, www.demographic-research.org, retrieved July 2001.

Opitz, W., and H. Nelson. 1996. "Short-Term Population-Based Forecasting in the Public Sector: A Dynamic Caseload Simulation Model." *Population Research and Policy Review* 15: 549–563.

Oregon Office of Economic Analysis. 2000. *Oregon Corrections Population Forecast.* Salem, OR: Oregon Department of Administrative Services, Office of Economic Analysis.

Pant, P., and W. Starbuck. 1990. "Innocents in the Forest: Forecasting and Research Methods." *Journal of Management* 16: 433–460.

Pflaumer, P. 1992. "Forecasting U.S. Population Totals with the Box-Jenkins Approach." *International Journal of Forecasting* 8: 329–338.

Pielou, E. C. 1969. *An Introduction to Mathematical Ecology.* New York: Wiley-Interscience.

Pignataro, L., and Epling, J. 2000. "The TELUS Story: Information Tool for Transportation Planning Makes Its Debut." *Transportation Research News* 210: 9–12, 25.

Pittenger, D. 1976. *Projecting State and Local Populations.* Cambridge, MA: Ballinger.

Pol, L., and R. Thomas. 2001. *The Demography of Health and Health Care,* 2nd ed. New York: Kluwer Academic/Plenum Press.

Putman, S. 1991. *Integrated Urban Models: II.* London, UK: Pion Limited.

Ravenstein, E. 1889. "The Laws of Migration." *The Journal of the Royal Statistical Society,* LII, 241–301.

Rogers, A. 1985. *Regional Population Projection Methods.* Beverly Hills, CA: Sage.

Rogers, A. 1995. *Multiregional Demography: Principles, Methods and Extensions.* Chichester, UK: John Wiley and Sons.

Rogers, A., and L. Castro. 1978. "Model Migration Schedules and Their Application." *Environment and Planning A* 10: 457–502.

Rogers, A., and P. Williams. 1986. Multistate demoeconomic modeling and projection. In A. Isserman (Ed.). *Population Change in the Economy: Social Science Theory and Methods* (pp. 177–202). Boston, MA: Kluwer-Nijhoff.

Rosenthal, N. 1999. "The Quality of BLS Projections: A Historical Account." *Monthly Labor Review* 122: 27–35.

Ryder, N. 1990. "What Is Going to HAPPEN to American Fertility?" *Population and Development Review* 16: 433–453.

Sanderson, W. 1999. "Knowledge Can Improve Forecasts: A Review of Selected Socioeconomic Population Projection Models." *Population and Development Review* 24: 88–117.

San Diego Association of Governments. 1998. "Urban Development Model," Volume 2: Technical description. San Diego, CA.

San Diego Association of Governments. 1999. "Demographic and Economic Forecasting Model," Volume 2: Technical description. San Diego, CA.

Schmidt, R., C. Barr, and D. Swanson. 1997. "Socioeconomic Impacts of the Proposed Federal Gaming Tax." *International Journal of Public Administration* 20: 1675–1698.

Schmitt, R., and A. Crosetti. 1951. "Accuracy of the Ratio Method for Forecasting City Population." *Land Economics* 27: 346–348.

Schnaars, S. 1986. "A Comparison of Extrapolation Models on Yearly Sales Forecasts." *International Journal of Forecasting* 2: 71–85.

Shryock, H., and J. Siegel. 1973. *The Methods and Materials of Demography.* Washington, DC: U.S. Government Printing Office.

Siegel, J. 2002. *Applied Demography: Applications to Business, Government, Law, and Public Policy.* San Dingo: Academic Prcss.

Smith, S. 1986. "Accounting for Migration in Cohort-Component Projections of State and Local Populations." *Demography* 23: 127–135.

Smith, S. 1987. "Tests of Forecast Accuracy and Bias for County Population Projections." *Journal of the American Statistical Association* 82: 991-1003.

Smith, S., and B. Ahmed. 1990. "A Demographic Analysis of the Population Growth of States, 1950–1980." *Journal of Regional Science* 30: 209–227.

Smith, S., and M. Shahidullah. 1995. "An Evaluation of Population Projection Errors for Census Tracts." *Journal of the American Statistical Association* 90: 64–71.

Smith, S., and T. Sincich. 1988. "Stability Over Time in the Distribution of Population Forecast Errors. *Demography* 25: 461–474.

Smith, S., and T. Sincich. 1991. "An Empirical Analysis of the Effect of the Length of Forecast Horizon on Population Forecast Errors." *Demography* 28: 261–274.

Smith, S., and T. Sincich. 1992. "Evaluating the Forecast Accuracy and Bias of Alternative Population Projections for States." *International Journal of Forecasting* 8: 495–508.

Smith, S., and D. A. Swanson. 1998. "In Defense of the Net Migrant." *Journal of Economic and Social Measurement* 24: 249–264.

Smith, S., J. Tayman, and D. A. Swanson. 2001. *State and Local Population Projections: Methodology and Analysis.* New York: Kluwer Academic/Plenum Publishers.

Spencer, G. 1989. "Projections of the Population of the United States by Age, Sex, and Race: 1988 to 2008." *Current Population Reports* P-25, No. 1018. Washington, DC: U.S. Bureau of the Census.

Statistics Canada, 2001. *Population Projections for Canada, Provinces, and Territories, 2000–2026.* Catalogue No. 91-520. Demography Division. Ottawa, Ontario: Statistics Canada.

Statistics Canada, 2002. *Annual Demographic Statistics, 2001.* Catalogue No. 91-213. Demography Division. Ottawa, Ontario: Statistics Canada.

Statistics New Zealand. 2000. *Subnational Population Projections: 1996 (Base) to 2021 (May 2000 Release).* Last accessed May 2002 online at www.stats.govt.nz.

Stoto, M. 1983. "The Accuracy of Population Projections." *Journal of the American Statistical Association* 78: 13–20.

Swanson, D., and D. Beck. 1994. "A New Short-Term County Population Projection Method." *Journal of Economic and Social Measurement* 20: 25–50.

Swanson, D., G. Hough, J. Rodriguez, and C. Clemans. 1998. "K-12 Enrollment Forecasting: Merging Methods and Judgment." *ERS Spectrum* 16: 24–31.

Swanson, D., and B. Klopfenstein. 1987. "How to Forecast VCR Penetration." *American Demographics* (December): 44–45.

Tabuchi, T. 1985. "Time Series Modeling of Gross Migration and Dynamic Equilibrium." *Journal of Regional Science* 25: 65–83.

Tayman, J. 1996a. "The Accuracy of Small-Area Population Forecasts Based on a Spatial Interaction Land-Use Modeling System. *Journal of the American Planning Association* 62: 85–98.

Tayman, J. 1996b. "Forecasting, Growth Management, and Public Policy Decision Making." *Population Research and Policy Review* 15: 491–508.

Tayman, J., B. Parrott, and S. Carnevale. 1994. "Locating Fire Station Sites: The Response Time Component." In H. Kintner, P. Voss, P. Morrison, and T. Merrick (Eds.), *Applied Demographics: A Casebook for Business and Government* (pp. 203–217). Boulder, CO: Westview Press.

Tayman, J., and D. Swanson. 1996. "On the Utility of Population Forecasts." *Demography* 33: 523–528.

Texas Water Development Board. 1997. "Water for Texas: A Consensus-Based Update to the State Water Plan," Vol. II, technical planning appendix. Austin, TX: Texas Water Development Board.

Thomas, R. 1994. "Using Demographic Analysis in Health Services Planning: A Case Study in Obstetrical Services." In H. Kintner, T. Merrick, P. Morrison, and P. Voss (Eds.), *Demographics: A Casebook for Business and Government* (pp. 159–179). Boulder, CO: Westview Press.

Thompson, A. 1999. "Industry Output and Employment Projections to 2008." *Monthly Labor Review* 122: 33–50.

Thompson, W., and P. Whelpton. 1933. *Population Trends in the United States*. New York: McGraw-Hill Book Company.

Treadway, R. 1997. "Population Projections for the State and Counties of Illinois." Springfield, IL: State of Illinois.

Treyz, G. 1993. *Regional Economic Modeling: A Systematic Approach to Economic Forecasting and Policy Analysis*." Boston, MA: Kluwer.

Treyz, G. 1995. "Policy Analysis: Application of REMI Economic Forecasting and Simulation Models." *International Journal of Public Administration* 18: 13–42.

Treyz, G., D. Rickman, G. Hunt, and M. Greenwood. 1993. "The Dynamics of U.S. Internal Migration." *Review of Economics and Statistics* 75: 209–214.

United Nations. 1973. *Manual VII. Methods of Projecting Households and Families*. New York: United Nations.

United Nations. 1998. *World Population Projections to 2150*. New York: United Nations Population Division.

United Nations. 1999. *World Population Prospects: The 1988 Revision*. New York: United Nations Population Division.

U.S. Bureau of Economic Analysis. 1995. *BEA Regional Projections to 2045: Volume I: States*. Washington, DC.

U.S. Bureau of the Census. 1957. "Illustrative Projections of the Population, by State, 1960, 1965, and 1970." *Current Population Reports*, P-25, No. 160. Washington, DC.

U.S. Bureau of the Census. 1966. "Illustrative Projections of the Population of States: 1970 to 1985." *Current Population Reports*, P-25, No. 326. Washington, DC.

U.S. Bureau of the Census. 1972. "Preliminary Projections of the Population of States: 1975–1990." *Current Population Reports*, P-25, No. 477. Washington, DC.

U.S. Bureau of the Census. 1979. "Illustrative Projections of State Populations by Age, Race, and Sex: 1975 to 2000." *Current Population Reports*, P-25, No. 796. Washington, DC.

U.S. Census Bureau. 2001. *International Data Base*. Last Accessed March 2002 online at www.census.gov/ipc/www/idbnew.html7/9/01.

U.S. National Center for Health Statistics. 1997. *U.S. Decennial Life Tables for 1989–91*. Volume 1, No. 1. Washington, DC.

Verma, R. B. P., and M. V. George. 1993. "Projecting the Age Distribution of Immigrants in Canada: An Alternative Approach by Linking Immigrants Flow and Stock Data." Paper prepared for the Conference of European Statisticians, Joint ECE/Eurostat Work Session on Migration Statistics, Geneva, Switzerland.

Verma, R. B. P., and M. V. George. 2002. "Application of Multiregional Migration Model for Interprovincial Migration Projections in Canada." Puper presented at the annual meeting of the Southern Demographic Association, Austin, Texas.

Verma, R. B. P., S. Loh, S. Y. Dai, and D. Ford. 1994. "Fertility Projections for Canada, Provinces and Territories, 1993–2016." Background Paper, Population Projections Section, Demography Division, Statistics Canada. Ottawa, Ontario.

Voss, P., and B. Kale. 1985. "Refinements to Small-Area Population Projection Models: Results of a Test Based on 128 Wisconsin Communities." Paper presented at the meeting of the Population Association of America. Boston, MA.

Waddell, P. 2000. "A Behavioral Simulation Model for Metropolitan Policy Analysis and Planning: Residential Location and Housing Market Components of UrbanSim." *Environment and Planning B* 27: 247–263.

Washington State Office of Financial Management. 2000. *Historical/Current Data Set: Total Resident Population by Year for County, Washington, 1960 to 2000*. Olympia, WA: Washington State Office of Financial Management. Last accessed March, 2002 online at www.ofm.wa.gov/pop6098/pop6098toc.htm12/28/01.

Washington State Office of Financial Management. 2001. *Forecast of the State Population by Age and Sex, 1990 to 2030, November 2001 Forecast*. Olympia, WA: Washington State Office of Financial Management. Last accessed May, 2002 online at www.ofm.wa.gov/popagesex19702020/popagesex19702020toc.htm.

Wetrogan, S. 1990. "Projections of the Population of States by Age, Sex, and race: 1989–2010." *Current Population Reports*, P-25, No. 1053. Washington, DC: U.S. Bureau of the Census.

Whelpton, P. 1928. "Population of the United States, 1925 to 1975." *American Journal of Sociology* 34: 253–270.

White, H. 1954. "Empirical Study of the Accuracy of Selected Methods of Projecting State Populations." *Journal of the American Statistical Association* 49: 480–498.

Yaffee, R. 2000. *Introduction to Time Series Analysis and Forecasting, with Applications of SAS and SPSS*. New York: Academic Press.

Yokum, J., and J. Armstrong. 1995. "Beyond Accuracy: Comparison of Criteria Used to Select Forecasting Methods." *International Journal of Forecasting* 11: 591–597.

Suggested Readings

General Works

Ahlburg, D., W. Lutz, and J. Vaupel. 1998. "Ways to Improve Population Forecasting: What Should Be Done Differently in the Future?" *Population Development Review* 24: 191–199.

Armstrong, J. 2001. *Principles of Forecasting: A Handbook for Researchers and Practitioners*. Norwell, MA: Kluwer Academic Publisher.

Makridakas, S., S. Wheelwright, and R. Hyndman. 1998. *Forecasting: Methods and Applications*. New York: Wiley.

Trend Extrapolation

Fildes, R. 1992. "The evaluation of Extrapolative Forecasting Methods. *International Journal of Forecasting* 8: 81–98.

Marchetti, C., P. Meyer, and J. Ausubel. 1996. "Human Population Dynamics Revisited with the Logistic Model: How Much Can Be Modeled and Predicted." *Technological Forecasting and Social Change* 52: 1–30.

McNown, R., A. Rogers, and J. Little. 1995. "Simplicity and Complexity in Extrapolative Population Forecasting Models." *Mathematical Population Studies* 5: 235–257.

Pearl, R., and L. Reed. 1920. "On the Rate of Growth of the Population of the United States Since 1790 and Its Mathematical Representation." *Proceedings of the National Academy of Science* 6: 275–287.

Schmitt, R., and A. Crosetti. 1953. "Short-Cut Methods of Forecasting City Population." *Journal of Marketing* 17: 417–424.

Swanson, D. A., D. Beck., and J. Tayman. 1995. "On the Utility of Lagged Ratio-Correlation as a Short-Cut Population Projection Method: A Case Study of Washington State." *Journal of Economic and Social Measurement* 21: 1–16.

Neural Networks

Adya, M., and F. Collopy. 1998. "How Effective are Neural Networks at Forecasting and Prediction: A Review and Evaluation. *Journal of Forecasting* 17: 481–495.

Hill, T., L. Marquez, M. O'Conner, and W. Remus. 1994. "Artificial Neural Network Models for Forecasting and Decision Making. *International Journal of Forecasting* 10: 5–15.

Wasserman, P. 1989. *Neural Computing: Theory and Practice.* New York: Van Nostrand Rheinhold.

Zhang, G., B. Patuwo, and M. Hu. 1998. "Forecasting with Artificial Neural Networks: The State of the Art." *International Journal of Forecasting* 14: 35–62.

Urban Systems Models

Hunt, D., and D. Simmons. 1993. "Theory and Application of an Integrated Land-Use and Transport Modelling Framework." *Environment and Planning B* 20: 221–244.

Kim, T. 1989. *Integrated Urban Systems Modeling: Theory and Applications.* Cambridge, MA: Harvard University Press.

Klosterman, R. 1994. "Large Scale Urban Models: Retrospect and Prospects." *Journal of the American Planning Association* 60: 3–6.

Landis, J. 1994. "The California Urban Futures Model: A New Generation of Metropolitan Simulation Models." *Environment and Planning B* 31: 399–420.

Landis, J. 1995. "Imagining Land Use Futures: Applying the California Urban Futures Model." *Journal of the American Planning Association* 61: 438–457.

Landis, J., M. Zhang, and M. Zook. 1998. "CUFII: The Second Generation of the California Urban Futures Model." Berkeley, CA: UC Transportation Center, University of California.

Lowry, I. 1964. "A Model of Metropolis." Report RM 4125-RC. Santa Monica, CA: The Rand Corporation.

Wegener, M. 1994. "Operation Urban Models: State of the Art." *Journal of the American Planning Association* 60: 17–30.

Forecast Uncertainty and Accuracy

Alho, J. 1997. "Scenarios, Uncertainty and Conditional Forecasts of the World Population." *Journal of the Royal Statistical Society A* 160, part 1: 71–85.

Armstrong, J., and F. Collopy. 1992. "Error Measures for Generalizing about Forecasting Methods: Empirical Comparisons." *International Journal of Forecasting* 8: 69–80.

Armstrong, J., and R. Fildes. 1995. "Correspondence on the Selection of Error Measures for Comparisons among Forecasting Methods." *Journal of Forecasting* 14: 67–71.

Cohen, J. 1986. "Population Forecasts and the Confidence Intervals for Sweden: A Comparison of Model-Based and Empirical Approaches." *Demography* 23: 105–126.

Keilman, N. 1998. "How Accurate Are the United Nations World Population Projections?" In W. Lutz, J. Vaupel, and D. Ahlburg (Eds.), *Frontiers of Population Forecasting* (pp. 15–41). New York: The Population Council. (A supplement to *Population and Development Review* 24.)

Makridakis, S. 1993. "Accuracy Measures: Theoretical and Practical Concerns." *International Journal of Forecasting* 9: 527–529.

Pflaumer, P. 1988. "Confidence Intervals for Population Projections Based on Monte Carlo Methods." *International Journal of Forecasting* 4: 135–142.

Shryock, H. S. 1954. "Accuracy of Population Projections for the United States." *Estadistica* 12: 587–597.

Smith, S., and T. Sincich. 1990. "The Relationship between the Length of the Base Period and Population Forecast Errors." *Journal of the American Statistical Association* 85: 367–375.

Swanson, D., and J. Tayman. 1995. "Between a Rock and a Hard Place: The Evaluation of Demographic Forecasts." *Population Research and Policy Review* 14: 233–249.

Tayman, J., E. Schafer, and L. Carter. 1998. "The role of Population Size in the Determination and Prediction of Population Forecast Errors: An Evaluation Using Confidence Intervals for Subcounty Areas." *Population Research and Policy Review* 17: 1–20.

Tayman, J., and D. Swanson. 1999. "On the Validity of MAPE as a Measure of Population Forecast Accuracy." *Population Research and Policy Review* 18: 299–322.

Subjective Methods

Dalkey, N., and O. Helmer. 1963. "An Experimental Application of the Delphi Method to the Use of Experts." *Management Science* 9: 458–467.

Lutz, W., P. Saariluoma, W. Sanderson, and S. Scherbov. 2000. "New Developments in the Methodology of Expert- and Argument-Based Probabilistic Population Projection." Interim Report 1R-00-020. Laxenburg, Austria: IIASA.

Lutz, W., W. Sanderson, and S. Scherbov. 1998. "Expert-Based Probabilistic Population Projections." In W. Lutz, J. Vaupel, and D. Ahlburg (Eds.), *Frontiers of Population Forecasting.* (pp. 139–155). New York: The Population Council. (A supplement to *Population and Development Review,* 24).

McNees, S. 1992. "The Uses and Abuses of 'Consensus' Forecasts." *Journal of Forecasting* 11: 703–710.

Rowe, G., and G. Wright. 1999. "The Delphi Technique as a Forecasting Tool: Issues and Analysis." *International Journal of Forecasting* 15: 353–375.

Projecting Mortality

Bennett, N., and S. Olshansky. 1996. "Forecasting U.S. Age Structure and the Future of Social Security: The Impact of Adjustments to Official Mortality Schedules." *Population and Development Review* 22: 703–727.

Budlender, D., and R. Dorrington. 2002. *ASSA AIDS and Demographic Models: User Guide.* Cape Town, South Africa: Center for Actuarial Research, University of Cape Town.

Horiuchi, S., and J. Wilmoth. 1998. "Deceleration in the Age Pattern of Mortality at Older Ages." *Demography* 35: 391–412.

Olshansky, S., B. Carnes, and C. Cassel. 1990. "In Search of Methuselah: Estimating the Upper Limits to Human Longevity." *Science* 250: 634–640.

White, K., and S. Preston. 1996. "How Many Americans Are Alive Because of Improvements in Mortality?" *Population and Development Review* 22: 415–429.

Projecting Fertility

Ahlburg, D. 1982. "How Accurate Are the U.S. Bureau of the Census Projections of Total Live Births." *Journal of Forecasting* 1: 365–374.

Ahlburg, D. 1983. "Good Times, Bad Times: A Study of the Future Path of U.S. Fertility." *Social Biology* 30: 17–23.

Akers, D. S. 1965. "Cohort Fertility versus Parity Progression as Methods of Projecting Births." *Demography* 2: 414–428.

Bloom, D., and J. Trussell. 1984. "What Are the Determinants of Delayed Childbearing and Permanent Childlessness in the United States?" *Demography* 21: 591–611.

Bumpass, L., and C. Westoff. 1969. "The Prediction of Completed Fertility." *Demography* 6: 445–454.

Easterlin, R. 1987. *Birth and Fortune: The Impact of Numbers on Personal Welfare*, 2nd ed. Chicago, IL: University of Chicago Press.

Friedman, D., M. Hechter, and S. Kanazawa. 1994. "A Theory of the Value of Children." *Demography* 31: 375–401.

Golini, A. 1998. "How Low Can Fertility Be? An Empirical Exploration." *Population and Development Review* 24: 59–73.

Lee, R. 1974. "Forecasting Births in Post-Transition Populations: Stochastic Renewal with Serially Correlated Fertility." *Journal of the American Statistical Association* 69: 607–617.

Lee, R. 1976. "Demographic Forecasting and the Easterlin Hypothesis." *Population and Development Review* 2: 459–468.

Lesthaeghe, R., and P. Wilhems. 1999. "Is Low Fertility a Temporary Phenomenon in the European Union?" *Population and Development Review* 25: 211–228.

Mason, K. 1997. "Explaining Fertility Transitions." *Demography* 34: 443–454.

Projecting Migration

Clark, D., and J. Cosgrove. 1991. "Amenities versus Labor Market Opportunities: Choosing the optimal distance to move." *Journal of Regional Science* 31: 311–328.

Clark, D., T. Knapp, and N. White. 1996. "Personal and Location-Specific Characteristics and Elderly Interstate Migration." *Growth and Change* 27: 327–351.

Clark, D., and C. Murphy. 1996. "Countywide Employment and Population Growth: An Analysis of the 1980s." *Journal of Regional Science* 36: 235–256.

Cushing, B. 1987. "A Note on the Specification of Climate Variables in Models of Population Migration." *Journal of Regional Science* 27: 641–649.

DaVanzo, J. 1978. "Does Unemployment Affect Migration? Evidence from Micro-data." *Review of Economics and Statistic* 60: 504–514.

Edmonston, B., and J. Passel. 1992. "Immigration and Immigrant Generations in Population Projections." *International Journal of Forecasting* 8: 459–476.

Evans, A. 1990. "The Assumption of Equilibrium in the Analysis of Migration and Interregional Differences: A Review of Some Recent Research." *Journal of Regional Science* 30: 515–531.

Graves, P., and P. Mueser. 1993. "The Role of Equilibrium and Disequilibrium in Modeling Growth and Decline." *Journal of Regional Science* 33: 69–84.

Greenwood, M. 1981. "*Migration and Economic Growth in the United States: National, Regional and Metropolitan Perspectives.*" New York: Academic Press.

Greenwood, M. 1997. "Internal Migration in Developed Countries." In M. Rosenzweig and O. Stark (Eds.), *Handbook of Population and Family Economics* (pp. 647–720). Amsterdam, Holland: Elsevier Science B.V.

Lee, E. 1966. "A Theory of Migration." *Demography* 3: 47–57.

Long, L. 1991. "Residential Mobility Differences among Developed Countries." *International Regional Science Review* 14: 133–147.

Massey, D. 1999. "International Migration at the Dawn of the Twenty-First Century: The Role of the States." *Population and Policy Review* 25: 303–322.

Massey, D., J. Arango, G. Hugo, A. Kouaouci, A. Pellegrino, and J. Taylor. 1998. *Worlds in Motion: Understanding International Migration at the End of the Millenium.* Oxford, UK: Oxford University Press.

McHugh, K., T. Hogan, and S. Happel. 1995. "Multiple Residence and Cyclical Migration: A Life Course Perspective." *Professional Geographer* 47: 251–267.

Meuser, P., and M. White. 1989. "Explaining the Association between Rates of In-migration and Out-migration." *Papers of the Regional Science Association* 67: 121–134.

Mohlo, I. 1986. "Theories of Migration: A Review." *Scottish Journal of Political Economy* 33: 396–419.

Morrison, P. 1971. "Chronic Movers and the Future Redistribution of Population: A Longitudinal Analysis." *Demography* 8: 171–184.

Plane, D. 1989. "Population Migration and Economic Restructuring in the United States." *International Regional Science Review* 12: 263–280.

Plane, D. 1993. "Demographic Influences on Migration." *Demography* 27: 375–383.

Rogers, A. 1992. Elderly Migration and Population Redistribution in the United States. In A. Rogers (Ed.), *Elderly Migration and Population Redistribution* (pp. 226–248). London, UK: Belhaven Press.

Rogers, A., and L. Castro. 1984. "Model Migration Schedules." In A. Rogers (Ed.), *Migration, Urbanization and Spatial Population Dynamics* (pp. 41–88). Boulder, CO: Westview Press.

Smith, S., and H. Fishkind. 1985. "Elderly Migration in Rapidly Growing Areas: A Time Series Approach." *Review of Regional Studies* 15: 11–20.

Steinnes, D. 1982. " 'Do People Follow Jobs' or 'Do Jobs Follow People'?" A Causality Issue in Urban Economics." *Urban Studies* 19: 187–192.

Vijverberg, W. 1993. "Labor Market Performance as a Determinant of Migration." *Economica* 60: 143–160.

Projecting Labor Force and Household Income

De Wolff, P. 1967. "Employment Forecasting by Professions." In United Nations, *World Population Conference* (pp. 109–114), 1965 (Belgrade), Vol. III.

Fullerton, H. 1997. "Labor Force 2006: Slowing Down and Changing Composition." *Monthly Labor Review* 120: 23–38.

Goldstein, H. 1966. "Projections of Manpower Requirements and Supply." *Industrial Relations* 5(3): 17–27.

Tilak, V. R. K. 1963. "The Future Manpower Situation in India, 1961–76." *International Labor Review* 80: 435–446.

United Nations. 1993. *Projection Methods for Integrating Population Variables into Development Planning. Volume 1: Methods for Comprehensive Planning. Module 3: Techniques for Preparing Projections of Household and Other Incomes, Household Consumption, and Savings and Government Consumption and Investment.* New York: United Nations.

Projecting Households and Families

George, M. V., and J. Perreault. 1993. "Projecting Households and Families in Canada by the Headship Rate Method. In K. Mahadevan and P. Krishnan (Eds.), *Methodology for Population Studies and Development* (pp. 385–402). New Delhi: Sage.

Siegel, J. S. 1972. "Development and Accuracy of Projections of Population and Households in the United States." *Demography* 9(1): 51–68.

Van Imhoff, E., A. Kuijsten, P. Hooimeijer, and L. van Wissen. 1995. *Household Demography and Household Modeling*. New York: Plenum Press.

Walkden, A. H. 1961. "The Estimation of Future Numbers of Private Households in England and Wales." *Population Studies* 15: 174–186.

Zeng, Y., J. Vaupel, and Z. Wang. 1998. "Household Projection Using Conventional Demographic Data. In W. Lutz, J. Vaupel, and D. Ahlbrrg (Eds.), *Frontiers of Population Forecasting* (pp. 59–87). New York: The Population Council.

22

Some Methods of Estimation for Statistically Underdeveloped Areas

CAROLE POPOFF AND D. H. JUDSON

BASIC DEMOGRAPHIC STATISTICS FOR LESS DEVELOPED AREAS

Demographic information in less developed countries varies in the level of accuracy and detail much more than it does in the more developed countries. This is primarily because the more developed countries support the conduct of periodic censuses and maintenance of vital registration systems or have population registers. Thus, virtually without exception the economically more advanced countries are able to describe the fundamental demographic processes taking place in their countries. At this writing almost all countries of the world have conducted at least one census, but most still lack adequate vital registration systems. Thus, there is still a need for alternate techniques that can produce meaningful demographic statistics essential to demographic analysis, which may be used to inform national development efforts.

An adequate description of the results of the basic demographic processes of fertility and mortality (hence population change) requires the combined use of two types of demographic data, stock and flow date. These data allow tabulations of the composition of the population and form the basis of rates of change that are used to create estimates and projections used for planning and other purposes. Analyses of military needs, educational requirements, labor force, family composition, migration, aging, and retirement will, at the least, require these basic data. The combined system of a periodic census and a vital registration that generates demographic information may be referred to as the "classical system." Both stock and flow data are used to estimate current rates of change and project them. At the most basic level, the minimum demographic information that would provide planners and others with the necessary information needed for economic and social development includes: (1) total population by age and sex and (2) birth, death, and net migration rates, all disaggregated by geographic regions, if feasible.

Stock data are the numbers of persons at a given date, classified by various characteristics, geographic area, and so on. Stock data are recorded from censuses and normally include such information as age, race, sex, marital status, and (sometimes) national origin. More detailed data are often collected from sample surveys of the population or a census that can include household relationships, home ownership, occupation, income, place of work, family relationship, and so forth. Flow data are the collection or summation of events. At the most basic level this includes births, deaths, and migration flows occurring to, or originating from, the population during some specified time period such as a calendar year. These data are used to illustrate the basic mechanisms that change a population's size, composition, and geographic distribution. Flow data that arise from vital registrations and other mechanisms provide the information to tabulate changes in the population. That is, rates of change can be derived from these data, such as rates of fertility, mortality, and migration.

SCOPE OF THE CHAPTER

The main focus of this chapter is on indirect methods of estimation because many less developed countries lack complete systems of vital registrations and censuses that allow direct estimation. Estimation methods for developing areas can be grouped into two general types (1) methods based on cross-sectional data, either from censuses, surveys, or both, and (2) methods utilizing data collected in sample registration areas, typically linked with census-type recording systems in various ways. One fundamental tool used is the model life table whose basic features are discussed in the first section. Short examples are given of various calculations using model life tables. Next, more examples using model life tables are shown in combination with various types of data the analyst might encounter in data from the less developed countries. These include (1) data from two successive censuses using model life tables and model stable populations, (2) data from a single census or survey including surveys of children ever born and children living, and (3) data from sample registrations. Examples are provided to demonstrate the estimation of overall rates of natural increase, death rates, and birthrates. Other examples include using life expectancy at birth to determine the appropriate model life table, life expectancy at age x > 0, and fertility rates and mean age using a standard age pattern of "natural" fertility from a stable population model, and so on. Whenever appropriate, comments on the results of applying alternative "regional" models to the same problem and comparing the results will be made. These examples are not exhaustive of the techniques that are available but are meant to be representative of general approaches to estimation using deficient data. The reader is encouraged to refer to Appendixes B and C in this volume for a more complete discussion of these topics. Preceding the two major sections in this chapter is a general discussion of data sources and data quality.

APROACHES TO OBTAINING DEMOGRAPHIC INFORMATION

Background

Vital statistics administrative-record systems came into use before other Demographic data systems. The problem early demographers faced was estimating rates from vital data only, a famous example being the astronomer Halley's attempt to construct a life table from death statistics alone. Consequently, new techniques were developed that used existing census or census-type data as inputs. These data typically came into use because, in statistically less developed countries, they were far more abundant and generally of much higher quality than were vital records data.

Implementing the "Classical" System

It is often thought that, in the long run, the best way to increase the supply of basic demographic information in the less developed countries is to bring census taking and vital registration record keeping up to the level that exists in the more developed countries. In other words, the less developed countries should adopt the so-called classical system as soon as possible. There are, however, fundamental reasons why this may not be feasible in the short run. First, data needs are immediate but implementing a vital registration system and a periodic enumeration that is accurate and

has complete or broad coverage takes time. Second, there is a need for more demographic detail than these systems often provide when they are first implemented. Finally, combining these two data sets to produce more detail exacerbates the biases that are inherent weaknesses in each. For example, putting a comprehensive vital registration system into operation may be unobtainable in the near term for many less developed countries because implementation often requires more resources than can be justified from an economic standpoint. Citizens' attitudes can also play a role; people may not see it in their interest to voluntarily cooperate with the registrar, even if intensive educational programs and strict enforcement of the registration laws are implemented at the same time. Also, gross errors have been observed in vital registration data, even in systems that have been in existence for many decades. Finally, highly developed countries' experience reveals that the attainment of full or nearly full coverage of vital events is a long and gradual process. Although, clearly, implementing a comprehensive vital registration system should be pursued, there are strong incentives to look for less costly methods that will produce demographic information in the near term while the system is being put into place.

There are additional considerations. Even when both censuses and vital registration systems are reasonably accurate, these two data sources often do not meet all needs for demographic information. For example, to be useful, both a census and a vital statistics registration system must have complete or, at least, widespread coverage. In addition, the demographic information needed for social and economic advancement must consist of more detail than is usually collected in a simple count or vital statistics registration system. However, this additional demographic information becomes a by-product because the ultinate objectives of enumerations and vital registration systems are legal and administrative. Further, there is always a strong, but understandable, resistance to collecting more information than is actually needed to support these legal and administrative requirements because of implementation and maintenance costs. Finally, the population may react negatively if they are asked to provide more detailed information.

Another consideration is the nature of records data collection itself. Because these two sets of records are typically generated by separate data-collecting agencies that have different agendas and data needs, combining these data sets is problematic. This results from the biases found in records data; they arise from both the collection process and respondent behavior as well as general random response and recording errors. While random errors tend to cancel each other out, biases create distortions; thus, combining two biased data sets simply exacerbates the problem. For example, it might be straightforward to calculate a simple measure of mortality (e.g., the crude death rate) from the combination of these two data sets by relating the total number of deaths in a single year (a flow) to the stock of the total population enumerated at the midpoint of that year or estimated for that date. To disaggregate a crude death rate by sex is also relatively easy to accomplish because sex is usually unambiguously defined; thus both data sets may be relatively accurate. Creating age data from these two data sets, however, may be far more difficult because age is less likely to be reported accurately. These problems multiply rapidly when one is trying to generate more specialized types of information (e.g., marital status, occupation, race, or religion) where the conceptualizations of these categories by respondents or the record-keeping agency may be subject to varying interpretations. In addition, the items may not exist in both data sets.

Deficiencies of Demographic Statistics in Less Developed Countries

It appears that the availability of data from the less developed countries has greatly improved in the past several years. Statistical offices in all countries have expanded or have been built, and at least one census has been conducted in all but two countries (Arriaga, Johnson, and Jamison 1994). However, collecting and warehousing data are not sufficient without accompanying analysis, which has been lacking. In addition, vital registration systems are still not reliable sources of vital statistics. Because these deficiencies are largely a feature of the broader problem of limited resources, one would suppose that economic and social development should generate the resources to overcome these deficiencies. However, social and economic advancement requires ever more detailed demographic information than the existing sources can supply. Hence there exists an urgent need to develop and disseminate methods for a better utilization of the statistical data that already exist in these countries. This can, in turn, provide the incentive to increase the supply of pertinent demographic information that will aid these countries' development efforts.

New Approaches

Even when systems of census-taking and vital registration are fully developed, there are still cost issues, organizational constraints, and issues of accuracy and coverage. This is why alternative sources of data and methods to develop demographic information have been developed. Two general approaches have emerged from these efforts. One approach relies on special sample surveys and census-type information alone, the other on sample registration systems, usually in combination with sample surveys. Techniques were developed using these data produced from sample registration systems or sample surveys to provide needed demographic information at the level of detail useful to a country's socioeconomic development efforts.

Making estimates from census data alone can produce reliable information. First, a cross-sectional view of the population provided by a census reflects the cumulative results of past demographic flows and offers a base for estimating such flows, particularly if more than one, not too widely spaced, censuses have been taken. Flow data can also be collected during a census by including questions about past events, with or without a specified reference period, that become a substitute for vital statistics information. In fact, efforts to improve or augment data sources have been aimed at utilizing precisely the capability of a cross-sectional survey to generate flow-type data. The traditional census has been used to collect this types of information by expanding the number and types of questions asked. However, the cost of a census rises with increases in the number and variety of questions asked. Also, obtaining retrospective information of reasonable quality requires intense fieldwork, and highly qualified field personnel that is seldom available for a full census in a less developed country. Thus, there has been a shift toward sample surveys that are more limited in size as a substitute for, or more typically as a complement to, a conventional census. Sample surveys can be administered in a timely manner, can be repeated with much less cost than an enumeration, and can be rich in content. However, one drawback is that sample surveys cannot provide detail at lower geographic levels without raising the cost greatly.

Using cross-sectional surveys as a remedy for the lack of complete vital registration data has required innovative analytical techniques. Demographic models have been developed that transform survey data into traditional demographic data. These models must be able to produce reasonable estimates of general population characteristics from sample data or fill in gaps in the existing information. A second type of methodological innovation is to collect vital registration data on a sample basis rather than have 100% coverage. Estimates can then be prepared using the sample data in conjunction with traditional census data or, more often, with data obtained from special cross-sectional sample surveys, where the survey record can be linked with the vital registration record or the census record. One notable feature is that they may incorporate techniques ensuring a higher level of control over omissions by matching or linking records from different sources.

In addition, these newer methods can provide the basis for generating more information than merely creating complete vital statistics from information derived from a sample or by comparing conventional flow or stock "rates" with "rates" derived from survey data alone. The refinement of these matching or record-linkage techniques, currently being developed and used, promise to provide a suite of demographic tools that would supply not only almost all information that can be obtained from the conventional methods but that in some respects might be superior. Unfortunately, these matching techniques require high levels of technical skill and sophisticated equipment that are generally more expensive than the those needed to generate estimates based on survey data alone.

The two main new approaches to generating data—surveys and sample registration—do not exhaust the full range of possible alternative methods to generate demographic data. Some examples of nonconventional approaches to data collection are continuous population registers, longitudinal panel studies, and intensive observation of small subsets of the population utilizing all available tools for recording demographic facts (for example, the information typically gathered in intensive anthropological fieldwork). As a general solution, however, these atypical techniques are limited because of their cost, their extremely specialized nature, or their narrow range of applicability.

ESTIMATION TECHNIQUES AND MODELS

Demographic models are generalized representations of demographic events or processes. This section focuses on some estimation models with a brief discussion relating to the use of limited data. Use of these models becomes particularly important when the available data are limited or otherwise defective. If reliable and comprehensive demographic data are available, these models are rarely needed. However, they can be indispensable in checking and adjusting data, in filling gaps in the available records, and in deriving reliable estimates from fragmentary pieces of evidence. There are two important types of models that will be discussed in some detail in this section because of their general usefulness in methods of demographic estimation for the statistically less developed areas. These are (1) model life tables and (2) model stable populations. Other techniques will also be discussed, including some basic techniques to verify the accuracy of, or improve data from, censuses or vital registrations briefly mentioned earlier.

Age and Sex Composition

Age and sex distributions are the most basic information that is needed for future planning. Thus, it is important that these data be as accurate or representative as possible. Normally, these data are secured by periodic population censuses; however, even basic information such as this can be misreported or incomplete, or a significant proportion of the population may simply not respond. For example, in many less developed countries people do not know their age with accuracy. Or there may be only one census from which to make inferences. Age and sex data also play a crucial role in the determination of mortality and fertility rates in the absence of a very accurate vital registration system.

Methods to analyze age and sex composition are important demographic tools to determine data deficiencies such as misreporting. Some of the more important analytic techniques for age analysis are graphical representation, evaluation using indices, and data smoothing techniques.

Age structure is a map of demographic history as well as a means to forecast the future. Graphical plots of the year of birth can reveal past fertility trends as well as indicate migration or age misreporting or even errors or omissions in a census. The age pyramid displays the surviving cohorts by age and sex. For example, a smooth cone–shaped pyramid suggests a population where fertility has not fluctuated in the past, population has been little affected by net migration, mortality is following a typical trend, and the age reporting appears to be accurate. A pyramid with bulges can indicate significant past events in certain age groups such as a sharp drop in fertility or a rise in mortality (caused by a war or a sudden outbreak of a total disease like AIDS, for example). A pyramid that shows uneven percentages of males to females in a particular age range, for example, may indicate the results of migration patterns. Overlaying plots of prior and current census data by age categories can show migration patterns. Age misreporting can be detected in a line graph of deviations of numbers reported at each age from the expected curve.

The main indices used to evaluate demographic data are (1) sex ratios, (2) age ratios, and (3) indices that can detect preference for certain digits in age reporting. If there has not been significant migration, age ratios constructed by dividing one age cohort by the average of the leading and following age cohorts can also indicate reporting errors or inconsistencies. The larger the fluctuations or deviations of these ratios from unity, the higher probability there has been misreporting of some type. Digit preference or heaping can be detected using one of several indices Chapter 7. Relatively large departures of sex ratios from 100 indicate misreporting. Although allowance should be made for the general decline of the sex ratio with age, any deviation can indicate either an event of note or misreporting. Recall that the United Nations developed a system of indices to evaluate population structure. It is composed of (1) an index of sex-ratio score (SRS), the mean difference between sex ratios for the successive age groups, averaged irrespective of sign, and (2) an index of the age-ratio score (ARSM and ARSF for males and females, respectively) or the mean deviation of the age ratios from 100%, irrespective of sign. The Joint Score Index (JS) is defined as JS = $3 \times$ SRS + ARSM + ARSF. Based on empirical analysis, if the JS is less than 20, the population structure is considered accurate; if the JS is between 20 and 40, the population structure is considered inaccurate; for any JS score greater than 40, the population structure is considered highly inaccurate.

Adjustment can be made for inaccuracies or irregularities in age distributions by smoothing techniques. There are numerous formulas. We can distinguish formulas that maintain the original 5-year totals and those that modify them, even though lightly, they do go only. These formulas give similar results. See Appendix C for a more complete discussion of smoothing and other data-adjustment techniques.

Mortality and the Effect of HIV/AIDS on Mortality Levels

Life expectancy is often used as an indicator of the viability of a country's basic ability to provide for its citizens' well-being. Reliable information on mortality levels and rates, particularly for age groups, is a necessary ingredient for tracking changes in mortality and understanding where there are improvements still to be made. With reliable demographic information on deaths and total population, direct estimation techniques can be used including the construction of a life table. When these data are not reliable or simply not available, some indirect techniques can be used, to be discussed here.

A significant development that characterizes the latter part of the 20th century is the global HIV/AIDS epidemic (U.S. Department of Commerce, 1999). Mortality has risen and growth has slowed in every world region, with the greatest impacts in many sub-Sahara African, Asian, and Latin American countries. Mortality levels in these countries have been seriously affected; current estimates indicate that more than 40 million people have become infected with HIV since about 1970, and 11 million of those have died. Deaths from AIDS has reversed the declines in infant mortality in many countries; however, two-thirds of AIDS deaths occur after the first year of life. Methodologies to incorporate AIDS into population analysis are discussed in detail in *World Population Profile: 1996* (McDevitt, 1996; Stanecki and Way, 1997).[1] The basic approach is to (1) establish criteria for selecting countries that require taking AIDS into account; (2) determine the trend and an estimate of prevalence for a specific date; (3) model the development and spread of AIDS and generate alternate scenarios; (4) use the empirical evidence from step 2 to establish a ranking for each country based on the scenarios from step 3; (5) project adult HIV seroprevalence for the total country by locating the country's weighted total adult seroprevalence on the total country epidemic curve implied by interpolation; and (6) interpolate AIDS-related mortality rates, by age and sex,

implied by the estimated speed and level of HIV infection from epidemiological results for a selected period. It should be noted that levels of mortality and values of life expectancy will change dramatically from those found in model life tables. However, the analyst should remember that model life tables represent consistent conditions over time, whereas epidemics or other disasters represent phenomena that will wax and wane and thus, in some respects, represent temporary and unreular events.

A Note on Direct Estimation Techniques

Direct techniques require reliable information on population and deaths, usually from censuses and registration systems, to measure the level of mortality. Crude death rates and life tables, with their life expectancies at birth, are the indices for the measurement of mortality levels. Infant mortality in particular, is considered an important measure of the state of development of a country. Life expectancy, a summary of mortality of every age expressed in a single number, and age-specific death rates also provide important information.

Model Life Tables

The history of demographic analysis has numerous examples of attempts to formulate generalizations about the age pattern of human mortality (Coale and Demeny, 1966, 1983). However, less developed countries may lack age-specific mortality data to the extent that a direct and reliable description of the pattern of mortality is not feasible. If it is useful to have an estimate of the true level of mortality, a viable solution is to select an actual life table from a country that has similar characteristics and reliably recorded mortality experience, possibly a neighboring country. A generalization of this approach is to construct a set of model life tables based on recorded data for a broad range of countries. A simple example is the construction of life tables from observed data, where graduation, interpolation, and extrapolation often replace the raw data with a descriptive model of reality. This technique, however, is justifiable only when the basic data are essentially reliable and the analyst wishes to remove the effects of random deviations from the observed values, to estimate the true underlying values, or needs to obtain estimates for age intervals different from those in the original data. (See Appendix C for further discussion.)

Regional Model Life Tables

A fundamental observation is that the level of mortality in any given age group can be closely predicted if the level of mortality in an adjacent age group is known. Several model-life-table systems exist. The best known, the Coale

---

[1] The reports referred to in this section were sponsored by the U.S. Agency for International Development; the World Health Organization, Bureau for Global Programs, Field Support, and Research, under the Center for Population, Health and Nutrition; the U.S. Department of Commerce's Economics and Statistics Administration; and the U.S. Census Bureau. The reader is encouraged to refer to the list of suggested readings as well as to access documents from these agencies for detailed reports.

and Demeny (1966, 1983) regional tables, first published in 1966 and reproduced in part by the United Nations in 1967, consists of four sets of model life tables labeled "West," "East," "North," and "South," each representing an individual mortality pattern. Originally, the "East" tables were based mainly on Central European experience, whereas the "North" and "South" tables were derived from life tables of Scandinavian and South European countries, respectively. The "West" tables, on the other hand, are representative of a broad residual group. This model set was based on some 125 life tables from more than 20 countries, including Canada, the United States, Australia, New Zealand, South Africa, Israel, Japan, and Taiwan, as well as a number of countries from Western Europe. The mortality experience in these countries did not show the systematic deviations from mean world experience found in the other three groups. The mortality levels shown in the male tables differ from the mortality level of the female tables with which they are paired; this difference reflects the typical relationship between male and female mortality occurring in a particular population. The original set (Coale and Demeny, 1966) contained 24 mortality levels corresponding to expectations of life at birth. These are calculated for males and females separately, with equal spacing of the values of the expectation of life at birth for females, ranging from an e_0 of 20 years (labeled as level 1) to an e_0 of 77.5 years (labeled as level 24). The second edition published in 1983 consists of 25 levels from life expectancy at birth from 20 to 80 years and ages in each table going up to 100. Using a large number of life tables of acceptable quality, primarily for European countries, Coale and Demeny (1983) used graphical and statistical analysis to identify the distinct patterns of mortality for the updated tables.

The United Nations Model Life Tables

The United Nations' 1955 set of model life tables were made available in a more elaborate form in 1956 (United Nations, 1956). These were constructed from parabolic regression equations indicating the relationships between adjacent pairs of life table $_nq_x$ values as observed in 158 life tables collected from a wide selection of countries and representing different periods of time. The basic method is to start from a specified level of infant mortality, q_0, from which a value for $_4q_1$ can be determined. From $_4q_1$ a value of $_5q_5$ is estimated, which in turn serves as an estimator of $_5q_{10}$, and so on, until the life table is completed. By repeating this procedure starting from various specified levels of q_0, a system of model life tables is obtained spanning the entire range of human mortality experience. The construction of these tables, however, has been subject to various questions. Apart from the statistical bias introduced by the iterative use of a series of regression equations to construct the life table, there are two main points of criticism. First, it may be argued that the collection of life tables used in the

analysis is not sufficiently representative of the whole range of reliably recorded human mortality experience. Moreover, some of the tables in the collection themselves incorporate a great deal of actuarial manipulation and the outright use of models. For example, the life tables for India have a heavy influence on the pattern of mortality at low levels of e_0, shown in the UN model tables (1956). But the childhood mortality values of these Indian tables are essentially extrapolations from mortality at more advanced ages and, thus, are not indicative of reliably recorded experience. Second, the suggestion implicit in the UN model life tables that a single parameter (such as q_0 or any other life table value) can determine all other life table values with sufficient precision is clearly dependent on the particular use of that life table. Although high mortality in one age group does tend to imply high mortality in all other age groups as well, the detailed age patterns of human mortality can display substantial variation. To assume away the existence of such variation may be legitimate for some applications but unacceptable for others. In 1982, the United Nations issued an updated and more sophisticated set of life tables that are used in some of the examples in this chapter.

The models developed by the United Nations (1982) display five distinct mortality patterns called "Latin American," "Chilean," "South Asian," "Far Eastern," and "General" They represent distinct geographic regions as named; "General" represents a common region. The life tables constructed representing each mortality pattern are arranged by life expectancy at birth for each life expectancy from 35 to 75 years. Statistical and graphical analyses of a number of evaluated and adjusted life tables for the less developed countries were used to identify the different patterns (United Nations, 1982; see also United Nations, 1990). After experimentation with several approaches, the basic technique used was a variation of the classical principle components analysis. Age patterns of mortality comprised the input data set that was clustered by statistical and graphical procedures by distinct average age patterns of mortality. The principle components model was fitted to the deviations from average mortality patterns for each age cluster. Life tables from countries in each of the named regions were used. The model life tables produced by the United Nations have proven useful in a wide range of practical applications, notably in preparing population projections with a specified pattern of mortality change.

The differences among the age (and sex) patterns of mortality in the four regional models of the Coale and Demeny system or the five models of the United Nations are slight in some respects and pronounced in others. These differences also vary in character as one moves from higher to lower levels of mortality. Thus, no simple rule can summarize the extent to which the use of one set, in preference to another, will affect the outcome in any particular application. In general, the use of the "East," "North," and "South" models or the "Latin American," "Chilean," "South Asian," and "Far Eastern" models are recommended only if there is some evidence suggesting that the mortality in the population is a close approximation to the model picked or has some of the peculiarities that also characterize these models. Otherwise the use of the "West" or the "General" model is preferred (United Nations, 1990).

The analyst must remember that the outcome of his or her analysis may be strongly affected by the choice of a particular model. Although the rule just given favors the use of the "West" or "General" model, there is no assurance that the pattern in these models represents the true pattern. However, lacking substantive evidence there exists no sound basis for deciding where a particular country's mortality fits within the range represented by any of these regional models. Any regional model may fail to span the range covered by mortality patterns in contemporary situations. In fact, the use of a regional model should serve as a constant warning that the model describes only a certain type of experience and that attempts to generalize from it can be risky. In reality, however, when the analyst has little or no reliable information concerning the true pattern of mortality, the model life tables can be very useful and may be necessary. The following example illustrates the varying estimates of mortality using different models.

Examples

Consider the problem of estimating infant mortality from given values of the expectation of life at age 5. In this example, the levels of q_0 for females are determined using the 1966 Coale and Demeny regional model life tables[2] and in the UN set, assuming an e_5 of 45, 55, and 65 years, respectively. The steps the analyst should follow are (1) locate those tables that bracket the given values for e_5; (2) find the corresponding values of q_0; and (3) then determine by interpolation the values of q_0, corresponding exactly to the given value of e_5. The results are demonstrated here:

Set of model tables	q_0 for $e_5 = 45.0$	q_0 for $e_5 = 55.0$	q_0 for $e_5 = 65.0$
"West"	.234	.126	.048
"East"	.331	.178	.070
"North"	.200	.112	.048
"South"	.238	.154	.092
United Nations	.210	.140	.058

[2] For the illustrations of the use of model life tables and model stable populations described in this chapter, we have used the earlier sets of model tables published by Coale and Demeny (1966) rather than their more recent ones (Coale and Demeny, 1983). Although this has been done in the interest of saving time and labor, it should be recognized that the new tables differ only slightly from the earlier ones and that the methodological exposition would be the same with either set. In dealing with an actual problem, the analyst is advised to use the more recent volume because of the greater scope of the tables with respect to the levels of life expectation and the age span and the greater availability of the more recent publication.

As can be seen from this example, the values for q_0 vary considerably; thus, any attempt to estimate infant mortality from an estimated value of e_5 is subject to the risk of considerable error. However, some applications will be more sensitive than others. For instance, given $e_5 = 45.0$, the "West" and the "South" tables result in very similar values for q_0. However, another measure of early childhood mortality, $_5q_0$, if derived from the same model tables ($e_5 = 45.0$), yields quite different figures: .357 if the "West" tables are used and .439 if the "South" tables are applied. Without some dependable indication of the true mortality pattern, the analyst must use caution in making estimates when the outcome will differ significantly on the basis of the chosen pattern. The analyst who has access to the sets of regional tables is encouraged to follow similar procedures routinely. If the estimates are not overly sensitive to the choice of model pattern, however, the analyst can have a high level of confidence in using either the "West" set or the "General" United Nations set.

Apart from the question of the reliability of the age pattern of mortality, recorded experience varies considerably with the level of mortality; thus, the reliability of the tables as representations of real experience will vary. Generally speaking, the tables are most reliable in a broad middle range of mortality. At very low expectations of life, the recorded experience is very sparse; hence the models should be considered as somewhat tentative approximations. Similar caution should be exercised in attributing significance to minor details of the age pattern shown in the models representing very low levels of mortality.

Table B.1 (in Appendix B) presents abridged life tables for females only, from the "West" model (Coale and Demeny 1966) at five different levels of mortality, namely levels 9, 11, 13, 15, and 17.[3] The corresponding table for males at level 9 is also shown. Table B.2 gives a more detailed description of mortality under age 5, in terms of the function l_x for 12 mortality levels, levels 1, 3, ... 21, and 23, separately for males and females. Given that estimates of l_x for x = 1, 2, ... 5 are often obtainable only for the two sexes together, this table also gives values for each sex, assuming a sex ratio at birth of 1.05. Tables in the Coale/Demeny system provide a sufficient density of information such that values at intermediate mortality levels can be obtained by interpolation. Simple linear interpolation can be expected to give sufficient precision in most applications. The following examples illustrate the method of calculating various life table values not directly available from the model life tables shown in the appendix. The "West" model is used in the following calculations, assuming that the age pattern of mortality is well described by this model.

[3] See footnote 2.

Example 1

Interpolate to find the proportion surviving from birth to age 27 among females assuming that the expectation of life at birth is 49.2 years. To find the answer, the analyst will have to interpolate between level 11 ($e_0 = 45$) and level 13 ($e_0 = 50$). Also, because abridged life tables do not contain information on l_{27}/l_0, interpolation is necessary between l_{25}/l_0 and l_{30}/l_0. From Appendix, Table B-1, we have the following figures (taking l_0 as equal to 100,000, as usual):

	$e_0 = 45.0$	$e_0 = 50.0$
l_{25}	69,022	74,769
l_{30}	66,224	72,326

There are two approaches to the interpolation procedure (for convenience, apply the easier interpolation first): (1) calculate both l_{25} and l_{30} for $e_0 = 49.2$, and then interpolate between l_{25} and l_{30} to obtain l_{27}; or (2) calculate l_{27} for $e_0 = 45.0$ and $e_0 = 50.0$, and then interpolate between $e_0 = 45.0$ and $e_0 = 50.0$ to obtain $e_0 = 49.2$.

The following is a demonstration of the second calculation. It should be noted that interpolation can be done either "up" from 45.0 or "down" from 50.0, in each case deriving the required weight; the sum of the two fractions equals 1.

Step 1. Perform interpolation for l_{27} "up" from 45.0:

$$\text{weight } 1 = \frac{49.2 - 45.0}{50.0 - 45.0} = \frac{4.2}{5} = .84$$
$$\text{weight } 2 = 1.00 - .84 = .16$$

Step 2. (*Alternate*). Perform interpolation for l_{27} "down" from 50.0:

$$\text{weight } 1 = \frac{50.0 - 49.2}{50.0 - 45.0} = \frac{0.8}{5} = .16$$
$$\text{weight } 2 = 1.00 - .16 = .84$$

Note that the weighted average of the "margin" ages will equal the target age; for example, $49.5 = (45.0 \times .16) + (50.0 \times .84)$.

Step 3. Obtain the figures for levels l_{25} and l_{30} for $e_0 = 49.2$ using these weighting factors:

$$l_{25} = (69,022 \times .16) + (74,769 \times .84) = 73,849$$
$$l_{30} = (66,225 \times .16) + (72,326 \times .84) = 71,350$$

Step 4. Interpolate between the levels 25 and level 30 to find the weights for level 27:

$$\text{For } l_{25}: \frac{27 - 25}{30 - 25} = 0.6 : \text{for } l_{30}: 1.0 - .6 = .4$$

Step 5. Calculate the number surviving birth at l_{27} for $e_0 = 49.2$:

$$l_{27} = (73,849 \times .60) + (71,350 \times .40) = 72.849$$

Example 2

Calculate the joint male and female mortality level. What is the value of e_{65} at mortality level 9, for males and females combined? In general, a simple arithmetic mean of the male and female 65 values will give a good approximation. A more exact answer can be obtained by finding a value of T_{65} for males and females together and dividing this figure by the corresponding value of l_{65}. Assuming a sex ratio at birth of 1.05, the calculation is as follows:

Step 1. Find T_{65} and l_{65} for males (adjusted for sex ratio) and females as follows:

	T_{65}	l_{65}
(1) Females, level 9	308,597	29,527
(2) Males, level 9	229,910	24,006
(3) Males, level 9, adjusted: line (2) × 1.05	241,406	25,206
(4) Males adjusted + females, level 9: line (1) + line (3)	549,918	54,733

Step 2. Calculate the value of e_{65} at mortality level 9, for males and females combined as follows:

$$e_{65} \text{ at level } 9 = T_{65}/l_{65} = 549,913/54,733 = 10.05$$

Example 3

Interpolate to find the level of mortality corresponding to the proportion dying under age 2. The value of $_2q_0$ is estimated as .270 for both sexes combined. What is the implied level of mortality? Proportions surviving to age 2 out of 100,000 births (males and females combined) are tabulated in Appendix Table B.2. In the present example, l_2 is $(1 - .270) \times 100,000 = 73,000$. This figure is bracketed by levels 7 and 9 in Table B.2:

Level	l_2
Step 7	71.112
Step 9	75,813

Step 1. Interpolate to find the weights as follows:

$$\text{weight } 1 = \frac{73,000 - 71,112}{75,813 - 71,112} = \frac{1,888}{4,701} = .402$$
$$\text{weight } 2 = 1 - .402 = .598$$

Step 2. Calculate the level:

$$\text{For } l_2 = 73,000; 7 \times (1 - .402) + (9 \times .402)$$
$$= (7 \times .598) + (9 \times .402) = 7.80$$

The level of mortality associated with any life table parameters corresponding to level 7.80 can now be obtained by applying the same weights to the appropriate values in level 7 and level 9 life tables.

Model Stable Populations

In demographic analysis, the assumption that current behavior can be used as a predictor of future behavior can be a useful concept. For instance, the analyst may want to find the ultimate level of vital rates in a closed population (i.e., where net migration is negligible) assuming current age-specific death rates and fertility rates remain fixed. The answer requires the calculation of stable values, the fundamental or stable rates to which current crude vital rates would converge if the current conditions of fertility and mortality remain constant. The assumption that age-specific fertility and mortality rates remain the same over time defines the conditions underlying the theory of stable populations. A special kind of stable population is a stationary population where the crude birthrate and the crude death rate are equal; thus, the population does not grow. Stable population theory relaxes the stationary population assumption such that the population can grow on decline even though the age-specific fertility and mortality rates remain stable.[4]

Although the theory of stable population and the computational routines required to determine stable population parameters had been worked out decades ago (Coale, 1988; Dublin and Lotka, 1925; Lotka, 1907), it was discovered that fertility and mortality schedules are consistent for a wide range of human populations and are, also, a close approximation for past schedules of fertility and mortality. This discovery implies that these populations as observed in the present must approximate a stable state. It provides demographers with a powerful tool for estimating population characteristics for populations where demographic statistics are deficient or erroneous but where the assumption of a stable population is realistic.

The essence of the stable population estimating procedure consists of two basic steps: (1) a stable population is constructed from the available evidence about a given population; and (2) the calculated parameters of the stable population are used as estimates of the corresponding parameters in the actual population being studied. The power of the technique is that the constructed stable population can be made with confidence, often even on the basis of fragmentary data. Second, the resulting calculating yield a series of sophisticated measures for which no accurate information exists. However, this method has some weaknesses. One is that the stable model may not represent the actual situation. For example, the age and sex distributions will be substantially different when a country experiences large migratory movements or some unique outbreak of a fatal disease such as AIDS. Likewise, substantial, if temporary, deviations from past fertility and mortality rates (e.g., those created by epidemics, wars, or other unusual conditions) will have the same effect, even if both fertility and mortality have been following unchanging trends. Systematic changes in the level of fertility or mortality will also change the schedule. Last, even if the true situation is close to a stable state, the available data may be too fragmentary or biased to permit the derivation of the appropriate stable population. In this situation, there will be no reliable basis for choosing a particular stable model.

Despite these potential problems, the method, or modifications thereof, has proven effective under many circumstances. A significant portion of our current knowledge on world demographic trends and characteristics comes directly from applications of stable population analysis. Although the volume and quality of demographic data in the less developed countries has been improving, these techniques will still be useful in the future because progress will come slowly and unevenly.

The two basic steps in preparing stable estimates can be made mechanically by following the detailed rules and examples set forth later in this chapter. Even though in practice the analyst might routinely use a precomputed set of stable populations such as the Coale/Demeny regional model life tables or the United Nations model life tables, it is important to have full understanding of the logic underlying the method in order to apply the model in unusual situations. This includes being familiar with the methods and data used to derive these stable models as well as how they can be used in combination with actual data to derive unique estimates of fertility, mortality, and the natural rate of increase.

The Stable Population Model

Suppose the analyst wants to estimate the number of persons by age in a particular population. Assume he or she knows that during the relevant past this population (1) has been closed to migration; (2) the number of births has been growing at a constant annual rate r; and (3) mortality, as described by a life table, has been constant. First, define the number of live births during some year, say 1980, in a female population as B_{1980}. Here, the number of children under 1 year of age at the end of 1980 will be the survivors of the birth cohort of 1980; the 1-year-olds will be the survivors of the births in 1979; and, in general, the number of x-year olds will be the survivors of all births that have occurred x years before 1980. (Ages are expressed as exact age at last birthday.) Thus, to answer the question posed earlier the analyst must calculate (1) the number of births in

---

[4] Because such an assumption appears to be unrealistic under most circumstances, it is sometimes charged that the assumption in question is at best of an academic interest. Such a judgment is based on the misinterpretation of the stable measures, however. Just as a speedometer reading of 60 miles an hour is a measure of the *current* speed, and the implied prediction (that the vehicle will be 60 miles away if current speed is maintained for an hour) is of secondary importance, so the calculated stable population and its various parameters are of primary interest as reflections of a *current* situation.

each of the 100 or so years preceding 1980 and (2) the survivors to the end of 1980.

Using the knowledge that in 1980 there were B_{1980} births and this number has been growing annually at the rate of r, we can generalize the calculation of the number of births.

The general calculation using 1980 as the base year is as follows:

Births in 19xx equals

$$B_{1980} \big/ (1+r)^{(1980-19xx)} \text{ or } B_{1980}e^{-(1980-19xx)r}$$

For example,

Births in 1980 = B_{1980}

Births in 1979 = $B_{1980} \big/ (1+r)$ or $B_{1980}e^{-r}$

Births in 1978 = $B_{1980} \big/ (1+r)^2$ or $B_{1980}e^{-2r}$

Births in 1942 = $B_{1980} \big/ (1+r)^{38}$ or $B_{1980}e^{-38r}$

The exponential function will be used in the following illustrations as it is computationally more convenient and also corresponds better to the continuous nature of population growth than the annual compounding formula. Of course, the two formulas yield results that are numerically very close to each other for values of r within the range of human experience, particularly when the absolute value of r is small.

Next we determine the numbers of survivors by age at the end of 1980. In general form (note that 1980 stands for any current year just ended):

Persons at age x = $B_{1980}e^{-xr} L_x/l_0$

For example,

Persons at age 0 = $B_{1980} L_0/l_0$

Persons at age 1 = $B_{1980}e^{-r} L_1/l_0$

Persons at age 5 = $B_{1980}e^{-5r} L_5/l_0$

The next step is to determine the rate of growth of the population, remembering that mortality within each age group is constant from year to year, but births have been growing at a constant annual rate. With the assumption of a closed population, the rate of natural increase is solely due to the relative level of the birthrate and the death rate. Now the analyst can determine age-specific rates of growth.

Step 1. Consider first the rate of growth at an arbitrarily selected age, for instance, those aged 38. The number of 38-year-olds at the end of 1980 (P_{1980}^{38}) is obtained by calculating first the size of the birth cohort for 1942 and multiplying that number by a factor indicating survival from birth to age 38. Perform the same calculation for 38-years-olds born in 1979:

$$P_{38}^{1980} = B_{1942} L_{38}/l_0 = B_{1980}e^{-38r} L_{38}/l_0 \qquad (22.1)$$

$$P_{38}^{1979} = B_{1941} L_{38}/l_0 = B_{1979}e^{-39r} L_{38}/l_0 \qquad (22.2)$$

Step 2. Calculate r, the rate of growth for 38-year-olds in 1980. Divide the right-hand side of Equation (22.2) into the right-hand side of Equation (22.1). The same reasoning holds for any other age group or any other time interval. Thus it can be seen that, because the rate of growth is constant across ages for any time interval, the population as a whole is also growing at the same annual rate. This also implies that the size of each age group relative to any other age group, or to the total population remains constant. In other words, the age distribution is "stable." Equation (22.3) is the general form to determine the population for any age group in 1980:

$$P_x^{1980} = B_{(1980-x)} L_x/l_0 = B_{1980}e^{-rx} L_x/l_0 \qquad (22.3)$$

Step 3. Find the total population P. Sum the number of people at each age group from age 0 to the highest age ω as follows:

$$P^{1980} = \sum_{x=0}^{\omega} B_{1980}e^{-rx} L_x/l_0 = B_{1980}\sum_{x=0}^{\omega} e^{-rx} L_x/l_0 \quad (22.4)$$

Next, obtain the expression of the proportion of the population at age x in a stable population by dividing the right-hand side of the Equation (22.4) into Equation (22.3). Note that the equation no longer contains a dated quantity because r is consistent across all age cohorts:

$$C_x = \frac{e^{-rx} L_x/l_0}{\sum e^{-rx} L_x/l_0} \qquad (22.5)$$

Step 4. Determine the birthrate in a the stable population under study. To obtain the birthrate for 1980, we must divide B_{1980} by the population at mid-1980. As before, we may obtain the total population by summing up individual age groups. Following the form of Equation (22.4), the number of those aged x at mid-1980 is expressed as follows:

$$P_x^{mid\ 1980} = B_{1980}e^{-r(x+1/2)} L_x/l_0 \qquad (22.6)$$

Note that the expression $B_{1980}e^{-r(x+1/2)}$ gives the number of births during yearly intervals, going backward from the midpoint of 1980, in terms of the number of births during the calendar year 1980 and the annual rate of growth. Thus, for $x = 0$, the expression yields the number of births from mid-1979 to mid-1980. For $x = 1$ the number of births calculated are those that took place between mid-1978 and mid-1979, and so on. Total population at mid-1980 is calculated as

$$P^{mid\ 1980} = \sum_{x=0}^{\omega} P_x^{mid\ 1980} = \sum_{x=0}^{\omega} B_{1980}e^{-r(x+1/2)} L_x l_0 \quad (22.7)$$

Next the birth rate is calculated as follows:

$$b = \frac{B_{1980}}{P^{mid-1980}} = \frac{B_{1980}}{\sum B_{1980}e^{-r(x+1/2)} L_x/l_0} = \frac{1}{\sum e^{-r(x+1/2)} L_x/l_0} \qquad (22.8)$$

Again, the expression does not contain quantities with a time subscript; in a stable population, the birthrate is constant. As the rate of growth of the population was shown to be also constant, the death rate d is constant as well. We derive d from the fundamental relationship between births, natural rate of increase, and deaths:

$$d = b - r \qquad (22.9)$$

The same calculations can also be carried out if the initial stable conditions specify a life table and a constant set of age-specific fertility rates, f_x, because this type of combination implies a rate of growth. This is so because the number of births in 1980 is the cumulative product of the age-specific fertility rates and the number of women over all the childbearing ages from w_1 to w_2 (roughly from ages 15 to 49):

$$B_{1980} = \sum_{x=\omega_1}^{\omega_2} P_x^{mid\ 1980} f_x$$

$$P_{1980}^{midyear} = \sum_{x=\omega_1}^{\omega_2} B_{1980} e^{-r(x+1/2)} L_x/l_0$$

$$B_{1980} = \sum_{x=\omega_1}^{\omega_2} B_{1980} e^{-r(x+1/2)} f_x L_x/l_0 \qquad (22.10)$$

$$1 = \sum e^{-r(x+1/2)} f_x L_x/l_0$$

Note that a set of age-specific fertility rates and a life table determine a unique stable population, with unique vital rates and with a unique age distribution. Thus, Equation (22.10) has a unique solution for r.

On the other hand, specification of a stable growth rate and a fixed life table is not sufficient to determine the series of age-specific fertility rates because, for any fixed growth rate and life table, an arbitrarily large number of f_x schedules can be constructed that would satisfy Equation (22.10). The determination of the f_x schedule (female both only) and of measures of the stable population such as the gross reproduction rate ($GRR = \Sigma f_x$) or the net reproduction rate [$NRR = \Sigma f_x(L_x/l_x)$] requires a specification of the age pattern of fertility as well as the rate of growth and the life table. Suppose that such an age pattern of fertility is described by a fertility schedule f_x^*, so that the true fertility schedule f_x is simply a multiple k of f_x^*, at each age: $f_x = kf_x^*$. If we know r, the life table schedule Lx/l_0, and the f_x^* schedule, equation (22.11) permits calculation of k as follows:

$$k = \frac{1}{\displaystyle\sum_{x=\omega_1}^{\omega_2} e^{-r(x+1/2)} f_x^* L_x/l_0} \qquad (22.11)$$

Once k is known, the true fertility schedule is kf_x^*, and consequently such summary indices of reproduction as the GRR and the NRR are easily calculated. The preceding discussion of the stable model is for the female population only.

A stable population model can be constructed for the male population as well once a fixed annual increase of male births and a male life table have been specified.

Regional Stable Population Models

Despite the essential simplicity of the stable population model, typical applications require time-consuming calculations if attempted without access to a set of model stable populations. For example, can the birthrate in a male stable population be determined given a proportion of persons under age 10 and a given death rate? Because there exists no convenient analytical expression from which such a birthrate could be directly calculated, the only feasible approach is to calculate a trial stable population, to observe its proportion under 10 and its death rate, and, using the difference between the observed values and the desired values, to calculate another stable population close to the desired one. This procedure will usually have to be repeated several times before the stable population can be obtained with exactly the desired proportion under 10 and with the desired death rate. Because actual populations are never exactly stable and because observed parameter values are often distorted by reporting errors, the analyst will need to perform a series of calculations to observe the range of estimates resulting from different combinations of observed parameters. The need for such exploration tends to make the set of needed computations prohibitively large.

Given that the task of calculating certain vital rates from one stable population is an iterative process that could be very resource-intensive, the ideal solution would be to have an existing tabulated network of stable populations spanning the entire feasible range of mortality and fertility experience. A tabulation of this type is illustrated in Appendix Table B.3, which presents a series of stable populations excerpted from the volume, *Regional Model Life Tables and Stable Populations* (Coale and Demeny, 1966). The tabulations printed in the appendix tables are all from the "West" family. They were obtained by combining various mortality levels in the "West" model life tables shown in Appendix Table B.1 (selected tables only), with 13 evenly spaced values of the rate of increase ranging from $r = -.010$ to $r = .050$ (whole array shown only for levels 9 and 11). The tables are computed separately for females and males. For each stable population, Appendix Table B.3 gives the proportionate age distribution, the cumulative age distribution (up to age 65), and various stable parameters, such as the rates of birth and death, and gross reproduction rates associated with four values of the mean age at maternity. The detailed characteristics of the life table underlying some of the stable populations can be established by referring to the model life tables in Table B.1. Linear interpolation may be used on any series of model life tables to obtain the desired information when the observed parameters fall "between" the parameters calculated in the model life tables. The method of calculating stable population parameters not directly available in Appendix Table B.3 is illustrated in the following examples.

Example 1

Calculate the birthrate (b), the proportion under age 35 [C(35)], and the gross reproduction rate (GRR) assuming a mean age at maternity (m) of 28.2 years, GRR (28.2), in a "West" female stable population with $e_0 = 48.7$ years and $r = .0263$. The sought-for stable population is bracketed by the four stable populations tabulated for level 11 and level 13 ($e_0 = 45.0$ and 50.0 respectively) at $r = .025$ and $r = .030$.

Step 1. Interpolate between $r = .025$ and $r = .030$ in Appendix Table B.3 (levels 11 and 13, females), to obtain columns 1 and 2, both representing stable populations with $r = .0263$.

Step 2. Interpolate between columns 1 and 2 to obtain a stable population having both $r = .0263$ and level 12.48 ($e_0 = 48.7$), shown in column 3. The gross reproduction rates are calculated in this exercise for $m = 27$ and $m = 29$.

Step 3. To obtain GRR (28.2), a final interpolation is required between GRR (27) and GRR (29). The result is given in the bottom line of column 3:

	Level 11	Level 13	Level 12.48
Parameter	$e_0 = 45.0$	$e_0 = 50.0$	$e_0 = 48.7$
	$r = .0263$	$r = .0263$	$r = .0363$
	(1)	(2)	(3)
b	.0456	.0421	.0430
C (35)	.7710	.7580	.7614
GRR (27)	2.94	2.71	2.77
GRR (29)	3.14	2.89	2.96
GRR (28.2)	3.06	2.82	2.88

Other parameter values of the same stable population can be obtained by similar interpolations. The reader may check his understanding by calculating values for C (10), the proportion under age 10, and l_2/l_0. (The answers are .3110 and .8399, respectively.)

Example 2

Find the sex ratio in the stable population defined by "West" level 9 mortality and a growth rate of .020. Find also the birth rate for the sexes combined assuming that the sex ratio at birth is 1.05. From Table B.3 we have $b_{female} = .0433$ and $b_{male} = .0456$.

Step 1. Determine the number of female births and male births given the parameters in Appendix Table B.3. (Note that the choice for the size of the current birth cohort is arbitrary and does not affect the final results.) For every female birth, there are 1.05 male births.

Female population	Male population
1,000 / .0433 = 23,095	1,000 / .0456 = 21,930
	21,930 × 1.05 = 23,027

Step 2. Determine the sex ratio.

$$\frac{23,027}{23,095} = .997$$

Step 3. Determine the births rate for the sexes combined.

$$\frac{2.05}{46.119} = .0445$$

Note that a sample anthentic mean of the male and female birth rates would give a very close approximation in most instances, as here.

Example 3

Find the net reproduction rate in a "West" female stable population with an $e_0 = 45.0$ and $r = .025$, assuming the mean age at maternity is 29 years. The needed calculation is summarized in Table 22.1. The expected person-years to be lived in the childbearing ages by an original cohort of 100,000 women shown in column 2 is taken from Appendix Table B.1 (females, level 11). The calculation in columns 2 and 3 indicates that, with a fertility schedule assuming GRR (29) = 1.00, 66,554 female children would be born to a birth cohort of 100,000 women by the end of their childbearing ages. However, Appendix Table B.3 shows that the actual GRR in the stable population defined earlier equals 3.03. Thus, the actual number of female children born to the cohort of 100,000 women will be 66,554 × 3.03 = 201,659, or 2.02 per woman. A good estimate of the NRR can be obtained directly, and much more easily, by using the approximation: NRR = GRR l_m/l_0. In this instance $m = 29$

TABLE 22.1 Calculation of the Net Reproduction Rate (NRR) in a Model Stable Population ("West" Females, $e_0 = 45.0$, $r = .025$) Assuming a Mean Age at Maternity of 29 years (Implied GRR is 3.03)

Age (x to x + 4)	Expected person-years (in birth cohort of 100,000) ($e_{0=45.0}$) (1)	Fertility schedule assuming GRR = 1.0 and m = 29[1] (2)	Expected births (2) × (1) = (3)
15 to 19 years	363,207	0.0180	6,538
20 to 24 years	351,543	0.0420	14,765
25 to 29 years	338,115	0.0560	18,934
30 to 34 years	323,525	0.0440	14,235
35 to 39 years	307,872	0.0280	8,620
40 to 44 years	291,388	0.0100	2,914
45 to 49 years	273,969	0.0020	548
Total	2,349,619	5*Σfa = 1.0000	66,554

$$\text{NRR} = \frac{66,554 \times 3.03}{100,000} = 2.02$$

Source: Coale and Demeny (1966), See Appendix B, Tables B.1 and B.3.

[1] Female births only.

and $l_{29}/l_0 = .6678$ (by interpolating between l_{25} and l_{30} in the appropriate life table). Thus, NRR = $3.03 \times .6678 = 2.02$.

EXAMPLES OF METHODS USING THE MODEL LIFE TABLE SYSTEMS AND DATA FROM CENSUSES AND SURVEYS

Indirect Estimation Techniques

In areas where vital registration systems are grossly deficient or nonexistent, that is, where it is impossible to apply the direct estimation procedures, indirect techniques are typically used to estimate mortality (see, for example, Coale, Cho, and Goldman, 1980; United Nations, 1983). These methods can be applied, for example, in the situation where vital statistics systems are deficient or nonexistent but the population has been enumerated in one or more censuses or one or more cross-sectional demographic surveys has been taken. This situation is fairly typical in many, if not most, of the less developed areas in the contemporary world. In this section, solutions are demonstrated to two broad questions demographers will be asked when these types of conditions exist. First, given the available census and survey data, what methods can be applied to derive measures of demographic flows such as birth and death rates, gross reproduction rates, life expectancy, and so on? The answer depends on the exact nature of the available data. The analyst will have to carefully consider the problems unique to estimating the variable of interest, given the condition of the data. Second, given the existing tool-kit demographers have available, what is the best advice the analyst can give to the census and survey taker as to the kinds of data to be collected? Again, no generally correct answer can be given because the answer will necessarily depend on weighing the needs of the users of the final estimates against the costs and efficiency of data-collecting in any particular situation. A fairly general ranking of the various pieces of data by order of importance can be suggested with some confidence, however.

In this section we demonstrate how estimates of growth rates can be made from two consecutive censuses. The first two steps will be taken using two different model life table systems; the United Nations model life tables (1983) and the Population Analysis with Microcomputers (PAS) software system, developed by the U.S. Census Bureau's International Programs Center (IPC) (Arriaga, Johnson, and Jamison, 1994).[5] The PAS system, based on the Coale and

Demeny West regional model life tables, was developed by the IPC to aid analysts in producing estimates of basic demographic information using available census data and, if available, the reported death rate.[6] The way in which model life tables are traditionally used in conjunction with two consecutive censuses to generate estimates of the birthrate, the death rate, and the natural rate of increase is demonstrated. Using the United Nations model life tables, estimates of the 1986 population of Fiji are constructed by varying the life expectancy at birth (e_0) until projections that bracket the actual census are obtained. A similar experiment is conducted using the PAS model in the same manner as the United Nations model life table example by varying one input, the crude death rate. The results from both model life table systems can be seen in Tables 22.3a and 22.4a for the United Nations model life tables and Tables 22.3b and 22.4b for the PAS. Note that the examples consider the female population only. Similar calculations can be done for the male population and then combined growth rates can be calculated by weighting the male and female rates.

Methods Based on Observed Intercensal Growth Rate and Census Survival Rates

Consider the information presented in Table 22.2 on the population of Fiji. It summarizes perhaps the most basic cross-tabulation likely to be available in any census—that is, population by age and sex. The table gives data for two consecutive censuses, those of 1976 and 1986. In this example we will estimate the annual growth rate, the death rate, and the birthrate using these data. Because, during the intercensal years, the population of Fiji was essentially closed to migration,[7] a comparison of the total female population figures yields the natural growth rate per annum (r) for the intercensal period t, for females only.

Derive the annual rate of growth, r, for the total female population.

$$\frac{351,679}{290,160} = 1.212018 = e^{rt} \qquad r = \frac{\log_e 1.212018}{t}$$

---

[5] The Population Analysis with Microcomputers (PAS) software and domumentation was developed by staff at the International Programs Center (IPC), Population Division, U.S. Census Bureau in collaboration with the International Institute for Vital Registration and Statistics and with financial support from the United Nations Population Fund (UNFPA) and the United States Agency for International Development (USAID) in

1994. The documentation and spreadsheets are available from the Population Division at the U.S. Bureau of the Census. Volumes I and II include descriptions of basic techniques, including the mathematical representations, and come with a set of diskettes containing the spreadsheets. These are not copyrighted and thus are available for public use. They may also be accessed from the IPC website at www.census.gov/ipc/www/idbnew.html.

[6] The PAS requires one set of census numbers by age and sex and a crude death rate. The output of the PAS model includes such summary statistics as life expectancy, infant mortality rate, the crude birthrate, the crude death rate, the rate of natural increase, and the total number of deaths.

[7] The reader should note that the United Nations model numbers used are from printed tables. Thus the results presented here differ from results using an electronic version becaused a lack of digits behind the decimal and rounding.

TABLE 22.2 Population of Fiji by Age and Sex as Enumerated: 1976 and 1986

Age (x to x + n)	Population[1] Female 1976 (1)	Female 1986 (2)	Male 1976 (3)	Male 1986 (4)	Proportionate age distribution Female 1976 (5)	Female 1986 (6)	Male 1976 (7)	Male 1986 (8)
Total, all ages	290,160	351,679	295,871	361,333	1.0000	1.0000	1.0000	1.0000
Under 5 years	39,764	49,242	41,542	52,044	0.1370	0.1400	0.1404	0.1440
5 to 9 years	38,249	45,302	39,719	47,850	0.1318	0.1288	0.1342	0.1324
10 to 14 years	40,994	38,667	41,586	40,358	0.1413	0.1099	0.1406	0.1117
15 to 19 years	36,339	36,546	36,829	37,070	0.1252	0.1039	0.1245	0.1026
20 to 24 years	28,975	36,997	27,833	36,731	0.0999	0.1052	0.0941	0.1017
25 to 29 years	22,644	31,456	22,435	31,988	0.0780	0.0894	0.0758	0.0885
30 to 34 years	18,567	25,371	18,753	25,337	0.0640	0.0721	0.0634	0.0701
35 to 39 years	16,063	20,682	15,931	21,035	0.0554	0.0588	0.0538	0.0582
40 to 44 years	12,591	17,199	13,191	17,570	0.0434	0.0489	0.0446	0.0486
45 to 49 years	10,386	14,351	10,827	14,451	0.0358	0.0408	0.0366	0.0400
50 to 54 years	7,987	11,162	8,657	11,502	0.0275	0.0317	0.0293	0.0318
55 to 59 years	6,610	8,320	7,114	8,749	0.0228	0.0237	0.0240	0.0242
60 to 64 years	4,716	5,845	5,227	6,198	0.0163	0.0166	0.0177	0.0172
65 to 69 years	2,926	4,581	2,934	4,609	0.0101	0.0130	0.0099	0.0128
70 to 74 years	1,849	2,911	1,889	3,097	0.0064	0.0083	0.0064	0.0086
75 years and over	1,500	3,047	1,404	2,744	0.0052	0.0087	0.0047	0.0076

[1] The population for which age was not stated is omitted from the tabulation as it represented a negligible fraction (0.2%) of the total.
Source: U.S. Census Bureau, International Data Base, Washington, D.C., www.census.gov/ipc/www/idbnew.html.

Given that the censuses were taken 10 years apart, t = 10:

$$r = \frac{\log_e 1.212018}{10} = 0.019229 \text{ or } 1.92\% \text{ annual growth rate}$$

If the actual enumerations did not take place on the same calendar day but within the same week or month, for example, the calculated growth rate will be a very close approximation. The exact annual growth rate could be calculated by use of a slightly different value of t.

Estimation of the Expectation of Life at Age x

Relying upon the data in Table 22.2 alone, crude death rates can be constructed for the population that was 0 to 4 years of age in 1976, and is now tabulated in the 10-to-14 age category because the censuses were taken 10 years apart. In a closed population, the reduced amount from 1976 to 1986 in each cohort indicates the number of persons in that cohort who died in the intervening 10 years. However, this simple calculation cannot be used to estimate the number of deaths in the population under age 10 because they were not alive at the 1976 census. Thus, comparison of two consecutive census counts gives only a partial picture of the number of deaths in infancy and at the early childhood ages that occurred in the intercensal period. However, a measure of the mortality at roughly age 5 and over is implicit in the data of Table 22.2. If that mortality is calculated, an extrap-

olation to ages 0 to 4 will successfully complete the task of stimating the level of overall mortality. The following discussion and Tables 22.3 through 22.8 present various examples of the types of estimates one can make from two consecutive censuses using the United Nations model life tables (1983).

First, derive the level of mortality over age 5. One possibility is to calculate 10-year census survival rates and construct a life table from such rates. Under the typical conditions of age misreporting and differential underenumeration that prevail in countries with inadequate statistics, this design is almost always unworkable. An alternative would be to derive age-specific death rates for age ranges of 10 to 14 and over and test for reasonableness using simple comparisons to expected or normal patterns to detect irregularities. If irregularities are found, there are two possible solutions. The age distributions or the calculated death rates can be smoothed to reduce the effect of age misreporting (and possibly correct for net omissions) prior to calculating the census survival rates. Alternatively, a smoothing of the highly erratic individual census survival rates can be attempted. Refer to Appendix C for a further discussion of smoothing methods.

A third solution uses the information provided in model life tables, assuming they are available and broadly representative of the country of interest. In general this method consists of identifying the life table that represents the life expectancy from birth (e_0) that correspond to reported

TABLE 22.3a Projections of the Female Population of Fiji from 1976 to 1986 Assuming Various Life Expectancies at Birth Using the United Nations "General" Model Life Tables

Age (years) (x to x + n)	Population 1976 (1)	10-year survival rates in "General" U.N. female model life tables for various life expectancies at birth			Projected population in 1986 using U.N. model life tables, assuming various life expectancies at birth		
		e = 40 (2)	e = 43 (3)	e = 46 (4)	e = 40 (1) × (2) = (5)	e = 43 (1) × (3) = (6)	e = 46 (1) × (4) = (7)
Under 5	39,764	0.8912	0.8935	0.9038			
5 to 9	38,249	0.9490	0.9479	0.9533			
10 to 14	40,994	0.9417	0.9375	0.9441	35,436	35,527	35,939
15 to 19	36,339	0.9231	0.9167	0.9254	36,299	36,255	36,464
20 to 24	28,975	0.9090	0.9032	0.9128	38,603	38,433	38,704
25 to 29	22,644	0.8939	0.8929	0.9027	33,545	33,314	33,627
30 to 34	18,567	0.8732	0.8839	0.8934	26,339	26,171	26,448
35 to 39	16,063	0.8459	0.8729	0.8819	20,242	20,219	20,441
40 to 44	12,591	0.8093	0.8509	0.8599	16,213	16,411	16,588
45 to 49	10,386	0.7611	0.8107	0.8206	13,587	14,022	14,167
50 to 54	7,987	0.6963	0.7496	0.7608	10,190	10,714	10,827
55 to 59	6,610	0.6067	0.6662	0.6785	7,905	8,420	8,522
60 to 64	4,716	0.4934	0.5579	0.5707	5,561	5,987	6,077
65 to 69	2,926	0.3721	0.4262	0.4389	4,010	4,404	4,485
70 to 74	1,849	0.2639	0.2928	0.3036	2,327	2,631	2,692
75 to 79	1,020	0.2223	0.2380	0.2492	1,089	1,247	1,284
80 and over	1,149	0.2053	0.2268	0.2351	951	1,045	1,086
Total, all ages	290,829	X	X	X	252,297[1]	254,799[1]	257,352[1]

Source: United Nations, *Demographic Yearbook, 1989*, New York: United Nations, 1991, Table 7. In U.S. Census Bureau, International Data Base, Washington, DC, http://www.census.gov/ipc/www/idbnew.html. United Nations, *Model Life Tables for Developing Countries*, New York: United Nations, 1982. Official Fiji national sources.

X Not applicable.

[1] 10 years and over.

TABLE 22.3b Projections of the Female Population of Fiji from 1976 to 1986 Assuming Various Crude Death Rates Using the PAS Model System

Age (years) (x to x + n)	Population 1976 (1)	10-year survival rates based on crude death rates estimated using the PAS model			Projected population in 1986 using U.N. model life tables, assuming various crude death rates		
		7.78 (2)	12.78 (3)	17.78 (4)	7.78 (1) × (2) = (5)	12.78 (1) × (3) = (6)	17.78 (1) × (4) = (7)
Under 5	39,764	0.9701	0.9276	0.8840			
5 to 9	38,249	0.9825	0.9626	0.9450			
10 to 14	40,994	0.9782	0.9561	0.9365	38,574	36,887	35,152
15 to 19	36,339	0.9718	0.9453	0.9221	37,578	36,818	36.144
20 to 24	28,975	0.9664	0.9366	0.9104	40,102	39,194	38,393
25 to 29	22,644	0.9611	0.9285	0.8996	35,314	34,353	33,510
30 to 34	18,567	0.9542	0.9198	0.8890	28,002	27,138	26,378
35 to 39	16,063	0.9443	0.9095	0.7879	21,763	21,025	20,371
40 to 44	12,591	0.9281	0.8920	0.8587	17,717	17,079	16,506
45 to 49	10,386	0.9020	0.8612	0.8234	15,169	14,610	14,102
50 to 54	7,987	0.8609	0.8119	0.7665	11,686	11,231	10,812
55 to 59	6,610	0.7965	0.7381	0.6842	9,368	8,944	8,551
60 to 64	4,716	0.7001	0.6357	0.5764	6,876	6,484	6,122
65 to 69	2,926	0.5662	0.5014	0.4421	5,265	4,879	4,522
70 to 74	1,849	0.2533	0.2141	0.1851	3,302	2,998	2,718
75 to 79	1,020				1,657	1,467	1,294
80 and over	1,149				931[1]	900[1]	866[1]
Total, all ages	290,829	X	X	X	273,304[2]	264,007[2]	255,441[2]

Source: United Nations, *Demographic Yearbook, 1989*, New York: United Nations, 1991, Table 7. In U.S. Census Bureau, International Data Base, Washington, DC, http://www.census.gov/ipc/www/idbnew.html. United Nations, *Model Life Tables for Developing Countries*, New York: United Nations, 1982. U.S. Census Bureau, *Population Analysis with Microcomputers*, Washington, DC, 1994. Official Fiji national sources.

X Not applicable.

[1] Survivors 80 years and over, including estimates of survivors 85 and over from Table 22.3a.

[2] 10 years and over.

"cumulative survival rates" (proportions surviving from age 0 and over at one census to age 10 and over at a census taken 10 years later; from age 5 and over to age 15 and over, etc.). These mortality levels will generally show a reasonably high level of consistency, hence an estimate of a single mortality level (e.g., the median of the series) can be generated with some confidence. First, calculate 10-year survival rates—that is, as $_5L_x + _{10} / _5L_x$ from several model life tables with various values of life expectancy at birth (e_0) that represent different mortality schedules. Table 22.3a displays three sets of 10-year survival rates calculated using the United Nations model life tables with values of life expectancy at birth of 40, 43, and 46. To finish this step, project the population to 1986 using the calculated 10-year survival rates (shown in columns 5 through 7). Note that we generate a similar table using the PAS system by varying the crude death rate.

The next step is to determine the accuracy of the projections in reflecting the 1986 census. That is, when the projected populations are cumulated (so as to show totals for age 10 and over, 15 and over, 20 and over, etc.), the cumulated totals will bracket the corresponding reported population totals in 1986. This procedure may involve iterative trials starting from an arbitrary mortality assumption and successively modifying the assumption to obtain projections consistent with the actual census figures. Naturally, the computation is likely to be much simpler if the projections based on the first set of 10-year survival rates are accurate estimates of the true number of survivors. Usually, several life tables will have to be used and the actual numbers of survivors will fall between the projected populations. As can be seen from Table 22.4a, the actual population in the various age groups corresponds to life expectancies at birth ranging from an e_0 of 40 to an e_0 of 46. Using the PAS system (Table 22.4b)

survival rates corresponding to a crude death rate of 17.3 generates estimates close to the actual 1986 census figures.

Calculation of the Crude Death Rate

The estimate of e_5 is of considerable interest for its own sake, but is itself not sufficient to obtain the crude death rate. For this calculation, model life tables are again employed. For that purpose, estimates of the age-specific death rates, including the death rate under age 5 are needed. Lacking other information, the $_nm_x$ values "found" in the median level could simply be assigned. These values are obtained by interpolation of values from the model life tables between $e_0 = 40$ and $e_0 = 46$ that "bracket" the last census ($e_0 = 47$ was also used; as the reader can see from Table 22.4a, not all values are completely bracketed by $e_0 = 40$ and $e_0 = 46$). The death rate under age 5 ($_5m_0$) is calculated from the model life tables as follows:

$$\frac{l_0 - l_5}{L_0 + _4L_1}$$

The calculation of the crude death rate as seen in Table 22.6 requires two inputs: (1) the mean population by age between 1976 and 1986 and (2) the imputed age-specific death rates ($_nm_x$) displayed in Table 22.5. These death rates now permit the calculation of the absolute total number of deaths per annum during the intercensal period. This calculation is shown in column 3 of Table 22.6. The crude death rate for females is then obtained as the ratio of the number of calculated deaths per annum to the mean population during the decade, as shown in this example: (4914)/ (320,170) = 0.0153 per head, or 15.3 per 1000 of the population.

TABLE 22.4a   Female Population of Fiji at Age x and Over in 1986 as Reported by the Census of 1986 and as Projected from 1976 Assuming Various Life Expectancies at Birth in the United Nations "General" Female Model Life Tables

| Age (years) (x to x and over) | Census Population | | Projected population assuming various life expectancies at birth | | | | | |
| | | | Projected population assuming various mortality schedules | | | Percent deviation of projected from actual population | | |
	1976	1986	e = 40	e = 43	e = 46	e = 40	e = 43	e = 46
10 and over	212,816	257,135	252,297	254,799	257,352	−1.9	−0.9	+0.1
15 and over	171,822	218,468	216,861	219,272	221,413	−0.7	+0.4	+1.3
20 and over	135,483	181,922	180,562	183,017	184,949	−0.7	+0.6	+1.7
25 and over	106,508	144,925	141,959	144,584	146,244	−2.1	−0.2	+0.9
30 and over	83,864	113,469	108,414	111,270	112,617	−4.5	−1.9	−0.8
35 and over	65,297	88,098	82,035	85,099	86,169	−6.9	−3.4	−2.2
40 and over	49,234	67,416	61,833	64,880	65,728	−8.3	−3.8	−2.5
45 and over	36,643	50,217	45,620	48,470	49,140	−9.2	−3.5	−2.1
50 and over	26,257	35,866	32,033	34,448	34,973	−10.7	−4.0	−2.5
Total	887,924	1,157,516	1,121,648	1,145,840	1,158,853	−3.1	−1.0	+0.9

Source: United Nations, *Demographic Yearbook, 1989*, New York: United Nations, 1991. In U.S. Bureau of the Census, International Data Base, Washington, DC, http://www.census.gov/ipc/www/idbnew.html. United Nations, *Model Life Tables for Developing Countries*, New York: United Nations, 1982.

TABLE 22.4b Female Population of Fiji at Age x and Over in 1986 as Reported by the Census of 1986 and as Projected from 1976 Assuming Various Crude Death Rates Using the PAS Model System

Age (years) (x to x and over)	Census population		Projected population assuming various crude death rates					
			Projected population assuming various mortality schedules			Percent deviation of projected from actual population		
	1976	1986	7.78	12.78	17.78	7.78	12.78	17.78
10 and over	212,816	257,135	273,304	264,007	255,441	+6.3	+2.7	−0.7
15 and over	171,822	218,468	234,730	227,120	220,289	+7.4	+4.0	+0.6
20 and over	135,483	181,922	197,152	190,302	184,145	+8.4	+4.6	+1.2
25 and over	106,508	144,925	157,050	151,108	145,752	+8.4	+4.3	+0.6
30 and over	83,864	113,469	121,736	116,755	112,242	+7.3	+2.9	−1.1
35 and over	65,297	88,098	93,734	89,617	85,864	+6.4	+1.7	−2.5
40 and over	49,234	67,416	71,971	68,592	65,493	+6.8	+1.7	−2.9
45 and over	36,643	50,217	54,254	51,513	48,987	+8.0	+2.6	−2.4
50 and over	26,257	35,866	39,085	36,903	34,885	+7.0	+2.9	−2.7
Total	887,924	1,157,516	1,243,046	1,195,917	1,153,098	+7.0	+3.3	−0.4

Source: Same as Table 22.3b.

TABLE 22.5 Levels of Mortality of Fiji Females and Corresponding Expectations of Life at Age 5 Derived from Proportions Surviving to Age x and Over in 1986 from Age x-10 and Over 10 Years Earlier

Age (x and over)	Actual value of e_0 (1)	Value of e_5 (2)
10 years and over	40.72	48.60
15 years and over	39.80	48.07
20 years and over	42.85	50.16
25 years and over	40.48	48.42
30 years and over	43.20	52.59
35 years and over	43.27	53.14
40 years and over	43.08	53.13
45 years and over	41.59	49.24
50 years and over	42.90	50.20
Median	42.85	50.16

Source: Same as Table 22.4a.

Calculation of the Crude Birthrate

The female crude birth rate now can be calculated as the sum of the observed rate of increase plus the death rate as estimated from census survival rates:

$$b_f = 0.0192 + 0.0153 = 0.0346$$

An exactly analogous but independent calculation may be followed with respect to the male population shown in Table 22.2. This calculation is left to the reader as an exercise. For the female population of Fiji during the 1976–1986 period, we then have the following estimates:

Rate of natural increase	0.0192
Death rate	0.0153
Birth rate	0.0346

TABLE 22.6 Calculation of the Crude Death Rate for the Female Population of Fiji in the Period 1976–1986 Corresponding to the Recorded Age Distribution and to a Life Expectancy at Birth Estimated from Cumulated Census Survival Rates

Age	Mean population 1976–1986 (1)	Death rate $e_0 = 42.85$ (2)	Mean annual deaths 1976–1986 (1) × (2) = (3)
Total	320,170	0.0153[1]	4,913.7[2]
Under 5 years	44,503	0.0307	1,364.8
5 to 9 years	41,776	0.0074	307.0
10 to 14 years	39,831	0.0043	172.7
15 to 19 years	36,443	0.0068	248.6
20 to 24 years	32,986	0.0094	311.1
25 to 29 years	27,050	0.0106	285.8
30 to 34 years	21,969	0.0119	261.7
35 to 39 years	18,373	0.0128	236.0
40 to 44 years	14,895	0.0138	205.1
45 to 49 years	12,369	0.0162	200.3
50 to 54 years	9,575	0.0210	201.2
55 to 59 years	7,465	0.0288	215.3
60 to 64 years	5,281	0.0405	213.8
65 to 69 years	3,754	0.0577	216.7
70 to 74 years	2,380	0.0843	200.7
75 years and over	1,524	0.1791	272.9

Source: Same as Table 22.4a.
[1] Derived by deviding 4,914 by 320,170.
[2] Derived by summelion.

Validity of Estimates Based on Observed Growth Rate and Census Survival Rates

In preparing any estimate, the analyst should be able to indicate to what extent his estimates are insensitive, or "robust," first, to the various assumptions incorporated in the estimating procedure and, second, to possible errors in the data themselves. The most convenient way to effect this is to calculate multiple sets of estimates by making alternative assumptions in applying the estimating procedure and by considering alternative hypotheses as to the accuracy of the basic data. Such procedures, guided by the knowledge of special local circumstances, should be routinely followed in order to validate the results. Following are brief comments made in the present context concerning this topic.

It is important to consider that the model life table pattern of mortality is a major assumption that is incorporated in the calculations based on census survival rates (apart from any assumption concerning completeness of data). The basic weakness of this method is that there exists no way to extract information on the entire mortality pattern from reported age distributions alone. What, then, are the consequences of selecting West model life tables in preference to other models? First, the estimates of mortality at age 5 and over, whether expressed in terms of the model life tables or of some other measure, are principally insensitive to the model pattern chosen. Therefore, even the selection of sharply differing life table patterns leaves the estimates of mortality over age 5 largely unaffected. However, the opposite is true when mortality estimated for age 5 and over is extrapolated to ages less than 5. The record indicates that historically very different levels of early childhood mortality are associated with a fixed level of mortality at higher ages. If the life table pattern chosen underestimates the level of infant mortality, for example, the estimated total death rate will be lower than actual experience. There will be an error of the same absolute magnitude and direction in the estimated birthrate.

Concerning errors in the basic data, the method of "cumulative census survival" is relatively insensitive to errors of age misreporting. No such statement can be made, however, about the effect of differential net under-or overenumeration of the population in two consecutive censuses. Obviously, such errors affect the observed intercensal growth rate, and censuses that are relatively close together with large differences in the level of error will produce more serious error.

Stable Population Estimates from Observed Age Distribution and Intercensal Growth Rate

The discussion of the stable population model earlier in this chapter indicated that, if some observed population's parameters closely resemble those of a particular stable population, then other parameters of that stable population may be reliable estimates of the corresponding parameters in the observed population. Ideally, derivation of stable population estimates should be attempted only if the existence of approximate stability can be verified by direct evidence. For example, if age distributions are consistent across consecu-

tive censuses and the intercensal growth rate is constant over successive census intervals, then using the stable population estimates would produce reliable results. Indications that fertility and mortality behavior is relatively stable may also present additional and important, if impressionistic, evidence to support the hypothesis that a population is approximately stable. (Note that when the data from censuses and the registration system are deemed accurate, there is no need to apply stable analysis to measure a population's basic parameters.)

Requirements for "proofs" of stability are, strictly speaking, not satisfied in the case of Fiji. Comparison of the 1976 and 1986 censuses shows some minor changes in the reported age distribution (refer to columns 6 to 9 in Table 22.2). There is evidence of an acceleration of the rate of population growth and of a decline in mortality.

Most, if not all, countries will exhibit anomalies in their demographic processes that cause the analyst to question the validity of applying stable population analysis. Yet the technique of stable analysis is useful under a wide range of circumstances provided that such analysis contains a reasonably full exploration of the conflicting evidence presented by the observed data. In fact, if the conditions of stability are not fulfilled, the results of the analysis themselves will show the differences.

In the instance of Fiji, the young age distribution does suggest that no sustained and substantial decline of fertility took place prior to 1986. The examination of census survival rates suggests some age misreporting and probably some omission of children under age 5. Variations in the observed age distributions thus may reflect differential occurrence of such errors of enumeration in the censuses of 1976 and 1986. It is also known that an orderly decline of mortality has only a relatively minor effect on the age distribution. Furthermore, a population that was initially stable but has undergone a decline of mortality is always closely approximated by a stable population having the current growth rate and the current life table of the actual population.

Given the considerations previously noted, an attempt to derive estimates of the vital rates for Fiji (or any like situation) by the stable technique can be justified. In this example, we will again demonstrate the estimation of the death rate and birthrate using the previously calculated rate of growth of .0192. Following that is an example of estimating a gross reproduction rate using a standard pattern of "natural" fertility. Again, the only data used in the analysis are those contained in Table 22.2. To determine stable populations corresponding to the recorded data, the observed intercensal rate of growth is combined with measures of the observed age distribution in 1976. Naturally a large number of indices of age distribution can be constructed, defining a more or less broad spectrum of stable populations, all characterized by the observed intercensal r. It is important to select indices of age distribution such that they will be least affected by errors of age reporting. At the same time the indices should reflect a broad range of observations. These and other considerations, plus experience, suggest the selection of proportions from the cumulative age distribution-aproportion under age 5, under age 10, under age x in general, denoted as C(5), C(10), C(x) for this purpose. Going beyond C(45) in the analysis is not recommended.

Computational Routine

The technique is illustrated in Table 22.7 for the female population of Fiji. For this illustration, the Coale and Demeny (1966) model stable population tables are used, examples of which are found in Appendix B (see Table B.3). Column 1 shows the observed values of C(5), C(10), . . . C(45). When each of these nine indices of the age distribution is combined with the same observed growth rate of .0192, they define nine different populations defined by 5-year age ranges within the tabulated network of a set of model stable populations.

First, locate these populations by constructing model populations having a growth rate of .0192 (by interpolating between columns with $r = .015$ and $r = .020$ for various levels of mortality). Select the mortality levels such that the various observed C(x) values are bracketed by the corresponding C(x) values in the models. (A similar process was used in constructing Table 22.4a.) The results of this part of the calculation are presented in columns 2 to 6. Note that the parameters to be estimated (the birthrate, the death rate, etc.) are shown along with the C(x) values in the bottom rows of Table 22.7.

Second, determine (for example) the birthrate in a "West" female stable population having an r of .0192 and a C(20) of .4827. The models shown in columns 4 and 5 bracketing this value of C(20) give the corresponding values for C(20) as .4916 and .4771, respectively. Appropriate linear interpolation, described earlier in this chapter, between these two bracketing populations yields the population with the required C(20). When the same interpolation factors used in this calculation are applied to the birthrates (.0354 and .0385), they yield the birth rate .0366, for the entry in column 7. Exactly analogous procedures result in various estimated parameter values (columns 7 to 13) corresponding to all C(x) values shown in column 1.

Validity of the Stable Estimates

The analyst must be cautious about the interpretation of the results of Table 22.7, especially if there is no additional outside information or knowledge of special conditions of the area under study to inform the analysis. The gradually increasing estimates of the birthrate associated with C(20) to C(45) tend to suggest higher fertility in the past. However, accepting these birthrates (ranging from about .037 to .047) and values of other parameters as truth would imply a high degree of confidence that the West model life tables describe the true mortality pattern of Fiji. In addition, the validity of this analysis depends on the precision of the intercensal growth rate. For these reasons, the results do not necessarily imply reliability of the estimates because the two methods are sensitive to similar biases.

The estimates associated with C(5) to C(15) show relatively lower levels of fertility (and mortality). This could be interpreted as evidence of fertility decline during the decade or so prior to 1986, or as a consequence of a tendency to exaggerate the ages of children in census reports or to omit children in the census, particularly in the youngest ages. Analysis of census survival rates suggests that the last explanation is correct or at least dominant.

These comments indicate the need for reliable age reports in stable population analysis. Alternatively, the analyst should endeavor to obtain all information that is helpful in determining the most reliable segments of the age distribution or in isolating particular errors that affect age reports. From such information, the analyst can select particular indices (e.g., C(10) or C(35)) of the age distribution as preferable to others or adjust the age distribution prior to stable analysis. In general, the former procedure is preferred. In the absence of particular reasons for preferring one index of the age distribution to another, and in the absence of very marked fluctuations in the estimates produced by various C(x) values, the median of the series should be selected as the single best estimate. The median of the birthrates is .0405 and of the death rates .0213. In the present instance, this rule favors the stable population associated with C(25) and mortality level 10.0 ($e_5 = 51.28$).

The application of similar procedures to the male population is straightforward, and it is left to the reader as an exercise. For the total female population of Fiji, we obtain the following stable estimates:

Rate of natural increase	.0192
Death rate	.0213
Birthrate	.0405

It should be noted that knowledge of local conditions often suggests that the estimates for one sex are more accurate than for the other sex. For instance, when ages are inadequately known and have to be estimated by enumerators, female age distributions are typically more amenable to correct interpretation than male age distributions. Under such circumstances it is preferable to derive the estimate for males, and for the total population, from stable analysis of the female population only.

Calculation of the Gross Reproduction Rate by Stable Population Analysis

In the preceding example (Table 22.7), two alternative values of the GRR were obtained corresponding to a mean age of the fertility schedule, GRR (m = 29) and

TABLE 22.7 Stable Population Estimates of Fertility and Mortality Based on the Age Distribution of the Female Population of Fiji as Reported in the Census of 1986 and on the Observed Intercensal Growth Rate ($r = 0.0192$)

Age x	Proportionate population up to age x (1)	Values of $C(x)$ and of various parameters in female stable populations with $r = 0.0192$ and levels of mortality as indicated					Parameter values in stable populations with $C(x)$ as shown in column (1) and $r = 0.0192$						
		Level 7 (2)	Level 9 (3)	Level 11 (4)	Level 13 (5)	Level 15 (6)	Birthrate (7)	Death rate (8)	Level of mortality (9)	e_0 (10)	e_5 (11)	GRR(29) (12)	GRR(31) (13)
5 years	0.1400	0.1681	0.1590	0.1512	0.1445	0.1385	0.0335	0.0155	13.5	51.28	56.58	2.45	2.59
10 years	0.2688	0.3036	0.2902	0.2787	0.2684		0.0355	0.0192	11.1	45.23	52.98	2.72	2.89
15 years	0.3788	0.4220	0.4058	0.3916	0.3788		0.0354	0.0193	11.0	45.01	52.85	2.73	2.90
20 years	0.4827	0.5256	0.5077	0.4916	0.4771		0.0366	0.0181	11.8	46.94	54.01	2.64	2.80
25 years	0.5879	0.6152	0.5965	0.5795			0.0405	0.0213	10.0	42.48	51.28	2.79	2.96
30 years	0.6774	0.6920	0.6734				0.0436	0.0273	8.6	38.93	49.08	2.97	3.16
35 years	0.7495	0.7574	0.7396				0.0453	0.0255	7.9	37.21	47.99	3.16	3.37
40 years	0.8083	0.8126	0.7962				0.0462	0.0246	7.5	36.30	47.42	3.26	3.48
45 years	0.8572	0.8589	0.8443				0.0470	0.0239	7.2	35.58	46.96	3.34	3.57
Birth rate (b)		0.0476	0.0425	0.0385	0.0354	0.0328							
Death rate (d)		0.0284	0.0233	0.0193	0.0162	0.0135							
e_0		35	40	45	50	55							
e_5		46.59	49.75	52.84	55.86	58.70							
GRR (29)		3.41	2.85	2.73	2.50	2.31							
GRR (31)		3.64	3.02	2.90	2.64	2.43							

Source: United Nations, *Demographic Yearbook, 1989*, New York: United Nations, 1991, In U.S. Bureau of the Census, International Data Base, Washington, D.C., www.census.gov/ipc/www/idbnew.html; A. Coale and D. Demeny, *Regional Model Life Tables and Stable Populations*, Princeton: Princeton University Press, 1966.

GRR (m = 31). The median estimates were 2.79 and 2.96, respectively.

To arrive at a single estimate of the GRR, a prior estimate of the true value of *m* is necessary. When age-specific fertility rates are not available, as is likely to be the case, a rough estimate can be made by various methods. The largely self-explanatory calculation shown in Table 22.8 illustrates one such method. Its application is based on the assumption that fertility outside marriage is negligible and that within marriage little or no contraception is practiced. A standard age pattern of "natural" fertility (i.e., without contraception) shown in column 2 can then be combined with the proportions of married women as reported in the census to give the likely pattern (but of course not the level) of age-specific fertility rates (column 3). The mean of this schedule is calculated as 31.5 years. The stable estimate of the gross reproduction rate for Fiji can now be calculated as 3.37 by interpolation between GRR (*m* = 31) and GRR (*m* = 33) to GRR (*m* = 31.5).

Quasi-stable Estimates

When an actual population is reasonably approximated by the stable model, it is often described as being in the "quasi-stable state," and the estimates derived from the model are referred to as "quasi-stable estimates." However, the two meanings of the term used by analysis should be distinguished. In one sense, the expression is intended merely as a reminder that the correspondence between the model and the actual population is imperfect, because of both inadequately fulfilled conditions of stability and distortions in the data. In this loose interpretation, all estimates described here

as "stable" should be considered "quasi-stable." Although use of the term is a matter of definition, it is preferable to refer to such estimates simply as stable estimates. It should always be understood that such estimates are subject to biases owing to deviations of the actual population from the stable model used and owing to erroneous measurements.

In a second more precise meaning, the term "quasi-stable" is applied only to populations that were initially stable (as always, only as a close approximation) but that have undergone a process of "destabilization", such as an orderly and sustained decline of mortality. Research has been conducted on the impact of the resulting decline on the age distribution and the values of other parameters, as well as on the biases in estimating population parameters for such a population under the assumption of strict stability. When the findings of this research are used to make appropriate numerical adjustments on the stable estimates, taking into account the decline of mortality, the final estimates are called quasi-stable in the more narrow, technical sense of the term.

The special interest in studying populations where mortality has declined while fertility remained stable is, of course, due to the prevalence of this condition in many contemporary populations. Proper quantitative adjustments for quasi-stability require information on the duration and rapidity of the mortality decline that is seldom available in the desired form and detail. Hence, the dimensions of the mortality decline itself have to be estimated from often fragmentary pieces of evidence. For discussions and illustrations of the estimating methods that have been worked out, the reader is referred to the specialized publications

TABLE 22.8 Calculation of the Mean of the Fertility Schedule for the Female Population of Fiji from Proportions Married as Reported in the 1986 Census and from a Standard Age Pattern of Fertility Rates Reflecting "Natural" Fertility

Age (x to x + 4)	Proportions married, females, Fiji, 1986[1] (1)	Age pattern of natural fertility rates (2)	Age pattern of marital fertility, Fiji (1) × (2) = (3)	Midpoint of age interval (4)	Weighted midpoint ages (3) × (4) = (5)
15 to 19 years	0.130	1.109 [2]	0.14417	17.5	2.52
20 to 24 years	0.425	1.0000	0.42500	22.5	9.56
25 to 29 years	0.746	0.9350	0.69751	27.5	19.18
30 to 34 years	0.864	0.8530	0.73699	32.5	23.95
35 to 39 years	0.892	0.6850	0.61102	37.5	22.91
40 to 44 years	0.898	0.3490	0.31340	42.5	13.32
45 to 49 years	0.880	0.0510	0.04488	47.5	2.13
Total, 15 to 49 years			2.97297		93.57

Mean age of fertility schedule = 93.57 ÷ 2.97297 = 31.5

[1] Source: Official census reports.
[2] Estimated as 1.2 − (.7 ∗ .130) = 1.109.
Source: Same as Table 22.2.

(United Nations, 1967). However, the general effect of mortality change is to introduce a downward bias into the stable estimates of the birthrate (and of the GRR) when such estimates are obtained from observed intercensal growth rates and from $C(x)$ values for x at 20 years and over. If the decline in mortality was very rapid, and if the decline lasted for several decades, this downward bias can be quite pronounced—for example, the stable estimate of the birthrate associated with $C(35)$ may be .0.025 when the true (quasi-stable) birthrate is in fact 0.029. On the other hand, estimates derived from $C(10)$ or $C(15)$ are likely to be only slightly affected by declining mortality.

Estimates Based on the Reverse Survival Technique

When two consecutive censuses contain no other demographic information but age and sex distributions and the population is not a stable one, the analyst may wish to apply the familiar reverse survival technique to estimate the crude birthrate in the 5- or 10-year period preceding the second census. The technique requires the construction of an appropriate life table by which the population is projected "backward" by 5 or 10 years. A by-product of such a reverse projection is the absolute number of births during the 5 or 10 years prior to the census. These quantities are obtained by dividing the populations under 5 and under 10 years old by the factors $_5L_0/_5l_0$ and $_{10}L_0/_{10}l_0$, respectively. Dividing the mean annual number of births during the given interval by the total population calculated at the midpoint of the interval yields the estimated birth rate.

Insofar as the life table is estimated from census survival rates (hence infant and early childhood mortality is essentially an extrapolation), the method is subject to a type of uncertainty that plagues the previously discussed estimates as well. In making reverse survival estimates, no assumption of stability is made; therefore, the method may appear attractive under many situations where the stable conditions do not exist. It can be shown, however, that regardless of the existence of stability or the lack of it, the results of reverse survival estimates and the stable estimates obtained from the population under age 5 or 10 are essentially identical. In fact, using a set of tabulated model stable populations is a quick and efficient way to obtain reverse survival estimates whether the population is stable or not. Thus, the first two lines of the example set forth in Table 22.7 illustrate the results of a reverse survival analysis for Fiji. This example calls attention to a weakness of the method. By necessity, the estimate of the birthrate is obtained primarily from the numbers under 5 and under 10 reported in the second census. However, frequent undercounting of the age group under 5 years old in censuses creates measures of the age distribution that are suspect. To avoid the pitfall of interpreting the level of fertility in the light of the recorded numbers in childhood ages only, the analyst again may find it advantageous

to examine a full set of computations, such as those summarized in Table 22.7, even if the stability conditions are very inadequately fulfilled.

Estimates Based on Data Collected in a Single Census or Survey

Fertility Measures Derived from a Single Recorded Age Distribution

The most conspicuous common feature of the methods discussed in the preceding sections was their reliance on the analysis of the age distribution recorded in the most recent census. However, a prior census is an essential requirement for the calculation of an intercensal growth rate or census survival rates, as demonstrated in the prior section. The question posed in this section is, can general magnitudes of fertility, mortality, and growth be derived from a single recorded age distribution alone? The answer is essentially negative.[8] If age and sex distributions have been tabulated for numerous geographical subdivisions of the country, however, and are available for other subpopulations as well, such as racial or ethnic groups, internal comparisons and checks may reveal sufficient consistency of age reporting so that various measures of the age distributions may be accepted as reliable. Because past fertility is the dominant factor determining the shape of the age distribution and, in particular, proportions in the youngest ages depend on recent fertility, a rough estimate of the level of the birthrate may be obtained by an examination of a single age structure. Alternative assumptions concerning the level of mortality (e.g., contrasting a plausible low and a plausible high hypothesis for early childhood mortality) might show, for instance, that either assumption leads to a birthrate of over 40 per thousand. In most cases it will be true, however, that the uncertainty about the level of mortality removes even qualitative "precision" from the estimate. Experimentation in the hands of a skilled analyst will normally result in determining nontrivial thresholds or ceilings for the birthrate, but the method will be unable to differentiate between, for example, "very high" or just "moderately high" fertility.

The explicit introduction of assumptions concerning probable mortality levels may be omitted if only comparative estimates of fertility levels are the aim. Thus, some indices of the age distribution that are, *ceteris paribus*, highly correlated with fertility levels may show sufficient regional contrasts to warrant valid conclusions concerning differential fertility. The most commonly used index of age distribution for such purposes is the ratio of children under age 5 to the number of women in the childbearing ages (usually defined as ages 15 to 49), i.e., the child-woman ratio. General indices of age distribution (e.g., proportions

---

[8] It appears, however, that the PAS system can be used for single surveys.

under age 5, 10, or 15) may perform as well or better for this purpose, and there is less temptation to interpret the results as a measure of fertility as such. The interest in differential patterns shown by such indices is greatly strengthened if analysis (easily performed by means of tabulated model stable populations) can show that mortality differentials, or plausible directions and magnitudes, do not qualitatively affect the patterns. Information on the age distribution alone is entirely insufficient to support meaningful estimates with respect to either absolute values or to differentials in growth rates and mortality rates.

Estimates of Fertility from Retrospective Reports on Childbearing

By tradition, censuses have been used primarily to record a cross-sectional view of the state of a population at a given moment in time. As we have seen, however, questions concerning past demographic events experienced by individuals can also be included in a census or survey. When vital registration is deficient, the recording and analysis of such events may be especially rewarding. With respect to fertility, two types of questions have appeared with increasing frequency in recent censuses and surveys. One type of question concerns the number of births that have occurred during a specified period, usually a year, preceding the survey. Another question inquires about the number of children ever born to each woman up to the time of the inquiry.

A priori reasoning as well as experience suggests, however, that reports by women on past births may be subject to serious biases. As to the question on births during a specified period, a chief problem lies in the difficulty on the part of the respondents of reporting the event in an exact time frame, especially when no written record of that event is available. Thus, the mean length of time covered by the reports may span more or less than the intended 12-month period, often by a margin of several months. Accordingly, age-specific fertility rates, and hence total fertility, calculated from such statistics, may be under- or overestimated.

With respect to children ever born, the possibility of overreporting is rather remote. On the other hand, understatement of the true number appears to be common, owing to various factors, such as memory failure and omission of deceased children or children who have already left home. In particular, these biases are likely to affect reporting by women of older age and higher parity. Thus the value of the information that is of greatest interest, namely the number of children ever born by the end of the childbearing age, is weakened by this circumstance. Clearly, under conditions of approximately constant fertility (and ignoring differential mortality and migration), the mean number of children ever born to women of about age 50 would direclty supply an estimate of the current total fertility rate.

Methods that would permit the evaluation and correction of distortions in retrospective fertility reports would, therefore, greatly enhance the usefulness of such information. A technique worked out by Brass (1968, 1975) to serve that purpose is illustrated next through data taken from the Philippines (U.S. Census Bureau, 2000). The data relate to a sample area covering the country; thus they also demonstrate the possibilities of retrospective fertility reports to generate information for subpopulations, as well as for a country as a whole.

Column 2 of Table 22.9 shows age-specific fertility rates calculated from 12-month retrospective reports. Note that, because women in a given 5-year age group at the time of the survey were on the average half a year younger at the time the births occurred, the age-specific fertility rates actually relate to the unconventional age groups bounded by exact ages 14.5 and 19.5, 19.5 and 24.5, and so on. The cumulative totals of these rates are shown in column 3 (0.2662 children up to age 19.5, 1.3510 children up to age 24.5, etc.). The cumulative total for the end of the childbearing period gives an estimate of the current (1974–1975) total fertility rate of the population in question, assuming, of course, that the reports are correct. The estimated total fertility rate from these "current" reports is different than the average number of children ever born reported by women at the end of the childbearing period, as shown in column 6. This comparison is, however, inconclusive as to the validity of the current fertility reports; the number of children ever born is often underreported by older women or, alternatively, past fertility may have been higher than current fertility.

These considerations suggest that a comparison of cumulated current fertility with corresponding reports on children ever born at younger age groups would provide more information. However, apart from the age at the end of the childbearing period, columns 3 and 6 are not directly comparable. Column 3 shows cumulated fertility up to ages 19.5, 24.5, and so on, whereas in column 6 cumulative fertility relates roughly to the midpoint of the age groups shown at the left (i.e., up to 17.5, 22.5, etc.). Adjusting to these ages the cumulated current fertility shown in column 3 by "linear" interpolation is a possibility, but assuming an even distribution of fertility within each age interval is clearly unrealistic. To eliminate an unnecessary source of bias, a more sophisticated adjustment is performed in columns 4 and 5 with the help of Appendix Table B.4. Here is found a set of adjustment factors w_i to obtain values of cumulated "current" fertility (F_i) directly comparable to average numbers of children ever born (P_i) calculated for the conventional 5-year age groups of women.

The correction factors reflect the curvature of an underlying set of model age-specific fertility rates. The appropriate model, hence the appropriate correction factor, is selected by either of two summary measures of the age-specific fertility rates. These are the mean of the fertility

TABLE 22.9 Estimation of Total Fertility for the Philippines from Survey Reports on Births During a 12-Month Period Preceding the 1975 Census

Age	Age interval (1)	Average number of births in 12 months preceding the survey per woman[1] (E_i) (2)[3]	Cumulative fertility to the beginning of interval age $5\sum_{j=0}^{i=1} f_j$ (3)	Adjustment factors for estimating average fertility[2] (W_i) (4)	Estimated average cumulative fertility $F_i = (3) + w_i f_i$ $(3) + [(4) \times (2)]$ $= (5)$	Average number of children ever born per woman (P_i) (6)[3]	$\dfrac{P_i}{F_i}$ (6)/(5) = (7)	Adjusted age-specific fertility rates $f_i' = f_i \dfrac{P_2}{F_2}$ $(2) \times .9622 =$ (8)
15 to 19 years	1	0.0532		1.7068	0.0908	0.1000	1.1073	0.0512
20 to 24 years	2	0.2170	0.2662	2.7964	0.8730	0.8400	0.9622	0.2088
25 to 29 years	3	0.2461	1.3510	2.9918	2.0873	2.2100	1.0588	0.2368
30 to 34 years	4	0.2360	2.5815	3.1018	3.3135	3.8200	1.1529	0.2271
35 to 39 years	5	0.1808	3.7617	3.2232	4.3445	5.1100	1.1762	0.1740
40 to 44 years	6	0.0914	4.6657	3.4556	4.9815	5.9400	1.1924	0.0879
45 to 49 years	7	0.0291	5.1228	4.2171	5.2452	6.1600	1.1744	0.0280
Total, 15 to 49 years		1.0537	5.2684					1.0138

[1] For age intervals one-half-year younger than shown in stub (i.e., in exact ages, 14.5–19.5, 19.5–24.5, etc.).
[2] From Appendix Table B-4 for f1/f2 = .2452; these are interpolated values.
[3] Source: Based on Philippines Bureau of the Census, 1975. In U.S. Census Bureau, International Data Base, Washington, D.C., www.census.gov/ipc/www/idenew.html.

schedule and the steepness of the take-off of the fertility curve measured by the ratio $fi/f2$ (in this instance .2452, using data in column 2). The two adjustments give somewhat different results; only the adjustment through factors selected on the basis of $fi/f2$ is illustrated in Table 22.9.

The values of P_i and F_i are compared in column 7 in term, of their ratio. Ideally, the ratio should equal one if there is no misreporting of births. The values calculated for ages 15 to 19 are always highly uncertain and best ignored because of the small base from which the average number of births in the preceding 12 months is calculated. If there was progressive forgetting of offspring with age, then the ratios would tend to decline. (This decline was demonstrated in the original edition of the *Methods and Materials of Demography* with 1966 data from Turkey.) However, this tendency is not apparent in this example. The interpretation of the P_i/F_i ratios between ages 20 and 35 is more problematical. Ordinarily, it could be assumed that reports on children ever born to women aged 20 to 24 tend to be reliable. By definition these reports are not affected by the problem of time-reference error, and forgetting children at such an age is highly unlikely. Hence, any discrepancy between the value of P_2/F_2 and the expected value of one reflects a period-reference error in the "current" fertility reports. Because there is no reason to expect that such time-reference errors are related to the age of the respondent, the correction factor P_2/F_2 could be used to adjust the entire series of reported

current fertility rates. Column 8 demonstrates the mechanics of adjustment through deflating the reported "current" age-specific fertility rates by the factor P_2/F_2 (.9622). Obviously the effect in the present case is trivial. The chief concluision that emerger is that retrospective fertility, reports strongly supportan estimate of a total fertility rate of 6.2, i.e., a gross reproduction rate of indent 3.0.

As mentioned in Chapter 17, the Arriaga technique is an alternative to the Brass technique for adjusting a set of age-specific fertility rates complied under the circumstances considered here (Arriaga, 1983).[9] Unlike the Brass technique, the Arriaga technique does not require an assumption of constancy of fertility levels in prior years.

The Arriaga technique involves use of data from two censuses or surveys. The first step is to derive the average number of children ever born per woman for exact single years of age (CEB_x^t) from the information on children ever born for 5-year age groups at census or survey years. That is,

$$CEB_x^t = F(_5 CEB_x^t) \qquad (22.12)$$

where CEB_x^t is the children ever born per women at exact single-year-of-age x at the census or survey year t, F is an

[9] The material on the Arriaga technique was prepared by A. Dharmalingam, University of Waikato, N.Z.

interpolation function, and $_5CEB_x^t$ is the children ever born per woman at age group x to $x + 4$.

To get the CEB_x^t values for single years of age, we need to find an appropriate interpolation function F. Although several functions follow the general pattern of children ever born per woman by age, a polynomial function that meets the following conditions seems to provide the best fit:

1. The polynomial is zero at age 15; the first derivatives of the polynomial at age 15 and at age 50 are zero.
2. The polynomial produces the average number of children ever born for the age groups 20 to 24, 25 to 29, 30 to 34, 35 to 39, 40 to 44, and 45 to 49 at stact ages 22.5, 27.5, 32.5, 37.5, 42.5, and 47.5, respectively. The value for the age group 45 to 49 can be ignored if it is smaller than for ages 40 to 44 years. In this case, the degree of the polynomial will be reduced by 1.
3. The integral of the polynomial between exact ages 15.0 and 20.0 reproduces the average number of children ever born per women for the age group 15 to 19.

Under these conditions, a ninth-degree polynomial can be fitted to the data on children ever born per woman for the 5-year age groups 15 to 19, 20 to 24, ..., 45 to 49. The fitted polynomial can then be used to obtain the average number of children ever born per woman for each single year of age, as in Equation 22.12.

Next, we estimate the average number of children ever born per women for the periods a year *after* the earlier census or survey date and a year *before* the latest census or survey year:

$$BA_x^{t+1} = \frac{n-1}{n} \cdot CEB_x^t + \frac{1}{n} \cdot CEB_x^{t+n} \qquad (22.13a)$$

and

$$BB_x^{(t+n)-1} = \frac{1}{n} \cdot CEB_x^t + \frac{n-1}{n} \cdot CEB_x^{t+n} \qquad (22.13b)$$

where BA_x^{t+1} is the average number of children ever born per woman at exact age x during the year *after the earlier census* or survey date, n is the number of years between the two censuses or surveys with information on children ever born, and $BB_x^{(t+n)-1}$ is the average number of children ever born per woman at exact age x during the year *before the latest census* or survey. By combining (22.12) and (22.13), the age-specific fertility rates can be derived as the cohort differences in the average number of children ever born per woman:

$$ASFR_x^{t+0.5} = BA_{x+1}^{t+1} - CEB_x^t \qquad (22.14a)$$

and

$$ASFR_x^{(t+n)-0.5} = CEB_{x+1}^{t+n} - BB_x^{(t+n)-1} \qquad (22.14b)$$

where $ASFR_x^{t+0.5}$ is the age-specific fertility rate at age x for the year *after* the earlier census or survey date, and

$ASFR_x^{(t+n)-0.5}$ is the age-specific fertility rate at age x for the year *before* the latest census or survey date. From (22.14), the 5-year age-specific fertility rates can be obtained as

$$_5ASFR_x^t = \frac{1}{5} \sum_{i=x}^{x+4} ASFR_i^t \qquad (22.15)$$

The 5-year age-specific rates can then be cumulated as

$$CF_{i+5}^t = 5 \cdot \sum_{x=15}^{i} {}_5ASFR_x^t \qquad (22.16)$$

Similarly, the age pattern of fertility (*APF*) derived from the number of births during the previous 12 months or from registration data can be cumulated as

$$CPF_{i+5}^t = 5 \cdot \sum_{x=15}^{i} {}_5APF_x^t \qquad (22.17)$$

Using (22.16) and (22.17), an adjustment factor is derived as

$$k_i = \frac{CF_i^t}{CPF_i^t} \qquad (22.18)$$

Assuming that the cumulated fertility rates obtained from using information on children ever born, derived from Equation (22.16), reflect the "true levels," a set of estimated fertility rates is obtained by applying the adjustment factor (k_i) to the age pattern of fertility (APF). In other words, the estimated fertility rates (F) are

$$_5F_x^t = k_i \cdot {}_5APF_x^t \qquad (22.19)$$

As k_i is likely to differ by age, it is recommended that one select the adjustment factor that corresponds to the age group whose mean is closest to the mean age of childbearing.

If the age pattern of fertility (APF) is not available, then one can accept the fertility rates obtained from children ever born (Equation 22.16) as the "true ones." However, the results may be affected by the tendency among older women to underreport children ever born. This can be avoided by re-estimating the single-year-of-age-specific fertility rates for ages 40 to 49 by an extrapolation of cumulative fertility rates for single years of age from 33 to 38. This involves fitting a Gompertz function to cumulative single-year-of-age-specific fertility rates (CFR, obtained from Equation 22.16) for ages 33 to 38 as follows:

$$k \cdot g^{c^x} = CFR^{t+5} \qquad for \; x = 33, 34, \ldots, 38 \quad (22.20)$$

From the fitted Gompertz function, the fertility rate for each age from 39 to 49 can be derived as

$$F_x^t = k \cdot g^{c^{x+1}} - k \cdot g^{c^x} \qquad for \; x = 39, 40, \ldots, 49 \quad (22.21)$$

As the fertility rate derived from Equation (22.21) for age 50 may not be zero, the extrapolated fertility rates for ages 39 to 49 can be adjusted as follows:

$$_{adj}F_x^t = F_x^t - F_{50}^t \cdot \frac{x-39}{11} \qquad for \; x = 39, 40, \ldots, 49 \quad (22.22)$$

Using Equation (22.15), fertility rates 5 year age group can be calculated.

If the information on children ever born is available for only one census or survey date, the Arriaga technique can still be applied. In this case, it is assumed that the average number of children ever born per woman by age of mother has been constant during the past, and Equation (22.13) becomes irrelevant. The single-year-of-age-specific fertility rates as in Equation (22.14) are obtained by taking the differences between the average numbers of children ever born per woman for two consecutive single years of age. Then by following Equations (22.16) to (22.19), a set of estimated fertility rates can be obtained.

Estimates of Mortality from Retrospective Reports on Deaths

Using the analogy of estimating fertility from survey reports on childbearing during a specified period prior to the survey, it seems intuitive to try to derive mortality estimates from survey data on deaths obtained from retrospective reports. In fact, a number of censuses as well as surveys have experimented with such ideas. In retrospective birth reports, the rate of omission or the degree of distortion with respect to the length of the reference period may reasonably be assumed to be insensitive to the age of the reporting women, hence the pattern of fertility shown by such reports can be accepted as approximately correct. In contrast, any assumption of uniformity of errors in reported deaths with respect to age at death appears to be patently false. Differential completeness is generated by the fact that the importance of death to the survivors varies with the personal attributes of the deceased, and such attributes are highly correlated with age. Also, although retrospective birth reports are supplied by a well-defined group, women in the childbearing age, directly connected with the event of birth and subject to low mortality, no such logical respondent category exists with respect to past deaths. Thus, retrospective death reports often contain not only errors of omission and of reference period, but also of duplicate reporting of the same event. Furthermore, unlike the case of retrospective birth reports, no technique exists by which the average degree of the erroneous lengthening or shortening of the reference period can be estimated. Hence, no correction is possible for reference-period errors. The assumption that the reference-period error is of the same magnitude as the one calculated for fertility by the method described earlier is unacceptable, because the distortion in the perception of time elapsed is likely to be different for the two events.

Estimates of Infant and Child Mortality from Proportions Living among Children Ever Born

Data on children ever born and children living allow the calculation of the proportion of children surviving and its complement, the proportion of deceased children. This can, in turn, provide measure of child mortality during the precensal period. Such a measure, by definition, contains no reference-period error. Apart from minor biases, such as those originating from a possible relation between the mortality of women according to the number of the children who have died, it is likely to be affected only by underreporting (but only if the degree of underreporting differs in the numerator and in the denominator of the measure.) The underreporting would also tend to vary inversely with the recency of the births concerned. It is almost always the case that proportionate underreporting affects the number of children ever born more than the number reported as surviving, because children already dead at the time of the survey are more likely to be omitted than children who are still alive. Thus, even if the magnitude of the bias in the value of the proportion dead is unknown, its direction is unambiguously defined and the resulting measure gives a minimum estimate of mortality.

Reported proportions dead (when specifice for age of the reporting women) supply a measure directly usable for purposes of roughly describing patterns of mortality differencer. But the usefulness of the measure as a measure of mortality is obviously limited unless it can be interpreted in terms of conventional mortality indices.

A method developed by Brass (1961, 1975) that permits such a translation is illustrated in Table 22.10 by data for the Philippines in 1977. Columns 2 and 3 present the raw statistics of children ever born (P) and children surviving (S) by age of women. Calculated proportions deceased are shown in column 4. Clearly these proportions reflect the chances of dying from the moment of birth to some age x (in standard life table symbolism, $_xq_0$), where the value of x is an average determined by the lengths of time elapsed during which births to women of various age groups were exposed to the risk of dying. If the age pattern of fertility and the age pattern of the risk of dying are known, or can be estimated, the value of x can be calculated. When such calculations are performed for typical age patterns of fertility and mortality, the value of x is found to be very close to 1 for proportions dead reported by women 15 to 19 years old, very close to 2 for reports by women 20 to 24 years old, and so forth (see column 6). Thus, for example, proportions dead reported by women 25 to 29 years old supply an estimate of $_3q_0$, the probability of dying between birth (age zero) and age 3. It can be demonstrated that such estimates are robust to known variations in the pattern of infant and child mortality. Very early or very late childbearing does affect the exact value of x, however. If childbearing is especially early, the true x is larger, and the converse is true if childbearing

TABLE 22.10 Estimation of Values of $_xq_0$ (Proportions Dead by Age x) from Survey Reports on Children Ever Born and Children Surviving

Age of woman	Age interval (i) (1)	Average number of children ever born per woman[1] (P_i) (2)	Average number of children surviving per woman[1] (S_i) (3)	Proportion of children dead $(1 - S_i/P_i)$ (4)	Multipliers for column (4) $P_1/P_2 = .0789$ (5)[2]	Years to age x (6)	Proportion dead by age x $(_xq_0)$ (4) × (5) = (7)
15 to 19 years	1	0.0600	0.0500	0.167	1.160	1	0.193
20 to 24 years	2	0.7600	0.7100	0.066	1.094	2	0.072
25 to 29 years	3	2.0900	1.9300	0.077	1.038	3	0.079
30 to 34 years	4	3.6800	3.3600	0.087	1.035	5	0.090
35 to 39 years	5	5.1700	4.6600	0.099	1.043	10	0.103
40 to 44 years	6	6.4100	5.6600	0.117	1.025	15	0.120
45 to 49 years	7	6.6100	5.7400	0.132	1.025	20	0.135

[1] Source: Same as Table 22.9.
[2] From Appendix Table B-5.

is very late. To obtain $_xq_0$ estimates for the desired round values of x shown in column 6, it is therefore desirable to correct reported values of proportions of dead children to take into account the age pattern of fertility prevailing in the population in question.

Multipliers that perform the needed correction are tabulated in Appendix Table B.5. The multipliers are to be selected on the basis of one or more of three alternative indices of the age pattern of fertility shown in the bottom three lines of Table B.5. These three indices are (1) the ratio, P_1/P_2, where P_1 and P_2 are the average number of children ever born reported by women aged 15 to 19 and 20 to 24, respectively; (2) the mean of the fertility schedule m; and (3) the median of the fertility schedule m. The first of these indices was used for determining correction factors in the example shown in Table 22.10. The value of P_1/P_2 is determined from column 2 of the table as the ratio the average number of children ever born per woman in successive age categories. The multipliers, obtained through linear interpolation from Table B.5, are given in column 5 of Table 22.10. The products of columns 4 and 5 give the final estimates for $_xq_0$, shown in column 7.

The original edition of this book recommended that the estimate of $_1q_0$ derived from reports of women aged 15 to 19 years old is "often affected by grave biases and is best ignored." Table 22.10 illustrates why: The proportion dead by ages 15 to 19 shown in Table 22-10 is .193; this value drops to .072 in the next age category. Obviously, a person's cumulative probability of dying between birth and exact age x cannot decrease as x increases. This anomaly is caused by the very small reporting base in the ages 15 to 19, which creates unstable estimates.

The $_xq_0$ values given in column 7 of Table 22.10 may be expressed in terms of mortality levels through locating model life tables (usually by interpolation) having the same $_xq_0$ values. Except for the age 15-to-19 category, the esti-

mates show an impressive consistency, suggesting a mortality level of roughly 18 (in terms of the "West" model life tables) (i.e., an expectation of life at birth in the neighborhood of 60 years). Naturally, a translation of child mortality into e_0 values implies an extrapolation to adult mortality using a particular model life table. The validity of such an operation should be, if possible, corroborated by additional evidence. Alternatively, various model life table patterns should be used to gauge the sensitivity of the estimate to plausible variations in the age patterns of mortality.

Consistency of the estimates obtained from women of various ages is not sufficient to assert that the model used is correct or that mortality has remained unchanged. It should be remembered that the various estimates refer to various time periods prior to the census, depending on the age of the women reporting. The older the women reporting, the longer the period represented. Thus, for $_2q_0$ the reference period is roughly 4 to 5 years; for $_3q_0$ it is 6 to 8 years prior to the census. For women over 30, the period is of course much longer. Accordingly, consistent estimates for mortality levels may be a fortuitous outcome of two biases pulling in opposite directions; increasing underestimation of mortality from retrospective reports of older women, and relatively higher child mortality in earlier years. The retrospective reporting may be subject to errors of memory and to errors arising from an aversion to mentioning dead children, especially those just recently deceased.

Reports of younger women, on the other hand, are likely to contain only minor errors due to memory failure, because the events reported are recent and parity is low. These reasons single out the estimates of $_2q_0$ and $_3q_0$ as the most reliable, as well as most interesting. In view of the fact that these estimates are to be regarded as minimum estimates of mortality (as dead children are more likely to go unreported), it is notable that for typical less developed countries such estimates tend to indicate higher levels of child mortality than estimates based on vital registration. Obtaining more precise estimates of child mortality is of great interest because of the interest in measuring child mortality itself and because of the use of such estimates as a tool in estimating fertility from a reported age distribution.

Estimates of Fertility from Child Mortality and Age Distribution

As noted earlier, a recorded age distribution reflects past processes of fertility and mortality. In particular, an accurate count of persons in childhood permits the reconstruction of births in recent years, provided a satisfactory correction for child mortality can also be obtained. Estimates of child mortality obtained by the method just described from census or survey reports supply the data needed for such a correction.

As before, a reported age distribution may be interpreted as arising from a stable population. If positive evidence exists to show that the population is not stable, the analyst may choose to rely on estimates based on reverse survival alone. Because stable analysis is also a simple way of making reverse survival calculations, the method displayed in Table 22.11 is illustrated for that assumption only. Column 1 shows the reported female cumulative age distribution for the Philippines for which mortality estimates in Table 22.10 were obtained. Accepting the value of $_3q_0 = .079$, from Table 22.10, column 7, as the most reliable estimate of the $_xq_0$ values, the "West" model tables (Appendix Table B-1) indicate a mortality level of about 18 for the two sexes combined. If the true sex pattern of mortality differs

from that shown by the model, as is likely to be the case in this instance, this procedure will give biased estimates for both males and females (such as estimates of the male and female birthrates). However, the biases will be equal in size and different in direction; thus, in the merged (average) estimates for both sexes, they will cancel out. Note that only the calculation for the female population is illustrated here.

Columns 2 to 6 show various parameter values in "West" female stable populations that share the characteristic of having a mortality level of 18 and that have proportions under age 5, 10, ... 45 as shown in column 1. The parameter values are obtained by linear interpolation from Appendix Table B.3; as the estimated $_3q_0$ corresponds to a round mortality level, only one set of interpolations is necessary.

An important difficulty arises here that the analyst should not miss. Using the stable population tables, one finds that no single pair of adjacent columns (e.g., $r = .025$ and $r = .030$) bounds the proportion of the female population for all of the age groups tabulated. Thus, it would not be possible to interpolate between only two adjacent columns. The solution in this case is to choose two columns that are not adjacent, specifically, $r = .025$ and $r = .035$. This means that the interpolations are much more suspect, because they take place between two points that are farther apart. This should also be considered evidence that the stable model may not be representative of this population.

An examination of column 2 of Table 22.11 shows a tendency toward lower birthrates when estimates are derived from increasingly larger segments of the cumulated age distribution. Explanations consistent with this finding include

TABLE 22.11 Stable Population Estimates of Fertility and Mortality Based on the Age Distribution of the Female Population of the Philippines and on a Level of Mortality Derived from Reported Child Survival Rates

| Exact age x | Proportionate population cumulate up to age x, $C_{(x)}$ (1)[1] | Values of various parameters in female stable population with $C(x)$ shown in column (1) and with mortality level of 18 | | | | |
| | | Birth rate (2) | Death rate (3) | Rate of natural increase (4) | Gross reproduction rate | |
					$m = 29$ (5)	$m = 31$ (6)
5 years	0.1937	0.0448	0.0125	0.0323	2.95	3.16
10 years	0.3032	0.0464	0.0124	0.0340	3.22	3.47
15 years	0.4290	0.0408	0.0127	0.0281	2.74	2.92
20 years	0.5411	0.0391	0.0127	0.0263	2.65	2.81
25 years	0.6345	0.0474	0.0123	0.0352	3.40	3.69
30 years	0.7081	0.0381	0.0128	0.0253	2.59	2.76
35 years	0.7690	0.0383	0.0128	0.0255	2.61	2.77
40 years	0.8215	0.0381	0.0128	0.0253	2.60	2.76
45 years	0.8652	0.0379	0.0128	0.0251	2.59	2.75

[1] Source: Same as Table 22.9.

gradually falling fertility in the decades prior to the survey or distortion due to falling mortality (i.e., to quasi-stability in the strict sense).

These pieces of evidence indicate that the Philippines population is poorly described by the stable model. Thus, a cautious analysis should rely on the reverse survival technique only, as summarized in the indices derived from proportions under age 5 and 10, and, to a lesser extent, under age 15. These parameters, in combination with the estimated $_3q_0$, suggest a crude birthrate between .045 and .046 per person, a crude deathrate between .013 and .012, and a growth rate somewhere between .032 and .034. The reliability of these estimates would be increased, and the range of uncertainty narrowed, if some additional information on age reporting were also available. Differences between the estimates of the crude birthrate derived from C(5) and C(10), for instance, may be explained by exaggeration of age of children under 5, by differential omission of infants, or by falling fertility. Elimination of some of these possibilities on the basis of local evidence or confirmation of one of the interpretations as the correct one would be most helpful for the analyst.

Estimates of Fertility and Mortality through Reconstruction of Pregnancy Histories

Attempts to obtain information on past flows of vital events through retrospective reports in a census or survey can be logically extended beyond the relatively simple goals of recording the number of children ever born and surviving or the number of children born (or dead) during a specified period. A small but substantial step in this direction may be to ask about vital events during a 24-month period, instead of a 12-month period, prior to the survey. Even in reports for such recent periods, however, survey experience has shown that the respondent often makes errors in placing the event in the correct time interval. Ideally, tabulation of such data would give a crude birthrate, as well as various age-specific fertility rates, for two consecutive years. (See Chapter 16.)

Increasing the detail of such questions may conceivably lead to the establishment of a full pregnancy history for each woman past age 15, specifically to the recording of the timing of each conception and its outcome: fetal loss, live birth, or death (Bogue and Bogue, 1967). If such records are accurate, a highly refined description of past fertility can be obtained, at least up to the point—perhaps 20 or 30 years before the date of the survey—where the effects of increasingly scarce survivors in the older ages and the correlation of fertility and mortality become strong enough to destroy the representativeness of retrospective reports.

Many persons, particularly in largely unsophisticated populations, are unfamiliar with the more developed countries' calendar or the concept of chronological age. They would, therefore, be unable to recall past events or to locate these events with some precision on a time scale. These facts make the collection of usable pregnancy histories not only costly but also an exceedingly difficult enterprise. Under many circumstances, in fact, even the most careful field work will fail to elicit the information sought. If the attempt is made, there may also be some danger that the results will primarily reflect the judgment of enumerators on what is "normal" (e.g., with respect to birth intervals) rather than the actual situation. Naturally even under such conditions various by-products of the pregnancy history, such as more reliable figures on children ever born and surviving, may still be highly useful and thus justify the extra costs.

The "own children" technique is a less ambitious effort to establish dated records of fertility performance of women with respect to children alive at the time of the census (Grabill and Cho, 1965). If almost all young children live with their mothers in a particular population—that is, if the extent of adoption (including de facto adoption) is limited—household schedules obtained in a census can be used to record the number of live "own children" by age for each mother even without asking any direct questions on fertility. If children are fully counted and their recorded ages (as well as their mothers') are accurate, age-specific birthrates for some 10 years prior to the survey can be calculated on a year-by-year basis for any suitable subgroup of women. Naturally, an allowance for mortality is necessary, specifically an estimate of infant and child mortality. As with reverse-survival estimates, a further problem with this method is that young children tend to be omitted from the census altogether or placed in the wrong age group. When these distortions are mild or controllable, the "own children" technique may be a useful addition to the tool kit of the demographer (Grabill et al., 1959: Grabill and Cho, 1965). Cho (1969) has applied this technique to an Asian population.

Data Requirements for Estimation in Censuses and Surveys

The analysis of existing census or survey data is largely circumscribed by prior decisions that cannot be modified by the analyst such as decisions about the questionnaire content, coding, tabulation, and publication. In the light of the state of analytical techniques discussed earlier, the contents of past surveys and their form of presentation often severely limit the possibilities of applying some of the more powerful methods of estimating demographic measures from survey data. Such limitations may result from the need to minimize the costs of a census or survey. One caveat to note is that too few data elements may restrict the analytical possibilities to such an extent that for some purposes, such as estimating vital rates, the data may no longer be useful at all.

On the other hand, deficiencies in survey content and in its form of presentation often arise simply from a lack of coordination between producers and users of the data. With better coordination such deficiencies could be easily avoided. At this point, a summary of the data requirements is provided.

In setting data requirements, obviously no general rules are possible. It should be stressed, however, that when the reliability of the basic data is demonstrably weak, or at least open to suspicion, it is highly desirable that the same measures be estimated on the basis of several methods. The same principle suggests that statistics should be collected and tabulated in sufficient detail to permit the application of various alternative methods and to facilitate checks within the methods themselves. For example, calculation of the birthrate from the age distribution should be based, if possible, on separate estimates of the male and female birthrates derived by means of sex-differentiated estimates of child mortality. The inconsistencies that are inevitably found when such procedures are applied will help the analyst to identify both strengths and weaknesses in the data. This enhances the ability of the analyst to arrive at more reliable estimates.

Some flexibility and ranking of priorities are nevertheless called for even within a so-called minimum program. A basic "menu" of tabulations determined by the data needs for the application of basic techniques to estimate vital rates follows:

Symbol Tabulation

A Population by age, sex, and marital status

B Women by age; and total number of children born alive, for each age group of women

C Women by age; and total number of children living, for each age group of women

BX Women by parity and by age

BB Women by age; and total number of children born alive, for each age group of women, by sex

CC Women by age; and total number of children living, for each age group of women, by sex

D Number of women who have had a live birth during the 12 months preceding the census, by age

DX Women by length of time that has elapsed since the birth of their last live-born child, by age; separately for currently married women and other women.

In all these tables, age classifications are assumed to be based on standard 5-year age groups: for all ages in tabulation A, and at least for ages 15 to 49 in the other tabulations. In tabulation BX, parities at least up through parity 7 should not be grouped. In tabulation DX, column headings might be "no live birth ever," 0 to 2 months, 3 to 5 months, . . . 15 to 17 months, 18 to 23 months, 24 to 29 months, and 30 months or more.

From the above list, variants of a minimum tabulation program may be selected. The number of meaningful com-binations is limited by needs of the various methods for joint tabulations. Tabulations BB, CC, and DX account for tabulations B, C, and D; given the former, the latter do not constitute separate tabulations. Tabulation BX accounts for tabulation B only if parities are given in full detail; this is seldom the case. (In practice, tabulation B would be independently tabulated rather than obtained from BX.) The five basic variants of a minimum tabulation program for obtaining estimates of vital rates from a census are as follows:

I	II	III	IV	V
A	A	A	A	A
B	B	BB	BB	BB
C	C	CC	CC	CC
	BX	BX	BX	
			D	DX

Although the analytical possibilities would differ appreciably depending on which of the five specific programs from the table has been carried out, the feasibility of deriving an accurate fertility estimate in each instance from the same source (e.g., from reported age distribution plus child mortality) gives underlying unity to the various approaches that would be adopted in the analysis. To have less than variant "I," which is suggested here as a minimum, would drastically curtail the ability of the analyst to estimate certain characteristics. On the other hand, to go beyond the program suggested in variant "V" (e.g., by introducing age at marriage as a variable or, preferably, by preparing parity-specific tabulations of tabulation DX) would certainly be desirable but would involve much greater complexity and appreciably higher cost.

METHODS OF ESTIMATION FROM SAMPLE REGISTRATION AREAS

The techniques relying on census or survey data described in the preceding section represent the least expensive, quickest, and most flexible approach toward generating estimates of vital rates in statistically underdeveloped countries. However, although estimates obtained by such techniques may be perfectly adequate for some purposes such as charting the basic parameters of the population situation in a given country, describing group patterns of demographic behavior, or for formulating general population policy, the precision needed for other, more complex, or detailed analyses is seriously lacking. For example, to measure the effects of a family planning program (particularly in the initial stages when the effects are small), survey data typically lack sufficient precision. Similarly, the effective management of a public health program would require detailed data on age at death by sex in combination with various other characteristics, notably cause of death. Such data cannot be reliably obtained from a survey, even if it is repeated at regular intervals.

Given these types of needs, reliance on survey and census data alone is merely a stopgap measure until such data may be combined with information obtained from a continuous vital registration system. However, as was pointed out earlier, the building up of a reliable vital registration system is both an expensive and necessarily long-drawn-out process for less developed countries. In addition, these techniques have been tested in comparative studies by sampling registrations and administering surveys (see, for example, Narasimhan *et al.*, 1997). Comparing results from both systems showed that misreporting, underregistration, and omission of births all occur.

Sample Registration

A possible solution for this dilemma is to substitute a sample registration scheme for the standard system of comprehensive registration. With such a sample, it may be possible to achieve a far higher level of accuracy than could be the case for the population as a whole. This can be done by a variety of administrative devices designed to compensate for the lack of motivation on the part of the populace to register vital events, and for the often inadequate motivated on the part of even the official registrars themselves. The relatively small size of a sample provides many opportunities for improvements, even within the confines of a limited budget. Some opportunities are (1) to select better registrars; (2) to provide them with more thorough training, better supervision, and greater remuneration; (3) perhaps to employ them on a full-time basis; and (4) to facilitate registration through organizing a continuous house-to-house canvass and through employing a network of informants who have particularly easy access to relevant local information. Within the sample these improvements may be effected through upgrading the existing deficient vital registration system or through introducing an entirely new system, possibly organized under a different agency from the one responsible for the general vital registration system. The optimal mix of the various methods for promoting more complete coverage and the specific administrative arrangements for the scheme will obviously vary depending on local circumstances.

If the sample is scientifically designed, it can be taken as a representation of the entire population, and vital rates observed in the sample may be used to estimate vital rates for the entire population within the limits of quantifiable errors. Taken in isolation, the statistics supplied by sample registration, even when of a high quality, are not adequate for a full description of demographic processes. For some purposes, however, incompleteness of vital registration may not be important when identification of a trend alone suffices. If the degree and type of incompleteness can be taken as roughly uniform over time, even grossly incomplete data may reliably reveal a fall or a rise in the birthrate. Moreover, careful examination of flows alone—sometimes referred

to as numerator analysis—may reveal processes normally described by indices based on both stock and flow data. For instance, shifts in the distribution of reported birth order of children may serve as an approximate index of changes in reproductive behavior. The obvious advantage of such measures is their simplicity of calculation and their lack of dependence on stock data. It remains true, however, that more sophisticated measures of fertility and mortality do require both data from continuous registration and stock data obtainable from a census or survey. For practical purposes, therefore, registration on a sample basis must generally be combined with periodic surveys based on a corresponding sample.

DUAL SYSTEMS BASED ON SAMPLE REGISTRATION AREAS AND SURVEYS

It follows from the proposition just made that the introduction of sample registration will require a dual system of measurement, including a sample survey, which can be used also to obtain all information necessary for applying the techniques that were discussed in the preceding section. Thus, the two approaches of estimation based on survey data, on the one hand, and sample registration, on the other, are not competitive alternatives. Rather, they are complementary and the letter may be considered a powerful extension of techniques using survey data only. Obviously this extension can only be achieved at the cost of a substantial increase in the resources invested in the operation of the system.

It will be recalled that estimates of vital rates from survey data alone can be generated by obtaining direct information on events (e.g., births) during a specified time period from a cross-sectional investigation. In a dual system, however, in addition to such information, the same events are also observed through continuous observation (i.e., through sample registration). Thus, dual-systems analysis provides a possibility for comparing numbers of births and deaths obtained by alternative means. If the independence of the two approaches is scrupulously maintained (e.g., by assigning the two tasks to two different organizations and by preventing their collaboration through suitable administrative controls), such comparisons will permit the evaluation of the quality of the system and possibly the correction of any deficiencies revealed.

The capacity of the analyst to make appropriate corrections will naturally depend on the nature of the comparisons between the results obtained from the two systems. Obviously, a simple comparison of the total number of births, for instance, would not be particularly illuminating. If a discrepancy was found, the reasons for the discrepancy may not be identifiable from the summary comparison. Similarly, if the two systems give essentially the same result, this circumstance alone cannot be interpreted as a confirmation of the validity of the estimates, because both systems may be affected by biases of identical magnitude and direction, even if originating from different sources.

If comparisons are performed for progressively smaller units (e.g., by comparing numbers of births reported by the two systems in small territorial subdivisions of the total sample), the pattern of the discrepancies found between the events registered by the two systems may turn out to be quite uneven, thus indicating the location and possible source of underlying weaknesses in the data. In any event, it is most likely that, by diminishing the size of the units compared, increasingly large discrepancies between the two sets of data will be revealed. Hence, the more detailed such comparisons are, the better the picture of the errors affecting the two systems will emerge.

Options for Evaluating Coverage of Censuses or Registration Systems

Obviously, a vital registration system and a census have much in common. Both are intended to be 100% enumerations of their events of interest. Both have undercoverage to various degrees. Fellegi (1984) cataloged the options for evaluating coverage. Because his labels of the approaches are so descriptive, they are repeated here:

• *Do it again, but better.* In this method, a sample of areas is selected from the intended population, and these sampled areas are energetically enumerated using the best interviewers, repeated follow-ups, and so on in an attempt to get a "true" result for these areas. The U.S. Census Bureau's "CensusPlus" test was a test of this method in the United States (Mulry and Griffiths, 1996; Robinson, 1996; Treat, 1996). While this approach is conceptually appealing, it appears to fail in practice; many of the people missed by the registration or census can also be missed by the coverage survey, even given heroic efforts.

• *Do it again, independently.* This is the approach of dual-systems estimation, which was briefly described in Chapters 3 and 4, but is described move fully here. Rather than presume that the coverage survey can find people that the census of registration system cannot, this approach presumes that the two systems are statistically *independent*, thus allowing the analyst to estimate the cases missed both by the census or registration system and the coverage survey.

• *Reverse record check.* In a reverse record check in the census context, previously noted in Chapters 3 and 4, four frames may be constructed: a time $t - 1$ census frame, a register of intercensal births, a list of legal immigrants, and a sample of persons missed in the $t - 1$ census. A sample of these four frames is obtained, and they are "traced" to their location in the time t (current) census, including a determination whether they died or emigrated. If a sampled person cannot be found (after careful follow-up), has not died, and has not emigrated from the country, then he or she is presumed missed in the current census and in counted in an estimate of under coverage. While this method appears to work well in Canada, with only 5 years between censuses, in the United States the 10-year gap, limitations of databases, and the difficulty of tracing each have limited the application of this method (to the 1960 census). A description of the Canadian experience can be found in Fellegi (1980).

• *The megalist method.* The megalist method (Eriksen and Kadane, 1986) is an attempt to cover all the events in the registration area by combining multiple lists. These lists are unduplicated, and the hope is that, since each list can only increase coverage and not decrease it, the number of missed events can be driven to zero. It is similar to both the "do it again, but better" and "do it again, independently" methods. However, it relies heavily on the existence of multiple lists, and on the ability to successfully unduplicate events in those lists.

• *Demographic analysis.* The method of demographic analysis attempts to rely on underlying regularities in demographic phenomena (such as sex ratios at birth and at various ages) to evaluate coverage (Robinson *et al.*, 1993). In the United States, demographic analysis is a key method used to evaluate, census undercoverage, at the national level. To apply it, one must have an estimates of the events over sevoral decades to evaluate the fundamental demographic corrponent equation—that is, births, deaths, international immigrants, and emigrants. (See Chapters 3, 4, and 7.)

Chandra Sekar and Deming's Method— Dual-Systems Estimation

When the results of two systems—such as a sample survey and sample vital registration—are matched on the level of persons and housing units—it is possible to obtain a numerical estimate of the degree of completeness of both systems and hence to estimate the true total number of persons or events on the basis of assumptions described next.

Case-by-case matching of data from a registration system and a survey were employed in connection with the 1940 and 1950 censuses of the United States and the Current Population Survey in 1969–1970 (to measure completeness of birth registration, or of both infant underenumeration and birth underregistration). It was employed in the 1970, 1980, 1990, and 2000 censuses of the United States, with increasing levels of sophistication (see, e.g., Hogan, 1992, 1993, 2000; Wolter, 1986), but also increasing levels of criticism (see, e.g., Darga, 1999, 2000; Freedman, 1991; and Wachter and Freedman, 2000).

This technique of estimating the total number of events was developed and first tested by Chandra Sekar (now known as "Chandrasekaran") and Deming (1949). More recent work in this area was done by Krótki (1977) and Marks, Seltzer, and Krótki (1974). The essential features of the Chandrasekaran-Deming procedure may be summarized as follows (using statistics of births as an example). Suppose that births are recorded for a given year in a sample vital registration system and in a corresponding sample survey (conducted at the end of the year) in which a question on births during the 12-month period preceding the survey is asked. Suppose further that the two sets of birth records so obtained are matched event by event. From the matching procedure for the ith birth, the classification may be represented in the following schematic table:[10]

List A (registration system)

	In registration system	Out of registration system	Total
List B (survey)			
In survey	p_{i11}	p_{i12}	p_{i1+}
Out of survey	p_{i21}	p_{i22}	p_{i2+}
Total	p_{i+1}	p_{i+2}	p_{i++}

Where P_{i11} denotes the probability that birth event "i" falls into cell 11 (i.e., is "captured" by both systems).

For any class of individuals, let there be N people in the "true" population. Then, assuming independence between people, we have a count of the persons in each cell (Wolter, 1986):

List A (Registration system)

	In registration system	Out of registration system	Total
List B (survey)			
In survey	N_{11}	N_{12}	N_{1+}
Out of survey	N_{21}	N_{22}	N_{2+}
Total	N_{+1}	N_{+2}	N_{++}

where

N_{11} is the number of people (events) counted in both the registration and the survey
N_{12} is the number of people counted only in the survey
N_{21} is the number of people counted only in the registration
N_{22} is the number of people missed by both the registration and the survey

N_{1+} is the total number of people counted in the survey
N_{+1} is the total number of people counted in the registration
N_{++} is the total number of people

Assuming the "capture" probabilities of people satisfy $p_{i1+} = p_{1+}$ or $p_{i+1} = p_{+1}$ for all $i = 1, \ldots, $ N, the following equation represents the standard Chandrasekaran-Deming model, or "dual systems estimator," from which the standard dual-systems estimate (DSE) can be made.[11]

$$\hat{N}_{++} = \frac{N_{+1}N_{1+}}{N_{11}} \qquad (22.23)$$

Adjusting the equation somewhat, the DSE can be thought of as

$$\hat{N}_{++} = N_{+1}\left(\frac{N_{1+}}{N_{11}}\right). \qquad (22.24)$$

The equation reminds the analyst that the total population for the class of people is estimated by the number captured in the registration system times the inverse ratio of those in *both* systems to those in the survey (i.e., the inverse of the coverage rate of the registration, as measured by the survey). From rearranging Formula (22.24), it can be seen that the Chandrasekaran-Deming formula estimates the completeness of the coverage of the registration system as the match rate of the survey, and estimates the completeness of the coverage of the survey as the match rate of the registration.

Readers should note that the results of the DSE, though developed from a sample of registration cases, can naturally be extended to the population of all cases using a version of synthetic estimation (discussed in Appendix C, "Selected General Methods"). The DSE will yield a DSE of the population of class j, as well as any sum of classes. In the context of the United States, "j" might be the household population of a state, of an ethnic group, or perhaps of an ethnic group within a state. Often, the DSE is combined with a synthetic assumption to produce estimates for areas of geography smaller than that defined by the estimator domain "j." Requirements for estimating small or local populations, for example, age by sex, by race, by town, often far exceed the capacity of even a very large sample. Using a synthetic assumption, a "correction factor" for the jth domain can be estimated (following the development in Hogan, 2000):

$$CF_j = \frac{\hat{N}_j}{C_j} \qquad (22.25)$$

where

CF_j is the net coverage correction factor for group j
$\hat{N}_j$ is the DSE of group j

---

[10] In the following section, we will use the term "registration system". However, one can think of the "registration system" as a "census." The analysys remains essentially unchanged.

[11] Strictly speaking, p_{i1+} and p_{i+1} need only be uncorrelated. Zero correlation is easily visualized if one or both systems have constant "capture" probabilities.

$C_j = \Sigma_k \Sigma_h C_{jkh}$, where C_{jkh} is the measure of the population available at the smaller level of geography k (i.e., town, tract, block) and finer demographic subclass h

C_j might not equal N_{+1} for the jth group in place k and subclass h if place k and subclass h are heterogeneous (that is, if their coverage factors for the jth group are not the same as the estimated coverage factors for the jth group). As we shall see, N_{+1} is the number of people correctly included in the census. It is estimated from sample data and is not available for all small areas. C is normally the census or registration count, including imputations and erroneous inclusions (duplicates, etc.). Presumably, only the census or registration count is available for *all* areas. So using the synthetic model,

$$\hat{N}^s_{jkh} = CF_j C_{jkh} \tag{22.26}$$

Summing over group and subclass yields a measured population for a given geographic area (state, county, town). This is the final synthetic estimate using both the coverage factor, estimated by the sample survey for group j, and the count of events from the registration system or census disaggregated by place k and h.

$$\hat{N}^s_k = \sum_j \sum_h \hat{N}^s_{jkh} = \sum_j \sum_h CF_j C_{jkh} \tag{22.27}$$

For example, j may define all zero- to 18-year-old Asians in the West region, while k may define Orange County, California, and h may define 11-year-old girls.

In reviewing estimates based on a single system (survey), it has been emphasized that comparisons of estimates based on alternative estimating procedures constitute essential checks on the quality of the results obtained. It is the great merit of the dual-systems method of estimating vital events that such checking is a built-in feature of the estimating procedure. Unfortunately, the simplicity of the estimating formulas conceals a number of difficulties in the practical application of the method. The nature of the major problems will be discussed briefly.

Suppose that in a dual system the number of births in a given year and in a given geographic area is found to be 1200 when recorded by birth registration, whereas the number registered in a retrospective survey is 1300. Suppose also that subsequent individual matching of the births recorded in the two systems is successful in 900 instances. Using the notation given earlier, we have

$$\hat{N}_{++} = N_{+1}\left(N_{1+}\Big/N_{11}\right) = 1200(1300)/900 = 1733$$

Hence the estimated total number of births is obtained as $N = 900 + 300 + 400 + 133 = 1,733$. For simplicity, we will round this number to the nearest integer.[12]

<hr>

[12] Important note: For large-scale (e.g., country-wide) applications of the DSE technique, this rounding can cause serious biases unless it is approached in a careful and mathematically principled way.

Inserting these figures in our schematic table, the following is obtained:

List A (Registration system)

	In registration system	Not in registration system	Total
List B (Survey) In survey	900	400	1300
Not in survey	300	133 (estimated)	933
Total	1200	533	1733

In other words, the completeness of the registration of births is estimated as 69.2% (1200/1733 or 900/1300), and the completeness of the listing of births in the survey is estimated as 75% (1300/1733 or 900/1200).

Consider now a mother matching situation, census and survay data on renters and homeowners. Suppose that the census coverage varies for these two groups (it might be the case that renters are harder to enumerate than homeowners because of their higher mobility). First, a (hypothetical) DSE table for renters is presented. Given $N_{+1} = 1400$, $N_{1+} = 1300$, and $N_{11} = 1200$: our DSE estimate of N_{++} is

$$\hat{N}_{++} = N_{+1}\left(N_{1+}\Big/N_{11}\right) = 1400(1300/1200) = 1516.67$$

List A (census)

	In census	Not in census	Total
List B (Survey) In survey	1200	200	1400
Not in survey	100	17	117
Total	1300	217	1517

Seconds we derive the table for homeowners (again, rounding for simplicity). Given $N_{+1} = 2700$, $N_{1+} = 2650$, and $N_{11} = 2500$:

List A (census)

	In census	Not in census	Total
List B (Survey) In survey	2500	200	2700
Not in survey	150	12	162
Total	2650	212	2862

From these two tables, we calculate two factors to adjust for undercoverage in the census, one for renters ($j = 1$) and one for homeowners ($j = 2$):

$$CF_1 = 1517/1300 = 1.167 \text{ and}$$

$$CF_2 = 2862/2650 = 1.080$$

That is, using the constructed DSE tables, it is estimated that about 16.7 more renters should be "captured" by the census than were actually enumereted. Similarly, 8.0% more homeowners should be "captured" by the census than were actually enumereted.

Now suppose the analyst wishes to examine a province that is *not* in the DSE sample; however, it is desirable to use the DSE sample results to estimate the number of persons who should be "captured" by the registration system in this other province. For the sake of this hypothetical illustration, it is presumed that there are 10,000 persons enumerated in the province, of which 20% are renters and 80% are homeowners. Using the synthetic assumption, we note that we have an "h-th" subclass in province k, and $j = 1$ or 2 as noted earlier. Thus, the estimated number of persons who should have been enumereted by the census is

$$\hat{N}_k^s = \sum_j \sum_h \hat{N}_{jkh}^s = \sum_j \sum_h CF_j C_{jkh} = \sum_{j=1}^{2} CF_j C_j$$
$$= 1.167(2,000) + 1.080(8,000) = 10,974$$

As can be seen, the DSE tables are used to construct coverage factors that are then applied to the enumerated population of each kind to generate a final estimated total number of persons who should have been enumereted in the census.

The validity of the preceding estimates will necessarily depend on the fulfillment of the following main conditions:

1. The matching procedure successfully identifies all true matches and, conversely, only true matches are identified as matches.
2. All events identified in either of the two systems are true events (i.e., occurred in the population under investigation and in the appropriate time period).
3. The two systems are independent (i.e., the probability of an event being omitted from one system is not related to the chance of the event being omitted from the other system).
4. The nonsampled population on which the estimate is being constructed (i.e., in the other province) can be unambiguously classified (i.e., into either "renter" or "homeowner" status).
5. The synthetic assumption (i.e., that every renter has the same coverage factor) holds for nonsampled areas.

Practical and General Considerations

Deviations from these conditions may seriously affect the accuracy of the estimates derived from the method. Yet these conditions are quite stringent and the degree of deviation from their fulfillment is at best difficult to ascertain. First of all, the notion of what constitutes a proper match is ambiguous in almost all practical applications. Events may be described through listing a variety of alternatives. In the instance of births, for example, the statistics may record the address of the head of the household in which the event has occurred, the name, date of birth, and sex of the newborn, the age and the parity of the mother, and related items. In general, the more stringent the definition for a match (i.e., the larger the number of the attributes that must coincide in order to establish a "true" match), the smaller will be the estimate of C, the larger will be N_1 and N_2, and, consequently, the larger will be the estimate of N. There is a danger that overly stringent matching criteria, apart from making the matching process especially laborious will result in inflated estimates of the true number of births. On the other hand, an estimate of N based on loose matching criteria may yield an underestimate. Ding and Feinberg (1996), developed a model of sensitivity to false match and false nonmatch probabilities; for an overview of record linkage theory, estimation of false match and false nonmatch rates, and specific applications in demographic and epidemiological settings, see Alvey and Jamerson (1997).

The task of finding the golden mean between such extremes is difficult. The obvious solution of investigating every suspected match in detail is limited by cost considerations. Usually, simple rules will have to be imposed, but the fact that such rules necessarily must take into account the peculiarities of the specific situation makes generalizations about them difficult. If, for instance, addresses are nonexistent or ambiguous, or if names have many variations or are shared by many people, the power of these otherwise most useful matching criteria is greatly diminished or at least the possibility of mechanizing the matching operation is greatly lowered. Uncertainty about dates and ages makes matching by these characteristics unrealistic; but here again, the middle road between too stringent and too loose requirements is difficult to establish. It should be emphasized, however, that the very act of matching and the problems revealed by adopting alternative matching criteria will provide analysts with valuable insights into the quality of the data and hence make their interpretations more informed.

When reasonable matching criteria are applied, it can be accepted without further investigation that matched records of events are correct unless both are "out of scope." This generalization does not apply to entries recorded in only one of the two systems. A failure to match a registered event may mean either that the event in question was erroneously omitted in the other system or that it was erroneously included in the first system. Such erroneous inclusions may originate, for instance, from errors of time reference in a retrospective survey. Insofar as no correction is possible or is carried out for such errors, the validity of the method will be affected. The preceding formulas imply that nonmatches are investigated and false entries are eliminated from the statistics. Various devices, notably the use of overlapping reference periods in consecutive surveys, may lessen the need for such investigations but only at the expense of carrying out a prior matching procedure for events reported for the overlapping survey periods themselves.

Possible false entries in one of the two reporting systems may also make their appearance because of inmigration to or outmigration from the area covered. The effects of such migrations are often particularly strong on the phenomena under observation. Thus, deaths and births in a sample population may commonly occur in a hospital outside the sample area, or the sample area may contain a hospital attracting outsiders. Similarly, many women often return to their parents' homes for the birth of a baby. Accordingly, if survey and registration data are based on a de facto definition of the population (which would be the simplest solution from an administrative viewpoint), there is a definite risk that the results will show false discrepancies and that total births and deaths will be overestimated. This risk can be reduced or eliminated if the same rules are applied in both collection systems. (If many events occur in hospitals and a de facto approach is used, then hospitals should be sampled separately to reduce sampling error.) By adopting a de jure concept instead, the method can solve this problem, but only at the cost of following up residents moving out of the area and keeping track of events affecting temporary residents. The technical difficulties involved in such a solution are formidable: The U.S. Census Bureau, having performed dual system estimation for decades, continues to struggle with the proper rules for handling in-movers, out-movers, and the like (Hogan, 2000).

Finally, the previous formulas provide no correction for the presumably not uncommon situation where certain events tend to be omitted from both systems for the same reasons. A simple application of the estimating formulas will then give an estimate of the completeness of coverage that is biased upward. If, for example, both systems missed the same 20% of births (e.g., all illegitimate births) but both included all other births, the method would erroneously indicate full coverage for both systems.

Another manifestation of lack of independence between the two systems may be that the general quality of each is influenced by the existence of the other. Although such influences are typically positive and hence would normally be welcome, they do make it difficult to derive conclusions as to the completeness of coverage that can be generalized for areas where only one system is in operation. It is by no means certain, however, that a dual registration system will tend to improve over time if maintained for a given area for a longer time period. Beyond the general difficulty of sustaining a complicated and demanding system at a high level of efficiency, it will be particularly hard to avoid the deleterious effects of a possible collusion between the officials responsible for the operation of the two systems. Such collusion will naturally tend to be established as soon as it is understood that the quality of the work done by the registrar and the survey takers can be evaluated by observing changes in the match rates achieved in the survey and the vital registration.

Experience with dual-systems analysis of vital records and survey results described earlier was building up rapidly during the decades of the 1960s and 1970s in Africa, Asia, and Latin America. Marks, Seltzer, and Krotki (1974) have summarized the results from a number of "population growth estimation" studies conducted in Canada, the United States, the former Soviet Union, Asia, Africa, Latin America, and the Caribbean. Although the underlying principles have generally been the same, a wide variety of specific attempts have been made seeking to minimize the biases just mentioned. Thus, attempts using sample registration differ not only in the size of the sample and in the design of the sampling scheme, but even more with respect to the following characteristics:

- The length of the reference period and the peculiarities of the field operation
- The frequency and scope of the periodic surveys
- The registrars' mode of operation
- In particular, the existence, detail, and quality of the matching operation and of the investigation of the validity of nonmatches.

Experience indicates that the measurement of coverage of either registration systems or censuses remains very difficult, even by means of dual systems. Dual systems estimation has been heavily criticized in the United States and elsewhere. However, in lieu of new approaches that are *demonstrably* superior, it remains a tool in the demographer's tool kit.

References

Alvey, W., and B. Jamerson. 1997. "Record Linkage Techniques—1997: Proceedings of an International Workshop and Exposition." Washington, DC: Federal Committee on Statistical Methodology.

Arriaga, E. E. 1983. "Estimating Fertility from Data on Children Ever Born, by Age of Mother." *International Research Document* No. 11. Washington, DC: U.S. Census Bureau.

Arriaga, E. E., P. D. Johnson, and E. Jamison. 1994. *Population Analysis with Microcomputers, Vol. 1 and 2.* Washington, DC: U.S. Census Bureau.

Brass, W. 1961. "The Construction of Life Tables from Child Ratios." International Population Conference, New York, 1961. Liège: International Union for the Scientific Study of Population, Vol. 1, pp. 294–301.

Brass, W., A. J. Coale, P. Demany, D. F. Heisel, F. Lorimer, A. Romaniuk, and E. van deWalk. 1968. *The Demography of Tropical Africa*, Princeton, NJ: Princeton University Press, pp. 89–104 and 140–142.

Brass, W. 1975. *Methods for Estimating Fertility and Mortality from Limited and Defective Data.* Chapel Hill, NC: The University of North Carolina.

Bogue, D. J., and E. J. Bogue. 1967. "The Pregnancy History Approach to Measurement of Fertility Change." In *Proceedings of the Social Statistics Section*, American Statistical Association, pp. 212–231.

Chandrasekaran, C., and Deming, W. 1949. "On a Method of Estimating Birth and Death Rates and the Extent of Registration." *Journal of the American Statistical Association* 44: 101–115.

Cho, L. J. 1969. "Estimates of Fertility for West Malaysia (1957–67), Kuala Lumpur." Research Paper No. 3. Malaysia, Department of Statistics.

Coale, A. J. 1988. "Convergence of a Human Population to Stable Form." *Journal of the American Statistical Association* 63: 395–435.

Coale, A. J., L. J. Cho, and N. Goldman. 1980. *Estimation of Recent Trends in Fertility and Mortality in the Republic of Korea*. Washington, DC: National Academy of Sciences.

Coale, A. J., and P. Demeny. 1966. *Regional Model Life Tables and Stable Populations*. Princeton, NJ: Princeton New Jersey Press.

Coale, A. J., P. Demeny, and B. Vaughan. 1983. *Regional Model Life Tables and Stable Populations*, (2nd Ed.) New York: Academic Press.

Darga, K. 1999. *Sampling and the Census*. Washington, DC: AEI Press.

Darga, K. 2000. *Fixing the Census Until It Breaks*. Lansing, MI: Michigan Information Center.

Ding, Y., and S. E. Feinberg. 1996. "Multiple Sample Estimation of Population and Census Undercount in the Presence of Matching Errors." *Survey Methodology* 22: 55–64.

Dublin, L., and A. J. Lotka. 1925. "On the True Rate of Natural Increase." *Journal of the American Statistical Association* 20: 305–339.

Ericksen, E. P., and J. B. Kadane. 1986. "Using Administrative Lists to Estimate Census Omissions." *Journal of Official Statistics* 2: 397–414.

Fellegi, I. 1980. "Should the Census Count Be Adjusted for Allocation Purposes: Equity Considerations." Conference on Census Undercount. Washington, DC: U.S. Government Printing Office.

Fellegi, I. 1984. "Notes on Census Coverage Evaluation Methodologies." Mimeographed, February 16, 1984.

Freedman, D. A. 1991. "Adjusting the 1990 Census." *Science* 252: 1233–1236.

Grabill, W., and L. J. Cho. 1965. "Methodology for the Measurement of Current Fertility from Population Data on Young Children." *Demography* 2: 50–73.

Grabill, W. H., C. V. Kiser, and P. K. Whelpton. 1959. *The Fertility of American Women*. New York: John Wiley and Sons.

Hogan, H. 1992. "The 1990 Post-Enumeration Survey: An Overview." *The American Statistician* 46: 261–269.

Hogan, H. 1993. "The 1990 Post-Enumeration Survey: Operations and Results." *Journal of the American Statistical Association* 88: 1047–1060.

Hogan, H. 2000. "Accuracy and Coverage Evaluation: Theory and Application." Paper presented at the 2000 Joint Statistical Meetings, Indianapolis, IN, August 2–5, 2000.

Krótki, K. J. (Ed.). 1977. *Developments in Dual System Estimation of Population Size and Growth*. Edmonton, Alberta, Canada: University of Alberta Press.

Lotka, A. J. 1907. "Relation Between Birth Rates and Death Rates." *Science* 26: 21–22.

Marks, E. S., W. Seltzer, and K. J. Krótki. 1974. *Population Growth Estimation: A Handbook of Vital Statistics Measurement*. New York: The Population Council.

McDevitt, T. M. 1996. *World Population Profile: 1996*. Washington, DC: UNAIDS/WHO.

Mulry, J. J., and R. Griffiths. 1996. "Integrated Coverage Measurement (ICM) Evaluation Project 12: Comparison of CensusPlus and Dual System Estimates." 1995 Census Test Results, Memorandum No. 42. U.S. Census Bureau.

Narasimhan, R. L., R. D. Retherford, V. Mishra, F. Arnold, and T. K. Roy. 1997. "Comparison of Fertility Estimates from India's Sample Registration System and National Family Health Survey." *National Family Health Survey Subject Reports*, No. 4. Honolulu, HI: East-West Center Program on Population.

Robinson, J. G. 1996. "Integrated Coverage Measurement (ICM) Evaluation Project 15: Evaluation of CensusPlus and Dual System Estimates with Independent Demographic Benchmarks." Census Test Results, Memorandum No. 43. U.S. Census Bureau.

Robinson, J. G., B. Ahmed, P. Das Gupta, and K. A. Woodrow. 1993. "Estimation of Population Coverage in the 1990 United States Census Based on Demographic Analysis." *Journal of the American Statistical Association* 88: 1061–1071.

Stanecki, K. A., and P. O. Way. 1997. "The Demographic Impacts of HIV/AIDS, Perspectives from the *World Population Profile: 1996*." U.S. Bureau of the Census. IPC Staff Paper No. 86.

Treat, J. B. 1996. "Integrated Coverage Measurement (ICM) Evaluation Project 9: Effect on the Dual System Estimate and the CensusPlus Estimate of the Adds and Deletes to the Census File." 1995 Census Test Results, Memorandum No. 40. U.S. Census Bureau.

United Nations. 1956. *Methods for Population Projections by Sex and Age*. Series A, Population Studies, No. 25.

United Nations. 1967. *Methods of Estimating Demographic Measures from Incomplete Data*. Manual IV. Manuals on Methods of Estimating Population, Series A. Population Studies. No. 42.

United Nations. 1982. *Model Life Tables for Developing Countries*. Population Studies, No. 77. New York: United Nations.

United Nations. 1983. *Manual X: Indirect Techniques for Demographic Estimation*. Population Studies, No. 81. New York: United Nations.

United Nations. 1989. *Demographic Yearbook*. New York: United Nations. U.S. Census Bureau, International Data Base. Accessed at www.census.gov/ipc/www/idbnew.html.

United Nations. 1990. *Step-by-Step Guide to the Estimation of Child Mortality*, Population Studies No. 107. New York: United Nations.

U.S. Bureau of the Census. 2000. International Data Base. Washington, DC. Found at www.census.gov/ipc/www/idbnew.html on November, 19, 2000.

U.S. Department of Commerce. 1999. *HIV/AIDS in the Developing World*. WP/98-2. Washington, DC.

Wachter, K. W., and D. A. Freedman. 2000. "Measuring Local Heterogeneity with 1990 Census Data." Demographic Research. Online document: www.demographic-research.org/Volumes/Vol3/10. Retrieved December 12, 2000.

Wolter, K. 1986. "Some Coverage Error Models for Census Data." *Journal of the American Statistical Association* 81: 338–346.

Suggested Readings

Agrawal, B. L. 1969. "Sample Registration in India." *Population Studies* (London) 23(3): 379–394.

Ahmed, N., and K. J. Krótki. 1963. "Simultaneous Estimations of Population Growth—the Pakistan Experiment." *Pakistan Development Review* 3(1): 37–65.

Alauddin Chowdhury, A. K. M., K. M. A. Aziz, and W. H. Mosley. 1969. *Demographic Studies in Rural East Pakistan: Second Year, May, 1967–April, 1968*. Dacca, Pakistan SEATO Cholera Research Laboratory. June 1969.

Arnold, F., and A. K. Blanc. 1990. "Fertility Levels and Trends." *Demographic and Health Surveys Comparative Studies* No. 2. Columbia, MD: Institute for Resource Development/Macro Systems.

Arriaga, E. E. 1967. "Rural-Urban Mortality in Developing Countries: An Index for Detecting Rural Underregistration." *Demography* 4(1): 98–107.

Blacker, J. G. C., and C. J. Martin. 1961. "Old and New Methods of Compiling Vital Statistics in East Africa." In International Population Conference, New York. Liège: International Union for the Scientific Study of Population, Vol. 1, pp. 355–362.

Bogue, Donald J., and Bogue, Elizabeth J. 1967. "The Pregnancy History Approach to Measurement of Fertility Change." *Proceedings of the Social Statistics Section*. Washington, DC: American Statistical Association, pp. 212–231.

Bourgeois-Pichat, J. 1958. "Utilisation de la notion stable pour mesurer la mortalité et la fecondité des populations des pays sous-developpés." *Bulletin de l'Institut international de statistique* 36(2): 94–121. (Proceedings of the 30th Session, Stockholm, 1957). Uppsala.

Brass, W. 1961. "The Construction of Life Tables from Child Ratios." In International Population Conference, New York, 1961 Liège: International Union for the Scientific Study of Population, Vol. 1, pp. 294–301.

Brass, W., and A. J. Coale, Ansley J. 1968. "Methods of Analysis and Estimation." In William Brass, A. J. Coale, P. Demeny, D. F. Heisel, F. Lorimor, A. Romaniuk, and E. van deWalle. *The Demography of Tropical Africa*, Princeton, Princeton University Press, Chapter 3, pp. 88–150.

Carmen, A. G., and J. L. Somoza. 1965. "Survey Methods, Based on Periodically Repeated Interviews, Aimed at Determining Demographic Rates." *Demography* 2: 289–301.

Cavanaugh, J. A. 1961. "Sample Vital Registration Experiment" In International Population Conference, New York, 1961. Liège: International Union for the Scientific Study of Population, Vol. 11, pp. 363–371.

Chandra, S. C., and W. E. Deming. 1949. "On a Method of Estimating Birth and Death Rates and the Extent of Registration." *Journal of the American Statistical Association* 44(245): 101–115.

Chandrasekaran, C. 1964. "Fertility Indices from Limited Data." International Population Conference, Ottawa 1963. Liège: International Union for the Scientific Study of Population, pp. 91–105.

Clairin, R. 1963. "Les données susceptibles d'etre utilisées pour une evaluation du mouvement de la population en Afrique au sud du Sahara." In International Population Conference, Ottawa, Liège, International Union for the Scientific Study of Population, 1964, pp. 107–120.

Coale, Ansley J., and E. M. Hoover. 1958. Population Growth and Economic Development in Low-Income Countries. Princeton, NJ: Princeton University Press, 1958, pp. 337–374.

Coale, A. J. 1961. "The Design of an Experimental Procedure for Obtaining Accurate Vital Statistics." In International Population Conference, New York, Vol. II, pp. 372–375. Liège: International Union for the Scientific Study of Population.

Coale, A. J. 1963. "Estimates of Various Demographic Measures through the Quasi-Stable Age Distribution." In *Emerging Techniques in Population Research*, New York, Milbank Memorial Fund, pp. 175–193.

Cooke, D. S. 1969. "Population Growth Estimation Experiment in Pakistan." *Statistical Reporter* (U.S. Bureau of the Budget), pp. 173–176.

Curtia, S. L. 1995. *Assessment of the Quality of Data Used for Direct Estimation of Infant and Child Mortality in DHS-II Surveys*. Calverton, MD: Macro International.

Demeny, P. 1965. "Estimation of Vital Rates for Populations in the Process of Destabilization." *Demography* 2: 516–530.

Demeny, P. 1967. "A Minimum Program for the Estimation of Basic Fertility Measures from Censuses of Population in Asian Countries with Inadequate Demographic Statistics." In International Population Conference, Sydney, Australia 1967, Liège: International Union for the Scientific Study of Population, pp. 818–825.

Demeny, P., and F. C. Shorter. 1968. "Estimating Turkish Mortality, Fertility, and Age Structure: Application of Some New, Techniques," Publication No. 218, Faculty of Economics, University of Istanbul, Istanbul, 1968.

El-Badry, M. A. 1955. "Some Demographic Measurements for Egypt Based on the Stability of Census Age Distributions." *Milbank Memorial Fund Quarterly* 33(3): 268–305.

El-Badry, M. A., and C. Chandrasekaran. 1961. "Some Methods for Obtaining Vital Statistics in India." International Population Conference, New York. Liège: International Union for the Scientific Study of Population, Vol. 11, pp. 377–386.

Goldberg, D., and A. Adlackha. 1968. "Infant Mortality Estimates Based on Small Surveys on the Ankara Area." Chapter 7 in *Turkish Demography: Proceedings of a Conference*, Izmir, February 21–24, 1968. Hacettepe University, Publication No. 7, Ankara, Turkey, 1969, pp. 133–145.

Grabill, Wilson H., and L. J. Cho. 1965. "Methodology for the Measurement of Current Fertility from Population Data on Young Children." *Demography* 2: 50–73.

Heligman, L., G. Finch, and R. Kramer. 1978. "Measurement of Infant Mortality in Less Developed Countries." *International Research Document* No. 5. Washington, DC: U.S. Census Bureau.

Holzer, J. 1967. "Estimate of the Age Structure of Ghana's Population. An Application of the Stable Population Model." In International Population Conference, Sydney, Australia. Liège: International Union for the Scientific Study of Population, pp. 838–849.

India, Office of the Registrar General. 1969. "Sample Registration in India: Report on Pilot Studies in Urban Areas: 1964–67."

Indian Statistical Institute. 1961. "The Use of the National Sample Survey in the Estimation of Current Birth and Death Rates in India." International Population Conference, New York. Liège: International Union for the Scientific Study of Population, Vol. 11, pp. 395–402.

Johnson, P. J. 1980. "Techniques for Estimating Infant Mortality." *International Research Document* No. 8. Washington, DC: U.S. Census Bureau.

Krótki, K. J. 1964. "First Report on the Population Growth Experiment." In International Union for the Scientific Study of Population, International Population Conference, Ottawa, 1963. Liège, International Union for the Scientific Study of Population, pp. 159–173.

Krótki, K. J. 1965. "Estimating Population Size and Growth from Inadequate Data." *International Social Science Journal* 17(2): 246–258.

Krótki, K. J. 1966. "The Problem of Estimating Vital Rates in Pakistan." In World Population Conference, 1965. Belgrade. Liège: International Union for the Scientific Study of Population.

Lauriat, P. 1967. "Field Experience in Estimating Population Growth." *Demography* 4(l): 228–243.

Liberia, Department of Planning and Economic Affairs. 1969. *Liberian Population Growth Survey Handbook*.

Marks, E. S., W. Seltzer, and K. J. Krotki. 1974. *Population Growth Estimation: A Handbook of Vital Statistics Measurement*. New York: The Population Council.

Mauldin, W. P. 1966. "Estimating Rates of Population Growth." In Family Planning and Population Programs, Proceedings of the International Conference on Family Planning Programs, Geneva, August 1965. Chicago: University of Chicago Press, pp. 635–653.

Myburgh, C. A. L. 1956. "Estimating the Fertility and Mortality of African Populations from the Total Number of Children Ever Born and the Number of these Still Living." *Population Studies (London)* 10(2): 193–206.

Pakistan Institute of Development Economics. 1968. *Report of the Population Growth Estimation Experiment*, Karachi.

Rele, J. R. 1967. "Estimation of Reproduction Rates for Asian Countries from Census Data." In International Population Conference, Sydney, Australia. Liège: International Union for the Scientific Study of Population, pp. 929–934.

Rele, J. R. 1967. Fertility Analyses through Extension of Stable Population Concepts, Berkeley, California. International Population and Urban Research, University of California, 1967.

Roberts, G. W. 1961. "Improving Vital Statistics in the West Indies." International Population Conference, New York. Liège: International Union for the Scientific Study of Population, Vol. 11, pp. 420–426.

Romaniuk, A. 1967. "Estimation of the Birth Rate for the Congo Through Non-conventional Techniques." *Demography* 4(2): 688–709.

Sabagh, G., and C. Scott, Christopher. 1967. "A Comparison of Different Survey Techniques For Obtaining Vital Data in a Developing Country." *Demography* 4(2): 759–772.

Siegel, J. S. 2002. *Applied Demogaphy: Applications to Business, Goverment, Law, and Public Policy.* San Diego: Academic Press. Chapter 4.

Seltzer, W. 1969. "Some Results from Asian Population Studies." *Population Studies (London)* 23(3): 395–406.

Som, R. K. 1967. "On Some Techniques of Demographic Analysis of Special Relevance to the Asian Countries." In International Population Conference, Sydney, Australia. Liège: International Union for the Scientific Study of Population, pp. 807–813.

Srivastava, M. L. 1967. "The Relationships between Fertility and Mortality Characteristics in Stable Female Populations." *Eugenics Quarterly* 14(3): 171–180.

Srivastava, M. L. 1967. "Selection of Model Life Tables and Stable Populations." In International Population Conference, Sydney, Australia. Liège: International Union for the Scientific Study of Population, pp. 904–911.

United Nations. 1949. *Methods of Using Census Statistics for the Calculation of Life Tables and Other Demographic Measures,* by Giorgio Mortara, Series A, Population Studies, No. 7.

United Nations. 1956. *Age and Sex Patterns of Mortality. Model Life Tables for Developing Countries,* Series A, Population Studies, No. 22.

United Nations. 1967. *Methods of Estimating Basic Demographic Measures from Incomplete Data,* Series A, Population Studies, No. 42.

United Nations Population Fund. 1993. *Readings in Population Research Methodology,* Vol. 2. Chicago: Social Development Center.

United States National Center for Health Statistics. 1969, March. "Methods for Measuring Population Change: A Systems Analysis Summary" by Forrest E. Linder. *Vital and Health Statistics,* Series 2, No 32.

Vallin. J., H. J. Pollard, and L. Heligman (Eds.). 1981. *Methodologies for the Collection and Analysis of Mortality Data.* Liège: Ordina Editions, Chapter 5.

Wells, H. B., and B. L. Agrawal. 1967. "Sample Registration in India." *Demography* 4(1): 374–387.

Zelnik, M., and M. R. Khan. 1965. "An Estimate of the Birth Rate in East and West Pakistan." *Pakistan Development Review* 5(1): 64–93.

A

Reference Tables for Constructing an Abridged Life Table by the Reed-Merrell Method

The tables in this appendix first appeared in Lowell J. Reed and Margaret Merrell, "A Short Method for Constructing an Abridged Life Table," *American Journal of Hygiene* 302 (2): 52–61, September 1939. (Copyright 1939 by the *American Journal of Hygiene,* now the *American Journal of Epidemiology*, The Johns Hopkins University.)

These tables provide a direct method for deriving the $_nq_x$ values, or probabilities of dying, from the observed $_nm_x$ values, or age-specific death rates, for constructing an abridged life table. The text of Chapter 13, "The Life Table," provides instructions to the reader on the steps in calculating the survivorship column (l_x) and the column of deaths ($_nd_x$) in the life table. The equations required for deriving the person-years columns ($_nL_x$ and T_x) by the Reed-Merrell method are given in the text. Once these values are known, it is a simple step to calculate the remaining basic column of the life table, e_x, from T_x and l_x.

Chapter 13 describes other methods of constructing abridged life tables in addition to the Reed-Merrell method. An Excel program for constructing an abridged life table that requires only population and deaths by age as input is available from George C. Hough, Jr., of the Population Research Center, Portland State University.

TABLE A.1   Values of q_0 Associated with m_0 by the Equation $q_0 = 1 - e^{-m_0(.9539-.5509m_0)}$

m_0	q_0	Δ	m_0	q_0	Δ	m_0	q_0	Δ	m_0	q_0	Δ
		0.000			0.000			0.000			0.000
0.000	0.000000	953	0.050	0.045261	857	0.100	0.085960	770	0.150	0.122510	691
0.001	0.000953	951	0.051	0.046119	855	0.101	0.086730	769	0.151	0.123201	690
0.002	0.001904	949	0.052	0.046974	854	0.102	0.087499	767	0.152	0.123891	688
0.003	0.002853	947	0.053	0.047828	852	0.103	0.088266	765	0.153	0.124579	687
0.004	0.003800	945	0.054	0.048679	850	0.104	0.089032	764	0.154	0.125266	685
0.005	0.004744	943	0.055	0.049529	848	0.105	0.089795	762	0.155	0.125951	684
0.006	0.005687	941	0.056	0.050378	846	0.106	0.090557	760	0.156	0.126635	682
0.007	0.006628	939	0.057	0.051224	845	0.107	0.091318	759	0.157	0.127317	681
0.008	0.007567	937	0.058	0.052068	843	0.108	0.092077	757	0.158	0.127998	679
0.009	0.008504	935	0.059	0.052911	841	0.109	0.092834	756	0.159	0.128677	678
0.010	0.009439	933	0.060	0.053752	839	0.110	0.093590	754	0.160	0.129355	676
0.011	0.010372	931	0.061	0.054591	837	0.111	0.094344	752	0.161	0.130031	675
0.012	0.011303	929	0.062	0.055429	836	0.112	0.095096	751	0.162	0.130706	673
0.013	0.012232	927	0.063	0.056264	834	0.113	0.095847	749	0.163	0.131379	672
0.014	0.013159	925	0.064	0.057098	832	0.114	0.096596	747	0.164	0.132051	670
0.015	0.014084	923	0.065	0.057930	830	0.115	0.097343	746	0.165	0.132722	669
0.016	0.015008	921	0.066	0.058761	829	0.116	0.098089	744	0.166	0.133390	667
0.017	0.015929	919	0.067	0.059589	827	0.117	0.098833	743	0.167	0.134058	666
0.018	0.016848	917	0.068	0.060416	825	0.118	0.099576	741	0.168	0.134724	664
0.019	0.017766	915	0.069	0.061241	823	0.119	0.100317	739	0.169	0.135388	663
0.020	0.018681	913	0.070	0.062064	821	0.120	0.101056	738	0.170	0.136051	662
0.021	0.019594	912	0.071	0.062886	820	0.121	0.101794	736	0.171	0.136713	660
0.022	0.020506	910	0.072	0.063705	818	0.122	0.102531	735	0.172	0.137373	659
0.023	0.021416	908	0.073	0.064523	816	0.123	0.103265	733	0.173	0.138032	657
0.024	0.022323	906	0.074	0.065339	814	0.124	0.103998	731	0.174	0.138689	656
0.025	0.023229	904	0.075	0.066154	813	0.125	0.104730	730	0.175	0.139345	654
0.026	0.024133	902	0.076	0.066967	811	0.126	0.105460	728	0.176	0.139999	653
0.027	0.025035	900	0.077	0.067778	809	0.127	0.106188	727	0.177	0.140652	651
0.028	0.025935	898	0.078	0.068587	808	0.128	0.106915	725	0.178	0.141303	650
0.029	0.026833	896	0.079	0.069395	806	0.129	0.107640	724	0.179	0.141953	649
0.030	0.027729	894	0.080	0.070200	804	0.130	0.108364	722	0.180	0.142602	647
0.031	0.028624	892	0.081	0.071005	802	0.131	0.109086	720	0.181	0.143249	646
0.032	0.029516	891	0.082	0.071807	801	0.132	0.109806	719	0.182	0.143895	644
0.033	0.030407	889	0.083	0.072608	799	0.133	0.110525	717	0.183	0.144539	643
0.034	0.031296	887	0.084	0.073407	797	0.134	0.111242	716	0.184	0.145182	641
0.035	0.032182	885	0.085	0.074204	796	0.135	0.111958	714	0.185	0.145823	640
0.036	0.033067	883	0.086	0.074999	794	0.136	0.112672	713	0.186	0.146463	639
0.037	0.033950	881	0.087	0.075793	792	0.137	0.113385	711	0.187	0.147102	637
0.038	0.034832	879	0.088	0.076585	790	0.138	0.114096	710	0.188	0.147739	636
0.039	0.035711	877	0.089	0.077376	789	0.139	0.114806	708	0.189	0.148374	634
0.040	0.036588	876	0.090	0.078165	787	0.140	0.115514	707	0.190	0.149009	633
0.041	0.037464	874	0.091	0.078952	785	0.141	0.116220	705	0.191	0.149642	632
0.042	0.038338	872	0.092	0.079737	784	0.142	0.116925	703	0.192	0.150273	630
0.043	0.039210	870	0.093	0.080521	782	0.143	0.117629	702	0.193	0.150903	629
0.044	0.040080	868	0.094	0.081303	780	0.144	0.118331	700	0.194	0.151532	627
0.045	0.040948	866	0.095	0.082083	779	0.145	0.119031	699	0.195	0.152159	626
0.046	0.041814	865	0.096	0.082862	777	0.146	0.119730	697	0.196	0.152785	625
0.047	0.042679	863	0.097	0.083639	775	0.147	0.120427	696	0.197	0.153410	623
0.048	0.043542	861	0.098	0.084414	774	0.148	0.121123	694	0.198	0.154033	622
0.049	0.044402	859	0.099	0.085188	772	0.149	0.121817	693	0.199	0.154655	620
0.050	0.045261	857	0.100	0.085960	770	0.150	0.122510	691	0.200	0.155275	

TABLE A.2   Values of q_1 Associated with m_1 by the Equation $q_1 = 1 - e^{-m_1(.9510-1.921m_1)}$

m_1	q_1	Δ	m_1	q_1	Δ
		0.000			0.000
0.000	0.000000	949	0.050	0.041847	725
0.001	0.000949	944	0.051	0.042572	721
0.002	0.001893	939	0.052	0.043293	717
0.003	0.002832	934	0.053	0.044009	712
0.004	0.003766	930	0.054	0.044722	708
0.005	0.004696	925	0.055	0.045430	704
0.006	0.005621	920	0.056	0.046134	700
0.007	0.006541	916	0.057	0.046833	696
0.008	0.007457	911	0.058	0.047529	691
0.009	0.008368	906	0.059	0.048221	687
0.010	0.009275	902	0.060	0.048908	683
0.011	0.010176	897	0.061	0.049591	679
0.012	0.011074	893	0.062	0.050270	675
0.013	0.011966	888	0.063	0.050945	671
0.014	0.012854	883	0.064	0.051616	667
0.015	0.013738	879	0.065	0.052282	663
0.016	0.014616	874	0.066	0.052945	658
0.017	0.015491	870	0.067	0.053603	654
0.018	0.016360	865	0.068	0.054258	650
0.019	0.017225	861	0.069	0.054908	646
0.020	0.018086	856	0.070	0.055554	642
0.021	0.018942	852	0.071	0.056196	638
0.022	0.019794	847	0.072	0.056835	634
0.023	0.020641	843	0.073	0.057469	630
0.024	0.021483	838	0.074	0.058099	626
0.025	0.022321	834	0.075	0.058724	622
0.026	0.023155	829	0.076	0.059346	618
0.027	0.023984	825	0.077	0.059964	614
0.028	0.024809	820	0.078	0.060578	610
0.029	0.025629	816	0.079	0.061188	606
0.030	0.026445	811	0.080	0.061794	602
0.031	0.027257	807	0.081	0.062396	598
0.032	0.028064	803	0.082	0.062994	594
0.033	0.028866	798	0.083	0.063588	590
0.034	0.029664	794	0.084	0.064177	586
0.035	0.030458	789	0.085	0.064763	582
0.036	0.031248	785	0.086	0.065345	578
0.037	0.032033	781	0.087	0.065924	574
0.038	0.032814	776	0.088	0.066498	570
0.039	0.033590	772	0.089	0.067068	566
0.040	0.034362	768	0.090	0.067634	562
0.041	0.035130	763	0.091	0.068196	558
0.042	0.035893	759	0.092	0.068755	554
0.043	0.036652	755	0.093	0.069309	551
0.044	0.037407	751	0.094	0.069860	547
0.045	0.038158	746	0.095	0.070407	543
0.046	0.038904	742	0.096	0.070949	539
0.047	0.039646	738	0.097	0.071488	535
0.048	0.040384	734	0.098	0.072023	531
0.049	0.041117	729	0.099	0.072555	527
0.050	0.041847	725	0.100	0.073082	

TABLE A.3   Values of $_3q_2$ Associated with $_3m_2$ by the Equation $_3q_2 = 1 - e^{-3_3m_2-.008(3)^3_3m_2^2}$

$_3m_2$	$_3q_2$	Δ	$_3m_2$	$_3q_2$	Δ
		0.00			0.00
0.000	0.000000	2996	0.010	0.029575	2911
0.001	0.002996	2987	0.011	0.032487	2903
0.002	0.005983	2979	0.012	0.035390	2895
0.003	0.008962	2970	0.013	0.038284	2886
0.004	0.011932	2962	0.014	0.041171	2878
0.005	0.014893	2953	0.015	0.044049	2870
0.006	0.017847	2945	0.016	0.046919	2862
0.007	0.020791	2936	0.017	0.049781	2854
0.008	0.023728	2928	0.018	0.052634	2845
0.009	0.026656	2920	0.019	0.055480	2837
0.010	0.029575	2911	0.020	0.058317	

TABLE A.4   Values of $_4q_1$ Associated with $_4m_1$ by the Equation $_4q_1 = 1 - e^{-4_4m_1(.9806-2.079_4m_1)}$

$_4m_1$	$_4q_1$	Δ	$_4m_1$	$_4q_1$	Δ
		0.00			0.00
0.000	0.000000	3906	0.020	0.072369	3316
0.001	0.003906	3875	0.021	0.075686	3289
0.002	0.007781	3843	0.022	0.078975	3262
0.003	0.011624	3812	0.023	0.082237	3235
0.004	0.015436	3781	0.024	0.085472	3209
0.005	0.019217	3750	0.025	0.088681	3182
0.006	0.022967	3720	0.026	0.091864	3156
0.007	0.026687	3689	0.027	0.095020	3130
0.008	0.030376	3659	0.028	0.098150	3105
0.009	0.034035	3629	0.029	0.101255	3079
0.010	0.037665	3600	0.030	0.104334	3054
0.011	0.041265	3571	0.031	0.107388	3028
0.012	0.044835	3541	0.032	0.110416	3003
0.013	0.048376	3512	0.033	0.113419	2979
0.014	0.051889	3484	0.034	0.116398	2954
0.015	0.055373	3455	0.035	0.119352	2929
0.016	0.058828	3427	0.036	0.122281	2905
0.017	0.062255	3399	0.037	0.125186	2881
0.018	0.065654	3371	0.038	0.128067	2857
0.019	0.069026	3344	0.039	0.130924	2833
0.020	0.072369	3316	0.040	0.133758	

TABLE A.5   Values of $_5q_x$ Associated with $_5m_x$ by the Equation $_5q_x = 1 - e^{-5_5m_x - .008(5)^3{_5}m_x^2}$

$_5m_x$	$_5q_x$	Δ	$_5m_x$	$_5q_x$	Δ	$_5m_x$	$_5q_x$	Δ
		0.00			0.00			0.00
0.000	0.000000	4989	0.050	0.223144	3953	0.100	0.399504	3115
0.001	0.004989	4966	0.051	0.227096	3934	0.101	0.402619	3100
0.002	0.009954	4943	0.052	0.231031	3916	0.102	0.405720	3085
0.003	0.014897	4920	0.053	0.234946	3897	0.103	0.408805	3070
0.004	0.019817	4897	0.054	0.238843	3879	0.104	0.411875	3056
0.005	0.024714	4875	0.055	0.242722	3861	0.105	0.414931	3041
0.006	0.029589	4852	0.056	0.246583	3842	0.106	0.417972	3026
0.007	0.034442	4830	0.057	0.250425	3824	0.107	0.420998	3012
0.008	0.039272	4808	0.058	0.254249	3806	0.108	0.424009	2997
0.009	0.044080	4786	0.059	0.258056	3788	0.109	0.427007	2983
0.010	0.048866	4764	0.060	0.261844	3770	0.110	0.429989	2968
0.011	0.053629	4742	0.061	0.265614	3753	0.111	0.432957	2954
0.012	0.058371	4720	0.062	0.269367	3735	0.112	0.435911	2940
0.013	0.063091	4698	0.063	0.273102	3717	0.113	0.438851	2925
0.014	0.067789	4676	0.064	0.276819	3700	0.114	0.441777	2911
0.015	0.072465	4655	0.065	0.280519	3682	0.115	0.444688	2897
0.016	0.077120	4633	0.066	0.284201	3665	0.116	0.447585	2883
0.017	0.081753	4612	0.067	0.287866	3647	0.117	0.450468	2869
0.018	0.086365	4590	0.068	0.291513	3630	0.118	0.453338	2855
0.019	0.090955	4569	0.069	0.295143	3613	0.119	0.456193	2842
0.020	0.095524	4548	0.070	0.298756	3596	0.120	0.459035	2828
0.021	0.100072	4527	0.071	0.302352	3579	0.121	0.461862	2814
0.022	0.104599	4506	0.072	0.305931	3562	0.122	0.464676	2800
0.023	0.109105	4485	0.073	0.309493	3545	0.123	0.467477	2787
0.024	0.113590	4464	0.074	0.313038	3528	0.124	0.470264	2773
0.025	0.118054	4443	0.075	0.316566	3511	0.125	0.473037	2760
0.026	0.122498	4423	0.076	0.320077	3495	0.126	0.475797	2746
0.027	0.126921	4402	0.077	0.323572	3478	0.127	0.478543	2733
0.028	0.131323	4382	0.078	0.327050	3461	0.128	0.481276	2720
0.029	0.135705	4361	0.079	0.330511	3445	0.129	0.483996	2707
0.030	0.140066	4341	0.080	0.333956	3429	0.130	0.486703	2693
0.031	0.144407	4321	0.081	0.337385	3412	0.131	0.489396	2680
0.032	0.148728	4301	0.082	0.340797	3396	0.132	0.492076	2667
0.033	0.153029	4281	0.083	0.344193	3380	0.133	0.494743	2654
0.034	0.157310	4261	0.084	0.347573	3364	0.134	0.497398	2641
0.035	0.161571	4241	0.085	0.350937	3348	0.135	0.500039	2628
0.036	0.165812	4221	0.086	0.354284	3332	0.136	0.502667	2616
0.037	0.170033	4201	0.087	0.357616	3316	0.137	0.505283	2603
0.038	0.174234	4182	0.088	0.360932	3300	0.138	0.507886	2590
0.039	0.178416	4162	0.089	0.364232	3284	0.139	0.510476	2577
0.040	0.182578	4143	0.090	0.367516	3268	0.140	0.513053	2565
0.041	0.186721	4123	0.091	0.370784	3253	0.141	0.515618	2552
0.042	0.190844	4104	0.092	0.374037	3237	0.142	0.518170	2540
0.043	0.194948	4085	0.093	0.377274	3222	0.143	0.520710	2527
0.044	0.199033	4066	0.094	0.380496	3206	0.144	0.523237	2515
0.045	0.203099	4047	0.095	0.383702	3191	0.145	0.525752	2503
0.046	0.207146	4028	0.096	0.386893	3176	0.146	0.528255	2490
0.047	0.211174	4009	0.097	0.390069	3160	0.147	0.530745	2478
0.048	0.215182	3990	0.098	0.393229	3145	0.148	0.533223	2466
0.049	0.219172	3971	0.099	0.396374	3130	0.149	0.535689	2454
0.050	0.223144	3953	0.100	0.399504	3115	0.150	0.538143	2442

(continues)

TABLE A.5   *(continued)*

$_5m_x$	$_5q_x$	Δ	$_5m_x$	$_5q_x$	Δ	$_5m_x$	$_5q_x$	Δ
0.150	0.538143	2442	0.200	0.646545	1904	0.250	0.730854	1477
0.151	0.540585	2430	0.201	0.648449	1894	0.251	0.732330	1469
0.152	0.543015	2418	0.202	0.650343	1885	0.252	0.733799	1461
0.153	0.545433	2406	0.203	0.652228	1875	0.253	0.735261	1454
0.154	0.547839	2394	0.204	0.654104	1866	0.254	0.736714	1446
0.155	0.550233	2382	0.205	0.655970	1857	0.255	0.738161	1439
0.156	0.552615	2371	0.206	0.657826	1847	0.256	0.739600	1432
0.157	0.554986	2359	0.207	0.659673	1838	0.257	0.741032	1424
0.158	0.557345	2347	0.208	0.661511	1829	0.258	0.742456	1417
0.159	0.559692	2336	0.209	0.663340	1819	0.259	0.743873	1410
0.160	0.562028	2324	0.210	0.665159	1810	0.260	0.745282	1402
0.161	0.564352	2313	0.211	0.666969	1801	0.261	0.746685	1395
0.162	0.566665	2301	0.212	0.668771	1792	0.262	0.748080	1388
0.163	0.568966	2290	0.213	0.670563	1783	0.263	0.749468	1381
0.164	0.571256	2279	0.214	0.672346	1774	0.264	0.750849	1374
0.165	0.573535	2267	0.215	0.674120	1765	0.265	0.752223	1367
0.166	0.575802	2256	0.216	0.675885	1756	0.266	0.753589	1360
0.167	0.578059	2245	0.217	0.677641	1747	0.267	0.754949	1353
0.168	0.580304	2234	0.218	0.679388	1738	0.268	0.756302	1346
0.169	0.582538	2223	0.219	0.681127	1730	0.269	0.757647	1339
0.170	0.584761	2212	0.220	0.682856	1721	0.270	0.758986	1332
0.171	0.586972	2201	0.221	0.684577	1712	0.271	0.760318	1325
0.172	0.589173	2190	0.222	0.686289	1704	0.272	0.761643	1318
0.173	0.591363	2179	0.223	0.687993	1695	0.273	0.762961	1311
0.174	0.593543	2168	0.224	0.689688	1686	0.274	0.764272	1304
0.175	0.595711	2158	0.225	0.691374	1678	0.275	0.765576	1298
0.176	0.597868	2147	0.226	0.693052	1669	0.276	0.766874	1291
0.177	0.600015	2136	0.227	0.694721	1661	0.277	0.768165	1284
0.178	0.602152	2126	0.228	0.696382	1652	0.278	0.769449	1278
0.179	0.604277	2115	0.229	0.698034	1644	0.279	0.770727	1271
0.180	0.606392	2104	0.230	0.699678	1636	0.280	0.771998	1264
0.181	0.608497	2094	0.231	0.701314	1627	0.281	0.773262	1258
0.182	0.610591	2084	0.232	0.702941	1619	0.282	0.774520	1251
0.183	0.612674	2073	0.233	0.704560	1611	0.283	0.775771	1245
0.184	0.614747	2063	0.234	0.706171	1603	0.284	0.777016	1238
0.185	0.616810	2053	0.235	0.707773	1594	0.285	0.778255	1232
0.186	0.618863	2042	0.236	0.709368	1586	0.286	0.779486	1226
0.187	0.620905	2032	0.237	0.710954	1578	0.287	0.780712	1219
0.188	0.622937	2022	0.238	0.712532	1570	0.288	0.781931	1213
0.189	0.624959	2012	0.239	0.714102	1562	0.289	0.783144	1206
0.190	0.626971	2002	0.240	0.715664	1554	0.290	0.784350	1200
0.191	0.628973	1992	0.241	0.717219	1546	0.291	0.785551	1194
0.192	0.630965	1982	0.242	0.718765	1538	0.292	0.786744	1188
0.193	0.632947	1972	0.243	0.720303	1530	0.293	0.787932	1182
0.194	0.634919	1962	0.244	0.721834	1523	0.294	0.789114	1175
0.195	0.636881	1952	0.245	0.723356	1515	0.295	0.790289	1169
0.196	0.638833	1943	0.246	0.724871	1507	0.296	0.791458	1163
0.197	0.640776	1933	0.247	0.726378	1499	0.297	0.792621	1157
0.198	0.642709	1923	0.248	0.727878	1492	0.298	0.793778	1151
0.199	0.644632	1913	0.249	0.729370	1484	0.299	0.794929	1145
0.200	0.646545	1904	0.250	0.730854	1477	0.300	0.796074	1139

(continues)

TABLE A.5   (*continued*)

$_5m_x$	$_5q_x$	Δ	$_5m_x$	$_5q_x$	Δ	$_5m_x$	$_5q_x$	Δ
0.300	0.796074	1139	0.350	0.846261	874	0.400	0.884675	667
0.301	0.797213	1133	0.351	0.847135	869	0.401	0.885342	663
0.302	0.798346	1127	0.352	0.848004	865	0.402	0.886005	660
0.303	0.799474	1121	0.353	0.848869	860	0.403	0.886665	656
0.304	0.800595	1115	0.354	0.849729	855	0.404	0.887321	653
0.305	0.801710	1109	0.355	0.850585	851	0.405	0.887974	649
0.306	0.802820	1104	0.356	0.851435	846	0.406	0.888623	646
0.307	0.803923	1098	0.357	0.852282	842	0.407	0.889269	642
0.308	0.805021	1092	0.358	0.853124	837	0.408	0.889911	639
0.309	0.806113	1086	0.359	0.853961	833	0.409	0.890549	635
0.310	0.807200	1081	0.360	0.854794	828	0.410	0.891184	632
0.311	0.808280	1075	0.361	0.855622	824	0.411	0.891816	628
0.312	0.809355	1069	0.362	0.856446	819	0.412	0.892444	625
0.313	0.810425	1064	0.363	0.857265	815	0.413	0.893069	621
0.314	0.811488	1058	0.364	0.858081	811	0.414	0.893690	618
0.315	0.812547	1053	0.365	0.858891	806	0.415	0.894308	614
0.316	0.813599	1047	0.366	0.859698	802	0.416	0.894922	611
0.317	0.814646	1042	0.367	0.860500	798	0.417	0.895534	608
0.318	0.815688	1036	0.368	0.861298	793	0.418	0.896141	604
0.319	0.816724	1031	0.369	0.862091	789	0.419	0.896746	601
0.320	0.817754	1025	0.370	0.862880	785	0.420	0.897347	598
0.321	0.818780	1020	0.371	0.863665	781	0.421	0.897945	595
0.322	0.819799	1014	0.372	0.864446	777	0.422	0.898539	591
0.323	0.820814	1009	0.373	0.865222	772	0.423	0.899131	588
0.324	0.821823	1004	0.374	0.865995	768	0.424	0.899719	585
0.325	0.822826	998	0.375	0.866763	764	0.425	0.900304	582
0.326	0.823825	993	0.376	0.867527	760	0.426	0.900885	578
0.327	0.824818	988	0.377	0.868287	756	0.427	0.901464	575
0.328	0.825806	983	0.378	0.869043	752	0.428	0.902039	572
0.329	0.826788	977	0.379	0.869794	748	0.429	0.902611	569
0.330	0.827766	972	0.380	0.870542	744	0.430	0.903180	566
0.331	0.828738	967	0.381	0.871286	740	0.431	0.903746	563
0.332	0.829705	962	0.382	0.872025	736	0.432	0.904308	560
0.333	0.830667	957	0.383	0.872761	732	0.433	0.904868	557
0.334	0.831624	952	0.384	0.873493	728	0.434	0.905424	553
0.335	0.832576	947	0.385	0.874221	724	0.435	0.905978	550
0.336	0.833523	942	0.386	0.874944	720	0.436	0.906528	547
0.337	0.834464	937	0.387	0.875664	716	0.437	0.907076	544
0.338	0.835401	932	0.388	0.876380	712	0.438	0.907620	541
0.339	0.836333	927	0.389	0.877092	708	0.439	0.908161	538
0.340	0.837260	922	0.390	0.877800	704	0.440	0.908700	535
0.341	0.838182	917	0.391	0.878505	701	0.441	0.909235	532
0.342	0.839099	912	0.392	0.879205	697	0.442	0.909767	529
0.343	0.840011	907	0.393	0.879902	693	0.443	0.910297	527
0.344	0.840918	902	0.394	0.880595	689	0.444	0.910823	524
0.345	0.841821	898	0.395	0.881284	685	0.445	0.911347	521
0.346	0.842718	893	0.396	0.881970	682	0.446	0.911868	518
0.347	0.843611	888	0.397	0.882652	678	0.447	0.912386	515
0.348	0.844499	883	0.398	0.883330	674	0.448	0.912900	512
0.349	0.845383	879	0.399	0.884004	671	0.449	0.913413	509
0.350	0.846261	874	0.400	0.884675	667	0.450	0.913922	

TABLE A.6 Values of $_{10}q_x$ Associated with $_{10}m_x$ by the Equation $_{10}q_x = 1 - e^{-10_{10}m_x - .008(10)^3{}_{10}m_x^2}$

$_{10}m_x$	$_{10}q_x$	Δ	$_{10}m_x$	$_{10}q_x$	Δ	$_{10}m_x$	$_{10}q_x$	Δ
		0.00			0.00			0.00
0.000	0.000000	9958	0.050	0.405479	6391	0.100	0.660404	3919
0.001	0.009958	9875	0.051	0.411870	6332	0.101	0.664324	3879
0.002	0.019833	9792	0.052	0.418202	6273	0.102	0.668203	3840
0.003	0.029624	9709	0.053	0.424475	6214	0.103	0.672043	3800
0.004	0.039334	9627	0.054	0.430689	6156	0.104	0.675843	3762
0.005	0.048961	9546	0.055	0.436845	6098	0.105	0.679605	3723
0.006	0.058507	9465	0.056	0.442943	6041	0.106	0.683328	3685
0.007	0.067972	9385	0.057	0.448984	5984	0.107	0.687012	3647
0.008	0.077356	9305	0.058	0.454969	5928	0.108	0.690659	3609
0.009	0.086661	9225	0.059	0.460897	5872	0.109	0.694268	3572
0.010	0.095886	9146	0.060	0.466769	5817	0.110	0.697840	3535
0.011	0.105033	9068	0.061	0.472585	5761	0.111	0.701375	3498
0.012	0.114101	8990	0.062	0.478347	5707	0.112	0.704874	3462
0.013	0.123091	8913	0.063	0.484053	5652	0.113	0.708336	3426
0.014	0.132004	8836	0.064	0.489706	5599	0.114	0.711762	3390
0.015	0.140840	8760	0.065	0.495304	5545	0.115	0.715152	3355
0.016	0.149600	8684	0.066	0.500850	5492	0.116	0.718507	3320
0.017	0.158283	8609	0.067	0.506342	5440	0.117	0.721827	3285
0.018	0.166892	8534	0.068	0.511781	5387	0.118	0.725112	3251
0.019	0.175426	8459	0.069	0.517169	5336	0.119	0.728363	3217
0.020	0.183885	8385	0.070	0.522504	5284	0.120	0.731579	3183
0.021	0.192270	8312	0.071	0.527788	5233	0.121	0.734762	3149
0.022	0.200583	8239	0.072	0.533021	5183	0.122	0.737911	3116
0.023	0.208822	8167	0.073	0.538204	5132	0.123	0.741027	3083
0.024	0.216989	8095	0.074	0.543336	5082	0.124	0.744110	3050
0.025	0.225084	8024	0.075	0.548419	5033	0.125	0.747160	3018
0.026	0.233107	7953	0.076	0.553452	4984	0.126	0.750178	2986
0.027	0.241060	7882	0.077	0.558436	4935	0.127	0.753164	2954
0.028	0.248942	7812	0.078	0.563371	4887	0.128	0.756118	2923
0.029	0.256754	7743	0.079	0.568258	4839	0.129	0.759041	2891
0.030	0.264497	7674	0.080	0.573098	4792	0.130	0.761932	2860
0.031	0.272170	7605	0.081	0.577889	4745	0.131	0.764793	2830
0.032	0.279775	7537	0.082	0.582634	4698	0.132	0.767622	2799
0.033	0.287312	7469	0.083	0.587332	4652	0.133	0.770422	2769
0.034	0.294782	7402	0.084	0.591984	4606	0.134	0.773191	2740
0.035	0.302184	7336	0.085	0.596589	4560	0.135	0.775931	2710
0.036	0.309520	7270	0.086	0.601149	4515	0.136	0.778641	2681
0.037	0.316789	7204	0.087	0.605664	4470	0.137	0.781321	2652
0.038	0.323993	7139	0.088	0.610134	4425	0.138	0.783973	2623
0.039	0.331132	7074	0.089	0.614559	4381	0.139	0.786596	2594
0.040	0.338205	7009	0.090	0.618941	4337	0.140	0.789190	2566
0.041	0.345215	6946	0.091	0.623278	4294	0.141	0.791757	2538
0.042	0.352160	6882	0.092	0.627572	4251	0.142	0.794295	2511
0.043	0.359042	6819	0.093	0.631823	4208	0.143	0.796806	2483
0.044	0.365862	6757	0.094	0.636032	4166	0.144	0.799289	2456
0.045	0.372618	6695	0.095	0.640197	4124	0.145	0.801745	2429
0.046	0.379313	6633	0.096	0.644321	4082	0.146	0.804174	2402
0.047	0.385946	6572	0.097	0.648404	4041	0.147	0.806576	2376
0.048	0.392518	6511	0.098	0.652445	4000	0.148	0.808952	2350
0.049	0.399029	6451	0.099	0.656445	3959	0.149	0.811302	2324
0.050	0.405479	6391	0.100	0.660404	3919	0.150	0.813626	2298

(continues)

TABLE A.6   (*continued*)

$_{10}m_x$	$_{10}q_x$	Δ	$_{10}m_x$	$_{10}q_x$	Δ	$_{10}m_x$	$_{10}q_x$	Δ
		0.00			0.00			0.00
0.150	0.813626	2298	0.200	0.901726	1289	0.250	0.950213	693
0.151	0.815924	2273	0.201	0.903016	1274	0.251	0.950905	684
0.152	0.818197	2248	0.202	0.904290	1259	0.252	0.951589	675
0.153	0.820445	2223	0.203	0.905549	1244	0.253	0.952264	666
0.154	0.822667	2198	0.204	0.906793	1229	0.254	0.952930	658
0.155	0.824865	2173	0.205	0.908021	1214	0.255	0.953588	649
0.156	0.827039	2149	0.206	0.909236	1200	0.256	0.954237	641
0.157	0.829188	2125	0.207	0.910435	1185	0.257	0.954878	633
0.158	0.831313	2101	0.208	0.911620	1171	0.258	0.955511	624
0.159	0.833415	2078	0.209	0.912791	1157	0.259	0.956135	616
0.160	0.835493	2055	0.210	0.913948	1143	0.260	0.956752	608
0.161	0.837547	2031	0.211	0.915090	1129	0.261	0.957360	601
0.162	0.839579	2009	0.212	0.916219	1115	0.262	0.957961	593
0.163	0.841587	1986	0.213	0.917334	1102	0.263	0.958554	585
0.164	0.843573	1964	0.214	0.918436	1088	0.264	0.959139	577
0.165	0.845537	1941	0.215	0.919524	1075	0.265	0.959716	570
0.166	0.847478	1919	0.216	0.920599	1062	0.266	0.960286	562
0.167	0.849398	1898	0.217	0.921661	1049	0.267	0.960848	555
0.168	0.851295	1876	0.218	0.922710	1036	0.268	0.961403	548
0.169	0.853171	1855	0.219	0.923746	1023	0.269	0.961951	541
0.170	0.855026	1834	0.220	0.924770	1011	0.270	0.962492	534
0.171	0.856859	1813	0.221	0.925780	998	0.271	0.963026	527
0.172	0.858672	1792	0.222	0.926779	986	0.272	0.963552	520
0.173	0.860464	1771	0.223	0.927765	974	0.273	0.964072	513
0.174	0.862235	1751	0.224	0.928739	962	0.274	0.964585	506
0.175	0.863986	1731	0.225	0.929701	950	0.275	0.965091	499
0.176	0.865717	1711	0.226	0.930651	938	0.276	0.965590	493
0.177	0.867428	1691	0.227	0.931590	927	0.277	0.966083	486
0.178	0.869120	1672	0.228	0.932516	915	0.278	0.966569	480
0.179	0.870792	1653	0.229	0.933432	904	0.279	0.967049	473
0.180	0.872444	1633	0.230	0.934336	893	0.280	0.967522	467
0.181	0.874077	1614	0.231	0.935228	882	0.281	0.967989	461
0.182	0.875692	1596	0.232	0.936110	871	0.282	0.968450	455
0.183	0.877288	1577	0.233	0.936981	860	0.283	0.968905	449
0.184	0.878865	1559	0.234	0.937840	849	0.284	0.969354	443
0.185	0.880424	1541	0.235	0.938689	838	0.285	0.969797	437
0.186	0.881964	1523	0.236	0.939528	828	0.286	0.970233	431
0.187	0.883487	1505	0.237	0.940355	817	0.287	0.970664	425
0.188	0.884992	1487	0.238	0.941173	807	0.288	0.971090	419
0.189	0.886479	1470	0.239	0.941980	797	0.289	0.971509	414
0.190	0.887949	1453	0.240	0.942777	787	0.290	0.971923	408
0.191	0.889401	1435	0.241	0.943564	777	0.291	0.972331	403
0.192	0.890837	1419	0.242	0.944341	767	0.292	0.972734	397
0.193	0.892255	1402	0.243	0.945108	758	0.293	0.973131	392
0.194	0.893657	1385	0.244	0.945866	748	0.294	0.973523	387
0.195	0.895043	1369	0.245	0.946614	738	0.295	0.973910	381
0.196	0.896411	1353	0.246	0.947352	729	0.296	0.974291	376
0.197	0.897764	1337	0.247	0.948081	720	0.297	0.974668	371
0.198	0.899101	1321	0.248	0.948801	711	0.298	0.975039	366
0.199	0.900421	1305	0.249	0.949511	702	0.299	0.975405	361
0.200	0.901726	1289	0.250	0.950213	693	0.300	0.975766	356

(*continues*)

TABLE A.6   (*continued*)

$_{10}m_x$	$_{10}q_x$	Δ	$_{10}m_x$	$_{10}q_x$	Δ	$_{10}m_x$	$_{10}q_x$	Δ
		0.00			0.00			0.00
0.300	0.975766	356	0.350	0.988667	176	0.400	0.994908	83
0.301	0.976122	351	0.351	0.988842	173	0.401	0.994990	82
0.302	0.976474	347	0.352	0.989015	170	0.402	0.995072	80
0.303	0.976820	342	0.353	0.989186	168	0.403	0.995152	79
0.304	0.977162	337	0.354	0.989354	166	0.404	0.995232	78
0.305	0.977499	333	0.355	0.989519	163	0.405	0.995309	77
0.306	0.977832	328	0.356	0.989682	161	0.406	0.995386	76
0.307	0.978160	323	0.357	0.989843	158	0.407	0.995462	74
0.308	0.978483	319	0.358	0.990001	156	0.408	0.995536	73
0.309	0.978802	315	0.359	0.990158	154	0.409	0.995609	72
0.310	0.979117	310	0.360	0.990311	152	0.410	0.995681	71
0.311	0.979427	306	0.361	0.990463	149	0.411	0.995752	70
0.312	0.979733	302	0.362	0.990612	147	0.412	0.995822	69
0.313	0.980035	298	0.363	0.990759	145	0.413	0.995891	68
0.314	0.980332	293	0.364	0.990904	143	0.414	0.995959	67
0.315	0.980626	289	0.365	0.991047	141	0.415	0.996025	66
0.316	0.980915	285	0.366	0.991188	139	0.416	0.996091	65
0.317	0.981200	281	0.367	0.991327	137	0.417	0.996156	64
0.318	0.981482	277	0.368	0.991463	135	0.418	0.996219	63
0.319	0.981759	274	0.369	0.991598	133	0.419	0.996282	62
0.320	0.982033	270	0.370	0.991731	131	0.420	0.996343	61
0.321	0.982302	266	0.371	0.991861	129	0.421	0.996404	60
0.322	0.982568	262	0.372	0.991990	127	0.422	0.996464	59
0.323	0.982831	259	0.373	0.992117	125	0.423	0.996522	58
0.324	0.983089	255	0.374	0.992242	123	0.424	0.996580	57
0.325	0.983344	251	0.375	0.992365	121	0.425	0.996637	56
0.326	0.983596	248	0.376	0.992486	119	0.426	0.996693	55
0.327	0.983843	244	0.377	0.992606	118	0.427	0.996748	54
0.328	0.984088	241	0.378	0.992723	116	0.428	0.996803	53
0.329	0.984329	238	0.379	0.992839	114	0.429	0.996856	53
0.330	0.984566	234	0.380	0.992953	112	0.430	0.996909	52
0.331	0.984800	231	0.381	0.993066	111	0.431	0.996961	51
0.332	0.985031	228	0.382	0.993177	109	0.432	0.997012	50
0.333	0.985259	224	0.383	0.993286	107	0.433	0.997062	49
0.334	0.985483	221	0.384	0.993393	106	0.434	0.997111	49
0.335	0.985704	218	0.385	0.993499	104	0.435	0.997160	48
0.336	0.985922	215	0.386	0.993603	103	0.436	0.997207	47
0.337	0.986137	212	0.387	0.993706	101	0.437	0.997254	46
0.338	0.986349	209	0.388	0.993807	100	0.438	0.997301	46
0.339	0.986558	206	0.389	0.993907	98	0.439	0.997346	45
0.340	0.986764	203	0.390	0.994005	97	0.440	0.997391	44
0.341	0.986967	200	0.391	0.994101	95	0.441	0.997435	43
0.342	0.987167	197	0.392	0.994197	94	0.442	0.997479	43
0.343	0.987364	194	0.393	0.994290	92	0.443	0.997521	42
0.344	0.987558	192	0.394	0.994383	91	0.444	0.997563	41
0.345	0.987750	189	0.395	0.994473	90	0.445	0.997605	41
0.346	0.987938	186	0.396	0.994563	88	0.446	0.997645	40
0.347	0.988124	183	0.397	0.994651	87	0.447	0.997685	39
0.348	0.988308	181	0.398	0.994738	85	0.448	0.997725	39
0.349	0.988488	178	0.399	0.994823	84	0.449	0.997763	38
0.350	0.988667	176	0.400	0.994908	83	0.450	0.997802	

APPENDIX

$$\boxed{B}$$

Model Life Tables and Stable Population Tables

Part I. Selected "West" Model Life Tables and Stable Population Tables, and Related Reference Tables[1]

TABLE B.1   Selected "West" Model Life Tables Arranged by Level of Mortality

Age interval (exact ages x to x + n)	l_x	$_nm_x$	$_nq_x$	$_nL_x$	$(_5L_{x+5})/ (_5L_x)$	T_x	e^o_x
			Level 9 Female				
0–1	100,000	.2010	.1777	88,447	.7835[1]	4,000,000	40.00
1–5	82,226	.0320	.1179	303,316	.9100[2]	3,911,553	47.57
5–10	72,530	.0069	.0338	356,520	.9698	3,608,237	49.75
10–15	70,078	.0054	.0264	345,762	.9694	3,251,718	46.40
15–20	68,227	.0071	.0350	335,172	.9606	2,905,956	42.59
20–25	65,842	.0090	.0440	321,964	.9533	2,570,784	39.04
25–30	62,944	.0102	.0495	306,933	.9474	2,248,820	35.73
30–35	59,829	.0115	.0559	290,781	.9412	1,941,886	32.46
35–40	56,483	.0128	.0618	273,690	.9355	1,651,105	29.23
40–45	52,993	.0139	.0673	256,043	.9291	1,377,415	25.99
45–50	49,424	.0155	.0747	237,894	.9144	1,121,372	22.69
50–55	45,733	.0205	.0975	217,525	.8891	883,478	19.32
55–60	41,277	.0268	.1257	193,410	.8481	665,953	16.13
60–65	36,087	.0400	.1818	164,037	.7895	472,543	13.09
65–70	29,527	.0560	.2457	129,500	.7100	308,507	10.45
70–75	22,272	.0845	.3488	91,943	.6006	179,007	8.04
75–80	14,505	.1235	.4772	55,221	.3657[3]	87,064	6.00
80 and over	7,584	.2385	1.0000	31,843		31,843	4.20

Age interval (exact ages x to x + n)	l_x	$_nm_x$	$_nq_x$	$_nL_x$	$(_5L_{x+5})/ (_5L_x)$	T_x	e^o_x
			Level 9 Male				
0–1	100,000	.2408	.2074	86,106	.7567[1]	3,730,053	37.30
1–5	79,263	.0321	.1183	292,227	.9088[2]	3,643,947	45.97
5–10	69,888	.0065	.0322	343,818	.9722	3,351,720	47.96
10–15	67,639	.0047	.0233	334,258	.9722	3,007,902	44.47
15–20	66,064	.0066	.0324	324,977	.9610	2,673,644	40.47
20–25	63,926	.0094	.0459	312,305	.9517	2,348,667	36.74

(continues)

[1] These tables were repreduced from Ansley J. Coale and Paul Demeny, *Regional Model Life Table and Stable Populations*, pp. 10, 12, 14, 16, 18, 42, 46, 50, 54, 58, 62, 66, and 138 (copyright © 1966 by Princetory University Press, Reprinted by permission of Princeton University Press).

TABLE B.1 *(continued)*

25–30	60,995	.0104	.0508	297,226	.9454	2,036,363	33.39
30–35	57,895	.0121	.0585	281,009	.9365	1,739,137	30.04
35–40	54,509	.0142	.0688	263,172	.9240	1,458,128	26.75
40–45	50,760	.0175	.0837	243,182	.9088	1,194,955	23.54
45–50	46,512	.0209	.0994	220,999	.8872	951,774	20.46
50–55	41,887	.0273	.1277	196,068	.8572	730,775	17.45
55–60	36,540	.0348	.1602	168,066	.8135	534,706	14.63
60–65	30,686	.0489	.2177	136,730	.7510	366,640	11.95
65–70	24,006	.0676	.2891	102,678	.6693	229,910	9.58
70–75	17,066	.0967	.3893	68,718	.5598	127,231	7.46
75–80	10,421	.1418	.5234	38,471	.3425[3]	58,514	5.62
80 and over	4,967	.2478	1.0000	20,043		20,043	4.04

Age interval (exact ages x to x + n)	l_x	$_nm_x$	$_nq_x$	$_nL_x$	$(_5L_{x+5})/$ $(_5L_x)$	T_x	e^o_x
			Level 11 Female				
0–1	100,000	.1615	.1461	90,502	.8219[1]	4,500,000	45.00
1–5	85,388	.0250	.0937	320,442	.9288[2]	4,409,498	51.64
5–10	77,389	.0055	.0272	381,683	.9758	4,089,056	52.84
10–15	75,285	.0043	.0212	372,430	.9752	3,707,373	49.24
15–20	73,687	.0058	.0284	363,207	.9679	3,334,942	45.26
20–25	71,596	.0073	.0360	351,543	.9618	2,971,735	41.51
25–30	69,022	.0083	.0405	338,115	.9569	2,620,192	37.96
30–35	66,224	.0094	.0459	323,525	.9516	2,282,077	34.46
35–40	63,186	.0105	.0510	307,872	.9465	1,958,552	31.00
40–45	59,963	.0116	.0562	291,388	.9402	1,650,680	27.53
45–50	56,592	.0131	.0636	273,969	.9267	1,359,291	24.02
50–55	52,996	.0175	.0837	253,884	.9309	1,085,322	20.48
55–60	48,558	.0232	.1095	229,493	.8669	831,439	17.12
60–65	43,239	.0347	.1596	198,946	.8127	601,946	13.92
65–70	36,339	.0495	.2203	161,682	.7367	403,000	11.09
70–75	28,333	.0758	.3184	119,112	.6304	241,319	8.52
75–80	19,311	.1144	.4448	75,083	.3856[3]	122,207	6.33
80 and over	10,722	.2275	1.0000	47,125		47,124	4.40

Age interval (exact ages x to x + n)	l_x	$_nm_x$	$_nq_x$	$_nL_x$	$(_5L_{x+5})/$ $(_5L_x)$	T_x	e^o_x
			Level 13 Female				
0–1	100,000	.1282	.1183	92,310	.8566[1]	5,000,000	50.00
1–5	88,169	.0188	.0717	335,996	.9453[2]	4,907,690	55.66
5–10	81,848	.0043	.0214	404,871	.9810	4,571,694	55.86
10–15	80,100	.0034	.0166	397,178	.9804	4,166,823	52.02
15–20	78,771	.0046	.0226	389,403	.9743	3,769,645	47.86
20–25	76,990	.0059	.0289	379,397	.9693	3,380,242	43.90
25–30	74,769	.0066	.0327	367,736	.9652	3,000,845	40.13
30–35	72,326	.0076	.0370	354,934	.9608	2,633,107	36.41
35–40	69,647	.0085	.0415	341,009	.9561	2,278,173	32.71
40–45	66,756	.0095	.0464	326,031	.9500	1,937,165	29.02
45–50	63,656	.0111	.0538	309,724	.9375	1,611,134	25.31
50–55	60,234	.0149	.0717	290,374	.9170	1,301,410	21.61
55–60	55,916	.0200	.0953	266,259	.8834	1,011,036	18.08
60–65	50,587	.0301	.1401	235,225	.8332	744,777	14.72
65–70	43,503	.0439	.1980	195,982	.7603	509,552	11.71
70–75	34,890	.0683	.2918	149,002	.6566	313,570	8.99
75–80	24,771	.1051	.4163	97,836	.4055[3]	164,568	6.66
80 and over	14,424	.2162	1.0000	66,732		66,732	4.63

(continues)

TABLE B.1 *(continued)*

Age interval (exact ages x to x + n)	l_x	$_nm_x$	$_nq_x$	$_nL_x$	$(_5L_{x+5})/(_5L_x)$	T_x	e^0_x
			Level 15 Female				
0–1	100,000	.0996	.0934	93,745	.8889[1]	5,500,000	55.00
1–5	90,661	.0129	.0500	350,729	.9613[2]	5,406,255	59.63
5–10	86,127	.0032	.0157	427,251	.9860	5,055,527	58.70
10–15	84,773	.0025	.0122	421,284	.9852	4,628,276	54.60
15–20	83,740	.0035	.0174	415,061	.9800	4,206,992	50.24
20–25	82,284	.0046	.0227	406,751	.9757	3,791,931	46.08
25–30	80,416	.0053	.0259	396,874	.9724	3,385,180	42.10
30–35	78,333	.0060	.0294	385,907	.9686	2,988,306	38.15
35–40	76,029	.0068	.0334	373,805	.9643	2,602,399	34.23
40–45	73,493	.0078	.0382	360,445	.9581	2,228,595	30.32
45–50	70,686	.0094	.0458	345,343	.9464	1,868,150	26.43
50–55	67,452	.0128	.0619	326,821	.9274	1,522,807	22.58
55–60	63,276	.0175	.0840	303,101	.8966	1,195,986	18.90
60–65	57,964	.0266	.1246	271,765	.8492	892,885	15.40
65–70	50,742	.0398	.1808	230,771	.7783	621,120	12.24
70–75	41,567	.0629	.2716	179,610	.6765	390,349	9.39
75–80	30,277	.0984	.3948	121,501	.4235[3]	210,740	6.96
80 and over	18,323	.2053	1.0000	89,239		89,238	4.87

Age interval (exact ages x to x + n)	l_x	$_nm_x$	$_nq_x$	$_nL_x$	$(_5L_{x+5})/(_5L_x)$	T_x	e^0_x
			Level 17 Female				
0–1	100,000	.0745	.0707	94,785	.9171[1]	6,000,000	60.00
1–5	92,934	.0085	.0332	363,755	.9744[2]	5,905,215	63.54
5–10	89,854	.0022	.0110	446,805	.9902	5,541,460	61.67
10–15	88,868	.0017	.0085	442,445	.9895	5,094,655	57.33
15–20	88,110	.0025	.0125	437,800	.9855	4,652,210	52.80
20–25	87,010	.0033	.0165	431,463	.9822	4,214,410	48.44
25–30	85,575	.0039	.0191	423,798	.9795	3,782,947	44.21
30–35	83,944	.0044	.0219	415,125	.9763	3,359,149	40.02
35–40	82,106	.0052	.0255	405,299	.9722	2,944,024	35.86
40–45	80,014	.0061	.0302	394,022	.9660	2,538,725	31.73
45–50	77,595	.0077	.0379	380,623	.9550	2,144,704	27.64
50–55	74,655	.0180	.0523	363,504	.9378	1,764,080	23.63
55–60	70,747	.0151	.0727	340,876	.9097	1,400,576	19.80
60–65	65,603	.0231	.1093	310,088	.8652	1,059,700	16.15
65–70	58,432	.0356	.1633	268,300	.7968	749,612	12.83
70–75	48,888	.0574	.2508	213,785	.6969	481,312	9.85
75–80	36,626	.0917	.3729	148,989	.4431[3]	267,528	7.30
80 and over	22,970	.1938	1.0000	118,539		118,538	5.16

[1] Proportion surviving from birth to 0–4 years of age, $_5L_0/_5l_0$.

[2] $_5L_5/_5L_0$.

[3] T_{80}/T_{75}.

Source: Table B.1 (pp. 523–525) in H. Shryock, J. Siegel, and E. Stockwell, 1976, *The Methods and Materials of Demography, Condensed Edition*, New York: Academic Press.

TABLE B.2   Values of the Function l_x for x = 1, 2, 3 and 5 in "West" Model Life
Tables at Various Levels of Mortality, for Females, Males, and Both Sexes
[l_0 = 100,000. The l_x values for both sexes assume that the sex ratio at birth is 1.05]

Level	l_1	l_2	l_3	l_5
Female				
1	63,483	55,000	51,199	46,883
3	69,481	61,829	58,399	54,506
5	74,427	67,671	64,643	61,205
7	78,614	72,765	70,145	67,169
9	82,226	77,271	75,051	72,530
11	85,388	81,300	79,468	77,389
13	88,169	84,939	83,492	81,848
15	90,661	88,364	87,324	86,127
17	92,934	91,419	90,709	89,854
19	95,006	94,143	93,724	93,201
21	96,907	96,559	96,385	96,160
23	98,484	98,377	98,321	98,248
Male				
1	58,093	50,308	46,898	43,005
3	64,868	57,690	54,546	50,957
5	70,454	64,015	61,195	57,976
7	75,183	69,537	67,064	64,242
9	79,263	74,425	72,307	69,888
11	82,835	78,800	77,032	75,015
13	86,058	82,912	81,534	79,961
15	88,864	86,523	85,498	84,327
17	91,379	89,790	89,056	88,184
19	93,713	92,796	92,338	91,774
21	95,909	95,508	95,285	94,989
23	97,856	97,719	97,636	97,521
Both Sexes				
1	60,722	52,597	48,996	44,897
3	67,118	59,709	56,425	52,688
5	72,392	65,798	62,877	59,551
7	76,857	71,112	68,567	65,670
9	80,709	75,813	73,646	71,177
11	84,080	80,019	78,220	76,173
13	87,088	83,901	82,489	80,881
15	89,740	87,421	86,389	85,205
17	92,137	90,584	89,862	88,999
19	94,144	93,453	93,011	92,455
21	96,396	96,020	95,822	95,560
23	98,162	98,040	97,970	97,876

Source: Table B.2 (p. 525) in H. Shryock, J. Siegel, and E. Stockwell, 1976, *The Methods and Materials of Demography, Condensed Edition*, New York: Academic Press.

TABLE B.3 Selected "West" Model Stable Populations Arranged by Level of Mortality and Annual Rate of Increase

| | | | | | | LEVEL 9 | | | | | | | |
| | | | | | | Female (e°₀ = 40.0 years) | | | | | | | |

Age & Parameter	Annual Rate of Increase												
	−.010	−.005	.000	.005	.010	.015	.020	.025	.030	.035	.040	.045	.050
Age Interval						Proportion in Age Interval							
Under 1	.0158	.0188	.0221	.0257	.0295	.0336	.0379	.0424	.0471	.0518	.0567	.0617	.0667
1–4	.0557	.0653	.0758	.0870	.0988	.1111	.1238	.1367	.1498	.1629	.1760	.1890	.2018
5–9	.0684	.0786	.0891	.1000	.1111	.1221	.1330	.1436	.1538	.1636	.1728	.1814	.1894
10–14	.0698	.0781	.0864	.0946	.1024	.1098	.1167	.1229	.1284	.1332	.1372	.1405	.1431
15–19	.0711	.0776	.0838	.0894	.0945	.0988	.1024	.1051	.1071	.1084	.1089	.1087	.1080
20–24	.0718	.0765	.0805	.0838	.0863	.0880	.0890	.0891	.0886	.0874	.0856	.0834	.0808
25–29	.0720	.0747	.0767	.0779	.0783	.0779	.0767	.0750	.0727	.0699	.0668	.0635	.0600
30–34	.0717	.0726	.0727	.0720	.0705	.0684	.0658	.0627	.0593	.0556	.0518	.0480	.0443
35–39	.0709	.0701	.0684	.0661	.0632	.0598	.0560	.0521	.0480	.0439	.0400	.0361	.0324
40–44	.0698	.0672	.0640	.0603	.0562	.0519	.0474	.0430	.0387	.0345	.0306	.0270	.0236
45–49	.0681	.0640	.0595	.0546	.0497	.0447	.0399	.0352	.0309	.0269	.0233	.0200	.0171
50–54	.0655	.0600	.0544	.0487	.0432	.0379	.0330	.0284	.0243	.0207	.0174	.0146	.0122
55–59	.0612	.0547	.0484	.0423	.0365	.0313	.0265	.0223	.0186	.0154	.0127	.0104	.0084
60–64	.0546	.0476	.0410	.0350	.0295	.0246	.0204	.0167	.0136	.0110	.0088	.0070	.0056
65–69	.0453	.0385	.0324	.0269	.0221	.0180	.0145	.0116	.0092	.0073	.0057	.0044	.0034
70–74	.0338	.0280	.0230	.0186	.0150	.0119	.0093	.0073	.0056	.0043	.0033	.0025	.0019
75–79	.0213	.0173	.0138	.0109	.0085	.0066	.0051	.0039	.0029	.0022	.0016	.0012	.0009
80 & over	.0131	.0103	.0080	.0061	.0046	.0035	.0026	.0019	.0014	.0010	.0007	.0005	.0004
Age						Proportion under given age							
1	.0158	.0188	.0221	.0257	.0295	.0336	.0379	.0424	.0471	.0518	.0567	.0617	.0667
5	.0715	.0842	.0979	.1127	.1284	.1448	.1617	.1791	.1968	.2147	.2327	.2506	.2685
10	.1400	.1627	.1871	.2127	.2394	.2668	.2947	.3227	.3507	.3783	.4055	.4321	.4579
15	.2097	.2408	.2735	.3073	.3419	.3767	.4114	.4456	.4791	.5115	.5427	.5725	.6010
20	.2809	.3185	.3573	.3968	.4363	.4755	.5137	.5507	.5862	.6198	.6516	.6813	.7090
25	.3527	.3949	.4378	.4806	.5227	.5635	.6027	.6399	.6747	.7072	.7372	.7647	.7898
30	.4247	.4697	.5145	.5585	.6009	.6414	.6794	.7148	.7474	.7771	.8040	.8282	.8498
35	.4963	.5423	.5872	.6305	.6715	.7098	.7452	.7775	.8067	.8328	.8559	.8762	.8940
40	.5673	.6124	.6556	.6966	.7346	.7696	.8012	.8296	.8547	.8767	.8958	.9123	.9265
45	.6370	.6796	.7197	.7568	.7908	.8214	.8487	.8726	.8933	.9112	.9264	.9393	.9501
50	.7052	.7436	.7791	.8115	.8405	.8662	.8885	.9078	.9243	.9381	.9497	.9593	.9672
55	.7707	.8036	.8335	.8602	.8837	.9041	.9215	.9363	.9486	.9588	.9671	.9739	.9794
60	.8319	.8583	.8819	.9025	.9202	.9354	.9481	.9586	.9672	.9742	.9798	.9843	.9878
65	.8865	.9059	.9229	.9374	.9497	.9600	.9684	.9753	.9808	.9852	.9886	.9913	.9934
						Parameter of Stable Population							
Birth rate	.0178	.0212	.0250	.0291	.0336	.0383	.0433	.0486	.0540	.0597	.0654	.0713	.0773
Death rate	.0278	.0262	.0250	.0241	.0236	.0233	.0233	.0236	.0240	.0247	.0254	.0263	.0273
GRR(27)	1.24	1.42	1.63	1.86	2.12	2.41	2.75	3.12	3.55	4.02	4.56	5.17	5.85
GRR(29)	1.25	1.44	1.66	1.91	2.20	2.53	2.91	3.34	3.83	4.38	5.01	5.73	6.54
GRR(31)	1.25	1.46	1.70	1.97	2.30	2.67	3.09	3.58	4.15	4.79	5.54	6.39	7.36
GRR(33)	1.25	1.47	1.73	2.04	2.40	2.81	3.30	3.86	4.52	5.28	6.17	7.20	8.39
Average age	36.2	33.9	31.6	29.5	27.4	25.5	23.7	22.0	20.5	19.1	17.8	16.7	15.6
Births/population 15–44	.042	.048	.056	.065	.075	.086	.099	.114	.130	.149	.170	.194	.221

(*continues*)

TABLE B.3 *(continued)*

LEVEL 9
Male (e°₀ = 37.3 years)

Annual Rate of Increase

Age & Parameter	−.010	−.005	.000	.005	.010	.015	.020	.025	.030	.035	.040	.045	.050
Age Interval						Proportion in Age Interval							
Under 1	.0168	.0198	.0231	.0267	.0305	.0346	.0389	.0433	.0480	.0527	.0576	.0625	.0675
1–4	.0583	.0680	.0783	.0894	.1010	.1131	.1255	.1382	.1510	.1639	.1768	.1895	.2022
5–9	.0718	.0818	.0922	.1028	.1136	.1244	.1350	.1453	.1552	.1647	.1737	.1821	.1899
10–14	.0733	.0815	.0896	.0975	.1051	.1122	.1187	.1247	.1299	.1344	.1383	.1414	.1438
15–19	.0750	.0812	.0871	.0925	.0972	.1012	.1045	.1070	.1087	.1097	.1101	.1098	.1089
20–24	.0757	.0801	.0837	.0867	.0888	.0902	.0908	.0907	.0899	.0885	.0866	.0842	.0815
25–29	.0758	.0781	.0797	.0804	.0804	.0797	.0782	.0762	.0737	.0707	.0675	.0640	.0604
30–34	.0753	.0757	.0753	.0742	.0723	.0699	.0669	.0636	.0599	.0561	.0522	.0483	.0445
35–39	.0741	.0727	.0706	.0678	.0644	.0607	.0567	.0525	.0483	.0441	.0400	.0361	.0324
40–44	.0720	.0689	.0652	.0611	.0566	.0520	.0474	.0428	.0384	.0342	.0303	.0267	.0233
45–49	.0688	.0642	.0592	.0541	.0490	.0439	.0390	.0344	.0301	.0261	.0225	.0193	.0165
50–54	.0642	.0584	.0526	.0468	.0413	.0361	.0313	.0269	.0230	.0194	.0164	.0137	.0114
55–59	.0578	.0513	.0451	.0392	.0337	.0287	.0243	.0203	.0169	.0140	.0115	.0094	.0076
60–64	.0495	.0428	.0367	.0311	.0261	.0217	.0179	.0146	.0119	.0096	.0077	.0061	.0048
65–69	.0390	.0330	.0275	.0228	.0186	.0151	.0121	.0097	.0077	.0060	.0047	.0037	.0028
70–74	.0275	.0226	.0184	.0149	.0119	.0094	.0074	.0057	.0044	.0034	.0026	.0020	.0015
75–79	.0162	.0130	.0103	.0081	.0063	.0049	.0037	.0028	.0021	.0016	.0012	.0009	.0006
80 & over	.0089	.0700	.0054	.0041	.0031	.0023	.0017	.0013	.0009	.0007	.0005	.0003	.0002
Age						Proportion under given age							
1	.0168	.0198	.0231	.0267	.0305	.0346	.0389	.0433	.0480	.0527	.0576	.0625	.0675
5	.0751	.0877	.1014	.1161	.1315	.1477	.1644	.1815	.1990	.2166	.2343	.2520	.2697
10	.1468	.1695	.1936	.2189	.2452	.2721	.2994	.3268	.3542	.3813	.4080	.4341	.4596
15	.2202	.2510	.2832	.3164	.3502	.3843	.4181	.4515	.4841	.5158	.5463	.5755	.6034
20	.2951	.3322	.3703	.4089	.4474	.4855	.5226	.5585	.5928	.6255	.6563	.6853	.7123
25	.3709	.4123	.4541	.4956	.5363	.5767	.6134	.6492	.6827	.7140	.7429	.7695	.7938
30	.4466	.4904	.5338	.5760	.6167	.6553	.6916	.7253	.7564	.7847	.8104	.8335	.8542
35	.5219	.5661	.6091	.6502	.6890	.7252	.7585	.7889	.8163	.8409	.8626	.8818	.8986
40	.5961	.6389	.6796	.7179	.7534	.7859	.8152	.8414	.8646	.8850	.9027	.9180	.9311
45	.6681	.7078	.7448	.7790	.8101	.8379	.8626	.8843	.9031	.9192	.9330	.9446	.9544
50	.7369	.7719	.8041	.8331	.8590	.8818	.9016	.9186	.9331	.9453	.9555	.9640	.9709
55	.8011	.8303	.8566	.8800	.9003	.9179	.9329	.9455	.9561	.9648	.9719	.9777	.9824
60	.8589	.8817	.9017	.9191	.9340	.9466	.9572	.9659	.9730	.9788	.9834	.9871	.9900
65	.9084	.9245	.9384	.9502	.9601	.9683	.9751	.9805	.9849	.9883	.9910	.9932	.9948
						Parameter of Stable Population							
Birth rate	.0194	.0229	.0268	.0311	.0356	.0405	.0456	.0510	.0566	.0623	.0682	.0742	.0804
Death rate	.0294	.0279	.0268	.0261	.0256	.0255	.0256	.0260	.0266	.0273	.0282	.0292	.0304
GRR(27)	1.29	1.47	1.68	1.92	2.19	2.49	2.84	3.22	3.66	4.16	4.71	5.34	6.04
GRR(29)	1.29	1.49	1.72	1.98	2.28	2.62	3.01	3.45	3.96	4.53	5.18	5.92	6.76
GRR(31)	1.29	1.51	1.76	2.05	2.38	2.76	3.20	3.71	4.29	4.96	5.73	6.61	7.62
GRR(33)	1.30	1.53	1.80	2.12	2.49	2.92	3.42	4.00	4.68	5.47	6.39	7.45	8.69
Average age	34.7	32.5	30.4	28.4	26.5	24.7	23.0	21.5	20.0	18.7	17.5	16.4	15.4
Births/population 15–44	.043	.050	.058	.067	.077	.089	.103	.118	.135	.154	.176	.201	.229

(continues)

TABLE B.3 *(continued)*

LEVEL 11
Female (e°₀ = 45.0 years)

Age & Parameter	Annual Rate of Increase												
	−.010	−.005	.000	.005	.010	.015	.020	.025	.030	.035	.040	.045	.050
Age Interval						Proportion in Age Interval							
Under 1	.0142	.0170	.0201	.0235	.0272	.0311	.0352	.0396	.0440	.0487	.0534	.0582	.0631
1–4	.0516	.0610	.0712	.0822	.0939	.1061	.1187	.1316	.1447	.1579	.1711	.1842	.1971
5–9	.0643	.0743	.0848	.0957	.1069	.1181	.1292	.1401	.1506	.1606	.1702	.1792	.1875
10–14	.0660	.0743	.0828	.0911	.0992	.1069	.1141	.1206	.1265	.1316	.1360	.1396	.1425
15–19	.0676	.0743	.0807	.0867	.0920	.0967	.1006	.1038	.1061	.1077	.1086	.1087	.1082
20–24	.0688	.0738	.0781	.0818	.0847	.0868	.0881	.0887	.0884	.0875	.0860	.0840	.0816
25–29	.0696	.0727	.0751	.0767	.0775	.0775	.0767	.0753	.0732	.0707	.0677	.0645	.0611
30–34	.0700	.0714	.0719	.0716	.0706	.0688	.0664	.0635	.0603	.0568	.0531	.0493	.0455
35–39	.0700	.0696	.0684	.0665	.0639	.0607	.0572	.0534	.0494	.0453	.0413	.0375	.0337
40–44	.0697	.0676	.0648	.0614	.0575	.0533	.0490	.0446	.0402	.0360	.0320	.0283	.0249
45–49	.0689	.0651	.0609	.0563	.0514	.0465	.0417	.0370	.0326	.0284	.0247	.0213	.0182
50–54	.0671	.0619	.0564	.0508	.0433	.0400	.0349	.0302	.0260	.0221	.0187	.0157	.0131
55–59	.0637	.0574	.0510	.0448	.0390	.0335	.0286	.0241	.0202	.0168	.0138	.0114	.0093
60–64	.0581	.0510	.0442	.0379	.0321	.0270	.0224	.0185	.0151	.0122	.0098	.0079	.0062
65–69	.0496	.0425	.0359	.0300	.0248	.0203	.0165	.0132	.0105	.0083	.0065	.0051	.0040
70–74	.0384	.0321	.0265	.0216	.0174	.0139	.0110	.0086	.0067	.0052	.0039	.0030	.0023
75–79	.0255	.0207	.0167	.0133	.0104	.0081	.0063	.0048	.0036	.0027	.0020	.0015	.0011
80 & over	.0170	.0134	.0105	.0081	.0062	.0047	.0035	.0026	.0019	.0014	.0010	.0007	.0005
Age						Proportion under given age							
1	.0142	.0170	.0235	.0235	.0272	.0311	.0352	.0396	.0440	.0487	.0534	.0582	.0631
5	.0658	.0780	.1057	.1057	.1210	.1371	.1539	.1711	.1887	.2065	.2245	.2424	.2602
10	.1301	.1523	.2014	.2014	.2279	.2552	.2831	.3112	.3393	.3672	.3947	.4215	.4477
15	.1961	.2266	.2926	.2926	.3271	.3621	.3971	.4318	.4658	.4988	.5306	.5611	.5902
20	.2637	.3009	.3792	.3792	.4191	.4588	.4978	.5356	.5719	.6065	.6392	.6698	.6984
25	.3325	.3747	.4610	.4610	.5038	.5457	.5859	.6242	.6604	.6940	.7252	.7539	.7800
30	.4021	.4474	.5377	.5377	.5814	.6231	.6626	.6995	.7336	.7647	.7930	.8184	.8411
35	.4721	.5188	.6094	.6094	.6519	.6919	.7290	.7630	.7938	.8215	.8460	.8677	.8867
40	.5421	.5884	.6758	.6758	.7158	.7527	.7862	.8164	.8432	.8668	.8874	.9052	.9204
45	.6117	.6559	.7372	.7372	.7733	.8060	.8352	.8610	.8835	.9028	.9194	.9335	.9453
50	.6806	.7211	.7934	.7934	.8247	.8525	.8769	.8980	.9160	.9313	.9441	.9547	.9635
55	.7476	.7829	.8443	.8443	.8700	.8925	.9118	.9282	.9420	.9534	.9628	.9705	.9766
60	.8114	.8403	.8891	.8891	.9090	.9260	.9404	.9532	.9622	.9702	.9766	.9818	.9859
65	.8695	.8913	.9270	.9270	.9411	.9530	.9628	.9708	.9772	.9824	.9865	.9897	.9921
						Parameter of Stable Population							
Birth rate	.0156	.0188	.0222	.0260	.0302	.0346	.0393	.0443	.0494	.0547	.0602	.0658	.0715
Death rate	.0256	.0238	.0222	.0210	.0202	.0196	.0193	.0193	.0194	.0197	.0202	.0208	.0215
GRR(27)	1.13	1.29	1.48	1.69	1.92	2.19	2.50	2.84	3.23	3.66	4.16	4.71	5.33
GRR(29)	1.13	1.30	1.50	1.73	2.00	2.30	2.64	3.03	3.47	3.98	4.55	5.20	5.94
GRR(31)	1.12	1.31	1.53	1.78	2.07	2.41	2.79	3.24	3.75	4.34	5.01	5.78	6.68
GRR(33)	1.12	1.32	1.56	1.83	2.15	2.53	2.97	3.47	4.07	4.76	5.56	6.48	7.56
Average age	37.6	35.2	32.9	30.6	28.5	26.4	24.6	22.8	21.2	19.7	18.4	17.2	16.1
Births/population 15–44	.038	.044	.051	.059	.068	.078	.090	.103	.118	.135	.155	.177	.201

(continues)

TABLE B.3 (*continued*)

Age & Parameter	LEVEL 13 Female $e^0_0 = 50.0$ Annual rate of increase			LEVEL 15 Female $e^0_0 = 55.0$ Annual rate of increase			LEVEL 17 Female $e^0_0 = 60.0$ Annual rate of increase			LEVEL 19 Female $e^0_0 = 65.0$ Annual rate of increase			LEVEL 21 Female $e^0_0 = 70.0$ Annual rate of increase		
	.025	.030	.035	.025	.030	.035	.025	.030	.035	.025	.030	.035	.025	.030	.035
Age Interval						Proportion in Age Interval									
Under 1	.037	.042	.046	.035	.039	.044	.033	.037	.042	.032	.036	.040	.030	.034	.039
1–4	.127	.140	.153	.123	.136	.149	.119	.133	.146	.116	.129	.143	.113	.126	.140
5–9	.137	.148	.158	.134	.145	.156	.131	.142	.153	.128	.140	.151	.126	.137	.149
10–14	.118	.125	.130	.117	.123	.129	.115	.121	.127	.113	.120	.126	.111	.118	.124
15–19	.103	.105	.107	.101	.104	.107	.100	.103	.106	.099	.102	.105	.097	.101	.104
20–24	.088	.088	.088	.088	.088	.088	.087	.088	.087	.086	.087	.087	.085	.087	.087
25–29	.075	.074	.071	.076	.074	.072	.075	.074	.072	.075	.074	.072	.075	.074	.072
30–34	.064	.061	.058	.065	.062	.059	.065	.062	.059	.065	.063	.060	.066	.063	.060
35–39	.054	.051	.047	.055	.052	.048	.056	.053	.049	.057	.053	.049	.057	.054	.050
40–44	.046	.042	.037	.047	.043	.039	.048	.044	.040	.049	.045	.041	.050	.046	.041
45–49	.039	.034	.030	.040	.035	.031	.041	.037	.032	.042	.038	.033	.043	.039	.034
50–54	.032	.027	.023	.033	.029	.025	.035	.030	.026	.036	.031	.027	.037	.032	.028
55–59	.026	.022	.018	.027	.023	.019	.029	.024	.020	.030	.025	.021	.031	.027	.022
60–64	.020	.017	.013	.022	.018	.014	.023	.019	.016	.024	.020	.017	.026	.021	.018
65–69	.015	.012	.009	.016	.013	.010	.018	.014	.011	.019	.015	.012	.020	.017	.013
70–74	.010	.008	.006	.011	.009	.007	.012	.010	.008	.014	.011	.008	.015	.012	.009
75–79	.006	.004	.003	.067	.005	.004	.008	.006	.004	.009	.007	.005	.010	.008	.006
80 & over	.003	.003	.002	.004	.003	.002	.005	.004	.003	.006	.005	.004	.008	.006	.004
Age						Proportion under given age									
1	.037	.042	.046	.035	.039	.044	.033	.037	.042	.032	.036	.040	.030	.034	.039
5	.164	.182	.200	.158	.175	.193	.153	.170	.187	.148	.165	.182	.143	.161	.178
10	.301	.329	.357	.292	.320	.349	.284	.312	.340	.276	.305	.333	.269	.298	.327
15	.420	.454	.487	.409	.443	.477	.398	.433	.468	.389	.424	.459	.380	.416	.451
20	.522	.559	.595	.510	.548	.584	.498	.537	.573	.487	.526	.564	.477	.517	.555
25	.610	.647	.682	.598	.636	.671	.585	.624	.661	.574	.613	.651	.562	.603	.642
30	.685	.721	.753	.673	.710	.743	.661	.698	.733	.649	.687	.723	.637	.677	.714
35	.750	.782	.811	.738	.771	.802	.726	.761	.792	.714	.750	.783	.703	.740	.774
40	.804	.833	.858	.793	.823	.849	.782	.813	.841	.771	.803	.832	.760	.794	.824
45	.850	.874	.895	.840	.866	.888	.830	.857	.880	.820	.848	.873	.810	.840	.866
50	.889	.908	.925	.880	.901	.919	.871	.893	.913	.862	.886	.906	.853	.878	.900
55	.920	.936	.948	.913	.930	.943	.906	.923	.938	.898	.917	.933	.890	.910	.928
60	.946	.957	.966	.941	.953	.963	.934	.948	.959	.928	.942	.954	.921	.937	.950
65	.966	.974	.980	.962	.970	.977	.957	.967	.974	.952	.963	.971	.947	.958	.967
						Parameter of Stable Population									
Birth rate	.041	.046	.051	.038	.043	.047	.035	.040	.045	.033	.038	.042	.032	.036	.040
Death rate	.016	.016	.016	.013	.013	.012	.010	.010	.010	.008	.008	.007	.007	.006	.005
GRR(27)	2.62	2.98	3.38	2.43	2.76	3.14	2.28	2.59	2.95	2.16	2.45	2.79	2.06	2.34	2.66
GRR(29)	2.78	3.19	3.66	2.58	2.96	3.39	2.41	2.77	3.17	2.28	2.61	3.00	2.17	2.49	2.85
GRR(31)	2.96	3.43	3.97	2.74	3.17	3.67	2.55	2.96	3.43	2.41	2.79	3.23	2.28	2.65	3.07
GRR(33)	3.17	3.71	4.34	2.92	3.42	4.00	2.71	3.18	3.72	2.55	2.99	3.50	2.41	2.83	3.31
Average Age (Births)/	23.5	21.8	20.3	24.2	22.4	20.8	24.8	23.0	21.3	25.4	23.5	21.8	26.0	24.1	22.3
(Pop. 15–44)	.095	.109	.124	.088	.101	.115	.082	.094	.103	.077	.089	.102	.073	.084	.097

Source: Table B.3 (pp. 526–529) in H. Shryock, J. Siegel, and E. Stockwell, 1976, *The Methods and Materials of Demography, Condensed Edition*, New York: Academic Press.

TABLE B.4   Table for Estimating Cumulated Fertility from Age-Specific Fertility Rates Calculated From Survey Reports on Births During a 12-Month Period Preceding the Survey[1]

Age interval	Exact limits of age interval	Adjustment Factors w_i for values of f_1/f_2 and m as indicated in lower part of table							
1	15–20	1.120	1.310	1.615	1.950	2.305	2.640	2.925	3.170
2	20–25	2.555	2.690	2.780	2.840	2.890	2.925	2.960	2.985
3	25–30	2.925	2.960	2.985	3.010	3.035	3.055	3.075	3.095
4	30–35	3.055	3.075	3.095	3.120	3.140	3.165	3.190	3.215
5	35–40	3.165	3.190	3.215	3.245	3.285	3.325	3.375	3.435
6	40–45	3.325	3.375	3.435	3.510	3.610	3.740	3.915	4.150
7	45–50	3.640	3.895	4.150	4.395	4.630	4.840	4.985	5.000
	f_1/f_2	.036	.113	.213	.330	.460	.605	.764	.939
	m	31.7	30.7	29.7	28.7	27.7	26.7	25.7	24.7

[1] See text in Chapter 22 that explains the use of this table.
f_1 = age specific fertility rate for ages 14.5 to 19.5.
f_2 = age specific fertility rate for ages 19.5 to 24.5.
m = mean age of childbearing.
Source: Table B.4 (p. 530) in H. Shryock, J. Siegel, and E. Stockwell, 1976, *The Methods and Materials of Demography, Condensed Edition*, New York: Academic Press.

TABLE B.5   Table for Estimating Mortality from Child Survivorship Rates[1]

Mortality measure estimated	Exact limits of age interval of women	Adjustment factors to obtain q(a) shown in col. 1 from proportion of children reported as dead by women (in 5-year age groups) as shown in col. 2; for specified values of P_1/P_2, m and m' as shown in the lower part of the table							
q(1)	15–20	0.859	0.890	0.928	0.977	1.041	1.129	1.254	1.425
q(2)	20–25	0.938	0.959	0.983	1.010	1.043	1.082	1.129	1.188
q(3)	25–30	0.948	0.962	0.978	0.944	1.012	1.033	1.055	1.081
q(5)	30–35	0.961	0.975	0.988	1.002	1.016	1.031	1.046	1.063
q(10)	35–40	0.966	0.982	0.996	1.011	1.026	1.040	1.054	1.069
q(15)	40–45	0.938	0.955	0.971	0.988	1.004	1.021	1.037	1.052
q(20)	45–50	0.937	0.953	0.969	0.986	1.003	1.021	1.039	1.057
q(25)	50–55	0.949	0.966	0.983	1.001	1.019	1.036	1.054	1.072
q(30)	55–60	0.951	0.968	0.985	1.002	1.020	1.039	1.058	1.076
q(35)	60–65	0.949	0.965	0.982	0.999	1.016	1.034	1.052	1.070
	P_1/P_2	0.387	0.330	0.268	0.205	0.143	0.090	0.045	0.014
	m	24.7	25.7	26.7	27.7	28.7	29.7	30.7	31.7
	m'	24.2	25.2	26.2	27.2	28.2	29.2	30.2	31.2

[1] See text in Chapter 22 that explains the use of this table.
P_1 = average number of children born to women by age 20.
P_2 = average number of children born to women by age 25.
m = mean age of childbearing.
m' = median age of childbearing.
Source: Table B.5 (p. 530) in H. Shryock, J. Siegel, and E. Stockwell, 1976, *The Methods and Materials of Demography, Condensed Edition*, New York: Academic Press.

Part II. Model Life Tables

C. M. SUCHINDRAN

For many of the countries with no reliable mortality data or no mortality data at all, models constructed on the basis of other countries' mortality experience can be used to infer parameters. With the increased use of demographic and health surveys and with continued improvements in vital statistics, many of these countries are now able to conduct improved analysis of the age pattern of mortality, at least in certain age segments (e.g., infancy and childhood, young adulthood). Improved data collection has helped in developing several new and better models to study the age pattern of mortality.

A model for mortality may be a mathematical representation of the age-specific mortality (or risk of death). When the mortality pattern is U- or J-shaped, mathematical representation of the age pattern is difficult. The Gompertz or Makeham curve may not depict the mortality pattern of the entire age span; these curves may fit only certain segments of the human life span (Gompertz, 1825; Makeham, 1860). Because of the difficulty of finding simple mathematical functions to represent the entire life span, model construction has taken different directions. One such direction is toward empirically based models in which typical patterns are extracted from a collection of real life tables. Once the patterns of mortality in these collections of life tables are identified, simple analytical procedures are used to generate models by varying the level of mortality within each identified pattern. Several model life tables of this type have been constructed. This chapter presents two in detail (Coale and Demeny, 1983; United Nations, 1982).

A second way of constructing model life tables is the relational model method. In this approach, a standard age pattern of mortality is specified and a mathematical equation is also specified to relate the standard pattern to a general class of age patterns of mortality. A pattern of mortality is generated by changing the parameters in the specified mathematical equation. This method has the advantage of being able to generate patterns of mortality that are not included in the empirically based procedures. The Brass logit system of model life tables, which is based on the relational principle (Brass et al., 1968), is presented in this appendix. This appendix also presents a simple extension of the Brass model.

Because of the relationship between age-specific death rates and life table functions such as the probability of dying in an age interval (q_x) or the proportion surviving to a specified age x (l_x), some models used to study age patterns of mortality are generated for these specific functions. Models constructed using these functions have the advantage of being easily manipulated to generate other life table functions.

With modern computer power, renewed attempts have been made to formulate complex mathematical (parametric) models to represent the mortality experience of the entire age span. A brief discussion of such parametric models is also included here (Di Pino and Pirri, 1998; Heligman and Pollard, 1980; Rogers and Little, 1994).

EMPIRICALLY BASED SYSTEMS OF MODEL LIFE TABLES

The two significant attempts using the empirical approach are the first United Nations model life tables and Ledermann's (1969) system of model life tables. The approach taken in these systems of life tables paved the way for new and improved systems, described in detail later in this section.

The Early United Nations System of Model Life Tables

The United Nations was the first to make a systematic attempt to construct model life tables with an empirical basis (United Nations, 1955). In this effort the key assumption was that the level of mortality in any age group was closely correlated with the level of mortality in an adjacent age group. Parabolic regression equations indicating the relationship between adjacent pairs of life table $_nq_x$ values were constructed using data from life tables of 158 countries. Thus, starting from a specified level of infant mortality, q_0, a value of $_4q_1$ could be determined. From the calculated value of $_4q_1$, a value of $_5q_5$ could be estimated using the regression equation. This process was continued in chain fashion to generate all the $_nq_x$ values for the entire life span. Thus, by specifying various levels of infant mortality (q_0), one could generate a set of life tables. This set of UN model life tables was criticized for several reasons. Using a series of regression equations in chain fashion introduced a bias into the estimated life table parameters because of the statistical errors in the estimated predictor variables. It was also argued that the collection of life tables that went into calculating the regression equation was not sufficiently representative of the whole range of reliably recorded human mortality experience. The system of life tables generated with a single parameter, the infant mortality rate, (q_0), also lacked flexibility because it could generate only one plausible age pattern of mortality from among the many potential patterns.

Ledermann's System of Model Life Tables

Ledermann and Breas (1959) used factor analysis to analyze variations in mortality in the set of actual life tables used to construct the first United Nations model life table. They concluded that five significant factors contribute to these variations in mortality: (1) the overall level of mortality, (2) the ratio of child to adult mortality, (3) old-age mortality, (4) pattern of infant and child mortality, and (5) sex differences in mortality from ages 5 to 70. Taking into account these factors in the variation of mortality, Ledermann (1969) constructed a system of life tables. The basis of these life tables, as in the case of the early United Nations life tables, is a system of regression equations predicting the logarithm of the $_nq_x$ with one or two independent variables. For example, the system of regression equations consisting of two independent variables is of the form

$$\ln {}_nq_x = \beta_0(x) + \beta_1(x)\ln Z_1 + \beta_2(x)\ln Z_2 \qquad (B.1)$$

where the pair of independent variables (Z_1, Z_2) can be any of the following pairs: $({}_5q_0, {}_{20}q_{45})$, $({}_{15}q_0, {}_{20}q_{30})$, $({}_{15}q_0, m_{50+})$.

Ledermann's system is much more flexible than the one-parameter system in the earlier United Nations set of model life tables because regression equations are available with several choices of independent variables. However, the regression parameters are estimated using the same set of life tables as that of the United Nations, which may not cover all the possible patterns. Moreover, reliable estimates of the independent variables used in these equations may not be available in the less developed countries. Because most of the current methods of estimating the demographic parameters for the less developed countries seldom use Ledermann's system of life tables, this system of life tables is not discussed in detail here.

Other Empirically Based Systems of Model Life Tables

Two sets of model life tables that have wider use in countries with limited mortality data are the Coale and Demeny system of model life tables and the new United Nations model life tables.

Coale and Demeny System of Model Life Tables

Coale and Demeny first published a system of model life tables in 1966 (Coale and Demeny, 1966). They published a revised system in 1983 (Coale and Demeny, 1983).

The basis of the Coale-Demeny life table system is the mortality patterns exhibited in 192 actual life tables by sex. They chose these life tables from an original collection of 326 male and 326 female life tables. The original set contained 23 pairs of life tables for the period before 1870, 189 between the years 1871 and 1945, and the remaining 114 the period after 1945. Two hundred and forty-six of the original 326 came from European and other developed countries. Of the original 326, those that exhibited large deviations from the "norm" were dropped. Only life tables derived from registration data and from the complete enumeration of the populations to which they refer were included. The final set of 192 life tables selected for the construction of model life tables contained only 16 from Asia and Africa. The remaining 176 came from Europe, North America, Australia, and New Zealand.

Analysis of these 192 life tables revealed four age patterns of mortality. These patterns were labeled North, South, East, and West. The characteristics of the age patterns of the four regions are as follows:

1. *North.* This region's age pattern of mortality is characterized by relatively low infant mortality, relatively high child mortality, and low mortality after age 50. The high adult mortality (age 20 to 50) in this mortality pattern is attributed to a high incidence of tuberculosis. The life tables that exhibited this pattern were derived from nine observed tables from Norway (1856–1880), Sweden (1851–1890), and Iceland (1941–1950).

2. *South.* The South mortality pattern is characterized by high mortality under age 5 (particularly among infants), low adult mortality from age 40 to age 60, and high mortality over age 65. The South model represents the age pattern of mortality of southern European countries such as Spain, Portugal, and Italy, from 1876 to 1957.

3. *East.* The East pattern of mortality exhibits relatively high infant mortality and high old-age mortality. This pattern appears mainly in the life tables of central European countries such as Austria, Germany, north and central Italy, Czechoslovakia, and Poland.

4. *West.* The West pattern is derived from the largest set of observed life tables (130) and is considered to represent the most general mortality pattern. Its mortality pattern does not deviate significantly from the mortality pattern derived when all the observed life tables are put together. This model is based only on the tables that were not included in the derivation of the other three patterns. Coale and Demeny recommended its use when reliable information is lacking for choosing one of the other patterns.

Constructing Model Life Tables

Coale and Demeny used regression modeling to construct the life tables. Regression equations relating the life table probability of dying ($_nq_x$) and a single predictor variable (e_{10}^0) were constructed for each of the four mortality patterns, separately for males and females. Specifically, the following type of regression model was constructed on the basis of the observed life table data:

$$_nq_x = A_x + B_x e_{10}^0 \tag{B.7}$$

$$\ln_{10}(10,000 \,_nq_x) = A'_x + B'_x e_{10}^0 \tag{B.8}$$

For illustration, the regression coefficient for the four mortality patterns for males and females aged 0 are given in Table B.5. For the purpose of constructing the life tables $_nq_x$ values were generated using various values of the independent variable e_{10}^0. Both the estimates obtained from the logarithmic equation and those from the equation based on the untransformed mortality rates were used in constructing the model life tables. Using simple criteria (Coale and Demeny, 1966), the logarithmic regression was used for one segment of the age range, the regression equation based on the untransformed mortality for another age range, and the mean of the two for the rest. The 1966 model system generated life tables with an upper age of 80. In 1983, Coale and Demeny (Coale and Demeny, 1983) extended the upper age to 100 years. They did this using the Gompertz model to fit mortality at the older ages.

The regression equations used to generate $_nq_x$ values depend on only one predictor variable, e_{10}^0. Values of e_{10}^0 for females were chosen to generate life tables with the assigned expectation of life at birth. With appropriate values of e_{10}^0, the 1966 Coale-Demeny life tables generated an expectation

of life at birth (e_0^0) ranging from 20 to 77.5, increasing in steps of 2.5 years. The 24 life tables generated were labeled levels 1 to 24. The 1983 revision of the life tables (Coale and Demeny, 1983) extended the range of e_0^0 to 80 years, labeled as level 25.

To preserve the typical relation between male and female mortality at each level, the values of e_{10}^0 for males were chosen using the relation exhibited by e_{10}^0 for females and e_{10}^0 for males in the life tables within the selected pattern. This relationship is given by the following equation:

$$\left(e_{10}^0\right)_{males} - \left(\bar{e}_{10}^0\right)_{males} = \frac{\sigma_{males}}{\sigma_{females}}\left[\left(e_{10}^0\right)_{females} - \left(\bar{e}_{10}^0\right)_{females}\right] \tag{B.9}$$

where σ_{males} and $\sigma_{females}$ are the standard deviations of life expectancy at age 10 for males and females, respectively, and $\bar{e}_{10}^0$ is the average e_{10}^0 for the region or pattern.

A Further Look at the Four Mortality Patterns

As mentioned earlier, the changes in age patterns of mortality can be examined either through the pattern implied in the age-specific death rates, through the life table quantities $_nq_x$, or through the survival function l_x. A plot of the $_nq_x$ values shows a pattern similar to that of the age-specific death rates. Alternatively, one can examine a plot of the ratio of $_nq_x$ values from two life tables. Figure B.1 shows a plot of the ratio of $_nq_x$ values calculated as $R(x) = \,_nq_x/\,_nq_x^W$ where the numerator is the $_nq_x$ value of a pattern other than the West pattern and the denominator is the $_nq_x$ value of the West pattern. This plot is calculated for level 15 of the model life tables. Deviations from one exhibit the difference in the $_nq_x$ value of a specified pattern from that of the West model. The plot in Figure B.1 clearly shows, for example, how the East pattern differs from the West pattern with its lower childhood mortality and higher old-age mortality. Similarly, one can also visualize in the figure the difference between the North and West patterns and the South and West patterns.

A plot of the survival function can also reveal the differences in the age pattern of mortality. Figure B.2 shows a plot of the l_x values of the four mortality patterns at level 15. Because of its higher child mortality, the curve for the South pattern shows a steep drop during childhood and the curve for the South crosses over the West curve (attaining larger values l_x) because of the lower mortality rate of the South pattern at older ages.

Occasionally one would like to see how the four regional mortality patterns differ in a selected age segment. Table B.6 shows infant mortality in the four patterns at selected levels. The table clearly shows that infant mortality differs by for the four regions. The South pattern continues to exhibit higher infant mortality even when $e_0^0 = 75$.

TABLE B.6 Regression Coefficients for the Model Equation for Age Zero by Type of Model, Sex, and Mortality Pattern

Model and sex	Untransformed mortality regression		Logarithmic regression	
	A_0	B_0	A'_0	B'_0
Females				
West	.53774	−.008044	5.8992	−.05406
North	.47504	−.006923	5.7332	−.05133
East	.78219	−.011679	5.8529	−.05064
South	.52069	−.007051	4.5097	−.02566
Males				
West	.63726	−.009958	5.8061	−.05338
North	.54327	−.008251	5.6151	−.05022
East	1.07554	−.017228	6.3796	−.06124
South	.61903	−.008974	4.7096	−.02980

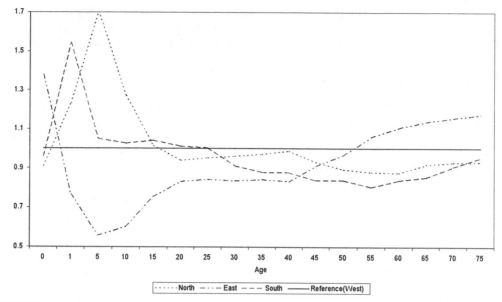

FIGURE B.1 Relative proportion dying in North, East, and South models in relation to the West model (Level 15).

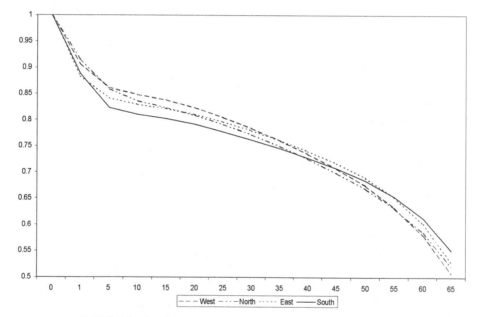

FIGURE B.2 Proportion surviving to a specified age by mortality pattern.

TABLE B.7 Values of Female Infant Mortality (q_0) at Selected Mortality Levels by Pattern

Pattern	Level 15 ($e_0^0 = 55$)	Level 19 ($e_0^0 = 65$)	Level 23 ($e_0^0 = 75$)
West	.093	.050	.015
North	.085	.048	.018
East	.116	.064	.021
South	.112	.077	.041

The 1982 United Nations Model Life Tables

The United Nations (1982) produced a set of model life tables that, like Coale and Demeny's (1983), are empirically based. However, unlike Coale and Demeny's, most of the life tables included in the UN set came from less developed countries. After carefully evaluating the available life tables from the less developed countries, 72 high-quality tables (36 males and 36 females) were chosen as the basis for the construction of model life tables. These life tables came from 22 less developed countries and cover the period 1920 to 1973. The female life expectancy at birth in these life tables ranged from 40.1 to 76.6 years.

Patterns of Mortality

An examination of the life tables selected by graphical and statistical procedures, such as cluster analysis, revealed four distinct age patterns of mortality. These patterns were labeled Latin American, Chilean, South Asian, and Far Eastern. A fifth general pattern was also constructed, which is an average pattern derived from all the original life tables selected. Each pattern is briefly described next.

The Latin American Pattern

The Latin American model has relatively high infant and child mortality (caused mainly by excess diarrheal and parasitic diseases). Adult mortality is also high (primarily because of accidents). Old-age mortality is low (primarily because of low cardiovascular mortality).

The life tables that exhibited this pattern came from Colombia, Costa Rica, El Salvador, Guatemala, Honduras, Mexico, and Peru, as well as three Asian countries—the Philippines, Sri Lanka, and Thailand.

The Chilean Pattern

The Chilean pattern has extremely high infant mortality (mainly because of deaths from respiratory diseases, and possibly related to early weaning). This pattern is distinctive, found only in life tables from Chile.

The South Asian Pattern

This pattern has high mortality under 15 and over 55 (attributed to diarrheal and parasitic diseases at young ages and to respiratory and diarrheal diseases at older ages) but relatively low mortality in the intermediate ages. The life tables included in this pattern came from India, Iran, Bangladesh, and Tunisia.

The Far Eastern Pattern

In this pattern, mortality at old ages was relatively high compared to other patterns, especially among males (probably due to a past history of tuberculosis). This cluster included life tables from Guyana, Hong Kong, Republic of Korea, Singapore, and Trinidad and Tobago.

The General Pattern

The general pattern is an average of the life tables considered. It is similar to the Coale and Demeny's West model life tables.

Construction of the Model Life Tables

The statistical method of principal component analysis was used for the construction of the model life tables. The age pattern of each life table analyzed was characterized by its $_nq_x$ values. Specifically, the logit transformation of $_nq_x$ was used. The form of the logit transformation used is

$$\text{logit}[_nq_x] = \frac{1}{2}\ln\left[\frac{_nq_x}{1 - _nq_x}\right] \qquad (B.4)$$

Denote $_nY_x^{ij}$ as the logit of the $_nq_x$ function for life table j of cluster i and $_n\overline{Y}_x^i$ as the average of the $_nY_x^{ij}$ within cluster i. Then the k-component principal component model is specified as

$$_nY_x^{ij} = _n\overline{Y}_x^i + \sum_{m=1}^{k} a_{mj}U_{mx} \qquad (B.5)$$

where U_{mx} equals the element of the *mth* principal component vector corresponding to age group $(x, x + n)$, k is the number of principal components, and a_{mj} equals the factor loading of the *mth* principal component vector for country j in the principal component analysis. When $k = 1$, the model is referred to as a one-component model. Similar references are made to two-component and three-component models. Note that in the fitted model, the factor loading, a_{mj}, and the principal component vector, U_{mx}, does not depend on the cluster pattern. In the United Nations' collection of life tables, for all ages combined, the percentage of variation in female mortality explained by the model is 91.3, 95.2, and 96.8, respectively for one-, two-, and three-component models. For male life tables, the corresponding percentages are 89.2, 94.7, and 96.7.

The average female patterns of mortality for specific cluster patterns defined by the logit values, $_n\overline{Y}_x^i$, are shown in Table B.8. The age pattern of mortality implied in each pattern is clearly reflected in the averages in Table B.8. As noted earlier, a three-component model captures nearly all the variations in mortality. Table B.9 presents the first three principal components ($U_{1x}, U_{2x}, and U_{3x}$) for females.

The first principal component captures the change from the average in the overall level of mortality at each age. These component values show that the change is greatest in childhood and young adulthood and decreases as age increases. The second component reflects the characteristic differences in changes in mortality under age 5 in relation to that of mortality over 5. For females, the third component reflects the mortality changes in the childbearing years.

As stated earlier, a life table for a particular pattern i can be produced from a one-component model by generating the logit values of $_nq_x$ (denoted as $_nY_x^i$) using the model equation

$$_nY_x^i = _n\overline{Y}_x^i + a_1 * U_{1x} \qquad (B.6)$$

where a_1 denotes the loading factor and U_{1x} denotes the first component factor for age x. The model construction can be extended to include the second and third component

TABLE B.8 Average Female Pattern of Mortality by Cluster

Exact age	Latin American	Chilean	South Asian	Far Eastern
0	−1.22452	−1.12557	−0.97055	−1.42596
1	−1.45667	−1.82378	−1.15424	−1.95200
5	−2.13881	−2.52319	−1.93962	−2.55653
10	−2.46676	−2.63933	−2.36857	−2.68018
15	−2.31810	−2.38847	−2.19082	−2.33095
20	−2.14505	−2.20417	−2.09358	−2.15952
25	−2.03883	−2.09701	−2.04788	−2.03377
30	−1.93294	−1.99128	−1.95922	−1.94554
35	−1.83147	−1.87930	−1.87311	−1.82299
40	−1.74288	−1.75744	−1.76095	−1.69084
45	−1.62385	−1.61558	−1.61425	−1.52189
50	−1.47924	−1.45886	−1.39012	−1.33505
55	−1.28721	−1.26115	−1.15515	−1.13791
60	−1.07443	−1.05224	−0.90816	−0.93765
65	−0.83152	−0.80346	−0.68011	−0.72718
70	−0.59239	−0.58202	−0.43231	−0.50916
75	−0.35970	−0.35093	−0.17489	−0.28389
80	−0.08623	−0.10587	0.05948	−0.01285

TABLE B.9 First Three Principal Components (Females)

Exact Age	1st Component U_{1x}	2nd Component U_{2x}	3rd Component U_{3x}
0	.18289	−0.51009	0.23944
1	.31406	−0.52241	−0.11117
5	.31716	0.08947	0.07566
10	.30941	0.03525	0.06268
15	.32317	0.03132	−0.26708
20	.32626	0.07843	−0.39053
25	.30801	0.06762	−0.28237
30	.29047	0.00482	−0.14277
35	.25933	−0.01409	−0.05923
40	.22187	−0.02178	0.18909
45	.19241	0.01870	0.24773
50	.17244	0.04427	0.33679
55	.15729	0.08201	0.34121
60	.14282	0.08061	0.38290
65	.12711	0.15756	0.26731
70	.11815	0.24236	0.14442
75	.11591	0.30138	0.09697
80	.09772	0.50530	−0.13377

$$_nY_x^i = {}_n\overline{Y}_x^i + a_1 * U_{1x} + a_2 * U_{2x} \quad \text{(two-component model)} \quad \text{(B.7)}$$

$$_nY_x^i = {}_n\overline{Y}_x^i + a_1 * U_{1x} + a_2 * U_{2x} + a_3 * U_{3x}$$
(three-component model) (B.8)

Empirical data can be fitted to a particular pattern by estimating the appropriate loading factor. In cases where available data include $_nq_x$ values for all 18 age groups, simple equations can be used to estimate the factor loading:

$$\hat{a}_1 = \sum_x \left({}_nY_x - {}_n\overline{Y}_x^i \right) U_{1x} \quad \text{(B.9)}$$

$$\hat{a}_2 = \sum_x \left({}_nY_x - {}_n\overline{Y}_x^i \right) U_{2x} \quad \text{(B.10)}$$

$$\hat{a}_3 = \sum_x \left({}_nY_x - {}_n\overline{Y}_x^i \right) U_{3x} \quad \text{(B.11)}$$

When data on $_nq_x$ are not available for all 18 age groups, special methods, as described in United Nations (1982, p. 16), should be used to estimate the loading factors.

The United Nations (1982) presents a one-component model for all four identified mortality patterns and for the general pattern. The published life tables include, for each sex, tables with life expectancy at birth from ages 35 to 75 in single-year intervals. Figure B.3a gives a comparison of the mortality patterns as observed in the calculated life tables. It depicts the ratio $q_x^i/q_x^{General\ pattern}$ for females corresponding to a life expectancy at birth of 55. A value of 1 for the ratio indicates that the $_nq_x$ values for a specific pattern are identical to that of the general pattern at this age. The

figure clearly shows the distinctive features of each mortality pattern.

Example 1: Fitting an Observed Life Table to a Selected Pattern

Table B.10 gives the observed values of $_nq_x$ from the 1995 female life table for Tunisia. This example illustrates fitting a one-, two-, and three-component model to these data on the basis of the Latin American pattern. The calculations are shown in Table B.10.

Fitting a One-Component Model

Step 1: Convert $_nq_x$ values (col.1) to logits as
$$_ny_x = \frac{1}{2} \ln \frac{_nq_x}{1 - {}_nq_x} \text{ (column 2)}.$$

Step 2: Take deviations from the average values $({}_n\overline{Y}_x)$ of logits for the Latin American pattern (column 3). Column 4 gives the deviations (col.2–col.3).

Step 3: Compute the loading factor of the first component as $\hat{a}_1 = \Sigma({}_ny_x - {}_n\overline{Y}_x)U_{1x}$. Multiply columns 4 and 5, then the products ($\hat{a}_1 = -2.38159$).

Step 4: Obtain the estimated logits for the model (column 6) as $_n\hat{y}_x = {}_n\overline{Y}_x + \hat{a}_1 U_{1x}$

Step 5: Convert the model estimated logit values to $_nq_x$ (column 7) as

$$_n\hat{q}_x = \frac{1}{1 + e^{-2_n\hat{y}_x}} \quad \text{(B.12)}$$

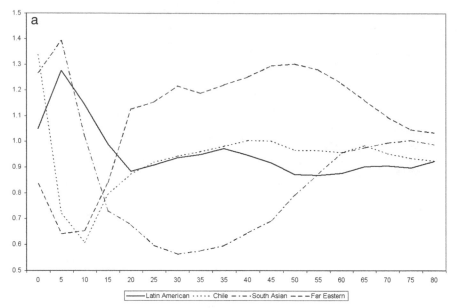

FIGURE B.3a   The ratio $q_x^i/q_x^{General\ pattern}$ by mortality pattern, (females at $e_0^0 = 55$).

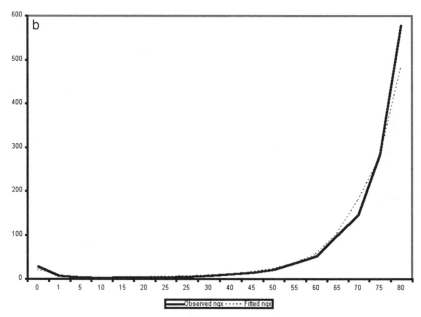

FIGURE B.3b   Observed and fitted $_nq_x$ values (three-component model): Latin American pattern.

Fitting Models of Two and Three Components

The two-component model is

$$_nY_x^i = {_n\overline{Y}_x^i} + a_1 * U_{1x} + a_2 * U_{2x} \tag{B.13}$$

The factor loading $\hat{a}_1$ is calculated as before in Table B.10. Similarly, the factor loading $\hat{a}_2$ is calculated as

$$\hat{a}_2 = \sum ({_ny_x} - {_n\overline{Y}_x})U_{2x}$$

For the Tunisia data in Table B.10, the estimated value of $\hat{a}_2$ is 0.52416.

The predicted logit values for the two-component models are calculated as

$$_n\hat{Y}_x = {_n\overline{Y}_x} + \hat{a}_1 * U_{1x} + \hat{a}_2 * U_{2x}$$

The logit values can be converted into $_n\hat{q}_x$ using the conversion formula in step 5 (B.11). The estimated $_n\hat{q}_x$ for the two-component model is shown in Table B.11.

Three-Component Model

A three-component model is specified as

$$_nY_x^i = {_n\overline{Y}_x^i} + a_1 * U_{1x} + a_2 * U_{2x} + a_3 * U_{3x} \tag{B.14}$$

TABLE B.10   Fitting the Latin American Model to Tunisian 1995 Female Life Table

Exact age	$_nq_x$ (1)[1]	$_ny_x$ (2)	$_n\overline{Y}_x$ (Latin American pattern) (3)[2]	$_nY_x - _n\overline{Y}_x$ (2) − (3) = (4)	U_{1x} (5)[3]	$_n\hat{y}_x = _n\overline{Y}_x + U_{1x}\hat{a}_1$ (3) + (5)(−2.38159) = (6)	$_n\hat{q}_x$ (7)[4]
0	.02715	−1.78943	−1.22452	−0.56491	0.18289	−1.66009	0.03488
1	.00657	−2.50932	−1.45667	−1.05265	0.31406	−2.20463	0.01201
5	.00295	−2.91150	−2.13881	−0.77269	0.31716	−2.89415	0.00305
10	.00220	−3.05854	−2.46676	−0.59178	0.30941	−3.20365	0.00164
15	.00280	−2.93767	−2.31810	−0.61957	0.32317	−3.08776	0.00207
20	.00310	−2.88662	−2.14505	−0.74157	0.32626	−2.92207	0.00288
25	.00374	−2.79246	−2.03883	−0.75363	0.30801	−2.77238	0.00389
30	.00479	−2.66821	−1.93924	−0.72897	0.29047	−2.63102	0.00515
35	.00683	−2.48979	−1.83147	−0.65832	0.25933	−2.44909	0.00740
40	.01055	−2.27051	−1.74288	−0.52763	0.22187	−2.27128	0.01053
45	.01391	−2.13057	−1.62385	−0.50672	0.19241	−2.08209	0.01530
50	.02031	−1.93806	−1.47924	−0.45882	0.17244	−1.88992	0.02231
55	.03589	−1.64537	−1.28721	−0.35816	0.15729	−1.66181	0.03477
60	.05112	−1.46055	−1.07443	−0.38612	0.14282	−1.41457	0.05577
65	.09872	−1.10576	−0.83152	−0.27424	0.12711	−1.13424	0.09376
70	.14614	−0.88260	−0.59239	−0.29021	0.11815	−0.87377	0.14835
75	.28289	−0.46509	−0.35970	−0.10539	0.11591	−0.63575	0.21900
80	.57791	0.15710	−0.08623	0.24333	0.09772	−0.31896	0.34571

Source: [1] United Nations, *Damographic Yearbook, 1996*, New York: United Nations, 1998.
[2] Table B.8.
[3] Table B.9.
[4] Formula B.12.

The factor loadings $\hat{a}_1$ and $\hat{a}_2$ are estimated as shown earlier. The factor loading $\hat{a}_3$ is estimated as

$$\hat{a}_3 = \sum (_ny_x - _n\overline{Y}_x)U_{3x}$$

For the Tunisia data in Table B.10, the factor loading $\hat{a}_3$ is estimated to be −0.11071. The estimated three-component logit model is obtained for the data as

$$_n\hat{Y}_x = _n\overline{Y}_x + 2.38159*U_{1x} + 0.52416*U_{2x}$$
$$- 0.11071*U_{3x}$$

The logit values are converted into $_n\hat{q}_x$ values as in step 5. These values are shown in Table B.11.

The fit of the model is examined by computing the sum of the squares(ss) of the deviations of the observed from the fitted values, divided by thermometer of age groups as

$$SS = \frac{1}{18} \sum_x (_n\hat{q}_x - _nq_x)^2 \qquad (B.14)$$

where 18 is the number of age groups involved.

The values of SS for the three fitted models are as follows:

Model	SS
One component	0.05814
Two components	0.01267
Three components	0.01076

TABLE B.11   Observed and Fitted $_nq_x$ Values for 1995 Tunisian Female Life Table

Age	Observed $_nq_x$[1]	Fitted $_n\hat{q}_x$ values based on Latin American pattern		
		One component[1]	Two components[2]	Three components[2]
0	0.02715	0.03488	0.02073	0.01968
1	0.00657	0.01201	0.00698	0.00715
5	0.00295	0.00305	0.00335	0.00329
10	0.00220	0.00164	0.00170	0.00168
15	0.00280	0.00207	0.00214	0.00227
20	0.00310	0.00288	0.00313	0.00341
25	0.00374	0.00389	0.00417	0.00444
30	0.00479	0.00515	0.00518	0.00535
35	0.00683	0.00740	0.00729	0.00739
40	0.01055	0.01053	0.01029	0.00988
45	0.01391	0.01530	0.01560	0.01478
50	0.02031	0.02231	0.02335	0.02171
55	0.03589	0.03477	0.03777	0.03512
60	0.05112	0.05577	0.06039	0.05575
65	0.09872	0.09376	0.10877	0.10316
70	0.14614	0.14835	0.18340	0.17866
75	0.28289	0.21900	0.27776	0.27348
80	0.57791	0.34571	0.47297	0.48036

[1] Source: Table B.10.
[2] See text.

The reduction in SS shows how additional components improve the fit of the model. However, a comparison of the observed and fitted values (Figure B.3b) indicates that the three-component model based on the Latin American pattern may not be the best-fitting pattern for the Tunisian data because the fitted values deviate widely from the observed values at older ages.

Example 2: Identification of Mortality Pattern in an Observed Life Table

In this example, a one-component model is fitted to the $_nq_x$ values of the 1995 Tunisian female life table using all four mortality patterns. The average of the squared deviations (SS) is calculated using the fitted $_n\hat{q}_x$ values for each pattern. The pattern with the smallest value of the average the squared deviations is chosen as the appropriate pattern for the data.

The calculations used for a one-component model in Example 1 are repeated, replacing the Latin American average pattern of mortality ($_n\overline{Y}_x^i$) with the Chilean, South Asian, and Far Eastern patterns. The fitted $_n\hat{q}_x$ values and the corresponding average of the squared deviations are shown in Table B.12. The table shows that the sum of squared deviations is the lowest for the South Asian pattern, suggesting that the Tunisia mortality graph is likely to follow this pattern.

RELATIONAL MODEL LIFE TABLES

Because of the restrictive nature of the data involved in the construction of model life tables, the mortality pattern of some countries may not fit very well into them. For example, because the United Nations database did not include any life tables from sub-Saharan Africa, the mortality pattern observed in these countries may not fit well into any of the four patterns identified in the UN life tables. To overcome this difficulty, Brass (1964, 1971) suggested model life table construction basing on the relational principle. In this system, a mathematical relationship is specified to relate pairs of life tables.

The Brass Relational Two-Parameter Logit System

Brass (1964, 1971) proposed a two-parameter logit system to construct model life tables. In this system, the model specifies a simple linear relationship between the transformed l_x values of two life tables. Specifically, this relationship is expressed as follows:

$$\frac{1}{2}\ln\frac{1-l_x}{l_x} = \alpha + \beta\frac{1}{2}\ln\frac{1-l_x^s}{l_x^s} \qquad (B.15)$$

TABLE B.12   Fit of One-Component Model of Selected Mortality Patterns to 1995 Tunisian Female $_nq_x$

Age	Observed $_nq_x$[1]	Fitting $_n\hat{q}_x$ values according to specified pattern			
		LA	Ch	SA	FE
0	0.02715	0.03488	0.04763	0.04924	0.02588
1	0.00657	0.01201	0.00720	0.01697	0.00528
5	0.00295	0.00305	0.00176	0.00351	0.00156
10	0.00220	0.00164	0.00144	0.00156	0.00126
15	0.00280	0.00207	0.00225	0.00206	0.00239
20	0.00310	0.00288	0.00321	0.00245	0.00332
25	0.00374	0.00389	0.00428	0.00298	0.00461
30	0.00479	0.00515	0.00568	0.00392	0.00591
35	0.00683	0.00740	0.00805	0.00553	0.00860
40	0.01055	0.01053	0.01192	0.00850	0.01308
45	0.01391	0.01530	0.01773	0.01337	0.02062
50	0.02031	0.02231	0.02609	0.02317	0.03223
55	0.03589	0.03477	0.04060	0.03966	0.05005
60	0.05112	0.05577	0.06382	0.06835	0.07717
65	0.09872	0.09376	0.10677	0.11218	0.11985
70	0.14614	0.14835	0.16180	0.17900	0.17950
75	0.28289	0.21900	0.23621	0.26977	0.25737
80	0.57791	0.34571	0.35219	0.39516	0.39164
$SS = \frac{1}{18}\sum_x \left(_nq_x - _n\hat{q}_x\right)^2$		0.00323	0.00300	0.00198	0.00211

[1] Source: Table B.10.
[2] Source: Table B.11.

where l_x^s denotes the survival function of a standard life table. Let

$$\lambda(l_x) = \frac{1}{2}\ln\frac{1-l_x}{l_x} \quad \text{and} \quad \lambda(l_x^s) = \frac{1}{2}\ln\frac{1-l_x^s}{l_x^s} \quad \text{(B.16)}$$

Then $\lambda(l_x)$ is the logit transformation of $1 - l_x$. The model equation (B.22) can be re-expressed as

$$\lambda(l_x) = \alpha + \beta\lambda(l_x^s) \quad \text{(B.17)}$$

The model equation contains two parameters α and β. By choosing a standard life table and values for parameters α and β, one can generate a set of life tables. The steps in constructing model life tables based on a standard life table are as follows:

1. Compute $\lambda(l_x^s)$, the logit transformation of $1 - l_x^s$ values taken form the chosen standard life table, using Equation (B.23).
2. Choose values of α and β.
3. Use Equation (B.23) to compute the logit transformation $1 - l_x$ of a life table, $\lambda(l_x)$.
4. Convert the computed $\lambda(l_x)$ (i.e., logit values of $1 - l_x$) to l_x values using the relation

$$l_x = \frac{1}{1 + e^{2\alpha + 2\beta\lambda(l_x^s)}}$$

Thus, for a given standard life table one can generate a set of life tables by varying the parameters α and β.

The Choice of Standard

Potentially, one can choose as a standard any life table that seems appropriate. Brass, in his earlier studies of Africa, proposed an African standard. This standard is characterized by relatively low infant mortality and relatively high child mortality. Later he proposed a general standard similar to the West-model life-table mortality pattern in the Coale-Demeny life tables. These Brass standards are widely used in many applications. Table B.14 reproduces the logit values at selected ages.

The Effect of Changing α and β Parameters

Figures B.4a and B.4b depict the effect that changing the α and β parameters has on the survival curve. When the intercept term α varies and β remains the same, the survival curves form a set of nonoverlapping curves (Figure B.4b). Values of l_x decrease with increasing values of α.

When the slope parameter β changes, keeping α same, the survival curves form a set of intersecting curves (Figure B.4a). It is easy to verify that the curves cross at the median

TABLE B.14 General and African Standard Life Table Logit Values

Age (x)	General standard $\lambda(l_x^s)$	African standard $\lambda(l_x^s)$
1	−0.8670	−0.9972
5	−0.6015	−0.6514
10	−0.5498	−0.5498
15	−0.5131	−0.5131
20	−0.4551	−0.4551
25	−0.3829	−0.3829
30	−0.3150	−0.3150
35	−0.2496	−0.2496
40	−0.1817	−0.1817
45	−0.1073	−0.1073
50	−0.0212	−0.0212
55	0.0832	0.0832
60	0.2100	0.2100
65	0.3746	0.3746
70	0.5818	0.5818
75	0.8611	0.8611
80	1.2433	1.2433
85	1.7810	1.7810

age of the standard life table. When β is greater than 1, the survival probabilities are greater than the corresponding survival probabilities of the standard curve until the median age of the standard life table and then the order is reversed.

Fitting the Brass Model to a Observed Life Table

The Brass relational model can be fit to an actual life table to capture the essential features of the mortality pattern in the observed data. The steps are

1. Convert observed life table l_x values (with $l_0 = 1$) into logit values $\lambda(l_x)$ using Equation (B.2).
2. Obtain the logit values of the standard life table $\lambda(l_x^s)$.
3. Fit the regression model $\lambda(l_x) = \alpha + \beta \lambda(l_x^s)$ using the least squares method.

The procedure is illustrated here using the 1995 Tunisian female life table and the Brass African pattern as the standard (shown in Table B.14). Table B.15 shows the necessary data to fit the model.

The model parameters estimated by the least squares procedure are $\hat{a} = -1.1194$ (standard error 0.0225) and $\hat{\beta} = 0.9644$ (standard error 0.0327). The fitted model has an adjusted R-square of 98.1%. A high negative intercept parameter reveals the improvement in the level of mortality compared to the standard. The closeness of the slope parameter to 1 ($\beta \approx 1$) suggests that the pattern of the curve has not changed drastically from the pattern of the standard. The survival probabilities predicted by the model are given in Table B.15. These predicted probabilities show that the model overestimates the l_x values at the very young and very old ages.

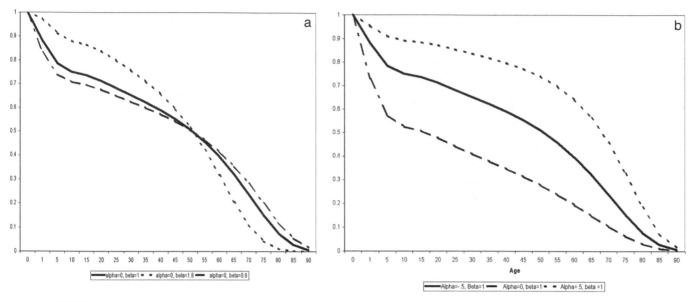

FIGURE B.4   Survival curves showing the effect of varing the α and β parameters. (*a* graph: α = 0 β varies; *b* graph: α varies, β = 1)

TABLE B.15   1995 Tunisian Female Life Table Values

Age	l_x[1]	$\lambda(l_x)$ logit $(1 - l_x)$	$\lambda(l_x^s)$ African standard	Predicted l_x
0	1.0000	X	X	1.0000
1	0.9728	−1.78848	−0.9972	0.9847
5	0.9664	−1.67953	−0.6514	0.9705
10	0.9636	−1.63805	−0.5498	0.9644
15	0.9615	−1.60892	−0.5131	0.9619
20	0.9588	−1.57362	−0.4551	0.9576
25	0.9558	−1.53691	−0.3829	0.9515
30	0.9522	−1.49587	−0.3150	0.9451
35	0.9477	−1.44852	−0.2496	0.9382
40	0.9412	−1.38651	−0.1817	0.9301
45	0.9312	−1.30264	−0.1073	0.9203
50	0.9183	−1.20974	−0.0212	0.9072
55	0.8997	−1.09695	0.0832	0.8888
60	0.8674	−0.93908	0.2100	0.8622
65	0.8230	−0.76840	0.3746	0.8200
70	0.7417	−0.52741	0.5818	0.7533
75	0.6334	−0.27342	0.8611	0.6406
80	0.4542	0.09186	1.2433	0.4602
85	0.1918	0.71918	1.7810	0.2320

X Not applicable.

[1] Source: United Nations *Demographic Year book, 1996*, New York: United Nations, 1998.

Extensions of the Two-Parameter Relational Model

Because of the failure of the two-parameter model to adequately fit several life table mortality patterns, several extensions to it have been proposed. This section briefly describes these extended models.

Following Ewbank *et al.* (1983), Namboodiri (1990) proposed the following five-parameter model:

$$\lambda(l_x) = \alpha + \beta_1 \frac{\left[e^{c\lambda\left(l_x^s\right)} - 1\right]}{c} \quad \text{if} \quad \lambda\left(l_x^s\right) < 0$$
$$= \alpha + \beta_2 \frac{\left[e^{d\lambda\left(l_x^s\right)} - 1\right]}{d} \quad \text{if} \quad \lambda\left(l_x^s\right) > 0 \tag{B.18}$$

where $\lambda(l_x)$ denotes the logit of l_x and l_x^s denotes the l_x value in the standard life table. If in the model $\beta_1 = \beta_2 = \beta$, the model reduces to the four-parameter model proposed by Ewbank *et al.* (1983). When $\beta_1 = \beta_2 = \beta$ and c and $d \to 0$, the model reduces to the two-parameter Brass relational model. Also note that when $\alpha = 0$, $\beta_1 = \beta_2 = \beta = 1$, and c and $d = 0$, the model specification reduces to $\lambda(l_x) = \lambda(l_x^s)$ (i.e., the observed life table is the same as the standard life table).

In the present model, the α and β parameters have the same interpretations as in the two-parameter relational logit model. Changes in the α parameter shifts the l_x curve vertically. Changes in β cause a pivoting around the median age of the standard curve. The changes in the c parameter affect the steepness of the survival curve at the young ages (see Figure B.5a). Similarly changes in the d parameter affect the older ages (see Figure B.5b). A positive value of c increases the mortality (or decreases survival chances) at the young ages compared to the standard, and a negative value decreases the mortality (or increases survival chances). Similarly, negative values of d increase the mortality (decrease the survival chances) at older ages, and positive values of d decrease the mortality (increase survival chances) at older ages.

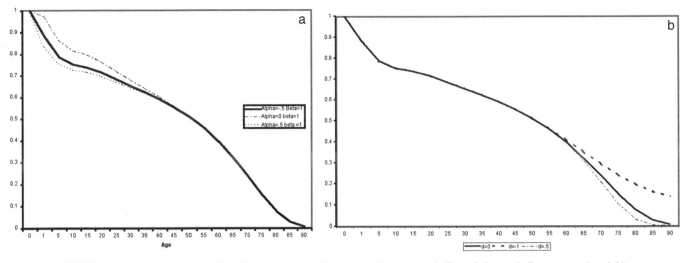

FIGURE B.5 Survival curves showing effect of changes in C parameter (graph a) and effect of changes in D parameter (graph b).

Fitting of the Five-Parameter Model

Because of the nonlinear nature of the model, iterative procedures are required to fit it to observed data. The iterative procedure "NLIN" in SAS (SAS Institute, 1997) was used to fit the model to the Tunisian data in Table B.15. The estimated parameter values are as follows:

Parameter	Estimate	Standard error
α	−1.7112	0.0117
β_1	1.3457	0.0952
β_2	1.0450	0.0373
c	1.8518	0.2136
d	0.0072	0.0400

The model fit indicated a sum of squares of the residuals of 0.00421 with 13 degrees of freedom and a corresponding extremely low residual mean square of 0.00032. Constraining $\beta_1 = \beta_2 = \beta$ reduces the model to the four-parameter model suggested by Ewbank *et al.* (1983). The fit of the four-parameter model yields a sum of the squares of the residuals of 0.00632 with a residual mean square of 0.00045. The difference in the sum of squares of residuals provides a one-degree-of-freedom test to see the improvement of the five-parameter model over the four-parameter model. In this example, the difference in the residual sum of squares is 0.00211. The test of the hypothesis, $\beta_1 = \beta_2 = \beta$, gives a value of 6.52 for the F-test statisticd with 1 and 13 degrees of freedom. In this case, the null hypothesis is rejected, favoring the five-parameter model.

The predicted values of l_x under the four- and five-parameter models as well as under the two-parameter model are given in Table B.16. The improvement in the fit of the five-parameter model over Brass's two-parameter model is clearly evident from the table. The five-parameter model shows better predicted values at the very young and very old ages.

TABLE B.16 Comparison of the Fitted l_x Values for the 1995 Tunisian Female Life Table under Five-, Four-, and Two-Parameter Models

		Predicted l_x		
Age	Observed l_x^1	Five-parameter model	Four-parameter model	Two-parameter model (Brass)
0	1.0000	1.0000	1.0000	1.0000
1	0.9728	0.9725	0.9734	0.9847
5	0.9664	0.9665	0.9662	0.9705
10	0.9636	0.9634	0.9628	0.9644
15	0.9615	0.9621	0.9614	0.9619
20	0.9588	0.9597	0.9589	0.9576
25	0.9558	0.9561	0.9552	0.9515
30	0.9522	0.9519	0.9510	0.9451
35	0.9477	0.9467	0.9462	0.9382
40	0.9412	0.9403	0.9402	0.9301
45	0.9312	0.9312	0.9320	0.9203
50	0.9183	0.9167	0.9199	0.9072
55	0.8997	0.8974	0.9009	0.8888
60	0.8674	0.8703	0.8727	0.8622
65	0.8230	0.8261	0.8266	0.8200
70	0.7417	0.7547	0.7522	0.7533
75	0.6334	0.6312	0.6252	0.6406
80	0.4542	0.4334	0.4279	0.4602
85	0.1918	0.1972	0.2002	0.2320

[1] Source: Table B.15.

OTHER PARAMETRIC MODELS

Modern computer power has facilitated fitting complex mathematical models to describe the age pattern of mortality. Three such models that have gained attention are briefly described here.

Additive Multicomponent Model

Helligman and Pollard (1980) proposed an additive multicomponent model to describe the age pattern of human mortality:

$$f(x) = A^{(x+B)^C} + De^{-E(\ln x - \ln F)^2} + \frac{GH^x}{1 + GH^x} \quad \text{(B.19)}$$

where $f(x)$ is the age-specific death rate at age x. The first component depicts infant and child mortality. The A parameter is the mortality at age 1, and B measures the difference in mortality between ages 0 and 1. An increase in the B value indicates convergence of the two mortality rates. The C parameter captures the decline in child mortality with age. The second component tracks mortality at young adulthood. The D parameter captures the intensity of mortality at very young adulthood, E captures the young adult mortality hump caused by accidents, and F captures the concentration of mortality in young adulthood. The third component describes mortality in older ages. The G parameter describes the level and the H parameter describes the shape of the old-age mortality pattern. The model is nonlinear and needs an iterative procedure to estimate the model parameters from data on age-specific death rates.

Multiexponential Model

Rogers and Little (1994) proposed a multicomponent exponential model to describe the age pattern of mortality. The specific model is as follows:

$$f(x) = a_0 + f_1(x) + f_2(x) + f_3(x) + f_4(x)$$

where $f(x)$ is the age-specific mortality rate, a_0 is a constant,

$$f_1(x) = a_1 e^{-\alpha_1 x} \quad \text{(a single exponential function)}$$

$$f_2(x) = a_2 e^{-\alpha_2(x-\mu_2) - e^{\lambda_2(x-\mu_2)}}$$

$$f_3(x) = a_3 e^{-\alpha_3(x-\mu_3) - e^{\lambda_3(x-\mu_3)}}$$

$$f_4(x) = a4 e^{-\alpha_4 x} \quad \text{(B.20)}$$

Note that $f_2(x)$ and $f_3(x)$ are double exponential distributions.

The first component describes childhood mortality and the last component describes mortality at older ages. The two middle components describe mortality at the middle ages, including the hump caused by accidental mortality.

Generalized De Moivre Function

Di Pino and Pirri (1998) suggested a generalized De Moivre function to describe the age pattern of mortality. The specific model is

$$\ln \frac{l_x}{1 - l_x} = a_0 + a_1 x + a_2 x^2 + a_3 x^3 + \ldots + a_k x^k \quad \text{(B.29)}$$

The right-hand side is a polynomial, that as the sum of a series of powers of age x. In practice it is found that a polynomial of degree 5 ($k = 5$) will fit the data well. The lower-power parameter influences the mortality of the young the most. The model is easy to fit to a set of data, and it does not require an iterative procedure.

CONCLUDING COMMENTS

This appendix presents several models that are used to describe age patterns of mortality. The empirically based ones such as the Coale-Demeny and the United Nations model life tables have seen widespread use in estimating demographic parameters from limited data. For the purposes of generating life tables for population projections where data are limited, any one of the models presented in this appendix can be used. The empirically based models may not always represent the mortality pattern of a country. On the other hand, some countries may not have the minimum data needed to estimate sophisticated relational models as well as the other parametric models.

References

Brass, W. 1964. "Uses of Census or Survey Data for Estimation of Vital Rates." *African Seminar on Vital Statistics*. Addis Ababa: U. N. Economic Commission for Africa.

Brass, W. 1971. "On the Scale of Mortality." In W. Brass (Ed.), *Biological Aspects of Demography*. London: Taylor & Francis: 69–110.

Brass, W., A. J. Coale, P. Demeny, D. F. Heisel, F. Lorimer, A. Rumaniuk, and E. van de Walle. 1968. *The Demography of Tropical Africa*. Princeton, NJ: Princeton University Press.

Coale, A. J., and P. Demeny. 1966. *Regional Model Life Tables and Stable Populations*. Princeton, NJ: Princeton University Press.

Coale, A. J., and P. Demeny. 1983. *With B. Vaughan. Regional Model Life Tables and Stable Populations*, 2nd ed. New York: Academic Press.

Demeny, P., and F. C. Shorter. 1968. *Estimating Turkish Mortality, Fertility and Age Structure*. Istanbul: Istanbul University, Statistics Institute.

Di Pino, A., and P. Pirri. 1998. "Analysis of Survival Functions by a Logistic Derivation Model: The 'Generalized de Moivre' Function." *Genus* LIV (3–4): 35–54.

Ewbank, D. C., J. C. Gomez de Leon, and M. A. Stoto. 1983. "A Reducible Four Parameter System of Model Life Tables." *Population Studies* 37: 105–127.

Gompertz, B. 1825. "On the Nature of the Function Expressive of the Law of Human Mortality. *Philos. Trans. R. Society* 115: 513–593.

Heligman, L., and J. H. Pollard. 1980. "The Age Pattern of Mortality." *The Journal of Institute of Actuaries* 10: 49–80.

Ledermann, S. 1969. "Nouvelles tables-type de mortalité." Travaux et documents, Cahier n.53. Paris: INED.

Ledermann, S., and J. Breas. 1959. "Les dimensions de la mortalité." *Population* 14 (4): 637–682.

Makeham, W. M. 1860. "On the Law of Mortality and the Construction of Annuity Tables." *Journal of Institute of Actuaries* 8: 301–310.

Merli. M. G. 1998. "Mortality in Vietnam, 1979–1989." *Demography* 35(3): 345–360.

Namboodiri, N. K. 1990. *Demographic Analysis: A Stochastic Approach.* San Diego, CA: Academic Press.

Rogers, A., and J. S. Little. 1994. "Parameterizing Age Patterns of Demographic Rates with the Multiexponential Model Schedules." *Mathematical Population Studies* 4: 175–195.

SAS Institute. 1997. *SAS/STAT Software: Changes and Enhancements through Release 6.12: The NLIN Procedure.* Cary, NC: SAS Institute.

United Nations. 1955. *Age and Sex Patterns of Mortality: Model Life Tables for Under developed Countries.* New York: United Nations.

United Nations. 1982. *Model Life Tables for Developing Countries.* New York: United Nations.

United Nations. 1983. *Manual X: Indirect Techniques for Demographic Estimation.* New York: United Nations.

United Nations. 1998. *Demographic Yearbook, 1996.* New York: United Nations.

Selected General Methods

D. H. JUDSON AND CAROLE L. POPOFF

This appendix treats a variety of topics concerned with methods of measurement and analysis. None is strictly demographic; yet all are applicable to many fields of demography. The methods and basic concepts presented are ones that the demographer will find useful regardless of his or her special subject interest, but they are especially pertinent for work in population estimates and projections.[1]

This appendix will proceed in the following order:

- The first section of this appendix will give an overview of sampling theory in demographic surveys and discuss both sampling and nonsampling error in surveys, and use of external information to add value to surveys, particularly Horvitz-Thompson estimation, poststratification, statistical matching, and synthetic estimation.
- The second and third sections describe standard methods for interpolating point and grouped data and curve fitting, and the general approach to parameterizing demographic models. Such methods are standard parts of the demographer's tool kit.
- The fourth section describes methods for adjusting distributions to marginal totals, both classical multiway adjustment methods and more modern loglinear methods. Such methods are frequently used in estimation contexts and when reconciling different estimation methods or data sources.
- The fifth section will present an overview of the growing role of computer models and databases in demographic research. In particular, the section discusses how file handling affects demographic analysis and common data configurations and describes the features of massive data

warehouses (also known as administrative records) for demographic work.
- The sixth section describes the features of and use of matrix methods in demography.
- The seventh section explores additional topics, such as microsimulations, system dynamics models, and regional demographic-economic models, that are relevant to the demographer's job, but for which space precludes a detailed exposition. This section will be necessarily brief on each specific topic.

SAMPLING, SAMPLING ERRORS, AND OTHER ERRORS IN SURVEYS

Sampling as an Alternative to "Complete" Data Collection

The basic principle that motivates the use of statistical sampling is that a large number of measurements taken poorly often yields less useful information than a small number of measurements taken well. A quintessential example is an event that occurred in the Office of Price Administration during World War II in the United States. At that time, rubber was an extremely important commodity for the war effort, but, because of the war, it was in short supply. The office attempted to send a survey to every automobile dealership in the United States, asking about automobile tires. As can be imagined, the response to this survey was sufficiently low that the estimates obtained by this "blanket survey" were extremely poor. The office instituted a sample, in which dealership data were vigorously pursued. By making sure that nonresponse was kept to a minimum and that data were recorded accurately, a better picture of the supply was obtained. Often, so-called complete data

---

[1] Spreadsheets and programs implementing the models described herein can be obtained from the authors.

collection is in fact less informative than a properly drawn and representative sample (Wallis and Roberts, 1962; Thompson, 1992).

Criteria for an Acceptable Sample Design

To draw acceptable inferences from the data collected from a sample, it is necessary that the sample have *measurable* reliability and that it be *efficient* and *practical*. The *measurability* requirement means that every member of the population must have a *known* probability of being selected in the sample; it is then possible to compute the reliability of the estimates made from the sample, using the sample data only. The *efficiency* requirement means that the sample design that is used should give the most reliable information possible, considering the time and money available. The *practicality* requirement means that it can be carried out, operationally, as specified. Adequate supervision and control are needed so that the methods specified are carried out correctly.

Variability in Surveys

Because a survey is based on a sample, the calculations (or estimates) generated from a particular sample design will differ from one sample to the next. If one took another sample at the same data, using differently randomly selected areas, households, establishments, or persons, one would obtain slightly different results from those based on the first sample. Moreover, if one took a second sample on the heels of the first, one would certainly obtain slightly different results than acquired from the first sample. There are two primary kinds of variability (or error) in sample results of interest: *sampling variability* refers to the variability caused only by sampling itself; *nonsampling variability* refers to the different responses repondents give over time, or limitations of the survey instrument itself, including question wording or varying patterns of nonresponse.

Sampling Variability

The sampling error of a sample survey can be measured in several ways. The first measure usually desired is the *variance* of the sample estimate. This is the average, over all possible samples, of the squared deviations of the estimates from their expected value. An estimate of the variance can be obtained from the sample survey data themselves. If there are nonsampling errors or the sample is biased, as is often the case, then the deviations are taken around the true value of the statistic and the measure is called the *mean square error (MSE)*. Typically, the variance is denoted σ^2 and the mean square error by MSE. Of these two measures, the MSE is more general, as illustrated by its formula. Suppose that

p is the value being estimated, and $\hat{p}$ is the estimator of p; then the MSE of $\hat{p}$ is given by:

$$
\begin{aligned}
MSE(\hat{p}) = E(\hat{p} - p)^2 &= E(\hat{p} - E(\hat{p}) + E(\hat{p}) - p)^2 \\
&= E(\hat{p} - E(\hat{p}))^2 + (E(\hat{p}) - p)^2 \qquad \text{(C.1)} \\
&= \operatorname{var}(\hat{p}) + bias(\hat{p})^2
\end{aligned}
$$

If $\hat{p}$ is unbiased, then the MSE is just the variance itself.

Nonsampling Variability and Error

In addition to the "error" of the estimates caused by sampling variability, there is another component of the total error in demographic data. *Nonsampling error* characterizes all surveys, whether sampling is used or not—including 100% surveys otherwise known as censuses. This component arises from mistakes made in the process of eliciting, recording, and processing the response of an individual unit in the surveyed population. Every operation in a census or sample survey, and every factor within an operation, may contribute to nonsampling error.

Because the nonsampling error arising from the respondent, in interaction with the interviewer and the questionnaire is more serious and less amenable to measurement than errors arising from other operations, it is often called response error. A typical example of response error arising from respondents is the tendency of persons in many countries to report their ages in years ending in zero and five (Ewbank, 1981). Often such response error requires special detection and smoothing methods; such methods are described in Chapter 7 and later in this appendix.[2]

An interviewer's tendency to change a respondent's answer to a question to conform more closely with his or her perception of the respondent's socioeconomic class is an example of response error arising from the interaction between respondent and interviewer. For example, in a working-class neighborhood, the interviewer may record total income as wage and salary income and fail to inquire about income other than wage and salary income (such as income from investments or property rent).

The most important feature of nonsampling error is that one often cannot reasonably assume that nonsampling error is the same across different respondent groups. As noted by Lessler and Kalsbeek (1992, p. 254), in the absence of any hard data on bias, the assumption is often made that although the measurements may be biased, the bias is the same for each subgroup, so that subgroup comparisons remain valid. This assumption can be very wrong and should only be made with extreme caution.

---

[2] Spreadsheets for performing detection and smoothing can be found at the U.S. Census Bureau, International Programs Center, at www.census.gov/ipc/www/pam.html.

Use of Internal and External Information to Add Value

As noted earlier, estimates derived from sample surveys will vary from the true population value because of both the sample itself and nonsampling errors. However, when extra information about the population is available, this information can be used to improve the survey estimates. The following section describes four methods for using extra information: the Horvitz-Thompson estimation theory (Horvitz and Thompson, 1952), poststratification, statistical matching, and synthetic estimation.

Horvitz-Thompson Theory

In any sampling plan where objects have nonequal probabilities of selection, a method for correcting for this nonequal probability must be devised. For example, if, in a sample survey, the sample design is such that households in rural areas are half as likely to be sampled as those in urban areas, then each sampled rural household actually represents twice as many potential respondents as an equivalent urban household. This intuition is the basis of Horvitz-Thompson (Horvitz and Thompson, 1952) sampling theory.

If a sample of size n is selected from a population of size N, each with equal probability n/N, then any total in the population can be estimated by multiplying the corresponding sample total by N/n. The quantity N/n is called the sampling weight or "raising" factor (Macro International, 1996) and, under equal probability sampling, corresponds to $1/p$, where p is the probability of selection. However, if selection probability varies across the i units, then the "raising" factor for the ith unit is $1/p_i$.

Consider estimating the mean of some quantity Y in the population. If each sampled unit responds with value Y_i, then the estimate of the population total is simply the sum over all responses:

$$\hat{Y} = \sum_{i=1}^{n} Y_i$$

where, as usual, the "hat" indicates that the calculated quantity is an estimate of a population parameter. However, when individual cases are sampled with unequal probability, the basic approach of Horvitz-Thompson is to weight the ith case by the inverse of its probability of selection, p_i. Thus, the Horvitz-Thompson estimator of the population total would be

$$\hat{Y} = \sum_{i=1}^{n} \frac{Y_i}{p_i} \qquad (C.2)$$

Consider what this implies: If a particular case is sampled with probability 1, then it adds its full value to the estimate; but if a particular case is sampled with probability $\frac{1}{2}$, then it adds twice its value to the estimate. This conforms to the intuition stated earlier: If a household has a $\frac{1}{2}$ chance of being selected, then because it was selected it represents two households, itself and the other household that was not selected. Hence, it is doubly weighted.

For fixed n and p_i known, and if p_{ij} is the probability that both unit i and unit j are included in the sample, the variance of the Horvitz-Thompson estimator is

$$Var(\hat{Y}) = \left[\sum_{i=1}^{n} \left(\frac{1 - p_i}{p_i} \right) Y_i^2 \right] + \sum_{i=1}^{n} \sum_{i \neq j} \left(\frac{p_{ij} - p_i p_j}{p_i p_j} \right) Y_i Y_j \qquad (C.3)$$

As noted by Thompson (1992, p. 49), if all the jointly included probabilities p_{ij} are greater than zero, an unbiased estimator of this variance is given by

$$\hat{Var}(\hat{Y}) = \sum_{i=1}^{n} \left(\frac{1}{p_i^2} - \frac{1}{p_i} \right) Y_i^2 + 2 \sum_{i=1}^{n} \sum_{i < j} \left(\frac{1}{p_i p_j} - \frac{1}{p_{ij}} \right) Y_i Y_j \qquad (C.4)$$

Thus, when the sample has known probabilities of selection and joint probabilities of selection, the researcher can always use this theory to estimate population means and the variance around those estimates. In cases where all units have equal probability of selection, the Horvitz-Thompson estimator reduces to the "usual" estimator. The strength of this method of estimation is that if the probability of selection can be known, it is an extremely general method of account for the sample design effects.

Poststratification to External Data

The Horvitz-Thompson theory is used to account for nonequal probability of selection. However, this does not account for nonsampling errors such as undercoverage of certain population segments in the original sample frame or response biases. To account for these factors, poststratification to external data or adjustment to independent "controls" is often used.

Effectively, poststratification has the effect of "upweighting" cases that, for one reason or another, are underrepresented in the sample, and "downweighting" cases that are overrepresented in the sample. But how is it determined whether some cases are over or underrepresented? Typically, the demographic characteristics of the sample survey are compared to estimated characteristics of those persons or households living in the comparable area. If a particular demographic group appears less often in the sample than it "should", on the basis of the external estimates, then that group is given a weight greater than 1. If that group appears more often in the sample than it "should," then it is given a weight less than 1. The poststratification estimator of a population total is then

$$\hat{Y}_{ps} = \sum_{i=1}^{n} w_i Y_i \qquad (C.5)$$

where w_i is the poststratification weight for the ith case. Note that if all weights are 1.0, then the poststratification estimator is the same as the usual estimator.

Note that postratification and unequal probability of selection can be incorporated simultaneously by including both weighting to external data via w_i and sampling weights via p_i. It is conceptually important, however, to maintain the distinction between them because they are intended to deal with different things. As noted by Lohr (1999, p. 115), post-stratification can be risky. One can obtain arbitrarily small variances if one chooses the strata after examining the data, just as one can always obtain statistically significant results if one decides on null and alternative hypotheses after looking at the data. Poststrata should be specified before examining the data.

Statistical Matching

A modern approach to adding value to a survey is to use statistical matching to add donated data to the existing data set. It has found particular application in the area of microsimulation (Cohen, 1991), which will be described later. Suppose the researcher has two populations, labeled the "target" population and the "donor" population. The target population has a collection of variables unique to it, labeled $\vec{Z}_1$. Both populations have a collection of common variables, which are labeled $\vec{X}_1$ for the target database and $\vec{X}_2$ for the donor database. Finally, the donor population has a collection of variables unique to it, which are labeled $\vec{Y}_2$. (When referring to the Y values in the target database, label their $\vec{Y}_1$.) The researcher takes samples from each population using some probability sampling mechanism (while this must be taken into account in practice, it is not important to this ex-position). Assume that the sample size of the target database is N_1, and the sample size of the donor database is N_2. To refer to the ith case in the target population, subscript the variables $\vec{Z}_1$, and $\vec{X}_1$ and $\vec{X}_2$; i.e. $\vec{Z}_{1i}$ refers to the variables unique to the target database for the ith case, while $\vec{X}_{1j}$ refers to the variables common to both databases, but for the jth case in the donor database.

With this terminology in mind, suppose that one wishes to add some variable Y from the donor population database to the target population database. The problem is to impute values for a variable that is missing in the target data set, but exists in the donor data set, i.e., to add value to the target data set. To simulate the variation in Y values that occurs in the donor population as closely as possible, an individual unique donor amount is found for each record rather than using an average or a simple distribution. The problem may be thought to be analogous to constructing a pseudo-control group for an experimental design study when a random assignment between treatment and control groups is not possible (Rubin, 1979). It is also analogous to "imputation" methods—estimating a response when it was not given in a survey.

There are essentially two methods for finding "donors" from one data set for the missing variable Y in the target data set. One method is to employ some distance-measure algorithm typically used in clustering techniques to find the "nearest neighbor" or single unique donor in the donor database, then set the value of the missing value Y in the target database equal to some function of the amount from the donor. (It is a "function" of the donor amount because there is additional uncertainty associated with the amount the donor should give to the target.) Another method is to employ a multiple regression model $\hat{Y} = \vec{X}\vec{\beta}$ to generate the expected value $\hat{Y}_2$ of the variable of interest from the donor data set; calculate the expected value $\hat{Y}_1$ for each record in the target data set; perform a simple match using a distance measure on each estimated value. Finally, set the value of the missing variable equal to some function of the actual amount recorded for the donor. Each of these methods uses a set of variables common to both data sets that are believed to be reliable indicators of the missing variable. For example, if the missing variable is the value of the person's occupied house, a set of reliable indicators might include household income, persons per household (as a proxy for number of bedrooms), and some set of neighborhood characteristics.

Statistical matching algorithms can be *constrained* or *unconstrained*. In *unconstrained* matching, each member of the target data set must appear in the final, matched data, but it is not required that each member of the donor data set appear; in addition, a donor record can be used more than one time. In *constrained* matching, either (1) all records from both files must appear on the final data set, replicated if necessary, or (2) donors can be used only one time each. For the purpose of illustrating a statistical match, the next section compares two unconstrained matching algorithms: a nearest-neighbor centroid method and a multiple regression model-based method (e.g., Rubin, 1986).

Nearest-Neighbor Centroid Method

In the nearest-neighbor centroid method, the centroid of a cluster (the set of indicator variables) is the average point in the multidimensional space defined by the variables chosen for matching. The difference—for example, simple or squared Euclidean distance between the two clusters—is determined as the difference between centroids. Standardized variables are used to mitigate different magnitudes of measure for each variable. The Mahalanobis distance is a standardized form of Euclidean distance wherein data are standardized by scaling responses in terms of standard deviations, and adjustments are made for intercorrelations between the variables. Using the centroid technique, each recipient would be paired to an unique donor based on the minimum Mahalanobis distance (Hair *et al.*, 1995).

Model-Based Method

The model-based method is also known as predictive mean matching (Ingram *et al.*, 2000; Rubin, 1986). Multiple regression modeling was described earlier in this section. In this technique, the researcher uses multiple regression to find the expected value of the variable of interest, then calculates the expected value for each record in both data sets. Then he or she performs a simple match using a distance measure on each estimated value and finally sets the value of the missing variable equal to some function of the actual amount recorded for the donor. Using this technique, the match would be performed on one variable, the expected value of each case under a regression model. To pick the minimum distance, the distance measure should be either Euclidean, Squared Euclidean or City-Block (Manhattan) distance (absolute value) as they eliminate negative distance values. For the purposes of this example, this section shall use squared Euclidean distance as the distance measure to minimize in the selection of donors.

Uses of Matched Data

The two most important criticisms of statistical matching are that (1) it relies on strong assumptions about the data, namely, that Y and Z are conditionally independent given the X data, and (2) because additional variability is not incorporated into the match, the matched data set may have lower variance than implied in the donor population. While results are often reasonably close (e.g., Ingram *et al.*, 2000), they can still fail statistical tests to determine that the distributions are the same (e.g., a chi-square test on a cross-tabulation). In simulations, several researchers (e.g., Draper, 1992; Kadane, 1978; Paass, 1985) have noted that often the statistically matched file does not reproduce the desired distributional properties well. However, as Cohen (1991) noted, the potential for novel uses of statistically matched data, particularly in microsimulations and imputation situations where direct data collection is not available, continues to generate research interest in the technique (e.g., Moriarty and Scheuren, 2001).

Synthetic Methods of Estimation

When one takes a survey designed to construct an estimate at a high geographic level (e.g., a state or province), various clients often desire to have similar estimates at lower geographic level (e.g., counties or cities). Often, the sample design or sample size will not support direct estimates. Either the sample size is too small to make reliable estimates, or the sample design itself omitted certain lower geographic levels, thus precluding direct estimates in these places.

However, there are methods that allow one to use higher-level survey data to generate lower-level estimates by "borrowing information" obtainable at the lower geographic level and using relationships between the obtainable information and the quantity one wishes to estimate. This methodology is known as *synthetic estimation*. Similar ideas

can be constructed by regression techniques such as the "empirical bayes" method employed by the U.S. Census Bureau in their Small Area Income and Poverty Estimates program (Citro *et al.*, 1997; U.S. Census Bureau, 2000). The basic description of a synthetic estimate is given in Gonzalez (1973, p. 33); see also Chattopadhyay *et al.*, 1999; Gonzalez and Hoza, 1978; Levy and French, 1977a, 1977b; and Siegel, 2002 (pp. 497–502). An estimate is obtained for a larger area; then the estimate is used to derive estimates for the subareas, on the assumption that, within specific groups, the small areas have the same characteristics as the larger areas.

A simple, archetypal situation is illustrated by the use of the public use microdata sample (PUMS) from the decennial census. This file is a 1% or 5% sample of households from the complete census record. It is a microdata file—that is, a file with virtually complete information on the household and the individuals in the household. Because it is a microdata file, it is potentially extremely useful for estimating the characteristics of certain kinds of persons and households. However, to protect confidentiality, the only geographic identifiers provided for the household are for areas with quite large populations. This means that if one wishes to estimate a smaller area's characteristics, say, the characteristics of the persons living in households in a small county, he or she simply does not have data from the PUMS file.

At this point enters the notion of synthetic estimation. The researcher uses the PUMS data at a higher level of geographical aggregation, ties them to data that can be obtained at the lower level of aggregation, and makes an estimate of the characteristics for the lower-level area. For example, if the researcher wishes to estimate the average income of a small county, she or he might have at hand the number of housing units of the four basic types (single family detached, single family attached, multifamily, and mobile home) from the local tax assessor's office. If he or she calculates the average income for households in each type of housing unit, using the higher-level PUMS data, she or he can then apply these averages to each type of housing unit in the county to derive a synthetic estimate of the average income in the county.

Such an approach rests, of course, on the assumption that there is some fairly stable relationship between the housing unit and the income of the household(s) residing there. Without that stable relationship, the estimate would have little validity. In general, because the relationships are not exact, researchers have found that such estimates are biased. However, if they apply the sample results to any particular group, they typically obtain unbiased estimates, but estimates with high sampling variability because the sample sizes for subgroups are so small (see, e.g., Heeringa, 1993). The research and analytic question at this point is which kind of "error", bias or variance, is more bearable.

How does this apply to adding value to survey data? First, later, define the phrase *formal research data*[3] to describe results or estimates in which the analyst has a great deal of confidence and the phrase *target database*[4] to describe data in which the analyst either has limited confidence, or in which the analyst does not have the particular data item of interest and onto which the analyst wishes to place the formal research's information. To summarize the procedure, the analyst wishes to use the information in the target database as an indicator variable to "project" the information obtained by formal research onto the target database. The target data will be the data used to make the projection; the formal research estimates will be "projected." Although the technique is most commonly used for small area estimation, instead of speaking only of larger and smaller "areas," one can think in terms of different sources of information and project from the one kind of group estimate onto other kinds of group estimates.

Following Gonzalez (1973), and Gonzalez and Hoza (1978); but modifying terminology to generalize to this new context, we wish to estimate a characteristic x in a group from our target database. Assume that there are N cases in the formal research database and A cases in the target database. Identify G subgroups of the population (in both databases) and index the groups $j = 1, 2, \ldots, G$; the subgroups must be exclusive and exhaustive. Further assume that one can identify C cells of the population and index the cells $i = 1, 2, \ldots, C$. Presume that for each cell i and group j, from the formal research database there is an estimate x_{ij}. From the latter we can also obtain estimates $x_{.j}$ for $j = 1, 2, \ldots, G$. Where the "dot" indicates that the sum is taken over all cells, so that $x_{.j} = \sum_{i=1}^{C} x_{ij}$.

A synthetic estimate is desired for the ith cell, which is contained in the population defined by the formal research database and in the target database. From the target database, one can calculate proportions that each group represents of the population—that is, the ith cell and the jth group in the population represents a proportion—and

$$\sum_{i=1}^{C} p_{ij} = 1 \quad \text{and} \quad \sum_{j=1}^{C} p_{ij} = 1$$

Finally, the analyst wishes to obtain a synthetic estimate of x for the ith cell, denoted x_i^*. This estimate is defined as

---

[3] Examples of "formal research" are a population survey performed with care; a sample of an administrative-records database for which we have verified the information with great care; or a carefully controlled census.

[4] The term applies to any database in which we have limited confidence and do not wish to use in a "count-based" or "direct" way. It could be an administrative-records database of uncertain coverage or quality, a compilation of age-race-sex-and-Hispanic-origin estimates, as we describe later; or a census itself (if the characteristic we wish to estimate is not measured in the census).

$$x_i^* = \sum_{j=1}^{G} p_{ij} x_{.j} \tag{C.6}$$

Thus, this method uses p_{ij} to project the characteristic of the ith cell from the population defined in the formal research database to the ith cell in the target database.

What assumptions are made in this estimate? Perhaps the most important one is that the $x_{.j}$ estimate for the jth group does not vary across the i cells in the formal research data. While this is a simple method for estimation, this assumption has proven to be problematic in synthetic estimates in actual use. Because the method applies averages to obtain a synthetic estimate, it does not account for variation (or heterogeneity) in the cells. As the borrowed information database moves further away from the formal research database (for example, if the formal research takes place at a specific date and the analysts makes estimates beyond this date; or if the formal research applies to a population that is dissimilar from the target population), the procedure becomes move problematic. This may lead to a biased estimate. Sarndal (1984) identified the bias in the estimator as

$$bias(x_i^*) = \sum_{i=1}^{G} N_{ij}(\bar{x}_{i.} - \bar{x}_{ij}) \tag{C.7}$$

where

N_{ij} = the number of cases in the ith cell and jth group
$\bar{x}_{i.}$ = the mean of the characteristic of interest for the ith cell, this average being taken over all groups
$\bar{x}_{ij}$ = the mean of the characteristic of interest for the ith cell and jth group

As Sarndal (1984) indicated, the bias of the synthetic estimator is zero if the mean for the ith cell is equal to the mean of the ith cell in the jth group. The hope in synthetic estimation, therefore, is that this quantity will be close to zero. Wachter and Freedman (2000) noted that, in the presence of heterogeneity within cells, increasing the sample size of the formal research database will not reduce the bias: The heterogeneity does not go away just because of a reduction in sampling variability.

To attempt to avoid the bias problem, an extension of this method was tested by Gonzalez and Hoza (1978) in which they used the synthetic estimate as an independent variable in a regression-based estimating method (leading to the term, *regression-synthetic estimate*). Heeringa (1993) discussed the possibility of developing composite estimators that are a weighted combination of the formal-research results (in his case, sample survey or design-based estimates) and the administrative-records results (in his case, the synthetic estimator). Both of these extensions are possible, and the reader should consult the extensive research publications for more details.

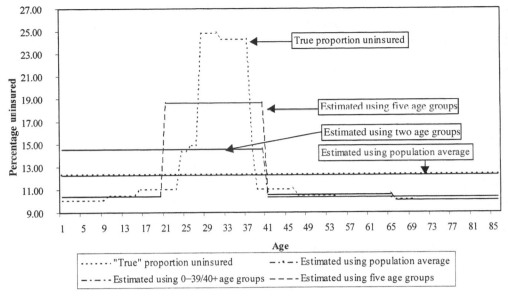

FIGURE C.1   Proportion uninsured across the age span: Hypothetical distribution illustrating advantage of finer detail in synthetic estimation.

An application of the synthetic methodology to generate estimates of the number of uninsured persons for counties in the United States was presented in Sigmund, Judson, and Popoff (1998), for Oregon, and in Popoff, Fadali, and Judson (2000) for Nevada. In each case, the state had state data on the uninsured; in Oregon, data were obtained from the Oregon Population Survey and in Nevada, from the U.S. Current Population Survey. In both states, age-race-sex-and-Hispanic-origin estimates were available for single years of age for counties. (Other specific examples of the use of synthetic methods for projecting information from one database to another can be found in Hogan, 2000; Levy and French, 1977a, 1977b; Reder, 1994; and Siegel, 2002).

The basic equation for synthetic estimation is

$$\hat{x}_{a,r,s,h} = P_{a,r,s,h} \cdot \hat{\mu}_{a,r,s,h}, \qquad (C.8)$$

where

$a \in \{0, \dots, 85+\}$ for ages

$r \in \{W, B, API, AI\}$ for whites, blacks, Asian and Pacific Islanders, and American Indians

$s \in \{M, F\}$ for the sexes

$h \in \{H, \sim H\}$ for household and nonhousehold population

$P_{a,r,s,h}$ = the number of persons of age a, race r, sex s, and ethnicity h

$\hat{\mu}_{a,r,s,h}$ = the proportion of persons of age a, race r, sex s, and ethnicity h that have the health-related characteristic of interest (in this case, who are uninsured), $\hat{\mu}_{a,r,s,h} \in [0, 1]$

$\hat{x}_{a,r,s,h}$ = the number of persons of age a, race r, sex s, and ethnicity h that have the health-related characteristic of interest (in this case, who are uninsured)

Thus, one uses the known age/race/sex/Hispanic *number*, and an estimated group-specific *proportion* who are uninsured, to estimate the *number* of uninsured persons of the specific group. The reduced form of synthetic estimation is, of course, to multiply an overall population by an overall proportion to get an overall number. Again, we use the "dot" notation to describe this method in this framework. For any variable $y_{a,r,s,h}$, we define: $y_{a.,s,h} = \sum_{r} y_{a,r,s,h}$. Define other sums similarly if a, s, or h are "dotted"; that is, when a subscript is "dotted," it merely indicates that one should sum over all elements of that subscript or, using more informal language, "collapse" that margin.

Using $P_{a,r,s,h}$ as an example, the total population of an area is equivalent to "collapsing" all margins, or

$$\text{Total population} = P_{.,.,.,.} = \sum_{a} \sum_{r} \sum_{s} \sum_{h} P_{a,r,s,h} \qquad (C.9)$$

If one wishes to multiply the total population by some overall uninsured proportion in the population, express this notion as

$$\text{Total population uninsured} = \hat{x}_{.,.,.,.} = P_{.,.,.,.} \times \hat{\mu}_{.,.,.,.} \qquad (C.10)$$

However, the synthetic methodology goes beyond this simple notion and instead makes the multiplication on a cell-by-cell basis.[5] Figure C.1 illustrates the advantage of

---

[5] The equation $\hat{x}_{.,.,.,.} = P_{.,.,.,.} \cdot \hat{\mu}_{.,.,.,.}$ implies that one is "summing first, then multiplying"; the synthetic method reverses the order: One "multiplies first, then sums" over the individual cells. The two methods are not equivalent.

making estimates by individual ARSH cells. For the purposes of this illustration, assume that the population can be broken into five age groups, 0 to 19, 20 to 39, 40 to 64, 64 to 79, and 80+. Further assume that 12% of the total population is uninsured. However, this proportion is not distributed uniformly across the age groups. This figure illustrates why breaking the population into finer groups must necessarily generate more correct estimates. Identify the dotted line in the figure as the "true" proportion uninsured for single years of age.

Now, suppose one wishes to use only the proportion uninsured for the total population, 12%, to make an estimate of the number uninsured. This proportion is dramatically incorrect for the age groups that deviate from this average, as identified by Sarndal's bias equation. A similar argument applies to the estimate using only two age groups, and as can be seen, using five age groups improves the estimate, although without the full original age detail the estimate will not be as good as achievable with age detail.

When these three synthetic estimates are compared to the (hypothetical) true data, the mean of absolute errors (estimated proportion minus true proportion by age, divided by 86 age groups) goes down as more detail is added to the synthetic computations. For example, using only the population average as the estimate, the mean absolute error is .061, while using two age groups to make the estimate reduces the mean absolute error to .049, and using five age groups to make the estimate reduces the mean absolute error to .03.

The advantage of the synthetic technique is that it is broadly applicable and, with the appropriate information in the target database, very flexible. Its disadvantage is that it does not account for heterogeneity within estimation cells; hence it has the bias noted earlier.

Connections between These Methods

Note that all of these techniques could be used together: For example, one might have a sample survey with probability weights, poststratify it to independent population estimates, then use the survey to generate a synthetic estimate at lower geographic levels. Of course, other combinations of techniques are possible as well.

INTERPOLATION OF POINT DATA

Introduction

Some Definitions

Interpolation is narrowly defined as the art of inferring intermediate values within a given series of data by use of a mathematical formula or a graphic procedure. Extrapolation is the art of inferring values that go beyond the given

series of data. Many of the techniques used for interpolation are suitable also for extrapolation; hence, the term interpolation is often used to refer to both types of inference. Broadly considered, interpolation encompasses mathematical and graphic devices not only for estimating inter-mediate or external values in a series (e.g., annual population estimates from decennial counts, survivors in a life table for single ages from survivors at every fifth age) but also for subdividing grouped data into component parts (e.g., figures for single years of age from data for 5-year age groups) and for inferring rates for subgroups from rates for broad groups (e.g., birthrates by duration of marriage). Typically, these devices reproduce, or are consistent with, the given values. In this case we say that the fit is exact. In other cases, modified interpolation formulas are used and the interpolated series does not pass through the original values or maintain the original group totals. Then, we say that the fit is approximate.

Interpolation is, in a sense, a form of estimation, but normally "interpolation" relates only to those forms of estimation that involve the direct application of mathematical or graphic devices to observed data. Sometimes, however, it is used loosely to include some forms of estimation involving a simple use of some external series of data suggestive of the pattern or trend in the range of interpolation. A principal type of "interpolation" of this kind is interpolation by prorating. We discuss this method later.

Though there is frequent need for interpolated estimates in demographic work, the degree of precision required by the user in practice or actually supported by the data is often too low to justify use of anything more than the more simple forms of interpolation. Indeed, for some purposes demographic data could satisfactorily be interpolated by running a smooth line by hand through a set of plotted points. For others, complex methods of interpolation are essential. Sometimes, however, where highly complex methods of interpolation appear necessary, the problem may be that the initial data are too defective or the number and spacing of the observations are inadequate.

Interpolation by mathematical formula has the quality of imputing a regularity or smoothness to the given series of data or even imposing these characteristics on the data. The regularity imputed or imposed may be unrealistic, however. There are often true fluctuations in population growth or in the age distribution due to past variations in births, deaths, and migration, especially if there have been wars, epidemics, population transfers, refugee movements, and so on. Interpolation may usefully serve to adjust defective data, even though some real fluctuations are removed, or to eliminate abnormalities from a series, such as those due to war, when the underlying pattern or trend is wanted.

This section first considers the methods of interpolating "point" values in a series, such as a time series; and among these we consider first those methods that can be employed to fit the given data exactly. These methods include polynomial interpolation, use of some types of exponential functions, osculatory interpolation, and use of spline functions.

Polynomial Interpolation

General Form of Equation

Polynomial interpolation is interpolation where the series is assumed to conform to an equation of the general type, $y = a + bx + cx^2 + dx^3 \ldots$. More or fewer terms may be used. As is well known, the equation $y = a + bx$ is a straight line, or linear equation, which can be passed through any two given points. The equation $y = a + bx + cx^2$ is a quadratic, or parabola, which can be passed through any three given points. The equation $y = a + bx + cx^2 + dx^3$ is a cubic, which can be passed through any four given points. More generally, a polynomial equation of the nth degree can be passed through $n + 1$ given points. Although one has decided to fit a polynomial of higher degree to the observed data and a polynomial of the nth degree will give an exact fit for $n + 1$ observations, one must still decide how many observations to use. The choice of the degree of the polynomial would depend on the nature of the data to be interpolated. Usually, the simplest equation that describes the data reasonably well and gives a smooth series is the one wanted. The criterion of a smooth fit of the given data normally requires use of a higher-degree equation than a straight line. Greater smoothness would normally be achieved by employing at least two observations before, and two observations after, the point of interpolation. This would seem to call for at least 4-point interpolation by a third-degree polynomial, where possible, but often 3-point or even 2-point interpolation will give about the same results.

In what follows, we will need symbols for given points. The symbol $f(a)$ means the value of the function when x equals a, $f(b)$ the value of the function when x equals b, and so forth. Hence, the symbol $f(a)$ will be the observed value of the y ordinate for the abscissa[6] $x = a$. The symbol $f(b)$ will be the observed value of $f(b)$ for $x = b$, and so on. The symbol $f(x)$ will be the desired interpolated value of the function f for any x.

Methods of Application

Polynomials that pass through the given data may be fitted in several different ways operationally while produc-

ing the identical results. One is by general solution of the polynomial equation and derivation of the values of the constants a, b, c, d, and so on; another is by use of interpolation coefficients; still another is by sequential linear interpolation; and a fourth is by use of "differences." Usually in polynomial interpolation by exact fit, the method involving the general solution of the polynomial equation is not employed because it is too cumbersome to perform "by hand." However, with the advent of computational tools, some computationally intensive forms of interpolation have become popular. One, cubic spline interpolation, will be described in detail with a computational example later in this section.

Waring's Formula

The formulas for polynomial interpolation can be set forth in the form of linear compounds—that is, as the sum of the products of certain coefficients or multipliers and certain given values. The Waring formula, also known as the Lagrange formula or the Waring-Lagrange formula, is used to derive the multipliers to interpolate for the $f(x)$ value corresponding to a given x value. The Waring formula for interpolating between four points by a polynomial, (i.e., for fitting a cubic) is as follows:

$$f(x) = f(a)\frac{(x-b)(x-c)(x-d)}{(a-b)(a-c)(a-d)}$$
$$+ f(b)\frac{(x-a)(x-c)(x-d)}{(b-a)(b-c)(b-d)}$$
$$+ f(c)\frac{(x-a)(x-b)(x-d)}{(c-a)(c-b)(c-d)} \quad \text{(C.11)}$$
$$+ f(d)\frac{(x-a)(x-b)(x-c)}{(d-a)(d-b)(d-c)}$$

This is equivalent to the polynomial $y = a + bx + cx^2 + dx^3$ passing through the four points $f(a)$, $f(b)$, $f(c)$, and $f(d)$ to derive $f(x)$. The points do not have to be equally spaced. By the formula, a particular value of (x) can be obtained from given values of $f(a)$, $f(b)$, $f(c)$, and $f(d)$.

The formula is especially suitable for computing the coefficients or "multipliers" to be applied to the $f(a)$, $f(b)$, $f(c)$, and $f(d)$ values to obtain $f(x)$. These multipliers may be used again and again so long as a y value on the same x abscissa is being sought and there are four given points spaced in the same way. In this way, for example, the same multipliers may be used for all the age-sex groups in a distribution or for all the states in a country to secure interpolated values at the same date. The multipliers for any particular interpolation formula add to 1.00.

Similarly, the formula

---

[6] As an aid to explanation, in a cartesian two-way graph of y against x, the "abscissa" is often referred to as the "x-axis" and the "ordinate" is often referred to as the "y-axis."

$$f(x) = f(a)\frac{(x-b)(x-c)}{(a-b)(a-c)} + f(b)\frac{(x-a)(x-c)}{(b-a)(b-c)}$$
$$+ f(c)\frac{(x-a)(x-b)}{(c-a)(c-b)} \qquad \text{(C.12)}$$

is equivalent to the polynomial $y = a + bx + cx^2$, a parabola passing through three points $f(a)$, $f(b)$, and $f(c)$. This is Waring's 3-point formula. By this formula, $f(x)$ can be obtain from given values of $f(a)$, $f(b)$, and $f(c)$. Extension to more points or fewer points should be obvious from an inspection of Formulas (C.11) and (C.12).

Suppose the population in 1980 is Pa, the population in 1990 is Pb, the population in 2000 is Pc, and one desires to use 3-point interpolation to estimate the population in 1995. Then,

$$\text{Population in 1995} = f(1995)$$

$$= \text{Pa}\frac{(1995-1990)(1995-2000)}{(1980-1990)(1980-2000)}$$

$$+ \text{Pb}\frac{(1995-1980)(1995-2000)}{(1990-1980)(1990-2000)}$$

$$+ \text{Pc}\frac{(1995-1980)(1995-1990)}{(2000-1980)(2000-1990)}$$

$$= \text{Pa}\frac{(5)(-5)}{(-10)(-20)}$$

$$+ \text{Pb}\frac{(15)(-5)}{(10)(-10)} \qquad \text{(C.13)}$$

$$+ \text{Pc}\frac{(15)(5)}{(20)(10)}$$

$$= -.125\text{Pa} + .750\text{Pb} + .375\text{Pc}$$

The reader should note that the computational work could have been simplified if, instead of using dates like 1980, 1990, 1995, and 2000, x (representing 1995) had been taken as "0" and the other dates as -3, -1, and $+1$, for 1980, 1990 and 2000, respectively. (The simplified recodes come by noting that 1980 is three units of 5 years each before 1995, 1990 is one unit of 5 years before 1995, and 2000 is one unit of 5 years past 1995.) Accordingly,

$$f(x) = f(0) = \text{Pa}\frac{(1)(-1)}{(-2)(-4)} + \text{Pb}\frac{(3)(-1)}{(2)(-2)} + \text{Pc}\frac{(3)(1)}{(4)(2)} \quad \text{(C.14)}$$

$$= -.125\text{Pa} + .750\text{Pb} + .375\text{Pc}$$

The a, b, c (and so forth) values may be recoded in any desired way so long as they maintain the same relative values. Thus, they can be multiplied or divided by a constant, and the differences between them can be divided by a constant without any effect on the results.

Aitken's Iterative Procedure

Aitken's (1932) iterative procedure is a system of successive linear interpolations equivalent to interpolation by a polynomial of any desired degree.[7] It is especially suitable for use with desk calculators or electronic computers.(C.11)

Waring's 2-point formula,

$$f(x) = f(a)\frac{(x-b)}{(a-b)} + f(b)\frac{(x-a)}{(b-a)} \qquad \text{(C.15)}$$

can be rewritten as

$$f(x) = \frac{f(a)(b-x) - f(b)(a-x)}{(b-x) - (a-x)} \qquad \text{(C.16)}$$

which is an expression that will appear in Aitken's procedure as outlined next. Aitken's system is set up in the following basic format for interpolation between four given points for the value of $f(x)$:

Given ordinates	Computational stages			Proportionate parts
	(1)	(2)	(3)	
$f(a)$				$(a - x)$
$f(b)$	$f(x; a, b)$			$(b - x)$
$f(c)$	$f(x; a, c)$	$f(x; a, b, c)$		$(c - x)$
$f(d)$	$f(x; a, d)$	$f(x; a, b, d)$	$f(x; a, b, c, d)$	$(d - x)$

Only the first two lines would be used for 2-point or linear interpolation, and there would be just one computational stage. The first three lines and two computational stages would be used for 3-point interpolation. Additional lines and computational stages are used as required for more points. As many points as desired can be used. The first column, "given ordinates," symbolizes the given data (i.e., the four observations). The "proportionate parts" in the extreme right-hand column are differences between the given abscissa and the one for which the interpolation is wanted. The abscissa values may be transformed into simplest terms in order to reduce the calculations, as in the case of the Waring formula.

The entries in computational stage 1 are each calculated by computing diagonal cross-products, "differencing" them, and dividing by the difference between the proportionate parts, as follows:

$$f(x; a, b) = \frac{f(a)(b-x) - f(b)(a-x)}{(b-x) - (a-x)} \qquad \text{(C.17)}$$

$$f(x; a, c) = \frac{f(a)(c-x) - f(c)(a-x)}{(c-x) - (a-x)} \qquad \text{(C.18)}$$

and

[7] Note: Other assumptions are possible.

$$f(x;a,d) = \frac{f(a)(d-x) - f(d)(a-x)}{(d-x) - (a-x)} \quad \text{(C.19)}$$

Each of the expressions $f(x; a, b)$, $f(x; a, c)$, $f(x; a, d)$, and so on is an estimate of $f(x)$ obtained by linear interpolation or extrapolation of $f(a)$ and one of the subsequent $f(b)$, $f(c)$, or $f(d)$ values. The general process of successive linear interpolations is repeated for computational stage (2), but this time we use the results of computational stage 1 and their associated diagonal multipliers. Thus,

$$f(x;a,b,c) = \frac{f(x;a,b)(c-x) - f(x;a,c)(b-x)}{(c-x) - (b-x)} \quad \text{(C.20)}$$

and

$$f(x;a,b,d) = \frac{f(x;a,b)(d-x) - f(x;a,d)(b-x)}{(d-x) - (b-x)} \quad \text{(C.21)}$$

Suppose, for example, one wants to interpolate the population of an area in 1975, given data on population in 1960, 1970, 1980, and 1990. The calculations are summarized in Table C.1. Table C.1 can be easily constructed in a spreadsheet; likewise, computation can easily proceed by hand or with a hand calculator. Our final interpolated figure for 1975, 40,002, is the result of computational stage 3. The given observations need not be equally spaced as they are in the example. Also, their order of arrangement in the table can be mixed; that is, they do not have to follow a prescribed order. This interpretation of the results assumes, however, that the given data are not too widely spaced for a reliable result. If the given data are widely spaced and have a high degree of curvature in the region of interpolation, none of the interpolation procedures, including Aitken's, will yield a reliable result: Observations closer to the desired abscissa must be used. In interpolations of demographic data, the computational stages should probably stop at about the point where it is clear that there is no longer a clear convergence from stage to stage.

Aitken's iterative procedure involves a relatively large amount of work to arrive at a single result if many observations are used, and the same amount of work must be repeated each time another interpolation is carried out. It is

efficient to use this procedure, therefore, when only a few interpolations at most are required. In contrast, it is more efficient to use the Waring formula when many interpolations are being carried out for the same abscissa or x-value, especially ones based on relatively few observations. Under these circumstances, the coefficients, once derived, can be used over and over again.

Osculatory Interpolation

One of the chief difficulties met in adjusting rough data by the usual (single polynomial) interpolation formulas, as described earlier, is that at points where two interpolation curves meet, there are sudden breaks in the values of the first-order differences. Various methods have been employed to effect a smooth junction of the interpolations made for one range of data with the interpolations made for the next (adjacent) range. Osculatory interpolation is a method that accomplishes that purpose. It involves combining two overlapping polynomials into one equation. One of the polynomials begins sooner and ends sooner than the other, and the interpolations are limited to the overlapping parts. The second of the two polynomials in the first range then becomes the first polynomial in the second range. The use of one polynomial in common for each pair of successive ranges permits a continuous welding of results from range to range. The two overlapping polynomials are generally forced to have specified conditions in common at the beginning and at the end of the range in which interpolation is desired. The specified conditions may include a common ordinate, a common tangent (slope), or a common radius of curvature, usually accomplished by making the first derivative or the first two derivatives equal for the two polynomials.

Illustrative Formulas

Although osculatory interpolation encompasses a wide variety of possible equations, only a few have seen much use. This section considers specifically Sprague's fifth-difference equation, Karup-King's third-difference equation, Beers' six-term formulas, and cubic spline interpolation.

Sprague's Fifth-Difference Equation

The fifth-difference equation developed by Sprague is expressed in terms of leading differences (Sprague, 1881). The equation is based on two polynomials of the fourth degree, forced to have a common ordinate, a common tangent, and a common radius of curvature at Y_{n+2} and at Y_{n+3}:

$$y_{n+2+x} = \frac{(x+2)}{1!}\Delta y_n + \frac{(x+2)(x+1)}{2!}\Delta^2 y_n + \frac{(x+2)(x+1)x}{3!}\Delta^3 y_n$$

$$+ \frac{(x+2)(x+1)x(x-1)}{4!}\Delta^4 y_n + \frac{x^3(x-1)(5x-7)}{4!}\Delta^5 y_n$$

$$\text{(C.22)}$$

TABLE C.1   Illustration of Aitken's Iterative Procedure

Interpolation date		1975			
		Computational stages			
Date	Population	(1)	(2)	(3)	Proportionate parts
1960	16,321				1960 − 1975 = −15
1970	30,567	37,690			1970 − 1975 = −5
1980	52,108	43,161	40,426		1980 − 1975 = 5
1990	87,724	52,023	41,273	40,002	1990 − 1975 = 15

Six given observations, designated Y_n, Y_{n+1}, Y_{n+2}, Y_{n+3}, Y_{n+4}, and Y_{n+5}, are involved in the leading differences, Δy_n, ..., $\Delta^5 y_n$. In the formula, n denotes any integral number, including 0, and x denotes any fraction less than unity. Thus, interpolation is to be limited to a middle range, from abscissa $n + 2$ to abscissa $n + 3$, or to "midpanel" interpolation. The six given observations must be equally spaced along the abscissa. Other procedures exist or can be developed for use with unevenly spaced observations and also for interpolation in other than a middle range, but midpanel formulas for use with equally spaced observations cover most situations.

Karup-King's Third-Difference Equation

As another example of an osculatory interpolation equation, we present a third-difference equation based on two overlapping polynomials of the second degree, with ordinates, tangents, and radius of curvature forced to be common to both polynomials at the abscissas $n + 1$ and $n + 2$. The equation is designed to interpolate between the abscissas $n + 1$ and $n + 2$; that is, it is limited to midpanel interpolation. The four given points Y_n, Y_{n+1}, Y_{n+2}, and Y_{n+3} must be equally spaced. The formula is again expressed in terms of leading differences:

$$
\begin{aligned}
y_{n+1+x} = y_n &+ \frac{(x+1)}{1!}\Delta y_n + \frac{(x+1)x}{2!}\Delta^2 y_n \\
&+ \frac{x^3(x-1)(3-2x)}{2!}\Delta^3 y_n
\end{aligned}
\tag{C.23}
$$

If only a common tangent is required but not a common radius of curvature, the corresponding equation would be

$$
y_{n+1+x} = y_n + \frac{(x+1)}{1!}\Delta y_n + \frac{(x+1)x}{2!}\Delta^2 y_n + \frac{x^2(x-1)}{2!}\Delta^3 y_n
\tag{C.24}
$$

The last equation is the Karup-King osculatory interpolation formula (Miller, 1946; Wolfenden, 1942).

The Beers Six-Term Ordinary and Modified Formulas

In most interpolation work, the interest is in the interpolated points themselves, and a procedure that yields smooth trends in terms of the interpolated points is logically sounder than one that forces a specified number of derivatives to be equal at junction points. The two overlapping curves can be fitted in a manner that minimizes the squares of a certain order of differences within the interpolation range. Beers did this by a minimization of fifth differences for a six-term formula. The resulting formulas generally yield smoother results than are possible from the usual osculatory interpolation formulas (Beers, 1944). "Ordinary" osculatory equations, such as the Beers six-term formula mentioned,

reproduce the given values. The requirement that the given values be reproduced sometimes causes undesirable undulations in the interpolated results. "Modified" equations relax the requirement that the given values be reproduced and yield smoother interpolated results than would otherwise be possible. The Beers six-term modified formulas is an example of a formula that combines interpolation with some smoothing or graduation of the given values (Beers, 1945). It minimizes the fourth differences of the interpolated results. This formula is recommended for use when smoothness of results is more important than maintenance of the given values. In the next section on "use of multipliers," procedures are described for applying both the ordinary and the modified interpolation formulas. The analyst has to decide for him or herself whether he or she wishes to maintain the original data unchanged at a cost of less smoothness for the interpolated results or prefers results that are smoother and only approximate the original data.

Use of Multipliers

The actual application of the equations given earlier takes a different form from that shown. The formulas for osculatory interpolation can be expressed in linear compound form—that is, in terms of coefficients or multipliers that are applied to the given data. An interpolated value can then be readily computed by multiplying the given data by the corresponding coefficients and by accumulating the products. In this way, the analyst has only to select the method of interpolation and to know how to use the multipliers; he or she does not need to be familiar with the formula itself or with the mathematical derivation of the multipliers. In effect, then, carrying out the interpolation becomes a purely clerical operation. This appendix presents selected sets of multipliers for point interpolation. The sets presented (see tables C.13 to C.17 at the end of the text of this appendix) are based on four different formulas:

1. Karup-King third-difference formula
2. Sprague fifth-difference formula
3. Beers six-term ordinary formula
4. Beers six-term modified formula

The Karup-King formula is applied to four points, the Sprague formula to six points (for midpanel interpolation), and the Beers formulas to six points (for midpanel interpolation). For all formulas the given points must be equally spaced, and the given values are maintained in the interpolation for all formulas except Beers's modified formula.

Table C.2 illustrates the application of the multipliers by interpolating to single ages between l_{45} and l_{50} by the use of the Karup-King formula in a 1989–1991 U.S. life table for the general population (presented in U.S. National Center for Health Statistics, 1997, p. 6). For these

TABLE C.2   Karup-King Interpolation of an Except from Life Table for the Total Population, United States: 1989–1991

x to x + 1	q_x	l_x	d_x	L_x	T_x	e_x	Karup-King interpolation between 5-year intervals
Years							
0–1	0.00936	**100,000**	936	99,258	7,536,614	75.37	100,000
1–2	0.00073	99,064	72	99,028	7,437,356	75.08	99,628
2–3	0.00048	98,992	48	98,968	7,338,328	74.13	99,355
3–4	0.00037	98,944	37	98,926	7,239,360	73.17	98,958
4–5	0.0003	98,907	30	98,892	7,140,434	72.19	99,004
5–6	0.00027	**98,877**	27	98,863	7,041,542	71.22	98,877
6–7	0.00025	98,850	24	98,839	6,942,679	70.23	98,790
7–8	0.00023	98,826	23	98,814	6,843,840	69.25	98,761
8–9	0.0002	98,803	20	98,794	6,745,026	68.27	98,763
9–10	0.00018	98,783	17	98,774	6,646,232	67.28	98,773
10–11	0.00016	**98,766**	16	98,758	6,547,458	66.29	98,766
11–12	0.00016	98,750	16	98,742	6,448,700	65.3	98,746
12–13	0.00022	98,734	21	98,723	6,349,958	64.31	98,729
13–14	0.00032	98,713	32	98,697	6,251,235	63.33	98,709
14–15	0.00047	98,681	46	98,658	6,152,538	62.35	98,680
15–16	0.00063	**98,635**	62	98,604	6,053,880	61.38	98,635
⋮							
40–41	0.00228	**95,373**	217	95,265	3,622,154	37.98	95,373
41–42	0.0024	95,156	228	95,042	3,526,889	37.06	95,156
42–43	0.00254	94,928	241	94,808	3,431,847	36.15	94,932
43–44	0.00271	94,687	256	94,559	3,337,039	35.24	94,695
44–45	0.00292	94,431	277	94,292	3,242,480	34.34	94,438
45–46	0.00318	**94,154**	299	94,005	3,148,188	33.44	94,154
46–47	0.00348	93,855	327	93,692	3,054,183	32.54	93,848
47–48	0.0038	93,528	355	93,350	2,960,491	31.65	93,526
48–49	0.00414	93,173	386	92,980	2,867,141	30.77	93,178
49–50	0.00449	92,787	417	92,579	2,774,161	29.9	92,795
50–51	0.0049	**92,370**	452	92,144	2,681,582	29.03	92,370
51–52	0.00537	91,918	494	91,671	2,589,438	28.17	91,910
52–53	0.0059	91,424	539	91,155	2,497,767	27.32	91,420
53–54	0.00647	90,885	588	90,591	2,406,612	26.48	90,889
54–55	0.00708	90,297	639	89,978	2,316,021	25.65	90,305
55–56	0.00773	**89,658**	693	89,311	2,226,043	24.83	89,658
⋮							
90–91	0.15135	**17,046**	2,580	15,757	76,698	4.5	17,046
91–92	0.16591	14,466	2,400	13,266	60,941	4.21	14,545
92–93	0.18088	12,066	2,182	10,975	47,675	3.95	12,172
93–94	0.19552	9,884	1,933	8,918	36,700	3.71	9,972
94–95	0.21	7,951	1,669	7,116	27,782	3.49	7,993
95–96	0.22502	**6,282**	1,414	5,575	20,666	3.29	6,282
96–97	0.24126	4,868	1,174	4,281	15,091	3.1	4,875
97–98	0.25689	3,694	949	3,219	10,810	2.93	3,740
98–99	0.27175	2,745	746	2,372	7,591	2.77	2,824
99–100	0.28751	1,999	575	1,711	5,219	2.61	2,070
100–101	0.30418	**1,424**	433	1,208	3,508	2.46	1,424
101–102	0.32182	991	319	832	2,300	2.32	922
102–103	0.34049	672	229	557	1,468	2.19	602
103–104	0.36024	443	159	364	911	2.05	407
104–105	0.38113	284	109	229	547	1.93	283
105–106	0.40324	**175**	70	140	318	1.81	175
106–107	0.42663	105	45	83	178	1.7	NA
107–108	0.45137	60	27	46	95	1.59	NA
108–109	0.47755	33	16	25	49	1.49	NA
109–110	0.50525	17	8	13	24	1.39	NA

Notes: Bolded cells are the "reference" cells for the Karup-King interpolation formula.
For interpolation of ages 0–1 to 4–5, the "first interval" coefficients are used.
For interpolation of ages 101–102 to 105–106, the "last interval" coefficients are used.
For interpolation of all other ages, the "middle interval" coefficients are used.
Because age 110 is not available, interpolations for 106–107 to 109–100 are not given (NA).
Source: U.S. National Center for Health Statistics. *U.S. Decennial Life Tables for 1989–1991*, Volume 1, Number 1, *United States Life Tables* Hyattsville, MD: U.S. National Center for Health Statistics, 1997.

interpolations, four points are used. The general form of the equation is simply

$$N_{2+x} = m_1 N_1 + m_2 N_2 + m_3 N_3 + m_4 N_4 \qquad (C.25)$$

where x is a fraction between 0 and 1; N_1, N_2, N_3, and N_4 represent four known values; and m_1, m_2, m_3, and m_4 are the four multipliers associated with the four given points. In this case, if one wishes to find l_{48}, a value 0.6 of the way between l_{45} and l_{50}, one has

$$N_{2.6} = m_1 N_{40} + m_2 N_{45} + m_3 N_{50} + m_4 N_{55} \qquad (C.26)$$

or

$$l_{48} = m_1 l_{40} + m_2 l_{45} + m_3 l_{50} + m_4 l_{55} \qquad (C.27)$$

The set of multipliers used for interpolating the middle interval is given in Table C.13, Section A.

Selecting the multipliers for $N_{2.6}$ from this table and the values of l_x from the NCHS life table, then

$$l_{48} = -.048(95,373) + .424(94,154)$$
$$+ .696(92,370) - .072(89,658) = 93,178$$

Using the same formula with different coefficients, one can derive the following values for l_{46}, l_{47}, and l_{49}

l_x	Computed by Karup-King formula	Published
l_{45}	94,154	94,154
l_{46}	93,848	93,855
l_{47}	93,526	93,528
l_{48}	93,178	93,173
l_{49}	92,795	92,787
l_{50}	92,370	92,370

As noted in Table C.2, the first group (ages 0 to 1 to 4 to 5) uses the "first interval" coefficients, the last group (ages 101 to 102 to 105 to 106) uses the "last interval" coefficients, and all others use the "middle interval" coefficients. While ages 106+ are not calculated because age 110 (l_{no}) is not available, if such interpolations were absolutely necessary, one could consider age 100 to 111 to be zero and use the "last interval" coefficients.

Once l_x is calculated for single ages, the remaining columns of the left table may be completed by use of standard formulas.

Cubic Splines

A method of interpolation of point data that has emerged strongly with widespread access to electronic computers (although it existed in mechanical form earlier) is that of cubic spline interpolation. Like other methods described previously, it fits a piecewise cubic polynomial of the form $y = a + bx + cx^2 + dx^3$ to a portion of the data. However, with cubic splines, one constrains the relationship of one cubic spline to the next one in the series, specifically, so that the slope of the top end of the first polynomial must match the slope of the bottom end of the next polynomial. This "complication" allows us to find a linear system of equations that is solvable, thus giving us the collection of cubic spline coefficients needed.

Begin by presuming that one has an ordered collection of points x_1, x_2, x_3, . . . , x_n, along a continuum. To each of these points is associated some $y_j - f(x_i)$. Following the derivation in Johnson and Percy (2000) and Burden and Faires (1993) closely, split the continuum into i intervals. In each interval the goal is to fit a cubic polynomial. Make the following definition: $h_i = x_{i+1} - x_i$; that is, h_i is just the difference between two successive x_i points in two successive intervals. In the ith interval, one wishes to fit a polynomial of the form

$$y = a_i(x - x_i)^3 + b_i(x - x_i)^2 + c_i(x - x_i) + d_i \quad (C.28)$$

where x_i is the first x-value in the ith interval. Recall that, to fit a third-order polynomial, the interval must contain at least four points.

The goal at this point is to find solutions for a_i, b_i, c_i, and d_i, in the ith interval. We will proceed to develop these solutions, writing each coefficient, as much as possible, in terms of observed x_i and y_i values. At the lower end of the interval, the polynomial is simple; it is just

$$y = a_i(x_i - x_i)^3 + b_i(x_i - x_i)^2 + c_i(x_i - x_i) + d_i = d_i \quad (C.29)$$

At the upper end of the interval, the polynomial is

$$\begin{aligned} y &= a_i(x - x_i)^3 + b_i(x - x_i)^2 + c_i(x - x_i) + d_i \\ &= a_i(h_i)^3 + b_i(h_i)^2 + c_i(h_i) + d_i \end{aligned} \quad (C.30)$$

Take first and second derivatives of this polynomial, and obtain

$$\frac{dy}{dx} = 3a_i(h_i)^2 + 2b_i h_i + c_i \qquad (C.31)$$

and

$$\frac{d^2 y}{dx^2} = 6a_i(h_i) + 2b_i \qquad (C.32)$$

Again following the derivation in Johnson and Percy and Burden and Faires, write the coefficients in terms of the second derivative at each end of the interval. Thus, at the lower end of the ith interval,

$$S_i = \left(\frac{d^2 y}{dx^2} \right)_i = 6a_i(x_i - x_i) + 2b_i = 2b \qquad (C.33)$$

and at the upper end of the ith interval,

$$S_{i+1} = \left(\frac{d^2 y}{dx^2} \right)_{i+1} = 6a_i(x_{i+1} - x_i) + 2b_i = 6a_i h_i + 2b_i \quad (C.34)$$

Substitute the lower-end equation into the upper-end equation, and obtain

$$S_{i+1} = 6a_i h_i + S_i$$

Solving for a_i:

$$a_i = \frac{S_{i+1} - S_i}{6h_i}$$

Now substitute a_i, b_i, and d_i into the upper-end equation, and obtain

$$y_{i+1} = \frac{S_{i+1} - S_i}{6h_i}(h_i)^3 + \frac{S_i}{2}h_i^2 + c_i h_i + y_i$$

Finally, solve this equation for c_i:

$$c_i = \frac{y_{i+1} - y_i}{h_i} - \frac{2h_i S_i + h_i S_{i+1}}{6} \qquad (C.35)$$

At this point, these substitutions have now given us equations for a_i, b_i, c_i, and d_i, in the ith interval, in which these constants are expressed in terms of known values (y_i, y_{i+1}, and h_i) and as yet unknown first derivatives ($S_i's$).

To find the first derivatives, use the aforementioned condition that slopes of two successive polynomials are the same at their common point. Using the definition of the derivative, $(dy/dx)_i = c_i$ and $(dy/dx)_{i-1} = 3a_i h_{i-1}^2 + 2b_i h_{i-1} + c_{i-1}$. Setting these two equal implies that

$$c_i = 3a_{i-1}h_{i-1}^2 + 2b_{i-1}h_{i-1} + c_{i-1} \qquad (C.36)$$

Now substitute for all quantities, c_i, a_i, b_i, and c_{i-1}, and solve to find the relation

$$h_{i-1}S_{i-1} + (2h_i + 2h_i)S_i + h_i S_{i+1} = 6\left(\frac{y_{i+1} - y_i}{h_i} - \frac{y_i - y_{i-1}}{h_{i-1}}\right) \qquad (C.37)$$

Now, this relation contains known quantities y_i, y_{i+1}, h_i, h_{i-1}, and unknowns S_i, S_{i-1}, and S_{i+1}. By combining all of the implied equations, for all i intervals, the system so constructed has the following form:

$$\begin{bmatrix} h_1 & 2(h_1+h_2) & h_2 & & & & \\ & h_2 & 2(h_2+h_3) & h_3 & & & \\ & & \ddots & \ddots & \ddots & & \\ & & & \ddots & \ddots & & \\ & & & & h_{n-2} & 2(h_{n-2}+h_{n-1}) & h_{n-1} \end{bmatrix}$$

$$\begin{bmatrix} S_1 \\ S_2 \\ \vdots \\ \vdots \\ S_{n-1} \\ S_n \end{bmatrix} = 6 \begin{bmatrix} \dfrac{y_3 - y_2}{h_2} - \dfrac{y_2 - y_1}{h_1} \\ \dfrac{y_4 - y_3}{h_3} - \dfrac{y_3 - y_2}{h_2} \\ \vdots \\ \dfrac{y_n - y_{n-1}}{h_{n-1}} - \dfrac{y_{n-1} - y_{n-2}}{h_{n-2}} \end{bmatrix} \qquad (C.38)$$

The linear system in Equation (C.38) contains $n-2$ equations and n unknowns. Two more equations are needed to make this uniquely solvable. If one applies end values $S_1 = S_n = 0$ (which implies that the polynomial is flat at the very bottom and very top points), one can solve this system of equations for all $S_i's$ in the system. Applying these two boundary conditions effectively eliminates two columns, the first and the last, in the matrix, and creates the system:

$$\begin{bmatrix} 2(h_1+h_2) & h_2 & & & \\ h_2 & 2(h_2+h_3) & h_3 & & \\ & \ddots & \ddots & \ddots & \\ & & \ddots & \ddots & \\ & & & h_{n-2} & 2(h_{n-2}+h_{n-1}) \end{bmatrix} \begin{bmatrix} S_2 \\ \vdots \\ \vdots \\ S_{n-1} \end{bmatrix}$$

$$= 6 \begin{bmatrix} \dfrac{y_3 - y_2}{h_2} - \dfrac{y_2 - y_1}{h_1} \\ \dfrac{y_4 - y_3}{h_3} - \dfrac{y_3 - y_2}{h_2} \\ \vdots \\ \dfrac{y_n - y_{n-1}}{h_{n-1}} - \dfrac{y_{n-1} - y_{n-2}}{h_{n-2}} \end{bmatrix} \qquad (C.39)$$

Equation (C.39) is the system which can be solved for $S_2 \ldots S_{n-1}$.

Consider a simple example. Table C.3 displays the percentages unemployed for the years 1982 to 1997 in the United States. The goal is to fit a series of four cubic splines to these data, with interval points at 1986, 1990, 1993, and 1997.

Fit four cubic polynomials to these data, with cutpoints (or "knots") at 1982, 1986, 1990, and 1994. Because, in general, the cubic spline matrix has a special form (known as a "tridiagonal" form), there are shortcuts to solving the system. The shortcut used here is described in Burden and Faires (1993, p. 136, algorithm 3.4). Using the shortcut methods described there, solve for a, b, c, and d within each interval [1982, 1986], [1986, 1990], [1990, 1994], [1994, 1997], and fit the polynomial within the interval, using these coefficients within each interval, to obtain the cubic spline interpolation across the entire series. Figure C.2 demonstrates the results of this fit. Note that, at the four cutpoints (1982, 1986, 1990, and 1994), the cubic is forced to fit exactly, and further, forced to fit so that the slope of the top end of the earlier cubic matches the slope of the bottom end of the later cubic.

What can be seen in this figure? Overall, the cubic spline fits the trend reasonably well. However, there is an anomalous result in the interval 1990–1994: Specifically, in this

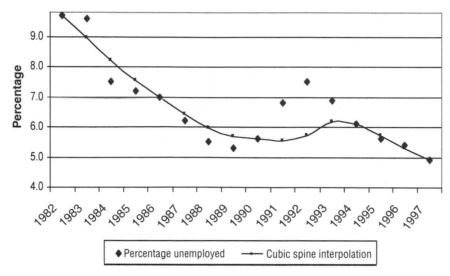

FIGURE C.2 Percentage unemployed, United States, 1982–1997, with cubic spline interpolation.

TABLE C.3 Employment Status of the Civilian Noninstitutional Population, United States: 1982–1997
(Figures in thousands. Annual averages of monthly figurs.)

Year	Civilian noninstitutionalized population[1]	Civilian labor force				Not in labor force	
		Total	Employed	Unemployed number	Percent of labor force	Number	Percentage of population
1982	172,271	110,204	99,526	10,678	9.7	62,067	36.0
1983	174,215	111,550	100,834	10,717	9.6	62,665	36.0
1984	176,383	113,544	105,005	8,539	7.5	62,839	35.6
1985	178,206	115,461	107,150	8,312	7.2	62,744	35.2
1986	180,587	117,834	109,597	8,237	7.0	62,752	34.7
1987	182,753	119,865	112,440	7,425	6.2	62,888	34.4
1988	184,613	121,669	114,968	6,701	5.5	62,944	34.1
1989	186,393	123,869	117,342	6,528	5.3	62,523	33.5
1990	189,164	125,840	118,793	7,047	5.6	63,324	33.5
1991	190,925	126,346	117,718	8,628	6.8	64,578	33.8
1992	192,805	128,105	118,492	9,613	7.5	64,700	33.6
1993	194,838	129,200	120,259	8,940	6.9	65,638	33.7
1994	196,814	131,056	123,060	7,996	6.1	65,758	33.4
1995	198,584	132,304	124,900	7,404	5.6	66,280	33.4
1996	200,591	133,943	126,708	7,236	5.4	66,647	33.2
1997	203,133	136,297	129,558	6,739	4.9	66,837	32.9

[1] Population 16 years old and over.

Source: U.S. Bureau of Labor Statistics, Bulletin 2307; and *Employment and Earnings*, monthly, January issues. Based on Current Population Survey.

See U.S. Census Bureau, *Statistical Abstract of the United States, 1999,* Section 1, "Population", and Appendix III, Washington, DC: U.S. Census Bureau, 2000.

interval, the unemployment rates are substantially higher than the smoothed cubic values. Why does this occur? If one examines the graph closely, one can see that the slope at the lower cutpoint (1990) is downward. One can also see that the slope at the higher cutpoint (1994) is also downward. This means that, in the interval 1990–1994, the calculation is attempting to fit a cubic that is forced, by construction, to slope downward at both ends. Needless to say, this, in combination with the limited number of data points available to us, limits how much "bend" the curve can have. Hence, while the cubic spline bends upward in the 1990–1994 period, it cannot bend upward too far. As with any interpolation method, cubic splines, while attractive, have their limits.

Curve Fitting

Exponential Functions

Exponential functions are another class of mathematical equations useful in interpolation and extrapolation of series of data. This class of curves is important in connection with the measurement and analysis of population growth. Exponential equations are used for many other demographic purposes. The discussion here is intended to describe the types of exponential functions and note their general relationship to one another.

An exponential function is one in which one or more of the variables is expressed as a power of some parameter or constant in the formula. Thus, $y = a^x$ is an exponential function because x is a power of the parameters. Exponential functions take many forms, as indicated here. One general form of an exponential function, the power function, is

$$y = ab^x \qquad (C.40)$$

With modifications, this general equation lends itself to many uses. Power functions are also known as growth curves.

Geometric Curve

The simple geometric curve is a special case of the power function. In the geometric curve, the given y values form a geometric progression while the corresponding x values form an arithmetic progression. The curve can be fitted exactly through two points. If there are more than two observations, the simple geometric curve may be fitted approximately by various methods (shown later). An example of the simple geometric curve is the "compound interest" curve. This curve commonly takes the form of annual compounding, semiannual compounding, or quarterly compounding. For a quantity (population) compounded annually, the formula is

$$y = a(1+b)^x \qquad (C.41)$$

When the frequency of compounding is increased without limit, we derive a quantity (population) compounded continuously. The formula is

$$y = ae^{bx} \qquad (C.42)$$

where

a is the initial amount
x is the period of time over which growth occurs
b is the growth rate per unit of time
e is the base of the system of natural logarithms
y is the amount (population) at time x

The formula for continuous compounding has several applications in demographic analysis. For example, it is the basis for Lotka's equations for a stable population. In con-

structing the stable population, to convert the life table survival $P(x)$ proportions into proportions for a stable population growing or decreasing at a constant rate r, the continuous compounding formula is used in a reverse fashion. The life table survival $P(x)$ values are taken as the "present values," or y values, and r is taken as the growth rate per year, in the continuous compounding formula $y = ae^{rx}$. Then, the coefficient a becomes the proportion that persons x years of age would constitute of the births (1.0000 birth per year in the stable population). There would be a different "a" value for each age x, so it is made a function of x, called $a(x)$. The formula can now be written in the form

$$P(x) = a(x)e^{rx} \qquad (C.43)$$

so that

$$a(x) = \frac{P(x)}{e^{rx}} \qquad (C.44)$$

or

$$a(x) = P(x)e^{-rx} \qquad (C.45)$$

This is the equation for computing the proportion $a(x)$ of the population at age x in a stable population growing (or declining) at a constant rate r, from a life table series of proportions $P(x)$.

Other Growth Curves

As noted earlier, there are many possible modifications of the general exponential equation $y = ab^x$ in addition to the geometric curves with annual or continuous compounding. These growth curves do not usually fit the given data exactly; hence, they also belong under the heading "curve fitting."

The equation

$$y = k + ab^x \qquad (C.46)$$

is a modified exponential equation that yields an ascending asymptotic curve when a is negative and b is a fractional value between 0 and 1. It describes a series in which the absolute growth in the y values decreases by a constant proportion. When $x = 0$, $y = k - a$. As x increases, y approaches k as an upper limit. In other variations, a is positive and b is between 0 and 1 or greater than 1.

More commonly used than the modified exponential equation just described is the Gompertz curve, the equation of which is

$$y = ka^{b^x} \qquad (C.47)$$

which reduces to the equivalent logarithmic form:

$$\log(y) = \log(k) + b^x \log(a) \qquad (C.48)$$

The Gompertz curve is exactly like the modified exponential curve except that it is the increase in the logarithms of the y values that decreases by a constant proportion. The Gompertz curve fits many types of growth data much better than the modified exponential curve.

Another type of growth curve that has the same general shape as the Gompertz curve is the logistic curve, also known as the Pearl-Reed curve. The logistic curve has the general equation

$$\frac{1}{y} = k + ab^x \qquad (C.49)$$

or when fitted by the method of selected points,

$$y = \frac{k}{1 + e^{a+bx}} \qquad (C.50)$$

The reader is cautioned that no matter how well an asymptotic growth curve fits observed data, projections that go beyond the observations will not necessarily be realized. No empirically fitted curve can magically anticipate future changes when these are dependent on circumstances that are beyond the ken of the curve. It is often easy to fit a variety of modified logistic curves to the same observations in a manner that will yield very different projections.

Curve Fitting

Although a series of demographic data may not be subject to any mathematical law, the data may follow a typical trend or pattern that can be represented empirically by some mathematical equation. Curve fitting consists of finding a suitable equation to represent that trend or pattern. Curves to be fitted might be polynomials, osculatory equations, exponential equations, trigonometric equations (useful for data that have periodic fluctuations or seasonal patterns), or still other curves. The aim may be to fit a curve to the data in an approximate fashion, in which case crude methods, such as graphic methods or moving averages, may be suitable, or to fit a curve by a more sophisticated method, as by the method of moments or by the method of least squares. Whether or not the fitted curve is suitable for interpolation or extrapolation depends on the nature of the given data, the choice of curve, and the goodness of fit. Probably demographers most often fit straight lines or polynomials of second or third degree in such applications.

Method of Least Squares

Curves are commonly fitted by the method of least squares or by the use of moments. Consider first the method of least squares illustrated by fitting a second-degree polynomial ($y = a + bx + cx^2$) to a time series of data on median household income in the United States for selected dates from 1967 to 1998. The method of least squares minimizes the sum of the squares of the differences between the observed or given points Y and the points calculated from the fitted curve $\hat{Y}$. That is, given n points of data, least squares finds the $\hat{Y}$ that minimizes the sum:

$$\sum_{i=1}^{n} w_i \left(Y_i - \hat{Y}_i \right)^2 \qquad (C.51)$$

where Y_i is the observed value of y at the ith point, $\hat{Y}_i$ is the corresponding value at the ith point from the fitted curve, and w_i is a weight for the ith value (1 for each observed value if all are assumed to be of equal precision, as in the present example). Three "normal" equations have to be solved. The normal equations in general form are

$$\sum Y = an + b\sum X + c\sum X^2 \qquad (C.52)$$

$$\sum XY = a\sum X + b\sum X^2 + c\sum X^3 \qquad (C.53)$$

$$\sum X^2 Y = a\sum X^2 + b\sum X^3 + c\sum X^4 \qquad (C.54)$$

In every case, the sum is taken over the n observations. The origin ($x = 0$) is arbitrarily taken at the year 1967, the first in the series. The following data, taken from Table C.4, is needed to solve the normal equations:

$$N = 31 \text{(observations)}$$
$$\sum Y = 1,141,362$$
$$\sum X = 496$$
$$\sum X^2 = 10,416$$
$$\sum X^3 = 246,016$$
$$\sum X^4 = 6,197,520$$
$$\sum XY = 17,990,484$$
$$\sum X^2 Y = 380,563,510$$

These values are now inserted in the normal equations as required to obtain the following of equations:

$$1,141,362 = a(31) + b(10,416) + c(246,016)$$
$$17,990,484 = a(496) + b(10,416) + c(246,016)$$
$$380,563,510 = a(10,416) + b(246,016) + c(6,197,520)$$

Solution of the three normal equations for a, b, and c by any of a number of methods yields:[8]

$$a = 36235$$
$$b = -164.08$$
$$c = 7,0206$$

---

[8] We used the commercial software package Maple VR4 (Waterloo, Inc.), but others such as Mathematica or MathCad could also be used. Of course, one could also solve such a system by hand using regular or matrix algebra. Because this is a standard regression equation solved by least squares, a statistics package or curve-fitting package is almost certainly the best choice for fitting such an equation.

TABLE C.4 Fitting a Second-Degree Polynomial by Least Squares to Median Income of All Households in the United States, in Constant (1998) Dollars

Year	Median income (1998 dollars)[1] Y	Calculations X^2	X^2	X^3	X^4	$X*Y$	X^2Y	Fitted $\hat{Y}$ Median income (1998 dollars)	Percentage difference
1967	32,075	0	0	0	0	0	0	36,235.0	12.97
1968	33,478	1	1	1	1	33,478	33,478	36,077.9	7.77
1969	34,706	2	4	8	16	69,412	138,824	35,934.9	3.54
1970	34,471	3	9	27	81	103,413	310,239	35,805.9	3.87
1971	34,143	4	16	64	256	136,572	546,288	35,691.0	4.53
1972	35,599	5	25	125	625	177,995	889,975	35,590.1	−0.02
1973	36,302	6	36	216	1,296	217,812	1,306,872	35,503.3	−2.20
1974	35,166	7	49	343	2,401	246,162	1,723,134	35,430.4	0.75
1975	34,224	8	64	512	4,096	273,792	2,190,336	35,371.7	3.35
1976	34,812	9	81	729	6,561	313,308	2,819,772	35,326.9	1.48
1977	35,004	10	100	1,000	10,000	350,040	3,500,400	35,296.3	0.83
1978	36,377	11	121	1,331	14,641	400,147	4,401,617	35,279.6	−3.02
1979	36,259	12	144	1,728	20,736	435,108	5,221,296	35,277.0	−2.71
1980	35,076	13	169	2,197	28,561	455,988	5,927,844	35,288.4	0.61
1981	34,507	14	196	2,744	38,416	483,098	6,763,372	35,313.9	2.34
1982[3]	34,392	15	225	3,375	50,625	515,880	7,738,200	35,353.4	2.80
1983	34,397	16	256	4,096	65,536	550,352	8,805,632	35,407.0	2.94
1984	35,165	17	289	4,913	83,521	597,805	10,162,685	35,474.6	0.88
1985	35,778	18	324	5,832	104,976	644,004	11,592,072	35,556.2	−0.62
1986	37,027	19	361	6,859	130,321	703,513	13,366,747	35,651.9	−3.71
1987[3]	37,394	20	400	8,000	160,000	747,880	14,957,600	35,761.6	−4.37
1988	37,512	21	441	9,261	194,481	787,752	16,542,792	35,885.4	−4.34
1989	37,997	22	484	10,648	234,256	835,934	18,390,548	36,023.2	−5.19
1990	37,343	23	529	12,167	279,841	858,889	19,754,447	36,175.1	−3.13
1991	36,054	24	576	13,824	331,776	865,296	20,767,104	36,340.9	0.80
1992	35,593	25	625	15,625	390,625	889,825	22,245,625	36,520.9	2.61
1993	35,241	26	676	17,576	456,976	916,266	23,822,916	36,714.8	4.18
1994	35,486	27	729	19,683	531,441	958,122	25,869,294	36,922.9	4.05
1995	36,446	28	784	21,952	614,656	1,020,488	28,573,664	37,144.9	1.92
1996	36,872	29	841	24,389	707,281	1,069,288	31,009,352	37,381.0	1.38
1997	37,581	30	900	27,000	810,000	1,127,430	33,822,900	37,631.1	0.13
1998	38,885	31	961	29,791	923,521	1,205,435	37,368,485	37,895.3	−2.55
Sum over 1967–98:	1,141,362	496	10,416	246,016	6,197,520	17,990,484	380,563,510		
1999 (Estimated)	39,934	32	1,024	32,768	1,048,576	1,277,883	40,892,416	38,173.5	
						Error in 1999 forecast		−1,760	416
						Percentage error in 1999 forecast		−4.41	

[1] Source: U.S. Bureau of the Census, *Current Population Reports*, P60-206, www.census.gov/hhes/www/income.html. Constant dollars based on CPI-U-X1 deflator. Households as of March of following year.

[2] Year−1967.

[3] In 1983 and 1987, changes in data collection procedures occurred, making direct comparison with prior years suspect.

The desired equation is, therefore,

$$\hat{Y} = 36235 - 164.08X + 7.0206X^2 \qquad (\text{C}.55)$$

Because this equation predicts or estimates Y for each value of X, we have inserted $\hat{Y}$ for the predicted value.

The actual values of Y and the computed values of $\hat{Y}$ are shown in Figure C.3. (Note that the Y-axis scale does not start at 0, thus making the income values appear to have more variability. We have focused the graph for the purposes of examining the shape and fit of the fitted polynomial.)

If the equation is also used to project or forecast a value for 1999, the result would be $38,173, as displayed in Figure C.3. The observed value for 1999 was (approximately) $39,934. The projection falls short of the observed value, therefore, by $1760, or about 4.1%. This percentage difference is one of the highest of any year within the range of the observed data and is noted as an example of the hazards of extrapolation.

We have skipped over illustrating the procedure for fitting a straight line by the method of least squares because the illustration just given encompasses the basic steps. Only two normal equations have to be solved:

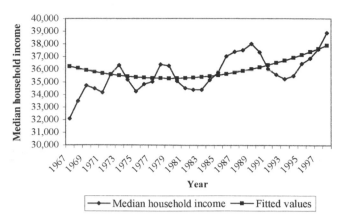

FIGURE C.3 Median household income versus values fitted by least squares 2nd degree polynomial.

$$\sum Y = an + b\sum X \qquad (C.56)$$

$$\sum XY = a\sum X + b\sum X^2 \qquad (C.57)$$

Hence, we need to compute only ΣY, ΣX, ΣXY, and ΣX^2. These have the same values as given previously. The normal equations, which we solve for a and b, then become

$$1,141,362 = a(31) + b(496)$$
$$17,990,484 = a(496) + b(10,416)$$

and the desired equation is

$$\hat{Y} = 36235 + 1.736X$$

The pattern of the normal equations is evident. For fitting a third-degree polynominal by least squares, the normal equations are

$$\sum Y = an + b\sum X + c\sum X^2 \qquad (C.58)$$

$$\sum XY = a\sum X + b\sum X^2 + c\sum X^3 \qquad (C.59)$$

$$\sum X^2 Y = a\sum X^2 + b\sum X^3 + c\sum X^4 \qquad (C.60)$$

$$\sum X^3 Y = a\sum X^3 + b\sum X^4 + c\sum X^5 + d\sum X^6 \qquad (C.61)$$

The least squares method is only one of many methods for fitting functions to data, for estimating population parameters from data, or for general maximization and minimization of functions. The least squares method has traditionally had the advantages that it is computationally simple to implement and often has a closed form solution. Readers who wish a full explanation of the principles of least squares and related methods of estimation (such as the method of moments or the maximum-likelihood method) may wish to consult any of a variety of textbooks specializing in these topics. An introduction to these methods is given by Kmenta (1986) Weisberg (1982) and Greene (1993). For a full account, including advanced topics, see Judge *et al.* (1985, 1988). Finally, for a mathematical development from

first principles (that is, from the axiomatic probability models that serve as their foundation), see Bickel and Doksum (1977), Dudewicz and Mishra (1988), or Bain and Engelhart (1987).

INTERPOLATION OF GROUPED DATA

Introduction

We have been concerned in the preceding part of this appendix with interpolation and curve fitting as applied to point data. We now consider interpolation as applied to grouped or "area" data. Interpolation of grouped data may serve any of several purposes. The most common purpose probably is the estimation of data in finer detail than is available in published data, as for estimating numbers of persons in single years of age from published data for 5-year age groups. Another purpose is the smoothing or graduation of data that are available in fine detail, as when interpolating 5-year age data to obtain smoothed estimates of data by single years of age. It should be noted that the methods to be described have one thing in common: They assume that the distribution pattern of grouped data is a valid indication of the distribution pattern within groups. There are some kinds of demographic data where the distribution within groups is known to have a special pattern that is not reflected by grouped data. In such instances, the methods described here may not apply. For example, in the United States it is common for persons to work either 40 or 48 hours a week—a fact that is not evident from broad groupings of hours worked.

"Interpolation" by Prorating

Sometimes the best estimates of the subdivisions of grouped data come not from elaborate mathematical techniques but rather from simple prorating. (In fact, in practice this is probably the most common technique for disaggregating grouped data.) In this procedure, a distribution taken from some other similar group that has satisfactory detailed information is used to split up a known total for a given group. Such a procedure depends for its accuracy on how well the distribution of the former group represents conditions in the latter group.

For example, a series of annual birth statistics for the years in which persons now 25 to 29 years of age were born may be a useful basis for prorating the number of persons 25 to 29 years of age so as to obtain estimates of the population for single years of age. It is not necessary to allow for deaths since the birth period or for net migration, if it is thought that the distribution of the annual births is a reasonably good indicator of how the population is distributed by age within the 25-to-29 year age group currently. Furthermore, the birth registration need not have been complete so long as the percent completeness was reasonably similar from year to year. Interpolations obtained in this manner may be superior to interpolations from a mathematical equation that involves an assumption of a smooth flow of events from age to age.

As another example of a type of problem where prorating may be superior, consider the task of securing the percentage married for single ages from the percentage married for a 5-year age group, say for ages 15 to 19. A suggested procedure is to (1) multiply the percentage married for age group 15 to 19 in the given population, by 5 to obtain an approximate value for the sum of the percentages for each of the 5 single years of age, and then to (2) estimate the percentages for single years of age by prorating this total according to known single-year-of-age percentages from some other population. In the United States, the decennial census provides data on marital status by single years of age, but the data from the Current Population Survey are usually tabulated only by broad age groups. The census data may be a good basis, therefore, for splitting up the current survey data. Additional applications of prorating procedures are discussed in the section on "adjustment of distributions to marginal totals."

Use of a Rectangular Assumption

The simplest and perhaps the most commonly used method of subdividing grouped data employs the assumption that the data are rectangularly (evenly) distributed within the interval to be subdivided. This assumption is that the values of the parts are all equal. They are derived, then, by dividing the total for the interval by the number of parts desired. A rectangular assumption is a useful basis for deriving rough estimates of detailed categories under many different circumstances in demographic studies. For example, it may be employed to derive life table d_x's in single years

of age from $_5d_x$'s or to derive the central d_x in each 5-year interval. We illustrate with data based on an abridged 1996 U.S. life table for the total population (U.S. National Center for Health Statistics/Anderson, 1998, Tables 1 and 2) in Table C.5 and Figure C.4.

As can be seen in this table and figure, the rectangular assumption works best when the underlying data are not changing rapidly. In later years, when the number of deaths is increasing substantially with age, the rectangular assumption overestimates the number of the younger ages in the interval, and underestimates the number of the older ages in the interval.

Births or deaths on a calendar-year basis may be shifted to a "fiscal-year" (i.e., July-to-June) basis by simply assuming that one-half the births or deaths of each year occurs in the first or second half of the year. Even if there is a pronounced seasonal variation and a sharp trend up or down through the 2 years split up, the 12-month estimate may be quite adequate because the excess or deficit in the estimate for the first half of the period may be largely offset by the deficit or excess in the estimate for the second half of the period.

Graphic Interpolation

Sometimes graphs are of special help in interpreting and solving an interpolation problem. Suppose, for example, one wishes to compute separation factors for apportioning annual birth data by age of mother into the births occurring to mothers who would be of given ages at some date during the period. Specifically, we may wish to determine the number of births in a 12-month period ending on April 1, 2000, which occurred to mothers who are x years of age on April 1, 2000. A diagram of the type shown as Figure C.5 may be helpful.

If the births are assumed to be uniformly distributed by date of occurrence and age of mother, then the desired separation factors can be figured from the proportionate parts

TABLE C.5 Excerpt of 1996 U.S. Life Table with Rectangular Interpolation

Age	Official data[1] d_x	$5d_x$	Rectangular interpolation	Age	Official data[1] d_x	$5d_x$	Rectangular interpolation
10	14	117	23.4	55	635	3,776	755.2
11	14		23.4	56	684		755.2
12	19		23.4	57	744		755.2
13	28		23.4	58	816		755.2
14	42		23.4	59	897		755.2
15	56	386	77.2	60	985	5,760	1152
16	70		77.2	61	1074		1152
17	81		77.2	62	1158		1152
18	88		77.2	63	1235		1152
19	91		77.2	64	1308		1152
20	95	499	99.8				

[1] Source: U.S. National Center for Health Statistics/Anderson, 1998.

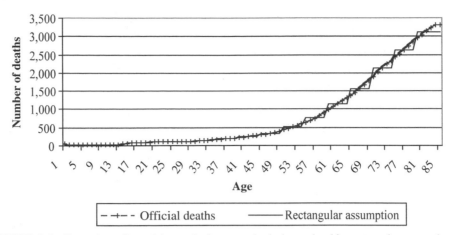

FIGURE C.4 Comparison of actual 1-year deaths versus deaths interpolated by rectangular assumption.

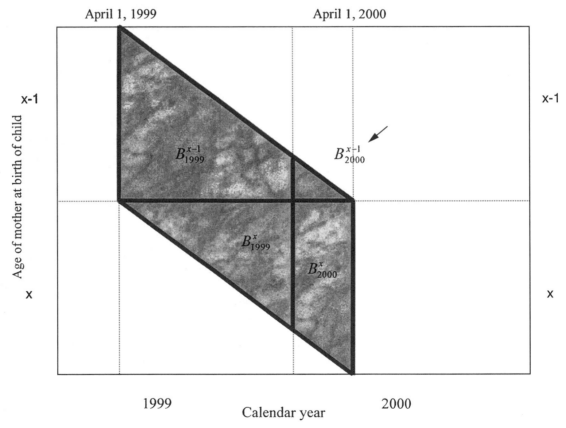

FIGURE C.5 Illustration of the graphic interpolation of births to mothers aged *x-1* on April 1, 1999 and aged *x* on April 1, 2000.

of the shaded areas. The procedure consists of estimating directly the triangular area included in the shaded area for each age and year; or estimating the rectangular area from April 1, 1999, to December 31, 1999 (3/4 year), and from January 1, 2000, to March 31, 2000 (1/4 year), and subtracting from it the triangular area that is not included in the shaded area.

Proportion of births occurring to mothers of age "x" in 2000 (the area labeled B_{2000}^x in the figure):

$$= \left[\frac{1}{4} - \frac{1}{2}\left(\frac{1}{4} \times \frac{1}{4} \right) \right] B_{2000}^x = \frac{7}{32} B_{2000}^x$$

Proportion of births occurring to mothers of age "$x - 1$" in 2000 (the area labeled B_{2000}^{x-1} in the figure):

$$= \left[\frac{1}{2}\left(\frac{1}{4} \times \frac{1}{4}\right)\right] B_{2000}^{x-1} = \frac{1}{32} B_{2000}^{x-1}$$

Proportion of births occurring to mothers of age "x" in 1999 (the area labeled B_{1999}^x in the figure):

$$= \left[\frac{1}{2}\left(\frac{3}{4} \times \frac{3}{4}\right)\right] B_{1999}^x = \frac{9}{32} B_{1999}^x$$

Proportion of births occurring to mothers of age "$x - 1$" in 1999 (the area labeled B_{1999}^{x-1} in the figure):

$$= \left[\frac{3}{4} - \frac{1}{2}\left(\frac{3}{4} \times \frac{3}{4}\right)\right] B_{1999}^{x-1} = \frac{15}{32} B_{1999}^{x-1}$$

The width of the interval from January 1 to March 31, 2000 is 1/4 year and the height of the January 1, 2000, vertical line is 3/4 year for the shaded area relating to age x and 1/4 year for the shaded area relating to age $x - 1$. Hence, the shaded areas for 2000 are computed at 7/32 of 2000 births to mothers x years old at childbirth plus 1/32 of 2000 births to mothers $x - 1$ years old at childbirth. In a similar manner, the desired proportions for the interval between April 1 and December 31, 1999, are 9/32 of 1999 births to mothers x years old at childbirth plus 15/32 of 1999 births to mothers $x - 1$ years old.

Midpoint and Cumulation-Differencing Methods

One general procedure for the interpolation of grouped data may be called, for want of a better term, the "midpoint" approach. Another, usually more reliable approach, involves a cumulation and differencing calculation. Polynomial interpolation, particularly in the form of Aitken's procedure, is then ordinarily combined with one of these approaches to obtain the final results. Both methods will be briefly explained in terms of illustrative examples.

Midpoint Method Using Data on Percentages

Suppose one has data on the proportion of women ever married for age groups 15 to 24, 25 to 34, 35 to 44, and 45 and over and wants an estimate of the proportion ever married for women 28 years of age. The lower limit of age group 15 to 24 is the 15th birthday (exact age 15.0) and the upper limit of that age group is the 25th birthday (exact age 25.0); the midpoint of age group 15 to 24 is, therefore, (15.0 + 25.0)/2, or 20.0. In a similar manner the midpoints of the other age groups in this example may be determined to be, respectively, (25.0 + 35.0)/2 = 30.0 for age group 25 to 34, (35.0 + 45.0)/2 = 40.0 for age group 35 to 44. The midpoint of the desired year of age 28 is 28.5. By equating the given percentages ever married with the corresponding midpoints of age groups and by interpolating among the

former, we can obtain an estimate of the percentage ever married corresponding to the midpoint of age 28 (i.e., for age 28).

In the following example of midpoint interpolation, Aitken's iterative procedure is applied to marital data for females in the United States in 1990. Note that the "midpoint" of the highest age group is problematic in this context; if one did not have a statement of the midpoint from another tabulation, one would either (1) use only the second computational stage and not the third or (2) estimate the midpoint of the highest age group using other methods, and use that estimate. (In fact, this illustrates a weakness of the midpoint method.) In this case, we take the midpoint to be halfway between 80.0 and 45.0, or 62.5. The interpolation table is presented in Table C.6.

The last figure in column 3 of the computations is the desired result: We estimate that 70.4% of women of exact age 28 were ever-married as of the 1990 U.S. Census. Because so much of the female population is "ever married" by the time they reach age 45, the upper age group midpoint makes only a small difference to the estimate: If we assumed the upper midpoint was (60 + 45)/2 = 52.5, the final estimate of percent of women of exact age 28 ever-married would be 70.6%.

Cumulation-Differencing Method Using Data on Absolute Numbers

The cumulation-differencing method has a sounder theoretical basis for interpolation of groups than the midpoint approach just described. This is because, in fact, group averages seldom apply exactly to the midpoints of groups, as is assumed in the midpoint approach; however, in the cumulation-differencing approach the observed data are associated with the precise points to which they actually apply.

Consider the numbers of women in the age groups 15 to 24, 25 to 34, 35 to 44, and 45 and older for the United States in 1990, as before. Tentatively, for illustrative purposes,

TABLE C.6 Illustration of Midpoint Method of Interpolation of Percents Using Aitken's Procedure

| Interpolation date | | 28.5 | | | |
| Midpoint | Percentage ever married | Computational Stages | | | Proportionate parts |
		(1)	(2)	(3)	
20	20.97				20 − 28.5 = −8.5
30	75.52	67.34			30 − 28.5 = 1.5
40	90.23	50.41	69.88		40 − 28.5 = 11.5
62.5[1]	94.85	35.75	68.80	70.43	62.5 − 28.5 = 34.0

[1] Based on arbitrary assignment of 80.0 as upper limit of age group 45 and over.

Source: 1990 U.S. census data.

assume that there are K females under age 15. (The number K will drop out as the work progresses, so that its value does not matter; it is used here simply to help clarify the exposition.) The upper limit of the age range under 14 is 15.0. The number of females aged 15 to 24 plus K (the females under 15) is then the cumulated number under 25 years old; the upper limit of that age range is 25.0. The population 25 to 34 years old, plus the population 15 to 24 years old, plus K, is the cumulated number under 35 years old; the upper limit of that age range is 35.0. Continuing this process, one obtains the cumulated numbers at exact ages 25.0, 35.0, and 45.0. The cumulated data represent the "ogive" transformation of the original data for groups into data for specific points along the age scale. The transformed data are thus associated with precise points of age.

Interpolation of the transformed data can now be performed by any appropriate method but must be done twice—once for the upper limit of the subgroup for which interpolation is desired and once for the lower limit. Thus, to estimate the population in age 28 from the data for age groups 15 to 24, 25 to 34, 35 to 44, and 45 and older, one estimates the population under age 28 and then estimates the population under age 29. The difference between the two estimates will be the population between the 28th and 29th birthdays. Because K is common to both the population under 28 and the population under 29, the subtraction causes K to vanish. This means that K can be taken as zero (instead of some other arbitrary number), thereby simplifying the operation. Table C.7 illustrates the calculation.

The figure of 24,577,639 in column 3 of the top table is the interpolated estimate of the number of women cumulated to exact age 28.0. We also need the cumulated number to age 29.0, and the figure of 26,793,458 in column 3 of the bottom table is that interpolated estimate. Therefore, the desired estimate of the population from exact age 28.0 to exact age 29.0 is the difference (2,215,819) between the 26,793,458 cumulated to age 29.0 and the 24,577,639 cumulated to age 28.0.

Cumulation-Differencing Method Using Data on Percentages

In applying the cumulation-differencing method to percentage data, the percentages require weighting by the class intervals associated with them as a first step. The work then proceeds in the same manner as for absolute numbers. The following example uses the same data as those used in the example of interpolation of percentages by the midpoint method, but in Table C.8 we interpolate for the value of the percentages ever married cumulated to age 29.0.

The figure of 416.72% in the last computational stage of the upper table is the interpolated estimate of percentages cumulated to age 28.0. We also need the cumulated figure for age 29.0, and it is presented in the last computational stage of the bottom table as 489.70%. The desired estimate of the percentage ever married for women from exact age 28.0 to exact age 29.0 is the difference (73.0%) between the figures for the upper (489.70%) and lower (416.72%) limits of the year of age.

These examples employ Aitken's iterative procedure. If one has many interpolations to make for the same spacings of the abscissas (ages in this case), it might save time to use

TABLE C.7   Illustration of Cumulation-Differencing Method of Interpolation of Absolute Numbers Using Aitken's Procedure

Age group	Number of women			Computational stages			Proportionate parts
	Upper limit	In age group	Cumulated from youngest group	(1)	(2)	(3)	
Interpolation age 28.0							
15–24	25.0	17,769,944	17,769,944				−3.0
25–34	35.0	21,757,561	39,527,505	24,297,212			7.0
35–44	45.0	19,012,425	58,539,930	23,885,442	24,585,452		17.0
45+	80.0	42,884,185	101,424,115	22,332,899	24,603,772	24,577,639	52.0
Interpolation age 29.0							
15–24	25.0	17,769,944	17,769,944				−4.0
25–34	35.0	21,757,561	39,527,505	26,472,968			6.0
35–44	45.0	19,012,425	58,539,930	25,923,941	26,802,385		16.0
45+	80.0[1]	42,884,185	101,424,115	23,855,884	26,821,913	26,793,458	51.0

Estimated number of women from exact age 28.0 to exact age 29.0: 26,793,458 − 24,577,639 = 2,215,819.

[1] Arbitrary assignment of upper limit of age group.
Source: 1990 U.S. Census data.

TABLE C.8 Illustration of Cumulation-Differencing Method of Interpolating Percentages Using Aitkon's Procedure

Age group	Upper limit	Number of single years in age group (1)	Percentage ever married (2)	In age group (3) = (1)*(2)	Cumulated from youngest group	Computational stages (1)	Computational stages (2)	Computational stages (3)	Proportionate parts
Interpolation age 28.0									
15–24	25.0	10.0	20.97	209.70	209.70				−3.0
25–34	35.0	10.0	75.52	755.21	964.91	436.26			7.0
35–44	45.0	10.0	90.23	902.30	1867.21	458.33	420.82		17.0
45+	80.0	35.0	94.85	3319.75	5186.96	481.19	429.27	416.72	32.0
Interpolation age 29.0									
15–24	25.0	10.0	20.97	209.70	209.70				−4.0
25–34	35.0	10.0	75.52	755.21	964.91	511.78			6.0
35–44	45.0	10.0	90.23	902.30	1867.21	541.20	494.13		16.0
45+	80.0	35.0	94.85	3319.75	5186.96	571.46	503.82	489.70	91.0

Estimated number of women from exact age 28.0 to exact age 29.0: 489.70 − 416.72 = 72.89%.

Source: 1990 U.S. Census data.

Waring's formula to derive interpolation multipliers that can be used for all the interpolations.

Osculatory Interpolation

Both Aitken's procedure and Waring's procedure use a single curve (i.e., polynomial) and, as mentioned earlier, this circumstance can give rise to a lack of smoothness in the junction between interpolated results when passing from one group to another. Because of this, osculatory interpolation or other smooth-junction procedures are often preferred for interpolating demographic data.

Tables of Selected Sets of Multipliers

As we noted earlier, formulas for interpolation can be expressed in linear compound form—that is, in terms of coefficients or multipliers that are applied to the given data. Tables C.13 to C.17 present selected sets of multipliers for "area" interpolation (i.e., for subdivision of grouped data). These sets of multipliers are based on five different formulas:

1. Karup-King third-difference formula
2. Sprague fifth-difference formula
3. Beers six-term ordinary formula
4. Beers six-term modified formula
5. Grabill's weighted moving average of Sprague coefficients

Sets of multipliers based on all five formulas are given for subdividing intervals into fifths, that being the most common need. These are suitable for subdividing age data given in 5-year groups into single years of age. For the first two formulas, sets of multipliers are also presented for subdividing grouped data into tenths and halves. They may be used for subdividing data for 10-year age groups into single years of age and into 5-year age groups.

The multipliers can be manipulated in various ways (e.g., used in combination) to meet special needs. For example, one set might be used to split 10-year groups into 5-year groups and then another set used to subdivide the 5-year groups into single ages. Or multipliers for obtaining three single ages might be added to obtain multipliers that would yield in one step an estimate for a desired 3-year age group. Or multipliers may be combined in a manner that enables one to derive estimates of average annual age-specific first marriage rates from data on the proportion of persons ever married by 5-year age groups, or to derive estimates of average annual age-specific birthrates from data on ratios of children under 5 years old to women by age. The possibilities for manipulation of the multipliers for demographic analysis are many and varied and not limited to the usual objective of subdividing grouped data on age into single years.

Application of Multipliers

The general manner in which the multipliers (or coefficients) are used with given data to obtain an interpolated result is illustrated by the following example employing the Karup-King third-difference formula. We will begin with these (hypothetical) data:

Age group (years)	Population
15–19	35,700
20–24	30,500
25–29	32,600

Suppose we wish to estimate the population 20 years old. Age 20 is the "first fifth" of age group 20 to 24. Age group 20 to 24 is a middle group. The table of coefficients based on the Karup-King formula has the following values for interpolating a middle group to derive the first fifth (Table C.13):

	Coefficients to be applied to:		
	G1	G2	G3
(1) First fifth of G2	+.064	+.152	−.016
(2) Population	35,700	30,500	32,600
(3) = (1)*(2)	2285	4636	−522

The population aged 15 to 19 is taken as G1, the population aged 20 to 24 as G2 and the population aged 25 to 29 as G3. The desired estimate (of the population 20 years old) is then computed as follows:

$$+.064(35,700) + .152(30,500) - .016(32,600)$$
$$= 2285 + 4636 - 522 = 6399$$

Note that the Karup-King formula has four multipliers for point interpolation and three for subdivision of grouped data. Similarly, some of the sets of multipliers for interpolation of groups are labeled as having come from six-term formulas but only five groups are employed in an interpolation.

Whenever possible, midpanel multipliers (i.e., the multipliers applicable to the middle group of three or five groups) should be used. End-panel multipliers make use of less information on one side of an interpolation range than on the other side and therefore are likely to give less reliable results than when the midpanel multipliers are used. For subdivision of the first group in a distribution (e.g., ages 0 to 4), the first-panel multipliers must be used and for subdivision of the last group (e.g., ages 70 to 74), the last-panel multipliers must be used. With the Sprague formula (Table C.14) and the Beers formulas (Table C.15), there are also special multipliers for the second panel from the beginning of the distribution (e.g., ages 5 to 9) and for the next-to-last panel from the end of the distribution (e.g., 65 to 69). Once the multipliers have been selected, they are applied in the same way as the midpanel multipliers.

For example, let us estimate the population 8 years old on the basis of the Sprague formula and the following data:

Age group (years)	Population
0–4	74,300
5–9	68,700
10–14	60,400
15–19	63,900

Age 8 is the "fourth fifth" of the age group 5 to 9. Age group 5 to 9 is the next-to-first panel. The table of coefficients based on the Sprague formula has the following values for interpolating a next-to-first panel to derive the fourth fifth (Table C.14):

	Coefficients to be applied to:			
	G1	G2	G3	G4
(1) Fourth fifth of G2	−.0160	+.1840	+.0400	−.0080
(2) Population	74,300	68,700	60,400	63,900
(3) = (1)*(2)	−1,189	12,641	2,416	−511

The four population groups are taken as G1, G2, G3, and G4, respectively. The desired estimate of the population 8 years old is then computed as follows:

$$-.0160(74,300) + .1840(68,700)$$
$$+ .0400(60,400) - .0080(63,900)$$
$$= -1189 + 12,641 + 2416 - 511 = 13,357$$

By contrast, the rectangular assumption discussed earlier in this appendix would estimate the population aged 8 as 68,700/5 = 13,740.

Subdivision of Unevenly Spaced Groups

Interpolation coefficients may also be derived for subdividing unevenly spaced groups. Suppose we wish to divide in half a group that has the same width as the two following groups but is twice as wide as the two preceding groups. Thus, G1 and G2 might represent 5-year age groups while G3, G4, and G5 represent 10-year age groups. The pattern of the available data to be subdivided into 5-year age groups is, therefore, 5-5-(10)-10-10, or 1-1-(2)-2-2:

	Coefficients to be applied to:				
	G1	G2	G3	G4	G5
First half of G3	−.0677	+.2180	+.4888	−.0737	+.0097
Last half of G3	+.0677	−.2180	+.5112	+.0737	−.0097

After a series of 5-year age groups is obtained by use of the above coefficients, the other sets of interpolation coefficients can be used further to subdivide the data into single years of age.

Interpolation multipliers can be derived for subdividing a group under many variations in the pattern of the available data. The data may follow the pattern 1-1-(2)-2-5, 1-5-(5)-5-5, 1-1-(5)-5-5, 1-2-(5)-5-10, or other pattern. The midpanel (circled group) may be subdivided into fifths, tenths, halves, or other fraction.

Comparison and Selection of Osculatory-Interpolation Formulas

As stated earlier, the choice of a method for interpolation is dependent on the nature of the data and on the purposes to be served. The several sets of interpolation coefficients presented in Appendix C are based on formulas that differ in their underlying principles. There is no one "best" method for all purposes.

Use of Ordinary Formulas

The Karup-King formula is the simplest one for which interpolation coefficients are actually presented here. It is "correct to second differences" and has an adjustment involving third differences. It uses four given points (or the four boundaries of three groups). It resembles the formula for an ordinary second-degree polynomial (expressed in differences) fitted to the first three points plus an adjustment involving the fourth point. If the third difference of the four given points is zero, then all four given points fall on the same second-degree curve and no adjustment results.

The three formulas discussed (Karup-King, Sprague, and Beers ordinary) reproduce the data. Specifically, the interpolated points fall on curves that pass through the given points, and the interpolated subdivisions of groups add up to the data for the given groups. Following are two examples of results from the use of the three methods described with certain kinds of regular well-behaved data. Results from rough data or data of erratic quality are considered later.

Suppose we are given the following data:

x	$y = x^2$	$y = x^4$
1	1	1
2	4	16
3	9	81
4	16	256
5	25	625
6	36	1296

We wish to find y for $x = 3.4$ by interpolation of the given values. We note that 3.4 is in the "middle" interval of the range of data, so, for the Karup-King method, we will use the middle interval table. We start at the $N_{2.0}$ position and read down to find the $N_{2.4}$ row for coefficients. The four x values preceding and following $x = 3.4$ are, of course, 2 and 3 preceding and 4 and 5 following. The $y = x^2$ values corresponding to these x's are $y = 4$, $y = 9$, $y = 16$, and $y = 25$, respectively. Using these four y-values and the coefficients in row $N_{2.4}$ of Table C.13, we obtain the interpolated value:

$$y_{KK \text{ interpolated}} = (-.072 * 4) + (.696 * 9) + (.424 * 16)$$
$$+ (-.048 * 25) = 11.5600, \text{ as desired}$$
$$(\text{i.e., } 3.4^2 = 11.56)$$

The Sprague interpolation is calculated similarly. Because 3.4 is in the "middle" interval of the range of data, we use the middle interval table. We start at the $N_{3.0}$ position and read down to find the $N_{3.4}$ row for coefficients. The six x values preceding and following $x = 3.4$ are, of course,

1, 2, and 3 preceding and 4, 5, and 6 following. The $y = x^2$ values corresponding to these x's are $y = 1$, $y = 4$, and $y = 9$ (preceding) and $y = 16$, $y = 25$, and $y = 36$ (following), respectively. Using these six y-values and the coefficients in row $N_{3.4}$ of Table C.14, we obtain the Sprague interpolated value:

$$y_{S \text{ interpolated}} = (+.0144 * 1) + (-.1136 * 4) + (.7264 * 9)$$
$$+ (.4384 * 16) + (-.0736 * 25) + (.0080 * 36)$$
$$= 11.5600, \text{ as desired}$$

Finally, the Beers interpolation is similar to the Sprague formula. We present it here without discussion, using the coefficients from row $N_{3.4}$ in Table C.15:

$$y_{B \text{ interpolated}} = (0.0137 * 1) + (-0.1101 * 4) + (0.7194 * 9)$$
$$+ (0.4454 * 16) + (-0.0771 * 25) + (0.0087 * 36)$$
$$= 11.5600, \text{ as desired}$$

We note that the same coefficients are used to interpolate y for $x = 3.4$ in the second equation $y = x^4$. We present the calculations here:

Karup-King formula:

$$y_{KK \text{ interpolated}} = (-.072 * 4) + (.696 * 9) + (.424 * 16)$$
$$+ (-.048 * 25) = 133.7680$$

Sprague formula:

$$y_{S \text{ interpolated}} = (+.0144 * 1) + (-.1136 * 4) + (.7264 * 9)$$
$$+ (.4384 * 16) + (-.0736 * 25) + (.0080 * 36)$$
$$= 133.6336$$

Beers ordinary formula:

$$y_{B \text{ interpolated}} = (0.0137 * 1) + (-0.1101 * 4) + (0.7194 * 9)$$
$$+ (0.4454 * 16) + (-0.0771 * 25) + (0.0087 * 36)$$
$$= 133.6336$$

The true value of 3.4^4 is 133.6336.

This example demonstrates empirically that the two fifth-difference formulas (Sprague and Beers) will reproduce the results of polynomials of low degree (e.g., $y = x^2$) when the observed data are of that form. It also demonstrates that the Karup-King third-difference formula can sometimes produce nearly correct results for a set of observed data in which fourth differences are not zero (as in the case of $y = x^4$).

Use of Modified Formulas

The modified formulas assume that the observed data are subject to error, and, in effect, they substitute weighted moving averages of the observed point or group data for the observed data. Thereby they obtain more smoothness in the interpolated results, although at a cost of some modification of the original data.

The extent to which the modifications alter the original data can perhaps best be seen by adding together the five coefficients for subdividing a central group into five equal parts according to the various interpolation schemes. These sums are as follows:

G1	G2	G3	G4	G5
Beers's modified six-term minimized fourth-difference formula				
−.0430	+.1721	+.7420	+.1720	−.0430
Grabill's modification of Sprague coefficients				
+.0164	+.2641	+.4390	+.2641	+.0164
Formulas that reproduce group totals without modification				
0	0	1.0000	0	0

Note that all of these coefficients sum to 1.0 across the rows. In this sense, they "weight" the different observations, G1 through G5, differently. These figures represent consolidated coefficients which, if applied to the given G1, G2, G3, G4, and G5 groups, would yield the sums of the five interpolated subdivisions of G3. It is apparent from the difference in weights assigned to the middle panel that the Beers modified formula involves a less drastic modification of the original group values than Grabill's coefficients.

Illustration of Comparative Results with Age Data

Comparative results for interpolating census data for 5-year age groups into single ages are shown in Table C.9, with graphical results in Figure C.6. In this table, we have collapsed 1960 census data for Mexico into 5-year age groups. Using only the 5-year age groups, we then interpolate to single years of age using the Karup-King coefficients, the Sprague coefficients, the Beers ordinary coefficients, the Beers modified coefficients, and the Grabill coefficients.

Finally, we display the interpolated distributions for comparison with the original, single-year-of-age data reported in the 1960 Census of Mexico. Figure C.6 shows that the enumerated data in single years fluctuate sharply as a result of the tendency of many persons to report ages that are multiples of five or two.

The table and the figure illustrate the digit preferences clearly. The Karup-King formula smoothes out only part of these undulations because the group totals are maintained. The Sprague and Beers ordinary formulas generate interpolations that are very similar to the Karup-King formula. Use of Grabill's coefficients shows how completely the undulations can be removed by a drastic smoothing procedure. The Beers modified formula is similar in its effect as the Grabill formula; it removes most of the undulations, at the cost of modifying the 5-year age groups' totals.

An alternative procedure for subdividing the last few regular groups in the age distribution (e.g., 75 to 79, 80 to 84 for Mexico, 1960) involves, first, splitting up the open-ended terminal group (e.g., 85 and over) into three groups (i.e., 85 to 89, 90 to 94, and 90 and over) and then applying midpanel coefficients for subdividing the groups just ahead of the terminal group. The precision of the results of subdividing the terminal group would have only a small effect on

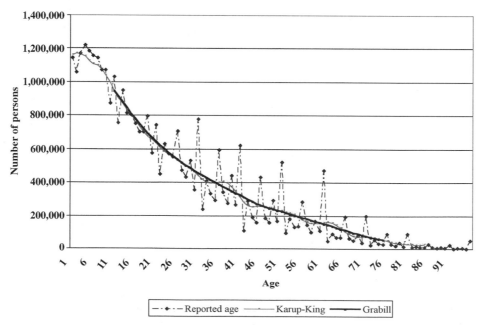

FIGURE C.6 Population of Mexico, 1960, by single years of age as enumerated and as interpolated from 5-year age groups by the use of the Karup-King method and the Grabill method.
Source: Table C.9 and unpublished calculations.

TABLE C.9   Results of Interpolating the Population of Mexico, 1960, for 5-year Age Groups under 20 and 65 to 84, by Single Years of Age, According to Several Methods (See text for explanation of various types of interpolation.)

Age group (years)	Enumerated Population[2]	Single ages (years)	Enumerated population	Interpolated population[1]				
				Karup-King formula	Sprague formula	Beers ordinary formula	Beers modified formula	Grabill modification of Sprague formula
Total, all ages	34,809,586	Total, all ages	34,809,586	34,809,586	34,809,586	34,809,586	34,809,586	(NA)
Under 5	5,776,747	**Under 5**	**5,776,747**	**5,776,747**	**5,776,747**	**5,776,747**	**5,776,747**	**(NA)**
5–9	5,317,044	**Under 1**	**1,144,187**	**1,160,188**	**1,146,846**	**1,162,002**	**1,165,090**	**(NA)**
10–14	4,358,316	1	1,059,321	1,169,745	1,160,676	1,163,085	1,165,241	(NA)
15–19	3,535,265	2	1,171,914	1,167,326	1,164,419	1,159,921	1,160,371	(NA)
20–24	2,947,072	3	1,219,205	1,152,930	1,159,093	1,152,185	1,150,479	(NA)
25–29	2,504,892	4	1,182,120	1,126,558	1,145,713	1,139,554	1,135,565	(NA)
30–34	2,051,635	**5–9**	**5,317,044**	**5,317,044**	**5,317,044**	**5,317,044**	**5,289,752**	**(NA)**
35–39	1,920,680	5	1,158,544	1,108,169	1,125,294	1,121,652	1,115,684	(NA)
40–44	1,361,324	6	1,143,140	1,097,766	1,098,851	1,098,155	1,091,005	(NA)
45–49	1,233,608	7	1,071,375	1,075,385	1,067,401	1,068,900	1,061,845	(NA)
50–54	1,063,359	8	1,070,475	1,041,028	1,031,959	1,033,994	1,028,728	(NA)
55–59	799,899	9	873,510	994,695	993,540	994,343	992,490	(NA)
60–64	744,710	**10–14**	**4,358,316**	**4,358,316**	**4,358,316**	**4,358,316**	**4,381,343**	**4,394,266**
65–69	414,164	10	1,029,718	946,191	952,303	951,714	954,046	945,840
70–74	333,371	11	756,819	905,671	908,406	908,621	914,517	912,389
75–79	187,773	12	948,976	868,407	867,150	867,900	875,130	878,716
80–84	128,338	13	814,823	834,399	831,264	831,478	836,935	845,217
85 and over	131,389	14	807,980	803,648	799,192	798,603	800,716	812,104
		15–19	**3,535,265**	**3,535,265**	**3,535,265**	**3,535,265**	**3,543,350**	**3,609,614**
		15	753,742	769,139	766,509	766,302	767,084	779,861
		16	703,138	732,460	733,929	734,004	736,000	749,206
		17	703,225	701,416	703,971	704,234	706,772	720,369
		18	798,608	676,010	677,396	677,471	679,461	693,091
		19	576,552	656,240	653,461	653,254	654,033	667,086
		. . .						
		65–69	**414,164**	**414,164**	**414,164**	**414,164**	**450,270**	**482,737**
		65	191,430	105,280	107,502	106,579	110,095	112,222
		66	60,826	88,063	88,888	89,223	98,187	103,968
		67	48,671	76,839	75,461	76,636	87,972	96,034
		68	78,878	71,609	70,750	71,085	79,923	88,671
		69	34,359	72,373	71,563	70,640	74,093	81,842
		70–74	**333,371**	**333,371**	**333,371**	**333,371**	**313,353**	**319,639**
		70	200,200	74,175	71,427	71,939	69,982	74,290
		71	20,313	71,980	71,924	71,738	66,754	68,679
		72	52,712	68,230	70,172	69,520	63,236	63,620
		73	31,757	62,924	64,177	63,991	59,106	58,834
		74	28,389	56,063	55,671	56,183	54,276	54,216
		75–79	**187,773**	**187,773**	**187,773**	**187,773**	**194,265**	**(NA)**
		75	88,484	47,824	48,619	47,921	48,970	(NA)
		76	28,812	40,621	42,518	40,749	43,524	(NA)
		77	19,474	35,487	36,865	35,562	38,288	(NA)
		78	36,715	32,420	31,902	32,507	33,633	(NA)
		79	14,288	31,421	27,869	31,034	29,850	(NA)
		80–84	**128,338**	**128,338**	**128,338**	**128,338**	**128,338**	**(NA)**
		80	88,484	29,044	25,008	30,362	27,016	(NA)
		81	7,520	25,288	23,562	29,567	25,239	(NA)
		82	13,514	23,600	23,771	27,681	24,564	(NA)
		83	9,537	23,980	25,877	23,782	24,993	(NA)
		84	9,283	26,427	30,121	16,947	26,526	(NA)

(NA) Not available.

[1] Slight discrepancies in the last digit between the sums of interpolated single ages and the 5-year totals are due to rounding.

[2] Total excludes "unknowns". Age was not reported for only 0.3 percent of the population.

Source of census data: México, Secretaría de Industria y Comercio, Dirección General de Estadística, *Censo de Población, 1960.*

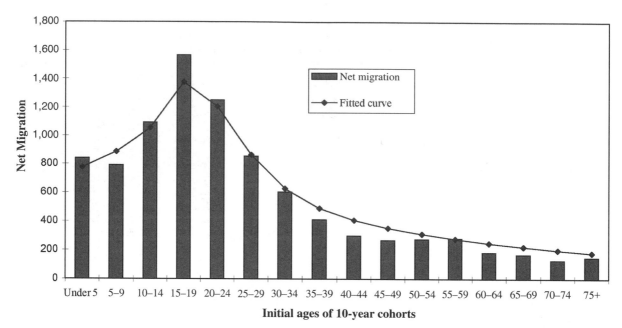

FIGURE C.7 Data and model net migration schedule for age cohorts of females, McCleennan County, Texas, projected 1980–1990.
Source: Bars: Basedon Murdock and Ellis (1991, p. 207) Fitted curve: Calculated by authors.

the interpolated single-year-of-age values for the preceding age groups. One device for subdividing the terminal group is to employ the distribution of L_x from an appropriate life table (e.g., a life table for Mexico, 1959–1961). Another is to fit a polynomial to the last several observed values and zero for 100 and over (e.g., a third-degree polynomial to values for 75 and over, 80 and over, 85 and over, and 100 and over). The appropriate population by age at the preceding census may be "aged" to the current census year, and the distribution of survivors may then be used to subdivide the current total for the terminal age group. At the beginning of the distribution, to the extent that the quality of the statistics permit, birth statistics, or birth statistics adjusted for deaths, may be employed to subdivide the 5-year totals into single ages, as suggested in Chapter 7.

Parameterizing Demographic Models

Many demographic models have a common form, consisting of a curve or sequence of age-specific (or age/race/sex specific) numbers, rates, or proportions. Figure C.7 illustrates this idea with an array of 16 net-migration values for 5-year age (birth) cohorts for a 10-year period (Murdock and Ellis, 1991, p. 207) and with an interpolated curve on top of the sequence of grouped data.

The interpolated curve provides the clue to simplifying the demographic model implied by the data. Instead of considering 16 age-specific migration rates or numbers, we can summarize the data by fitting a single curve with a limited

number of parameters that define its level and shape.[9] We refer to this as "parameterizing" the model. Once a model has been parameterized, it is then potentially broadly applicable—again because we are not calculating numerous age-specific numbers or rates, but can plot and manipulate the curve itself, similar to working with model life tables.

As an example of the power of parameterizing a demographic model, Castro and Rogers (1983) developed model schedules for migration for a variety of cities and nations of the world. Instead of calculating a series of disconnected age-specific migration counts or rates, they presumed that the age distribution of migrants could be split into three components: A child/dependent component, an independent/adult component, and an older-age component.[10] They simply added components together:

$$N(x) = N_1(x) + N_2(x) + N_3(x) \qquad (C.62)$$

where

N_1 is the proportion of migrants in the dependent component

---

[9] The details of the curve-fitting technique are more advanced than this appendix warrants. Programs and data are available from the authors.

[10] Rogers and Castro (1986) later introduced a fourth component to account for post–labor force migration. We will not deal with that fourth component here except to note that it illustrates that migration propensities are in fact quite difficult to model adequately. Migration as a sequence of events is simply not as regular and easy to model as fertility or mortality.

N_2 is the proportion of migrants in the independent component

N_3 is the proportion of migrants in the older adult component

$N(x)$ is the proportion of migrants at age x

Up to this point, the model is quite simple; it is merely the sum of three conceptually different components. It is here, however, that parameterization adds value. Castro and Rogers then proposed the following three functions for each component:

$$N_1(x) = a_1 e^{-\alpha_1 x} \qquad (C.63)$$

$$N_2(x) = a_2 e^{-\alpha_2(x-\mu_2) - e^{-\lambda_2(x-\mu_2)}} \qquad (C.64)$$

$$N_3(x) = c \qquad (C.65)$$

One can always simply count up the number of migrants in a particular group and divide by the total population at risk, generating a rate for each age group. However, with these models, the age-specific migration rates have been "summarized" by seven parameters, a_1, a_2, α_1, α_2, λ_2, μ_2, and c. If one can assume that older migration does not require its own parameter, one can set $c = 0$ and reduce the load to six parameters. Figure C.8 displays these three curves individually and their sum, using parameters for Rio de Janeiro Castro and Rogers. The older adult component is assumed to be zero, so the model migration schedule is the sum of only two schedules, the independent and the dependent schedules. Obviously, by fitting the curves to different age-specific migration data, one can generate a wide variety of plausible migration schedules.

This procedure illustrates the power of parameterizing a demographic model: Once the shape of the overall curve (or collection of curves) has been established, the analyst can use the parameters of the curve in modeling and analysis. Further, for this particular application (migration), one can then cast the events in a traditional life-table framework for

further analysis (see, e.g., Long, 1984). Similar analyses, in the context of mortality probabilities, are given in Heligman and Pollard (1993). This observation is not unique to demography, but is true in statistical studies in general. By parameterizing a relationship, one gains analytic power.

ADJUSTMENT OF DISTRIBUTIONS TO MARGINAL TOTALS

There are many instances where available distributions of demographic data do not satisfy certain desired marginal totals. The distribution(s) in question may be a univariate distribution or multivariate cross-tabulations. The need to adjust to marginal totals, whether for a single distribution or for a two-dimensional table, may arise in connection with the following:

- The adjustment of sample data to agree with complete-count data or independent estimates
- The estimation of the frequencies in a distribution for a given year on the basis of data for prior years and a total or totals for the given year
- The adjustment of the detailed data for a given year(s) and area(s) to presumably more accurate marginal totals for the same year(s) and area(s) obtained from a different source
- The adjustment of the frequencies in reported categories of the variables to absorb the categories designated as not reported

Commonly, the detailed data and the marginal total or totals are all positive numbers—that is, neither zero nor negative. Zero cells may be encountered frequently in sample data, and negative frequencies appear occasionally in demographic data, as for example in a series on net migration. Although the procedures for adjusting distributions

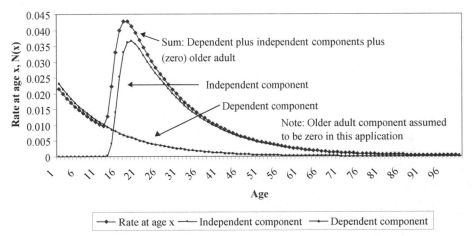

FIGURE C.8 Model migration rate schedule for males, Rio de Janiero.
Source: Based on Rastro and Rogers (1983).

with negative cells are logical extensions of those with only positive or zero cells, somewhat different arithmetic steps are involved. We shall therefore consider this case separately. We may then outline the types of situations considered here as follows:

1. Single distribution
   a. Frequencies all positive or zero
   b. Frequencies include negatives
2. Two-dimensional table
   a. Frequencies all positive or zero
   b. Frequencies include negatives
3. General multiway tables

In the case of 1b, 2b, and 3, the marginal totals may be positive, negative, or zero. The marginal totals are not likely to be negative or zero if the basic distribution has only positive frequencies or a combination of positive and zero frequencies.

Single Distribution

Distributions with All Positive or Zero Frequencies

The simplest case involves a single distribution with only positive frequencies, or positive and zero frequencies, and a positive assigned total. It is illustrated by a distribution of preliminary postcensal population estimates for states for which there is an independent estimate of the national population, or a distribution of births by order of birth including a category "order not stated." In the first case, we wish to adjust the preliminary state figures to the independent national total; in the second case, we wish to eliminate the "unknowns" by distributing them over the known categories in such a way that the adjusted frequencies will add to the required total. Assuming in the first case that we do not have any information regarding the errors in the preliminary estimates, we may further assume that the discrepancy between the sum of the preliminary state estimates and the independent national estimate has a distribution proportionate to the preliminary state estimates. Similarly, assuming in the second case that we have no special information regarding the distribution of the "unknowns", we may further assume that the "unknowns" have the same relative distribution as the "known" categories.

Suppose that N is the required total, n is the sum of the groups excluding the unknowns, and each ith group in the distribution has n_i cases. Then the simplest way of applying the "proportionate" assumption to obtain adjusted figures N_i is to multiply each known category in the distribution (n_i) by a factor representing the ratio of the required total (N) to the sum of the frequencies excluding the unknowns (Σn_i). Or

$$N_i = \left(\frac{N}{\Sigma n_i} \right) n_i \qquad (C.66)$$

Such an adjustment of a distribution is known as prorate adjustment but is sometimes refined to informally as "raking." In multiway contexts, the term "iterative proportional fitting" is used. It is a standard and very commonly used tool for distributing one group among all the rest, proportional to the recipient group's representation in the whole, and it is regularly used to "control" subarea or subgroup populations to the total area or combined group. (See, e.g., Citro, Cohen, Kalton, and West, 1997, for its use in the U.S. Census Bureau's Small Area Income and Poverty Estimates program.)

The adjustment of the reported distribution of deaths by age for Mexico in 1990 to include deaths of age not reported is shown in Table C.10. The required total number of deaths is 422,803 for both sexes combined and the total of the distribution excluding the cases not reported is 419,972 (= 422,803 − 2,831). The adjustment factor (for both sexes combined) is equal to 422,803/419,972, or 1.006741. Given a fixed adjustment strategy, the results obtained for a particular category (N_i) are unaffected by the number of categories in the distribution. For example, the adjusted number of deaths for ages 0 to 4 and 5 to 9 combined would be the same whether the deaths were adjusted separately or in combination. However, as can be clearly seen in the table, when two different groups are adjusted separately and then added together, their sum will not necessarily add up to the value when they are summed and adjusted as a total. This can be seen in columns 6 and 7; in column 6, males and females were added together after being adjusted separately, while in column 7, males and females were added together and then adjusted. To simultaneously adjust two distributions so that both fit, iterative multiway proportionate adjustment must be performed; it will be described later.

Distributions with Some Negative Frequencies

Occasionally a distribution that requires adjustment to a marginal total includes negative as well as positive values. This arises when a distribution of an element that "operates" negatively (e.g., deaths, outmigration) is superimposed on the distribution of an element that "operates" positively (e.g., births, inmigration). Distributions such as those of net migration or population change for the states of a country, or natural increase for the counties of a state, may have negative cells.

The marginal total for a "plus-minus" distribution may be positive, negative, or zero. In this case, the use of a single adjustment factor applied uniformly to all values would yield the required total but the original data would be subject to excessive modification. A procedure, originally proposed by Akers and Siegel (1965), that minimizes the adjustment requires the use of two factors, one for the positive items and one for the negative items. The formulas for the factors are as follows:

TABLE C.10 Number of Deaths, by Age and Sex, Mexico: 1990

| | Registered deaths | | | Not reported allocated | | | |
| | | | | | | Both sexes (adjusted separately) | Both sexes (adjusted together) |
Age (years)	Both sexes (1)	Male (2)	Female (3)	Male (4) = (2) × 1.00746	Female (5) = (3) × 1.00581	(6) = (4) + (5)	(7) = (1) × 1.00674
All ages	422,803	239,574	183,229	239,574.0	183,229.0	422,803.0	422,803.0
0–4	85,635	47,575	38,060	47,929.7	38,281.0	86,210.8	86,212.3
5–9	6,485	3,610	2,875	3,636.9	2,891.7	6,528.6	6,528.7
10–14	5,417	3,272	2,145	3,296.4	2,157.5	5,453.9	5,453.5
15–19	9,587	6,688	2,899	6,737.9	2,915.8	9,653.7	9,651.6
20–24	11,702	8,584	3,118	8,648.0	3,136.1	11,784.1	11,780.9
25–29	12,023	8,829	3,194	8,894.8	3,212.5	12,107.4	12,104.0
30–34	11,890	8,526	3,364	8,589.6	3,383.5	11,973.1	11,970.1
35–39	13,196	9,010	4,186	9,077.2	4,210.3	13,287.5	13,285.0
40–44	13,282	8,786	4,496	8,851.5	4,522.1	13,373.6	13,371.5
45–49	15,754	10,216	5,538	10,292.2	5,570.2	15,862.3	15,860.2
50–54	17,475	10,754	6,721	10,834.2	6,760.0	17,594.2	17,592.8
55–59	21,439	12,733	8,706	12,827.9	8,756.6	21,584.5	21,583.5
60–64	24,424	13,852	10,572	13,955.3	10,633.4	24,588.7	24,588.6
65–69	27,884	15,463	12,421	15,578.3	12,493.1	28,071.4	28,072.0
70–74	27,501	14,816	12,685	14,926.5	12,758.7	27,685.1	27,686.4
75–79	32,195	16,861	15,334	16,986.7	15,423.1	32,409.8	32,412.0
80–84	31,567	15,404	16,163	15,518.8	16,256.9	31,775.7	31,779.8
85+	52,516	22,822	29,694	22,992.2	29,866.5	52,858.6	52,870.0
Not reported	2,831	1,773	1,058				
Adjustment factor =	1.00674	1.00746	1.00581				

Source: Based on United Nations, 1994, *Demographic Yearbook* 1992, New York, United Nations, Table 22.

Factor for the positive values of n_i:

$$\frac{\sum_i |n_i| + (N - n)}{\sum_i |n_i|} \quad \text{(C.67)}$$

Factor for the negative values of n_i:

$$\frac{\sum_i |n_i| - (N - n)}{\sum_i |n_i|} \quad \text{(C.68)}$$

In these factors, $\sum_i |n_i|$ represents the sum of the absolute values (i.e., without regard to sign) of the original distribution, N the assigned total, and $n = \sum_i n_i$ the algebraic sum of the original observations. The factor for adjusting the positive items represents the ratio of (1) the sum of the absolute values in the distribution plus the net amount of adjustment required in the distribution to (2) the sum of the absolute values. The factor for adjusting the negative items in the distribution represents the ratio of (1) the excess of the sum of the absolute values over the net amount of adjustment required in the distribution to (2) the sum of the absolute values. The formulas are applied in the same way if the assigned total is zero. Akers and Siegel called this procedure the plus-minus proportionate adjustment procedure.

The application of this procedure is illustrated in Table C.11. This table presents estimates of net migration for the nonmetropolitan counties of Louisana, separately for the white and nonwhite populations, for the decade 1950–1970, derived by the residual method. Specifically, the estimates were derived by applying national census survival rates to the population distributed by age, sex, and color in 1960 and births by sex and color for 1960–1970 and by subtracting the survivors from the 1970 population. As explained in Chapter 19, this method yields only estimates of net migration for age (birth) cohorts over the decade. Different figures for all-ages net migration are obtained if the residual method is applied with actual death statistics instead of national census survival rates. Theoretically, the latter estimates (the vital statistics estimates) are viewed as more accurate than the sum of the preliminary age estimates. Accordingly, the task is to adjust the preliminary estimates of net migration distributed by age, separately for the two race groups, to the vital statistics estimates of net migration. The distributions contain both plus entries and minus entries.

To generate net migration estimates for age cohorts adjusted to the all-ages vital statistics estimates, we use the

Table C.11   Illustration of the Plus-Minus Proportionate Adjustment Procedure for Estimates of Net Migration by Race for the Nonmetropolitan Counties of Louisiana, 1960–1970 (A minus sign denotes net outmigration; the absence of a sign denotes net inmigration)

	Preliminary estimates[1]			Total		Adjusted estimates[2]	
Age in 1970	Total[3] (1)	White (2)	Black and other races (3)	Direct calculation[4] (4)	By summation[5] (5)	White (6)	Black and other races (7)
All ages	−97,731	14,253	−111,984	−95,644	−95,644	15,086[6]	−110,730[6]
0–4	−2,739	1,792	−4,531	−2,685	−2,660	1,821	−4,481
5–9	−5,641	5,502	−11,143	−5,530	−5,428	5,591	−11,019
10–14	−7,454	4,190	−11,644	−7,307	−7,257	4,258	−11,515
15–19	−10,898	3,242	−14,140	−10,683	−10,689	3,294	−13,983
20–24	−34,806	−8,331	−26,475	−34,120	−34,377	−8,196	−26,181
25–29	−33,541	−9,836	−23,705	−32,880	−33,119	−9,677	−23,442
30–34	−3,920	5,102	−9,022	−3,843	−3,738	5,184	−8,922
35–39	−406	3,220	−3,626	−398	−314	3,272	−3,586
40–44	280	2,239	−1,959	285	338	2,275	−1,937
45–49	2	1,595	−1,593	2	46	1,621	−1,575
50–54	335	1,325	−990	342	367	1,346	−979
55–59	397	1,322	−925	405	428	1,343	−915
60–64	547	1,232	−685	558	575	1,252	−677
65–69	1,907	1,370	537	1,945	1,935	1,392	543
70–74	635	800	−165	648	650	813	−163
75 and over	−2,430	−511	−1,919	−2,382	−2,401	−503	−1,898

[1] Derived as residuals by use of national census survival rates, census populations for 1960 and 1970, and births for 1960 to 1970. These particular figures represent arbitrary reconstructions. As a result, these are slight discrepancies between the preliminary and the adjusted estimates when the adjustment factors are applied.

[2] Source: U.S. Economic Research Service (U.S. Department of Agriculture) and Institute of Behavioral Research (University of Georgia), "Net Migration of the Population, 1960–70, by Age, Sex, and Color, Part 7–Analytical Groupings of the Counties," by G. K. Bowles and E. S. Lee, Athens, Georgia: University of Georgia, 1977.

The (imputed) adjustment factors are:

	Net inmigration (+)	Net outmigration (−)
Total	1.019700	.980300
White	1.016141	.983859
Black and other races	1.011092	.988908

[3] Obtained by summing the preliminary estimates for race groups in columns 2 and 3.

[4] Obtained by direct plus-minus adjustment of preliminary estimates in column 1.

[5] Obtained by summing the adjusted estimates for race groups in columns 6 and 7.

[6] Independent estimates derived by the vital statistics residual method.

Note: This illustration of the plus-minus proportionate adjustment procedure was provided to the authors in a personal communication from J. S. Siegel.

plus-minus proportionate adjustment procedure, as shown in formulas C.67 and C.68. We plan to allocate the difference between the pairs of totals by age in accordance with the age distribution of the preliminary estimates. Thus, for the white population, we have a distribution that sums to 14,253 and we wish to make the distribution sum to 15,086; that is, we need to increase the figures by +833. For blacks and other races, we have a distribution that sums to −111,984 and we wish to make the distribution sum to −110,730; that is, we need to increase the figures by +1254. We lay out the computation of the factors only for the second (i.e., nonwhite) distribution. The first factor, applied to the positive items, is

$$\frac{\sum_i |n_i| + (N-n)}{\sum_i |n_i|} = \frac{113,059 + (-110,790 + 111,984)}{113,059}$$
$$= 1.011092$$

The second factor, applied to the negative items, is

$$\frac{\sum_i |n_i| - (N-n)}{\sum_i |n_i|} = \frac{113,059 - (-110,790 + 111,984)}{113,059}$$
$$= 0.988908$$

The last two columns of Table C.11 show the results of the adjustment. The adjustment factor is 1.011092 for the cases of net inmigration and .988908 for the cases of net outmigration. In effect, the procedure distributes the amount of adjustment among the items in proportion to their absolute values. The farther away from zero the estimated net migration for an age cohort is, more (or fewer) persons are allocated to the net migration cohort. For example, age group 70–74, which had a net outmigration of only 165, is almost unaffected by the plus-minus procedure and thus (almost) neither gains nor loses persons from the 1254 added to the age distribution as a whole.

The plus-minus proportionate adjustment procedure described suffers from at least three weaknesses. First, the detail of the given distribution affects the results—that is, the combination of cells adjusted separately would not show the same result as when the combined category is adjusted directly. As illustrated in the original *Methods and Materials of Demography* (Shryock and Siegel *et al.*, 1971), if the adjustment procedure was applied to geographic divisions instead of 50 states and the District of Columbia, one would obtain substantially different adjusted estimates of net migration for divisions when the adjusted state figures are added. Table C.11 also presents illustrative evidence showing that adjusted estimates obtained by direct calculation differ from those obtained by summing adjusted estimates for its component groups. In this case the direct adjustment of the figures in column 1, "total population" (obtained by summing the preliminary estimates for the white the nonwhite populations), shown in column 4, do not agree, except approximately, with the figures obtained by summation of the figures for the racial groups shown in column 5.

A second weakness of the procedure is that zero cells in the distribution cannot receive any of the adjustment. A third weakness is that, in the event that the net amount of adjustment required in the distribution $(N - n)$ exceeds the sum of the absolute values in the distribution $\sum_i |n_i|$, one of the adjustment factors will have a negative sign and, hence, will cause all the items in the distribution to which it is applied to reverse signs. The larger positives could become the larger negatives or the larger negatives could become the larger positives. This is untenable because the pattern of the original distribution would thereby be sharply altered. One procedure for avoiding this type of result is to "translate" the original data into a more acceptable form by adding or subtracting a fixed amount to or from each item in the distribution, apply the formulas, and then translate the numbers back by the same amount as used in the first translation (Akers and Siegel, 1965).

Two-Dimensional Tables

Situations differ with regard to the availability of marginal totals for two-dimensional tables (bivariate distributions), hence, the adjustment procedures may vary somewhat. In some cases, the marginal totals in two dimensions differ from the sums of the distributions. In other cases, marginal totals in two dimensions are known but differ in only one dimension from the sums of the distributions. In still other cases, marginal totals in neither dimension are known at first but emerge in the process of adjustment, and these totals differ from the sums of the original distributions. We also have the case of a bivariate distribution where only the grand total is fixed, none of the column or row totals being known, and the

sum of all the cells differs from the required grand total. Any of these cases may be complicated by a mixture of positive and negative signs in the body of the table, with associated positive, negative, or zero marginal totals.

Tables with All Positive or Zero Frequencies

The common situation where the sums of both the rows and columns differ from the required marginal totals is that where the cross-tabulations were obtained only for a sample of the population and marginal totals are available from a complete census count. Let us consider the specific case, drawn from the 1990 Oregon Population Survey, where we have sample statistics for the population by age and sex and complete-count statistics only for age groups and sex groups separately. In this typical example, we wish to "calibrate" the sample survey data to the independently derived census data.

We will employ the following symbols:

i = age group, consisting of $j = 1$ (for age <5 years), 2 (for age 5 to 14), 3 (for age 15 to 44), 4 (for age 45 to 64), 5 (for age 65+) and 6 (for age unknown)

j = sex group, consisting of $j = 1$ and $j = 2$

n_{ij} = sample count for a the ith age and jth sex group

$n_{i.} = \sum_{j=1}^{2} n_{ij}$ = sample count for total number of persons in the ith age group

$n_{.j} = \sum_{i=1}^{6} n_{ij}$ = sample count for total number of persons in the jth sex group

$n = n_{..} = \sum_{j=1}^{2} \sum_{i=1}^{6} n_{ij}$ = sample count for all age and sex groups (the total sample size)

N_{ij} = estimated complete count for a particular sex and age group

$N_{i.}$ = complete count for total number in the ith age group

$N_{.j}$ = complete count for total number in the jth sex group

$N = N_{..} = \sum_{j=1}^{2} \sum_{i=1}^{6} N_{ij}$ = complete count for all age and sex groups (the total population size)

Using these quantities, we can set up the following chart:

Age group	Sample figures on:		Sample total	Complete count
	Sex			
	1	2		
1	n_{11}	n_{12}	$n_{1.}$	$N_{1.}$
2	n_{21}	n_{22}	$n_{2.}$	$N_{2.}$
3	n_{31}	n_{32}	$n_{3.}$	$N_{3.}$
4	n_{41}	n_{42}	$n_{4.}$	$N_{4.}$
5	n_{51}	n_{52}	$n_{5.}$	$N_{5.}$
6	n_{61}	n_{62}	$n_{6.}$	$N_{6.}$
Sample total	$n_{.1}$	$n_{.2}$	$n_{..}$	
Complete count	$N_{.1}$	$N_{.2}$		$N_{..}$

Method of Iterative Proportional Fitting

The adjustment of the sample data to sum to the complete-count marginal totals may be achieved by iterative sequential "raking" of the original matrix, alternating with rows and columns, that is, first horizontally, then vertically, then horizontally, and so on, or first vertically, then horizontally, then vertically, and so on. The procedure is illustrated in Table C.12 with sample data on age cross-classified by sex, and complete-count data on age and sex, separately, drawn from the 1990 Oregon Population Survey (for sample data) and the 1990 census of the United States (for complete count data). Each step in the calculations is like that for adjusting single distributions proportionately to an assigned total. This procedure is called the method of iterative proportional adjustment or fitting, originally described in Deming and Stephan (1940) and Deming (1948).

Iterative proportional fitting proceeds as follows: Begin with proportionate adjustment along each row to the marginal row totals in Table C.12 (labeled "First proration by age"), then follow with proportionate adjustment of the results along each column to the marginal column totals (labeled "First proration by sex"). The vertical adjustment throws the figures out of line with respect to the marginal row totals; so adjust the figures to the marginal row totals once again (labeled "Second proration by age"). The readjustment of the rows to the marginal row totals then throws the figures out of line with respect to the marginal column totals, and so adjust figures to the marginal column total once again (labeled "Second proration by sex").

This sequence of adjustments is continued until it produces complete convergence to a final unchanging matrix of numbers that add to the required row and column totals at once; at this point further proration merely replicates the numbers within a few digits. The convergence to marginal row and column totals is usually rapid, requiring only a few cycles (each consisting of a vertical adjustment and a horizontal adjustment) to achieve close agreement in one dimension and precise agreement in the other. As this example shows, convergence to within a decimal occurs by the fourth proration, or two cycles.

The procedure is clearly laborious by hand calculation, but the operation is quite simple to carry out by electronic computer without concern for the number of cycles required. The calculation can be stopped at any required degree of agreement with marginal totals, merely by setting a stopping rule such as STOP when $N_{ij}^{(n+1)} - N_{ij}^{(n)} < .01$ for all i and j cells.

Deming does not give the mathematical proof that the same results are obtained whether the columns or the rows are "raked" first, but empirical testing indicates that the order of raking is immaterial. In the case, however, where one is attempting to "fit" a zero "margin", the process may not converge; see Bishop, Feinberg, and Holland (1975, pp. 90–91) for discussion. Note in the example given about that the "unknown" age group had a zero *cell* in the complete census count, but the "*margin*" was not all zeros. Thus, it was possible to fit the "margin" even when one of its cells was zero. If, however, the *entire margin* were zeros, the procedure would not have worked. This is a general principle for iterative proportional fitting. (For extra details on zero cells and methods for handling them, see Agresti, 1990, pp. 245–250.)

Tables with Some Negative Frequencies

An earlier discussion indicated some of the complexities of the situation when single distributions with negatives are to be adjusted. Adjustment of bivariate distributions including negative values may be accomplished by an extension of procedures already described. For example, the method of iterative proportions may employ a two factor plus-minus proportionate procedure for each column and row.

General Multiway Tables

Since publication of the original *Methods and Materials of Demography* (Shryock Siegel and Associates, 1971), a generalization of the method of iterative proportions has emerged, known as "loglinear" analysis in social science or as "analysis of cross-classifications" or even as "poisson regression." This generalization allows the analyst to fit general multiway cross-classifications of two, three, or even more variables—for example, age and race and sex simultaneously. A comprehensive introduction to these methods can be found in Agresti (1990), with a simpler exposition in Agresti (1996). This methodology puts the analysis of categorical data in the framework of a generalized linear model (McCullagh and Nelder, 1990).

There are several key questions regarding the strategy for analyzing a cross-classification of categorical data:

1. Is there a clear *dependent* variable?
   a. If NO (i.e., all one has is a three-way classification of data), then "loglinear analysis" is an appropriate choice to consider.
   b. If YES, then "loglinear analysis" is not the best choice. Go to the next question.
2. Is the dependent variable categorical?
   a. If YES, then one would look at techniques like logistic regression, multinomial logit or probit, ordinal logit and probit, discriminant analysis, and the like.
   b. If NO, then one would look at ordinary regression, tobit/censored normal, Heckman models, and the like.

The most important point, of course, is to choose the estimation method that corresponds to the sampling and other properties of the variables one has measured.

TABLE C.12 Sample Data from the 1990 Oregon Population Survey by Age and Sex;
Adjusted to Complete Count Data from the 1990 Census of Population, by the Method
of Iterative Proportional Fitting

Original data table

Age group	Sex Male	Sex Female	Sample total, $n_{i.}$	Complete count, $N_{i.}$	$N_{i.}/n_{i.}$
Age < 5	285	334	619	201,421	325.40
Age 5–14	667	615	1,282	411,140	320.70
Age 15–44	1,658	1,742	3,400	1,305,492	383.97
Age 45–64	812	856	1,668	532,944	319.51
Age 65+	562	711	1,273	391,324	307.40
Unknown	11	21	32	0	0.0
Sample total, n_j	3,995	4,279	8,274		
Complete count, N_j	1,397,073	1,445,248		2,842,321	
N_j/n_j	349.71	337.75			

First proration by age: $Nij^{(1)} = Nij^{(0)}*(Ni.)/(ni.)$

Results of first iteration

Age group	Sex Male	Sex Female	Sample total, $n_{i.}$	Complete count, $N_{i.}$	$N_{i.}/n_{i.}$
Age < 5	92,738	108,683	201,421	201,421	1.00000
Age 5–14	213,908	197,232	411,140	411,140	1.00000
Age 15–44	636,619	668,873	1,305,492	1,305,492	1.00000
Age 45–64	259,443	273,501	532,944	532,944	1.00000
Age 65+	172,760	218,564	391,324	391,324	1.00000
Unknown	0	0	0	0	X
Sample total, n_j	1,375,469	1,466,852	2,842,321		
Complete count, N_j	1,397,073	1,445,248		2,842,321	
N_j/n_j	1.01571	0.98527			

First proration by sex: $Nij^{(2)} = Nij^{(1)}*(N.j)/(n.j)$

Results of second iteration

Age group	Sex Male	Sex Female	Sample total, $n_{i.}$	Complete count, $N_{i.}$	$N_{i.}/n_{i.}$
Age < 5	94,195	107,082	201,277	201,421	1.00072
Age 5–14	217,268	194,327	411,595	411,140	0.99889
Age 15–44	646,618	659,021	1,305,640	1,305,492	0.99989
Age 45–64	263,518	269,473	532,991	532,944	0.99991
Age 65+	175,474	215,345	390,818	391,324	1.00129
Sample total, n_j	1,397,073	1,445,248	2,842,321		
Complete count, N_j	1,397,073	1,445,248		2,842,321	
N_j/n_j	1.00000	1.00000			

Second proration by age: $Nij^{(3)} = Nij^{(2)}*(Ni.)/(ni.)$

Results of third iteration

Age group	Sex Male	Sex Female	Sample total, $n_{i.}$	Complete count, $N_{i.}$	$N_{i.}/n_{i.}$
Age < 5	94,262	107,159	201,421	201,421	1.00000
Age 5–14	217,028	194,112	411,140	411,140	1.00000
Age 15–44	646,545	658,947	1,305,492	1,305,492	1.00000
Age 45–64	263,495	269,449	532,944	532,944	1.00000
Age 65+	175,701	215,623	391,324	391,324	1.00000
Sample total, n_j	1,397,031	1,445,290	2,842,321		
Complete count, N_j	1,397,073	1,445,248		2,842,321	
N_j/n_j	1.00003	0.99997			

Second proration by sex: $Nij^{(4)} = Nij^{(3)}*(N.j)/(n.j)$

Results of fourth iteration

Age group	Sex Male	Sex Female	Sample total, $n_{i.}$	Complete count, $N_{i.}$	$N_{i.}/n_{i.}$
Age < 5	94,265	107,156	201,421	201,421	1.00000
Age 5–14	217,034	194,106	411,141	411,140	1.00000
Age 15–44	646,565	658,928	1,305,492	1,305,492	1.00000
Age 45–64	263,503	269,442	532,944	532,944	1.00000
Age 65+	175,706	215,617	391,323	391,324	1.00000
Sample total, n_j	1,397,073	1,445,248	2,842,321		
Complete count, N_j	1,397,073	1,445,248		2,842,321	
N_j/n_j	1.00000	1.00000			

Third proration by age: $Nij^{(5)} = Nij^{(4)}*(Ni.)/(ni.)$

Source: Based on Oregon Progress Board, 1990 Oregon Population Survey; and U.S. Census Bureau, 1990 Census of Population and Housing, STF-1 tabulation for Oregon.

X Not applicable.

For the analysis of cross-classifications, assume that the analyst has observations on N cases on K discrete variables $A_1, \ldots, A_k$.

Let

A_1 take on $0, 1, 2, \ldots, n_1$ values (e.g., 0 = male, 1 = female);
A_2 take on $0, 1, 2, \ldots, n_2$ values;
$\ldots$
A_k take on $0, 1, 2, \ldots, n_k$ values.

These observations are arranged in a contingency table or cross-classification table.

As a classic example (originally analyzed by Radalet, 1981, and discussed in Agresti, 1990, p. 136, or Long, 1997, p. 260), let A_1 take on two values, A_2 take on two values, and A_3 take on two values, where A_1 represents race of defendant (0 = white, 1 = nonwhite), A_2 represents race of victim (0 = white, 1 = nonwhite), and A_3 represents death penalty (0 = no death penalty sentence, 1 = death penalty sentence). These data are arranged in a typical table:

	Death penalty = NO Race of victim		Death penalty = YES Race of victim	
Race of defendant	White	Nonwhite	White	Nonwhite
White	(0,0,0)	(0,1,0)	(0,0,1)	(0,1,1)
Nonwhite	(1,0,0)	(1,1,0)	(1,0,1)	(1,1,1)

When the count of cases is inserted in each cell, the following table appears:

	Death penalty = NO Race of victim		Death penalty = YES Race of victim	
Race of defendant	White	Nonwhite	White	Nonwhite
White	132	9	19	0
Nonwhite	52	97	11	6

Or, stretched out a little:

Count	A1	A2	A3
132	0	0	0
19	0	0	1
52	1	0	0
9	0	1	0
0	0	1	1
11	1	0	1
97	1	1	0
6	1	1	1

Now, the table contains data on three variables, A_1, A_2, and A_3, but obviously there is actually a fourth variable, the most important variable, in this table. The fourth variable, in fact, is the count of cases in each cell. In loglinear analysis, the analyst is particularly interested in modeling the distribution of cell counts and does so by forcing the dates to fit certain marginal totals, just as with iterative proportional fitting before. However, because of the generalized

framework allowed by loglinear analysis, the analyst can fit more general models, and answer analytical questions like these:

1. Do nonwhite defendants receive the death penalty more often than expected given the rest of the table?
2. Do nonwhite defendants who murder white victims get the death penalty more often than expected?

Thus, substantive research questions are transformed into questions about the distribution of cell counts.

Theory

To develop the loglinear model, this section will describe the mathematical framework on which it is built. Let $Y_{n1,n2,\ldots,nk}$ be independently distributed POI($\mu_{n1,n2,\ldots,nk}$); that is, each cell count is independently Poisson distributed with its own parameter $\mu_{n1,n2,\ldots,nk}$. In elementary statistical theory, one method of estimating such parameters is known as the method of maximum likelihood. Under the assumption that the cell counts are independently distributed, the likelihood function is

$$L(\mu|Y) = \prod_{j=1}^{n_1 n_2 \ldots n_k} \frac{e^{-\mu_j} \mu_j^{Y_j}}{Y_j!} \quad (C.69)$$

and the log likelihood function is

$$\ln L(\mu|Y) = \sum_{j=1}^{n_1 n_2 \ldots n_k} -\ln(Y_j!) - \mu_j + Y_j \ln(\mu_j) \quad (C.70)$$

This specifies the stochastic component of the table; if the analyst estimated these parameters using the cell frequency data, there would be one unique parameter for each cell. This would perfectly reproduce the table, but would not be particularly informative, because a table with k cells would have k parameters. So the goal is to simplify the description. In loglinear models, one specifies a structural component to answer the question: What is the effect of race of victim, race of murderer, and so forth on the distribution of counts inside the table? A specification is the following:

Let $\ln \mu = X\beta$, where

- X is a $(n_1 \cdot n_2 \cdot \ldots \cdot n_k \times v)$ "design matrix" of nonstochastic variables, with $v \leq n_1 \cdot n_2 \cdot \ldots \cdot n_k$
- β is a $(v \times 1)$ vector of design parameters
- $\ln \mu$ is a $(n_1 \cdot n_2 \cdot \ldots \cdot n_k \times 1)$ vector of logarithms of cell parameters

Note that $\ln \mu_j = X_j^{\circ} \beta = X_{j,1}\beta_1 + X_{j,2}\beta_2 + \ldots + X_{j,v}\beta_v$; that is, each row of the matrix X times the parameter vector β determines the natural logarithm of the cell parameter μ.

This substitution results in

$$\ln L(\mu|Y)$$
$$= \sum_{j=1}^{n_1 \ldots n_k} -\ln(Y_j!) + \sum_{j=1}^{n_1 \ldots n_k} Y_j(X_j \cdot \beta) - \sum_{j=1}^{n_1 \ldots n_k} e^{(X_j \cdot \beta)} \quad (C.71)$$

and, taking partial derivatives with respect to each parameter β_m and setting them to zero, generates a system of equations, one for each parameter β_m, each of the form:

$$0 = \frac{\partial}{\partial \beta_m} = -\sum_{j=1}^{n_1...n_k} Y_j X_{j,m} - \sum_{j=1}^{n_1...n_k} e^{X_j \cdot \beta} X_{j,m} \qquad (C.72)$$

(Note: $\frac{\partial^2}{\partial \beta_m^2} = -\sum_{j=1}^{n_1...n_k} X_{j,m}^2 e^{X_j \cdot \beta} < 0$ ensures that this is a maximum.)

The root of this equation in each β can be found iteratively using, for example, the Newton-Raphson algorithm. When that root is found, it is the maximum-likelihood estimates of the β's that are then used to generate expected cell counts under the model.

The key to this model is the design matrix X; it specifies what "margins" in the table the analyst wishes to control, interaction effects between marginal variables, and any other model-related aspects. So the question at this point becomes: What is X and how is it specified?

Because the only explanatory variables are $A_1, \ldots, A_k$, the table margins, X is a matrix of indicator variables specifying unique parameters for specific cells. Consider the example of the $2 \times 2 \times 2$ death penalty table. Suppose the analyst wished to specify the model that all the cell frequencies are the same. This means that

- All the Poisson counts are governed by the same parameter
- Under the model the expected cell counts will all be the same
- P[death penalty|nonwhite murderer] = P[death penalty|white murderer]

To do this, the analyst specifies X as a $(n_1 \cdot n_2 \cdot \ldots \cdot n_k \times 1)$ matrix and β as a 1×1 vector. Thus,

$$\ln(\mu) = \begin{bmatrix} 1 \\ 1 \\ \vdots \\ 1 \end{bmatrix} \cdot [\beta] = \begin{bmatrix} \beta \\ \beta \\ \vdots \\ \beta \end{bmatrix}$$

If this model fits the data well, the analyst has simplified the structure of the table, from a maximum of eight parameters, one per cell, to this minimum of one. The analyst has, in effect, "fit" each observed cell count to be the same across the table. This is, of course, a baseline model, and few real-world applications will be so simplistic. So consider a more sophisticated model. Suppose the analyst wished to specify the following:

- A baseline level of occupants in each cell (a constant)
- Plus an additional amount in all death penalty cells (to let that variable affect the counts)

- An additional amount in all nonwhite victim cells (to let that variable affect the counts)
- An additional amount in all nonwhite murderer cells (to let that variable affect the counts)

This results in

A1	A2	A3		PARAMETERS		
0	0	0	β_0			
0	0	1				β_3
0	1	0			β_2	
1	0	0	β_0+	β_1		
0	1	1	β_0+		β_2+	β_3
1	0	1	β_0+	β_1+		β_3
1	1	0	β_0+	β_1+	β_2	
1	1	1	β_0+	β_1+	β_2+	β_3

This is represented in the matrix:

$$\begin{bmatrix} (0,0,0) \\ (0,0,1) \\ (0,1,0) \\ (1,0,0) \\ (0,1,1) \\ (1,0,1) \\ (1,1,0) \\ (1,1,1) \end{bmatrix} = \begin{bmatrix} 1 & 0 & 0 & 0 \\ 1 & 1 & 0 & 0 \\ 1 & 0 & 1 & 0 \\ 1 & 0 & 0 & 1 \\ 1 & 1 & 1 & 0 \\ 1 & 1 & 0 & 1 \\ 1 & 0 & 1 & 1 \\ 1 & 1 & 1 & 1 \end{bmatrix} \cdot \begin{bmatrix} \beta_0 \\ \beta_1 \\ \beta_2 \\ \beta_3 \end{bmatrix}$$

or, equivalently, the equation:

$$\hat{Y} = \beta_0 + \beta_1 \cdot A_1 + \beta_2 \cdot A_2 + \beta_3 \cdot A_3$$

This is known as the "independence" model because no interaction is specified between the margins $A1$, $A2$, and $A3$. It does not specify that all cell probabilities and conditional probabilities are the same; rather, it forces the expected cell frequencies under the model to fit the $A1$ margin in the table, the $A2$ margin in the table, and the $A3$ margin in the table. Thus, the expected cell frequencies will reproduce the three marginal distributions. This is exactly what the earlier example of iterative proportional fitting did.

The "Loglinear" Model Versus Iterative Proportional Fitting for Multiway Tables

It should be clear at this point that the loglinear model is effectively doing the same thing that the iterative proportional fitting model did earlier. In fact, Bishop, Feinberg, and Holland (1975) and earlier, Birch (1963) demonstrated that the two approaches generate equivalent results under a variety of sampling models. In practice, iterative proportional fitting might be used for simpler tables or models because of its easy interpretability, while a loglinear model might be used for a more complex model or a higher-dimensional table because of its flexibility. In addition, because the loglinear model is placed in a regression-like framework, it is possible to evaluate standard errors of coef-

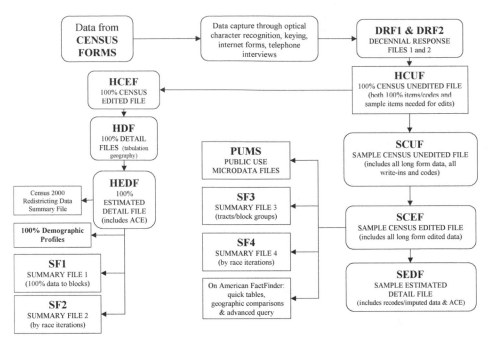

FIGURE C.9 A summary of U.S. census 2000 file construction: From original census forms to data products.

COMPUTER USAGE, MODELS, AND METHODS

Use of Electronic Computers in Demographic Studies

Data Collection and Processing

Data collection in the demographic field has been dramatically altered by new technologies, in particular those offered by computerized data collection systems. The original *Methods and Materials of Demography* (Shryock, Siegel, and Associates, 1971) made reference to the use of optically scanned ("FOSDIC") data collection forms in the 1970 and 1980 U.S. censuses. In 2000, the U.S. Census Bureau invested in optical scanning of handwritten forms, and optical character recognition technology for processing these handwritten responses.

Figure C.9 describes (approximately) the flow of files in the U.S. 2000 Census.[11] The original responses are collected and maintained in the Decennial Response File (DRF1 and

2). These receive minimal editing, but most important, are unduplicated and compiled into the Hundred Percent Unedited File and Sample Census Unedited File (HCUF and SCUF). At this point, edits and imputations are applied. As the reader may recall from Chapter 3, these edits and imputations are not trivial; the edits cannot be applied in isolation (independent of one another) but instead must reflect the covariance structure actually present in the data.

The HCUF and SCUF are easily the primary files for analyses that are tied closely to respondents (although some studies attempt to get even closer to the respondent via the DRF files or, closer yet, by reinterviews). As the reader knows, the U.S. Census Bureau uses a dual-systems methodology for measuring differential census undercounts. The impact of this methodology is reflected in the HCEF and SCEF files, where coverage factors for undercounts are applied. Further downstream, tabulation geography (e.g., city boun- daries that split collection blocks) is added back in (via the HEDF file), and tabulation products begin to be produced.

One might dismiss these processes as merely "data handling." In fact, most users of census data work directly with the tabulation products as if they were simply the "truth" and ignore the process of data handling. However, the transformations that these files require are not merely a matter of moving data around a computer system, but at each step of the process decisions must be made about the characteristics of persons and households, and these decisions are demographically substantive. People are "created" and "deleted," their characteristics (e.g., income) are estimated, their ages are edited and other such operations are performed. Demographers should pay attention to these opera-

[11] Mai Weismantle of the Housing, Household, and Economic Statistics Division of the U.S. Census Bureau developed the prototype for this graphic.

tions. For example, Darga (1999, 2000) made a strong case against some of these adjustments on the grounds that they create demographically unrealistic results for small geographic areas.

Analysis and Research

The computer has become almost indispensible for the analysis of demographic data. However, because database technology has advanced at the same time as demographic techniques, new ways of representing data have emerged. This section describes three data structures in common use and how they are handled.

Consider that we have three kinds of objects: persons, housing units, and blocks. Each has properties not enjoyed by the other; for example, a housing unit does not have a "sex," while a person does not have a "number of residents." Some aspects of one relate to the other, though: An "address" is a property of a housing unit, and, while a person resides there, that same address can also be considered a property of the person. If the person moves, the housing unit does not change address status, but the person does. Furthermore, if the housing unit resides in a block, the block will have its own unique properties, but the housing unit will be related to the block. While the person lives in that housing unit, the person will also share the properties of the block.

In data handling, it is a common problem to determine how to represent such relations between objects. Let us consider a concrete example. Suppose a person has four measured characteristics: FULL NAME, AGE, RACE, and SEX, and an identifier telling us which housing unit the person lives in, ID. For the purposes of this example, it is not important to specify the exact coding scheme used in these variables. A housing unit also has four measured characteristics: HOUSE NUMBER, STREET NAME, ZIP CODE, NUMBER OF BEDROOMS, the aforementioned ID, and a BLOCK NUMBER. Finally, a block has a BLOCK NUMBER and an ESTIMATED POPULATION residing in the block. For the purposes of this example, we shall suppose that we are dealing with a single block, block 9876, which has 200 persons living in it. We shall also suppose that we are dealing with two housing units, one at 101 Main Street and one at 300 Elm Street. Within these two housing units, we shall suppose that Tom James and Betty James live at 300 Elm, and Joseph Smith lives at 101 Main.

Many traditional statistical packages represent such data in a "flat file" form. This form is displayed as follows

Record #	FULL NAME	AGE	RACE	SEX	ID	HOUSE NUMBER
1	Tom James	31	black	male	12346	300
2	Betty James	32	black	female	12346	300
3	Joseph Smith	42	white	male	12345	101

Record #	STREET NAME	ZIP CODE	NUMBER OF BEDROOMS	BLOCK NUMBER	ESTIMATED POPULATION
1	Elm	97701	2	9876	200
2	Elm	97701	2	9876	200
3	Main	97701	3	9876	200

As shown, the simple rectangularity of the "flat file" layout is appealing; however, this simplicity is obtained at the cost of significant amounts of duplication in the data. Because Tom James and Betty James, reside at the same ID housing unit, they each receive the same data. This is a very inefficient way to store data. However, if one wished to use data at the housing-unit level to predict some characteristic of the person, this form would allow such an analysis to be performed with little extra processing work.

Alternatively, when geographical hierarchies are involved, the "hierarchical" form is popular. This form is displayed as follows:

Record #	Record type	FULL NAME HOUSE NUMBER ESTIMATED POPULATION	AGE STREET NAME
1	B	200	
2	H	300	Elm
3	P	Tom James	31
4	P	Betty James	32
5	B	200	
6	H	101	Main
7	P	Joseph Smith	42

Record #	ZIP CODE	RACE NUMBER OF BEDROOMS	SEX	ID BLOCK NUMBER
1				9876
2	97701	2		9876
3		black	male	12346
4		black	female	12346
5				9876
6	97701	3		9876
7		white	male	12345

In the "hierarchical" record layout, except for identifiers used for linking different levels, data are not duplicated. However, there is a cost of processing because one must determine the record type before one can know how to interpret the individual fields. Is the third column FULL NAME, HOUSE NUMBER, or ESTIMATED POPULATION? It depends on what the record type is. The advantage of the approach is that it compactly holds data that are, implictly, hierarchical.

A final approach, which is becoming very common in the database community, is the "relational" layout. In the "relational" layout, each object has its own separate table. The tables are related to each other using a "key" variable. The following illustrates such a layout. The "key" between the block table and the housing-unit table is the BLOCK

NUMBER field, while the "key" between the housing unit table and the person table is the ID field.

Block table

Record #	Record type	ESTIMATED POPULATION	BLOCK NUMBER
1	B	200	9876

Housing unit table

Record #	Record type	HOUSE NUMBER	STREET NAME
1	H	300	Elm
2	H	101	Main

Record #	ZIP CODE	NUMBER OF BEDROOMS	ID	BLOCK NUMBER
1	97701	2	12346	9876
2	97701	3	12345	9987

Person table

Record #	Record type	FULLNAME	AGE	RACE	SEX	ID
1	P	Tom James	31	black	male	12346
2	P	Betty James	32	black	female	12346
3	P	Joseph Smith	42	white	male	12345

It is easy to see that there is again almost no duplication of data; furthermore, there is not the varying field meanings that the hierarchical record layout creates. The relational layout form has become very popular because of these advantages. However, it has one notable disadvantage, particularly when dealing with large data sets: If one wants to analyze data across different tables, one must perform a "table join." For example, if one wanted to analyze how the number of bedrooms in a house relates to a person's age, race, or sex, one must join the housing unit table with the person table, using the ID as the joining device. Even more, if one wished to examine how a block size relates to a person's age, race, or sex, the join is more complicated (from person ID to housing unit ID, then from housing unit ID to BLOCK NUMBER), to finally attach the ESTIMATED POPULATION of the block to the person. This is a computationally intensive process.

Administrative Records Databases and Data Warehousing

In the late 20th and early 21st centuries, the growth of administrative records and computing power and storage has made massive databases available for demographic use. However, the principles of data collection and analysis have not changed—only the (lowered) intensity of the data collection effort and its widespread dissemination among many collectors.

In response to this technological opportunity, the field of "data warehousing" has emerged (Inmon, 1996). Figure C.10 diagrams the basic features of a data warehouse, which is the central concept in the "modern" use of administrative records. On the left are symbols representing the ongoing, operational databases: client contact records, tax returns, quarterly business reports, unemployment insurance records, credit card purchase data, insurance and medical treatment records, building permits, and so on. These databases are typically produced to support the ongoing operations of the organization: Accounting (in the broadest sense of that term) is perhaps the most important use. They have not been, and typically are not, designed for research analytic use.

In the center is the data warehouse itself. This is a repository of recoded and maintained data and can be designed for analytic access. The Oregon Shared Information System (Judson, 1993) and the U.S. Census Bureau's Statistical Administrative Records System (Judson, 2000) are examples of "set up" data warehouses designed for research analyses. The data warehouse serves the following functions, different from operational data:

- Developing common data definitions and maintaining a record of those definitions as they evolve over time
- Matching operational data to create a master record of the object(s) of interest
- Maintaining panels or a time series of data (a most important function, which operational databases may or may not do)
- Summarizing data (creating decision-support reports)
- Providing a flexible access structure (as opposed to the quite rigid structures of many operational data bases)
- Allowing users to construct ad hoc analyses of data

On the right of the figure is the end user of these data. The demographer, statistician, or geographic information systems expert is typically considered the end user.

Challenges with Using Administrative Records

Despite their now widespread use, administrative records are not without pitfalls. Figure C.11 illustrates the process of data collection in the administrative records context (taken variously from Judson and Popoff, 1996; Ma, 1986; and Redman, 1996):

This figure identifies how records are created and used, and, at each step, where there is potential for error. A record begins as an event or an object in the "real world" outside the database. Some of these are actually identified (note already that some events and objects that are really there do not get identified) as observed events and objects. Some of

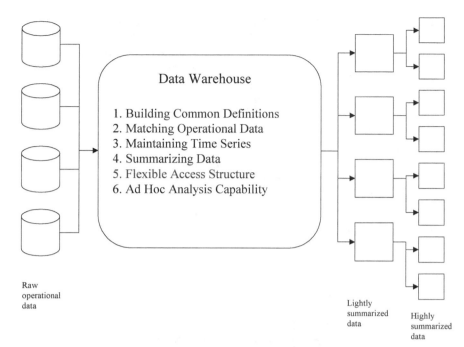

FIGURE C.10   An illustration of the data warehouse concept.

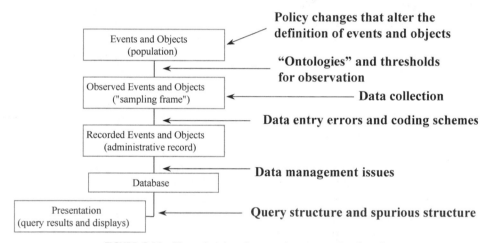

FIGURE C.11   How administrative records are created and used.

these observed events and objects get recorded (again, some do not) and become part of the administrative record. These are then arranged in some form of database. Later, when the analyst approaches these records, he or she develops analyses ("queries" in the language of data mining) and makes presentation of the results. Finally, using either the usual statistical framework or policy-making framework, some decision is made.

At each step in this process there is potential for error or misinterpretation. At the event/object level, policy changes can change the definition of an event or object (as when the U.S. welfare program Aid to Families with Dependent Children [AFDC] ceased to exist or when a mobile home is recoded from "real" property to "personal" property). As events and objects become observed, the "ontologies" that

observers use to categorize the world (that is, the schema that they use) enter in. Likewise, some events and objects do not reach a threshold for official notice (as where the "officer on the beat" makes a determination whether to identify an event as a problem or not; see, e.g., Laudon, 1986; Light, 1990). Some of those observed events become recorded, and there are the possibilities of data entry errors and limitations of coding schemes for mapping the real-world events into their database representations. As data are moved from place to place in computer systems, data management problems (corruption in transit, changes in formatting, and so forth, documented in Stevens, Richmond, Haenn, and Michie, 1992, pp. 171–178) arise. Finally, as the analyst extracts data using queries of various kinds, he or she may discover that the query is either syntatically incorrect in a nonobvious way, or the query generates results whose structure itself is spurious.

Models for Use with Administrative Records

In virtually all cases, the administrative records analyst has no control over the data-collection process in administrative records use—that is, the analyst does not control how the administrative form asks a question or records a datum. As noted earlier, as with all data sets, random errors will occur; but in the administrative records context, demographers are most concerned with detecting biased data collection.

Because the analyst does not control data collection, there are two contexts in which administrative records analyses take place: after data collection, but prior to analysis, and during analysis. In the first context, the analyst is handling data and catching errors and anomalies when they occur. Tools used in the data-handling context include record linkage, editing and imputation, and direct testing for bias. During analysis, the strategies for dealing with the anomalies in administrative records may change. Tools used in the context of analysis include: poststratification and synthetic estimation, dual systems analysis, measurement error models, and direct evaluations of bias.

Each of these tools has generated a substantial literature on its own (Judson and Popoff, 1996).

MATRIX METHODS

Matrix Methods of Population Analysis

Matrix methods have been employed in the development of a number of recursive models, those where some mathematical relationship representing change in the population is assumed to be repeated again and again. A matrix is an array of data in one or two dimensions to which the special procedures of matrix algebra can be applied. The basic population matrix changes according to the rates or probabilities, called transition probabilities, given in a transition matrix. The process of change in a model whose population moves from one state to another according to the probabilities in the transition matrix is called a *Markov process*, and a model that has this characteristic is called a *Markovian model*. The population in the model may move in the direction of and attain a state of equilibrium (i.e., invariant once it has been reached) that is completely independent of the initial distribution.

Markovian Models

There are two basic kinds of Markov processes, *discrete*-time and *continuous*-time (Schoen's, 1988). Continuous time models can usually be identified by the presence of integrals and differential equations, which indicate that time is considered in a continuous fashion. Discrete time models are distinguished by the fact that events take place in distinct jumps rather than occur continuously. A Markov process in discrete time is often called a *Markov chain*. It usually requires conventional algebra and matrix algebra for understanding rather than the calculus and differential equations. For the purpose of describing matrix methods of analysis, this section shall focus on discrete time models.

Imagine a population whose members are divided into K distinct states, which may be age "grades", positions in an organization, locations in a region, or some other status of interest. Each member falls into one and only one state at any time. Represent the numbers of persons in each state by a $1 \times (K + 1)$ row vector N_t, where time takes on the values 0, 1, 2, 3, . . . , T, and movement between states occurs at the time jumps.

Assume that for each person there exists a fixed probability of moving from his or her current state into another state. This is p_{ij}, which denotes the probability of moving from state i to state j. However, some of the states cannot be exited (because the person is dead or because the person has "left the system"). Let there be a $K + 1$st state that represents leaving the system. This can be represented by a $(K + 1) \times (K + 1)$ matrix P of p_{ij}'s. The exit state is known as an *absorbing state* because people who enter it never leave. Hence, the probability of going from an absorbing state to itself is 1. Note also that there may be more than one absorbing state (exit due to death and exit due to migration or marriage, for instance). Recall that a life table that has this property is referred to as a "multiple decrement" life table.

When the matrix P contains probabilities representing the probability of a birth occurring to a female (thus generating a new "entrant" to the system) and the probability of each person dying, then this matrix can be used to project population growth under the fixed fertility and mortality regime implied by the matrix. Leslie (1945) provided the best known and most detailed analysis of this case, and the matrix he constructed is often referred to as a "Leslie" matrix. (See discussion later, Pollard, 1973, and Rogers, 1975, 1995, for extensive details and continuous time extensions.)

Stable Theory

If we temporarily ignore the absorbing state and only consider the $K \times K$ matrix P by dropping the $K + 1$st row and column vectors, then there exists some machinery to assist in assessing the stable population implied by the matrix P. A "stable population" is a population in which the transition probabilities for fertility and mortality do not vary over time. A "stationary population," which is stable, also has the feature that entries into and exits from it are equal in absolute numbers, as in a standard life table.

In a population without absorbing states, and satisfying certain conditions of regularity needed for a Markov chain, over time the population will tend toward a limiting distribution called stable.[12] This limiting distribution will be independent of the starting distribution and will have members in each state in fixed proportions. That is, the fraction of persons in each state will not change from time period to time period. In this case, the limiting distribution can be found simply using the following eigenvalue and eigenvector methods.

In a stable state, the population matrix will obey the following equation:

$$PN' = \lambda N' \qquad (C.73)$$

where N' is a $K \times 1$ column vector, the transpose of the row vector N_t, ignoring the "exited" state, with the desired limiting distribution. This equation indicates that, in the stable limit, if we begin with the population in distribution N' and apply the transition probabilities to each member, we end with a population in the same distribution (hence the terminology: "stable" population). This equation implies

$$(P - \lambda I)N' = 0 \qquad (C.74)$$

In this form, N' is an *eigenvector* of the matrix P corresponding to the dominant (largest) *eigenvalue* of that matrix. Brown (1993, p. 172) noted that this dominant eigenvalue has a demographic interpretation: It will be $\lambda = e^{nr}$, where n is the size of the age groups, and r is the "intrinsic" rate of growth when in a stable state. Methods for finding eigenvalues and eigenvectors corresponding to those eigenvalues are standard (Press *et al.*, 1989) and implemented in numerous computer packages.

Models with Entry and Exit Variation

In standard population models, a demographer typically specifies that each female has children that fall into the youngest age category. In multiple increment-decrement models, one need not make any such specification. Instead, new members of the population can enter into *any* of the states. If states are age grades in a closed population, new members must enter at the youngest age grade; if states are school grades, however, new members can enter at higher grades due to inmigration.

For now, assume that members enter the states in fixed *proportions*, although the *number* varies by time. Let E be a $1 \times (K + 1)$ row vector representing the proportion of new members who enter state j in any time period, and let r_t be the number of new recruits at time t.

<hr>

[12] Strictly speaking, in order for the following theory to hold, a stable population must satisfy three additional conditions of regularity: the states must be recurrent with positive probability, all states must be reachable one from another, and the transitions must be aperiodic. Such a Markov chain is called irreducible and ergodic, and that is a necessary condition for a limiting distribution to exist (Ross, 1997, p. 173).

To summarize:

P = a $(K + 1) \times (K + 1)$ matrix consisting of the probability of moving from state i to state j, where state $K + 1$ means "leaving the system"

E = a $1 \times (K + 1)$ row vector consisting of the proportion of new entrants that enter a particular state

r_t = a scalar, the number of new recruits that enter at each time period

t = time, measured in discrete increments 0,1,2,3,4, and so on

In matrix algebra, the number of people in each state at any time can be represented by

$$N_t = N_{t-1} \cdot P + r_t \cdot E \qquad (C.75)$$

where N_t = the $1 \times (K + 1)$ row vector representing the number of people in each state at time t, and the other elements are as defined earlier.

Now, to find a solution to this process, apply the equation repeatedly until reaching N_0, which is the starting value. So

$$N_t = N_{t-1} \cdot P + r_t \cdot E, \qquad \text{as in C.75}$$

$$N_{t-1} = N_{t-2} \cdot P + r_{t-1} \cdot E \qquad (C.76)$$

and so on.

Starting at any arbitrary time t, and continuing substituting backward until reaching time $t = 0$,

$$N_t = N_{t-1} \cdot P + r_{t-1} \cdot E$$
$$= (N_{t-2} \cdot P + r_{t-1} \cdot E) \cdot P + r_t \cdot E \qquad (C.77)$$
$$= ((N_{t-3} \cdot P + r_{t-2} \cdot E) \cdot P + r_{t-1}) \cdot P + r_t \cdot E$$

and so on, which results in the general equation:

$$N_t = N_0 \cdot P + E \cdot \left(\sum_{t=0}^{t-1} r_{t-t} P^t \right) \qquad (C.78)$$

(For more details, see Bartholomew, 1982, pp. 50–53.)

What does this mean? Simply this: If the analyst knows

1. The number of persons that start in each state (N_0),
2. The probability transition matrix P,
3. The proportion that enter each state at each time period (E), and
4. The number of new entrants at each time period (r)

then the analyst can calculate exactly how many people will be in each state at any time in the future. The analyst needs to know a lot of information to work with this model, but much of it is easily assumable from past trends (number 3 or number 4, for example) or could be statistically estimated from existing data (number 2 and number 3).

Note two important facts:

1. When the $K + 1$st state, the "dead" or "exited" state, is included, then the proportions in each state do not

converge toward a stable value; the number of dead/exited people keep increasing as the system keeps going. In a computer simulation, one could ignore this cell by just dropping the dead/exited people and calculating the relative proportions of the remainder. However, the eigenvalue/eigenvector methods used earlier would not apply, because including the "exited" state in the matrix violates an assumption needed for eigenvalue/eigenvector methods. (Specifically, it violates the assumption that every state is reachable from every other state; once a person enters the exited/dead state, no other "alive" state is reachable by that person.)

2. If r is a constant value, then there exists a "closed form" solution to equation 79. "Closed form" means that one does not have to compute numbers iteratively, but one can solve the system for any time using a single calculation. Judson (1990) included a program written in the GAUSS programming language, which allows the user to specify how these equations should interact and displays line graphs indicating the numbers of persons who are in each state over time.

The Leslie Matrix

Using the theory developed in the previous section, and basic life table concepts, we are able to derive the Leslie matrix for population projection, following closely the development in Plane and Rogerson (1994, pp. 160–169) and Brown (1993, pp. 168–176). This development shall ignore entrants to the system other than births. In particular, it ignores migration, although migration shall return in the multiregional context. In addition, it represents only a one-sex model, although in practice, of course, a two-sex model is more realistic.

Suppose that the analyst has a life table for his or her population in 5-year age increments, from age 0 to 4, 5 to 9, and so on to age 85+; then, as we know, for each age group x to $x+4$ (except the last one), the probability that the person will survive 5 years (and thus appear in the next age group) can be defined as

$$_5s_x = \frac{_5L_{x+5}}{_5L_x} \qquad (C.79)$$

The last age group requires special attention. Because surviving 5 years means that the person returns to the same state, its treatment of probability must take that fact into account. The ratio of the stationary population aged 85 and over (T_{85}) to the stationary population aged 80 and over (T_{80}) is the appropriate probability measure:

$$s_{80+} = \frac{T_{85}}{T_{80}} \qquad (C.80)$$

This specifies transition probabilities, the probability that a person of age x will survive into the next age group. Now the analyst must specify how new entrants (births) come into

the system. The goal is to specify the probability that a person of age x to x+4 will generate a birth in the next 5 years, not necessarily the rate at which such births occur. Data on age-specific fertility rates can often be obtained from vital registration. Note that for a particular cohort of women starting in the interval beginning at age x, during the first half of the period they will be bearing children at the rate of their current group, age x to $x+4$, but, during the second half of the period (for those that survive) they will be bearing children at the rate of their new age group, age $x+5$ to $x+9$. Finally, the analyst will also need to account for infants born during the 5-year period that do not survive into the $6-4$ age group.

Combining these two concepts, estimate the average fertility rate for the cohort at age x to $x+4$ by taking the average of the two group-specific rates:

$$_5\hat{F}_x = \frac{1}{2}\left(_5F_x + \frac{_5L_{x+5}}{_5L_x} F_{x+5} \right) \qquad (C.81)$$

and account for mortality in the 0-to-4 age group by the ratio $_5L_0/_5l_0$. Combining these two terms, the probability that a female of age x to x+4 generates a birth during the 5-year interval and that that birth survives to age 0–4, is given by

$$_5b_x = \left(\frac{_5L_0}{_5l_0} \right)\left[\frac{1}{2}\left(_5F_x + \frac{_5L_{x+5}}{_5L_x} {_5F_{x+5}} \right) \right] \qquad (C.82)$$

With these equations, all terms are accounted for, and the Leslie matrix **L** is

$$\mathbf{L} = \begin{bmatrix} 0 & _5b_5 & _5b_{10} & _5b_{15} & \cdots {_5b_{45}} & 0 & 0 \\ _5s_0 = \frac{_5L_5}{_5L_0} & 0 & & & & & \vdots \\ 0 & _5s_5 = \frac{_5L_{10}}{_5L_5} & 0 & & & & \vdots \\ \vdots & 0 & _5s_{10} = \frac{_5L_{15}}{_5L_{10}} & & & & \vdots \\ \vdots & \vdots & 0 & \ddots & & & \vdots \\ \vdots & \vdots & \vdots & & 0 & & 0 \\ 0 & 0 & 0 & & _5s_{75} = \frac{_5L_{80}}{_5L_{75}} & _5s_{80+} = \frac{_5T_{85}}{_5T_{80}} \end{bmatrix}$$
$$(C.83)$$

Now, to project the population one time period into the future, simply apply the Markovian model described earlier:

$$\mathbf{N}'_{t+5} = \mathbf{L} \cdot \mathbf{N}'_t \qquad (C.84)$$

where, as before, N_t is the row vector containing population counts at time t, and N'_t is the corresponding column vector (this equation uses column vectors with this matrix to conform to a standard description for the Leslie matrix). There are no new entrants in this equation because they have already been accounted for in the Leslie matrix itself.

Multiregional Models

With the development of matrix methods and the generation of a wider array of data sources for demographic analysis, multiregional demography has emerged (Rogers, 1975, 1995). Migration is clearly not a component in the Leslie matrix presented earlier. In the context of a one-region model, net migration can be included in the Leslie matrix by adding a net migration fraction to each survival cell. Thus, for example, to account for migrants entering into the age group x to $x + 4$, the term $_5s_x = \dfrac{_5L_{x+5}}{_5L_x}$ is replaced with $_5s_x = \dfrac{_5L_{x+5}}{_5L_x} + _5n_x$, where $_5n_x$ is the net migration rate for age group x to $x + 4$. A similar term can be added to the first row to account for migrants in the youngest age group. This method, while conceptually simple, can lead to serious biases in projection (Smith, 1986, and Isserman, 1993). This is because, while the region of interest may be growing in population due to inmigration, the regions contributing migrants are declining, thus exposing fewer members of their population to the risk of migration. That reduction in population at risk is not accounted for in this simple method.

In place of the simple model, Rogers (1975, 1995) and others have proposed the *multiregional* model, which directly accounts for the flows from one region to another, thus avoiding the biases of a one-region, net migration model. Space precludes a full discussion here, but the development is similar to that of the Leslie matrix, with the addition of migrants from place to place, each of whom bring their mortality and fertility experience with them.

OTHER TOPICS CONSIDERED BRIEFLY

This section will briefly touch on areas that have developed substantially since the original *Methods and Materials* (Shryock, Siegel, and Associates, 1971), appeared but for which space precludes a full exposition. In each case, this section provides readers with references to the substantial body of putacatime the topic has generated.

Microsimulation Methods

With the emergence of computing power and databases sufficient to handle the task, analysts in the early to mid-1960s began to develop microsimulation models of demographic and economic behavior. As defined by Citro and Hanushek (1991, p. 101), a *microsimulation* model is intended to model the impact of a program at the level at which it actually operates, usually the household or individual level, rather than at an aggregate level. An example will illustrate. A standard demographic model of welfare reform might multiply an aggregate tabulation of households by a presumed "take up" rate of welfare participation. This result would generate an implied demand for the welfare program. A microsimulation model, in contrast, would model the behavioral response of individual households to a variety of economic factors, including the benefits and costs of welfare receipt. Typically, in the United States this model would use microdata from such data sources as the U.S. Survey of Income and Program Participation or the U.S. Current Population Survey (Citro, 1991). After this behavioral model is designed, the program changes would act as input to the behavioral model, which would then generate the predicted takeup of welfare. The behavioral model could be *deterministic*, in which case a probability model is not used and there are no random components, or *stochastic*, in which case a probability model is estimated, and, in the simulation phase, a process of randomness is used to simulate whether a particular household or person participates in the program.

System Dynamics Models

The success of many demographic models has been, in no small part, due to the fact that most basic demographic phenomena, particularly at a high level of geographical aggregation, are very predictable, with few discontinuities and system shocks. War and AIDS notwithstanding, mortality is, in fact, a very predictable process in aggregate.

However, as one moves down the geographical scale, or into social and household demography, complexity increases. The smooth relationships that could be assumed at higher levels no longer hold. As noted by Pool (1964, p. 64), "The nemesis of applied social science up to now has been the hideous complexity of the systems of variables—nonlinear and discontinuous ones at that—with which they deal."

System dynamics modeling (developed by Forrester, 1968) is an attempt to handle the dynamic complexity of systems, including social systems. It is an exceptionally general tool and has been used both for research and applied purposes. As examples of the former, applications include exploration of hypothetical systems, thorough and critical review of knowledge concerning a phenomenon, and simulation experiments. As examples of the latter, applications include forecasting, system control and management, stability under disturbances, and policy analyses.

System dynamics models consist of three main components: stocks, flows, and "intermediates". Stock (quantity or level of something as people or firms) and flow (amount of movement between two levels, as births and migrants) have the usual demographic meanings. An "intermediate" is a quantity that exists between stocks and flows, but is neither of them. For example, the maximum potential birthrate puts a limit on achieved birthrates. Intermediates typically convey information about parameters or external states of a system or about intervening variables that may be theoretical.

There are two positive features of these concepts: extreme generality and "structural" nature. Extreme generality means that anything that can be represented as a quantity, even if unmeasurable, can be included. As a theory or model-generating tool, it does not limit the researcher to concrete quantities, nor to observable variables.

The "structural" nature of these concepts is also a positive feature. According to Mayhew (1980, p. 349), in structural sociology the unit of analysis is always the social network, never the individual. In systems dynamics models, the unit of analysis is always the set of stocks, flows, and intermediates. These elements are structural quantities: They may or may not refer to individuals, and they may or may not refer to components presumed to exist in persons.

Once the structure of systems dynamics models is determined, the flow diagram is converted into a set of difference equations approximating differential equations. From some starting state consisting of the starting levels of each stock, the future dynamics of the system of difference equations is simulated iteratively into the future. A diagrammatic example of a system dynamics model representing the basic demographic estimating equation is given in Figure C.12 (from Alfeld and Graham, 1976, p. 99):

In this figure, one can see that the basic "stock" is represented by population size. Two "flows" generate added members: births and inmigration. The star-shaped figures represent people coming from or going to "outside the system." Two "flows" generate losses: deaths and outmigration. To illustrate the added value of the system dynamics approach, note that "population density" is a function of area and population, and that, finally, the "attractiveness multiplier" decreases as density increases; this causes lower inmigration. The "attractiveness multiplier" is a real, but not easily measurable, concept that can be directly incorporated into the model even if it is not measurable in a conventional way. This system as developed by Alfeld and Graham is expressed as the following difference equations:

Equation number	Equation
(1)	$Pop_t = Pop_{t-1} + dt\,[B_{(t-1,t)} + D_{(t-1,t)} + IM_{(t-1,t)} - OM_{(t-1,t)}]$
(2)	$B_{(t-1,t)} = Pop_{t-1}*BN$
(3)	$D_{(t-1,t)} = Pop_{t-1}*DN$
(4)	$OM_{(t-1,t)} = Pop_{t-1}*OMN$
(5)	$IM_{(t-1,t)} = Pop_{t-1}*AMM_t*IMN$
(6)	$PD_t = Pop_t/AREA$
(7)	$AMM_t = f(PD_t)$

Parameters
BN Birthrate normal = .03
DN Death rate normal = .015
IMN Inmigration normal = .1
OMN Outmigration normal = .07
AREA Land area = 9000
P_0 Starting population = 50000

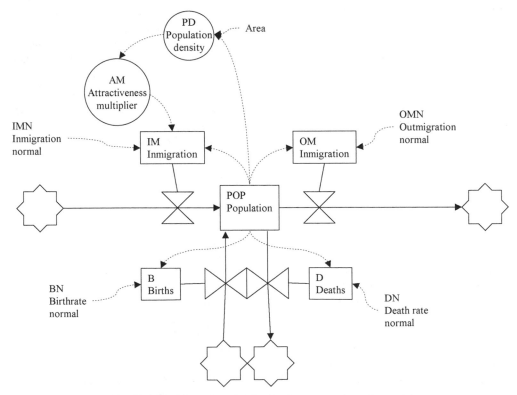

FIGURE C.12 Illustration of a simple urban system dynamics model.
Source: Alfeld and Graham (1976, p. 99)

Given these equations, once the function relating the attractiveness-for-migration multiplier (AMM) to population density (PD) is specified, and the degree of approximation represented by $dt < 1$ is specified, the system is completely specified. (Note that if $dt = 1$, we obtain the usual population component equation.) By using numerical integration techniques, the computer iterates these equations into the future in fine increments of dt. The system can then be simulated at will; parameters can be modified to reflect different growth scenarios, and, the structure of the diagram and the equations it represents can also be changed.

This illustration provides an overview of the system dynamics approach to modeling. Standard software packages exist to specify and simulate such models (e.g., High-Performance Systems, 1996), and excellent, albeit dated, introductions to the methods can be found in Goodman (1974) or Randers (1980).

Demographic-Economic and Econometric Models

A major advance in the mid- to late 20th century was the explicit exploration of the interaction between demographic phenomena (particularly migration, but also fertility, mortality, and population composition) and economic phenomena (see, e.g., Isard, 1960). For example, it became clear that any account of migration, to be complete, needed an account of job growth and income disparities between regions. Likewise, fertility behavior could be understood as responding to micro and macroeconomic forces (such as women's labor force participation opportunities). At the same time, econo-

mists realized that the demand side (for both private and public goods) of their models was heavily affected by the composition of the population making demands. It is easy to understand that older persons demand different public services than younger persons and young families; likewise, they demand different consumer goods and approach consumption with different disposable incomes.

In response to this new understanding, economists and demo-graphers began developing models that became known as "economic-demographic" or "demographic-economic" models. The main focus of such models is to show how the two sectors interact with one another. A typical model has the following sectors:

1. A "basic" economic sector. In this case "basic" refers to those goods and services, produced within the region, that are primarily sold outside the region and hence bring money in from outside.
2. A "nonbasic" economic sector. "Nonbasic" refers to those goods and services, produced within the region, that are primarily sold inside the region and hence are dependent on the basic sector for their livelihood, but are also dependent on the demographic composition of the regional population.
3. A "demographic" sector, in which fertility and mortality assumptions are made. Typically these assumptions are fixed (and hence "exogenous" to the model), although occasionally fertility is allowed to vary as a function of economic conditions.
4. A "labor market" sector, in which the growth or decline of the basic and nonbasic sectors are translated into labor market demand.

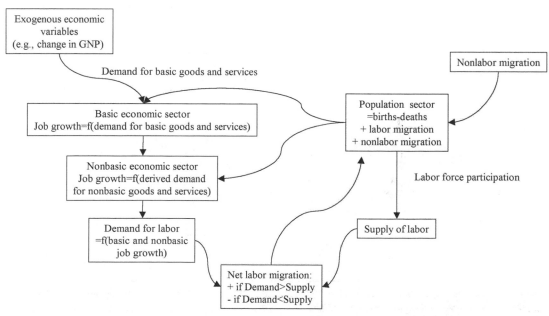

FIGURE C.13 Illustration of the form of a regional demographic-economic model.

5. An "exogenous" sector, typically representing neighboring regions or the economy as a whole.

6. A "migration" sector. The migration sector is important because it is the mechanism by which calibration between labor market demand and labor market supply is achieved; a certain proportion of in- or outmigrants are presumably labor-market oriented, while others are presumably nonlabor-market oriented (e.g. retired migrants).

These sectors are presented diagrammatically in Figure C.13.

A review of the usefulness of the basic/nonbasic distinction in economic-demographic models is given in

TABLE C.13   Interpolation Coefficients Based on the Karup-King Formula (The Karup-King formula is a four-term third-difference osculatory formula. It maintains the given values. Given points or groups must be equally spaced.)

A. For interpolation between given points at intervals of 0.2

Interpolated point	Coefficients to be applied to			
	$N_{1.0}$	$N_{2.0}$	$N_{3.0}$	$N_{4.0}$
First interval				
$N_{1.0}$	+1.000	.000	.000	.000
$N_{1.2}$	+.656	+.552	−.272	+.064
$N_{1.4}$	+.408	+.856	−.336	+.072
$N_{1.6}$	+.232	+.984	−.264	+.048
$N_{1.8}$	+.104	+1.008	−.128	+.016
Middle interval				
$N_{2.0}$	.000	+1.000	.000	.000
$N_{2.2}$	−.064	+.912	+.168	−.016
$N_{2.4}$	−.072	+.696	+.424	−.048
$N_{2.6}$	−.048	+.424	+.696	−.072
$N_{2.8}$	−.016	+.168	+.912	−.064
Last interval				
$N_{3.0}$	.000	.000	+1.000	.000
$N_{3.2}$	+.016	−.128	+1.008	+.104
$N_{3.4}$	+.048	−.264	+.984	+.232
$N_{3.6}$	+.072	−.336	+.856	+.408
$N_{3.8}$	+.064	−.272	+.552	+.656
$N_{4.0}$	.000	.000	.000	+1.000

B. For subdivision of groups into fifths

Interpolated subgroup	Coefficients to be applied to		
	G_1	G_2	G_3
First panel			
First fifth of G_1	+.344	−.208	+.064
Second fifth of G_1	+.248	−.056	+.008
Third fifth of G_1	+.176	+.048	−.024
Fourth fifth of G_1	+.128	+.104	−.032
Last fifth of G_1	+.104	+.112	−.016

B. For subdivision of groups into fifths (Continued)

Interpolated subgroup	Coefficients to be applied to		
	G_1	G_2	G_3
Middle Panel			
First fifth of G_2	+.064	+.152	−.016
Second fifth of G_2	+.008	+.224	−.032
Third fifth of G_2	−.024	+.248	−.024
Fourth fifth of G_2	−.032	+.224	+.008
Last fifth of G_2	−.016	+.152	+.064
Last Panel			
First fifth of G_3	−.016	+.112	+.104
Second fifth of G_3	−.032	+.104	+.128
Third fifth of G_3	−.024	+.048	+.176
Fourth fifth of G_3	+.008	−.056	+.248
Last fifth of G_3	+.064	−.208	+.344

C. For subdivision of subgroups into tenths or halves

Interpolated Subgroup	Coefficients to be applied to		
	G_1	G_2	G_3
First tenth of G_2	+.0405	+.0640	−.0045
Second tenth of G_2	+.0235	+.0880	−.0115
Third tenth of G_2	+.0095	+.1060	−.0155
Fourth tenth of G_2	−.0015	+.1180	−.0165
Fifth tenth of G_2	−.0095	+.1240	−.0145
Sum of coefficients for first five-tenths = coefficients for first half of G_2	+.0625	+.5000	−.0625
Sixth tenth of G_2	−.0145	+.1240	−.0095
Seventh tenth of G_2	−.0165	+.1180	−.0015
Eigth tenth of G_2	−.0155	+.1060	+.0095
Ninth tenth of G_2	−.0115	+.0880	+.0235
Last tenth of G_2	−.0045	+.0640	+.0405
Sum of coefficients for last five-tenths = coefficients for second half of G_2	−.0625	+.5000	+.0625

Source: The interpolation coefficients in Tables C.13, C.14, and C.17 were originally computed by Wilson H. Grabill, of the U.S. Bureau of the Census, from the basic formulas. Interpolation coefficients in Tables C.15 and C.16 are reproduced from the sources cated in these tables.

TABLE C.14 Interpolation Coefficients Based on the Sprague Formula (The Sprague formula is a six-term fifth-difference osculatory formula. It maintains the given values. Given points or groups must be equally spaced.)

A. For interpolation between given points at intervals of 0.2

Interpolated point	Coefficients to be applied to					
	$N_{1.0}$	$N_{2.0}$	$N_{3.0}$	$N_{4.0}$	$N_{5.0}$	$N_{6.0}$
	First interval					
$N_{1.0}$	+1.000	.0000	.0000	.0000	.0000	
$N_{1.2}$	+.6384	+.6384	−.4256	+.1824	−.0336	
$N_{1.4}$	+.3744	+.9984	−.5616	+.2304	−.0416	
$N_{1.6}$	+.1904	+1.1424	−.4896	+.1904	−.0336	
$N_{1.8}$	+.0704	+1.1264	−.2816	+.1024	−.0176	
	Next-to-first interval					
$N_{2.0}$	.0000	+1.000	.0000	.0000	.0000	
$N_{2.2}$	−.0336	+.8064	+.3024	−.0896	+.0144	
$N_{2.4}$	−.0416	+.5824	+.5824	−.1456	+.0224	
$N_{2.6}$	−.0336	+.3584	+.8064	−.1536	+.0224	
$N_{2.8}$	−.0176	+.1584	+.9504	−.1056	+.0144	
	Middle interval					
$N_{3.0}$	.0000	.0000	+1.000	.0000	.0000	.0000
$N_{3.2}$	+.0128	−.0976	+.9344	+.1744	−.0256	+.0016
$N_{3.4}$	+.0144	−.1136	+.7264	+.4384	−.0736	+.0080
$N_{3.6}$	+.0080	−.0736	+.4384	+.7264	−.1136	+.0144
$N_{3.8}$	+.0016	−.0256	+.1744	+.9344	−.0976	+.0128
	Next-to-last interval					
$N_{4.0}$		.0000	.0000	+1.000	.0000	.0000
$N_{4.2}$		+.0144	−.1056	+.9504	+.1584	−.0176
$N_{4.4}$		+.0224	−.1536	+.8064	+.3584	−.0336
$N_{4.6}$		+.0224	−.1456	+.5824	+.5824	−.0416
$N_{4.8}$		+.0144	−.0896	+.3024	+.8064	−.0336
	Last interval					
$N_{5.0}$		.0000	.0000	.0000	+1.000	.0000
$N_{5.2}$		−.0176	+.1024	−.2816	+1.1264	+.0704
$N_{5.4}$		−.0336	+.1904	−.4896	+1.1424	+.1904
$N_{5.6}$		−.0416	+.2304	−.5616	+.9984	+.3744
$N_{5.8}$		−.0336	+.1824	−.4256	+.6384	+.6384
$N_{6.0}$		.0000	.0000	.0000	.0000	+1.0000

B. For subdivision of groups into fifths

Interpolated Subgroup	Coefficients to be applied to				
	G_1	G_2	G_3	G_4	G_5
	First panel				
First fifth of G_1	+.3616	−.2768	+.1488	−.0336	
Second fifth of G_1	+.2640	−.0960	+.0400	−.0080	
Third fifth of G_1	+.1840	+.0400	−.0320	+.0080	
Fourth fifth of G_1	+.1200	+.1360	−.0720	+.0160	
Last fifth of G_1	+.0704	+.1968	−.0848	+.0176	
	Next-to-first panel				
First fifth of G_2	+.0336	+.2272	−.0752	+.0144	
Second fifth of G_2	+.0080	+.2320	−.0480	+.0080	
Third fifth of G_2	−.0080	+.2160	−.0080	.0000	
Fourth fifth of G_2	−.0160	+.1840	+.0400	−.0080	
Last fifth of G_2	−.0176	+.1408	+.0912	−.0144	
	Middle panel				
First fifth of G_3	−.0128	+.0848	+.1504	−.0240	+.0016
Second fifth of G_3	−.0016	+.0144	+.2224	−.0416	+.0064
Third fifth of G_3	+.0064	−.0336	+.2544	−.0336	+.0064
Fourth fifth of G_3	+.0064	−.0416	+.2224	+.0144	−.0016
Last fifth of G_3	+.0016	−.0240	+.1504	+.0848	−.0128
	Next-to-last panel				
First fifth of G_4		−.0144	+.0912	+.1408	−.0176
Second fifth of G_4		−.0080	+.0400	+.1840	−.0160
Third fifth of G_4		.0000	−.0080	+.2160	−.0080
Fourth fifth of G_4		+.0080	−.0480	+.2320	+.0080
Last fifth of G_4		+.0144	−.0752	+.2272	+.0336
	Last panel				
First fifth of G_5		+.0176	−.0848	+.1968	+.0704
Second fifth of G_5		+.0160	−.0720	+.1360	+.1200
Third fifth of G_5		+.0080	−.0320	+.0400	+.1840
Fourth fifth of G_5		−.0080	+.0400	−.0960	+.2640
Last fifth of G_5		−.0336	+.1488	−.2768	+.3616

C. For subdivision of subgroups into tenths or halves

Interpolated Subgroup	Coefficients to be applied to				
	G_1	G_2	G_3	G_4	G_5
First tenth of G_3	−.0076	+.0510	+.0660	−.0096	+.0002
Second tenth of G_3	−.0052	+.0338	+.0844	−.0144	+.0014
Third tenth of G_3	−.0022	+.0154	+.1036	−.0195	+.0027
Fourth tenth of G_3	+.0006	−.0010	+.1188	−.0221	+.0037
Fifth tenth of G_3	+.0027	−.0133	+.1272	−.0203	+.0037
Sum of coefficients for first five-tenths = coefficients for first half of G_3	−.0117	+.0859	+.5000	−.0859	+.0117
Sixth tenth of G_3	+.0037	−.0203	+.1272	−.0133	+.0027
Seventh tenth of G_3	+.0037	−.0221	+.1188	−.0010	+.0006
Eigth tenth of G_3	+.0027	−.0195	+.1036	+.0154	−.0022
Ninth tenth of G_3	+.0014	−.0144	+.0844	+.0338	−.0052
Last tenth of G_3	+.0002	−.0096	+.0660	+.0510	−.0076
Sum of coefficients for last five-tenths = coefficients for first half of G_3	+.0117	−.0859	+.5000	+.0859	−.0117

Source: See source note for Table C.13.

Klosterman, Brail, and Bossard (1993); a particularly comprehensive regional economic model is the REMI model (Treyz, 1993; or see Treyz, Rickman, and Shao, 1992, for a summary analysis), and the Bureau of Economic Analysis has also maintained the RIMS model (Bureau of Economic Analysis, 1997). The IMPLAN model, primarily an input-output model, has been used in this context as well (See www.mig-inc.com). These models are important to the demographer because population composition affects both the labor market sectors by supplying labor and the nonbasic economic sectors by demanding goods and services—and it is well known that different age, sex, race, and ethnic-origin groups demand different kinds of goods and services (Smith *et al.*, 2002, pp. 185–214; Siegel, J. S., 2002, pp. 232–237)

TABLE C.15 Interpolation Coefficients Based on the Beers "Ordinary" Formula (The Beers formula is a six-term formula that minimizes the fifth differences of the interpolated results. It maintains the given values. Given data must be equally spaced.)

A. For interpolation between given points at intervals of 0.2

Interpolated point	Coefficients to be applied to					
	$N_{1.0}$	$N_{2.0}$	$N_{3.0}$	$N_{4.0}$	$N_{5.0}$	$N_{6.0}$
First interval						
$N_{1.0}$	+1.000	.0000	.0000	.0000	.0000	.0000
$N_{1.2}$	+.6667	+.4969	−.1426	−.1006	+.1079	−.0283
$N_{1.4}$	+.4072	+.8344	−.2336	−.0976	+.1224	−.0328
$N_{1.6}$	+.2148	+1.0204	−.2456	−.0536	+.0884	−.0244
$N_{1.8}$	+.0819	+1.0689	−.1666	−.0126	+.0399	−.0115
Next-to first interval						
$N_{2.0}$	.0000	+1.000	.0000	.0000	.0000	.0000
$N_{2.2}$	−.0404	+.8404	+.2344	−.0216	−.0196	+.0068
$N_{2.4}$	−.0497	+.6229	+.5014	−.0646	−.0181	+.0081
$N_{2.6}$	−.0389	+.3849	+.7534	−.1006	−.0041	+.0053
$N_{2.8}$	−.0191	+.1659	+.9354	−.0906	+.0069	+.0015
Middle interval						
$N_{3.0}$	.0000	.0000	+1.000	1.0000	.0000	.0000
$N_{3.2}$	+.0117	−.0921	+.9234	+.1854	−.0311	+.0027
$N_{3.4}$	+.0137	−.1101	+.7194	+.4454	−.0771	+.0087
$N_{3.6}$	+.0087	−.0771	+.4454	+.7194	−.1101	+.0137
$N_{3.8}$	+.0027	−.0311	+.1854	+.9234	−.0921	+.0117
Next-to-last interval						
$N_{4.0}$	.0000	.0000	.0000	1.0000	.0000	.0000
$N_{4.2}$	+.0015	+.0069	−.0906	+.9354	+.1659	−.0191
$N_{4.4}$	+.0053	−.0041	−.1006	+.7534	+.3849	−.0389
$N_{4.6}$	+.0081	−.0181	−.0646	+.5014	+.6229	−.0497
$N_{4.8}$	+.0068	−.0196	−.0216	+.2344	+.8404	−.0404
Last interval						
$N_{5.0}$	.0000	.0000	.0000	.0000	+1.0000	.0000
$N_{5.2}$	−.0115	+.0399	−.0126	−.1666	+1.0689	+.0819
$N_{5.4}$	−.0244	+.0884	−.0536	−.2456	+1.0204	+.2148
$N_{5.6}$	−.0328	+.1224	−.0976	−.2336	+.8344	+.4072
$N_{5.8}$	−.0283	+.1079	−.1006	−.1426	+.4969	+.6667
$N_{6.0}$	.0000	.0000	.0000	.0000	.0000	+1.0000

B. For subdivision of groups into fifths

Interpolated subgroup	Coefficients to be applied to				
	G_1	G_2	G_3	G_4	G_5
First panel					
First fifth of G_1	+.3333	−.1636	−.0210	+.0796	−.0283
Second fifth of G_1	+.2595	−.0780	+.0130	+.0100	−.0045
Third fifth of G_1	+.1924	+.0064	+.0184	−.0256	+.0084
Fourth fifth of G_1	+.1329	+.0844	+.0054	−.0356	+.0129
Last fifth of G_1	+.0819	+.1508	−.0158	−.0284	+.0115
Next-to-first panel					
First fifth of G_2	+.0404	+.2000	−.0344	−.0128	+.0068
Second fifth of G_2	+.0093	+.2268	−.0402	+.0028	+.0013
Third fifth of G_2	−.0108	+.2272	−.0248	+.0112	−.0028
Fourth fifth of G_2	−.0198	+.1992	+.0172	+.0072	−.0038
Last fifth of G_2	−.0191	+.1468	+.0822	−.0084	−.0015
Middle panel					
First fifth of G_3	−.0117	+.0804	+.1570	−.0284	+.0027
Second fifth of G_3	−.0020	+.0160	+.2200	−.0400	+.0060
Third fifth of G_3	+.0050	−.0280	+.2460	−.0280	+.0050
Fourth fifth of G_3	+.0060	−.0400	+.2200	+.0160	−.0020
Last fifth of G_3	+.0027	−.0284	+.1570	+.0804	−.0117
Next-to-last panel					
First fifth of G_4	−.0015	−.0084	+.0822	+.1468	−.0191
Second fifth of G_4	−.0038	+.0072	+.0172	+.1992	−.0198
Third fifth of G_4	−.0028	+.0112	−.0248	+.2272	−.0108
Fourth fifth of G_4	+.0013	+.0028	−.0402	+.2268	+.0093
Last fifth of G_4	+.0068	−.0128	−.0344	+.2000	+.0404
Last panel					
First fifth of G_5	+.0115	−.0284	−.0158	+.1508	+.0819
Second fifth of G_5	+.0129	−.0356	+.0054	+.0844	+.1329
Third fifth of G_5	+.0084	−.0256	+.0184	+.0064	+.1924
Fourth fifth of G_5	−.0045	+.0100	+.0130	−.0780	+.2595
Last fifth of G_5	−.0283	+.0796	−.0210	−.1636	+.3333

Source: Hensy S. Beers, "Discussion of Papers Presented in the Record, No. 68: 'Six-Term Formulas for Routine Actuarial Interpolation,' by Henry S. Beers," *The Record fo the American Institute of Actuaries* 34, Part I(69): 59–60, June 1945.

TABLE C.16 Interpolation Coefficients Based on the Beers "Modified" Formula (The Beers "modified" formula is a six-term formula that minimizes the fourth differences of the interpolated results. This formula combines interpolation with some smoothing or graduation of given values; end panels maintain the given values, however. Given data must be equally spaced.)

A. For interpolation between given points at intervals of 0.2

Interpolated point	Coefficients to be applied to					
	$N_{1.0}$	$N_{2.0}$	$N_{3.0}$	$N_{4.0}$	$N_{5.0}$	$N_{6.0}$
First interval						
$N_{1.0}$	+1.000	.0000	.0000	.0000	.0000	.0000
$N_{1.2}$	+.6668	+.5270	−.2640	+.0820	−.0140	+.0022
$N_{1.4}$	+.4099	+.8592	−.3598	+.1052	−.0173	+.0028
$N_{1.6}$	+.2196	+1.0279	−.3236	+.0874	−.0136	+.0023
$N_{1.8}$	+.0862	+1.0644	−.1916	+.0464	−.0066	+.0012
Next-to first interval						
$N_{2.0}$	.0000	+1.000	.0000	.0000	.0000	.0000
$N_{2.2}$	−.0486	+.8655	+.2160	−.0350	+.0030	−.0009
$N_{2.4}$	−.0689	+.6903	+.4238	−.0442	+.0003	−.0013
$N_{2.6}$	−.0697	+.5018	+.5938	−.0152	−.0097	−.0010
$N_{2.8}$	−.0589	+.3233	+.7038	+.0578	−.0257	−.0003
Middle interval						
$N_{3.0}$	−.0430	+.1720	+.7420	+.1720	−.0430	.0000
$N_{3.2}$	−.0270	+.0587	+.7072	+.3162	−.0538	−.0013
$N_{3.4}$	−.0141	−.0132	+.6098	+.4708	−.0477	−.0056
$N_{3.6}$	−.0056	−.0477	+.4708	+.6098	−.0132	−.0141
$N_{3.8}$	−.0013	−.0538	+.3162	+.7072	+.0587	−.0270
Next-to-last interval						
$N_{4.0}$	.0000	−.0430	+.1720	+.7420	+.1720	−.0430
$N_{4.2}$	−.0003	−.0257	+.0578	+.7038	+.3233	−.0589
$N_{4.4}$	−.0010	−.0097	−.0152	+.5938	+.5018	−.0697
$N_{4.6}$	−.0013	+.0003	−.0442	+.4238	+.6903	−.0689
$N_{4.8}$	−.0009	+.0030	−.0350	+.2160	+.8655	−.0486
Last interval						
$N_{5.0}$	.0000	.0000	.0000	.0000	+1.0000	.0000
$N_{5.2}$	+.0012	−.0066	+.0464	−.1916	+1.0644	+.0862
$N_{5.4}$	+.0023	−.0136	+.0874	−.3236	+1.0279	+.2196
$N_{5.6}$	+.0028	−.0173	+.1052	−.3598	+.8529	+.4099
$N_{5.8}$	+.0022	−.0140	+.0820	−.2640	+.5270	+.6668
$N_{6.0}$	.0000	.0000	.0000	.0000	.0000	+1.0000

B. For subdivision of groups into fifths

Interpolated subgroup	Coefficients to be applied to				
	G_1	G_2	G_3	G_4	G_5
First panel					
First fifth of G_1	+.3332	−.1938	+.0702	−.0118	+.0022
Second fifth of G_1	+.2569	−.0753	+.0205	−.0027	+.0006
Third fifth of G_1	+.1903	+.0216	−.0146	+.0032	−.0005
Fourth fifth of G_1	+.1334	+.0969	−.0351	+.0059	−.0011
Last fifth of G_1	+.0862	+.1506	−.0410	+.0054	−.0012
Next-to-first panel					
First fifth of G_2	+.0486	+.1831	−.0329	+.0021	−.0009
Second fifth of G_2	+.0203	+.1955	−.0123	−.0031	−.0004
Third fifth of G_2	+.0008	+.1893	+.0193	−.0097	+.0003
Fourth fifth of G_2	−.0108	+.1677	+.0577	−.0153	+.0007
Last fifth of G_2	−.0159	+.1354	+.0972	−.0170	+.0003
Middle panel					
First fifth of G_3	−.0160	+.0973	+.1321	−.0121	−.0013
Second fifth of G_3	−.0129	+.0590	+.1564	+.0018	−.0043
Third fifth of G_3	−.0085	+.0260	+.1650	+.0260	−.0085
Fourth fifth of G_3	−.0043	+.0018	+.1564	+.0590	−.0129
Last fifth of G_3	−.0013	−.0121	+.1321	+.0973	−.0160
Next-to-last panel					
First fifth of G_4	+.0003	−.0170	+.0972	+.1354	−.0159
Second fifth of G_4	+.0007	−.0153	+.0577	+.1677	−.0108
Third fifth of G_4	+.0003	−.0097	+.0193	+.1893	+.0008
Fourth fifth of G_4	−.0004	−.0031	−.0123	+.1955	+.0203
Last fifth of G_4	−.0009	+.0021	−.0329	+.1831	+.0486
Last panel					
First fifth of G_5	−.0012	+.0054	−.0410	+.1506	+.0862
Second fifth of G_5	−.0011	+.0059	−.0351	+.0969	+.1334
Third fifth of G_5	−.0005	+.0032	−.0146	+.0216	+.1903
Fourth fifth of G_5	+.0006	−.0027	+.0205	−.0753	+.2569
Last fifth of G_5	+.0022	−.0118	+.0702	−.1938	+.3332

Source: Henry S. Beers, "Modified Interpolation Formulas that Minimize Fourth Differences," *The Record of the American Institute of Actuaries* 34, Part I(69): 19–20, June 1945.

TABLE C.17 Interpolation Coefficients Based on Grabill's Weighted Moving Average of Sprague Coefficients (See text for derivation. Used for drastic smoothing. Given groups must be equally spaced.)

Interpolated subgroup	Coefficients to be applied to				
	G_1	G_2	G_3	G_4	G_5
First fifth of G_3	+.0111	+.0816	+.0826	+.0256	−.0009
Second fifth of G_3	+.0049	+.0673	+.0903	+.0377	−.0002
Third fifth of G_3	+.0015	+.0519	+.0932	+.0519	+.0015
Fourth fifth of G_3	−.0002	+.0377	+.0903	+.0673	+.0049
Last fifth of G_3	−.0009	+.0256	+.0826	+.0816	+.0111

Source: See source note for Table C.13.

CONCLUDING NOTE

In so many pages, with so many applications and examples, we have merely scratched the surface of the variety of tools now available to the demographer. Readers interested in more details may consult the eight-volume set, *Readings in Population Research Methodology* (Bogue, Arriaga, and Anderton, 1993) or any of a number of specialized texts.

References

Agresti, A. 1990. *Categorical Data Analysis*. New York: John Wiley and Sons.

Agresti, A. 1996. *An Introduction to Categorical Data Analysis*. New York: John Wiley and Sons.

Aitken, A. C. 1932. "On Interpolation by Iteration of Proportionate Parts, without the Use of Differences." *Proceedings of the Edinburgh Mathematical Society, Series 2*, 3: 56–76.

Akers, D. S., and J. S. Siegel. 1965. "National Census Survival Rates, by Color and Sex, for 1950–1960." *Current Population Reports*, Series p. 23, No. 15. Washington, DC: U.S. Bureau of the Census.

Alfeld, L. E., and A. K. Graham. 1976. *Introduction to Urban Dynamics*. Cambridge, MA: Wright-Allen Press.

Bain, L. J., and M. Engelhart. 1987. *Introduction to Probability and Mathematical Statistics*. Boston: Duxbury Press.

Bartholomew, D. J. 1982. *Stochastic Models for Social Processes*, 3rd ed. New York: John Wiley and Sons.

Beers, H. S. 1944. "Six-Term Formulae for Routine Actuarial Interpolation." *Record of the American Institute of Actuaries* 33: 245–260.

Beers, H. S. 1945. "Modified-Interpolation Formulae that Minimize Fourth Differences." *Record of the American Institute of Actuaries* 34: 14–20.

Bickel, P. J., and K. A. Doksum. 1977. *Mathematical Statistics: Basic Ideas and Selected Topics*. Engelwood Cliffs, NJ: Prentice Hall.

Birch, M. W. 1963. "Maximum Likelihood in Three-Way Contingency Tables." *Journal of the Royal Statistical Society B* 25: 220–233.

Bishop, Y. V. V., S. E. Feinberg, and P. W. Holland. 1975. *Discrete Multivariate Analysis*. Cambridge, MA: MIT Press.

Bogue, D. J., E. E. Arriaga, and D. H. Anderston. 1993. *Readings in Population Research Methodology, Volumes 1–8*. Chicago: Social Development Center and United Nations Population Fund.

Brown, R. L. 1993. *Introduction to the Mathematics of Demography*, 2nd ed. Winsted, CT: ACTEX Publications.

Burden, R. L., and J. D. Faires. 1993. *Numerical Analysis*, 5th ed. Boston: PWS.

Bureau of Economic Analysis. 1997. *Regional Multipliers: A User Handbook for the Regional Input-Output Modeling System (RIMS II)*. Washington, DC: U.S. Government Printing Office.

Castro, L. J., and A. Rogers. 1983. "What the Age Composition of Migrants Can Tell Us." *Population Bulletin of the United Nations* 15: 63–79.

Chattopadhyay, M., P. Lahiri, M. Larsen, and J. Reimnitz. 1999. "Composite Estimation of Drug Prevalences for Sub-State Areas." *Survey Methodology* 25: 81–86.

Citro, C. F. 1991. "Databases for Microsimulation: A Comparison of the March CPS and SIPP." In C. F. Citro and E. Hanushek (Eds.), *Improving Information for Social Policy Decisions: The Uses of Microsimulation Modeling, Volume II: Technical Papers* (pp. 11–61). Washington, DC: National Academy Press.

Citro, C. F., M. L. Cohen, G. Kalton, and K. K. West (Eds.). 1997. *Small-Area Estimates of School-Age Children in Poverty: Interim Report 1: Evaluation of 1993 County Estimates for Title I Allocations*. Washington, DC: National Academy Press.

Citro, C. F., and E. Hanushek (Eds.). 1991. *Improving Information for Social Policy Decisions: The Uses of Microsimulation Modeling, Volume 1*. Washington, DC: National Academy Press.

Cohen, M. 1991. "Statistical Matching and Microsimulation Models." In C. F. Citro and E. Hanushek (Eds.), *Improving Information for Social Policy Decisions: The Uses of Microsimulation Modeling, Volume II: Technical Papers* (pp. 62–85). Washington, DC: National Academy Press.

Darga, K. 1999. *Sampling and the Census*. Washington, DC: AEI Press.

Darga, K. 2000. *Fixing the Census Until It Breaks*. Lansing, MI: Michigan Information Center.

Deming, W. E. 1948. *The Statistical Adjustment of Data*. New York: John Wiley and Sons.

Deming, W. E., and F. F. Stephan. 1940. "On a Least Squares Adjustment of a Sampled Frequency Table When the Expected Marginal Totals Are Known." *Annals of Mathematical Statistics* 11: 427–444.

Draper, D. 1992. *Combining Information: Statistical Issues and Opportunities for Research*. Washington, DC: National Academy Press.

Dudewicz, E. J., and S. N. Mishra. 1988. *Modern Mathematical Statistics*. New York: John Wiley and Sons.

Ewbank, D. C. 1981. *Age Misreporting and Age-Selective Underenumeration: Sources, Patterns, and Consequences for Demographic Analysis*. Washington, DC: National Academy Press.

Forrester, J. W. 1968. *Principles of Systems*. Cambridge, MA: Wright-Allen Press.

Gonzalez, M. E. 1973. "Use and Evaluation of Synthetic Estimates." In American Statistical Assocation, *Proceedings of the Social Statistics Section*. Washington DC: American Statistical Association.

Gonzalez, M. E., and C. Hoza. 1978. "Small-Area Estimation with Application to Unemployment and Housing Estimates." *Journal of the American Statistical Association* 73: 7–15.

Goodman, M. R. 1974. *Study Notes in System Dynamics*. Cambridge, MA: Wright-Allen Press.

Greene, W. H. 1993. *Econometric Analysis*, 2nd ed. Englewood Cliffs, NJ: Prentice-Hall.

Hair, J. F., R. E. Anderson, R. L. Tatham, and W. C. Black. 1995. *Multivariate Data Analysis*, 4th ed. Upper Saddle River, NJ: Prentice Hall.

Heeringa, S. G. 1993. "Statistical Models for Small Area Estimation." In D. J. Bogue, E. E. Arriaga, and D. L. Anderton (Eds.), *Readings in Population Research Methodology, Volume 5: Population Models, Projections, and Estimates* (pp. 20.58–20.64). Chicago: Social Development Center and United Nations Population Fund.

Heligman, L., and J. Pollard. 1993. "The Age Pattern of Mortality." In D. J. Bogue, E. E. Arriaga, and D. L. Anderton (Eds.), *Readings in Population Research Methodology, Volume 2: Mortality Research* (pp. 7.98–7.104). Chicago: Social Development Center and United Nations Population Fund.

High Performance Systems. 1996. *An Introduction to Systems Thinking.* Hanover, NH: High Performance Systems.

Horvitz, D. G., and D. J. Thompson. 1952. "A Generalization of Sampling without Replacement from a Finite Universe." *Journal of the American Statistical Association* 47: 663–685.

Ingram, D. D., J. O'Hare, F. Scheuren, and J. Turek. 2000. *Statistical Matching: A New Validation Case Study.* Paper presented at the 2000 Joint Statistical Meetings, Indianapolis, IN, August 5–11.

Inmon, W. H. 1996. *Building the Data Warehouse.* New York: Wiley.

Isard, W. 1960. *Methods of Regional Science: An Introduction to Regional Analysis.* Cambridge, MA: MIT Press.

Isserman, A. 1993. "The Right People, the Right Rates." *Journal of the American Planning Association* 59: 45–64.

Johnson, A., and D. Percy. 2000. *Cubic Splines.* Online document at www.geol.pdx.edu/Courses/G423/Handouts/Spline/Derivation.html. Retrieved December 23, 2000.

Judge, G. G., W. E. Griffiths, R. C. Hill, H. Lutkepohl, and T-C. Lee. 1985. *The Theory and Practice of Econometrics,* 2nd ed. New York: John Wiley and Sons.

Judge, G. G., R. C. Hill, W. E. Griffiths, H. Lutkepohl, and T-C. Lee. 1988. *Introduction to the Theory and Practice of Econometrics,* 2nd ed. New York: John Wiley and Sons.

Judson, D. H. 1990. *Discrete Increment-Decrement Population Models: A Demonstration and Simulation.* Sociological Data Processing Center Technical Report, Washington State University, April 25.

Judson, D. H. 1993. *Performance Standards in the Shared Information System: An Evaluation of the Uses of the Mobility Continuum Concept for the Workforce Quality Council.* Salem, OR: Oregon Employment Department.

Judson, D. H. 2000. *The Statistical Administrative Records System: System Design, Challenges, and Successes.* Paper presented at the NISS/Telcordia Data Quality Conference, Morristown, NJ, November 30–December 1.

Judson, D. H., and C. L. Popoff. 1996. *Research Use of Administrative Records.* Paper presented at the 6th International Conference on Applied and Business Demography, Bowling Green State University, Bowling Green, OH, September 19–21.

Kadane, J. B. 1978. "Statistical Problems of Merged Data Files." In *Compilation of OTA Papers, Vol. 1* (pp. 159–179). Washington, DC: Office of Tax Analysis, U.S. Department of the Treasury.

Klosterman, R. E., R. K. Brail, and E. G. Bossard. 1993. *Spreadsheet Models for Urban and Regional Analysis.* New Brunswick, NJ: Rutgers, the State University of New Jersey.

Kmenta, J. 1986. *Elements of Econometrics,* 2nd ed. New York: MacMillan.

Laudon, K. C. 1986. "Data Quality and Due Process in Large Interorganizational Record Systems." *Communications of the ACM* 29: 4–11.

Leslie, P. H. 1945. "On the Use of Matrices in Certain Population Mathematics." *Biometrika* 33: 183–212.

Lessler, J. T., and W. D. Kalsbeek. 1992. *Nonsampling Error in Surveys.* New York: John Wiley and Sons.

Levy, P. S., and D. K. French. 1977a. *Synthetic Estimation of State Health Characteristics Based on the Health Interview Survey.* Hyattsville, MD: National Center for Health Statistics.

Levy, P. S., and D. K. French. 1977b. *Synthetic Estimation of State Health Characteristics Based on the Health Interview Survey.* U.S. Department of Health, Education, and Welfare, National Center on Health Statistics Series #275. Washington, DC: U.S. Government Printing Office.

Light, S. C. 1990. "Measurement Error in Official Statistics: Prison Rule Infraction Data." *Federal Probation* 54: 63–68.

Lohr, S. L. 1999. *Sampling: Design and Analysis.* Pacific Grove, CA: Brooks/Cole.

Long, L. 1984. *Migration and Residential Mobility in the United States.* New York: Russell Sage Foundation.

Long, J. S. 1997. *Regression Models for Categorical and Limited Dependent Variables.* Thousand Oaks, CA: Sage.

Ma, J. M. 1986. *A Modeling Approach to System Evaluation in Research Data Management.* Ph.D. thesis, University of North Carolina, Chapel Hill, NC.

Macro International. 1996. *Sampling Manual.* DHS-III Basic Documentation No. 6. Calverton, MD: Macro International.

Mayhew, B. H. 1980. "Structuralism versus Individualism: Part 1, Shadowboxing in the Dark." *Social Forces* 59: 335–375.

McCullagh, P., and J. Nelder. 1990. *Generalized Linear Models,* 2nd ed. London: Chapman and Hall.

México, Dirección General de Estadística. 1962. *Censo General de Población—1960.* Mexico City, Mexico: Secretaría de Industria y Comercio, Dirección General de Estadística.

Miller, M. D. 1946. *Elements of Graduation.* Chicago: Actuarial Society of America and American Institute of Actuaries.

Moriarty, C., and F. Scheuren. 2001. *Statistical Matching: Pitfalls of Current Procedures.* Paper presented at the 2001 Joint Statistical Meetings, Atlanta, GA, August 5–11.

Murdock, S., and D. Ellis. 1991. *Applied Demography: An Introduction to Basic Concepts, Methods, and Data.* Boulder, CO: Westview Press.

Paass, G. 1985. "Statistical Record Linkage Methodology: State of the Art and Future Prospects." In *Proceedings of the 100th Session of the International Statistical Institute* (pp. 9.3.1–9.3.16). Amsterdam: International Statistical Institute.

Plane, D. A., and P. A. Rogerson. 1994. *The Geographical Analysis of Population with Applications to Planning and Business.* New York: John Wiley and Sons.

Pollard, J. H. 1973. *Mathematical Models for the Growth of Human Populations.* Cambridge: Cambridge University Press.

Pool, I. 1964. "Simulating Social Systems." *International Science and Technology* 27: 62–72.

Popoff, C. L., E. Fadali, and D. H. Judson. 2000. Methodology Explanation and Documentation for Nevada-Specific Estimates of the Uninsured. Online document at www.gbpca.org/Documents/methodology.htm. Retrieved December 12.

Press, W. H., B. P. Flannery, S. A. Teukolsky, and W. T. Vetterling. 1989. *Numerical Recipes in Pascal: The Art of Scientific Computing.* New York: Cambridge University Press.

Radelet, M. 1981. "Racial Characteristics and the Imposition of the Death Penalty." *American Sociological Review* 46: 918–927.

Randers, J. 1980. *Elements of the System Dynamics Method.* Cambridge, MA: MIT Press.

Reder, S. 1994. *Synthetic Estimates of NALS Literacy Proficiences from 1990 Census Microdata.* Portland, OR: Northwest Regional Education Laboratory.

Redman, T. J. 1996. *Data Quality for the Information Age.* Norwood, MA: Artech House.

Rogers, A. 1975. *Introduction to Multiregional Mathematical Demography.* New York: Wiley Interscience.

Rogers, A. 1995. *Multiregional Demography: Principles, Methods and Extensions.* New York: John Wiley and Sons.

Rogers, A., and L. Castro. 1986. "Migration" (pp. 157–210). In A. Rogers and F. Willikens (Eds.). *Migration and Settlement: A Multiregional Comparative Study.* Dordrecht, Netherlands: D. Reidel Publishing Company.

Ross, S. M. 1997. *Introduction to Probability Models,* 6th ed. New York: Academic Press.

Rubin, D. B. 1979. "Using Multivariate Matched Sampling and Regression Adjustment to Control Bias in Observational Studies." *Journal of the American Statistical Association* 74: 318–328.

Rubin, D. B. 1986. "Statistical Matching Using File Concatenation with Adjusted Weights and Multiple Imputations." *Journal of Business and Economic Statistics* 4: 87–94.

Sarndal, C. E. 1984. "Design-Consistent Versus Model-Dependent Estimation for Small Domains." *Journal of the American Statistical Association* 79: 624–631.

Schoen, R. 1988. *Modeling Multigroup Populations*. New York: Plenum Press.

Shryock, H. S., J. S. Siegel, and Associates. 1971. *The Methods and Materials of Demography*. Washington, DC: U.S. Government Printing Office.

Siegel, J. S. 2002. *Applied Demography: Applications to Business, Government, Law, and Public Policy*. San Diego: Academic Press.

Sigmund, C. L., D. H. Judson, and C. L. Popoff. 1998. *A System for Synthetic Estimates of Health-Related Characteristics: Linking a Population Survey with Local Data*. Paper presented at the 1999 meetings of the Population Association of America, New York.

Smith, S. K. 1986. "Accounting for Migration in Cohort-Component Projections of State and Local Populations." *Demography* 23: 127–135.

Smith, S. K., J. Tayman, and D. Swanson. 2001. *State and Local Population Projections: Methodology and Analysis*. Boston: Kluwer Academic.

Sprague, T. B. 1881. "Explanation of a New Formula for Interpolation." *Journal of the Institute of Actuaries* 22: 270.

Stevens, D. W., P. A. Richmond, J. F. Haenn, and J. S. Michie. 1992. *Measuring Employment Outcomes Using Unemployment Insurance Wage Records*. Washington, DC: Research and Evaluation Associates.

Thompson, S. K. 1992. *Sampling*. New York: John Wiley and Sons.

Treyz, G. I. 1993. *Regional Economic Modeling: A Systematic Approach to Economic Forecasting and Policy Analysis*. Boston: Kluwer Academic Publishers.

Treyz, G. I., D. S. Rickman, and G. Shao. 1992. "The REMI Economic-Demographic Forecasting and Simulation Model." *International Regional Science Review* 14: 221–253.

U.S. Census Bureau. 2000. *Statistical Abstract of the United States: 1999*. Washington, DC: U.S. Government Printing Office.

U.S. National Center for Health Statistics. 1997. *U.S. Decennial Life Tables for 1989–91*, vol 1 no 1. Hyattsville, MD: National Center for Health Statistics.

U.S. National Center for Health Statistics. 1998. "United States Abridged Life Tables, 1996." By R. N. Anderson. *National Vital Statistics Reports* 47(13): 1–20.

Wachter, K. W., and D. A. Freedman. 2000. "Measuring Local Heterogeneity with 1990 Census Data." *Demographic Research*. Online document at www.demographic-research.org/Volumes/Vol3/10. Retrieved December 12.

Wallis, W. A., and H. V. Roberts. 1962. *The Nature of Statistics*. New York: The Free Press.

Weisberg, S. 1982. *Applied Linear Regression*, 2nd ed. New York: John Wiley and Sons.

Wolfenden, H. H. 1942. *The Fundamental Principles of Mathematical Statistics*. New York: The Actuarial Society of America.

Suggested Readings

Sampling, Sampling Errors, and Other Errors in Surveys

Biemer, P. B., R. M. Groves, L. E. Lyberg, N. A. Mathiowetz, and S. Sudman (Eds.). 1991. *Measurement Errors in Surveys*. New York: Wiley-Interscience.

Fink, A. (Ed.). 1995. *The Survey Kit, Volumes 1–9*. Thousand Oaks, CA: Sage.

Groves, R. M. 1989. *Survey Errors and Survey Costs*. New York: Wiley-Interscience.

Kish, L. 1965/1995. *Survey Sampling*. New York: John Wiley and Sons.

Siegel, J. S. 2002. *Applied Demography: Applications to Business, Government, Law, and Public Policy*. Chapter 4. San Diego: Academic Press.

Interpolation

Brass, W. 1960. "The Graduation of Fertility Distributions by Polynomial Functions." *Population Studies* 14: 148–162.

Keyfitz, N. 1966. "A Unified Approach to Interpolation and Graduation." *Demography* 3(2): 528–536.

Keyfitz, N. 1977. "Interpolation and Graduation." Chapter 10 in *Introduction to the Mathematics of Population, with Revisions*. Reading, MA: Addison-Wesley.

U.S. Census Bureau. 1994. *Population Analysis with Microcomputers, Volumes I and II*. By E. Arriaga, P. Johnson, and E. Jamison. Washington, DC: U.S. Bureau of the Census.

Adjustment of Distributions to Marginal Totals

Deming, W. E. 1948. *Statistical Adjustment of Data*. New York: John Wiley & Sons.

Deming, W. E., and F. F. Stephan. 1940. "On a Least Squares Adjustment of a Sampled Frequency Table When the Expected Marginal Totals are Known." *The Annals of Mathematical Statistics* 11(4): 427–444.

Feinberg, S. 1981. *The Analysis of Cross-Classified Categorical Data*. Cambridge, MA: MIT Press.

Computer Usage and Data Warehousing

Brackstone, George J. 1988. "Statistical Uses of Administrative Data: Issues and Challenges." In J. W. Coombs and M. P. Singh (Eds.), *Statistical Uses of Administrative Data : An International Symposium* (pp. 5–16). Ottawa: Statistics Canada.

Coombs, J. W., and M. P. Singh (Eds.). 1988. *Statistical Uses of Administrative Data: An International Symposium*. Ottawa: Statistics Canada.

English, L. P. 1999. *Improving Data Warehouse and Business Information Quality: Methods for Reducing Costs and Increasing Profits*. New York: John Wiley and Sons, Inc.

Kilss, B., and W. Alvey (Eds.). 1984. *Statistical Uses of Administrative Records: Recent Research and Present Prospects, Volumes I and II*. Washington, DC: Department of the Treasury, Internal Revenue Service, Statistics of Income Division.

Naus, J. I. 1975. *Data Quality Control and Editing*. New York: Marcel Dekker.

Silverston, L., W. H. Inmon, and K. Graziano. 1997. *The Data Model Resource Book: A Library of Logical Data Models and Data Warehouse Designs*. New York: John Wiley and Sons.

Other Topics

Citro, C. F., and E. A. Hanushek. 1991. *Improving Information for Social Policy Decisions: The Uses of Microsimulation Modeling. Volume II: Technical Papers*. Washington, DC: National Academy Press.

Forrester, J. W. 1971. "Counter-Intuitive Behavior of Social Systems." *Technology Review* 73: 52–68.

Klir, G. J. 1991. *Facets of Systems Science*. New York: Plenum Press.

Geographic Information Systems

KATHRYN NORCROSS BRYAN AND ROB GEORGE

How can geographic information systems (GIS) be useful to demographers? At first glance this question seems trivial, in that the importance of maps, the fundamental GIS product, is immediately obvious. Moreover, approximately 85% of all databases contain some sort of geographic information (MapInfo Corporation, 1998, p. 2). However, at a deeper level, the question is not trivial—is it worthwhile to learn something about GIS capabilities? This appendix attempts to answer the latter question by providing an overview of GIS, briefly describing its origins, discussing basic GIS concepts and issues, and giving examples of its use. Because of the highly technical nature of GIS, this appendix is not designed to be a GIS user's manual. Such information can be found in the works listed in the References and Suggested Readings provided at the end of this appendix.

Aronoff (1989, p. 39) describes GIS as "a computer-based system that provides the following four sets of capabilities to handle 'geo-referenced data:' (1) input; (2) data management; (3) manipulation and analysis; and (4) output." To operate a GIS one needs a computer, data with geographic identifiers, and a software program that can manipulate and display such data.[1] The geographic identifiers may be based on physical or administrative geography and may be as specific as latitude/longitude or a street address.

However, GIS should be thought of as more than a utility that can create maps. It can be used as a research tool to help explore demographic data and search for patterns and relationships. Social scientists have often used maps for descriptive purposes, but rarely for other applications. Prior to the arrival of high-powered computers and mapping software,

creating maps was a costly and time-consuming task. With GIS, not only is map making inexpensive and fast, but the way is clear to conduct both spatial analysis and predictive modeling quickly and efficiently (Fotheringham and Rogerson, 1994).

Spatial analysis affords one the ability to see geographic trends. For example, if there is an outbreak of sickness in a community, a map could be used in two ways. First, by showing the location of each incident, a pattern of dispersal may be revealed. Second, if a pattern is found, a map with layers of additional features, such as water supply, wind direction, and other natural phenomena, can be easily created in a GIS, which can then be used to evaluate patterns and correlations.

An advanced application of spatial analysis is *predictive modeling*. With each type of data in a GIS system, certain geographic characteristics can be gathered. Distance is one such key characteristic. Calculating the distance between two points, the length of a line, or the distance between a point and the centroid of a polygon can all be useful in predictive modeling. GIS can be used to measure the distance from a point to a particular shopping center, rather then from the centroid of a geographically defined area, such as a zip code.

ORIGINS OF GIS

For the most part, GIS theory originated with researchers interested in spatial analysis. In the 1950s and 1960s, demand for powerful analytical tools to address "real" problems initiated GIS development. Fueled by such geography-oriented industries as public utilities, transportation, retail marketing, and environmental management, GIS developed rapidly through the 1970s and 1980s, primarily in the United States. Many projects contributed to the development of

---

[1] MapInfo, ArcView, Arc Info, GeoMedia, Infomark, Maptitude, Atlas GIS, and so forth.

733

what we know as modern GIS systems. Some of these projects were taking place in the academic setting, some in the private sector, and some in various parts of government. Unfortunately, because all were in an evolutionary stage, little documentation of the simultaneity of ideas exists. As GIS has become more popular and easier to use, a greater interest developed in its origins. The National Center for Geographic Information and Analysis (NCGIA), established in 1988, began a comprehensive "GIS History Project" in 1996. The project is an attempt to document the history and origins of GIS. NCGIA intends to research and document not only the development of today's GIS software and data, but also the precursors and preconditions for its development, as well as a history of its applications in different cultural, political, and economic practices.

In early 1966, the Census Small Area Data Advisory Committee began working on a case study in preparation for the 1970 Census of the United States. A test census was taken in New Haven, Connecticut, in 1967. With the information gathered, the committee began computer mapping experiments and "geographic base file" (GBF) research. They found that converting the analog maps to numerically encoded files was redundant. Streets were being digitized multiple times at the beginning of the project. Fortunately for the Census Bureau, the problem was overcome by census mathematician James Corbett. Based on the principles of map topology, his encoding scheme became known as "DIME" (dual independent map encoding). This laid the groundwork for thematic mapping of census data and "GBF-DIME" files were digitized for U.S. cities during the 1970s. These were key components of the Census Bureau's current digital database used to support its mapping system, now known as the "Topologically Integrated Geographic Encoding and Referencing (TIGER) Line files." The TIGER/Line files were developed to support the data tabulating function of the Census Bureau. Files for public use include digital data for map features, boundaries, names, coordinates, and (for populous areas) address ranges and zip codes. Coverage is for all of the United States, including Puerto Rico and U.S. territories. They are grouped by state (or sets of states), by county (or sets of counties), and by statistical equivalents in the territories. Census information is further disaggregated into census tracts and block groups.

Although much of the literature on the history of GIS focuses on developments in the United States, important research was conducted elsewhere. Researchers in Canada, for example, played an important role in GIS development. One of the earlier systems developed in Canada resulted from the need to manage land and natural resources (Tomlinson, 1997, p. 38). In 1964, a team representing the Agricultural Rehabilitation and Development Act (ARDA) began work on the Canada Geographic Information System (CGIS). The system aimed to facilitate the inventory of land use and land capability across Canada. By 1971, the system was already fully operational. As a result, the early 1970s saw a boom in the use of GIS for various governmental projects in Canada.

The U.S. Geological Service developed "DLG" (digital line graphs) in the early 1970s. This development occurred about the same time as the U.S. Census bureau developed "DIME." These two federal agencies were among the first organizations to experiment with data formats that could serve many people for many purposes. Commercial data vendors soon followed, and by the 1980s, vendors began to develop file translation and conversion software. This enabled data to be imported and exported between certain systems and simplified the process of data acquisition. One of the most important standard file types is .dxf (drawing exchange format). The dxf standard (developed by Autodesk) is an ASCII format that describes the contents of a CAD (computer-assisted drawing) file in a way that can be interpreted by other software systems. Translators are available for all the major software. There are translators that convert .dxf files into MapInfo table files or to Arcview shape files, and vice versa. Translators are available from private vendors as well as the software companies themselves, and many of the GIS software available can recognize multiple file formats without going through the translation process. For example, in MapInfo one can open Dbase, Excel, Lotus, ASCII, and Access file formats, in addition to the MapInfo specific format.

BASIC GIS CONCEPTS AND ISSUES

Data

The data used in a GIS are of two types: spatial and nonspatial. Spatial data represent the geographic location of features. The nonspatial data describes variables such as names, addresses, type of feature, and so forth. When data are entered in a GIS, the two types of data need to be linked. There are five types of data entry systems that can be used in GIS: (1) keyboard entry, (2) coordinate geometry, (3) manual digitizing, (4) scanning, and (5) transfer of existing files. As technology improved and demand increased, more data much of which have already been scanned, digitized, or otherwise placed in digital form have become available. Existing digital data, of all types, are available at varying degrees of detail and accuracy from many sources. Many governmental agencies, such as the Census Bureau, provide much of their data to the public (some free; some for a fee). In addition to governmental agencies, many private companies also generate various types of data. The principles that affect the cost of data are level of detail, size of coverage, and timeliness.

With the voluminous amount of data available today, the results of primary research are virtually the only data that need to be entered manually by keyboard. Keyboard entry is used to add additional variables or observations to the spatial data that are being used. Information can easily be updated and edited using the keyboard. In most cases, it is possible to edit databases directly within the GIS software. GIS systems have the ability to add or delete fields and records and to edit existing information. It also is possible to edit data in a spreadsheet program, and then bring the data back into a GIS.

Another technological component that increases precision is provided by the global positioning system (GPS). GPS technology has evolved through efforts of the U.S. Department of Defense. It involves 24 satellites that orbit the earth at an elevation of 12,000 miles and continuously beam their locations and temporal positions toward the earth's surface. A GPS receiver can be used to collect data from at least three satellites so that the receiver's latitude and longitude can be calculated for two-dimensional readings. It is even possible to get three-dimensional accuracy (latitude, longitude, and altitude) if the receiver gets signals from at least four satellites. With a GPS receiver, it is possible to record the precise coordinates of any point on earth. The coordinates can then be entered into a GIS and a point can be located at its exact point in space. The coordinates may be recorded manually, although the data in most GPS receivers can be downloaded digitally.

It is important to understand census geography when talking about GIS. In the United States, for example, the Census Bureau collects data for many types of geographic regions. Although discussed in greater detail earlier (Chapters 2, 4, and, particularly, 5), the following is a list (from largest to smallest) of the census statistical units for which one can gather information:

Regions
Divisions
Urban/rural areas
Metropolitan statistical areas (MSA)
Primary metropolitan statistical areas (PMSA)
Consolidated metropolitan statistical areas
Urbanized areas
Census designated place (CDP)
Census tracts
Block groups
Blocks

The following is a list (from largest to smallest) of the census political units for which one can gather information:

United States
States (all states, District of Columbia, Puerto Rico, and the Virgin Islands)
Counties
County subdivisions (townships)
Places (boroughs, cities, and CDPs)

Accuracy

Considering that a GIS has the ability to collate and cross-reference many types of data by location, every time a new data set is added, a GIS has the potential to inherit and propagate errors. Data errors can make the results of a GIS analysis worthless.

There are many sources of error that can affect the quality of a GIS data set. It is largely the user's responsibility to prevent and manage error. Particular care should be devoted to checking for errors because a GIS is quite capable of fooling the user into a false sense of accuracy existence. The existence of error, and especially a level of error that is intolerable, must be acknowledged and accounted for by users. Data errors result from errors in field measurements, errors in existing maps, errors in any of the additional data used, or the incorrect recording and input of information. Reliability is affected by the number of observations used in the analysis. An insufficient number of observations (as in any statistical analysis) may not provide the level of resolution required to adequately perform spatial analysis and determine the patterns one is hoping to find. Data storage also is a concern. A storage format may have insufficient numerical precision and insufficient spatial precision. If latitude and longitude numbers are rounded at too high a level, for example, precision will be lost. Data manipulation errors can happen for many reasons. If boundary files are incorrect, results may be less precise. Inappropriate class intervals are also a concern. Methods of formatting digital information for transmission, storage, and processing may introduce error in the data. Multiple conversions from one format to another may create an effect similar to making copies of copies on a photocopying machine—the more they are copied, the less clear and less precise it becomes. Data output errors may be caused by the output device or the instability of the medium; scaling may become slightly inaccurate when printing is done directly from a computer screen.

Sources of errors can be grouped into two classes: quality of individual data elements and quality of data sets. Individual data element quality is related to *positional accuracy and precision*, *attribute accuracy and precision*, *logical consistency*, and *resolution*. Data set quality is affected by completeness, time, and lineage (Aronoff, 1989, p. 138). We begin with a discussion of individual data element quality.

The *positional accuracy and precision* of a data element applies to both horizontal and vertical positions. Positional accuracy refers to any difference between the represented geographic position (on the map) of a point or feature and its true position on the earth. The geographic level (scale) determines the level of precision needed. For example, a point showing Providence, Rhode Island, on a national map does not need to be as precise as it would on a map of Providence county. The lower the geographic level, the more positional accuracy will be important. Maps D.1a, b, and c

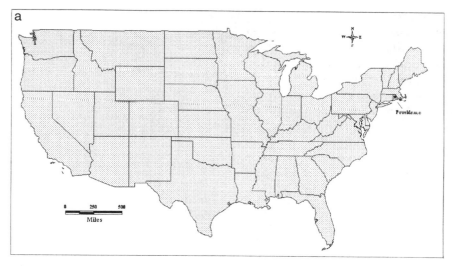

MAP D.1a   Providence, Rhode Island, on map of Continental United States.
Source: Made using MapInfo version 5.0. All data provided by MapInfo.

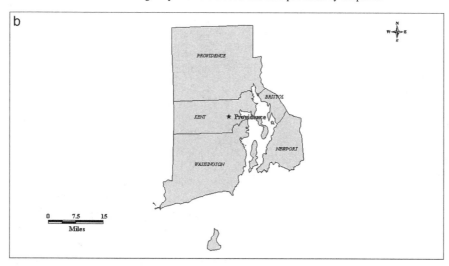

MAP D.1b   Map D.1a zoomed in to show state of Rhode Island and counties.
Source: Made using MapInfo version 5.0. All data provided by MapInfo.

MAP D.1c   State of Rhode Island and counties showing more precise location of Providence.
Source: Made using MapInfo version 5.0. All data provided by MapInfo.

illustrate this point. Map D1-a shows Providence on a map of the continental United States. Map D.1b shows that same position on a map of the state of Rhode Island. It is not very accurate, but it is sufficient for the national view. Map D.1c shows a more precise location of Providence on the state map. GIS allows a user to "pan" and "zoom" at will to a different scale and, as has been illustrated by the maps, this can be problematic. Accuracy and precision are tied to the original map scale and do not change even if the user zooms in and out. Zooming in and out can mislead the user into believing that the accuracy and precision have improved when in fact they have not.

Accuracy and precision of nonspatial data refers to the quality of the data about the places on a map. The location of a data element may be correct, but if the data attached to it are wrong, having a correct location may be a moot point. Misclassified or incorrect data can affect the outcome of the analysis and the visual effect of the map. Incorrect data may not always be obvious when looking at the map. For example, a pine forest may be incorrectly labeled as a spruce forest, thereby introducing error that may not be known or noticeable to the map or data user. Mistakes made in the field (such as errors in digitizing, processing, measurement, or keyboard entry) may be undetectable in the GIS project unless the user has conflicting or corroborating information available. If an error is not noticed, it very well may affect the decision making in a project, report, or research.

Logical consistency refers to how well logical relations among data elements are maintained. In other words, do the boundaries in the county file match up with the boundaries of the states in a file of the entire United States? How well do the edges line up? Logical consistency can be a problem in performing proportional queries or calculations. Areas of comparison may not be equal, and results may not add up.

The smaller the geographic unit being used, the greater the consideration required. Map D.2 illustrates this point. If the user ran a query to count the number of points in the state, points would be missed because of the fact that the boundaries for states and counties are not the same in all places. This problem may result in the omission of data in an analysis. This may or may not have an impact on results, but it is a problem of which a user should be aware when using two or more boundary files to conduct analysis.

Resolution is the smallest discernible unit or the smallest unit represented on the map. Resolution will be affected by the purpose of the map, legibility (how many variables or features are being represented), and the accuracy of the source data. If the data are not especially accurate, the result may not be noticeable, depending on the scale. One may want to use such a database only in its entirety rather than in small parts for, if one were to zoom in closer, the inaccuracies of the data would be more noticeable. Geographic data can be presented at any scale, and scale can be adjusted to fit the map, as is shown on Maps D1.a, b, and c.

Turning from the quality of individual data elements to the quality of data sets, we again note that the latter is affected by *lineage, completeness*, and *time* (Aronoff, 1989, p. 138). The *lineage* of a data set refers to its source and the steps taken to produce it. When one is using primary data, one would know exactly what the sources are and the steps taken to produce them. This becomes more of an issue when the data are from a secondary source. It is important to know where the data came from, when they were collected, and which methods and assumptions, if any, were used to produce the data. Finding this information is not always easy. Lineage information should be available for all data you acquire (and that you create). If it is not available, there are questions you should try to answer before using them:

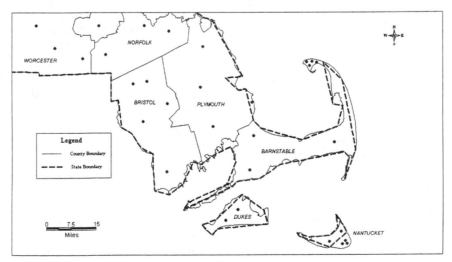

MAP D.2 Eastern Massachusetts: Differences in boundaries of state and county files.
Source: Made using MapInfo version 5.0. All data provided by MapInfo.

What is the age of the data?

Where do they come from?

In what medium were they originally produced?

What is the areal coverage of the data?

To what map scale were the data digitized?

What projection and coordinate system were used in drawing maps?

What was the density of observations used for their compilation?

How accurate are the data on positional and substantive features?

Do the data seem logical and consistent?

Do cartographic representations look "clean"?

Are the data relevant to the project at hand?

In what format are the data kept?

How were the data checked?

Why were the data compiled?

What is the reliability of the provider?

Completeness refers to the proportion of data available for an area. Complete coverage would mean 100% data for a given area. Data for an area may be completely lacking, or only partial information may be available. For example, a comparison of counties that have varying degrees of data completeness may not be as accurate as if they all had complete information. Uniform, essentially complete coverage may not be available and the user must decide what level of generalization is necessary or whether further collection of data is required.

The quality of a data set is also effected by *Classification* issues. Any GIS depends on the abstraction and classification of real-world phenomena. A user determines the amount of information to be used and its classification. Sometimes a user may use inappropriate categories or misclassify information. Even if the correct categories are employed, individual data may be misclassified. On occasion, definitions, and have the counter, of categories may overlap. The way classes are defined will affect how consistently and accurately the features can be assigned to classes and how analytically useful the classes are. For instance, assigning a cause of death to males between 18 and 24 years old would probably be significantly different from assigning it to a class interval 18 to 39 years old. Data are most accurately displayed and manipulated in smaller class intervals.

Timeliness is often important Many demographic data are very time-sensitive, and data values can change significantly over short periods of time. Attributes of a population and the geographic areas they occupy can change quickly. Past collection standards may be unknown, nonexistent, or not currently acceptable. Timeliness can become a problem when multiple data sets are used together. When using data sets collected at different times, especially when making comparisons of measures, extra caution must be used. In such cases, not only is it likely that the total population six

has changed, but its composition as well. Changes and shifts in the economy may have taken place, as well as in geographic boundaries. Reliance on old data may unknowingly bias or negate results.

Failure to control and manage sources of error can limit severely or invalidate the results of a GIS analysis. We give a few simple guidelines that will help limit the error in GIS. Standards should always be set from the start. Standards should be established for both the spatial and nonspatial data of the data set. Issues to be addressed include the accuracy and precision of the data, conventions for naming geographic features, criteria for classifying data, and related issues. Everyone involved with the database should be aware of the established standards, and the database should be checked occasionally. Standards for procedures and products should always be documented in writing. Data documentation should include information about how the data were collected and from what sources, how they were preprocessed and geocoded, how they were entered into the database, and how they were classified and coded. Without clear documentation a data set can neither be expanded nor knowledgeably used by others.

GIS data sets should be checked regularly against reality. Nonspatial data should also be checked either against reality or a source of equal or better quality. The type of data will determine how often this must be done. Solutions reached by GIS analysis should be checked or calibrated against reality. The best way to do this is to check the results of a GIS analysis against the findings produced from completely independent calculations.

Portrayal

Data can be illustrated and analyzed in a GIS as a point, line, or polygon. Point data represent a geographic phenomenon that is generally too small to be represented by a polygon, such as cities on a large national map. Line data represent connected points that are too small to be presented as an area, or features that have an imperceptible width, such as roads or highways. Polygons are data features that represent areas of substantial size, such as regions. Examples of data typically portrayed as a polygon are states and large geographic features such as lakes (Aronoff, 1989, pp. 38–39). The portrayal of a feature is often relative to the scale of the map. A city on a national map may be portrayed as a point, but it may be portrayed as a polygon on a county map. Lines that are created by common points bound polygons. Map D.3 displays points, lines, and polygons.

Media

The term "media" refers to how data are presented to the viewer. There are three formats of data media: soft copy, hard copy, and electronic. Soft-copy output is the data

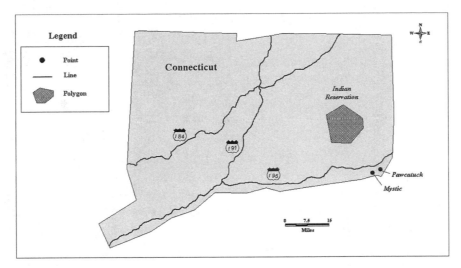

MAP D.3   Points, lines, and polygons.
Source: Made using MapInfo version 5.0. All data provided by MapInfo.

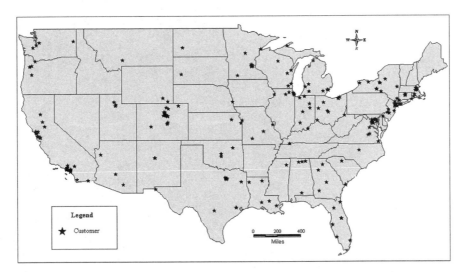

MAP D.4   Company XYZ customers by state.
Source: Made using MapInfo version 5.0. All data provided by MapInfo.

as viewed on a computer's monitor. A hard-copy output is a permanent form of display. The most common hard-copy output is a printed map. Electronic output formats are computer compatible files, which are stored on electronic media such as a CD-ROM, and can be used at another location with other files or to produce hard or soft copies at that site.

Mapping

Maps present data in ways spreadsheets and graphs cannot. Not only does a map provide a visual representation of data but it also shows the location of the data and their relationship to other geographic units or their characteristics over time. GIS is not just useful for creating maps, however.

GIS is much more than just a computer mapping device; it is a set of principles, methods, and tools that can be used to capture, store, transform, analyze, model, simulate, and display spatial and nonspatial data jointly (Aronoff, 1989, p. 39). In addition to various types of maps, GIS also has the capability to produce reports, statistics, graphs (area, bar, pie, and line graphs), and other types of figures. These functions have become more and more versatile in recent years. Users can produce different types of graphs on the variable(s) they choose. Users have the ability to edit graphs by changing font sizes, colors, scaling, and so forth. User can choose the setup of reports, can perform grouping and sorting on the data, and can insert graphs and images. For example, Map D.4 shows customer data for states. Figure D.1 is an example of a bar graph showing the amount of

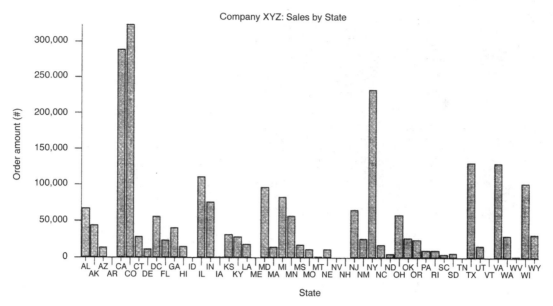

FIGURE D.1   Bar graph of Company XYZ sales by state.
Source: Made using MapInfo version 5.0. All data provided by MapInfo.

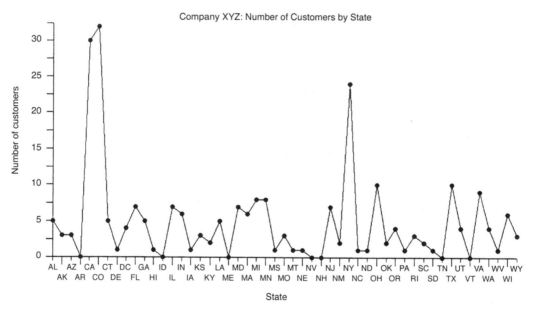

FIGURE D.2   Line graph of Company XYZ customers by state.
Source: Made using MapInfo version 5.0. All data provided by MapInfo.

sales for states. Figure D.2 is a line graph detailing the number of customers for states.

Map making is a skill. Not everyone can master the art of map making, but with GIS, effective maps can be easily made. Numerous studies have been conducted to determine the best way to make a map. One good rule to follow is to view the map from the user's perspective. If the reader of the map cannot understand your map, the map is not effective. Another consideration is the amount of data being por-

trayed on a map. If you are going to make a map showing the major highways of the United States, inclusion of surface streets would complicate the map to a degree that would render it virtually useless. Following these simple considerations, maps can be efficiently made to clearly portray the right amount of information.

Two complementary types of maps (of the many types proposed) meet most needs in the social sciences: graduated-point-symbol maps and thematic maps (also called choropleth maps). Graduated-point maps use vertical bars or circles to show variation in magnitude. Thematic maps use graduated colors or patterns to show variation in intensity of specific themes (Monmonier, 1993, p. 159). Other maps frequently used include flow maps and time series maps.

The type of map to use is determined by the type of data being portrayed. Count and intensity data are best represented by different types of maps. "Count" data represent the total number of occurrences, such as the total population of a state or the number of reported cases of cancer. "Intensity" data relate the counts to another set of data; examples are the total population of the state in relation to the total population of the country or population in relation to areas.

The graduated-point-symbol approach can be effectively used to show points graduated in size relative to their actual magnitude. For example, on maps of the United States, cities are often shown as points of varying size. The size of the point (shape does not matter) may represent the size of the population, income levels, race, and so on. On a map representing population of state capitals, it is likely that Phoenix, Arizona, and Boston, Massachusetts, would have larger points than Tallahassee, Florida, and Salem, Oregon (see Map D.5). Many databases, including data collected in the census and surveys of the Census Bureau, report aggregated data (data for areas, such as states, counties, tracts, etc.) as counts. These counts are magnitude data, and effective cartographic portrayal requires a graduated-point-symbol map. This is because size is the principal visual variable in this case.

A graduated-point-symbol map can be most useful when combined with a thematic map with intensity data. Graduated-point-symbol maps alone can be less meaningful because the pattern of large and small circles will reflect population distribution. Two maps may be more likely to

indicate the need to examine other factors, such as race or income, than one map.

A thematic map is one that uses a variety of styles (colors, shading patterns, or both) to graphically display information about the map's underlying theme. A thematic map may be made from points, lines, or polygons. It is a very useful and informative type of map. For example, a thematic map of poverty may use two colors to show whether a region is above or below the poverty level. Patterns can also be used in addition to color to show more specific ranges of poverty. This provides more information than if only one or the other was displayed. Map D.6 shows the percentage of the population of each state that is urban. In only five states 0% to 50% of the total population lives in an urban area, and in seven states 85% to 100% of the population lives in an urban area. This map "speaks" to us right away. Before we even read the legend, we can see the differences between the states.

A flow map is another type of map that can be useful to demographers, especially for showing migration flows. A simple straightline or a curved line with arrowheads can show direction, origin, and destination. This type of map can help users to visualize actual or potential routes. Multiple arrows can illustrate separate flows, multiple destinations, and an ultimate destination. Flow lines can vary in thickness to show differences in volume, or they can vary in color or pattern to show qualitative differences. The greater the size of the flow, the thicker the arrow. Solid and dashed flow lines can differentiate routes. Flow symbols also can show patterns that split or merge (Monmonier, 1993, p. 190). Map D.7 is a very simplified example of a flow map. It is a generalization of wintertime flows from the Northeast and Northwest to the Southwest and Southeast. The flow from the Northeast to the Southeast is greater than the flow

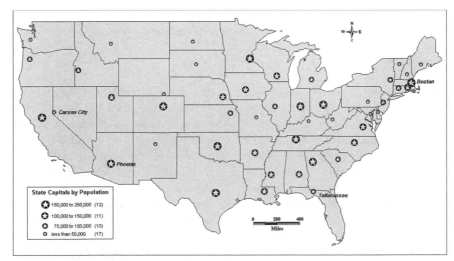

MAP D.5 Graduated point symbol map of U.S. capitals.
Source: Made using MapInfo version 5.0. All data provided by MapInfo.

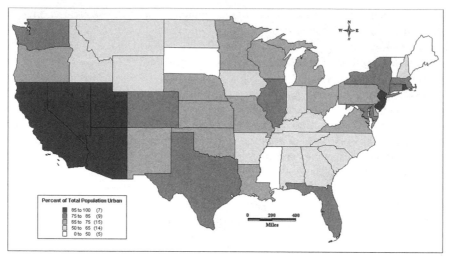

MAP D.6   Thematic map of percentage of population urban by state.
Source: Made using MapInfo version 5.0. All data provided by MapInfo.

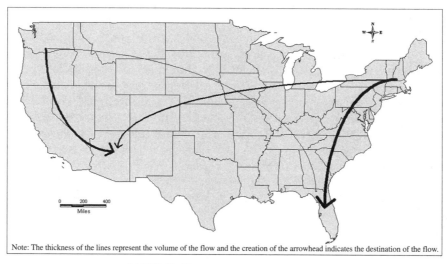

Note: The thickness of the lines represent the volume of the flow and the creation of the arrowhead indicates the destination of the flow.

MAP D.7   Flow map.
Source: Made using MapInfo version 5.0.

to the Southwest. The mirror image of the movement from the Northeast is seen in the movement from the Northwest.

Many demographers are interested in the changes that take place over time and a series of maps can be useful to demonstrate such changes. A series of maps showing the trend in some characteristic or event through space and over time is known as a spatiotemporal series. This is a sequence of maps showing how the incidence of an event, such as the spread of AIDS, is changing over space and time (Gould, 1993). Such a series of maps allow the reader to assess the general direction and rate of change of the event, as well as to examine the geographic pattern of "counts" and "intersi-

ties" for individual dates. To make this type of display more effective and more easily understood, the scale, format, symbols, and classifications should be kept the same from map to map if at all possible (see later).

Maps can be very useful in examining health indicators. When we examine them in relation to other factors, such as changes in population, we can interpret the changes more insightfully. For example, it may be disturbing to observe a large number of deaths from heart attacks and cancer in Florida. If we map the deaths spatiotemporally and in terms of age-specific rates, we may find that the mortality level has been increasing but is not so different from that in other states and that an increase takes place mainly in the winter months, when the population of Florida grows considerably because of the inflow of "snowbirds" and visitors.

The characteristics of a map determine its clarity, ease of use, and effectiveness. Features such as its intensity, scaling, and formats must be considered.

Areas or regions having values that vary are most often used for mapping intensity measures/rates (population density, percent urban, infant mortality rate, etc.). A map that displays raw data may not be very informative. Most demographic and economic data appropriate for mapping are based on censuses or surveys and the social scientist may wish to relate the raw counts to other data, to take account of variation in land area, total population, or some other relevant magnitude.

A very important concept in map creation is "data scaling." For graduated-point maps, this refers to the size of the point for each count portrayed and the number of different-size points (the number of categories). For the thematic maps, data scaling refers to deciding how many categories are necessary to ensure that the map reflects significant differences or trends in the data. Experimentation is often the best way to determine if a scale results in a pattern of symbols that are too small, too cluttered, or too large. Sometimes fewer categories can be better than many. Carefully chosen boundaries between categories can identify areas having values above or below a meaningful value, such as a national or state average rate (Monmonier, 1993, p. 169). Class boundaries separating significantly high or low data values may also be informative in some instances. The mean and standard deviation of an array are often used as dividers of the data. When creating a thematic map, a given GIS may offer the option of using an equal-interval strategy, natural clusters, or a quantile approach to create breaks in the data. These options, although easy to apply

(with a click of the mouse), do not necessarily make the best choice of breaks in data and should be examined closely before being used.

Finally, if one is creating a series of maps that are making comparisons for the same area, identical scaling should be used so that differences will be indicated clearly. When a comparison of different areas is being made, if at all possible, scaling should also be the same. If the same scaling is not possible, be sure to point this anomaly out in the legend so as not to mislead the viewer. Maps D.8 and D.9 demonstrate how a map can be changed when different data scaling is used. Map D.8 uses the "default" scale that the program created. It really does not tell the reader very much. A large number of states fall within the 10 to 45% category. Of course, 10% is much smaller than 45%; even 20% is much smaller. This category is worthless if the reader is looking for detailed information. Map D.9 was made with custom scaling. The data scale was increased by two categories to give more specific information on a state's level. The states with the largest and smallest population change fall into their own category. It is a good idea to do this when differences between values are significant.

The two fundamental digital map formats are raster and vector. Vector images are tied to a coordinate system. Every feature is defined as a point (or multiple points) on the image and has an "x" and a "y" attached to it. Raster images are divided into adjacent polygons of equal size, oftentimes resembling a grid. Each polygon is assigned a value based on the attribute that is the subject of the map. A raster map of rivers and streams would typically assign a value of one to a square in which such a watercourse occurs and a zero to any square where it does not occur. Unless the map is high-resolution with small polygons, the depiction of surface features on a raster map will often be inaccurate and

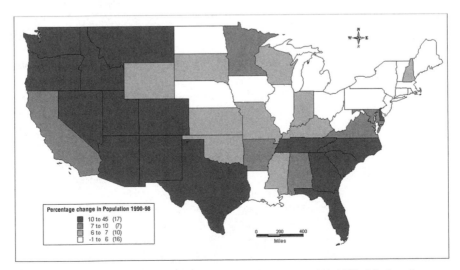

MAP D.8   Thematic map of percentage population change, 1990–1998, default scale.
Source: U.S. Bureau of the Census data, MapInfo version 5.0.

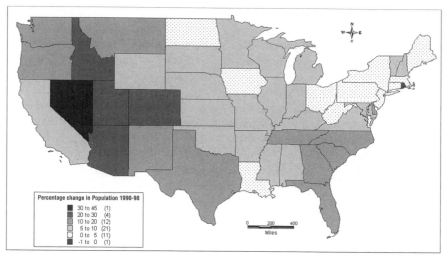

MAP D.9   Thematic map of percentage population change, 1990–1998, custom scale.
Source: U.S. Bureau of the Census data, MapInfo version 5.0.

unnatural. The location of an item on a raster map is typi-cally considered to be the center of the polygon in which it resides. It is more effective to use to raster maps for mapping features that have extent, such as types of crops or soils or population concentrations. Because of its ease of use, fre-quent application, and smaller storage requirements, GIS software most often displays data as a vector image rather than a raster image.

GIS EXAMPLES

One of the best ways to learn about GIS applications in demography is to review already completed and ongoing projects. One can find many articles and books on topics that integrate GIS with demographic data. The following exam-ples come from sources ranging from medical journals and GIS journals to business journals. GIS is being used in such fields as anthropology, archaeology, environmental studies, biology, real estate, marketing, and urban planning, among others. The individual interests of demographer vary, but GIS can be a helpful tool for those working in most spe-cialized areas of demography.

Political Redistricting

An example of exploiting data by spatial analysis is polit-ical redistricting. The U.S. Decennial Census of Population enumerates persons at the block level although the total pop-ulation of the states determines the number of Congressional representatives from each state. Based on specified criteria of size, compactness, and contiguity, the state legislatures use maps and spatial analysis to determine which block groups make up a district.

After each decennial census, the U.S. Census Bureau pro-vides new population figures that are used to redraw various federal, state, and local political districts. Because of the substantial population shifts that occur between each census and the impact of these changes on political representation and fund allocation, there is usually a high level of interest in these population changes. Three major considerations influence the current redistricting process: the shape and size of the districts, fair representation for minority groups, and political interests. To prevent gerrymandering (designing voting districts so that a political party or racial group has an unfair advantage in electing representatives) when the state governments are drawing up the new congressional dis-tricts they are obligated to follow certain guidelines. They must delineate one congressional district for each represen-tative, delineate districts that are contiguous and compact geographically, and allocate each piece of territory to one and only one district (Astroth, 1991, p. 34). Fundamental criteria are population equality, political equality and minor-ity representation (Siegel, 1996). Other criteria likely to be factors for local governments are preservation of communi-ties of interest and incumbent protection.

Milwaukee, Wisconsin, provides a simple example of how a GIS can be beneficial in drawing new districts. Prior to 1980, the population of the 8000 census blocks was hand-written on a wall-sized map of the city. The population totals for all the blocks within the voting wards were added to get total population per ward. If any of the populations were significantly different, boundaries would be moved and the population totals recalculated. Following this, these wards had to be assigned to one of 16 alderman districts. Each ward must be wholly within one district. This was a slow, tedious process as lines were drawn and populations calculated. In

1970, this process took 6 months and cost more than $60,000.

In 1980, the city began using a GIS to help with the redistricting process. The Census Bureau provided new population figures on a computer tape that could be matched with a file of the block boundaries. No longer was there a need for writing on a wall map. With GIS software, the numbers were easily added to secure the population of the wards. Boundaries could be modified with a few clicks of a mouse and numbers recalculated in a matter of minutes. After the boundaries for the wards were determined, the same process was used to create the alderman districts. GIS cut the time to complete the process in half and costs to $24. As time and cost decreased, it is likely that accuracy and precision increased.

The previous example is rather simplified. GIS was used to make the process quicker and easier; it did not create the wards for the city. In most cases, redistricting is much more complicated and there are many more guidelines to follow. Much has changed since 1980, and it is now possible to have the GIS do more, or all of it, for you. MapInfo, for example, has a specific redistricting function. Not only can this function be used for redistricting in the traditional sense, but also for determining school districts, sales territories, service regions—dividing any area into separate districts. The most dynamic aspect of redistricting using a GIS is the ability to see on-the-fly updates of record counts and data totals. Performing "what if" analyses in a matter of seconds, can be especially useful for areas that are changing often. With the computer you can move a segment from one district to another and observe what effects this change has on population totals and characteristics. These changes can be seen on the map and in the table browser. The map shows the districts shaded by colors and the browser window shows the demographic data for the districts. Until the file is saved, the redistricting function does not change the map or permanently change its style. Any "mappable" table containing region, line, or point objects that share the same district information as a group can be (re)districted.

Epidemiology

Epidemiology focuses on geographic clusters, patterns, and the spread of disease. GIS can be a useful tool for displaying these clusters and patterns. Maps enable us comprehend quickly, as well as see, the factors that may be important in understanding a health problem. One of the first known examples of using maps to help in analysis of a health problem occurred in 1849 when John Snow used a map to discover a distinct pattern of cholera cases in London, England. Snow learned that most cases were clustered around a particular water pump. When the pump was closed, the number of cholera cases declined. Snow used the map alone, without benefit of the automated spatial analysis now possible with a GIS. Yet the map was all he needed to investigate the problem and find a solution. A reproduction of the map he created is shown as Map D.10.

The regional distribution of disease(s) will naturally raise questions about the cause and will often suggest possibilities for intervention; this information is essential for effective and preventive education. In some cases, once the pattern of disease is identified, control and prevention measures can be instituted. One of the first large-scale applications of GIS in epidemiology occurred in the 1980s, during the spread of the AIDS virus. By using GIS to identify where AIDS cases were increasing the most, and by learning the characteristics of these populations and how those infected had contracted the disease, targeting measures could be developed and prevention and treatment resources could be assigned in the most efficient way possible.

Wartenberg (1992) gave a good example of how GIS can help in an epidemiological study. He analyzed screening programs for lead overexposure, which typically target high-risk populations, by identifying regions with common risk markers (older housing, poverty, etc.). A GIS can make screening programs more effective and more cost-efficient by mapping cases of overexposure and identifying high-incidence and high-risk neighborhoods.

Kitron et al. (1994) demonstrated the use GIS for malaria surveillance in Israel, where there is a risk for localized outbreaks due to infection of local mosquitoes by imported cases.

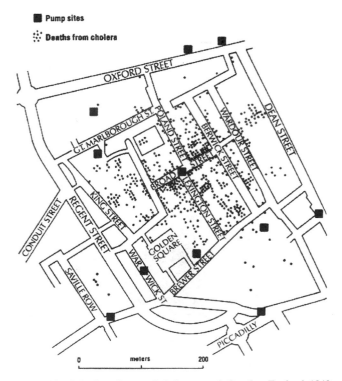

MAP D.10   John Snow's map of cholera cases in London, England, 1849. Source: www.nationalgeographic.com/resources/ngo/education/ideas912/912choleraho3.html.

A national computerized surveillance system of breeding sites and imported malaria cases was established in 1992 using a GIS. Distances between population centers and breeding sites were calculated, and maps associating epidemiological and entomological data were generated. Risk of malaria transmission was assessed with consideration of vector capacity and flight range of each species. The GIS-based surveillance system ensures that if a localized outbreak does occur, it will be associated rapidly with a likely breeding site, a specific vector, and a probable human source, so that prompt and effective control measures can be instituted. This cost-effective GIS-based surveillance system would be especially useful for countries with indigenous malaria transmission.

There are several reasons why spatial analysis serves as a valuable research tool. Kitron *et al.* (1994), for example, observed that different health outcomes necessitate specialized statistical and spatial analysis to carry out an overall risk assessment because many disease-carrying vectors disperse and spread disease spatially. The dispersal of infected individuals also spreads the disease spatially. Kitron *et al.* (1994) went on to note that although one strives to incorporate all of the known variables in the model, inevitably some will be missed and, given this, spatially contiguous observations can serve as effective proxies for such missing variables.

Vital Rates and Socioeconomic Characteristics

GIS can also be an effective tool in analyzing fertility or mortality rates. A particularly good example is a study conducted by Rushton *et al.* (1995) on geographic analysis of infant mortality rates. Originally a study of infant mortality in Des Moines, Iowa, by census tract, the project was expanded to map infant deaths and births using a spatial pattern of grid points. A local newspaper article stated that infant deaths were clustered in the southern part of the city. By analyzing births and deaths for small areas in the city, it was determined that this was not the case. When the results were overlaid with a census tract map, the initial indication was found to be misleading. Inappropriate choice of the geographic unit used in the analysis and of the variable to be mapped may result in misleading or incorrect analysis. This result indicated not only how GIS can be used but that the geographic units being analyzed can make a dramatic difference in the results.

An example of how different geographic units can affect one's interpretation is suggested by Map D.11. This map illustrates how more information can be learned by choosing smaller geographic units. The reader can learn much more about per capita income in New England by looking at the

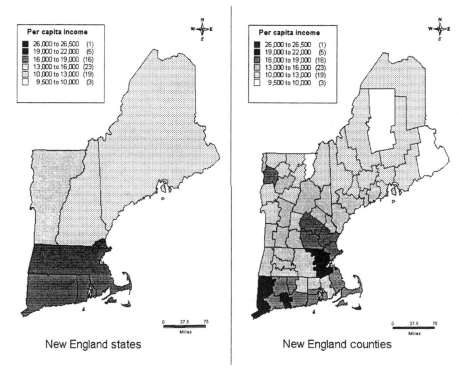

MAP D.11   New England states and counties, per capita income, 1989.
Source: Created using MapInfo version 5.0. Boundary and income data from the U.S. Bureau of the Census TIGER/Line files and STF3.

county map rather than the state map. Depending on the issue one is trying to explore, it is normally wise to show the lowest geographic units possible (the lowest one can afford or has access to, that is).

The United Nations Statistics Division has recognized the importance of using GIS to portray and analyze population statistics. In 1997, the division published "Applications of Geographical Information Systems for Population and Related Statistics." The project assists the less developed countries in setting up GIS as a tool for analyzing population statistics. The publication provides examples of GIS techniques in demographic studies in Nepal. It demonstrates the capabilities of GIS to old in visualizing complex demographic data sets, the use of digital maps and a linked database of characteristics and events to facilitate the exploratory analysis of demographic data sets, and the ability of a GIS to model and aid policy planning.

First discussed is Nepal's distinct physiographic patterns (topography) and their relation to the culture and demographic characteristics of the country. The mountains, glaciers, rivers, and poor roads hinder accessibility to the five regions of Nepal. The impact of physiographic patterns can be seen by mapping the population distribution between 1966 and 1991. Despite migration and urbanization, the highest concentration of people remains in the same area (although magnitudes have changed). This can also be said of economic patterns, literacy ratios, and religious affiliations.

Information on social and economic patterns is useful for planning related decisions and understanding the distinct cultures and regional variations of the society. For example, family planning may be affected by religion, literacy, or economic status. These, along with the age distribution and fertility rates, can easily be mapped and analyzed. An examination of the maps alone provides insight as to these patterns in Nepal. Fertility rates have risen in the more urbanized area of Kathmandu, where the population is relatively young. Female literacy ratios are significantly lower than those for males throughout all regions of Nepal. The highest literacy ratios are around Kathmandu. Maps illustrate variables that may be relevant in explaining the change in fertility in Nepal.

The UN generated statistics externally rather than with the GIS. This is not always necessary; some GIS and statistical software packages are compatible (for example, MapInfo and SPSS for windows). The researchers were particularly interested in the regions where both female literacy ratios and contraceptive prevalence ratios (CPR) were low. They used a bivariate analysis to determine whether CPR and literacy ratios were related. When they had determined the areas with low ratios of both, they conducted a multiveriate regression analysis using CPR as the dependent variable. Though the model was simple, the regression analysis indicated that values of CPR are associated with all variables but one. The results are important for the next section that describes the second half of the UN publication.

Planning/Decision Making

The UN project stresses the planning and modeling possibilities offered through GIS. To do this, the UN gives a hypothetical example using spatial data for the analysis of the demand for health services. This type of analysis is especially important for countries with limited resources (doctors and nurses, medical equipment) and access to the facilities.

Matching the supply of health services to demand is important in any society. However, in less developed countries, there is often insufficient information on how many persons are being served and what services they are seeking. The UN study estimates the number of people served by the existing hospitals (as well as determining if there is a large portion of people not being served at all). The first step is defining the areas from which people come to the hospitals, called "catchment" areas. GIS is helpful in this regard as it can determine time and difficulty of travel, in addition to distances.

The next step is to estimate the number of people living within each catchment area. The district boundaries did not match the catchment boundaries, so the catchment boundaries were overlaid with the detailed population information by the GIS. A "needs assessment" was then made, based on number and characteristics of persons in the catchment. Although some of the areas looked smaller than others on the map, they have much higher population densities than other areas and thus a much greater demand for services.

CONCLUDING NOTE

GIS is a new resource for compiling, analyzing, and presenting data. Its ease of use and applications are growing rapidly with improvements in technology; yet development is always being outpaced by the demands of GIS users. Support groups around the country are growing, and data sources are becoming more abundant and less expensive. While GIS has already enjoyed substantial advances, it requires substantial development before its use will be as common as word-processing and spreadsheet software.

The challenges to GIS development include improvements in presentation, analytical capabilities, and flexibility. Mapping in GIS systems need to be much more cartographically sound than they are so that a person with no training in cartography can produce maps that make sense to the reader. Analysis needs to be simplified to layperson's terms so that the novice can not only do simple tasks within a GIS system but also perform some complex spatial analysis. Flexibility needs to be integrated into GIS systems to allow the users to customize their software to their needs. Many software packages are moving in these directions. Maps from the first GIS software systems and the maps from today's software systems are not comparable; the analysis that is available to the novice today is much more powerful. The software companies have almost all created a programming language for users' to customize their software to the users' needs, although some of the programming languages are difficult to learn and use. GIS has become an important research and application tool. As both its flexibility and its ease of use increase, more and more people are expected to incorporate GIS into their work.

References

Aronoff, S. 1989. *Geographic Information Systems: A Management Perspective*. Ottawa, Canada: WDL.

Astroth, J. 1991. "The Role of GIS in Redistricting: A Case Study in Missouri." *Geo Info Systems* 1: 34–42.

Fotheringham, S., and P. Rogerson. 1994. *Spatial Analysis and GIS*. London: Taylor & Francis.

Gould, P. 1993. *The Slow Plague: A Geography of the AIDS Pandemic*. Oxford: Blackwell Publishing.

Kitron, U., H. Pener, C. Costin, L. Orshan, Z. Greenberg, and U. Shalom. 1994. "Geographic Information System in Malaria Surveillance: Mosquito Breeding and Imported Cases in Israel, 1992." *American Journal of Tropical Medicine & Hygiene* 50: 550–556.

MapInfo Corporation. 1998. *MapInfo Professional User's Guide, V. 5.0*. Troy, NY: MapInfo Corporation.

Mark, D. M., N. Chrisman, A. U. Frank, P. H. McHaffie, and J. Pickles with contributions from M. Curry, J. Goss, F. Harvey, K. Hillis, R. Miller, E. Shepard, and D. Varanka. 1997. "The GIS History Project." National Center for Geographic Information and Analysis (NCGIA), www.geog.buffalo.edu/ncgia/gishist.

Monmonier, M. 1993. *Mapping It Out: Expository Cartography for the Humanities and Social Sciences*. Chicago: The University of Chicago Press.

Niemann, B. J., Jr., and S. Niemann. 1998a. "Allan H. Schmidt: GIS Journeyman." *Geo Info Systems* 8(5): 42–45.

Niemann, B. J., Jr., and S. Niemann. 1998b. "Thomas Karl Poiker: Algorithms and Academics." *Geo Info Systems* 8(2): 36–39.

Rushton, G., D. Krishnamurti, R. Krishnamurti, and H. Song. 1995. "A Geographic Information Analysis of Urban Infant Mortality Rates." *Geo Info Systems* 5: 52–56.

Siegel, J. S. 1996. "Geographic Compactness vs. race/ethnic Compactness and other criteria in the delineation of legislative districts." *Population Research and Policy Review* 15: 147–164 (April).

Tomlinson, R. F. 1997. "Federal Influences in Early GIS Development in Canada." *Geo Info Systems* 7: 38–39.

Wartenberg, D. 1992. "Screening for Lead Exposure Using a Geographic Information System." *Environmental Research* 59(2), 310–317.

Suggested Readings

GIS History

American Cartographer. 1988. Special Issue. "The Development of GIS Technology." *American Cartographer* 15(3): 245–322.

Cartographic Journal. 1991. Special Issue. "British Cartography 1987–1991: An Overview." *Cartographic Journal* 28: 30–54.

Foresman, T. (Ed.). 1998. *The History of GIS: Perspectives from Pioneers*. Englewood Cliffs, NJ: Prentice Hall.

Mark, D. M., N. C. A. U. Frank, P. H. McHaffie, J. Pickles, with contributions from M. Curry, J. Goss, F. Harvey, K. Hillis, R. Miller, E. Shepard, and D. Varanka. 1997. "The GIS History Project." The National Center for Geographic Information and Analysis (NCGIA), www.geog.buffalo.edu/ncgia/gishist.

GIS General

Bernhardsen, T. 1996. *Geographic Information Systems*. New York: John Wiley & Sons.

Berry, J. K. 1993. *Beyond Mapping: Concepts, Algorithms, and Issues in GIS*. Fort Collins, CO: GIS World Books.

Clarke, K. 1998. *Getting Started with Geographic Information Systems*. Englewood Cliffs, NJ: Prentice Hall.

Congalton, R. G., and K. Green. 1992. "The ABC's of GIS: An Introduction to Geographic Information Systems." *Journal of Forestry* 90: 13–20.

Cressie, N. 1991. *Statistics for Spatial Data*. New York: John Wiley & Sons.

Daniel, L., and J. Slezak. 1995. "Street Talk: The Word on Address Matching." *Business Geographics* 3: 53–59.

DeMers, M. 1996. *Fundamentals of Geographic Information Systems*. New York: John Wiley & Sons.

DeMers, M. 1996. "Dictionary of Abbreviations and Acronyms in Geographic Information Systems, Cartography, and Remote Sensing," www.lib.berkeley.edu/EART/abbrex.html#a.

ESRI. 1999. *Getting to Know ArcView GIS*. Redwood, CA: ESRI.

Goodchild, M. F. 1992. "Geographical Information Science." *International Journal of Geographical Information Science* 6: 31–45.

Heywood, I. 1990. "Geographic Information Systems in the Social Sciences—Introduction." *Environment and Planning* 22: 849–852.

Kaplan, E. D. 1996. *Understanding GPS: Principles and Applications*. Boston: Artech House.

Martin, D. 1996. *Geographic Information Systems: Socioeconomic Applications*. New York: Routledge.

Openshaw, S. 1990. "Spatial Analysis and Geographical Information Systems: A Review of Progress and Possibilities." Pp. 153–163. In H. J. Scholten and J. C. H. Stillwell (Eds.), *Geographical Information Systems for Urban and Regional Planning* (pp. 153–163). Boston: Kluwer Academic.

Pickles, J. 1995. *Ground Truth: The Social Implications of Geographic Information Systems*. New York: Guilford Press.

Rogerson, P. A., and A. S. Fotheringham. 1994. *Spatial Analysis and GIS*. London: Taylor and Francis.

Spitzer, T. 1996. "A Database Perspective on GIS: Part I." *DBMS* 9: 95–102.

Star, J., and J. Estes. 1990. *Geographic Information Systems: An Introduction*. Englewood Cliffs, NJ: Prentice Hall.

General Mapping and Geography Sources

Clarke, K. 1995. *Analytical and Computer Cartography*. New York: Prentice Hall.

Fisher, H. T. 1982. *Mapping Information: The Graphic Display of Quantitative Information*. Cambridge, MA: ABT Books.

Garson, G. D., and R. S. Briggs. 1992. *Analytic Mapping and Geographic Databases*. New York: Sage.

Griffith, D., and C. Amrheun. 1997. *Multivariate Statistical Analysis for Geographers.* Englewood Cliffs, NJ: Prentice Hall.

Kraak, M.-J. 1996. *Cartography: Visualization of Spatial Data.* Reading, MA: Addison-Wesley.

MacEachren, A. 1995. *How Maps Work: Representation, Visualization and Design.* New York: Guilford Press.

Plane, D. A., and P. A. Rogerson. 1994. *The Geographical Analysis of Population.* New York: John Wiley & Sons.

Robinson, A. H., J. L. Morrison, P. C. Muehrche, A. J. Kimerling, and S. C. Guptill. 1995. *Elements of Cartography.* New York: John Wiley and Sons.

Shaw, G., and D. Wheeler. 1994. *Statistical Techniques in Geographical Analysis.* New York: John Wiley & Sons.

Wood, C., and C. P. Kellers. 1996. *Cartographic Design: Theoretical and Practical Perspectives.* New York: John Wiley & Sons.

Wood, D. 1992. *The Power of Maps.* New York: Guilford Press.

Case Studies in GIS

Braddock, M., G. Lapidus, E. Cromley, R. Cromley, G. Burke, and L. Banco. 1994. "Using a Geographic Information System to Understand Child Pedestrian Injury." *American Journal of Public Health* 84: 1158–1161.

Danziger, J. N., W. H. Dutton, R. King, and K. L. Kraemer. 1982. *Computers and Politics: High Technology in American Local Government.* New York: Columbia University Press.

Davenhill, W. F. 1995. "Is There a Doctor in the Area?" *Business Geographics* 3: 34–35.

De Lepper, M., H. Scholten, and R. Stern. 1995. "The Added Value of Geographical Information Systems in Public and Environmental Health." *Geojournal Library*, Volume 24. New York: Kluwer Academic Publishers.

Del Valle, J. C. 1996. Thesis: *Retail Site Selection: An Integrated Approach.* Gainesville, FL: University of Florida.

Friel, C. A. 1991. "A Zip Code-Based GIS Reveals the Geography of Retirement." *Geo Info Systems* 1: 48–56.

Gesler, W. 1986. "The Uses of Spatial Analysis in Medical Geography: A Review." *Social Science & Medicine* 23: 963–973.

Glass, G., *et al.* 1994. "Environmental Risk Factors for Lyme Disease Identified with Geographic Information Systems." *American Journal of Public Health* 85: 944–948.

Gobalet, J., and R. Thomas. 1996. "Demographic Data and Geographic Information Systems for Decision Making: The Case of Public Health." *Population Research and Policy Review* 15: 537–548.

Gould, P. 1993. *The Slow Plague: A Geography of the AIDS Pandemic.* Oxford: Blackwell.

Lam, N. S. 1986. "Geographical Patterns of Cancer Mortality in China." *Social Science & Medicine* 23: 241–247.

Levine, J., and J. D. Landis. 1989. "Geographic Information Systems for Local Planning." *Journal of the American Planning Association* 55: 209–220.

Longley, P., and G. Clarke. 1996. *GIS for Business and Service Planning.* New York: John Wiley & Sons.

Maltz, M., A. Gordon, and W. Friedman. 1991. *Mapping Crime in Its Community Setting: Event Geography Analysis.* New York: Springer-Verlag.

Martin, D. 1991. *Geographic Information Systems and Their Socioeconomic Applications.* Oxford: Routledge.

Plane, D., and P. Rogerson. 1994. *Geographical Analysis of Population; with Applications to Planning and Business.* New York: John Wiley & Sons.

Rushton, G., *et al.* 1995. "A Geographic Information Analysis of Urban Infant Mortality Rates." *Geo Info Systems* 5: 52–56.

Scholten, H., and J. Stillwell. 1990. *Geographical Information Systems for Urban and Regional Planning.* New York: Kluwer Academic.

Stallones, L., J. Nuckols, and J. Berry. 1992. "Surveillance around Hazardous Waste Sites: Geographic Information Systems and Reproductive Outcomes." *Environmental Research* 59: 81–92.

Yeh, A. G. 1991. "The Development and Applications of Geographic Information Systems for Urban and Regional Planning in Developing Countries." *International Journal of Geographical Information Systems* 5: 5–27.

Data-Related Issues

Adam, N., and A. Gangopadhyay. 1997. *Database Issues in Geographic Information Systems.* New York: Kluwer Academic Publishers.

Bolstad, P. V., and P. Gessler. 1990. "Positional Uncertainty in Manually Digitized Map Data." *International Journal of Geographical Information Systems* 4: 399–412.

Goodchild, M., and S. Gopal. 1990. *Accuracy of Spatial Databases.* London: Taylor & Francis.

Guptill, S., and J. Morrison. 1995. *Elements of Spatial Data Quality.* Oxford: Pergamon Press.

Scott, L. M. 1994. "Identification of GIS Attribute Error Using Exploratory Data Analysis." *The Professional Geographer* 46: 378–386.

Spitzer, T. "A Database Perspective on GIS, Part I," www.dbmsmag.com/9611d15.html.

U.S. Census Bureau and GIS

Broome, F. R., and L. Godwin. 1988. "The Census Bureau's Publication Map Production System." *Cartography and Geographic Information Systems* 17: 79–88.

Broome, F. R., and D. B. Meixler. 1990. "The TIGER Data Base Structure." *Cartography and Geographic Information Systems* 17: 39–48.

Carbaugh, L. W., and R. W. Marx. 1990. "The TIGER System: A Census Bureau Innovation Serving Data Analysts." *Government Information Quarterly* 7: 285–306.

Trainor, T. F. 1990. "Fully Automated Cartography: A Major Transition at the Census Bureau." *Cartography and Geographic Information Systems* 17: 21–26.

U.S. Census Bureau. 1977. "Mapping for Census and Surveys." Washington, DC: U.S. Bureau of the Census.

U.S. Bureau of the Census. 1990. "Strength in Numbers: Your Guide to 1990 Census Redistricting Data from the U.S. Bureau of the Census." Washington, DC: U.S. Bureau of the Census.

U.S. Census Bureau. 1992. "What Do I Need to Map Out 1990 Census Data?" Washington, DC: U.S. Bureau of the Census.

U.S. Census Bureau. 1993. "1992 TIGER Line Files: Helping You Map Things Out." Washington, DC: U.S. Bureau of the Census, Geography Division.

U.S. Census Bureau. 1994. "Maps and More: Your Guide to Census Bureau Geography." Washington, DC: U.S. Bureau of the Census.

GIS Software Vendor Information

This is a selected list of GIS software packages with contact information. Given the rapidly changing nature of GIS software with respect to price and function, no attempt has been made to describe or compare these packages.

MapInfo. MapInfo was the first company to develop and market PC-based mapping software for business applications. www.mapinfo.com

ESRI (Environmental Systems Research Institute). A privately held consulting group, building software tools and products. ESRI's first commercial GIS product was ARC/INFO (1981). Later products include PC ARC/INFO, ArcView GIS, ArcCAD, and MapObjects, ESRI also offers data sets to compliment its products.www.esri.com

Intergraph Corporation. This global company offers a variety of hardware and software products for Windows NT.www.intergraph.com

IDRISI (The Clark Labs). A research organization located within the Graduate School of Geography at Clark University. IDRISI is a raster GIS and image processing software developed at the lab. The lab has also developed a digitizing and editing software, CartaLinx. www.clarklabs.org

Caliper. Caliper produces transportation GIS software called Trans CAD, Maptitude GIS+, and Maptitude for Redistricting. www.caliper.com

GRASS. The U.S. Army Construction Engineering Research Laboratory's (USA-CERL) Geographic Resources Analysis Support System (GRASS) was developed to provide management tools to army environmental planners and land managers. GRASS can handle different representations of data (raster, vector, and point). www.cecer.army.mil/grass/GRASS.main.html

Northwood Geoscience, Ltd. Vertical Mapper add-on program for MapInfo. www.northwoodgeo.com

Tydac Technologies, Inc. / PCI Geomatics Group—SPANS 7 and PAMAP. SPANS 7 is a complete spatial analysis software system that provides modeling and analysis capabilities, data management, and professional map output. www.pci.on.ca

ComGrafix. MAPGRAFIX was the first desktop GIS complete with digitizing, printing/plotting, and analytical tools. The map elements are linked to the demographic data in databases using AppleScript to create automatic thematic maps. It has the built-in capability of importing ESRI files and supports many standard vector formats. www.comgrafix.com

Smallworld. www.smallworld-us.com

Compusearch/Market Math. www.esri.com/partners/gissolutions/compusrc/marketm.html

Private Sources

Many software vendors (listed earlier) repackage and sell data in the proprietary forms used by their software products. Because the data are usually checked and corrected as they are repackaged, the use of these converted datasets can save time.

Geographic Data Technology, Inc. (GDT) sells geographic databases specializing in street network data. Formats compatible with ARC/INFO, ArcView, MapInfo, Tactician, AtlasGIS, and SAS/GIS are provided. www.gdt1.com

Cartotech of San Antonio, Texas, and GDT of New Hampshire, among others, are "conversion" firms that will build datasets to a user's specifications.

ADC (American Digital Cartography) Worldmap. www.adci.com

Claritas sells marketing data, demographic data, and boundary files for GIS. Claritas provides formats for MapInfo, ArcView, Intergraph's MGE, SAS/GIS and Tactician software.www.claritas.com

Equifax National Decision Systems is a major provider of demographic, geographic, business, consumer behavior, and industry-specific data. www.ends.com

Etak offers precise street map data, navigation technology, and geocoding tools. www.etak.com/corporate.html

The POLK Company offers a variety of data relating to motor vehicles, lifestyles, population, neighborhoods, businesses, geography, and purchasing behavior. www.polk.com

ACXIOM combines public record information with data from a variety of other national information providers to produce comprehensive data sets on consumers and businesses. www.acxiom.com

Mediamark Research, Inc. offers comprehensive data on population and lifestyle. Custom studies are available using the Internet, telephone, and mail samples. www.mediamark.com

Spatial Logic maintains current district boundaries for mapping and GIS. Congressional, State legislature district boundaries are available. File formats available include Atlas GIS (AGF) , Atlas ASCII (BNA), AutoCAD (DXF), MapInfo Interchange Format (MIF), Arcview Shapfiles (SHP), and MapInfo files (TAB). www.spatialogic.com

Infotech. InfoTech offers comprehensive services in GIS conversion (digitization), mapping, and Software. http://infotech.stph.net/infotech.html

Center for International Earth science Information Network (CIESIN, Columbia University) provides demographic data, metadata, resources, interactive applications. www.ciesin.org

Public Sources

USGS (U.S. Geological Survey). www.usgs.gov

U.S. Census Bureau. www.census.gov

Federal Geographic Data Committee, Manual of Federal Geographic Data Products. Washington, D.C.: Environmental Protection Agency, Office of Information Resources Management, 1992.

The Historical United States Boundary Files (HUSCO) Home page offers various historical boundaries ranging from the years 1790 to 1970. www.cadgis.lsu.edu: 80/geoscipub

Oregon State Service Center for Geographic Information Systems. www.sscgis.or.gov

Connecticut Map and Geographic Information Center. http://magic.lib.uconn.edu

Geostrategies. Extensive data for Central and Eastern Europe. www.geo.strategies.ro

Australia Survey and Land Information Group (AUSLIG). Australia's National Mapping Agency; digital map infomation and more. www.auslig.gov.au/welcome.htm

ESRI Canada. www.esricanada.com

European Umbrella Organisation for Geographic Information. www.eurogi.org

GIS Data Depot. www.gisdatadepot.com

Indonesian Land Use Databank. www.geocities.com/Tokyo/2439

Glossary

DAVID A. SWANSON AND G. EDWARD STEPHAN[1]

ABORTION The expulsion of a fetus from the uterus. An induced abortion is the intentional removal of a fetus from the uterus. A spontaneous abortion is the premature and naturally occurring expulsion of a fetus from the uterus. In popular usage, the term is restricted to the former meaning. See also BIRTH and FETAL LOSS.

ABORTION RATE The estimated number of abortions per 1000 women aged 15 to 44 years in a given year.

ABRIDGED LIFE TABLE See LIFE TABLE.

ACCEPTOR A person receiving service or advice from a family-planning program.

ACCESSION RATE The entry rate of persons into a given status, a function often shown in specialized life tables, such as tables of working life.

ACTIVITIES OF DAILY LIVING (ADLs) Measures of functioning that typically are concerned with limitations in the ability, or the inability, to carry out certain personal care routines, such as eating, dressing, toileting, transferring into and out of bed, and bathing. See INSTRUMENTAL ACTIVITIES OF DAILY LIVING.

ACTUARIAL SCIENCE The science of risk, premium, and benefit analysis, involving the preparation of life and actuarial tables that form the foundation of the business of insurance and related activities.

ACUTE CONDITION A health condition of rapid onset and a relatively short duration that usually ends with either recovery or death.

ACUTE DISEASE A disease that has a rapid onset and generally lasts for only a short period of time. See also CHRONIC DISEASE.

ADJUSTED RATE See STANDARDIZATION.

ADJUSTED INFANT MORTALITY RATE This takes into account the change in the number of births from the preceding year by the use of appropriate separation fuctors. See also INFANT MORTALITY RATE.

ADMINISTRATIVE AREA A geographic area used in censuses for collection, tabulation, and analysis that corresponds to a political and or other administrative unit.

ADMINISTRATIVE RECORDS Data collected by governmental (and sometimes private) organizations for taxation, registration, fee collection, and other administrative purposes that indirectly provide demographic information. These data are used by demographers for analyses, estimates, projections, and the evaluation of data specifically collected for demographic purposes. See also ADMINISTRATIVE RECORDS METHOD.

ADMINISTRATIVE RECORDS METHOD In the United States, a member of the family of component methods for estimating population that relies on a past census, vital statistics data, and migration data derived from tax returns. See also POPULATION ESTIMATE.

AGE The length of time that a person has lived. A distinction is made between completed age and exact age, with completed age usually defined in terms of the last birthday and exact age

[1] The authors thank Dean Judson, Nancy McGirr, Jerry McKibben, and Peter Morrison for their comments and suggestions. Sources of information used in compiling this Glossary include, but are not limited to, the following publications:

Namboodiri, K. 1991. *Demographic Analysis: A Stochastic Approach.* New York: Academic Press.

Peterson, W., and R. Peterson. 1986. Dictionary of Demography: Terms, concepts, and Institutions. Wisport , CT Greenword Press.

Population Reference Bureau. 2001. *Glossary of Population Terms,* accessed in August 2001 at www.prb.org/template.cfm?Section=Glossary.

Ross, J. A. (Editor). 1992. International Encyclopedia of Population. New York: Free Press.

Shryock, H., and J. Siegel. 1973. *The Methods and Materials of Demography,* Rev. ed. Washington, DC: U.S. Government Printing Office.

Smith, S. K., J. Tayman, and D. A. Swanson. 2001. *State and Local Population Projections: Methodology and Analysis.* New York: Kluwer Academic/Plenum.

United Nations. 1953. *The Determinants and Consequences of Population Trends.* New York: United Nations.

United Nations. 1999. *Dictionary of Demographic and Reproductive Health Terminology,* accessed in August 2001 at www.popin.org/~unpopterms/.

United States Census Bureau. 2001. *Glossary,* last accessed in August 2002 at www.census.gov/main/www.glossary.html.

being the exact time since birth. Conventions for determining age vary somewhat between cultures and countries.

AGE ACCURACY INDEX The arithmetic average of the absolute values of the differences between observed age ratios and expected age ratios. See also AGE RATIO.

AGE CUMULATIVE FERTILITY RATE See CUMULATIVE FERTILITY RATE.

AGE DEPENDENCY RATIO A ratio in which the numerator represents the total number of people not of working age (too young or too old to work and therefore "dependent" on those who do), and the denominator represents the population of working age; often multiplied by 100, which yields the number of dependents per 100 persons of working age. See ALSO DEPENDENCY RATIO.

AGE DISTRIBUTION See POPULATION COMPOSITION.

AGE EFFECT An analytical perspective that attempts to determine the effect of age on a variable of interest. Age effects are often considered simultaneously with cohort and period effects. See also AGE-PERIOD-COHORT EFFECTS, COHORT EFFECT, and PERIOD EFFECT.

AGE GROUP Multiyear categories into which single years of age are assembled for purposes of data presentation or analysis. The most frequently found age grouping is 0 to 4, 5 to 9, 10 to 14, and so on.

AGE HEAPING A higher-than-expected proportion of ages with certain terminal digits and a lower than expected proportion with other terminal digits, often adjacent, because of digit preference or digit avoidance. See also AGE MISREPORTING, AGE PREFERENCE, DIGIT AVOIDANCE, and DIGIT PREFERENCE.

AGE MISREPORTING The tendency for people to not report their correct age because they do not know it exactly or because they prefer to report another age, often an adjacent age or age group. See also AGE HEAPING.

AGE PARITY GRID See FERTILITY PATTERN METHOD.

AGE-PERIOD-COHORT EFFECT The joint and separate effects of age, period, and cohort membership on a dependent variable of interest. See also AGE EFFECT, COHORT EFFECT, and PERIOD EFFECT.

AGE PREFERENCE The tendency for people to report an age different than their actual age because of cultural, social, or personal reasons. See also AGE-HEAPING.

AGE RATIO The ratio of a given age group to the average found by summing the age group in question and two adjoining age groups and dividing this sum by three. See also AGE-HEAPING.

AGE-SEX DISTRIBUTION See POPULATION COMPOSITION.

AGE-SEX POPULATION PYRAMID See POPULATION PYRAMID.

AGE-SEX STRUCTURE See POPULATION COMPOSITION.

AGE-SPECIFIC PROPORTION A ratio that relates the persons with a given demographic characteristic at a specific age (or age group) to the corresponding population in the same age (or age group). Examples include the age-specific propor-

tion married and the (age-specific) labor force participation ratio. See also GENERAL PROPORTION.

AGE-SPECIFIC RATE A rate that relates a given demographic event at a specific age (or age group) to the corresponding at-risk population in the same age (or age group). Examples include age-specific birthrate, age-specific marital birthrate, and age-specific death rate. See also CRUDE RATE, GENERAL RATE, and RATE.

AGE STRUCTURE See POPULATION COMPOSITION.

AGED The latter stages of adulthood, usually specified by law or culture in terms of a certain minimum age (e.g., those 75 years and over are "aged").

AGGREGATION The process of assembling individual elements into summary form for purposes of presentation or analysis. For example, to assemble census records for individuals in a given area into a summary for the area as a whole.

AGGREGATION BIAS A type of distortion that can result by attributing relationships found among summaries to the individual elements from which the summaries were obtained.

AGING The process of growing older. For an individual it is simply measured in terms of age; for a population it is measured by one of several indices. For example, the percentage age 65 years and older, median age, or mean age.

ALIEN See FOREIGNER.

ALLIANCE INDEX A measure of male-female unions.

ALLOCATION The assignment of values to cases for which "item nonresponse" is found in a sample survey or census. Many allocation methods are available, including automated algorithms. See also IMPUTATION, NONRESPONSE, and SUBSTITUTION.

AMENORRHEA The temporary cessation of menstruation, for normal or pathological reasons, usually the latter. It is not used to refer to old age or prepuberty, but may be used to refer to pregnancy or the post-partum condition. See also POST-PARTUM AMENORRHEA.

AMERICAN COMMUNITY SURVEY (ACS) In the United States, an ongoing household survey conducted by the Census Bureau on a "rolling" geographic basis that is designed to provide demographic characteristics for counties, places, and other small areas. It may replace the long form in the 2010 census.

ANNEXATION In the United States, the legal act of adding territory to a governmental unit, usually an incorporated place, through the passage of an ordinance, court order, or other legal action.

ANNUITY A term used in actuarial science for a type of cash distribution (e.g., payments on a life insurance policy) in which the distribution is fixed at a certain amount and date over a given period of time. See also ACTUARIAL SCIENCE.

ANTENATAL See PRENATAL.

APPLIED DEMOGRAPHY A field of demography concerned with applications of demographic data, methods, and perspectives to the practical problems of business, government, and other institutions, aiding in the formulation and implementation of decisions and policies by these institutions.

AREA ANALYSIS Measurements collected on a number of variables for each of many administrative/statistical areas that are usually analyzed using multivariate techniques.

ARRANGED MARRIAGE A union arranged by relatives (or other influential parties) of the couple to be married, with or without the agreement of the couple.

ASYLEE In the United States, an alien already in the country or at a port of entry who is found to be unable or unwilling to return to his or her country of nationality, or to seek the protection of that country because of persecution or a well-founded fear of persecution based on his or her race, religion, nationality, membership in a particular social group, or political opinion. For an alien with no nationality, the country of nationality is considered to the country in which he or she last habitually resided. An asylee is eligible to adjust to lawful permanent residence status after 1 year of continuous presence in the United States. See also INTERNALLY DISPLACED PERSON and REFUGEE.

AT-RISK POPULATION The persons to whom an event can potentially occur. In the form of the population at the middle of a given period, such as a year, it is used as an approximation of "person-years lived." See also EXPOSURE, PERSON-YEARS LIVED, and PROBABILITY.

AVERAGE FAMILY SIZE The mean number of living children of an individual or couple.

BABY BOOM The dramatic increase in both birthrates and absolute numbers of births in the United States, Canada, Australia, and New Zealand that started after World War II and lasted for nearly 20 years. In the United States, for example, it lasted from approximately 1946 to 1964. See also BABY BUST.

BABY BUST The rapid decline in fertility rates to record low levels during the period immediately after the baby boom. See also BABY BOOM.

BACHUE MODELS A method primarily designed by the International Labor Organization in the 1970s to integrate demographic variables into the planning process for developing countries. Although they have fallen into disuse, the models were designed to study the relationship between population growth and spatial distribution while controlling for the effects of other variables.

BALANCING EQUATION A term attributed to A. J. Jaffe that describes the basic population relation: $P_t = P_0 + I - O$, where P_t equals a given population at time $= 0 + t$, $P_0 =$ the given population at time $= 0$, $I =$ the number of persons entering the population through birth and immigration between time $= 0$ and time $= 0 + t$, and $O =$ the number of persons exiting the population through death and emigration between time $= 0$ and time $= 0 + t$. See also COHORT-COMPONENT METHOD, COMPONENT METHOD, ERROR OF CLOSURE, and RESIDUAL METHOD.

BASE PERIOD In a population projection, this is the period between the initial year for which data are used to generate the projection and the last year, which is known as the launch year.

See also LAUNCH YEAR, POPULATION PROJECTION, PROJECTION HORIZON, and TARGET YEAR.

BASELINE SURVEY A collection of data used for subsequent comparison or control.

BELOW REPLACEMENT FERTILITY The level at which the total fertility rate is too low for the numbers of women of childbearing ages to be replaced in a generation. See also TOTAL FERTILITY RATE.

BIAS The deviation of an estimate or set of estimates from the correct value(s) in one direction (i.e., above or below the correct value(s)). See also TOTAL ERROR.

BIRTH This refers only to a live birth and is referenced by the issuance of a birth certificate in the United States. As defined by the World Health Organization and allied organizations, a live birth is the complete expulsion or extraction from its mother of a product of conception, irrespective of the duration of pregnancy, which, after such separation, breathes or shows any other evidence of life such as beating of the heart, pulsation of the umbilical cord, or definite movement of voluntary muscles, whether or not the umbilical cord has been cut or the placenta is attached; each product of such a birth is considered "live-born." According to this definition, the period of gestation, or the state of life or death at the time of registration, are not relevant. The U.S. standard contains this definition plus a statement recommended by the American College of Obstetricians and Gynecologists to assist in the determination of what should be considered a live birth: "Heartbeats are to be distinguished from transient cardiac contractions; respirations are to be distinguished from fleeting respiratory efforts or gasps." See also ABORTION and FETAL LOSS.

BIRTH COHORT Members of a population born in a given period (e.g., 1950, 1975–1979).

BIRTH CONTROL An attempt to regulate the timing or occurrence of births.

BIRTH HISTORY The date and outcome of each birth experienced by a woman.

BIRTH INTERVAL The period between two successive live births. In the case of the first birth interval, the period between time of entry into sexual union (e.g., marriage) and the first live birth. In the case of the most recent live birth, it is the period between it and a subsequent date (e.g., the date of a birth history interview). Where a period is bounded by either birth or time of entry into sexual union, the interval is known as closed; where a period is bounded only on one side, the interval is known as open.

BIRTH ORDER The location of a given birth in the sequence of births to a woman, starting with the first and ending with the most recent (e.g., first, second, third).

BIRTH-ORDER RATE Births of a given order during a given period, divided by the number of women exposed during the same period.

BIRTH REGISTRATION AREA In the United States, the states and local governments complying with federal standards for the registration of births. It was established in 1915 and by 1933 encompassed all states. See also DEATH REGISTRATION AREA.

BIRTH SPACING See CHILDSPACING.

BIRTH WEIGHT The amount that an infant weighs at birth, usually expressed in grams.

BIRTHS EXPECTED The number of births that a woman or couple expects to have in a specified future period or by the end of childbearing, usually obtained in a census or survey. See also DESIRED FAMILY SIZE.

BLOCK In the United States, the lowest level of geography for which census data are compiled. It is a typically a city block, but specifically is a small area bounded on all sides by identifiable features (e.g., roads, rivers, and city limits) that does not cross the boundaries of a given census tract. Each block is numbered uniquely within census tracts. See also BLOCK GROUP, BLOCK NUMBERING AREA, CENSUS GEOGRAPHY, and CENSUS TRACT.

BLOCK GROUP In the United States, a cluster of blocks within a census tract that have the same first digit in their identifying numbers. See also BLOCK, BLOCK NUMBERING AREA, CENSUS GEOGRAPHY, and CENSUS TRACT.

BLOCK NUMBERING AREA In the United States, these are clusters of block groups used in the 1990 census as the framework for grouping and numbering blocks in counties that did not have census tracts and provided coverage only for the block-numbered portion of a county. Starting with the 2000 decennial census, all U.S. counties have census tracts. See also BLOCK, BLOCK GROUP, CENSUS GEOGRAPHY, and CENSUS TRACT.

BONGAART'S DECOMPOSITION An equation named after its developer, J. Bongaarts, that expresses the total fertility rate as the product of variables affecting fertility.

BRASS RELATIONAL MODEL LIFE TABLES A family of life tables developed by W. Brass that is based on an age invariant linear function (logarithmic) of the ratio of the probability of dying to the probability of not dying before a given birthday. See also MODEL LIFE TABLE.

BRASS TECHNIQUE One of many methods of estimating the level and pattern of both fertility and mortality from limited demographic data, devised by W. Brass.

CASE-FATALITY RATE The ratio of deaths from a health condition per year to persons who have that health condition at midyear. Alternatively, the population base can be the number of persons who have that condition at any time during the year.

CAUSE-DELETED LIFE TABLE A life table calculated after removing one or more specific causes of death.

CAUSE-SPECIFIC DEATH RATE The ratio of the number of deaths due to one or more causes to the at-risk population.

CENSAL-RATIO METHOD A set of population estimation techniques found within the "change in stock method" family that uses crude rates (e.g., birth and death) as measured at the most recent census date(s) and post-censal administrative records. For example, a population estimate for 2002 can be obtained by dividing reported deaths for 2002 by the crude death rate measured in 2000 or by a crude death rate projected from 2000 to 2002. Often a series of censal-ratio estimates are averaged together. D. Swanson and R. Prevost showed in 1985 that the ratio-correlation method is algebraically equivalent to a weighted average of censal-ratio estimates in which regression slope coefficients serve as weights. See also CHANGE IN STOCK METHOD, POPULATION ESTIMATE, RATIO-CORRELATION METHOD, and WEIGHTED AVERAGE.

CENSORED A condition affecting time-ordered data because the time frame for which data are collected does not cover the entire time span over which an event of interest may occur (e.g., a pregnancy at future point beyond the time frame in which data were collected). "Left-censored" is used to described the period preceding the data collection time frame and "right-censored," the subsequent period.

CENSUS The count of a given population (or other phenomena of interest) and record its characteristics, done at a specific point in time and usually at regular intervals by a governmental entity for the geographic area or subareas under its domain. See also CENSUS COVERAGE, CENSUS DEFINED RESIDENT, POPULATION, POPULATION ESTIMATE, and SAMPLE.

CENSUS COVERAGE An estimate of how complete a census was of a given population. See also COVERAGE ERROR, NET CENSUS UNDERCOUNT ERROR, and TRUE POPULATION.

CENSUS COVERAGE ERROR See COVERAGE ERROR.

CENSUS COUNTY DIVISION In the United States, a statistical subdivision of counties in states established cooperatively by the Census Bureau and local groups in which minor civil divisions (e.g., townships) are not suitable for presenting census data. See also CENSUS GEOGRAPHY.

CENSUS DEFINED RESIDENT The concept of defining persons counted in a census in order to count each and every person once and only once. One of two counting bases is used: (1) de jure, which attempts to locate persons at their usual residence, and (2) de facto, which counts people where they are found. The U.S. decennial census is based on the de jure method. See also CENSUS, DE FACTO POPULATION, DE JURE POPULATION, DOMICLE, RESIDENCE, and USUAL RESIDENCE.

CENSUS DESIGNATED PLACE (CDP) In the United States Census, a concentration of population enumerated during the decennial census in an area lacking legal boundaries, but recognized by the residents (and others) as a distinctive area with a name. A CDP is defined cooperatively by local officials and the Census Bureau. CDPs have been used since the 1980 census; from 1940 to 1970, they were called unincorporated places. See also CENSUS GEOGRAPHY.

CENSUS ERROR See COVERAGE ERROR.

CENSUS GEOGRAPHY In the United States, this refers to the hierarchical system of geographic areas that is used in conjunction with each decennial census. It consists of two major components: (1) areas defined by political or administrative boundaries (e.g., states, counties, townships, and cities) and (2) areas defined by "statistical" boundaries (e.g., block, census designated place, census tract). The areas so defined are used for analytical, political, and administrative purposes. Any country conducting a census uses some type of census geography. See also BLOCK, CENSUS COUNTY DIVISION,

CENSUS DESIGNATED PLACE, CENSUS TRACT, CITY, COUNTY. METROPOLITAN AREA.

CENSUS SURVIVAL RATE   See NATIONAL CENSUS SURVIVAL RATE.

CENSUS TRACT   In the United States, this is the lowest level of "statistical geography" found in the decennial census designed to be homogenous with respect to population and economic characteristics (note that blocks and block groups, while at a lower level, are not designed with respect to population or economic homogeneity). Once established it is designed to be consistent in its boundaries for a long period of time. Starting with the 2000 census, all areas in the United States are tracted. See also BLOCK, BLOCK GROUP, BLOCK NUMBERING AREA, and CENSUS GEOGRAPHY.

CENTRAL CITY   Within the U.S. Census Bureau's geography system, the core area in a metropolitan area. However, in other contexts, it is usually viewed as the concentrated inner area of a city consisting of business districts and urban housing.

CENTRAL RATE   An event-exposure ratio where the numerator is the number of events in a given period and the denominator is the number of people taken as the population as of the midpoint of the period.

CHAIN MIGRATION   One migration leading to another, whether within a single migration cycle (a migrant) or among multiple cycles (among migrants).

CHANGE IN STOCK METHOD   A family of techniques for estimating population that is based on the measuring the total change in population since the previous census rather than the components of change. Examples include the censal-ratio method, the housing unit method, and the ratio-correlation method. See also COMPONENT METHOD, CENSAL-RATIO METHOD, HOUSING UNIT METHOD, and POPULATION ESTIMATE.

CHILD MORTALITY   Deaths to children between the ages of 1 year and puberty.

CHILD SPACING   The Pattern of intervals between successive births to a woman. Also the practice of controlling the spacing of one's births.

CHILD SURVIVAL   Number of survivors of a cohort of births past their fifth birthday.

CHILD-WOMAN RATIO   A measure formed by dividing the number of children (aged 0 to 4) by the number of women of child-bearing age (aged either 15 to 49 or 15 to 44). See also EFFECTIVE FERTILITY.

CHILDREN EVER BORN   The number of children born alive to a woman, reported usually in a census or sample survey.

CHRONIC DISEASE   A disease having a slow onset and lasting for a long period of time, usually refers to diseases associated with later life such as cardiovascular diseases, malignont neoplasms, and diabetes. See also ACUTE DISEASE.

CITIZEN   A legal national of a given country. Citizenship may be acquired by birth or naturalization.

CITY   In the United States, a type of incorporated place. See also CENSUS GEOGRAPHY.

CIVILIAN LABOR FORCE   See LABOR FORCE.

CIVILIAN NONINSTITUTIONAL POPULATION   In the United States, persons 16 years and over who are not inmates of institutions and who are not on active duty in the armed forces. See also CURRENT POPULATION SURVEY.

CIVILIAN POPULATION   Persons who are not members of the armed forces, including dependents of members of the armed forces.

CLOSED POPULATION   A population for which inmigration and outmigration are minimal, if they occur at all. For example, the population of the world as a whole is "closed," whereas the population of New York City is not.

COALE-DEMENY MODEL LIFE TABLES   Sets of life tables developed by A. Coale and P. Demeny that represent the age patterns of mortality of four different "regions" of the world. See also MODEL LIFE TABLE.

COALE-MCNEIL NUPTIALITY METHOD   A mathematical model developed by A. Coale and D. R. McNeil that is designed to estimate and analyze age patterns of first marriage by cohorts of women.

COALE-TRUSSELL FERTILITY MODEL   A mathematical model developed by A. Coale and J. Trussell that is used to estimate the relationship between marital fertility and natural fertility by age of woman.

COALE'S FERTILITY DECOMPOSITION   A method developed by A. Coale that can be used to estimate marital birth patterns over time.

COEFFICIENT OF POPULATION CONCENTRATION   A measure of urbanization based on the Gini index. See also GINI INDEX.

COHABITATION   An unmarried couple living together in what may or may not be a stable union. See also CONSENSUAL UNION.

COHORT   A group of people who experience the same demographic event during a particular period of time such as their year of marriage, birth, or death. Cohorts are typically defined on the basis of a initiating signal event (e.g., birth), but they also can be defined on the basis of a terminating signal event (e.g., death). See also COHORT ANALYSIS, COHORT EFFECT, COHORT MEASURE, and PERIOD.

COHORT ANALYSIS   An analysis that traces the demographic history of a cohort as it progresses through time. See also AGE-PERIOD-COHORT EFFECT, COHORT, LEXIS DIAGRAM, and PERIOD ANALYSIS.

COHORT CHANGE METHOD   See HAMILTON-PERRY METHOD.

COHORT CHANGE RATIO   See HAMILTON-PERRY METHOD.

COHORT-COMPONENT METHOD   A projection technique that takes into account the components of population change, births, deaths, and migration, and a population's age and sex composition. See also BALANCING EQUATION, COMPONENT METHOD, and POPULATION PROJECTION.

COHORT EFFECT An analytical perspective that attempts to determine the effect of cohort membership (as distinct from age and period effects) on a variable of interest. See also AGE-EFFECT, AGE-PERIOD-COHORT EFFECT, COHORT, and PERIOD EFFECT.

COHORT LIFE TABLE See GENERATION LIFE TABLE.

COHORT MEASURE A summary measure of data collected for a given cohort that typically represent more than one period. It also refers to a one-year rate structured in cohort form (e.g., a probability rather than a central rate). See also COHORT ANALYSIS and PERIOD MEASURE.

COMMUTING A regular journey (typically one that occurs daily) between the place of residence and place of work. See also MIGRATION.

COMORBIDITY Multiple chronic conditions experienced by one individual at the same time.

COMPARATIVE MORTALITY INDEX A measure designed to indicate mortality change to a given population that is based on a ratio of the population-weighted sum of age-specific death rates at the end of the period to the population-weighted sum of age-specific death rates at the start of the period.

COMPARATIVE STUDY Method of relating two or more sets of data.

COMPLETE LIFE TABLE See LIFE TABLE.

COMPLETED FAMILY SIZE Total number of children born by end of the reproductive period of an individual or couple.

COMPLETED FERTILITY RATE The total number of children born to women by the end of the childbearing years (e.g., aged 45 to 49 years) per 1000 women at these ages (e.g., 45 to 49 years), usually obtained from censuses or surveys. When the measure is obtained by adding age-specific fertility rates, whether on a period basis or a cohort basis, it is usually called the total fertility rate. See also TOTAL FERTILITY RATE.

COMPONENT METHOD In general, this refers to any technique for estimating population that incorporates births, deaths, and migration. Also known as a "flow method." See also BALANCING EQUATION, CHANGE IN STOCK METHOD, COMPONENT METHOD I, COMPONENT METHOD II, and POPULATION ESTIMATE.

COMPONENT METHOD I A component method of estimating population that uses the relationship between local and national school enrollment data to estimate the net migration component. See also COMPONENT METHOD, COMPONENT METHOD II, and POPULATION ESTIMATE.

COMPONENT METHOD II A component method of estimating population that uses the relationship between expected (survived) and actual local school enrollment data to estimate the net migration component. See also COMPONENT METHOD, COMPONENT METHOD I, and POPULATION ESTIMATE.

COMPONENTS OF CHANGE There are four basic components of population change: births, deaths, inmigration, and outmigration. The excess of births over deaths results in natural increase, while the excess of deaths over births results in natural decrease. The difference between inmigration and outmigration is net migration. In an analysis of special characteristics or groups, the number of components is broadened to include relevant additional factors (e.g., aging, marriages, divorces, annexations, and retirements), depending on the group. See also BALANCING EQUATION.

COMPOSITE METHOD A technique for estimating total population that is based on independent estimates of age or age-sex groups that are summed to obtain the total population. See also POPULATION ESTIMATE.

CONCEPTION The act of fertilization.

CONCEPTION PROBABILITY See FECUNDABILITY.

CONSANGUINITY A family relativeship based on blood; descended from the same ancestor.

CONSENSUAL UNION An unmarried couple who live together in what is thought of as a stable union. See also COHABITATION.

CONSOLIDATED METROPOLITAN STATISTICAL AREA See METROPOLITAN AREA.

CONTRACEPTION. The act of preventing pregnancy when sexually active.

CONTRACEPTIVE EFFICACY The extent to which contraction reduces the likelihood of becoming pregnant, usually measured by comparing the pregnancy difference between contraceptive users and nonusers. A distinction is made between use-effectiveness and clinical effectiveness.

CONTRACEPTIVE EFFECTIVENESS See CONTRACEPTIVE EFFICACY.

CONTROLLING The act of adjusting a distribution to an independently derived total value. See also CONTROLS.

CONTROLS Independently derived estimates of a "total value" to which distributions are adjusted for purposes of improving accuracy, reducing variance and bias, or maintaining consistency. Controls can be univariate (one-dimensional) or multivariate (n-dimensional). Many methods may be used, including those that take account of whether the distributions have only positive values or both positive and negative values. See also CONTROLLING, ITERATIVE PROPORTIONAL FITTING, and PLUS-MINUS METHOD, and PRORATA ADJUSTMENT.

CORRECTED CENSUS POPULATION A census population count that includes an adjustment for net census undercount error. See NET CENSUS UNDERCOUNT ERROR.

COUNTERSTREAM The movement in the opposite direction of a migration stream. See also MIGRATION STREAM.

COUNTY In the United States, a type of governmental unit that is the primary administrative subdivision of every state except Alaska and Louisiana. See also CENSUS GEOGRAPHY.

COUNTY BUSINESS PATTERNS In the United States, an annual report compiled by the Census Bureau that summarizes economic information about each county.

COUNTY EQUIVALENT In the United States, a geographic entity that is not legally recognized as a county but referred to by the Census Bureau as the equivalent of a county for purposes of data presentation. Boroughs and certain statistically defined areas are county equivalents in Alaska and parishes are county equivalents in Louisiana. See also COUNTY, and CENSUS GEOGRAPHY.

COVERAGE ERROR   In principle, this refers to the difference between the "true population" and the number reported in a set of data such as a census, survey, or set of administrative records. In practice, it is the difference between an *estimate* of the true number and the number reported in a set of data such as a census, survey, or set of administrative records. See also CENSUS, NET CENSUS UNDERCOUNT ERROR, TOTAL ERROR, and TRUE POPULATION.

CROSS-SECTIONAL ANALYSIS   Studies that focus on phenomena that occur during a short time interval (such as a calendar year) among several cohorts. See also COHORT ANALYSIS and PERIOD ANALYSIS.

CRUDE RATE   A rate that relates a demographic event to the total population and makes no distinction concerning different exposure levels to the event. Examples include the crude birth rate, crude death rate, crude divorce rate, crude marriage rate, and crude rate of natural increase. See also AGE-SPECIFIC RATE, GENERAL RATE, and RATE.

CUMULATIVE FERTILITY RATE   The cumulative number of births a hypothetical cohort of 1000 women would have had each year of their lives at a given set of age-specific fertility rates or ratios of children ever born. Alternatively, ratios of children ever born to women at each childbearing age. The latter is problematic because it refers to surviving births rather than all births.

CURRENT POPULATION SURVEY (CPS)   In the United States, a sample survey conducted monthly by the Census Bureau designed to represent the civilian noninstitutional population that obtains a wide range of socioeconomic-demographic data. See also CIVILIAN NONINSTITUTIONAL POPULATION.

CURVE   A mathematical function, usually continuous and otherwise "well behaved," that can be used as a model for a demographic process such as the change in the size of a population over time. Examples include the exponential, Geometric, gompertz, linear, logistic, and polynomial.

CURVE-FITTING   The process of finding a mathematical function that serves as a model for a given demographic process.

DATA AGGREGATION   Compounding primary data into an aggregate to express data in summary form or compiling tabular data into broader groups.

DATA LINKAGE   See MATCHING.

DEATH   The permanent disappearance of all evidence of life at any time after a live birth has taken place. The loss of a member of a population, as recorded by a death certificate.

DEATH DENSITY FUNCTION   The probability that a death (or more generally, an event) occurs during a given time interval, no matter how small the interval. It is a probability density function, where the random variable is time. It is one of three algebraically related functions broadly dealing with the issue of "survival," the other two being the "hazard function" and the "survivorship function." The death density function is found by multiplying the survivorship function by the hazard function. See also HAZARD FUNCTION and SURVIVORSHIP FUNCTION.

DEATH REGISTRATION AREA   In the United States, the states and local governments complying with federal standards for the registration of deaths. It was established in 1900 and by 1933 encompassed all states. See also BIRTH REGISTRATION AREA.

DECREMENT   The exit of an individual or set of individuals from a "population" of interest, where the population is often defined by a model. In the case of a model such as the standard life table, such an exit would be due to death. See also INCREMENT and INCREMENT-DECREMENT LIFE TABLE.

DE FACTO POPULATION   A census concept that defines an enumerated person on the basis of his or her actual location at the time of the census. See also CENSUS DEFINED RESIDENT and DE JURE POPULATION.

DE JURE POPULATION   A census concept that defines an enumerated person on the basis of a person's usual place of residence at the time of a census. See also CENSUS DEFINED RESIDENT and DE FACTO POPULATION.

DEMOGRAPHIC ACCOUNTING   The process of analyzing the change in a population using "stocks" (e.g., conditions such as the number of people in a given age-sex group) and "flows" (e.g., events such as births and deaths by age and sex) to show how the flows affect stocks over time. Ideally the stocks and flows should be measured without error and form mutually exclusive and exhaustive categories.

DEMOGRAPHIC ANALYSIS   Generally, this refers to the methods of examination, assessment, and interpretation of the components and processes of population change, especially births, deaths, and migration. In the United States, it also refers to a specific method of estimating net census undercount using the components and process of population change.

DEMOGRAPHIC TRANSITION   In general, this refers to a change from high birth and death rates to low birth and death rates resulting from industrialization or modernization. See also DEMOGRAPHIC TRANSITION THEORY, and LOGISTIC CURVE.

DEMOGRAPHIC TRANSITION THEORY   This theory posits three stages in the evolution of a population experiencing the demographic transition: (1) pre-industrial, characterized by high birth and death rates and low growth; (2) early industrial, characterized by high birth rates low death rates, and high growth; and (3) mature industrial, characterized by low birth and death rates and low population growth. This theory can be quantitatively expressed using the logistic model of population change. See also DEMOGRAPHIC TRANSITION.

DEMOGRAPHICS   A popular term for demography also used to represent demographic data and the application of demographic data, methods, and perspectives to activities undertaken by nonprofit organizations, businesses, and governments. See also DEMOGRAPHY and APPLIED DEMOGRAPHY.

DEMOGRAPHY   The study of population, typically focused on five aspects: (1) size, (2) geographic distribution, (3) composition, (4) the components of change (births, deaths, migration), and (5) the determinants and consequences of population change. This term is usually used to refer to human populations, but it also is used to refer to nonhuman, particularly wildlife, populations. See also APPLIED DEMOGRAPHY DEMOGRAPHICS, FAMILY DEMOGRAPHY, HOUSEHOLD DEMOGRAPHY, MATHEMATICAL DEMOGRAPHY ORGANIZATIONAL DEMOGRAPHY, and POPULATION.

DENSITY   The number of people per unit area (e.g., persons per square kilometer).

DEPENDENCY BURDEN   See DEPENDENCY RATIO.

DEPENDENCY RATIO   The ratio of the number of persons in a given "dependent" age group of interest to the number in a different age group considered to contain those persons providing support to those dependent (e.g., the number of persons less than 15 years of age divided by the number aged 15 to 64). See also AGE DEDENDENCY RATIO and ECOMONIC DEPENDENCY RATIO.

DESIRED FAMILY SIZE   The total number of children desired by a woman or a couple. See also BIRTHS EXPECTED.

DESTINATION   The place of residence of a migrant at the conclusion of a given (migration) period. See also MIGRANT, MIGRATION, and ORIGIN.

DEVELOPED COUNTRIES   Those nations that have a developed industrial infrastructure. The United Nations' compilations recognize a specific list of such countries. See also DEVELOPING COUNTRIES.

DEVELOPING COUNTRIES   Those nations that do not have a developed industrial infrastructure. The United Nations' compilations recognize a specific list of such countries. See also DEVELOPED COUNTRIES.

DIFFERENCE-CORRELATION METHOD   See RATIO-CORRELATION METHOD.

DIGIT AVOIDANCE   A tendency for people to avoid reporting ages with certain terminal digits. See also AGE HEAPING and DIGIT PREFERENCE.

DIGIT PREFERENCE   A tendency for people to prefer reporting ages with certain terminal digits. See also AGE HEAPING and DIGIT AVOIDANCE.

DIRECT ESTIMATION   The measurement of demographic phenomena using data that directly represent the phenomena of interest. The term also is used by survey statisticians to describe estimates obtained by survey sampling. See also INDIRECT ESTIMATION.

DIRECT STANDARDIZATION   The adjustment of a summary rate (e.g., the crude death rate) for a population in question found by computing a weighted average of group-specific rates (e.g., age-specific death rates) for the population in question, where the weights consist of specific groups (e.g., the proportion in each age group) found in a "standard" population. This procedure is designed to produce a summary rate that controls for the effects of population composition (e.g., age) and is usually used for purposes of comparison with directly standardized rates for other populations computed using the same standard population. To standardize a crude death rate by the direct method, multiply the age-specific death rates for the population in question by the age-specific proportions in a standard population and sum the products. See also INDIRECT STANDARDIZATION, STANDARD POPULATION, and STANDARDIZATION.

DISEASE   A morbid condition that is sufficiently pronounced to require treatment or cessation of usual activity.

DISSIMILARITY INDEX   See INDXEX OF DISSIMILARITY.

DIURNAL FLUCTUATION   For a given area, the change in its de facto population over the course of a day (i.e., a 24-hour period). See also DE FACTO POPULATION.

DIVORCE   A complete, legal termination of a marriage. See also MARRIAGE.

DOMESTIC MIGRATION   The movement of people within a given country across political or administrative boundaries. People leaving an area are outmigrants and those entering an area are inmigrants. It is a synonym for internal migration. See also FOREIGN MIGRATION and MIGRATION.

DOMICILE   A person's fixed, permanent, and principal home for legal purposes. See also HOUSEHOLD, HOUSING UNIT, RESIDENCE, and USUAL RESIDENCE.

DUAL CITIZENSHIP   The state of having citizenship in two countries simultaneously.

DUAL RESIDENCE   The state of having two usual places of residence over a given period of time, which must be resolved in a de jure census through the use of a set of procedures designed to count persons once and only once.

DUAL-SYSTEMS ESTIMATION   Estimation of the total number of events or persons by matching the individual records in two data collections systems. See also MATCHING.

EASTERLIN HYPOTHESIS   A hypothesis proposed by R. Easterlin that the level of income and consumption in parental households influences fertility decisions, with the result that large birth cohorts tend to give birth to small birth cohorts and vice versa.

ECOLOGY   The science and practice dealing with the interrelationships between population factors and their environments.

ECONOMICALLY ACTIVE POPULATION   The segment of a population that engages in or attempts to engage in the production of goods and services during a given period. It includes both civilians and military personnel. See also LABOR FORCE.

ECONOMIC DEPENDENCY RATIO   The ratio of economically inactive population to the economically active population regardless of age. See also DEPENDENCY RATIO.

EDUCATIONAL ATTAINMENT   The highest grade completed within the most advanced level attended in the educational system of the country where the education was received, where grade is defined as a stage of instruction, usually a school year.

EFFECTIVE FERTILITY A concept related to the number of offspring who are likely to survive sufficiently long to reproduce. The child-woman ratio is an example of a measure that can be used to measure this concept. See also CHILD-WOMAN RATIO.

EMIGRANT A resident of a given country who departs to take up residence in another country. See also DOMESTIC MIGRATION, FOREIGN MIGRATION, and MIGRATION.

EMIGRATION See FOREIGN MIGRATION.

EMIGRATION RATE An outmigration rate for a country as a whole. See also FOREIGN MIGRATION and OUTMIGRATION RATE.

EMPLOYED PERSON In the United States, persons 16 years and over who worked for pay during the "reference week," or who worked unpaid for 15 hours or more in a family-owned business, or those who were temporarily absent from their jobs due to illness, bad weather, vacation, labor dispute, or personal reasons. See also EMPLOYMENT.

EMPLOYMENT State of being engaged in an activity for compensation, with the exact definition dependent on whether it is subsumed under the economically active concept or the labor force concept. See also EMPLOYED PERSON.

EMPLOYMENT STATUS The classification of an individual exercising an economic activity; as to whether he or she is employed or unemployed.

ENUMERATION The act of counting the members of a population in a census.

ENUMERATION DISTRICT The area assigned to an enumerator during a census or survey of a given area.

EQUILIBRIUM MODEL A model used in labor force and employment analysis to project employment in which projections of labor supply (labor force) and projections of labor demand are reconciled.

EPIDEMIOLOGIC TRANSITION The shift in population disease patterns and causes of mortality from infectious and parasitic diseases to degenerative and chronic conditions.

EPIDEMIOLOGIC TRANSITION THEORY Based on the work of Omran (1971, 1982) this theory posits three stages in the epidemiologic transition: (1) the age of pestilence and famine, (2) the age of receding pandemics, and (3) the age of degenerative and "man-made" diseases.

EPIDEMIOLOGICAL STUDY Research that is concerned with the distribution of diseases and injuries in human populations and the possible risk factors associated with these diseases.

EPIDEMIOLOGY The study of the distribution and spread of diseases in a population, and the application of this study to control diseases.

ERGODICITY A process whereby a closed population subject to fixed or nearly fixed fertility and mortality schedules eventually acquires a constant or nearly constant age composition that is independent of its starting age composition. See also STABLE POPULATION.

ERROR OF CLOSURE The difference between the change in population implied by census counts at two different dates and the change implied by an estimate not dependent on both census counts. This also can refer to a term added to the demographic balancing equation to account for errors in the components of change that cause them not to exactly match the change in measured independently for the population to which they apply. See also BALANCING EQUATION and RESIDUAL METHOD.

ESTIMATE See POPULATION ESTIMATE.

ETHNICITY A common cultural heritage that sets a group apart on the basis of national origin, ancestry, language, religion, and similar characteristics. In the U.S. decennial census, ethnicity is self-identified. See also RACE.

EVENT A change in condition or status (e.g., single to married.

EVENT-EXPOSURE RATIO See OCCURRENCE-EXPOSURE RATIO.

EVENT HISTORY ANALYSIS The study of longitudinal-event data using survival analysis and regression analysis with explanatory variables. It typically examines transition rates from one "status" to another over time (e.g., life to death, non-married to married to divorced, household with children to empty-nest household.

EVER MARRIED Persons who have at any time in their lives been married, as opposed to "never married," those who have never been married.

EXACT AGE The difference between one's birthday and the date of observation, expressed in a exact number. It refers to a single point in the age continuum, such as a birthday, as compared with age in completed years, which expresses age in a band between two exact ages.

EXCESS MORTALITY Relatively high death rates among a particular group or subpopulation.

EXPECTATION OF LIFE A statistical measure of the average amount of time (usually measured in years) remaining for a person or group of persons before death, usually estimated using a life table.

EXPECTED FAMILY SIZE Number of children a person or couple anticipates raising See also BIRTHS EXPECTED.

EXPOSURE The condition of a population being at risk of having an event occur to it during a specified period. See also AT-RISK POPULATION.

EXTENDED FAMILY A group within a specified degree of consanguinity or marriage who tend to collaborate in support activity for one another.

EXTINCT GENERATIONS A technique introduced by P. Vincent in the early 1950s that is designed to estimate the number of extremely old persons in a population at a given date by cumulating deaths (to include, as needed, reported, estimated, and projected deaths) to given cohorts to the point where all members of the given cohorts have expired.

EXTRAPOLATION The process of determining (estimating or projecting) values that go beyond the last known data point in a series (e.g., the most recent census or estimate). It is typically accomplished by using a mathematical formula, a graphic procedure, or a combination of the two. See also INTERPOLATION.

FAMILY In the United States, defined by the U.S. Census Bureau as those members of a household who are related through blood, adoption, or marriage. See also HOUSEHOLD.

FAMILY DEMOGRAPHY The study of the size, distribution, and composition of families, along with their components of change and the determinants and consequences of family change. See also DEMOGRAPHY, FAMILY, HOUSEHOLDS and HOUSEHOLD DEMOGRAPHY.

FAMILY LIFE CYCLE The evolution of a family through various critical stages (e.g., marriage, birth of first child, birth of last child, divorce, widowhood).

FAMILY PLANNING Voluntary planning and action by individuals to have the number of children they want and to space their births as they wish.

FAMILY SIZE See AVERAGE FAMILY SIZE.

FECUNDABILITY Generally defined as the probability that a woman capable of conception (i.e., neither using contraception nor sterile) will conceive in a given menstrual cycle. See also FECUNDITY.

FECUNDITY The physiological capacity of a woman, man, couple, or group to reproduce. See also FECUNDABILITY, FERTILITY, STERILITY, and SUBFECUNDITY.

FERTILITY The reproductive performance of a woman, man, couple, or group. Also a general term for the incidence of births in a population or group. One of the components of population change. See also COMPONENTS OF CHANGE and FECUNDITY.

FERTILITY DETERMINANTS Factors influencing births.

FERTILITY PATTERN METHOD A method of analyzing changes in age-parity-specific birthrates in the presence of deficient data.

FERTILITY SCHEDULE A set of age-specific age-marital specific or marital-duration-specific fertility rates.

FERTILITY TRANSITION See DEMOGRAPHIC TRANSITION.

FERTILIZATION See CONCEPTION.

FETAL See FETUS.

FETAL LOSS The loss of a fetus *in utero*, where the reason for the loss usually excludes abortion when abortion in the same context is limited to induced pregnancy termination. See also ABORTION and FETUS.

FETUS The product of conception from a given period, such as the end of the eighth week of development up to the moment of birth.

FETAL LOSS RATE The ratio of (late) fetal losses during a year to the sum of births plus late fetal losses during the year.

FETAL LOSS RATIO The ratio of (late) fetal losses during a year to births during the year.

FIPS CODE In the United States, one of a series of codes issued by the National Institute of Standards and Technology for the identification of geographic entities. FIPS stands for "Federal Information Processing Standards."

FIRST BIRTH The first child born to a woman or couple.

FIRST BIRTH INTERVAL The length of time between the first birth and a prior relevant "event" such as marriage.

FIRST TRIMESTER PREGNANCY See PREGNANCY.

FLOW METHOD See COMPONENT METHOD.

FOLLOW-UP STUDIES A collection of data in which the same group of persons or households is tracked over time by means of repeated visits or other contacts.

FORCE OF MORTALITY Generally defined as the rate of death during the smallest possible interval over which deaths can be measured (approaching a limit of zero), equivalent to the first-order differential of a continuous mortality function. See also HAZARD RATE.

FORCED MIGRATION See ASYLEES, INTERNALLY DISPLACED PERSONS, and REFUGEES.

FORECAST See POPULATION FORECAST.

FOREIGN MIGRATION See INTERNATIONAL MIGRATION.

FOREIGNER A person in a given country who is a citizen of another country or otherwise owes allegiance to another country.

FORMAL DEMOGRAPHY See MATHEMATICAL DEMOGRAPHY.

FORWARD SURVIVAL METHOD A method that involves survival of a population group from a younger age to an older age. Where a survival rate method is not further labeled, forward survival is to be assumed. See also FORWARD-REVERSE SURVIVAL METHOD, REVERSE SURIVAL METHOD and SURVIVAL RATE.

FORWARD-REVERSE SURVIVAL METHOD A technique used in estimating both intercensal populations and net migration between two censuses in which an "average" is taken between the results of using forward and reverse survival rates to age and "young" a given population, respectively, over the period between the two censuses. See also FORWARD SURVIVAL RATE, REVERSE SURVIVAL RATE, and SURVIVAL.

FORWARD SURVIVAL RATE A type of rate that expresses survival of a population group from a younger age to an older age. Where a survival rate is not further labeled, forward survival is to be assumed. See also REVERSE SURVIVAL RATE and SURVIVAL.

GENERAL RATE A rate that relates a demographic event to a set of people in a given population generally thought to be exposed to the event of interest, but one for which no distinction is made regarding different exposure levels to the event. A GENERAL RATE is distinguished from a CRUDE RATE because of the former's attempt to limit the population at risk to those actually exposed to the event in question, typically on the basis of age. Examples include the general activity rate, general divorce rate, general enrollment rate, and the general fertility rate. See also AGE-SPECIFIC RATE, CRUDE RATE, and RATE.

GENERATION   Often used as a synonym for "cohort" in demographic analysis, but can refer to other concepts as well, such as the mean age of childbearing in years. See also COHORT and MEAN LENGTH OF GENERATION.

GENERATION LIFE TABLE   A type of life table based on the mortality rates experienced by an actual cohort from the time of its birth to its extinction. See also LIFE TABLE and PERIOD LIFE TABLE.

GENERATION REPRODUCTION RATE   A group of measures of reproductivity based on the fertility and mortality experience of a cohort of women during its reproductive years. See also REPRODUCTIVITY.

GEOCODING   The assignment of geographic or spatial information to data, such as coordinates of latitude and longitude. It is the most fundamental operation in the development of a "GIS," a geographic information system. See also GEOGRAPHIC INFORMATION SYSTEM.

GEOGRAPHIC INFORMATION SYSTEM (GIS)   A chain of operations involving the collection, storage, manipulation, and display of data referenced by geographic or spatial coordinates (e.g., coded by latitude and longitude).

GINI INDEX   A measure developed by C. Gini of the distributional equality of two variables (e.g., the distribution of income across a population, the relative geographic distribution of the Hispanic population relative to the distribution of the non Hispanic population over the same geography). It is based on the proportion of the total area under a diagonal that lies in the area between the diagonal and the Lorenz curve, where the diagonal represents a condition of equality in the distribution of two variables and the Lorenz curve represents the actual distribution of the same two variables. See also COEFFICIENT OF POPULATION CONCENTRATION, INDEX OF DISSIMILARITY, and LORENZ CURVE.

GIS   See GEOGRAPHIC INFORMATION SYSTEM.

GOMPERTZ CURVE   A mathematical formulation of a "law" of mortality introduced by B. Gompertz in the early 19th century that describes the variation of the force of mortality with age. It assumes that the force of mortality increases in geometric progression with advancing age. At the highest ages, Gompertz proposed a formula that assumes a less rapid rise in the force of mortality, specifically, that the growth increments of age-specific mortality rates decline at a constant proportion with advancing age. See also GOMPERTZ FERTILITY MODEL and LOGISTIC CURVE.

GOMPERTZ FERTILITY MODEL   Application to the analysis of fertility of the mathematical function developed by B. Gompertz for mortality analysis. See also GOMPERTZ CURVE.

GRADUATION   See SMOOTHING.

GRAVIDITY   The state of pregnancy. See also PREGNANCY RATE.

GRAVITY MODEL   A model (borrowed from classical physics) based on the hypothesis that movement (migration, commuting, retail purchasing, etc.) between two areas is directly related to the population size of each area and inversely related to the distance between the two areas.

GROSS INMIGRATION   The total number of inmigrants to an area during a given period.

GROSS MIGRATION   The sum of inmigration and outmigration for a given area. See also MIGRATION and NET MIGRATION.

GROSS OUTMIGRATION   The total number of outmigrants from an area during a given period.

GROUP QUARTERS   In the United States, a term used by the Census Bureau for places in which people reside that are not considered "housing units." Such places include prisons, long-term care hospitals, military barracks, and school and college dormitories. See also HOUSEHOLD POPULATION and HOUSING UNIT.

GROWTH RATE   Often used as a general expression to describe the rate of change in a given population, even one that is declining. See also RATE and RATE OF CHANGE.

HAMILTON-PERRY METHOD   A technique developed by H. Hamilton and J. Perry used in population projections that refers to a type of survival rate calculated for a cohort from two censuses. It includes not only the effects of mortality, but also the effects of net migration and relative census enumeration error. See also SURVIVAL RATE.

HAZARD FUNCTION   One of three algebraically related functions used in survival analysis, the other two being the "Death Density Function" and the "Survivorship Function." The hazard function is found by dividing the death density function by the survivorship function. See also DEATH DENSITY FUNCTION, HAZARD RATE, and SURVIVORSHIP FUNCTION.

HAZARD RATE   The probability that an event occurs within a given time interval, no matter how small the interval, given that the event has not occurred to the subject of interest prior to the start of the interval. Typically, the event of interest is a "decrement" such as death. See also DECREMENT, FORCE OF MORTALITY, and HAZARD FUNCTION.

HEAD OF HOUSEHOLD   A "marker" for a household, its type and structure. It is usually defined as the principal wage earner or provider for a multiperson household or, alternatively, as the person in whose name the housing unit is rented or owned. Persons living alone also are designated as heads of households. In principle, the number of households is equal to the number of household heads. See also HOUSEHOLD.

HEADSHIP RATE   Usually defined as the proportion of the (household) population who are "heads" of households (i.e., divide the number of households by the household population), often by age. It is often used in conjunction with population projections to obtain household projections. See also HEAD OF HOUSEHOLD, HOUSEHOLD, and POPULATION PROJECTION.

HEAPING   See AGE HEAPING.

HELIGMAN-POLLARD MODEL   A refinement of the Gompertz curve developed by L. Heligman and J. Pollard, positing that after the age of 50 the odds of dying in a given age interval increase exponentially with age. See also GOMPERTZ CURVE, LEE-CARTER MODEL, and MCNOWN-ROGERS MODEL.

HETEROGENEITY The presence of variation among the members of a population with respect to a given characteristic of interest. See also HOMOGENEITY.

HISPANIC A person of Spanish or Latin American origin (also known as "Latino"). In the U.S. decennial census, persons of Hispanic origin are self-identified. Persons of Hispanic origin may be of any race. See also ETHNICITY and RACE.

HISTORICAL DEMOGRAPHY A specialized branch of demography dealing with the study of populations in the past; more particularly concerned with the period before vital registration was introduced or modern censuses were taken.

HOMELESS PERSON Member of a population without a home or an official address usually found in shelters, on the streets, in vacant lots, or vacant buildings.

HOMOGENEITY Lack of variation among the members of a population with respect to a given characteristic of interest. See also HETEROGENEITY.

HORIZON See PROJECTION HORIZON.

HOT DECK IMPUTATION See IMPUTATION.

HOUSEHOLD Either a single person or a group of people making provision for food and other essentials of living, occupying the whole, part of, or more than one housing unit or other provision for shelter. The definitions vary by country. See also DOMICLE, FAMILY, GROUP QUARTERS, HEAD OF HOUSEHOLD, HOMELESS PERSON, HOUSEHOLD POPULATION, and HOUSING UNIT.

HOUSEHOLD DEMOGRAPHY The study of the size, distribution, and composition of households, along with their components of change and the determinants and consequences of household change. Sometimes called HOUSING DEMOGRAPHY. See also DEMOGRAPHY, FAMILY DEMOGRAPHY, and HOUSEHOLD.

HOUSEHOLD POPULATION Members of a population living in housing units (as opposed to those who are homeless or living in group quarters—e.g., prisons, long-term care hospitals, military barracks, and school and college dormitories). See also GROUP QUARTERS, HOMELESS PERSONS, HOUSEHOLD, and HOUSING UNIT.

HOUSING DEMOGRAPHY See HOUSEHOLD DEMOGRAPHY.

HOUSING UNIT Generally a shelter intended for "separate use" by its occupants, such that there is independent access to the outside and the shelter is not a group quarters. A housing unit may be occupied or vacant. See also DOMICLE, FAMILY, GROUP QUARTERS, HOMELESS PERSONS, and HOUSEHOLD.

HOUSING UNIT METHOD A population estimation technique found within the "change in stock method" family that uses current housing unit counts, vacancy estimates, and estimates of the number of persons per household to estimate the total household population, to which can be added an estimate of the group quarters population to obtain an estimate of the total population. See also CHANGE IN STOCK METHOD, HOUSEHOLD, HOUSING UNIT, GROUP QUARTERS, and POPULATION ESTIMATE.

ILLEGAL ALIEN A person illegally in a given country who either is a citizen of another country or otherwise owes allegiance to another country.

ILLEGAL MIGRANT A person who illegally enters a country with the intention of residing there.

ILLEGITIMACY State of being born of parents not married to each other. Toward the end of the 20th century, this term began to be replaced in many countries by others, such as "non-marital birth."

ILLEGITIMACY RATE The number of illegitimate births per 1000 nonmarried women. See also ILLEGITIMACY, ILLEGITMACY RATIO, and NON-MARITAL BIRTH.

ILLEGITIMACY RATIO The number of illegitimate live births per 1000 total live births. See also ILLEGITIMACY and ILLEGITIMACY RATE.

ILLEGITIMATE BIRTH See ILLEGITIMACY and NON-MARITAL BIRTH.

IMMIGRANT Residents of a given country entering another country in order to take up permanent residence. See also DOMESTIC MIGRATION, FOREIGN MIGRATION, and MIGRATION.

IMMIGRATION See FOREIGN MIGRATION.

IMPAIRMENTS Chronic health conditions involving abnormalities of body structure and appearance, the most common being chronic sensory and musculoskeletal conditions.

IMPUTATION In a sample survey or census, a general term used to describe the assignment of values to cases for which one or more variables have missing values due to "nonresponse." Four common methods are (1) deductive imputation, which is based on other information available from the case in question; (2) hot-deck imputation, which is based on information from "closest-matching" cases; (3) mean-value imputation, which uses means of variables as the source of assignment; and (4) regression-based imputation, in which models are constructed using cases with no missing values and a dependent variable is the one whose missing values will be imputed and the independent variables are those that yield acceptable regression equations. See also ALLOCATION, NONRESPONSE, and SUBSTITUTION.

INCIDENCE RATE The frequency with which an event, such as a new case of illness, occurs in a population at risk to the event over a given period of time.

INCREMENT The entry of an individual or set of individuals into a population of interest, where the population of interest is often defined by a model. In the case of a model of nuptiality, such an entry would be marriage. See also DECREMENT and INCREMENT-DECREMENT LIFE TABLE.

INCREMENT-DECREMENT LIFE TABLE A life table in which there are both entries and exits to the population of interest. It is often used in reference to multiple increments and multiple decrements. That is, when there is more than one way to enter and exit a population of interest (e.g., enter via marriage and inmigration and exit via divorce, death, and outmigration). In such a life table it is potentially possible to exit and reenter the population of interest. See also DECREMENT, INCREMENT, LIFE TABLE, and MULTISTATE LIFE TABLE.

INCOME Revenues or receipts accruing from business enterprise, labor, or invested capital.

INCOME DISTRIBUTION The way income is divided among various societal groups.

INDEX OF CONCENTRATION A measure of population concentration based on the Lorenz curve introduced by O. D. Duncan in 1957. It is algebraically equivalent to the index of dissimilarity. See also INDEX OF DISSIMILARITY.

INDEX OF DISSIMILARITY An index with a potential range from 0 to 1 that became accepted as a standard measure of segregation due to work reported by O.D. and B. Duncan in 1955. It is designed to measure the distributional equality of two variables (e.g., the distribution of income across a population; the geographic distribution of the Hispanic population relative to the distribution of the non-Hispanic population over the same geography). It is algebraically equivalent to the value that provides the maximum vertical distance from the diagonal to the Lorenz curve. It represents the proportion of cases for one variable that would have to be redistributed to achieve the same distribution of the other variable. It is used in many applications, but particularly as an index of residential segregation. As such, it is most identified with the "evenness" dimension of segregation. See also GINI INDEX, LORENZ CURVE, RESIDENTIAL SEPARATION, SEGREGATION, and SEGREGATION INDEX.

INDIRECT ESTIMATION The measurement of demographic phenomena using data that do not directly represent the phenomena of interest. See also DIRECT ESTIMATION.

INDIRECT STANDARDIZATION The adjustment of a summary rate (e.g., the crude death rate) for a population in question found in part by computing a weighted average of group-specific rates (e.g., age-specific death rates) of a "reference" population, where the weights are the specific groups (e.g., proportion in each age group) of the population in question. This procedure is designed to produce a summary rate that controls for the effects of population composition (e.g., age) and is usually used for purposes of comparison with indirectly standardized rates for other populations computed using the same reference population. To standardize a crude (death) rate by the indirect method, first multiply the age-specific (death) rates in the reference population by the population in the corresponding age groups of the population in question and sum the products to get the "expected" total (deaths) for the population in question. Then divide the expected total (deaths) into the total reported (deaths) for the population in question and multiply this ratio by the crude (death) rate of the reference population. See also DIRECT STANDARDIZATION and STANDARDIZATION.

INDUCED ABORTION See ABORTION.

INDUSTRY An economic product or activity (e.g., the making of automobiles, the design of software, the selling of insurance), usually grouped by the type of product made or activity undertaken. See also NORTH AMERICAN INDUSTRIAL CLASSIFICATION SYSTEM and OCCUPATION.

INFANT A child under one year of age.

INFANT MORTALITY RATE The number of deaths to infants before they reach one year of age, per 1000 live births in the same time period. See also ADJUSTED INFANT MORTALITY RAIE.

INFECUNDITY See STERILITY.

INFERTILITY A general term indicating an inability or diminished ability to produce children. See also FECUNDITY, STERILITY, and SUBFECUNDITY.

INFLATION-DEFLATION METHOD A technique that compensates for census coverage error by adjusting the demographic composition of the population of interest, but not its total number. It is sometimes used in conjunction with the cohort-component method of population projection, with the population in the launch year subject to "inflation" and the subsequent projection(s) subject to a compensating "deflation." It also is employed in the preparation of the official estimates of the population of the United States by age, sex, race, and ethnicity (Hispanic and non-Hispanic). See also COHORT-COMPONENT METHOD, COVERAGE ERROR, LAUNCH YEAR, and POPULATION ESTIMATE.

INMIGRANT A person who takes up residence within a "migration-defined" receiving area (the destination) after leaving a residence at a location outside of the receiving area (the origin), but one within the same country. For most countries, the destination and origin must be in different areas as defined by a political, administrative, or statistically defined boundary. In the United States, the destination must be in a different county than the origin for a person to be classified as an in-migrant by the Census Bureau. See also DESTINATION, IMMIGRANT, INMIGRATION RATE, MIGRANT, MIGRATION, MOVER, NET MIGRATION, NONMIGRANT, ORIGIN, and OUTMIGRANT.

INMIGRATION See INMIGRANT.

INMIGRATION RATE The ratio of the number of inmigrants to a receiving area (the destination) over a given period to any one of a number of measures of the population of the receiving area, including the population at the end of the period, the population at the beginning of the period, and so on. Sometimes the denominator is formed by using an approximation of the population at risk of migrating (e.g., the national population outside of the destination). See also DESTINATION, INMIGRANT, MIGRATION, NET MIGRATION RATE, and OUTMIGRATION RATE.

INSTANTANEOUS DEATH RATE See FORCE OF MORTALITY.

INSTRUMENTAL ACTIVITIES OF DAILY LIVING (IADLs) Measures of functioning that include certain more complex routines associated with independent living, such as using the telephone, going shopping, and handling one's own money. See ACTIVITIES OF DAILY LIVING.

INTERCENSAL The period between two successive censuses.

INTERMARRIAGE Marriage between members of different cultural, ethnic, racial, or religious groups.

INTERMEDIATE VARIABLES The biological and behavioral factors through which social, economic, psychological, and environmental variables affect demographic outcomes.

INTERNAL MIGRATION See DOMESTIC MIGRATION.

INTERNALLY DISPLACED PERSON A person similar in status to a refugee except that he or she is not outside his or her country of nationality. See also ASYLEE and REFUGEE.

INTERNATIONAL MIGRATION The movement across an international boundary for the purpose of establishing a new permanent residence. See also DOMESTIC MIGRATION.

INTERPOLATION The calculation of intermediate values for a given series of numbers. It is typically accomplished by using a mathematical formula, a graphic procedure, or a combination of the two. It typically imparts or even imposes a regularity to data and can, therefore, be used for smoothing, whether or not the imposed regularity is realistic. See also EXTRAPOLATION and SMOOTHING.

INTERVENING OPPORTUNITIES A theory of migration introduced in 1940 by S. Stouffer in which it is postulated that the level of movement between two places is dependent on the number of intervening opportunities between them. The theory suggests that the nature of places is more important than distance in determining where migrants end up.

INTRINSIC RATE (OF NATURAL INCREASE) A rate that would eventually be reached if a given population were subject to fixed mortality and fertility schedules, such that it became a "stable population" in the formal demographic sense. Intrinsic rates include the intrinsic birth rate, intrinsic death rate, and the intrinsic rate of increase. See also BIRTH RATE, DEATH RATE, and RATE OF NATURAL INCREASE.

ITEM NONRESPONSE See NONRESPONSE.

ITERATIVE PROPORTIONAL FITTING A method for adjusting a multiway distribution to a set of independently derived total values that approximates a least-squares approach. See also CONTROLLING, CONTROLS, and PLUS-MINUS METHOD.

J-INDEX A measure of the intrinsic growth of a population in a generation developed by A. J. Lotka that approximates the net reproduction rate and that, in turn, is approximated by the replacement index. When divided by the mean length of a generation it yields an estimate of the intrinsic rate of increase. See also MEAN LENGTH OF A GENERATION, NET REPRODUCTION RATE, REPLACEMENT INDEX, and INTRINSIC RATE.

JUMP-OFF YEAR See LAUNCH YEAR.

KAP SURVEY A survey assessing "knowledge," "attitude," and "practice" (KAP) in regard to issues such as family planning or disease prevention.

KARUP-KING METHOD A technique used to interpolate between given points or to subdivide groups based on a polynomial osculatory formula. See also INTERPOLATION.

KINSHIP NETWORK A family support system that operates both within and outside of a household.

LABOR FORCE Persons employed for pay or profit plus those who are unemployed but seeking work. In the United States, the total labor force of a given area includes the civilian labor force and members of the armed forces, as counted by their usual residence. See also ECONOMICALLY ACTIVE POPULATION and USUAL RESIDENCE.

LABOR FORCE PARTICIPATION RATE A conventional term for the proportion of a given age group in the labor force. See LABOR FORCE PARTICIPATION RATIO.

LABOR FORCE PARTICIPATION RATIO The proportion of a given age group (or age-sex group, etc.) in the labor force.

LATINO See HISPANIC.

LAUNCH YEAR The year in which a population projection is launched, typically the year of the most recent census. Sometimes referred to as the "jump-off" year, it is the starting point of the projection horizon. See also BASE PERIOD, PROJECTION HORIZON, TARGET YEAR, and POPULATION PROJECTION.

LEE-CARTER MODEL A relational model developed by R Lee and L. Carter for projecting mortality. See also GOMPERTZ CURVE, HELIGMAN-POLLARD MODEL, and MCNOWN-ROGERS METHOD.

LEFT-CENSORED See CENSORED.

LESLIE MATRIX An approach to population projection developed by P. H. Leslie in the late 1940s. It represents the calculations for cohort-component projections of the age distribution of the population in terms of a square matrix incorporating age-specific birth rates and survival rates and a vector containing the initial age composition of the population.

LESS DEVELOPED COUNTRIES See DEVELOPING COUNTRIES.

LEXIS DIAGRAM A graphic technique developed apparently independently by several people, but largely attributed to Wilhelm Lexis (hence, the name "Lexis diagram"), that is designed to reveal the relationship between age, time, and population change, with particular applications to cohort analysis, life table construction, and population estimation. See also COHORT ANALYSIS and LIFE TABLE.

LIFE CYCLE A sequence of significant events through which an individual or group (e.g., family, household), passes over time.

LIFE EXPECTANCY The average number of years of life remaining to a group of persons who reached a given age, as calculated from a life table. See also LIFE SPAN, LIFE TABLE, and SURVIVAL RATE.

LIFE SPAN The extreme upper limits of human life. The maximum age that humans as a species could reach under optimum conditions. See also LIFE EXPECTANCY.

LIFE TABLE A statistical model composed of a combination of age-specific mortality rates for a given population. A period life table (also known as a cross-sectional life table) is constructed using mortality and age data from a single point in time; a generation life table (also known as a cohort life table) is based on the mortality of an actual birth cohort followed over time (to its extinction). A complete or unabridged life table contains mortality information for single years of age, while an abridged table contains information by age group. See also GENERATION LIFE TABLE, INCREMENT-DECREMENT LIFE TABLE, LIFE EXPECTANCY, PERIOD LIFE TABLE, STANDARD LIFE TABLE, and SURVIVAL RATE.

LIFE TABLE FUNCTIONS   The fundamental elements of a life table, to include the number surviving to a given age, the number of deaths to those surviving to a given birthday before they reach a subsequent birthday, the probability of dying before reaching a subsequent birthday for those who survived to a given birthday, the number alive between two birthdays, and the years of life remaining for those who survive to a given birthday (including birth). Life table functions can be interpreted in two ways: (1) as a depiction of the lifetime mortality experience of a cohort of newborns and (2) as a stationary population that would result from a fixed mortality schedule and a constant number of annual births equal to the constant number of annual deaths resulting from the fixed mortality schedule. See also LIFE TABLE.

LIFE TABLE SURVIVAL RATE   See SURVIVAL RATE.

LIFETIME MIGRATION   Migration that has occurred between birth and a given point in which a census or survey is conducted.

LIVE BIRTH   See BIRTH.

LIVE-BIRTH PREGNANCY RATE   The ratio of live births to conceptions.

LOGISTIC CURVE   A mathematical model that depicts an S-Shaped curve indicative of three stages of population change: (1) an initial period of slow growth, (2) a subsequent period of rapid growth, and (3) a final period in which growth slows and comes to a halt. See also DEMOGRAPHIC TRANSITION.

LOGIT   A mathematical transformation, often used in event history analysis. For a number between 0 and 1, its logit is usually defined as the natural logarithm of the number divided by one minus the same number: $\text{logit}(n) = \ln[n/(1 - n)]$, where $0 < n < 1$. Sometimes it is defined as $\text{logit}(n) = (.5)\{\ln[n/(1 - n)]\}$. See also EVENT HISTORY ANALYSIS, ODDS RATIO, and PROBIT.

LOGIT LIFE TABLE SYSTEM   A system of model life tables initially developed by William Brass that relies on forming logits of the proportion of deaths to those who survived to a given birthday before reaching a subsequent birthday. See also LOGIT.

LOGIT TRANSFORM   See LOGIT.

LONG FORM   In the United States, the decennial census form given on a sample basis (approximately one in six households) that is designed to collect a wide range of population and housing data. The data collected go well beyond the basic information collected in the short form, which is given to the remaining households. Note, however, that the questions on the short form are contained in the long form. See also SHORT FORM.

LONG-TERM CARE   The provision of health, personal care, and social services over time to individuals who have functional limitations.

LONGEVITY   See LIFE SPAN.

LONGITUDINAL STUDIES   Those studies in which variables relating to an individual or group of individuals are assessed over a period of time.

LORENZ CURVE   Named after M. Lorenz, who introduced it in 1905, it is used to measure the distributional equality of two variables (e.g., the distribution of income across a population; the geographic distribution of the Hispanic population relative to the distribution of the non-Hispanic population over the same geography). To plot the curve, units in both variables are aggregated and the cumulative proportion of one variable is plotted against the corresponding cumulative proportion of the other (e.g., $x\%$ of the people have $y\%$ of all income). See also GINI INDEX, INDEX OF DISSIMILARITY, and SEGREGATION INDEX.

LOW BIRTH WEIGHT   Birth weight of 2500 grams or less.

MAJOR CIVIL DIVISION   A "primary" subnational political area established by law or a related process. See also CENSUS GEOGRAPHY and MINOR CIVIL DIVISION.

MALTHUSIAN GROWTH   The hypothesis that unless negative checks (i.e., T. Malthus's idea of "moral restraint") are introduced, a population increases geometrically until some type of positive check is imposed (i.e., famine, war, pestilence).

MALTHUSIANISM   Doctrine based on the theory of population growth proposed by T. space Malthus in the early 19th century. It is based on the idea that population growth must be limited in order to maximize economic welfare. See also NEO-MALTHUSIANISM.

MARITAL FERTILITY   The reproductive performance of married couples.

MARITAL SEPARATION   See SEPARATION.

MARKOV PROCESS (also known as a MARKOV CHAIN)   A systems model named after A. A. Markov that is specified by transition probabilities between the different states of the system, where the transition probabilities are dependent solely on the present distribution of the population in these states. See also MULTISTATE LIFE TABLE and TRANSITION PROBABILITY.

MARRIAGE   The social institution involving legal or religious sanction whereby men and women are joined together for the purpose of founding a family unit. In some countries, marriage includes couples joined for purposes other than founding a family unit. See also DIVORCE, SINGLE, and WIDOWED.

MARRIAGE COHORT   The set of marriages occurring at a given point in time.

MARRIAGE POSTPONEMENT   Delaying marriage beyond the early reproductive years.

MARRIAGE SQUEEZE   An imbalance in the number of suitable marriage partners, as defined by social convention and custom.

MASTER ADDRESS FILE (MAF)   In the United States, the set of records maintained by the Census Bureau for purposes of conducting the decennial census. It is intended to represent the geographic location of every housing unit.

MATCHED GROUPS   A group constructed on a case-by-case basis through matching of sets of records according to a limited number of characteristics.

MATCHING (of records)   Assembly of data in a common format from different sources but pertaining to the same unit of observation (e.g., a person, household, or an event such as death). Also known as record matching and data linkage. See also DUAL SYSTEMS ESTIMATION.

MATHEMATICAL DEMOGRAPHY   The field of demography that applies mathematical analysis to the interpretation, analysis, and solution of issues in demography, particularly with respect to population structure and population dynamics.

MATERNAL MORTALITY   Deaths to women in a given population resulting from complications of pregnancy or childbirth.

MATERNAL MORTALITY RATE   Deaths due to puerperal causes during a year per 100,000 births during the year.

McNOWN-ROGERS METHOD   A parameterized time series model developed by R. McNown and A. Rogers for mortality projections. See also GOMPERTZ CURVE, HELIGMAN-POLLARD MODEL, and LEE-CARTER METHOD.

MEAN AGE AT DEATH   The arithmetic mean age at death of the reported deaths in a given year. In the life table the mean age at death of life table deaths is equal to the life expectancy at birth in the same life table.

MEAN GENERATIONAL LENGTH   See MEAN LENGTH OF A GENERATION.

MEAN LENGTH OF A GENERATION   A concept used in stable population theory and reproductivity analysis to represent the mean age of mothers at the birth of their daughters. See also STABLE POPULATION.

MEAN POPULATION AGE   The average age of all members of a population.

MEDIAN LENGTH OF LIFE   The age by which half of an original cohort of births has died according to a particular set of age-specific death rates. Corresponds to the median age at death in a life table. See also LIFE TABLE.

MEDIAN POPULATION AGE   The age at which a population is divided into two equally sized groups.

METROPOLITAN AREA   In the United States, this refers to a family of specific census geographies intended to represent a large population nucleus and aggregations thereof. Specific types of include "primary metropolitan statistical area" and "standard consolidated statistical area." See also CENSUS GEOGRAPHY, PRIMARY METROPOLITAN STATISTICAL AREA, and STANARD CONSOLIDATED STATISTICAL AREA.

METROPOLITAN STATISTICAL AREA   A statistical area defined in the censuses of some countries consisting of a central city and the surrounding political areas linked to the central city by economic and urban bonds. In the United States it is a family of geographic entities consisting a large population nucleus and the densely populated aggregations thereof. Specific types include "primary metropolitan statistical area" and "standard consolidated statistical area." See PRIMARY METROPOLI-

TAN STATISTICAL AREA and STANDARD CONSOLIDATED STATISTICAL AREA.

MIGRANT   A person who makes a relatively permanent change of residence from one country, or region within a country (an origin), to another (the destination) during a specified (migration) period. For most countries, the change must be across a political, administrative, or statistically defined boundary for a person to be classified as a migrant. In the United States, the origin and destination must be in different counties for a person to be classified as a migrant. See also DESTINATION, EMIGRANT, IMMIGRANT, INMIGRANT, MIGRATION, MOVER, NONMIGRANT, ORIGIN, and OUTMIGRANT.

MIGRATION   A general term for the incidence of movement by individuals, groups or populations seeking to make relatively permanent changes of residence. One of the components of population change. See also ASYLEE, COMMUTING, COMPONENTS OF CHANGE, DESTINATION, DOMESTIC MIGRATION, EMIGRANT, FOREIGN-BORN, GROSS MIGRATION, IMMIGRANT, INMIGRANT, INTERNALLY DISPLACED PERSONS, INTERNATIONAL MIGRATION, MIGRANT, MOBILITY, MOVER, NATIVE, NET MIGRATION, NONMIGRANT, ORIGIN, OUTMIGRANT, and REFUGEE.

MIGRATION EFFECTIVENESS INDEX   A measure of the "economy" of movement into an area or between two areas, representing the gap between the volume of movement actually achieved and the volume of movement required to effect the redistribution achieved. One such measure is the ratio of net migration to a given area to the total number of interarea migrants.

MIGRATION HISTORY   Information obtained in a census or a sample survey that provides lifetime migration data. See also LIFETIME MIGRATION.

MIGRATION PREFERENCE INDEX   As defined by R. Bachi in 1957, the ratio of the actual to the expected number of migrants to a given area, where the expected number is directly proportional to both the population at the origin and the destination.

MIGRATION STATUS   See MOBILITY STATUS.

MIGRATION STREAM   A group of migrants with a common origin and destination over a given period. See also COUNTERSTREAM.

MILITARY DEPENDENT POPULATION   Persons who are dependents of members of the armed forces.

MILITARY POPULATION   Persons who are members of the armed forces.

MINOR CIVIL DIVISION   A "secondary" subnational political area established by law or a related process. See also CENSUS GEOGRAPHY and MAJOR CIVIL DIVISION.

MINORITY GROUP   A group constituting a numerical minority within the general population, with characteristics that distinguish it from the general population (e.g., race, ethnicity).

MISCARRIAGE   A type of fetal loss occurring early in pregnancy that is spontaneous. See also ABORTION, FETALLOSS.

MOBILITY, GEOGRAPHIC Any move resulting in a change of residence. See also DOMESTIC MIGRATION and MIGRATION.

MOBILITY, OCCUPATIONAL See OCCUPATIONAL MOBILITY.

MOBILITY, SOCIAL See SOCIAL MOBILITY.

MOBILITY RATE The ratio of the number of movers over a given time period to the population at risk of moving over the same period. In practice, the usual choice of base population is the census (or estimated) population at the end of the period. See also INMIGRATION RATE, MIGRATION, and OUTMIGRATION RATE.

MOBILITY STATUS A classification of people based on their residential locations at the beginning and end of a given time period.

MODEL A generalized representation of a demographic process, set of demographic relationships, pattern of mortality, fertility, migration, or marriage, or method of population estimation or projection.

MODEL LIFE TABLE A life table based on the generalization of empirical relationships derived from a group of observed life tables. See also BRASS RELATIONAL MODEL LIFE TABLES and COALE-DEMENY MODEL LIFE TABLES.

MOMENTUM OF POPULATION GROWTH The tendency of a population to increase for as many as 70 years after reaching replacement level fertility. It may be measured as the projected percentage increase in the population between the current level and the level when it is projected to reach stationarity in the absence of migration. See also STATIONARY POPULATION.

MORBIDITY A general term for any health condition that encompasses diseases, injuries, and impairments in a population or group.

MORTALITY A general term for the incidence of deaths in a population or group. One of the components of population change. See also COMPONENTS OF CHANGE.

MOTHER TONGUE The language used in the household during earliest childhood; the initial language learned by a person.

MOVER A person who reports in a census or survey that he or she lived at a different address at an earlier date (e.g., 5 years before the census or survey). In the United States, a mover is classified by the Census Bureau as a person who changed residence, but continued to reside within the same county. See also MIGRATION.

MULTIPARITY The state of a woman who has given birth to more than one child.

MULTIPLE BIRTH More than one birth resulting from the same pregnancy.

MULTIPLE DECREMENT TABLE See MULTISTATE LIFE TABLE.

MULTIPLE INCREMENT TABLE See MULTISTATE LIFE TABLE.

MULTIPLE INCREMENT-DECREMENT LIFE TABLE See MULTISTATE LIFE TABLE.

MULTIPLE INCREMENT-DECREMENT TABLE See MULTISTATE LIFE TABLE.

MULTIREGIONAL ANALYSIS An analysis of multiregional systems in which spatial and demographic factors are linked.

MULTISTATE LIFE TABLE An extension of the standard life table in which multiple transitions between states are possible and the transitions are expressed in terms of transition probabilities between states. See also DECREMENT, INCREMENT, INCREMENT-DECREMENT LIFE TABLE, and MARKOV PROCESS.

MYER'S INDEX A measure of age heaping introduced by R. Myers in 1940 that involves a comparison of expected proportions of population at ages with each terminal digit and the "reported" proportions of the population at the ages with these terminal digits. See also AGE HEAPING and WHIPPLE'S INDEX.

NAICS See NORTH AMERICAN INDUSTRIAL CLASSIFICATION SYSTEM.

NATALITY A general term for the factor of birth in population change. See also FERTILITY.

NATIONAL CENSUS SURVIVAL RATE A ratio that purports to express the probability of survival from one age group to another and from one date to another on the basis of two national censuses. In addition to the effects of mortality, it also can include the effects of net immigration and net census undercount error where these latter two effects exist and for which no special adjustments are made. See also HAMILTON-PERRY METHOD, NET CENSUS UNDERCOUNT ERROR, and SURVIVAL RATE.

NATIONALITY Political nationality refers to citizenship of a specific nation. In some countries, ethnic nationality also is recognized, whereby residents are identified by ethnicity.

NATIVE Persons born in a particular country or region as distinguished from foreign-born.

NATURAL DECREASE See NATURAL INCREASE.

NATURAL FERTILITY The level of fertility in a population in which deliberate control of childbearing (e.g., contraception, abstinence) is not practiced.

NATURAL INCREASE The excess of births over deaths in a population is defined as natural increase; an excess of deaths over births is defined as natural decrease.

NATURALIZATION In the United States the conferring, by any of a variety of methods, of citizenship upon a person after birth.

NEO-MALTHUSIANISM The theory that only through the limitation of births by the use of artificial contraceptives can the size of a population be controlled to maximize economic welfare. See also MALTHUSIAN.

NEONATAL The period of life from birth to 28 days.

NEONATAL DEATH RATE Deaths during the first 28 days of life, per 1000 live births.

NET CENSUS UNDERCOUNT ERROR The estimated level of coverage and reporting error in a census computed by algebraically adding estimated overcounts and estimated undercounts for population groups (e.g., age-sex-race) and summing them. See also CORRECTED CENSUS POPULATION, COVERAGE ERROR, NONRANDOM ERROR, and TRUE POPULATION.

NET MIGRATION The difference between the number of inmigrants and the number of outmigrants for a given area (e.g., a county) over a given period of time: Net = In − Out. See also GROSS MIGRATION, INMIGRANT, MIGRATION, NET MIGRATION RATE, and OUTMIGRANT.

NET MIGRATION RATE The ratio of net migration for a given area (e.g., a county) over a given period to any one of a number of measures of the population of the area, including the population at the end of the period, the population at the beginning of the period, and so on. Sometimes the denominator is formed by using a population outside of the area (e.g., the national population outside of the county). See also INMIGRATION RATE, MIGRATION, NET MIGRATION, and OUTMIGRATION RATE.

NET NUMBER OF MIGRANTS See NET MIGRATION.

NET RATE OF REPRODUCTION See NET REPRODUCTION RATE.

NET REPRODUCTION RATE Average number of daughters born per woman (or per 1000 women) by the end of her childbearing years, subject to the age-specific birthrates and survival rates of a given year. Takes into account that some women will die before completing their childbearing years. See also POPULATION REPLACEMENT.

NONINTERVIEW See NONRESPONDENT.

NONMARITAL BIRTH State of being born of parents not married to each other. Toward the end of the 20th century this term began to replace "Illegitimacy" in many countries. See ILLEGITIMACY.

NONMETROPOLITAN POPULATION The number of people living outside large urban settlements. In the United States, this represents the population outside metropolitan statistical areas. See also CENSUS GEOGRAPHY.

NONMIGRANT In a census or survey, an individual who resided in an area both at the beginning and end of the designated migration period. Alternatively, an individual who has neither migrated into nor migrated out of his or her area of residence. See also INMIGRANT, MIGRATION, MOVER, NET MIGRATION, and OUTMIGRANT.

NONRANDOM ERROR All errors not due to the effects of random sample selection (i.e., random error). It can occur both in a sample survey and in a population census. Examples include nonresponse, incorrect answers by a valid respondent and answers given by a nonvalid respondent, as well as coding and other processing errors. Statistical inference can only be used to estimate random error, not nonrandom error. See also NET CENSUS UNDERCOUNT ERROR, NONRESPONSE, POPULATION, RANDOM ERROR, SAMPLE, and TOTAL ERROR.

NONRENEWABLE EVENT Something that can, in principle, be experienced only once by a member of a population of interest. See also RENEWABLE EVENT.

NONRESPONDENT In a sample survey or census, a respondent who refuses to be interviewed or is otherwise unable to take part. See also NONRESPONSE.

NONRESPONSE Missing data on a form used in a survey or census due to a number of reasons, including the refusal of a respondent to answer, the inability to locate a potential respondent, the inability of a respondent (or informant) to answer questions, or the omission of answers due to a clerical or some other form of error. Total nonresponse refers to a case (i.e., an observation) in which all variables have missing values, and item nonresponse refers to a case in which fewer than all variables have one or more missing values. Imputation is often used to estimate values for cases in which they are missing. See also IMPUTATION, NONRANDOM ERROR, and NONRESPONDENT.

NONRESPONSE ERROR See NONRESPONSE.

NORTH AMERICAN INDUSTRIAL CLASSIFICATION SYSTEM (NAICS) In the United States, the standard classification system for coding the industry reported by employed persons in censuses and surveys, applicable since the 1997 economic census when it replaced the 1987 Standard Industrial Code. See also INDUSTRY, OCCUPATION, STANDARD INDUSTRIAL CODE, and STANDARD OCCUPATIONAL CODE.

NUCLEAR FAMILY A family composed of husband and wife with their children.

NULLIPARITY The state of a woman who has never given birth to a child.

NUMBER OF CHILDREN See FAMILY SIZE.

NUPTIAL AGE See MARRIAGE AGE.

NUPTIALITY A general term for the incidence of both marriage formation and marital dissolution in a population. See also MARRIAGE.

NUPTIALITY TABLE An extension of the standard life table that incorporates increments and decrements such as first marriage, first divorce, second marriage, second divorce, and so on. Nuptiality tables may deal with marriage or marital dissolution or combination of both. See also LIFE TABLE and NUPTIALITY.

OCCUPATION The type of work done (e.g., firefighter, laborer, librarian, teacher), a position in the labor force, usually grouped by similarity of work done or the skills and training required. See also INDUSTRY, OCCUPATIONAL STATUS, and STANDARD OCCUPATIONAL CODE.

OCCUPATIONAL STATUS The classification of an individual or group of persons with respect to their occupation. For example, one broad category of occupations is sales, another is protective service. This also can refer to the position of an individual or group in relation to the social ranking of occupations. See also OCCUPATION.

OCCURRENCE-EXPOSURE RATIO   The ratio of the number of events occurring during a given period to the population at risk during the same period. The population at risk may be measured in different ways.

ODDS RATIO   As defined for a dichotomous variable, the ratio of the proportion of the population having a characteristic of interest to the proportion not having the characteristic. For example, the proportion of the population in poverty to the proportion not in poverty. The logarithm of the odds ratio is termed a logit. See also LOGIT.

OPEN-ENDED INTERVAL   A class interval in a distribution of grouped data that is not bounded on one end. For example, in a distribution of data on income, the highest income class may be given as $100,000 or more; in a life table, the last age interval may be given as 85 years and over. In a longitudinal analysis, the period between the most recent occurrence of an event of interest (e.g., a live birth) and a subsequent time point. For example, in a survey of birth histories, the period between the second birth and the survey would constitute an open-ended interval for a woman reporting two births, whereas the periods between her first and second birth would be a closed interval.

OPEN INTERVAL   See OPEN-ENDED INTERVAL.

OPEN LIVE-BIRTH INTERVAL   The time elapsed since the most recent birth, typically measured as an average for a group of women; an index that directly reflects the effect of increased spacing between births.

ORGANIZATIONAL DEMOGRAPHY   The study of the size, distribution, and composition of organizations (e.g., corporations, book clubs, university alumni groups, farm cooperatives, the military), to include the organizations themselves, their members, dependents, or even combinations thereof, along with their components of change and the determinants and consequences of change. See also DEMOGRAPHY.

ORIGIN   The place of residence that a migrant left at the start of a given (migration) period. See also DESTINATION, MIGRANT, and MIGRATION.

ORPHAN   A child who has been abandoned or whose parents are deceased.

ORPHANHOOD METHODS   A set of survey and census-based techniques for estimating adult mortality in a population that lacks reliable mortality data. It is based on identifying the proportion of respondents with living mothers and fathers. See also SIBLING METHODS.

OSCULATORY INTERPOLATION   An interpolation method that involves combining higher-order polynomial formulas into one equation, designed to provide a smooth junction between two adjacent groups of data (e.g., age group 5 to 9 and age group 10 to 14). See also INTERPOLATION.

OUTMIGRANT   A person who leaves his or her residence in a "migration-defined" sending area (the origin) to take up residence at a location outside of the sending area (the destination) but within the same country. For most countries, the origin and destinaiton must be in different areas as defined by a political, administrative, or statistically defined boundary. In the United States, the origin must be in a different county than the desti-

nation for a person to be classified as an outmigrant by the Census Bureau. See also DESTINATION, EMIGRANT, INMIGRANT, MIGRANT, MIGRATION, MOVER, NET MIGRATION, NONMIGRANT, ORIGIN, and OUTMIGRATION RATE.

OUTMIGRATION   See INTERNAL MIGRATION.

OUTMIGRATION RATE   The ratio of the number of outmigrants from a sending area (the origin) over a given period to some measure of the population of the sending area, including the population at the beginning of the period, the population at the end of the period, and so on. See also INMIGRATION RATE, MIGRATION, NET MIGRATION RATE, ORIGIN and OUTMIGRANT.

OVERCOUNT   In a census, this can be due to counting some people more than once, counting people in a census who are not members of the population in question, or a combination of both. See also NET CENSUS UNDERCOUNT ERROR and UNDERCOUNT.

OWN-CHILD METHOD   A census or survey-based method for measuring fertility that uses counts of children living with their mothers.

PALEODEMOGRAPHY   See PREHISTORIC DEMOGRAPHY.

PARITY   The number of live births born to a woman.

PARITY PROGRESSION RATIO   The proportion of women of a given parity who proceed to have at least one additional live birth. See also PARITY.

PARITY SPECIFIC BIRTH RATE   Live births to women of specific parities. See also PARITY.

PARTIAL MIGRATION RATE   The number of inmigrants from a particular origin to a given destination relative to the population of either the origin or destination.

PARTICIPATION RATE   The proportion of a population or segment of a population with a certain characteristic, usually social or economic (e.g., the proportion aged 10 to 14 who are enrolled in school).

PEARL'S FORMULA   A measure of contraceptive effectiveness developed by R. Pearl defined as the pregnancy rate per 100 women-years of contraceptive use.

PERCENTAGE   See PROPORTION.

PERINATAL DEATH RATE   See PERINATAL MORTALITY RATE.

PERINATAL MORTALITY RATE   The number of fetal losses of 28 weeks gestation or more plus neonatal deaths in the first seven days after birth, per 1000 live births in a given year. See also DEATH RATE, FETAL LOSS, and POSTNEONATAL DEATH RATE.

PERIOD ANALYSIS   The analysis of demographic data observed during a brief period of time (usually one year), such as death registrations, or a single date, such as census data on marital status, and sometimes at several points of time. The data are typically composed of more than one cohort. See also AGE-PERIOD-COHORT EFFECT, COHORT ANALYSIS, PERIOD EFFECT, and PERIOD MEASURE.

PERIOD EFFECT An analytical perspective that attempts to determine the effect of a period event (e.g., a war, famine, or natural disaster) on a variable of interest (as distinct from an age or cohort effect). See also AGE EFFECT, AGE-PERIOD-COHORT EFFECT, COHORT EFFECT, and PERIOD ANALYSIS.

PERIOD LIFE TABLE A life table based on mortality data collected at a given point in time (1 year) or a short period (2 or 3 years) for a given population. See also GENERATION LIFE TABLE and LIFE TABLE.

PERIOD MEASURE A summary measure of data collected during a brief period of time (usually 1 year) that typically represent more than one cohort. See also COHORT MEASURE and PERIOD ANALYSIS.

PERSON-YEARS LIVED The total number of years (and fractions thereof) lived by a given population or population segment during a given period of time. It is approximated by computing the product of (1) the number of persons in the population or population segment and (2) the amount of time in years (and fractions thereof) lived by these same persons during the time in question. See also AT-RISK POPULATION and LIFE TABLE.

PLACE In United States census geography, either an incorporated area with a general purpose government or other concentration of population with recognized boundaries called a census designated place.

PLACE OF RESIDENCE See USUAL RESIDENCE.

PLUS-MINUS METHOD A "controlling" technique that attempts to compensate for both increasing and decreasing subsets of a population of interest by using two separate adjustment factors. For example, one might use the plus-minus method in adjusting post-censal population estimates of census tracts to an estimate of the county containing the tracts if some tracts show growth since the last census and others show decline. See also CONTROLLING, CONTROLS, and ITERATIVE PROPORTIONAL FITTING.

POPULATION In the demographic sense, the "inhabitants" of a given area at a given time, where inhabitants could be defined either on the de facto or de jure basis (but not a mixture of both). Note that the concept of "area" can be generalized beyond the geographical sense to include, for example, formal organizations. In the statistical sense, the term "population" refers to the entire set of persons (or phenomenon) of interest in a particular study, as compared to a sample, which refers to a subset of the whole. See also CENSUS, DE FACTO POPULATION, DE JURE POPULATION, DEMOGRAPHY, SAMPLE, and SPECIAL POPULATION.

POPULATION AT RISK See AT-RISK POPULATION.

POPULATION CHANGE Change in the number of inhabitants of an area. The change may be an increase, a decrease, or zero.

POPULATION COMPONENT EQUATION See BALANCING EQUATION.

POPULATION COMPOSITION The classification of members of a population by one or more characteristics such as age, sex, race, and ethnicity. It can be presented in either absolute or relative numbers. "Population distribution" and "population structure" are often used as synonyms. See also POPULATION DISTRIBUTION.

POPULATION DECREASE Reduction in the number of inhabitants in an area.

POPULATION DENSITY Number of persons per unit of land area.

POPULATION DISTRIBUTION Usually refers to the location of a population over space at a given time, but sometimes used as a synonym for population composition. See also POPULATION COMPOSITION.

POPULATION DYNAMICS Changes in population size and structure due to fertility, mortality, and migration, or the analysis of population size and structure in these terms.

POPULATION ESTIMATE An approximation of a current or past population of a given area at a given time, or its distribution and composition, in the absence of a complete enumeration, ideally done in accordance with one of two standards for defining a population, de facto or de jure. See also ADMINISTRATIVE RECORDS METHOD, CENSAL-RATIO METHOD, CENSUS, CENSUS DEFINED RESIDENT, CHANGE IN STOCK METHOD, COMPONENT METHOD, COMPOSITE METHOD, DE FACTO POPULATION, DE JURE POPULATION, HOUSING UNIT METHOD, POPULATION PROJECTION, RATIO-CORRELATION METHOD, RATIO ESTIMATION, SYNTHETIC METHOD, and VITAL RATES METHOD.

POPULATION FORECAST An approximation of the future size of the population for a given area, often including its composition and distribution. A forecast usually is one of a set of projections selected as the most likely representation of the future. See also POPULATION ESTIMATE and POPULATION PROJECTION.

POPULATION MOMENTUM See MOMENTUM OF POPULATION GROWTH.

POPULATION POTENTIAL A measure of the influence of population on a given point (or alternatively, the accessibility of a population to a given point). Influence is assumed to decline with the distance from the point, so population potential is measured as the sum of the reciprocals of the distances of individuals from the selected point. Points of equal influence may be joined on a map to show contours. See also SITE POTENTIAL and WORKPLACE POTENTIAL.

POPULATION PROJECTION The numerical outcome of a particular set of implicit and explicit assumptions regarding future values of the components of population change for a given area in combination with an algorithm. Strictly speaking, it is a conditional statement about the size of a future population (often along with its composition and distribution), ideally made in accordance with one of the two standards used in defining a population, de facto or de jure. See also BASE PERIOD, CENSUS, CENSUS DEFINED RESIDENT, COHORT-COMPONENT METHOD, DE FACTO POPULATION, DE JURE POPULATION, LAUNCH YEAR, POPULATION ESTIMATE, POPULATION FORECAST, PROJECTION HORIZON, and TARGET YEAR.

POPULATION PYRAMID A graphic device that shows the age-sex composition of a given population and possibly other characteristics as well. It is in pyramidal form, ranging from an equilateral triangle to a near-rectangle, with the shape determined by the effects of the components of population change on a prior age-sex composition.

POPULATION REGISTER An administrative record system used by many countries (e.g., China, Finland, Japan, and Sweden) that requires residents to register their place of residence, usually at a local police station. By itself, such a system provides limited demographic information (e.g., total population), but where it can be matched to other administrative record systems (e.g., tax, social and health care services), the result is often a system that provides a wide range of longitudinal and cross-sectional demographic information.

POPULATION REPLACEMENT In general, the process of renewal by which a population replaces losses from deaths by means of births. In stable population theory, it refers to the extent to which women in the population are being replaced over the course of a generation or a year. It is measured by the net reproduction rate for a generation and by the intrinsic rate of increase on an annual basis. These measures allow for both the level of fertility and the level of mortality through the childbearing ages. Exact replacement requires a net reproduction rate of 1.00. See also NET REPRODUCTION RATE.

POPULATION SIZE The number of persons inhabiting a given area at a given time. See also CENSUS and POPULATION.

POPULATION STATISTICS These are generally comprised of vital statistics, migration statistics, and census and survey data, but they vary by country in that not all countries collect all types of data. They also may include administrative record data, including population register data.

POPULATION STRUCTURE See POPULATION COMPOSITION.

POST-NEONATAL MORTALITY RATE Deaths to those aged 28 to 364 days, per 1000 live births.

POST-PARTUM AMENORRHEA The temporary cessation of menstruation following childbirth; including both normal and prolonged periods of cessation. See also AMENORRHEA.

POSTPONED CHILDBEARING See DELAYED CHILDBEARING.

POVERTY An economic and social condition for an individual, family, or household in which the level of living is below the standard of the community or some other reference. In the United States, the poverty level set is by the federal government for families and their members on the basis of dollar thresholds based on money income received, size of family, number of children, and age of family head (above and below age 65). A minimum standard is set for a family of four and the other thresholds are determined in relation to this standard.

PREGNANCY Condition of a woman having a developing embryo or fetus in the body after the union of a spermatozoon and an ovum. A first-trimester pregnancy is the period of pregnancy from the first day of the last normal menstrual period through the completion of the 14th week (98 days) of gestation.

A second-trimester pregnancy is the period of pregnancy from the beginning of the 15th week through the completion of the 28th week (99 to 196 days) of gestation. A third-trimester pregnancy is the period following completion of the 28th week.

PREGNANCY HISTORY A record of all pregnancies experienced by a woman, or group of women, either followed on a panel basis or reporting in a single survey.

PREGNANCY INTERVAL The period of time between two consecutive pregnancies.

PREGNANCY OUTCOME The end result of a given pregnancy, including spontaneous abortion, induced abortion, fetal loss, and live birth.

PREGNANCY RATE The ratio of the number of conceptions occurring during a given time period to some measure (e.g., the mean) of the number of women of reproductive age calculated for the same period.

PREGNANCY WASTAGE See FETAL LOSS.

PREHISTORIC DEMOGRAPHY The study of populations that existed prior to recorded history and the set of methods developed for this type of study.

PREMATURE BIRTH See PREMATURE INFANT.

PREMATURE INFANT A birth occurring before the normal 38 weeks of gestation.

PREMATURE MORTALITY The years of potential life lost—that is, a death that occurs to a person prior to reaching the life expectancy applicable to him or her. See also LIFE TABLE.

PREVALENCE The number of persons who have a given characteristic (e.g., disease, contraceptive use, impairment, labor force participation) in a given population at a designated time or who had the characteristic at any time during a designated period, such as a year. See also PREVALENCE RATE.

PREVALENCE RATE (RATIO) The proportion of persons in a population who have a particular disease or attribute at a specified time (point prevalence) or at any time during a designated period, such as a year (period prevalence). See also PREVALENCE.

PRIMARY METROPOLITAN STATISTICAL AREA In the United States, a census-based piece of geography defined by the Office of Management and Budget that is comprised of a central city and county and adjoining counties linked to the central city by social and economic interactions that meet prescribed standards. See also CENSUS GEOGRAPHY, METROPOLITAN AREA, and STANDARD CONSOLIDATED AREA.

PRIMIPARITY The state of a woman who has given birth to her first and only child.

PROBABILITY A ratio in which the numerator consists of those in a population experiencing an event of interest (e.g., death) over a specified period of time, while the denominator consists of the at-risk population. See also AT-RISK POPULATION, PROPORTION, RATE, and RATIO.

PROBIT A mathematical transformation, often used in event history analysis, for "linearizing" the cumulative normal distribution of a variable of interest. The probit unit is $y = 5 + Z(p)$, where p = the prevalence of response at each dose level and $Z(p)$ = the corresponding value of the standard cumulative normal distribution. See also EVENT HISTORY ANALYSIS and LOGIT.

PROJECTED BIRTHS   In reference to a population projection, this refers to the numerical outcome of a particular set of implicit and explicit assumptions regarding future values of fertility for a given population in combination with an algorithm. However, it is sometimes used as a synonym for "births expected." See BIRTHS EXPECTED and POPULATION PROJECTION.

PROJECTION   See POPULATION PROJECTION.

PROJECTION HORIZON   In a population projection, the period between the launch year and the target year. See also BASE PERIOD, LAUNCH YEAR, and TARGET YEAR; also see POPULATION PROJECTION.

PROPORTION   A ratio used to describe the status of a population with respect to some characteristic (e.g., married), where the numerator is part of the denominator. When multiplied by 100, a proportion is known as a "percentage." See also PROBABILITY, RATE, and RATIO.

PROPORTIONAL HAZARDS   The examination of "exogenous" explanatory variables in the analysis of survival time and related data. See also PROPORTIONAL HAZARDS MODEL and SURVIVAL.

PROPORTIONAL HAZARDS MODEL   A regression-based approach to the analysis of survival or duration data designed to examine survival time, failure time, or other duration data in terms of the effect of exogenous explanatory variables. See also PROPORTIONAL HAZARDS.

PRORATA ADJUSTMENT   Adjustment of a distribution to an assigned total in proportion to the frequencies in this distribution. See also CONTROLS.

PROXIMATE DETERMINANTS OF FERTILITY   See INTERMEDIATE FERTILITY VARIABLES.

PUBLIC USE MICRODATA SAMPLE (PUMS)   In the United States and elsewhere, this usually refers to a hierarchically structured data set that contains individual, family, and household information in a given record and for which confidentiality is maintained by deleting identifying information. It is typically obtained by sampling from census records.

QUASI-STABLE POPULATION   A population not affected by migration with constant fertility and gradually changing mortality. It also is used to refer specifically to a formerly stable population in which fertility remains constant but mortality is gradually changing. See also STABLE POPULATION.

RACE   In theory, classification of the members of a population in terms of biological ancestry, in which a range of physical characteristics, such as hair structure, cephalic index, and so on, is employed to assign persons to one category or another (one of three principal races or unclassified). In demographic practice, classification of the members of a population in terms of socially constructed definitions of membership in categories in which skin color and other characteristics, including national ethnic affiliations, may be the basis of assignment by census

or survey enumerators or by self-enumeration. In the U.S. decennial census, persons are self-identified by race. See also ETHNICITY.

RADIX (OF A LIFE TABLE)   A hypothetical cohort of newborns used as the starting point of a life table, typically 100,000.

RAKING   See   CONTROLLING   and   PRORATA ADJUSTMENT.

RANDOM ERROR   The difference between a statistic of interest (e.g., mean age) found in a sample unaffected by nonrandom error and its corresponding parameter (e.g., mean age) found in the population from which the sample was drawn. Random error can only occur in a sample, never in a population. It is often referred to as sample error or sampling error. See also NONRANDOM ERROR, POPULATION, SAMPLE, and TOTAL ERROR.

RANK-SIZE RULE   An empirical regularity in the distribution of cities by population size, whereby that the number of cities in a population size interval tends to be inversely related to the size level; given its most complete expression in the writings of G. K. Zipf.

RATE   Technically, this type of ratio is the same as a probability. However, the term is often applied to the type of ratio known as a proportion, as in the case of "vacancy rate," which is the ratio of unoccupied housing units to all housing units. It is also applied to other types of ratios in which the denominators are not precisely the "at-risk populations," as is the case of the crude birthrate. See also AT-RISK POPULATION, PROBABILITY, PROPORTION, and RATIO.

RATE-CORRELATION METHOD   See RATIO-CORRELATION METHOD.

RATE OF CHANGE   The change of population during a given period expressed as a rate. The rate may relate to the entire period, in which case the denominator is usually the initial population. Alternatively, it may be an average annual rate—in which case the rate may assume annual compounding, continuous compounding, or some other function. See also POPULATION CHANGE.

RATE OF NATURAL INCREASE   The result of subtracting the crude death rate from the crude birthrate. For a population closed to migration, it provides the rate of increase (or the rate of decrease if the crude death rate exceeds the crude birthrate). See also CRUDE BIRTH RATE, CRUDE DEATH RATE, and INTRINSIC RATE.

RATIO   A single number that expresses the relative size of two other numbers (i.e., a quotient, which is the result of dividing one number by another). See also PROBABILITY, PROPORTION, and RATE.

RATIO-CORRELATION METHOD   A regression-based subnational population estimation technique included within the "change in stock method" family. Introduced by R. Schmitt and A. Crosetti in the early 1950s: (1) the dependent variable consists of the ratio formed by dividing the most recent population proportion for a set of subareas (e.g., proportion of a state population in each of its counties at the most recent census) by the population proportion for the same subareas at an earlier time (i.e., the previous census); and (2) the independent variables consist of corresponding ratios of proportions for symptomatic indicators of population (e.g., school enrollment, automobile registrations, births, deaths) available from administrative records. Variations of the ratio-correlation method include the difference-correlation method, introduced by R. Schmitt and J. Gier in 1966, and the rate-correlation method, introduced by D. Swanson and L. Tedrow in 1984. See also CENSAL-RATIO METHOD, CHANGE IN STOCK METHOD, POPULATION ESTIMATE, and WEIGHTED AVERAGE.

RATIO ESTIMATION A set of techniques used to estimate population based on ratios across geographic areas, variables, or both. See also POPULATION ESTIMATE.

RECORD LINKAGE See MATCHING.

RECORD MATCHING See MATCHING.

REFERENCE POPULATION See STANRARD POPULATION.

REFUGEE An alien outside of his or her country of nationality who is unable or unwilling to return to his or her country of nationality, or to seek the protection of that country, because of persecution or a well-founded fear of persecution based on his or her race, religion, nationality, membership in a particular social group, or political opinion. Unlike an asylee, a refugee applies for and receives this status prior to entry into the United States. See also ASYLEE and INTERNALLY DISPLACED PERSON.

RELATIONAL MODEL LIFE TABLES See BRASS RELATIONAL MODEL LIFE TABLES.

RELATIVE MORTALITY INDEX A weighted mean of the ratios of age-specific death rates in a population of interest to the age-specific death rates of a reference population.

REMARRIAGE Marriage after divorce or death of a previous spouse.

RENEWABLE EVENT Something that can, in principle, be experienced more than once by a member of a population of interest. See also NONRENEWABLE EVENT.

REPLACEMENT FERTILITY See REPLACEMENT LEVEL OF FERTILITY.

REPLACEMENT INDEX A measure approximating the net reproduction rate and related to the intrinsic rate of increase through the mean length of a generation. It is typically computed by dividing the ratio of children to women of childbearing age in a population of interest by the corresponding ratio in a reference stationary population (e.g., a life table) or a reference stable population. See also INTRINSIC RATE, J-INDEX, NET REPRODUCTION RATE, STABLE POPULATION, and STATIONARY POPULATION.

REPLACEMENT LEVEL OF FERTILITY In the absence of migration, the (fixed) level of fertility and mortality in a population of interest at which women will replace themselves in a generation. It corresponds to a net reproduction rate of 1.0 and a total fertility rate in the range of 2.04 to 2.10. See also INTRINSIC RATE, J-INDEX, NET REPRODUCTION RATE, STABLE POPULATION, and STATIONARY POPULATION.

REPRODUCTION The production of offspring.

REPRODUCTIVE BEHAVIOR Actions that reflect the reproductive performance of a person or a group.

REPRODUCTIVE PERIOD Women's childbearing years, usually assumed as the ages from 15 to 44 for purposes of analysis, but 15 to 49, and 10 to 54 also are used.

REPRODUCTIVITY Field of analysis and measures describing the joint contribution to population growth, particularly to generational population replacement, of both fertility and mortality.

RESIDENCE The place where a person lives. Defined differently in different censuses, but often interpreted as "usual residence," which is the case in the U.S. decennial census based on the de jure method. See also CENSUS, CENSUS-DEFINED RESIDENT, DE JURE, DOMICLE, and USUAL RESIDENCE.

RESIDENTIAL MOBILITY A change of residence, either in the same city or town, or between cities, states, countries, or communities.

RESIDENTIAL SEGREGATION See SEGREGATION and RESIDENTIAL SEPARATION.

RESIDENTIAL SEPARATION Spatial separation or isolation of a race, ethnic, or socioeconomic group by residence. Preferred to "segregation" as a value-free expression encompassing the several causes of spatial separation and isolation of groups.

RESIDUAL METHOD A technique that estimates intercensal net migration for a given area by subtracting from the most recent census count the algebraic sum of intercensal births and deaths added to the population counted at the preceding census. Resulting estimates are confounded by differences in net census undercount error. See also BALANCING EQUATION, COMPONENT METHOD, ERROR OF CLOSURE, and NET MIGRATION.

RETIREMENT The permanent withdrawal of a person from the labor force, usually in older age, but also for medical and other reasons. It is measured variously on the basis of responses to questions on labor force participation or information on receipt of benefits from a disability or a retirement system, or a combination thereof.

RETURN MIGRATION A move back to point of origin, whether domestic or foreign. See also MIGRATION.

RETURNEES Persons who have been forced to move from their homes, such as internally displaced persons, who have returned. The term is limited to "international" movements, such as those of refugees, asylees, and other persons of interest to the international refugee organizations.

REVERSE RECORD CHECK A technique used to estimate census coverage error that attempts to match a sample drawn from a reliable source of records independent of the census with data collected in the census. For example, a reverse record check may attempt to match a sample of births over a 10-year period with children under 10 in the census, or a sample of enrollees under Medicare with the elderly population in the census. See also CENSUS and COVERAGE ERROR.

REVERSE STREAM   See COUNTERSTREAM.

REVERSE SURVIVAL METHOD   Any method of estimating population or migration involving backward "survival" of a population to an earlier date. See also SURVIVAL RATE.

RIGHT-CENSORED   See CENSORED.

RISK ASSESSMENT   The qualitative or quantitative estimation of the likelihood of adverse effects attributable to exposure to specified health hazards or medical procedures or treatments, such as contraceptives.

RURAL POPULATION   Usually defined as the residual population after the urban population has been identified. See also URBAN POPULATION.

RURAL-URBAN MIGRATION   The migration from rural to urban areas, both internal and international.

SAMPLE   A subset of a population (in the statistical sense) for which data are typically collected in a "survey," which is a way of providing respondents with questions to be answered (e.g., through personal interviews, telephone interviews, mail-out/mail-back questionnaires). Samples may also be selected from administrative and other records such that interviews are not needed because data are taken directly from the records themselves (e.g., from Medicare files). Samples may be defined in a number of ways, but if statistical inference is to be used, a sample's elements should have a known probability of selection, or at least a reasonable approximation thereof, so that "random error" can be estimated. See also CENSUS, NON-RANDOM ERROR, and POPULATION, RANDOM ERROR, and SAMPLE SURVEY.

SAMPLE ERROR   See RANDOM ERROR.

SAMPLE SURVEY   Collection of data from a subset of the population, preferably a probability sample, through, for example, personal interviews, telephone interviews, and mail out/mail back questionnaires. See also CENSUS and SAMPLE.

SCHOOL-AGE POPULATION   Children of school age, usually defined by the ages for which school attendance is compulsory, which varies from country to country and sometimes within a given country.

SEASONAL ADJUSTMENT   A statistical modification to a data series to reduce the effect of seasonal variation. See also SEASONAL VARIATION.

SEASONAL VARIATION   Seasonal differences in the occurrence of data collected over time and reported at least quarterly. See also SEASONAL ADJUSTMENT.

SEGREGATION   There are many different interpretations of the term "segregation" and at least five dimensions of segregation have been identified: (1) centralization, (2) concentration, (3) clustering, (4) evenness, and (5) exposure. In demography, segregation usually refers to the spatial separation or isolation of a race, ethnic, or socioeconomic group by residence. See also SEGREGATION INDEX.

SEGREGATION INDEX   At least 20 indices have been developed to measure the different dimensions of segregation, many of which are algebraically related to one another. Those typically used in demography are concerned with residential segregation, with the most common being the index of dissimilarity. See also GINI INDEX, INDEX OF DISSIMILARITY, LORENZ CURVE, and SEGREGATION.

SELF-ENUMERATION   A method of conducting a census or sample survey in which respondents fill out questionnaire themselves, usually in connection with a mail-out/mail-back design for distributing and retrieving the questionnaires.

SEPARATION FACTORS   The proportions used to assign deaths at each age in each calendar year to birth cohorts in connection with the calculation of probabilities of dying, especially for constructing life tables. Special separation factors are applied to infant deaths because of the tendency for deaths to be concentrated in the earliest days, weeks, and months of infancy. See also INFANT MORTALITY RATE and LIFE TABLE FUNCTIONS.

SEPARATED   Related to a married person who does not live with his or her spouse because of marital discord. See also SEPARATION.

SEPARATION   The process of a married person becoming separated from his or her spouse. See also SEPARATED.

SETTLEMENT AND RESETTLEMENT   The relocation of refugees and other displaced persons in a new place. See also ASYLEES, INTERNALLY DISPLACED PERSONS, and REFUGEES.

SEX COMPOSITION   See POPULATION COMPOSITION.

SEX DISTRIBUTION   See SEX COMPOSITION.

SEX RATIO   The ratio of males to the number of females in a population, usually computed for age groups and expressed per 100 females.

SEX STRUCTURE   See POPULATION COMPOSITION.

SHORT FORM   In the United States, the decennial census form asking a limited range of basic population and housing questions and distributed to about five-sixths of the households, with the so-called long form being distributed to the remaining households. Note, however, that the questions on the short form are contained in the long form, so in effect all households receive the short form. See also LONG FORM.

SIBLING METHOD   A set of survey and census-based techniques for measuring mortality in a population that lacks otherwise reliable mortality data. It is based on asking respondents for dates of birth and ages at death (if applicable) of brothers and sisters with living mothers and fathers. See also ORPHAN-HOOD METHODS.

SIC   See STANDARD INDUSTRIAL CLASSIFICATION.

SINGLE   A general term for a person not currently married. It could be applied to a person who has never been married or a person who is divorced or widowed and not yet remarried. See also MARRIAGE.

SITE POTENTIAL   A concept related to population potential. See POPULATION POTENTIAL.

SMALL AREA   The subdivisions of the primary political subdivisions of a country. In the United States, counties and their subdivisions are usually considered small areas, although some limit the term to subcounty areas such as census tracts, block groups, and blocks and the areas that can be aggregated from them. See also CENSUS GEOGRAPHY.

SMOOTHING The adjustment of data to eliminate or reduce irregularities and other anomalies assumed to result from measurement and other errors. A common application of smoothing procedures is in connection with single-year-of-age data that appear to be affected by age heaping. See also AGE-HEAPING and INTERPOLATION.

SOC See STANDARD OCCUPATIONAL CODE.

SOCIAL MOBILITY The movement or shifting of membership between or within social classes by individuals or groups.

SPECIAL POPULATION Population groups identified separately for purposes of a census and or sample survey because of their distinctive living arrangements, such as college students, prison inmates, residents of nursing homes, and military personnel and their dependents. Special populations usually are characterized by components of change very different from the broader populations in which they are found, sometimes because of laws or regulations governing them. See also COMPONENTS OF CHANGE and POPULATION.

SPONTANEOUS ABORTION See ABORTION.

SPOUSE A marriage partner.

STABLE POPULATION (MODEL) A population with an unchanging relative age composition and a constant rate of change in its total size, resulting from conditions of constant fertility and mortality rates over an extended period, about 70 years. See also QUASI-STABLE POPULATION, POPULATION COMPOSITION, STABLE POPULATION METHOD, and STATIONARY POPULATION.

STABLE POPULATION METHOD The use of a "reference" stable population and its parameters approximating the conditions of an observed population to evaluate and estimate the composition and the fertility and mortality levels of an observed population of interest. See also STABLE POPULATION.

STANDARD CONSOLIDATED AREA In the United States, a combination of primary metropolitan statistical areas, with a total population of at least 1,000,000, established by the Office of Management and Budget. See also CENSUS GEOGRAPHY, METROPOLITAN AREA, and PRIMARY METROPOLITAN STATISTICAL AREA.

STANDARD INDUSTRIAL CODE (SIC) In the United States, the standard classification system for coding the industry reported by employed persons in censuses and surveys, applicable up to 1997. Since the 1997 economic census this system has been replaced by NAICS, the North American Industrial Classification System. See also INDUSTRY, NORTH AMERICAN INDUSTRIAL CLASSIFICATION SYSTEM, OCCUPATION, and STANDARD OCCUPATIONAL CLASSIFICATION.

STANDARD LIFE TABLE A life table against which values from another life table are compared, or from which a life table for a population of interest is constructed. The term also is used to refer to the conventional life table, representing the diminution of a cohort of births through age-specific death rates of a

particular year or short group of years without additional decrements or any increments. See also LIFE TABLE.

STANDARD METROPOLITAN STATISTICAL AREA See PRIMARY METROPOLITAN AREA.

STANDARD OCCUPATIONAL CLASSIFICATION (SOC) In the United States, the standard classification system for coding the occupations reported by employed persons in censuses and surveys. See also OCCUPATION and STANDARD INDUSTRIAL CODE.

STANDARD POPULATION A "reference" population used for purposes of analyzing a population of interest. Also, specifically, a population whose age distribution is employed in the calculation of standardized rates by the direct method. See also DIRECT STANDARDIZATION and STANDARDIZATION.

STANDARDIZATION The adjustment of a summary rate (e.g., the crude death rate) to remove the effects of population composition (e.g., age), usually done to compare rates across populations with different compositions. There are two general types of standardization, direct and indirect. The type selected is dependent on the data available for the population(s) of interest. See also CRUDE RATE, DIRECT STANDARDIZATION, INDIRECT STANDARDIZATION, POPULATION COMPOSITION, STANDARD POPULATION, STANDARDIZED RATE, and WEIGHTED AVERAGE.

STANDARDIZED RATE A rate that results from the standardization of a crude or general rate. See also STANDARDIZATION.

STANDARDIZED MORTALITY RATIO A measure of relative mortality calculated by dividing the number of deaths in a population of interest by the number of deaths expected in this population if it had the age-specific death rates of a reference population. It is a form of indirect standardization. See also INDIRECT STANDARDIZATION and STANDARDIZED RATE.

STATIONARY POPULATION A stable population in which the rate of increase is zero and the total size and both the absolute and relative age composition are constant. It also represents the number of Person-years lived by the survivirs in each age group in a life table. See also MOMENTUM OF POPULATION GROWTH, PERSON-YEARS LIVED, and STABLE POPULATION.

STATIONARITY The condition where a population is stationary. See also STATIONARY POPULATION.

STATISTICAL AREA A geographic area defined for census purposes having boundaries that do not correspond to those of a particular political or administrative area. Used for tabulation and presentation of data and useful for spatial analysis.

STERILITY A condition in which reproduction is not possible because of reasons not related to contraception. See also FECUNDITY and SUBFECUNDITY.

STILLBIRTH See FETAL LOSS.

SUBFECUNDITY A limited physiological capacity to bear children, illustrated by the inability to have another child after bearing one. See also FECUNDITY and STERILITY.

SUBSTITUTION In a sample survey or census, the process of assigning values for a case in which there is "total nonresponse." Many substitution methods are available, including automated algorithms. See also ALLOCATION, IMPUTATION, and NONRESPONSE.

SUBURBAN A popular term referring to the residential area surrounding a central city. Such an area may follow the transportation lines and be dependent on the central city both economically and culturally but, increasingly, such areas are becoming the equivalent of central cities to suburbs of their own. See also URBAN FRINGE.

SUBURBANIZATION The spatial diffusion of population growth affecting areas adjoining a city.

SURVEY See SAMPLE.

SURVIVAL Primarily a condition where an individual or group remains alive after a specified interval, and secondarily a condition where an individual or group maintains membership in the group of interest, such as a school enrollment cohort, marriage cohort, or the nonpoor population. See also SURVIVAL RATE.

SURVIVAL CURVE A graph depicting a survivorship function. See also SURVIVORSHIP FUNCTION.

SURVIVAL RATE A rate expressing the probability of survival of a population group, usually an age group, from one date to another and from one age to another. A survival rate can be based on life tables or two censuses. When based on two censuses, the rate includes not only the effects of mortality, but also the effects of net migration and relative census enumeration error. See also FORWARD SURVIVAL RATE, HAMILTON-PERRY METHOD, LIFE TABLE, SURVIVAL, and SURVIVORSHIP FUNCTION.

SURVIVORSHIP See SURVIVAL.

SURVIVORSHIP FUNCTION The probability that an individual survives to time = t before an event of interest (e.g., death) occurs. It is one of three algebraically related functions used in survival analysis, the other two being the "death density function" and the "hazard function." The survivorship function is found by dividing the death density function by the hazard function. See also DEATH DENSITY FUNCTION, HAZARD FUNCTION, and SURVIVAL RATE.

SURVIVORSHIP RATIO See SURVIVAL RATE.

SYNTHETIC METHOD A member of the family of ratio estimation methods that is used to estimate characteristics of a population in a subarea (e.g., a county) by reweighting ratios (e.g., prevalence rates or incidence rates) obtained from survey or other data available at a higher level of geography (e.g., a state) that includes the subarea in question. See also POPULATION ESTIMATE, RATIO ESTIMATION, and WEIGHTED AVERAGE.

TARGET YEAR In a population projection, the final year for which a population is projected. It is the end point of the projection horizon. See also BASE PERIOD, LAUNCH YEAR, and POPULATION PROJECTION, and PROJECTION HORIZON.

TEMPORARY MIGRATION A type of migration, both internal and international, in which the duration of stay is temporary. Data for temporary migration are not normally included in the official data on internal or international migration and are usually obtained from a special sample survey.

TIGER See TOPOLOGICALLY INTEGRATED GEOGRAPHIC ENCODING AND REFERENCING SYSTEM.

TOPOLOGICALLY INTEGRATED GEOGRAPHIC ENCODING AND REFERENCING SYSTEM (TIGER). A digital database of geographic features (e.g., roads, rivers, political boundaries, census statistical boundaries, etc.) covering the entire United States. It was developed by the U.S. Census Bureau to facilitate computerized mapping and areal data analysis. See also GEOGRAPHIC INFORMATION SYSTEM.

TOTAL DIVORCE RATE An age-adjusted period measure of lifetime divorce, derived by summing age-specific divorce rates over the age range from age 15 on in a given year (i.e., with equal weighting of the rates). The age-specific rates are computed as the ratio of divorces to total population in the age group. Analogous to the total fertility rate. See also TOTAL FERTILITY RATE and TOTAL MARRIAGE RATE.

TOTAL ERROR In a sample, the theoretical sum of random error and nonrandom error, which in practice can at best only be roughly approximated because of the difficulty of estimating nonrandom error. Also known as total sample error. In a census, total error is composed solely of nonrandom error. See also BIAS, NONRANDOM ERROR, RANDOM ERROR, and TRUE POPULATION.

TOTAL FERTILITY RATE An age-adjusted, period measure of lifetime fertility, derived by summing age-specific birthrates in a given year over all ages of childbearing (i.e., with equal weighting of the rates). When the rates for the individual ages are combined (or rates for 5-year age groups are multiplied by five and combined), the resulting figure represents the average number of children a hypothetical cohort of 1000 women would have in their lifetimes, in the absence of mortality before the end of childbearing. See also COMPLETED FERTILITY RATE and PERIOD MEASURE.

TOTAL FIRST MARRIAGE RATE A measure of lifetime first marriages, derived by adding age-specific first marriage rates over all the adult ages for a given year (i.e., equal weight is given to each rate). The first-marriage rates are computed by dividing first marriages by the total population in each age group. Analogous to the total fertility rate. See also TOTAL DIVORCE RATE, TOTAL FERTILITY RATE, and TOTAL MARRIAGE RATE.

TOTAL MARRIAGE RATE A measure of lifetime marriage, derived by adding age-specific marriage rates over all the adult ages for a given year (i.e., equal weight is given to each rate). The age-specific marriage rates are computed by dividing marriages by the total population in each age group. Analogous to the total fertility rate. See also TOTAL DIVORCE RATE, TOTAL FERTILITY RATE, and TOTAL FIRST MARRIAGE RATE.

TOTAL REMARRIAGE RATE The difference between the total marriage rate and the total first marriage rate. See TOTAL FIRST MARRIAGE RATE and TOTAL MARRIAGE RATE.

TRADITIONAL METHODS OF FAMILY PLANNING Methods of family planning that were available before the advent of modern scientific methods (e.g., the rhythm method, abstinence, coitus interruptus, breast feeding, and herbal preparations).

TRANSITION PROBABILITY The probability of moving from one state to another during a specified time interval in a multistate transition matrix. The probabilities of moving from any one state to all others (including the same state) must sum to one.

TREND EXTRAPOLATION See EXTRAPOLATION.

TRUE POPULATION In theory, the population that would be counted if there were no errors in a census. In practice, it is a value representing the theoretical actual number for the population at a given date, which cannot be precisely measured but which can be roughly approximated by adjusting a census for net census undercount error. See also CENSUS CORRECTED POPULATION, CENSUS POPULATION, and NET CENSUS UNDERCOUNT ERROR.

TRUNCATION BIAS Distortion of results due to the systematic omission from an analysis of values that fall below or above a given range.

TURNOVER A term sometimes employed to refer to the sum of the components of change during a period (i.e., births plus deaths plus immigrants/inmigrants plus emigrants/outmigrants).

UNABRIDGED LIFE TABLE See LIFE TABLE.

UNDERCOUNT In a census, the omission of valid members of the population in question. See also NET CENSUS UNDERCOUNT ERROR and OVERCOUNT.

UNDER-ENUMERATION See UNDERCOUNT.

UNDER-REGISTRATION The omission of persons or events from a registration system or other administrative record system.

UNDOCUMENTED IMMIGRANT Often used as a synonym for illegal immigrant. For formal usage the latter term is preferred as complementing the term legal immigrant.

UNEMPLOYED PERSON According to the labor force concept used in the United States, a member of the labor force who was not working or with a job and was actively looking for work during the week or other specified period prior to the collection of data (e.g., a sample survey). Under the gainful worker concept used in the United States, a worker who at the time of data collection (e.g., a sample survey) is lacking a gainful activity that he or she normally exercises.

UNINCORPORATED PLACE See CENSUS DESIGNATED PLACE.

URBAN FRINGE The densely settled area surrounding the core city of an urbanized area. Sometimes population referred to as the suburban area. See also SUBURBAN.

URBAN POPULATION Usually defined as a large population in a densely packed area that meets criteria derived from geographic, social, and economic factors, which, in turn, may vary by country. See also PLACE, RURAL POPULATION, and URBANIZED AREA.

URBANIZATION Growth in the proportion of persons living in urban areas; the process whereby a society changes from a rural to an urban way of life.

URBANIZED AREA In the United States the combination of an urban core and the surrounding closely settled territory or "urban fringe." See also URBAN FRINGE.

USUAL RESIDENCE The place where one usually eats and sleeps, a concept associated with a de jure census. See also CENSUS, CENSUS-DEFINED RESIDENT, DE JURE, DOMICILE, LABOR FORCE, and RESIDENCE.

VERY LOW BIRTHWEIGHT A birthweight less than 1500 grams.

VITAL EVENTS Births, deaths, fetal losses, abortions, marriages, annulments, divorces—any of the events relating to mortality, fertility, marriage, and divorce recorded in registration systems. See also VITAL STATISTICS.

VITAL INDEX A term attributed to R. Pearl that represents the ratio of birth to deaths for a given population over a given period, such as a year.

VITAL RATES METHOD A censal-ratio method of population estimation introduced by D. Bogue in the 1950s that uses crude birth and crude death rates. See also CENSAL-RATIO METHOD and POPULATION ESTIMATE.

VITAL RECORDS See VITAL STATISTICS.

VITAL STATISTICS Data on births, deaths, fetal losses, abortions, marriages, and divorces usually compiled through registration systems or other administrative record systems. See also VITAL EVENTS.

WASTAGE See FETAL LOSS.

WEIGHTED AVERAGE Usually an arithmetic mean of an array of specific rates or ratios, with variable weights applied to them representing the relative distribution of the populations on which the rates or ratios are based. More generally, a summary measure of a set of numbers (absolute numbers or ratios), computed as the cumulative product of the numbers and a set of weights representing their relative importance in the population. An unweighted average is one in which each number in the set has the same weight (e.g., 1 or 1/n, where n is the total set of numbers). See also CENSAL RATIO METHOD, STANDARDIZATION and SYNTHETIC METHOD.

WHIPPLE'S INDEX A measure of age heaping, calculated as the ratio of the sum of populations ending in terminal digits 0 and 5 in the range 23 to 62 years to one-fifth the total population 23 to 62 years. See also AGE HEAPING and MYER'S INDEX.

WIDOWED The state following the death of a spouse. See also MARRIAGE.

WOOFTER'S METHOD A technique developed by T. J. Woofter in the early 1950s designed to estimate a fertility measure he called the generation gross reproduction rate. See also GENERATION and GENERATION REPRODUCTION RATE.

WORK FORCE See LABOR FORCE.

WORKING AGE POPULATION The population ranging variously from 15 to 64, 18 to 64, 15 to 59, or similar ages, designed to represent the principal ages at which members of a population work. It includes a substantial number of persons who are not in the labor force and excludes a substantial number of persons, particularly above the range given, who are in the labor force. See also LABOR FORCE.

WORKING-LIFE EXPECTANCY The average remaining years a person will be in the labor force, as measured by a table of working life. See also MULTISTATE LIFE TABLE and WORKING LIFE TABLE.

WORKING-LIFE TABLE A life table with increments of birth and labor force entry and decrements of death and labor force exit. It discribes the life history of a birth cohort in terms of its labor force porticipution and its work life and nonwork life expctancy. It may be computed by the prevalence-ratio method, cohort-exposure method, or as a multistate life table. See also MULTISTATE LIFE TABLE and WORKING-LIFE EXPECTANCY.

WORKPLACE POTENTIAL A concept related to population potential. See POPULATION POTENTIAL.

YEARS OF SCHOOL COMPLETED See EDUCATIONAL ATTAINMENT.

ZERO POPULATION GROWTH A condition where a population does not grow (or decline) in total numbers. The concept is not defined with respect to those cases where amounts of increase or decrease for sexes, ages, or other component demographic categories offset one another.

ZIP CODE Administrative areas set up by the U.S. Postal Service as postal delivery areas and used for marketing and related purposes in the United States. They have fluid boundaries that do not correspond to any established political area or statistical area of the decennial census but may approximate some small areas defined by the census. See also CENSUS GEOGRAPHY.

A Demography Time Line

DAVID A. SWANSON AND G. EDWARD STEPHAN*

_3800 B.C. Babylonian census (for taxation purposes).

_1400 Egyptians begin to regularly register their citizens.

_1055 King DAVID (reign 1055–15) takes a census of Israel; II Samuel 24:9 reports 800,000 men, I Chronicles 21:5 reports 1,100,000.

_578–34 Reign of SERVIUS TULLIUS, who ordered the first Roman census (from "censere" to assess); 83,000 citizens counted and grouped for military, taxation, and voting purposes.

_520–479 KONG FUZI (Confucius) writes on optimal population numbers and related principles.

_360 PLATO Laws, IV, relates population pressure to colonial emigration.

_354 ARISTOTLE considers optimal population size and related issues in Politica.

_28 Rome enumerates 4,063,000 (some scholars believe this included women and children, though other indications in primary sources suggest this was the total of adult male citizens, implying vast extension of citizenship in the empire).

1 WORLD POPULATION: 200 Million.

6–7 Census ordered by QUIRIMINUS, governor of Syria, associated with Jesus's birth (Luke 2:2).

230 Domitius ULPAINUS, Roman jurist, produces a table of annuity values that remain in use until 1814, considered the best annuity table in Europe until the end of the 17th century.

645 Koseki (Japanese family records) introduced as part of the Taika Reforms.

1320 Eruption of the Black Death in the Gobi desert spreads to China, where the population declines from around 125 million to 90 million.

1347 October Black Death arrives in Messina, Sicily; Marseilles, January 1348; Paris, July 1348; England, September 1348.

1347–52 Population of Europe declines from 75 to 50 million due to the Black Death.

1375–79 IBN-KHALDUN: Muqaddimah (an introduction to history, including role of population in culture and history and extensive development of theories on cyclical variations of population in relation to psycho-socal, political, and economic conditions); the impact of the Black Death.

1558 Giovanni BOTERO: Delle cause della grandezza della città (first of several publications, includes discussion of factors limiting the growth of population, anticipates Malthusian ideas regarding population).

1603 December 29 ff. Weekly London Bills of Mortality begin (earlier bills, 1592–4, but so discontinuous that GRAUNT ignored them).

1612 Felix PLATTER: Beschreibung der Stadt Basel 1610 und Pestbericht 1610/11 (first demographic field study—plague in Basel).

1620 First English colonial census in the New World (Virginia).

1625 Francis BACON: "Of Seditions and Troubles," essay that includes "it is to be foreseen that the population of a Kingdom . . . do not exceed the stock of the Kingdom which should maintain them." Bacon may have been the first to use the word "population" in its modern sense.

1635 Census of the Virginia Colony.

1650 WORLD POPULATION: 500 million.

1661–1680 Census activities undertaken in British Colonies, including Jamaica, Newfoundland, Barbados.

1661 Giovanni Battista RICCIOLI: "De verisimili hominum numero," Geographiae et Hydrographiae Reformatae (scholarly estimate of the earth's population and in various states).

* Sources of information used in compiling this Demography Time Line include:

Anderson, M. J. 1988. The American Census: A Social History. New Haven, CT: Yale University Press.

De Gans, H. A. 1999. Population Forecasting 1895–1945: The Transition to Modernity. Dordrecht, Netherlands: Kluwer Academic.

Lee, R. D. 1995. "History of Demography in the U.S. Since 1945." Paper presented at the Celebration of the 50th Anniversary of INED, Paris, France, October 25–27.

Stigler, S. M. 1986. The History of Statistics: The Measurement of Uncertainty before 1900. Cambridge, MA: The Belknap Press of Harvard University Press.

Weeks, J. R. 2000. "Population Association of America Timeline." Unpublished document prepared for the Population Association of America.

1662 January 25 John GRAUNT: *Natural and Political Observations . . . Made upon the Bills of Mortality with Reference to the Government, Religion, Trade, Growth, Ayre, Diseases, and the Several Changes of the Said City* [London] editions: 2nd, 1662; 3rd, 1665; 4th, 1665; 5th (by PETTY), 1676.

1665 First census in New France (now Québec).

1665 The Great Plague of London, last and worst outbreak of the Black Death in England, killed 70,000 out of 460,000, from autumn 1664 to February 1666.

1670 ff. Annual reports begin for births, marriages and deaths in Paris.

1693 Edmund HALLEY: *An Estimate of the Degrees of Mortality of Mankind* (first empirical life table based on births and deaths for age groups in Breslaw, Silesia, recorded by Kasper NEUMANN, transmitted to HALLEY by LIEBNITZ).

1693 General census for France ordered as an aid to distributing food during a severe shortage.

1703 Complete census of Iceland.

1707 Sebastian VAUBAN: *Projet d'une Dîme Royale* (first published population of France, by parishes, with methods of enumeration).

1741 Johann SÜSSMILCH: *Die Göttliche Ordnung in den Veränderungen des menschlichen Geschlechts, aus der Geburt, dem Tode und der Fortplanzung desselben erwissen* (The Divine Order . . . , most painstaking estimate of world population to his time, editions: 2nd, 1761; 3rd, 1765).

1747 James HODGSON constructed life tables from London mortality records.

1748 Swedish law requiring national compilation of parish vital statistics records.

1751 Population of Sweden completely enumerated.

1752 David HUME: "Of the Populousness of Ancient Nations," *Political Discourses*.

1753 Robert WALLACE: *The Numbers of Man in Ancient and Modern Times* (French ed., 1760).

1755 Benjamin FRANKLIN: *Observations Concerning the Increase of Mankind, Peopling of Countries, etc.*

1756 Victor Marquis de MIRABEAU: *L'ami des hommes ou traité de la population* (stirred debate over relation of national strength to population structure).

1760 Leonhard EULER: *A General Investigation Into The Mortality and Multiplication of the Human Species* (seminal work on the mathematical conditions that hold under stable population theory).

1761 Robert WALLACE: *Various Prospects for Mankind, Nature, and Providence* (argues that any "perfect government" will produce overpopulation; stimulus for GODWIN).

1762 Abbé Jean D'EXPILLY: *Dictionaire géographique, historique, et politique des Gaules et de la France* (included vital statistics for two-thirds of the parishes of France).

1765 Johann SÜSSMILCH constructed mortality tables for all of Prussia.

1766 Wilhelm WARGENTIN: *Mortaliteten i Sverige, i adledning cef Tabell-Verket* (Swedish mortality tables, first sex- and age-specific death rates for any nation).

1767 Thomas SHORT: *A Comparative History of the Increase and Decrease of Mankind*.

1770 Annual account of vital statistics for each French généralité.

1776 Adam SMITH: *An Inquiry into the Nature and Causes of the Wealth of Nations* (among other seminal ideas, an early statement of human capital theory).

1778 Baron de MONTYON (via MOHEAU): *Rechecres et considérations sur la population de la France* (most precise and general treatise on demography in France up to its time).

1787 The U.S. Constitution is established, in which Article 1, Section 2, calls for the world's first regular national census: "the actual enumeration shall be made within three years after the first meeting of the Congress of the United States, and within every subsequent term of ten years in such manner as they shall by law direct."

1790 March 1 In accordance with Article 1, Section 2, of the U.S. Constitution, the first United States census began; the world's first continuous, periodic national census.

1793 William GODWIN: *Enquiry Concerning Political Justice and Its Influence on Morals and Happiness* (possible ways to limit population growth; response to WALLACE, stimulus for MALTHUS).

1798 June 7 MALTHUS: *An Essay on the Principle of Population, As It Affects the Future Improvement of Society* (geometrical population growth outstrips arithmetic expansion in resources).

1800 WORLD POPULATION: 1 billion.

1801 Periodic census begins in England and France.

1803 MALTHUS's essay, 2nd ed.: *An Essay on the Principle of Population; or a View of Its Past and Present Effects on Human Happiness; with an Inquiry into Our Prospects Respecting the Future Removal or Mitigation of the Evils Which It Occasions* (primarily an attack on the English Poor Laws), editions: 3rd, 1806; 4th, 1807; 5th, 1817; 6th (last) 1826.

1812 Pierre Simon de LAPLACE: *Théories analytiquse des probabilités* (a study using sampled ratios of populations to births, from 1802 onward, to estimate total births).

1819 U.S. Congress requires passenger lists of all arriving vessels.

1825 Benjamin GOMPERTZ: *On the Nature of the Function Expressive of the Law of Human Mortality* (a treatise on the development of mathematical models of mortality).

1830 Michael SADLER: *The Law of Population* (used census-based indices of fertility).

1830–42 Auguste COMTE: *The Positive Philosophy* (society driven forward by "the demographic tendency" toward increased size).

1832 Charles KNOWLTON: *The Fruits of Philosophy: or The Private Companion of Young Married People* (methods of birth-control).

1833 France established the office of Statistique Générale.

1837–40 Henry C. CAREY: *Principles of Political Economy* (first statement of "gravity model" of migration).

1839 ff. *Annual Report of the Registrar-General* (summary of vital statistics produced under the direction of William FARR).

1839 American Statistical Association founded in Boston.

1840 U.S. Census becomes the focus of controversy regarding "findings" that the black population in the North was beset with epidemic rates of insanity.

1841 Lemuel SHATTUCK: *The Vital Statistics of Boston.*

1841 ff. *Massachusetts State Registration Report.*

1846 Belgian census conducted by Adolphe QUETELET (influential, it introduced a careful analysis and critical evaluation of the data compiled).

1850 U.S. census collected individual-level data for the first time.

1850 ff. Otto L. HÜBNER: *Geographisch-statistiche Tabellen* (until 1919).

1850 7th U.S. census (new tabulation methods to enable more detailed analyses; use of census data to provide vital statistics for preceding year).

1851 Adolphe QUETELET: *Nuvelles tables de la mortalité pour la Belgique* (influential construction of life tables).

1853 Adolphe QUETELET: Organized a series of international conferences on statistics, pushed data-gathering for quinquennial age groups.

1854 James DeBOW: *Statistical View of the United States* (a summary of the 7th U.S. census, including results of all earlier censuses).

1854 George DRYSDALE: *Elements of Social Science* (first comprehensive book outlining and defending the birth control movement on broad sociological and economic grounds).

1854 Dr. John SNOW maps wells and cholera incidence for areas of London, and although subject to flaws, it was one of the first times "geographic information systems" were used to shape public policy (the closing of certain wells).

1855–65 Complete enumerations for 24 sovereign nations.

1855 Achille GUILLARD: *Eléments de statistique humaine ou démographie comparée* (coins the term "démographie").

1855 Frédéric LePLAY: *Les ouvriers européens* (comprehensive statement of the relation of family structure to demographic characteristics).

1856–59 William FARR works on indirect age standardization, culminating with its appearance in the 1859 annual report of the Registrar General of England and Wales.

1859 Charles DARWIN: *Origin of the Species by Means of Natural Selection* (esp. Chapter 3, "The Struggle for Existence," which shows the influence of MALTHUS).

1860 W. M. MAKEHAM: "On the Law of Mortality and Construction of Annuity Tables," *J. Inst. Actuaries* (development of general mortality formulas).

1861 Karl MARX: *Theories of Surplus Value* (esp. Chapter XIX—DARWIN's demonstration that plants and animals increase geometrically, contradicts MALTHUS).

1868 Georg KNAPP: *Über der Ermittlung der Sterblichkeit aus den Auszeichnungen der Bevölkerungs-Statistik* (a treatise on the theoretical aspects of life table construction).

1868 Meniji restoration reinstitution of Koseki (household registration system) in Japan.

1871 Census of British India, the first modern census for a large non-European country.

1874 Registration of vital events becomes obligatory in England and Wales.

1875 Wilhelm LEXIS: *Einleitung in die Theorie der Bevölkerungs-Statistik* (a theoretical treatise on demographic statistics; mortality in older ages).

1876 Georg von MAYR: *Die bayerische Bevölkerung nach der Gebürtigheit* (a study of internal migration using census data from Bavaria).

1877 George DRYSDALE founds England's Malthusian League.

1877 Annie BESANT: *The Law of Population* (influential treatise on population control).

1878 Dr. Aletta JACOBS: World's first birth-control clinic, Amsterdam, Netherlands.

1882 4th (or 5th) international congress on hygiene, at Geneva, newly titled "Congrès international d'Hygiène et Démographie," includes a section on demography.

1882 Chinese Exclusion Act (first nationality exclusion in the United States; followed by ban on Japanese, 1907, and on all Asians, 1917).

1883 Francis GALTON: *Natural Inheritance* (emphasis on differential fertility).

1884 Columbia College offers the course "Statistics of Population" covering such demographic topics as density, age, sex, birth, death, marriage, mortality tables, emigration.

1884 Richard BÖCKH: *Statistisches Jahrbuch der Stadt Berlin* (first appearance of the net reproduction rate in a publication).

1885 Ernst Georg RAVENSTEIN: *Laws of Migration* (a treatise that introduces the "gravity model" of migration).

1885 International Statistical Institute organized; Luigi BODIO is its first secretary-general.

1889–92 Êmile LEVASSEUR: *Le Population françoise* (a comprehensive survey of population trends in France that includes comparisons with other nations).

1889 Ernst Georg RAVENSTEIN: *Laws of Migration* (II).

1890 First census tabulated using electricity—mechanically punched holes in cards are counted by a machine using electrical flows, designed and patented by Herman Hollerith; sets the stage for the emergence of electronic computers and IBM.

1890 Arsène DUMONT: *Dépopulation et civilisation* (declining fertility in France).

1891 director of 1890 census, Francis WALKER: "Immigration and Degradation," *Forum* (argued that foreign influx led to decline in native fertility).

1892 Office of Immigration established in the United States.

1893 Émile DURKHEIM: *On the Division of Labor in Society* (this book includes the hypothesis that demographic trends drive history).

1893 John S. BILLINGS: "The Diminishing Birth-Rate in the United States," *Forum* (native versus immigrant fertility).

1895 Edwin CANNAN: "The Probability of a Cessation of the Growth of Population in England and Wales during the Next Century" *Economic Journal* (an early use of the cohort-component method of population projection).

1896 director of 1890 census, Francis WALKER: "Restriction of Immigration," *Atlantic Monthly* (another influential argument that foreign influx led to a decline in native fertility).

1897 Karl PEARSON: *The Chances of Death and Other Studies of Evolution* (mortality patterns in old age).

1897 Vilfredo PARETO introduces what comes to be known as the "80/20" or "Pareto" principle, which specifies a predictable imbalance in the joint distribution of many two-variable sets.

1900–33 The US death registration area is extended from 10 states, D.C., and 134 cities to the whole nation.

1900 First use of sampling in national census operations, Norway.

1901 Rodolfo BENINI: *Principi di demografia* (stimulated academic interest in demography in Italy).

1902 U.S. Bureau of the Census becomes a permanent office and moved to the newly established department of Commerce, shortly thereafter.

1903 Charles BOOTH: *Life and Labour of the People of London* (a report on "social surveys" begun in 1886).

1906 David HERON: *On the Relation of Fertility in Man to Social Status and on the Changes in This Relation That Have Taken Place during the Last Fifty Years* (studies in "national deterioration"—differential fertility, eugenics).

1907 The highest number of U.S. immigrants reported in a single year, through 2003: 1,285,349.

1907 U.S. Federal Immigration Commission founded amid movements aimed at restricting immigration from eastern and southern Europe; actions ultimately lead to the immigration restriction bill of 1921 assigning quotas based on the 1910 census.

1908 Giorgio MORTARA: La Mortalita Secondo l'eta et la Durata della Vita Economicamante Produttiva.

1908 Giorgio MORTARA: *Le Popolazioni della grandi città italiane* (student of BENINI; demographic characteristics of Italian cities).

1908 Corrado GINI: *Il sesso dal punto di vista statistica; le leggi della produzione dei sessi* (statistical determination of sex in humans).

1908 Harald WESTERGAARD: "The Horoscope of the Population in the Twentieth Century," *Bulletin de l'Institut International de Statistique* (seminal article on demographic transition and future population).

1911 E. C. SNOW: "The Application of the Method of Multiple Correlation to the Estimation of Postcensal Population," *Journal of he Royal Statistical Society* (first known use of linear regression to estimate population).

1912 Corrado GINI: *Demographic Factors in the Evolution of Nations.*

1913 The 16th amendment to the U.S. Constitution is ratified, which fundamentally alters a balance established in Article 1 regarding the costs and benefits of "larger" populations to states; unwittingly sets the foundation for highly contentious census counts in the latter part of the 20th century when there is only perceived "benefit" and no "cost" to states (and local governments) associated with higher population counts.

1913 Gustav SUNDBÄRG: *Emigrationsutredningen Betänkande* (detailed study of migration using Swedish registration data).

1915 National birth registration area established in United States; extended to the entire country by 1933.

1915 Warren THOMPSON: *Population: A Study in Malthusianism.*

1917 Margaret SANGER founds national birth-control league in the United States.

1917 Raymond PEARL and Lowell REED: "On the Rate of Growth of the Population of the United States Since 1790 and Its Mathematical Representation," *Proceedings of the National Academy of Sciences* (the "logistic" curve as populations approach an upper limit).

1920 U.S. census results of urban/rural, native-born/foreign-born, and so forth spark a crisis, with the result that the 1920 census was not used to reapportion Congress.

1921 Margaret SANGER organized the first American birth-control conference.

1921 First immigration quota system in the United States (3% by nationalities in 1910 census).

1921 Malthusian League established first birth-control clinic in London, England.

1922 Foundation for Research in Population established by E. W. SCRIPPS, Miami University, Oxford, OH; hires Warren THOMPSON as director, then P. K. WHELPTON as associate director.

1922 A. M. CARR-SAUNDERS: *The Population Problem* (Comprehensive eugenics statement).

1924 Second immigration quota system in the United States (2% by nationalities in 1890 census).

1924 A. L. BOWLEY: "Births and the Population of Great Britain," *The Journal of the Royal Economic Society* (believed to be the first published account of the complete cohort-component method of population projection, although related independent work was under way in Holland by G. A. H. WIEBOLS and in the United States by P. K. WHELPTON).

1925 Robert WOODBURY: *Causal Factors in Infant Mortality: A Statistical Study Based on Investigations in Eight Cities* (one of the first large-scale demographic field studies in the United States).

1925 Alfred J. LOTKA: *Elements of Physical Biology* (first major work on the mathematics of population dynamics).

1925 Margaret SANGER organized the first international birth-control conference.

1925 Hugh WOLFENDEN: *Population Statistics and Their Compilation* (published by the Society of Actuaries, it focused on the compilation of census data and vital statistics and on mortality measures from an actuarial standpoint).

1925 Louis DUBLIN and A. J. LOTKA: "On the True Rate of Natural Increase, as Exemplified by the Population of the United States, 1920" *Journal of the American Statistical Association* (first complete statement of the stable population model).

1925 G. A. H. WEIBOLS: *De Toekomstige Bevolkingsgroote in Nederland* (a treatise on the cohort-component method of population projection that includes the use of net reproduction).

1925–34 Complete enumerations for 49 sovereign nations.

1927 August 31 Margaret SANGER organizes first World Population Conference, Geneva, which leads to formation of the IUSSP; attended by statisticians, biologists, economists; ended September 2; papers included PEARL: "Biology of Population Growth," F. A. E. CREW: "Concerning Fertility and Sterility in Relation to Population," Edward EAST: "Food and Population"; SANGER's name is kept off the program.

1928 International Union for the Scientific Study of Population (IUSSP) founded, Paris, Raymond PEARL first president.

1928 P. K. WHELPTON: "Population of the United States, 1925 to 1975," *American Journal of Sociology* (influential work on the cohort-component method of population projection).

1928 Milbank Memorial Fund hires Frank NOTESTEIN, begins population studies.

1929 Margaret SANGER formed National Committee on Federal legislation for birth control.

1929 Warren THOMPSON: "Population," *American Journal of Sociology* (seminal article that classifies nations into three groups of nations based on different fertility-mortality patterns).

1929 Guy BURCH founds Population Reference Bureau, New York City.

1930 WORLD POPULATION: 2 billion.

1930 U.S. census is used to reapportion Congress for the first time in 20 years, reapportionment crisis resulting from the 1920 census is finally resolved.

1930 Louise KENNEDY: *The Negro Peasant Turns Cityward: Effects of Recent Migrations to Northern Centers* (review and interpretation of black migration studies).

1930 December 15 Population Association of America (PAA), offshoot of the American National Committee of the IUSSP, conceived at a "preliminary conference" of 13 people, Town Hall, New York City.

1931 May 7 Population Association of America (PAA) officially organized, Town Hall Club in New York City, Henry Pratt FAIRCHILD first president, William Ogburn vice president, Alfred LOTKA secretary-treasurer; 38 attending, "Second Conference" includes Louis DUBLIN, Frederick OSBORNE, Warren THOMPSON; paid for by a $600 grant from Milbank Memorial Fund; OSBORNE opposed naming SANGER to the board in order to emphasize the scientific character of the PAA.

1931 Louis DUBLIN named chairman of the American National Committee of the International union for the successive study of population (IUSSP).

1932 Stewart BROOM sues the state of Mississippi for violating usual districting requirements in its redistricting following the 1930 census; case goes before the U.S. Supreme Court, which, in effect, declared gerrymandering to be legal, setting the stage for the reapportionment revolution of the 1960s.

1932 April 22–23 First annual meeting of the PAA, Town Hall, New York City, 67 attending.

1933 Warren S. THOMPSON and P. K. WHELPTON: *Population Trends in the United States*.

1933 May 12 Second annual meeting of the PAA, New York City, 17 attending.

1934 Frank LORIMER and Frederick OSBORN: *The Dynamics of Population* (emphasis on eugenics).

1934 May 11 Third annual meeting of the PAA, New York City, 20 attending.

1934–39 Alfred LOTKA: *Théorie analytique des associations biologiques, Deuxième partie: Analyse démographique avec application particulière à l'espèce humaine* (definitive exposition of his mature demographic theory by "the Newton of demography").

1934 Raymond PEARL, at a Milbank Memorial Fund symposium, presented data that led him to say, "Gentlemen, you realize that this evidence destroys the basis of most of my life's work," thus signaling a shift of emphasis from biological to sociocultural factors in demography.

1935 May 2 Frank LORIMER produces first issue of *Population Index*, until 1937 called *Population Literature*.

1935 May 2–4 Conference on Population Studies in Relation to Social Planning, Washington D.C., Eleanor ROOSEVELT attended.

1936 Louis DUBLIN and Alfred LOTKA: *The Length of Life* (a comprehensive treatise on the methodology and applications of the life table).

1936 Robert KUCZYNSKI: *The Measurement of Population Growth* (a monograph on fertility and mortality and their relation to population growth).

1936 Frank NOTESTEIN directs population studies from Office of Population Research at Princeton University through League of Nations' sponsorship.

1936 A. M. CARR-SAUNDERS: *World Population: Past Growth and Present Trends* (a comprehensive empirical examination of the world's population).

1937 Large, successful International Population Conference, Paris.

1938 ff. Italian demography journal, *Genus*.

1939 Alfred J. LOTKA: *Théorie Analytique des Associations Biologiques* (Analytical Theory of Biological Populations, considered to be the first modern introduction to population mathematics; an 1998 English language translation by David P. SMITH and Hélène ROSSERT is available).

1940 U.S. census first employed sampling, 1 in 20 households received "supplemental questions," based on experience gained from unemployment surveys done in the 1930s and the first "Current Population Survey," which itself preceded the 1940 census; participants include W. Edwards DEMING, Philip HAUSER, Morris HANSEN, William HURWITZ, and William MADOW, who collectively would make important contributions to the theory and practice of sampling.

1940 First indications of a rise in the number of births in the United States that is subsequently recognized as the baby boom.

1941 Margaret HAGOOD: *Statistics for Sociologists* (first statistics text in the United States with a section on demographic methods).

1941 Indianapolis study: A comprehensive early fertility survey that examined social and psychological factors and set the stage for subsequent studies.

1944 Dudley KIRK, Frank NOTESTEIN, and Ansley COALE, with Irene TAEUBER and Louis KISER: *The Future Population of Europe and the Soviet Union: Population Projections, 1940–70* (comprehensive quantitative treatment of demographic analysis using limited data).

1945–54 Complete enumerations for 65 sovereign nations.

1945 Ernest BURGESS and L. COTTRELL: *Predicting Success or Failure in Marriage* (comprehensive work on family demography).

1945 Institut National d'Études Démographiques established in France.

1945 Charter of the United Nations adopted, which includes a provision for a Commission on Population.

1945 Frank NOTESTEIN: "Population: the Long View," *Food for the World*, ed. T. W. Schultz (uses the phrase "demographic transition," based on THOMPSON's work in 1929).

1945 Kingsley DAVIS: "The World Demographic Transition," *Annals of the American Academy of Political and Social Science* (first comprehensive overview of demographic transition theory).

1945 Sept. ff. Population Reference Bureau begins publication of *Population Bulletin* (first issue, eight pages, on the labor market in the postwar world).

1946 U.S. Congress enacts federal programs that use statistical formulas in conjunction with census and other data for funding purposes; sets the stage for a tremendous expansion of the use of such formulas from the 1950s to the 1990s.

1946 Recognition begins to take hold of postwar baby boom in the United States (see 1940, 1957, and 1961, and 1964), similar postwar booms subsequently recognized in Australia and Canada.

1946 ff. French demography journal, *Population*.

1946 P. H. LESLIE: "On the Use of Matrices in Certain Population Processes," *Biometrika* (seminal paper on population projection using matrix algebra).

1947 ff. *Population Studies* (Population Investigation Committee, London School of Economics, first regularly published English-language journal devoted to demography).

1948 ff. United Nations: *Demographic Yearbook*.

1949 Louis DUBLIN, Alfred J. LOTKA, and Mortimer SPIEGELMAN: *Length of Life*, revised edition of the book that first appeared in 1936 (comprehensive and seminal work on mortality, demography, and actuarial science).

1949 George ZIPF: *Human Behavior and the Principle of Least Effort: An Introduction to Human Ecology* (detailed observations on empirical regularities in population distribution and migration).

1949 United Nations: *Problems of Migration Statistics* (seminal work on data on overcoming data flaws in conjunction with the analysis of migration).

1950 U.S. Census "supplemental questions" sampling frequency increased from 1 in 20 to 1 in 5 households. "FOSDIC" optical scanning system introduced as a means of electronically capturing data on census forms.

1950 Peter COX: *Demography* (although oriented toward actuaries, the first comprehensive textbook on demography).

1950 Amos HAWLEY: *Human Ecology: A Theory of Community Structure* (comprehensive theoretical work on human ecology).

1951 Kingsley DAVIS: *The Population of India and Pakistan* (seminal work on population and development).

1951 UNIVAC I, first commercially available computer, delivered to the U.S. Bureau of the Census for processing 1950 census tabulations.

1951 A. J. JAFFE: *Handbook of Statistical Methods for Demographers*, preliminary edition, 2nd printing (published under the auspices of the U.S. Bureau of the Census "in response to the many urgent requests received by the Bureau from technicians in foreign countries and the United States," it is aimed at the analysis of census and related data).

1952 International Planned Parenthood Federation founded.

1952 United Nations: *Methods of Estimating Total Population for Current Dates, Manual I.*

1953 Frank W. NOTESTEIN: *Economic Problems of Population Change* (comprehensive neo-Malthusian work).

1953 United Nations: *The Determinants and Consequences of Population Trends.*

1954 Robert C. SCHMITT and Albert H. CROSETTI: "Accuracy of the Ratio-Correlation Method for Estimating Postcensal Population," *Land Economics* (seminal work on subnational population estimation).

1954 P. K. WHELPTON: *Cohort Fertility: Native White Women in the United States* (a comprehensive presentation of the cohort approach to fertility analysis).

1954 Hugh WOLFENDEN: *Population Statistics and Their Compilation* (comprehensive book on demographic methods).

1954 United Nations: *Handbook of Population Census Methods.*

1954 First World Population Conference, sponsored by United Nations, Rome; notable for the fact that participants were experts in their own right and did not represent countries.

1955 Mortimer SPIEGELMAN: *Introduction to Demography* (a textbook using mathematical formulations, and weighted heavily toward the study of mortality).

1955 United Nations: *Age and Sex Patterns of Mortality, Model Life Tables for Underdeveloped Countries.*

1955 United Nations: *Methods of Appraisal of Quality of Basic Data from Population Estimates, Manual II.*

1955 United Nations: *Handbook of Vital Statistics Methods* and *Principles for a Vital Statistics System.*

1955–60 Growth of American Families (fertility survey, Rockefeller Foundation, initial investigators: Arthur CAMPBELL, John PATTERSON, and P. K. WHELPTON).

1956 Kingsley DAVIS and Judith BLAKE: "Social Structure and Fertility: An Analytic Framework," *Economic Development and Cultural Change* (seminal work on the social analysis of fertility).

1956 United Nations: *Methods for Population Projections by Sex and Age, Manual III.*

1956 United Nations: *The Aging of Population and Its Economic and Social Consequences.*

1957 Peak year of U.S. baby boom.

1957 Princeton Fertility Survey (with re-interviews in 1960 and 1963–1967).

1958 UNITED NATIONS: Multilingual Demography Dictionary.

1958 George BARCLAY: *Techniques of Population Analysis* (widely used as a text in demographic methods courses for many years).

1958 Ansley COALE and Edgar HOOVER: *Population Growth and Economic Development in Low Income Countries* (highly influential neo-Malthusian analysis of the relationship between development and population growth).

1958 Sidney GOLDSTEIN: *Patterns of Mobility* (comprehensive empirical and theoretical work on domestic migration in a capitalistic system).

1958–59 United Nations: *Principles and Recommendations for National Population Censuses; Handbook of Population Census Methods, Vol. I; General Aspects of a Population Census, Vol. II; Economic Characteristics of the Population, Vol. III; Demographic and Social Characteristics of the Population, Studies in Methods Series F.*

1959 Wilson GRABILL, Clyde KISER, and P. K. WHELPTON: *The Fertility of American Women.*

1960 WORLD POPULATION: 3 billion.

1960 U.S. Census is the last in which 100% door-to-door canvassing was attempted; self-enumeration introduced on a massive scale; the "long form" is introduced and this becomes the first census in which the sample segment is asked more questions than the 100% segment.

1960 May 9 U.S. Food and Drug Administration approves marketing "the pill" for birth control.

1960 Gary S. BECKER: "An Economic Analysis of Fertility," *Demographic and Economic Change in Developed Countries* (seminal work on the economic approach to fertility).

1961 Beginning of steep decline in U.S. births.

1961 Birth control pill comes on the market.

1961 Otis D. DUNCAN, Ray CUZZORT, and Beverly DUNCAN: *Statistical Geography* (a pioneering treatment of the statistical analysis of demographic and related data aggregated by area).

1962 U.S. Supreme Court ruled malapportioned state legislatures unconstitutional, setting the way for numerous lawsuits and the reapportionment revolution of the 1960s.

1963 Ansley COALE and Melvin ZELNIK: *New Estimates of Fertility and Population in the United States* (seminal work on evaluating census and vital statistics data and developing estimates from deficient census and vital statistics data).

1963 ff. *Studies in Family Planning*.

1964 ff. *Demography* (Population Association of America; Donald BOGUE, first editor).

1964 Recognition that the baby boom ends in the United States and a "baby bust" begins—the last continuous year in which the number of births exceeded 4 million.

1964–68 The United States enacted federal civil rights, voting, and fair housing employment laws that rely on high-quality census and other data for enforcement and compliance needs.

1965 Gladys BOWLES and James D. TARVER: *Net Migration of the Population, 1950–60, By Age, Sex, and Color* (seminal empirical work on domestic migration).

1965, 1970, 1975 National Fertility Surveys (NICHD).

1965 Norman RYDER: "The Cohort as a Concept in the Study of Social Change," *American Sociological Review* (seminal work on the analytical utility of the cohort perspective).

1966 Ansley COALE and Paul DEMENY: *Regional Model Life Tables and Stable Populations* (comprehensive set of model life tables and model stable populations for use in evaluating and adjusting demographic data that are defective).

1966 P. K. WHELPTON, Arthur CAMPBELL, and John PATTERSON: *Fertility and Family Planning in the United States*.

1967 United Nations: *Methods of Estimating Basic Demographic Measures from Incomplete Data, Manual IV*.

1968 William BRASS et al.: *The Demography of Tropical Africa* (important methodological developments for dealing with missing and defective demographic data).

1968 Garrett HARDIN, "The Tragedy of the Commons," *Science* (seminal prelude to popular concern over global population growth and use of resources).

1968 Paul EHRLICH: *The Population Bomb* (another seminal prelude to popular concern over global population growth and neo-Malthusian ideas).

1968 Nathan KEYFITZ: *Introduction to the Mathematics of Population*.

1968 Mortimer SPIEGELMAN: *Introduction to Demography*, 2nd edition (compact introduction to demography written with mathematical formulation, based on the original edition published in 1955).

1968 United Nations: *The Concept of a Stable Population: Applications to the Study of Populations of Countries with Incomplete Demographic Statistics*.

1969 ff. *Family Planning Perspectives* (Alan Guttmacher Institute, NY).

1970 Census Bureau releases census data on machine readable tapes (first count through fourth count, etc.) with file documentation and COBOL processing software written by Gary K. Hill and others at DUALABS, Inc.).

1970 First case in U.S. federal court regarding census undercount.

1970 United Nations: *Methods of Measuring Internal Migration, Manual VI*.

1971 Controversy arose over privacy in the census of the Netherlands, leading to indefinite postponement of the 1981 census; mirrors privacy concerns elsewhere.

1971 Henry S. SHRYOCK, Jacob S. SIEGEL, and ASSOCIATES: *The Methods and Materials of Demography* (important comprehensive text book and reference work on demography).

1971 Norman CARRIER and John HOBCRAFT: *Demographic Estimation for Developing Societies: A Manual of Techniques for the Detection and Reduction of Errors in Demographic Data* (seminal work on methods of estimation using deficient data).

1971 U.S. National Academy of Sciences: *Rapid Population Growth: Consequences and Policy Implications*.

1971 United Nations: *Methods of Projecting the Economically Active Population, Manual V*.

1972 MEADOWS et al.: *The Limits to Growth: A Report for the Club of Rome's Project on the Predicament of Mankind* (opening neoMalthusian salvo that helps kick off environmentalism movement).

1972 Ansley COALE: *The Growth and Structure of Human Populations: A Mathematical Investigation* (influential mathematical treatment of demography).

1972 Samuel PRESTON, Nathan KEYFITZ, and Robert SCHOEN: *Causes of Death Life Tables for National Populations* (appearance of a comprehensive set of cause-specific life tables).

1972 U.S. Commission on Population Growth and the American Future: *Population and the American Future* (assessment of U.S. population policy, concluding that it would be advantageous for the U.S. population to have lower fertility and a lower maximum population than anticipated under prevailing trends).

1973 Evelyn KITAGAWA and Philip HAUSER: *Differential Mortality in the United States: A Study in Socio-Economic Epidemiology* (comprehensive treatment of socioeconomic factors and mortality).

1973 United Nations: *Determinants and Consequences of Population Trends*.

1973 United Nations: *Methods of Projecting Households and Families, Manual VII*.

1973 National Survey of Family Growth (National Center for Health Statistics; cycle II, 1976; III 1982, IV 1988).

1973 Mindel C. SHEPS and Jane A. MENKEN: *Mathematical Models of Conception and Birth* (comprehensive treatment of fertility that includes an extensive listing of computer models of human reproduction).

1974 Leo GOODMAN, Nathan KEYFITZ, and Thomas PULLUM: "Family Formation and the Frequency of Various Kinship Relationships," *Theoretical Population Biology* (seminal demographic paper on kinship).

1974 World Fertility Survey begins and runs for a number of years, with a comprehensive appraisal in a book edited by J. CLELAND, C. SCOTT, and D. WHITELEGGE, published in 1987.

1975 WORLD POPULATION: 4 billion.

1975 Andrei ROGERS: *Introduction to Multiregional Mathematical Demography* (comprehensive introduction to the multiregional theory and methods).

1975 ff. *Population and Development Review* (Population Council).

1975 ff. *International Family Planning Digest*—evolved into *International Family Planning Perspectives and Digest* 1978 and *International Family Planning Perspectives*, 1979.

1978 Brian ARTHUR and Geoffrey McNICOLL: "Samuelson, Population, and Intergenerational Transfers," *International Economic Review* (seminal paper contributing ideas to complexity theory).

1979 Roland PRESSAT: *The Dictionary of Demography* (in French).

1979 ff. *American Demographics* (the first periodical devoted to commercial applications of demography; Peter FRANCESE, founder).

1979 United Nations: *Manual IX: The Methodology of Measuring the Impact of Family Planning Programmes on Fertility.*

1980 U.S. Census becomes the focus of substantial litigation and related actions over "undercounts," marking the start of highly contentious census counts.

1980 Evelyn KITAGAWA *et al.* (editors): *Estimating Population and Income for Small Places* (comprehensive treatment of small area population estimation).

1981 Louis HENRY: *Dictionnaire Demographique Multilingue.*

1981 Gary S. BECKER: *A Treatise on the Family* (comprehensive economic approach to family and household microdemography).

1981 Ester BOSERUP: *Population and Technological Change: A Study of Long-Term Trends* (a strong statement against the Malthusian thesis that more people yield more misery).

1981 Julian SIMON: *The Ultimate Resource* (another very strong statement against the Malthusian thesis that more people yield greater misery).

1982 J. ROSS (ed.): *International Encyclopedia of Population.*

1983 John BONGAARTS and Robert G. POTTER: *Fertility, Biology, and Behavior: An Analysis of the Proximate Determinants* (comprehensive framework for analyzing fertility using the "proximate determinants" framework).

1983 United Nations: *Indirect Techniques for Demographic Estimation, Manual X.*

1984 Chin Long CHIANG: *The Life Table and Its Applications* (comprehensive stochastic treatment of the life table and its functions).

1984 Charles MODE: *Stochastic Processes in Demography and Their Computer Implementation* (comprehensive stochastic treatment of fertility, mortality in conjunction with population projections).

1985 Karen MASON OPPENHEIM: *The Status of Women: A Review of Its Relationships to Fertility and Mortality* (seminal work on the relationship of the status of women to fertility and mortality).

1985 William PETERSON and Renee PETERSON: *Dictionary of Demography* (first comprehensive English language demography dictionary to appear; in the same year, however, a translation of PRESSAT's French language dictionary of demography also appears, with Christopher WILSON as editor).

1987 WORLD POPULATION: 5 billion.

1987 Jerry WICKS and Jose PEREIRA DE ALMEIDA: IPSS population projection system released (commercial appearance of "point and click" demographic software).

1987 Douglas MASSEY, Rafael ALARCON, Jorge DURAND, and Humberto GONZALEZ: *Return to Aztlan: The Social Process of International Migration from Western Mexico* (comprehensive theoretical and empirical response to the human capital approach to migration—an argument for the importance of social factors in the migration process).

1987 Richard EASTERLIN: *Birth and Fortune* (comprehensive theory concerning economic opportunity and variation in the size of birth cohorts).

1990 U.S. Census results distributed on diskettes along with processing software for use on "personal" computers. Results subject to contentious litigation and related actions over "undercounts."

1990–1991 Number of legal U.S. immigrants exceeds 1.5 million in each year.

1990–2000 Substantial efforts made by U.S. Census Bureau to improve accuracy and quality in 2000 while reining in costs, leads to a proposal that "statistical adjustment" be used to reduce differential net undercount error; proposal is subject to intense litigation and related actions; U.S. Supreme Court rules that the direct count must be used for apportionment and cannot be statistically adjusted for this purpose.

1994 International Conference on Population and Development in Cairo, attendance on a national basis and theme is more political than technical.

1996 American Community Survey initiated, starting the process that could lead to collecting in a "continuous measurement" sample survey of the long form of the U.S. Census.

1999 WORLD POPULATION: 6 billion.

2000 full "democratization of U.S. Census data" with worldwide access to census results through American Fact Finder in graphic and tabular forms via the Internet; electronic versions of reports and maps replace paper copies.

2001 American Community Survey results available on the Internet, with worldwide access.

Author Biographies[1]

Thomas A. Bryan is lead statistician for Third wave Research. He has a master's degree in urban studies from Portland State University and a master's degree in information systems technology from George Washington University. Mr. Bryan's research interests are in developing small-area population estimates and statistical evaluation techniques.

A. Dharmalingam is a lecturer in population studies at the Department of Sociology and Social Policy and an associate of the Population Studies Centre, University of Waikato, Hamilton, New Zealand. He is editor of the *New Zealand Population Review*. He has an MSc. in Mathematical Economics from Madurai Kamaraj University (India) and a Ph.D. in demography from the Australian National University. His research interests include the demography and status of women in India, family formation in New Zealand, and household demography.

Barry Edmonston is director of the Population Research Center and a professor in the School of Urban Studies and Planning, Portland State University. He has a Ph.D., with a specialization in population studies, from the University of Michigan. He has been a faculty member at Stanford University and Cornell University and served as a researcher at the Urban Institute and the National Academy of Sciences. His current research interests are in the demographic effects of immigration, immigration statistics, internal migration of the foreign-born, and demographic changes in homeownership.

Sharon Estee is research supervisor in the Research and Data Analysis Division of the Washington State Department of Social and Health Services. While completing the chapter

on natality measures using vital statistics, she was manager of research for the Washington State Center for Health Statistics. Dr. Estee has managed research units in government agencies for more than 20 years and is currently investigating the social service needs of homeless families and medical cost offsets associated with drug and alcohol treatment. She has a Ph.D. in sociology from Ohio State University.

Kimberly Faust is associate professor of Sociology at Fitchburg State College in Massachusetts. She has an M.A. and Ph.D. from the University of North Carolina at Chapel Hill. Dr. Faust has published numerous articles on marriage and family issues.

Linda Gage is liaison to demographic programs for the State of California after serving as chief of the state's Demographic Research Unit for two decades. She has managed and evaluated California's demographic programs, administered the state's Census Data Center, and served as the governor's liaison for Census 2000. Ms. Gage serves on the U.S. Secretary of Commerce's Decennial Advisory Committee and the National Academy of Sciences' Panel on Formula Allocations. She has an M.A. in sociology from the University of California, Davis.

M. V. George has been chief of the Population Projections, Demography Division, Statistics Canada, since 1979. He is also adjunct professor of the Department of Sociology at the University of Alberta. He holds a Ph.D. in demography from the Australian National University.

Robert George is geographic business manager at Sonic Industries. He is responsible for all day-to-day demographic, geographic, and cartographic needs within the company. He has an M.S. in geography from the University of Alabama.

Robert L. Heuser served in a number of capacities for many years with the U.S. National Center for Health Statistics. He is perhaps best known for his service as chief of the Natality, Marriage and Divorce Statistics Branch of the Division of Vital Statistics.

---

[1] Not listed here are authors of chapters in the original two-volume set of the *Methods and Material of Demography*, from which, however, material was drawn in different ways by the authors of the current edition. The original authors are identified in Table 1-1. Author disclaimer: The views expressed in this book are those of the individual authors and do not reflect views or positions held by their respective employers.

Frank Hobbs is chief of the Special Projects Staff in the Population Division of the U.S. Census Bureau. He has specialized in age and sex composition (particularly ages 65 and over) and in international demography, especially analyses of developing countries (mainly in South Asia and the Middle East). He served 6 years (1981–1984 and 1995–1998) as the demographic statistics advisor to the Central Department of Statistics, Riyadh, Saudi Arabia. He has a B.S. in mathematics from the University of Maryland and an M.S. in sociology/demography from Florida State University.

George C. Hough, Jr., is coordinator of the Oregon State Data Center, Population Research Center, Portland State University, and research associate professor in the School of Urban Studies and Planning at Portland State University. He received a Ph.D. in sociology from the University of Texas at Austin. Dr. Hough's research interests include demographic and statistical methods, race and ethnic demographic behavior, and urban sociology.

Dean H. Judson is group leader of the Administrative Records Evaluation and Linkage Group at the U.S. Census Bureau. Formerly, he was the Nevada state demographer and has worked as a private consultant with Decision Analytics, Inc. Dr. Judson received an M.S. in mathematics from the University of Nevada and an M.A. and a Ph.D. in sociology from Washington State University.

Hallie J. Kintner is a staff research scientist in the Enterprise Systems Laboratory of General Motors Research and Development Center. She has published extensively on mortality and applied demography, including co-editing *Demographics: A Casebook for Business and Government*, the first collection of real-life case studies in applied demography. Dr. Kintner has chaired the Census Advisory Committee on Population Statistics for the U.S. Bureau of the Census. She received an M.A. and a Ph.D. in sociology/demography, as well as an M.S. in biostatistics, from the University of Michigan.

Vicki L. Lamb is a research scientist at the Center for Demographic Studies, Duke University. She also is affiliated with the Howard Odum Institute for Research in Social Science at the University of North Carolina, Chapel Hill. Dr. Lamb has numerous publications on estimates of healthy life expectancy and other measures of health and disability, particularly of older adults. She has a Ph.D. in sociology from Duke University.

Douglas S. Massey is the Dorothy Swaine Thomas professor and chair of the Department of Sociology at the University of Pennsylvania. He holds a Ph.D. in sociology from Princeton University and has published widely on topics related to migration, human ecology, race, and ethnicity.

Mary A. McGehee is a researcher with the University of Texas, San Antonio. Her current research involves the investigation of social, economic, demographic, and environmental factors related to health disparities between race/ethnic populations in the United States. She has a Ph.D. from Texas A&M University.

Jerome N. McKibben III is a visiting professor of sociology at Eastern Connecticut State University. He holds a master's degree in criminal justice from Syracuse University and received a Ph.D. in applied demography from Bowling Green State University. Dr. McKibben has been a visiting professor at the Helsinki School of Economics.

Margaret Michalowski is chief of Development and Demographic Methods for Statistics Canada. She has led major research projects on internal and international migration in Canada and Poland. She has published extensively on different aspects of international migration, ethnicity, and demographic estimates and projections. She has a Ph.D. in statistics and demography from the Warsaw School of Economics, Poland.

Peter A. Morrison is the founding director of RAND's Population Research Center, where he is a resident consultant. He has published extensively on the consequences of demographic trends for public policy and business. He has taught at The RAND Graduate School and Helsinki School of Economics. Dr. Morrison has been elected president of the Southern Demographic Association and served as advisor to the National Academy of Sciences. He holds a Ph.D. in sociology from Brown University.

Kathryn Norcross-Bryan was the lead mapping specialist for Washington, D.C.-based Cogent Communications. In addition to telecommunication experience, she has done retail site location analysis for Blockbuster Entertainment. She has an M.A. in sociology/demography from Florida State University.

William O'Hare directs the KIDS COUNT program at the Annie E. Casey Foundation. He has published widely in the areas of applied and social demography. He was a contributing editor to *American Demographics* magazine, director of Policy Studies at the Population Reference Bureau, and president of the Southern Demographic Association. Dr. O'Hare obtained a Ph.D. in sociology from Michigan State University.

Stephen Perz received a Ph.D. in sociology with a specialization in demography from the University of Texas at Austin in 1997. He is now an assistant professor in the Department of Sociology and faculty affiliate to both the Center for Latin American Studies and the College of Natural Resources and Environment, University of Florida. Dr. Perz conducts interdisciplinary and international research on population and the environment, focusing on the demographic and other social forces affecting land use and land-cover change in the Brazilian Amazon.

David Plane is a professor in the Department of Geography and Regional Development at the University of Arizona, where he served as head of department from 1990 to 1997. His research has focused primarily on modeling the changing geographic patterns of U.S. interregional migration and on developing new methods for analyzing systems of geographic movement. Dr. Plane is co-author (with Peter Rogerson) of the textbook, *The Geographical Analysis of Population*. He has served as president of the Pacific Regional Science Conference Organization and co-edits the *Journal of Regional Science*. Dr. Plane received his Ph.D. from the University of Pennsylvania.

Kelvin M. Pollard is a research demographer at the Population Reference Bureau, Washington, D.C. He is the author of PRB's *United States Population Data Sheet* and has authored numerous articles for PRB publications. He provides data analysis and technical assistance for the Annie E. Casey Foundation's KIDS COUNT program. Mr. Pollard received a master's degree in applied social research from the University of Michigan.

Carole L. Popoff is chief of the Modeling and Outreach Branch in the Housing and Household Economic Statistics Division at the U.S. Census Bureau, the primary focus of which is to model program eligibility using household surveys. Formerly, she was the associate director for research at the Bureau of Business and Economic Research, University of Nevada, Reno, as well as president of Decision Analytics, Inc., a consulting firm that provides economic and demographic analysis for various state-level programs. Ms. Popoff has an M.S. in economics from Arizona State University and is currently finishing her dissertation for a Ph.D. in political science at the University of Nevada, Reno.

Thomas Pullum has a master's degree in statistics and a Ph.D. in sociology from the University of Chicago. He has taught courses on demographic methods there as well as at several other universities, including the University of Texas at Austin, where he is professor of sociology and research associate in the Population Research Center.

Amy R. Ritualo was a data analyst in the International Programme on the Elimination of Child Labour at the International Labour Organization in Geneva. In this capacity, she carries out in-depth analyses of child labor data in order to develop indicators of child labor, identify general and regional patterns of child labor, evaluate child labor collection methodologies, and provide assistance in establishing priorities and recommendations for policy and program development. Ms. Ritualo holds a master's degree in demography from Georgetown University.

Jacob S. Siegel is currently a private consultant with interests in methods of demographic analysis, applied demography, and gerontological demography. He was formerly senior statistician for demographic analysis and research at the U.S. Census Bureau and senior research scholar and professorial lecturer in demography at Georgetown University. He is a former president of the Population

Association of America and was a co-editor of the former editions of *The Methods and Materials of Demography*. He holds an M.A. in sociology from the University of Pennsylvania.

Stanley K. Smith is professor of economics and director of the Bureau of Economic and Business Research at the University of Florida. His research unit produces the official state and local population estimates and projections for the state of Florida. His research interests include the methodology and analysis of population estimates and projections, the determinants of population forecast accuracy, and the demography of Florida, subjects on which he has published widely. He has a Ph.D. in economics from the University of Michigan.

G. Edward Stephan is professor emeritus at Western Washington University. He has published widely on the size of territorial divisions, work summarized in his online book *Division of Territory in Society*. He received a Ph.D. in sociology from the University of Oregon.

C. M. Suchindran is professor of biostatistics and a fellow at the Carolina Population Center, University of North Carolina at Chapel Hill. He heads the demography training program in the Department of Biostatistics. He is also a member of the statistical services core of the Carolina Population Center. Dr. Suchindran is a fellow of the American Statistical Association.

David A. Swanson Professor of Sociology and Chair of the Department of Sociology and Anthropology, University of Mississippi. He has published more than 50 journal articles on various demographic topics and is co-author of several books and monographs, including *State and Local Population Projections: Methodology and Analysis* (with Stanley K. Smith and Jeff Tayman). He holds a Ph.D. in sociology (population studies) from the University of Hawaii.

Jeff Tayman is the director of Research and Information Systems for the San Diego Association of Governments. He has published extensively in the areas of estimates and projections, focusing on methodology and the measurement of error. Dr. Tayman has led major research projects on integrating geographic information systems into the development of demographic and economic estimates and projections for census tracts, blocks, and other spatially defined areas. He has a Ph.D. in sociology/demography from Florida State University.

Janet Wilmoth is associate professor of sociology at Syracuse University and senior research associate for the Center for Policy Research. Her published research examines the older adult population, with an emphasis on migration, living arrangements, social support, and health status. She has a Ph.D. in sociology/demography, with a minor in gerontology, from Pennsylvania State University.

Author Index

Subject Index